HOLY PLACES
AND TEMPLES IN

INDIA

JOHN HOWLEY, JADA BHARATA DASA

SPIRITUAL GUIDES   PRACTICAL
TRAVEL

Holy Places and Temples of India Credits

Writer: John Howley (Jada Bharata Dasa)
Editor: Pundarika Vidyanidhi Dasa
Proofreader: Vegavati-devi Dasi

Published by John Howley (Jada Bharata Dasa) and Spiritual Guide.

If you interested in purchasing a copy or copies of this book you can contact:

Jada Bharata Dasa
Krishna Balarama Mandir,   Bhaktivedanta Swami Marg
Vrindavana, Mathura District, UP India
Phone 0565-442-400 Fax 91-565-442-952   Com Jada Bharata Dasa (SDG)

Krishna Culture
P.O. Box 12380
Philadelphia, PA 19919 USA
Phone (215) 242-2579   Fax (215) 247-4230

BBL
PO Box 324
Borehamwood, Herts, WD6 1NB UK
Phone 44-81-905-1244   Fax 44-81-905-1108

The publisher and writers of Holy Places and Temples of India have done their
best to make sure that the facts in this book are accurate and up to date, however
the publisher, Spiritual Guide, and the writers can accept no responsibility for any
loss, injury, or inconvenience sustained by anyone reading this book.

ISBN 0-9653858-0-9

The first edition published in March, 1996 by Spiritual Guide.

Printed in India at Indira Printers, New Delhi-110 020.

Jada Bharata Das (John Howley)

Jada Bharata Dasa was born in America and for the first 23 years of his life never went more than 200 miles from his home town. He grew up in a hotel that his mother managed, and worked for a year in a restaurant. He studied to be an accountant at Drexel and Rutgers University, but dropped out of school at the end of his Junior year to become a member of ISKCON, the International Society for Krishna Consciousness.

He spent 10 years traveling in America visiting 42 of the 50 states. He has been in India ten different times spending over four years in India, a year of that traveling around to the different holy places and temples in India.

The way this book was compiled

First I talked to a few people and made up a list of all the holy places and famous temples that I knew or they knew. I then got any travel book I could find on India. I added some more places by reading these books. I then collected whatever books that I could find about the holy places and temples in India and took information from them. For the health section I got a few books by doctors about health while travelling. Also many guide books have good health sections, which I got information from.

Then I made the big step for me and that was to go to most of the places in this book. I went to all the major holy places and temples. I went from one end of India, both north to south, and east to west. I visited many of the hotels and restaurants in this book. I also got information from the local tourist offices in each town. At many places I got literature about the holy places and temples that could only be gotten at those places.

I talked to hundreds of people about their travels and what places they liked, and their experiences. I also discussed with them the problem that they had, and what they would have done or not done next time. Also for 19 years I studied the Vedic literature.

The total time spent to write this book was two and a half years.

Warning and Request

Nothing stays the same. Places change and close, a good place can become bad or raise their prices, and phone numbers or addresses change. If you find something that is changed please write me and let me know. If you know some information about a place that I do not know, please let me know so I can add it to the next edition of this book. If you know some story or information about a temple or holy place let me know.

I really appreciate any letters that are sent in. Thank you for you help.

ACKNOWLEDGEMENTS

I would like to thank the people that gave me information or inspiration for this book. First I would like to thank my spiritual teachers, Satsvarupa Dasa Goswami and His Divine Grace AC Bhaktivedanta Swami Srila Prabhupada.

Other people who have made contributions or suggestions are: Krishnadas Kaviraja Dasa, Braja Bihari Dasa, Abhaya Dasa, Chandra Dasi, Narmada Dasi, Kaushika Dholakia, Viprahita Dasa, Ananga Manjari Dasi, Acyuta Dasa, Padmanabha Goswami, Rai Krishna Dasa, Nama Sankirtana Dasa, Dhritarastra Dasa, Mahamantra Dasa, Bhakta Steve, Markandeya Dasa, Vedavyasa Dasa, Gitanagari Dasa, Rukmavati Dasi and Yasmin Tabib. I would like to especially thank Krishnadas Kaviraja Dasa (Kaushik Rajani) who was not only helpful by giving useful information, but also gave me much practical help.

I would also like to thank my editor Pundarika Vidyanidhi who helped get rid of many of my factual and English mistakes. He is proficient in English, Hindi and Sanskrit. He also has lived in India for over 15 years. My proof-reader, Vegavati Dasi not only helped to keep this book from having many mistakes, but also straightened me out on a few points in the way I was presenting things in a very polite and helpful manner.

I also would like to thank my mother who taught me what a good hotel and restaurant is, and also to be in the mood of trying to help people.

Contents

Introduction

A question that could be asked is: What is the need of another tourist book about India? There are already so many good travel guides. A few years ago I purchased my first travel guide to India. I found it very useful, and when I traveled around India to write this book I used it, along with other books, many times. When I read the book, I thought I could do the same thing. The problem with all the tourist books that I have—and I have about ten of them—is that they give little or no information about the holy places and temples in India. I had to travel around with a suitcase full of books to have full information about all the places I went to.

Most India travel books have a lot of information, but little or nothing on the spiritual aspect, the real wealth of India. Many of the books I read were written from the standpoint of an observer, not a believer. I have personally studied the Vedic literature for over 15 years, and I believe the stories in them to be actual facts. They are not myths or legends. They are actual historical facts that happened, in some cases, beyond the concept of recorded history. Krishna is an actual personality who lived on earth 5000 years ago. To worship the Deity of Krishna in a temple is as good as worshiping Krishna directly.

Many travellers who come to India are coming to experience something spiritual or to see the temples. Many of them realize that spiritual life is the answer to many of their problems, but they do not know which path to follow. So this book also gives an introduction to Vedic and Vaishnava philosophy.

Many travellers come to India to feel spiritual and happy, but when they get to India they just find cheaters and people who want to rip them off. Many of them lose all their money in the first week. Then they just want to leave India immediately and never come back. So this book gives many hints on how to avoid problems and enjoy India. If you have never been to India, I would recommend that you read the section entitled "Your first day in India." There are some good practical lessons to be learned therein.

This book also has some valuable information for people that have been to India many times and know the Vedic philosophy. Based on over two years of research and travel, there is a good deal of information in this book about what holy places and temples there are to see in India. Not only is this book the most detailed book on the holy places and temples in India, it is also full of practical information. There is a listing of the different places to see at each place, hotels in different price ranges, information about pure vegetarian restaurants, and valuable travel information for travelers on all budgets.

India is a big country with many holy places. If you travel nonstop, you can go to most of the major places in six months, but you will really tire yourself out. If you travel for too long at one time you can get totally exhausted. If you really have to move fast, even then it is best to stop in a nice place every three weeks and take three days rest. The public transportation in India, especially the buses, can be murder. But if you really want to see many of these places, you are going to have to use the buses. So you have to give yourself a rest sometimes. Because India is so big, many times travel is not very straight forward, and a 24-hour train ride or a four hour ride on a crowded bus is typical. For long distances, trains are usually the best way to travel. Many places cannot be reached by plane.

It is a good idea to select an area of India to see in detail. In this way you can cut down your travel time. Over the years you can select different areas and see the entire country. One person told me "India isn't a vacation, it's an experience." If you go to the right places and do not travel too quickly you will have a great time.

You can find someone who speaks English mostly everywhere in India. Many of the shopkeepers and hotel people speak English.

The best time to come to India, for most areas, is between October and March. The summer can be unbelievably hot and the monsoons in July and August can make travel difficult. If you are going to the Himalayas, then the best time to go is May/June or September/October. The Himalayas are the best place to be weather-wise in the summer months of May and June.

Despite many of the negative things I say about the people you may meet in India, I feel the people in India for the most part are much better than most other people in the world. They have a sense of hospitality that is excellent. They really treat you like a guest. They can go out of their way a hundred times over to help you.

On the hundreds of bus trips I took

on extremely crowded buses, only once did I have to stand up for more than five minutes. Because I was a foreigner and therefore a guest to the Indian country, I was always treated as special. Quite frankly, I needed it, because I was not used to traveling in such crowded situations.

At times it may seem that most of the people in India have no brains. Often many of the problems experienced are just a communication problem. Behind the mass of bureaucracy and apparent inefficiency are many of the most intelligent people in the world. If you just accept the fact that there is someone intelligent making everything happen, intelligent people will almost always come to your aid and make your life much easier. An Indian can often do in a few minutes what will take a foreigner two days to do.

Much of my time is spent at the Krishna Balarama Temple (ISKCON temple) in Vrindavana. If you would like to speak to me personally about the subject matter in this book, please feel free to do so. Much of the information compiled in this book was brought to real-life by hundreds of conversations with people while traveling. Also if you are new to the Indian philosophy and would like someone to show you around Vrindavana, I most likely can help you.

Please forgive me for any mistakes that may be in this book. This is the first book I have ever written. If you find any mistakes and would like to correct them please write me. In this way the readers of the future editions of this book will benefit.

Please Help Us

As the subject matter of this book is extremely complex and detailed it is very difficult to include everything relevant. So if you have some information that would be valuable to the readers of this book please send it to us, so they may be benefited.

Whatever you can tell about any temple, the story behind the Deity, what Deities are in a particular temple, or other interesting facts may be valuable information. Also of interest is your opinion on hotels, restaurants or dharamshalas, especially ones missed in this book. Travel information is also valuable. Please refer to the page number in this book in reference to the place that you are writing about.

Please give as detailed information as possible.

For temples or holy places please send:
Temple name, location, Deities' names
What is especially interesting about the temple or place
Story about the temple or Deities
Opening or closing hours
How to get there, what bus or train
Potential problems such as guides, hard climbs, or monkeys

For hotels and restaurants please send :
Name, address, phone number, opening hours of a restaurant
Tariff card or room rates
Location, distance from a land-mark either walking or by rickshaw.
How close to a railway or bus station.
How to get there and how much it cost.
Your comments on why this place stood out.
For a restaurant, any recommended preparations or things to be avoided

The writers of the ten best letters will receive an updated edition of this book.

Thank you very much for your help.

Write to

Spiritual Guides   Jada Bharata Dasa
Krishna Balarama Mandir
Bhaktivedanta Swami Marg
Vrindavana, Mathura Dist. UP, India

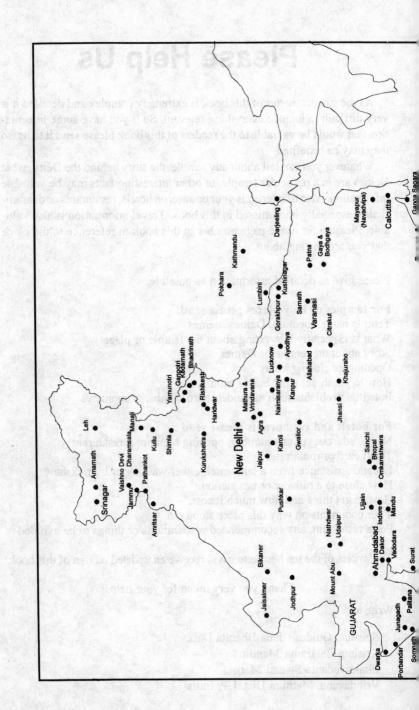

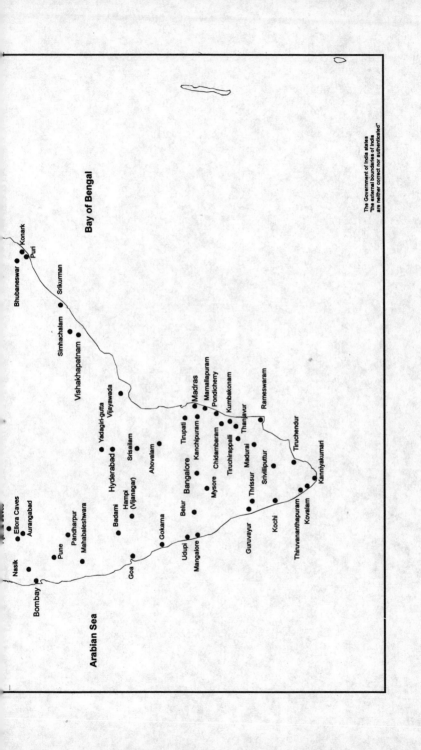

The Government of India states
"the external boundaries of India
are neither correct nor authenticated"

CHAPTER ONE

SPIRITUAL INFORMATION

Important Holy Places

There are thousands of holy places throughout India. Some have more spiritual significance than others, and the benefits and spiritual advancement for a person going there is increased. There are four *dhamas*, or kingdoms of God, which are Badrinath, Rameswara, Puri, and Dwarka. There are seven sacred cities known as the Saptapuris (Mokshapuris), which are Ayodhya, Mathura, Mayapuri (Haridwar), Kasi (Varanasi), Kanchi (Kanchipuram), Avantipuri (Ujjain), and Dwarka. The seven most sacred rivers are the Ganges, Yamuna, Godavari, Saraswati, Narmada, Sindhu, and Kaveri. There are four Kumbha-melas at Allahabad, Haridwar, Ujjain, and Nasik.

There are eight self-manifested holy places (Svayam Vyakta Ksetras), out of a list of 108 major Vishnu temples (108 Vaishnava Divya Desams), which are Sri Rangam, Tirumala, Sri Mushnam, and Thotadri in South India; and Shalagram, Pushkara, Naimisaranya, and Badrinath in North India.

The most important holy places for Gaudiya Vaisnavas are Vrindavana, Mathura, Puri, and Mayapur. Other important holy places are Dwarka, Ayodhya, Kurukshetra, Naimisaranya, Nasik, Ujjain, Rameswaram, Gaya, Gangotri, Yamunotri, Kedarnath, Badrinatha, Varanasi, and Prayaga. Vrindavana and Mathura are important because Lord Krishna appeared and had His childhood pastimes there. Dwarka is important because Lord Krishna lived there.

The Himalayas are considered a holy mountain range. The Himalayan Range is about 2500 km long and 350 km wide, and there are hundreds of peaks over 20,000 feet high.

Important Temples and Deities

Each region has one or two favorite incarnations of Lord Vishnu or other gods that they especially worship. From Uttar Pradesh to Bihar is Lord Rama, in Western India is Lord Krishna, in Maharashtra and northern Karnataka is Vitthala, in Tamil Nadu is Lord Vishnu, and in Andhra Pradesh is Narasimha.

Each region has one or two important religious shrines. There are the Guruvayur and Padmanabha temples in Kerala; Sri Meenakshi (Madurai) and Srirangam in Tamil Nadu; Chamundeswari and Udupi in Karnataka; Tirupati in Andhra Pradesh; Pandharpur in Maharashtra, Dakor and Dwarka in Gujarat; and Nathdwar and Radha-Govinda (Jaipur) in Rajasthan.

Throughout the provinces of India, the Supreme Lord is worshiped in various forms. At each different temple the Vishnu Deity is given a special name. Vishnu is know by various names. In Tamil Nadu He is worshiped as Varadaraja Perumal in Kanchipuram, Ranganatha Swami in Sri Rangam, and Kallalagar in Madurai. In Andhra Pradesh

He appears as Tirupati Balaji, in Kerala as Guruvayurappan, in Karnataka as the beautiful Udupi Krishna, in Gujarat as Dwarkadhisa and Rancoraji, and in Pandharpur as Sri Vitthala. Often the names of the Deity are in reference to a pastime of Vishnu or Krishna.

Some places have become important pilgrimage spots because of the important temples located in those places such as Tirupati, Trivandrum, Kanchipuram, and Pandharpur, which are all famous because of the Vishnu temples located there. Kedarnath, Bhubaneswara, Madurai and Rameswaram are famous for having important Siva temples.

Worshipers in a temple comes under three main groups: Vaishnavas, or worshipers of Lord Vishnu or Lord Krishna; Shaivites, or worshipers of Lord Siva; and Shaktas, or worshipers of Durga, Kali, or Parvati.

Temples

In India there are many temples dedicated to Lord Vishnu in His various forms, such as Govinda, Madhusudhana, Narasimha, Madhava, Kesava, Narayana, Padmanabha, Parthasarathi, and many others. The Lord expands Himself into innumerable forms, but all of them are non-different from one another.

Lord Vishnu has four hands, and each hand holds a particular item—conch shell, wheel, club, and lotus flower. Of these four emblems, the *cakra,* or wheel, is the chief. Lord Krishna, being the original Vishnu form, has only one emblem, namely the wheel, and therefore He is sometimes called Cakri. The Lord's *cakra* is the symbol of the power by which the Lord controls the whole manifestation. The spires of Vishnu temples are marked with the symbol of the wheel so that people may have the chance to see this symbol from a very long distance and at once remember Krishna.

The purpose of building very high temples is to give people a chance to see them from a distant place. This system is carried on in India whenever a new temple is constructed, and it appears that it is coming down from a time before recorded history.

The Deities can be moving (*dhruvabera*) or unmoving (*cala*). The unmoving ones are usually big and made of stone. The moving images are usually made of metal such as bronze or an alloy of five metals (*pancaloha*). The moving Deity is taken out on festive occasions and is used for bathing, ritualistic worship, etc. A third type of Deity is *cala-acala* (both movable and immovable). This would be the case with Lord Jagannatha in Puri who goes out once a year for a chariot ride (Ratha-yatra).

Temple worship usually consists of bathing the Deity in the morning, offering food stuffs, dressing, *arati*, processions and festivals.

The priests who worship the Lord in the temple are called *pujaris*.

Temple Priests

The worship of deities in the temple is done by the priests (*archaka*) and their assistants (*paricharaka*). These priests must be *Brahmins* to go inside the altar room (in the inner sanctum) to worship and touch the deity.

The priests are mostly born in *Brahmin* families, but a person can also become a *Brahmin* by initiation, although this is not accepted by many orthodox *Brahmins,* who believe that one can only become a *Brahmin* by being born into a *Brahmin* family.

Only the temple priest can enter the inner sanctum. None of the administrative staff, even the person in charge or persons who give large donations, can enter the inner sanctum. Even among the temple priests not all of them can enter the sanctum. Only the head priest and a few assistants can actually touch the deity.

Only the priest can go onto the altar to clean the floor and walls. Also only qualified *Brahmin* priests can cook for the deities.

Temple Worship

In Sri Vaishnava Vishnu temples they mainly follow the mode of worship established by Ramanujacarya called *pancharatra,* which is according to texts such as *Padma samhita, Paramesvara samhita, Sri prasna,* and *Jayakhya samhita.* The more ancient Vaikhanasa mode of worship is also used in some of the South Indian temples.

The fifteen most common forms of worship are: 1) offering a seat (*asana*) for the moveable deity, which represents the main deity, 2) welcome (*svagata*), 3) offering water for the feet (*padya*), 4) water offering (*arghya*), 5) sipping of water (*acamana*), 6) bathing the deity (*snana*), 7) presenting garments and ornaments (*vasana-bhushane*), 8) offering sandal paste, 9) offering flowers, 10) offering incense (*dhupa*), 11) offering lamps (*dipa*), 12) offering food (*naivedya*), 13) offering water to rinse the mouth (*punar achamaniya*), 14) reciting prayers to the Lord, and 15) offering prostrated obeisances (*namaskriya*).

Other forms of worship are cleaning the altar, offering a mirror, offering *arati* or various items to the Lord, offering instrumental music, reciting Vedic hymns, and offering food several times a day to the Lord.

Worship of the Lord begins early in the morning (usually between four or five am) and continues straight through the day (usually to nine or ten pm).

The water that is distributed in the temple is usually the water that is used to bathe the deity in the morning. Bathing the deity is done every morning in an elaborate ritual. Various items such as milk, yogurt, ghee, sugar, honey (these five items are known as *panchamrita*), and water may be used to bath the Deity. Prayers are recited during the bathing.

After the bathing, the Deity is decorated with fresh clothes and ornaments, which may include valuable jewelry. Food is then offered to the Lord and an *arati*, presentation of different items, is performed.

Besides the daily worship, festivals are celebrated to worship the Lord. There may be an annual Rathotsava festival in which the processional deity is brought out of the temple and pulled on a cart around the streets. Many festivals are on fixed dates and cannot be missed for any reason. In South India usually the major festival of the year is called Brahmotsava.

Main Deity's Consort

Usually beside the shrine (altar) of the main temple deity there is a shrine for the deity's consort. In a Krishna temple this could be Radharani or Rukmini, in a Vishnu temple, Laksmi, and in a Siva temple, Parvati. Also in a Krishna temple Radha could be standing right next to Krishna; and on the main altar of a Vishnu temple Laksmi could be at the feet of Lord Vishnu.

Sometimes, as in Tirupati, the consort of the main deity could be in another temple some distance away. The consort of Sri Venkateswara, Sri Padmavathi, is in the town of Tiruchanur, 23 km from the main temple in Tirumala. Also the temple dedicated to Rukmini, the wife of Sri Krishna, is located just outside the town of Dwarka, a few km away from the temple dedicated to Krishna in Dwarka.

Tirtha

A *tirtha* is a sacred place that is holy because a pastime of God took place there, it is a holy river, a temple of God is there, or a holy sage (saint) lived there. The confluence of two holy rivers is especially holy.

It is a general rule to shave your head at a place of pilgrimage. You can especially notice this at Tirupati, where even many of the women have their heads cleanly shaven. One is not supposed to take gifts when he goes to a *tirtha*, rather one is supposed to give religious charity. It is recommended that as far as possible one should go to a *tirtha* by foot. The journey to a pilgrimage place is called a *tirtha-yatra*. When you bath in a holy river it is best to face the direction from which the river flows.

Ganges and Yamuna Rivers

The Yamuna River and the Ganges are considered the most sacred rivers in India. The Yamuna begins at Yamunotri in the Himalayas. The Ganges starts near Gangotri, where it is called the Bhagirathi River. When the Bhagirathi meets the Alakananda River it takes the name Ganges. The Ganges meets the Yamuna and the invisible, or underground, Saraswati at Allahabad (Prayaga).

Several other important rivers meet the Ganges such as the Gandaki, Kosi, Son, and Karnali on its way to the Bay of Bengal. About 450 km before reaching the Bay of Bengal, the Ganges divides into several rivers. The widest river goes into Bangladesh, and another branch heads south through Mayapur and Calcutta before reaching the Bay of Bengal at Ganga-sagara. It is called the Hugli when it passes through Calcutta. The numerous holy places along the Ganges include Gangotri, Haridwar, Kankhal, Prayaga (Allahabad), Varanasi, Mayapur, and Gangasagara.

The *Srimad Bhagavatam* (5.17.1) glorifies the Ganges in the following words: "Sukadeva Gosvami said: My dear King, Lord Vishnu, the enjoyer of all sacrifices, appeared as Vamanadeva in the sacrificial arena of Bali Maharaja. Then He extended His left foot to the end of the universe and pierced a hole in its covering with the nail of His big toe. Through the hole, the pure water of the Causal Ocean entered this universe as the Ganges River. Having washed the lotus feet of the Lord, which are covered with reddish powder, the water of the Ganges acquired a very beautiful pink color. Every living being can immediately purify his mind of material contamination by touching the transcendental water of the Ganges, yet its waters remain ever pure. Because the Ganges directly touches the lotus feet of the Lord before descending within this universe, she is known as Vishnupadi. Later she received other names like Jahnavi and Bhagirathi."

Srila Prabhupada writes in his purport to the above verse: "The water of the Ganges is called *patita-pavani*, the deliverer of all sinful living beings. It is a proven fact that a person who regularly bathes in the Ganges is purified both externally and internally. Externally his body becomes immune to all kinds of disease, and internally he gradually develops a devotional attitude toward the Supreme Personality of Godhead. Throughout India, many thousands of people live on the banks of the Ganges, and by regularly bathing in her waters, they are undoubtedly being purified both spiritually and materially. Many sages, including Sankaracarya, have composed prayers in praise of the Ganges, and the land of India itself has become glorious because such rivers as the Ganges, Yamuna, Godavari, Kaveri, Krishna, and Narmada flow there. Anyone living on the land adjacent to these rivers is naturally advanced in spiritual consciousness."

Water from the Ganges does not get contaminated, even if stored for years. The purity of the Ganges is documented through Mr Henkin's research in the book *The Ganga Trail*. Water was taken from the mouth of a sewer as it emptied into the Ganges and after six hours all the germs were dead. A corpse floating in the Ganga was towed to the shore and the water taken from beside it was found to be swarming with cholera germs, but after six hours all the germs died. When water was taken from a pure well and a few cholera germs were put in the water, within six hours there was a multitude of cholera germs in the water.

"In India there are five sacred rivers, but the Ganges is the most sacred. The River Ganges and *Bhagavad-gita* are chief sources of transcendental happiness for mankind, and intelligent persons can take shelter of them to go back home, back to Godhead. Even Sripada Sankaracarya recommends that a little knowledge in *Bhagavad-gita* and the drinking of a little quantity of Ganges water can save one from the punishment of Yamaraja." *Srimad Bhagavatam* (3.5.41 purport)

And from the purport to *Srimad Bhagavatam* (1.19.6): "Lord Krishna's lotus feet are always besmeared with *tulasi* leaves, and thus as soon as His lotus feet contact the water of the Ganges and the Yamuna, the rivers become at once sanctified. The Lord, however, contacted the River Yamuna more than the Ganges. According to the *Varaha Purana*, as quoted by Srila Jiva Goswami, there is no difference between the water of the Ganges and the Yamuna, but when the water of the Ganges is sanctified one hundred times, it is called the Yamuna."

While taking bath in the Ganges or other holy rivers one should not make the water impure by spitting into or throwing any dirty substance in it. One should not wash clothes on its bank.

Importance of Visiting Holy Places

The *Srimad Bhagavatam* (7.14.30-33) states: "The sacred lakes like Puskara and places where saintly persons live, like Kurukshetra, Gaya, Prayaga, Pulahasrama, Naimisaranya, the banks of the Phalgu River, Setubandhu, Prabhasa, Dwarka, Varanasi, Mathura, Pampa, Bindu-sarovara, Badarikasrama, the places where the Nanda River flows, the places where Lord Ramacandra and mother Sita took shelter, such as Citrakuta, and also the hilly tracts of land known as Mahendra and Malaya—all of these are to be considered most pious and sacred. Similarly, places where Radha-Krishna Deities are worshiped must all be visited and worshiped by those who want to be spiritually advanced. One who intends to advance in spiritual life may visit all these places and perform ritualistic ceremonies to get results a thousand times better than the results of the same activities performed in any other place."

In his purport to *Srimad Bhagavatam* (4.8.42) Srila Prabhupada states: "Places of pilgrimage yield a special advantage for a devotee in quickly advancing his spiritual life. Lord Krishna lives everywhere, but still it is very easy to approach Him in holy places of pilgrimage because these places are inhabited by great sages. Lord Sri Krishna says that He lives wherever His devotees are chanting the glories of His transcendental activities. There are many places of pilgrimage in India, and especially prominent are Badarikasrama, Dwarka, Rameswara, and Jagannatha Puri. These sacred places are called the four *dhamas*. *Dhama* refers to a place where one can immediately contact the Supreme Lord. To go to Badarikasrama one has to pass through Haridwar. Similarly, there are other holy places of pilgrimage, such as Prayaga (Allahabad) and Mathura, and the topmost of them all is Vrindavana. Unless one is very advanced in spiritual life, it is recommended that he live in such holy places and execute devotional service there."

"In the material world the Lord is situated in different *arca-murtis* (Deities) in the temples, just to decrease the material activities of the conditioned soul and increase his spiritual activities. Particularly in India there are many temples throughout the country. Devotees may take advantage of them and go see the Lord at Jagannatha Puri, Vrindavana, Prayaga, Mathura, Haridwar and Vishnu-kanci (Kanchipuram). When the devotees travel to these places and see the Lord, they become very happy in devotional service." (Cc. Madhya.20.219)

"There are four dhamas, or kingdoms of God, which represent the planets of the spiritual sky, which consists of the *brahmajyoti* and the Vaikunthas. These are Badarikasrama, Rameswara, Jagannatha Puri, and Dwarka. Faithful Hindus visit these holy places for perfection of spiritual realization." (purport to *Srimad Bhagavatam* 3.4.22)

Kumbha-mela

Kumbha-mela takes place every 12 years at four different holy places in India. These four places are Prayaga (Allahabad), Haridwar, Nasik, and Ujjain. The Kumbha-mela at Prayaga (Allahabad) is the largest attended event in the world, with about 15 million people. Many different sects of holy men gather for Kumbha-mela. There is a procession on the main bathing days, the order of which is very strictly enforced. There can be a riot over protocol, and people have been killed in the past during these riots. The Naga Babas, who are Siva worshipers, are famous because they walk around naked. They are the first ones to bath on the major bathing days.

The time for Kumbha-mela is judged by the astrological positions of Jupiter and the Sun. In Prayaga (Allahabad) the Kumbha-mela takes places during January-February when Jupiter is in Taurus and the Sun enters Capricorn. Kumbha-mela takes place in Haridwar in April-May when Jupiter is in Aquarius and the Sun is in Aries. In Nasik the Mela is in July-September when Jupiter is in Leo and the Sun is in Leo. In Ujjain it is in May-June when Jupiter is in Scorpio and the Sun is in Aries.

Kumbha-mela lasts for one month while the Sun transits the particular sign of the zodiac. During this month there are certain important bathing days such as the Sankranti (when the Sun enters the next sign), Ekadasi, and Amavasya. The most important bathing day is when the nectar actually falls from the sky. It is considered especially auspicious to bathe at a particular place, at just the correct time.

Six years before each Kumbha-mela is an Ardha Kumbha, which takes places only at Haridwar and Prayaga.

Kumbha-mela Story

The demigods and demons made a truce so they could churn the ocean of milk to get the nectar that would give immortality. The rope that was used was Vasuki, the largest serpent, and the churning rod was Mandara Mountain. As they were churning the milk ocean many things were generated. First poison was produced, and it was drunk by Lord Siva. This is why he has a blue throat.

Eventually Dhanvantari, who is a partial incarnation of Lord Vishnu, appeared carrying a jug containing the nectar.

The demigods (*devas*) entrusted the nectar (*amrita-kalasha*) to Brihaspati, Surya, Chandra, and Shani. The demigods ran away with the *amrita-kalasha* from the demons (*asuras*), because the demons were more powerful than they were. When the asuras learned of the conspiracy, they got extremely angry and chased the four demigods. The chase lasted 12 days (of the demigods, which is a year by our time) during which time the *devas* and *asuras* went around the earth and drops of the nectar fell at Haridwar, Prayaga, Ujjain, and Nasik.

Another way the story is told is that the demons snatched the jug of nectar from Dhanvantari and began to fight amongst themselves. During this fight some nectar fell at these four places. Kumbha-mela is held at each of these four places every 12 years.

Shalagram-shilas

Shalagram-shilas are self-manifested Deities of Lord Vishnu or Krishna appearing as stones. They are forms of Lord Krishna that require no installation ceremony. *Shalagram-shilas* are considered always nondifferent from Krishna Himself. Sri Caitanya told Gopal Bhatta Goswami to go to the Gandhaki River from Vrindavana to find Sri Hari in the form of *shalagram-shilas*. The *Padma Purana* says: "Lord Vishnu may be worshiped in the form of a Deity made of eight kinds of material: stone, wood, metal, mud, written word, earth, jewels, and words within the mind. But you should know that the worship of *shalagram-shila* is worship of Sri Krishna Himself, since the Lord exists eternally in the *shalagram-shila*."

In the *Bhavisya Purana*, Lord Krishna says to His devotee, Tulasi: "In the form of small stones, I live always on the banks of the Gandhaki River. The millions of worms who live in that place adorn those stones with the sign of My *cakra*, by carving Them with their small teeth."

According to the their markings, or *cakras*, one can identify the *shalagrams* as one of the many incarnations of the Lord, such as Narasimha, Matsya, Kurma, Varaha, etc.

The Vedas

According to the *Bhavisya Purana*, the *Vedas* includes the original four *Vedas*—*Rig*, *Atharva*, *Yajur*, and *Sama*—the *Upanisads*, the *Mahabharata* (which includes the *Bhagavad-gita)*, the *Pancaratna*, the *Ramayana*, and the *Puranas*. Many scholars say that only the original four *Vedas*: *Rig*, *Atharva*, *Yajur*, and *Sama* are real Vedic literatures. This is neither accepted by the *Vedas* themselves nor by the important Vedic teachers such as Sankara, Ramanuja, or Madhvacarya. The *Chandogya Upanisad* says that the *Puranas* and *Itihasas* are the fifth *Veda*.

The main criterion for a literature to be accepted as Vedic is that it must have the same purport as the original Vedic scriptures. Any work that expands on the Vedic conclusion without change of meaning may be accepted as a Vedic writing.

The Vedic scriptures are huge. The *Mahabharata* has 110,000 couplets, the *Rig Veda* contains 1,017 hymns, and the 18 main *Puranas* contain hundreds of thousands of verses.

The Vedic literature gives knowledge of self-realization and liberation (*moksa*) from material bondage and suffering. They teach that the material body is temporary and that one should not resign himself to this temporary and miserable world, but try to get permanent happiness. This is done by serving the Supreme Personality of Godhead, who is known in the *Vedas* as Krishna or Vishnu.

The *Vedas* are considered eternal. They do not come from any materially conditioned person, but from the Supreme. They cannot be understood by logic or experimentation, as they are inconceivable. They must be understood by hearing from an authoritative source.

The *Puranas* establish the meaning of the *Vedas*, as they are the natural commentaries on the *Vedas*. The highest *Purana* is the *Srimad Bhagavatam*. This is the history of various incarnations of Lord Vishnu and His devotees. It also gives the history of Lord Krishna.

Guru Parampara

Technically guru means "heavy", and the guru should be heavy with knowledge. He has to come in a bona fide disciplic succession and have complete knowledge of the Absolute Truth. The faithful student of the guru becomes the next guru, and his relationship is not therefore just with his guru or teacher, but also with his spiritual master's spiritual master and so on down the line in an unbroken chain of masters. This chain of disciplic succession is called *sampradaya*

or *parampara*.

The disciple must completely surrender himself and be the humble servant of the guru. He has to make the instructions of his guru his life's mission. The most important attributes of a disciple, or servant of the guru, are faith, service, and submissive inquiry. The disciple should not just serve the spiritual master blindly, but must also inquire from the spiritual master about the ultimate solution to the problems of life and about the Absolute Truth.

The secrets about the goal of life given by the bona fide guru are open to everyone regardless of caste, creed, or nationality, but they remain secrets unless one has sincerity and an honest desire to know the goal of life. To understand the goal of life the follower must follow regulations of purification given by the guru.

Karma

This is the scientific law of cause and effect. Whatever someone does will come back at a later date, if not in this lifetime, then in the next or future births. From time immemorial, the individual soul has been acting in the material world and enjoying or suffering the reactions. His actions bring about his transmigration from one material body to another. Both pious and impious actions bind a person to the wheel of transmigration, because both cause a reaction. Each person creates his own karma out of his particular desires to enjoy this world in different ways. Neither God nor other persons are responsible for the karma of a person; one makes his own destiny.

The goal of life is to be free from karma. A person cannot be free from karma by just refraining from work. One must engage in transcendental activities. This is done by serving the Supreme Personality of Godhead, who then intervenes and frees one from previous karmic reactions.

Reincarnation

This is the science of repeated birth and death. The logic is that the soul is eternal and the body is temporary. So when a person dies only his body dies, and his soul takes another body according to his karma. As a result of karma, a person may take birth in a family of wealthy merchants or in a family of insects. The *Padma Purana* says there are 8,400,000 species of life, and that the fallen soul has to undergo birth in every one of them. The Vedic conclusion does not agreed with Darwin's Theory of Evolution. According to the *Vedas*, all species were created at the same time and did not evolve over a period of time. Rather, the soul evolves through all of them, until he reaches the human form of life when there is a chance to cultivate self-realization and become liberated.

Mahabharata

The *Mahabharata* is about the five sons of Maharaja Pandu—Yudhisthira, Bhima, Arjuna, Nakula and Sahadeva, and the Battle of Kurukshetra. There were two brothers—Pandu and Dhritarastra—who were the heirs to the throne of India. Dhritarastra, the oldest brother, was blind and therefore could not rule. Therefore his younger brother, Pandu, became the king. When Maharaja Pandu died, Duryodhana, the oldest of the one hundred sons of Dhritarastra, did not like the fact that the sons of Pandu were the heir to the throne. Duryodhana felt this way because his father was the elder brother, and if his father had not been blind he would have been the normal heir to the throne.

The five Pandavas, sons of Pandu, were eventually forced into exile because of court intrigues. During this time the five Pandava brothers married Draupadi and many of the adventures took place which led to their names being attached to many temples and places around India.

After a period of time the Pandavas came back and asked that the kingdom be divided. Duryodhana did not want to do this, but the court ministers convinced Dhritarastra to split the kingdom evenly between the two parties. The Kauravas, sons of Dhritarastra, got Hastinapur as their capital, and the Pandavas got Indraprastha, which is now greater Delhi.

Over a period of time there were petty quarrels that finally culminated in a dice game in which the Pandavas lost their entire kingdom, including their wife Draupadi. The Kauravas attempted to strip Draupadi in public, but she was protected by Krishna. The Pandavas then had to go into exile for 12 years.

After the exile was over, the Pandavas came back and demanded just five small towns to rule, but they were refused. This led to the battle of Kurukshetra, where the *Bhagavad-gita* was spoken. The battle lasted for 18 days and millions of soldiers were killed. Most of the Kauravas were killed in this battle. With the help of Lord Krishna, the Pandavas won and got back their kingdom .

Ramayana

This is the story of Lord Rama, the seventh incarnation of Lord Vishnu. Rama's father, King Dasaratha, decided to retire as the King of Ayodhya and to crown Rama, his eldest son, as king. King Dasaratha had four sons Rama, Laksmana, Bharata and Shatrughna from three different wives. On the eve of the coronation, Kaikeyi, the youngest wife of Dasaratha, was manipulated by her servant and given bad advice. Accordingly, she asked her husband to crown her son Bharata as king and exile Rama to the forest for 14 years. Dasaratha was unwillingly obliged to comply, as he had previously promised Kaikeyi to fulfill any desire that she wanted.

In this way, Rama, along with His devoted wife, Sita, and brother Laksmana, went in exile to the forest. When Bharata, who was away at the time, returned to Ayodhya, he did not want to be king out of affection for Rama. He followed Rama to the forest to beg Him to come back and rule the kingdom. Rama refused, however, in order to maintain His father's promise.

While in the forest, Ravana, the king of Lanka, kidnapped Sita and brought her to his kingdom. Rama and Laksmana then went out to search for Sita. During this time They met Sugriva, the king of the monkeys, and Hanuman, his minister. The devoted Hanuman eventually found Sita in Lanka. Rama and Laksmana along with Their allies, the monkey army, attacked Lanka. After much fighting, the ten-headed Ravana was killed and Sita was saved. Rama then returned to Ayodhya and became the king there.

Bhagavad-gita

In the *Gita*, Arjuna accepts Krishna as his spiritual master, while they are on the battlefield of Kurukshetra. Their discussion takes place just before the huge battle. Seeing his friends and relatives on the other side, Arjuna suddenly loses his desire to fight and becomes confused about his duty. At this time Bhagavan Sri Krishna begins His great instructions, which are the conclusion of Vedic knowledge.

The *Gita* is like the Indian Bible. Its first instruction is you are not your body, but an eternal spirit soul temporarily encaged within a material body. It concludes that the perfection of life is to totally surrender to God and act according to His desire.

His Divine Grace A.C. Bhaktivedanta Swami Prabhupada writes that the *Gita* is "the essence of Vedic knowledge. Because *Bhagavad-gita* is spoken by the Supreme Personality of Godhead, one need not read any other Vedic literature." If one reads the *Gita* without motivated interpretation, he surpasses all studies of Vedic wisdom and all scriptures. *Bhagavad-gita* is highly recommended reading for one who wants to have an understanding of the essence of Vedic teachings.

Hindu

The words "Hindu" and "Hinduism" are not mentioned in the Vedic literature. These words have never been used in any scripture or by any *acarya,* or spiritual teacher. To indicate Vedic society, the scriptures use the word *"Aryan"* or *"sanatana-dharma"*.

The Sindhu River divides what was at one time the Middle East and India. Because of problems with pronouncing the initial "S", the river was called "Hindu," so the people who lived on the other side of the Sindhu River, in India, were called Hindus.

Now the word Hindu is used to describe worshipers of Vishnu or Krishna, Siva, or Durga, etc.

Jainism

The word Jain comes from *jina,* the conqueror. Jains are followers of the Conqueror, the first teacher Adinatha. There is a line of twenty-four great teachers, which are called *tirthankaras*, or "Finders of the Path". Mahavira (the great hero) was the 24th teacher. He died in 526 BC, so this religion is very old. Jain temples are dedicated to one of the *tirthankaras*. The Jain religion has about 4 million followers.

Jains believe in *ahimsa* (nonviolence). Orthodox Jains are strict vegetarians and do not eat onions or garlic. They are not supposed to farm so they can avoid killing insects and small animals.

Jains do not believe in the *Vedas*. They believe in reincarnation, that the universe is infinite and that one can eventually attain *moksa*, liberation, by following the path of the *tirthankaras*. They do worship Lakshmi and Ganesha. But the *tirthankaras* are the supreme object of worship.

Jains are pious. They cannot lie, they must avoid useless actions, talk, or thoughts, and they must eat only pure food. Mahavira taught one's state of consciousness was directly influenced by the food he eats. Jains must also give charity, either in the form of knowledge or money.

Buddhism

Lord Buddha is one of the ten major incarnations of Lord Vishnu. So he is worshiped both by the Buddhists and Hindus. Buddhism is practiced in many countries all over Southeast Asia, but it was first established in India.

Buddhism was a major religion in India 2000 years ago, but declined until according to a 1951 census there were only 181,000 Buddhists in India. The present number in India is approximately 5 million.

Siddhartha Gautama, who was later called the Buddha, appeared around 563 BC (the Mahabodhi Society accepts 624 BC) in a warrior caste. He got married when he was 16, and he had one son. He left home when he was twenty-nine in search of the answer to life. After about six years he went to Bodh Gaya and sat under the Bodhi tree. While meditating he was tempted by the demon Mara, who offered him all the desires of the world. Not taking these temptations, he received enlightenment. You can see these scenes in many of the Buddhist carvings around India.

There are four important places connected with the Buddha's life—**Lumbini** in Nepal, where he was born; **Bodh Gaya** in Bihar, where he received enlightenment; **Sarnath** near Varanasi, where he preached his first major sermon; and **Kushinagar** in UP, where he left his body. When the Buddha left his body, his body was cremated and the ashes were given to people to whom he had preached. Some of these ashes were buried under Stupas throughout India.

At **Rajgir**, Buddha converted King Bimbisara to Buddhism and the First Buddhist Council was held there. At **Vaishali**, Buddha preached his last sermon and announced his approaching *nirvana*. At **Nalanda** there is the remains of an ancient Buddhist University. These three places are all in Bihar near Patna. Other places in India are famous Buddhist places because of monuments, temples, or cave temples built there. The finest of these are at Ajanta and Ellora in Maharashtra, Sanchi in Madhya Pradesh and Amaravati in Andhra Pradesh.

Buddha preached Four Noble Truths: (1) life is painful because nothing in this material world is permanent or reliable; (2) this suffering is caused by desire, attachment, and ignorance; (3) there is a state beyond this suffering which is called *nirvana*; and (4) this state of *nirvana* is reached by the eight-fold path, which is: right understanding, thought, speech, action, livelihood, effort, mindfulness, and concentration. Buddha also believed in karma. He rejected the teachings of the Vedic scriptures and the Vedic gods. He did this because when he appeared, people were using the *Vedas* to slaughter animals and eat them in the name of performing sacrifices. So even though followers of the *Vedas* accept Buddha as an incarnation of Lord Vishnu, they reject his philosophy.

Buddhism spread over a good part of India during the time of Emperor Ashoka (272-232 BC), after he became a Buddhist. He sent people all over South Asia to preach the doctrines of Buddhism and spread it all over this area. From the 7th to 12th centuries AD Buddhism started to decline in India due to the influential preaching of Sankaracarya, Ramanujacarya, and Madhvacarya, who gradually reintroduced the Vedic conclusion. As a final blow to Buddhism, the Muslims carried out large scale slaughters of monks and destroyed their monasteries and places of worship.

108 Divya Desams & the Alwars

The Alwars were twelve Vaishnava saints (devotees of Lord Vishnu) in Tamil Nadu. There are 108 important temples glorified by hymns composed by the Alwars. If an Alwar praised a temple or Deity of Vishnu, it could be a single verse or even part of a verse, then that temple and Deity is regarded in a class apart from the rest. All these temples are considered special. Different Alwars have visited these temples and sung the glories of the presiding Deities. Alagia Manavala Dasa (also known as Divya Kavi Pillai), who was a devotee of Lord Vishnu and a Tamil poet, has compiled a list of 108 Divya

Desams in his *108 Tirupati – Anthaadi*. This has been accepted as an authentic list ever since.

The Divya Desam temples can be grouped broadly into six geographical locations—Thondai Nadu, which is in the Madras and Chengalput area; Chola Nadu (Chozha Naattu); Nadu Naattu; Pandya Nadu; Vada Nadu; and Paraloka. Many times it is possible to visit several Divya Desam temples in one day. In the area of Kanchipuram there are 14 different Divya Desam temples, which can be visited in a day or two.

The 12 Alwars are Kulasekhara Alwar, Pey Alwar, Tirumalisai Alwar, Thirumangai Alwar, Tondaradippadi Alwar, Bhutatt Alwar, Poygai Alwar, Nammalwar, Periy Alwar, Andal, Tiruppan Alwar, and Madhurakavi. Four of the Alwars were born within 80 km of Kanchipuram.

Siva Lingas & Jyotirlingas

A Siva-linga is usually made of stone and has three parts. The base is square with an oval or octagonal platform with a cylindrical, round topped stone on top. It is common to have a temple of Siva without a form of Siva and just a Siva-linga. The *linga* may either be carved or natural. The natural *lingas* are usually gotten from a riverbed, usually the Krishna River. A Siva-linga is bathed, given flower garlands, covered with milk, and offered food as part of its worship.

Lord Siva is worshiped as five element *lingas* at five different major temples in South India. These are the 1) sky or space (ether), Akash-linga, in Chidambaram, Tamil Nadu; 2) water, Appu-linga at the Jambukeswaram temple near Tiruchirappalli (Trichy), Tamil Nadu; 3) fire, Agni-linga in the Arunachaleswar Temple, in Tiruvannamalai, Tamil Nadu; 4) earth, Prithvi-linga in Kanchipuram, Tamil Nadu, or some people say Gokarna, Karnataka; and 5) air, Vayu-linga, in Sri Kalahasti, Andhra Pradesh.

There are also twelve Siva *jyotirlingas*, which are symbols of creation and power. They are said to be self-manifested. Temples where they are installed are considered very important Siva temples.

Siva Jyotirlingas

(1) Sri Somnatha in Saurastra, Gujarat

(2) Sri Mallikarjuna on Srisailam Hill in the Kurnool district, Andhra Pradesh

(3) Sri Mahakaleswara in Ujjain, Madhya Pradesh

(4) Sri Omkareswara on the bank of the Narmada River, Madhya Pradesh

(5) Sri Vaidyanatha in Chitabhumi (Deoghar), near Patna, Bihar

(6) Sri Nageswara near Dwarka, Gujarat

(7) Sri Viswanatha in Varanasi, Uttar Pradesh

(8) Sri Bhima Sankara in Mahabaleswara, Maharastra

(9) Sri Rameswara in Rameswaram, Tamil Nadu

(10) Sri Trimbakeswara near Nasik, Maharashtra

(11) Sri Kedarnatha in the Himalayas, Uttar Pradesh

(12) Sri Ghrisneswara in Sivalaya near the Ellora Caves, Maharashtra

Varnasrama Dharma

According to the Vedas, the system of *varnasrama-dharma* has been existing since time immemorial. There are four *varnas* (social orders): *Brahmins*, or teachers and spiritual advisors; *ksatriyas*, or administrators and warriors; *vaisyas*, or farmers and businessmen; *sudras*, or laborers and craftsmen. These *varnas* are not political or social factions; they are natural categories to be found in every human civilization.

The present system generally practiced in India is a corrupt form. People claim to be *Brahmins* and *ksatriyas* by birth alone, even though they may not personally possess the qualities of *Brahmins* or *ksatriyas*. A person should be accepted as belonging to a particular caste by his activities, not by birth. At the present time there is virtually no pure system of *varnasrama-dharma*.

There are also four spiritual orders of life: *brahmacarya*, or celibate student life; *grihasta* life, or married life; *vanaprastha*, or retired life; and *sannyasa*, or the renounced order of life. The *brahmacari* is trained to control his senses by austerity and service to the guru. In the *grihasta*, or married life, there is some license for sense pleasure, but everything is regulated so that one can fulfill his desires and yet become spiritually purified. After going through married life one is supposed to give up family life and engage full time in spiritual life. First one enters the *vanaprastha* life in which the husband and wife discontinue sexual relations, but the wife may remain with the husband as his assistant. Ideally, they travel together to holy places of pilgrimage such as Puri, Haridwar, Rishikesh, and Vrindavana. Finally, the man breaks all family connections and takes up *sannyasa*, the renounced order, to fully dedicate himself to the cultivation of spiritual life.

Vaishnava Philosophy

Vaishnava philosophy accepts that there is only one God. He takes many names and forms in different religions. Christians may call him Jehovah, Muslims–Allah, or the Hindus–Vishnu or

Krishna. Krishna is the Supreme Personality of Godhead and all other gods and living entities are His servants. This is the essential difference between material life and spiritual life; spiritual life means that God is the object of our service, and material life means our service is devoid of relationship with God.

A common misconception is that Krishna is an incarnation of Vishnu. But in actuality Krishna is Supreme. Even though Lord Vishnu is nondifferent in one sense, still He is an expansion of Krishna. The analogy is that when one candle lights another, they are both the same, but one was the origin of the other. Vishnu is the administrative form of Lord Krishna, who is always engaged in enjoying with His devotees.

A major misconception is the belief that God is ultimately formless. But if one accepts that God is all-powerful, then why can He not be a person? Rather, it is everywhere seen that behind all energy is a person. A common idea is that Lord Siva is supreme, but even Lord Siva, who is very powerful, is the servant of Lord Vishnu, or Krishna.

Krishna

Krishna is the Supreme Personality of Godhead. He is the son of Vasudeva and Devaki. He is the source of Lord Vishnu, who is the source of all other incarnations of God. Krishna is unborn and eternal as confirmed in the *Bhagavad-gita* and other Vedic literatures.

His complexion is blackish, like the color of a new rain cloud. He stands in a three-fold bending form, dancing and playing on His flute. On the altar many times He will be with His consort, Radha. In paintings, He will be seen dancing with the cowherd girls (*gopis*), playing with the cowherd boys, or as Arjuna's chari-

oteer on the battlefield of Kurukshetra.

He appeared in Mathura in Uttar Pradesh about 5000 years ago.

He killed the evil king Kamsa and many other demons to protect His devotees. He is the speaker of the *Bhagavadgita*, which is considered like the Bible of Indian philosophy.

Vishnu

Lord Vishnu is the Supreme Personality of Godhead. He is the maintainer of the material creation. Another name for Him is Narayana. As Garbodakasayi Vishnu, Brahma appears from His navel and creates the universe. His consort is Lakshmi. His other consort is Bhudevi, who carries a lotus flower. If both consorts are with Lord Vishnu, Lakshmi is on the His right and Bhudevi on His left.

He usually has four hands which hold a conch shell, or *sankha*; a disc, or *chakra*; a club, or *gada*; and a lotus flower, or *padma*. He is carried by Garuda, who is half bird and half man. Garuda is seen in many Vishnu temples kneeling reverently in front of the temple.

Lord Vishnu is often seen reclining on a bed made of the coils of the serpent Ananta Sesa with Lakshmi and Bhudevi at His feet. There are unlimited incarnations of Lord Vishnu, but ten major incarnations.

INCARNATIONS OF VISHNU

Vishnu has ten major incarnations. They are Matsya, the fish; Kurma the tortoise; Varaha, the boar, who killed Hiranyaksa and saved the earth; and Narasimha, who was half-man and half-lion. Narasimha killed the demon Hiranyakasipu and saved His pure devotee Prahlada. The fifth incarnation was Vamana who begged three paces of land from Bali Maharaja, the king of the demons, to reclaim the world for the demi-gods.

Next was Parasurama, who although born a *Brahmin,* killed the *ksatriyas* (warrior caste) 21 times. Rama was the seventh incarnation. He saved His wife from Ravana, the king of Lanka. The famous *Ramayana* narrates his activities. Balarama was the eighth incarnation, and Lord Buddha the ninth. The tenth incarnation is Kalki, who kills the demoniac population at the end of Kali-yuga.

Besides the major incarnations there are innumerable other ones. The Lord manifests in many species of life for the maintenance of the faithful and the annihilation of the unfaithful.

Matsya

He is the fish incarnation. When Lord Brahma sleeps during the night, annihilation takes place and the three worlds are covered by the water of the ocean. At the end of the past millennium (the end of Brahma's day) as Brahma felt sleepy and desired to lie down, the *Vedas* were emanating from his mouth and the great demon named Hayagriva stole the Vedic knowledge. Understanding this, Lord Vishnu then assumed the form of a fish and saved the *Vedas* by killing the demon.

When the entire world was covered with water, the Lord again took the form of a fish and saved Satyavrata, keeping him on a boat which was attached to the fish's horn, to save him and the rishis, herbs, seeds, and other living entities.

Kurma

Kurma is Lord Vishnu in the form of a tortoise. His shell served as a pivot for Mandarachala Hill, which was used as a churning rod by the demigods and demons. The demons and demigods were producing nectar from the sea by churning it with Mandarachala Hill. This is the same nectar that drops during Kumbha-mela which is said to give eternal life. To churn the ocean, the gods needed a churning stick. They used a mountain. In the form of a tortoise, Lord Vishnu became the support for this mountain.

Varaha

Lord Varaha appeared as a giant boar to save the earth planet and to kill the demon Hiranyaksa, who was terrifying the universe. Varaha is often seen as a half-man with the face of a boar engaged in picking up the earth.

Vamana

Lord Vishnu appeared as Vamana, a dwarf-*Brahmin,* and went to the sacrifice that Bali Maharaja, the grandson of Prahlada Maharaja, was performing. He begged three steps of land from Maharaja Bali. As it is the duty of a king to give charity to the *Brahmins,* Maharaja Bali replied, "Why take so little? I can give you much more than that."

Lord Vamana replied "O my dear King, even the entirety of whatever there may be within the three worlds to satisfy one's senses cannot satisfy a person whose senses are uncontrolled. One should be satisfied with whatever he achieves by his previous destiny, for discontent can never bring happiness. A person who is not self-controlled will not be happy even with possessing the three worlds."

Vamana then expanded His body to take up the earth and all the heavens in His first two steps. There was nothing left for Bali Maharaja to give for the third step, so he offered his head. After taking everything from him, Lord Vamana then made Bali the king of the underworld.

Vamana holds a water-pot in one hand and an umbrella in the other. He wears either a loincloth or deer-skin. He is also called Trivikrama. *Tri* means three, and *vikrama* means victory. Lord Vishnu, as Vamana, is seen stretching His leg to take a step.

Parasurama

He is seen in a human form holding a battle axe in one hand. Sometimes he is seen with four hands carrying a sword, axe, bow, and arrows. Parasurama was born as a *Brahmin*, but he acted like a *ksatriya*. There are just a few temples dedicated to Parasurama in India.

One time the powerful *ksatriya* king Kartaviryarjuna stole Parasurama's father's Kamadhenu cow. Parasurama then killed the king to get the cow back. After killing the king, Parasurama's father, Jamadagni, told him that killing a king is sinful and that as a *Brahmin* he should have tolerated the offence. Jamadagni advised Parasurama to atone for his sin by traveling to various holy places.

While Parasurama was traveling, the king's sons killed Jamadagni to revenge. Parasurama then killed the *ksatriya* race twenty-one times to avenge the killing of his father.

Lord Rama

He is also known as Raghunath and Ramacandra. He is the hero in the famous story, the *Ramayana*. Rama is the husband of Sita. The Lord appeared in His full quadruple expansions as the four brothers: Rama, Laksmana, Bharata, and Satrughna. He appeared in Ayodhya as the son of King Dasaratha.

If you see Lord Rama on an altar, many times He will be with His consort, Sita, His brother Laksmana, and His monkey servant Hanuman.

His father, Maharaja Dasaratha, had three wives. From these three wives Maharaja Dasaratha had four sons. One of his wives, Kaikeyi, served Dasaratha very nicely and received a benediction from him. She said she would ask for the benediction at another time. At the time of the coronation of Ramacandra, Kaikeyi asked her husband to enthrone her son Bharata and send Ramacandra to the forest for 14 years. Maharaja Dasaratha ordered Ramacandra to go to the forest. Rama left everything without hesitation, just as a liberated soul or great yogi gives up his life without material attraction.

He went to the forest with Laksmana and Sita. When Marica assumed the form of a golden dear, Lord Ramacandra wanted to capture the deer to please Sita. While He was trying to capture the deer, the ten-headed demon Ravana kidnapped Sita. As Rama and Laksmana were searching through the forest for Sita, They met the bird Jatayu who had tried to stop Ravana from kidnapping Sita. Rama then killed the monkey Vali and made friendship with Sugriva, the monkey king.

The monkeys were sent out to find Sita. Hanuman, the eternal servant of the Lord, was able to find Sita at Ravana's capital, Lanka. Hanuman jumped across the sea, but when Lord Ramacandra came with the monkey army they made a bridge with rocks that floated on the water so they could get to Lanka from the coast of India. This happened at Rameswaram.

With the help of Laksmana and the monkey army, Rama was able to kill all of Ravana's army. He then personally killed Ravana. Lord Rama then crowned Vibhisana, Ravana's brother, the king of Lanka, as Vibhisana had surrendered to Rama and helped defeat Ravana. Rama then returned to His kingdom in Ayodhya and was enthroned as king.

Narasimha

Lord Vishnu appears in this form as a half-man, with a lion's head to kill the king of the demons, Hiranyakasipu. Lord Narasimha tore apart the body of the great demon Hiranyakasipu, the older brother of Hiranyaksa.

Hiranyakasipu became very powerful. After doing extreme austerities, he received a benediction from Lord Brahma. He asked to be immortal, but Brahma told him that was not possible, for he himself was not immortal. So Hiranyakasipu got the benediction that he would not be killed by any man, beast or demigod or any kind of weapon or by hands. He would not die in the air, water, or on the ground, nor be killed either inside or outside and would not die either during the day or during the night.

The Lord assumed the incarnation of a half-man, half-lion and killed Hiranyakasipu. He killed him on His lap, so that he was not killed either on the land nor on the water nor in the sky. The demon was torn apart by Narasimha's nails, which were not a weapon nor hands. He was killed at dusk, which was neither day nor night. He was killed in the doorway of the assembly hall, which was neither inside nor outside a building.

Prahlada Maharaja was the son of Hiranyakasipu, and because the boy was a great devotee of Lord Vishnu, his father tortured him. To save His devotee Prahlada Maharaja, Lord Narasimha appeared to killed Hiranyakasipu.

Lord Buddha

He appeared in Lumbini, which is now in Nepal, preached his own conception of nonviolence, and deprecated the animal sacrifices sanctioned in the *Vedas*. During the time when Lord Buddha appeared, animal killing was done unrestrictedly on the plea of Vedic sacrifice. Lord Buddha preached nonviolence. He preached that he did not believe in the tenets of the *Vedas* and stressed the adverse psychological effects of animal killing.

Technically Lord Buddha's philosophy is called atheistic because there is no acceptance of the Supreme Lord and he denied the authority of the *Vedas*. But that is an act of camouflage by the Lord, because he is an incarnation of the Lord. He rejected the *Vedas* outwardly because people were supporting cow-killing and animal-killing from the pages of the *Vedas*. Lord Buddha preached the preliminary principles of the *Vedas* in a manner suitable for the time.

Kalki

At the end of Kali-yuga, Kalki appears. He rides a white horse and carries a flaming sword with which he kills the demoniac populace of the world who have degraded to atheism.

VEDIC PERSONALITIES

Balarama

He is the older brother of Krishna. He is white and has two hands and sometime carries a plough or club and sometimes both. He is often seen in pictures with Krishna and with the cowherd boys. He usually wears a blue *dhoti*.

Lakshmi

She is the consort of Lord Vishnu and the goddess of wealth and good fortune. She may be at the feet of Lord Vishnu or standing next to Him. She usually has two arms, but sometimes she has four. She sits or stands on a lotus and often holds a lotus flower. When she has four arms, she often holds lotuses in her two upper hands. Gold coins may be seen dropping from her lower two hands, or they may be in a boon-giving position. She is normally a bright golden color.

There are no temples dedicated exclusively to just her, but she is worshiped in most homes. Many times she is worshiped alone in someone's home to attain wealth. People do not know that Lakshmi is flickering and unless she is worshiped with her consort, Lord Vishnu, her mercy will be only temporary.

Radharani

She is also known as Radha. She is the most important of the *gopis* of Vrindavana. She is the main consort of Krishna and is often seen standing with Lord Krishna on the altar in temples.

Garuda

He is the half-bird half-man (half eagle) carrier of Lord Vishnu. Many times he is seen kneeling outside a Lord Vishnu temple.

Siva

He is the destroyer in the Hindu trilogy. He may hold a trident, as do many of his followers. He may also hold a mace or battle-axe, or an hour-glass drum called a *damru*.

He has three eyes. The third one, which is between the eyebrows, is normally closed. He has a crescent moon in his matted hair, and his body is smeared with ashes. He wears a cobra around his neck. He has fair colored skin. Lord Siva has a blue throat, because he drank poison when the ocean was churned by the demigods and demons. His carrier is Nandi, the bull, who is seen in many of his temples. Usually there is a trident on top of a Siva temple.

He is worshiped as a Siva-linga, or phallus, in most temples. He resides at Mt Kailash, which is located in the Himalayas in Tibet.

He is known as Nataraja, the cosmic dancer. He has other names, such as Rudra, Mahadeva, Sankara, Pashupati (the lord of the beasts), and Bhairava, which is his terrible form. Siva is also known as Gangadhara, or one who bears the weight of the Ganges River as it falls down to earth. Hari Hara is a form that is half Vishnu and half Siva.

His consort is Parvati, who is also known as Kali or Durga. Parvati is Lord Siva's wife and the mother of his sons Karttikeya (Subrahmanya) and Ganesh. Parvati lives with Siva on Mount Kailash. Her carrier is a lion.

Durga

She is also known as Kali, Parvati, or Uma. As Durga, she is in her punishing or threatening mode. This is the darker form of Siva's consort. Her carrier may be a tiger or a lion. She may be carrying weapons to destroy the demons.

Kali is a very fierce form of Lord Siva's consort. She may ride a tiger, breathe fire, and wear a garland of skulls and snakes. She is black. She may have four or eight arms holding knives and severed heads. With her other hands she makes a gesture of "Fear not," and she grants boons.

In this form she is also called Bhadrakali or Mahakali. Kali represents the ingredients of matter which are counted as twenty-three: the total material energy, false ego, sound, touch, form, taste, smell, earth, water, fire, air, ether, eye, ear, skin, evacuating organ, speech, mind, etc. All these are combined together by the influence of time and are again dissolved in the course of time.

She is also called Mahishasura-mardini, because she killed the buffalo demon. In the form of Chamunda she has a terrifying look and wears a garland of skulls. Snakes and scorpions adorn her body. Chamunda was created to kill the demons Chanda and Munda.

Brahma

He is the god of creation, and he sits on a lotus sprouted from Lord Vishnu's navel. He is one of the three main Hindu gods, which include Lord Vishnu and Lord Siva. He has four heads and is the father of Lord Siva. He holds a spoon, a pot of holy water, beads (*mala*), and a part of the *Vedas.* He may also hold a bow, lotus, or sceptre. Sometimes two of his hands are in a protective and boon-giving attitude.

There are few Brahma temples in India. The one at Pushkar in Rajasthan is the main one. He rides on a swan or sits in a lotus position in a chariot pulled by seven swans. His consort is Saraswati, but in Pushkar Gayatri is also worshiped as his consort. His consort Saraswati is supposed to have cursed him at Pushkar, and you can read the story in the section about Pushkar.

One day of Brahma is a thousand cycles of the four *yugas*, which equals 4.32 billion years. His night is the same time. In this way he lives for 100 years.

Saraswati

She is the goddess of learning and the consort of Lord Brahma. She holds a lotus and vina. She sits on a peacock or a lotus flower. She holds different objects: a book, beads (*mala*), an elephant hook, and a vina. She is the deity for scholars, students, and artists.

Ganesh

He is the god of prosperity and wisdom. Ganesh has an elephant head. Siva and Parvati are his parents. It is said that he received the elephant head from his father, Lord Siva. When Lord Siva came back from a long trip, he found his wife Parvati with another man. Not realizing that his son could have grown up since he was gone, he cut his head off. Parvati made Siva bring her son back to life, but Siva had to give him the head of the first living being he saw, which was an elephant. Another story says that he was guarding the door of his mother, Parvati. When Lord Siva returned from being away he wanted to enter, but was stopped by Ganesh. Lord Siva then cut his head off.

He is the eldest of Lord Siva's two sons. He is worshiped to remove all obstacles in an endeavor. He is seen on the altar in many businesses and at the entrances of temples. In South India he is known as Vinayaka.

He aided Vyasadeva in writing the *Mahabharata*. He is also called Ganapati, or Lord of the *ganas*, or head of the army of demigods. He is called Ekadanta because he has one broken tusk. His trunk usually turns toward the left. He wears a snake around his waist like a belt or across his chest. His carrier is a rat.

He has four to ten arms. He holds in his hands an axe, a goad, a rope, a dish of sweet-balls, etc. His fourth hand is in the boon giving position.

Kartikkeya

He is the god of war and the younger son of Siva and Parvati. He is also known as Subrahmanya, Kumar, Murugan, and Skanda. He has six heads and rides a peacock. In South India he is usually worshiped as Subrahmanya, the pious and sacred one. In his hands he carries a conch shell, sword, bow, arrows, spear, noose, shield, and a discus. He may have one hand in a protective pose and the other in a charitable pose.

Hanuman

He is a monkey and Lord Rama's eternal servant in the *Ramayana*. He helped Rama defeat Ravana and save Sita. He jumped from the mainland of India to Lanka to discover Sita there. Hanuman was captured, but he escaped and set Lanka on fire.

He flew to the Himalayas to collect medicinal herbs to help the wounded Laksmana, brother of Lord Rama. He has many temples of his own and is also worshiped along with Sita and Rama. He is often painted bright orange.

Demigods (Universe Administers)

Indra

He is the chief of the administrative demigods and the king of the heavenly planets. He rides a white elephant. He holds a thunderbolt (*vajra*) in one hand, as he is the lord of thunder and lighting. He may have two or four arms. He may be shown with eyes all over his body.

Surya

He is the sun-god, who rides across the sky on a chariot drawn by seven horses. His charioteer is Aruna, the older brother of Garuda. There are several temples dedicated to Surya in India.

Kuvera (Kubera)

He is the god of wealth and the treasurer of the demigods. He carries a money bag and a bowl. He has a white dwarfish body. He rides on a chariot called Pushpak.

Soma

He is the moon-god. He has two hands, one holding a mace and the other in a protective mode.

Four Main Schools of Thought

1. Vaishnavas, who worship Lord Vishnu and Krishna.
2. Shaivites, who worship Lord Siva.
3. Shaktas, who worship the goddess Durga.
4. Smartas, who worship five major deities: Vishnu, Siva, Shakti, Ganesha, and Surya, the sun-god.

Vaishnava or Shaivite Markings

You can tell the difference between them by the marks on their foreheads. Vertical marks mean devotees of Lord Vishnu and horizontal marks mean devotees of Lord Siva. Also devotees of Lord Siva usually wear *rudraksa* beads and devotees of Lord Vishnu or Krishna wear *tulasi* beads around their necks.

Cows

One may ask why the cow is protected, even more than people. Cows are sacred because they are very dear to Lord Krishna, the Supreme Personality of Godhead. Also the cow is important because she supplies the most important food, milk. Because of this, the cow is consider one of mankind's mothers. Another reason is that the cow is helpless like a child and should be protected as such.

The urine and dung (stool) of the cow are considered pure and are used in worship. In science labs they have been found antiseptic. According to the *Vedic* culture eating of beef is strictly forbidden and is considered extremely sinful. If a person must eat meat, they definitely should not eat cow, and therefore beef is never sold publicly on the streets in India.

Sankaracarya (788-820)

When he was only eight years old, he completed his study of all the scriptures and took *sannyasa* from Govinda, who was residing on the banks of the Narmada River. After accepting *sannyasa*, Sankaracarya stayed with his spiritual master for some days. He then took permission to go to Varanasi, and from there he went to Badrinath, where he stayed until his twelfth year. While there he wrote a commentary on *Brahma-sutra*, ten *Upanisads* and the *Bhagavad-gita*. He traveled widely all over India and died when he was thirty-two.

He wrote two major works, *Sariraka-bhasya* and *Vivekacudaani*. For many, his *Sariraka-bhasya* is the definitive rendition of Vedanta. He established four main maths in Puri. Joshimath, Dwarka, and Sringeri.

Sankara taught that the living entities are themselves the Absolute Truth and that there is ultimately no variety, individuality, or personality in spiritual existence. He said that the individuality of both the Supreme Being and the individual is false.

During his time Buddhism had spread all over India. Sankara sought to reform and purify religious life by reinstating the authority of the Vedic scriptures, which Buddha had totally rejected. Since it would have been impossible to restore the Vedic literature's theistic conception just after the Buddha's complete atheism, Sankara made a compromise to fit the time and circumstance. His interpretations resembled Buddhism, but unlike Buddhism, they were based on the authority of Vedic literatures. His philosophy is totally rejected by the personal school of thought which was propounded by Ramanujacarya, Madhvacarya and Sri Caitanya Mahaprabhu.

Ramanujacarya

He was born in 1017 AD in a small village near Kanchipuram. Ramanujacarya founded the Sri-sampradaya, one of the four main Vaishnava *sampradayas*. This *sampradaya* propounds the *visistadvaita-vada* philosophy, qualified monism.

He was initiated by Mahapurna, the disciple of Yamunacarya. He took the *sannyasa* name Yatiraja. Ramanuja lived the later part of his life in Srirangam, a large temple located on an island by Tiruchirappalli. He established 74 Sri Vaisnavas centers and converted thousands of people, including several kings. Beside householders, his followers included 700 *sannyasis*, 12,000 *brahmacaris*, and 300 *ketti ammais* (ladies who have taken a vow of renunciation). He left his body in the month of Magha, 1137 AD, in Sri Rangam at the age of 120.

He taught that there is a difference between the Supreme Brahman and the individual soul. Ramanujacarya taught that by God's grace the *jiva* (individual soul) can get out of the material world and attain the eternal abode of Lord Vishnu. Ramanuja accepts three classes of *jivas* (living souls): eternally liberated, forever bound, and those freed by devotion and devotional practices. He taught serving God in Vaikuntha with awe and reverence. He always defeated any scholar who preached the impersonal school of thought.

Ramanuja initiated anyone regardless of caste. He established that the position of a Vaishnava surpasses all social considerations.

Madhvacarya (1239-1319)

He was a Vaishnava (devotee of Vishnu) and devoted himself to defeat-

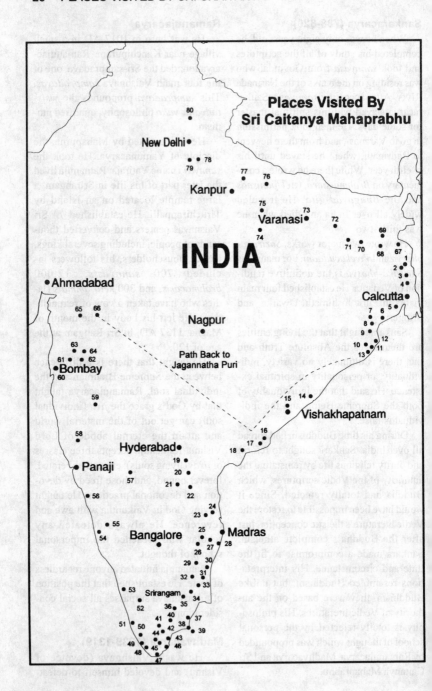

Places Visited By
Sri Caitanya Mahaprabhu

INDIA

New Delhi

Kanpur

Varanasi

Ahmadabad

Nagpur

Path Back to
Jagannatha Puri

Bombay

Calcutta

Vishakhapatnam

Hyderabad

Panaji

Bangalore

Madras

Srirangam

Places Visited By Sri Chaitanya Mahaprabhu

Northern India

1   Sri Mayapur (Antardwipa)
2   Kulia (Town of Navadwip)
3   Santipur
4   Panihati
5   Jaleswar
6   Remuna
7   Bhadrak
8   Jajpur
9   Cuttack
10 Bhubaneswar
11 Puri
12 Konark
13 Alalanatha

South India

14 Kurmachalam
15 Simhachalam
16 Vidyanagar
17 Kovur (Goshpada Ghat)
18 Vijayawada (Mangalagiri)
19 Srisailam
20 Ahovaiam
21 Falgutirtha
22 Siddhavata
23 Tirupati
24 Srikalahasti
25 Kanchipuram
26 Skandashetra
27 Pakshitirtha
28 Briddhakolatirtha
29 Bridhachalam
30 Chidambaram
31 Shiyali (Sirkazli)
32 Gosamajtirtha
33 Kumbakonam
34 Tanjore
35 Srirangam
36 Madurai
37 Durbasayanam
38 Rameswaram
39 Dhanuskoti Tirtha
40 Tilakanchi
41 Anilitala
42 Sri Vaikuntham
43 Vetapani
44 Mahendrasaila
45 Navatirupati
46 Malayaparvata
47 Kanniyakumari
48 Tiruvattar
49 Gajendramokshanatirtha
50 Thiruvananthapuram
51 Varkala (Janardana Temple)
52 Tritakupa
53 Matsyatirtha
54 Udupi
55 Sringeri
56 Gokarna
57 Dandakaranya Forest
58 Kolhapur
59 Pandarpur
60 Bombay
61 Surparaktirtha
62 Kushavartagiri
63 Nasik
64 Brahmagiri
65 Dhanustirtha
66 Omkareshwara

North India

67 Ramakeli
68 Mandar Hill
69 Kanai Natsala
70 Gaya
71 Rajgiri
72 Punpuntirtha
73 Varanasi (Kasi)
74 Arail
75 Allahabad (Prayag)
76 Ayodhya
77 Naimisaranya
78 Mathura
79 Govardhana Hill
80 Kurukshetra

ing the impersonal philosophy. He named his explanation of the Vedas *dvaita-dvaita-vada* (pure dualism). He taught that there is the Supreme Lord, the individual souls, and the material world. He taught that the individual souls are superior to matter and are distinct from the Lord as His servitors. He also taught that each person moulds his own karma, and that by serving the Supreme Lord one can eliminate karma and return to his position of serving the Lord in the eternal spiritual world.

He possessed an unusually strong body and extraordinary intellectual power. It is said there was no limit to his bodily strength. He went to almost every sacred place of pilgrimage, where he defeated scholars of rival schools and won them over to his faith.

Madhvacarya went to the Himalayas to meet Srila Vyasadeva. Vyasadeva gave him a *shalagram-shila* called Astamurti and approved his *Bhagavad-gita* commentary.

Sri Caitanya Mahaprabhu

He appeared in Navadvipa, West Bengal, in 1486. He took the renounced order of life when He was 24. He then left Navadvipa and went to Puri in Orrisa. His spiritual master, Iswara Puri, came in the line of Madhavendra Puri, who came in the line of Madhvacarya.

Gaudiya Vaishnavas accept Sri Caitanya to be non-different from Lord Krishna, in the form of a devotee. He taught that by chanting the holy names of the Lord, specifically the mantra, Hare Krishna, Hare Krishna, Krishna, Krishna, Hare Hare, Hare Rama Hare Rama, Rama Rama, Hare Hare one could attain transcendental devotion to God.

He taught the philosophy that the Supreme Lord and the individual souls are inconceivably simultaneously one and different. He explained the direct meaning of the *sastras* (scriptures) as devotion (*bhakti*) to Lord Krishna.

Sri Andal

She wrote two works, *Tiruppavai* and *Nachiar Tirumozhi*, which express her burning love of God. There is a major temple dedicated to her in Srivilliputtur and a shrine dedicated to her in the Srirangam Temple.

She was the daughter of Periya Alwar, also known as Vishnucittar, who was one of the 12 Alwars. According to tradition, Periya Alwar used to take care of the flower garden at the Vishnu temple in Srivilliputtur. While tending the garden he found Andal as a baby and then brought her up. This was around the 8th century. When her foster father tried to find a husband for her, she refused any mortal man and said that she would only marry the Lord.

Periya Alwar used to make flower garlands for Lord Vishnu. One day he was shocked to find a human hair in the basket of flowers. The next day he watched and saw Andal standing in front of her dressing mirror with a garland on. He scolded her and sent a fresh garland for the Lord. That night the Lord told him in a dream that He only likes the garlands first worn by Andal. He also requested him to bring Andal to Srirangam so He could marry her. When she saw the image of Sri Ranganatha she was absorbed in Him. The incarnation of the goddess of fortune known as Godadevi (Andal), was married to the Deity, Sri Ranganatha.

Bhaktivedanta Swami Prabhupada

He was born in 1896 in Calcutta. He was initiated by Bhaktisiddhanta Saraswati Maharaja into the Gaudiya Vaishnava sampradaya, followers of Sri Caitanya Mahaprabhu. He went to New York in 1965.

Between the years 1965 and 1977 he spread the teachings of Krishna consciousness to every major city in the world and formed an international society comprising thousands of members. He established 108 temples spread over six continents and circled the globe twelve times.

He also translated, wrote, and published 51 volumes of books in twenty-eight languages, tens of millions of which have been distributed throughout the world. He is known as Srila Prabhupada by his followers.

Vaishnava Sampradayas

There are four Vaishnava *sampradayas* (lines of disciplic succession): namely, the Brahma-sampradaya, the Sri-sampradaya, the Kumara-sampradaya, and the Rudra-sampradaya. These *sampradayas* are also known respectively as the Madhva-sampradaya, the Ramanuja-sampradaya, the Nimbarka-sampradaya, and the Vishnuswami-sampradaya after the four major *acaryas* in each *sampradaya*.

FESTIVALS

Makara Sankranti (Pongal)

It falls on the first day of the month of Magh (Mid-January). This is the day the sun enters the sign of Makara, or Capricorn. It is considered an auspicious day.

Siva-ratri

This is the appearance day of Lord Siva in Feb/March. Special festivals are held in Varanasi, Kalahasti, Chidambaram, Srisailam, and other places where there are important Siva temples.

Caitanya Mahaprabhu's Appearance Day

This important Gaudiya Vaishnava festival falls at the same time as Holi in Feb/March. On this day there is a large festival at the birthplace of Sri Caitanya in Sri Dhama Mayapur, which is located about 150 km north of Calcutta in West Bengal. About a quarter of a million people come to Mayapur on Lord Caitanya's appearance day.

Holi

Holi is celebrated on the full moon day in February-March. People throw powdered dye and colored water on each other.

This is joyfully celebrated in Vraja (the area around Vrindavana), especially at Varsana and Nandagram. In Varsana the festival may include colorful processions with music, song, dance, and some boisterous scenes around the temples. If you go to these festivals you have to expect to be totally covered in dye and never to be able to use the clothes that you are wearing again, at least until next year's festival.

One story about Holi is that Prahlada Maharaja refused to worship his father and wanted to worship his father's enemy, Lord Vishnu, instead. His father's sister, Holika, who was immune to being burned, sat with the boy in a big fire, in an attempt to kill the boy. Prahlada's devotion was so great that Holika was burnt to death and Prahlada was unharmed. Huge bonfires are lit on the eve of Holi, and the grains of the harvest are thrown into the fire.

Warning You should be careful if you are in India during Holi (Feb/March). During this time the locals throw a pink dye on anyone they can. Many times it does not come out, and the more you resist, the worst it gets for you. During this time if you walk on the street expect to get covered with dye and to take it with a smile.

Rama-naumi

This is the appearance day of Lord Rama, which usually falls in April.

Narasimha's Appearance Day

This is in April/May.

Buddha Purnima

This is the celebration of the birth, enlightenment, death, and salvation of Lord Buddha in May. There is a special festival at Bodh Gaya in Bihar.

Ratha-yatra Festival

The main Ratha-yatra festival is at Puri in Orissa on the first day of the waxing moon in Asadha (June/July). Lord Jagannatha, Balarama, and Lady Subhadra are pulled on their giant chariots along the main road in Puri. About a half a million people come for this festival. Lord Jagannatha is non-different than Lord Krishna.

The ISKCON temples in Calcutta, Baroda, and Bhubaneswara also organize Ratha-yatra on the same day as the original in Jagannatha Puri. The ISKCON Calcutta festival reportedly draws larger crowds than Puri.

Janmastami

This festival celebrates the appearance day of Lord Krishna in Mathura about 5000 years ago. It is celebrated in an elaborate way in Vrindavana and at all Krishna temples, such as at Nathdwar. Rasa-lila is performed depicting different pastimes of Lord Krishna. There is a huge *arati* at 12 midnight in Krishna temples across India.

This festival is celebrated all over India, especially in Gujarat, Rajasthan, Mathura and Vrindavana. Janmastami falls on the 8th day of the dark half of Bhadra (August/Sept).

Ganesh Chaturthi

It is held during the month of Bhadra (August/Sept).

Dussera

This festival celebrates the victory of Lord Rama over Ravana, the king of Lanka who kidnapped Rama's wife Sita. This festival goes on for 10 days. On the tenth day a large effigy of Ravana is shot and killed (actually burnt) by Rama.

The victory of Durga (consort of Siva) over the buffalo demon, Mahisasura, is also celebrated at this same time. This festival goes on for 10 days. On the tenth day there may be a big parade in different cities. The Dussera processions in Mysore and Jaipur are big events.

Dipawali (row of lights)

It is celebrated 20 days after Dussera. It celebrates the return of Lord Rama to Ayodhya, after His victory over Ravana. This is celebrated by burning lamps and candles in temples and homes and by fireworks.

Navratri

This is a nine day festival. In Gujarat, women, and sometimes men, dance the *garbha* dance. They dance around in a big circle with swaying steps and rhythmically clap to music. It is a big social and spiritual event.

Camel Festival

The Camel Festival at Pushkar draws a couple of hundred thousand people and a lot of camels too. This festival takes place for three days around the full moon day of Kartika (Oct/Nov), which is considered a very auspicious day at Pushkar. It is considered especially auspicious to bathe in the lake at Pushkar on the full moon day of Kartika.

Onam

It is a major festival in Kerala. It celebrates the memory of the king of the demons, Bali Maharaja, who was removed as king of the earth by Vamanadeva, an incarnation of Lord Vishnu, and sent to the underworld. The king is so attached to his subjects that he returns once a year to see them. In Trichur there is a large festival with colorfully decorated elephants. At Kottayam, Arnmula, and Champakulam there are snake boat races, with large crews of oarsmen rowing to the rhythm of drums and cymbals.

TEMPLE DESIGN

The principles of temple design culminate in the vast and rich knowledge laid down by the *sastra*, religious scriptures, such at the *Silpa-sastra* and *Sthapana-veda*. A temple is traditionally designed by a *stapati*, a traditional Indian architect coming in *parampara*, which is a direct line from teacher to teacher. The different stages in building a temple are started at auspicious times, which are astrologically calculated.

The most important part of the temple is the sanctum sanctorum, or *garbha-griha*, which is where the main deity of the temple is located. In a South Indian temple the room is usually square with a low roof and no windows or doors, except the front door.

Over the deity is a tower. In North Indian temples the tower is usually quite high, and in South Indian temples the tower is usually low or medium height. The main entrance of the temple is usually from the east.

Inside the *prakara* (walls surrounding the temple) there will usually be minor temples that contain deities who are connected to the main deity. In a Lord Vishnu temple these deities may include Sita, Laksmi, Hanuman, or Garuda. In a Lord Siva temple these deities may include Parvati, Ganesh, or Subrahmanya.

Parts of a Temple

1. *Garbha-griha,* which contains the main deity of the temple. It has a tower called a *vimana* over it.
2. The *ardha-mandapa* and *maha-mandapa* are in front of the *garbha-griha* (inner sanctum).
3. The *gopurams* are entrance towers.
4. The veranda next to the inside walls of the *pradakshina* path.
5. Tanks and wells, which are either sacred or for bathing purposes.
6. Subsidiary deities and shrines dedicated to minor gods.

Vertical Construction of Temples

The temple is divided into six main vertical divisions, which are:

1. The lower part of the temple, basement or foundation (*adhishthana, adhara*).
2. Stone walls with columns embedded in the walls and also projecting out.
3. Roof above the columns.
4. The molding.
5. The spherical top, which is a small tower over the molding (*sikhara*, also called *sirah* and *mundaka*) that covers the sanctum (altar).
6. The pinnacle and the spire.

The last three items constitute the tower over the *garbha-griha* (altar), called the *sikhara*. *Vimana* refers to the entire sanctum from the basement to the pinnacle. *Sikhara* commonly refers to the superstructure over the sanctum, not the superstructure over the entrances of the surrounding walls.

Dravidian Temple Design

The Dravidian style is the typical South Indian style temple that is usually made from stone. The temple shape may be rectangular, square, star-shaped, or octagonal. These temples usually have *gopurams*, which are large towers over the entrances; a *vimana*, which is the tower over the *sanctum* (the Deities); and large pillared halls and corridors. The *gopurams* were in the past always the tallest structures in town.

The most sacred place is the *pitha* (altar), or pedestal, of the Deity. The *pitha* is in the sanctum sanctorum (inner sanctum) called the *garbha-griha* (womb house). This is where the altar of the main deity of the temple is located. The *garbha-griha* or inner sanctum of the main shrine is usually semi-dark and has no sculptures, except the main deity. This part of the temple must be constructed first, and before construction begins there has to be a significant ceremony known as impregnating (*garbhadhana* or *garbha-nyasa*). There is usually a *pradakshina* path that enables pilgrims to go around the deities.

The sanctum sanctorum (central shrine) is topped by a pyramidal tower several stories high called *vimana* or *sikhara*. It is crowned by a cakra in a Lord Vishnu temple and a trident in a Lord Siva temple.

The inner sanctum is surrounded by subsidiary shrines, *mandapas* (halls), and pillared corridors. *Mandapa* (*mantapa* in Kannada) means any roofed, open or enclosed pavilion (hall) resting on pillars, standing independently or connected to the sanctum of the temple. *Mandapas* are one or more entrance porches or halls that lead to the inner *sanctum*.

The inner sanctum and the pavilion in front of the main altar is connected by a vestibule or porch called *ardha mandapa* or sometimes *antarala*. There is a rectangular hall in front of the sanctum (*mukha mandapa*) where the devotees stand and view the main deity of the temple. The *nityarchana mandapa* is where the daily worship of the small (moveable) representative of the main deity is done. The flight of stairs that connects the first *prakara* with the sanctum sanctorum is called *sopana*. In front of this flight of stairs is the main *mandapa*.

The subsidiary shrines or altars contain other deities, including the consort of the main deity (Lakshmi or Parvati). The shrine dedicated to the consort of the main deity usually has her own sanctum (*garbha-griha*) and ambulatory pathway (*pradakshina-patha*). In some larger temple they have their own halls and pavilions.

Many temples have several halls such as: *ranga-mandapa*—usually a large hall with intricately carved pillar used as a large audience pavilion, *yajna-sala*—hall for occasional sacrifices, *nrittya mandapa*—hall for dance recitals, *vahana-mandapa*—place where the festival vehicles are kept, *kalyana-mandapa*—marriage hall, *asthana-mandapa*—where the processional deity holds court, *alankara-mandapa*—where the processional deity is dressed before being taken on procession, *vasanta-mandapa*—hall in the middle of the temple tank used for festivals, and the *utsava manadapa*—hall used on festive occasions. Temples will also usually have a treasury, a kitchen (*paka-sala*), store room (*ugrana*), dining hall (*Ramanuja-kuta* in a Vaishnava temple and *Siva-kuta* in a Siva temple).

In the temple yard outside the main entrance of the inner sanctum is the flagpost (*dhvaja-stambha*) and a platform for food-offerings (*bali-pitha*). Both of these are usually right next to each other directly in front of the doorway. Near here is the *vahana-mandapa*, where the carrier (*vahana*) of the deity, Garuda in a Vishnu temple or Nandi in a Siva Temple.

Each temple usually has a temple tank (*teppakulam*), flower garden (*nanda-vana*), and temple chariot (*ratha*). On festival days the processional deity is paraded around town on the chariot. Many thousands of people join the festival.

This entire area is surrounded by high walls (*prakara*) with entrances through towering gateways (*gopurams*). The gateway facing the sanctum is called *maha-dvara* and is usually the main entrance to the temple. These rectangular, pyramidal towers are often 50 metres high with intricate sculptures of gods, demons, humans, and animals on them. They can also be painted very bright colors.

Dravidian Temple Enclosures

The main area of the temple, plus the halls, tanks and gardens may be surrounded by a single wall (*prakara*) or a series of walls. This is especially a feature of South Indian temples. The *prakara* contributes to the security and beauty of the temple. Even two hundred years ago it was not uncommon for a temple to be attacked and destroyed, so the walls enabled the temple to be protected.

The *garbha-griha* (inner sanctum) is encircled by the first *prakara* called *antara-mandala*. This is a passage-way, often narrow, which permits the devotees to go around the sanctum in a customary act of devotion. The flight of stairs that connects the first *prakara* with the sanctum sanctorum is called the *sopana*. In front of the *sopana* is the main *mandapa*.

Around the main *mandapa* and *antara-mandala* is the second *prakara* called *antahara*. This forms a broad veranda with doorways on all four sides. The *antahara* leads out into an enclosure containing the main *bali-pitha*.

The next enclosure is called *madhya-hara*. Beyond this and just outside the main *bali-pitha* is the flagstaff (*dhvaja-stambha*).

The fourth enclosure is called *bhayahara*. It forms the pathway for the processions within the temple. The fifth *prakara* (enclosure) is the *maryada* (limit), last wall.

Andhra Pradesh Temples

In Andhra Pradesh the main deity is generally found in the center of the temple. The accessory buildings are usually inside a rectangular wall which has high *gopurams* (towers) that can be seen from a great distance. The eastern entrance is typically the main entrance and the deity usually faces east.

The tower over the main deity is called a *vimana*, and it is generally covered with sculptures from top to bottom. The deity room is called the *garbha-griha*, which is in a circular or square building surrounded by a *pradakshina-patha* (path), so devotees can go around the deities. In front of this area is the *ardha-mandapa*, which may be square or rectangular. The *maha-mandapa* is in front of the *ardha-mandapa*. It consists of a building with pillars in it with an entrance and space on three sides. There may be other *mandapas* like the *nrittya mandapa* and *kalyana-mandapa*.

Usually on either side of the main entrance of the *ardha-mandapa* are two *dwarapalakas* (carvings of temple guards). In front of the sanctum is located either Garuda, in a Vishnu temple, or Nandi, the bull, in a Siva temple.

In most temples there are usually two sets of deities: One is permanent and is called the Mulabera and the other is taken on processions and is called the Utsavabera. In some temples there are different deities for *abhisheka* (bathing) and *utsava* (festivals).

Kerala Temple Design

Most temples in Kerala face east, but some face west and a few south. The central shrine or altar is called the *srikoil* and it may be square, oblong, or circular in shape. It may be one or two stories. Within it is the *garbha-griha*, or the altar in which the Deity is installed. In front of the central shrine is a *namaskara-mandapa*, or hall that is used for the devotees to view the Lord and to pay obeisances. Surrounding this is a corridor or pillared hall called either the *nalambalam* or *chuttambalam*, the outer portico of which is called the *belikkalpura*, which contains the *belikkal* or platform for food offerings. In front of the belikkal is the *dwajasthamba* (flag-staff). Around the *nalambalam* could be the *vilakkumatam*, which is rows of lamps that are lit during festivals.

Outside of this structure is a paved processional path. Normally the temple well is situated in the northeast corner of this area. The temple kitchen, called *madappalli*, is usually in the nalambalam. There are usually smaller shrines in the temple dedicated to the goddess of the temple and other deities.

North India Temples

The North Indian temple style is called *nagara*. The North India temple towers tend to be curved. The superstructure

(tower) of a *nagara* style temple is square from the base to the pinnacle (*stupi*).

The parts of the temple are the *garbha griha, prakara, upa-tirtha, khanda, main tirtha, kshetra, mandala* and/or the *desha*. The inner sanctum (altar) is called *deul*.

Orissan Style Temples

The Orissan temple consists of two apartments. The *deul* corresponds to the *vimana*, or towered sanctum. It is a cubical inner apartment where the main deity is located, with a tower over it.

In some temples there is a *pradakshina-patha* or *bhrama* (circumambulatory path), which goes around the sanctum sanctorum (altar) so the devotees can go around the deity.

In front of the sanctum is the *mukhamandapa* or *mukhashala*. Sometimes it is called *ardha-mandapa* or *sukanasi*, depending on how big it is compared to the sanctum. It is used as a passage and sometimes to keep food offerings on special occasions.

After this is the *antarala*, which connects the sanctum and *mukha-mandapa* to the *mandapa*, or pavilion hall. The *antarala*, which is usually square and has a pyramidal roof, is also called the *jagmohana* (world-delighter). In many cases the *antarala* is the same as the *mukha-mandapa*. Sometimes one or two pavilions are added in front of the *antarala*, such as the *nat-mandir* and the *bhog-mandir*.

A *mandapa* (*nritta-mandapa* or *navaranga*) is a big hall that is used for spiritual classes, singing, dancing, or chanting.

In front of these is the *dhvajastambha* (flagpost). The *lanchana* (insignia), which is made of brass or copper, is different depending on the deity in the temple. This is usually the carrier of the deity. For Lord Vishnu it would be Garuda, and for Lord Siva it would be Nandi.

The *bali-pitha* (pedestal of sacrificial offerings), which usually has the footprint of the deity or a lotus on it, is near the *dhvaja-stamba*.

The entire temple is surrounded by a high wall (*prakara*), which usually has a main gate and three subsidiary gates opening in the four directions. Sometimes there is a *gopuram* (high tower) over the gate.

Inside the *prakara* there will usually be minor temples that contain deities which are related to the main deity. In a Lord Vishnu temple these deities may include Sita, Laksmi, Hanuman or Garuda. In a Lord Siva temple these deities may include Parvati, Ganesh, or Subrahmanya.

Within the temple's wall there may also be a kitchen, *yajnashala* (sacrificial arena), a well or tank called *puskarini*, flower gardens, a processional cart and other buildings for worship or management of the temple.

Tulasi

Tulasi is an extremely sacred plant and is considered worshipable. Many Vishnu temples have *tulasi* gardens. When food is offered to Lord Vishnu or Krishna, *tulasi* leaves are put on each individual preparation offered. Many people have *tulasi* plants in their home. It is considered inauspicious to brush against a *tulasi* plant by mistake. *Tulasi* plants look like basil plants, but have smaller leaves.

Non-Hindus Not Allowed

In many temples throughout India there is no entry for non-Hindus. This means if you are not Indian you'll not be allowed in. This also means if you are from India, but are Muslim you cannot enter the temple. This restriction mainly applies in Varanasi, Orissa, Kerala, and Tamil Nadu. You can enter many of the temples in Tamil Nadu, but you can not enter the inner sanctum where the deity is located.

If you are an ISKCON devotee or a converted Hindu, you can enter most temples in the South. This is because you are considered a Hindu, by their definition. Some temples may request an official letter from you saying that you are a Hindu. I know someone who was asked to show a letter at a major temple in Madras, the Parathasarathi temple. To increase your chances of entering a temple you should dress in devotional clothing, a *dhoti* and *kurta* for men and a sari for ladies. In some temples in South India you must wear a *dhoti* and also enter with no shirt. Also some temples insist that you have *tilaka* (sacred clay) on your forehead.

Bharata Natyam Dance

This is one of four classical styles of South India temple dancing. Each gesture and movement has a meaning. Dancers never turn their back to the gods that they are honoring. *Devadasis*, or servants of God, traditionally perform this type of dance in temples. *Bharata* means India, and *natya* means dance.

It is performed by a solo woman. It begins with *alarippu*, which symbolizes the body as an offering to the gods. She then combines *nritya*, emotions, with *nritta*, pure dance. They use heavy face and hand expressions. They are accompanied by musicians and a *nattuvanar*.

Madras is the main place for Bharata Natyam dance. There are regular performances at the Kalaksetra center, Music Academy, Raja Ananmalai Hall, Museum

Theater, and other places.

Kathakali Dance

It means literally, story-play. The performance is worship. It is only performed by men. Boys take the part of women. The dance is accompanied by a vocalist and drummers. They tell stories of the *Mahabharata* and *Ramayana*. Dialogue is combined with the dance. The costumes are very decorative with huge skirts and headdresses and the dancers wear heavy make-up. There is much movement of the limbs and eyes and every gesture has a specific meaning.

There are five primary distinct characters which you can tell by their make-up and costumes. *Pacha* (green) represents the noble-hearted hero or god; *kathi* (knife) represents a mixture of the nobility and evil; both of them have their face painted green, but the *kathi* has a knife pattern on the cheek in red pigment and a small white ball is on the tip of the nose and the middle of the forehead. The other characters are *tati* (beard), *kari* (black), and *minukku* (polished). Bad guys usually have black faces with white spots on their cheeks or nose. They may have a red beard (*thadi*), a false nose and a big frill. They put a cunlappuva seed inside the eye-lid to turn the white part of the eyes red. Hanuman's face is red.

The orchestra consists of the *maddalam*, *edakka*, *chenta*, cymbals, and the gong. There is also a singer who directs the play, and the actors take their cue from him.

Dances can last for hours. Originally Kathakali used to be an all-night performance in temples during festivals. Dancers train for six to twenty years to learn the dance steps and movements. It demands extraordinary muscle control to contort the face and make the sudden leaps and spins.

It takes four hours to prepare for a performance, to put on the make-up, elaborate costumes, and head dress. Everything is put on in a fixed order.

Chatunni Paniker and Guru Gopinath are considered two of the best dancers. Cochin in Kerala is the best place to see this type of dance, as there are daily performances at the Cochin Cultural Centre. The India Foundation and Art Kerala, both near Ernakulam Railway Station, have regular performances from 7 to 10:30 pm.

Other Dance Styles

Manipuri style dancing is considered a religious ritual. Many of the dances have themes based on Krishna's pastimes. Manipur is a hilly tract of land in the extreme northeastern part of India.

Krishnayattam is a predecessor of Kathakali which is done at the Guruvayur temple. The performances starts around 10 pm, from October to April if it does not rain.

Odissi is classical Orissan temple dancing. The dance is a ritual offering, which is performed in the temples. There are strict rules of position of feet, body, and hands. Jayadeva's *Gita Govinda*, which is about Krishna's great love for Radha, is a favorite subject of this dance.

CHAPTER TWO

Practical Information

The Country

India is the ninth largest country in the world. It has a land border of 15,174 km (9,425 mile), a land area of 3,287,263 square km (1,261,000 square miles) and a coastline of 6083 km (3,535 miles). It is 3218 km (2000 miles) from the north of Kashmir to the extreme south at Kanniyakumari (Cape Comarin). From the border of Pakistan to the easternmost town of Kahan near Myanmar is also about 3218 km (2000 miles). It is three-fifths the size of the United States, 20 times the size of Britain, or the size of Europe without Russia.

To the north of India is Nepal. The Himalayas separate India from China and Bhutan. Pakistan is on the western border and Bangladesh and Myanmar on the east. The Arabian Sea is to the west and the Bay of Bengal to the east. The Ganges, which is the main river in India, is 1000 miles long.

Facts

India has a population of about 920 million that is increasing every day. About 75% of the population live in villages. There are 14 major languages spoken in India and about 250 regional dialects. Even though Hindi is the official language, many people in India do not speak it at all. Hindi is spoken by about half the population, mostly in North India. English is the second major language spoken in India and used for much of the official business. In the Indian Air Force all business is done in English. Each state in the South has its own language—Tamil in Tamil Nadu; Telegu in Andhra Pradesh; Kanada in Karnataka; and Malayalam in Kerala. Each of these languages has its own script.

BEFORE YOU GO

Planning Your Trip

It is best to plan your trip in advance. India is a big country and the distances between places can be great. While traveling, it is a good idea to take a break every 7 or 10 days and just relax. You can catch up on your rest and laundry, which can be a problem if you are always traveling. Otherwise you can really tire yourself out.

It is best not to have too tight of a schedule, as things do not usually go on schedule in India.

Visas

Residents of most countries need a visa to enter India. The normal tourist visa is valid for six months. You can also get a one month, three months, one year, or even five years tourist visa. Normally you will be given a six month tourist visa, which begins the day you get the visa. The visa usually starts from the date of issue—not the date you enter India. If you have a six month visa and enter India three months after you got your visa, your visa is good for only three more months. If you enter India one day after you get your visa it will be good for the full six months. A tourist visa is usually multiple entry, but you should specifically ask to have a multiple entry visa when you apply, as it is no extra cost. You never know if you will want to go to Nepal or some other country.

In New York you can go to the office in the morning to submit your application and pick up your visa in the afternoon after 4 pm. You must submit two passport photos of yourself with your application form.

You can also get a visa by mail. It is best to send in for your visa at least three weeks in advance. If you do not receive your visa within two and half weeks, call up the Indian Visa Office and ask if there is a problem. There might be one, and there is a good chance they will not contact you if there is.

If you apply for a visa outside of your home country it can take up to two weeks. This is because they have to fax your name back to your home country, supposedly to check up on you. If you are from the USA, traveling through England to get to India, do not try to get your visa there, unless you want to wait one or two weeks in London. Although US citizens can get a visa in one day in New York, do not expect to get it in less than a week in London.

The price of the visa varies from country to country and also changes regularly. If you are from the USA you should expect to pay more than people from other countries.

Indian Embassies & Consulates

Australia
   3-5 Moonah Place, Yarralumla, ACT 2600 (06-273-3999)
   153 Walker St, 11th Floor, North Sydney, NSW 2060 (02-9955-7055)
   13 Munro St, Coburg, Vic 3058 (03-9384-0141)
Austria
   Karntner Ring 2, 1015 Wien (01-505-8667)
Bangladesh
   House 120, Road 2, Dhanmodi Residential Area, Dhaka (02-503-606)
Belgium
   217 Chaussée de Vleurgat, 1050 Brussels (02-640-9802)
Canada
   10 Springfield Rd, Ottawa K1M 1C9 (613-744-3751)
   2 Bloor St W. #500, Toronto, ON M4W 3E2 (416-960-0751)
   325 Howe St, 2nd Floor, Vancouver, BC V6C 1Z7 (604-662-8811)
Denmark
   Vangehusvej 15, 2100 Copenhagen (045-3118-2888)
France
   15 rue Alfred Dehodencq, 75016 Paris (1-4520-7070)
Germany
   Adenauerallee 262, 53113 Bonn (228-54050)
   Mittelweg 49, 60318 Frankfurt (069-153-0050)
   Raboisen 6, 20095 Hamburg (040-338-036)
Ireland
   6 Leeson Park, Dublin 6 (01-970-843)
Israel
   4 Kaufman St, Sharbat House, Tel Aviv 68012 (03-584-585)
Italy
   Via XX Settembre 5, 00187 Rome (6-488-4642)
   Via Larga 16, 20122 Milan (02-869-0314)
Japan

2-11 Kudan Minami 2-Chome,
Chiyoda-ku, Tokyo 102 (3-262-2391)

Kenya
Jeevan Bharati Bldg, Harambee Ave,
Nairobi (02-222-566)

Malaysia
2 Jalan Taman Dlita, 50480 Kuala
Lumpur (03-253-3504)

Myanmar (Burma)
545-547 Merchant St, Yangon
(01-82550)

Nepal
Lainchaur, GPO Box 292,
Kathmandu (071-411-940)

Netherlands
Buitenrustweg 2, 252 KD, The Hague
(70-346-9771)

New Zealand
180 Molesworth St, Princess Towers,
Wellington (4-499-0665)

Norway
Niels Juelsgaten 30, 0244 Olso 2
(443-194)

Pakistan
India House, 3 Fatima Jinnah Rd,
Karachi (021-522-275)

Russia
6 Ulitsa Obukha, Moscow
(095-297-0802, fax 975-2337)

Singapore
India House, 31 Grange Rd
(737-6777)

South Africa
Sanlam Centre, Johannesburg
(011-333-1525)

Spain
Av Pio XII 30-32m 28016 Madrid
(91-345-0406)
C/T Roviraita 21-23, 08022
Barcelona (93-212-0422)

Sri Lanka
36-38 Galla Rd, Colombo 3
(1-421-605)

Sweden
Adolf Fredriks Kyrkogata 12, Box

1340, 11183 Stockholm (08-107-008)

Switzerland
Effingerstrasse 45, CH-3008 Berne
(31-382-3111)

Thailand
46 Soi 23 (Prasarnmitr), Sukhumvit
Rd, Bangkok 10110 (2-258-0300)

UK
India House, Aldwych, London
WC2B 4NA (071-836-8484)
8219 Augusta St, Birmingham
B18 6DS (21-643-0366)

USA
3 East 64th St, New York, NY 10021
(212-879-7800)
2107 Massachusetts Ave NW, Washington DC 20008 (202-939-7000)
540 Arguello Blvd, San Francisco,
CA 94118 (415-668-0662)
150 N Michigan Ave, Suite 1100,
Chicago, IL 60601 (312-781-6280)
1100 Huntingdon Bldg, Cleveland,
OH 44155 (216-696-1100)
201 St Charles Ave, New Orleans, LA
70170 (504-582-8106)
2051 Young St (PO Box 15683),
Honolulu, HI 96826 (808-947-2618)

Passport

According to law you must have your
passport with you at all times. To check
into a hotel you must show your passport to the hotel clerk and fill out a form
with your passport and visa information.
If the police ask to see you passport you
must show it to them. They have the right
to ask you for it at any time, for no reason.

Visa Extensions

If you plan to stay in India more than
the period for which your visa was issued, then you will have to extend your
visa. You need four photos. Depending
on the office you apply at and your per-

sonal circumstances, you may get a extension. The Delhi office is tough and is best avoided for visa extensions. They have a sign that says it is not possible to extend a three or six months tourist visa. You are more likely to get an extension on a three months visa than on a six months visa. One woman told me she saw seven people turned down in the Delhi office. She got a one month extension because she had gone to Nepal for a part of her visa period.

Usually the only reason that you will get an extension is because you were or are sick (you need a doctor's letter saying this was a fact), or you have some very special circumstance. The official policy is that a tourist visa cannot be extended.

You can apply to extend your visa in all state and district capitals at the office of the Superintendent of Police or in New Delhi, Bombay, Madras, or Calcutta at the Foreigners' Regional Registration Offices. Usually officials are more friendly in the smaller towns than in the big cities. You should try to extend your visa at least a week before your visa expires. In case you do not get the extension, you should have your plane trip scheduled to leave India within the time that your visa is scheduled to expire. Over extending your visa is taken very seriously by Indian officials.

Many people go to Nepal to get a new visa. It seems fairly routine to get another visa in Nepal.

Foreign Registration Office

Visa extensions are issued at some Foreign Registration Offices. If you plan to stay in India for more than six months you must register with the Foreign Registration Office within two weeks of your arrival. You need to turn in four photo-graphs when you register. If you come on a student visa or entry visa, you have to report any change of address or travel for more than 15 days from the place where you are registered. You also have to get an AIDS test within one month of registration. If you are found positive, you will be asked to immediately leave the country.

Main Foreign Registration Offices
New Delhi
    1st Floor, Hans Bhavan, Tilak Bridge, by the Tilak Bridge Railway Station (011-331-9489)
Calcutta
    237 Acharya J C Bose Rd (033-247-3301)
Bombay
    Special Branch II, Annexe 2, Office of the Commissioner of Police, Dadabhoy Naoroji Rd (022-262-0446)
Madras
    Shashtri Bhavan Annexe, 26 Haddows Rd (044-827-8210)

Tourist Offices
There are three types of tourist offices. The Indian Tourist Development Corporation (ITDC), state tourist offices, and national tourist offices. Each state has its own tourist offices, and there are also national offices. In some cities the national office is larger than the state office, if the state office exists at all. I have usually found the tourist offices in India to be helpful, especially if questioned properly. But you definitely cannot expect too much from them.

Many tourist offices, however, can be downright inefficient. When you ask for information they may hand you one brochure, when they may have ten hand-outs or brochures on the subject you want to know about, and then try to get rid of you.

The general rule is that you have to struggle to get every bit of information you want. I guess they are trying to save money. So whatever information they give you, they may have 10 times more. Be specific. What about this city? What about this tourist site? If one person just won't help you, politely try someone else.

The Indian Tourism Development Corporation (ITDC) also runs bus tours to different tourist sites, and the tourist offices sell tickets for these tours. They also operate a chain of hotels that operate under the name Ashok. Some of these hotels can be a good value for budget travelers, and others can be very high-class.

Overseas Tourist Offices

The Government of India has tourist offices in other countries where you can get information, brochures, maps, and leaflets about India. Many times you can get a lot of information from them. For the most part the overseas tourist offices will be more efficient than the offices in India.

Australia
    Level 1, 17 Castleregh St, Sydney NSW 2000 (02-9232-1600)
Canada
    60 Bloor St West, Suite No 1003, Toronto, Ontario M4W 3B8 (416-962-3788)
Germany
    Kaiserstrasse 77-III, D-6000 Frank furt Main-1 (069-235-423)
Italy
    Via Albricci 9, 20122 Milan (02-804-952)
Japan
    Pearl Bldg, 9-18 Ginza, 7-Chome, Chuo ku, Tokyo 104 (03-571-5062)
Malaysia

Wisma HLA, Lot 203 Jalan Raja Chulan, 50200 Kuala Lumpur (03-242-5285)
Netherlands
    Rockin 9-15, 1012 KK Amsterdam (020-620-8991)
Sweden
    Sweavagen 9-11, S-III 57, Stockholm 11157 (08-21-5081)
Switzerland
    1-3 rue de Chantepoulet, 1201 Geneva (022-732-1813)
Thailand
    62/5 Thaniya Rd, Bangkok 10500 (02-235-2585)
UK
    7 Cork St, London W1X 2AB (0171-437-3677)
USA
    30 Rockefeller Plaza, 15 North Mezzanine, New York, NY 10112 (212-586-4901)
    3550 Wilshire Blvd, Suite 204, Los Angeles, CA 90010 (213-380-8855)

There are also promotion offices in Dallas, San Francisco, Washington DC, and Miami.

Tourist Offices In India:
Agra
    191 The Mall (363-377)
Aurangabad
    Krishna Vilas, Station Rd (31217)
Bangalore
    KFC Building, 48 Church St (558-9517)
Bhubaneswar
    B21, B J B Nagar (0674-412-203)
Bombay
    123 Maharishi Karve Rd, Churchgate (022-203-2932)
Calcutta
    4 Shakespeare Sarani (242-1402)
Jaipur
    Rajasthan State Hotel (327-200)

Khajuraho
  Near Western Group Temples (2047)
Madras
  154 Anna Salai Rd (869-685)
New Delhi
  88 Janpath (011-332-0005)
Panaji, Goa
  Communidade Building, Church
  Square (0832-43412)
Varanasi
  15B The Mall (0542-43744)

Tax Clearance

If you stay in India for more than four months, you are supposed to get a 'tax clearance certificate' before leaving the country.

To get one you go to the Foreign Section of the Income Tax Department in Delhi, Calcutta, Madras, or Bombay and show them your passport, visa extension form (if any), and whatever bank exchange receipts you have, so you can prove that you have changed your foreign currency officially. You fill in a form and wait anywhere from 15 minutes to a few hours. This is supposed to prove that you did not work in India.

The Foreign Section of the Income Tax Department in New Delhi is in the Central Revenue Building, near Hans Bhavan and the Tilak Bridge Railway Station.

I have heard of two people that have been asked for this certificate and did not have it. Therefore they had to miss their flight. In practice, they very seldom ask for it.

If you are in India for education or other business with a long term visa (one year or more), you can get a letter from the organization that you are with. This letter must say that you have been supported by the organizations while you were in India.

Consulates and Embassies

If you have a problem, like your money or ticket was lost or stolen, you can go to your consulate and they will often help you out. This is definitely true of the USA and British Embassies. They usually have a good list of doctors to see if you need one.

Customs

If you bring more than US$10,000 in cash or traveler's cheques, you are supposed to declare this to the customs officials when arriving in India. If you bring a video camera or computer, you are supposed to declare them, and they may be marked on your passport to insure that you bring them out of the country. When I recently came into the country and tried to declare my laptop computer, they told me it was not necessary.

I do know of cases where people have not declared their computer or printer and had to pay a $200 fine. They can also legally seize what you were supposed to have declared, and I have heard of cases where this has happened. They X-ray your check-on and carry-on baggage when you come off the plane. They then put a big chalk "X" on the bags that contain electronic equipment. When you come to the door to leave the airport they check to see if there are any chalk "X" marks on your bags. The reason why they are so strict about electronic wares is because they charge a high duty on imported goods.

Valuables

When you travel there are three things that are very valuable to you—your money, passport, and plane ticket. It is best to keep these things with you at all times. Carry your valuables in a money belt, a pouch under your shirt, or a pocket sewn into your clothing, not in your pockets or exposed bags. You can also get a money belt that attaches to the calf of your leg, or you can get a special pocket sewn inside of your clothes. You should try to never let anyone see your money belt in public, as thieves will try to cut it. You should not even think of putting any valuables in your check-in baggage on plane flights.

Valuables should not be left in your hotel room if possible, especially in low-class places where you use the hotel's lock. It is best to always carry valuables on you. Most hotel rooms have extra keys for all the rooms. Your $1,000 could be worth two years of work for someone. You can leave valuables at the front desk at respectable hotels. If you are carrying a lot of money it could be a good idea to carry two money belts. When I go into a crowded situation, for example, a railway station, I put my money belt in my underwear.

It is a good idea not to carry all your money in one place. If you do get robbed, what will you do if you are on a train to Madras with no money. It is best to carry at least $20 or $100 somewhere else all the time.

Travel bags should be made of a strong material so they cannot be cut open. You should also be able to put a lock on them if possible. The external pockets of a bag should not be used to carry valuables. Women should not keep their valuables in their pocket-book as they would in America. They are easily slit with a razor or pickpocketed. You should also not carry valuables in your back pockets or kurta pockets. Carry them in your front pants pockets or upper shirt pockets or in a money belt. It is best to keep your valuables in the front part of your body.

MONEY

Changing Money

The State Bank of India is usually the place to change money, but major branches of all Indian banks can usually change money. Indian banks, especially the State Bank of India, can complicate your life by making it very hard to change money. What takes 30 seconds in London can take an hour in India. US dollars are the easiest currency to convert, and the British pound is second. In many cases, especially in smaller cities, banks will not accept certain currencies, and in some cases they will only accept US dollars or British pounds. I went to one bank that would only take American Express travellers' cheques (checks).

You get a slightly higher bank rate for travellers' cheques than cash. Travellers' cheques can very seldom be used as direct payment, so they usually have to be changed in banks or hotels. In a lot of cases only certain banks will change travellers' cheques. You can also buy travellers' cheques in Indian rupees when you get to India. These are more widely accepted, especially in small towns.

It is a good idea to change a good amount at one time in the bigger cities. A few times I have spent two hours changing money in a small bank. Banks usually give a much better rate than hotels. Many large hotels change money 24 hours a day. Usually it is much quicker to change money at the airport than at a bank.

A good place to change money is at the American Express or Thomas Cook offices, which usually only take five minutes. They are efficient and easy to deal with.

There is a black market in India, and you can get up to two rupees more than the official bank rate for a dollar on the streets. They usually only want $50 or $100 bills or large British pounds. If you do this, however, it is illegal and there is a chance you will be ripped off. As you are changing the money, suddenly the "police are coming" and you have to put away the rupees you just received before you can count them. When you turn around everyone is gone, and later when you count your money you find out only the first few bills are real and the rest are just pieces of paper. This is more common in Bombay than anywhere else.

Travellers' Cheques (checks)

They are the safest way to carry your money. Besides safety, another advantage with travellers' cheques is you get a slightly higher exchange rate at the bank when you exchange them for rupees. If you live in America and belong to AAA you can purchase American Express travellers' cheques with no service charge. On the other hand, it is not a good idea to bring all your money in traveller's cheques because cash often comes in handy. Many banks do not accept traveller's cheques.

It is best to use US dollar or pound sterling traveller's cheques. Both American Express and Thomas Cook have several offices in India. It is best to use the well-known brands like Visa, Citibank, Barclays, American Express, and Thomas Cook. I've seen that American Express cheques are not accepted by some Indian banks, while Thomas Cook cheques are usually accepted everywhere. American Express and Thomas Cook are known to be the most efficient in replacing your cheques in case you lose them or have them stolen. With some travellers' cheques you can only get a refund when you get home. When you purchase cheques you should get the addresses of the refunding agents in India.

You should keep your proof of purchase receipt and cheque serial numbers. Don't throw away your receipt or leave it at home. Bring it with you and keep it separate from your cheques. If you lose your cheques the proof-of-purchase receipt will highly speed up the process of getting replacements. You are supposed to report loss or theft of your cheques within 24 hours to the company from which you got them. American Express's 24 hour number in Delhi is (011-687-5050).

If you lose your cheques you need a photocopy of the police report, your photo, proof-of-purchase receipt, and the cheque numbers. If you do not have the cheque numbers they will have to contact the place where you purchased them. So at least make sure you have that address.

American Express refunding agents are in New Delhi, A Block, Connaught Place (332-4119); Calcutta, 21 Old Court House Street (248-4464); Bombay, Regal Cinema Building, Chatrapati Shivaji Road, Colaba (285-1820); and Madras, G-17, Spencer Plaza, Anna Salai (852-3638).

Thomas Cook offices are in New Delhi, Hotel Imperial, Janpath (332-7135); Calcutta, 21 Old Court House St (248-8096); Bombay, Dr Dadabhai Naoroji Rd (204-8556); Madras, 112 Nungambakkam High Road (827-4941); Bangalore, 55 MG Rd (558-6742); and Hyderabad, Nasir Arcade, 6-1-57 Saifabad (231-988).

Credit Cards

In India, most major credit cards are accepted in big hotels, high-class restaurants, major shops, and Indian Airlines.

Visa, Master Card, and Diners are widely accepted. It is a good way to pay your hotel bill. The exchange rate you receive is the same as you receive with travellers' cheques. A lot of people who come to India do not bring enough money with them, so a credit card can be a good source of needed cash. You can also purchase travellers' cheques with a credit card.

Don't let your credit card out of your sight, as duplicate forms can be made and billed to you for fictitious purchases. This is not unusual in India.

Encashment Certificates

When you change money at the bank they give you a piece of paper called an encashment certificate. It's a record of the amount of money you exchanged. To change money back to foreign currency when you leave India you need to turn in your encashment certificate. It is illegal to bring rupees in or out of India, and if you are searched by customs when you are leaving or entering they will take them from you.

Always keep this certificate. If you want to get an extension on your visa you have to show enough encashment certificates to prove that you legally changed enough money to have supported yourself in India. If you stay in India longer than 120 days you need an income tax clearance. You have to show an encashment certificate to get this.

If you want to purchase a railway ticket using the tourist quota, you may have to present an encashment certificate. If you use excess baggage or export something from India you have to show an encashment certificate at least for the amount of the shipping and maybe the cost of the goods.

If you take things out of India in your check-in luggage you do not need an encashment certificate.

How Much Money To Bring

You get a good value for your money in India. But even though things are cheap, they do add up. You may have medical expenses. You may suddenly find out about some wonderful place that you just have to go to. You may want to stay an extra month, or you may want to purchase something you always needed and can't do without. Also it really can be much more expensive than you think. So, if possible, it is a good idea to bring about 50% more than you were planning to bring.

It you are constantly traveling it will cost you about double what it would cost if you stay in one place. For about $20 a day you can live and travel in India at close to an American standard.

If you always stay at the cheapest hotels, travel second-class on the trains, take cheap buses, and eat in simple places, you can spend less than Rs 150 (US$5) a day, or US$150 in a month. If you stay in a standard place with attached bath (like government tourist bungalows), travel first-class on the trains, take luxury buses or auto rickshaws instead of ordinary buses, and eat in a fancy place now and then, it will cost you about US$15 to US$25 a day, or US$450 to US$750 a month. If you travel at the highest standard, staying in the best hotels and flying everywhere, you can easily spend more than US$100 a day.

Transferring Money

Although over the last few years it has become much easier, it can still be difficult to send money to India. Never send cash by mail as there is a high rate of theft, and the postal system is inefficient. It can take months to receive a letter from England. You should cable the money. Transferring money to India can be very time-consuming and difficult if a slight mistake is made.

It is a good idea to deal with a foreign bank or company. Bank of America, American Express, ANZ Grindlays, Citibank, and Thomas Cook have branches in India. If you have an American Express credit card, wiring money is very efficient. The person wiring the money just has to go to any American Express office, give them the money, and tell them which branch in India they want it wired to and who will receive it. Within 24 hours the money can be picked up. The person wiring the money can also just call American Express and use their credit card to pay them. They charge about 8% to transfer money to India.

Western Union can transfer money to one of their 43 offices in India in fifteen minutes for a fee of 9.5 percent of the amount sent.

Indian banks such as the State Bank of India and Bank of Baroda can wire money from their branches in your country to large branches in India in two working days.

The money should be transferred in hard currency (your own currency or dollars) because you will get a better exchange rate in India than from the place from which the money is being transferred.

Small Change

When you exchange money, it is a good idea to ask for a good amount of small bills, such as five or ten rupee notes. Many times it will be impossible to find change for a 50 or 100 rupee note. You should also check the notes for large holes and even small tears, as damaged bills are not generally accepted. If your money is really damaged, you have to bring it to the bank to exchange it. When I make any decent sized purchase I use a large bill so I can get change. Places that sell cold drinks usually have change, especially if you pay after you drink one.

Emergency Numbers

Police 100
Fire 101
Ambulance 102

These are the numbers in Delhi, but they are usually the same in other places too.

Tipping

In India you tip to get things done, not just for services rendered. Tipping is not necessary for taxis, especially if you have set the price in advance. If a taxi driver goes out of the way for you, such as he carries your bags, it is a good idea to tip the driver. If you arrange a taxi for the day, it is normal to give the taxi driver something for lunch, say Rs 25 or Rs 50. In more expensive hotels a tip of Rs 5 to carry a bag is appropriate, and in cheaper hotels it is less.

In expensive tourist restaurants or hotels a service charge is sometimes tacked on to the bill at a 10% rate. So before you tip, look to see if a service charge has already been added to your bill. Giving small tips can make the most difficult things suddenly easy. You do not have to tip, but it can really help when you need something done quickly or efficiently.

Laundry

Laundry men are called dobhis in India. They do an excellent job on your laundry and will more than likely clean your cloth better than you could ever imagine. If you change your clothes every day, then bring at least four sets, as it takes at least one or two days to get your clothes back. I have never seen a washing machine in India and never even heard about dryers. So either you have to wash your clothes by hand or have a dobhi do your laundry. If you have the dobhi do your laundry, it can cost more than having your clothes washed in America, but they do a much better job. They can even get blood stains out. However, they can also beat your clothes, especially socks, until they get holes in them, and in the process they knock no shortage of buttons off your shirts.

Generally the hotel you stay at can arrange to get your laundry done. At least they will know where to find the local dobhi.

Business Hours

Shops are usually open from 10 am to 5 pm, Monday to Saturday. Post offices are usually open 10 am to 5 pm, Monday to Friday, and Saturday till noon. The Delhi post office is open from 8 am to 6 pm. Banks are open from 10 am till 2 pm and until noon on Saturday. Offices and shops are usually closed on Sunday, but this can be different depending on the town. The off day for the shops in Loi Bazaar, Vrindavana, is Wednesday, and in Bhubaneswar shops are closed on Thursday.

Phone

To call long distance you go to a STD/ISD phone booth. They can be found in most cities in India. They are not phone booths, but small shops. Billing rates for a call are recorded by a computer.

There are three different billing rates for long distance calls in India. Normal (8 am to 7 pm), half rate (7 pm to 10 pm and 6 am to 8 am), and quarter rate (10 pm to 6 am). On Sundays and Holidays calls are half rate between 6 am and 9 pm and quarter rate between 9 pm and 6 am. Calls to other countries are the same rate all the time.

To get a telephone number, dial 191 for Directory Enquiry. To get the operator (assistance) dial 199. There is also Home Country Direct service that enables you to reach your home country operator. You can then make a collect (reverse charges) or credit card call. The numbers for the countries that you can call this way are:

Australia	0006117
Canada	000167
Italy	0003917
Germany	0004917
Japan	0008117
Netherlands	0003117
New Zealand	0006417
Singapore	0006617
Spain	0003417
UK	0004417
USA	000117

The codes for some important cities are: Bangalore 080, Bhubaneswar 0674, Bombay 022, Calcutta 033, Jaipur 0141, and New Delhi 011.

To dial internationally from India first dial "00," then dial the country code, then the area code, and then the telephone number. The codes for some frequently called countries are Argentina 54, Australia 61, Bangladesh 880, Belgium 32, Brazil 55, Canada 1, Chile 56, China 86, Denmark 45, Germany 49, Singapore 65, France 33, Guyana 592, Hong Kong 852, Hungary 36, Ireland 353, Italy 39, Japan 81, Spain 34, Sri Lanka 94, Sweden 46, Switzerland 41, Thailand 66, Kenya 254, Malaysia 60, Mauritius 230, Mexico 52, Russia 7, United Kingdom 44, and United

States (Excluding Hawaii) 1.

If you dial from your home country to India, you dial an access code before the number. Some numbers are Australia 0011 91, UK 00 91, USA and Canada 011 91, Ireland 00 91, and New Zealand 00 91.

You can use an AT & T calling card to call America from India by dialing 000-117. This enables you to use your calling card or call collect.

The Indian government has 24-hour communications centers in four major cities. Videsh Sanchar Nigam Ltd (VSN Ltd) is the name of the company that runs these centers. Their addresses are as follows:

New Delhi

Videsh Sanchar Bhavan, Bangla Sahib Rd, (011-374-6769; fax 011-374-6769)

Bombay

Videsh Sanchar Bhavan, Mahatma Gandhi Rd, (022-262-4001; fax 022-262-4027)

Calcutta

Poddar Court, 18 Ravindra Sarani, (033-303-266; 033-303-218)

Madras

Videsh Sanchar Bhavan, 5 Swami Sivananda Salai, (044-561-994; fax 044-583-838)

Warning Be careful about making phone calls at hotels. The service charges can be outrageous. If the normal rate to call America is Rs 75 a minute, you may be charged Rs 300 a minute when you use a phone in your hotel room.

Fax and Telex

You can send faxes from the main post office in many cities. You can also have a fax sent to the local post office and delivered at the address you are staying at.

Faxes can be sent to and from better hotels, often with a hefty service charge. Telexes can be a good way to reserve hotels and flights, as this gives you a record of a hotel reservation or airline confirmation.

Mail (Post)

It usually takes at least 10 days to receive a letter from the USA or Europe, but two weeks is normal. Letters can arrive even two or three months after they are mailed, either coming to or going from India. Make sure you write AIR MAIL all over your letter.

Foreign air mail rates are Rs 11 for a letter, Rs 6.50 for aerogrammes, and Rs 6 for postcards. Letters mailed within India cost Rs 1, and postcards cost Rs .75.

When you send things in India you must make sure the letter or postcard is stamped right in front of you. The major reason why letters are not delivered from India is because the postal employees steal the stamps that are not cancelled and resell them. Also if you send postcards with nice pictures of Krishna, etc., they could be stolen just to get the photograph.

You can purchase aerogrammes with stamps printed on them from the post office which you do not have to worry about it being cancelled.

Speed Post Service is much faster and secure. If there is a delay in delivery you are supposed to get a refund. It costs Rs 200 to send a 200 gram letter to the United States.

The main post office in every town is called the **General Post Office (GPO)**. You can have Poste restante letters sent there. **Poste restante** is when you send the letter to a post office and it is stored under your name until you come and pick it up.

You can receive mail at Post Restante,

GPO (care of the postmaster), Baba Karak Singh Marg, New Delhi 110001 (be sure to put New Delhi and not just Delhi) or at the Tourist Office, 88 Janpath, New Delhi 110001. If you mail to the Delhi GPO, the letter will be sent to the GPO in Old Delhi, as there is a GPO in both Old Delhi and New Delhi. The main Post Office is located in New Delhi, where the important offices in town are located and where most tourists stay.

Poste restante letters can be pigeon-holed under the first initial of either your first or last name, so ask for both.

The address should be written like:

John RAMA
Poste Restante
G.P.O.
Bangalore India

You can have your poste restante letter forwarded from the place where it will arrive. You go to the place where the letter is being sent and fill out an instruction slip with the forwarding address.

Parcels

There is a good chance that a package sent to you in India by mail will not arrive.

To send a parcel, you first take it to a tailor and have him stitch cheap linen around it and seal the seams with wax. The parcel is supposed to be pressed with a seal that cannot be copied. If you have nothing else a foreign coin will do. Many times there is someone outside major post offices that does this. You can also have the person that you purchased the goods from arrange to seal and pack the package. It is not a good idea to have them ship the goods, unless you know them extremely well.

Take the parcel to the post office and fill out the customs declaration forms. You write your passport number, nation-ality, and the words "bona fide tourist" across the top of both forms. You are also supposed to list the contents of the package. To get lower duty when sending a package, it is best to write that it is a gift. If the parcel costs more than Rs 1000 you are supposed to show an encashment certificate, so you may want to write down the value as less than Rs 1000. Have the parcel weighed, and make sure they cancel the stamps in front of you. Each package shipped has to be less than 10 kilos.

You can send books and printed materials at bookpost rates. The package has to be packed in a certain way. Basically the postmen have to be able to see that there are only printed materials inside.

Warning Often shops that offer to send goods home for you send a cheap substitute instead. This is a common complaint. Sometimes they don't send the goods at all.

Guides and Tours

Many times the tourist offices in whatever city you are in offer guided tours. Often they are good, but they are usually somewhat rushed. Mostly Indians take the guided tours, as most foreigners find them to be to rushed. I found them to be a good cheap way to see places quickly. Sometimes the guide for the tour does not speak English.

You can often get a good private guide for the area by contacting the local tourist office. Travel agents in town can usually arrange a good guide for you. If the travel agent cannot speak good English, then there is a good chance that the "English speaking" guide he arranges will not speak good English either, because the agent's standard of what is good English is different than yours. You may want to test your guide on some basic information and his ability to speak good English. Sometimes they may be able to speak a few things in good English to trick you. Also many times a rickshaw or taxi driver can give you a good tour.

I have often found guides to be useful for information. On the other hand they may not really be guides at all, but commission agents. They may charge you a low price to guide you around town, say Rs 50, and just take you around to shops all day along with the few places you want to go. You should become suspicious if they want to charge you an unusually low price. The first impression of the guide is usually correct. If you do not trust the guide at all, do not hire him. A guide who manipulates you in order to be hired is usually nothing but trouble.

Travels Guides

Lonely Planet's *India* guidebook is by far the best practical travel guide. Besides good information they also have excellent maps. They also have a good book on Nepal and *Southeast Asia On a Shoestring*. *India, The Rough Guide* is also excellent. They have some cities that Lonely Planet does not mention in detail and can have much better tourist information for certain places. They are not as good, however, when it comes to finding a hotel.

Trade & Travel Handbooks' *India Handbook* is a very detailed guidebook which is over 1400 pages long. It lacks the personality and good advice of the Lonely Planet guide, but they cover a lot of additional places, so it is a good second book to get.

A *Handbook for Travellers in India, Pakistan, Nepal, Bangladesh, and Sri Lanka*, by John Murray (1982, 22nd edition), is almost like a history book, describing the history of each place. The first edition dates back to the 19th century. It is like a Victorian travel guide, but it is difficult to find and is expensive.

South India, Tamil Nadu, Kerala, Goa as well as *Western India, Karnataka, Bombay, Maharashtra,* by Philip Ward are two good general books about traveling in the respective areas. He describes the places to you as he is actually going to them, so they give you a feeling of what it is like to be there.

Insights Guides' *Rajasthan* and *India* by APA Productions, and Nelles Guides' *Northern India* and *Southern India* are good photo essays on India. They have excellent photographs and general descriptions of places, but their practical sections are limited. *India by Rail,* by Royston Ellis, is a good book about traveling by train. *Garhwal-The Devbhoomi,* published by Nest and Wings, is a good detailed book about traveling in the Himalayas.

If you are going to Nepal, the best practical guide to get is Lonely Planet's *Nepal* guide. Rough Guides' *Nepal* is also very good.

Books of India, 45 Museum Street, London WC1 by the Museum, has the best selection of books on India in the UK.

Books On Holy Places & Temples

The Penguin Guide to the *Monuments of India, Volume 1: Buddhist, Jain, Hindu* is a good technical book about the temples in India.

The Bharatiya Vidya Bhavan in Bombay publishes a good selection of spiritual books. You really have to fight past the hard-to-understand English. They have a series of books on temples in different parts of India. The best of these is *Temples of Tamil Nadu*, by R.K. Das. It is a detailed book about the temples there.

They also publish a good book about the temples in Andhra Pradesh. Their books about the temples in Kerala, Maharashtra, Bengal, and Bihar are not as good. They have a four-book series called Immortal India that describes the holy places of India. Sri Krishna, *The Lord of Guruvayur*, by KR Vaidyanathan, is an informative book about this important temple.

Temples of South India, by R.S. Ramaswami, is a good detailed book. *Yatra, Pilgrimages in the Western Himalayas* is a good book on visiting Char Dhama, Vaishno Devi, and Amarnath. *Vaishnavite Divya Desams*, by RS Ramesh, is a good detailed book with stories about these important temples. It is a multi-volume book, but only the first volume has been written as of 1996. This is about the Divya Desam temples around Madras and Kanchipuram.

Most of these books are not so easy to find, and you may have to look in many bookshops to find them.

Recommended Reading

To have a correct understanding of the spiritual culture of India it is necessary to read the *Bhagavad-gita*, which was spoken by Lord Sri Krishna to Arjuna. The most authoritative version in English is *Bhagavad-gita As It Is* by His Divine Grace A.C. Bhaktivedanta Swami Prabhupada.

Sri Navadwipa Mahatmya by Bhaktivinode Thakur is a book about the places in Navadwipa Dhama. *Radha Kunda Mahima Madhuri* by Mahanidhi Swami is a good book about Radha Kunda in Vrindavana. *Srimad Bhagavatam* contains many of the stories in this book.

Maps

The *Bartholomews map* is an excellent map. It is plastic and lasts a long time I used it myself and after two years it is still in good shape. The Nelles Verlag series has more detail, but takes 5 maps to cover India. You cannot usually buy them in India. *Nelles South India map* is far superior to any other map. It marks most of the holy cities and towns where there are major temples, and will enable you to find some smaller places that are not on any other map. The *Lascelles map of India, Pakistan, Nepal, Bangladesh, and Sri Lanka* is a useful map of India.

The Government of India tourist offices have some good city maps and a decent India map that they give away for free.

The Government Map Office has some good detailed city maps, including: Mathura, Varanasi, Allahabad, and Rishikesh. Their sales office in Delhi is opposite the tourist office on Janpath.

Weather

The weather in India can vary greatly. For the most part it is hotter in the south, but during the summer months it can be much hotter in the north. There are five seasons in India: winter, December to the middle of February; spring, middle of February to middle of April; summer, middle of April to middle of July; monsoon, middle of July to middle of September; and fall, middle of September to end of November.

The winter can be extremely cold in the north and pleasant in the south. During the spring the weather in the north is very nice. By the end of April, India is very hot everywhere but in the Himalayas. The weather in June is extremely hot, sometimes going above 45°C (113°F). It is not really possible to travel too much at this time. May and June is a good time to visit the Himalayas and to do the Himalayan Char Dham Yatra.

The monsoon season (July/Aug/beginning of Sept) is not an ideal time to travel in India, as it rains a lot. India has typical tropical rain, very hard for short periods of times. Sometimes, however, it can rain steadily for days. In Delhi during the monsoon it does not rain that much, while in Bombay it rains a lot. Other times of the year it may not rain for eight months straight, except an occasional shower. In September the rains stop in the north and it can still be pretty hot, but is not usually unbearable. October and November are ideal weather. It is still hot, but pleasant, and the rains have stopped, except in some areas in the south.

In Delhi, Agra, and Vrindavana, winter (December, January, February) is cold, especially at night, but it can be good during the day. If you are going to be traveling in the north during this time you should bring warm clothing. It does not get as cold as Europe or the USA, but there is virtually no heating system or hot water for showers in India, so you cannot escape from the cold.

If you are staying for a while, you can purchase an electric heater, which is efficient to heat up a small room. You can also get an electric coil water heater to heat up water for your bath.

Summer in Delhi and Vrindavana is extremely hot. The best season to go to Delhi and Vrindavana is spring and fall. There is no rain and the weather is perfect. October, November, and March are the best months.

The temperature in Bombay, Jagannatha Puri, and Mayapur is nice all year around, but they have a lot of rain during the monsoon. In Puri you can swim in the ocean all year around.

The Himalayas are extremely cold in the winter time, so it is not advised to go there then. The summer months, May and June, are great times to go there. Even though it rains in July and August it is still a good time to go to the Himalayas. The weather is good in September in the Himalayas, but by the middle of October it starts getting cold. Even in the summer the nights can be cool, and you may need warm clothes all year around, depending on how high up you go.

It is good to visit Nepal in October and November; western Himalayas from April to June; and the Indian peninsula and Sri Lanka from November to March.

South Indian Weather

The best time to go to South India is December to mid-February. It is hot and sunny, there is little or no rain, and the temperature rarely goes above 30°C (86°F) or below 13°C. This is the best time to travel, but the hotels may be full and the prices will be higher than normal. Especially the Christmas-New Years time is a crowded time for traveling.

From the end of February to May the weather gets hotter and hotter. From April 15 till the end of June is a bad time to travel as it is oppressively hot.

The summer monsoon (rainy) season is June to the end of August. It is still hot, but the rain makes it more refreshing. All day torrential rain is uncommon. It does not rain much in Tamil Nadu in June and July. The weather is fine in Mysore and Bangalore, but there is a lot of rain in Bombay.

In Tamil Nadu and Andhra Pradesh they have a southeast monsoon season in October and November. The rainiest months of the year in Madras and Madurai are October and November.

Hotels

It is always best to ask to see some

rooms in a hotel before paying. In hotels there can be a vast different between one room and another in the same price range. If you do not like the first room you are shown, ask to see another room. You may notice the next room is slightly, or even much better. Usually you will be shown a sub-standard room first, and if you do not like that one you will be shown a better room. This has happened to me hundreds of times.

When I come into a room I check if the sheets are clean, and I check the bathrooms to see if they have been cleaned in the last month. I expect the room to be cleanly swept. These are my minimum standards to stay in a room. It is best to see if things work in the room, such as the fan or the air-cooler. They may say they have hot water, but often it does not work.

An important thing with me about a hotel is the management. I prefer not to stay in a place where the hotel clerk is drunk or I cannot communicate with them. Good hotel managers can really make your life easier in a town. They can give you good information. They can do things for you such as arrange transportation. In short, they can generally make you feel much better about your stay in India.

Depending on the season and day of the week, in many hotels you can bargain for a lower price. Often hotels have discount rates for the off-season, but they might not tell you about them unless you ask. Many times you can get at least a 10% discount. A hotel has a fixed expenditure to have someone in a room—the cost of electricity, maid service, linen, etc. This may be Rs 30. If the hotel is only going to be 50% full that day, then anything over Rs 30 is profit for them. So if you don't mind shopping around, you may be able to get a Rs 300 room for Rs 150 on off-days and off-seasons.

In big cities like Bombay, Madras, or Calcutta, it can be very difficult to find a room at any price. Especially during the high seasons such as December or January. It is best to arrive early in the morning and find a room immediately. Even better is to reserve a room in advance.

Before checking into a hotel, it is a good idea to find out the checkout time, which is usually 12 noon. In some hotels it is 8 or 9 am instead of 12 noon. Many times you can get the checkout time extended before you move into the room. If the checkout time is 9 am, you can tell them you want to leave at 11 am. If they refuse, tell them you can't stay there then. They will usually adjust at that point. Some places have a 24-hour checkout, which means if you arrive at 7 pm you do not have to check out until 7 pm the next day.

Do not believe your rickshaw or taxi driver when they tell you the hotel you want to go to is full or closed. Or they may say that they have a much better hotel for you to go to. Actually they are probably only interested in taking you to a hotel in which they receive a commission, which in turn will be added onto your bill. When you arrive in a town it is best to use a rickshaw driver that you choose rather then one who runs up to you with enthusiasm. You have to pay for the extra work he is doing.

Even the most expensive hotels may try to overcharge you. This can particularly happen with groups. You should be careful when making long distance phone calls, as the price can be over three times the normal price. It is best to check and pay your hotel bill the night before, not when you are rushing to the airport the next morning.

Tip It is a good idea to take a business card from the hotel where you are staying and keep it with you. You may forget exactly where your hotel is located. Also many times the taxi drivers cannot understand your English when you tell them the hotel's name. If you just show them the card, they will immediately figure out how to get you to your hotel.

Railway Retiring Rooms

These are often hotel or dormitory rooms right at the railway stations. You are supposed to have a train ticket to stay in them. In a busy station they can be noisy. They can be very cheap and a good place to stay, especially if you have an early morning train. They are usually rented on a 24-hour basis.

Room Taxes & Service Charges

There are different types of taxes on hotel rooms imposed by the state government. It is usually called expenditure tax or luxury tax, and it is different from state to state. At most cheap hotels you do not have to pay this tax. The percentage rate of the tax usually goes up as the price of the room increases. A room that costs Rs 200 may have a 10% tax, and a room that costs Rs 500 will have a 15% tax. Luxury hotels usually have a tax of over 20%, with some having up to 35%.

Besides the above tax, a service charge may be added to your hotel bill. This is usually 10%. In some hotels, this is only added to food, room service, and the use of telephones. At others, it is added to the total bill. Expenditure tax is not supposed to be paid if you settle your hotel bill in foreign currency.

Seasonal Prices

Depending on the season and whether there is a festival going on, prices for hotels will vary. The main tourist season is from November to February, and prices for hotels at beaches can be two to four times inflated at this time. During the Christmas-New Year rush the prices can be even higher. During a festival, beside the price going up, it may be difficult, if not impossible, to find a decent room at all. If you are going to a big religious festival you have to take this into consideration and if possible book a room in advance. If you go to Puri in the off season you can get 20% to 50% off on your room, but to get a room during the Rathayatra you may have to reserve it months in advance. During the off season, unless you ask for a room discount, you may not get it.

World Times

Great Britain -5.30, Eastern USA -11.30, Central USA -12.30, Pacific USA -14.30, Germany -4.30, Thailand +1.30, Australia Perth +2.30, Sydney, Melbourne +4.30, Malaysia +2.30, Mauritius -5.30, Nepal is 15 minutes different, South Africa -3.30, Singapore +2.30. During the summer, Great Britain time is just -4½ hours different.

Months

The Indian lunar months and the western equivalents (Indian Calendar)

Magha	January-February
Phalguna	February-March
Chaitra	March-April
Vaishaka	April-May
Jyaistha	May-June
Asadha	June-July
Sravana	July-August
Bhadra	August-September
Asvina	September-October
Kartika	October-November
Aghan	November-Dec
Pausa	December-January.

Holiday and Festival

Holidays and Festivals normally follow the Indian lunar (Vikramaditya) calendar, and therefore each year they fall on a different day of the normal western calendar. The calendar is based on lunar months, which begin with the full moon. The lunar calendar adds a thirteenth month every thirty months to make sure the months stay the same as the seasons. It is 57 or 58 years ahead of the Christian calendar.

Electricity

The electrical current is 230-240 volts AC 50 cycles. This is different from America and England, so to use your tape record, etc., you need a converter and an adapter for your plug, which you can get at certain Indian appliance stores in your own country. Socket sizes in India vary, so it is a good idea to get an universal adapter which is available at airports and at special travel stores.

Photography

The best cameras you can buy now have automatic focus and automatic light meters, which enable even an amateur to take perfect pictures. I met an excellent professional photographer in Varanasi who used an automatic camera. I asked him how much he used it on automatic, and he told me 90% of the time. He said if he did it manually, he would miss so many good pictures.

It is a good idea to have a camera case, a cleaning brush, lens cleaning paper, polarizing filter, and a skylight filter to keep the lens from being scratched.

A lead bag to carry film protects your film from X-ray machines in the airports. Lens caps can easily get lost, so it is a good idea to bring a spare one.

I was told by a professional photographer that because of the harshness of the sun in India you get your best pictures in the early morning and late afternoon. I was advised by another professional photographer to use a polarizing filter when taking pictures in direct sunlight in the middle of the day to kill the glare of the sun. I also read this in a photography book.

Many times the film developing places are not very good in India. It is best to process your film in the big cities. Mahattas and Kinsey Bros, both in Connaught Place, New Delhi, are good for film development. Mitter Bedi Studio, by the Taj Mahal Hotel in Bombay, does one of the best jobs at processing black and white film.

Permission is often needed to use a video camera or a tripod for photography at archaeological sites. Advance permission can be obtained from the office of the Director General, The Archaeological Survey of India, Janpath, by the National Museum in New Delhi. Many spots such as the Taj Mahal do not like people to use video cameras and may charge as much as Rs 500 for their use.

Very seldom will you be allowed to take pictures inside temples, especially of the deities. The priest may get violent if you try to do so and may grab your camera out of your hand. Many people do not want their photos taken and may even get violent if you take a picture of them without permission.

You are not allowed to take pictures of anything remotely military such as railway stations, bridges, dams, border crossings, radio stations, and of course military ships or bases. I know someone who was seen by an army officer taking a picture of his friend, with a bridge in the background by the Tibet border. He was immediately detained until he could convince the army officials that he was not a spy, which took hours.

Film

The X-ray machines do not usually ruin your film the first few times, but the effect is cumulative and can cause fogging after about the fifth time. Processed film is not harmed by X-rays, nor will the archway metal-detectors or hand-held devices harm your film. So you can carry some film in your pocket.

If possible you should bring whatever film you need with you. A general rule is to bring twice the amount of film that you think you will need. If you run out of film and have to purchase some in India, make sure you check the sell-by date to confirm that it is not old stock. It is best to buy as much film as you need in the big cities, as in the small towns it can be expensive and is often past the sell-by date. Heat increases the decay of film. After taking your photos you should try to get them developed as soon as possible, especially in the summer.

Used film is more sensitive than unused film. If you are taking most of your pictures outside in bright sunlight it is best to use 100 speed film. If you will take some pictures with not such good light you should use 200 speed film. 200 speed film is a good overall film. In bad light you need 400 speed film or faster.

Antiques

Despite what you may be told and how ancient the item may look, it is unlikely that an item said to be an antique is one.

Antiques over 100 years old cannot be taken out of India unless you have an export clearance certificate from the Archaeological Survey of India, which is difficult to get. If you are discovered taking an antique out of the country without a clearance certificate, it will be taken from you.

To attempt to get an export clearance certificate for antiques you can contact the Director, Antiquities, Archaeological Survey of India, Janpath, New Delhi; Archaeological Survey of India, Sion Fort, Bombay; Superintending Archaeologist, Eastern Circle, Archaeological Survey of India, Narayani Building, Brabourne Road, Calcutta; Archaeological Survey of India, Fort St George, Madras.

Clothes

Most of the time in India you should wear loose fitting cotton cloth. In India you can get good comfortable cotton clothes, which are specially made for the weather. Artificial materials can be extremely uncomfortable as they tend to stick to your skin.

If you go to India between mid-November and mid-February it can be very cold in northern India, especially in the Himalayas. You definitely need a warm sweater or two. If you are staying for a few months it is a good idea to bring extra socks, because if you have a laundry man wash them, they wear out very quickly. A warm hat in the early morning is necessary. Thermal underwear could also be a good thing to bring. It is hard to get good winter clothes and socks in India.

Sandals are good to wear because they go on and off easy. At Bata Shoe Store for about Rs 100 you can get good cheap leather-less sandals, which are comfortable and sturdy. It is a good idea to purchase cheap sandals for temple visits. If you leave an expensive pair of shoes outside a temple unguarded they may be stolen.

Acceptable Dress

In you are well dressed, you will usually be treated better in India, especially when you are doing official business.

When going to temples you should dress very conservatively. Transparent and low-cut dresses, bare shoulders, short skirts, and shorts are not acceptable for women, except in big cities like Bombay. Women can wear trousers. Indian women on the beach bathe with their clothes on and never swim in bathing suits. Men should usually always wear a shirt in public. Men wearing *lungis* or *gumshas* away from beaches or rivers is not regarded very highly.

Many temples will not let you take leather items like bags and belts into the temple, and some will not allow socks.

Lost Passport or Ticket

If you lose your passport or plane ticket, you can expect a big hassle. If they are stolen, you must report the theft to the police immediately. You must show this police report to the airlines to get another ticket and to your local embassy to get a new passport. A USA passport is valuable in India.

If your ticket is lost, the travel agent where you purchased the ticket may have to request a new one. So it is a good idea to have the phone number and address of the travel agent that you got your ticket from. Depending on the type of ticket you had, you may have to pay again for the ticket and then wait for a refund, which can take a while. A photocopy of your passport and ticket will come in very handy if they are stolen.

Theft

If you stay in a cheaper hotel use your own lock. You can be certain that someone in the hotel has a set of spare keys. I asked several hotel managers to show me a room in their hotel while researching this book. If the hotel was full, they opened a room that had someone's things in it.

Be careful of theft in crowded places such as train stations and airports when you might be in a hurry. I have heard of cases of people having their money belt cut by thieves with razor blades underneath their fingernail. Also one person got fibreglass, which itches like hell, put down the back of his shirt. He dropped the bags he was carrying, someone bumped into him, and before he knew it, his bags were gone. One person went to sleep in his first-class compartment on a train with the doors locked. When he woke up the next morning the door of the compartment was open and all his bags were gone.

A woman may drop some coins and you may bend down to help her retrieve them. When you turn around, your camera bag is gone. You may be sitting at a train station and someone turns to you and points and says did you drop that ten rupee note by your foot. You think of course it was me, otherwise how could it have got there. You bend to pick it up and next thing you know your bag with your camera is gone. These are some actual incidents I have heard of.

If you are taking a train be careful of any bags that you place above your head. I have heard of two people who had their bags taken from there. In both cases the bags were taken before the train even left the station. It can be very hectic trying to catch a train, and when you finally sit down in your seat, you want to just relax. This is a likely time to get robbed. Be especially careful if someone wants to adjust yours bags above your head on a train so they don't fall. If someone handles your bags it is advised to watch them at every second. Even better is not to let anyone touch your bags for any reason.

If someone you do not know is overly friendly and especially helpful it is advised not to trust them. An old saying is "too much devotion is the sign of a thief."

Don't leave things lying around in a temple room. I know several cases of people putting down their bag during *arati* and later finding the bag or something from the bag missing. They couldn't believe that it happened, and I couldn't believe that they left it lying around.

When you go into a temple, you have to leave your shoes outside. A good security measure is to separate your shoes so it will be difficult for a thief to find both of them quickly. A shoe thief will not wear one shoe while he is looking for the other. The best thing is not to bring expensive shoes to temples at all, especially a good new pair of sneakers (trainers) or Berkenstocks.

Be careful of changing money on the street. A few persons I heard about were handed rupees in a paper bag. When they opened the bag they found only some newspapers with a few real bills on top. This is normal in Bombay.

On overnight trains it is best to travel with a bag or trunk that can be locked. Also it is a good idea to bring a bicycle or regular chain with you so you can lock your bag to something. Regular chains can be purchased at larger train stations.

Never take drinks or food from strangers when traveling by train or bus, as there are many known cases of drugging like this.

Also be careful that your credit card is not run off more than once when you purchase something with it. It should not be out of your sight at any time.

If someone has stolen your passport, ticket, or other important documents that are only valuable to you, you can go to the police and offer a reward for the items. The police usually have good contact with the criminal elements and may be able to get your documents back. You can also ask your hotel manager, touts, guides, and taxi drivers.

Some practical advice coming from someone who lived in New York for ten years. The most likely time for someone to get robbed is when they are intoxicated, especially totally drunk. Also, if you are by yourself on a secluded street and someone comes up to you to ask a stupid question such as, "What time is it?" or "Do you have a match?" do not even think to stop. Just keep walking like you did not hear them. And when you turn street corners at night always stay away from the buildings and turn the corner wide. Thieves always look for easy customers and the element of surprise. Make it hard for them.

Baggage Theft

I saw a show on TV about how bad theft of check-in baggage was in the USA. I also heard that the theft at Heathrow airport is very high. In a third world country, such as India, it can be outrageous. After seeing the TV show, I purchased a hard, lockable suitcase. It is a good idea to purchase a small lock to put on a cloth or soft bag to make it harder for thieves. It is best to never put valuables in check-in luggage on a plane, but to carry them with you.

Astrologers

Panditji S Nanjundiah (011 687-2312) 4-B Basant Goan, New Delhi, is a good experienced astrologer. He is located in southwest Delhi off Ring Road by the airport, next to a temple with a huge Hanuman deity. The local people know him as Panditji, the astrologer.

Food

There can be a huge difference between what you will get in most restaurants in India and what is cooked in an Indian home. The food in an Indian home is usually excellent, while most restaurant food is fair at best. In the smaller cities or when doing some heavy traveling it can be difficult to get decent food.

In South India, Bengal, and Orissa the main food is rice. The average Bengali would not know how to eat without rice. In the North they eat much more breads and wheat preparations. South India is famous for its cuisine. The main delicacies are *dosas, masala dosas, idlis*, and *uttapam*.

A *thali* meal usually consists of a number of preparations, sometimes ten or more, and often you can eat all you like for a set price. It is usually the most economical and filling thing to get on the menu, and some people think they can be very tasty.

To get good western food in India is difficult. Getting a good pizza or vegiburger is unlikely. Most attempts are not even close to being good by western standards. For India, they may still be the best thing on the menu. The food at the New Yorker in Bombay is an exception. It is usually best to eat the Indian style food in most restaurants.

Most restaurants in India put onions and garlic in many of the preparations. In South India almost everything has a great quantity of onions—sometimes five times what there is in North Indian cooking. Many people could not even imagine eating something without onions. If you do not like onions in your food, you may have to tell the waiter at least three times that you do not want any onions. I have told waiters 5 times I did not want onions and I still got them. One time in South India the waiter told the person who takes the orders back to the kitchen that I did not want onions. The man couldn't believe it, and he had to come up to me and confirm it.

It can also be difficult to communicate that you do not want chilies or heavy spicing in your food. You have to make this desire very clear to the waiter.

Food Types

Rice is the basic food in most parts of India, and many Indians will not have a meal without it. Basmati rice, which grows in the Dehra Dun area, is the best rice in the world. It has long grains and tastes great. The difference between basmati rice and the lowest grade rice is enormous. *Pulao* rice is specially cooked rice, usually with vegetables added, and it is usually a good bet in most restaurants. *Biryani* is also a special rice with nuts and dried fruit, but the standard is inconsistent.

Chapatis, flat unleavened wheat bread, are the most commonly eaten and most healthy bread for you. The deep fried variety of chapatis are called *puris*. A *nan* is bread that you bake in a clay tandoori oven and is usually excellent.

Dal is a lentil (pea) soup, which is included in most meals. In some small towns *dal* and rice may be the only thing you find on the menu or the only thing worth eating, as everything else may be too spicy.

A meal will usually also include one or two *subjis*, or vegetable preparations. A normal side dish is *raita*, cucumber mixed with curd (yoghurt). *Dahi* (curd or yoghurt) is also a normal addition to a meal.

Samosas are the most commonly eaten snack. It is vegetable covered by pastry bread and fried. It is a good item to travel with as it does not go bad right away. *Bhelpuri* is a famous Bombay snack and is very good. *Channa* means chickpeas.

Restaurants In This Book

Most of the restaurants in this book are pure vegetarian. Pure vegetarian means there is no meat, fish, or eggs cooked in the kitchen or served in the restaurant.

There are three reasons why only pure-veg restaurants are listed in this book. When you go to holy places it is suggested not to eat fish, meat, eggs, or impure food. That is why in some holy cities such as Haridwar, Rishikesh, and Pushkar, the eating of meat, fish, and eggs is forbidden. Another reason is because I am a vegetarian and believe meat should not be eaten. Therefore, unless mentioned otherwise, the restaurants listed in this book are pure-veg.

If you have any trouble with that, I can objectively warn you that the way meat is handled in India can be very unhealthy for you. There is no standard or laws that deal with meat in India, so it is potentially highly hazardous for your health.

Women Traveling Alone

It is best for women not to travel alone, especially if they have never been to India before. Many men in India think western women to be easy.

I met a woman on the plane coming back from India who traveled by herself. She told me she never wanted to come to India again, it was a total nightmare. She took a second-class train and was the only woman on the train. She said, "All the men just stared at me. I finally fell asleep and when I woke up, I was still alive. I then arrived in Mathura during Holi and a bunch of men surrounded me and threw red dye on me. The more I told them to go away, the more they bothered me. Things really got bad for me when my Deities were stolen in Calcutta from my room. Someone put their hand through the window and took them. I made a phone call to America from my hotel room and the bill was $600. They charged me ten dollars a minute."

There are some advantages to being a woman in India. Women can request a ladies compartment in a 2nd class carriage of a train. Many trains have such a compartment. Also, most of the time there is a special ladies' queue (line) for purchasing train tickets. This means that ladies can go to the front of a queue to purchase tickets for trains and no one will say anything. Most railway stations have ladies' waiting rooms.

If you are a woman traveling alone, it can be a good idea to travel by air-conditioned or first-class. There are much less passengers on these carriages, and they have usually had more contact with foreigners, so they are easier to deal with. It is important that women dress modestly. Women in India do not normally show their shoulders or knees, or wear tight fitting clothes or shorts. It is best not to wear clinging or low cut clothes.

Women usually do not shake hands with men, and certainly any physical contact beyond this is asking for trouble. Gropers are a normal thing. It is standard for women to be groped (handled) on the local trains in Bombay. That is why there are separate compartments for women.

Even just walking in the station women can be handled. If a woman goes into a very crowed situation with many men, such as a bus, especially if she is a by herself, it is not unusual for her to be groped. This happens with Indian ladies too.

Shopping

If you want to get a good idea of what the local area offers, you can go to the government emporiums. Their price may be a little higher than other shops, but they have a good selection of quality products at fixed prices. Their prices are usually fixed at the high end, so it is advised not to pay more for a product than the price at a government emporium.

On the streets you have to bargain hard to get anything at a fair price. Never accept the first price given. Many times it can be four to five times the normal price. Many times it is a matter of pride to bargain for a lower price.

Jaipur and Agra are known for marble work, Mysore and Bangalore for incense and sandalwood, Varanasi for brasswork and silk, Jaipur for gems, Hyderabad for silver work, and Udaipur for miniature painting.

To check if cloth is silk, you burn a thread. Silk smells like burnt hair. Synthetics do not burn, but melt, and other materials smell differently. Silk burns and disappears, while synthetics become a round plastic ball. Marble cannot be scratched with your fingernail, unlike the cheaper soapstone.

In your travels you will see what appears to be old jewelry, boxes, or other items. Very seldom are these items actually antiques. They may put some chemical, bury them, beat the items, or treat them in some way to make them look old. In many cases the items look great, but

don't be tricked into paying a higher price for the items because they are antique. I know people who purchase painting in America, spray some chemical on them, and sell them as paintings that look antique, and people love them. So I am not saying don't buy the items, but I am saying bargain the shop owner down at least 50% for the item.

You should make sure you get a receipt for any expensive item. You may have to produce a receipt for customs when you return home. Many countries encourage imports from developing countries, so there may be special customs treatment for Indian goods.

It is a good idea to bring a bag when you go shopping for fruits, etc. as you may either not get a bag or get one made of newspaper. It is also good to carry a shopping bag so as not to increase the number of plastic bags littering the terrain.

How to Bargain

It is important to know in advance the price of something you want to purchase. If you want to buy some fruit, ask a local person what the price is before purchasing. If you do not know the price, then assume they will charge 20% to 200% more than you should pay. If the price seems outrageous, just walk away and don't even answer them. Check other shops and if you cannot get a cheaper price, then go back to one of the shops you walked away from. They think nothing of it.

To shop properly in India you have to give yourself at least 50% more time than in the West, so you can bargain properly. The longer a merchant spends with you, the more likely you are to work the price down. A merchant does not like to totally waste his time, he wants to make the sale. So sometimes it pays to just stall. If the merchant sees you are in a big hurry, they will almost certainly try to charge you a high price. So even if you are in a hurry, you should still act like you have all the time in the world.

If you are a foreigner you should expect to pay more than the locals. One person came up to me and asked me to come to his uncle's shop. I said let me bring my friend, who happened to be Indian. He said to me "Oh, your friend is Indian." He then walked away because he realized he could not rip me off, because I was with an Indian who knew the prices of everything.

For a large purchase I would suggest that you never buy anything the first time you go to a shop. Go around and check out the prices in other shops and find the best deal. You can be reasonably assured you are getting ripped off if a shopkeeper is trying to force you to buy an expensive item immediately, without shopping around. Unless you are highly experienced, it is best to never purchase any item over US$100 the first time you come to a shop. Indians are expert at the hard sale and are sometimes down-right cheaters and liars.

Never allow your taxi driver or guide to bring you to a shop, as they always get a large commission on anything you buy. I have never found a decent deal in this way, and I have tried a number of times just to see what would happen. This way of buying is a total dead end.

If you really like something, it is usually a good idea to purchase the item right there on the spot, as it may be impossible to find the same product again. Especially if it is a regional product.

You can almost always bargain on the street. Government emporiums, expensive shops, and department stores often have fixed prices, and you can not bargain. When there is a fixed price, many times you can get a price discount if you purchase more than one item.

If you are going to Nepal, you can get most Tibetan items there at a lower price than in India. Most Tibetans will not bargain. They would rather lose the sale than give a lower price.

Buying Warning

It is not a good idea to purchase things for resale, unless you know what you are doing. You may be told that you can purchase gems and resell them outside of India for at least double, if not ten times, the price. They may even give you a fake customer's address in your home country who they say will buy from you. I heard of a case where two women purchased gems for US $2,500. When they sent them to Israel to be resold, they were valued at less than $250.

I do know people that are doing this business out of India and making good money, but they have years of experience. In the section on Jaipur I suggest a few gem people that you can purchase from for personal use. Even from these people, I would be careful.

If you purchase goods from a shop, be careful about having them ship the goods back to your own country. If you are buying with a credit card, they may tell you they will not forward your credit slip for payment until you receive the goods at home. Do not believe this. If you do not know the shop owner you are buying from, how do you know they will ever ship the goods? Even if you have to pay a good amount for overweight, it is usually better than shipping them.

Very seldom do you have to pay duty when you bring goods with you back to your home country. If you ship the goods, however, there is a good chance you will have to pay duty. You may also have to pay clearing charges, VAT or sales tax, storage, and airport charges. Many times it can cost you more than double the shipping cost to get what you purchased home.

It is not unusual for merchants to incorrectly add up bills, and the mistake is almost always in favor of the merchant. Seldom will the bill ever be added correctly, unless you are going to the same person year after year. In this case the bill will usually be correct every time. I check every bill thoroughly, unless I have been dealing with someone for years. In that case I already checked them, and even then I still randomly check them.

Buying Fake Things

Many times gems that are offered to you on the street are fake or only worth one-tenth of what you are told. Items sold as sandalwood are often not real sandalwood. Sandalwood oil is put on other wooden items to make them smell like sandalwood. Real sandalwood items are expensive.

Ivory and Restricted items

Ivory items are banned in most countries of the world, and if you are caught bringing them into your local country, not only may they be confiscated, but you may also face a fine.

Animal skins are not supposed to be taken out of India. Peacock feathers in reasonable quantities can be brought out of India.

Gold jewelry up to Rs 2,000 and other jewelry (set with precious stones) up to Rs 10,000 can be exported out of India. Items purchased above these amounts are supposed to be declared when departing the country.

Ants

They love anything sweet. It is a good idea to bring zip-lock plastic sandwich bags to store sweet things. If ants attack your room, you can get rid of them by cleaning the room with eucalyptus oil.

Notice There are many power failures in India. So it is a good idea to have a good torch (flashlight).

Touts (Commission Agents)

They meet you at the train station, bus station, or airport and are paid a commission by a hotel to bring you there. They pick up unsuspecting tourists and either bring them to a hotel, where they charge up to double the normal price, or to some shop, where they try to sell tourist items for double to ten times the normal price. They can get 30% to 100% commission on the price of the room, which just means that you pay more. Taxi or auto-rickshaw drivers often engage in such activities. If you ask to go to a particular hotel, they might tell you it is full or many people get robbed there. One tout jumped into my taxi in Jaipur and offered to show us around. He told me the hotel I wanted to stay at was full, and when we got there the hotel was totally empty.

They will say they are taking you to their uncle's or father's shop, where you will get an unbelievable deal. Don't believe it. If a tout does bring you to a shop and you want to purchase something, a good idea is to act like you do not like anything in the shop and just leave. You could then come back a half hour later without the tout and purchase the item that you liked at a much lower price.

There are touts in Jaipur who offer to take you on an all-day tour for Rs 50, which doesn't pay for their petrol (gas) to get around. They actually know the town and give you a good tour, but in between each place they show you great spots to purchase clothes, jewels, or whatever else. I know two ladies who did this. They purchased a ring that was an all right deal and paid double the correct price for some clothes. Considering that they got a good tour of the town, they were more than satisfied.

One way to get rid of touts is to hire one. If most of the hotels in town are full, they always know where there is a hotel with a room. They can be useful if there is a special festival and the town is packed, as they will know the hotels that still have rooms. They can save you a lot of time and hassle.

Social Behavior

In India people use their right hand to eat, as well as to offer and take things from people. The left hand is considered unclean, as that hand is used for the toilet. It is considered impolite to give or accept something from someone with your left hand. It is considered dirty to serve food with the left hand or to put your left hand in your mouth.

Women do not generally shake hands with men. Also men and women should not touch each other in public, especially in holy places and temples.

To greet someone, it is good manners to put your palms together and say "Namaste" or "Hare Krishna." You can also shake hands, but this is not usually done in India unless you are doing a business deal or someone wants something from you. Orthodox Hindus consider themselves polluted if they touch a person from a lesser caste, which Westerners are considered. Usually the more enthusiastically someone greets you the more likely they are to rip you off.

When you enter someone's home you should take off your shoes. It is all right to wear shoes inside a house as long as they are never taken outside the house. Most Indians take a bath and brush their teeth every day, if not several times a day. It is a religious duty to take a daily bath.

Serving spoons should never touch the plate of the person being served. After someone has begun eating, they should wash their hands before serving themselves or others food. If someone drinks from a bottle, they should not touch the mouth of the bottle and give it to someone else. This is considered unclean and unhealthy. Also you do not take a bite out of something and then hand it to someone else to eat, or eat off the same plate as someone. After eating, Indians always wash their hands and mouth.

Indian Toilets

You may be bewildered when you first go into an Indian toilet, because there may not be any toilet paper or a seat to sit on. Indians, even the highest class Indians, usually clean themselves with water instead of using toilet paper. They usually then take a full bath with soap and water. Also Indians do not sit down, they squat when they go to the toilet. It is actually a much more healthy and effective system. Only the left hand is used for the toilet.

Begging

There are beggars and then there are sadhus or saintly persons who accept donations. I do not think it is a good idea to give anything to the average beggars, unless you give them food. Giving to a saintly person is actually to the benefit of the giver. The difficulty with giving to a saintly person is to know who is actually saintly.

One problem about giving to beggars

by temples or holy places, especially if they are children, is that if you give to one, you may have a hundred persons surround you and ask you for money. Also it is a bad policy to give any money to small children, because they usually give all the money to their parents or some other adult. In this way the parents do not have to work nor is it profitable for the parents to give their children an education.

General Information

Geckoes, the little lizards in your room, are not only harmless, but also very helpful, because they eat mosquitoes and other insects. Their skin is poisonous, so they should not be touched.

If you have a problem understanding what is being said, you can ask the person to spell out the word, especially if it is a name.

Before you hire a guide make sure you can understand his English and he can understand yours. Many times they will say a few words that they know so you think they speak good English, then later you find you cannot communicate with them at all.

If I cannot communicate with someone, I immediately go on to the next person and do not waste my time.

Many times the word hotel is used for a restaurant.

Shaking of the head to the side, as you would do if you were saying no in America, can mean yes in India. Sometimes nodding the head can mean "no."

Measurements and Numbers

India uses the metric system. In this book, distances are usually given in kilometres. A kilometre is 0.62 of a mile. Eight kilometres equal five miles. There are 1000 metres in a kilometre and 100 centimetres in a metre. A metre is just over 3.3 feet and a centimetre is .4 inches. A litre is equal to 1.06 quarts.

Temperature in India is measured by the Centigrade system. To convert from Centigrade to Fahrenheit you multiply the Centigrade temperature by 9/5 and add 32. A kilo is 2.2 pounds.

A hundred thousand is called a *lakh* (1,00,000), and ten million is called a *crore* (1,00,00,000). A million would be referred to as 10 *lakhs* and not as a million.

Indian English & Communication

Unless a person is highly educated, it is best to not speak in complete sentences. If you want a post office or the bus stand, it is usually best to just ask "Post Office?" or "bus stand?" and not "Where is the bus stand?" You could also say "Where Post Office?" It is best to mainly speak in one-to-three word sentences. Even if you speak to a highly educated person it is best to speak with an Indian accent if you can (I can't) and speak very slowly. What Indians are taught in school has little to do with the language that is spoken in America.

If you want to get directions to the train station, and you say "Where is the train station?" there is a good chance all you will get is blank stares. You have to ask "railway station?" Many people do not know what a train station is. Sometimes a bus station is called the "bus stand" in a particular town. If you ask for the bus station, no one will know what you are talking about.

If people cannot understand you when you speak, try to say the same thing in another way. Sometimes you will have to rephrase your question five or six times before it will be understood.

Mandir is another name for temple.

In Sanskrit sometimes the letter 's' is pronounced as 'sh' and sometimes simply as 's.' The letter 'b' and 'v' are used interchangeably. It can be either Braja or Vraja, or it can be Vrindavana or Brindavana.

Temple Rules

1. It is best to dress conservatively. Women should not overly expose themselves. Women should also ideally have their head covered in a temple. This can be done by a simple shawl or a piece of cloth.

2. You have to leave your shoes outside temples. Shoes are not supposed to be carried into the temple in a bag or purse. You can purchase a cheap pair of sandals for temple visits. In this way you can easily slip them off and on, and you will not have to worry about them being stolen. You should not leave an expensive pair of shoes (especially brand new ones) outside a temple unless they are guarded by a person, as there is a good chance they will be stolen. There is usually someone who will look after your shoes for a rupee or two. In most temples it is all right to keep your socks or stockings on, but not always.

3. A number of temples are off limits to non-Hindus. Other temples may allow non-Hindus to enter parts of the temple, but not the inner sanctum where the deity is located. Temple authorities can be very strict about this and can be violent if you do not follow the rules.

4. You may have to pay a small fee to take pictures of a temple. Many times you can take pictures of the temple building itself, but not the deities. You should ask for permission to take pictures of the deities. You should also ask to take pictures of persons, as they may not like it at all.

5. Smoking is strictly prohibited on temple grounds.

6. You may be approached by persons asking for donations or a fee to take photographs. Do not blindly accept that these persons are bona fide.

7. Leather items should not be taken in temples. At Jain temples they are strictly forbidden.

8. Men and women should never touch each other in a temple and deep respect should be shown in the temple.

9. You do not have to make a donation in a temple, but a small donation will help both yourself and the temple. You can consider it like an admission fee.

10. If you take any items in the temple from a priest, such as a flower, *prasada* (food), *tilaka*, etc., expect to give a donation. In many cases no matter how much you give it will not be enough. So give what you think is correct and smile.

11. It is traditional to circle the temple, *stupa*, or deities. This should always be done clockwise.

12. If you bow down before the deities (pay obeisances) you should bow down with your left side to the deities, not your right side.

13. If you are walking in a crowded temple room you should not walk over people to get somewhere. This is considered extremely impolite. Better to alert them to your presence and desire to get through and ask them to move, no matter how much trouble this takes.

14. While sitting in a temple, you should not point your legs towards the deities.

Temple Tour, Pandas & Donations

It you are having someone guide you, it is best to work out a price in advance. Expect when you get fairly close to the altar (inner sanctum) of the temple to be approached for a donation. What you give is really up to you. Depending on the temple, a rupee or two may be enough, or for a major temple you may be approached for Rs 100 or more. I have found that when I give a donation to the temple priest on the altar I get treated much better. I definitely will be able to have *darshan* for a longer period, and I usually receive some *maha-prasada* or a garland of the deity.

When you enter some temples the temple *pandas* (*brahmin* guides) may accost you and offer to guide you around the temple, especially if you look like you have some money. Sometimes these guides can be extremely aggressive. They will gladly bring you to see every deity in the temple complex and explain to you how much you, your family members, and everyone in the world will benefit if you give a large donation. Many times these guides receive back over 50% of each donation you give to the temple as a cut for getting you to give.

I have actually found the brahmin temple guides to be very useful for getting information for this book, and I didn't mind giving a decent donation to them for helping me. Giving Rs 50 to a brahmin is a good donation for showing you around for an hour, and most guides will be more than satisfied with this even though they may not appear to be. If they are really good, I may give Rs 100.

Indian Culture

1. Don't overload your plate, you are expected to finish everything.

2. Never put objects on a temple or someone's personal altar in their home or on sacred items, such as a religious book.

3. Never point the soles of your feet towards an altar in a temple, other people, or holy sites.

4. Remove your shoes when entering

someone's home, even if they tell you it is all right to wear your shoes. It is almost never all right.

Problems & Indian Bureaucracy

Do not be annoyed if you have a problem getting something done, just be patient. If the person that you are dealing with can't do what you need or is just plain unhelpful, ask to see the next higher official or the manager. Make sure you tell the person how important and competent he is and the organization he is working for is. It is amazing how proud Indians are about working for the government. Many things can happen just by waiting and letting the system fall into place.

If all else fails, ask to see the complaint book, which no one can refuse to give you. If someone is treating me in a way that I consider totally unfair, I demand that the person writes down his name so I can complain to his superior. This usually breaks the person out of their dream world and makes them do things efficiently and quickly. I do actually complain if I am unfairly treated and have usually received what I consider justice when I complained. Also small personal gifts such as a western pen or lighter or a devotional item such as a picture of Krishna or a spiritual book can really help.

WHAT TO BRING

It is a good idea to make a list of all the things that are needed for a trip to India at least a month before departure. It is amazing how fast your life can start moving just before you go to India and how many valuable things you can forget. It is best to have everything you need at least a week before you go to India, which will usually never happen.

There is a high duty (changes all the time) on goods imported into India. So even though things are usually cheap in India, anything imported is very expensive, even by western standards. Also the quality of many products made in India is highly inferior to that of the same item made in the USA or Europe.

A **sturdy backpack** or a strong plastic or **cloth bag** is usually better than a sturdy suitcase. If you plan to travel a good deal by bus, two small bags could be better than one large one because the small bags can fit under the sit and you do not have to put them on top of the bus.

Clothing

Cotton clothing is usually best in India. It is not a good idea to bring clothes that have to be specially laundered, as it will be difficult to find some place in India to clean them, unless you are staying in first-class hotels. In India you can get good clothes that are made for the weather. The same Indian style clothes you find in the West can be one tenth the cost in India.

It is a good idea to bring modest type clothing. Wearing shorts or not wearing a shirt in formal situations is not well received in India. Except in beach towns, big cities such as Bombay, and major tourist towns, women wearing shorts, short skirts, or low cut dresses is not a good idea and is just asking for trouble.

If you are going to be in North India during the winter, from the end of November to the middle of March, you will need some warm clothing. It can get very cold in Delhi and Vrindavana, going close to freezing. In the Himalayas it can be cold at night even in the summer time. You should bring a **warm sweater** and maybe a **jacket** or **thermal underwear** if you are going to be in North India in the winter. I bring a sweater, sweatshirt, and thermal underwear and sometimes wear all of them on a cold morning. It can seem a lot colder than it is because there is no central heating at all, and the cold weather can wear on you. You should bring more than enough **socks**, as it is difficult to get a good pair of socks in India and laundry men tend to ruin your socks.

Sandals are useful in India because you will have to take your shoes off to go into temples or people's homes.

Personal Items

Soap, toothpaste, and other toiletries are easily gotten in India. You can get a good Ayurvedic soap called Candrika and good Ayurvedic toothpastes like Vicco or Neem. It is still a good idea to bring whatever toiletries you might need, as the quality of shampoos, lotions, razors, and some other personal items is not as good as in the West. You can get good Gillette **temporary razors** cheaply in India. **Dental floss** and **shaving cream** are important things to bring from the West. **Bandages** and **anti-infection creams** are also very useful. A small cut can easily become infected, so it should immediately be treated and bandaged. A cream to kill the pain of insect bites is very useful. Calamine lotion is good for this.

Imported **cosmetics** are expensive, and the Indian brands are often highly inferior. Bring your own **tampons**, as the ones in India are usually not very good.

Bring your **eye-glass prescription** if you have a sight problem and ideally an extra pair of glasses. If you wear contact lenses, it is best to bring your own **contact lens solution** and another set. A friend of mine told me that he had a problem with his contacts because it is often very dusty in India and he would often have to wear his glasses instead. **Earplugs** can be essential, as India is a very noisy country. It is not unusual for people to blast loud-speakers at an unbelievable level all night. Buses have very loud horns that can be blown almost continuously, and the music on private buses can be so loud you would think that half the country must be totally deaf.

Mosquito repellent is a necessity. Spray cans are good because you can spray them over your body and clothing. Also some liquid repellent is necessary to put on your face. If you can get a roll-on repellent, it can save you from having to touch the repellent.

Sunscreen lotion or sunblock cream is useful, as the sun in India is like nowhere else in the world. You can get it in India at beach resorts, but it is expensive.

The **towels** in India are not usually very good, so it is a good idea to bring your own. I read in one book where the author tested whether dark towels dry faster than light colored towels. He found that the dark towels dried faster, which is important when you travel, as often your towel drying time will be limited.

Food

I found that it is a good idea to bring some good **nuts** and **dried fruit** to India. Both these items are expensive in India and are often not very good quality. These items are nice to have for traveling and also just for taste. Many times the meals in India can be very dull and a handful of cashews and dried fruit can be just what you need.

If you are used to drinking herbal tea, bring it with you, as you won't find it in India. **Herbal teas** are a good source of clean water, because you boil the water which kills the germs. You might also want to bring some **honey** as it is hard to find good honey.

Water Purification Devices

A **water purifier pump** can be a very useful item to have. The *Pur* water purifier is excellent because it also contains an iodine filter that is supposed to kill anything. Then it has another filter that filters out the iodine. The *Trekker Travel Well* also works the same way with an iodine resin complex. The problem with a water purifier is it is one more thing to carry around.

Water purification tablets are useful both to purify drinking water and also to purify water to wash salads and fruit. Good water purification pills cannot be found in India.

Bring a **canteen** or **water bottle**, as it is difficult to find a water container in India that does not leak.

Others

I've found a **pocket knife** (preferably Swiss Army) to be totally essential in India. It is very difficult to find a pocket knife in India that can cut properly and does not rust. When you purchase a knife it can be so dull that it's difficult to figure out which side of the knife is the cutting side.

A **flashlight (torch)** is needed in India. The lights go out often in India, even in the big cities. A decent flashlight can be purchased in India very cheaply, but not an excellent one.

A **money belt** is an absolute necessity. It is best to always carry your money with you, but never in your outer pockets. There are no shortage of pickpockets in India. A friend of mine told me he was pickpocketed of all his money on a Delhi bus and didn't even know it until he got home. You may consider having two money belts. You carry your main supply of money underneath your clothing in one money belt, and in the other money belt you carry a small amount of money that you might need immediately.

Tape can be useful. I use it for taping up ripped bills, among other things. Five **passport photos** are a good thing to bring with you when you travel. A **sewing kit** and **sunglasses** can also be useful.

Bring two strong **locks**. One should be a combination lock in case you share a room with someone. Locks in India are of very poor quality. Also many times the key from one lock can open up other locks made by the same company. This is especially true with small locks. I consider a good lock essential. A **bicycle chain** to chain your luggage to something on a train or bus can be useful.

Plastic **zip-lock bags** to carry food may come in handy. The ants love raisins and sweets. **Clothespins** can be useful if you plan to wash your own clothes. If you are going during the monsoon season (July/Aug), an **umbrella** may be necessary. A good universal **sink plug** can be handy, as most sinks in India do not have plugs.

You should try to bring whatever **film** you need with you. Bring more than you plan on using, as India is a very interesting country. A **lead bag** to protect your film from the X-ray machines could be a good idea. You can get many imported films in India, but they are expensive and sometimes sold past the sell-by date.

Tissue paper and **paper towels** are not good quality in India.

Sleeping Gear

You may or may not want to bring a **sleeping bag**. If you are going to be in North India during the winter months, November to March, it is a good idea to have a good sleeping bag, especially if

you like to be warm at night. Sometimes it can go into the thirties (5°C), so even with a few blankets it can be cold. A sleeping bag can also be useful to avoid dirty sheets in cheap hotels and to sit on while riding on a train. If you are going to be traveling in the South or during the summer months in the North and sleeping on a bed all the time, you may not need a sleeping bag.

If you are going to be sleeping on the floor in cold weather it could be a good idea to bring an **insulation mat**, as the floors in India are usually made of stone. A Therm-a-Rest self-inflating one is recommended. Much body heat can leak out when you sleep on the floor even with the best sleeping bag. An insulation mat can make you 50% warmer when you sleep, especially on bare ground. It can also be useful and more comfortable to sleep on if it is too hot to use a sleeping bag. The problem with these mats is that they are big and hard to carry around.

If you do not bring a sleeping bag, a **sleeping bag liner** can be useful to insulate you while sleeping on trains or on dirty beds in lower-end hotels and guesthouses. It is a good idea to try to get one made of the finest cotton possible so you carry less bulk around.

Introduction to India

India can be the greatest paradise or the worst nightmare for a visitor. It is important to start your trip off right from the moment you come off the plane. The first time I went to India, I was part of a tour. Everything was arranged for me—transportation, eating and accommodation. The trip was very easy for me, and it was possible for me to gradually get used to India while being totally protected.

So my first suggestion to a person on

his or her first trip to India is don't go alone. Go with someone who knows the country. Or when you get there join up with someone for the first week or two. If you are going with other first-time visitors, or by yourself, then I would suggest that you take your time while doing things. I would say about 10% of the newcomers to India that don't come with a tour group experience a nightmare for the first week. After a few days they just want to leave, and many of them do just that. The first three days can be the toughest. For many people India is a culture shock.

Newly Arrived in India

As you walk up to immigration there is a large line that takes an unbelievably long time, especially after such a long trip. This is your first experience with Indian bureaucracy. Get used to it. This is normal in India.

You get through immigration and are waiting for your bags. What an opportunity to get some help. Everyone waiting for their bags is friendly and just waiting to help you. There is no shortage of people who know the exact price of the transportation to wherever you want to go. Many of them know a good hotel to stay at, in your price range. Maybe one of them wants to go to the same place. Only airline passengers are allowed in the terminal. In general everyone is your friend.

Educated older gentlemen are usually very helpful because they usually speak good English and don't need anything from you, except maybe an interesting conversation. This is not always true if you are a single woman. Be careful of people who speak too hip English, unless they are from Bombay.

You then go through customs. If you are in Delhi on your right is a prepaid

taxi booth. There are two prepaid taxi booths in Delhi airport—one inside the terminal and one outside. The one outside is cheaper. When you get outside the terminal, go to the prepaid taxi booth and ask them how much it is to where you want to go. Do you know where that is? Your first lesson is, always have a good idea what you are going to do when you arrive at a new place. If you are going downtown, you should already know the price by asking other passengers on your flight. In Delhi for long distance trips, such as to Vrindavana or Jaipur, you should be able to get a taxi for 30% cheaper than whatever price you are told at the prepaid taxi stand. In Bombay and Calcutta it is usually best to arrange a taxi at the prepaid taxi stand.

When you first come out of the terminal, you hit the moment of truth. You are in INDIA. People are rushing everywhere. It seems as if hundreds of people are coming up and asking if you need a taxi or some help in some way. Hundreds of people want to help you. Need a taxi? Where do you want to go? If you say you don't need any help, then they want to help you even more. Second lesson. Always be prepared for these experiences.

Just stand there calmly and ask how must it costs to go to where you want to go. If you already know the price, tell the taxi driver the price you are willing pay. Why waste time? As the taxi drivers can tell you are a newcomer, it will be hard to get that price. Don't worry too much about getting ripped off, you are obviously a tourist. Pay a price that is reasonable and get going. This might take you ten minutes, but don't worry about the time. Third Rule: Always be patient. If you are in a hurry, pay the price and don't worry about it. But don't get totally ripped off. Once you start being ripped off, it's hard to get out of the habit. Don't wait till you are broke to get cheap.

A major rule is to always have the taxi driver quote you the price in Indian Rupees. You can be certain that a taxi driver (or anyone else for that matter) is trying to rip you off if they quote prices in dollars. The usual line is "It is just $50, in your country the price would be $200". Well, you are not in your own country.

Once you are in the taxi do not listen to any advice the taxi driver may give you. He is not your friend. He is only interested in one thing, your money. You arrive at your hotel and it is full. What do you do now? You could not sleep on the plane, and you are really tired. Open this book or another tourist book you have and look for another hotel. You can ask the hotel clerk if he thinks your next choice will be full. Why not call up the hotel and see if it is full? Show the hotel clerk whatever tourist books you have and ask him to choose a hotel in your price range, but do not totally trust him. If possible, don't let the taxi driver choose a hotel for you. He will only be interested in bringing you to a hotel where he will get a commission.

If you arrive late at night, you may have to pay an outrageous amount the first night or you may have to stay in a real dump. In big cities many of the hotels will be full by evening time. If you plan to stay in a higher class hotel, you could arrange a room with the tourist booth at the airport. For the budget traveler arriving in Delhi, there are many cheap hotels in the Paharganj area.

Fourth lesson: When you arrive in your hotel go to sleep and do not talk to any Indians that come to give you advice. Do not make any important or even minor decisions about your trip. Just rest. Why not spend your first day walking around the city and feel the place out? When you walk out onto the street, suddenly someone walks up to you and just wants to know how he can help you. Do you need to find a rug or painting shop? Maybe you need some handicrafts? If you are not interested, politely say, "no thank you." Or if someone will not go away, firmly ask him to leave. Fifth lesson: Anyone who wants to help you when you do not really need any help usually doesn't want to help you at all, they usually only want to exploit you. It is a good idea not to talk to anyone on the street. These people can be very expert at what they do. They can even throw a big guilt trip on you by saying something like, "You mean you will not be even decently polite and speak to an Indian interested in meeting someone from another country. I don't want to hurt you. I just want to help you. I have all the time in the world to help you."

The key is to block these people out and not even acknowledge their existence. Especially if you are a woman, no man should approach you for any reason. It is against Indian culture for a man to come up unsolicited to an unknown woman. It is considered extremely bad manners. If you are a woman, you do not have to be even slightly polite, and every person walking by will stand up for you. After a few days they will not exist any more. They know who is easy and who isn't. As one woman who lived in India for five years told me, "You mean people really get ripped off?"

If you really do need help and someone offers it, there is a good chance the person is sincere. The proof of this is that he just deals with the problem on hand and then walks away, maybe after asking what country you are from.

When you see some other westerners

that look like they have the same interest and are presently in the same economic status, stop them and ask for advice. You will find that westerners will be more than willing to help you in any way. They usually love to talk about their experiences, and that's what you need, experience.

Tourist offices, as well as hotel clerks, are also good sources of useful information. If you are on a city street, just stop an intelligent-looking man, especially if he is older, and ask him if he speaks English. If he does, ask him to help you. You'll be amazed how helpful they can be. Sometimes they will walk with you for five blocks to get you to where you want to go. Or go to a shop that sells expensive items and ask for advice. I found that shops that sell cigarettes, cold drinks, and pan are good sources of information. The shopkeepers in these shops usually speak English and know where everything is located. Remember: stop the person of your choice. It is usually best not to take advice from someone who suddenly appears to help you.

SUGGESTED HOLY PLACES

Vrindavana and Mathura This is the birthplace and childhood home of Lord Krishna. The entire place has a totally spiritual atmosphere. It is a very peaceful place, and it is a highly recommended.
Mayapur This is the birthplace of Lord Caitanya Mahaprabhu. It is therefore considered along with Vrindavana as the most important pilgrimage place for Gaudiya Vaisnavas. It is a beautiful and peaceful place out in the middle of beautiful tropical Bengali villages about four hours north of Calcutta.
Puri This is the home of Lord Jagannatha and His transcendental brother and sister, Lord Balarama and Lady Subhadra. Lord Caitanya spent a good part

of His life here. It is a beach town in Orissa and has many western visitors. It is a good place to stay for a week or two, even though most of the holy places can be seen in two days.
Dwarka This is a small town on the west coast of Gujarat where Lord Krishna spent the later part of His time on earth, 5000 years ago. It is a peaceful town and some people consider it their favorite place in India.
Varanasi Many people would consider their tour of India incomplete without coming to Varanasi. It is a town very dear to Lord Siva. It is a maze of very crowded small streets and temples. Also the *ghats* are interesting, and some of them are very busy. A boat ride on the Ganges during the early morning is a must.
Pushkar This small desert town has a pleasing atmosphere with no vehicle traffic on the main street. It has a holy lake and one of the only Brahma temples in India. It is popular with young travelers.
Rishikesh It is a peaceful town on the bank of the Ganges, where the Ganges first leaves the Himalayas and reaches the plains. It is famous for having many yoga ashramas. During the summer it is a nice place to come and stay for a while.
Himalayan Char Dham These are the four holy towns of Yamunotri, Gangotri, Kedarnath, and Badrinath, high in the Himalayas. Going to these holy places you can experience the beauty of the Himalayas. It is a tough trip, but well worth the experience.

TEMPLES AND TEMPLE TOWNS
Tirupati This is the home of Sri Venkateswara (Sri Balaji). This is one of the most visited temples in all of India with over 25,000 people visiting on an average day. It is on top of a spiritual hill and has an unbelievably tranquil atmo-

sphere. It is an important temple to visit if you are in South India. Foreigners are allowed to enter the temple.

Sri Rangam It has the magnificent temple of Sri Ranganatha. I consider the Deities here to be the most impressive in all of India. Non-Hindus are not allowed to enter, but the temple is still impressive.

Govindaji Temple in Jaipur Radha-Govinda are two of the most beautiful Deities in all of India. Govindaji is around 5000 years old. The impressive thing about this temple is the extreme enthusiasm of the worshippers. The *mangala-arati* at 5 am is an interesting experience.

Madurai The Meenakshi Temple is a temple dedicated to Lord Siva and his consort Meenakshi. It is a huge ancient temple with very impressive architecture and carvings.

Mayapur ISKCON Temple This temple is located about a kilometre from the birthplace of Lord Caitanya Mahaprabhu in Sri Dhama Mayapur. Mayapur is about four hours north of Calcutta, across the Ganges from Navadvipa. The extreme devotion and mood of worship are the interesting things to see here, as well as the beautiful larger than life size Deities of Radha Krishna and the eight principal *gopis*.

Udupi Krishna This temple has the beautiful Deity of Lord Krishna originally installed by the great Vaishnava *acarya*, Madhvacarya. Almost nightly there is a cart procession in which the processional Deity is put on a cart and pulled around the main street.

The **Guruvayur Temple** in Kerala is one of the most visited temples in all India. The Deity is said to have been worshiped by Lord Krishna Himself. Every night there is a Deity procession in which Lord Krishna is carried by a huge elephant.

Ahovalam is a small town between Hyderabad and Madras in Andhra Pradesh. There are numerous temples here dedicated to the nine forms of Lord Narasimha. It has two impressive ancient temples—one at the bottom of the hill and another at the top.

The **Nathaji Temple** in Nathdwar is about 60 km north of Udaipur, Rajasthan. This Deity of Lord Krishna was originally worshiped at Govardhana Hill in Vrindavana. The extreme devotion to Nathaji is unique in all of India.

INTERESTING PLACES

Hampi (Vijayanagar) This deserted city used to be one of the greatest Hindu cities in all of India. A visit here is like going back 500 years in the past. If it were not so hard to reach, it would be one of the most popular tourist places in India.

Ellora There is an ancient series of temples here carved into a hill. The Kailash Temple is very impressive.

Kovalam It is a nice beach town by Trivandrum, which is a good place to take a break from your travels for a few days.

Mamallapuram (Mahabalipuram) is a nice beach town by Madras, with some of India's oldest temples and rock carvings. It is a nice peaceful place and is a good place to take a break for a few days.

POSSIBLE SPIRITUAL TOURS

Delhi To Calcutta

You can start in Delhi and from there go to Jaipur in Rajasthan, which is about five hours away by bus or train. From there you can take a six-hour bus or train to Mathura and Vrindavana, the land of Lord Krishna. From there you can go by train to Lucknow and then to Naimisaranya, where the *Srimad Bhagavatam* was spoken by Suta Goswami. From Lucknow you then take a four hour bus to Ayodhya, the birthplace of Lord Rama.

From there it is a six hour bus to Allahabad, where the famous Kumbha-mela is held at the confluence of the Ganges, Yamuna, and Saraswati Rivers. From Allahabad you can take a five-hour side trip to Chitrakut, where Lord Rama is said to have lived 11 years in exile. Then from Chitrakut you can take an overnight train or a bus (7 hr) to Varanasi.

You can skip going to Chitrakut and from Allahabad you can take a three-hour bus or one of the many trains to Varanasi. From Varanasi you can make a side trip to the famous Buddhist pilgrimage site of Sarnath, which is a half hour away. From Varanasi you can go to Gaya and Bodh Gaya, where the Buddha attained enlightenment. Gaya is about seven hours away by train. From Gaya there is an overnight train to Calcutta. From there you can go to Puri or Mayapur, the birthplace of Sri Caitanya.

North

The Char Dhama Yatra takes 11 to 18 days and includes Haridwar, Yamunotri, Gangotri, Kedarnath, and Badrinath. Many people go just to Haridwar and Rishikesh and then take a side trip to Badrinath. On the way coming or going to Haridwar you can stop at Kurukshetra where the *Bhagavad-gita* was spoken.

An interesting trip is to go to Amritsar to see the Golden Temple and then to Dharamshala, the home of the Dalai Lama. From Dharamshala you can go further north to the Vaishno Devi temple.

Rajasthan and Gujarat

You can start in Jaipur, which has some interesting temples and palaces to see. From there you can take a three-hour

bus ride to Pushkar, which has a sacred lake and one of the only temples dedicated to Lord Brahma. From Pushkar it is a seven-hour bus ride to Udaipur or a six-hour bus ride to Nathdwar, which is the home of the famous Nathaji Deity. From Udaipur it is a seven-hour bus to Mount Abu, which has some holy places and is a nice peaceful hill station. From there it is another seven-hour bus ride to Ahmedabad. It is a two hour side trip from Ahmedabad to Dakor, where there is the famous temple dedicated to Krishna called the Ranchorji Temple.

From Ahmedabad you can take a 10-hour train to either Dwarka or Somnath. Lord Krishna lived at Dwarka and is said to have left this material world at Somnath. You can then take a side trip to Junagadh and Girnar Hill. From Udaipur you could also head to Nasik, which is a pastime place of Lord Rama.

Andhra Pradesh

You could start in Puri in Orissa and maybe stop at Bhubaneswara. From there you can head south to Visakhapatnam and go to the famous Narasimha temple at Simhachalam. On the way to Visakhapatnam you could stop at Srikurman and visit the only Kurma temple in India. From Visakhapatnam you can go to Vijayawada and visit the Narasimha temple at Mangala Giri. You could then go to Hyderabad. There is an interesting Narasimha temple 60 km north of Hyderabad at Yadagiri-gutta. You could then go to the interesting Siva temple at Srisailam, which is six hours by bus south of Hyderabad. You could also go directly to Ahovalam, where there are the nine Deity forms of Lord Narasimha.

South

If you start in Madras you could first

go to Tirupati, where there is the famous Sri Venkateswara (Balaji) Temple. From there you could go to Kanchipuram, which is a famous temple town. From there you can go to Mamallapuram, which is a nice shore town with some ancient rock carvings and temples. You could then head south by train or bus to Srirangam (Tiruchirappalli), where there is one of the major Vishnu temples in India. You can stop in Chidambaram, which has a famous deity of Lord Siva dancing on one foot. You could also stop at Thanjavur, which has a famous Lord Siva temple, or Kumbakonam, which is an interesting temple town. From Srirangam you could head to Madurai to see the Meenaksi Temple. There are also a few important Vishnu temples there. You can make a side trip to Rameswaram, which is where Lord Rama crossed the ocean to go to Lanka. There is a famous Siva temple there that has a Siva-linga said to have been installed by Rama and Sita.

You can then go to Thiruvananthapuram (Trivandrum), seven hours from Madurai, where there is a famous Vishnu temple. You could make a side trip to Kovalam or Kanniyakumari, the southern most point in India. From here you head north to the one of the most important Vishnu temples in India at Guruvayur, which is by Thrissur. From Thrissur it is a seven-hour bus ride to Mysore. From there you can visit some old temples in the area. You can then go to Bangalore.

An interesting town to visit is Udupi, by Mangalore, which has the famous Udupi Krishna Deity, installed by Madhvacarya. You could then go up to Hampi and maybe stop at Badami and the other temple towns by Badami. This entire trip takes at least a month.

Lord Balarama & Vidura's Tours

According to *Srimad Bhagavatam,* five thousand years ago Lord Balarama, the brother of Lord Krishna, went on tour of the holy places of India. He went to Prabhasaksetra by Somnath and Naimisaranya. Other places He went to are Prayaga at Allahabad; Gaya; Gangasagara, where the Ganges mixes with the Bay of Bengal; Setubandhu by Rameswaram; Gokarna; and the Dandakaranya forest.

Important temples that Balarama visited were Lord Venkateswara (Balaji), the temples in Visnukanci (Kanchipuram), Sri Rangam, and Kanniyakumari. The temple of Kanniyakumari was also visited by Lord Ramacandra, and therefore it is to be understood that the temple has been existing for an extremely long time.

According to the *Srimad Bhagavatam*, Vidura, the uncle of the Pandava brothers, also toured India 5000 years ago. He visited many holy places and temples in India. Srila Prabhupada writes in his purport to *Srimad Bhagavatam* (3.1.23), "The foolish propaganda by atheists that temples were constructed only in later days is refuted because Vidura visited many temples at least five thousand years ago, and the temples of Vishnu were in existence long, before Vidura visited them."

CHAPTER THREE

Travel

AIR

Most international flights arrive in Delhi or Bombay. There are also international airports in Madras, Calcutta, Thiruvananthapuram, Tiruchirappalli and Goa. Some airlines allow you to fly into one airport and out from another.

Airfare To India

It is usually best to purchase your ticket from a travel agent, as they will probably give you a greater discount than purchasing directly from the airlines. Airlines may quote you twice the price a travel agent will. If you are taking a connecting flight, it is usually best to purchase this connecting flight when you purchase your ticket to India. For example, if you are flying Houston-New York-India, the Houston-New York ticket should be purchased along with the New York-India ticket. Sometimes you can get this connecting flight for half price or even free.

The airfare from New York to India is between $950 and $1500, depending on which airline you take and how long the ticket is valid for. You can be quoted double these prices. The price of a flight to India has for the most part remained the same for the last 10 years.

To find the cheapest price for a ticket to India, you can pick up the travel section in the Sunday newspaper. They will usually have some ads for cheap tickets to India. If your local newspaper does not have any prices advertised, get a paper from the nearest major city. In this way you can get an idea of what the price should be. If you have a friend who is from India, there is a good chance that they will know a good Indian travel agent to purchase a ticket from. Usually travel agencies run by Indians have the best prices for tickets to India

A good place to get a cheap ticket is from a "Bucket Shop" travel agent. These are special agents that are given cheap tickets by the airlines so they can fill up their planes. You have to look in your local newspaper to find these travel agents. The best way to find a good travel agent is to get a reference from someone who has been dealing with them.

You should be careful to buy your ticket from a reputable ticket seller. A group of my friends once purchased tickets from someone who had by far the best price. When it came time to get on the plane they were told that they were not reserved for the flight, because the person who had sold them the tickets never paid the airlines. For the same reason, be careful of ads that give prices too good to be true, because they probably aren't.

If you are flying into Delhi and plan to fly from Delhi to Calcutta and back, it is usually cheaper and easier to arrange for these tickets when you purchase your international ticket. You should check this with your travel agent when you purchase your ticket.

Seasonal Prices

Depending on the time of the year, flight prices change. During the Christmas holidays and during the summer (June to August) airfares are usually more expensive, as more people travel to India at these times. Often flying on a weekend can increase the price of a ticket by $100.

Airlines

British Air, Air India, and Thai Air all have direct flights from London. Aeroflot or one of the other former Soviet states airlines usually have the cheapest tickets. I did not have a good experience with Aeroflot, and I know many people who had a problem with them. I would not suggest them. But if money is your most important consideration, they are cheap and not unbearable. One of the reasons their prices are so cheap is no one would take them otherwise.

A major problem with taking a cheap airline is if you want to change your return flight from India, it may be impossible to get a flight out of India. It may be difficult to arrange your flight even two months before you want to leave. Because they are so cheap, they are usually heavily booked. Also they usually have a long stopover, sometimes 12 hours or more at the Moscow airport or some other enjoyable place. You can also expect service on their flights to be very bad. They might not even have drinking water on the plane.

The Middle East airlines are a little more expensive than former Soviet Bloc airlines. I personally have taken both Kuwait and Gulf Air and found them to be good. Gulf Air is $1050 for a four month ticket and $1280 for a one-year ticket from New York. The problem with Gulf Air, as well as most of the other Middle-East airlines, is you have to change planes in London if you are coming from America. Then you have to stop in the Gulf for a couple of hours before you reach Delhi. Otherwise they are good airlines.

From my experience, Air India is a good airline and has the advantage of having a lot of flights out of several cities. You can fly into Delhi and fly out of Bombay. From New York the flight stops only a few hours in London before flying direct to Delhi. Because Air India flies between the major cities in India, you may be able to add discount flights between these cities. So if you are taking some internal flight in India, even though Air India is normally more expensive than other airlines, all your flights together may be cheaper than a more economical airline. A friend of mine got an Air India ticket for $1250 that went from New York to Delhi with two connecting flights between Delhi to Calcutta and then Calcutta to Bombay. He then flew back to New York from Bombay. To fly a Middle East airline would have cost $1050, plus $300 for the internal flights. So the total cost would have been $1350.

Return Flights

Even if you are not sure when you are going back to your home country, it is a good idea to book a date, as sometimes it can be very difficult to get a flight back to America or Europe. This is especially true on discount airlines, or if a good airlines has a special discount, as more people take the cheaper flights. I have been told that I could not get a flight out for three months on one airline. I have experienced that if you have a problem and you have to leave India in a week, you may be able to get a travel agent to arrange to get you on an earlier flight.

This is not true with all airlines.

The general rule is to book your return flight out of India as early as you can. It is not something to leave for the last minute, even with the best airlines

Flight Reconfirmation

You must confirm your return flight at least 72 hours before your departure date. This can be done much sooner. I have stayed in India for three months and confirmed my ticket back to America the day I arrived in India. If you do not confirm your return flight, your booking will usually be automatically cancelled.

Type of Ticket

Usually a ticket to India will be valid for four months. This means you have to use the ticket within four months or it is useless. You can also purchase a ticket that is valid for year. If a four month ticket costs $1000, a one year ticket on the same airlines will usually cost at least $1200 and sometimes much more. Some airlines have tickets that are valid for a year for the same price as a four-month ticket.

With some tickets the return date cannot be changed unless you pay $50 or $100 extra, while with other tickets you can change the return date as many times as you want with no charge. On some airlines, if you do not want to fly on your scheduled departure date, you just don't show up for the flight and it is automatically cancelled. Other airlines, however, insist that you inform them if you are not taking your scheduled flight, and if you don't you have to pay an extra $100. On some airlines you have to pay extra to get a ticket that you can change the date of your return flight. When you purchase your ticket you should ask your travel agent what the rules are concerning your ticket.

Flying From the USA

Prices are the most competitive in New York. You can get a ticket for around a thousand dollars on Aeroflot or other former Eastern European countries' airlines. Tickets are under $1100 on some of the good Middle East airlines. For a ticket on a good airline that flies direct, such as Air India, the price will be about $1250 to $1400. To depart from Washington and Miami it is slightly more expensive, and from the mid-west the price can be $200 more. The price for a flight departing from the west coast will be a little more than the flights from New York. Flights over the Pacific Ocean take about the same amount of flying time over the Atlantic.

A reliable travel agent in New York is Radha Travel (212-719-3244), Suite 903, 110 West 40th Street, by Sixth Avenue. They are one of the biggest sellers of tickets to India, and they always have good prices. Even if you decide to go with another travel agent they will give you a good idea of what the ticket prices should be. You can purchase a ticket from them by mail.

Flights From London and Europe

There are direct flights to India from London, Frankfurt, Rome, Paris, Geneva, Amsterdam, Moscow and Zurich. A direct flight from London to Delhi takes about 9 hours. If you take a flight on a Middle Eastern airlines from London the flight will take at least 11 hours (usually longer), because the flight will stop in the Middle East and then continue on to India.

London is known to be one of the best places to get discount tickets to India. It is by far the cheapest place in Europe to fly from. There are many bucket shops in London that deal with cheap tickets.

You can find cheap tickets by looking at the ads in the City Limits, Time Out, or TNT. You can also look at the travel section of the Times and Business Traveler. You should be able to get a round trip ticket for less than 400 pounds.

Trailfinders Travel Centre (071-938-3366), 46/48 Earls Court Road, London, is a complete travel service. They mainly deal only with the major airlines, so they will not be the most economical, but they are reliable. They can also give great discounts on good hotels and help arrange vaccinations. STA (071-937-9962), 74 Brompton Rd, London, or 117 Euston Rd, London NW1, is a good travel agency.

Palm Beach Travel (071-287-5803, fax 071-287-5774), Suite 112, Premier House, 77 Oxford St, London, is a reliable economical travel agent.

The cheapest airlines are usually the Middle East airlines and the former Soviet airlines. I would not recommend the Soviet airlines, but they are cheap. I have had good experiences with Middle East airlines such as Gulf Air and Kuwait.

From London the cheapest round trip flight you can get on a discount airline is about £340. A direct flight on a better airline will cost about £440. Air India, British Airways, and Thai Air fly direct to Delhi. British Airways and Air India fly direct to Bombay daily, and Singapore Airlines flies twice a week. British Airways flies direct to both Madras and Calcutta. There are no direct flights to India from cities in Britain other than London. If you are leaving from a city other than London, you do not have to fly to London to get to India. You can route your flight through another country, often more economically. The Air India office (071-493-4050) in London is located at 17/18 New Bond Street.

Special Needs

If you want a vegetarian meal on the plane, you have to ask the travel agent you purchase your ticket from to request the airlines for it. Often the travel agent forgets to reserve the vegetarian meal with the airlines, so if you do not want to take a chance call the airlines and confirm it. When you check-in you should again remind them that you want a vegetarian meal. On some airlines you can also request a fruit plate. You should be suspicious of whatever they give you. Many times they believe that eggs are vegetarian.

Children between 2 and 12 travel for one-half to two-thirds the full fare and also get a baggage allowance. Children under two travel for 10% of the full fare or free on some airlines, as long as they don't use a seat. You can get a little bed for them, if you request one in advance.

TIP: Before you travel, it is a good idea to photocopy your passport and ticket. Also write down your ticket number, flight number, and other information. If you then lose either your ticket or passport, it will be much easier to get replacements.

Departure Tax

When you leave India you have to pay a Rs 300 departure tax just before you check-in for your departing flight. The departure tax is Rs 150 if you are going to a neighboring SAARC country. This amount must be paid in rupees.

Air Travel Within India

Indian Airlines flies to many cities within India as well as some neighboring countries. Besides their international routes, Air India flies between a few major cities in India, like Bombay-Delhi,

Calcutta-Bombay, Bombay-Madras, and Delhi-Calcutta. There are a several other domestic airlines such as Modiluft, Jagson, Jet, and East-West.

Indian Airlines is one of the most inefficient airlines in the world. They will tell you that you are booked on a flight, and when you come to the airport you will not be booked on the flight. If you book any flight with them outside of India, you should reconfirm all your flights when you arrive in India. You usually have to go into their office, as doing it over the phone can be very difficult. I have heard of people who called 20 times trying to get through to their office before they gave up.

The most reliable travel agents are those that display the IATA organization logo. This means they have been approved by this international organization after scrutiny of their competence and financial reliability. These agencies have given financial guarantees to the airlines against default. A travel agency cannot get commissions directly from an international airline until they are approved by IATA.

Previously you had to purchase your ticket with foreign currency, but now you can purchase your tickets with rupees.

For Indian Airlines flights you should purchase your ticket as far in advance as possible, as most flights are fully booked with a long waiting list. If a flight is fully booked, you should put your name on the waiting list, as there is a good chance you can get on the flight even if the list is long. If you do not have a confirmed seat you should arrive as early as possible to the airport.

If you lose your Indian Airline ticket, it is just like cash and you are not supposed to be issued a replacement. But I have heard of cases where replacements were issued for lost tickets.

Indian Airlines does not allow batteries, sharp objects, scissors, or nail files in your carry-on baggage. *Excel, Perfect Media* and *Divan* are three publications that list all Indian domestic flights and their fares on the different airlines.

You can get some good fares for internal flights in India if you fly Air India to India and have them add on internal flights for you. You may be able to add a flight from Delhi to Calcutta onto a London-Delhi flight for considerably less than a separate Delhi-Calcutta flight would be. You can often get a cheaper fare if you purchase your internal flights along with your international ticket.

Discover India Ticket

On an Indian Airlines Discover India ticket you can go anywhere in India for 21 days for $500. The ticket must be purchased with US dollars or British pounds. You cannot go to the same airport twice, unless you are going there to catch a connecting flight. The problem with this ticket is that even if the place you are going to has an airport, often there will be no direct flight. To go from Trivandrum to Cochin you might have to fly from Trivandrum to Madras and wait two days in Madras to fly to Cochin.

You cannot fly back and forth across the country. You can not fly from Bhubaneswara to Bombay and then to Madras and then to Delhi. You are supposed to fly the shortest route possible. You have to go from Bhubaneswara to Madras and then to Bombay and then Delhi. You are supposed to go in a circle.

You can lengthen the validity of your ticket if the last flight you book does not have a daily flight. The ticket is then extended to the next available flight. If you are doing even a fair amount of flying and you don't mind the limitations this is a very good deal.

India Wonderfares

India Wonderfares is an airfare costing $200 for unlimited travel for one week within the north, south, east, or west regions.

All your flights within one week have to be within the same area. You cannot go to the same city twice, except for transfers or connections.

Youth Fare

Persons between 12 and 30 receive a 25% discount on all Indian Airlines flights—both domestic and to Nepal. This is for persons who are not Indian citizens and for Indians who permanently live outside of India.

Indian Airlines Cancellation Rules

To cancel a flight, the ticket has to be returned to the booking office. Persons residing other than where the flight departs from, may cancel their booking by letter or telegram, but not by phone. There is no cancellation charge if the ticket was purchased with foreign currency. If you purchase your ticket outside of India, the refund will not be given in India.

If you do not report at the check-in counter at least 30 minutes before the flight is scheduled to depart, that is considered a "No Show".

Cancellation charges are:

48 hours or more before flight departure—Rs 20
Less than 48 hours and more than 24 hours—10% of basic fare
Less than 24 hours—25% of basic fare
Less than one hour or "No Shows"—100% of basic fare

Check-in

You should check-in an hour to an hour and fifteen minutes before the flight. Many times the check-in counter closes 30 minutes before the flight departs. One time I missed a flight because I arrived 29 minutes before a flight took off.

For security reasons, you are supposed to identify your bags after checking them in, just before you board the plane. If you don't identify them, they will not be put on the plane.

You should not confuse Air India, which departs from the international terminal, with Indian Airlines.

Reconfirmation of Flights

When there is a break of more than 72 hours between flights, passengers should reconfirm their onward and return reservations. If you do not confirm your flight within 72 hours of its departure, your reservation may be cancelled. This is true for both internal and international flights. You do not have to reconfirm your flight personally. You can have a travel agent or friend do it for you.

It can be a good idea to later check that your flight was really confirmed, as many times in India, your confirmation is never recorded. This happened to me on Malaysia Airlines.

Can't Get a Flight Out of India

If it seems hopeless, go to a good travel agent—money talks. Many times the travel agent knows someone in the airline office who can help you out. This does not work for Aeroflot.

Indian Airlines Offices
Agra
  Hotel Clarks Shiraz, 54 Taj Rd
  (0562-360-948)
Ahmedabad

Airlines House, Lal Darwaja (353-333)
Aurangabad
  Dr Rajendra Prasad Marg (02432-24864)
Bangalore
  Housing Board Bldg, Kempegowda Rd
  (080-221-1914)
Bhubaneswara
  Unit 1, Raj Path, Bapuji Nagar
  (0674-400-533)
Bombay
  Air India Bldg, 1st Floor, Madam Cama
  Rd, Nariman Point (022-202-3031)
Calcutta
  Airlines House, 39 Chittaranjan Ave
  (033-263-390)
Delhi
  Malhotra Bldg, Connaught Place
  (011-331-0517)
  Barakhamba Rd (331-3732)
Hyderabad
  Saifabad, near Legislative Assembly
  Bldg (0842-243-333, 236-902)
Jaipur
  Nehru Pl, Tonk Rd (0141-514-407)
Kathmandu, Nepal
  26 Durbar Marg (419-649)
Kochi (Cochin)
  Durbar Hall Rd, Ernakulam (370-242)
Lucknow
  Clarks Avadh, 5 Mahatma Gandhi
  Marg (0522-240-927)
Madras
  19 Marshalls Rd, Egmore (825-1677)
Madurai
  Pandyan House, 7A West Veli St
  (0452-37234)
Mangalore
  Moti Mahal Hotel, Falnir Rd
Mysore
  Hotel Mayura Hoysala, 2 Jhansi
  Lakshmi Bai Rd (0821-516-943)
Rajkot
  Angel Chamber, Station Rd (27916)
Thiruvananthapuram (Trivandrum)
  Mascot Hill Bldg, Museum Rd

(438-288)
Tiruchirappalli
  Railway Co-op Credit Society Bldg,
  Dindigul Rd (0431-42233)
Tirupati
  Hotel Vishnupriya, Ranigunta Rd
  (22349)
Udaipur
  LIC Bldg, outside Delhi Gate (410-999)
Vadodara (Baroda)
  University Rd, Fateh Ganj (329-668)
Varanasi
  Mint House Motel, Vadunath Marg,
  Cantonment (45959)
Visakhapatnam
  Jeevan Prakash, LIC Bldg Complex
  (46503)

Flight Information Numbers
Bangalore: 566-233, 564-433
Bombay: 202-3262, 287-6363, 142,143
Calcutta: 263-390, 262-657
Delhi, Departures: 143, Arrivals: 142
Hyderabad: 844-422, 844-443
Madras: 234-4433, 142
Trivandrum: 451-537

Flight Problems
If you have ear pain when flying, you can relieve the pain by eating some candy while descending. Yawning, moving your chin from side to side, swallowing, and pinching your nose combined with gentle blowing can help. If you have a cold or hay-fever, the pain can be even worst.

It is a good idea to bring some warm clothes onto the plane as it can get very cold on long flights.

Two Bags on Plane
I usually carry two bags onto the plane with me and have never had a problem. On flights to and from Europe you are only allowed 20 kg check-in baggage al-

lowance. On flights from America you can take two 30 kg bags. I have found that you can check-in bags that are two or three kilos overweight for cheaper airlines and five or six kilos overweight on more expensive airlines without being questioned about overweight. This is far from an absolute rule. Certain airlines will not allow you to have even one kilo overweight.

A solution to a potential overweight problem is to take your heavy items in one or two pieces of carry-on baggage. I have carried 30 kilos onto the plane in my carry-on baggage.

Excess Luggage

If you are flying to countries other than the USA, you are only allowed 20 kg total weight for your check-in bags. I know one person who was about 30 kg overweight when flying from England to India, and they wanted to charge him more for his extra baggage than he paid for his ticket.

If you are flying between India and the USA and you want to stop in Europe, you can often bring the US baggage allowance of 60 kg, if you do not stopover for longer than a week. This is true if you fly the entire way with the same airlines and with many of the Middle East Airlines. You should arrange this in advance with the airlines. It is best to confirm this with the airlines before you purchase your ticket.

If you are overweight, on many airlines you can send your luggage as excess baggage. This can be almost one tenth the price of checking in the extra baggage when you are boarding the plane. On one airline the price was Rs 550 a kilo for checking in extra baggage and Rs 65 to send extra baggage by excess luggage.

To send your luggage as excess baggage in Delhi you have to take your baggage to the cargo department at the Delhi airport a day or two before your flight. The entire process will take about three hours. The bag may be shipped the same day that you leave, but you will not be able to get it when you come off the plane. You will have to pick it up later. When you arrive, get a phone number and the location of where you pick up the bag.

You are only supposed to send as excess baggage personal things, such as your clothes and books. They may check your bag thoroughly. So if you are bringing other things, put them in the bags you check onto the plane and put your personal things in excess baggage. The customs officials are more strict about inspecting excess baggage than check-on bags.

TRAINS

The first passenger train in India ran in 1853. The rail system in India is the second largest in the world with about 62,000 km of track. There are over 7000 stations, and over 11 million people a day travel by train.

Trains can be very cheap in India if you take second-class. From Delhi to Mathura (150 km) is just 42 rupees.

For long-distance travel (over 8 hours) trains are usually better than buses.

Train Classes

First-class A/C is the most expensive. This is a private four-person compartment with a locking door in an air-conditioned car. Only people that have a reservation are allowed on the carriage. It is a nice way to travel, but it is expensive. It is almost the same price as flying. Many trains do not have first-class A/C.

Two-tier A/C (2nd-class A/C) has two sets of two beds facing each other with two seats in the hall, in an air-conditioned carriage. There are curtains that you can pull to get some privacy. The big advantage of two-tier A/C over regular second-class, besides the air-conditioning, is that no one is allowed on the car without a reservation, so it is much less crowded than second-class. It is a relatively painless way to travel. Many people think this is the best way to travel. Often the air-conditioning is up extremely high and it can be freezing at night. This class is about five times the price of normal second-class and 25% more than first-class. **Three-tier A/C** is less expensive than two-tier A/C, but it is slightly more crowded. On air-conditioned cars don't get Seat 1, 2, 5, or 6 as you will be right next to the door that people will be opening and closing all night.

In **First-class** you ride in a private two-berth or four-berth compartment, with no air-conditioning. It is fairly comfortable and only people who have a first-class tickets can come onto the carriage. It costs about three and a half times what a second-class ticket costs. One problem with this class is that people are allowed to smoke, while there is no smoking allowed in the air-conditioned classes. On some express trains there are no first-class carriages, just two-tier A/C.

A/C chair cars are air-conditioned and have airplane-like reclining seats. There are also **non-A/C chair cars**, which are comfortable during the day. The problem with these carriages is that you cannot lie down at night and you have to sit upright the whole journey. As these cars are cheaper than two-tier A/C sleeper class, some people take them instead of second-class.

Second-class sleeper cars have compartments with three berths across from each other. There are also two berths in

the hall. At night you have your own bunk to sleep on, but during the day anyone can get on your carriage and sit next to you. Sometimes the carriage can get extremely crowded and uncomfortable and sometimes it will be all right, but very seldom will it be as comfortable as A/C or first-class.

Second and third-class unreserved is usually very crowded and is best used only for short distances. You are not guaranteed a sleeping berth, so this is a painful way to travel overnight.

Types of Trains

There are two different types of train tracks—broad and metre gauge. The broad gauge trains go much faster than the metre gauge because the rails are wider. In South India only a few of the trains run on the faster broad gauge. Where there are no broad gauge trains, many times a bus can be faster.

Passenger trains stop at most stations, so they are very slow and should be used only for short trips. It is better to try to avoid them altogether, as they tend to be very crowded. They usually have only crowded second or third-class facilities.

Express or Mail trains are considerably faster. An advance reservation is essential for overnight sleeping facilities. Reservations often have to be made weeks in advance unless you use the tourist quota, so you should plan your train trips as far ahead as possible.

Superfast Trains

There are superfast trains that are named either **Rajdhani** or **Shatabdi** Express. These trains are fully air-conditioned and go much faster than any other train on the same route. They are given right of way, and they stop only at major stations. They are more expensive than other trains. You must book these trains in advance, as these trains are in high demand.

The Rajdhani Express goes from Delhi to Bombay in 16 hours 45 min. The Rajdhani Express from New Delhi to Calcutta takes 18 hours and the next fastest train takes 24 hours. The Shatabdi Express departs from Delhi at 6.15 am and arrives in Agra two hours later. The same train returns from Agra at 8.15 pm, arriving in Delhi two hours later at 10.20 pm. Other trains between Delhi and Agra takes 3½ hours or more.

Train Reservations

If you are taking an overnight train, you must reserve a berth so you will have somewhere to sleep at night. When you purchase a ticket you must fill out a sleeper reservation form, which you should get before you get into the queue. The demand for second-class sleepers is usually greater than the demand for first-class or A/C sleepers.

At most stations there is a special counter or place for tourists to get their tickets. It is often called the "Tourist Cell". It only deals with tourists. This may be the only counter where foreigners can purchase a ticket, and almost certainly it will be the only place to get tourist quota tickets.

Your reserved ticket has the name of the train, your carriage number, your berth number, and the time of departure written on it. There will usually be a sheet of paper at the entrance of each carriage that lists each passenger's name and their berth number. A list of the people getting on at that station is posted on a notice board, usually on the same platform that the train leaves from.

There is a small reservation charge for each class of ticket. The charge is more for higher-class tickets. Many times a travel agent or someone at the hotel where you are staying can arrange to get you a train ticket for a Rs 30 to Rs 100 fee. Anything over Rs 100 to get you a ticket is too high a charge.

Each station has a certain quota of seats allocated to it. If you are going from Calcutta to Delhi there may be 10 seats allocated to Howrah station in Calcutta. Burdwan, a station about two hours outside of Calcutta, may have only 1 first-class ticket allocated to it.

If you purchase a ticket departing from Howrah station in Calcutta to Delhi you must get on the train at Howrah station. If you do not present your ticket to the ticket collector within a half hour after leaving the station that you are reserved from, your reservation may be cancelled. You are not supposed to get on the train at Burdwan, two hours outside of Calcutta, because when you get on the train, you may find that your reservation was cancelled, because you did not board at Calcutta.

The most crowded time to travel in India is during the summer—May and June. This is not a good time to travel anyway because it is so hot. Also March, October, early November and during the Christmas holidays can be crowded.

Waiting List

There are different types of reservations. There are confirmed reservations. Then there is reservation against cancellation, or RAC, which guarantees you a seat and probably means you will get a berth. If a berth becomes available you get it and pay the sleeper surcharge.

If all the reservations are full on a train, you can be put on the waiting list. Then if someone cancels, you can get on the train. It seems that if your waiting list number is below 20, you will get on most trains. When you get a waiting list ticket you should ask what your chances of getting on the train are. Usually the person selling the ticket will know. Sometimes extra carriages are put on a train.

If you are on the waiting list you should arrive early for the train and look for the reservation board, which has a list of all the passengers on the train. This board will be either by the entrance or at the beginning of the platform from where your train departs. If you have gotten a seat, your name will be listed along with the carriage that you are on. If you do not see your name on any list, immediately go to the person in charge of the station and ask for help. There is a good chance he can help you, because he is in charge of emergency and VIP quota seats that he releases an hour before the train departs. I personally would have gone to the station superintendent before purchasing a waiting list ticket in the first place.

If you have a waiting list ticket and cannot get a reservation or seat on the train, you can get a refund for a small fee.

Tourist Quota

This is a facility for foreign tourists to get train reservations on short notice. Especially during certain seasons many trains are fully booked for weeks in advance. So to enable foreign tourists to get tickets, there is an allotment of tickets set aside for them on well-traveled tourist routes. These tickets are purchased in a special office in the bigger cities and at a special counter in some stations. You must show your passport to purchase a ticket this way. Also you are supposed to have a tourist visa.

You can also have a travel agent purchase your ticket for a fee. This is usu-

ally easier and is a good way to do it, if you have time. Generally you have to write a letter empowering the travel agent to use your passport to purchase a ticket.

If there is no tourist quota office, one of the windows in the reservation hall may be allocated for tourists' use. If you are in a town that does not have a tourist quota or a special window for tourists, you may have to see the Station Superintendent, the Deputy Superintendent, the Chief Reservation Supervisor, or the Station Master, depending on the station. This is usually the person in charge of the station. They can allocate a ticket to you from the tourist quota, emergency quota, or VIP quota. They may have you purchase a waiting list ticket for the train and then send you to someone else to give you the needed reservation.

Tourist Quota Office Locations
New Delhi

First floor, New Delhi Train Station, International Tourist Bureau
Indira Gandhi International Airport
It is open from 12 midnight to 8 am.
Bombay

Western Railway, Churchgate
Railway Tourist Guide, Central Railway, Victoria Terminus
Bombay International Airport
Madras

Central Reservation Office, Southern Railway, Madras Central
Calcutta

Railway Tourist Guide, Eastern Railway, 6 Fairlie Place near BBD Bagh
14 Strand Rd

How To Get a Ticket

You walk into the station and find the Enquiry Counter. You go up to the counter and ask where to purchase a ticket for the place you want to go. Tell them you would like to get a ticket using the tourist quota. Also tell them what class you want to travel. You then go to the counter to which they direct you. When you get to the counter, if you are lucky they will sell you the ticket that you want. There is good chance, however, that this will not happen.

If you are not sold a ticket, you then ask the person at the counter what you should do. They may tell you to go see someone else in another office. If they do not send you anywhere, just go see the station superintendent, the person in charge of the station. He may have a different title, depending on the size of the station.

An important point to know is that the station manager or station superintendent is usually highly educated and expects people to treat him with respect. Do not just burst into his office. Knock at the door to his office and get his attention before entering his office. Ask him meekly "Sir, I need your help, could I talk to you?" He will then answer, "Yes, of course you may." You then say "Sir, I would like to go on the 5 pm train, and I was told to come to you for help. Can you please help me?" He will answer, "Of course I can." He definitely can help you, because, besides the tourist quota, he also controls the VIP and emergency quotas. He may tell you to go back to the ticket counter and get your ticket. His words are not good enough. You should get something in writing or have someone come with you. Remember the key is to treat the station manager with a lot of respect. He really can make your life much easier.

One important point is to always make getting your train ticket a priority. If you are on a tight schedule it is best to immediately purchase a train ticket to the next

place that you are going to as soon as you arrive in town.

Security

If you have a backpack or cloth bag it is a good idea to put a small lock on it to stop the casual theft. I have heard about and seen cases of people cutting open cloth bags. You should also carry a regular chain or bicycle chain to lock your bag to your seat. If you travel in the higher class cars there is much less chance of anything being stolen, because the persons in your carriage are usually more well-to-do. Also only persons who have reservations are allowed in that carriage. This is usually strictly enforced, especially at night.

I like the upper berths, because they give you better protection from theft. If you are on the lower berth of a 1st Class or AC Sleeper, you have to fold down the back-rest over the seat. You can leave your valuables under the seat while you sleep. Never put any valuables near the window at night, because it is common for someone to put their hand through the window and take things.

Train Conductor

The train conductor is in charge of the train. He is usually an older gentleman who wears a black jacket. If there are any spare sleeping berths or seats on the train, he is in charge of allotting them. While the train is in a station, he usually stands on the platform with a group of people surrounding him trying to get a seat on the train. If you purchase a tourist quota, first class, or a VIP quota ticket you may be sent to him to be allotted a seat.

Information

When you purchase a train ticket it is a good idea to ask the person selling the ticket from which track the train departs.

A handkerchief or *gumsa* will save your seat while you go to the bathroom. The best seats on the train are in the middle of the carriage, that are not over the wheels.

When you get off the train, you will probably have to show your train ticket to get out of the station. If you do not have your ticket, you can be charged the maximum fare for the train that you just got off.

During the monsoon season, trains can be badly affected by floods, especially in Andhra Pradesh, where major rivers come to the sea and the Ganges Basin.

Air-conditioned carriages can be very cold at night, so you may need bedding at night. On air-conditioned carriages you can normally rent bedding for Rs 15. You are supposed to book it with your ticket or before you get on the train.

Often rickshaw drivers know a train station as the "railway station". If you ask for the "train station" they might not know what you are talking about.

A train is called *rel gaari* in Hindi

Warning The general rule is to not get on a train without reservations for an overnight train ride, unless it is an emergency. After 10 pm no one but people who have sleeper reservations are allowed in the sleeping area. So your only option is to sit or stand by the bathroom. There is a chance that you can pay the train conductor or ticket collector and get a berth, but they can only give you a berth if one is available. If you had a problem getting a berth for that train, that usually means the train was fully booked. If it was not full, the station manager of the station where you purchased your ticket could have already given you a berth.

When the train pulls into the station you can ask the conductor if he can give you a sleeping berth.

Ladies' Queue & Compartments

To buy tickets, there are often ladies' queues with a sign (often in Hindi) that says "Ladies' Queue." If there are no ladies, men will be lined up there. A woman can usually go to the front of the line and immediately get her ticket.

On a second-class sleeper carriage there is sometimes a compartment reserved just for ladies. So if you are a woman traveling alone, it is a good idea to request the ladies' compartment. It is normal for western ladies traveling alone to be hassled by young Indian men. If you have a problem, do not waste your time telling the person to act like a human being. Appeal for help from your fellow passengers, especially older respectable looking gentlemen. Tell them what is happening, and they will immediately protect you.

Train Schedules

If you travel a lot by trains it could be a good idea to get a train schedule. Indian Railways publishes *Trains At A Glance* twice a year. Also the *Newman's Indian Bradshaw* is published monthly. Each of the local railway zones publishes its own schedule that you can purchase at station bookstalls within their area. The *TTK Map and Guide to India's Railways* can be helpful.

Thomas Cook publishes a good train schedule called *Overseas Timetable*.

Fares

Fares are calculated at a fixed price per kilometre from the station of origin to the station of destination. Two different trains going to the same place may have different prices if they go different routes, which is very typical. For two trains leaving from and going to the same place, there can be a ten-hour difference in travel times. This means you can pay more for a train that takes longer because it goes a longer route.

Each class of travel, train type, and seating is a different price. There are extra charges for faster trains and sleeper reservations.

Lost Tickets and Refunds

If you lose a reserved berth ticket you can have a new ticket issued by paying a 25% surcharge. It could be a good idea to record the number, date, train, berth, and date of travel in case you lose your ticket.

If you realize that you lost your ticket on the way to the train station and it is a reserved ticket, just get on the train without the ticket. Your name is reserved with the conductor on the train and no one else will be in your seat. At most you will just have to pay some extra money.

Ticket Cancellations

If you cancel your ticket more than a day before it is scheduled to depart, there is a Rs 10 to Rs 50 cancellation fee, depending on the class of the ticket. You get back 75% of the fare between a day and four hours before departure time. You get back 50% if you turn in your ticket within 12 hours after the train departs on a journey over 500 km and three hours for a shorter journey.

Breaking The Journey

If you are going at least 400 km, you can break your journey after you have gone 300 km. When you stop, the ticket has to be endorsed by the Station Master with the station code, date, and SM's initials. You can stop one day for every 200 km traveled.

Luggage

You are only allowed a certain amount of luggage according to the ticket you have. This is 70 kg in A/C First-class, 50 kg in First-class or A/C Sleeper, 40 kg in Chair Car, and 35 kg in Second-class. If you have more than this you are supposed to weigh your luggage in advance and book your bags in the luggage van attached to the train, so it reaches the destination along with you. There is an extra fee per kilo for luggage over the allotted weight. I read about a person who checked in his baggage. It took him 45 minutes to retrieve it when he reached his destination. To check in overweight baggage can take a half hour to do all the paper work, and it can cause you to miss your train.

I have heard of a case where someone was fined over a thousand rupees because they were 50 kg over the weight limit. If you have five trunks you may be checked.

I have seen and heard of people who had half their baggage on the train and the other half on the train platform when the train took off. In the case I witnessed, one of the persons I was with asked the conductor to stop the train, which he did, and we loaded the rest of the luggage on. In another case I heard about, the train took off and one of the two persons stayed with the luggage and had to get the next train. Of course the luggage left on the platform was his friend's.

Bed Rolls

They are supplied to First-class and A/C Sleeper passengers for a Rs 15 fee. You are supposed to order them with the Station Superintendent/Master. Usually you can order them on the train.

Cloak Room (Luggage Storage)

Persons with onward tickets can store their bags in cloak rooms at major stations. If you want to ask someone where the baggage storeroom is you must ask for the "cloak room", because that is what Indians call it. Make sure the cloak room will be open when you want to pick up your bags. Also be very careful not to lose your ticket, because if you do, you will have to go though hours of red tape to get your bag back. Indians just do not lose things like this. If you do lose your ticket, go directly to the Station Superintendent/Master and ask him to help solve your problem.

All your bags are supposed to be locked to leave them in the cloak room. In some cases they will not take backpacks.

Retiring Rooms & Waiting Rooms

Indian Railways provides retiring rooms in many stations. Some may be as good as a nice hotel, and others may be really run-down. Dormitory rooms are also often available. These retiring rooms are supposed to be used only by train passengers for a 24-hour period, and you are supposed to show a train ticket.

For upper-class ticket holders most stations have an upper-class waiting room, which has decently clean showers and toilets. There is also usually a waiting room for ladies only.

Indrail Passes

This pass enables you to travel wherever you like, whenever you like, and by whatever train you like, within the period of validity. You pay one fee based on the duration of validity and class of travel, and there are no surcharges. For children age 5 to 12, fares are half the adult price. Children under five travel for free.

The pass does not mean you have a reserved spot on any train, unless you have confirmed everything in advance when you purchased the ticket. It is best to confirm your ongoing reservations when you arrive at each destination. You are given preferential booking treatment and are eligible for tourist quota and other special quotas. The Indrail pass can be purchased 360 days in advance, and reservations can be made at the same time.

Indrail passes can only be purchased by foreign nationals who are not resident in India and Indians living overseas. A foreign resident in India is treated as an Indian and cannot purchase an Indrail pass. The pass can only be purchased with foreign currency, either US dollars or British pounds.

A first-class air-conditioned Indrail pass is not really worth the price, as it costs a lot more than other classes, and this class does not exist on most trains other than superfast express trains.

From a financial point of view an Indrail pass may not be worth having unless you are taking a train almost every day. The shorter the pass the less economical it is. First-class and A/C class passes are a better deal than second-class passes.

The Railway officials are told to give Indrail pass holders special considerations concerning reservations. The main advantage is you can get a sleeper when there is normally none available. I have seen this to be true with my own eyes. It makes it easier to get a railway retiring room, and you can use the Upper-class waiting rooms.

When you get the pass you can also get a copy of Indrail India Rail Rovers booklet, which you get from the general sales agents who sold you the ticket. It lists all trains and helps you plan your itinerary.

When you purchase your ticket overseas you can make all your train reservations at that time. You may be advised by the person you get your ticket from about following a particular schedule. I have heard they tend to give a schedule that is impossible to follow, as it moves too quickly.

If you decide to change a schedule you reserved when you purchased your ticket you are supposed to cancel it and pay a fee (Rs 50). Unless you cancel your bookings, you cannot book another ticket at a place that does computer reservations, as you cannot have two different reservations on the same day.

A high percentage of people that get Indrail passes overseas regret it. Often it is easier and cheaper to take a bus than the train, especially in South India. With an Indrail pass you are obliged to take the train.

Also I believe that many budget travelers who purchase First-class or A/C passes would have purchased a sleeper class pass instead, because it is much cheaper and some people like it better. My suggestion would be to come to India for at least a week and then purchase a pass.

Indrail Pass Prices

The following prices are in US dollars. The left side is the adult price and the right is children.

Days	1st A/C	2-Tier A/C	Sleeper
1	65/32	39/20	17/9
7	300/150	150/75	80/40
15	370/185	185/95	95/45
21	440/220	220/110	100/50
30	550/235	275/140	125/65
60	800/400	400/200	185/95
90	1060/530	530/265	235/120

Main offices to get Indrail Passes

New Delhi
  Railway Tourist Guide, first floor,
  New Delhi Railway Station
Bombay
  Railway Tourist Guide,
  Western Railway, Churchgate.
  Railway Tourist Guide,
  Central Railway, Victoria Terminus
Madras
  Central Reservation Office,
  Southern Railway, Madras Central.
Calcutta
  Central Reservation Office,
  Esplanade Mansion
  Railway Tourist Guide,
  Eastern Railway, 6 Fairle Place

You can also get an Indrail pass at the central reservation offices in Jaipur, Bangalore, Hyderabad, Trivandrum (Thiruvananthapuram), Gorakhpur, and Rameswaram. Also some tourist agents are authorized to sell Indrail passes.

Some places outside of India where you can get an Indrail pass are:

England: SK Enterprises Ltd (081-903-3411, Fax: 081 903-3411), 103 Wembley Park Drive, Wembley, Middlesex, HA9 8HG. They sell passes and can make train and hotel reservations for you. Dr S. Dandapani, the sales agent, has a great deal of practical knowledge about train travel in India.

USA: Hariworld Travels Inc (212-957-3000, Fax: 495-2383), 30 Rockefeller Plaza, Shop 21, North Mezzanine, New York.

Canada: Hariworld Travels Inc. (366-2000, Fax: 062-3918), Royal York Hotel, 100 Front Street West, Arcade Level, Toronto, Ontario M5J 1E3.

Australia: Adventure World (290-3222, Fax: 22680), 37 York Street, Sydney, NSW.

Penthouse Travel (233-11455, Fax 107-18892), 5th Level, 72 Pitt Street, Sydney, NSW.

Porters (Coolies)

They have red shirts and badges and carry your bags in the train stations. If you are not an Indian and you have a lot of bags, they will want to charge you at least double if not 20 times the normal price to carry your bags. If the real price is five rupees to carry a bag, they may try to charge you 50 rupees and absolutely refuse to do it for Rs 10. You should fix a price for putting your bags on the train, never accept "as you like". "As you like" means they will want you to pay at least double the normal "rip off rate". The amount that you negotiate for is usually to put your bags on the train at the correct seat. When the train arrives in the station, the porter is supposed to come back and put your bags on the train. The fact that you are paying for the porter to put your bags on the train and not just to carry your bags to the correct train platform has to be established in advance, before the porter carries your bags to the train platform.

There is usually a board in the station that lists the official rate for porters at that station. The official rate is usually about Rs 5 for 40 kg. If you can move your bags, it might be possible to get that rate, but unlikely. If you have so many bags it would take an elephant to move them, expect to pay much more than the official rate.

Show the porter your ticket and ask him to take you to your train carriage. Do not try to explain what train and carriage you want, just show them your ticket. If the train is not at the station when you arrive, ask the porter to leave your bags where the train carriage will most

likely stop. Confirm this with a few people before he goes. The porters usually know everything about all the trains and are valuable for finding your seat. They are expert at adjusting everyone else's baggage so yours fits perfectly, no matter how crowded the train is.

Be careful, as they do steal. They are also expert at putting your baggage in a taxi that you do not want.

BUS

Usually for long distances (more than 6 hours) it is better to take a train. For shorter distances and certain routes taking a bus may be better than the train. This is especially true if you get a luxury or express bus. If the only train available is a narrow gauge passenger train, a bus may be much faster. Buses do not usually have delays, but passenger trains can be delayed for hours. A big advantage of buses over trains is they run much more frequently and they are easy to arrange, in many cases you just get on and pay on the bus.

It is best to get a seat near the front of the bus as the back is extremely bumpy. If you sit in the back of the bus you have to be careful not to get knocked out when your head hits the ceiling when the bus hits a big pothole. One time I was dazed in the back seat of a mini-bus. Some people do not like to sit too far in front of the bus as they have really loud horns, and you might have a heart attack by seeing how the bus is driven. Many people think the seat of honor is the front seat near the driver, and they may ask you to sit there for your convenience.

If you get off the bus to answer the call of nature or get a drink, you have to keep an eye on the driver all the time. You have about 5 seconds to get on the bus after the bus driver gets back in. The driver may get off the bus and say you will be stopped for 10 minutes. Two minutes later he may jump back in the bus, start the engine, and drive off without caring whether everyone is in the bus. I have had to stop the bus twice for friends who almost got left behind like this.

When I get on a local bus, I ask in a loud voice, "Is the bus going to (wherever I am going)?" In this way I find out if the bus is actually going where I want to go. Also when many people know where I am going, then someone usually helps me get off the bus at the correct place. It also solves the problem of having to answer the question "Where are you going?" Often it pays to make friends with someone on the bus who can help you.

When it is time to get on a crowded bus, you may have to push and shove your way on. Be prepared for this. You cannot be too polite. I saw one old lady literally climbing over another lady, who was so old she had to struggle up the steps.

You should be careful when getting on and off crowded buses, especially in a tourist area, as many pick-pockets work the buses. They use razor blades to cut money belts.

Buses usually make regular stops at roadside *dhabbas* (tea or cold drink stalls). If you are a woman or have diarrhoea, a bus trip can be unpleasant, as it is rare to see even a slightly decent toilet at one of these places.

A bus station in India is often called a "Bus Stand". If you use any other name than this, often no one will know what you are talking about.

Types of Buses

A local bus can be painful in India. They can be extremely crowded to the point of unbelievable. They have five seats across that were made for very small people. Usually when you get a local bus, you pay the conductor of the bus for the distance you are traveling. The express buses are also crowded, but stop less often.

There are semi-luxury buses between the big cities. These are also not so comfortable because they have five seats across instead of four, so you are sitting tightly. In many cases there is reserved seating. The main problem with these buses is they may have extremely loud sound systems. If you get an all-night bus they may blast cinema music all-night long. The deluxe buses are the best because they have only four seats across, which also recline. A deluxe bus is suggested for long-distance travel. All-night deluxe buses are uncomfortable, but in many cases this is the easiest and fastest way to get somewhere. Some people like to travel by all-night deluxe buses. If you can sleep on a bus, they are not so bad. Deluxe buses are often better than trains for journeys of less than 8 hours.

It is a good idea to reserve an express bus in advance, if it is possible. You can do this at the bus terminal (terminus), which is often called a bus stand in India. Express buses sometimes depart from a different place than normal buses. So check in advance where your bus departs from. For an overnight deluxe bus journey, you have to reserve your seat in advance. For crowded routes you may have to reserve the bus a few days in advance.

At many places there are both state bus and private bus services. Usually the private bus services will have better buses. But if the private bus has a video you may consider whether you want to tolerate the unbelievable noise. There is a good chance they will blast the video on high volume for most of the night. This is when ear plugs come in handy.

Getting a Seat

If you are with someone else, one person can jump on the bus and get seats for both, while the other watches the bags. You can place a cloth through a window of the bus on an empty sit to reserve it. Or you can have one of the passengers on the bus reserve a seat for you in this way. If you get off the bus to go to the bathroom, you can place a cloth on your seat to reserve it. No one would even think to move it and steal your seat.

It is a good idea to find someone who is taking the same bus you are taking and ask them to help you get on the bus. When they make a run for the bus you just follow them. A few extra steps can be the difference between sitting and standing.

Many times there are young boys or porters in the bus station who will help you get on the bus. For five rupees, they will find your bus, help you with your luggage, and get you a seat, which may be difficult for you.

Many times you can make advance reservations for deluxe or luxury buses, which can save you the trouble of fighting for a seat. You should always book private buses in advance.

I have found that if I am standing on a bus, most of the time someone will help me get the first available seat. Indian people really try to help foreigners for the most part.

Baggage

Usually if you have a large bag (that cannot fit under the sit), it is supposed to go on top of the bus. When you are getting off the bus you should make it clear to the bus driver that you have luggage on top, so he knows you need time to get

it off. Otherwise he can just drive off.

You should be careful about leaving your bag under your seat, even while you are on the bus, as people will steal from your bag, especially if you have a camera or something valuable. It is best to put your bag under the seat in front of you, so you can see the bag at all times. If your bags are on the roof, keep alert that no one takes them off when the bus stops. People may take your bag or cut it if it is locked.

If someone puts your bags on the roof, you should expect to pay something for this service. Personally I do not like to put my bags on the roof of the bus. I usually try to get on the bus early and find a place to put my bag, usually in the front of the bus by the bus driver.

Taxis and Motor Rickshaws

Taxis are about twice as expensive as auto-rickshaws, which are motorcycle type vehicles having two passenger seats. In big cities like Delhi, taxi and auto-rickshaw drivers are supposed to use the meter, but often they do not. Many drivers just will not use them. They will say it does not work, and when you walk away, suddenly it will work. Metered cabs are mostly black with a yellow roof.

To get an idea of the correct fare, ask at your hotel or any intelligent-looking person how much it should cost to go to your destination. Many times when I ask someone how much an auto-rickshaw costs to get somewhere, they will say they are not sure. I then suggest a number "Do you think it will cost Rs 50?" They may still have a blank look on their face, and at that point I give up. But they often answer no, it should not cost more than Rs 25. I then know I should pay Rs 30 or Rs 35, being a tourist.

Sometimes when you use the meter

the taxi driver will drive you all over town. I had it happen to me a couple times that I know about. I personally like to have a map of the city I am in, so I know where I am going.

Many times your driver will pull out a fare adjustment chart or just tell you that the meter is not up to date and the actual price is 25% higher than what the meter says. In Bombay the taxi rate is actually 9 times the meter price. The price increase is because every time they raise the fuel price they do not change the meter to adjust for this increase. If you do not know the correct fare adjustment, do not argue with the driver. First confirm with the person you are going to see if this is true or ask someone walking by. If a policeman is around, ask them. They are usually helpful, but are not usually around.

In many places the cabs are not metered. The fare is supposed to be calculated by either a distance or time basis. In actuality it is what price you can work out with the taxi driver. If you do not know the exact price, you can assume that at a railway station the price will be at least double the actual fare, especially if you have that real tourist look. Some of the worst places for overcharging are Delhi (the sky is the limit), Varanasi (as much as ten times the real price), and Puri (three times the real price).

In many cities it is difficult to get a taxi or auto-rickshaw to use their meters, even if they are required by law to do so. Several times I have gotten into a motor rickshaw and the driver immediately put the meter on without asking. Of course, in some of these cases the meter did not work. In Bombay they routinely use the meter, even without your asking.

If possible it is a good idea not to get an auto rickshaw or taxi at a tourist-trap or expensive hotel. There is a class of drivers who prey on tourists by asking outrageous prices. A good idea is to walk a block or two away.

If a taxi driver tries to charge you a higher price than you arranged, do not get angry, as this will not help. The best thing is to just put the money on the seat of the rickshaw or taxi and walk away, not turning around. The main times that I have seen a problem is when you make an unarranged stop.

If a taxi driver is totally unreasonable, it is a good idea to take his license plate number and threaten to complain to the police. Taxi drivers usually become much more reasonable if they believe you will complain about them to the police. Taxi drivers can lose their license for mistreating a tourist.

In some cities you pay 15% to 50% extra for night surcharge.

Long-distance taxi rates for each km driven are about Rs 4. More than Rs 5 a km would be outrageous. If you go a long distance, to another city, you are charged for both coming and going. This is because the driver will have difficulty getting a return fare back to his home city. For instance if you are going from Delhi to Vrindavana the trip is 150 km. You are charged for 300 km or the distance from Delhi to Vrindavana and back.

Taxi From Stations or Airports

When you come out of a railway station or airport expect to be quoted an outrageous price, sometimes ten times the normal price. Usually the first price quoted will be at least double the normal price. There is a class of English speaking taxi drivers who rush to greet tourists with the hope of getting more money.

Unless you definitely know the price, your best bet is to get out of the station and approach a taxi driver that looks mellow, or get a local person to negotiate the price for you. For instance a taxi driver quotes you a price. You can then turn to an intelligent looking person standing nearby and ask him how much it should be to go to that place. Usually he will then ask the taxi driver how much he wants to take you there. The driver will then probably quote the same price as he told you before, and the person who is negotiating for you will be astonished and tell him that the price is totally outrageous. He will insist that he gives you a decent price and you will most likely get it. Many times people will come up and help you even without you asking.

When you get into the taxi or rickshaw the driver may start suggesting other places or hotels to go to. He may even say that the hotel you are going to is closed or full. I do not even listen to them. I just tell them to take me to where I first asked to go. They want to get a commission by bringing you to a hotel. I am usually polite with rickshaw or taxi drivers, because several times I actually had to take their suggestion, because all the hotels I tried were full.

Prepaid Taxi Stands

At some airports and railway stations they have prepaid taxi stands. In some places everyone is required to use this stand. You tell them where you want to go and how many bags you have, and you pay in advance a set fee for the taxi or auto-rickshaw. They then give you a slip that you are to give the taxi driver. When you reach your destination (not before) you give the driver the slip that you received. Using the prepaid taxi stand is recommended in most cases.

In theory it is a good system, but the problem is that many times the price you

are charged at a prepaid taxi stand is higher than the meter price or price you could negotiate yourself. When there is a prepaid taxi and rickshaw stand you can ask what price they charge and then try to negotiate a cheaper price yourself. At least you know what the maximum price you should pay is. Also at some railway stations the prepaid rate is so low that no driver will want to take you at that rate. They will insist that you ride with another passenger going in the same direction.

If you go up to the Tourist Taxi Stand at the airport to get a taxi from Delhi to Vrindavana (about 150 km away) they will tell you Rs 1500, and when you negotiate yourself you may pay Rs 1000 (maximum Rs 1200). For long distances your best bet is to find out the correct price and negotiate yourself. At the Calcutta Airport the fare charged at the prepaid Taxi Stand to go downtown is cheaper than what most people can negotiate themselves. But to go to Mayapur (130 km away), you can usually negotiate for a cheaper fare than the prepaid taxi-stand. Depending on the airport or railway station, the prepaid taxi stands may be a bargain or slightly above the meter price. Usually for a taxi into the city it is cheaper and for a long distance taxis they are more expensive. At least you will not get totally cheated when using a prepaid taxi.

Tip If you are driving to some place in the middle of nowhere and the driver realizes that he is taking you further than he thought, he may tell you he wants another 200 rupees or more for the trip. Just nod your head as if you perfectly understand that he should get the extra fare. The last thing you need is to get into a fight with a taxi driver in the middle of a field in West Bengal at 9 o'clock at night.

When you arrive at your destination, take your bags out of his car and bring them into the hotel or wherever you are staying. Then ask the driver to come inside so you can pay him. Then pay him the amount that you originally set. You might then pay him another 50 rupees to satisfy him.

Bargaining with Rickshaw Drivers

If possible find out the price of where you are going in advance. There is no shortage of people who will help you. You should ask what is the regular price. Tourists will almost always pay a higher price. It is best to always settle the price in advance or use the meter. Often you will ask a taxi driver to bring you to a particular place and he will agree. You get in and he does not turn on the meter. He then drives you to your destination. When you get there he insists that you pay three times the normal price. This is typical. Try not to get mad, it will only make matters worse. I have seen people ruin their entire India trip by arguing with rickshaw or taxi drivers over a few rupees.

If there is a group of rickshaws in one place, as a rule do not take the first one that runs up to you. If someone is working harder to find customers usually they want a higher price.

Walk up to a group of rickshaw drivers and ask them how much they want, as if you know exactly what the price is (hopefully you do). If someone quotes you a totally outrageous price, do not even waste your time negotiating with him, just go to the next driver. You will almost always be quoted a higher price than the actual price, say Rs 7 rupees if the actual price is Rs 5. You then say I will pay you Rs 5. Usually they say no. At this point you immediately turn to the next rickshaw driver and ask him if he will take you for five rupees. If he says no then ask the next rickshaw driver. Usually one of the other drivers you have asked will then say, "I will do it." I then confirm the price by showing my hand with five fingers up and say five rupees and ask him to confirm that he understands by shaking his head yes. This might not be the best way to bargain with rickshaw drivers, but it definitely works.

A problem comes up if you see something you want on the way and ask the rickshaw driver to stop. It is best to work out something extra with the driver before you get out of the rickshaw. Ask him how much extra it will cost to stop for 10 minutes. When you stop like this and do not work out a price there is a good chance you will get into an argument with the driver. Sometimes they want double the negotiated price.

Sometimes at the end of the trip the rickshaw driver wants a higher price than you agreed to pay. You may try to hand him the money and he will not take it. At this point you can just put the money on the seat of the rickshaw and walk away, making sure you do not look back.

Never argue with a driver. The angrier you get, the more determined they get. He is used to seeing people get mad at him. Just act as if you know the price and there is not a problem in the world. If you are going to a shop the local shopkeeper will often help you with any dispute.

Communication Problems

When getting a motor or bike rickshaw, you may ask to go somewhere, the driver says that he will take you, and you work out a fair price. After you go two blocks the driver asks you where you want to go and you tell him again. You then realize he has no idea where you want to go. He is usually overcharging you enough that he can bring you anywhere in town and still make a profit. He will just tell you a price to get you on his rickshaw, knowing that once you are in, more than likely you will not get out at that point. He then tries to figure out where you want to go.

When I get a rickshaw, I first tell them where I want to go and make them repeat the name of the place. If they cannot repeat the name, I say it a few more times. If they still cannot understand where I want to go, I ask another rickshaw driver. Many times no one can understand what I am saying. I then stop a man who speaks English and ask him to tell the driver where I want to go. Usually when this man tells the driver he understand immediately. Sometimes I have to write down where I want to go and show it to the driver or someone passing by. Many people have a problem understanding my accent. I have been told that American English is hard for the average person to understand, because Americans speak too quickly.

It is important to speak as slowly as possible.

Bicycles

In many towns you can hire a bike. Bikes are cheap, around Rs 20 a day. Indian bikes are heavy and do not have gears, but they are good for short distances. When you rent a bike you should check a few, as there can be a big difference between one bike and another. Also make sure you get a bike that has a bell, so you can warn people that you are coming. You can purchase a new bike for about Rs 1200.

If you get a hole in your tire, don't worry. There are many bicycle repair shops. If you want to get the tire repair done quickly, offer a little more than the normal Rs 3 repair charge.

Average Temperatures and Rainfall in mm

		Jan	Feb	Mar	Apr	May	Jun	Jul	Aug	Sep	Oct	Nov	Dec
Bangalore	min	15	16	20	21	21	20	19	19	19	19	17	15
	max	28	31	32	33	33	30	28	28	28	28	27	26
	rain	4	12	6	41	118	72	110	132	141	190	51	16
Bombay	min	17	19	21	24	26	26	25	25	24	24	20	19
	max	31	31	32	32	33	32	30	30	30	32	32	31
	rain	1	1	0	1	18	580	825	555	305	98	15	2
Calcutta	min	13	16	21	25	27	26	26	26	26	24	18	14
	max	27	29	34	36	36	34	32	32	32	31	30	27
	rain	14	23	28	45	125	261	306	308	280	152	33	3
Delhi	min	6	10	15	21	26	28	27	26	24	17	11	7
	max	21	24	30	36	41	40	35	34	34	34	30	23
	rain	25	22	17	7	8	65	211	173	150	31	1	5
Goa	min	19	20	23	25	27	25	24	24	24	23	22	21
	max	31	32	32	33	33	31	29	29	29	31	33	33
	rain	2	0	4	17	18	520	892	341	277	122	20	37
Hyderabad	min	15	17	20	24	26	24	22	22	22	20	16	13
	max	29	31	35	37	39	34	30	30	30	30	29	28
	rain	2	10	12	24	30	105	163	145	165	70	25	5
Jaipur	min	8	11	15	21	26	27	26	24	23	18	12	9
	max	22	25	31	37	41	39	34	32	33	33	29	24
	rain	14	8	9	4	10	54	193	239	90	19	3	4
Kathmandu	min	2	4	7	11	16	19	20	20	19	14	8	3
	max	18	20	25	27	30	29	29	29	28	27	23	19
	rain	16	40	25	60	120	250	375	345	155	40	8	2
Madras	min	20	21	23	25	28	28	26	25	24	24	23	21
	max	29	31	33	35	38	37	35	35	34	32	28	28
	rain	24	7	15	25	52	53	84	124	118	267	309	139
Madurai	min	21	22	23	25	26	26	26	25	25	24	23	22
	max	30	32	35	36	37	37	36	35	35	33	31	30
	rain	26	15	20	81	59	30	48	117	123	179	161	43
Puri	min	18	21	25	27	27	27	27	27	27	25	21	18
	max	27	28	30	31	32	31	31	31	31	31	29	27
	rain	10	23	16	12	63	201	296	276	268	252	65	7
Trivandrum	min	22	23	24	25	25	24	23	23	23	23	23	22
(Kovalam)	max	31	32	33	32	32	29	29	29	30	30	30	31
	rain	20	20	44	122	249	331	215	164	123	271	207	73
Varanasi	min	9	11	17	22	27	28	26	26	25	21	13	9
	max	23	27	33	39	41	39	33	32	32	32	29	25
	rain	23	8	14	1	8	102	346	240	261	38	15	2

CHAPTER FOUR

History

EARLY RECORDED HISTORY

Modern recorded history begins with the life of Gautama Buddha between 563 and 483 BC. But there is little recorded about this period. Alexander the Great's armies reached India in 326 BC, but refused to go further than the Beas River, the easternmost part of the Persian Empire. They did not gain any real control in India.

A large part of northern India was controlled by the Maurya Empire, under Chandragupta, who came to power in 321 BC. They had a well managed empire with a huge standing army, an efficient system to collect taxes, and a good agricultural society. It reached its peak and controlled much of India under Emperor Ashoka (273-232 BC), who converted to Buddhism. He established many pillars, rock carved edicts, and *stupas* all over India. The pillars and edicts of Ashoka can be seen in Delhi, Gujarat, Orissa, Sanchi in Madhya Pradesh, near Varanasi at Sarnath, and many other places. Ashoka was a major factor in spreading Buddhism all over India. He also sent missionaries abroad to spread Buddhism. After his death in 232 BC the empire started falling apart until it collapsed in 184 BC.

Different empires rose and fell after the Mauryas. In 319 AD Chandragupta II founded the Gupta Empire, which controlled most of northern India. They ruled from Patna and later from other capitals,

such as Ayodhya. Their power lasted until 606 AD. When their empire broke up, a number of smaller Hindu kingdoms were established, until the Muslims started coming into India.

MUSLIMS PERIOD

Mahmud of Ghazni conducted the first major Muslim attacks on India. He destroyed no shortage of temples in the early 11th century. Between 1001 and 1027 Mahmud of Ghazni attacked India 17 different times. He would kill, ransack cities, and destroy temples. He made an attempt to take over India, but he just robbed and never ruled India.

Mohammed of Ghori was the first Muslim to actually conquer and rule a part of India. One of his generals, Mohammed Khilji, destroyed many Buddhist monasteries and killed many of the priests. This had a great effect in destroying Buddhism in India. In 1192 Mohammed of Ghori took Ajmer. The next year his general, Quib-ub-din, captured Varanasi and Delhi. Quib-ub-din became the first Sultan of Delhi after Mohammed of Ghori died in 1206. The Sultans of Delhi did not have a consistent territory that they ruled. Depending on the ruler, the kingdom would either expand or reduce. In 1297 Ala-ud-din extended the borders into Gujarat, but he could not maintain the expansion. The Mongol Timur the Lame (Tamerlane) made a ruinous raid into India in 1398, which weakened the

Delhi Sultan's rule.

Different rulers had different religious tolerances; some would destroy whatever temples that they could. Pherose Khan Jughalak (1351-1388) destroyed all the temples in his territory. When Sekandar Lodi was the emperor of Delhi, he would destroy all temples in the areas that he conquered.

Babur, from Kabul, Afghanistan, established the Moghul empire when he defeated the Sultan of Delhi at the battle of Panipat in 1526. Sher Shah defeated his son Humayan in 1540. Humayan lived in exile for 15 years, but again returned to the throne. The Moghuls had the most influence over India of all the Muslim rulers. There were six important Moghul emperors. The best of these was Akbar (1556-1605) who became the emperor in 1556 at the age of 13. He allowed freedom of religion, and his general, Man Singh of Jaipur, built the Govindaji temple in Vrindavana during his rule. His son Jehangir maintained his father's tolerance of other religions. The next ruler, Shah Jahan, built the famous Taj Mahal in Agra, but did not maintain the religious tolerance of his grandfather.

The next and worst of the Moghul emperors was Aurangzeb (1658-1707), who destroyed temples all over India and then built mosques at the same sites. He destroyed many temples in Vrindavana and Mathura including the temple at Lord Krishna's birthplace. Aurangzeb spread the Moghul Empire over a good part of India, but actually caused its downfall because of his religious intolerance. In 1739 India was invaded by Nadir Shah from Iran, who destroyed Delhi and killed over 100,000 people.

Mathura was first destroyed by Mahmud of Ghazni in 1018. At that time Mathura was considered one of the richest cities in the world. Both Sikander Lodi, in about 1500, and Aurangzeb, in 1669, destroyed temples in Mathura and Vrindavana. The Muslims would sometimes take the deities from the temple and bury them under the steps of a mosque. The steps of the Nawab Kudsia Begum Mosque had deities taken from Mathura buried under its steps. In 1803 when the British took over India, no harm came to the temples or deities.

After ruling India for 800 years the Muslims were able to convert only 25% of the population to Islam. The Muslims also could not rule without the assistance of Hindus. Despite repeated efforts to convert the so-called infidels, they were largely unsuccessful.

The Rajputs and Marathas

The Rajputs of Rajasthan are a warrior class who are fanatical in battle. The Rajputs fought every foreign attack on their land. Their problem was that they never united and could not organize amongst themselves to defeat the Muslims. If they were not fighting the Muslims, they would often fight amongst themselves. Therefore, for the most part, they were defeated one by one and became vassal states of the Moghul Empire.

Jaipur (Amber) was a Rajput kingdom in Rajasthan. Akbar's general, Man Singh of Jaipur, built the Govindaji temple in Vrindavana. His grandson, Maharaja Jai Singh II (1699-1744), who had the city of Jaipur built, moved different Deities, including Govindaji, from Vrindavana and Mathura to protect Them from Muslim attacks.

The Maratha, from Maharashtra in central India, became a major force in India between 1646 and 1680 under Shivaji. He was a devotee of Lord Vitthala. Over the years the Maratha took over much of the weakening Moghul Empire. Their expansion was halted when they were defeated at Panipat, on January 13, 1761 by Ahmad Shah Durani from Afghanistan. They still maintained their control over central India, but eventually they fell under the rule of the British.

The British

The Portuguese were the first European power to come to India. In 1498, Vasco da Gama came to Kerala. In 1510 the Portuguese captured Goa and controlled it right up to 1961. They did not expand much past this point. In 1672 the French established a trading post in Pondicherry.

The British first came to India in 1612, establishing a trading post at Surat in Gujarat. For the next 240 years Britain's interest in India was ruled by the London-based East India Company, not by the British government. They established English as the language for government and administration purposes. Madras was founded in 1639, Bombay in 1668, and Calcutta in 1690. The turning point for the British was the Battle of Plassey in Bengal in 1757, when they gained a real foothold in India.

The British practised tolerance of all religions. This enabled them to get the support of the local people who wanted to see the current leaders out of office. The British were mainly interested in trade, not in ruling the country. After defeating the Muslim ruler Tipu Sultan at Srirangapatnam near Mysore in 1799, the British gave control back to the former Hindu king of Mysore.

In 1803 the British were able to defeat the Marathas, thus leaving only Punjab free from their control. Then in 1849 Punjab also fell, after the two Sikh Wars.

By the beginning of the 19th century virtually all of India was in the control of the British. They continued keeping many of the princely states under the rule of the local maharajas and nawabs all the way to Independence. But they also maintained strict control over these states.

In 1857 there was an uprising by the Indian battalions of the Bengal Army. It never spread past northern India, however, and just died out after a while. After the uprising of the Indian troops, the British Crown took control of India from the East India Company and ruled India directly.

The British slowly began handing power over to the local people. Higher positions in the government that used to be held by British began opening up for the Indians. In 1885 the India National Congress was founded. In 1919 Mahatma Gandhi started his policy of passive resistance. He led movements against the salt tax and British textiles. In July 1945, when the Labour Party won in the British elections, it was just a manner of time before India became independent.

After Independence

On August 15th 1947 India's independence from England was proclaimed by Lord Mountbatten. At that time India was split into two countries, Pakistan and India. India was to be mainly Hindu, and Pakistan was to be mainly Muslim. Over 10 million people from both sides moved to the country of their choice. During this time there was wholesale violence, resulting in the death of about half a million people. At first the present countries of Pakistan and Bangladesh were one country, but it was difficult to manage two tracts of land so far apart. In 1971 Pakistan was divided into Pakistan, to the west of India, and Bangladesh, to the east.

SOUTH INDIA (DECCAN)

Until independence in 1947, India was never a totally united country. The empires in North India were totally different than those in the South. The rise and fall of empires in different parts of India often had no influence on empires in other parts of India.

In recent history several different Hindu powers ruled over South India. These include the Pallavas (550-869), the Cholas (850-1173), Hoysalas, Chalukyas, Pandyas, and Cheras. The Chalukyas ruled much of the Deccan area of central India. They ruled from their capital at Badami in Karnataka from 550 to 753 AD. They were replaced by the Rashtrakutas, but they regained power from 972 to 1190. The Pallavas were ruling further south at this time. They were the first builders of Dravidian temples. Around 850 AD the Cholas gradually took control of South India from the Pallavas.

From about 1000 to 1300 AD the Hoysala Empire ruled the area around Bangalore from the cities of Belur, Halebid, and Somnathpur.

The Muslims first arrived in South India between 1296 to 1347. The Vijayanagar Empire was a powerful Hindu kingdom that ruled from Hampi between 1336 to 1565. At the same time, from 1347 to 1489, the Muslim Bahmani kingdom had much power in the north part of South India. It split into five separate kingdoms at Bijapur, Golconda, Berar, Ahmednagar, and Ahmedabad. In 1565 at the battle of Talikota the five Bahmani kingdoms combined to destroy the city of Vijayanagar.

Later the Bahmani kingdoms fell to the Moghuls. Aurangzeb used a large quantity of men and money to conquer South India. After Aurangzeb's death the Moghul empire started to disintegrate, partly because of overexpanding and partly because of his bigotry in destroying the Hindu temples.

The Portuguese led by Vasco de Gama first arrived in 1498. The British first started trading in South India at Madras in 1640 through the East India Company. Eventually the British took over South India and then the rest of India. The Muslim rulers Haider Ali and his son Tipu Sultan from Mysore, were the last power in South India to fall to the British in 1799.

Ancient Temples in the South, but not the North.

To know a little history helps one to understand why South India is much more rich with ancient temples than the North. Militarily, the Hindu kingdoms were more united in the south, so the Muslims did not maintain power very long there, if at all. Some of the Muslim rulers would destroy temples wherever they conquered. Aurangzeb was one of the worst. He destroyed temples in Vrindavana, Varanasi, and many other places all over India. He was the cause of many of the original Deities of Vrindavana going to other cities in India, and he destroyed part of the Govindaji temple in Vrindavana. Maharaja Jai Singh II, a general in Aurangzeb's army, whose ancestor built the Govindaji temple, was the man responsible for saving the Deities.

The fact that the Muslims would destroy temples is the reason why many ancient deities were hidden and suddenly found in bushes or in a *kund* (lake). Not only would the Muslims destroy the temples, but in many cases they would also kill the priests of the temple and destroy the deities. Therefore after a priest hid the deities of the temple, he could have been killed or captured and the deities would be lost.

TEMPLE HISTORY

The earliest temples in North and Central India are from the Gupta period 320-650 AD. Some places where Gupta period temples are located are Nachna, Rajasthan; Sanchi, Madhya Pradesh; Bhumara, Madhya Pradesh; and Deogarh, Uttar Pradesh.

Some of the first temples were rock-cut Buddhist cave temples. The caves temples at Ajanta date from about 200 BC to 650 AD.

The Pallavas of Kanchi, the Pandyas of Madurai, and the Calukyas of Badami built the first major temples in South India. Some of the Badami temples were built between 450 and 466 AD. These temples include both free-standing and cave temples. The Rastrakutas of Malkhed came to power in the 8th century and are responsible for the Kailasanantha Temple in Ellora.

Some of the temples in Aihole and Pattadakal in Karnataka were built between the 5th and 7th centuries by the Chalukya kings. The Huchimalligudi, Durga, and Lad Khan temples were all built in Aihole between 450 to 650 AD. Some of the Calukyan temples are a combination of northern and southern styles.

The Pallavas (600-900 AD) built the Mahabalipuram temples, such as the Shore Temple. They also built the Vaikuntha Perumal and Kailasanatha Temple in Kanchipuram between 700 and 800 AD. They started the Dravidian school of temples, which are big and more complex stone temples with intricate sculptures. The earliest Dravidian temples are at Mamallapuram (Mahabalipuram), located about 85 kilometres south of Madras, and at Kanchipuram, about 70 kilometres southwest of Madras.

The Dravidian style was developed in Tamil Nadu and Andhra Pradesh and evolved over a thousand-year period. It covered different dynasties—the Pallavas (600-900), Cholas (900-1150), Pandyas (1152-1350), Vijayanagar (1340-1565), and the Nayaks of Madurai (1550-1750). The Dravidian style has large towers, concentric walls, a main shrine, and large halls with up to a thousand pillars.

The Chola kings built temples in about 70 cities between 900 and 1200 AD that were even larger than the temples built before them. The two most famous temples they built are at Tanjore (Thanjavur) and Gangaikondacholapuram in Tamil Nadu.

The Pandyas did not build many new temples, but they improved and added to the existing temples. They added extra walls and large elaborate gates with many ornamental sculptures, many-pillared halls, annexes to the shrines, and elaborate gateways.

The Hoysala kings built temples in the 12th and 13th century in southwest Karnataka. The temples they built have elaborate sculptures. They built the Chennakesava Temple in Belur, the Hoysaleswara Temple in Halebid, and the 13th century Kesava Temple at Somnathpur (40 km from Mysore).

The Vijayanagar kings (1350-1565) expanded many temples and built the Pampapati, Vitthala, and many other temples in Hampi. The Nayaks of Madurai (1600 to 1750) made the *gopurams* even more huge and intricate and added pillared corridors within the temple walls.

In the north many of the ancient temples (built from 750 to 1250) were destroyed by the Muslims. Some of the chief temples that are left are in Orissa. These include the Jagannatha Temple in

Puri, the Lingaraja Temple in Bhubaneswara, and the Surya Temple in Konark. The Chandellas built the famous temples in Khajuraho between 950 and 1050. There were important temples built in the 10th and 11th centuries in Rajasthan and 11th to 13th century in Gujarat. There are some interesting temples built with terra-cotta tiles in Vishnupur in Bengal. Temples were built in the 16th century by the followers of Sri Caitanya in Vrindavana, including the Govindaji and Madana Mohana Temples.

History of the Vedic Literature

According to the *Vedas*, Indian civilization has existed for millions of years. Modern history dates back to the time of death of Buddha, 483 BC. Archaeologists and anthropologists cannot accept the Vedic conclusion that civilization flourished in India long before fifty thousand years ago, which is the date that scientists give as the earliest possible appearance of Homo Sapiens (human beings) on earth. The *sastras* state that the Vedic literature was written down about 5000 years ago, at the beginning of Kali-yuga. These literatures describe the activities of sages and yogis who lived many millions of years ago.

The earliest Indus civilizations accepted by modern historians are the cities of Harappa and Mohenjaro, which are now located in Pakistan. According to modern Indian history books, the Dravidians, the then residents of India, were invaded by the Aryan barbarians, who brought with them their tales of Indra (*Rig Veda*). This account enjoys wide circulation in the history books, but it is by no means a scientific conclusion. It is a hypothetical creation set forth to explain what would otherwise be inexplicable to their frame of accepted knowledge.

According to the Vedic *acaryas* (teachers) the oral transmission of the *Vedas* began simultaneous to the cosmic creation, when God spoke the Vedic knowledge to the first living being, Brahma. Vyasadeva, the literary incarnation of the Supreme Person, wrote down the *Vedas* at the beginning of Kali millennium, about 5000 years ago.

CHAPTER FIVE

Health

Few people have a serious health problem when they visit to India. If you are careful most health problems can be avoided. If you stay in reasonably clean hotels or dharamshalas, and are careful about the water you drink and what you eat, there is a good chance you will not have a problem. The list of potential diseases that can be gotten can seem frightening, but most people will not encounter anything more than an upset stomach.

There are many qualified doctors in India, especially in the bigger cities. It is important to see a doctor immediately if any serious disease is suspected.

There are many health risks in India that would not normally be encountered in Europe or North America. Also there are still many diseases that are fairly common in India which are rarely found in Western countries. Therefore it could be a good idea to get some vaccinations as protection.

Good Books to Read

How To Stay Healthy Abroad (earlier editions were called *Travellers' Health*), by Dr Richard Darwood, is a good detailed book about staying healthy while traveling and is recommended. It is written by different doctors on the subjects they are expert in and is highly informative.

Staying Healthy in Asia, Africa & Latin America, Moon Publication, is an informative book about staying healthy in the tropics. It is an easy-to-understand book. *The Traveller's Health Guide*, written by Dr. Anthony C. Turner, who is a consultant in tropical and travel medicine, is an informative and easy-to-read book. *Travel with Children*, Maureen Wheeler, Lonely Planet. It has basic advice about travel health for young children.

Before You Go

You should have a dental check-up, as the dentists in India are usually not very good except in the big cities, or they just might not have modern equipment, like an X-ray machine. Also many times they do not properly clean their equipment.

You should also bring your glasses prescription. An extra pair of glasses would be useful, as you may lose your glasses in the middle of nowhere, and it can be very difficult to get another pair. I know a few people that went through this experience.

If you have a health problem or have not seen a doctor in a while, get a medical check-up before you leave. Find out from your doctor if there are any precautions you should take. If you are taking a **prescription medicine**, make sure you bring enough for the entire trip. You never know, you may decide to stay an extra month or two. People often stay much longer than they had planned in India. There is a good chance that it will be impossible to get the medicines you need in India, or even if you could, it might be an inferior quality. You should also get the generic name of the medicine, because in India it will most likely be sold under a different name.

Immunization

In health books (written by doctors) that I have read, they suggest that a person gets an injection for hepatitis A, polio, tetanus, and typhoid. They also suggest that you take malaria preventative pills.

Few vaccines give 100% protection, so care should still be taken regarding drink, food, and personal hygiene, no matter how many shots you get.

For recommendations on what shots to take, it is a good idea to go to a doctor who is familiar with common Indian diseases and tropical medicine. Many doctors know very little about this subject. A doctor trained in India or a tropical disease center would be your best option. It is best to get your vaccinations about two weeks before you leave. This gives time for the shots to take effect and also gives you some time to get over any side-effects.

A gamma globulin injection is given for infectious **hepatitis A**, but even so, you may still get the disease. The injection loses its potency steadily over a six month period. So, for a long-range stay it would be almost useless. This shot should be gotten just before departure. Havrix Vaccine is effective up to 10 years, but is expensive.

The first of two **cholera** injections should be taken six months before you leave. You need a second shot about six months later. For protection against **typhoid** two shots are needed, the first one six weeks before you leave. Protection from typhoid lasts for about two or three years.

According to one book I read, the US Health Service said that shots for cholera are only 50 percent effective. Another health book written by a doctor said that cholera shots give poor protection. I have heard that typhoid shots can cause considerable discomfort. Typhoid is easier to get when there is poor sanitation. You have a better chance of getting typhoid outside the major cities.

To prevent **polio,** you usually have to takes 3 doses of a live vaccine with a booster every 3 to 5 years.

If you take pills to prevent **malaria,** you should begin taking them two weeks before you go; and you should continue to take them at least six weeks after you return from India, as the disease takes a while to become active in your system. Many mosquitoes have built up a resistance to certain malaria pills, so it is important to contact a doctor to find out what pills to take for malaria.

Many times the pills you take to keep from getting malaria have side-effects and can ruin your vacation. Many people I talked to stopped taking them because of the side-effects. The sure way to keep from getting malaria is to not get bitten by mosquitoes. This is possible if you are very careful. Definitely take insect repellent with you, as the repellents in India are not as effective as the ones in the West.

At a commercial travel clinic in London a full set of shots costs about 40 pounds. Beside your local GP in the UK there are some good vaccinating centers. Some are: London Hospital for Tropical Diseases, 4 St Pancras Way, London (071-637-9899); West London Vaccinating Centre at 53 Gt Cumberland Place, London (071-262-6456); British Airways Travel Clinic at 156 Regent St, London (071-439-9584); Thomas Cook at 45

Berkeley St, London (071-408-4157); and Trailfinders, 194 Kensington High Street, London (071-938-3939). In the USA, for the latest advice on what shots to get and what malaria pills to take, contact the Center for Disease Control, Atlanta (404) 332-4555.

Advice for the Plane Journey

When you fly, gases in the body, especially the intestines, will expand and can cause discomfort and sometimes an earache. Because of this it is best to wear loose fitting clothes and not to eat too much on the aircraft. It is best not to smoke just before getting on the plane or on the aircraft because there is a slight decrease of oxygen, which can cause symptoms from excessive carbon monoxide. Because of the dry atmosphere on the plane there is a tendency for dehydration, therefore you should drink plenty of liquids. Because of the tendency for intestinal gases, fizzy or carbonated drinks should be avoided.

You should be careful of jet lag when you first come off the aircraft, as there are tests to prove that reaction time and decision time are affected for a day or two. It is best not to make any important decisions right away, especially if you have no advance plans. If you are too much in a hurry, there is a good chance you will make a mistake in judgment.

Water

In India most people should drink at least two quarts a day, if not much more. I read in a book about traveler's health that for every 10 degrees Fahrenheit, you should drink one pint of water. Under this rule, if it is 80°F (28°C) you should drink four quarts (litres) of water. Healthy urine should be almost totally clear, not dark yellow. The general rule is to drink water beyond the point of thirst-quenching.

It is advised by Ayurvedic doctors to avoid drinking water for at least one hour after eating. If you drink just after eating, it kills the fire of digestion in your stomach. You should also not drink too much just before you eat. You can drink a little bit of water while you eat, to wash your food down.

Alcohol, coffee, and tea increase dehydration, not decrease it.

Water As a Source of Disease

Be very careful of the water, as it is the main cause of disease in India. Bottled water is plentiful now. It is a good idea to use bottled or purified water even to brush your teeth. For most people it is not a good idea to put tap water in your mouth, as you may swallow some. Cold drink companies, such as Limca, purify the water they use. So they should be a good clean source of water.

If you are in a place where many foreigners drink the water, find out where they get their water and drink that. All tap water is not the same in India. Water from one source may be safe and from another may not be.

It is a good idea to purify the water you drink with a portable water purifier, boil it, or chemically treat it. Water should be boiled for at least five minutes to kill all the germs. It is best to filter your water before you boil it. Only fill up a sterilized bottle about 2/3 with the boiled water. When you boil water it loses the contained gases and the taste becomes flat. There will be some absorption of lost gases in a partially filled bottle, so flavor (taste) is regained. Hot water, even though not boiled, kills many disease organisms. Cholera bacillus is killed at 140°F. The container which holds your clean water also has to be kept clean. You can clean it by pouring boiling water in it.

Iodine tablets kill all kinds of germs, but too much iodine is not good for you. It takes 4 to 8 drops of iodine to purify a litre of water. You have to mix it well. Let the treated water sit for 30 minutes before drinking it. If exposed to air or dampness, iodine loses its power.

Chlorine tablets will kill most organisms in water. Contact time with the water should be as long as possible. If the water is very cold it may need more chlorine tablets, and you may have to let it sit for thirty minutes instead of 10 minutes. Chlorine tablets do not kill cryptosporidiosis, which is a cause of diarrhoea. Micropur is a completely tasteless water purification pill that is not available in India. It kills bacteria, but not all viruses, so it is not totally effective.

You can get water purification pills in the West, but they are not sold in India. If you chemically treat your water, it tastes horrible and you might not want to drink it. Tang or other flavored powders can be used to kill the taste. Also limes and sugar cover the taste. Many people prefer the taste of iodine to chlorine tablets.

Water purifiers can also be good. I have a water purifier that first treats the water with iodine to kill the germs and then purifies the water. It has another purifier to take out the iodine, as the iodine tastes terrible. I have read a few books by doctors that question some of the claims about water purification device. They say that most purifiers will not kill viruses. They consider boiling water as the safest solution.

In hotels or restaurants they may tell you that they filter the water. The local water filters get rid of solids, but they do not kill bacteria. So don't believe the water is absolutely safe. Many times fruit juice is mixed with regular tap water.

Avoid the local street vendors and be careful of ice, as you don't have any idea where the water came from. After the ice is cut up it may be transported on a dirty hand-cart or rickshaw and then broken up on the dirty pavement on the side of the street. I have seen this personally. There is usually no standard of cleanliness in regards to ice.

Water is more dangerous during the monsoon season than in the dry season. Green coconut is a good source of clean water. Green coconut is available in Bengal, Orissa, Bombay, and South India.

Food

It is best to eat boiled foods such as rice, *dal* (beans), and boiled vegetables. Fried foods are much harder to digest. Food should always be well cooked. Food in India can be dangerous if it cools and is later reheated.

Raw salads and ice creams can be potentially harmful things to eat in India. Ice creams may have melted and refrozen, giving many germs a chance to enter. Also frozen milk for some people is very hard to digest and can cause stomach disorders. Raw salads are dangerous because they are washed with potentially dangerous water. If the water is purified the salads will not usually be harmful.

Foods on display should be avoided, and you should be careful of restaurants that have a lot of flies.

The way meat is processed in India makes it potentially extremely dangerous to eat, and it is much heavier to digest in the hot climate, so it is best to eat vegetarian foods. There is virtually no health standard in meat preparation or storage in India. If meat is only half cooked or rare it is extremely dangerous. So for health reasons it is best to be totally avoided. When one smells a really disgusting smell, it usually comes from meat or fish. This is nature's way of warning us that there could be something wrong with it. In many holy places of India meat is totally banned, as meat is considered detrimental for spiritual life.

I heard one story about a person who was drinking some rose milk that was a pretty pink color. He thought it tasted really good. So he asked the person who made the milk to tell him how it got its pink color. He was then shown a container of industrial dye which said on it "NOT FOR HUMAN CONSUMPTION" in big letters. In India you can be fed anything that has been banned in the West for 50 years.

Papaya is a healthy food to eat. It is easy to digest, rich in vitamins (it has more vitamin C than oranges), and also helps with your digestion. It can also help you to have regular bowel movements. Mango season is from April to July. Coconut milk is good for most people.

Milk

Drinking milk in India can be risky. Milk must be boiled or pasteurized to be safe. Much of the milk you get in India is from buffaloes and not cows. Buffalo milk has a higher fat content than cow milk, but it is not as healthy.

Ice cream is usually all right, but not if it has melted and refroze, which happens when the electricity has been out for hours.

Raw milk must be is boiled properly to make it safe. The milk should be boiled for a while to kill all the germs. A good idea is to bring milk to a boil three times. Milk should be drunk as soon as possible after boiling, as germs quickly breed again. Bad milk can be the cause of tu-

berculosis, typhoid, dysentery, and other diseases. Because of the way yoghurt is processed it is safer than milk, but it can still be unhealthy if it has not been stored properly.

Washing Fruits and Vegetables

Fruits and vegetables should be peeled if possible. Many health books recommend that no raw fruits or vegetables should be eaten unless the skins are taken off. If you wash fruit with the local tap water this can be like drinking the local tap water.

Ideally fruits and raw vegetables (such as tomatoes) should be washed first with clean soapy water and then rinsed with treated water or dipped in boiling water. A good idea is to purchase water purification pills in your home country and wash your fruit with treated water.

Drinking Glasses on the Street

Be careful of drinking glasses used for juice, tea, etc. because they are seldom cleaned properly. I have yet to see one cleaned to my standards. Even if it looks clean, all they usually do is rinse it out in a bucket of local tap water in which 100 other glasses were already washed. You can get hepatitis (jaundice) and many other diseases from dirty glasses. If you like to drink fruit juice, it could be a good idea to carry your own glass with you.

Salt

In a hot climate people sweat more. Besides a loss of more fluids than usual, there is also a loss of salt. This must be replaced just like the fluids. The normal European diet contains about 10 grams of salt per 24 hours. You may need 15 to 25 grams of salt in your diet in the tropics, depending on the amount of physical work you do and how much time you spend in the sun. It is important that you do not increase your salt intake without increasing your fluid intake also. If you do this, it will be worse for you than not taking the extra salt that your body needs.

Digestion

In India many people experience some problem with digestion. Ayurvedic medicine suggests that food items like lime, ginger, and fresh coriander can be mixed with your food to help you digest better.

It is also a good idea to eat less, as overeating even once can result in immediate sickness. You should not drink water immediately after eating. It is better to wait for at least an hour before drinking, and two hours is even better. You should also not drink too much water just before you eat or while eating. Fried foods are much harder to digest than boiled foods. Also some people will find raw food to be indigestible in India.

It is best not to keep eating until you are full. You should eat only until you are three-fourths full. It is best to let your meal be totally digested before eating anything else. This takes about four hours. It is usually not good to eat between meals. If you stuff yourself, it is very normal to get sick within a few hours.

Fasting is a good cure for many digestion problems. A natural cure for indigestion is drinking water. Many times digestive problems in India are caused by a bad liver. There are Ayurvedic medicines that can help you digest your food better in India.

Ayurvedic Medicine

According to Ayurvedic medicine, by controlling your diet and taking herbal medicines you can cure or totally avoid most diseases. Ayurvedic medicine aims to not only cure the symptoms of a disease, but the cause of the disease. It takes into consideration that each person has a different bodily nature and so should be treated differently, even if they have the same disease. People come under three basic categories: Kapha, Pitha, and Vata. Ayurvedic medicine is much more effective than any other kind of medical treatment for digestive diseases and many of the typical diseases you find in India. Ayurvedic medicine can cure hepatitis (jaundice), while there is no cure according to conventional medicine practiced in the west.

You can also take Ayurvedic medicine to keep from getting sick. Many diseases in India are caused by the fact that a person's liver or digestive system does not work properly. You can take Ayurvedic medicine to help your digestive system work perfectly. This reduces the amount of undigested food in your digestive system that can cause disease. If your food is properly digested you have sufficient or at least more energy in your body to fight diseases.

There are also Ayurvedic massages which can help cure various afflictions of the body.

The main problem with taking Ayurvedic treatment to cure disease is finding a competent doctor. I would always try to get a recommendation from someone about which Ayurvedic doctor is good. Only if I had total faith in the Ayurvedic doctor would I trust him to treat me if I had malaria or a similar disease.

Dr Triguna and His Son

Dr Triguna is an excellent Ayurvedic doctor, one of the best in India. His office is by the Nizamuddin train station in southeast Delhi. He personally helped me when I was extremely sick at least three times. One time my digestion totally shut down, and I did not eat for five days. After taking his medicine I was back to normal in ten days. One friend of mine had a bad case of hepatitis (jaundice) and was told at the hospital that there is no known cure for this disease. After his visit to Triguna, he was up and moving around after a few days and normal in a week.

To get to his clinic you first go to the Nizamuddim train station. If you are walking out of the train station you turn left and go by rickshaw or walking about half a km (8-10 minute walk). When you come to the Y-intersection, take the left fork, by some vegetable stands, which brings you over the train tracks. After the train tracks, you walk about 150 feet and turn right at the intersection. His office is on the right at the end of the road, a minute away. You should arrive there before noon, as that is the usual closing time.

He is closed on Mondays, and sometimes he is not there, as he travels all over the world helping people.

Work out any question that you have before you see him, as you will only be given a few seconds to ask questions. If you do not ask anything right away, a rush of new patients will be in the room before you know it. One important question is how long you should continue to take the medicine. Another question to ask is what foods you should eat or avoid. Also you should ask when you should come back. With Ayurvedic medicine it is usually best to take the medicine over a long period of time.

Often the medicine is a powder that can taste horrible. Many people do not take the medicine because of this. If you will not take the medicine because of its bad taste, it is best to request pills. You can also often take the medicine with honey.

Dr Triguna is highly recommended.

Alternative Medicine

The Tibetan Clinic (Men-Tsee-Khang-Exports, 11-621-2604) is located at 13 Jaipur Estate, near the Nizamuddin train station in New Delhi. They treat people by natural herbal methods and have been recommended to me by many people. To get there you can ask a rickshaw driver at the Nizamuddin train station to take you to Jaipur Estate, where it is located.

There is a well-known homeopathic doctor called Dr R S Pareek (52786, 54422), 4/10 Bagh Farzana, Civil Lines in Agra. He is supposed to be especially effective in treating skin disorders.

Doctors

Indian doctors can be excellent. Doctors in the private clinics and large hospitals can be much better at curing tropical diseases than doctors in the USA and Europe. As a class, however, it is best to not totally trust doctors in India, unless they are in big cities. They are best saved for emergencies.

Before choosing a doctor it is advisable to get a few recommendations. The doctors recommended by the embassies usually have the best reputation.

In case of any serious illness, it is best to go to a big city to get treatment. A great fear about medical treatment in India is poor sanitation.

See a Doctor Immediately

If you get sick don't wait too long to go to a doctor. A good rule in India is to give one day for a heavy illness. If you are extremely sick two days in a row, it is best to go to see a doctor. If you think that you are too sick to get up and go see a doctor, you almost certainly need to see one.

Advice that most long-term visitors in India give people when they hear the question, "My friend (or husband) has been in bed for three days and hasn't eaten anything. What should I do?" The answer will always be, "Bring him to a doctor."

Medicine Tip

You get most medicines without a prescription (check the sell-by date). Private and mission hospitals are usually better than state-run ones, but may not have as good facilities. The hospitals in the big cities are usually the best, and university or medical schools are usually the best of all. In many hospitals you are expected to pay in advance for services, but charges are much lower than in the West.

You should be careful about the medicines given to you in India. The same medicine that may have been banned in the West for years can be prescribed to you by a doctor with complete conviction that the medicine is safe.

Hospitals

A few excellent hospitals are the *Christian Medical College Hospital* in Vellore, Tamil Nadu, the *All India Institute of Medical Sciences* in Delhi, and the *Breach Candy Hospital* in Bombay.

The *Hinduja Hospital* in Bombay is one of the best in India. If you have a serious problem and do not need immediate attention and you can get to Bombay, then this is a good place to go.

Dentist

If you are going to be in India for a while, it is best to see a dentist before going. Dentists as a class are not very trustworthy, but in an emergency I have found them to do a decent job. If you must see a dentist in India, try to see one that had some training outside of India or one that is recommended to you. For any major work, it is best to see a dentist in a big city, such as Bombay or Delhi.

I have gone six times to dentists in India and had varying success. I got a good filling put in once. But one dentist tried to glue a cap on and it came off after a few days. The next dentist glued the cap on properly. Another dentist tried to repair a cracked tooth with no success.

In the Bombay section of this book, I recommend one dentist, who is very good. He did a root canal, put some caps on my teeth, and repaired some cavities. He did a good job, as good as any I have had done in the West, for about one third the cost.

The **Delhi Dental Centre** (644-4918, 644-2398), C-565 Extension II, has been recommended to me as a good place to have dental work done. It is best to call for an appointment. Dr Chopra is said to be good.

Cures

The antibiotic Tinidazole is a good remedy for giardiasis.

Western medicine has no real cure for hepatitis, but a good Ayurvedic doctor can cure it. Hepatitis rarely kills someone, but it can be very uncomfortable.

Rabies is very dangerous and can kill you. If an animal bites you and draws blood, you should go immediately to a hospital. It takes 14 days to administer a cure, and the series of injections is unpleasant. Besides dogs, you should also be especially careful of monkeys, because they will bite. You can even be bitten while feeding monkeys.

It is a good idea to bring medicine for fungal infection, athlete foot, if you have this problem.

Cuts

The smallest cut that you would not even think about elsewhere can become infected in a day in India. If you get cut, a bandage is not enough. You immediately have to put some antiseptic on it, or even consider seeing a doctor if it is a big cut. It is a good idea to bring a good antiseptic cream from your home country, but Dettol is a good Indian alternative. You should closely observe the healing process of even the smallest cut to see if it gets infected. The slightest infection should be dealt with immediately.

Diarrhoea

Many people get diarrhoea for a variety of reasons. If that is the only symptom, many times it will go away in just a day or two, especially if you skip a meal or two. Most cases will go away in 48 to 72 hours. If diarrhoea lasts for more than a week or it is very heavy, even for a day or two, it is best to see a doctor. It may be the symptom of a much more severe disease. Severe results are more common with children and may cause death. Diarrhoea that lasts more than 10 days or that contains blood should always be taken seriously.

Diarrhoea is usually caused by food poisoning. It can be caused by bacteria, viruses, amoebas, salmonella, or cholera organisms.

Drinking large amounts of water is the most important part of treatment. Most people should drink at least two or three litres a day. It is also a good idea to take oral rehydration salts, called Electrolyte in India. If there is a severe water loss, Electrolyte is highly recommended. A substitute for this is a half teaspoon of salt and three teaspoons of sugar in a litre of water. The main defense against any serious outcome is drinking a good quantity of water and not just taking antibiotics or antidiarrhoeal agents.

The cure for diarrhoea may be simply a change of diet. You should not take milk products, except yoghurt or buttermilk, when you have diarrhoea. A good diet is plain rice and curd (yoghurt). Mung bean *kicharee*, which is a mixture of rice and mung bean, is for most people the best food to eat. It gives a good amount of energy and is easy to digest. Papaya and pomegranate are good fruits to eat. Good spices are ginger, long pepper, coriander, nutmeg, cardamom, and saffron. No fried food should be eaten. Fasting for a day cures many cases of diarrhoea.

Isabbael, which is a brown color, is a good medicine to take for diarrhoea. It helps to clog up your system. Ayurvedic medicines that contain *kutaja* are usually good for curing diarrhoea. Unless you have to take them, antibiotics and other powerful medicines should be avoided, as many times the side-effects of the drugs can be more dangerous than the disease. In some cases there is no choice but to take antibiotics and other such medicine. In one test it was found that streptomycin/sulphatriad marketed as Streptotriad was best at curing diarrhoea.

Many anti-diarrhoea medicines such as codeine-phosphate and loperamide (Imodium, Arret) may be dangerous for children.

Dysentery

Many people think every case of diarrhoea is dysentery. Actually, normal diarrhoea is commonly experienced by travelers, while dysentery is a potentially severe illness and should be treated by a doctor. If you have blood or mucus in your diarrhoea, you may have amoebic or bacillary dysentery. The symptoms of bacillary dysentery are diarrhoea, stomach pains, fever, and blood or mucus in the stool. It usually lasts for about a week. Amoebic dysentery is rarer and may take a while to develop, at least three weeks. It can last for a long time, and it can infect the liver if it is not treated. There is also giardiasis dysentery. The symptom of giardiasis dysentery is your stool will be frothy and yellow. Your stomach is usually uncomfortable and you fart a lot. It can also last a long time. A good Ayurvedic doctor can cure dysentery, as can a doctor experienced with tropical diseases.

Insanitation Diseases

These diseases are caused by shellfish, unwashed foods, contaminated ice cream, food that flies have landed on, water or milk that has been contaminated by sewage, and infections that have been spread to the kitchen from a toilet. This may happen when someone did not wash their hands properly after going to the bathroom.

Typhoid fever is the worst of these types of diseases. After you get typhoid, symptoms take about seven days to appear. Symptoms are a headache, fever, vomiting, a sore throat, diarrhoea, constipation, and abdominal pains. If a person has a pulse of 80 beats per minute or less, even though they have a high fever, typhoid is likely. It begins like a cold or flu and then there is a gradually increasing fever. If these symptoms appear it is best to seek medical treatment immediately.

Typhoid is a serious disease and may cause death if not treated. If you had a typhoid inoculation, it does not guarantee that you will not get it, but will usually help prevent it.

Cholera

It is a heavy dehydrating disease that causes dramatic fluid loss that for adults can excel half a litre (about a quart) of water per hour in the beginning stages. The average water content of an adult is about 45 litres; and a loss of more than 10 per cent, five litres, is usually fatal. Cholera may be fatal in just nine hours, unless rehydration is dealt with vigorously.

The symptom of this disease are a sudden onset of an extreme case of diarrhoea, muscular cramps, vomiting, and weakness. Medical attention is essential. It is important to drink a large amount of water.

If there is a delay in getting to a doctor, then you can take tetracycline. It is not recommended for pregnant women or children. Ampicillin could also be taken.

How To Avoid Disease

1. All water should be purified or boiled.
2. All milk should be boiled three times.
3. Beware of ice cream.
4. Mineral water may be refilled, so be careful.
5. Food should be well-cooked, recently cooked, and cooked only once.
6. Fruit should be peeled.
7. Do not eat cooked food that has been sitting uncovered.
8. Be careful of fly-infested eating places.

Snake and Poisonous Bites

If you get a bite, you should get a good description of the snake so the doctor will know what medicine to give you. If possible you should catch the snake so you will know exactly what kind of snake bit you. Snakes do not like light, so if you walk outside at night, a good idea is to shine a light in front of you when you walk. Even if you are bitten by a poisonous snake half the time there will be little or no poison.

Scorpion bites are very painful, but will rarely be fatal. A dog or monkey bite can be very dangerous and should be treated immediately by a doctor.

Antibiotics

If you get some disease, do not take just any antibiotic. Antibiotics are specific for different types of infections, so it is best to always get a doctor's advice.

Some of the side-effects of antibiotics can be much worse than the diseases they cure. If you use antibiotics too much, your body may build up a resistance and make other infections difficult to treat.

Hepatitis (jaundice)

This is a common disease in India. The symptoms of hepatitis are nausea, lack of appetite, headaches, fatigue, weakness, experiencing aches and pains and chills. Your eyes and skin turn yellow, and you may get a right upper abdominal pain. Your urine may also turn a very dark yellow, and your stool may turn grey or white. You should definitely not drink any alcohol if you have it.

There is no cure for jaundice according to conventional Western medicine. If you go to a good Ayurvedic doctor such as Dr Triguna it may be cured in a week or two. I have experienced this personally. If you get hepatitis you should rest, drink plenty of liquids and avoid fried foods, which are difficult to digest.

Hepatitis A is usually spread by bad water, raw vegetables, and poor personal hygiene. Hepatitis B, which is more severe and much less common, can be caused by sexual contact or any source of skin penetration, which includes a blood transfusion. If you have had hepatitis before, you may be immune to the disease.

Malaria

The symptoms of malaria are headaches, then fever and sweating, then chills, and then again fever. The symptoms subside then recur, usually in the evening. You may feel terrible one day, the next day you feel all right, and then the next day you feel terrible again. When you realize you have malaria, you should treat it immediately. If you even think you have it, go see a doctor or have one come see you. Certain types of malaria can be fatal, but in India malaria seldom causes death.

The disease develops at least five to ten days after one is bitten by the offending mosquito. It may take up to a year for symptoms to develop, especially if anti-malaria drugs were taken. Malaria is detected by taking a blood sample and examining it. It takes experience and skill to detect it. The symptoms usually just get worse, unless they are treated. Vivax Malaria, which is most common in India, is not usually fatal, but if you do not treat it the illness will recur and cause general bad health.

Malaria is caused by being bitten by the female anopheles mosquito, which usually bites only at night. Between 200 and 300 million people get malaria each year worldwide and about one million people die from it.

Many doctor say that Paludrine once a day and Maloprim once a week are good preventative pills. You can take pills to keep you from getting malaria, but they do not always work and often have bad side-effects.

Chloroquine and Doxycycline are medicines for malaria. They can have serious side-effects if used improperly, so follow the directions. I have seen people who have taken malaria medicine improperly have to go to the hospital because of the medicine, not the malaria. Chloroquine is also used to prevent someone from getting malaria, but there is now a strain of malaria that is resistant to this drug. So it may not help you.

Possible side-effects of malaria medicine are sight problems, itching, rashes, and hair loss. I have been told by an expert Ayurvedic doctor that taking malaria pills ruins the liver and spleen. I take an Ayurvedic malaria-prevention pill that is available from Dr Triguna.

Pregnant women should be especially careful about getting malaria, as their child may also get the disease.

Avoiding Mosquito Bites

The best way to avoid malaria is to avoid the cause by not getting bitten by mosquitoes. Mosquitoes mainly start biting at dusk. You avoid them by covering your skin and using insect repellent. Aerosols are the best way to put repellent on your clothes. Spray cans are good because you can spray them over your body and clothing, as the Indian mosquitoes bite right through your clothing.

Mosquitoes especially like to bite you on your feet and ankles, so it is a good idea to at least put repellent on your feet. Repellents containing deet are effective in stopping mosquitoes from biting and in tests have been found to be harmless to humans. Deet lasts a few hours on the skin and can lasts for weeks on cloth.

It is best to bring camping repellent (sportsmen's formula), as it lasts much longer and so is more effective. Normal brands may wear off before the night is over. An America brand called Cutters is the best repellent I have used.

Citronella is supposed to be a good natural way to keep mosquitoes from biting you, as is lavender oil. I read in one book that Avon Skin So Soft bath oil is an excellent repellent.

Sleeping under a mosquito nets gives protection. You can also burn a mosquito coil, which is effective. I have seen it empty out a room full of mosquitoes. Also you can use an electric mosquito device, which emits some kind of vapor, usually pyrethroid, that the mosquitoes don't like.

I have been told if you eat neem leaves or neem pills for two months, mosquitoes will not bite you because it makes your skin bitter. Calamine cream kills the pain of mosquito bites. It usually stops the itching almost immediately.

Electronic buzzers, which are supposed to simulate the sound of a male mosquito, have proven useless in experiments according to a book I read by a doctor.

Insects, Bedbugs, and Spiders

Bedbugs usually live in dirty mattresses. If you see spots of blood on the wall or on the sheets of the bed in your hotel room, it is time to find another place to stay. You can use calamine lotion to relieve the pain if they bite you. If you get bitten by a spider, you should get treated by a doctor, as some spiders are poisonous.

Benzyl Benzoate is good for scabies and Gamma Benzene hexachloride is good for lice.

Malathion lotion 5% gets rid of lice, but you have to be careful not to use it at full strength, as it is highly toxic. Crotamiton cream gets rid of itching and also kills some skin parasites.

AIDS and Blood

Some reports say that Aids is spreading faster in India than anywhere else in the world. Over 30% of the Bombay prostitutes were found to be HIV positive, and this is getting worse every year. Aids is probably spreading faster in India than any other country in the world. Some say that over 25% of the blood used in Indian hospitals may be infected with Aids. Sometimes the blood in India is not properly tested for Aids and other diseases.

It is best to purchase your own needle and bring it to the hospital for a blood test. The way blood is taken can be extremely unhygienic. Vaccinations, acupuncture, and tattooing can be dangerous. If you must have a blood transfusion, contact your local embassy, as they may have a list of "clean" blood donors.

Other

The head has about 25% of the sweat area of the body, so it is best that the head is not covered unnecessarily.

It is best to wear a clean change of clothes every day. In hot weather it is best never to wear nylon.

When you first go to the tropics, it is wise not to get too much sun the first few days. The first day you can get 15 minutes, then 30 minutes, an hour, two hours, three hours, then an extra hour per day thereafter.

In tropical countries it is much more important than in the West for a mother to breast-feed her child.

Prickly heat is an itchy rash that is especially common in the summer time. Washing frequently and wearing loose cotton clothes helps to avoid it. The use of talcum powders and drying thoroughly after washing also helps.

After Returning Home

It is not unusual to get sick on the return trip home or immediately upon returning home. When you return home it is advised to take a few days' rest before returning to your normal routine. If you do get sick, it is important to know that many doctors in non-tropical countries have little or no experience with tropical diseases. Therefore it is best to go to a tropical disease specialist or a doctor who was trained in India.

If you go to a doctor or a hospital, it is a good idea to take a stool sample. They will probably need to test a stool sample to find out what is wrong with you. If you can not go at the hospital, you may have to come back another day.

In London, normally the best place to get treated is at the Hospital of Tropical Diseases, 4 St Pancreas Way, London. This hospital has a travel health hotline to answer travel questions. MASTA, Ross Institute of Tropical Hygiene (071-631-4408), Keppel Street, (Gower Street), London, is also a good place for treating tropical diseases. I had a friend who had a digestive problem for a month after coming back from India. After going to her regular doctor a number of times, she went to the Hospital of Tropical Diseases and they immediately knew what was wrong with her and cured her in a week. If you go to this hospital make sure you bring some extra money, as you may have to purchase a prescription that can only be purchased there.

In the USA, the International Association for Medical Assistance to Travelers, 745 5th Ave, New York 10022, can give advice about what doctors have experience with tropical diseases.

Please Help Us

As the subject matter of this book is extremely complex and detailed it is very difficult to include everything relevant. So if you have some information that would be valuable to the readers of this book please send it to us, so they may be benefited.

Whatever you can tell about any temple, the story behind the Deity, what Deities are in a particular temple, or other interesting facts may be valuable information. Also of interest is your opinion on hotels, restaurants or dharamshalas, especially ones missed in this book. Travel information is also valuable. Please refer to the page number in this book in reference to the place that you are writing about.

Please give as detailed information as possible.

For temples or holy places please send:
Temple name, location, Deities' names
What is especially interesting about the temple or place
Story about the temple or Deities
Opening or closing hours
How to get there, what bus or train
Potential problems such as guides, hard climbs, or monkeys

For hotels and restaurants please send :
Name, address, phone number, opening hours of a restaurant
Tariff card or room rates
Location, distance from a land-mark either walking or by rickshaw.
How close to a railway or bus station.
How to get there and how much it cost.
Your comments on why this place stood out.
For a restaurant, any recommended preparations or things to be avoided

The writers of the ten best letters will receive an updated edition of this book.

Thank you very much for your help.

Write to

Spiritual Guides   Jada Bharata Dasa
Krishna Balarama Mandir
Bhaktivedanta Swami Marg
Vrindavana, Mathura Dist. UP, India

CHAPTER SIX

New Delhi

Population: 8.5 million, STD Code 011

Delhi is the capital and third largest city of India. There are two parts of the city—Old Delhi, the old Muslim capital, and New Delhi, which was mainly built by the British.

Delhi is considered to be the site of Indraprastha, the capital of the Pandavas of the *Mahabharata*, 5000 years ago. So it is a very ancient city. According to one book, *Immortal India,* Indraprastha was located about 3 km south of modern Delhi between the tomb of Humayun and the kotla of Firoz Shah. The Yamuna River, which used to flow by there, has since moved east from this point.

Delhi was invaded many times from outside of India. Delhi was the capital of the Muslim Moghul Emperors. The British moved their capital from Calcutta to Delhi in 1931.

There are no important holy places in Delhi, but it has the closest international airport to Vrindavana, Jaipur, and Agra. It is also important because it has many important government buildings and travel facilities. Delhi, along with Bombay, are the main cities in India to be used for international travel.

Getting Your Bearings

Connaught Place is in the center of the city, and most of the airlines offices, tourist information offices, and travel agents are located there. It is also the main shopping area in Delhi. The Government of India tourist office and many interesting shops are on Janpath Road, which run south from Connaught Place. Several blocks north is the New Delhi Train Station, which is the main railway station in town and the location of the Tourist Booking Office. Near here is Paharganj, where most of the budget hotels are located.

About 20 minutes north by car is Old Delhi, where the crowded Chandni Chowk shopping area is located. The Red Fort, the long distance bus station, and the Old Delhi train station are located there.

The Foreign embassies are mainly in the Chanakyapuri area, about a twenty minute drive southwest of Connaught Place. Nizamuddin Train Station is southeast of Connaught Place, and it is a good place to get a train to Mathura, as it is much less crowded than the other stations. Further south in southeast New Delhi is the ISKCON Temple. The airport is a 40-minute drive southwest of the city center.

The A to Z Road Guide to Delhi has 200 pages of very detailed maps of Delhi.

Tourist Offices and Information

The **Government of India tourist office**, 88 Janpath, has information about places all over India. They also give away a good map of Delhi and India. If you go and ask them to give you some information about all of India, they may hand you a map of Delhi and tell you that is all they have (it happened to me twice). My friend then insisted that they had more information, so after five minutes they finally gave us about 30 brochures about different places.

The **India Tourism Development Corporation** (ITDC), L Block, Connaught Place runs tours of Delhi and some other places in India. The ITDC office at Jeevan Vihar Bldg, 3rd Fl, 3 P Street, can book reservations for all over India for ITDC hotels, which usually go under the name "Ashok".

Delhi Tourism Dev. Corp. (Delhi Tourism) has offices at N Block, Connaught Place (331-3637); the International Airport; New Delhi Railway Station; Delhi Railway Station; Inter-State Bus Terminal; and at the Coffee House on Baba Kharak Singh Marg (345-358).

There is a tourist counter open all the time at the international airport.

Bihar, Maharashtra, Tamil Nadu, Orissa, Manipur, and **Gujarat** state tourist offices are on the upper floors of their respective state emporiums on Baba Kharak Singh Marg. Their entrances are located in the back of the emporiums. The Tamil Nadu and Orissa tourist offices are very helpful.

Haryana, Himachal Pradesh, West Bengal, and **Uttar Pradesh** offices are located in the Chandralok Building at 36 Janpath.

The offices for **Madhya Pradesh, Punjab, Jammu & Kashmir,** and **Kerala** are in the Kanishka Shopping Center between the Yatri Niwas and Kanishka Hotels at 19 Ashoka Rd.

The **Rajasthan** tourist office (389-525) is on Bikaner Rd by India Gate. The **Andhra Pradesh** office (381-293) is at 1 Ashok Rd.

The magazine *Here Delhi* has good detailed information about Delhi, including a calendar of events in Delhi and throughout India.

Tours

ITDC runs a half-day tour of **Old Delhi** (Rs 80, 2.15 to 7 pm) or **New Delhi** (Rs 90, 8 am to 1 pm). They also run a full-day tour of New Delhi and Old Delhi from 8 am to 7 pm for Rs 150. ITDC has a one-day tour of Agra that goes to the Taj Mahal, Agra Fort, and Sikandra from 6.30 am to 10 pm for Rs 425. They also have a tour to Vaishno Devi for Rs 500 that departs at 8.30 pm on Friday and returns on Monday morning. You can book these tours at the ITDC office at L Block at Connaught Circus, at their counters in the airports, or at ITDC Hotels.

The **Government of India Tourist Office,** 88 Janpath, organizes a morning tour of **New Delhi** (9 am to 2 pm, Rs 70) and an afternoon tour of Old Delhi (2.15 to 5.15, Rs 70). They can also arrange a guide for you. American Express Travels Service, A Block, Connaught Place, and Royal Express, 16 K G Marg, Connaught Place, both run tours of Delhi.

The Haridwar-Rishikesh tour departs 7.15 am on Wednesday and Saturday and returns the next day at 8 pm. It goes to Har-ki-Pauri, Mansa Devi Temple, *arati* at the Ganga Temple, and some ashrams in Rishikesh. This tour costs Rs 375. It is run by Delhi Tourism, which has many offices all over town. The main one is at N-36, Bombay Life Building, Connaught Place (Middle Circle).

There is a one-day and two-day tour of Jaipur and a two-day tour of Agra and Fatehpur Sikri. There is also a two day tour of Mathura, Agra, and Fatehpur Sikri.

Uttar Pradesh Tourism (332-2251), 36 Janpath, operates an overnight tour to

Haridwar and Rishikesh for Rs 700.

Weather

Delhi is most comfortable between October and March. Daytime temperatures are around 22°C (72°F) between November and the beginning of March. It is cold at night from December to February, with temperature going down to 3°C (37°F). During May and June it can be extremely hot with temperature going up to 46°C (114°F). The rainy season is from the middle of July to the middle of September. During this time it rains every few days and does not usually rain for more than an hour or two at a time.

Travel Agents

Tripsout Travels (332-2654), 7217 Janpath, behind the India Tourist Office, are reliable, but very busy, so you may have to wait a while. I know people who have been using them for years and recommend them. They are a good discount travel agent.

Aerotrek Travels (371-5966), E-1 Mercantile Building, 2nd Floor, Connaught Place, are trustworthy, have discount prices and are efficient. It is run by two brothers. One of the brothers lives in Mathura (0565-404361). They are highly recommended and I use them myself.

Maharani Travels (331-3917), 1 Scindia House, on Janpath near Air India, is a recommended discount travel agent. They are honest and have cheap prices. More upscale are Cox & Kings (332-0067), Indra Palace, H Block, Connaught Circus, and Sita World Travels (301-1122), 4 Malcha Marg, Diplomatic Enclave.

Medical and Dental

The *East West Medical Centre* (699-229), 38 Gold Link Rd, is a recommended place. They charge higher prices than normal for India. Also good is the *All India Institute of Medical Sciences* (661-123), at Ansari Nagar, and the *Dr Ram Manohar Lohia Hospital* (345-525), Baba Kharak Singh Marg. By phoning 102 you can get an ambulance.

Bhandari Homeopathic Store (373-2450), 43-44 Municipal Market, opposite the York Hotel, Connaught Circus, has an excellent selection of German, Swiss, and Indian made homeopathic medicines.

The *Tibetan Clinic* (Men-Tsee-Khang-Exports) (11-621-2604) is located at 13 Jaipur Estate, Nizamuddin East, New Delhi. They treat people by a natural herbal method and have been recommended to me by several people. To get there you can ask most of the rickshaw drivers at the Nizamuddin train station to take you to the nearby Jaipur Estate where it is located.

The *Delhi Dental Centre* (644-4918, 644-2398), C-565 Extension II, has been recommended to me as a good place to have dental work done. It is best to call for an appointment. Dr Chopra is supposed to be good.

You can have an Aids test done at the *National Institute of Communicable Diseases*, 22 Sham Nath Marg, across from IE College, north of the Red Fort in Old Delhi. You are supposed to have the test done between 10 and 11 in the morning. You then pick up the test results between 3 and 4 in the afternoon, ten days later. If you are having the test done because of registration requirements, you should bring your passport and a letter from the organization sponsoring you.

You can get a good massage at the Raveena Health Club (355-4818), down a side street off the main bazaar in Paharganj.

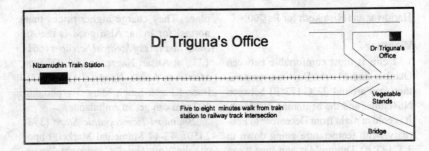

Dr Triguna's Office

Nizamudhin Train Station

Five to eight minutes walk from train
station to railway track intersection

Dr Triguna's Office

Vegetable Stands

Bridge

Dr Triguna

Dr Triguna (461-1221) is an excellent Ayurvedic doctor, one of the best in India. His office is by the Nizamuddin Train Station in southeastern Delhi. He personally helped me when I was extremely sick three times, and I know of many other people that he has helped. He is highly recommended

To find his office you go to the Nizamuddim Train Station. If you are walking out the door of the train station, you turn left and go by rickshaw or walking about a half a km. When you come to the Y-intersection, you take the left fork, by some vegetable stands, which brings you over the train tracks. After the train tracks, you walk about 150 feet and then turn right at the intersection. His office is at the end of the road, a minute away. You should arrive there before noon, as that is the usual closing time. He is closed on Mondays and sometimes he is not there for a week or two, as he travels all over the world helping people.

Places To Shop

You can get good Tibetan goods at *Tibetan Market*, Janpath. *Palika Bazaar*, underground at Connaught Place, has 300 shops.

Good places to shop are the government *Cottage Industries* on Janpath and the *government emporiums* on Baba

Karak Singh Marg near Connaught Place. They have an excellent selection of items at fixed prices, which may be more expensive than other places. At least you know you are getting what you paid for.

You can get good, very detailed maps of India and individual cities from the *Map Sales Office*, Survey of India, which is near the Central Cottages Emporium, 1st floor, Janpath.

Post and Phone

The GPO is on Baba Kharak Singh Marg, about a ten-minute walk from Connaught Place. **Poste restante mail** can be gotten at the Foreign Post Office on Market Rd (now called Bhai Vir Singh Marg). It is around the back and up the stairs. Letters with just "Delhi" on them will go to the Old Delhi post office and not this one, as this is the New Delhi post office. The New Delhi post office is more convenient for most people. There is a small post office at 9 A Block, Connaught Place.

It is easy now to call in India. There are many STD/ISD phones where you can call for a set fee per minute. They are all over Delhi. You can make international calls from the Central Telegraph Office on Janpath.

Collect and credit card calls can be made from Videsh Sanchar Bhavan, Bangla Sahib Rd. They can be made to

USA, UK, Italy, and Japan.

Money

American Express (332-7602), A Block, Connaught Place, changes money quickly and efficiently. They have a 24-hour telephone number (687-5050) for lost or stolen checks. Through them you can also have money wired from overseas, which takes 24 hours. The charge is about 8%. *Thomas Cook* (332-8468), in the Imperial Hotel on Janpath, also changes money in just five minutes.

Some banks are the State Bank of India, Sansad Marg; Bank of America (331-3883) Hansalaya Building, Barakhamba Rd; Citibank (332-8989), Parliament St; ANZ Grindlays (331-9643) Kasturba Gandhi Marg; Banque Nationnale de Paris (331-3883); and Hong Kong Bank (331-4355). Banks are usually open 10 am to 2 pm Mon to Fri and 10 am to noon on Saturday. The international banks are usually located by Connaught Place.

Changing money at the State Bank of India can take more than an hour, so it is best to change your money at the American Express office or Thomas Cook, where it will usually take less than five minutes. The money changing facilities at the *Ashok Hotel* are open 24 hours a day.

Visa Extension & Special Permits

At the Foreigners' Registration Office (331-9489), Hans Bhavan, Bahadur Shah Zafar Marg, near the Tilak Bridge Railway Station you can extend your visa. You need four photos for visa renewal. There is a photographer outside the building to do this. It is closed from 1 to 1.30 pm. They have a sign that says it is not possible to extend a three-month or six-month tourist visa. I have heard that the Delhi Office turns you down for an ex-tension more often than most other places, so it is probably best to apply in another city.

A tax clearance certificate is issued around the corner at the Foreign Section of the Income Tax Department (331-7826) in the Central Revenue Building, Hans Bhavan. You have to bring exchange certificates with you to show that you changed money legally and did not work in India. The office is closed from 1 to 2 pm.

Some areas are restricted for travel in India. You can apply for permits at Indian embassies overseas. Usually the Ministry of Home Affairs (694-828), Lok Nayak Bhawan, Khan Market, issues the permits to travel to prohibited areas.

Bookshops

Piccadilly Book Stall, Shop No. 64, Shankar Market, which is on a side road going off M Block from Connaught Place, has the best selection of astrology and spiritual books that I saw in Delhi and one of the best in all of India.

There are many good book stores by Connaught Place, including the Oxford Book Shop at N Block; New Book Depot at 18 B Block; Bookworm at 29B Radial Rd, No 4; and the English Book Depot. ED Galgotia & Sons, B Block, has a good selection of spiritual, travel, and Ayurvedic books.

At *BPB Publications* on B Block, Connaught Place, you can get **computer books**. They have many of the latest titles from the US, and you can get a $25 book here for $7.

In the center of Palika Bazaar there are two good book shops across from each other, ***Book World*** and *Rajiv Book House*, which mainly have books about India.

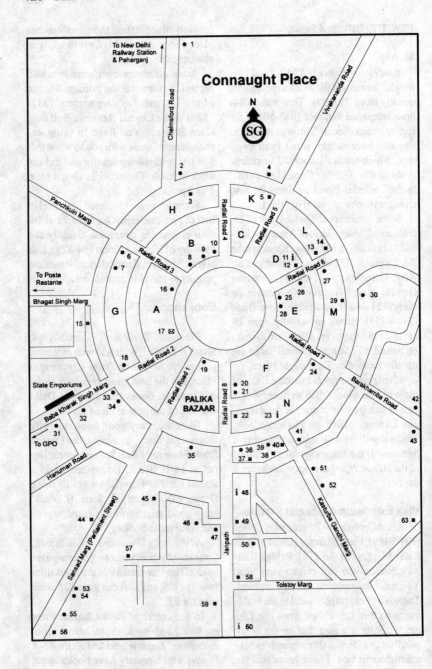

Connaught Place

To New Delhi
Railway Station
& Paharganj

Chelmsford Road

Vivekananda Road

N
SG

Panchkuin Marg

Radial Road 4

Radial Road 5

H

K

C

L

B

Radial Road 3

10

9

8

13 14

D

11 12

Radial Road 6

27

To Poste
Restante

6

7

Bhagat Singh Marg

16

26

25

28

E

M

29

30

G

A

17

Radial Road 7

24

15

18

Radial Road 2

Barakhamba Road

Radial Road 1

19

F

State Emporiums

Baba Kharak Singh Marg

33

34

32

PALIKA
BAZAAR

Radial Road 8

20

21

22 23

N

42

41

31

To GPO

35

43

Hanuman Road

36 39 40

37 38

51

52

45

48

44

46

49

63

47

50

57

Sansad Marg (Parliament Street)

Janpath

Kasturba Gandhi Marg

58

53

54

Tolstoy Marg

59

55

56

60

PLACES TO STAY

3	Hotel 55
5	York Hotel
6	Hotel Marina
11	Hotel Palace Heights
13	Jukaso Inn
14	Nirula's Hotel
15	Alka Hotel
22	Hotel Metro
29	Hotel Bright
37	Ringo Guest House
38	Sunny Guest House
40	Asia Guest House
44	Park Hotel
45	Mrs Coloco's Guest House
49	Janpath Guest House
56	YWCA International Guest House
57	Mr SC Jain's Guest House
59	Imperial Hotel
63	Hotel Hans Plaza

WHERE TO EAT

8	Zen
14	Nirula's Restaurant
15	Vega
25	Kovil
29	Lido
58	Sona Rupa

OTHER

1	Railway Booking Office
2	Cycle Rickshaw Stand
4	Bhandari Homeopathic Store
5	Libyan Arab Airlines
7	Gulf Air, Singapore Airlines
12	ITDC Booking Office
16	American Express
17	Post Office
18	Jordanian & Malaysian Airlines
19	Tempos to Old Delhi
20	EAT Bus
21	Indian Airlines
23	Delhi Tourism Corporation
24	Aeoflot
26	Aerotrek Travels
27	Mahatta & Co
28	Grindlays & Bank of Baroda
30	Super Bazaar
31	Hanuman Mandir
32	Mohan Singh Place
33	Khadi Gramodyog Bhavan
34	Regal Cinema
35	Air India & Citibank
36	Air France & Oxford Bookshop
39	Delhi Transport Corporation
41	HongKong Bank
42	Indian Airlines & Emirates Air
43	Saudia Arabian Airlines & Bank of America
46	Central Cottage Industries Emporium
47	Map Sales Office
48	Government of India Tourist Office
50	Tripout Travel
51	Pakistan International Airlines
52	American Centre
53	Bus 620 to Chanakyapuri & Youth Hostel
54	Jantar Mantar
55	Bus 433 to Bahai Lotus Temple
58	Royal Nepal Airlines
60	Haryana, HimachalPradesh, Uttar Pradesh & West Bengal Tourist Offices

Motilal Banarsidass (291-8335 Fax: 99-11-293-0689), 41 UA Bungalow Rd, has a good selection of books on Indian philosophy, the *Puranas*, astrology, and Ayurvedic medicines. They are big wholesalers, but also sell retail.

Munshiram Manoharlal Publishers (777-1668, Fax: 99-11-751-2745), 54

Rani Jhansi Road, has a good selection of Indian philosophy books and is also a big publisher. *Sagar Publications* (332-0648), 72 Ved Mansion, down a side road just off Janpath, has a good selection of astrology, Vedic, and Ayurvedic medicine books.

Photography

Mahatta & Co (332-9769), across the street from Nirula's on M Block, is a recommended professional camera store. Their prices are above average, but they do one of the best jobs in India. The *Delhi Photo Company*, 78 Janpath, by the tourist office, does a good job of processing film quickly.

National Museum

This museum has an excellent collection of old deities and ancient sculptures dating from the 7th to 17th century. The sculptures are from the Pallava period, Chalukya period (Badami and Aihole), and other periods.. There are also sculptures from the Konark Temple. There is an Indian Bronze Gallery with a famous Kaliya Mardan deity. It has a good collection of terracottas dating back to the fifth century. There are also ancient paintings showing Krishna's pastimes. The museum has a collection of rare and precious antique jewelry.

It is on Janpath, just south of Rajpath. It is open daily from 10 am to 5 pm, except Mondays and major government holidays. The Archaeological Survey of India's office is right next door.

Archaeological Survey of India

It is next to the National Museum on Janpath, just south of Rajpath. It has the most authoritative maps and guides of the major archaeological sites in India. You cannot get some of these publications at the sites themselves, as they are sometimes sold out.

Laksmi Narayana Temple (1938)

This Vishnu temple was built by Raja Baldeo Birla in 1938 and is very popular. It is located about 2 km west of Connaught Place. It is also called the Birla Mandir.

Connaught Place

This is a circle in the middle of New Delhi where most of the airlines, travel agents, and other important offices and stores are located. All the blocks are assigned letters, so when you have to go to some place at Connaught Place you should find out what block it is on, such as "A" Block or "D" Block. It is an interesting place to walk around and check out shops.

Chandni Chowk

This is a very crowded shopping area in Old Delhi. There are many jewelers, cloth and other shops here. You can get harmoniums here. Most shops are closed on Sunday.

Red Fort

This is a huge fort in Old Delhi, right next to Chandni Chowk. It was built by Shah Jahan. Aurangzeb ruled from here. King Yudhishthira is said to have performed a Horse Sacrifice here at the Dasaswamedha Ghat to celebrate the Pandava victory at Kurukshetra. It is an interesting place.

Iron Pillar

At the Qutab Minar, which is 15 km south of New Delhi, there is a tall victory town (1193) built by the Muslims. In the courtyard there is an interesting seven metres (23 feet, 8 inch) high Iron

Pillar. A six-line Sanskrit inscription says that it was originally in a Vishnu temple, maybe in Bihar. After 1500 years the pillar has not rusted. Scientist cannot understand how 1500 years ago there could have been such technology to cast such an exceptional pure iron pillar. It is said that if you can encircle the pillar with your arms, while standing with your back to the pillar, your wishes will be fulfilled.

ISKCON Temple

This beautiful new temple was finished in 1996. There is also an interesting museum here that explains the Krishna conscious philosophy. The Deities in this temple are Radha-Parthasarathi. The phone number is 642-9577, fax 011-644-1306.

To get to this temple ask for the Sant Nagar area by Nehru Place. There are two Sant Nagar areas in Delhi. So if you do not ask for "by Nehru Place" they may bring you to the other area in north Delhi. Once you get to the Sant Nagar area, everyone will know where the temple is located. The temple is located in the southeast part of Delhi by Mathura Road. It is about a half-hour auto-rickshaw ride from Connaught Place.

If you wish to stay here, there is not much facility at the present time, but there are plans to make guest facilities in the future. There are some rooms for life patrons that should be reserved in advance.

Foreign Embassies

Most embassies are open 9 am to noon, Monday to Friday. It usually takes at least 24 hours to get a visa. If you are going to an embassy to get a visa, you should make sure you have some passport photos with you.

Australia

1/50G Shantipath, Chanakyapuri (688-5673)
Bangladesh
56 Ring Rd, Lajpat Nagar III (683-4668)
Brazil
8 Aurangzeb Road (301-7301)
Canada
7-8 Shantipath, Chanakyapuri (687-6500)
China
50-D Shantipath, Chanakyapuri (600-328)
Czech
50-M Niti Marg, Chanakyapuri (611-0205)
Denmark
11 Aurangzeb Rd (310-0900)
France
2/50-E Shantipath, Chanakyapuri (604-004)
Germany
6/50-G Shantipath, Chanakyapuri (604-861)
Guyana
85 Poorvi Marg, Vasant Vihar (674-194)
Hungary
2/50-M Niti Marg, Chanakyapuri (611-4737)
Indonesia
50-A Chanakyapuri (602-352)
Iran
5 Barakhamba Rd (332-9600)
Ireland
13 Jor Bagh Rd (617-435)
Israel
3 Aurangzeb Road (332-3869)
Italy
50E Chandragupta Marg (600-071)
Kenya
E66 Vasant Marg, Vasant Vihar (687-6538)
Japan
50G Shantipath, Chanakyapuri

(687-6564)

Malaysia
50M Satya Marg, Chanakyapuri
(601-291)

Mauritius
5 Kautilya Marg (301-1112)

Mexico
10 Jor Bagh (469-7991)

Myanmar
3/50F Nyaya Marg, Chanakyapuri
(600-251)

Nepal
Barakhamba Rd (332-8191)

Netherlands
6/50-F Shantipath, Chanakyapuri
(688-4951)

New Zealand
50 Nyaya Marg, Chanakyapuri
(688-3170)

Pakistan
2/50-G Shantipath, Chanakyapuri
(600-601)

Poland
50-M Shantipath, Chanakyapuri
(608-321)

Russia
Shantipath, Chanakyapuri
(606-026)

Singapore
61-E Chandragupta Marg,
Chanakyapuri (604-162)

South Africa
B-18 Vasant Marg, Vasant Vihar
(611-9411)

Spain
12 Prithiviraj Rd (301-5892)

Sri Lanka
27 Kautilya Marg, Chanakyapuri
(301-0201)

Sweden
Nyaya Marg, Chanakyapuri
(604-961)

Switzerland
Nyaya Marg, Chanakyapuri
(604-227)

Thailand
56-N Nyaya Marg, Chanakyapuri
(605-679)

Trinidad & Tobago
131 Jor Bagh (461-8187)

Ukraine
176 Jor Bagh (461-6086)

United Kingdom
50 Shantipath, Chanakyapuri
(601-371)

USA
28 B Institutional Area,
Chanakyapuri (600-651)

Where to Stay

The hotels in Delhi are more expensive than in most other cities in India. Most budget hotels are in the Connaught Place area or the Paharganj area, near the New Delhi Railway Station. The Paharganj area can be very noisy and crowded, but many people think it is an interesting place.

Where to Stay – Paharganj Lower

One of the first hotels you get to when coming from the train station is the *Kiran Hotel* (526-104), which has rooms for Rs 150 with common bath, Rs 175 with bath, or a room on the 5th floor for Rs 105 with common bath. Next door is the *Kailash Guest House*, which has rooms for Rs 150/160 with attached bath and rooms with common bath for Rs 125. Both of these places are decent.

The *Hotel Bright* (752-5852), No 1089-90, is a cheap place with rooms for Rs 90/100 with common bath and Rs 120 with bath. It is a good value.

Hotel Namaskar (752-1234, 752-2233), 917 Chandiwalan, Main Bazaar, is located down a side alley. If you are coming from the New Delhi train station, you go about 100 feet past the Hotel Bright, then make a right at the alley,

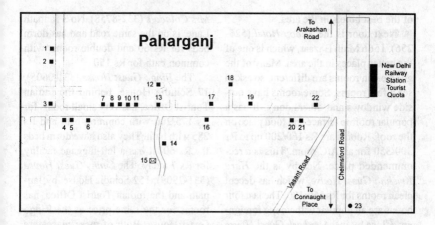

Paharganj

To Arakashan Road

To Connaught Place

New Delhi Railway Station Tourist Quota

Vasant Road

Chelmsford Road

which has some urinals in it. You then walk another 200 feet to the end of the alley. Rooms are Rs 175/225, and there are rooms with three beds for Rs 300. There are a few A/C rooms for Rs 400. For the Paharganj area it is a very nice place run by two brothers who are extremely friendly and helpful. I would suggest that you go to this place first, especially if you have heavy luggage. If it is full, as it usually is in the evening, you can leave your luggage there and walk around and find another place. A big advantage of this hotel is it is set off from the main road and is quiet. It is a highly recommended place. The problem with a place this good is that it is usually full. Book it in advance if you can.

The popular *Vivek* (777-7062), No 1534-50, about a ten minutes walk from the railway station, has rooms with common bath for Rs 130/150, Rs 130/160 with attached bath, and Rs 180/200 for a deluxe room. Some rooms have color TV and most of the rooms have bath. Some rooms do not have windows, so it is best to ask to see a few rooms. Nearby the *Hotel Vishal* (527-629) has rooms with bath for Rs 150/170 and dorm beds. It has a roof garden and is considered one

PLACES TO STAY

1	Chanakya Hotel
2	Hotel Kelson
3	Metropolis Tourist Home
4	Hotel Satyam
5	Sapna Hotel
6	Kesri Hotel
7	Hotel Vishal
8	Hare Krishna Guest House
9	Anoop Hotel
10	Ankush Guest House
11	Hotel Vivek
12	Navrang Hotel
13	Hotel Payal
14	City Lodge
16	Hotel Relaxo
17	Camran Lodge
18	Hotel Namaskar
19	Hotel Bright
20	Kiran Guest House
21	Kailash Guest House
22	Hotel Kanishta

OTHER

| 15 | Post Office |
| 23 | Railway Booking Office |

of the best hotels in the area.

Next door is the *Anoop Hotel* (526-256), 1566 Main Bazaar, which is one of the better places in the area. Many of the good clean rooms are different, so ask to see a few rooms. Some rooms have outside windows and others don't. It has a popular rooftop terrace and food place on the roof. Rooms are Rs 160/200 up to Rs 300/350 for an A/C room. This is a recommended place. Nearby is the *Hare Krishna Guest House,* which has decent clean rooms for Rs 150/180. The last four hotels are all popular with young foreigners. Close by is the *Ankush Guest House* (751-9000), which has rooms with common bath for Rs 100 and Rs 120 with bath.

The *Hare Rama Guest House* (529-273), 298 Main Bazaar, down the side room near the Khanna Cinema, has good rooms for Rs 170 and rooms with three beds for Rs 225. It is a popular place.

Metropolis (753-5766), 1634 Main Bazaar, is a decent place with hot water for Rs 350 and Rs 700 with A/C. *Hotel Chanakya* (751-8823), Rajguru Road, has rooms with common bath for Rs 120/175 and Rs 150/200 with attached bath. If you have a lot of baggage you can easily drive to the front door with a taxi. On the same road is the *Hotel Kelson* (752-7070), 2267 Rajguru Road. It is a clean place, but the rooms are a bit small and many do not have windows. Rooms are Rs 225 with a TV and Rs 325/375 with A/C. *Maden Guesthouse* has hot water. Rooms with common bath are Rs 175 and with attached bath are Rs 200.

Where to Stay – Connaught Place

Mr S C Jain's Guest House (353-484), 7 Pratap Singh Building, Janpath Lane, has simple rooms with common bath for Rs 160/190. It is clean and in a quiet area.

Mrs Colaco's (332-8758), No 3 Janpath Lane, is on the same road and has dorm beds for Rs 60 and double rooms with common bath for Rs 150.

The *Ringo Guest House* (331-0605), 17 Scindia House, behind the Indian Tourist Office, has very small rooms for Rs 175/200 with common bath and Rs 285 with bath. They also have dorm beds for Rs 60. It has a left-luggage facility for Rs 7 a day. The *Sunny Guest House* (331-2909), 152 Scindia House, by Janpath and the Indian Tourist Office, has rooms for the same price as the Ringo Guest House. Both of these places are popular with backpackers and have a good atmosphere, but the single rooms are really small. Both these places are owned and managed by the same people, and they are friendly and trustworthy.

Where to Stay – Other Lower

The *International Youth Centre* (Vishwa Yuvak Kendra, 301-3631), Circular by Chanakyapuri area, has good rooms for Rs 350. It is located about 20 minutes by car from Connaught Place, just behind the Chinese Embassy. The rooms are good and there are also dorms with beds for Rs 50.

The *New Delhi Tourist Camp* (327-2898), J Nehru Marg, by Jai Prakash Hospital, has a garden and clean rooms with common bath for Rs 100/140 and up. The *Gandhi Guest House*, 80 Tolstoy Lane, is a popular place.

There are *retiring rooms* at both the New Delhi and Old Delhi train stations. The Old Delhi station has rooms for Rs 150 and Rs 25 for a dorm bed. New Delhi has regular rooms for Rs 150/250 and A/C rooms for Rs 250/500. Both places are so noisy it can be difficult to sleep.

There are also retiring rooms at both the *Domestic Terminal* (329-5126) and

International Terminal (545-2011). You must have a confirmed departure within 24 hours to stay in the retiring rooms. The Domestic Terminal has rooms for Rs 175 and Rs 250 with A/C. Dorm beds cost Rs 80. The International Terminal has rooms for Rs 175/250 and dorm beds for Rs 80. Many times the rooms are full, but you can get a dorm bed. The dorms at the International Terminal are outside the terminal, on the other side of the parking lot. Some dorms have six beds in them, so you could rent all six beds and get a private room. It is best to call and reserve a room in advance.

In Old Delhi, The *Hotel New City Palace* (327-9548), by the Jama Masjid mosque, is a modern place with clean rooms with hot water for Rs 275 and Rs 325 with A/C. This is one of the better places in the area. The *Hotel Bombay Orient* (328-6253), by the Jama Masjid, is a well maintained place with clean rooms for Rs 100/175 with common bath, Rs 225 with bath, and Rs 350 with A/C.

Where to Stay – Paharganj Middle

There are many hotels on Arakashan Road, which is two blocks from the train stations. Most of these hotels are good and are used by travelers and Indian businessmen. Many of the other hotels on the street are as good as the ones mentioned here, so you will have no problem finding a good room here. For the same room you get here for Rs 250, you would have to pay Rs 500 in Connaught Place, which is just a five-minute auto-rickshaw ride away.

The *Hotel Ajanta* (752-0925, fax 752-0229), 36 Arakashan Rd, is a recommended and popular place. Economy rooms are Rs 185/265, standard rooms Rs 275/345 and an A/C room with a TV is Rs 545/645. All rooms have bathrooms

with hot water. They also have a travel agent who offers reasonable prices for local and long-distance tourist buses. I would suggest that you come to this place first, as the management is good. Since many of the hotels in the area are just as good, if it is full you can easily find another place to stay.

The *Hotel Syal* (751-0091), 43 Arakashan Road, has good rooms for Rs 275/350. Also good is the *Hotel Crystal* (753-1639) at 8501Arakashan Rd. It has rooms with TV for 295/375.

The *Krishna Hotel* (751-0252) has very good rooms for Rs 250/300 or Rs 475 with A/C and is a recommended place.

The *Hotel Soma* (752-1006), 33 Arakashan Road, has rooms for Rs 200/250 and Rs 350/400 with A/C. The *Hotel Yuvraj* (752-0423), 38 Arakashan Road, has nice rooms for Rs 300/350.

Where to Stay – Middle

The *YMCA* (374-6668), Jai Singh Rd, near Regal Cinema, is a recommended place with rooms for Rs 295/500 with common bath and Rs 525/880 with A/C and hot water. There is a 5% tariff charge and Rs 10 membership fee. This place has a swimming pool and garden. You have to pay in foreign currency, and they accept both men and women. It is a good value and is often full.

The *YWCA Blue Triangle Family Hostel* (310-202), Ashoka Rd, by Sansad Marg (Parliament St), is a good place with rooms for Rs 400/600 and Rs 425/750 with A/C and private bath. There is a 5% tariff charge. It is a 10 minute walk from Connaught Place.

The *YWCA International Guest House* (311-561), 10 Sansad Marg (Parliament St), has rooms for Rs 450/650 plus a 10% service charge. It is near Connaught Place.

The *Hotel Broadway*, Asaf Ali Road in Old Delhi, is a recommended place with rooms for around Rs 750.

Where to Stay – Janpath Area & Connaught Place

Usually middle-class hotels in Connaught Place are more expensive than the same hotel would be in another part of Delhi.

The *ITDC Ashok Yatri Niwas* (332-4511), Ashoka Rd and Janpath, is about a 10-minute walk from Connaught Place. It is a giant place, and it can take a long time to check in and out. It has rooms for Rs 375/500. The rooms are definitely run down and the place is impersonal, but for the price it is sufficient for most middle-class travelers. Some people like the place, and others cannot stand it. You should ask to see three or four rooms, as some of the rooms can be really run down. Usually the rooms with the cement beds are better than the ones with regular beds.

The *Alka Hotel* (334-4328, fax 373-2796), P Block, Connaught Circus, has A/C rooms for Rs 1050 up to Rs 1450 for a double deluxe room. It has a good vegetarian restaurant. The regular rooms are not a very good value, but the deluxe rooms are good. The *Hotel 55* (332-1244, fax 332-0769), 55 H Block, has A/C rooms for Rs 600/850.

The *Roshan Villa Guest House* (331-1770), 7 Babar Lane by Babar Rd, is a good place in a quiet area, with rooms for Rs 450/500 with common bath and Rs 500/600 with bath.

The *Janpath Guest House* (332-1935), next to the tourist office at 82 Janpath, is a popular place with rooms for Rs 240/275 with air-cooling and Rs 450/500 with A/C. Some of the rooms do not

have windows.

Jukaso Inn (332-4451), L-1 Connaught Circus, has rooms with bath for Rs 950/1200. The *Hotel Metro* (331-3805), N-49 Connaught Circus, has rooms for Rs 900/1000 and Rs 1050/1200 with A/C.

Where to Stay – Other Middle

The *Master Paying Guest House* (574-1089), R-500 New Rajendra Nagar, is a recommended place with large well-furnished rooms from Rs 300 up to Rs 600. It is about a 15 minute ride west of Connaught Place. It is in a quiet area. The *Puri Yatri Guest House* (752-5563), 3/4 Rani Jhansi Rd, by the junction of Mandir Marg and Panchkuin Marg, about 1 km west of Connaught Place, is a recommended place. It has clean rooms with bath for Rs 600/700 and Rs 750 with A/C. It is a well-managed place.

The *Classic Palace Hotel*, Chanakyapuri, is a good place with rooms for Rs 700. The *Hotel Ashoka Place* (677-308), 3 km from the domestic airport terminal, is the cheapest hotel by the airport. Even so, with rooms for Rs 900, it is not such a good value.

The B-57 Inn (469-4239), B-57 South Extension Part 1, just north of Ring Road, has good rooms with TV for Rs 550/650 and Rs 650/750 with A/C.

Where to Stay – Higher

The four-star *Nirula's Hotel* (332-2419, fax 332-4669), L Block, Connaught Place next to Nirula's restaurant, has good rooms for Rs 1200/2000 up to Rs 2395 for a deluxe suite. It is a well-managed place.

The four-star *Ambassador Hotel* (463-2600, Fax 463-2252), Sujan Singh Park, has rooms for $55/75. I was told that you had to reserve a room at least a week in advance. It also has an excellent South Indian restaurant, the Dasaprakash.

The four-star *Hotel Kanishka* (332-4422, fax 332-4242), at Ashoka Rd and Janpath Rd, has a swimming pool. Rooms are Rs 1950/2100. The *Hotel Marina* (332-4658), G Block, Connaught Place, has good rooms, some without windows, for Rs 1190/1600. It looks like a dump from outside, but looks very good inside. The *Connaught Palace Hotel* (344-225, fax 310-757), Bhagat Singh Marg, west of Connaught Place, has rooms for Rs 2100/2500.

The five-star *Imperial Hotel* (332-5332, fax 332-5332), Janpath Rd, has rooms for $120. It is a good value and is a quiet place with a nice garden. The five-star *Claridges Hotel* (301-0211, fax 301-0625), 12 Aurangzeb Rd, is a good place with rooms for $120/130. It has a swimming pool and is centrally located.

Where to Stay – Luxury

Besides the prices given here, most of these places also have more expensive suites.

The *Park Hotel* (373-2477, fax 352-025), 15 Sansad Marg (Parliament St), next to Connaught Place, has a swimming pool. Rooms are $160/175. The *New Delhi Hilton* (332-0101, 332-5335), Barakhamba Rd, southeast of Connaught Place, has rooms for $270/290, with all the facilities you would need. It is centrally located and has a swimming pool.

Hotel Maurya Sheraton (301-0101, fax 301-0908), Sardar Patel Marg, between Chanakyapuri and Connaught Place, is a huge luxury place with rooms for $210/235 up to $1,000. The *Taj Mahal Hotel*, (301-6162, fax 301-6162), 1 Man Singh Rd, is centrally located, but still quiet. The luxurious rooms are $245/280. The *Taj Palace Hotel* (301-0404),

2 Sardar Patel Marg, Diplomatic Enclave, is a first-class place with rooms for $230/250.

The *Ashok Hotel* (600-0121, fax 687-3216), 50B Chanakyapuri, is a huge place that is loaded with facilities. Rooms are $108/140. The *Hotel Oberoi New Delhi* (436-3030, fax 436-0484), southern New Delhi, has a swimming pool and rooms for $275/300.

The *Hotel Hyatt Regency* (688-1234, fax 688-6933), Bhikaji Cama Place, Ring Road, in south New Delhi, has excellent rooms for Rs 7250. This place has first-class facilities, including a pool and fitness center. The *Centaur Hotel* (545-2223, fax 545-2256), Gurgaon, just 2 km from the airport, is a big place with a swimming pool and health club. Rooms cost $80/90. It is the closest hotel to the airport.

Where to Stay – ISKCON Area

PGH (Purewal Guest House, 41-5005), 27 Sant Nagar, near the Centennial House, is a small (four rooms) family-run rest house with rooms for Rs 250 a night. It is in a quiet safe area and is a ten-minute walk from the temple.

Where To Eat

Dashprakash, at the Ambassador Hotel, Sujan Singh Park, in southeast Delhi, is considered by many to be the best vegetarian South Indian restaurant in Delhi. The service is excellent and the food is very good, but high priced. *Sagar Ratna Restaurant*, in the Lodhi Hotel, Lala Lajpat Marg, is an excellent popular South Indian restaurant. It has good **thalis**. It is a recommended place, but out of the way.

The *Vega*, in the Alka Hotel across the street from G Block, Connaught Place, is a good place. The food here does not have onion or garlic in it. It has a good all you can eat *thali* for Rs 110. If you are at Connaught Place, it is recommended, but not cheap. The very popular *Sona Rupa* (3326807), 40 Janpath, near Connaught Place, is an economical South Indian fast-food type restaurant.

Kovil, E Block-2, Connaught Place, is a recommended higher priced South Indian restaurant with good dosas. *Shudh,* in the Regal Building at Connaught Place, has a *thali* for about half the price of most of the other nearby places. *Lido Restaurant* is at M Block, Connaught Place. *Nirula's* has an excellent ice cream shop.

Nathus, at Bengali Market, has good fast food and sweets. It is located about a five-minute auto-rickshaw ride from Connaught Place. Ask to go to Bengali Market and you can't miss it. *Bengali Sweet Shop*, Bengali Market, has good pizza, fast foods, and of course, Bengali sweets.

Keventers, a milk bar, located at the corner of A Block and the inner circle, next to B Block, is frequented by many people I know who like to eat well.

The *Brindavan Restaurant*, 45 M Block Market, Greater Kailash, is a good South Indian restaurant. *Morning Stores*, also in M Block Market, is about as close as you'll get to a western supermarket.

An excellent selection of fruits and vegetables (for India) can be found in *Khan Market* in South Delhi. You can get avocados, pears, broccoli, lettuce, and much more. Two good stores are *Allied Fruit & Florist* at 58-B Khan Market and *Nathi Ram Rajora* at 72-B Khan Market. The prices are high. *Oriental Fruits Mart*, 23E Connaught Place, at the beginning of Barakhamba Rd, has a good selection of fruits, vegetables, and imported foods.

WARNING Be careful of travel agents

at the railway station, the airport, and in Connaught Place that have unofficial Government Tourist Office signs on them. If you read the signs closely you will see in small print "Approved by J & K" or some other government office, in small letters and in huge letters **GOVERNMENT TOURIST OFFICE.** A friend of mine saw the sign on one of these travel agencies that someone that worked for them pointed out to him and thought that since they were a tourist office, they must be bona fide and honest. When he got in the travel agency they told him it would cost US$30 to get to Mathura by train. The real cost is US$1.25 (Rs 42). They told him considering all the trouble, plus how much it would cost, it would be much better for him to pay $60 for a taxi to Vrindavana (150 km from Delhi). He thought since they are a tourist office they must be telling the truth, so he took the taxi for $60. The real price for the taxi was Rs 800 ($25).

I have also heard a case in which a travel agent had two women pay $235 each to share a taxi to Jaipur, Pushkar, Agra, and then back to Delhi. This is a total cost of $470. The real cost was a maximum of $235 for both of them. On top of that the taxi driver brought them to highly overpriced hotels, where he got a commission on the price of their room. He also brought them to places to shop where they were charged more than double the normal price for different items. As one woman who got totally ripped off told me, "I really thought I knew what I was doing, until all my money was gone in less than a week."

Around Delhi by Taxi or Rickshaw

It is a good idea to carry small notes with you because many times taxi and rickshaw drivers will tell you they have no change and try to keep your big bill. You should insist that the driver uses the meter and you should check that the meter is cleared.

Often auto rickshaw drivers in Delhi will not use the meter and you may have to negotiate the fare. Especially for short distances and in Connaught Place rickshaw drivers will often refuse to use their meters. If they use their meter they may drive you all over town before taking you to your destination. This has happened to me several times. You should ask what the fare should be at your hotel or at a shop and then bargain for that price. Luggage charges can be levied if your bags weight more than 20 kg. This charge should be worked out in advance.

Auto-rickshaw drivers will be more reluctant to use the meter for short distances. From the New Delhi railway station to Connaught Place by the meter is Rs 5 or 6, but few rickshaw drivers will bring you there for less than Rs 15. For the same trip you could be asked to pay Rs 50 or more.

The flagfall for taxis is Rs 7 and for auto-rickshaws Rs 4.40. Besides what shows on the meter an extra 50% is added as a fare adjustment, because the meters are not regularly adjusted. You can ask to see your driver's updated rate card, which they must show you on request. If they do not have a rate card, you can ask a local. An extra night charge of 20% for auto-rickshaws and 25% for taxis is added between 11 pm and 5 am. For complaints call 331-9334.

Metropole Tourist Service (469-2212), 294 Defence Flyover Market, is a reliable place to hire a luxury car. A good source for a long-distance taxi (taxi to Vrindavana, Jaipur, etc.) is Gaurav Tours (753-5062), 5212 Basant Road, Paharganj.

Prepaid Taxi Stands

There are prepaid taxi stands at the airport and railway station where you pay in advance a fixed fee for taxis and auto-rickshaws. At the train station I found them to be much cheaper than the price I could arrange myself. It is Rs 25 from the New Delhi railway station to Nizamuddin Station in southeast Delhi. The problem with going at this rate is that many of the motor rickshaw drivers will not want to take you at this rate. At the Nizamuddin Station they wanted to have me travel with two other people for Rs 25. After fighting for 15 minutes, finally a driver took me to the New Delhi railway station. For Rs 10 more I could have avoided all this trouble. On the other hand, going from New Delhi station to Nizamuddin I immediately got someone to take me for the prepaid price of Rs 25. Everyone else wanted at least Rs 40 or Rs 45. An advantage of using a prepaid taxi is you pay a set fee, and you will not be driven all over town so the driver can increase the meter price.

To and From the Airports

The Indira Gandhi International Airport is 16 km southwest of the city center. The domestic airport is 7 km from city center. The domestic airport is between the international airport and city center. Both Delhi Transport Corporation (DTC) and the Ex-Servicemen's Airlink Transport Service (EATS) operate buses between the airport, some hotels, and the city center. The DTC bus goes to the New Delhi Railway Station and the Interstate Bus Station. To go to the airport, the EATS bus departs from near the Wimpy restaurant, Palika Bazaar, Connaught Place. This is a safe, easy way to go for the budget traveler. Public bus No 780 goes from Super Bazaar at Connaught

Place to the airport.

It costs about Rs 180 ($6, Rs 250 at night) by taxi or Rs 90 by uncomfortable (for this distance) auto-rickshaw to get to Connaught Place, the Paharganj area, or the New Delhi Train Station.

As you come out of the International airport there are three prepaid taxi stands, which charge a fixed rate based on the distance to your destination. You tell them your destination and pieces of luggage. The first counter to your right is for limousines, which are expensive, and next is for a so-called luxury taxi (which basically means you pay more for nothing extra). Outside, straight and then to your right, is the lowest priced pre-paid taxi stand. Keep your receipt and give it to the driver at your destination, not before. A tip or further payment is not required.

Sometimes the pre-paid taxis are more expensive than if you bargain yourself. By finding out the price from the pre-paid taxi stands, you know what the price is that you have to beat. I was quoted Rs 1500 from the pre-paid taxi stand to go to Vrindavana (3½ hr from Delhi) and eventually paid Rs 900.

Warning If you get a taxi to a hotel in Delhi, you may be repeatedly asked whether you want to go to a different hotel. You may even be brought to a different hotel. Don't listen to the taxi driver, as they only want to bring you to a place where they get a percentage of the amount you pay for a room. Just go to where you want to go.

If you are arriving at night, it is highly advised to have a destination in mind and get a pre-paid taxi. It is advised to not talk too much with taxi drivers, because the end conclusion of 90% of the conversations is what they can get from you.

They often totally lie to you and act insulted if you don't believe them.

If you are traveling alone (especially women) you are more likely to have a problem. I have heard of several cases of women having problems with taxi drivers in Delhi. If you have a problem, take the taxi driver's license plate number, as drivers can lose their permits if they attempt to cheat. I have seen taxi drivers take very seriously a threat of taking their license plate number and reporting them. They are highly afraid of the police and will not harass you if they know you will report them.

Never pay a local taxi driver in advance. If you are going a long distance (Vrindavana or Jaipur) you may be requested to pay Rs 300 in advance for the gas (petrol). This is all right.

Travel

Air There is a State Bank of India (open 24-hours) before you leave customs, which is the best place to change money at the airport. I have found that the taxi drivers at the airport will take American dollars at slightly inflated prices. Many international flights come in and out of Delhi at the worst times. Most flights leave and depart between 12 midnight and six in the morning. If you have to get a 4 am flight departing from Delhi, you should book a taxi through your hotel in the afternoon, as it will be very difficult to get a taxi at 12 o'clock at night.

There is a departure tax of Rs 300 to leave the country. There are free shuttle buses between the two terminals every 30 minutes.

There are dormitories on the other side of the parking lot, which are a good place to stay. Some of the rooms have six beds, and you can rent the entire room. There are supposed to be rooms for passengers in the airport, but they seemed to be reserved for government officials. You can also sleep on the floor of the airport, if you have a sleeping bag. No one minds. When you go through immigration before getting to security, there are nice bed-like chairs where you can sleep an hour or two between checking in and getting on the plane.

International Airlines

Aeroflot
BMC House, 1st floor, 1-N Block, Connaught Place (331-0426)

Air Canada
105 Indra Prakash Building, 21 Barakhamba Rd (332-5876)

Air France
6 Scindia House, Connaught Place (331-0407)

Air India
Himalaya House, 23 Kasturba Gandhi Marg (331-3685)

Air Mauritius
Jeevan Bharti Building, Connaught Circus (331-1225)

Air Lanka
Room 1, Hotel Janpath, Janpath (332-6843)

Alitalia
19 Kasturba Gandhi Marg (331-1019)

American Airlines
78/1 Janpath (332-9349)

Bangladesh Biman
N-40 Connaught Place (331-2119)

British Airways
1A Connaught Place (332-7428)

Cathay Pacific
Tolstoy House, Tolstoy Marg (332-1286)

Continental Airlines
Hotel Janpath, Janpath (372-2162)

Delta Airlines
G-37, East of Kailash (683-3832)

Druk Air
415 Antriksh Bhavan, 22 Kasturba Gandhi Marg (371-2031)

Emirates
Kanchenjunga Bldg, 18 Barakhamba Rd (332-4665)

Ethiopian Airlines
Hotel Janpath, Janpath (372-2162)

Iran Air
Ashok Hotel, Chanakyapuri (604-397)

Gulf Air
G-12 Marina Arcade, Connaught Place (332-2018)

Japan Airlines
Chandralok Building, 36 Janpath (332-7724)

KLM
Prakash Deep Bldg, 7 Tolstoy Marg (331-1747)

Kuwait Airway
2C DCM Building, 16 Barakhamba Rd (331-4223)

Lot Polish Airlines
G-55 Connaught Place (332-4482)

Lufthansa
56 Janpath (332-3310)

Malaysian Airline System
G Block, Connaught Place (332-1605)

North West Airlines
Indra Prakash Building, Barakhamba Rd (371-6006)

Pakistan International Airlines (PIA)
Kailash Building, 26 Kasturba Gandhi Marg (331-3161)

Quantas Airway
Mohandev Building, 13 Tostoy Marg (332-9732)

Royal Jordanian Airlines
G-56 Connaught Circus (332-7418)

Royal Nepal Airlines
44 Janpath (332-0817)

SAS
B-1 Block, Connaught Place

(332-7503)

Saudi Arabian Airlines
Hansalaya Building, 15 Barakhamba Rd (331-0464)

Singapore Airlines
G-11 Connaught Circus (332-0145)

Swiss Airlines
56 Janpath (372-2993)

Thai International
Ambadeep Building, 14 Kasturba Gandhi Marg (332-3608)

United Airlines
66 Janpath (371-1226)

US Air
622 Indra Prakash Building, 21 Barakhamba Rd (371-4621)

Domestic Flights

The main domestic carrier in India is Indian Airlines, which is a government airline that flies to many of the major cities in India. Check-in time is an hour (best to be there an hour and half) before the flight. If you do not arrive within a half hour of the flight, your seat may be given to someone else. It is a good idea to reconfirm your reservation, especially if you purchased your ticket overseas. Air India also has domestic flights to the major cities, such as Calcutta and Bombay. These flights depart from the international terminal, not the domestic one.

The Indian Airlines office is at the Malhotra Building (331-0517), F Block, Connaught Place. It is crowded, but there is a special counter for foreign tourists. There is another office at the PTI Building (371-9168) on Sansad Marg, which is open 10 am to 5 pm, except Sunday. It could be a good idea to hire a travel agent to arrange your ticket, so you can avoid the long lines.

Indian Airlines also flies internationally to Bangkok, Singapore, Kathmandu (daily $170), Karachi, Kabul, Colombo,

and Dhaka. Many times they offer the cheapest flights to these places. The office at Barakhamba Rd (331-3732) handles the international flights, and also domestic flights. This office is open 10 am to 5 pm except Sunday.

There is a 24-hour flight information phone at the domestic airport (141, 144). The Indian Airlines office at the airport is a good place to make reservations, but is out of the way. You could arrange your booking here, when you fly into Delhi. For recorded flight information, the numbers are 142 for arrivals and 143 for departures. They may not allow you to take batteries onto the plane with you, including computer batteries. You are supposed to check these in.

The domestic airlines that have flights departing from Delhi are Indian Airlines, Jet Airways, Damania, Air India, East West, Archana, Sahara India, and Modiluft. Some of the flights from Delhi are: Agra (2 daily, $40), Ahmedabad (5 Daily, $98), Aurangabad (4 weekly, $110), Bangalore (6 daily, $195), Bhubaneswara (daily, $170), Bombay (15 daily, $165), Calcutta (7 daily, $155), Dharamshala (3 weekly, $100), Goa (3 daily, $200), Hyderabad (3 daily, $160), Jaipur (3 daily, $50), Khajuraho (daily, $75), Leh (daily, $100), Madras (5 daily, $200), Trivandrum (daily, $280), Udaipur (daily, $74), and Varanasi (4 daily, $100).

Domestic Airlines

Archana Airway
41A Friends Colony East, Mathura Rd (684-2001)

Damania Airways
Somdatt Chambers, 5 Bhikaji Cama Place (673-440)

East West Airlines
DCM Bldg, 2nd Fl, 16 Barakhamba Rd (332-4665)

Jagson Airlines
  12E Vandhana, 11 Tolstoy Marg
  (371-1069)
Jet Airways
  3E Hansalya, 15 Barakhamba Rd
  (372-4727)
Modiluft
  2 Commercial Complex, Masjid
  Moth, Greater Kailash II (643-1128)
Sahara India
  7th fl, Ambadeep Building, Kasturba
  Gandhi Marg (332-6851)

Rail There are two main train stations. The **New Delhi Station**, near Paharganj, about five minutes from Connaught Place in the center of town, and the **Delhi Station**, in Old Delhi. The New Delhi Station is on the broad gauge network and connects Delhi with most of the major cities in India. Old Delhi Station is on the metre gauge line of the Western Railway and connects Delhi with Jaipur, Ajmer, Udaipur, Nathdwar, Jodhpur, Ahmedabad, and many more places. They are a half-hour apart by auto-rickshaw, so you should make sure you find out which station you depart from when you purchase your ticket. The No 6 bus goes between the two stations for a few rupees.

The **Nizamuddin Station** in southeast Delhi is a good place to get trains, as it is much less crowded. You can get trains to Mathura or Puri from here. If you are coming from Mathura or Agra and are going to the airport, South Delhi, or the ISKCON Temple, it is better to get off the train here instead of the New Delhi station. There is also another station called **Sarai Rohilla St Station**, a ten-minute rickshaw from the New Delhi Station and Connaught Place on Guru Govind Singh Marg. From here trains to Rajasthan depart and arrive.

You can book trains at the Tourist Booking office, upstairs in the New Delhi Train Station. It is open from 7.45 am to 1.50 pm and 2 to 9 pm Monday to Saturday, and on Sunday it is open to 1.50 pm. If you book a ticket here you must pay in foreign currency or have an exchange certificate. Your change will be given in rupees. One of the queues (lines) is for paying in foreign currency and the other is for paying in rupees with an exchange certificate. You can purchase an Indrail pass here. The computerized booking office for Western Railway only (not all India) is in a separate building about 200 metres from the New Delhi Station. Waiting time may be a couple of hours here.

The 7.05 am Taj Express #2180 (2¾ hr) is a fast train to **Agra**. It also stops in Mathura (2¼ hr). The Shatabdi Express #2002 (2 hr, 6.15 am) to Agra is even faster. It continues on to Jhansi (4½ hr) to meet the express bus to Khajuraho. The Punjab Mail #1038 (7.15 am) takes three hours and the AP Express #2734 (5.55 pm) two and a half hours to reach Agra.

Fifteen trains each day go to **Mathura** (the train junction for Vrindavana) from either the New Delhi station or the Nizamuddin train station. These trains take between 2½ and 3½ hours, if there are no major delays. There is a detailed list of trains to and from Mathura in the Mathura section.

The fully A/C Shatabdi Exp (6.20 am) takes just 4½ hours to reach Jaipur. The Pink City Express #2901 going to **Jaipur** leaves from the Sarai Rohilla station, as do some other trains going to Rajasthan. It departs at 6 am and arrives at 11 am. It continues on to **Udaipur** (15½ hr). The New Delhi-Howrah Express # 2382 (4 pm) takes 14 hours to reach **Varanasi**. There are several other trains to Varanasi leaving on various days. The Ashram Express #2905 (6 pm, 17 hr) is a good train to **Ahmedabad**.

The fully air-conditioned Rajdhani Express #2952 is the fastest train to **Bombay** (17 hr, daily except Tues, 4.05 pm). There are several other trains to Bombay which take from 21 to 31 hours. A Rajdhani Express also goes to **Calcutta** (18 hr, daily except Sun, 5.15 pm). The Kalka-Howrah Mail #2312 (8 am) takes 25 hours to reach Calcutta.

The Rajdhani Exp #2430 (9.30 am) departs to **Bangalore** on Saturdays (36 hr). The Karnataka Exp #2628 (9.15, 41 hr) departs daily to Bangalore

The Rajdhani Express goes to **Madras** on Monday (30 hr). The Tamil Nadu Exp leaves daily to Madras #2622 (34 hr, 10.30 pm).

Trains from Delhi go to Agra (2-4½ hr, 15 daily), Lucknow (7-10 hr, 5 daily) Gorakhapur (13½ hr, one daily), Haridwar (7-10 hr, one or two a day), Jhansi (4½ to 9 hr, 15 daily), Allahabad (7-14 hr, 9 daily), and Varanasi (13½-18 hr, 6 daily) in Uttar Pradesh. Trains go to Jaipur (5-13 hr, 8 daily), Udaipur (15½-20 hr, 2 daily), and Ajmer for Pushkar (9 hr, 5 daily) in Rajasthan. Trains go to many other places in India such as Bombay (17-29 hr, 8 daily), Ahmedabad (17-25 hr, 4 daily), Amritsar (8-12 hr, 9 daily), and Puri (32-40 hr, two daily).

Some major places in South India that trains go to are Bangalore (40 hr, one daily), Madras (36 hr, 2 or 3 daily), Thiruvananthapuram (54 hr, one daily), Hyderabad (25-28 hr, 2 or 3 daily), and one train a week to Kanniyakumari (58 hr).

Bus The main bus station is the **Inter-state Bus Terminal** at Kashmir Gate, 1 km north of the Old Delhi Railway Station. Local buses to all over Delhi as well as many interstate buses leave from here. You can get a deluxe or semi-deluxe bus from here to Agra (5 hr) and Jaipur (5 hr). You can get a bus to Haridwar (6 hr), Dharamsala (13 hr), Shimla (10 hr), Manali (17 hr), Chandigarh (8 hr), Amritsar (9 hr), and many other places. There are regular buses to **Mathura** (3½ hr), every half-hour or hour. You should allow about 30 minutes to purchase your ticket and find the right bus, as it is a big place.

There is a State Bank of India, a post office, and a 24-hour left luggage counter (cloak room) in the terminal.

To get to many places such as **Haridwar** and **Manali** you can arrange a deluxe bus from a private company. These buses are usually much better than a local state bus. You should try to book your bus trip as far in advance as possible. Private deluxe buses usually depart from Chelmsford Rd, the street that the New Delhi train station is on. This is usually a much more convenient place to get a bus than at the Inter-state Bus Terminal. Tickets can be purchased from agents on Chelmsford Rd or Paharganj, or sometimes your hotel manager can get a ticket for you. It pays to shop and ask around before buying a ticket from a travel agent, as many will try to charge you double the normal fare.

Think twice before taking an all-night video bus, they are extremely loud throughout a good part of the night. An overnight local bus is a good way to understand how painful life can be, but the all night-luxury buses are not so bad.

You can get a **deluxe bus to Jaipur** and some other places in Rajasthan at Bikaner House, at the Rajasthan tourist office, just south of Rajpath by the India Gate.

CHAPTER SEVEN

Uttar Pradesh

Population: 152 million

Uttar Pradesh has some of the most important holy places in India. Mathura was where Lord Krishna was born, and Vrindavana is where He had His childhood pastimes. Ayodhya is where Lord Rama ruled. At Allahabad the Ganges, Yamuna, and Saraswati Rivers meet and there is the Kumbha-mela festival every twelve years. South of Allahabad is Citrakut, where Lord Rama is said to have spent 11 years in the forest while He was in exile. There is also Naimisaranya, which is located about 100 km from Lucknow.

In northern Uttar Pradesh are the important pilgrimage cities of Haridwar and Rishikesh. Further up into the mountains is the source of the Yamuna at Yamunotri and the source of the Ganges at Gangotri. Near these two places are Badrinath where there is an important Vishnu temple, and Kedarnath, where there is an important Siva temple.

Also in Uttar Pradesh are two important places in reference to Lord Buddha's life—Sarnath, where He preached His first important sermon, and Kushinagar, where he left his body.

NORTHERN UTTAR PRADESH

HARIDWAR
Population: 190,000; STD Code 0133

Haridwar is on the west bank of the Ganges, at the foot of the Himalayan Mountains. Haridwar means the gateway to Hari (Lord Vishnu). It is also called **Ganga-dwara,** because the holy Ganges enters the plains here. This is one of the seven holy cities in India. It is called Mayapuri Kshetra in the *Puranas*. Haridwar is about 225 km northeast of Delhi.

Uddhava instructed Vidura to go to Haridwar to be instructed by Maitreya Muni. It is also called Kapilasthan, because it is said that Kapiladeva performed penances here. The great sacrifice of Daksa Prajapati took place near here, where Sati burned herself alive. Nearby, at Sapta Sarovara, the Ganges splits into seven streams to please the seven Rishis doing austerities there. Lord Nityananda came here about 500 years ago.

Haridwar is hot in the summer, but the Ganges water is always icy cold. The river is fed by melting glaciers and snow peaks. The Ganges is split by a barrage just north of Haridwar. The water that flows next to the city of Haridwar is actually a fast-moving big canal. The main natural rivulet of the Ganges, called Neel Dhara, flows about a half km east of the city. The Ganges is known as the **Ganga** in India.

Haridwar is a busy, fairly fast moving town. Most people stay here for a day or two and then move on to Rishikesh or some other place in the mountains. If you want a peaceful place to stay for a few weeks, Rishikesh is much better. Meat, fish, and all intoxications are banned in Haridwar.

Information and Tours

The **Tourist Office** is on the main street by the Lalta Rao Bridge. There is also a **tourist information booth** at the railway station. The **UP Tourist Bureau** is near the bus stand at the Rahi Motel, Station Rd.

There is a tour from Haridwar that goes to many places in **Rishikesh** starting at 9.30 am and lasts about 8 hours. This can be arranged through one of the many tourist agents in Haridwar for about Rs 40. There is an overnight **Haridwar-Rishikesh tour** from Delhi that usually leaves every Wednesday and Saturday during the season. It departs at 7.15 am and returns 8 pm the next day. You book it at the Delhi Tourism Office (345-358), C/o Coffee House I, Baba Kharak Singh Marg, or at other Delhi Tourism offices around the city.

The main seasons are the summer, from May 15 to June 20, and autumn, from September 15 to the last week of October. The full moon day during the month of Kartika is very crowded. About 70% of the tourist and pilgrims come during the summer months.

You can change money at the **State Bank of India** (426-103), near Chitra Talkies on Sadhu Bela Marg.

Kumbha-mela

Haridwar is one of the four places where Kumbha-mela is held every 12 years. The other places are Allahabad (Prayag), Nasik, and Ujjain. It is said that some nectar fell at this place when the nectar pitcher was being carried by Jayanta (son of Lord Indra). Over 2 million people come to the Kumbha-mela here. The bathing takes place at Hari-ki-Pairi Ghat.

The next Kumbha-mela here is in April/May, 1998. Every six years Ardha Kumbha (half Kumbha) is held. The astrological timing of Kumbha-mela at Haridwar is when Jupiter is in Aquarius and the Sun is in Aries.

On April 14, 1986 over 50 people were trampled to death and many more injured when the crowd became so huge that they stampeded. There have been many deaths because of congestion at this Kumbha-mela.

One of the main bathing days is the 1st of Vaisakha (April-May), when the Hindu solar year begins. It is also said that the Ganges appeared on this day. Every year about a hundred thousand people come to Haridwar to bath in the Ganges on this day.

Har-ki-Pauri Ghat (Brahma Kund)

The name Har-ki-Pauri means the feet of Hari (Lord Vishnu). This *ghat* is also called Brahma Kund because it is said that Raja Shveta performed austerities here and received blessings from Brahma. Kumbha-mela is held here, as this is where the nectar fell. The **footprints of Lord Vishnu** are imprinted on the wall underneath the water at this *ghat*. You need to ask one of the priests to be able to touch it. There are temples dedicated to the goddess **Ganga** and **Haricharan** here. This *ghat* is supposed to be the exact spot where the Ganges enters the plains after leaving the mountains.

Every night at about 6 pm there is an *arati* to the sacred Ganges. The *arati* consists of offering some large lamps to the Ganges and the loud banging of gongs and other instruments. It is a dramatic and interesting event. Non-Hindus are not allowed on the actual Har-ki-Pairi Ghat, but can take bath or view the Ganga *arati* from the platform-like island with the clock tower on it.

Before starting their "Char Dhama yatra," pilgrims are supposed to come and bathe in this *ghat*. Four hundred thousand people can bathe here at one time. There are chains and rails that enable people to have a safe bath here, as the Ganges flows very quickly at this spot.

Hundreds of thousands of people come to bathe at this *ghat* on the first day of Vaisakha in April/May. On Gangadashera, at the beginning of the rainy season, the Ganges is said to have come down from the heavens. Other important bathing days are on Purnimas (full moon days, especially Kartika Purnima), Ekadasis, Amavasyas (new moon days), Sankrantis (when the sun enters the next zodiac sign), and solar and lunar eclipses.

The ashes of the dead are supposed to be cast into the Ganges at the southern part of the *ghat*.

Mansa Devi Temple

This temple is situated on Vilwa Parvat, the hill above the city. Mansa Devi is a form of Shakti Durga. There is a cable car that goes to the top of the hill, which you board close to Ratan Cinema, just off the main road. There is a beautiful garden in the stretch of land along the ropeway. From on top of the hill you get a bird's eye view of Haridwar, the Ganga valley, and the Himalayan peaks. It is open from 8 am to noon and 2 to 5 pm. It takes about a half hour to walk up the hill.

Other Places

Bhimgoda Kund is said to have been created by Bhima, one of the Pandavas, with a blow of his knee. It is about half a km upstream from Har-ki-Pauri Ghat, just off the road on the way to Sapta Rishi

Ashram. You can get shared rickshaws to Rishikesh from here.

There is a small **ISKCON preaching center** (0133-425-417) a five-minute walk down the road from Bhimgoda Kund. There are no guest facilities there, but the devotees are helpful.

Kushavarta Ghat, about half a km south of Har-ki-Pairi Kund, is said to be the place where Dattatreya did penance by standing on one foot for a thousand years.

By bathing at **Gau Ghat**, between Har-ki-Pairi and Kushavarta Ghat, it is said one can be freed from the curse of killing and eating a cow. Lord Vishnu is said to have bathed at **Vishnu Ghat**.

Sapta Rishi Ashram, about 6 km from Haridwar on the banks of the Ganges, is where the Ganges is said to have divided to avoid displeasing the seven rishis (yogis) meditating there.

About four and a half km from Haridwar on the eastern summits of the Siwaliks Hills are the Chandi Devi and Anjani Devi Temples. At the foot of the hills are the Gauri-Sankara and Neeleswara temples.

Gaurikund is a holy well about 4 feet wide, which is one of the four main *tirthas* (bathing places) in Haridwar. The other three are Hari-ki-Pairi, Neel Dhara (the main branch of the Ganges), and Kankhal, by the Daksa Mahadeva Temple.

There are three old temples in Haridwar called Narayana-shila, Mayadevi, and Bhairava. Mayadevi is a three-headed, four-armed female, who is killing a prostrated figure.

Kankhal

Kankhal is said to have been the capital of Prajapati Daksa. Kankhal is about 4 km south of the Haridwar railway sta-

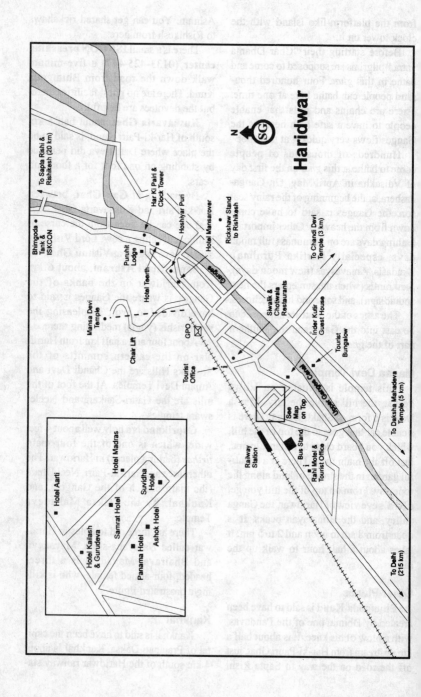

tion.

Daksa, the son of Lord Brahma and father of Sati, once performed a *yajna* (great sacrifice) at this place. When Daksa entered the assembly of great sages, philosophers, and demigods, all the participants in that great assembly, with the exception of Lord Brahma and Lord Siva, stood in respect. Daksa was very much offended to see Lord Siva sitting and not showing him any respect. He considered Lord Siva inferior to him because Siva was married to his daughter Sati. Therefore he cursed Lord Siva: "The demigods are eligible to share in the oblations of sacrifice, but Lord Siva should not have a share." Daksa then went back home, and Lord Siva's followers cursed his supporters. Lord Siva then left the assembly with his followers.

At the next *yajna* (sacrifice) that Daksa performed he did not invite Sati's husband, Lord Siva. Lord Siva did not go to the sacrifice, but Sati went. When her father would not even talk to her because she was the wife of Lord Siva, Sati felt insulted and burnt herself in a blazing fire by meditation on the fiery elements. Hearing about his wife's death, Lord Siva then created Virabhadra, a fearful black demon as high as the sky, who had thousands of arms and was equipped with various weapons. Lord Siva sent Virabhadra and his followers to ruin the sacrifice and cut off Daksa's head. On fulfilling his assignment, Virabhadra threw Daksa's head in the sacrificial fire. Later, at the request of Lord Brahma, Siva restored Daksa to life; but because his head was destroyed by the fire, Siva gave him the head of a goat.

The Dakseswara Mahadeva Siva Temple (also called Daksa Prajapati Temple) is said to have been built in commemoration of Lord Siva coming down to help Sati. Next to this temple on the bank of the Ganges is Daksa Ghat. Sati Kund, on Kankhal Jwalapur Road, is said to mark the spot where Sati actually burnt herself.

In the Area

Dehra Dun is said to be the place where Rama and Laksmana performed austerities to kill the demon Ravana. It is said that Drona came to **Tapovan**, about 6 km from Dehra Dun, in search of self-realization.

Lakhamandal (the palace of the Kauravas) is located at Chakrata about 92 km from Dehra Dun. At this place are the remains of what is supposed to be the shellac palace that was burned down to kill the Pandavas.

Where To Stay – Dharamsalas

Punjabi Ksetra Ashram and *Bharata Ashram* are extremely basic and cheap, about Rs 15. If you travel in the mountain area there are several *Punjabi Ksetra Ashrams* to stay at. Other dharamsalas are *Vishnu Bhavan, Gujran-wale*, and *Arya Samaj*. *Paramanand Ashram* has rooms with a good view of the Ganges. These ashrams are all close to Birla Ghat.

The *Karnataka Dharamsala* at Birla Ghat is a well-maintained clean place where you can stay for a donation. It is centrally and conveniently located by the river. *Jayaram Ashram* is one of the best dharamsalas in Haridwar. It has almost 500 rooms, many of which have a bathroom and are furnished.

Where To Stay – Lower

You can expect hotel prices to be higher here in May and June, which is the busy season. The budget places are mainly located near the railway station. The *Hotel Madras,* which is the cheapest place, has run-down basic rooms with common bath for Rs 60/90. The *Hotel Samrat* is across the street and has rooms for Rs 80/120 with bath. The *Hotel Ashok* and *Hotel Panama*, located on a side road close to the railway station, are both good values with rooms for Rs 65/85. The *Arya Niwas*, near Modi Bhawan, has recommended budget rooms.

Where to Stay – Middle

UP Tourism's *Rahi Motel* (426-430), Station Rd, next to the bus stand, has comfortable rooms in a quiet garden at Rs 275/325 for an air-cooled room and Rs 425/475 with A/C. It also has dorm beds for Rs 40.

The *GMVN Tourist Bungalow* (426-379) is peacefully situated across the river from the main part of town. Rooms are Rs 225/250 up to Rs 425/500 with A/C. Dorm beds are Rs 40. It has a garden and there is good view of the river from the rooms. You can take a good peaceful walk on this side of the river.

The *Hotel Kailash* (427-789), on the main road near the railway station, has rooms for Rs 140/175 and Rs 250 with A/C. Nearby, the *Hotel Aarti* (427-456), Railway Rd, is a good place with rooms for Rs 175/250 and air-cooled rooms for Rs 300/350. Do not get a room by the front desk, as the TV is blasted till late at night. The *Hotel Gurudev* (427-101), nearby on the main road, has rooms for Rs 250/350.

Hotel Mansarover International (426-501), Upper Rd, is one of the best places in town with comfortable rooms for Rs 250/300 and Rs 500/550 with A/C. The *Suvidha Hotel* (427-423), behind Chitra Talkies Cinema in Sharwan Nath Nagar, is in a peaceful location. It is a comfortable place with clean rooms that are about the same price as the Hotel Mansarover

International. It is one of the best hotels in town. It is a recommended place.

The *Hotel Teerth* is right on the river not far from Har-Ki-Pairi. It has rooms for Rs 400/450. Next to it is the cheaper *Gyan Niketan,* which has good rooms facing the Ganges for Rs 300 and not such good rooms in the back for Rs 200. You should see the room before you stay here. The large *Puruhit Lodge* (426-850), right next to Hari-ki-Pauri Ghat, has rooms for Rs 250 up to Rs 400 that are not a very good value, but you are right in the middle of all the action.

The popular newish *Tourist Villa*, Himalaya Depot Gali, Sharwan Nath Nagar, has an assortment of budget to mid-range rooms. The rooms on the ground floor can be noisy. The *Inder Kutir Guest House* (426-336), Sharwan Nath Nagar, near the Ganges, is a comfortable well-managed family-run place. It is a recommended clean place with rooms for Rs 90/160.

Where To Eat

Meat, fish, and eggs are banned within the city limits, so there are only vegetarian restaurants here.

Gurudev is between the railway station and the Tourist Office. The *Bestec Restaurant*, near the Hotel Panama, serves Chinese and South Indian food. The *Hotel Hoshiyar Puri*, on the main road by Hari-ki-pauri *ghat*, is one of the busiest places in town and is over 50 years old. The *Satkar*, Vishnu Ghat, has good Indian and Chinese food.

The *Chotiwala Restaurant*, opposite the Tourist Office, is popular and recommended. The *Siwalik Restaurant*, a few shops down from Chotiwala Restaurant, is also good. *Ahar*, near Chotiwala, is a good medium priced place serving Continental, Punjabi, and Chinese meals.

These three places are probably the best places in town.

The *Hotel Mansarover International* has a good restaurant, but is more expensive than the other places.

Punjabi Ksetra Ashram serves a basic meal at 8 am in the morning, and the *Nepali Ashram* serves free food for pilgrims at around 5 pm.

Travel

Air Jolly Grant Airport is 22 km northwest of Haridwar. There are daily flights to Delhi on Indian Air and Jagsons (except Thu). During the season there are daily helicopter flights to Badrinath and Kedarnath for Rs 13,500 return, 45 min.

Rail The Mussoorie Express #4042 departs from the **Old Delhi** station (7 hr, 262 km) at 10.25 pm and arrives in Haridwar at 6.20 am before continuing on to Dehra Dun. It departs from Haridwar at 10.50 pm to return to Delhi. Other trains to Delhi are the Bombay Express #3009 and the Dehra Dun Express #9020 (daily 12.50 pm, 10 hr). To Mussoorie is the Mussoorie Express #4041 (daily, 6.15 am, 1¾ hr).

You can get a direct train to Bombay (40 hr), Calcutta (35 hr), Varanasi (20 hr, 850 km, Janata Express), Lucknow (11 hr), Ujjain, and Gaya. The Doon Express #3009 goes to Calcutta via Lucknow and Gaya. The Ujjain Dehradun Exp #4310 (6.48 am) departs to Mathura (9 hr) via Delhi (6½ hr) on Wednesday and Saturday. From Mathura the Ujjain Dehradun Exp #4309 (8.20 am) goes to Haridwar on Thursday and Sunday.

Bus There are many buses to and from **Delhi** (6 hr, 222 km), both local and express. Buses to Delhi leave from the Station Bus Stand almost every half hour.

There are direct semi-luxury buses that depart in the morning for Delhi. They can be booked at the many travel agents or your hotel in advance. There is an air-conditioned luxury bus that departs from Haridwar to Delhi at around 8 am in the morning for Rs 200. This same bus, which departs from Delhi for Haridwar at 3 pm, can be booked in Delhi at the Delhi Tourism Development Corporation office (345-358), C/o Coffee House, Baba Kharak Singh Marg or at one of Delhi Tourism's other offices. This bus should be booked at least a day in advance. Buses to Haridwar depart from the Interstate Bus Terminal at Kashmiri Gate in Delhi. Private luxury buses to Haridwar from Delhi should be booked in advance with a travel agent.

From Haridwar, you can get buses to Manali (13 hr), Kullu, Agra, Chandigarh, Shimla, Badrinath (14 hr), Gangotri, and Uttarkashi. There are hourly buses to Dehra Dun, where you can get a connection to Mussoorie. There are regular local buses to Kurukshetra (4 hr).

There is a semi-luxury (five seats across) overnight bus from Vrindavana via Mathura that departs at around 8 pm. It is a good idea to purchase tickets in advance. If you want to get any sleep at all you should purchase two seats, because the seats of this bus are very close together. The bus costs about Rs 100 a seat and takes about 10 hours to arrive in Haridwar.

You can and should purchase a ticket one day in advance for a Char Dhama destination. Buses to Kedarnath and Badrinath depart in the early morning.

To and From Rishikesh There are frequent buses to Rishikesh (45 min, 24 km). You can get a shared taxi at the bus stand for Rs 25. Near Bhimgoda Kund, on the

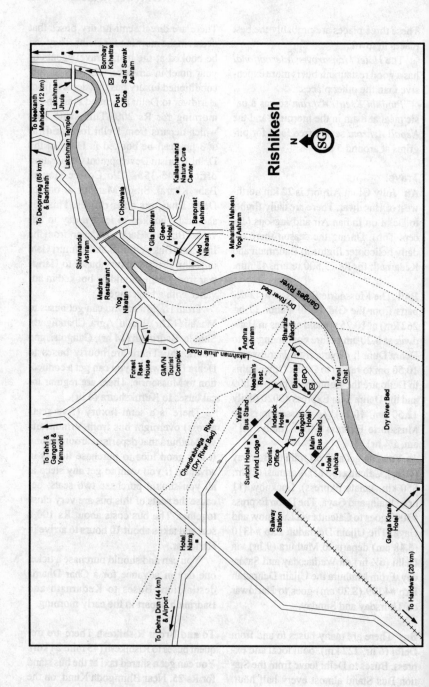

Rishikesh

N

SG

To Neekanth
Mahadev (12 km)

Bombay Kshetra

Lakshman
Jhula

Post
Office

Sant Sewak
Ashram

Lakshman Temple

To Deoprayag (65 km)

To Tehri & Badrinath

Chotiwala

Kailashanand
Nature Cure
Center

Shivananda
Ashram

Gita Bhavan

Green
Hotel

Banprast
Ashram

Maharishi Mahesh
Yogi Ashram

Madras
Restaurant

Yog
Niketan

Ved
Niketan

Forest
Rest
House

GMVN
Tourist
Complex

Lakshman Jhula Road

Andhra
Ashram

Bharata
Mandir

Ganges River

Dry River Bed

To Tehri &
Gangotri &
Yamunotri

Chandrabhaga River
(Dry River Bed)

Dry River Bed

Neelam's
Rest.

Baseraa

GPO

Triveni
Ghat

Yatra
Bus Stand

Surichi Hotel

Arvind Lodge

Inderlok
Hotel

Gangotri
Hotel

Main
Bus Stand

Tourist
Office

Hotel
Ashoka

Railway
Station

Ganga Kinare
Hotel

Hotel
Natraj

To Dehra Dun (44 km)
& Airport

To Haridwar (20 km)

road about half a km upstream from Har-ki-Pauri Ghat, you can get shared motor rickshaws (tempos) to Rishikesh. If you walk across the bridge a few blocks from Hari-ki-Pauri Ghat there are shared motor rickshaws (Rs 10 or Rs 100 for the entire rickshaw, 40 min) that regularly go to Rishikesh. These rickshaws go to the near end of Rishikesh, and from there you have to get another rickshaw to Shiva-nand Jhula or Laksman Jhula for Rs 3 or 4. You can get a shared motor rickshaw direct from Shivanand Jhula in Rishikesh to Haridwar (Rs 10 per person).

RISHIKESH

Population: 75,000, STD Code 01364

Located 24 km from Haridwar and 245 km northeast of Delhi is Rishikesh, where the clear Ganges leaves the Hima-layan Mountains. It is at an elevation of 356 metres (1080 ft). Rishikesh is famous as a place to study yoga and meditation, and there are many ashrams here. It is not nearly as crowded with pilgrims as is Haridwar. Rishikesh is a very peaceful place. Many foreigners come here, and many of them stay in ashrams to learn yoga. Most day trippers spend little time in the downtown, but spend their time across the river or at Laksman Jhula.

It is said that Bharata, the brother of Lord Rama, did severe penances here. A temple of Bharata was constructed at this site, and the town of Rishikesh grew up around it. The town got its name when Raibhya Rsi performed *tapasya* (austerities) here. Lord Hrishikesh, another name for Lord Vishnu, came before him and granted him *darshan*. Lord Vishnu is said to have killed the two demons Madhu and Kaitabha here.

Rishikesh is where most pilgrims begin their Char Dhama pilgrimage of going to Badrinath, Kedarnath, Yamunotri,

and Gangotri. Rishikesh is at the meeting point of the Ganges and Chandra-bhaga Rivers.

Orientation and Information

Most of the religious spots are along the banks of the Ganges or Chandrabhaga Rivers.

There is a good **tourist office** (30209) on Railway Station Rd. The tourist officer there was very knowledgeable and helpful when I went. **GMVN** (30372), Muni-ki-Reti, runs buses and tours to the pilgrimage places in the north.

The main tourist season is May and June. September and October are also crowded. During July and August it rains a lot, and from December to March it is very cold.

The State Bank of India, Railway Lok, near the Inderlok Hotel, and the Bank of Baroda, Dehra Dun Rd, **change money**.

Bharata Temple

Despite the name, the presiding Deity at this temple is Lord Narayana, not Bharata, Lord Rama's brother. It is a very old temple with a high wall around it. It is located in the heart of Rishikesh, about a half km from Triveni Ghat. There is an inscription on the temple that says the temple was renovated by Adi Sankara. It is open from 5 to 11 am and 1 to 9 pm.

Laksman Jhula

Laksman Jhula is about 3 km north of downtown Rishikesh. At this place Laksman, Rama's younger brother, is said to have performed penance. There is a **Laksman Temple** here by the bridge. It is said that near this temple at **Risha Kund** is where Lord Rama and Laksman took bath to atone for the sin incurred for killing Ravana, who was a Brahmin. There is also a seven story temple housing dioramas depicting spiritual subject manners.

There was a hanging jute rope bridge here until 1889. It was rebuilt with iron ropes in 1939. This is a very peaceful area, but can be crowded during the day.

There is a nice peaceful area with a small sandy beach where you can bathe in the Ganges. It is just south of the bridge, on the other side of the river from the main part of town.

Places To See

Triveni Ghat is the main bathing *ghat* where the Ganges and the subterranean Yamuna and Saraswati are said to flow together. *Pinda sraddha*, or offering to the forefathers, is performed here. There is a daily evening **Ganges** *arati* (offering of lamps) at around 6 pm. It is a well-attended, interesting event.

Shatrugna Temple, Muni-ki-Reti, is about 4.5 km from downtown Rishikesh. It is dedicated to Shatrugna, the youngest brother of Lord Rama. At Muni-Ki-Reti (abode of the Rishis) the Ganges emerges out of the Himalayan foothills.

The **Balaji and Chandramouleswara Temple** is constructed in the South Indian style. It is run by the same board that runs the temple in Tirupati, and the temple rituals are the same as at Tirupati. It is north of the Bharata Mandir beyond the Chandrabhaga River.

Neela Kantha Mahadeva Temple is situated at a height of 5,500 feet above sea level and is about 11 km from Laksman Jhula. It takes four hours to walk there from Laksman Jhula. There are regular shared jeeps to this temple from Rama Jhula.

Where To Stay

There are two areas of Rishikesh to stay at—the main part of town and the more mellow area on the other side of the Ganges or at Laksman Jhula. There are some nice peaceful places north of town across the river, which are good for long term stays. Most of the places in this area are ashrams or fairly basic places. This is a good area to stay a week or two, especially during the hot summer months. Vehicles do not go to the other side of the river. You either have to walk across the bridge or take a boat across the river.

Where to Stay – Ashrams

Ved Niketan, Swarag Ashram, is south of the bridge on the east bank of the river. It is a popular place with low-budget travelers. It is in a peaceful location and good for a long stay. I would suggest that you ask to see a few rooms before you choose one. Rooms are Rs 50 to Rs 80.

Banprast Ashram, which is next to Ved Niketan, has well-maintained rooms for just Rs 95, in pleasing grounds surrounded by a wall. It is a good value, but is totally booked except from November to March.

There are several ashrams where you can stay cheaply and also get free food if you are a pilgrim. Baba Kali Kamli Wale, Punjab Sindh Kshetra, Jaipuriwale, Gopal Kutir, and Khurjarawale are some dharamshalas. You can get a cheap room in the Andhra Ashram. The problem with many of the ashrams is they do not allow foreigners to stay.

The ashram run by the *League of Devotees* has some good rooms for around Rs 100 that were recommended to me. This ashram is by the place where all the tourist buses park, between the main part of town and Shivanand Jhula.

Where to Stay – Lower

A recommended place for a long time stay is the *Sant Sewak Ashram*, Laksman

Jhula. It has a selection of rooms ranging from Rs 70 to Rs 150. There are a few rooms for Rs 100 that have balconies directly above the Ganges. The Rs 150 rooms are clean, modern, and have balconies. It is a peaceful place.

Close by is the *Bombay Kshetra*, Lakshman Jhula, which has basic rooms with common bath for Rs 40/80 up to Rs 100. It is popular with long-time stayers on a budget. *Shikar*, Laksman Jhula, is a new peaceful budget place on the west bank of the river, 500m from the bridge. It is clean and has a good view from the roof. The restaurant is also supposed to be good.

The popular *Green Hotel* (31242), Swarag Ashram, across the river, is a good place in a quiet area. It has rooms for Rs 100 up to Rs 150 for a room with a bath.

The *Hotel Ashoka* (30715), by the main bus stand, is a good place to stay if you have to get an early bus. Rooms with bath are Rs 75/85. Also the cheap *Hotel Menka* and *Hotel Gaurev* are by the bus stand.

Swiss Cottage, Chandra Bhaga, near the bridge and down some side streets, is a peaceful place with nine rooms, popular with long-term stayers. It is a very good value with rooms for Rs 35 and Rs 50. It is often full.

The *GMVN's Tourist Bungalow* (30373), Tourist Complex Rishilok, is in a peaceful location by the ashrams. It has dorm beds for Rs 60 and rooms with bath for Rs 200/265 and Rs 125 with common bath. It has a garden and cottages. It has been recommended to me as a good place to stay, but is a little out of the way.

The *Arvind Lodge*, Yatra Bus Stand, is a decent basic place, convenient for an early morning Yatra bus. Double rooms are Rs 160. Next door is the *Adarsh Ho-*tel with rooms for Rs 140/160. Both these places are about the same.

Where to Stay – Middle

The *Surichi Hotel* (30356), across from the Yatra Bus Stand, is a recommended mid-range hotel if you plan to get an early morning Char Dhama bus. Rooms are Rs 200/275 and Rs 275/375 for a deluxe air-cooled room.

In the center of town, close to Triveni Ghat, is the *Baseraa Hotel* (30767). It is a nice place, but the rooms are overpriced at Rs 400/500 and Rs 550/600 with A/C.

The *Inderlok Hotel* (30555), Railway Road, is a good place with rooms for Rs 350/450 up to Rs 550/650 with A/C. It is better than the other hotels in the center of town and is a recommended place. For mid-range hotels, it is the best place in town and also has a good vegetarian restaurant. Across the street, the *Gangotri Hotel*, is a bit run-down. Rooms are Rs 200/275, but for the price it isn't so bad.

The *Hotel Ganga Kinare* (30566) has a good location next to the river with its own private *ghat*, but charges for the location. Rooms here are overpriced at Rs 940/1140, and it is inconvenient to get to. The *Hotel Natraj* (30099) has a pool and charges Rs 650/900 for a room.

The relatively new *Nanda Tels Mandakini Rishikesh* (30781), 63 Haridwar Rd, on the way to Haridwar, is a nice place with a vegetarian restaurant, pool, and health club. It has rooms for Rs 700/800 during the off-season. During the peak season the same rooms are Rs 1400/1600.

Where To Eat

Meat, fish, eggs, and alcohol are prohibited here, so all the places are vegetarian. Some do serve eggs, even though they are not supposed to.

Chotiwala, across the Sivanand Jhula bridge, on the other side of the river, is the most popular places in town. It has a good menu at reasonable prices. I was told that the place is run by two brothers and is divided into two different restaurants, each with a separate kitchen and separate cooks. In the restaurant on the right side you have to get up and order. In the restaurant on the left side a waiter takes your order. The left side place also has a larger menu. I have been told by long time stayers that the food in the left side restaurant is much better than the right side. I have also found this to be true. There is an A/C section upstairs that only serves individual orders.

The *Madras Restaurant*, at the boat landing north of town, has good *masala dosas* and noodles and is a recommended place. Near the Madras is the very small, just two tables, *Amrita*, which has real grilled cheese sandwiches.

The *Indrani Restaurant* at the Hotel Inderlok is one of the better places in town. The *Baseraa Hotel* is also good.

Neelam's, off Haridwar Rd in the main part of town, toward the bridge and Muni-ki-Reti, is frequented by young foreign travelers. It is cheap and the food is good. The restaurant at the *Shikar Hotel*, Laksman Jhula, is supposed to be good. *Vaishal* is a recommended place and is popular with the locals.

Travel

Air The Jolly Grant Airport is 18 km west of Rishikesh. There are daily flights to **Delhi** on Indian Airlines and Jagsons (except Thur). During the season, there are daily helicopter flights to **Badrinath** and **Kedarnath** for Rs 13,500 return (45 minutes).

Rail There is a train from Haridwar to Rishikesh, but the bus is a better way to go. From Haridwar you can get a train to Delhi and many other major cities.

Bus From the Main Bus Stand there are regular buses to **Haridwar** and **Dehra Dun**. There are also some direct buses to **Delhi** (6 hr). An A/C deluxe bus (Rs 200) departs from the Daseraa Hotel at 7 am to Delhi. From Vrindavana, you have to get a bus to Haridwar and from there get another bus to Rishikesh.

The buses for the Garhwal Hills (Char Dhama) depart from the Yatra Bus Stand, off Dehra Dun Rd. In the summer there are regular buses to **Gangotri** (250 km, 12 hr, Rs 110), **Badrinath** (297 km, 13 hr, Rs 130), Gaurikund (near **Kedarnath**, 210 km), Hanuman Chatti (for **Yamunotri**, 210 km, 9 hr, Rs 97), and other pilgrimage places. It is best to get an early morning bus (5 or 6 am), as the buses do not travel at night in the mountains.

Taxi and Rickshaws You can get a shared taxi from the bus stand in Rishikesh to Haridwar for Rs 25. There are also shared rickshaws (tempos) to Haridwar. In Haridwar, if you walk across the bridge a few blocks from Hari-ki-Pauri Ghat there are regular shared motor rickshaws (Rs 10 or Rs 100 for the entire rickshaw, 40 min) that go to Rishikesh. These rickshaws go to the end of town, and from there you have to get another rickshaw to Shivanand or Laksman Jhula for Rs 3 or 4.

GARHWAL (HIMALAYA MOUNTAINS) AND CHAR DHAMA

Pilgrimages go to the four holy places—Yamunotri, Gangotri, Kedarnath, and Badrinath which are called "Char Dhama." Char Dhama means four Ksetras or shrines. They are in the

Garhwal region of Uttar Pradesh. This area is called "Dev Bhoomi" or "Uttarakhand." In the *sastras* they are known as Kedarkhand. Jesus Christ is said to have spent time in his youth in the Himalayas.

It is customary to go to Rameswaram and get some sand at the beach at Setu to put in the holy Ganges before doing Char Dhama Yatra. Then the pilgrim collects some Ganges water to bathe Lord Siva at Rameswaram, after completing Char Dhama.

In *Bhagavad-gita* Krishna says, "Out of all immovable things, I am the greatest mountains in the world, the Himalayas." Lord Siva resides in the Himalayas at Mt Kailash, and his wife, Parvati, is known at Himavati, the daughter of the Himalayas.

The Himalayan range extends west to east in an arc shape, stretching from Pakistan, through northern India to Nepal. The length of the northern mountain wall, from west to east is approximately 5,000 km. The western wing is 1,500 km, the eastern Himalayas are 1,000 km, and the central Himalayas arc are 2,500 km. The tallest peaks are Mt. Everest, (Sagarmatha) at 8,848m (29,028 feet), Mt Godwin Austin, at 8,611m (28,250 feet), and Kanchanjangha, at 8,598m (28,216 feet).

A recommended book to get for your Himalaya Char Dhama trip is *Garhwal, The Dev Bhoomi* published by Nest & Wings. It is informative and detailed. Another good book is *Char Dhama Yatra, Ecstatic Flight Into Himalayas* by G R Venkatraman.

Distance Between Places

Delhi to Rishikesh	245 km
Rishikesh to Hanuman Chatti	209 km
Rishikesh to Gangotri	240 km
Hanuman Chatti to Gangotri	215 km
Gangotri to Gaurikund	334 km
Gaurikund to Badrinath	233 km
Rishikesh to Gaurikund	209 km
Badrinath to Rishikesh	301 km

Transportation for Char Dhama

There are a few types of transport you can choose from. You can go by taxi, which is fairly comfortable, but also expensive. Taxis can be arranged with the Nigam Tourist Office, which can also arrange places to stay. You can also go as part of a tour. Taking a 2 X 2 luxury bus is a good way to travel.

If you do not go by a tour or taxi, you are stuck with going on the **GMOU buses**, which have five, fairly soft seats across. The problem with these buses is that the seats are much too close together, so you have almost no leg room. For a 12-hour bus ride they are extremely uncomfortable.

If you want to take the first bus and guarantee yourself a seat, you must reserve a seat the evening before, regardless of what you are told. Reservation for early morning buses usually starts at 5 pm the day before. If you are told to purchase your ticket an hour before the 6.30 am departure, do not believe this for a second. You can be almost totally certain that the bus will be full when you arrive at 5.30 am. Get your ticket the night before.

The bus from Rishikesh to Yamunotri leaves about 6 am and arrives in Hanuman Chatti (220 km) about 9 hours later, around 3 pm. To go to Yamunotri, Gangotri, Kedarnath, or Badrinath from Rishikesh you must come at 5 pm the night before to insure yourself a seat on an early morning bus from the Yatra Bus Stand. I would advise you to arrive at 4.15 pm, as there can be a long queue (lines), and you may not get a seat for the bus if

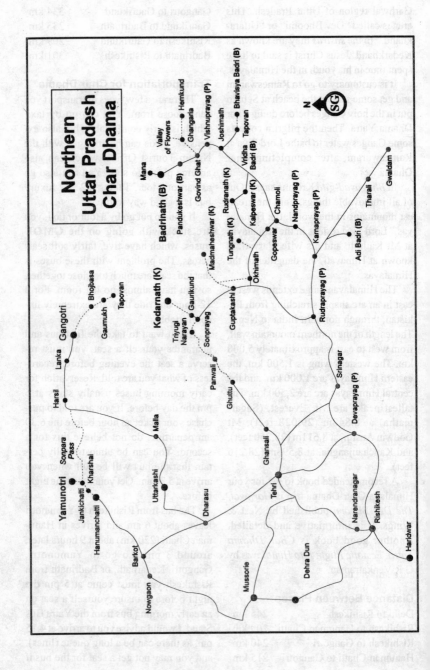

Northern
Uttar Pradesh
Char Dhama

N SG

you arrive too late (especially in June). You can also pay a travel agent in Rishikesh a commission to reserve a seat for you. This could be a good idea, as I was asked for just Rs 15 commission, which would have saved me two and a half hours of waiting in line. They need a few days to arrange a ticket.

Organized Tours

The **Garhwal Mandal Vikas Nigam Office (GMVN)** offers 18 different options for tours to the Char Dhama locations. Tours depart from Delhi and the Tourist Rest House in Muni-ki-reti, Rishikesh. Tours can be taken by 3 X 2 buses (which are very uncomfortable), 2 X 2 luxury buses, or taxis. Besides arranging your transportation, these tours also arrange your accommodations, which can be difficult to arrange yourself, as you often arrive late at night when most of the places are full. With the cheaper tours you will get a decent room with a common bath. With the more expensive tours you get a room with an attached bath. If you can tolerate being on a restrictive schedule, this is the most comfortable way to travel.

Tours vary from the 4-day Rishikesh to Badrinath tour (Rs 1200) to the 13 day tour on a 3 X 2 bus that starts in Delhi and goes to the four *dhamas*, plus a trek to Gaumukh for Rs 3305.

A good tour is the 12-day tour on a 2 X 2 bus, which starts in Rishikesh and goes to the four *dhamas*. Besides a nicer bus, you also get the best accommodation available in the Tourist Bungalows, which are the best places to stay while doing Char Dhama.

You can reserve a tour at the **GMVN office** in Rishikesh (01364/31793, fax 30372), at the Haridwar office (0133/ 424240) located at the UP Tourism office at Lalta Rao Bridge, and at the UP Tourism Office (011-332-6620, fax 011-371-1296) in the Chandralok Building, 36 Janpath, Delhi.

At the GMVN office in Rishikesh you can also **reserve rooms** for the Tourist Bungalows that they manage. You should reserve a room at least a week in advance.

Exchanging Money

When you head north from Rishikesh there is not much facility to change foreign currency. There are money changing facilities at the bank in Joshimath, which is a fairly large town on the way to Badrinath. Other than this bank, most of the banks on the Char Dhama route do not change money. There is also little facility to change money on the street. If you can find someone to do it, you will most likely be offered less than the bank rate. So it is important to bring enough rupees for your entire tour. You should also take into consideration the fact that hotels and food are 50% to 100% more than other places in India.

Guides

If you want to do some trekking in the mountains, it is a good idea to get a guide. There is a Nepali gentleman named Lambu, who lives at Hanuman Chatti, the village on the way to Yamunotri, who I have been told is a good guide. If you want to go to Sapta Rsi Kund from Yamunotri, it is best to get a guide. I have been told that at one of the tea stalls at Gaumukh you can get a guide who can take you over the glacier to Badrinath (6 days).

How Long Char Dhama Takes

As a crow flies, the four shrines are about 100 km from each other. But as the mountains are impassable, you will have to travel 1,500 km to visit these four places beginning and ending at Haridwar. You will have to walk about 60 km. If you go to Gaumukh, you have to walk another 40 km. Before starting you are first supposed to wash all your sins away by bathing in the holy Ganges at Har-ki-Pauri in Haridwar. It is then customary to first go to Yamunotri and then in order to Gangotri, Kedarnath, and Badrinath.

The entire trip will take 10 to 15 days, depending on the weather and how fast you want to travel. Sometimes the road can be blocked because of an avalanche. You have to move at a quick pace to complete the trip in 10 days, spending 6½ days on a bus.

What To Bring

It is best to bring good walking shoes with you: boots or sneakers (trainers). Walking in the mountains is not a good time to break in a new pair of shoes. If you are going to Gaumukh, you may have to walk through snow. A staff with a pointed metal end, woollen clothing, a rain jacket, dry food, and a first aid kit are all advisable. It is cold at night even in the summer. It is advisable to bring a warm sleeping bag, as the hotel facilities are not always so good. It can start raining at any time, so it is a good idea to have a rain jacket with you on the walks to Kedarnath and Yamunotri.

In June, which is the hottest time of the year, a warm sweater is sufficient, even at night. During early May and October it is much colder than in June.

Where To Stay and Eat

Along the Char Dhama route there is no shortage of places to stay, but many of them lack modern amenities. For what you get, the accommodations along the Char Dhama Yatra are the worst values in all of India. Except for the tourist bungalows it is difficult to find a clean place, and a clean sheet just does not exist. I would suggest that you bring your own sheets, if this matters to you. The Garhwal Mandal Vikas Nigam (GMVN), a UP government undertaking known as the Nigam, runs good tourist bungalows and lodges. They are by far the best places to stay, but should be booked at least a week in advance (especially in June) at their offices in Rishikesh or Delhi. Unless you are taking one of their tours, it may be difficult to get a room in one of the tourist bungalows.

Food in the mountains is more expensive than normal, because transportation is expensive. I found it difficult to find any decent food on the trip. Badrinath has a few decent places to eat, but for the most part all the places are really basic.

You can usually get bottled water along the route. In Hanuman Chatti, on the way to Yamunotri, it may not be possible to get bottled water.

Best Times To Go

The temples open the last week of April or the first week of May and usually close the second week of November because of severe weather. The opening day is called Akhand Jyoti Darshan. May and June is the peak season, and next is September and October. September is right after the rainy season has ended and the area is very green and beautiful. More people do Char Dhama Yatra in June, which makes the buses and accommodations more crowded.

All the mountain places are fairly cold at night, even in the summer. During the summer (late May/June) it is fairly warm during the day. Rishikesh is hot at night in the summer, but it can be cold in the winter.

The rainy season goes from the last week in June to the beginning of September. During this period it can start raining at any time. When you get wet it can get cold really fast. During October the sky is very clear, but it can be cold. As far as the weather is concerned, the middle of June and the end of September are the best times to go.

Himalayan Rivers

There are seven holy rivers in the Himalayas (called Sapta Samudrik Tirtha): the Alakananda (Vishnu Ganga), Dhauli Ganga, Nandakini, Bhagirathi, Pinder Ganga, Mandakini (Pinder), and Nayar. They are said to have all come down on Lord Siva's head, but they fall in different places. The Yamuna River begins near Yamunotri.

There are five confluences (*prayags*) of the Ganges on the way to Badrinath. A confluence is when two rivers meet. This is considered to be an especially auspicious place. The main branch of the Ganges is the Bhagirathi, which originates at Gaumukha, 18 km east of Gangotri. The five confluences are located on the route between Rishikesh and Badrinath and many pilgrims bathe at all five *sangams* (confluences) before having *darshan* at Badrinath. To bathe in all five places would be difficult without your own transport.

Deva Prayag (Deoprayag) (610m) is the confluence of the Bhagirathi and Alakananda. It is 90 km from Rishikesh. At this point the river takes the name Ganges. It is the second most important confluence in India, next to Prayag (Allahabad), where the Yamuna, Ganges, and Saraswati meet. In Treta-yuga, Lord Rama and Laksmana performed a *yajna* (sacrifice) here to atone for killing Ra-

vana, who was a Brahmin. There is an ancient **Raghunath Temple** here with a 15 foot tall deity of Sri Rama (Sri Raghunath). It was installed about 1,250 years ago and is one of the 108 most important temples in India (Divya Desams). In front of the temple is Garuda and to the left is Annapurna. Behind the temple and slightly up a hill is **Vamana's cave**. Nearby is Lord Rama's **stone throne**.

Rudra Prayag (618m) is where the Mandakini from Sri Kedarnath meets the Alakananda. There is a large temple of **Rudranath** here. Nearby is a place where **Narada Muni** is said to have performed austerities. At this point the river is very forceful and moves very quickly. Rudra Prayag is 70 km from Deoprayag. The Alakananda has flowed 159 km from Badrinath to reach here.

Karna Prayag (788m) is where the Alakananda meets the Pindar Ganga (from the Pindar Glacier). **Karna**, the half brother of the Pandavas from the *Mahabharata*, is said to have performed austerities here to please Surya Deva and Rudra. Karna Prayag is 34 km from Rudraprayag.

Nanda Prayag (914m) is a small confluence of the Nandakini and Alakananda. Ravana is said to have done austerities here, and Nanda Maharaja is said to have performed a great sacrifice at this spot. Dushyantha married Sakunthala here, and Kanva Rishi had his ashram at this place. There is a Gopalji temple here. Nanda Prayag is 21 km from Karna Prayag.

Vishnu Prayag (1,372m) is where the Dauli Ganga (from Niti Valley) meets the Alakananda river (from Badrinath). One road here, via the Niti Pass, leads to Mount Kailash in Tibet, Lord Siva's abode. Vishnu Prayag is 10 km past Joshimath on the way to Badrinath.

In the *Srimad Bhagavatam* (5.17.9) it is said: "The branch of the Ganges known as Alakananda flows and falls down with fierce force upon the peaks of the Himalayan mountains. Then the Ganges flows into the ocean of salt water (Bay of Bengal). Persons who come and bathe in this river are fortunate."

YAMUNOTRI

This is where the holy Yamuna River begins. Yamunotri is about 234 km north of Haridwar. The Yamuna River flows west to east at Yamunotri. Yamunotri is the source of the Hanuman Ganga and the Tons River, which are tributaries of the Yamuna.

Yamunotri is near a hot spring, at the foot hill of Kalinda Parvata, on the bank of the Yamuna at an elevation of 3,185 metres (10,000 ft). Yamunotri stands on the western flank of the always snow-covered Bandarpoonch mountain 6,315 metres (20,730 ft).

The hard climb from Hanuman Chatti, where the road ends, takes five or six hours. On the way up is the confluence of the Yamuna and Nil Ganga, called Shani Prayag. There is a temple here dedicated to Shani. Worship at this temple is supposed to rid one of the ill-effects of unfavorable stars.

Technically the source of the Yamuna is Saptarishi Kund, a glacial lake. To get there you have to climb right up the mountain, a very hard 12 km trek to the base of Kalinda Parbat.

You need a guide and at least one day's acclimatization at Yamunotri to reach Saptarishi Kund.

Yamunotri Temple

This temple is dedicated to the goddess Yamuna. It was constructed in 1839 by the Tehri, Naresh Sudarshan Shah.

The deity of Yamuna is carved from black stone, and there is also a deity of Gangadevi, who is white. Yamuna is the daughter of Surya (the sun-god) and Sangya. She is the twin sister of Yamaraja, the "Lord of Death." If you bathe in her waters, you are spared a painful death.

The temple usually opens the last week of April or the first week of May. It closes around the second week of November.

Saptarishi Kund

The Yamunotri Temple is built at the foot of Kalinda Parvata (4,421 m/ 14,505 feet). The actual source of the Yamuna is located at the very difficult to reach Saptarishi Kund. To reach it you must have a guide. It is believed that seven great Rishis—Kasyapa, Atri, Bhadravaj, Visvamitra, Gautama, Jamadagni, and Vasistha— performed austerities for millions of years here in Satya-yuga.

It takes 16 hours to go up and get back down. You have to deal with the high altitude, climbing up hills and over rock, ice, snow, and water. The *kund* is about a half km in diameter, and its water is dark blue with slushy snow. Very few people go there, as it is a difficult place to reach.

Other Places

Close to the temple are some hot water springs where the water gushes out at boiling point. At **Surya Kund**, which is said to be the most sacred, pilgrims wrap rice and potatoes in a cloth and place it in the hot water. Within a few minutes the rice and potatoes are cooked.

You can slowly get in and bathe in **Yamuna Bai Kund**, which is about 50 feet from the temple.

Right next to the temple is **Dibya Shila**, which is worshiped before *puja* is offered to Yamunaji.

Hanuman Chatti to Yamunotri

You have to walk the good part of a day, 14 km uphill, to reach Yamunotri. It takes five or six hours to walk from Hanuman Chatti. At a distance of 6.4 km from Hanuman Chatti there are sulphur springs. It is a steep and continuous climb to the top, just wide enough for two horses or a *dandi* to pass. The views are fantastic. The last half kilometre is almost vertical. The walk up is very difficult, but it is easy to walk down. It is advised not to carry too much up the hill.

If you cannot walk up the hill there is other transportation. A *dandi* (Rs 1500 up and back) is like a palanquin carried by four persons. It is the most comfortable form of transportation, as you can stretch your legs out. Pony rides (Rs 500 up and back) are uncomfortable for most people. Going by *khandi* (Rs 300 up and back), being carried in a back pack by one person, is uncomfortable.

Where To Stay

Yamunotri is a small town of about 100 buildings. Most of the places are very basic. In Yamunotri there are several dharamsalas to stay at. The *Nigam Tourist Bungalow*, up the hill to your right as you enter the town, has dorm beds for Rs 60. You can expect a basic double room in Yamunotri to be at least Rs 200. It is not such a big town, and most people stop for the night on the way up at Janaki-chatti.

On the way from Hanuman-chatti to Yamunotri, is the town of Janaki-chatti. Just past the halfway point, there is a *Nigam Tourist Rest House* with dorm beds for Rs 90 and rooms for Rs 175 to Rs 310. It is best to book a room here in advance. The *Hotel Ganga Yamuna* has rooms for Rs 250. There are several other private inns in Janaki-chatti. A decent

room is Rs 100/150. In Janaki-chatti there are just basic food places. Janaki-chatti is a much nicer town for staying the night than Hanuman Chatti.

There is a *Nigam Tourist Bungalow* with rooms for Rs 175 a night in the town of Sayana-chatti, two-thirds of the way to Yamunotri from Rishikesh. It is usually fully booked.

A flashlight (torch) is needed because many of the places do not have electricity. Most of the places, however, will supply a candle.

Hanuman Chatti

If you are going to Yamunotri, this is where the road ends. You then have to walk the last 14 km to Yamunotri. Hanuman Chatti is at an elevation of 2,400 metres (8,300 ft). This is a small town with basic accommodation, and food places. It is a place that most people would want to spend as little time as possible in.

In this town is the *Nigam Tourist Rest House*, down a flight of stairs by the river, which has dorm beds for Rs 90 and double rooms for Rs 375. This place must be booked in advance in June. The rest of the places in town are real dumps. They are dirty, expensive, and they may have no water. Rooms are Rs 200 to Rs 300 for two beds with a dirty common bath. You may have to be satisfied with floor space. Except for the Tourist Rest House, there are no other decent places in town.

There is a good chance that there will be no bottled water in this town. I did find bottled water (Rs 20 a bottle) on the route up to Yamunotri. As you are coming back down from Yamunotri, it could be a good idea to get a bottle of water on the way down. I have heard that the supposed drinking water in this town is highly polluted.

Travel

Bus From Haridwar or Rishikesh (Rs 97) you first take a bus to Hanuman Chatti, which is where the road ends. The distance is about 220 km, depending on the route, and takes 9 to 11 hours. The 6 am GMOU bus arrives in Hanuman Chatti at around 3 pm. If you take a later bus from Rishikesh you may have to stop on the way to Hanuman Chatti.

The first bus to Gangotri (11 hr) leaves at 5.30 am and must be reserved the night before. After the 5.30 am bus, then the buses to Gangotri leave when they are full. The next bus is scheduled to depart at 7 am, and that bus should arrive the same day. I took this bus and it left on time. There is no sign or booth to indicate where to reserve buses in advance. The people reserving the morning buses sit near a building that looks like a shack, right next to the parked buses.

If you arrive in the afternoon it is a good idea to immediately start walking to Janaki-chatti (3 hr). Janaki-chatti is a much nicer and cleaner town than Hanuman-chatti, and there are many more decent places to stay. You can leave your bags at the Nigam Guest House or one of the other guest houses for Rs 4 a bag.

Uttarkashi

Uttarkashi is located 100 km from Gangotri. The main temples here are the **Viswanath** and **Annapurna** **Temples**, like in Varanasi. There is also a Parasurama temple here. This a major junction town going and coming to Gangotri and has many hotels. Many of the places are totally booked early in the day.

About a five-minute walk from the main bazaar is *Ceeway Resort*. It is a recommended place with nice double rooms for Rs 175. The *Akash Ganga* is a better place for Rs 475 and Rs 575 with A/C.

The *Hotel Kashmeri* has basic rooms for Rs 85/170. The *Hotel Shekar* has good rooms for Rs 375. The *Hotel Bhandari* has rooms for Rs 70/135 and A/C rooms for Rs 135/235.

There is a *Nigam Guest House* here with rooms for Rs 140 up to Rs 425 for an A/C room. Dorm beds are Rs 70. The *Hotel Shivom* (2525) has good rooms for Rs 600.

At the *Birla Dharamshala*, a 10 minute walk from the bus stand, there is free accommodation, and for Rs 40 you can get a furnished room.

GANGOTRI

Gangotri is at an elevation of 10,500 feet (3140 metres). The actual source of the Ganges is Gaumukh, a hard 19 km climb from Gangotri. Bhagiratha is said to have prayed at Gangotri to save his relatives. The Pandavas are said to have visited this place to atone for the sin of killing their relatives during the Kurukshetra war. At this point the Ganges River flows north, giving this village its name, Gangotri, which means "Ganga turned north." Lord Krishna says in *Bhagavadgita,* "Of flowing rivers I am the Ganges."

Gangotri is a very nice town and is fairly popular with foreign tourists, many who have come to make the trek to Gaumukh, or further. Unlike most of the other towns on the Char Dhama route it is a nice place to stay for a while. The Bhagarathi River rushes by and is extremely loud, giving the place a peaceful atmosphere.

Gangotri is located about 250 km from Rishikesh and 230 km from Yamunotri. The bus trip via Tehri and Uttarkashi from Rishikesh takes 10 to 12 hours. At Gangotri the Kedar Ganga merges with the Bhagirathi. There is a falls called **Sahasradhara** about 100 yards below this confluence. Just before the falls the river squeezes itself into a narrow gorge about one metre wide.

Gangotri Temple

The Gangotri Temple is dedicated to the goddess Ganga. It is erected near a sacred stone, called Bhagiratha Shila, which is about 50 feet to the left of the temple. King Bhagiratha is said to have sat here to worship Siva, so Lord Siva would take the Ganges on his head. Soon after *arati* to the deities in the temple, an *arati* is performed to the holy Ganges River. The temple is open from May to early November.

Ganges Story

During Satya-yuga, King Sagar performed a horse sacrifice (Ashvamedha yajna) to prove his supremacy. Lord Indra, the leader of the demigods, became fearful over the results of the *yajna*, so he decided to steal the horse. He left the horse at the ashram of Kapiladeva, who was in deep meditation. King Sagar's 60,000 sons born of Queen Sumati and his son Asamanjas, born of Queen Kesoni, were then sent to find the horse. When the 60,000 sons found the horse at Kapiladeva's ashram, they thought he stole the horse. When they prepared to attack the meditating rishi (sage), Kapiladeva was disturbed. He opened one eye and burned the 60,000 sons to ashes.

Asamanjas was not burned and returned to tell the story to King Sagar, who then sent his grandson Amsuman to get the horse back. Kapiladeva returned the horse and told the king that his sons were burnt because they disturbed his meditation. He said his sons could be saved if the goddess Ganga descended to earth and bathed them in her waters.

King Sagar's great great grandson,

Bhagiratha, eventually pleased mother Ganga and asked her to come down to the earth. Mother Ganga told Bhagiratha that the force of the Ganges falling from heaven would be too great for the earth to handle, and that she needed someone to buffer the fall. After being worshiped by Bhagiratha, Lord Siva agreed to accept the powerful force of the descending river on his head. King Bhagiratha then preceded the holy river with his chariot and ripped open a gorge to allow the Ganges to flow. The river followed the king to Ganga Sagar at the Bay of Bengal, where Lord Kapiladeva resides. The Ganges River then bathed the remains of the 60,000 sons and returned them to their eternal positions.

When To Go

The temple here opens on **Aksaya-tritya**, during the last week of April or first week of May, with a formal *puja* to Gangaji. It closes on Diwali, in the midst of an array of oil lamps. During the winter months, Gangotri is covered with snow.

Where To Stay

Gangotri is divided into two areas, which are on either side of the river. Most of the nicer places are on the opposite side of the river from the temple and bus stop. Most of the places in town are fairly basic and can be totally booked by the late afternoon. Later in the day you may have to take whatever you can, at any price. If you plan to stay for a few days, you can take whatever is available the first night and get a nicer room the next morning. You should expect to pay more here than other places in India.

The best place in town is the *Nigam Tourist Lodge*, near the bus stand, which has dorm beds for Rs 85 and rooms from

Rs 225 up to Rs 475. It is best to book a room here a week in advance. The popular *Ganga Niketan*, by the bridge and across the river, has double rooms for Rs 200. It is a decent place. The *Birla Mangal Niketan*, near Ganga Niketan, has big rooms with attached bath for Rs 120. There are many basic no-name places in town.

Meat is banned in Gangotri. The open air eating place at the *Ganga Niketan* and the *Manisha* restaurant, pass the bus stand going out of town, are decent places. There are just basic eating places here.

Travel

Gangotri is 240 km from Rishikesh and 219 km from Hanuman Chatti (Yamunotri). Buses from Hanuman Chatti (13 hr) go directly to Gangotri, via Uttarkashi. There is an early morning bus from Hanuman Chatti (Rs 100) at 5.30 am, that must be reserved the night before. After that there are a few buses that depart from Hanuman Chatti when full. There is a bus scheduled to leave at 7 am, which arrives the same day. Later buses usually stop for the night at Uttarkashi, which has plenty of places to stay. You can also take an all day bus from Haridwar or Rishikesh. From Gangotri to Kedarnath there are regular buses that take a day and a half. No matter how early you leave, you cannot travel the 334 km in one day.

GAUMUKH

This glacier is the actual source of the Ganges. Gaumukh means cow's face, which the glacier is supposed to look like. It is a hundred metres (328 ft) high wall of grey snow. It is 30 km (18.85 miles) long and two to four km wide. Years ago the glacier is said to have reached all the way down to Gangotri.

The best time to visit is between June to September. Before June and after the second week of October there is too much ice and snow on the path to be able to reach it. There is a rocky path, marked white on one side. It is 19 km (some say 23 km) northeast of Gangotri at a height of 4,200 metres (14,000 ft). Mount Shivling, 6,543 metres (21,470 ft), towers above the source of the Ganges. The waters of the Bhagirathi gush out from the glacier with great force and cut a fantastic gorge out of the mountains. The climb is difficult and treacherous.

Getting There

There is a flight of stairs by the Gangotri Temple that leads to the path that goes to Gaumukh. After 8 km you reach **Chirbasa**, which is basically a few tea shops and some tents with mattresses for staying overnight. From here the path leads to a mountain desert. Just pass Chirbasa, where the cliff face has deteriorated, there have been quite a number of accidents, so you have to be really careful at this point.

Most people stay the night in Bhojbasa, where there is no electricity. If you plan to cross the glacier, you can get a guide here. From Bhojbasa it is a good 5 km track to Gaumukh (2 hr). The path is marked by stones, but it is not clear-cut. Usually people take one day to reach Bhojbasa. The next day they go from Bhojbasa to Gaumukh and then return to Bhojbasa the same day. Then the next day they return to Gangotri. Most people spend a day or two in Gangotri in order to get used to the altitude before making this trek. Past Gaumukh is Tapovan.

Practicalities

There is no place to stay in Gaumukh,

but you can camp out there if you have proper equipment. I know of people who have stayed there for days. There are some tea stalls where you can get basic food.

Five km from Gaumukh, at Bhojbasa, there is a *Tourist Bungalow* with four rooms, dorm beds, and two-person tents (Rs 180). It has a basic restaurant and hot water in a bucket for Rs 10. There is also the *Bhojbasa Ashram* of Lal Baba, who provides free food and lodging for pilgrims. This is basically some floor space. There is the very basic *Forest Rest House* at Chirbasa, 8 km from Gangotri and 3 km before Bhojbasa.

You should bring a warm sleeping bag, a torch (flashlight), and good shoes or boots.

Tapovan

Tapovan is at an altitude of 4463 metres, by a natural Siva-linga peak that rises 6,554 metres. It is called Tapovan because sadhus have performed penances there to realize the Absolute Truth. If you want to go there, you should have a guide, a good tent, food, a warm sleeping bag, and warm winter clothes. To get there without a guide can be extremely dangerous, as there can be huge holes in the glacier totally hidden by snow. But I do know of people who have gone there without a guide. Tapovan is four hours past Gaumukh (5 km).

The Tapovan trek takes four days.

Day 1	Gangotri to Bhojbasa	14 km
Day 2	Bhojbasa to Tapovan	10 km
Day 3	Tapovan to Bhojbasa	10 km
Day 4	Bhojbasa to Gangotri	14 km

There is a lady ascetic and a sadhu who host visitors in their caves at Tapovan, but you should definitely bring your own food.

Srinagar

Many people stay overnight here while going from Gangotri to Kedarnath. It is an active town with a number of hotels. The best place is the *Nigam,* which has rooms for Rs 200 up to Rs 400. It should be booked in advance. On the main road are the *Hotel Alpine,* with rooms for Rs 300, the *Hotel Menka,* with rooms for Rs 250, and the *Hotel New Rajhans,* with rooms for Rs 225. By the evening most of these places will be booked. The *Hotel Uttarakhand,* down a side-road, is a decent place that has rooms with common bath for Rs 175 and with bath for Rs 250. If all the hotels on the main road are full, this place will probably still have a room available.

Guptakashi

The Pandavas went to Kasi (Varanasi) to get Lord Siva's blessings, but Lord Siva fled here to Guptakashi and lived incognito. Eventually the Pandavas found him here, and Lord Siva then turned himself into a bull to hide from them. Because Lord Siva disappeared from the Pandavas here, the place was given the name Guptakashi.

Guptakashi has two main temples dedicated to **Ardhanareeswara** (Gaurishankar) and **Viswanath**. In front of the Viswanath Temple is a small *kund* called **Manikarnika**. Water coming from a Ganesh head and from a cow's head flow into the *kund*. Water from one is called the Ganges, and water from the other is called the Yamuna. It is believed that the water comes from Gangotri and Yamunotri. Guptakashi is 45 km south of Kedarnath.

If you arrive here after dark there is a good chance you will have to stop here, as the road is closed for the night at this point. There are a few basic lodges and a

GMVN Tourist Lodge. The *Mandakini Lodge* has decent doubles for Rs 200. The *Rajhans Tourist Lodge* has decent rooms for Rs 150. The *Nigam Tourist Guest House* has rooms for Rs 200 to Rs 250 and dorm beds for Rs 50. There is also a rest house here run by the Badari-Kedar temple committee.

The town of Agastmuni, 25 km before Guptakashi, is where Agastya Muni is said to have meditated. There is an Agastya temple there.

Triyugi Narayana

Triyugi Narayana is located on the mountain road between Gangotri and Kedarnath. Triyugi Narayana is about 5 km off the main road and can be reached from Sitapur or Sonprayag. It is said that the marriage of Lord Siva and Parvati took place here at Brahma Shila during Satya-yuga. Brahma was the priest who conducted the marriage, and Lord Narayana offered His sister, Parvati, to Lord Siva. It is said that the **marriage havan (fire) kund** has been kept burning for 3 *yugas*. Pilgrims offer pieces of wood in the *havan kund* and take the ashes as *prasada*.

It is said that the present **Akhand Dhuni Temple** was built by Adi Sankaracarya about 1200 years ago. In this temple there is a two-foot silver Deity of **Lord Narayana** (Vishnu) with Laksmi and Saraswati on either side. There is a stone outside the temple that marks the spot where the marriage was performed. There are also four holy *kunds* here called Vishnu Kund, Rudra Kund, Brahma Kund, and Saraswati Kund.

KEDARNATH

Kedarnath is on the bank of the Mandakini River between Gangotri and Badrinath. As the crow flies Kedarnath is only 42 km from Badrinath. Over 100,000 pilgrimage come here each year. It is believed that Sankaracarya attained *samadhi* here about 820 AD. Kedareswara is the presiding Deity.

Kedarnath Temple

This Lord Siva temple at Kedarnath is said to have been built by the Pandavas to atone for their sins procured during the Kurukshetra war. It is believed that this temple was originally constructed by the Pandavas, and the present temple was reconstructed by Sankaracarya in the 8th century. One of the 12 *jyotirlingas* is in this temple. The temple is dedicated to Lord Sada Siva and is considered to be one of the major Siva temples in India.

Inside the temple there is an irregular three-faced *linga*, representing the hump of Lord Siva when he took the form of a bull. It is about 9 ft long, 3 feet wide, and 4 feet high. Pilgrims are allowed to touch the *linga*, perform worship, *abhisheka* (bath), and massage the *linga* with ghee. There are deities of goddess Parvati and Ganesh in front of the main altar door. Outside the second door are Lord Krishna, the five Pandavas, their wife, Draupadi, and their mother, Kunti. In the temple is a Laksmi-Narayana Deity, which was installed by Adi Sankaracarya.

The temple faces south, which is an unique feature, as most temples face east. This temple is very solidly built. The temple opens the first week of May and closes either the last week of October or the first week of November. May-June is the busiest time of the year. Worship of Sri Kedarnath is continued at Okhimath in the winter by the priest from the Kedarnath Temple.

The waiting time to enter the temple in the afternoon is about 15 minutes, otherwise if you go at 7 am the waiting time may be two hours or more.

Temple Story

The story of the temple is that the Pandavas felt contaminated by sinful reactions from killing so many people during the Kuruksetra war. They decided to ask Lord Siva for his blessings to relieve them from these sinful reactions. The Pandavas first went to Kasi (Varanasi) to get Lord Siva's blessings, but the Lord fled to Uttarakhand (Guptakasi) and lived there incognito. Eventually the Pandavas found him there, and Lord Siva turned himself into a bull to hide. Bhima recognized his disguise and grabbed the bull by the tail. The bull slowly sank into the ground, and Lord Siva then appeared before them on account of their great determination. Lord Siva instructed them to worship the remaining hump of the bull (*pinda* form).

A temple was then constructed and worship has been going on here ever since. Other parts of Lord Siva's body appeared in other places in the area. It is said that the Pandavas also built temples at these places. They are known as the Panch Kedars: Kedarnath, hump (*pinda*); Tungnath, arm (*bahu*); Rudranath, face (*mukh*); Kalpeswara, hair (*jata*); and Madhyamaheswara, navel (*nabhi*).

Other Places

There is a marble staff behind the temple to commemorate **Sankaracarya**. It is believed that Sri Sankara left his body here. There is another school of thought that says he left his body in Kanchipuram, Tamil Nadu.

Just behind the Kedarnath Temple is the **Mahapanth Trail** (Gate of Heaven). It is said that from this place there is a path that goes north up to Swarga-rohini (path to heaven). It is said the five Pandavas took this path after performing a huge *yajna* (sacrifice). Other people said that the Pandavas ascended from Badrinath.

Where To Stay

The *Nigam Tourist Bungalow* has rooms for Rs 265, but you have to book in advance. There are also dharamshalas and the Birla Guest House. The *Bharat Seva Ashram*, a large red building left of the temple, is a nice clean place with rooms for Rs 135. There are a number of private no-name lodges. Rooms are typically Rs 300 or Rs 400 a night for a decent room. Rooms are expensive for what you get.

There are some basic places to stay at Rambara, at the halfway point walking up to Kedarnath. Food in Kedarnath is basic and expensive, as it all has to be brought up by horseback.

Travel

The road to Kedarnath ends at a town named Gaurikund (1,981 m). A bus from Haridwar or Rishikesh (295 km) takes all day to reach Gaurikund. It is best to catch the early morning bus at 6 am. If you get a later bus you will definitely have to stop for the night on the way. The bus from Gangotri to Gaurikund (334 km) takes a day and a half. From Gaurikund the bus usually takes a full day to get to Joshimath (Rs 100), which is 44 km south of Badrinath; but you could reach Badrinath the same day if you get the 6 am bus and nothing goes wrong. Otherwise from Joshimath the same bus goes the next morning to Badrinath.

From Gaurikund you should make sure you reserve early morning buses the night before. Even if you are told you can get a ticket the next morning, do not believe it.

You have to walk 14 km, at least 4 hours, up a steep incline to get to Kedarnath from Gaurikund. The trek along the Mandakini River to Kedarnath is slow and tiresome. If the sky is clear, at the 10 km stone you can view the Kedarnath mountain peak at 6,640 m (22,770 ft). As the walk is very tough, it is advised to carry as little as possible up the hill. Even the smallest load can feel like a lead weight after a few km. If you cannot walk, you can rent a horse for about Rs 250 one way. To be carried by four people up the hill costs Rs 900 one way. You should be prepared to stay the night at Kedarnath, as it is difficult to go both up and down in the same day.

Some people stop for the night halfway up at Rambara (7 km), which has several simple eating places and some basic rest houses.

Gaurikund

Gaurikund is said to be the place where Gaurimata (Parvati) took birth and did austerities for hundreds of year to be able to marry Lord Siva. It is 210 km from Rishikesh and 334 km from Gangotri. Gaurikund is the last bus stop on the way to Kedarnath.

There is a hot sulphur water spring here, also named Gaurikund, where you can take bath. It said to mark the place where Parvati did austerities. It is a great place to take bath after returning from your walk to Kedarnath. Next to the springs is a Gauri Devi Temple, dedicated to Parvati.

There is a temple called Sirkata Ganesh, the beheaded Ganesh, about a half km from Gaurikund. The Skanda Purana says this was the place where Lord Siva beheaded his son Ganesh and then gave him an elephant head. The story

says that Ganesh was guarding his mother, Parvati, who was bathing in Gaurikund. When Siva came, he was stopped by Ganesh. Siva, not recognizing his own son, then became angry and cut off the head of Ganesh. When Parvati found out this had happened, she requested Siva to bring him back to life and give him another head. Siva said he would give him the head of the first creature that came by, which happened to be an elephant. So he gave Ganesh the head of an elephant.

Places to Stay and Eat

In Gaurikund there are many private guest houses. For what you get most of them are way overpriced, usually at least Rs 250 for a dirty, run-down double room.

The *Bharat Seva Ashram* and *Punjab Sindh* are basic places and some of the rooms have bathrooms.

The *Shivlok*, next to Gaurikund and the Mandakini River is a decent place with double rooms for Rs 250. It is decently clean and conveniently located to be able to take a bath in Gaurikund. There are many other places to choose from, but do not expect any bargains.

The best place in town is the well located *GMVN Tourist Centre*. This place should be booked at least a week in advance at the GMVN office in Rishikesh. It has double rooms for Rs 375 and dorm beds for Rs 85.

The *Hotel Pavan Hansh Restaurant*, next to Gaurikund, is a well-managed, good vegetarian place. The manager was one of the few people that I met who was able to understand exactly what I wanted, and everything I ordered was well-cooked.

You can leave your extra luggage at a cloakroom to your left, just after going up the steps from where the buses park.

There is a *Nigam Tourist Lodge* in Sonprayag, which is six km south of Gaurikund. Sonprayag is much more mellow than Gaurikund, but you need your own transportation to stay there.

Panch (Five) Kedars

Parts of Lord Siva's body appeared at five places in the Kedarnath area. It is said that the Pandavas built temples at each of these places—Kedarnath, Madhyamaheswara, Rudranath, Tungnath, and Kalpeswara. They are at altitudes from 1,500 to 3,680m. It takes about 14 days to go to all five places. They can all be reached by a long circular trek. For the most part you have to walk from temple to temple. A bus leaves Gaurikund, near Kedarnath, every morning at 5 am and stops at access points for the Panch Kedar temples. A local bus goes between Gopeswara and Guptakashi.

You start at Kedarnath. From there you return to Guptakashi and then go to Ukhimath and continue on to Mansuna village. From Mansuna village it is a 24 km trek to **Madhyamaheswara** (3,497m), which is 30 km from Guptakashi. You can stop at Ransi overnight, and then you go to Gondhar (3 km) and climb 10 km to Madhyamaheswara. The temple here is a small stone temple dedicated to the middle (*madhya*) part of the bull-Siva.

Tungnath (3,680 m or 12,065 ft) is the highest (in altitude) temple in India. It is surrounded by striking mountains such as Neelkanth, Kedarnath, and Nanda Devi. The Siva temple here is on a stone paved platform overlooking a cliff. Tungnath represents the arm of Lord Siva. There are five silver faces of the Pandavas along with deities of Vyasadeva and Kalabhairava in the temple. There is

a small Parvati temple here. You get here by trekking from Chopta (7 km, 4 hr), which is 37 km from Ukhimath. At Chopta there is a *GMVN Tourist Bungalow* that has rooms with attached baths.

To get to **Kalpeswara Temple** (2100m), you first travel by bus to the village of Helang, 14 km south of Joshimath. From Helang you walk 9 km to the village of Urgam, which has basic accommodation and food. From there it is a 1.5 km walk to Kalpeswara Temple, which is dedicated to the *jata* (hair) of Lord Siva. It is a rock temple that is entered through a cave.

Next you go to Gopeswara by road and then to Sagar. From there it is a 24 km trek to **Rudranath**, dedicated to the mouth of Lord Siva. The Rudraganga flows by this temple. There are some good views of the Trisul, Nandadevi, and Parbat peaks and down below there are small lakes. To get to Rudranath you can also walk from Kalpeswara.

JOSHIMATH (1,845 M)

When Badrinath closes during the winter, the priests from the Badrinath Temple come to Joshimath and continue worship at the Narasimha Temple. The *utsava-murti* of Badri Vishal is brought to Pandukeswara for worship. There is the ancient Vasudeva Temple, which is dedicated to Lord Krishna, in Joshimath.

One of the four main Sankaracarya maths is located here. It is said that Adi Sankaracarya meditated in a cave here and attained *samadhi* (enlightenment) about 1200 years ago under the **Kalpavriksa tree** (Shahtoot/Mulberry).

Joshimath is between Rishikesh (11 hr) and Badrinath (2½ hr, 44 km). There is a good chance that you will have to stop here for the night on the way to Badrinath, as the road to Badrinath closes at 4.30 pm. The road then reopens the next morning at 6.30 am.

There is a bank in this town where you can **change money**.

Narasimhadeva Temple

In this temple is a Deity of Lord Narasimha, which is self-manifested from a *shalagram-shila*. He is about ten inches high and remarkably detailed, sitting in a lotus position. To the right of Lord Narasimha are Sita, Rama, Hanuman, and Garuda. Against the left wall is a deity of Chandika, which is another name for Kali. On the altar to the right of Lord Narasimha are deities of Kubera, Uddhava, and Badri Vishal. There is an altar for Laksmi Devi just outside the door of the temple.

Sankaracarya is said to have installed this Narasimha Shaligram. The left wrist of Narasimha is incredibly thin and gets thinner every day. It is said that when Kali-yuga overtakes the world, the wrist (arm) will break and the mountains Jaya and Vijaya (near Vishnu Prayag) will collapse and block the present road to Badrinath. The new Badrinath will be relocated at Bhavisya Badri, about 23 km southeast of Joshimath.

If you want to get a good view of Lord Narasimhadeva's wrist you can come when He is bathed between 7.30 and 8.30 in the morning.

This temple is said to be over 1200 years old. It is open from 5 am to 8.30 pm. This temple and the Vasudeva Temple, just thirty yards away, are located in the bottom part of the town, about a three minute walk from the Kedar Holy Home Guest House. Everyone knows where this temple is located.

Vasudeva Temple

This temple is one of the 108 Divya Desams, recognized by the Tamil Nadu Vaishnava saints as being a very important Vishnu temples. The black carved stone Deity of Lord Vasudeva is about six feet tall. He stands with His associates Sri, Bhu, Nila, and Kama. This temple is about thirty yards from the Narasimhadeva Temple. To the left of the main entrance is a deity of dancing Ganesh, which is said to be one of only two such deities in India. This temple is very ancient, and no one knows exactly how old it is.

Sankaracharya Math

This is a temple located on the ridge above the upper part of the town. If you enter the temple and follow the signs to your left, you come to the cave where Sankaracharya is said to have meditated. If you go up the stairs to the right of the temple entrance, you come to the Kalpavriksa tree, where Sankaracharya is said to have attained self-realization. This 125 foot tall tree has a huge trunk and is said to be more than 2,400 years old. Sankaracharya wrote the *Sankara Bhasya* in Joshimath.

Practicalities

The *Nigam Tourist Bungalow* has dorm beds for Rs 70 and rooms from Rs 175 up to Rs 425. There is a *Birla Guest House* and several private lodges in town.

Around the main square is the basic *Kamet*, where the rooms facing the square are cheaper than the other side. There is also the basic *Marwari*, which has a popular vegetarian restaurant below it. The *Jyoti Lodge* is a good middle value hotel. The older *Neelkanth* has nice rooms with a view of the valley.

In the lower part of town is the good *Kedar Holy Home Guest House*, which has good doubles for Rs 250 a night.

There are many places to stay here. The road to Badrinath is closed at 4.30 pm, so if you arrived after that time you must stay here.

Between Joshimath and Badrinath

The drive takes between two and a half to three hours to go about 45 km. **Vishnuprayag**, 10 km past Joshimath, is where the Alakananda and Dhauli Ganga join together. Ten km further is Govind Ghat, which is where the treks to the Valley of Flowers and Sri Hemkund Sahib begin.

Pandukeswara is 4 km further up the road. This town is the site of the **Yogadhyan Badri Temple**, one of the five Badri temples. The *utsava-murti* of Badri Vishal is brought here from Badrinath during the six winter months, from November to May.

Hanuman Chatti is 9 km further up the road. It is said that Bhimasena and Hanuman tested each others' strength in the Gandhamadhana Hills and realized that they were both sons of Vayu and therefore brothers.

Hanuman Chatti

There is a story of how the town got this name. Bhima was travelling on the road here, when he came upon an old monkey lying in his way. Bhima requested the monkey to move his tail, which was blocking his path. The monkey replied that he was very old and had no strength to personally move his tail, but welcomed Bhima to try to move it. After repeated attempts to move the tail, the powerful Bhima became humbled and gave up. The monkey then revealed himself as Hanuman.

There are two Hanuman Chattis, this one and another one by Yamunotri. This Hanuman Chatti is 27 km from Badri-nath and 9 km from Pandukeswara.

BADRINATH (BADARIKASHRAM)
Population: 3500

Badrinath is the abode of the Nara-Narayana sages and is a great place of pilgrimage. According to the *Srimad Bhagavatam* even five thousand years ago this holy place was being visited by such holy persons as Uddhava, and even at that time the place was known to be very old. It is one of the eight self-manifested holy *tirthas* in India (Svayam Vyakta Kshetras).

There are four *dhamas*, or kingdoms of God, which represent the planets of the spiritual sky, consisting of the *brahmajyoti* and the Vaikunthas. These are Badrinath, Rameswara, Jagannath Puri, and Dwarka. Faithful Hindus visit all these holy places for perfection of spiritual realization. Badrinath is a very important pilgrimage place and is very dear to Lord Krishna. Badri is the name of the Ilandai tree, which is a favorite of Maha-Laksmi.

The statement from the *Srimad Bhagavatam* (3.4.22) is: "There in Badrikashram the Personality of Godhead, in His incarnation as the sages Nara and Narayana, had been undergoing great penance since time immemorial for the welfare of all living entities."

Uddhava was sent to Badrikashram by Lord Krishna. It is stated in the *Srimad Bhagavatam* (11.29.44): "The Supreme Lord said: My dear Uddhava, take My order and go to My ashram called Badarika, purify yourself by touching and also bathing in the holy waters there, which have emanated from My lotus feet, rid yourself of all sinful reactions with the sight of this sacred Alakananda River."

The *Skanda Purana* says: "There are

several sacred shrines in heaven, on earth, and in hell; but there is no shrine like Badrinath so far in the future."

Badrinath is also called "Narada Kshetram" since Narada Muni attained liberation here in five days. Gautama Rishi, Kapila, and Kasyapa are said to have come here, and Sankaracarya established a temple here. Sankaracarya visited some 1,225 years ago; Ramanujacarya visited 955 years ago; Madhvacarya visited twice some 735 years ago; and Lord Nityananda visited 500 years ago.

During the season about 1,800 pilgrims a day come to Badrinath, 3,000 a day during May and June, which adds up to about 250,000 pilgrimages a year. Pilgrims chant "Bolo Badri Visal ki jai" and "Bolo Badri Narayana ki jai."

Badrinath is at an elevation of 10,244 feet, on a small plateau between Narayana Parbat and the Alakananda River. The Nara and Narayana peaks tower over Badrinath. It is located 301 km north of Rishikesh. Gaurikund (by Kedarnath) to Badrinath by road is 233 km.

Badrinath Temple

The *murti* of Lord Badrinath is self-manifested from a two-foot-high black *shalagram-shila*. He is also called Badri Vishal or Badarinarayana.

His details are not very distinct due to weathering, since He was thrown into Narada Kund for several years during the Buddhist period. Lord Badrinarayana is said to have been installed by Sankaracarya, who recovered the Deity from Narada Kund.

Lord Badrinath is sitting meditating in the *padmasana* (lotus posture). Badrinarayana is seen in His yogic pose, sitting erect with His palms closed. As you look at the Deities, standing to the right side of Badrinarayana is Uddhava.

To the far right side are **Nara and** Narayana. Narada Muni is kneeling in front on the right side and is difficult to see. On the left side is Kubera, the god of wealth, and a silver Ganesh. Garuda is kneeling in front, to the left of Badrinarayana.

The canopy over the Deities is covered with a sheet of pure gold. The temple is full of ancient stone carvings.

Within the temple enclosure, to the left of the main temple building, is a separate shrine dedicated to Laksmi Devi and the Gaddi (sitting place) of Adi Sankaracharya, just outside the exit door of the temple. The Laksmi Temple is painted red in front. The temple dedicated to Sankaracharya is said to mark his sitting place when he was in Badrinath.

The temple is open six months of the year, May to October. The priests of the temple perform their worship (*puja*) in Joshimath, 50 km south, the rest of the year. Before they close the temple in November, they perform one last *puja* and leave the ghee lamps in the temple lit. Six months later, in the month of May, they return to open the temple and find the ghee lamps still lit. It is said that the great sage Narada Muni along with other demigods come during the winter months to carry on the worship.

The **Nirmalya darshan** of Badarinarayana in the early morning is the most auspicious time to view the Deity. The present temple is about 400 years old. The temple is open from 6.30 am to 1 pm and 4 to 9 pm. Waiting time to enter the temple in the afternoon is a half hour or more. If you come in the morning, you can expect to wait an hour in line to enter the temple.

It is only possible for several people to view the Deities at one time. You are allowed to stand to the side once you are in the temple and view the Deities as long as you like.

Other Places

Near the temple are a number of *kunds* filled with hot sulphur water. Pilgrims bath in the *kunds* before taking *darshan* of Sri Badrinath. Each hot spring is a different temperature and some are very hot.

Before entering the temple it is customary for one to bath in **Tapta Kund,** which is a hot water tank at the base of the temple steps near the river. The temperature is around 45°C (115°F). Bathing in Narada Kund and Tapta Kund is considered especially auspicious. **Narada Kund** is where Adi Sankaracarya recovered the *murti* of Sri Badra Vishal. It is a small *kund* a few feet from the Alakananda River, on the temple side of the Alakananda. Panch Shilas—Narada, Narasimha, Varaha, Garuda, and Markendeya—are located by Tapta Kund. They are large rocks near the river.

You have to climb 600 feet to reach **Deva Darshini**. From here it is said the demigods come to have *darshan* of the holy town of Badrinath.

About 100 metres north of the Badrinath Temple, on the bank of the Alakananda, is **Brahma Kapal Ghat**. It is customary to offer *pinda* (*sraddha*) to departed ancestors here. When Lord Siva cut off Lord Brahma's fifth head, it is said to have fallen here at Brahma Kapal.

The Five Badri Temples

There are five Badri temples—Adi Badri, Vriddha Badri, Bhavisya Badri, Yogadhyan Badri, and the temple of Badri Vishal at Badrinath itself. To reach **Adi Badri village** you go 18 km south from Karna Prayag toward Gwaldam. There is a small 16 temple complex (15 m by 30 m) located here, which was built during the Gupta Dynasty in the tenth century. The main temple contains a beautiful three foot carved black stone *murti* of the Lord called Adi Badri Narayana. He holds a mace, chakra, and lotus. Not many people visit here

Vridha Badri is located in the village of Animath, which is on the way to Joshimath from Helang. It is 17 km from Joshimath on the way to Pipalkoti. When Narada performed *tapasya* here, Lord Vishnu appeared before him as Vridha Badri (Old Badri).

Bhavisya Badri is located in the small village of Subhain (2,744 m), which is beyond Tapovan. Tapovan is about a 15 km jeep ride from Joshimath, and from there it is a hard nine km walk.

Yogadhyan Badri is located in the town of Pandukeswara (1,955 m), 24 km from Badrinath and 20 km from Joshimath. **King Pandu**, the father of the Pandavas, performed penances here to atone for the curse he received for killing two mating deer, who were sages in their previous lives. It is said that the Pandavas were born here. King Pandu installed a bronze *murti* called Yogadhyan Badri.

In The Area

Near Keshava Prayag there is a temple dedicated to **Mata Murti**, mother of Nara and Narayana Rishi. Near this temple is a mountain called **Maninag Parvat**. It is said that near this mountain is where Yudhisthira was able to answer all the questions asked by a *yaksa* to bring his brothers back to life. They lost their lives when they did not answer the *yaksa's* questions.

Pancha Dhara (five Waterfalls): Kurma, Prahlada, Urvasi, Bhrigu, and Indra are waterfalls all located around Badrinath. **Sesha Netra** is a large stone marked with one eye of Ananta Sesa, who is watching over everyone.

Urvasi Temple is where Indra's pride was shattered by Urvasi, the most beautiful Apsara. At **Caranpaduka** a boulder bears the footprints of Lord Vishnu when He descended from Vaikuntha.

Nara and Narayana Mountains: **Nara Parvata** is opposite the main temple, and **Narayana Parvata** is behind. They are named after Nara and Narayana Rishis who did meditation here. **Neelkantha Peak** (6,596m/21,635 ft), is to the left of Narayana Parvata. It changes color at sunrise and sunset, so it is called the Queen of the Himalayas or the shining pyramid.

Mana

Mana is four km northwest of Badrinath near the Tibet border. This is where **Vyasadeva's cave** is located. He is said to have divided the *Vedas* into four parts and wrote many *Puranas* here. The front of the cave is painted white, and there is a deity of Vyasadeva in the cave. Nearby is **Ganesh's cave**. There are rocks here that look like layers of paper and are said to represent his works of writing down the *Mahabharata* and *Srimad Bhagavatam*. Vyasadeva narrated these works, and Ganesh wrote them down, under the condition that Vyasadeva would not stop reciting.

Near this location, Lord Siva narrated to the sage Skanda, who wrote the *Skanda Purana*, the glories of the Himalayas. The **Bhima** and **Mucukund caves** are located just above the cave of Vyasadeva. Down below is **Bhima Pul** (Bhima's bridge), which Bhima is said to have made from a huge stone slab, so his brothers and Draupadi could cross the Saraswati River safely. The **Saraswati River** emerges from a glacier north of Mana, touches

Vyas Gupha, merges into the Alakananda at Keshav Prayag and finally meets the Ganga and Yamuna at Prayag (Allahabad).

About three km from Bhima Pul is **Vasudhara Falls**, which are more than 44m (135 feet) high. To get to Mana is an easy climb. Foreigners have to get special permission to go to Mana, as it is a restricted area. This rule could change at any time.

Satopanth Lake

At Satopanth (4,402 m/14.442 ft), the Lake of the Divine Trinity, is a glacial lake. It is 25 km from Badrinath. Lord Brahma, Lord Siva, and Lord Vishnu are said to meditate at the three corners of this crystal clear green water lake. On Ekadasi, Lord Vishnu is said to come and take bath here.

Satopanth Lake is in a restricted area. To get here you walk past Mana. After leaving Mana you walk across a meadow full of flowers before reaching the 44m **Vasudhara Falls**. The path becomes more difficult until you reach the source of the Alakananda River, which is near where the Bhagirath Kharak and Satopanth glaciers meet. You then walk across the Chakra Tirtha meadow and over the steep rise of the glacier to get to Satopanth Lake. At this point you are surrounded by the mountains Swargarohini (7.898m), Chaukhamba (7,164m), and Nilkanth (6,558m), which make a sensational sight.

Beyond Mana

Laksmivan is where Laksmi is said to have meditated in a forest of Bhoj Patra trees. **Cakra-tirtha** is where Arjuna is said to have taken bath and received Lord Siva's Pashupati Astra, which helped him defeat the Kauravas.

Swargarohan Mountain (Stairway to Heaven) is said to be where the Pandavas, after visiting Badrinath, ascended to the spiritual world.

Where To Stay

During June, Badrinath can be a very crowded place, and it can be difficult to find a room at any cost. I looked for two hours before I found an extremely basic room at an ashram for Rs 100. So if comfort is important to you, it is best to book a room at the GMVN Tourist Bungalow in advance. When you arrive late in the day, people will come and offer you a room for Rs 300 to Rs 500. It could be a good idea to accept their offer rather than searching for three hours for a room. In Badrinath you can expect to pay at least double the price a similar room would cost anywhere else in India. During the weekends in June it will be more difficult to find a room than at other times.

The Badrinath's Temple Committee manages some pilgrim guest houses. The *Modi Bhavan* has rooms for Rs 60 and the *Gujarat Bhavan* is slightly more expensive. They are close to the river, on the opposite side of the river from the temple. You can book rooms for these guest houses at the Information Centre, at the main intersection in town not far from the guest houses and the bridge. You can also book rooms in advance at the Badrinath Temple Committee offices in Delhi or Rishikesh.

The *Hotel Garhwal*, near where the bus let you off, has rooms for Rs 300.

There are over 30 dharamshalas in Badrinath. The *Paramarth Lok* is a large well-maintained ashram like a modern lodge. Some rooms have attached bath, and double rooms are Rs 225. During the busy season there is a good chance that this place will be fully booked.

The *Garhwal Mandal Vikas Nigam Tourist Bungalow* has dorm beds for Rs 110 and ordinary rooms for Rs 175 up to Rs 500 with A/C. It is the best place in town. The GMVN has a cheaper lodge on the same road where the buses stop. It has rooms with common bath for Rs 165. It is best to book both of these places at least a week in advance at their office in Rishikesh.

Where To Eat

There is a group of good restaurants at the main intersection in town, near the bridge to cross the river to the temple. The best of the places seemed to be the *Kwality Restaurant*, but the *Vijay Laxmi* and *Saket* both have good menus. The paper *masala dosas* at the Saket are good. All the places here seem to be pure vegetarian.

Travel

To get to Badrinath you first have to go to either Haridwar or Rishikesh. From there you catch a bus to Badrinath. The bus starts early in the morning and, depending on what time it departs, may reach in the early evening. Usually the trip takes one and a half days. Buses do not drive at night, because the roads are so dangerous.

After 4.30 pm no buses can go past Joshimath, because the road is closed. So there is a good chance you will have to stop in Joshimath for the night. Often buses stop for the night at Rudraprayag, before reaching Badrinath.

Buses leave Badrinath at 6.30 am in the morning and arrive in Rishikesh about 8.30 pm and Haridwar at 9 pm. If buses departing from Badrinath to Rishikesh leave later in the day they have to make a night stop on the way.

There are buses to and from Kedarnath (14 hr) and Gangotri. It takes 8 days to walk from Kedarnath to Badrinath, 80 km on the mountain roads. Before the roads were built in the 1960s this was the only way to go from place to place.

Valley of Flowers and Hemkund

The beautiful **Valley of Flowers National Park**, 5 km from Ghangaria, has a large variety of flowers after the rainy season, between mid June and mid September. Other times of the year there are usually very few flowers. The valley is about 10 km long and 2 km wide. No camping is allowed, because too many tourists wreck all the flowers, so you have to make a day trip from **Ghangaria**. To enter the national park you have to get a permit at the police post at Govindghat for a small fee.

From Ghangaria, if you follow the Laxma Ganga, you reach **Lake Hemkund** (4,340m). In the *Granth Sahib*, the Sikh Guru Gobind Singh writes that in his previous life he meditated on the shore of a lake, that was surrounded by seven snow-capped mountains. The bank of Hemkund Lake is accepted as this place.

There is a large gurdwara (Sikh temple) and a small Laksman (Lord Rama's younger brother) temple at this place. Laksman is said to have meditated by the lake and regained his health here after he was seriously wounded by Meghnath, the son of Ravana. You cannot stay here overnight, but have to stay at Ghangaria.

To reach either the Valley of Flowers or Hemkund, you start from **Govind Ghat**, which is about 30 km south of Badrinath on the road to Joshimath. You then walk 15 km from Govind Ghat to Ghangaria, where there are some basic lodges, gurdwaras, and a *GMVN Tourist Bungalow* with a dormitory. From there it is a four km walk to the Valley of Flowers. To get to Hemkund you leave the main path to the Valley of Flowers and take a path 4 km to the right.

Jogeswara

One of the 12 *jyotirlingas* is located at Jogeswara. It is 34 km north of Almora. The temple here was constructed in the 7th century.

Dhudi Prayag

This is the birthplace of Ganesh. Dhudi Prayag is where the Pundavati River meets the Alakananda.

CENTRAL UTTAR PRADESH

AGRA

Population: 1,000,000, STD Code 0562

The main reason for coming here is to see the Taj Mahal. The other main tourist sites are the Agra Fort and 40 km away, Fatehpur Sikri. Agra is located on the west bank of the Yamuna, 200 km southeast of Delhi.

Sikander Lodi, the Sultan of Delhi, moved his capital here in 1504. Babur, the founder of the Moghul Dynasty, defeated the then Sultan of India, Ibrahim, at Panipat in 1526. He then sent his son Humayun here to capture the city. In the 16th and 17th century, Agra was the capital of the Moghul Empire, which was spread over most of India. Akbar constructed the Agra Fort during his reign.

It is convenient to make a day trip to Agra from Delhi by train. An express train leaves Delhi in the morning and returns in the evening.

Agra is one of the worst cities in all of India for touts (commission agents) and rip-offs. It seems like everyone in the entire city gives commissions. It is best to be prepared for this from the minute you get off the train or plane. If you want to go to a hotel that does not give commissions, it can be difficult to get a rickshaw driver to take you there. When I went to Agra, I never experienced any problems, but I have heard some bad stories about the place.

Tourist Offices and Tours

The **Government of India Tourist Office**, 191 The Mall, is open from 9 am to 5.30 pm weekdays, 9 am to 1 pm Saturdays, and is closed on Sundays. The **Uttar Pradesh Government Tourist Office** (75034) is on Taj Rd, near the Clarks Shiraz Hotel. There is also a tourist counter at the railway station.

You can book an organized tour on either the Taj Express, which arrives at 10 am, or the Shatabdi Express, which arrives at 8.30 am. The tours last all day and go to the Taj Mahal, Fatehpur Sikri, and the Agra Fort. You can book a tour at the **tourist office** at The Mall or at **platform 1** in the Cantonment Railway Station. The tour begins when you get off the train.

Information

The post office is opposite the Government of India tourist office on the Mall. The Modern Book Depot (363-133), Sadar Bazaar, is a good bookshop. The banks are on Taj Road.

Shopping

Agra is one of the worst cities for touts, rickshaw drivers, and guides, who want to show you the best possible shops. Usually you will pay more for your purchases, and a percentage is given to the person who brings you there. I was told one story in which two people were each convinced to purchase $800 rugs. When they came back the next day to ask for their money back, they were asked to show their receipt. The owner then tore up the receipt and told them they had no proof of purchasing anything from him. They left in dismay. These types of stories are normal for Agra. If you are making a purchase of over $100, it is best to think about it for a day, as the shop owners here are extremely aggressive salesmen.

There are of course some good shops in Agra, including the Oswal Emporium, 30 Munro Road, and Subhash Emporium, 18/1 Gwalior Road, which are good marble shops. Mangalick and Co, 5 Taj Road, Sadar Bazaar, has a good selection of rugs. Munshi Ganeshi Lall and Sons, 13 MG Road, and Kohinoor Jewellers, MG Road, are reputable jewellers.

The Taj Mahal

This beautiful marble tomb was built between 1631 and 1653. Inside are the tombs of Shah Jahan and his wife Mumtaz Mahal. Shah Jahan built the Taj in memory of his beloved wife. It took over 20,000 persons 22 years to build. Experts were brought from all over the world, including Italy and France. The Taj is made mainly of white marble, and many semiprecious stones from all over the world are embedded in the walls.

The ceiling of the inner tomb is 80 feet high. The Taj Mahal is flanked by four **minarets** that are 39m (130 ft) high. They are built leaning outwards so they will not damage the tomb if they collapse. The main gateway has **22 domes** on it, supposedly to represent the amount of years it took to build. The inlay work is so fine that no joints can be seen, even by looking through a magnifying glass.

You can get a good view of the Taj

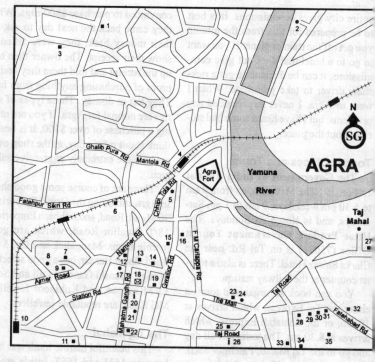

AGRA

Yamuna River

Agra Fort

Taj Mahal

from the Agra Fort. The Taj looks most beautiful at dawn and dusk. It is not open at night, even for the full moon. It is open from 6 am to 7 pm. Admission is Rs 100 before 8 am, Rs 10.50 after 8 am, and free on Fridays. You can enter from the east, south, and west sides, but tickets are only sold at the eastern and western gates. During the early morning, only the western ticket office is open.

Agra Fort

This fort was originally built by Emperor Akbar. Later it was expanded by Aurangzeb. You enter through Amar Singh Gate in the south. Aurangzeb overthrew his father, Shah Jahan, who built the Taj Mahal, and imprisoned him here in the Red Fort. He did give his father a room with a view of the Taj Mahal. It is

an interesting fort and is worth seeing.

Homeopathic Doctor

There is a well-known homeopathic doctor named Dr R S Pareek (52786, 54422), 4/10 Bagh Farzana, Civil Lines, Agra, who has been recommended to me. He is supposed to be especially effective in treating skin disorders.

Where To Stay

There are two areas where there are cheap hotels—the Taj Ganj area, just south of the Taj, and the Sadar area, by the Cantonment Railway Station.

Where to Stay – Lower Taj Ganj

The *Shanti Lodge* is a good value and also has a view of the Taj. It has rooms for Rs 70/90 with common bath, Rs 90/

PLACES TO STAY		33	Highway Inn
		34	Safari Hotel
1	Youth Hostel	35	Akbar International
3	Tourist Bungalow		
6	Kapoor Tourist Rest House	WHERE TO EAT	
7	Rose Hotel		
9	Sakura Hotel	17	Dasaprakash
11	Grand Hotel	21	Zorba the Buddha
12	Lauries Hotel		
13	Major Bakshi's Tourist House	OTHER	
14	Basera Hotel		
15	Tourist Rest House	2	Chini Ka Rauza
16	Agra Hotel	4	Agra Fort Railway Station
19	Agra Ashok Hotel	5	Agra Fort Bus Stand
22	Jaiwal Hotel	8	Idgah Bus Station
23	Akbar Inn	10	Agra Cantonment Railway
25	Clark Shiraz Hotel		Station
27	Taj Kheema	18	GPO
28	Mumtaz & Amar Hotels	20	Government of India Tourist
29	Shahanshah Inn		Office
30	Taj View Hotel	24	Archaeological Survey of India
31	Mayur Tourist Complex	25	Indian Airlines Office
32	Mughal Sheraton Hotel	26	UP Tourist Office

110 with bath, and Rs 130 with bath and hot water. The rooms here are varied, so it is best to see a few rooms before choosing one. The *Shahjahan Lodge* has rooms for Rs 50/60 where you share a bathroom with one other room. Rooms are Rs 80 to Rs 100 with bath and hot water.

The *Safari Hotel* (360-013), Shamsabad Rd, is a very good value with air-cooled rooms with hot water for Rs 100/130. A good choice is *Sheela Hotel* (361-794), East Gate, 200m from the east gate of the Taj, which has a nice garden and rooms for Rs 90. There are some rooms with baths for Rs 100/150.

Kamal (360-926), Chowk Kagzi, South Gate, is a new place with clean rooms for Rs 70 with common bath and Rs 100/120 with bath. There is a good view of the Taj from the roof.

Where to Stay – Lower Sadar

The *Tourist Rest House* (363-961), Kachahari Rd, near the Mall, has rooms with bath and hot water for Rs 75/85. It is popular with travelers and has a basic vegetarian restaurant. It is built around a small garden and is well-managed. Make sure you are at Kachahari Rd, because there are two other hotels with similar names, and the rickshaw drivers will want to take you to them to get commissions.

The *Hotel Akbar Inn* (363-212), between Taj Ganj and Sadar, has a good location and a large garden. Rooms are Rs 40/55 and Rs 100/120 with bath. The rooms here are a good value.

The *Agra Hotel* (363-331), Field

Marshal Cariappa Rd, is a good place with rooms for Rs 125/175 with bath and Rs 375/450 with A/C. It has old-world charm with a garden and a view of the Taj Mahal, but it looks a little aged.

The *Hotel Akbar* (363-312) is just next door. It has rooms for Rs 80/100 and rooms with bath for Rs 110/135.

The *Jaggi Hotel*, 183 Taj Rd, is popular with young travelers. The *Jaiwal Hotel* (363-716) is a good value at Rs 225/325 with bath, air-cooling, and TV.

The *Major Bakshi's Tourist Home* (672-043), 33-38 Ajmer Rd, is a recommended place. It is a well-managed, clean and pleasant place that has comfortable rooms for Rs 175/275 with bath and hot water. It is in a peaceful location.

Where to Stay – Middle

Lauries (364-536), Mahatma Gandhi Rd, is a recommended place. It is well run with a nice garden and swimming pool. Rooms are Rs 475/600.

Mayur Tourist Complex (360-302), Fatehabad Road, is also a good place with very nice cottages from Rs 450/600 up to Rs 750/1000 for an A/C deluxe room. It has a swimming pool and lawn. It is a well-managed place.

The *New Bakshi House* (368-159), 5 Laksman Nagar, is a recommended place with nice management. Rooms are Rs 450/550. The rooms are clean and comfortable. They are often booked. The *Hotel Amar* (360-695) has a swimming pool and health club. The A/C rooms are Rs 800/1000.

The *Grand Hotel* (364-014), near the railway station, is a nice place with a big garden. Rooms are Rs 500/600 and Rs 700/800 with A/C.

Where to Stay – Higher

The opulent *Moghal Sheraton* (361-701, fax 361-730), Fatehbad Rd, Taj Ganj, is an excellent place that looks like a fort. The rooms are $180/200 up to $700. You can get an elephant or camel ride at this hotel.

The five-star *Taj View Hotel* (361-171, fax 361-179), Taj Ganj, is lavish but tastefully done. Most of the rooms have views of the Taj. Standard rooms with no view are $100/125. Rooms with view are $140/150.

The well-managed ITDC *Agra Ashok Hotel* (361-223, fax 361-428), The Mall, has nice gardens and a swimming pool. The large rooms are Rs 1300/2100.

The *Clarks Shiraz Hotel* (361-421, fax 361-428) has a swimming pool and large gardens. There is a good choice of rooms starting at $80/90.

The new *Novotel Agra* (368-282), Fatehbad Rd, has a lawn and swimming pool. Rooms are $40/75.

Where To Eat

Zorba the Buddha, Gopi Chand Shivhare Road, run by the Rajneesh people, is one of the better restaurants in India. It is a recommended place, but the prices are higher than normal. It is open from 12 noon to 3 pm and 6 to 9 pm.

The *Dasaprakash Restaurant*, by Meher Cinema, around the corner from the Hotel Agra Ashok, is a good South Indian restaurant open for lunch and dinner.

Travel

Air Indian Airlines flies to Delhi (40 minutes, $55) and Khajuraho ($55) with a connection to Varanasi ($80). The Indian Airlines office (360-948) is at the Clarks Shiraz Hotel. It is open daily from 10 am to 1.15 pm and 2 to 5 pm. There is also an office for Lufthansa and Jet Air at the Clarks Shiraz.

Train There are six train stations in Agra. **Agra Cantt Station**, in the southwest, is the most convenient for most hotels. The best station to get a train to Rajasthan is **Agra Fort Station**, where trains depart for various places in Rajasthan, including **Jaipur** (Agra Fort-Jaipur Express #2921, 5 pm, 5 hr). The station before this, Agra City Station, is a good distance from town. Rickshaw drivers may try to persuade you to get off there, so they can charge you a high fare to get to a hotel.

There are many trains from **Delhi** to Agra. One of the best trains to take from Delhi is the fully air-conditioned Shatabdi Express #2002 (2 hr), which departs from Delhi at 6.15 am. The Shatabdi Exp #2001 returns from Agra at 8.15 pm, arriving in Delhi two hours later at 10.25 pm. The Taj Express leaves at 7.15 am from the Nizamuddin Station. It arrives in Agra at 10.15 am. It returns from Agra the same day at 6.45 pm and arrives in Delhi at 9.45 pm. To see the sites in Agra, you can get a tour bus at the station that brings you back in time to get a train back to Delhi at night.

There are 12 trains daily to **Mathura**. There are direct trains to Varanasi, Goa, Thiruvananthapuram (Trivandrum, 51 hr), Calcutta via Patna (30 hr), Bombay (29 hr, Punjab Mail #1038), and Madras (35-40 hr). To get to Khajuraho, you first take a train to Jhansi (at least 3 hr) and then a bus to Khajuraho (5 hr).

At Agra Cantt Station, there are only a limited number of tourist quota seats to Varanasi, so it is best to book a ticket as far in advance as possible.

Bus Buses usually depart from the **Idgah bus stand**, near Agra Cantt railway station. Rajasthan Roadways buses can and should be booked in advance at the station. Deluxe buses leave from in front of the Seetal Lodge on Ajmer Rd, close to the Idgah bus station. There is a booking office for deluxe buses in the lodge. There are deluxe buses every hour to Jaipur. There are buses to Delhi (hourly, 5-6 hr via Mathura), Gwalior (5 daily, 3½ hr), a morning bus to Lucknow (9 hr) and Khajuraho (5 am, 12 hr). It is better to get the Shatabdi Express train to Jhansi (3 hr) and then a five-hour bus to Khajuraho, rather than taking the direct bus to Khajuraho.

Buses to and from Mathura, onwards to Delhi, also depart from **Agra Fort Bus Stand**, just west of the fort. The buses to Mathura leaving from Idgah bus station are slightly better than the ones from Agra Fort bus stand.

Fatehpur Sikri

This was the temporary capital of Emperor Akbar, of the Moghul Empire, between 1570 to 1586. It was deserted because of lack of water. It is 40 km west of Agra. It is a perfectly preserved deserted city. The tour buses stop only for an hour here. You can get a bus from Agra's Idgah bus station to here, which takes about an hour. If you have bags you can leave them at the bus station restaurant.

Practicalities

Shree Tourist Guest House, Dargah Gali, near the bus stand, is a basic place. The *Maurya Rest House*, Buland Darwaza, is a little more up-market. The government run *Gulistan Tourist Complex*, Agra Rd, is a comfortable mid-range place.

There are buses every half hour from Agra (1 hr) between 5.45 am to 6.30 pm.

Runkata

About ten km from Agra on the way

to Delhi is Runkata. The town is named after Renuka, the wife of Jamadagni. The **ashram of Jamadagni**, the father of **Parasurama,** is said to have been here. Maharaja Sahasrabahu (Kartaviryarjuna) came here while hunting in the forest. After he and his men were sumptuously fed, the king asked the sage how he was able to feed them so well. Jamadagni told the king that this was possible because he had a Kamadhenu cow, which could fulfill all desires. The king then stole the cow. When Parasurama, the son of Jamadagni, found out about this, he fought with the king and his men. He killed the king and got back the Kamadhenu cow. For killing all these men, the sage requested his son to go off and do penance.

There is a temple here on a hill near the Yamuna with deities of Jamadagni and Renuka. At the bottom of the hill are temples of Laksmi-Narayana and Parasurama.

NAIMISARANYA

This is where the *Srimad Bhagavatam* was spoken. It is said that a pilgrimage to Badrinath and Kedarnath is incomplete without a visit to Naimisaranya. In the *Mahabharata* it is said, "Anyone who fasts, prays, and attains perfection at Naimisaranya finds happiness in all the worlds." According to the *Varaha Purana*, by performance of *yajna* (sacrifice) at this place, the strength of demonic people is curtailed. Therefore Brahmins prefer Naimisaranya for such sacrificial performances.

When Lord Brahma contemplated a great wheel that would span the entire universe, the wheel's center was at Naimisaranya. Naimisaranya has a *parikrama* (circumambulation) path of 16 km, in which all the sacred places in In-

dia are believed to be located.

Lord Balarama, Dadhici Muni, the Pandavas, Lord Nityananda, and Ramanujacarya all came here. The Pandavas are said to have come here when they were in exile. This is the place where the demigods came to ask Dadhici for his body, to be able to create a weapon, to be able to kill the demon Vrittrasura. Lord Rama is said to have performed sacrifice here for killing Ravana.

It is said that if you bathe in Chakratirtha Kund and make an offering to the presiding deity, Lalita, on a full moon day that falls on a Monday, you will wash away all the sins committed in a lifetime. Whoever bathes in Cakra-tirtha Kund on the twelfth lunar day attains the abode of Vishnu, even if he has committed the worst sins. About 10,000 people come for this. Lalita Devi, the presiding female deity of Naimisaranya is said to grant fulfillment of desires.

Information

It takes about two or three hours to see the major places here. I hired a guide for Rs 100 for the two hours. He did not speak very good English, but he knew all the places I wanted to go to. They would have been difficult to find without him, as almost no one there spoke English and the places are spread out.

If you would like to walk around Chakra-tirtha, which is what most of the pilgrims do when they come here, make sure that you bring some bathing gear.

Chakra Tirtha Kund

At the junction of Dvapara and Kaliyuga, 80,000 sages headed by Saunaka Rsi wanted to perform a sacrifice to hold off the effects of the oncoming age of Kali. They asked Lord Brahma where they should hold the sacrifice, and he told them he would send his disc to the earth and they should perform the sacrifice where it hits. It struck the earth at Naimisaranya. The disc passed through the earth at this spot, Chakra-tirtha.

The *Bhagavata Purana* says there is no holy place on earth that compares to this one.

Chakra-tirtha is said to be the center of the universe. It is said that the huge sweet water spring that marks the location of Chakra-tirtha has no bottom. The British wanted to disprove this as mythology, so they brought a cable and attempted to find the bottom. After more than 1000 metres (3200 ft) they ran out of cable and gave up.

In the *Vayaviya Tantra* it is said that Brahma contemplated a great wheel that could enclose the universe. The hub of this great circle is found at Naimisaranya.

Vyasa Gaddi

Close to Chakra-tirtha is where Vedavyasa is said to have divided the *Vedas* into four parts and written the *Puranas*. There is a big banyan tree said to be over 5000 years old and the place where Vyasa sat. In the temple there is a deity of Vyasadeva.

Hanuman Garhi (Panch Pandava)

There is an 18-foot self-manifested Hanuman deity here. In the *Ramayana* it says that Ravana captured Rama and Laksmana and kept them in Patalaloka at the bottom of the universe. Hanuman came and rescued them. When he came back to earth he arrived at Naimisaranya. There is a deity of Hanuman, with Rama on one shoulder and Laksmana on the other. Pilgrims buy big sweets and put them in his mouth.

Panch Pandava is a temple dedicated to the Pandavas.

Suta Gadi

This is where Suta Goswami sat while instructing the sages, headed by Saunaka, 5,000 years ago. He spoke the *Srimad Bhagavatam* here.

This is the place where Lord Balarama killed Romaharshana Suta for not standing and paying homage to Him when He came to Naimisaranya. Balarama then decided that the son of Romaharshana, Ugrasrava Suta, should recite the *Puranas* in his place. This is mentioned in the *Srimad Bhagavatam*.

Other Places

There is a **Gaudiya Math Temple** here that was opened by Bhaktisiddhanta Goswami. The Deities are Radha-Vinoda Vihari and Lord Caitanya.

There is the **Narada Deva Temple** with 108 altars and the **1008 Siva-linga Temple**, containing copies of the four *Vedas* and *Puranas*, including *Srimad Bhagavatam* (*Bhagavata Purana*). There is small temple of the Ramanuja-sampradaya.

Where To Stay and Eat

You would normally come here for a day trip from either Lucknow or Sitapur. It is best to bring your own water, as I did not see a place that sold water or cold drinks. There is a decent basic government bungalow here, which usually does not have electricity.

Travel

Naimisaranya is situated on the bank of the Gomati River about 80 km northwest of Lucknow and 60 km from Sitapur. To get here you would normally go first to Lucknow or Sitapur.

From Lucknow there are regular buses (3 hr) from the **Kasierbagh Bus Stand**. It could be a good idea to take a taxi to

Naimisaranya from Lucknow, as the bus trip is long and painful. It takes at least 3 hours each way for the bus alone, plus waiting for the bus and taking two 8 minute rickshaws that have no seats. You can also take a passenger train from Lucknow to Sitapur, and then get a bus to Naimisaranya from there. This complete trip would take four or five hours one way.

There are regular buses to and from Sitapur (2 hr). The bus stand in Naimisaranya is about an eight minute rickshaw ride from Cakra-tirtha. The bus stand is a little off the road.

LUCKNOW

Population: 1,700,000, STD Code 0522

Lucknow is the capital of Uttar Pradesh. It used to be the capital city of the Nawabs of Oudh (Avadh), Muslim rulers who controlled a part of north-central India after the decline of the Moghul Empire.

In 1856 the British annexed Oudh, exiling the then Nawab Wajid Ali Shah with an annual pension of 120,000 pounds. The annexation was one of the reasons for the Indian Uprising in 1857, in which the British residents held out in the Residency. After 87 days Sir Henry Havelock broke through to relieve the besieged British, only to be surrounded again for two more months. The hole-marked ruins of the Residency and the mausoleums of the Nawabs are interesting tourist sites here.

Lucknow can be used as a base to get to **Naimisaranya**.

Information

The **tourist office** (242-144), 10/4 Station Rd, is down an alley, opposite the Hotel Kohinoor. You can get tourist information at the Hotel Gomti from **UP Tours**, which runs a half-day tour of the city starting at 8.30 am.

Universal Bookseller, 82 Hazratganj, and British Bookshop, opposite Universal, are good bookshops.

The Residency

The Residency, built in 1800 for the British residents, was where some of the most dramatic events of the Indian Uprising in 1857 took place. The Residency has been kept the same as when the final relief arrived in the form of Sir Colin Campbell and his men on November 17. The walls are scarred by cannon shots. In the cellars you can see where many of the women and children lived.

There is a cemetery where 2,000 men, women, and children were buried during the siege. It is open from 9 am to 5.30 pm.

Where to Stay – Lower

Most of the hotels have 24 hour checkout. The *railway retiring rooms* are the best value in the station area. Dorm beds are Rs 25 and double rooms range from Rs 75 to Rs 150. Many of the hotels in the area can be very noisy.

The *Mohan Hotel* has a range of cheaper rooms ranging from Rs 100/150 and dorm beds for Rs 50. The *Hotel Mayur*, opposite the station, has rooms for Rs 130/150 and Rs 300/350 with A/C. It is not a good value.

On the way to the Hazratganj area from the station is the *Deep Hotel* (236-521), which has rooms for Rs 150/200 and Rs 300/380 with A/C. The nearby *Hotel Raj* is about the same.

Many of the cheaper hotels are in the Hazratganj area. The *Chowdhury Lodge* (241-911), 3 Vidhan Sabha Marg, down an alley by the GPO, has singles for Rs 75, with bath for Rs 140, and a room with an air-cooler for Rs 160/200. It is a popular place with good valued nice rooms. The *Hotel Ram-Krishna* has air-cooled rooms for Rs 140/185.

The *Baba Tourist Lodge* (54357), by the Charbagh Railway Station, is a clean, nice place with a range of cheaper rooms.

Capoors (243-958, 234-023), 52 Hazratganj, has good rooms with hot water for Rs 200/275 and A/C rooms for Rs 500. It is a suggested place.

The *Avadh Lodge* (282-861), 1 Ram Mohan Rai Marg, is an atmospheric old place with big rooms, but it is showing its age. It is in a quiet area of town. The rooms are Rs 175/225 to Rs 325/400.

The popular *Hotel Elora* (231-307), in the center of town at 3 Lalbagh, has rooms for Rs 175/225 and Rs 350/400. It is a good value.

Where To Stay – Middle and High

The UP Tourism *Hotel Gomti* (234-708), 6 TB Sapru Marg, has large rooms for Rs 275/300 to Rs 600/700. The *Hotel Kohinoor* (232-715), a km from the railway station, has modern, pleasant, clean rooms for Rs 500/700 with A/C.

The *Charans Hotel* (247-219), 16 Vidhan Sabha Marg, is a mid-range place with a selection of rooms for Rs 220/290 and A/C rooms for Rs 350/425. The *Deep Avadh* (236-521), Aminabad Rd, close to the station, is a new modern place with rooms for Rs 250/300 and A/C rooms for Rs 400/450.

The *Carlton Hotel* (244-021) Shah Najaf Rd, in the Hazratganj area, was once a palace and has a large relaxing garden. It is popular with foreigners and is often full. Rooms are Rs 350/450 to Rs 550/900 with A/C.

The *Hotel Clarks Avadh* (236-500, fax 236-507) is the best hotel in Lucknow. The rooms are Rs 1620/2400.

Where To Eat

The *Ritz Continental*, by the Hotel Ram-Krishna, is a recommended higher class place that serves Indian food and pizza. On the same road, right next to each other, at Vinay Palace, 11 Ashok Marg, are two high-class vegetarian restaurants, the *Viranjan* and *Ruchika*.

Travel

Air The Indian Airlines office (240-927, airport 256-327) is at the Hotel Clarks Avadh.

There are daily flights to Delhi and Varanasi, three flights a week to Calcutta (Mon, Wed, Fri) via Patna and three flights a week to Bombay (Tue, Thu, Sat).

Train There are two main stations, next to each other in the Charbagh area— Lucknow and Lucknow Junction which is mainly metre-gauge There are regular trains to Delhi (7 to 9 hr). There are trains to Gorakhpur (6 hr), Bombay (30 hr), Calcutta (23 hr), Faizabad (3 hr), Allahabad (4½ hr), and Varanasi (7 hr). There are overnight trains to Haridwar (13 hr) and Agra (7 hr).

Bus There are two bus stations— **Kaiserbagh**, which is in the center of town and **Charbagh**, which is near the railway stations.

To get to Naimisaranya, you get a three-hour local bus from Kaiserbagh Bus Stand. From Kaiserbagh there are buses to Faizabad (for Ayodhya, 3 hr), Delhi (12 hr), Gorakhpur (7 hr), and Sunauli (11 hr).

From the Charbagh station there are early morning buses to Varanasi (9 hr) and evening buses to Agra (10 hr). Buses also go to Allahabad (6 hr) and Kanpur (2 hr).

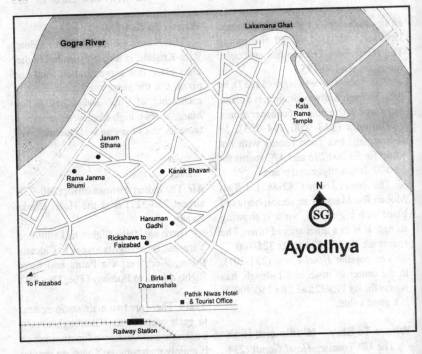

Sitapur

Sitapur is located about 60 km east of Naimisaranya and 100 km north of Lucknow. It is a possible city to stay at while going to Naimisaranya. Sitapur is one of those towns that really has nothing in it, and you would only use it as a stopover. At least Lucknow is a little interesting.

There is the *Mayur Hotel* here. It takes about two hours by local bus to get to Naimisaranya.

To get to Lucknow by local train takes between two and a half to four hours, as the train is often delayed.

AYODHYA

Population: 41,000

Lord Rama was born and had many of His pastimes here. It is a very holy city and is an important pilgrimage site. It is said to have once had a perimeter of 96

miles and was the capital of Koshala. It is on the banks of the **Gogra (Ghaghara or Saryu) River**, bathing in which is supposed to destroy even the sin of killing a Brahmin.

Ayodhya is 6 km from the town of Faizabad, about 150 km due east of Lucknow, and 200 km northwest of Varanasi.

The **UP Tourist Office** is by the railway station at the Pathik Niwas Saket Tourist Bungalow.

Janmabhoomi

Rama Janma Bhoomi is where Lord Rama was said to have taken birth. There is a small Lord Rama Temple here. At this location there used to be the Babri Mosque, which was constructed in the 15th century by the Moghuls. The mosque was destroyed in 1992, and at the present time there are plans to built a grand Rama Temple here.

There is a heavy security check here, they even ask to see your passport. They search you thoroughly, even worse than at an airport. You are not supposed to bring even a pen in with you. A steady stream of pilgrims come here each day.

Guptar Ghat

At Guptar Ghat there are some nice temples, and nearby there is a nice park. *Gupta* means disappearance. It is said that Rama left His body at this place. There are a few nice temples here, one called Chakra Harji Vishnu and Gupta Harji, and another called Raja Mandir. There are many Deities in the **Chakra Harji Vishnu Temple**, including what appears to be a very old carved Chakra Harji Vishnu Deity. There is also an imprint of Sri Rama's feet here. Guptar Ghat is located about 20 minutes by rickshaw from the bus station in Faizabad. You have to negotiate a price with the rickshaw-wala to take you there and back, plus waiting time, as few people come here.

Places To See

There are over 100 temples in Ayodhya. **Janma Sthana** is where Lord Rama was said to have been brought up.

There is a popular temple dedicated to Hanuman called **Hanuman-gadhi**. It is located right by the main road where the tempos from Faizabad stop. **Kanak Bhavan**, which is an interesting temple, and **Kala Rama Temple**, by the river, both have Deities of Sita-Rama.

There is a nice area by the river surrounding **Laksman Ghat**. Laksman, the brother of Rama, is said to have bathed at Laksman Ghat.

Vasistha Kund is a temple with a small round *kund* like a well.

Rama is said to have performed a *yajna* (sacrifice) at **Treta Ka Mandir**. There are Sita-Rama Deities in this temple.

Kaushalya, the mother of Rama, is said to have established the **Kshireswara Nath Temple** for Sita.

Bharata Kund, at Nandigram, 20 km from Ayodhya, is said to be the place where Bharata ruled while Rama was in exile for 14 years.

A half km north of Janmabhoomi is **Swarga Dwara**, or **Ram Ghat**, which is an important bathing ghat.

Where To Stay – Ayodhya

The *Pathik Niwas Saket* (05273-2007), next to the rail station, is a good simple place run by the UPTDC. It has rooms for Rs 90/110 and Rs 275/350 for an air-con room. It is the best place to stay in Ayodhya. There are also simple dharamshalas, such as the one at the *Kanak Mandir*, which has simple rooms for Rs 20, and the *Birla Dharamshala*.

Where To Stay – Faizabad

Population: 190,000, STD Code 0527.

You can also stay in the city of Faizabad, which is just 6 km away from Ayodhya and has better facilities. There are three places on a side street by the Moti Bagh (downtown) area in Faizabad. The *Abha Hotel*, Moti Bagh, has good rooms with hot water for Rs 110/130. For the price, it is a nice place and is suggested. The *Hotel Priya*, which has rooms for Rs 60/80, and the *Hotel Amber* are cheaper places, but not as nice.

The *Hotel Alka Raja*, Rekabganj area, is a decent place that has rooms with bath for Rs 100/150.

The best place in Faizabad is the *Hotel Shane Avadh* (813-586), Civil Lines, by the bus stand, a little outside of town.

It has rooms for Rs 125/150 and Rs 185/225 for a deluxe room. The A/C rooms are Rs 350/400. The rooms on the ground floor are noisy, as noise carries from the lobby, so it is best to stay upstairs.

Next door is the equally good *Hotel Tirupati* (813-231), which has rooms for Rs 200/250 and Rs 325/400 with A/C. The front rooms of both these hotels are noisy, as they are on a very busy street. Both of these hotels are good places to stay.

Where To Eat

Because Ayodhya is a holy place, meat, fish, or eggs cannot be sold in the town. The only real restaurant I saw in town was at the *Pathik Niwas Saket Guest House*, by the railway station in Ayodhya. It is a simple *thali* type place with almost no business. There are a few simple restaurants and street stands in town. As far as I could tell, there are no pure-veg restaurants in the city of Faizabad.

Faizabad to Ayodhya There are many buses and tempos going the 6 km between these two towns for Rs 3. You get the tempos in downtown Faizabad, at the Gudari Bazaar Crossing.

Travel

Ayodhya is located just 6 km from the city of Faizabad, so getting to Faizabad is the same as Ayodhya. It is usually more convenient to travel to Faizabad and from there go to Ayodhya. Ayodhya is on your way to Nepal from Varanasi or Allahabad.

Air The closest airports are in Lucknow (135 km) and Varanasi (190 km).

Train Faizabad is three hours from both Varanasi and Lucknow by train on a broad gauge railway line. From Faizabad trains depart to Lucknow, Haridwar, Varanasi, Calcutta, Gaya, Delhi, Ujjain and Ahmedabad.

From Ayodhya to Varanasi two trains are available—the Farakka Exp #3884 (11 am, 6 hr, Tues, Thu, Fri, Sun) and the Saryu Yamuna Exp #4650 (9.12 am, 3½ hr, Mon, Wed, Sat). There is a local train between Faizabad and Ayodhya.

Bus From Faizabad there are many buses to Lucknow (3 hr), Allahabad (5 hr), and Gorakhpur (3 hr). There is an early morning direct bus to Sunauli, for Nepal, from the Faizabad bus station. The bus station in Faizabad is located a few km from downtown and about 8 km from Ayodhya.

Gorakhpur

Population: 600,000, STD Code 0551

One may come here because it is the closest major rail junction to the Nepal border, or it may be used as a base to get to **Kushinagar** (53 km), where Buddha left his body. Gorakhpur is named after a Shaivite yogi, Gorakhnath. It is also known for being the home of **Geeta Press**, which is a huge publisher of Hindu religious literature. Gorakhpur is 230 km north of Varanasi.

Information

There are **tourist offices** at Park Rd and the railway station. An **Indrail Pass** can be purchased at the railway station with foreign currency.

Be careful of the ticket touts (commission agents) at the train and bus stations. Their through tickets to Kathmandu are not always reliable and cost two to four times more than doing it yourself. Also you are stuck with what they get for you, rather than going at your own pace and arranging it yourself, which is easily done. There is absolutely no reason to buy a bus ticket to Kathmandu from them. They are total rip-offs. During the high seasons, however, they can be useful to get you a hard-to-get train ticket and to change Nepali rupees.

You can **change money** at the State Bank of India on Bank Rd.

Where To Stay

To catch the 5 am bus to Sunauli it is convenient to stay at a hotel across from the train station. The *retiring rooms* at the station have dorm beds for Rs 35, standard rooms for Rs 75/110, and A/C room for Rs 135/225. They are recommended if you plan to catch an early morning train.

The *Modern Hotel Raj* and *Hotel Gupta* both have very basic rooms with bath for about Rs 70/110. The *Standard Hotel* (336-439) is the best budget place with rooms for Rs 80/135.

The *Hotel Raj* has air-cooled rooms for Rs 150. The *Hotel Siddhartha* (334-976) has rooms for Rs 95/150 and Rs 250/300 with A/C.

The *Elora* (330-647) is one of the better hotels by the station. It has rooms for Rs 85/125 with bath and TV and Rs 250/325 with A/C.

Shalimar (337-502), Ghosh Company Chowkha, is a very good value budget place in the center of town. The *Ganges* (333-530), Tarang Cinema Crossing, is one of the best hotels in town with all the modern comforts.

The *Hotel Marina* (337-630), in the center of town, is a good place with rooms for Rs 140/175 and Rs 250 for a room with A/C and TV.

Nearby is the *Hotel President* (337-654), Golghar area, off the main road, which is the best place in town. The rooms are Rs 200/225 and Rs 325/425 with TV. Of these two places the Hotel Marina is a better value, with almost similar rooms.

Travel

Train Gorakhpur is an important railway junction. Trains to Delhi are the Vaishali Exp #2553 (5.40 pm, 14½ hr, 780 km) via Lucknow (5 hr, 278 km) and the Barauni-Amritsar Exp #5207 (12.45 pm, 17 hr). There are four trains daily to Varanasi that take between 6 and 9 hours. To Bombay is the Dadar Exp #1028 (via Allahabad and Varanasi, 4.30 am, 35 hr) and the Kushinagar Exp #1016 (7 pm, 30 hr). There is a 1.30 pm train to Agra, which arrives at Agra Fort Station the next morning.

Bus There are three bus stands in Gorakhpur. From the bus stand near the train station (three minute walk from the station) there are regular buses to the border town of **Sunauli** (3 hr). To guarantee getting a morning bus to Kathmandu or Pokhara you have to get the 5 am bus from Gorakhpur. Private buses to Sunauli leave from in front of the train station. Travel agents offer through buses to Kathmandu. You still have to change buses at the border, and it is cheaper and more reliable to do it yourself. They often charge two to three times the normal price.

The buses to Kushinagar (1½ hr) depart from the bus stand by the train station.

Some buses to Varanasi (6½ hr) and all the buses to Lucknow, Patna, and Faizabad (right next to Ayodhya) leave from the Katchari bus stand, 1 km south of the train station. The main bus stand for Varanasi (6½ hr) is at Pedlleyganj, 2 km southeast of the train station.

Kushinagar

Kushinagar is 55 km east of Gorakhpur, not far from the Nepal border. This is said to be the place of **Lord Buddha's Mahaparinirvana**. He left his body at this place and His body was cremated here. There is a 50 foot high isolated brick *stupa*, called **Ramabhar Stupa**, on the west edge of the Ramabhar Tal, about 1.5 km from the main site. It is said to be the original **Mukutabandhana Stupa** that marked the spot of Lord Buddha's cremation. The **Kunwarkakot Matha**, about a mile and a half west of Ramabhar Stupa, is a temple with a huge seated Buddha.

The **Nirvana Stupa** dates back to 413-55 AD and was rebuilt in 1927 by the Burmese Buddhists. Near this *stupa* is a huge reclining figure of Buddha in the **Mahaparinirvana Temple**.

There are also some modern international temples here. There are temples built by Buddhists from Tibet, Japan, Burma, and China.

Practicalities

The *International Buddhist Guest House* is a nice budget place. The *UP State Tourist Bungalow*, the *Pathik Nivas*, has rooms for Rs 175/225. You can stay at some of the monasteries for a small donation. There is an ITDC hotel called *Ashok Traveler's Lodge*.

There are frequent buses to and from Gorakhpur (1½ hr, 55 km west). Buses to Varanasi take eight hours. The shared taxis and jeeps to and from Gorakhpur are not as comfortable as the buses.

Sunauli

Sunauli is a very small Indian border town next to Nepal. It is about 25 km from Lumbini, Nepal, the birthplace of Buddha.

Practicalities

The UP State *Hotel Niranjana* (4901) is a good clean place with rooms for Rs 50/75 and Rs 15 for a dorm bed.

There are buses to Gorakhpur (3 hr) every half hour between 5 am and 7 pm. There are directs buses to Varanasi (9 hr) in the early morning and evening. There are also buses to Lucknow (11 hr) and Allahabad (12 hr).

ALLAHABAD (PRAYAGA)

Population: 850,000, STD Code 0532

Allahabad is one of the oldest cities in India. It is located 135 km west of Varanasi, at the confluence of India's two most important rivers—the Yamuna and Ganges. It is 585 km southeast of Delhi and 160 km south of Ayodhya. The main spiritual reason for coming here is to take bath in the **Sangam,** or confluence (where rivers meet), of the Yamuna, Ganges, and the underground Saraswati Rivers. It is one of the major pilgrimage sites in all of India.

The **Prakrista Yajna** was performed here by Lord Brahma. That is how it received its ancient name, Prayag. Allahabad is also called **Tirtha-Raja**, king of all holy places. It is said that Lord Rama visited Allahabad when He was in exile.

Sri Caitanya instructed Rupa Gosvami in Allahabad at Dasasvamedha Ghat.

Information

The **tourist office** (601-873) is at the UP Tourist Bungalow, 35 Mahatma Gandhi Rd (MG Road), by the bus stand. There are a few decent bookstores on Mahatma Gandhi Rd, close to the Hotel Harsh. Right next to each other are the Universal Book Store and Chugh Publication, which also has Universal on their sign.

Sangam Bath

This is where the Ganges, Yamuna, and Saraswati meet. This place is considered to be the most important holy bathing place in India. The muddy-colored Ganges is shallower and more rapid. The Yamuna is bluer and deeper. The most auspicious time to bathe in the Sangam is during **Kumbha-mela**. It is also especially auspicious to bathe here during the month of Magh (January-February).

To get to the place where you get the boat to the Sangam is a Rs 20 bicycle-rickshaw ride from the downtown area. Ask to go to the Sangam, which is on the same side of the Fort as the Bare Hanuman Temple.

Most people take a boat out to the middle of the river and bathe from a platform there. You can also walk from the road and bathe on the shore. There are many boats here and the boat *ghat* here is closest to the Sangam. You can take a boat with other people that will cost Rs 6 to Rs 20 per person, depending on how many people you go with. A private boat to the Sangam is Rs 50 to Rs 100.

When you reach the Sangam, your boat docks on a little platform in the middle of the river. There is a good chance that a *pandit* (priest) will jump on your boat and start doing *puja* (worship) for you and your family. He will then expect anywhere from Rs 10 to Rs 500, to who knows what. My understanding is that there is a small docking fee at these platforms, from Rs 1 to Rs 50 depending on who you are (how rich you look). The boat ride and bath takes about 40 minutes to an hour, and it is an enjoyable experience.

You can also get a boat from Saraswati Ghat and the other *ghats* along the river, but they are much further away and therefore more expensive. This is the way to go, if you want a nice peaceful boat ride.

Kumbha-mela

Kumbha-mela is held here every 12 years. It also takes place in three other holy places in India every 12 years—Haridwar, Ujjain and Nasik. The Kumbha-mela in Prayag (Allahabad) is considered especially auspicious. It draws about 15 million people and is the largest attended event in the world. This is a very interesting event.

There are several especially auspicious bathing days. A huge temporary city is created for the millions of pilgrims that arrive for the most auspicious bathing days.

Every 6 years there is an **Ardha-mela** (half mela), which draws about 7 million people. Each year there is a regular Mela during the month of Magha, January-February, which draws one or two million people. The next Kumbha-mela is January, 2001. One of the most auspicious bathing days is Amavasya, the new moon day.

Kumbha-mela is like a "Yogi Convention," where yogis, sadhus (saints), holy people, and pilgrims come from all over India. Many sadhus come from various holy places, the most remote forests, and mountain caves in the Himalayas. The most famous are the Naga Babas, Siva worshipers who are completely naked. They cover their bodies only with ash and wear their hair in dreadlocks.

On the most auspicious bathing days there is a big parade, and the bathing order is very strictly observed. Not only are there especially auspicious days, but there are especially auspicious times of the day to bathe, and people are willing to die to bathe at the most auspicious time. The

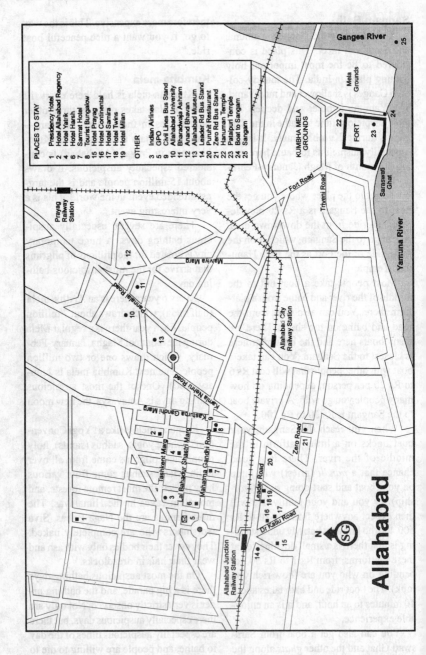

PLACES TO STAY

1 Presidency Hotel
2 Hotel Allahabad Regency
4 Hotel Yatrik
6 Hotel Harsh
7 Samrat Hotel
8 Tourist Bungalow
15 Hotel Prayag
16 Hotel Continental
17 Hotel Samira
18 Hotel Twins
19 Hotel Milan

OTHER

3 Indian Airlines
5 GPO
9 Civil Lines Bus Stand
10 Allahabad University
11 Bharadwaja Ashram
12 Anand Bhavan
13 Allahabad Museum
14 Leader Rd Bus Stand
20 Zero Rd Bus Stand
21 Purohit Restaurant
22 Hanuman Temple
23 Patalpuri Temple
24 Boat to Sangam
25 Sangam

Ganges River

Mela Grounds

KUMBHA MELA GROUNDS

FORT

Saraswati Ghat

Yamuna River

Fort Road

Triveni Road

Prayag Railway Station

Malviya Marg

Panniar Road

Allahabad City Railway Station

Kamla Nehru Road

Kasturba Gandhi Marg

Tashkent Marg

Lal Bahadur Shastri Marg

Mahatma Gandhi Road

Allahabad Junction Railway Station

Leader Road

Dr Katju Road

Zero Road

N

Allahabad

first to enter the water are the Naga Babas, who arrive dancing with enthusiasm. Then each different religious group enters the water in a prearranged order.

Hanuman Temple

Hanuman is in a reclining posture, a few feet below the ground, instead of his usual standing posture. It is said that every year the Ganges floods until it touches the sleeping Hanuman's feet and then it starts receding.

This temple is located by the Sangam side of the Fort and is a busy small temple open to non-Hindus. There are nice carvings on the nearby Sri Adi Shankara Temple, which has a Sri Tirupati Balaji Deity.

Fort

There is a huge fort built by Akbar in 1583, on the Yamuna River by the Sangam. Inside the fort there is a 35 ft high Ashoka pillar that dates back to 230 BC. The fort is in the control of the army, so unless you get advance written permission, you cannot enter the fort. It is a huge fort that cost 25 million rupees and took over 45 years to build.

Patalpuri Temple (Undying Tree)

It is located through a small doorway, in the wall of the fort, on the way to the boats that go to the Sangam. It is an underground temple with many different deities carved in stone.

The Akshayavata Tree is said to never die, even when the entire world is destroyed. It is located in the underground temple. The tree is on a deep niche, above an underground hole that is said to lead to the Triveni.

It is said that both Lord Rama and Prahlada visited this temple. This is an interesting temple

Bharadwaja Ashram

This ashram is mentioned in the *Ramayana*. Allahabad University now occupies the place where the ashram of Bharadwaja Rishi and his 10,000 disciples is said to have been located. There are the temples of Bharadwajeswara Mahadeva, Rishi Bharadwaja, and Kali here. It is said that Lord Rama and Sita visited this place when they began Their 14-year exile.

Anand Bhavan

This is the former home of the Nehru family, which includes: Motilal Nehru, Jawaharlal Nehru, India's first prime minister, Indira Gandhi, and Rajiv Gandhi. It is a beautiful house with many of the family's personal effects. You can also see the rooms where Mahatma Gandhi stayed and the place where he worked. It is open daily 9.30 am to 5 pm, except Monday.

Allahabad Museum

This interesting museum has many old archaeological treasures. It has an interesting ivory Krishna Arjuna on a carved sandalwood chariot in the Nehru collection. It is open 10.30 am to 4.30 pm and is closed on Mondays. You can get a free guided tour of the museum if you ask at the desk where you check-in your bags. It takes about an hour to see the whole place.

Sri Rupa Gaudiya Math

There is a Gaudiya Math temple, the Sri Rupa Gaudiya Math, on South Mallaca Street, in the Madhavapur area. This temple is by the Ganges River on the way to the Sangam from downtown. Srila Prabhupada took initiation here from Srila Bhaktisiddhanta Saraswati Maharaja.

Srila Prabhupada came to Allahabad in 1977 for Kumbha-mela and also in 1971 for Ardha Kumbha-mela.

Nearby Places

At **Ramchaura-Shringverpur** (40 km), on the bank of the Ganges, there is a platform called **Ram Chabutara**, which marks the spot where Lord Rama is supposed to have stayed before going to the forest in exile. It is said that before Lord Rama crossed the Ganges here, the boatman washed His feet. There are also temples dedicated to Panchmukhi (five-faced) Hanuman and Shring Rishi.

Lakshagriha (45 km) is said to be the place where the *house of lac* of the Pandavas was located. A big mound marks this spot.

Where To Stay – Lower

South of the Allahabad Junction Station there are some cheaper places, which are convenient if you have to catch a train. The *Hotel Samira* is a cheap place with rooms for Rs 70/100 with bath. The *Hotel Prayag* has rooms for Rs 90/110 to Rs 90/160 with bath. The *Hotel Continental*, which is most likely the best of these hotels, has clean rooms with bath for Rs 100/120 and A/C rooms for Rs 250/300.

The *Hotel Tepso*, by the railway station, has rooms for Rs 60 and deluxe rooms with bath for Rs 170/200. The *Raj Hotel* (54684), 6 Johnstonganj, about a 20 minute walk from the railway station, has rooms with bath for Rs 80/100 and with A/C for Rs 250.

The *UP Tourist Bungalows* (601-440), 35 MG Marg, Civil Lines, next to the bus station, is a good place to stay as long as you do not get a room on the bus station side or front side of the hotel, as they can be noisy. Rooms are Rs 175/

225 and Rs 400/450 with A/C. It has dorm beds for Rs 20. For a middle income hotel, it is recommended.

If you like older places, the Hotel Harsh (622-197) is the place for you. It has large rooms with high ceilings, but is totally run-down. Rooms are Rs 120/150, but they are not a good value.

The *Hotel Twins* (54554), 53 Leader Road, has rooms for Rs 160/175 with bath and Rs 325/375 with A/C. Also on Leader Road is the *Hotel Milan* (56021), which has rooms with bath and windows in the hall for Rs 200/265 and Rs 340/400 with A/C. Leader Road can be a little noisy, as it is a busy street.

Where To Stay – Middle & High

There are no luxury hotels in town. The *Samrat Hotel* (604-888, fax 604-987) is near the intersection of Mahatma Gandhi Rd and Sardar Patel Marg. It has rooms for Rs 500/600 and Rs 600/800 with A/C.

The popular *Hotel Yatrik* (601-713), 33 Sardar Patel Marg, has rooms for Rs 400/450 and Rs 650/800 with A/C. It has a pool and garden.

The two-star Hotel *Allahabad Regency* (601-519), 16 Tashkent Marg, Civil Lines, has a pool and comfortable rooms with A/C for Rs 575/700. It is a good value.

The comfortable two-star *Presidency Hotel* (623-308, fax 623-897) is north of Civil Lines in a quiet area. It has A/C rooms for Rs 600/675. It has a swimming pool and is popular, so it is best to book a room here in advance.

Where To Eat

The *Purohit Restaurant* is just off Leader Road in the Johnstonganj area, in the south of town. It is a good clean looking place with reasonable prices.

Travel

Air There are flights from Bamrauli Airport (15 km west) to Delhi, three days a week. The Indian Airlines office (624-105) is at Tashkent Marg, Civil Lines. Taxis from the airport to downtown are about Rs 150.

Train Allahabad has four railway stations. The main train station is **Allahabad Junction**, in the center of town. Allahabad is on the broad gauge route between Delhi and Calcutta, so many express trains stop here. There are express trains to Delhi (10 hr, 2 daily), Calcutta (15 hr, 3 daily), Lucknow (3½ hr), Bombay (24 hr), and Satna (4 hr) for Khajuraho.

Most trains for Varanasi leave from the **Allahabad City Station** at Ram Bagh, which is a metre gauge line. The 135 km trip takes three or four hours.

Bus There are buses to **Varanasi** that take 3½ hours from the Civil Lines (MG Marg) bus stand, by the Tourist Bungalow. There are also buses to Gorakhpur (8 hr), Agra, Sunauli (9 hr), and Faizabad (4½ hr) for Ayodhya. At 3 pm there is a deluxe bus to Lucknow (5 hr).

Buses to Jhansi and Satna leave from the Leader Rd bus stand, which is besides the railway station. Buses to western destinations such as Lucknow, Kanpur, Agra, and Delhi leave and arrive here.

Buses to **Citrakut** depart from the Zero Road bus stand. Beside the government buses to Citrakut you can get higher quality private buses. You can ask at the local travel agents, or there is a good chance someone will approach you with an offer to take a private bus to Citrakut when you arrive at the Zero Road bus stand. Buses to Satna and Mahoba also leave from here.

CHITRAKUT (CITRAKOOT)

Lord Rama and Sita are said to have stayed in the forest here during Their 14 year exile. Chitrakut is by the border of Uttar Pradesh and Madhya Pradesh, due south of Lucknow. It is 132 km south of Allahabad.

It is a nice peaceful place at which to stop for a day or two while going between Khajuraho and either Allahabad or Varanasi via Satna. This town is one of the nicer towns in India.

Lord Rama and Sita lived here for 11 years of Their 14 year exile. *Citra* literally means "beautiful" and *kut* means "mountain," so it means "the beautiful mountain."

Bharata, the brother of Rama, came to Chitrakut and begged Rama to return to Ayodhya, but Rama would not disobey His father's order. Rama stayed on **Kamadgiri**, which means the hill which can fulfill all desires.

Nearby lived the *sage* Atri and his wife Anusuya. Brahma, Vishnu, and Siva are said to have taken incarnations here. It is said that Anusuya made the Ganges appear as the **Mandakini River**, because holy water was needed for her husband's penance. Lord Rama would daily bathe in that river. Sita's footprints are said to be on the rocks at Janaki Kund, where Sita took bath.

There are over 30 temples in the town, and there are bathing *ghats* along the Mandakini River (also called Payasvini or Paisuni River).

Chitrakut is an extremely peaceful place. It is a place that is untouched by the foreign tourist trail and is relatively hassle free. On a major festival day over 100,000 people are said to come to Chitrakut. This place is mainly visited for the day by poorer Indian pilgrims. Every day busloads of pilgrims come here.

Information

The UP tourist office is next to the UP Tourist Bungalow. They have no literature about Chitrakut in English, but they can be a little helpful. You can also get more useful tourist information at the Madhya Pradesh Tourist Bungalow and a brochure in English about the sites in the area.

How To Get Around Town

The central part of town is the Ramghat area by the Madhya Pradesh Tourist Bungalow. You can see the town in three sections. One is the Ramghat area. Then you can take an auto-rickshaw to both Hanuman Dhara and Kamadgiri Hill. In the morning there are buses leaving every half hour on Char Dhama that go to Janaki Kund, Sati Anusuya, Sphatik Shila, and Gupta Godavari. You get the bus about a hundred metres from the Madhya Pradesh Tourist Hotel. To get on the right bus you ask for the Char Dhama bus, which costs about Rs 25. Buses also go to Hanuman Dhara. You can also hire a jeep to take you to all these places.

Ramghat

Ramghat, the main bathing *ghat* in town, is located in the center of Chitrakut, on the banks of the Mandakini River. It is a peaceful *ghat* where you can take a tranquil boat ride.

Kamadgiri Hill

Kamadgiri Hill is also called old Chitrakut or the original Chitrakut. It is a forest-covered hill that is surrounded by a 5 km *parikrama* path, with temples all the way around the hill. Every day many people walk around the hill barefoot. Rama is said to have lived here, and it is therefore considered the embodiment of

Rama. One of the major temples here is the **Shree Kamatanath Temple**. The **Bharat Milap Temple** is located on the back side of the hill. It marks the spot where Bharat, the brother of Rama, is said to have tried to convince Rama to return to be king of Ayodhya.

Right after you past the Bharat Milap Temple there is a path that leads to **Laksman Pahadi**. On this hill Laksman is said to have maintained guard for Rama and Sita. There is a Laksman Temple on top of the hill.

Janaki Kund

This is a peaceful place, located 2 km upstream from Ramghat on the bank of the Mandakini River. Sita, who is also known as Janaki, the daughter of Janaka, is said to have bathed here. The Rama Janaki Raghuveer Temple is situated here. There is also the **Sankat Mochan Hanuman** deity here. You can reach this place by road or a 2 km boat ride from Ramghat.

Sphatik Shila

Sphatik Shila is a few km upstream from Janaki Kund, on the banks of the Mandakini River. There is a boulder here that is supposed to have the footprints of Rama on it. Sita was also supposed to have been pecked by Jayant, who was in the form of crow, while standing on this boulder.

Sati Anusuya

Sati Anusuya is upstream from Janaki Kund, about 16 km from the center of town. It is said that at this place **Atri Muni** and his wife, **Anusuya**, had their ashram with their three sons, who were incarnations of Brahma, Vishnu, and Siva. There is a temple here that has a deity of Anusuya swinging her three babies. There are also nice dioramas (statues), which tell the story of Atri Muni and Anusuya, but the captions are just in Hindi. There are many hungry monkeys at this place who will grab anything they see to eat.

Gupta Godavari

Gupta Godavari is about 18 km from the town. Located here are two caves. One is wide and high and has an entrance that is hard to enter. At the end of this cave is a small pond, which is said to be the same as the Godavari River. The other cave is long and narrow with water in it. Rama and His brother Laksmana are said to have held court here at the end of the cave.

Hanuman Dhara

There is a spring several hundred feet up the hillside, on the rock-face, that is said to have been made by Rama to relieve Hanuman when he returned after setting Lanka on fire. It is a hard walk up the hill, which has many monkeys on it. The **Panch Mukhi** (five-headed) **Hanuman Dhara** deity is on this hill. You get a great view of the Chitrakut town from here. Sita Rasoi (the kitchen of Sita) is on top of the hill here.

Bharata Koop

This is where Bharata, the brother of Rama, is said to have stored water collected from all the pilgrimage places in India. It is at an isolated place, about a half hour from town.

Where To Stay

The *Annapurna Hotel*, by Ramghat, has simple rooms for Rs 75/100 a night. The *Yatrika*, outside of town by Janaki Kund, also has simple rooms for about the same price. There are many simple cheap dharamshalas in town such as the *Pramod Van* Dharamshala. Many do not have beds.

The *Madhya Pradesh Tourist Hotel* (0519768/326), by the Satna bus stand in near Ram Ghat, is the best place to stay. Rooms here are Rs 150/175 a night. When I stayed here, there was a helpful manager. This place along with the *UP Tourist Bungalow* (0519768/219), Karbi Rd, Sitapur, which has rooms for Rs 225/300, are the nicest places in town to stay. The UP Tourist Bungalow also has dorm beds. The Madhya Pradesh Tourist Hotel is cheaper, more centrally located, and also quiet at night.

The *Shree Kamadgiri Bhawan*, on Ratnavali Marg, between the two Tourist Bungalows, is a nice place that has rooms with common bath for up to three people for Rs 75 and Rs 150 with attached bath.

The *Jaipuriya Hotel* is also a good place with rooms for about Rs 150.

Where To Eat

Being a holy place, no meat, fish, or eggs are sold in Chitrakut. There are restaurants at both the Madhya Pradesh and UP Tourist Bungalows. The *Madhya Pradesh Restaurant* has meat and eggs on the menu, but does not serve these items. The *Shree Kamadgiri Bhawan* has *thalis* for Rs 20. The *Jaipuriya Hotel* also has a restaurant, as does the *Annpurna Hotel*.

When I went to Citrakut there was **no bottled water** or cold drinks sold there. I asked the hotel manager where I was staying to have some water boiled for drinking.

Travel

Air The nearest airports are Khajuraho (175 km) and Varanasi (260 km). Neither is very easy to reach.

Train The closest train station is at **Chitrakoot (Chitrakut) Dhama Karvi** on the Jhansi-Manikpur main line about 10 km from Chitrakut. From there you can get a train to Allahabad, Delhi, Lucknow, Mathura and Varanasi. There is a 12.30 am train that goes to Allahabad and then onto Varanasi arriving in the morning. The Mahakosal Exp #1449 departs to Delhi (14 hr) via Mathura (11 hr) and Agra in the afternoon. The Mahakosal Exp #1450 departs from Mathura to Chitrakut.

Bus There are many buses going to Chitrakut from places in the area, including Allahabad, Satna, Mahoba, and Jhansi. The bus station is located next to the UP Tourist Bungalow, slightly north of town.

In Allahabad the buses to Chitrakut depart from the bus station on Zero Road. In the morning you can get direct luxury buses from private companies in the Zero Road area.

VARANASI (BENARES, KASHI)

Population: 1,000,000, STD Code 0542

Varanasi is said to be the oldest inhabited city in the world. There are supposed to be 2,000 temples in Varanasi. It is on the bank of the Ganges between Delhi (710 km) and Calcutta (680 km). It is 125 km east of Allahabad. Millions of pilgrims a year come to Varanasi. The name Varanasi most likely stems from the two rivers, Varana and Assi, which join the Ganges on the north and south borders of the city. Varanasi is a very fast-moving place and at times can seem unbelievable crowded. In the old part of the city there are numerous mazes of thin very crowded streets, which makes the place very interesting.

The city was originally called **Kashi,** or the city of lights. It is said that the first *jyotirlinga*, the fiery pillar of light, çame through the earth here and flared into the sky. Therefore Varanasi is also called Kashi, City of Light. Kashi is mentioned in the *Mahabharata, Ramayana, Srimad Bhagavatam,* and the *Puranas,* which date back 5000 years, as the foremost city of Siva. The Muslims gave it the name Benares. At independence, the old name, Varanasi, was given to the city again.

Many older people come to Varanasi to die and be burned at the burning *ghats* along the river. It is believed that anyone who dies in Varanasi attains *moksha* (liberation). It is said that being burned at Varanasi adds to the pious credits of someone, therefore many bodies are brought here to be cremated. Many widows come here to die.

Many saints and sages have come to Varanasi including Sri Caitanya Mahaprabhu, Lord Buddha, Sankaracharya, and Sri Ramanuja. Lord Caitanya met Sanatana Gosvami here and converted the Mayavadi Prakasananda Sarasvati and his followers here. He bathed at Panchaganga (Panchanada) Ghat.

For many it is one of the highlights of a trip to India to get on a boat at 6 am and see the city on the waters of the Ganges at sunrise. Six o'clock in the morning is the best time to visit the waterfront. It is a good idea to rent your own boat and not go with many other people.

Varanasi was looted numerous times by Muslim invaders beginning from the 11th century. Aurangzeb destroyed most of the temples during his reign. This is why most of the temples are not more than 300 years old. In 1669 the Bindu Madhava Vishnu Temple and the Siva Visvanath Temple were destroyed. Mosques were built in their place.

The Ganges, which normally flows southeast, reverses its course and flows north for a while at Varanasi, which is considered very auspicious. There is a five-mile *parikrama* path that goes around this sacred city. There are 81 bathing *ghats* and other holy *kunds,* or sacred tanks. It is said that it is important to bathe at Manikarnika, by the cremation *ghat.*

The three most important *ghats* are **Manikarnika, Dasaswamedha, and Pancha-ganga**. To bath at these three *ghats* is called **tri-tirthi yatra**. Also important are **Asi Sangam and Varana Sangam**. To bath in these five places is call **pancha-tirtha yatra**. You are supposed to bathe in these five *ghats* in a certain order. First you bathe in Asi Ghat, then Dasaswamedha Ghat, then the *ghat* by the Adi Kesava Temple near the Varana River, then Pancha-ganga, and then Manikarnika. After taking bath at these five places, most pilgrims then go for *darshan* of Visvanath, Annapurna, and Sakshi Vinayaka (the witnessing Ganesh). It is said that if you bathe in these five places, all in the same day and in this order, you will not get another material body. You can do *pancha-tirtha yatra* by boat, but it is better to do it by foot.

The **Panchakroshi road** goes around the city of Varanasi. Many pilgrims walk the 58 km around Varanasi starting at Manikarnika Ghat. They then walk to Asi Ghat and then proceed around the city. You are supposed to visit 108 shrines along the way. Following this procedure is said to be the same as circling the entire world.

The **Adi Keshava Vishnu Temple** is located where the Ganges meets the Varana River, in the north of town. Tulsi Das translated the *Ramayana* from Sanskrit into Hindi in Varanasi, and there is a temple in his honor.

Sarnath is 10 km away and is famous for where Buddha first preached about enlightenment. You can see all the principal places in Varanasi and Sarnath in two days, but it is not unusual for people to spend a week or two in Varanasi.

Getting Your Bearings

The city of Varanasi is on the west bank of the Ganges River. The tourist office and the big hotels are located in the Cantonment area. The roads are much wider here. The railway station is south of the Cantonment area and north of the old part of the city, about a twenty minute auto-rickshaw ride from either area.

The old section of the city by the river is where the bathing *ghats* and temples are located. The streets can be very narrow and crowded, so much so that a bike rickshaw cannot get by. The main bathing *ghat* is Dasaswamedha, right in the middle of the old part of the city.

Information

A good source of information is the **Tourist Office** at 15B, The Mall, in the Cantonment, by the Hotel de Paris. You can hire a guide there for either four or eight hours. There is an **Information Counter** at the airport. The **UP state tourist office** is located in the Tourist Bungalow at Parade Kothi and there is a good tourist counter at the railroad station. The **Bihar State Tourist Office** is at Englishiya Market, Sher Shah Suri Marg, Cantt.

Some good guide books about Varanasi are *Banaras,* by S N Mishra, *Kashi The City Luminous* by K Chandramouli and *Glimpse of Varanasi,* by K Jaycees.

I found a good knowledgeable guide for information about the temples and holy places in Varanasi named Shobhit Shankar, who is a priest at the Visvanath Temple. He lives on the same small alley

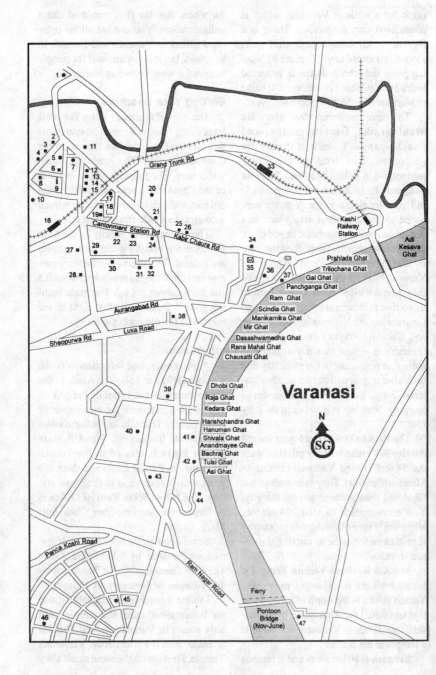

Grand Trunk Rd

Cantonment Station Rd

Kabir Chaura Rd

Aurangabad Rd

Luxa Road

Sheopurwa Rd

Panca Koshi Road

Ram Nagar Road

Kashi
Railway
Station

Adi
Kesava
Ghat

Prahlada Ghat
Trilochana Ghat
Gai Ghat
Panchganga Ghat
Ram Ghat
Scindia Ghat
Manikarnika Ghat
Mir Ghat
Dasashwamedha Ghat
Rana Mahal Ghat
Chausatti Ghat

Dhobi Ghat
Raja Ghat
Kedara Ghat
Harishchandra Ghat
Hanuman Ghat
Shivala Ghat
Anandmayee Ghat
Bachraj Ghat
Tulsi Ghat
Asi Ghat

Varanasi

N

SG

Ferry

Pontoon
Bridge
(Nov-June)

47

PLACES TO STAY		WHERE TO EAT	
2	Hotel Surya	34	Sindhi Restaurant
3	Clarks Varanasi	39	Sona Rupa
4	Ashok		
6	Tourist Dak Bungalow	**OTHER**	
8	Hotel de Paris		
11	Taj Ganges	1	Tempos to Sarnath
12	Hotel Vaibhav	5	TV Tower
13	Hotel Temples Town	7	Central Telegraph Office
14	Hotel Shalimer	9	Govt of India Tourist Office
15	Hotel India	10	Indian Airlines
18	Hotel Relax	16	Varanasi Junction Railway
19	Tourist Bungalow		Station
21	Pradeep Hotel	17	Bus Station
22	Hotel Avaneesh	20	Sanskrit University
23	Hotel Hindustan International	29	Bharat Mata Temple
24	Hotel Vaishal	33	City Railway Station
25	Hotel Natraj & Ajay	35	GPO
26	Hotel Gautam	36	Bus Stand
27	G M Guest House	37	Bindu Madhava Temple
28	Hotel Garden View	40	Vijaynagaram Palace
30	Hotel Varuna	42	Hanuman Temple
31	Hindusthan	43	Durga & Tulsi Manas
32	Pallavi		Temple
38	Sun Shiv Hotel	45	Bharat Kala Bhavan
41	Sandhya Guest House	46	New Visvanath Temple
44	Hotel Temple on Ganges	47	Ram Nagar Fort & Museum

as where the temple is located, at 35/15 Vishwanath Gali. I personally liked and trusted him, but I wouldn't let him do my shopping for me.

Conducted Tours

UPSRTC has a daily tour of the river, temples, and Benares Hindu University in the summer from 5.30 to 11.45 am and winter 6 am to 12.15 pm. They also have a tour to Sarnath and Ramnagar Fort daily from 2.30 to 6.25 pm in the summer and 2 to 5.55 pm in the winter. The bus starts at the Govt of India Tourist Office, at the Tourist Bungalow in the Mall.

Shopping

Varanasi is a good place to buy silks. You have to be careful, as many items sold as silk are not pure silk. It is also a good place to get musical instruments.

Visvanath Temple (Golden Temple)

This present temple dedicated to Lord Siva was built by Rani Ahalyabai Holkar of Indore in 1776. The old temple was destroyed by Aurangzeb in 1669. It is called the golden temple because of the gold plating put on the *shikharas* (roof over the altar) by Maharana Ranjeet Singh in 1835. Non-Hindus (non-Indians) are not allowed in the temple, and this is strictly enforced. The *linga* is on a golden altar. There has been a Siva temple at this site for over 1000 years. Beside the Siva-linga of Visvanath, there are many other shrines. To the left as one enters the temple is the Deity of Vishnu, who is supposed to be worshiped along with Visvanath.

Behind the temple is the **Jnana Vapi**, or the Wisdom Well, which is said to be the liquid form of enlightenment. It is said to have been in Varanasi before the Ganges came to this earth. Pilgrims give their *sankalpa*, or statement of intent, here before beginning their *pancha-tirthi yatra*.

Non-Hindus can look inside the temple through a hole in the wall, in the alley between the front of the temple and the Jnana Vapi.

You can see the roof of the temple from the roof of the Trimurti Guest House or some shops across the street from the temple for Rs 10.

Area Temples

Right outside the Golden Temple is the shrine of **Sanichar (Saturn)**, which is worshiped to get rid of misfortune.

A major temple, dedicated to **Annapurna**, is located in the same alley as the Visvanath Temple. *Anna* means "food," and *purna* means "who fills."

Dhundhiraj Ganesh is a small important Ganesh temple on Visvanath Lane, about a five-minute walk from the Visvanath Temple.

Sakshi Vinayaka is a Ganesh deity. *Sakshi* means "the witness." After finishing the Panch Kosi circuit, pilgrims come before this deity so that Ganesh can witness the completion of their pilgrimage.

When pilgrims visit Varanasi they register their arrival at the temple of

Bhairava. Bhairava is known as the policemen-magistrate and guardian protector of the city. Bhairava is the terrifying aspect of Lord Siva, who chopped off the fifth head of Brahma.

Benares Hindu University

This university was established at the beginning of the century and is famous for having an excellent Sanskrit school. It has over 150,000 rare manuscripts. The **New Visvanath Temple** here was build in 1966 by the Birla Family and is open to everyone. It is about 11 km from the center of the city. The school covers an area of 2 square miles.

It also has one of the best museums in India, the **Bharat Kala Bhavan Museum**, which has ancient sculptures and deities in it. The museum has various sections—bronze and cast metal, terracotta, and stone sculptures. There is also a painting gallery that contains a big statue of Krishna holding Govardhana Hill, dating from the fourth century. There are also two 18th century paintings on the same subject. This museum is open from 11 am to 4 pm, July to April, and 7.30 am to 12.30 pm in May and June. It is closed on Sunday.

Dasasvamedha Ghat

This is the main bathing *ghat* in town, so it can be extremely crowded. The area around this *ghat* is the main center of activity in the city, especially for pilgrims and tourists. This *ghat* is full of pilgrims bathing in the holy Ganges.

It is said that Lord Brahma performed a *Ten Horse Sacrifice* here for king Divodasa. *Das* means 'ten,' *aswa* means 'horse,' and *medha* means 'sacrifice.' It is said that bathing here is supposed to give the same merits as received by doing the 'ten horse sacrifice' that were performed here.

On certain auspicious days up to 30,000 pilgrims may take bath here. Right next to this *ghat* there is a **Shitala Temple**, which is dedicated to the goddess that protects against smallpox.

Manikarnika Ghat and Kund

The **Manikarnika Kund** is said to be so ancient that it was present before King Bhagiratha brought the Ganges to Varanasi. This *kund* is also called **Chakra-pushkarini Kund** or "Discus Lotus-Pond." Manikarnika means "Jewelled Earring". It is said that this name was given because Lord Siva's earring fell into the well. It is said that at one time this *kund* was a very large lake. Manikarnika Kund is right next to the Manikarnika Ghat and is surrounded by an iron railing, about sixty feet square. In October or November, there is a good chance the *kund* will be covered by dirt, because when the Ganges flows during the rainy season (June-September), dirt from the Ganges covers up the *kund*. I was told the *kund* is dug out each year in November-December.

The well is said to come from a source separate from the Ganges, an underground river that comes directly from Gaumukh, which is the source of the Ganges. It is said that this well was dug by Lord Vishnu with His disc (chakra) and filled by water as His first act of creation. There is an image of Lord Vishnu in the northern wall of the *kund*. Offerings of milk, sandalwood, sweets, and *bilva* flowers, which are sacred to Siva, are thrown in the well.

Lord Vishnu's footprints are located at **Chakra-pushkarini**, which is between Manikarnika Kund and the river. This is said to be the holiest spot in Varanasi.

Manikarnika Ghat is considered the holiest of all the *ghats*. There is a major cremation ground right next to this *ghat*. Normally the cremation ground is outside of town, as it is polluted. Here the burning *ghat* is in the middle of the city, because death in Kasi is considered a great blessing. It is said to be bad luck to mourn or cry for the dead. The cremation ground is under the supervision of the Doms, an untouchable caste, who have been doing it for a very long time. They sell the wood, tend the ever-burning sacred fire from which each pyre is lit, and tend individual pyres. You can see the burning *ghats* from a boat or from a tower next to the burning place. At any given time there may be half a dozen bodies burning here. The bodies are first placed in the Ganges before being burned.

There is an interesting **Durga Temple** by the *ghat* with good sculptures on it. There is no photography allowed at the burning *ghats,* and this is very strictly enforced.

Harishchandra Ghat

Dead bodies are brought here for cremation. It is believed that those who leave their bodies in Varanasi attain *moksha* (liberation) at once. Bodies are brought from thousands of miles away to be burned here. This *ghat* is named after King Harishchandra, who is said to have had to work as a Dom (caretaker of the crematorium) in order to keep his word.

Kings Harishchandra was famous for never refusing a guest and never telling a lie. He was a worshiper of Brahma. Indra told Brahma that he believed that Harishchandra's devotion was not as strong as he made it appear to be. So in order to prove that it was, Brahma disguised himself as a Brahmin priest and asked the king for his entire kingdom. Harishcandra gave it. In order to give the

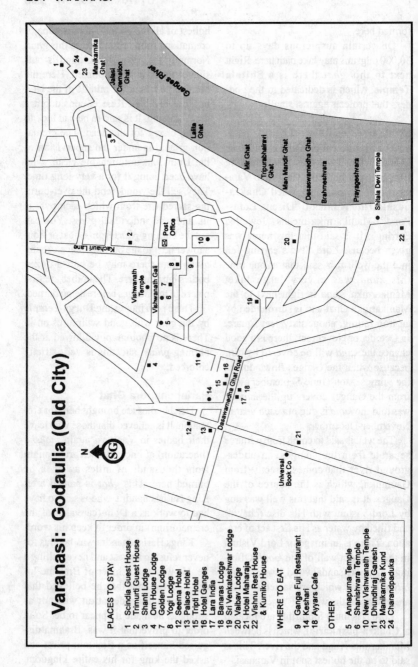

Varanasi: Godaulia (Old City)

PLACES TO STAY
1 Scindia Guest House
2 Trimurti Guest House
3 Shanti Lodge
4 Om House Lodge
7 Golden Lodge
8 Yogi Lodge
12 Seema Hotel
13 Palace Hotel
15 Tripti Hotel
16 Hotel Ganges
17 Lara India
18 Banaras Lodge
19 Sri Venkateshwar Lodge
20 Valbav Lodge
21 Hotel Maharaja
22 Vishnu Rest House
   & Kumiko House

WHERE TO EAT
9 Ganga Fuji Restaurant
14 Keshari
18 Ayyars Cafe

OTHER
5 Annapurna Temple
6 Shanishvara Temple
10 New Vishwanath Temple
11 Dhundhiraj Ganesh
23 Manikarnika Kund
24 Charandpaduka

priest payment (*daksina*) for performing some rituals the king became a worker at the crematorium at this ghat.

His wife was sold to a seller of flowers. When his son died of a snakebite his wife brought him to the burning ghat where her husband was working. Because she had no money to pay the cremation fee, she ripped her sari in half to pay the fee.

Brahma then restored the son back to life and gave the king back his kingdom. He also told Harishcandra that this ghat would be especially sacred and that it would be named after him.

Pancha-ganga Ghat

Beneath this *ghat* the Ganges, Yamuna, Sarasvati, Kirana, and Dhutapapa Rivers are said to meet. It is one of the five main *ghats* in Varanasi. It is considered especially auspicious to bathe here during the month of Kartika (Oct-Nov), and even more so on the full moon day of Kartika.

Other Ghats

Beside the main *ghats* there are many more *ghats*. The southern-most *ghat* is **Asi Ghat**, which is one of the five special *ghats* in Varanasi. This is the first place to bath at when you do Panchatirthas. From this *ghat* you can get a boat across the Ganges to Ramnagar, the Maharaja of Varanasi's palace.

Next is **Lala Misra** Ghat, and then **Tulsi Ghat**, named after Tulsi Das. He translated the *Ramayana* into Hindi and died in Varanasi in 1623. At **Hanuman Ghat** there is a temple dedicated to Hanuman. Hanuman Ghat is where Vallabha Acarya is said to have been born in the 16th century. **Harishchandra Ghat**, also called Smashan (Masan) Ghat, is a major burning *ghat* using electric ovens. At

Kedar Ghat there is a well half-way up the *ghat* called Gauri Kund, after Lord Siva's wife, which is said to have healing properties. At **Someswara Ghat** there is a temple of the moon, and every kind of disease is supposed to be healed here.

Maharajah Man Singh of Jaipur built the old **Man Mandir Ghat** in 1600. Man Mandir Ghat has an Observatory built by Raja Sawai Jai Singh, the founder of the city of Jaipur. At **Rama and Laksman Ghat** there is a Rama and Laksman Temple.

Bindu Madhava & Adi Kesava Temples

These are both important Vishnu temples. **Bindu Madhava Temple** used to be a very major temple, and it was visited by Lord Caitanya when He came to Varanasi. It was destroyed by the Muslims in the 17th century and a mosque was built in its place. The present Deity of Bindu Madhava is in a small temple by the mosque. It is located just above the Pancha-ganga Ghat. If you are taking a boat by yourself, you can have the boat stop here and walk up to the temple.

The **Adi Kesava Temple** is located where the Varana River flows into the Ganges. Lord Vishnu is said to have first put His feet here when He came to Varanasi.

Durga Temple and Sankat Mochan Temple

They are both located in the southern part of town, between Asi Ghat and the University. The Durga Temple was built in the 18th century and has many intense monkeys. The Sankat Mochan Temple is dedicated to Hanuman, the "Liberator from Troubles." Many people consider this to be one of the three major temples in Varanasi.

Other Places

The **Sanskrit University** has over 150,000 rare manuscripts. Varanasi is the chief center for learning Sanskrit in India. At **Augharki Takiya** you can drink sacred water from a well that is said to heal various diseases.

Across the river is the interesting **Ramnagar Fort** (9 am to 12 noon & 2 to 5 pm, except Friday) built by Maharaja Balwant Singh. The Royal Museum (summer 5.30 to 11.45 am, winter 6 am to 12.15 pm), in the fort, displays arms and outfits of former maharajas of Varanasi. There is a temple dedicated to **Veda Vyasa** in the Ramnagar Fort. It is said that Veda Vyasa stayed at Ramnagar for a short time.

Festivals

During the month of April pilgrims perform circumambulation of Kasi Dharmaksetra (Varanasi). **Ganga Dasara** in May celebrates the day the Ganges reached Haridwar. In Oct/Nov **Nagnathaiya** at Tulsi Ghat reenacts Krishna dancing on the head of the Kaliya snake in the Yamuna.

Bharat Milap at Nati Imli is the celebration of the meeting of Rama and Bharata after 14 years of separation. The Maharaja of Varanasi attends this interesting festival and rides on the back of an elephant.

Where To Stay

There are three main areas to stay. The old part of the city, by the *ghats*, captures the true atmosphere of the city. Many of the budget hotels are in this area. The other two areas are around the railway and bus station and the spacious Cantonment area, north of the railway station, where most of the higher class hotels are located.

Where To Stay – Lower & Middle

Cantonment Area

This area is north of the Varanasi Junction railway station.

The *Hotel Surya* (385-930) is a recommended place that has rooms with bath for Rs 85/100 and rooms with A/C for Rs 275/325. It is a peaceful place with a nice garden and a philosophical manager who used to be a tourist guide. So he is very helpful.

The *Tourist Dak Bungalow* (42182), on The Mall, is a little run down, but it has a nice garden. The rooms are Rs 100/250 and the dorm beds are Rs 20.

The *Hotel Temples Town* (46582), Patel Nagar, by the station, is a good quiet place with rooms for Rs 125/175 with bath and hot water. The *Hotel India* (43309), 59 Patel Nagar, is a recommended place with rooms for Rs 225/300 and Rs 400/500 with A/C. The nearby *Hotel Vaibav* (46588) is also good, but slightly cheaper, with rooms for Rs 200/250 and Rs 375/450 with A/C.

City Centre – Lahurabir Area

The *Hotel Barahdari* (330-346), east of Lahurabir, at Maidagin, has air-cooled rooms for Rs 250/300 and A/C rooms for Rs 400/450. It has a garden and a good vegetarian restaurant. The *Hotel Varuna* (358-524), between the railway station and the *ghats*, opposite Sigra Police Station, is a recommended place with rooms for Rs 150/275 and Rs 400/475 with A/C.

The *Hotel Ajaya* has rooms for Rs 100/120 and Rs 150/170 with air-cooling. It is one of the best hotels in the area and is recommended for budget travelers. It has 24-hour checkout.

The two-star *Pradeep Hotel* (44963), at Jagatganj, has rooms for Rs 250/300 and Rs 400/500 with A/C. *Hotel Gautam* is a good place with clean rooms from Rs 225/275 to Rs 350/400 with A/C. It is a bit overpriced.

Railway and Bus Station Area

There are many cheaper hotels in this area. There are no shortage of places with basic rooms such as the *SN Lodge* with rooms for Rs 50/60 to Rs 60/70 with bath.

The *Tourist Bungalow* (43413), off Parade Kothi, Grand Trunk Rd, is the best place in the area. It has rooms from Rs 100/125 to Rs 150/200 and dorm beds for Rs 20. An A/C room is Rs 275/350. It is a popular place and is often full. It has a nice garden and is within walking distance of the railway and bus stations.

The *Hotel Relax*, by the Tourist Bungalow, has rooms with common bath for Rs 60/95 and with bath for Rs 125/175. It is a good alternative if the Tourist Bungalow is full. The *Raj Kamal Hotel* has rooms for Rs 75/110. The *Hotel Sandona* has recently renovated good rooms for Rs 90/130.

Old City and Ghats Area

The streets are so narrow here that cycle rickshaws cannot fit down the lanes, so you have to be able to carry all your baggage to get a room here. This is where the real budget places are. Many of the places in this area are very basic.

The *Yogi Lodge* (322-588) is a very popular place. It has basic rooms with common bath and hot showers for Rs 50/75. If you are a backpacker, this is the place to stay and meet people. This place, however, is often full. People often do not like this place because it is too basic. Often rickshaw drivers or a tout (commission agent) will bring you to some place with a similar name, where they will get a commission. Three different people wanting to come here told me they were brought to three other places by commission agents.

Near the Yogi Lodge is the *Sadhu Lodge,* which is good clean place for about the same price. Also nearby, is the *Golden Lodge* (323-832), D8/35 Kalika Lane, which is popular and has a rooftop patio.

The *Scindhia Guest House* (320-319), by Manikarnika Ghat, has a good view of the Ganges. Rooms are Rs 80 and Rs 100 with bath. It also has dorm beds for Rs 20. To get there you have to walk to the *ghat* and up a dirt hill by the river. The *Shanti Lodge* (322-568), Manikarnika Ghat, is a popular budget place by the burning *ghat* with rooms for Rs 40/60 and Rs 100 with bath.

The *Trimurti Guest House* (322-616), near the Visvanath Temple, is a good place with rooms for Rs 40/55 and higher priced rooms that have a bathroom.

The *Vishnu Rest House* has a great view of the Ganges from the roof. The rooms here are Rs 65/85 with bath and Rs 55/65 with common bath. You can get to this hotel by turning right at the Dasaswamedha Ghat. Next to it is *Kumiko House*, which also has a good view and is about the same price.

Sri Venkateshwar Lodge (322-357), 5/64 Dasaswamedha Ghat Road, near the Dasaswamedha Ghat, is a good place with clean rooms for Rs 45/75.

The *Sun Shiv Hotel* (52468), 54/16-D Ravi Niketan, Jaddumandi Road, is a few blocks from the Old City area. It is a good place in a quiet area. It has rooms for Rs 100/175. The owner is a very knowledgeable and helpful person, and if this is important to you, this is the place to stay. It is a recommended place, if you don't mind staying out of the main Old City area.

The *Hotel Ganges* (321-097), Dasaswamedha Road, has rooms for Rs 150/200 and Rs 300/350 with A/C. It is set back a little from the road.

Other Areas

The *GM Guest House* (361-292), 1 Chandrika Colony, Sigra, is a little away from the old town area. It has large, clean, budget and middle range rooms and is a very good value. The *Hotel Faran* is a good place.

Hotel Temple on Ganges (312-340), Asi Ghat, is a recommended place with a good peaceful location. Some of the rooms have a great view of the Ganges. It has nice rooms for Rs 250/400. It is a good distance from the Old City area.

Where To Stay – High End

The *Hotel de Paris* (46601), The Mall in the Cantonment area, has a spacious garden and good large rooms for Rs 550/760 with A/C.

The *Hotel Clarks Varanasi* (348-501, fax 348-186), The Mall in the Cantonment area, is an old famous building with atmosphere, dating to the British era. It also has a modern extension and a swimming pool. Rooms cost Rs 1195/2250. It is the best place in town. Next to the Hotel Clarks is the new *Hotel Ideal Tops* (348-091, fax 348-685), which has comfortable rooms for $30/35.

The *Hotel Taj Ganges* (345-100, fax 348-067), Nadesar Palace Grounds, is the most opulent place in town with rooms from $88/95 up to $200. It has excellent facilities. The *Hotel Best Western Ideal* (348-091), The Mall, has rooms for Rs 995/1195.

The *Hotel Varanasi Ashok* (46020, fax 348-089), The Mall, Cantonment area next to Hotel Clarks, has a quiet location with air-conditioned rooms for Rs 1195/2000. The four-star *Hotel Hindustan International* (351-484, fax 352-374) has a swimming pool and rooms for Rs 1150/2000.

Where To Eat

Keshari is one of the best places in the Dasaswamedha Ghat area. It is down a small alley, off Dasaswamedha Ghat Rd. *Ayyar's Cafe* on Dasaswamedha Road serves South Indian food. It is a small, cheap place, open from 8 am to 9 pm. The *Madhur Jalpan Grih* on Dasaswamedha Road, is famous for its sweets, as is Varanasi.

The popular *Sindhi Restaurant*, Bhelupura area, near the Lalita Cinema, has good food. To get there ask to go to the cinema, as the rickshaw drivers (Rs 20) know the cinema, but not the restaurant. *Sona Rupa*, which is in the basement of a building across from the GPO, has good food at a reasonable price. It serves South Indian and Chinese food.

The *Gujarati Restaurant*, up a flight of stairs, across from the KVM Hotel, is a good clean place. The *Hotel Barahdari*, east of Lahurabir, at Maidagin, has a good Jain vegetarian restaurant.

Travel

Air There are three flights daily to Delhi, three direct flights to Bombay weekly ($179), two direct flights to Calcutta weekly, and three flights weekly to Bhubaneshwar. Indian Airlines has a daily flight to Kathmandu, which is heavily booked in the winter. There is a daily Indian Airlines flight to Delhi ($90) via Khajuraho ($54) and Agra ($76). The airport is about 22 km out of town. There is an Indian Airlines bus into town that goes to the Indian Airlines office in the Cantonment area.

The **Indian Airlines office** (Mon-Fri, 10 am to 1 pm & 2 to 5 pm, tel: 45959) is

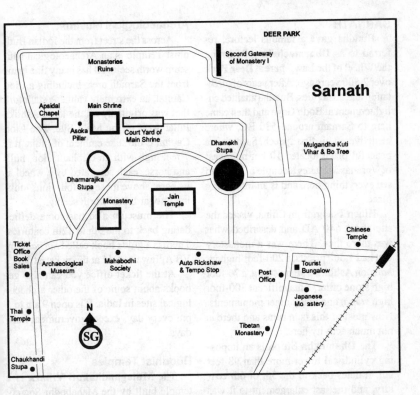

DEER PARK

Second Gateway
of Monastery I

Monasteries
Ruins

Sarnath

Apsidal
Chapel

Main Shrine

Court Yard of
Main Shrine

Asoka
Pillar

Dhamekh
Stupa

Mulgandha Kuti
Vihar & Bo Tree

Dharmarajika
Stupa

Jain
Temple

Monastery

Chinese
Temple

Ticket
Office
Book
Sales

Archaeological
Museum

Mahabodhi
Society

Auto Rickshaw
& Tempo Stop

Tourist
Bungalow

Post
Office

Thai
Temple

Japanese
Mo astery

Tibetan
Monastery

Chaukhandi
Stupa

N

SG

---

behind Hotel de Paris, Cantt, and there is an office at the airport (43742). The Air India office is in the Hotel Clarks (46326).

Train There are two train stations in the Varanasi area. There is **Varanasi Cantt** and a big train station in the suburbs called **Mughal Sarai Station**, which is 14 km from the center of the city. The main Delhi-Calcutta line trains stop at Mughal Sarai station. There are several trains daily to both Delhi and Calcutta that take about 15 hours to get to either city. The Amritsar Howrah Mail #3006 is the fastest train to Calcutta (15 hr). There is one train daily to Agra (10½ hr) and six trains a day to Gaya.

There are three passenger trains daily to Gorakhpur, which take 8 to 10 hours, with frequent delays. It is usually better to take a bus. There is a daily direct train to Haridwar (20 hr). There are three trains weekly to Puri and four trains daily to Bombay. The Mahanagri Express #1094 is the fastest train to Bombay (28 hr, 11.35 am).

The only decent place to stay near the Mughal Sarai station is the railway retiring rooms (Rs 70 for a double).

Bus Most buses arrive near the railway station. There are deluxe buses from Varanasi to Allahabad and normal buses to Khajuraho. Buses depart from the Cantonment Bus Stand to Gaya, Gorakhpur (7 hr), and Sunauli (9-11 hr) to get to Nepal.

SARNATH

Buddha gave a famous lecture, referred to as **Dharmachakra**, "Turning the Wheel of the Law," here at **Deer Park** over 2,500 years ago. After years of meditation and austerities, Buddha attained enlightenment at Bodh Gaya and then came here to Sarnath around 530 BC, where he delivered his first speech. Sarnath is a peaceful place located 10 km northeast of Varanasi. It takes a couple of hours to see everything here and is an interesting place.

Hiuen Tsang, from China, visited the site about 640 AD and described what was there then. There was a monastery that had 1,500 priests, a 200-foot-high *vihara*, an **Ashoka's stone stupa**, a 70-foot high stone pillar, a magnificent 300-foot high *stupa*, and many other monuments. Now most of this is in ruins and there is not much activity here.

The **Dhamekha Stupa** is an imposing cylindrical tower more than 98 feet tall. It dates back to the 5th or 6th century, and the last enlargement to it was supposed to be have been made in the 12th century. It is believed to mark the place of Lord Buddha's sermon. Slightly to the west is the **Ashoka Column**, dating back to the 3rd century.

The **Dharmarajika Stupa,** which is a short distance to the west of the Dhamekha Stupa, is attributed to Ashoka. In its core is a green marble casket containing pieces of human bone, decayed pearls, gold leaf, and other precious objects. It has been enlarged six times, the last time being in the 12th century.

The main shrines date from the 3rd century BC to the 5th century AD. There is the excavated ruins of a Buddhists monastery here, where there are four pillars that are said to mark the room where Buddha stayed.

Archaeological Museum

Across the street from the Indian Buddhist Temple is an Archaeological Museum worth seeing. It has many fine items from the Sarnath area, including a Lion Capital, an extremely valuable sculpture that was originally on the large Ashoka Pillar west of the Main Site. The Lion Capital is the state emblem of India. It is 7 feet high with an elephant, lion, bull, and horse, each separated by a wheel at its base; above these are four lions looking outward. It is worth seeing.

The museum also has some deities dating back to the 9th to 12th centuries. There is a guide book called *Sarnath,* by VS Agrawala, sold at the ticket office.

At the ticket office you can also get books about some of the other archaeological sites in India. It is open 9 am to 5 pm every day, except government holidays.

Buddhist Temples

The **Mulagandhakuti Vihara** is a temple built by the Mahabodhi Society in 1931. The silver casket in the temple is said to have the original relics of the Buddha in it. It was recovered from the ruins of the first century temple. The temple has interesting murals depicting the life story of Buddha. The murals were painted by a well-known Japanese artist, Kosetsu Nosu, in 1936. Outside the temple is an **Aswatha tree** transplanted from Sri Lanka. It is said to be a descendant of the original tree under which Buddha sat.

There are two Buddhist temples—a Chinese one with a nice garden and a highly decorated Tibetan one, with a picture of the Dalai Lama on the altar.

Festivals

The full moon of Vaisakha (April-

May) is observed as the anniversary of Buddha's birth, enlightenment, and death. The full moon in the month of Asadh (July-August) is considered the anniversary of his first sermon.

Tours

A tour goes to Sarnath first and then Ramnagar Fort, if there's time, departing from Varanasi. Hours are 2.30 to 6.25 pm in the summer and 2 pm to 5.55 pm in the winter.

Where To Stay

The UPTDC *Tourist Bungalow* (42002) has rooms for Rs 75/175 with bath. There are also dorm beds for Rs 20. There is a tourist office here.

It is possible to stay at some of the monasteries, such as the pleasant very basic *Burmese Vihara*. The basic *Birla Rest House* is near Mulagandhakuti Vihara.

Travel

There are many buses from Varanasi (Rs 4). It costs Rs 35 to go the 20 minutes from Varanasi by rickshaw. There are shared auto-rickshaws from the stand by the Civil Court and from the stands in Godaulia or Lahurabir areas for Rs 10.

Please Help Us

As the subject matter of this book is extremely complex and detailed it is very difficult to include everything relevant. So if you have some information that would be valuable to the readers of this book please send it to us, so they may be benefited.

Whatever you can tell about any temple, the story behind the Deity, what Deities are in a particular temple, or other interesting facts may be valuable information. Also of interest is your opinion on hotels, restaurants or dharamshalas, especially ones missed in this book. Travel information is also valuable. Please refer to the page number in this book in reference to the place that you are writing about.

Please give as detailed information as possible.

For temples or holy places please send:
Temple name, location, Deities' names
What is especially interesting about the temple or place
Story about the temple or Deities
Opening or closing hours
How to get there, what bus or train
Potential problems such as guides, hard climbs, or monkeys

For hotels and restaurants please send :
Name, address, phone number, opening hours of a restaurant
Tariff card or room rates
Location, distance from a land-mark either walking or by rickshaw.
How close to a railway or bus station.
How to get there and how much it cost.
Your comments on why this place stood out.
For a restaurant, any recommended preparations or things to be avoided

The writers of the ten best letters will receive an updated edition of this book.

Thank you very much for your help.

Write to

Spiritual Guides   Jada Bharata Dasa
Krishna Balarama Mandir
Bhaktivedanta Swami Marg
Vrindavana, Mathura Dist. UP, India

CHAPTER EIGHT

Braja—Vrndavana & Mathura

Braja Mandala covers an area of 1453 square miles surrounding Vrindavana and Mathura. Braja is where Sri Krishna performed His pastimes 5000 years ago. There are **twelve principle forests** in Braja and all of them are considered places of pilgrimage. Other major places in the Braja area are **Nandagrama, Varsana, Gokula, Govardhana Hill**, and **Radha Kund**.

Vrindavana and Mathura are the most important Vaishnava holy places in all of India. This is because Mathura is the birthplace of Lord Krishna and Vrindavana is where He had His childhood pastimes.

For a spiritual tour of India it is an extremely important and highly recommended place to visit. It is said in the *Padma Purana* that "Simply by residing for one day in Mathura one will attain Hari-bhakti, devotion to Hari (Vishnu)".

ISKCON (International Society for Krishna Consciousness) has one of its major centers in Vrindavana called the Krishna Balarama Mandir. Other important and especially interesting temples in the town of Vrindavana are the Govindaji, Madana Mohana, Banke Bihari, Radha-Damodara, Radha-Raman, and Sri Raghunath Temples. All the places in Vrindavana are considered important because they are transcendental.

"All the results of traveling on all the pilgrimages within the three worlds can be achieved simply by touching the holy land of Mathura." (NOD)

In the Adi-varaha Purana it is stated: "Any person who dies in any place within Mathura—a holy place, a home, or even a courtyard—certainly attains salvation. In this world Mathura is the best of all holy places beginning with Kashi."

Krishna's Pastimes

Krishna was born of Vasudeva and Devaki while they were in prison in Mathura, because their eighth son (Krishna) was destined to King Kamsa. Because the evil King Kamsa wanted to kill Krishna, He was transfer to Gokula to be looked after by His foster parents Nanda and Yasoda.

Krishna killed many demons sent by King Kamsa to kill him such as Putana, Trinavarta, Aghasura, Aristasura and Kesi. He also had many pastimes with the cowherd boys, cows, and *gopis* (the cowherd girls).

Deities Carved by Vajranabha

It is said that Vajranabha, the great-grandson of Krishna had 16 deities carved. It is said that these deities were carved from a rare imperishable stone called Braja.

The four presiding Deities of Braja Mandala are Sri Harideva of Govardhana, Sri Keshava Deva of Mathura, Sri Baladeva of Baladeo, and Govinda Deva of Vrindavana, who has now been moved to Jaipur.

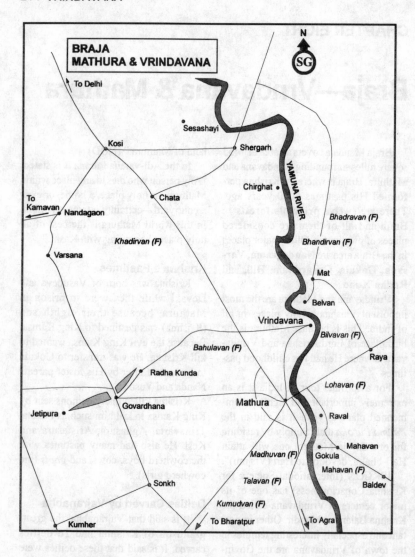

BRAJA MATHURA & VRINDAVANA

To Delhi

Sesashayi

Kosi

Shergarh

YAMUNA RIVER

Chirghat

Bhadravan (F)

To Kamavan

Nandagaon

Chata

Khadirvan (F)

Bhandirvan (F)

Varsana

Mat

Belvan

Vrindavana

Bahulavan (F)

Bilvavan (F)

Radha Kunda

Raya

Lohavan (F)

Jetipura

Govardhana

Mathura

Raval

Raval

Mahavan

Madhuvan (F)

Gokula

Mahavan (F)

Sonkh

Talavan (F)

Baldev

Kumudvan (F)

Kumher

To Bharatpur

To Agra

There are two Naths—Sri Nathji, who was originally at Govardhana and is now in Nathdwar, Rajasthan, by Udaipur, and Sri Gopinath, who is now in Jaipur.

The two Gopals are Sri Madana Gopala, renamed Sri Madana Mohana, who is now in Karoli, and Saksi-gopal, who is now in the town of Saksi-gopal, Orissa, near Puri.

The four Mahadevas (deities of Lord Siva) are Chakleswara at Govardhana, Kameswara at Kamavana, Bhuteswara at Mathura, and Gopiswara in Vrindavana. The four goddesses carved are Manasi Devi at Govardhana, Vrinda Devi at Kamavana, Pathal Devi at Mathura, and

Yogamaya Devi at Vrindavana.

It is said that Vajranabha first had three Deities of Krishna carved. He never saw Krishna, so they were carved from the description of Uttara, the mother of Maharaj Parikshit. He had three different images carved, but none of them were perfect. **Govindaji** resembled the face (Mukharabinda), **Madana Mohana** resembled the navel down to the lotus feet, and **Gopinath** resembled the trunk of the body, from the navel to the neck.

In one book I read about the temples of Vrindavana, it quoted the *Padma Purana* as saying that to get the full vision of Sri Krishna, you have to visit and pay obeisances to all three Deities in a single day, while the sun is still up.

Sri Govinda and Sri Gopinath are now in Jaipur and Madana Mohana is in Karoli, a small town in Rajasthan. If you are departing from Vrindavana or Delhi and want to see these three Deities all in one day you have to take a taxi to Karoli in the morning and from there go to Jaipur. It would be difficult to see all three Deities in a one day by public transportation.

Six Goswamis of Vrindavana

The six Goswamis of Vrindavana were sent by Sri Caitanya Mahaprabhu to establish the places of pilgrimage in Vrindavana. These six Goswamis were bona fide spiritual masters situated on the highest platform of devotional service to God, and for that reason they were called *goswamis*.

They are Sanatana Goswami, Rupa Goswami, Raghunath Dasa Goswami, Gopala Bhatta Goswami, Jiva Goswami, and Raghunath Bhatta Goswami. Sri Rupa and Sanatana Goswami first came to Vrindavana in 1515 to uncover the lost places of Krishna's pastimes.

They followed the strictest standard of devotional service or spiritual practices. Sri Raghunath Dasa Goswami's daily activities included chanting 64 rounds of *japa*, worshiping his Govardhana *shila*, bathing thrice in Radha Kund, offering 1,000 obeisances to Krishna, and offering 2,000 obeisances to the devotees, plus embracing them. He rested ninety minutes a day and some days not at all. Throughout his life, Raghunath Dasa Goswami never ate anything for sense gratification.

VRINDAVANA
Population: 50,000

Vrindavana is 135 km south of Delhi and 55 km north of Agra, just off the Delhi-Agra Road. It is 12 km or a 25-minute auto-rickshaw ride from Mathura. It has a small-town type atmosphere with narrow streets and not much motor traffic. There are said to be over 5000 temples in Vrindavana.

Orientation and Information

The Krishna Balarama Mandir (ISKCON temple) is in a peaceful area called Raman Reti, about a 15-minute bicycle rickshaw ride from the main downtown area. In the middle of the downtown area is Loi Bazaar, a main shopping bazaar to get devotional items. The road in front of the ISKCON temple is called Bhaktivedanta Swami Road. It is also referred to by its old name Chatikara Road.

Mathura-mandala Parikrama describes the glories of the Mathura area. *Radha Kund Mahima Madhuri* is a good book with detailed descriptions of Radha Kund and Syama Kund. *Madhurya Dhama* describes the Govardhana Hill area. And *Cintamani Dhama* describes the Vrindavana area.

Tours

There is a **Braja Darsana bus tour** (Rs 40, 8.00 am to 6 pm) departing from the Vrindavana bus stand. It goes to Nandagram, Varsana, Govardhana town, Manasi Ganga, and Radha Kund. There is no guide. It is a good, fast, cheap way to go to these places.

There is also a tour that goes to Agra, including the Taj Mahal, Red Fort, and Fatehpur Sikri for Rs 70. It leaves in the morning.

Braja Mandala Parikrama

Every year in Kartika (Oct/Nov) ISKCON puts on a Braja Mandala *parikrama*. It is a one-month walking tour that goes to all 12 forests in Vrindavana. The *parikrama* visits most of the major places in the Braja area including Mathura, Radha Kund, Varsana, Nandagrama, Gokula, Vrindavana, and Govardhana Hill. It is traditional to do this walk in bare feet, although shoes are permitted.

For further information contact the Centennial House (11-646-9633, Fax: 91-11-647-0742), 62 Sant Nagar, New Delhi - 65.

Krishna Balarama Mandir

This beautiful temple has Deities of Gaura-Nitai (left altar), Krishna Balarama (middle altar), and Radha-Shyamasundara (Radha-Krishna on right altar). In front of the temple is the Samadhi Mandir of His Divine Grace A.C. Bhaktivedanta Swami Prabhupada, the Founder Acarya of the International Society for Krishna Consciousness (ISKCON). This is where his body was laid to rest after he left this world and returned to the spiritual world. Normally the bodies of dead people are burned and the ashes are put in a holy river. But in the case of a *paramahamsa*, a highly elevated devotee of Lord Krishna, the body is not burned, but buried in *samadhi*. This is because the body of a pure devotee is spiritual.

By the guest house entrance are the actual rooms that Srila Prabhupada lived in while in Vrindavana. The bed that you see here is where Srila Prabhupada left his body in November 1977. In these rooms there are many of his personal items that he used while in Vrindavana and traveling around the world.

The guest house and restaurant are the best facilities in Vrindavana. Regrettably the guest house is usually full, so it is essential to book in advance. Even if the guest house is full, ISKCON life patrons are still given free places to stay in some other guest facilities, close to the temple.

Also there is a traditional *gurukula*, or school of the guru, which can sometimes be visited with prior permission. Students here are trained in an ashram situation. They get both spiritual and material education.

About a km from the temple is a *goshala*, where over a hundred cows are protected. It is located in a very peaceful place and has a nice garden. This can be visited.

The phone number for the guest house is (0565) 442-478. If you call from outside of India you call 00 91-565-442-478. The temple address is Krishna Balarama Mandir, Bhaktivedanta Swami Marg, Raman Reti, Vrindavana, Mathura District, UP.

ISKCON Temple Schedule

The Deities' doors are open from 7.15 am to 12.30 pm. They close for a half hour to offer *bhoga* to the Deities a half hour before each arati. The temple is closed between 12.30 and 4.30 pm (4 pm in the winter). The temple reopens at 4.30 pm (4 pm in the winter) and stays open until 8.45 pm (8.15 pm in the winter). Sandhya arati is at 6.30 pm in the winter.

Samadhi Mangala Arati	4.10 am
Temple Mangala Arati	4.30 am
Altar Closed	5.00 am
Greeting the Deities	7.15 am
Guru-puja	7.25 am
Srimad Bhagavatam Class	7.50 am
Puspa Arati	8.30 am
Noon Arati	12.00 pm
Temple Closes	12.30 pm
Temple Reopens (Arati)	4.30 pm
Sandhya Arati (6.30 winter)	7.00 pm
Shayan Arati (8 pm winter)	8.30 pm
Temple Closes for Night	8.45 pm

Places To See

Yamuna River

This is the most sacred river in Indian. The main reason it is so sacred is because it flows through Vrindavana and Mathura, and was thus intimately connected to Lord Krishna's pastimes. One who bathes in the Yamuna can be purified of all sinful reactions and attain love of Godhead.

Kesi Ghat

Lord Krishna killed the Kesi demon here. Kesi Ghat is on the bank of the Yamuna. If you bath here you get the benediction of bathing in all of the holy places. There is an *arati* performed here every day at sunset.

Govindaji Temple

This temple was built in 1590 and took several thousand men five full years to build. The original Govindaji Deity was found about 450 years ago by Rupa Goswami. Govindaji was removed from this temple when the Muslim emperor Aurangzeb tried to destroy it. The original Deity is now in Jaipur, in a temple right outside the King of Jaipur's palace.

This temple was originally seven stories high, with an altar of marble, silver, and gold. A sculptured lotus flower weighing several tons decorates the main hall. On meeting Rupa Goswami, Man Singh from Jaipur, a general in Emperor Akbar's army, built this magnificent temple. Aurangzeb and his army later destroyed part of the temple. When a few stories remained, all of a sudden the ground began to shake violently and Aurangzeb's men were terrified and ran for their lives, never to return.

The Deities on the altar in this temple are Govindaji in the middle, to His left is Lord Caitanya, and to His right is Lord Nityananda. Below are small Radha and Krishna Deities. Below Them are Lord Jagannath and a Govardhana-*shila*.

Since this temple was partially destroyed by Muslims, it is considered that worship can not be done in this temple. Therefore behind the temple another temple was established where worship is performed to the Deities that were installed after Govindaji was removed and brought to Jaipur.

Purusottama, the son of King Prataparudra, sent the deity of Radharani from Jagannath Puri to be installed next to Govindadeva. This was the first deity of Radharani to be installed in Vrindavana.

There are two small temples on two sides of the Jagmohan, the main audience hall (temple room). Inside the small temple on the southern side, down 12 steps is a cave in which the Deity of Govinda was found and where Rupa Goswami used to meditate. A deity of eight-armed Yogamaya sitting on a lion is also there. There is also a stone slab

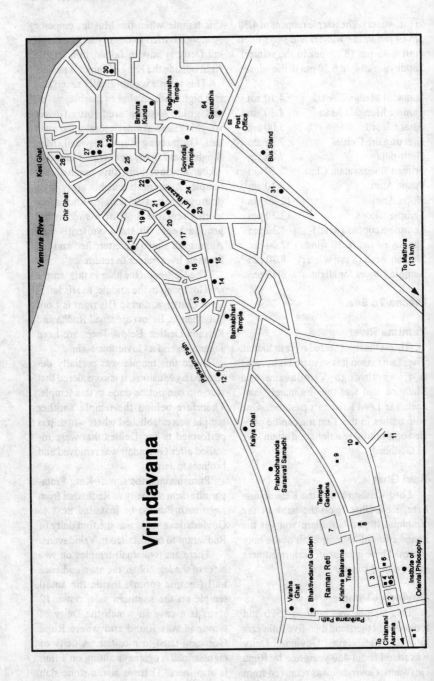

PLACES TO STAY

1   Citrakut Dham Ashram
2   Guest House
3   MVT
4   ISKCON Guest House
6   Shanti Ashram
8   Maheshwari Ashram
9   Krishna Nivasa Rohtak Wali
10 Fogal Ashram
11 Govinda Bihar

TEMPLES & HOLY PLACES

5   Krishna Balarama Temple
12 Madana Mohana Temple &
    Sanatana Goswami's Samadhi
13 Radha Vallabha Temple
17 Seva Kunja
18 Imli Tala
19 Radha Damodara Temple
20 Radha Syamasundara Temple
21 Syamananda Prabhu Samadhi
25 Nidhuban
26 Vamsi Gopala Temple
27 Radha Gokulananda Temple
28 Radha Raman Temple
29 Radha Gopinatha Temple
30 Gopisvara Temple

OTHER

7   ISKCON Goshala
14 Sriji Jewelers
15 Doctor Narottama
16 Shyamasakhi
22 Ganga Prasad
23 Heera Jeweler
24 State Bank of India
31 Rickshaw Stand to Mathura

with the footprint of Krishna on it. Vrinda Devi, who is now in Kamavana, used to be in the northern temple.

Madana Mohana Temple

The original Deity of Madana Mohana was discovered at the base of an old *vat* tree by Advaita Acarya, when he visited Vrindavana. He entrusted the worship of Madana Mohana to His disciple, Purusottama Chaube, who then gave the Deity to Sanatana Goswami. Sanatana Goswami spend 43 years in Vrindavana. Worshiped along with Madana Mohana are Radharani and Lalita, who were sent to Vrindavana by Purusottama Jena, the son of Maharaja Prataparudra.

This 60 foot high temple was opened in 1580 on a 50 foot hill called Aditya Tila, next to the Yamuna. Ram Das Kapoor paid to build the temple. One day a ship he owned, loaded with merchandise, went aground in the Yamuna. He was advised by Sanatana Goswami to pray to Madana Mohana for help. The ship came free and the owner of the ship made a big profit, which he used to built this temple.

The original Madana Mohana Deity was moved from Vrindavana to Jaipur when the Moghul Emperor Aurangzeb attacked Vrindavana in 1670. That Deity is now in Karoli, which is southeast of Jaipur in Rajasthan. There is a new Madana Mohana Temple, built by Sri Nanda Kumar Bose of Bengal, at the bottom of the hill, where the Madana Mohana Deities are now being worshiped. It is said that worship was moved to this new temple because the old temple was contaminated by the Muslims.

On the side of the temple is the *bhajana kutir* (meditation place) of Sanatana Goswami.

In back of the temple is the *samadhi* of Sanatana Goswami. On the side of the *samadhi* are the *puspa-samadhis* of Candrasekhara Acarya and Tapana Misra, two of Sri Caitanya's associates. There is also a sweet water well here that Sanatana Goswami used. Behind Sanatana Goswami's *samadhi* is a *grantha samadhi*, which contains some of the original manuscripts of the Goswamis.

Radha-Ballabha Temple

This popular temple was founded by Hit Harivamsa Goswami, a disciple of Gopala Bhatta Goswami. *Darshan* is from 6 to 11 am and 6 to 9 pm.

Radha-Damodara Temple

This temple was founded by Jiva Goswami. The main Deities here are Sri Sri Radha-Damodara. Other Deities worshiped here are the Radha-Vrindavana Candra Deities of Krishna Dasa Kaviraja Goswami, the Radha-Madhava Deities of Jayadeva Goswami, and the Radha-Chalacikana Deities of Bhugarbha Goswami. The original Deities were all moved to Jaipur. When the original Deities are moved, the replacement Deity is called a *pratibhu-murti* and is considered as good as the original Deity.

The *samadhis* of Jiva Goswami, Krishnadasa Kaviraja Goswami, Rupa Goswami and the *puspa-samadhi* of Bhaktisiddhanta Goswami are here. The *bhajan kutirs* (meditation place) of Rupa Goswami and Bhaktivedanta Swami Prabhupada are also here.

There is a **Govardhana Shila** in this temple that was worshiped by Sanatana Goswami. It has Lord Krishna's footprint on it, and it was given to Sanatana Goswami by Krishna Himself. For a small donation the *pujari* will show you this *shila*. You can see the imprints of Krishna's footprint, walking stick, flute, and the hoof-print of a calf imbedded in the *shila*. This temple was built by Maharaja Man Singh of Amber (Jaipur). The doors of the altar are open from 8.30 am to 12 pm and 5.30 to 8 pm.

Srila Prabhupada lived here for six years from 1959 to 1965. He translated and wrote commentaries on the first three volumes of the *Bhagavatam* here. Every day at 1 pm there is distribution of the *maha-prasada* that was offered to him. When you enter the courtyard of the temple, Srila Prabhupada's rooms are to your right. The small kitchen has a window through which you can see Srila Rupa Goswami's *samadhi*.

Jiva Goswami's *samadhi* is to the left of the Deities through a doorway. It is then directly to your right against the temple walls. Bhaktisiddhanta's *puspa samadhi* is the white marble *samadhi* fifteen feet in front as you cross the doorway. It is the first one in the second row. Rupa Goswami's *samadhi* is on the right side of the temple across from his *bhajana kutir*.

Radha-Gokulananda Temple

In this temple you can see the Radha-Vinod Deities of Lokanath Goswami, Radha-Gokulananda Deities of Viswanath Cakravarti, Caitanya Mahaprabhu Deity of Narottama Dasa Thakur, Vijaya Govinda Deities of Baladeva Vidyabhusana, and the Govardhana-*shila* given by Lord Caitanya to Raghunath Dasa Goswami. The *samadhis* of Lokanath Goswami, Narottama Dasa, and Viswanath Cakravarti are in front of the temple. Viswanath Cakravarti arranged to have this temple built.

Radha-Gopinath Temple

The Deity of Gopinath was discovered at Vamsivat by Paramananda Bhattacarya, who entrusted the Deity's worship to his disciple Madhu Pandita. On the altar are deities of Srimati Radharani and Her sister, Ananga Manjari. Madhu Pandita's *samadhi* is next to the temple.

Gopinathji was originally installed in Vrindavana by Vajranabha, the great-grandson of Krishna. When the Muslims raided Vrindavana, the original Gopinath Deity was taken to Jaipur. The Gopinath Deity in Jaipur and Lord Krishna are said to exactly resemble each other from Their shoulders down to the waist.

Radha-Raman Temple

Gopal Bhatta Goswami established this temple. The Deity of Sri Radha-Raman was manifested from one of Gopal Bhatta Goswami's *shalagram-shilas* on the full moon day of Vaisakha (April/May) in 1542. This event is celebrated every year (May) by bathing the Deity with 100 litres of milk and other auspicious items. The remnants of this **abhiseka** (bathing) are like nectar. Gopal Bhatta Goswami's other *shalagram-shilas* are worshiped on the altar here. The appearance place of the Sri Radha-Raman Deity is next to the temple. Radha-Ramanji is one of the few original Deities of the Goswamis still in Vrindavana. The standard of worship in this temple is very high..

Sri Caitanya Mahaprabhu's *kaupina* (cloth) and *asana* (seat), which Gopal Bhatta Goswami brought from Jagannath Puri, are also in this temple. They are brought out to be seen by the public three or four times a year. The *asana* is black wood about 12" by 10". Gopala Bhatta Goswami's *samadhi* is to the left after you enter the first gate from the street into the temple compound.

The fires for cooking in the temple kitchen have been burning continuously for over 435 years, since the Deity was installed. This is so no foreign elements, such as matches, are used for ignition

purposes.

Darshan is usually 9 to 11 am and 6 to 8 pm. According to the season, times may change.

Radha-Syamasundara Temple

These are the Deities of Syamananda Prabhu. *Darshan* is from 8.30 to 11 am and 5 to 8 pm. It is one of the seven major temples in Vrindavana. Syamananda's *samadhi* is across the street and down from the entrance of the temple.

Seva Kunja (Nikunjavan)

Krishna would massage Radharani's feet and decorate Her hair with flowers here. Once Krishna pushed His flute into the ground here and created a small *kund*, called Lalita Kund, to satisfy Lalita Sakhi's thirst. No one is allowed within the enclosure at night. The numerous monkeys that are there during the day also leave at night.

Nidhivana

Radha and Krishna take rest here after dancing and other conjugal affairs. *Nidhi* means "sleep". There is a small temple here which has a bed where Radha and Krishna are supposed to take rest. The *samadhi* of Haridasa Swami is here. He was a contemporary of the six Goswamis, and he discovered the Banke Bihari Deity here.

Sixty-four Samadhis

Opposite the post office near the Radha-Govinda Temple is a garden that contains the *puspa* (flower) *samadhis* of 64 Gaudiya Vaishnava Acaryas. These include Madhavendra Puri, Iswara Puri, the six Goswamis, Ramananda Raya, Swarupa Damodara, etc. There is also a well here, called Venu Kupa, which was manifest from the sound of Krishna's flute. The well is now covered by grass, so you may have to ask someone where it is located.

Sona Gauranga Temple

These Deities were worshiped by Jagannath Dasa Babaji. They are located in a person's house next to Prema Talkies cinema in the lane opposite the Radha-Gopinath Temple.

Banke Bihari Temple

This temple was established by Haridas Swami, a contemporary of the six Goswamis. He discovered the Banke Bihari Deity at Nidhivana, where Banke Bihari was originally worshiped. Banke Bihari was moved here when this temple was constructed in 1864. This is the most popular temple in Vrindavana, especially in the month of Sravana, during Jhulan Yatra.

The curtain before the Deities is not left open like at other temples. Every few minutes the curtain is pulled shut and then opened again. The Deities do not get up until 9 am. The temple has *mangala-arati* only one day a year. Only one day a year can the lotus feet of the Deity be seen, on Akhyaya Tritiya. The priests of the temple belong to the Nimbarka-sampradaya. *Darshan* is from 10 am to 12.30 pm and from 6 to 9 pm.

Vamsivata Area

In the *Srimad Bhgavatam* it is said that the *rasa* dance started from this place on the full moon night of the Sarat season.

Gopiswara Mahadeva Temple

The Siva-linga in this temple was installed by Vajranabha, the great grandson of Krishna. Every morning from 4 am to noon, thousands of people pour Yamuna water over the *linga*. It is said that the big pipal tree here is a *kalpa-vriksya* tree and will fulfil all desires. This temple is in the Vamsivata area.

Chir Ghat

Krishna rested here after killing the Kesi demon. Lord Caitanya also rested here. Some people say that the Gopis' clothes were stolen here by Krishna and other say that this pastime happened 14 km up the river.

Imli Tala

Sri Caitanya Mahaprabhu would come daily to **Imli Tala** to chant *japa*, when He was living in Vrindavana. Imli Tala means the shade of the tamarind tree. *Imli* means 'tamarind' and *tala* mean 'tree'. There is a small temple here with Gaura-Nitai and Radha-Krishna Deities.

Kaliya-hrada

At **Kaliya-hrada**, there is a *kadamba* tree that Krishna jumped from to chastise the Kaliya snake.

Vrindavana Parikrama

It is customary for devotees to walk around the town of Vrindavana. There is a *parikrama* path that goes around the town. This path is one street over from the ISKCON temple. It takes two or three hours to go around the town.

PRACTICALITIES

Phone and Post

There are STD phones across the street from the ISKCON Temple. There is also an STD phone in the front of the Gurukula building, by the front gate. Downtown there is an STD phone by the Banke Bihari Temple.

There is a good post office in the front of the ISKCON Gurukula building, near the street. The person working there is efficient. The main post office is on the same road as the Govindaji Temple.

Water

Most of the tap water in Vrindavana is dangerous to drink and tastes horrible. Even if the water tastes all right, unless you are used to drinking it, there is a good chance you will get sick. It is best to drink bottled water, purified water, or boiled water. The main cause of serious diseases in India is from bad water. If you do drink water from the tap or a well, you should only drink water that you see the locals drinking. It is best to ask the locals what water is safe to drink.

Directly across the street from the ISKCON Temple there is a tap that many people drink from and do not usually get sick. This water tastes good and is suggested, if you choose to drink tap water. Some of the wells in Vrindavana have sweet water and could be all right to drink. There is a well at the ISKCON *goshala* that many people drink from and do not usually get sick.

Photography

The best place in Vrindavana for developing and purchasing film is *RK Studio*. Most of the rickshaw-walas know where it is located.

Travel Agents

Aerotrek Travels is run by two brothers who work out of both Mathura (0565-404361) and Delhi (371-5966). The Delhi address is E-1 Mercantile Building, 2nd Floor, Connaught Place. This is across the street from Nirula's on E Block. They can book plane tickets anywhere in the world at discount prices. They are highly recommended. One of the brothers lives in Mathura and goes to the ISKCON Guest House almost every night during the busy times in Vrindavana. At other times he usually comes three days a week. If you have problems getting a flight out of India because the flights are all booked, they may be able help you get a reservation. You can ask in the ISKCON Guest House how to get in contact with them.

Radha Travels (Off: 82512, Res: 82474) Agrawal Market, Mandir Lane, Loi Bazaar, have been coming to the ISKCON Temple for years. During the busy times of the year someone from the travel agency normally comes to the temple every night. There is no problem with giving them your passport to arrange a tourist quota train booking. I have not heard of any case of them losing important documents.

If you arrange a train ticket with them it is a good idea to give them optional choices in case they cannot get the train and date you want. Sometimes they may tell you that they cannot get a particular train ticket for you. Often if you then give them your passport and ask them to access the tourist quota for that particular train, they are then able to get you the ticket. They also can arrange to reconfirm your plane reservation.

Doctors and Hospitals

There is an Ayurvedic doctor named Kaviraj Partap Singh Chauhan who comes to the ISKCON Temple every Sunday, 10 am to 2 pm. He usually charges Rs 50 a visit. There is also a decent Ayurvedic doctor on the road going to Banke Bihari Temple from Loi Bazaar, called Dr Narottama. A good western doctor is Doctor Nangia, who is located across from the Loi Bazaar post office.

If you have jaundice (hepatitis) there is a good doctor in downtown Vrindavana who is a disciple of **Shyamasakhi**.

You can ask the rickshaw-walas outside the ISKCON Temple to bring you to Shyamasakhi, as many of them know how to get there. One person told me that he was almost dead and was saved by this doctor. His house is down a side street right next to the STD phones on the road between Banke Bihari Temple and Loi Bazaar.

For any long-term illnesses I would highly recommend that you go see **Dr Triguna** in Delhi. He is one of the best Ayurvedic doctors in India, if not the best. Directions on how to get to his office are in the Delhi and Health sections.

Saraf Hospital, Bhaktivedanta Swami Rd (also called Chatikara Road), the road going out of town past the ISKCON Temple, and **Ram Krishna Hospital** are two places that can be used in an emergency. Better than these two places is **Methodist Hospital** in Mathura. If there is a serious illness it is suggested to go to a hospital in Delhi.

Monkeys

You have to be careful of the monkeys, because they will steal anything they can from you, if you give them a chance. They go especially for your eye glasses, bananas (small surprise), and other fruit. They can jump down from a roof and snatch your glasses off your face in one swipe. While you are trying to get the glasses of your friends back, another monkey can come and steal your glasses too (true story). On the Vrindavana *parikrama* path there is a spot by the Ya- muna River where you have to duck down to go through a doorway. This is a favorite spot for the monkeys to steal a pair of glasses. They also bite, especially small children. Children like to bother monkeys, and the monkeys won't take any nonsense from them. Monkeys also sometimes carry rabies.

Most of the time monkeys are sneak thieves and will not try to steal from a formidable opponent. Keep your eyes open for them, and never let them get too close to you without looking at them. Give them a look to let them know that you know they are there. Never turn and run from them, as they are extremely fast. If they go for your bananas and challenge you, renounce the bananas. This is a life and death situation for them. They are willing to die for a banana.

Security

You have to be careful about leaving your shoes in front of temples. If you have a new expensive pair of Birkenstocks or sneakers (trainers), there is a good chance you will lose them if you leave them un- protected in front of temples in India. It is a good idea to separate your shoes and to hide them. A good idea is to get a cheap pair of Indian shoes to wear to the temples. When you visit temples in Vrin- davana it is a good idea to pay someone a rupee or two to look after your shoes.

Do not leave any items lying around in the temple room. This includes a bead bag or carry bag. I have seen people amazed that someone stole their bag, which included their money and plane ticket. I have heard of a case where some- one had his money belt stolen off his body during a *kirtana* in a temple.

Changing Money

You can change money in the bank on the front side of the Gurukula build- ing, by the front entrance of the ISKCON Temple. This bank will usually only change American dollars and British pounds. They may not take Thomas Cook Travellers' cheques or American Express cheques. You may have to give them a day or two advance notice. At Shishu Kumar Agarwal, next to Ganga Prasad, you can change money and get an exchange certificate. There is a State Bank of India branch on the road to the right at the end of Loi Bazaar, but they can be very inefficient and take a long time.

Income Tax Clearance

The office to get an income tax clearance is by KR College, in Mathura. If you have a student or entry visa you need to bring a letter from the organization sponsoring you.

Where To Buy

I learned about buying in Vrindavana when I purchased goods for a store and spent weeks in Loi Bazaar. If one merchant tells you he will give you the exact same items as another merchant, but at a much cheaper price, I would not normally believe them. More than likely you will be getting an inferior quality product. Most of the time these merchants are working on a very low profit margin and cannot afford to give you a large discount.

The important judgment for me on which merchant to purchase from is good communications and consistent good quality. This means getting what I asked for without wasting any time. I also demand a money back guarantee, in case there is a defect in any of the products. A good merchant will gladly do this, as they will not want to ruin their reputation.

Ganga Prasada, end of Loi Bazaar, is by far the best place to get devotional clothing. It is run by four brothers who are easy to communicate with and they quickly give you what you want, without trying to push anything else on you. They have an excellent selection of items, and the quality is guaranteed or you can

return it. Their prices are not that cheap, but they are reasonable. They are highly recommended.

Rasbihari Lal & Sons are directly across from Ganga Prasada in Loi Bazaar. They have a good selection of devotional items and pictures at good prices. From looking at their shop they do not seem to have very much, but upstairs there are many more items. There is another shop that sells many of the same items a few shops down on the left from this shop. Often their prices are cheaper for the exact same items, but they do not have as good a selection.

Dinesh Cloth Merchant (82363), Loi Bazaar, has good quality and is fairly easy to communicate with. A lot of people deal with them.

Mahesh Cloth Merchant has a good selection of items and is fairly easy to communicate with. He usually has some new items that no one else has and can have good bags and bead bags.

Khadi Bhavan is a government undertaking that sells good *khadi* (hand-woven cotten) products at a fixed price. The month of Gandhi's birthday, October, they have a 30% off sale. This shop is at the beginning of Loi Bazaar, as you enter from the ISKCON Temple side. Many of the merchants in Loi Bazaar buy from them during their sale and later sell these same *khadi* items at a higher price. They also sell some other items besides *khadi*.

Rajendra Tulasiwala, Loi Bazaar, has good quality and prices on *tulasi* and other beads. They can make custom orders of beads that you design yourself. It is a father and son business. The son understands English much better and is easy to deal with.

Radheyshyam Puja Bhandar, Loi Bazaar, across from the two *tulasi* shops, sells good brass *puja* goods. They are a little hard to communicate with, but they have been dealing with devotees for years and have a good selection of goods.

Heera Jewellers, in the beginning of Loi Bazaar by the Loi Bazaar Post Office, have been dealing with devotees for years and know what they like to buy. They are good people to purchase from, but because they have a good location and a lot of customers, their prices can be high. If you are buying for resale, they are good to buy from because they can help you choose the items that sell well. They also offered to me the right to return whatever I did not sell. I did not return anything. They sell good silver shoes for Deities, silver *tulasi* necklaces, silver *puja* items, and much more.

Gopaldas Emporium and **Shriji Jewellers,** both on the left side of the road as you go from Loi Bazaar to Banke Bihari Temple, are honest silver jewellers. They have many of the items that other jewellers have, but 10% or 20% cheaper. Many of the local devotees buy from them. There are two Shriji Jewellers on this road. The one I am suggesting is closer to the Banke Bihari Temple.

Six Fingers Narayana is known to be one of the best tailors in Vrindavana. To get to his shop, go to the end of Loi Bazaar, make a right at the T intersection, and go down about 10 shops. His shop is on the right. During the festival times you should put your order in as early as possible, as he is very busy.

Matang Perfumers, across the street from the ISKCON Temple, has a good selection of incense and oils. Some people think he has the best incense in India, and other people do not like this variety of incense.

Vidya Dasi is expert at getting Deity outfits made. She has been doing it for over ten years and can make sure everything is done perfectly. If you go directly to the outfit makers there is a good chance you will receive an inferior product. She has a very good reputation.

Radhika (85252), Sant Colony, Raman Reti, owned by Shyam, makes Deity clothes and wedding dresses. He has been in the business for years.

Shipping: Shishu Kumar Agarwal, who has a trunk shop next to Ganga Prasad, also ships things out of India. His prices are reasonable, and he was recommended to me. He has been dealing with foreigners for years and has a good reputation.

Rambabu Bartan Bhandar, at the beginning of Loi Bazaar, as you come from Raman Reti, has a good selection of steel cups, plates, and pots.

Weather

During the summer the temperature is between 22°C (71°F) and 50°C (122°F). The winter has a low of 4°C (40°F) and a high of 25°C (77°F). The rainy season is from the end of June to September.

It is one of the hottest places in the world in the summer, during May and June. It is very cold in the winter time, from the end of November to mid-February. During the winter you need warm woolen clothing or thermal underwear in the morning, but the weather is all right during the day.

The weather is perfect from late September to the middle of November, during the month of Kartika. Also the month of March and the first half of April is good.

Where To Stay

Maheswari Ashram (442-043) is a recommended place, about an ten-minute walk from the ISKCON Temple. Basic rooms with bath are Rs 60, and there are rooms for Rs 80 in the new building that have small kitchen areas. It is a popular place and will definitely be full during the festival times. You can have a rickshaw driver bring you to Maheswari Ashram for Rs 3.

Santi Ashram (442-227) is a decent place, right next to the back-side of the ISKCON property. Rooms here are Rs 100 and Rs 150 for a big room. *Krishna Nivasa Rohtak Wali Dharamshala*, behind Fogal Ashrama, is a new place that has rooms with bath for Rs 60. It is a recommended place, but is not very conveniently located. The rooms here are a very good value.

Fogal Ashram (442-319), a third of the way to the downtown from the ISKCON Temple, is a large place that has very basic rooms with bath for Rs 50 and Rs 70. The Rs 70 rooms are a little newer. For location and quality this is not a very good choice, but because of its size a room is usually available, even when Vrindavana is very crowded and everything else is full.

Between the ISKCON Temple and Fogal Ashrama is *Bhaktivedanta Swami Ashram* (442-620), which has decent rooms for Rs 120 a night. I was told it can be noisy at night because of loud-speakers blasting.

If you go down the side road, across the street from Fogal Ashram, on your right you come to *Govinda Bihar*, which has good rooms for Rs 100 and Rs 150. I didn't see the difference between the two rooms. It has A/C rooms for Rs 500.

Temple & Garden (also called *Temple Gardens*, 442-225) is a nice place that has big rooms with a little kitchen area for Rs 200 a night. It is a suggested place in a quiet area, but it is a little hard to find. If you go down the street toward downtown from the ISKCON Temple to-wards Fogal Ashram, after an eight-minute walk you come to Bhaktivedanta Swami Ashram, where there is a sign directing you. You turn left there and go to the end of the road. The easiest way to get there is just have a rickshaw driver bring you there for about Rs 4.

The *ISKCON Guest House* (442-478) is the best place to stay in town. The problem with this place is that it is almost always full, so you have to reserve a room months in advance. Even then, during the festival times and Kartika (Oct/Nov) you most likely will not get a room here. Smaller rooms are Rs 175 and standard doubles are Rs 250 or Rs 275. There are more expensive rooms, which are more likely to be available, some with hot water and an air-cooler for up to Rs 400.

Chintamani Kunj (442-503) is a ten-minute walk from the ISKCON Temple on Bhaktivedanta Swami Marg, going away from the downtown. It has good rooms for Rs 125 and Rs 200 during the high seasons. It is a recommended place. On the other side of the street is the nearby *Citrakut Dhama* (442-729), which has basic rooms for Rs 100 to Rs 150.

Nandavana Hotel (442-517), a 15 minute walk from the ISKCON Temple (3 minute by motor rickshaw), has rooms for Rs 500 and Rs 700 with A/C. The rugs really need a cleaning. It is a good place, but inconveniently located.

Jagat Guru Dhama (442-717), on the way to the Nandanvan Hotel, has good clean rooms from Rs 200 to Rs 400. This place does not allow foreigners to stay here. It is a popular place.

Meera Mohan Atithi Bhawan (442-233), beginning of the downtown, has rooms with hot water and an air-cooler for Rs 200 and Rs 500 for an A/C room. Unless you want to be in the downtown, this place is inconveniently located, and the rooms are also over-priced.

Where To Eat

The best place to eat in town is at the restaurant in the *ISKCON Guest House*. There is a good selection of reasonably priced items that include an all-you-can-eat thali for Rs 40. Some good items on the menu are fried rice, dal fried, mixed vegetable, matar alu, chips (french fries) and the cheese (panir) preparation. They also sometimes have pizza and vegiburgers.

There is a booth at the ISKCON Temple that serves pizza and other snacks. You can also purchase a good selection of *maha-prasada* in the temple room. You can eat temple *prasada* breakfast (Rs 10) and lunch (Rs 20).

You can get cold drinks and good *lassi* across the street from the ISKCON Temple at *Biharilals*. This place is also a good general store.

There are a few good fruit and vegetable stands across the street from the ISKCON Temple. They are conveniently located, but they usually charge from 20% to 50% more than what you pay for the same items downtown. They may also overcharge you, so it is a good idea to add up the bill yourself.

Getting Around Vrindavana

A bike rickshaw to Loi Bazaar costs Rs 6 for one person and Rs 7 for two people, and anything over Rs 10 is overpaying. People have been charged Rs 100 and more. Sometimes at night and during festivals there are just no rickshaws around, so you may be forced to pay Rs 10 to Rs 15 to get to Loi Bazaar. This should not happen very often.

To get to Fogal Ashram is Rs 4, Maheshari Ashram is Rs 3, Vrindavana bus stand Rs 8 or Rs 10. Locals may pay

lower prices.

To visit the major temples in Vrindavana takes about three hours and costs Rs 75 by bicycle-rickshaw, or Rs 25 an hour. Many of the rickshaw-*walas* know where all the major temples are located.

Taxi Fares

To Radha Kund and back with a two hours waiting time is Rs 400. To go to Varsana and Nandagram is Rs 500. To go to Varsana, Nandagram, and Radha Kund is Rs 600. To go to Gokula and Raval is Rs 450. To do a local trip in Braj is about Rs 400 for 4 hours and Rs 500 for 6 hours. To go to Mathura and back by taxi is Rs 150, and one way it is Rs 100. To take an auto-rickshaw to Mathura is Rs 70 one way and Rs 120 round-trip.

Travel

Air The closest airport is in Delhi (150 km, 3½ hr).

Train There is no long-distance train station in Vrindavana. The closest major train station is in Mathura, about 14 km away or a half-hour taxi ride. There is a passenger train between Mathura and Vrindavana.

Bus There are buses to Delhi that you can get in front of the ISKCON Temple or at the Vrindavana bus stand at 5 am, 7 am, 9 am, 12 noon, 2.30 pm, and 4 pm. If you get the bus in front of the temple there is a good chance you will not get a seat (except the 5 am bus). So you could get a rickshaw to the Vrindavana bus stand (Rs 9) and guarantee yourself a seat.

Buses to Vrindavana or Mathura from Delhi depart from either the Interstate Bus Terminal near Kashmiri Gate, in Old Delhi, or from the Ashram bus stop in the southeast part of Delhi. There are a few direct buses from Delhi to Vrinda-vana, but most of the buses go to Mathura (every half hour). If you take the Mathura bus, you get down at Chatikara Road and from there get a motor rickshaw or a very crowded tempo. A tempo is a big motor rickshaw that picks up passengers like a bus. If you miss this stop, you can get down at Mathura and pay Rs 50 for a motor rickshaw to the ISKCON Temple. You could ask the conductor of the bus to inform you when you reach Chatikara Road, or ask a few passengers to help you get off at the correct place. After dark it may be difficult to get a rickshaw at Chatikara Road.

The Ashram bus stand is in the southeast part of Delhi, 30 minutes closer to Vrindavana than the Interstate Bus Terminal by Kashmiri Gate (Old Delhi). The problem with getting the Vrindavana or Mathura bus here is the signs on the buses are in Hindi, and there is a good chance there will be standing room only when you get on the bus. If you cannot read Hindi, you can ask people at the bus stand if they are going to Mathura. When you find someone, follow them closely and get on the same bus they get on, while at the same time confirming with other passengers that the bus is going to Mathura (Vrindavana).

A cheap way to get to Vrindavana from the airport is to take the Delhi Transport Corp. (DTC) bus to the Interstate bus station, and from there take a local bus to Mathura or Vrindavana.

There is a direct bus to **Jaipur** at 5.45 am from the Vrindavana bus stand. You can also get buses to Agra (1 hr). There is an overnight bus, with thin seats, that goes to Haridwar at around 8.30 pm. To be decently comfortable you could book two seats for this bus in advance, at the bus stand. The bus stand is about a twenty minute cycle rickshaw from the ISKCON Temple (Rs 8 or 10).

There are many buses to Haridwar, Jaipur, Agra, and Delhi that depart from the bus stands in Mathura.

Taxi Taking a taxi is the suggested way to reach Vrindavana from **Delhi** if you have a few people in your group, a family with children, or you just want to be decently comfortable. From the airport it is Rs 1000 to Rs 1200 direct to Vrindavana. At the "Paid Taxi Stands" you will be told Rs 1200 to Rs 1500, but you should not pay more than Rs 1200, even late at night. Coming by taxi is the fastest and most comfortable way. It will take you about three and a half hours. To get to the ISKCON center you must turn onto Bhaktivedanta Swami Marg (also called Chatikara Road), which is about 15 km before Mathura. There is a sign on the road pointing to the temple. If you have to ask directions and the local persons do not know the ISKCON Temple, ask for the Krishna Balarama Mandir or the Angrasi Mandir (Englishmen's temple).

A taxi from Vrindavana to **Jaipur** costs Rs 1500, if you go and come back the same day. The taxi is Rs 600 for each additional day. A taxi to the train station in **Tundla** costs Rs 550 from Vrindavana. From the Tundla train station it will cost about Rs 600 to Vrindavana. A taxi to Agra or Aligarh costs Rs 500 from Vrindavana.

The standard per km fee for a long distance taxi is Rs 3 for a vehicle that uses diesel fuel, such as an Ambassador, or Rs 3.5 for a vehicle that used gas, such as a Maruti van. From Delhi the rate will usually be Rs 4 per km for an Ambassador. From Delhi to Mathura is about 150 km. If you take a long-distance taxi you will be charged for both going and returning, as it will be difficult for the taxi driver to get a return fare.

Mathura to Vrindavana

The easiest transport to take between Mathura and Vrindavana is a taxi (25 min, Rs 80 to Rs 100 from the Mathura train station and Rs 100 from Vrindavana to the Mathura train station) or a motor rickshaw (30 min, Rs 40 to Rs 50 from Mathura and Rs 50 to Rs 70 from Vrindavana).

From the train station there are often very crowded shared motor rickshaws (tempos) that go to Vrindavana (Rs 4). To get a tempo you may have to take a bike rickshaw to the main road and from there get a tempo. From the main road tempos leave every few minutes. Once you reach Vrindavana you have to take a bike rickshaw. To the ISKCON temple a rickshaw should cost Rs 7 or Rs 8.

Buses from Mathura to Vrindavana leave infrequently from the old bus stand. There is a small train that leaves Mathura Junction at 9 am and 8 pm that goes to Vrindavana. It returns from Vrindavana at 9.30 am and 8.30 pm. Unless you are tight for money, it is best to take a Rs 40 or Rs 50 auto rickshaw ride from Mathura to Vrindavana.

Between Vrindavan and Mayapur

Air The closest airport to Vrindavana is in Delhi. There are seven flights a day between Delhi and Calcutta that cost around $150, depending on what airlines you take.

Train The fastest train from Delhi to Calcutta is the Rajdhani Exp #2302 or #2306 (5.15 pm, 18½ hr). The Rajdhani Exp leaves Calcutta at 4.30 pm via Gaya (Mon, Tue, Wed, Fri, Sat) and via Patna at 1.45 pm (Thu, Sun). The Rajdhani has three classes you can travel by: First class air-con, two tier A/C (second-class A/C), and three tiers A/C. It is expensive, but quick and comfortable.

If you travel from Vrindavana to Mayapur, you can get a train ticket from the travel agent who comes regularly to the ISKCON Guest House.

The Kalka Mail #2312 departs from Aligarh at 9.35 am and Tundla at 10.50 am (Rs 550 by taxi). The train takes about 20 hours to go from Tundla to Burdwan (also called Barddhaman). Burdwan is about two hours northwest of Calcutta. From Burdwan it will cost from Rs 750 to 850 by taxi to get to Mayapur. You could also get a local bus from Burdwan to Navadwipa and then take a boat and rickshaw to Mayapur, which is an uncomfortable way to go. Both the taxi stand and the bus station are a short walk outside and to the left from the train station. Burdwan is a mellow station, especially compared to Howrah. Also it is cheaper to take a taxi from there than from Calcutta.

If you take the Kalka Mail from Calcutta (7.15 pm) or Burdwan, you get down at Tundla, which is about an hour before Agra. You can board the Kalka Mail at either Calcutta (7.15 pm) or Burdwan (Barddhaman), which is two hours northwest of Calcutta. It is about Rs 750 or Rs 850 by taxi from Mayapur to Burdwan. The stop before Tundla is Firozabad, which is just five minutes before. This train takes 25 hours to go from Calcutta to Delhi. From Calcutta to Tundla takes 22 hours and from Burdwan to Tundla 20 hours. The train arrives in Tundla at 4 pm and Aligarh at 5.15 pm. From Tundla a taxi to Vrindavana costs Rs 550 to 600 rupee.

The Poorva Express #2304 or # 2382 departs from Delhi at 4.30 pm, Aligarh at 6.15 pm, and Tundla at 8 pm. It arrives in Burdwan (Barddhaman) at 2.36 pm and Calcutta at 4.15 pm. It is about the same as the Kalka Mail, but it departs Tundla in the evening rather than in the morning. The Poorva Express departs Howrah in Calcutta at 9.15 am and Burdwan (Barddhaman) at 10.30 am. It arrives in Tundla at 4.30 am, Aligarh at 5.30 am, and Delhi at 8.05 am.

The Toofan Express, which departs from Howrah in Calcutta (1.45 pm) goes via Agra. It takes 35 hours to reach Mathura (6 pm). This is the slowest and cheapest way to go. The Toofan Express departs from Mathura at 11 am and arrives in Burdwan (Barddhaman) at 3.20 pm (32 hr) and Calcutta at 6.15 pm. Being a local train this train stops frequently and can get extremely crowded.

Road It is too far to take a bus between Vrindavana and Mayapur. Your only options are to go by air or train.

BRAJA MANDALA AREA

Radha Kund and Syama Kund

This is a very tranquil and peaceful place. It is the most holy place in the Braja area, so Gaudiya Vaishnavas consider it the most sacred place in India. It is a very important place to visit. There are two holy tanks here right next to each other. For years Radha Kund and Syama Kund were lost and no one knew exactly where they were located. When Lord Caitanya came to Vrindavana in 1514 He rediscovered these two important *kunds*. Part of the *parikrama* of Govardhana Hill is going around Radha and Syama Kund.

The story of Radha Kund is that one demon named **Aristasura**, in the body of a bull, was killed by Krishna. The *gopis* (cowherd girls) told Krishna that for killing a bull He had to purify Himself by visiting every single holy place in the three worlds. Krishna then said, "Why should I visit all these places, I will just bring the water from all these places here and then bathe in them." Krishna then struck His heel on the ground and all the waters of the holy places entered into Syama Kund. The *gopis* led by Radharani then dug another pond nearby with their bangles. Then a representative of all the sacred places told Radharani, "Our lives would be successful if we could enter Your pond." The holy waters from Syama Kund then flowed into Radha Kund with the permission of Radha. So Radha Kund is the holy waters from all the sacred places.

When **Raghunath Dasa Goswami** first stayed at Radha Kund the two *kunds* were only 12 feet by 12 feet in size. At that time one rich man went to Badrinath to offer Lord Narayana a large donation. In a dream the Lord told the man to go to Radha Kund and give the money to Raghunath Dasa Goswami to renovate the *kunds*, which he did. Raghunath Dasa Goswami and Jiva Goswami supervised the expansion of the *kunds* around 1554.

In the center of Radha Kund is a small walled-in area called **Kancana-kund**. This *kund* is said to mark the location of the original *kund* that Srimati Radharani and the *gopis* dug with their bangles. In the eight directions surrounding Radha Kund are the *kunjas* of Sri Radha's *asta-sakhis* (eight main *gopis*). They are the *kunjas* of Lalita, Vishakha, Citra Devi, Indulekha Sakhi, Campakalata, Ranga Devi, Tungavidya, and Sudevi. Sri Ananga Manjari *kunja* is in the center of Radha Kund.

Radha Kund appeared at 12 midnight on Bahulastami, the eighth day (*astami*) of the waning moon in the month of Kar-

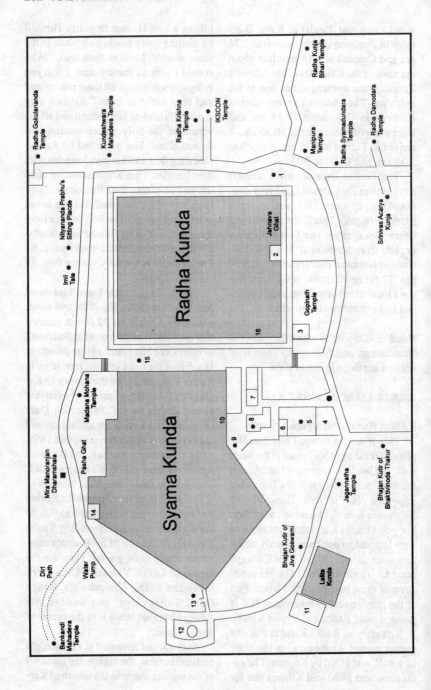

Radha Gokulananda
Temple

Kundeshwara
Mahadeva Temple

Radha Krishna
Temple

IKSCON
Temple

Radha Kunja
Bihari Temple

Manipura
Temple

Radha Syamasundara
Temple

Srinivas Acarya
Kunja

Radha Damodara
Temple

Nityananda Prabhu's
Sitting Placde

Imli
Tala

Jahnava Ghat

Radha Kunda

1

2

Gopinath
Temple

3

16

15

Madana Mohana
Temple

Pasha Ghat

7

10

8

6

5

4

9

Mira Manoranjan
Dharamshala

Syama Kunda

Jagannatha
Temple

Bhajan Kutir of
Bhaktivinoda Thakur

Bhajan Kutir of
Jiva Goswami

Dirt
Path

Water
Pump

Bankandi
Mahadeva Temple

Lalita
Kunda

14

12

13

11

1	Jhulan Sthali
2	Sitting Place of Jahnava Devi
3	Samadhi of Raghunath Dasa Goswami
4	Radha Govinda Temple
5	Tongue of Govardhana
6	Krishnadasa Kaviraja Goswami Bhajana Kutir
7	Teen Goswami Samadhi
8	Bhajana Kutir of Raghunatha Das Goswami
9	Pandava Tree
10	Manasa Pavan Ghat
11	Lalita Bihari Temple
12	Gopkuwa Well
13	Madhavendra Puri's Sitting Place
14	Sri Caitanya Mahaprabhu's Sitting Place
15	Ratna Vedi & Sri Carana Cinha
16	Govinda Ghat

tika (Oct/Nov). On that day thousands of people come and bathe at 12 midnight in Radha Kund. It is an ecstatic and exciting event.

There are many people who will try to guide you around the area and give you things. If you take anything from them or talk to them, expect to pay something. The problem I experienced was no matter how much you give them, it will not be enough. Do not get angry, it will not help. Also if you give some charity to the children here, you may attract an immediate crowd of twenty or thirty kids, who will not leave you alone. A good idea here is to not talk to anyone and not even acknowledge their existence, if possible. People that walk up to you will usually quickly go away if you politely ignore them. Any donations given at temples

will be politely accepted. If you like to give donations to anyone else, it is advised to give as you are leaving.

The cheapest way to Radha Kund is to take a tempo (many) to the end of Chatikara Rd. From there you get another tempo to Radha Kund. There are several direct buses to Radha Kund that can be boarded in front of the ISKCON temple.

You can get a motor rickshaw for Rs 250 or a taxi for Rs 400 round trip which includes a two hours waiting time. It takes about forty-five minutes to get to Radha Kund by taxi. From Vrindavana, the road to Radha Kund is very bumpy, and a motor rickshaw is very uncomfortable, so I would suggest taking a taxi. Radha Kund is much too far to go by bike rickshaw.

There are fairly decent rooms at the *Manoranjan Dharamshala*. To get there you walk from where the bus or taxi lets you off near Radha Kund. When you first see Radha Kund there is a road that goes straight and one that goes right. You take the road to the right and walk a few minutes. The dharamshala is a yellow building on the right.

Tour of Radha Kund

From where you arrive by taxi or bus you walk down the road toward Radha Kund. Just past the small hospital on the left is the **Radha-Gokulananda Temple**. This temple contains the *pratibhu-murtis* of Radha-Gokulananda. The original Deities are at Radha-Gokulananda Mandira in Vrindavana. In 1670 many of the original Deities of Vrindavana were moved to Jaipur. Their first stopping place was Radha Kund. Small replica temples of the original temples in Vrindavana were built at Radha Kund. *Pratibhu-murtis* (expanded forms, nondifferent from the original Deities) were established at Radha Kund to honor the Lord's visit here, and the worship has been continued for centuries. The residents of Radha Kund can visit the seven major temples of Vrindavana without leaving Radha Kund.

As you continue walking to Radha Kund you come to the small white marble roadside temple of **Sri Kundeswara Mahadeva** on the left. This is just before you see Radha Kund on your right. There are four Lord Siva temples in the four directions, surrounding Radha Kund, to protect Radha Kund from intrusion of unqualified persons.

As you continue on this road, Radha Kund is on your right. Another 200 feet from the Sri Kundeswara Mahadeva Temple is a stone structure shaped like an upside down U on the right side. This marks the site of Radha and Krishna's swing pastimes. If you walk up the small alley sloping up the hill to your left you come to the blackish pyramid-shaped **Radha-Krishna Temple**. This temple is the oldest temple at Radha Kund. Raghunath Dasa Goswami re-discovered the Radha-Krishna Deities in this temple when he excavated Radha Kund. They are said to be the presiding Deities of Radha Kund. There is a large neem tree and banyan tree entwined together in the courtyard of the temple, which are worshiped as Radha and Krishna. Next to this temple is a small **ISKCON Temple**, which has a good view of the *kund* from the roof.

You return to the *parikrama* path, turn left and walk 20 metres. The next road you see is the Govardhana *parikrama* path. Just after this junction on the left is the red stone **Gopala Manipur Mandira**. In 1994 Bhakti Swarupa Damodara Maharaja took possession of this temple. The white building opposite this temple houses the *pratibhu* Deities of **Radha-Kanta**. The original Deities were worshiped by Sri Vakreswara Pandita in Jagannath Puri. There is a *murti* of Vakreswara Pandita on the right side of the altar.

Coming out of the Radha-Kanta Temple you turn left, walk 20 feet, and turn right going backwards on the Govardhana *parikrama* path. After a five minute walk (100 metres) you come to the red stone **Radha-Kunja Bihari Temple**. This temple is on the Govardhana *parikrama* path. Located here are the Deities of Radha-Kunja Bihari and Caitanya Mahaprabhu. There is also the *puspa-samadhi* of **Gaurakisora Dasa Babaji Maharaja**. He lived in Vrindavana for 30 years and was the spiritual master of Srila Bhaktisiddhanta. This temple was founded by Srila Bhaktisiddhanta in 1935.

Back at the Radha Kund parikrama path, just pass the Gopala Mandira, you turn down a small lane on the left. Fifteen feet down this lane on the left hand side is the **Radha-Syama-sundara** Temple. Syamananda Prabhu's sitting place and *puspa-samadhi* are here. Further down this lane (30 metres), on the left, is the small red-colored **Radha-Damodara Temple**. Across the street from this temple is the sitting place of **Srinivas Acarya.**

If you go back to the main road and continue down the road 30 seconds just pass the water taps, you come to the **Radha-Gopinath Temple** on the right. This temple is right next to Radha Kund. On the altar of this temple the Deity of Gopinath is in the center and on His right hand side is Srimati Radharani and on His left hand side is Ananga Manjari, the younger sister of Radharani. Some of the ashes of Raghunath Dasa Goswami are entombed in this temple, and there is 24 hour *kirtana* at this spot. Behind the *samadhi*, is a small movable stone. Under this stone is *caranamrita* from **Raghunath Dasa Goswami's** *samadhi-murti*. You can also get some of Raghunath Dasa Goswami's buttermilk *maha-prasada*, which is kept behind the *kirtana* party in a small niche in the wall.

If you exit out the door to the left of the altar containing Gopinath it leads to a small platform jutting out into Radha Kund. This is where Jahnava-devi (in 1582), the wife of Lord Nityananda, stayed. This spot is known as **Jahnava Baitak**, the sitting place of Jahnava. There is a tamal tree and a small shrine here. Next to this is **Jahnava ghat**.

You then return to the *parikrama* path and continue down the path 15 metres. On your left is the red stone **Mahadeva Siva** Temple. Lord Mahadeva protects the northern side of Radha Kund. Right next to this temple is the **Radha-Raman Temple**. In 1879 the Deities of Sri Radha-Raman and Sri Sri Revati Balarama were installed in this temple.

Across the street from the Radha-Raman Temple and down a little is the **Radha-Govinda Temple** on the right. This temple contains the *pratibhu* Deities of Rupa Goswami. In the outer compound of this temple is the **Tongue of Govardhana**. Turn left immediately after leaving Govindaji's temple, before you reach the path. Walk up some steps and you come to a small garden with a small white temple in it. Raghunath Dasa Goswami saw the need of a water source other than Radha Kund, so he decided to have a well dug. As the workers dug down, they struck a rock and blood flowed from it. That night in a dream it was revealed to Raghunath Goswami that the stone was the tongue of Govardhana

and should be worshiped. It is said that if you walk seven times around any Govardhana-shila you can get the same benefit as by doing Govardhana *parikrama*, if time and circumstance do not allow you to do a full *parikrama* of Govardhana Hill.

If you proceed to the left from the Radha-Govinda Temple entrance on the path toward Syama Kund and walk straight 20 metres you come to the **Teen (three) Goswami Samadhi** of Raghunath Bhatta (left side), Krishna Dasa Kaviraja (center), and Raghunath Dasa Gosvami (right side). Each of these devotees left this world on the same day, but in different years: Raghunath Bhatta Goswami (1563), Raghunath Dasa Goswami (1583), and Krishna Dasa Kaviraja (1588). **Gopal Bhatta Gosvami's bhajana kutir** is twenty feet—to the right as you face the Teen Gosvami Samadhi.

To the left of this *samadhi* is the *bhajana kutir* of **Krishnadasa Kaviraja Goswami**. It is set back about 40 feet from the side of Syama Kund. This is where he wrote the *Caitanya-caritamrita*. The **bhajana kutir** of **Raghunath Dasa Goswami** is directly opposite Kaviraja Goswami's *bhajana kutir* and down a few steps toward Syama Kund. At this place Raghunath Das Goswami would speak three hours a day about the ecstatic pastimes of Sri Caitanya. He lived at Radha Kund for 41 years. On the left side of the same building is the **bhajana kutir** of **Sri Visvanath Cakravarti Thakura**.

Also near here is where the **Pandava trees** meditated on the bank of Syama Kund. When Raghunath Dasa Goswami was excavating Syama Kund, the Pandavas appeared to him in a dream. They told him not cut the trees because they, the Pandavas, were living in that form meditating on the banks of Syama Kund. He therefore dug around the trees, giving Syama Kund its irregular shape. Local authorities say the Pandavas have left and only a dead tree marks the place of their previous residence. At **Manas Pavan Ghat** Radharani and her girlfriends are said to bathe every day at noon.

Bhaktivinoda Thakura's house, which was built in the beginning of the century, is located down a side road going away from Syama Kund. After leaving the Govinda Temple and turning right back onto the *parikrama* path, you continue walking straight when the *parikrama* path turns right, about 40 feet from the Govinda Temple. Bhaktisiddhanta Sarasvati would come here during the month of Kartika (Oct/Nov). The *puspa-samadhis* of both Bhaktivinoda Thakur and Bhaktisiddhanta Sarasvati are located here. There are personal articles of Srila Bhaktisiddhanta in this house: his wooden shoes, walking stick, bed, chair, and table.

If you proceed back to the *parikrama* path from Bhaktivinoda's house and make a left, you come to the **Jagannath Temple** on the left. A little further down, on the left side of the road is **Lalita Kund**. Next to this *kund* is the **Lalita Mohana Temple**, where there are deities of Krishna and the *gopi* Lalita. To take some water from Lalita Kund on your head you have go through this temple to reach the *kund*. Directly across the road from Lalita Kund is the **bhajana kutir** of **Jiva Goswami** and a small temple dedicated to Radha-Damodara. Jiva Goswami did much of the practical work of excavating and managing Radha Kund. Also inside the *kutir* is the impression of Caitanya Mahaprabhu's footprints.

Thirty metres down the *parikrama*

path from Lalita Kund is the **Radha-Vinoda Bihari Temple**, which is a small temple on the right side. These are pratibhu Deities of Lokanath Goswami's Radha-Vinoda Deities. About 15 metres down the path and on the left is the well where the tongue of Govardhana was found, called **Gopi Kupa**. The well was never used. Behind the building opposite the well is where **Madhavendra Puri** sat while doing Govardhana *parikrama*, several years before Lord Caitanya revealed Radha Kund. If you continue around the path you come to a water pump on the left. Just before the path bends to the right, 10 metres further on the left hand side is a small dirt path which leads to the **Bankhandi Mahadeva** Siva Temple. This Siva Deity protects Radha Kund on the eastern side.

If you continue about 10 metres around Syama Kund you come to the place where **Lord Caitanya sat** when He came to Radha and Syama Kund. This spot, called Tamala Tala (Mahaprabhu Baithaka, sitting place), is on a platform with a tree on it, on the bank of Syama Kund. Lord Caitanya's footprints are enshrined here. When Lord Caitanya came here, Radha Kund and Syama Kund were small ponds surrounded by forest and fields. All the buildings here have been built since Lord Caitanya discovered Radha Kund, almost 500 years ago.

About 20 metres further down the path is the Manoranjan Dharamshala. Directly opposite, by Syama Kund, is **Pasa Ghata**, where Radha and Krishna are said to play *pasha kela* (a board game with dice). In this compound is a temple that commemorates **Vallabhacarya's** stay here. About 30 metres down the path on the left is the **Laksmi-Narayana Temple**, which is an old temple, about 500 years old.

A little distance from here on the right is the **Madana Mohana** Temple. Just past this temple are the stairs that lead to the path where Radha and Syama Kund meet. There are slits in the stone of the path between Radha and Syama Kund that allows mixing of the waters of Radha and Syama Kund. On this path, just past the mini-mountain of Govardhana-shilas, is a small open air shrine honoring the lotus footprints of Radha-Syamasundara. The **Sri Banke Bihari Temple** is an old temple on the right, just beyond the Sri Carana Cinha. About five metres north is a neem tree hanging over the path beside Radha Kund. This area is called **'Govinda Ghata'** and is where Radha and Krishna are said to sometimes enjoy *jhulana* (swing) pastimes.

If you come back up the stairs and continue to the right down the path after 30 metres you come to the **Radha-Gopinath Temple** on the left side. These are the *pratibhu* Deities of Madhu Pandita's Deities, which are now worshiped in Jaipur. In this compound, just opposite the temple, is a small building that marks the place where **Nityananda Prabhu** sat, called Nityananda Baithaka. By here is the **Imli Tala tree** where Rupa Goswami sat. About 20 metres more down the path is a Deity of Hanuman, on the right side, in between some shops. This completes the *parikrama* of Radha Kund and Syama Kund.

Kusuma Sarovara

A 25 minute walk from Radha Kund is Kusuma Sarovara, which is the best swimming spot in Vrindavana. *Kusuma* means "flower," and here the Gopis would pick flowers for Krishna. Also at this place is a temple dedicated to Uddhava that was established by Krishna's great-grandson about 4700 years ago.

Uddhava remains here in the form of grass. After you go to Radha Kund you could spend a relaxing hour or two here. It is a peaceful place.

GOVARDHANA TOWN

Manasi Ganga Kund is traditionally the starting and ending point of the circumambulation of Govardhana Hill. It is a large lake located in the middle of the town of Govardhana, and it is in the center of Govardhana Hill. One starts by bathing and ends by bathing here. This *kund* is a million times more potent than the Ganges River, because by bathing in the Ganges River one gets liberation and by bathing here one gets "Krishna prema," love of Krishna.

Mana means "mind" and *ganga* refers to the Ganga River. Once Nanda and Yasoda, hearing of the glories of the Ganges River, had a desire to bathe in it. All the cowherd boys did not want to leave Vrindavana, though Krishna was willing to take them there despite the great distance. They wishfully said, "I wish mother Ganga would come here." To fulfil the desires of His devotees, Krishna entered into meditation and from His mind sprung the *kund* known as Manasi Ganga.

The **bhajana kutir of Sanatana Goswami** is at Manasi Ganga. He would perform Govardhana *parikrama* as a daily vow. Next to the *bhajana kutir* is the **Chakaleswara Siva-linga**. It is one of the five presiding Siva-lingas worshiped in Vrindavana. It protects this part of the holy *dhama*. **Chakra Tirtha**, which was created by the Sudarsana Chakra, is embedded in the northern bank of Manasi Ganga.

On the bank of Manasi Ganga is the **Mukharavinda Temple**. There are two *shilas* in this temple. One *shila* is marked with the outline of Krishna's crown (Mukut-shila). According to Bhaktisiddhanta Maharaja the other *shila* is the mouth of Govardhana (Mukharavinda-shila).

The **Harideva Temple**, near Manasi Ganga, was established by Krishna's great-grandson 4800 years ago. Harideva is one of the four presiding Deities of Vrindavana, so one should ask His blessings before doing *parikrama*. The temple is a three-minute walk from the southern bank of Manasi Ganga. Lord Harideva is the presiding Deity for the western petal of the lotus of Braja Dhama. He is the lifter of Govardhana Hill. The temple was built by King Bhagandas of Jaipur, whose son, Raja Man Singh, built the Govindaji Temple in the sixteenth century during the reign of Emperor Akbar. The original Deity of Harideva was moved to the town of Rajdhani near Kanpur, when Aurangzeb tried to destroy the Deities and temples of Vrindavana. Lord Caitanya danced before this Deity.

Brahma Kund is the water that collected after Lord Brahma bathed Lord Krishna. This is where Lord Brahma offered his prayers after he took the cowherd boys away and hid them to test the power of Krishna. It is located on the southern bank of Manasi Ganga. Both Lord Caitanya and Lord Nityananda visited here. **Manasi Devi Temple** is located on the bank of Brahma Kund. Manasi Devi is the presiding deity of Manasi Ganga and one of the four main goddesses of Braja Dhama. The others are Vrinda Devi, in Kamyavana; Yogamaya Devi in Vrindavan; and Pataleswari in Mathura.

After taking bath in Manasi Ganga and *darshan* of Harideva, one returns to the *parikrama* path and continues on through the market. One will then come to a busy crossing where you should turn right on the road that goes over Govardhana Hill about three hundred meters ahead. Just before reaching the top of the hill, you will come to the **Laksmi Narayana Temple** on your left. This is one of the 108 Divya Desam Temples mentioned by the Alwars as being one of the most important temples in India. These Deities are considered to be the *utsava* (festival) Deities of Govardhana Hill. Just after the Laksmi Narayana Temple, before the top of the hill is a left turn to continue the *parikrama* of Govardhana.

ISKCON Temple (Govardhana)

There is an ISKCON property about 500m out of the town of Govardhana on the left side of the Govardhana Hill *parikrama* path. It is a peaceful place to spend the day, or a good place to rest while doing Govardhana *parikrama*. It is an old palace with a good size yard and a new stone boundary wall. There is a small white stone sign saying ISKCON in the wall. There are some very basic living facilities here.

Govardhana Hill Parikrama

Govardhana Hill was about two miles high 5000 years ago, but because of the curse of Pulastya Muni, it is sinking the height of a mustard seed daily.

The *parikrama* (circumambulation) route is 25 km (14 miles). It is a form of worship to walk around Govardhana Hill. Of all the devotees of Lord Krishna, Govardhana Hill is the best because it supplies Krishna and Balarama with all types of necessities. In the *Varaha Purana* it is said "Anyone who performs Govardhana *parikrama* will never have to take birth in this world again." Presently at its highest point the hill is just 80 feet high. Rupa

Goswami stated in his *Mathura Mahatyam* that one should first bathe in **Manasi Ganga** and then take *darshan* of **Harideva** before starting *parikrama*. There are many important spots that can be visited while going around Govardhana Hill.

After leaving the town of Govardhana you come to the village of Aniyora. In this village there is a **Balarama Temple** by Sankarsana Kund. The Balarama Deity was originally installed by Vajranabha nearly 5000 years ago. The present temple is about 200 years old. Balarama is black and about five feet high. This temple is open from 8 to 11 am and 4 to 8 pm. Next to the Balarama Deity, on His right, is a small Deity of Krishna.

Govinda Kund is just after the village of **Aniyora**. This is where Lord Indra bathed Krishna after Krishna lifted Govardhana Hill. This *kund* was made by the bathing ceremony. **Madhavendra Puri** found the Gopalji Deity while staying here. This Gopalji Deity is now known as **Sri Nathji** and is worshiped at Nathdwar in Rajasthan. **Indra Tila** is a small hill on the southern bank of Govinda Kund. This is where Lord Indra and mother Surabhi are said to have bathed Lord Krishna.

Dan Nivartana Kund is where the tax collection pastimes of the Lord took place.

The **Radha-Govinda Temple** is located between Nipa Kund and Govinda Kund. The Govinda Deity is playing a flute.

At the tail end of Govardhana is **Apsara Kund**, which is said to have been created when the seven main Apsaras came and bathed Lord Krishna. Govardhana Hill is said to resemble a peacock, so the *kund* next to Apsara Kund is called **Punchari Kund**, as this area is the tail

(*punch*) of Govardhana. Next to these two *kunds* is a Narasimha Temple.

Jatipura is named after Madhavendra Puri, who was a *sannyasi*, or *jati*. He worshiped the Deity of Gopal (Sri Nathji) here. In the town of Jatipura, at **Sringa Stali**, at the middle of the hill, devotees pour milk over a Govardhana *shila*. The *samadhis* of Vallabha acarya and his son Viththala, to whom Madhavendra Puri entrusted the worship of Gopala, are located here.

Devotees take rocks from Govardhana Hill and worship them exactly as they worship the Deity of Krishna in the temple. This worship is as good as Deity worship. Lord Krishna has appeared as Govardhana-*shila* (a stone from the hill), so that His devotees may render service to Him. It is important that not just anyone takes a rock from Govardhana Hill. The right to worship a Govardhana-*shila* should be given only by the guru (spiritual teacher). So his permission should be taken before beginning worship.

NANDAGRAM

Krishna lived here from the age of 8 to 16. Nanda Maharaja built his house on top of the large hill here to protect Krishna from the demons sent by King Kamsa to kill Him. It is 50 km northwest of Vrindavana town. The town surrounding the hill is called Nandagaon. The *panda* guides here are very persistent. If you talk to any of them or take anything from them, you should expect to give a donation.

Pavana Sarovara

This lake is located at the bottom of Nandagram Hill. Mother Yasoda used to bathe Lord Krishna here. The *bhajan kutir* of Sanatana Goswami is near the bank of the *kund*. There is also the *puspa-*

samadhi of Prabhupada's Godbrother, Akincina Krsnadas Babaji, who passed away at Nandagram.

Radharani would come to cook for Krishna every morning on the bank of this *kund*. There is a well here from which Srimati Radharani drew water when She would cook for Krishna.

Nandagram Temple

There are two black marble Deities of Krishna and Balarama in this temple. They are both in three-fold bending forms, holding flutes. On Their left and right are two tall deities of Yasoda and Nanda Maharaja. Next to mother Yasoda is a deity of Srimati Radharani and next to Nanda Maharaja are two of Krishna's friends, Sudama and Madhumangala. On the ceiling of the inner dome are many murals depicting Krishna's pastimes.

On the side altar there is a *linga* of Siva called Nandeswara, who is said to have been installed by Vajranabha. This *linga* of Siva resides eternally in Nandagram performing *bhajan* (worship) to Sri Krishna. This is one of the five presiding Siva-lingas of Braja. These Siva-lingas protect the holy *dhama* from any disturbing elements. This temple is on top of the hill.

Narasimhadeva Temple

At the bottom of the hill is a Narasimhadeva temple. Nanda Maharaja worshiped the Narasimha and Varaha Deities that are seen in this temple. It is on the opposite side of the Nandiswara Hill from Pavan Sarovara. The Deities are worshiped in a small house in the village. Nanda Maharaja's Lord Narayana Deity is also here, but it is not on the altar or worshiped because it is disfigured.

Close to this place is a **yoghurt pot** used by mother Yasoda. It is sunk into the ground in a broken down stone hut. It is 4½ feet across and five feet deep. One hundred fifty metres from the Narasimha Temple is **Yasoda Kund**. Mother Yasoda would bathe Krishna here.

Vrinda Kund

Vrinda Kund is where Srimati Vrinda Devi is said to contemplate how she will arrange the daily pastimes of Radha and Krishna. Next to Vrinda Kund is Gupta Kund, which is where Radha is said to secretly meet Krishna. There is a beautiful deity of Vrindadevi in the temple here. The *kund* and small temple are now entrusted in the care of ISKCON. Vrinda Kund is about one km from Nandagaon (Nandagram), not far from Pavana Sarovara.

To get to Vrinda Kund you can take a taxi and stop at Varsana and Nandagram on the way. To get there by public transportation you first take a public bus to the town of Kosi and from there you take a tempo to Nandagaon and then walk the remaining km from there. You can contact the mailout department at the ISKCON Vrindavana Temple to get more information about Vrinda Kund. The living facilities are very basic as there is no electricity.

VARSANA (BARSANA)

This is where Srimati Radharani lived and had many pastimes with Krishna. It is 42 km from Mathura and has a 7 km *parikrama* path around it. There are four peaks that make up Varsana, each one of these peaks is a head of Lord Brahma. Lord Brahma wanted to do some personal service for Radha and Krishna, so he incarnated himself as these hills.

On top of one of these hills is the **Larily Lal Temple** (Sriji Mandira), the temple of the beloved, which is where the original Radha-Krishna Deities of Varsana reside. The Deities in this temple were installed by Vajranabha. There are colorful pictures on the walls and ceiling, depicting the loving pastimes of Radha and Krishna. This temple is an important place to visit.

At **Pila Pokhar** Srimati Radharani washed Her hands. Because of Her touch, the *kund* turned a golden-yellow color. *Pila* means "yellow." This *kund* is still a golden-yellow color.

At **Mayur Kutir** (Mor Kutir) there was a dancing contest between Krishna and a peacock. Srimati Radharani judged their abilities. In the small temple of Mayur Kutir there are painted pictures of Krishna dancing as a peacock. There is a splendid painting done by a blind saint who used to live here.

On the hill next to the main temple, is the **Kushal Behari Temple**, built by the king of Jaipur at the turn of the century. You should be careful when you pass this temple because if you disturb the bees here they will attack you.

Sakara Gully (Sankari Kor) is the spot where Krishna would stop the *gopis* to steal their yoghurt. Krishna would stand in the middle of the ravine and would demand a tax from the *gopis* to get by. *Sakari* means "narrow."

Between Varsana and Nandagram

One time as Krishna and Radharani were sitting together a bee was disturbing Radharani by flying near Her. Krishna requested a friend to chase away the bee, and after finishing the task the friend came back proclaiming that *madhu* was gone. As *madhu* is a name for both a bee and Krishna, Radharani took the name as meaning Krishna and She began to cry, thinking Krishna was gone. Seeing Radharani cry, Krishna also began to cry, and their tears mingled together and became the *kund* known as **Prema Sarovara**.

At **Saket**, midway between Varsana and Nandagrama, the midnight or night time pastimes between Krishna and the *gopis* take place. All of the Goswamis have come to this place, at least for some time, to relish these pastimes. Radha and Krishna first met here. There is a temple here of **Yogamaya**. Her temple is here because she arranges the meetings between Radha and Krishna.

Uddhava Kyari is where Uddhava met the *gopis* when he was sent by Krishna to pacify them.

Forests of Vrindavana

In the **Madhuvana forest**, Dhruva Maharaja attained the *darshan* of Lord Vishnu during Satya-yuga. Satrughna, the brother of Lord Rama, made His capital in Madhuvana. There is a Deity of Satrughna on the bank of Krishna Kund. **Krishna Kund** was made by Krishna striking His flute on the ground. The village Deity is Balarama. His right hand is raised, and He is pitch black. There is a temple dedicated to **Narayana** and **Dhruva Maharaja** here. There is also a cave in which the demon Lavanasura lived.

Krishna appeared in Madhuvana in all four *yugas*. In Satya-yuga He appeared before Dhruva Maharaja. In Treta-yuga He came as Satrughna and killed the demon Lavanasura. He came as Lord Krishna in Dwapara-yuga and as Lord Caitanya in Kali-yuga.

In the **Talavana** forest Balarama killed Dhenukasura. There is a Deity of Balarama and His consort, Srimati Revati here.

At **Kumudvana** forest, on the bank

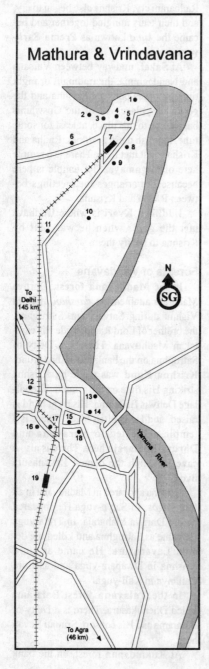

Mathura & Vrindavana

1	Kesi Gha
2	Madana Mohana Temple
3	Banki Bihari Temple
4	Loi Bazaar
5	Govindaji Temple
6	Krishna Balarama Temple
7	Vrindavana Railway Station
8	Bus Station
9	Rickshaw Stand to Mathura
10	Bhataron
11	Akrura Ghat
12	Krishna Janmabhumi Temple
13	Vishram Ghat
14	Dwarkadhish Temple
15	Archaeological Museum
16	Hotel Nepal
17	New Bus Stand
18	Old Bus Stand
19	Mathura Railway Station

of **Padma Kund**, is a small temple dedicated to Lord Kapila, who performed austerities here during Treta-yuga. *Kumud* means "water-lilies". During Krishna's time, beautiful water lilies grew here. If one takes bath here he acquires all the knowledge of the Vedic literature.

At **Bahulavana** there is a small temple with Deities of Krishna, Yamaraja, and Bahula carved in the wall.

Krishna killed **Bakasura** in the **Khadiravan** forest. On the bank of **Maduri Kund** (Sangam Kund) are the *bhajana kutirs* of Lokanath Goswami and Bhugarba Goswami.

At **Bhadravana** Krishna killed the demon Vatsasura. There is a **Bhadriswara Siva Temple** here founded by Vajranabha. In the **Bhandirvana** forest, Balarama killed the demon **Pralambasura.** Lakshmi, the goddess of fortune, being desirous of attaining the position of a *gopi* in Vrindavana, stays in the **Bilvavana** forest performing austerities.

Lohavana is where Jarasandha was defeated 18 times. There is a Radha-Gopinath Temple here. There is also the cave where the demon Lohasura lived. Krishna killed this demon.

Santanu Kund

This is the place where King Santanu performed austerities to get Bhismadeva as his son. There is a temple situated on a hill in the center of town. The Deity in this temple is a black Krishna, standing alone with His flute. At His feet is a collection of *shalagram-shilas*. Many childless couples come to worship this Deity and pray for children.

Badarikasrama and Kedarnath

Because Braja Dhama is the original abode of Lord Krishna, all the holy *tirthas* in the universe originally exist here. Badarikasrama originally exists in Braja Dhama and the one in the Himalayas is an expansion of the original in Braja. There is a cold *kund* here called Tapasa Kund.

About 10 km from Badarikasrama is Kedarnath Dhama. There is a Siva temple here, which you have to climb 270 steps to reach. Both of these places are in the middle of nowhere.

Kamavana

The town of Kamavana is 37 miles from Mathura and has a *parikrama* of 22 km.

Vrindadevi, the presiding deity of Vrindavana, is in the **Govinda Temple** in the town of Kamavana. This deity was discovered by Rupa Goswami on the bank of Brahma Kund in Vrindavana. He installed the deity in a small temple next to the Radha-Govinda Temple. Later, due

to fear of the Muslims, the king of Jaipur decided to take Vrindadevi, Radha-Gopinath, Radha-Madana Mohan, and Radha-Govinda to Jaipur. But when they reached Kamavana, Vrindadevi refused to go any further. She is a red deity with big black eyes.

Another important temple here is **Kameswara**, a Siva-linga, which is one of the four Mahadevas (deities of Lord Siva) that were installed by Vajranabha. Kameswara means one who fulfills all desires. It is said that with just a little worship of this *linga*, one gets all his devotional desires fulfilled.

The **Pandavas** lived here during their period of exile. The Caurasi-khamba Temple has eighty-four ancient beautifully carved pillars that resemble the ones at Gokula.

At **Bimal Kund**, Durvasa Muni bathed with his 60,000 disciples.

Vyomasura cave is a few km out of town in the side of a hill. In this cave Vyomasura put the cowherd boys after stealing them. Krishna apprehended and fought with Vyomasura here.

During this fight Krishna's helmet and necklace fell and there are indentations of them in the rocks on top of the hill. During the fight Krishna fell from the sky and landed on His feet and hands. Imbedded in the rock are perfectly legible footprints and handprints. The battle was so heavy that the earth began to shake. To steady the wobbling earth, Balarama pressed His foot into the rock. His footprint is enshrined nearby.

There is a **rock slide** near the cave that Krishna and the cowherd boys would slide down. Across the road from here, at **Bhojan-sthali**, Krishna would take lunch with the cowherd boys. There are imprints of the bowls and plates used by Krishna here.

On the other side of town at **Charana Pahadi** Krishna's footprints are enshrined. Krishna performed a sacrifice here for killing Vyomasura, the son of a Brahmin.

Unchagaon

Lalita-sakhi grew up here, and there is a Lalita Temple here. There is a set of Radha-Krishna Deities, and next to them a little deity of Lalita. It is Lalita's duty to pacify Srimati Radharani when She is feeling separation from Krishna.

Sesa Sayi Temple

In this temple there is a five-thousand year old Deity of **Garbhodaksayi Vishnu** and Laksmidevi.

Once the *gopis* told Krishna that they would like to enjoy His pastimes as Vaikunthanath, the Lord of Vaikuntha. Lord Krishna agreed to this proposal and transformed Himself into Garbhodaksayi Vishnu and Lord Balarama transformed Himself into Ananta Sesa, Lord Vishnu's eternal bedstead. Srimati Radharani transformed into Laksmi Devi.

Finally all the *gopas* and *gopis* were transformed into 33 million demigods and demi-goddesses. From the navel of Lord Krishna sprouted a lotus flower and all the *gopas* and *gopis* witnessed the pastime of Lord Brahma being generated.

Shergarh

This is where Lord Balarama performed His *rasa* dance. There is a small temple here with a white marble Lord Balarama.

Akrura Ghat

At this place Krishna and Balarama revealed Their forms of Maha-Vishnu and Ananta Sesa to Akrura, when Akrura was taking Them from Vrindavana to Mathura. Krishna also showed the residents of Vrindavana the Vaikuntha planets here. Caitanya Mahaprabhu stayed here when He visited Vrindavana.

The **Yajna-sthala**, where the wives of the Brahmins fed Krishna and Balarama, is near this place. This place is located halfway between Vrindavana and Mathura.

Across the Yamuna

GOKULA

Gokula is where Krishna lived until He was seven years old. The pastimes of Damodar, the stealing of butter, and other childhood pastimes took place here. There are small mud and straw temples on the side of the hill that mark the places where Krishna killed the demons Putana, Trinavarta, and Sakatasura. The **house of Nanda Maharaja** was built over 5000 years ago by the architect Visvakarma. It is on a hill and has 84 pillars.

Utkhal (Grinding Mortar) is where Krishna was tied to the grinding mortar by mother Yasoda. It is in a small hut, a km from the town of Mahavana. Nanda Maharaja's well is across the road from here.

Nearby, at **Brahmanda Ghat**, on the bank of the Yamuna River, is where Krishna ate dirt. When forced by mother Yasoda to open His mouth, He revealed to her the entire cosmic manifestation.

Raval

Raval is the birthplace of **Srimati Radharani**. It is 9 km from Mathura on the other side of the river. Once King Vrishabhanu went to the Yamuna River to take bath. He saw a golden lotus flower that shone like a million suns in the middle of the river. In the middle of the lotus flower was baby Srimati Radharani.

Lord Brahma appeared before King Vrishabhanu and told him that in his previous life he and his wife, Kirtida, had performed great austerities to get the consort of Lord Vishnu as their daughter.

King Vrishabhanu took the child home, but found Her to be blind. Narada Muni appeared before the king and told him that despite the child's blindness he should go ahead and perform all the auspicious birth ceremonies. Nanda Maharaja brought baby Krishna along for the ceremonies. When baby Krishna crawled before Srimati Radharani, She could smell the wonderful aroma of His body, and at that moment She opened Her eyes. The first person She saw was Her eternal consort, Sri Krishna.

Baldeva (known as Dauji)

There is a temple here with a two metre (6'6") Balarama Deity that was installed by Vajranabha, about 5000 years ago. This is the largest Deity in Braja Mandala. Balarama is black, with huge eyes, and His right hand is raised. In His left hand is a cup full of Varuni beverage. He is one of the four presiding Deities of Vrindavana. This Balarama Deity is the only original presiding Deity left in Braja.

The Deity was lost for a long time, but was rediscovered in a *kund* behind the Dauji Temple called Shiv Nagara (also called Khisagar or "sea of milk"). It is said that Gusain Gokul Nath had a dream that the Deity of Baladeva was in the tank.

This place is 18 km southeast of Mathura, on the other side of the river.

MATHURA

Population: 235,000, STD Code 0565

Mathura is the extremely important pilgrimage city where Lord Kr'shna was born. It is 150 km south of Delhi and 14 km from Vrindavana. Mathura is on the main train line between Delhi and Agra.

Information and Tours

There is a useless tourist office on the first floor of a building in the back of the old bus stand. Maybe if you speak Hindi you can get some information.

There is a **daily tour** to the towns of Vrindavana, Nandagram, Varshana, Govardhana Hill, Radha Kund, and Krishna Janma Bhumi that leaves from the old bus stand at 6 am.

You can **change money** at the State Bank of India on Railway Station Rd.

Krishna Janmasthan

The main temple here is called the **Keshava Deo Temple**. The Deities in the temple are Radha-Krishna. Lord Kesava, one of the four presiding Deities of Vrindavana, was installed here by Vajranabha, but the original Deity is now in Rajdhani, a small village near Kanpur. The central Deities in the temple are Radha-Kesava. On the left altar, by the entrance door, are Lord Jagannath, Balarama, and Subhadra, being looked at by Sri Caitanya. On the right altar are Sita, Rama, and Laksman. Across from them is Hanuman. There is a Siva-linga called Sri Keshaveshwar in front of the Deities of Sita-Rama. Directly across from this Siva-linga is Durga Devi.

The Deities can be viewed from (April to October) 5 am to 12 noon and 4 pm to 9 pm and from (November to March) 5.30 am to 12 noon and 3 pm to 8 pm.

There have been several major temples built on this site. The first temple here was constructed almost 5000 years ago by Vajranabha, the great-grandson of Lord Krishna. The next big temple was constructed here during the time of the

Gupta Emperor Chandragupta Vikramaditya around 400 AD. This temple was
so grand that it was said that neither painting nor description could describe it. This
temple was destroyed by Mahmud of
Ghazni.

Another temple was built here in
1150. Lord Caitanya Mahaprabhu visited this temple. This temple was destroyed in the sixteenth century during
the reign of Sikandar Lodi.

During the reign of Jahangir, Raja
Veer Singh Deva Bundela of Orchha constructed another temple about 250 feet
high at the cost of Rs 3.3 million. In 1669
Aurangzeb had this temple destroyed and
had a mosque, which is still there, built
from the materials of the temple.

Construction started on the present
temple in 1951, and the Deities were installed in 1958. The temple cost Rs 15
million to construct.

Next to the temple is a small room that
looks like a prison cell, where it is said
that Lord Krishna appeared.

Others say that Krishna's appearance
place is about 250 yards away, at a small
temple near Potra Kund. At this other
temple there are deities of Vasudeva,
Devaki, and four-armed Krishna. *Darshan* is from 8 am to 8 pm at this temple.
Just behind this place is **Jnana Vapi**
where Lord Caitanya stayed while in
Mathura.

Visrama Ghat

This is a bathing *ghat* on the bank of
the Yamuna where Krishna rested after
killing King Kamsa. It is said that Lord
Varaha also rested here after killing
Hiranyaksa. There are 5000 year old deities of **Yamuna devi** and her brother
Yamaraj here. Every day there is a sunset *arati* offered to the Yamuna River.
This *ghat* was reconstructed in 1814.

Ranga Bhumi

Krishna killed Kamsa here on the hill
called **Kamsa-tila**. Behind this hill is
where Krishna crowned Ugrasena the
king of Mathura. Next to this place
Krishna killed the wrestlers. Ranga
Bhumi is located just opposite the Main
Post Office.

Nearby is the **Rangeswara Mahadeva Temple**, which houses the Siva-
linga worshiped by Kamsa before the
wrestling match.

Kesava Gaudiya Math

This temple is located just next to
Ranga Bhumi. The presiding Deities are
Radha-Vinoda-Vihari. This temple is
managed by His Holiness Narayana Ma-
haraja. This is where Srila Prabhupada
took *sannyasa* from His Holiness Kesava
Maharaja in 1959. There is a Deity of
Lord Caitanya on the altar here that Srila
Prabhupada donated.

The Government Museum

Mathura has an excellent museum. It
has many ancient sculptures of Lord
Krishna and Vishnu. Many of the sculptures here are of Buddha. Many ancient
sculptures in museums throughout India
and in London are originally from
Mathura. This museum is located on
Museum Road by Dampier Park and is
open from 10 am to 5 pm, except on government holidays.

Other Places

Many pastimes from the *Srimad
Bhagavatam* and other *Puranas* took
place in Mathura. Ambarish Maharaja
waited at **Ambarish-tila** in Mathura for
Durvasa Muni to return, from being
chased by Lord Vishnu's disc. At **Bali-
tila**, Bali Maharaja performed his great
yajna to take over the universe. **Lord Va-**

manadeva begged three steps of land from Bali Maharaja at this place. Narada Muni instructed **Dhruva Maharaja** in Mathura. **Ravana** performed austerities to acquire his mystic powers here.

The **Dwarkadish Temple**, built in 1814, is a popular temple in the center of town.

Dentist

Dr Atul Kumar Agarwal is located across the street and down a little way from the Kesava Gaudiya Math, opposite the Kwality Hotel at 67 Vikas Bazaar in Mathura. I went to him a few times and he did a good job. I also know other people who were satisfied with his work. I would not advise you to have him do anything too complicated. Some of the auto-rickshaw drivers in front of Krishna Balarama Mandir know how to get to him. He is open in the morning and from 6 to 9 pm. He will do in an emergency.

Where To Stay

At the *International Guest House* (405-888), which is located right next to Sri Krishna Janmastham, you can get a clean double room with bath for Rs 70 to Rs 100 or a very basic room for Rs 20/ 30. There is also a vegetarian restaurant called *Bhojanalaya* in the Guest House. The *Hotel Brijraj*, opposite Sri Krishna Janmastham, has rooms with hot water for Rs 110 and Rs 200 for a room with A/C.

The *Hotel Nepal* (404-308), Delhi Rd, opposite the new bus stand, has decent rooms with common bath for Rs 120, with private bath for Rs 175, and a bigger room with an air cooler for Rs 250. The *Kwality Hotel* (406-195), near the old bus stand, is about the same price, but run down. The *Modern Guest House*, opposite the old bus stand, is a basic place

with rooms from Rs 90/130 up to Rs 120/ 170. The rooms are all right, but they have very small windows, if you can call them that. The *UPSTDC Tourist Bungalow* is at Civil Lines, Bypass Rd. The *Agra Hotel*, Bengali Ghat, has a view of the Yamuna.

The *Hotel Surya* (408-344) has good rooms for Rs 225/300. Nearby, the *Mansarovar Palace* (0565/408-686), State Bank Crossing, has modern rooms for Rs 350/450 and Rs 450/550 with A/C. The *Hotel Madhuvan* (404-064), Krishna Nagar, is the best place in town, with a pool and good modern rooms for Rs 500/ 600 and Rs 750/850 with A/C. The *Hotel Radha Ashok* (405-557), Masani Byepass Rd, a little out of town, is a good place with rooms for Rs 1090 and suites for Rs 2375.

Where to Eat

Most of the places in Mathura are vegetarian. *Brijraj*, across from Sri Krishna Janmasthan, serves snacks and dosas. *Deepak*, Delhi Road, next to Hotel Nepal, is one of the best places in Mathura.

Travel

Air The closest airport is in New Delhi (3½ hr, 150 km).

Train Mathura is a major stop on the Delhi–Agra and Delhi–Bombay broad-gauge lines. It is a hectic station, so it is hard to miss. From Delhi it takes two to four hours, usually three, to reach Mathura. It is not a good idea to take a train from Delhi to Mathura too late at night, after 8.00 pm, as it is not safe. Plus it will be hard to find a room in Vrindavana if you arrive after 10 pm.

Many trains depart each day for Mathura from both the New Delhi train station, by Connaught Place, and the

Mathura to Delhi Trains

Train	Train #	Mathura	Nizzamudhin	New Delhi
AP Exp	#2723	6.18 am	8.21 am	8.40 am
Paschim Exp	#2925	7.35 am	10.13am	10.35 am
GT Exp	#2615	8.35 am	11.27am	11.45 am
Rajdhani Exp	#2953	8.50 am		10.55 am
Janata Exp	#9023	9.20 am	12.47 pm	1.10pm
Mahakoshal	#1449	11.25 am	2.20 pm	
Kerala Exp	#2625	12.50 pm	2.57 pm	3.20 pm
Mangalore Exp	#2617	1.23 pm	3.40 pm	
Samta Exp	#8543	2.20 pm	4.45 pm	
Visakha-Niza	#8543	2.25 pm	4.45 pm	
Frontier Mail	#2903	4.40 pm	6.40 pm	7 pm
Toofan Express	#3007	4.50 pm		9.30 pm
Link Exp	#8516	5.05 pm	8.08 pm	8.30 pm
Punjab Mail	#1037	5.40 pm	7.55 pm	8.15 pm
Chhatisgarh Exp	#8237	5.05 pm	8.10 pm	8.30 pm
Jhalum Exp	#1077	6.22 pm	8.56 pm	9.15 pm
Madras-Jammu Exp	#6031	8.05 pm	10.40pm	11.05 pm

Delhi to Mathura Trains

Train	Train #	New Delhi	Nizzamudhin	Mathura
Chhattisgarh Exp	#8236	5 am		7.25 am
Link Exp	#8517	5 am	5.19 am	7.25 am
Punjab Mail	#1038	6 am		8.23 am
Taj Exp	#		7.17 am	8.55 am
Toofan Express	#3008	7.50 am		10.55 am
Niza-Visakh Exp	#8544		8.45 am	10.34 am
Frontier Mail	#2904	8 am		10.20 am
Nizs-Mangalore Exp	#2618		9.56 am	11.40 am
Jhelum Exp	#1078	10.50 am		12.44 pm
Kerala Exp	#2626	11.30 am		1.24 pm
Kalinga-Utkal Exp	#8478		12.50 pm	3.30 pm
Janata Exp	#9024	2 pm		5.10 pm
Jammu-Madras Exp	#6032	2.55 pm		5.16 pm
Rajdhani Exp	#2954		4.55 pm	6.35 pm
Paschim Exp	#2926	5 pm		7.15 pm
GT Exp	#2818	6.40 pm		8.37 pm
Intercity Exp			7.35 pm	9.40 pm
Mahokosal	#1450		7.45 pm	9.50 pm
Niz-Hyderabad Exp	#7022		8.30 pm	10.30 pm

Nizamuddin train station. Trains leave more often from the New Delhi Station, but the Nizamuddin station is closer to the airport and the ISKCON Temple. If you take an evening train (after 5 pm) it may be difficult to get a seat, and you cannot purchase First-class or A/C-class tickets. If you want to travel higher class to Mathura in the evening you can purchase a second-class ticket and get on a First-class or A/C carriage. You can then ask the ticket collector or the train conductor if you can upgrade your ticket to a higher class. They will often allow this. A second-class unreserved ticket from Delhi to Mathura is Rs 42. This class is very crowded and uncomfortable. When you get on the train you can pay an extra Rs 40 and ride in the second-class sleeper class, which is less crowded.

From Mathura many trains go to and from Agra (1 hr). There are direct trains to Jaipur (6 hr), Ujjain (12 hr), Bombay, Calcutta (32 hr), Ahmedabad, and Baroda.

The Toofan Exp #3008 (11 am) goes to **Calcutta** (32 hr) via **Allahabad** (12 hr). This train arrives at 3.20 pm the next day in **Barddhaman** (Burdwan), 5.05 pm in Bandel, and 6.15 pm in Calcutta. The Malwa Express #4668 (8.20 pm) goes to **Ujjain** (12½ hr). The Kalinga-Utkal Exp #8478 (3.35 pm) goes to **Puri**. The Jammu-Ahmedabad Sarvodaya #2474 (12 midnight) takes 14½ hours to get to **Ahmedabad**. There are several trains to **Vadodara** and **Bombay**.

There are direct trains to Madras (35 hr), Hyderabad (33 hr), Visakhapatnam (44½ hr), and Vijayawada (28 hr). The Kerala Exp #2626 goes all the way to **Trivandrum** (1.30 pm, 53½ hr).

There is a direct train to **Chitrakoot Dham** called the Mahakoshal Exp #1450 (9.50 pm, 11 hr). The #5314 Exp (7 pm)

goes to Lucknow (14 hr) via Sitapur.

The Lucknow-Jodhpur Exp #2463 (11.05 pm) arrives in Jaipur at 4.50 am. This is the only train to Jaipur, and it must be reserved in advance. The Jodhpur-Lucknow Exp #2464 returns from Jaipur (10.20 pm) and arrives in Mathura at 3.30 am.

Bus There are two bus stations in Mathura. From the Old Bus Stand buses depart to **Agra** (hourly), **Vrindavana**, and to the town of **Govardhana**. The tour of Govardhana, Nandagram, Radha Kund, Vrindavana town, and Varsana leaves from the Old Bus Stand at 6 am. There are regular buses to Haridwar (9 hr) from here. There is also a semi-luxury bus to **Haridwar** that departs at 10 pm and arrives around 6 am.

From the New Bus Stand, a couple of km west of the Old Bus Stand, buses depart to **Delhi** (3½ hr), **Jaipur** (6 hr, Rs 70), and **Agra** (1 hr). Buses to Jaipur leave almost every hour and to Agra every half hour. A luxury bus goes to Jaipur at 10.30 pm. For Delhi there are both regular buses (3½ hr, Rs 40) and some deluxe buses (Rs 70). The deluxe buses come from Agra, and if there is a seat available when it reaches Mathura, you can get a seat. There is a bus to **Aligarh** every hour (1½ hr, Rs 50).

Taxi Company

Some good taxi companies and drivers in Vrindavana are Raja Kumara Goswami (442-242, 442-515). Puran is a very good driver who knows both Delhi and Jaipur beside the Braj area. Gopal (4420493) is also very good and knows both Delhi and Jaipur. You can also hire a taxi from Ram Das at the tulasi bead shop across the street from the ISKCON temple.

Dinesh hires out taxi for the Vrindavana area, Delhi, Jaipur and other places. To get to his shop, if you are coming out of the ISKCON temple, you make a right and walk half a block. His shop is on the right. He has several taxis and he charges the same price for both day and night travel. He charges Rs 800 to go to Delhi, Rs 100 to go to Mathura and Rs 400 to go to Radha Kund with two hours waiting time. He has been in business for years. The name of the shop is K B Travels and Gift Shop (442-223). You usually can hire a taxi from here without any advance notice.

Temple Guest House Shop

Inside the ISKCON Guest House is a well stocked shop with different devotional and gift items. There is a good selection of quality Rajasthani goods. There is a good selection of devotional books, semi-precious jewelry, gift items, and exported western goods. Everything is sold at fixed prices.

CHAPTER NINE

Rajasthan

JAIPUR

Population: 1,500,000, STD Code 0141

Jaipur is the crown jewel of Rajasthan and one of the most visited places in all of India. This city was built by Maharaja Jai Singh II (1699-1744), according to the Shilpa Sastra, an ancient Hindu composition on architecture. He began the construction in 1727. Many of the buildings within the walled city are painted pink, hence the city is also known as the "Pink City." When one enters this city one is charmed by the old-world and picturesque atmosphere.

You need two full days to see all the temples and sites in the area. If you are in a hurry you can see the important temples in half a day. The Govindaji Temple is especially interesting during the *mangala-arati* ceremony at five in the morning. Govindaji is the original Deity of Srila Rupa Goswami. Srila Prabhupada came to Jaipur in January, 1972.

Getting Your Bearings

The Radha-Govinda Temple and the City Palace are located within the walled, older section of the northeastern part of the city. The new parts of the city are to the south and west. The temples and most of the tourist places are within the gates of the old city. Johari Bazaar, the jewelry market, is also in the old part of the city. The Amber fort is 11 km northeast of the city going toward Delhi. MI Rd, where many of the restaurants are located, runs east-west, just south of the walled part of the city.

Information

The helpful Government of India tourist office in the Khasa Kothi Hotel has some brochures, but nothing of much value. It is open 9 am to 6 pm Monday to Friday and 9 am to 1 pm Saturday.

The main tourist office, on platform No 1 in the railway station, has some good literature and can give you good information. It is open 6 am to 8 pm daily. There is also a tourist counter at platform 2 at the bus station.

Guides can be hired from the tourist offices. It could be a good idea to get a government-approved tourist guide. Other guides will just want to bring you shopping all day, as they get a commission on everything you buy.

Money

Most of the banks are open only on weekdays 11 am to 2 pm. Some of the main banks are the State Bank of India, Sanganeri Gate, MI Rd; the State Bank of Bikaner and Jaipur (noon to 6 pm); the Punjab National Bank, near Hawa Mahal; and the Bank of Baroda, Johari Bazaar. The State Bank of India at Sanganeri Gate on MI Road changes money efficiently. Most of the higher class hotels exchange money, although the rates they give are usually below that of the local banks.

Arrival and Touts

When you arrive by train or bus there will be no shortage of *rickshaw* and taxi drivers who will want to take you to a hotel practically for free. This is because the hotels they take you to will give them a high commission. If you ask to go to another hotel, you will be told it is full, or it had a fire, or whatever. They told me the hotel I wanted to go to was full, and when I got there it was totally empty.

The *rickshaw* drivers get a commission from the hotel that they bring you to, which is at least 20% of the cost of the room. This means you pay a higher price. If you insist on going to the hotel of your choice, the *rickshaw* driver will then want to charge you at least double the normal fare.

Tours

The RTDC has half-day and full-day tours of Jaipur and Amber. The tour goes to the City Palace and Museum (except Friday), Amber Fort, Hawa Mahal, and Jantar Mantar. The half-day tour is rushed, so it is better to take the full-day excursion tour.

The tour departs from the railway station, but you can be picked up at any RTDC hotel. The full day tour goes from 9 am to 6 pm and costs Rs 60. The hours for the half day tour are: 8 am to 1 pm, 11.30 am to 4.30 pm, and 1.30 to 6.30 pm.

Places To Shop

Bapu Bazaar and Nehru Bazaar are the main places to buy cloth. Johari Bazaar is famous for jewelry and gems. Also on two alleys off Johari Bazaar, Gopalji Ka Rasta and Haldiyon Ka Rasta, there are semi-precious stone shops and assorted silversmiths. Rajasthan Government Handicrafts Emporium on MI Rd has fixed prices and gives you a good idea of

what everything should cost. Normally this place is more expensive than other shops, so paying more than these prices is definitely a no-no.

Jaipur is a main market for gems in India. Gem prices in Jaipur are about 50% of what the prices are in London. Gem Palace, MI Road; Lall Gems, MI Road; Jewels Bhuramal Rajmal Surana, off Haldion-ka-Rasta; Beg Gems, Mehdi-ka-Chowk near Hawa Mahal; and Yogi Durvabhji's Emerald House, Subhash Marg, C-Scheme are reputable jewelry shops. Silver and Art Palace is a recommended place. Surana, Ratnasangam, and D.Y. Durlabhji are well-known places in Johari Bazaar. Silver bangles are rarely over 50% silver, even if the shop owner swears they are 100% silver. A good silver shop is Balaji Silvercraft, 102 Siredeori Bazaar, just off Johari Bazaar.

Manglam Arts has a good selection of jewelry, antiques, and good Rajasthani paintings. A visit there is like going to a museum. Their prices are a little high, but they are friendly and can be bargained to a reasonable discount. Some of the more precious items in their collections are so highly valued that they have an armed guard to protect them.

The marble carvers are in the Khajane Walon ka Rasta area. You can get carpets cheaper in Pushkar than Jaipur, but you will not get as good a selection of expensive items in Pushkar. You can get miniature Krishna paintings cheaper in Udaipur or Nathdwar than Jaipur, but the facility of finding all type of Rajasthani products in one city, though at higher prices, outweighs the sometimes tedious traveling necessary to get discounts.

Gem Testing Laboratory

At this place off MI Rd, near New Gate, you can have gems tested for quality and value for a small fee. You can ask for a money-back guarantee when you purchase gems and then get them tested. Any of the more reputable dealers will allow you to return items within a few days.

Post

The GPO, or main post office, is on MI Rd. Outside the GPO is a man who sews up parcels. His rates are quite reasonable.

Book Shops

There is a good selection of English books at *Books Corner* by Niro's Restaurant on MI Rd. There are also a good book shop at the *Rambagh Palace Hotel,* and there is a small decent selection of books at the *Arya Niwas Hotel* by Sansar Chandra Rd.

Jaipur Deities and Temples

It is said that Vajranabha, the great-grandson of Krishna, had three Deities of Krishna carved. He never saw Krishna, so the Deities were carved according to the description given by Uttara, the mother of Maharaja Parikshit. He had three different images carved, but none of them were perfect. Govindaji resembled Krishna's lotus face (Mukharavinda), Madana Mohana resembled Krishna from the navel down to the lotus feet and Gopinatha resembled Krishna from the naval to the neck. In one book about the temples of Vrindavana, it quotes the *Padma Purana* saying that to get the full vision of Sri Krishna, you have to visit and offer obeisances to all three Deities during a single day, while the sun is still up. Sri Govinda and Sri Gopinatha are now in Jaipur, and Madana-Mohana in Karoli, a small town in Rajasthan. The temples in Jaipur are not very impressive

architecturally, but the Deities in the Govindaji, Gopinatha and Radha-Damodara temples are very important Deities, which were originally installed in Vrindavana.

Radha Govindaji Temple

Sri Govinda was originally installed nearly 5000 years ago by the great grandson of Lord Krishna and is one of the four presiding Deities of the Braja-mandala (greater Vrindavana). The other three are Keshavadeva, situated at Sri Krishna Janmasthana, Harideva at Govardhana, and Dauji (Balarama) situated in Baladev.

Govinda was worshiped by Srila Rupa Goswami and installed at the Radha Govinda Temple in Vrindavana. For years the Deity of Govindaji had been lost. Then one night, about 450 years ago, the Govindaji Deity appeared to Rupa Goswami in a dream and revealed to him where He lay buried. Rupa Goswami then excavated Govindaji and personally took charge of His regular worship.

Govindaji was later brought to the city of Amber, near Jaipur, by Maharaja Jai Singh II to keep the Deity from being destroyed by the Muslim emperor Aurangzeb. His grandfather had originally built the Govindaji Temple in Vrindavana. Govindaji was moved to the present temple in Jaipur around 1728 (some say 1735). Maharaja Jai Singh created his "City of Victory," the city of Jaipur, as a dedication to Lord Govindaji. The temple is in a garden of the palace complex, and when the temple doors were opened, Maharaja Jai Singh could see his beloved Deity from the royal quarters.

On the altar are full size Deities of Govinda, a beautiful black marble Deity, and Radha. There is also a small Deity of Krishna named Gaura-Govinda, which was worshiped by Kasiswara Pandit. On the wall to the right of the Deities is a picture of Lord Caitanya and Lord Nityananda. There is beautiful tile work on the altar. The *maha-prasada* booth is located to the left of the Deities. It is customary that devotees purchase *maha-prasada* and then distribute it to the other devotees, who eagerly rush to get it. We gave a 50-rupee donation to the *pujari* and received four garlands from the Deities. Behind the temple is a large garden.

Mangala-arati, drawing around 5000 people a day, is an absolute must. The devotees of Govindaji rush eagerly at 5 am in the morning to see their beloved Lord. The devotees chant prayers enthusiastically in praise of Lord Govinda. After the *arati* the devotees circle the Deities, while different devotees pass out Govindaji's *maha-prasada*. This sight is a truly magnificent one to behold.

Srila Prabhupada had asked several devotees to carefully observe the Deity worship at the Radha-Govinda temple. Srila Prabhupada said the devotional practices were standard. The Deities' clothes are changed in the morning, afternoon and at night. The priest also offers oils on cotton-tipped sticks, and flower garlands from the Deities are given to the worshipers in exchange for fresh garlands.

The translation to the *mantra* that is chanted in front of Govindaji is: "We hunger for the sight of Your face and we wish to fix You constantly in our thoughts while meditating on Your lotus face. This life is full of responsibilities and now we are in the middle of the ocean; please give us Your blessing so that we can relieve ourselves of life's burdens and understand the meaning of life."

Arati Times: During Kartika (Oct-Nov) the times were 5, 8, 10, and 11.30 am and 5.15, 6.15, and 8.15 pm. Every month the times for all the *aratis* change, so it is important to ask someone what time *mangala-arati* will be or just get there before 5 am.

How to get there Everyone in town knows how to get there. It is located right next to the City Palace within the innermost wall of the old city.

Radha-Gopinatha Temple

These are the Deities worshiped by Madhu Pandita Goswami and discovered at Vamsivata in Vrindavana by Paramananda Bhattacarya, the disciple of Gadadhara Pandita. Gopinathaji was originally installed in Vrindavana by Vajranabha. This Deity was brought to Jaipur from Vrindavana when the Muslims raided Vrindavana. Gopinatha is said to exactly resemble Lord Krishna from the shoulders down to the waist.

This temple has beautiful carved silver doors and beautiful paintings on the wall. On the ceiling are paintings of *rasalila*. A unique embroidered *tulasi* bead jacket and *tulasi* japa beads, both of which belonged to Madhu Pandita, are displayed in the courtyard here. *Arati* times are 5, 8.30, 10, 11.15 am and 5, 5.20, 6, 7.30, 8 pm during Kartika (Oct-Nov).

How to get there The temple is located in the Topkhanadesh area of Jaipur by Chandpol Bazaar. If you are on Tripoliya Bazaar Road, you go west until you get to Gangori Bazaar Road. Tripoliya Bazaar Road is the main road right, next to the inner wall. You make a right and go down a few streets and then you make a left and go about a half km down the road. The temple will be on your left.

Radha Damodara Temple

There are two sets of Deities on the main altar. The smaller set of Deities are

Jiva Goswami's original Deities from Vrindavana, Radha Damodara. To the left of the Deities is a Govardhana-*shila* said to have been worshiped by Sanatana Goswami. On an altar, left of the main one, are Deities of Laksmi-Narasimha and Prahlada Maharaja. You have to look closely to see Prahlada Maharaja. There are beautiful paintings of Krishna's pastimes in this temple. The Goswami here, named Mahiman Goswami and his daughter Meetali, said they are members of the same Goswami family who run the Radha-Damodara Temple in Vrindavana. They are very friendly. This is an important temple to visit.

I was told the Deities were brought to Jaipur 260 years ago during the reign of Aurangzeb. We gave a 50-rupee donation and received 5 garlands and some plates of *maha-prasada*. We were also allowed to enter the fenced-off area and stand right next to the Deity door and to take a picture of the Deities. Any questions we had were gladly answered by the priest. Cows are kept in the courtyard of the temple, adding to the peaceful and very devotional atmosphere of the temple.

In the month of Kartika (Oct-Nov) *arati* times are 4.30, 6, 10, 11.30 am and 5, 6.45, 8.15 pm. During the summer months the *arati* times are later.

How to get there Coming from Tripoliya Bazaar Road, the temple is located about 200 feet down Chaura Rasta Road on the right side. It takes about 10 minutes to walk there from the Radha-Govinda temple. There is another temple next to the Radha Damodara Temple. Radha-Damodara is on the left while facing the temples.

Vinodilal Temple

This is a small temple up some stairs on Tripoliya Bazaar Road. Vinodilal was installed by Lokanatha Goswami, who is mentioned in the *guru-vandana*. He was the first devotee sent to Vrindavana by Lord Caitanya. He has one famous disciple, Narottama dasa Thakura, who was a great poet and composed many beautiful Vaishnava songs in praise of the Supreme Lord. Vinodilal is a beautiful Deity about 12 inches tall. There are at least 15 *shalagrama-shilas* to the left of the Deities.

Lokanatha Goswami resided in Vrindavana near the place called Chatravan. While staying near Kishora Kund in Umara village, he received the Deities of Radha-Vinoda whom he established in the Gokulananda Temple. These Deities were later moved to this temple in Jaipur. *Arati* times are 5.30, 7, 11 am and 6, 8.30 pm. At night the Deity *darshan* is from 4.30 to 8.30 pm, except when food is offered.

How to get there It is a very difficult temple to find, as few people go there. Even the shopkeepers right outside the temple do not know where it is. From Radha-Damodara Temple you walk back to Tripoliya Bazaar Road and make a left. Walk 50 big steps and you will find a flight of stairs to your left. To the right of the stairs is a hose shop, which is shop number 295. If you look at the building, it will not look like a temple. The temple is situated one flight up.

Radha Madhava Temple, Kanak Vrindavana, Birla Mandira

There are two temples here. In the Radha-Madhava Temple, to your right as you drive in, are the original Deities of Jayadeva Goswami. They were brought to Jaipur in 1560, almost 450 years ago. There is a set of four-foot-tall black marble Krishna and brass Radharani Deities and a small set of Deities here.

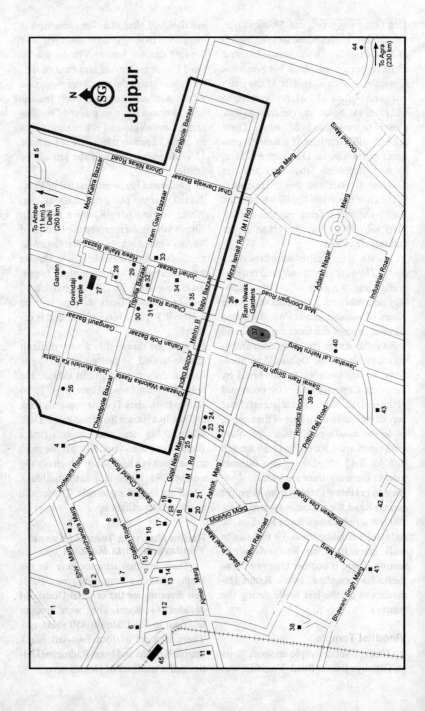

PLACES TO STAY

1	Madhuban Guest House & Marudhara Hotel
2	Hotel Jaipur Ashok
3	Jaipur Inn
4	Bissau Palace & Khetri Hotels
5	Samode Haveli Hotel
6	RTDC Swagat
7	RTDC Teej
9	Hotel Mangal
10	Arya Niwas Hotel
11	Jai Mangal Palace
12	Rajputana Palace
13	Hotel Khasa Kothi
14	Gangaur Tourist Bungalow
15	Atithi Guest House & Aangam Travellers Home
16	Hotel Natraj
17	Mansingh Hotel
20	RTDC Jaipur Tourist Hotel
21	Evergreen Guest House
33	Kailash
34	LMB Hotel & Restaurant
38	Rajmahal Palace Hotel
39	Diggi Palace Hotel
41	Youth Hostel
42	Rambagh Palace Hotel
43	Narain Niwas Hotel

WHERE TO EAT

19	Temptations
22	Annapurna
23	Natraj
24	Surya Mahal
25	Canakya
34	LMB Restaurant

OTHER

8	Bus Station
13	Government of India Tourist Office
18	GPO
22	Raj Mandir Cinema
26	Gopinatha Temple
27	City Palace and Museum
28	Jantar Mantar Observatory
29	Hawa Mahal
30	Vinodilal Temple
31	Radha Damodara Temple
32	Gopalji ka Rasta
35	Cycle Rental Shop
36	Zoo
37	Central Museum
40	Museum of Indology
44	Sisodia Rani Palace
45	Railway Station

The Natwarji Temple was established in the 18th century. In this temple are the Deities of Jaya Singh's sister, Amarkuar. There is beautiful silver work (known as *meena* work, done with mirrors and colored glass based in silver or white metal) around the altar. The temple is closed in the afternoon.

How to get there It is on the way to the Amber Fort on Amber Road, about 5 km from the downtown. You pass a large building in the middle of the lake and about a km later you see a sign for "Kanak Vrindavana and Govinda Deoji, Birla Restored" on the right.

City Palace and Museum

There is a great collection of over 2000 old weapons here dating from 1580 onwards. The sword of Maharaja Man Singh, the king of Jaipur in the 17th century, weighs about 11 pounds. For the artistically inclined, the palace has a wealth of artifacts and textiles that will enchant the eye of the beholders. There is a clothing museum which houses traditional old clothing and an art museum containing huge Moghul carpet and some beautiful Rajasthani paintings. The Radha Govinda Temple is next to the palace. The palace is open from 9 am to 4.30 pm. It is an interesting place that takes about an hour or two to see.

Jantar Mantar

Across from the City Palace is an observatory built by Maharaja Jai Singh in 1728. Each huge instrument is used to make intricate astronomical calculations. It is the largest stone observatory in the world.

Hawa Mahal (Palace of the Winds)

This five-story building, built around 1799, is very intricately built and is a major tourist site. It was built by Raja Sawai Pratap Singh to allow the royal ladies to overlook the city, as they were usually confined to the *zenana* quarters. This *mahal* enabled them to climb to the top and get a good view of the city. It is open from 9 am to 4.30 pm. The entrance of the building is in the rear. To get in, you go to the intersection on your left, as you face the Hawa Mahal, and make a right. At the first archway you make a right and you will see the entrance sign.

Galta

At Galta there is a temple dedicated to Surya, the sun-god, and natural springs said to have curative properties. There is a tank here which is constantly being filled by spring water coming out of a stone-carved cow. There are about 30 *shalagrama-shilas* here. You can get a good view of the city in the valley below from the temple here. There are many red-faced monkeys here.

Amber Fort

Amber, or Amer, was formerly the capital of the Rajput Princes before it was moved to the main city of Jaipur. It is situated 11 km northeast of the city on Amber Road, the road that goes to Delhi.

At the bottom of the hill is the Yajnastambha, a stone column that commemorates an Asvamedha-yajna (sacrifice) performed by Sawai Jai Singh.

This fort was begun in the beginning of the 17th century by Maharaja Man Singh (1589-1614), who was the commander-in-chief of Emperor Akbar's army. Mirza Raja Jai Singh (1621-1667) and Sawai Jai Singh (1666-1743) added to the palace. There is a beautiful marble **Kali temple** to the right of the entrance to the Maharaja's residence. The style of the fort is predominantly done in the Moghul architectural fashion, which was most commonly used during this era in Jaipur's history.

When you go up the stairs from the courtyard you first see the **Diwan-i-Am,** or the Hall of Public Audience, which is open on three sides. East of the inner court, toward the main road, is the **Jai Mandira** (Sheesh Mahal). Built by Mirza Raja Jai Singh, it has mosaic panels inlaid with glass, mirrors, and marble carvings. The **Jas Mandira**, Hall of Glory, is on the roof of the Jai Mandira. Across from the Jai Mandira, on the side away from the road, is the **Sukh Niwas,** or the Hall of Pleasure. It has a narrow channel in which water flowed from a tank on the roof to cool the room down in the burning desert summer heat.

The fort is open from 9 am to 4.30 pm. A highlight of coming to the fort is the elephant ride, to the top of the hill, where the fort is located. If you take the elephant ride you are expected to ride the elephant back down the hill in 40 minutes. This is not enough time to see everything at a leisurely pace, so you should ask for more time. It costs Rs 250 for up to four people to ride the elephant up and down the hill. It is a good idea to hire a guide to show you around the fort, as there are many interesting places here. They will give you a quick tour, and if you like you can walk around for a while longer by yourself.

How To Get There You can get a shared three-wheeler tempo (a big motor rickshaw like a mini-bus) or the green bus from Hawa Mahal up to the Amber Fort.

Jaigarh Fort

Above the Amber Palace, high on the hill, is another palace called **Jaigarh Fort,** which dates back to the 11th century. It has two ancient temples in it: the temples of Ram Harihar (10th century) and Kal Bhairava (12th century).

It has a weapon museum with a large collection of swords and small arms and a good photograph exhibit. The huge 50 ton **Jai Ban cannon** is said to be the largest cannon on wheels in the world. It has a range of 20 km.

The best way to get up to Jaigarh Fort is by jeep, but this a little expensive; to walk there is a steady half-hour climb. It is open 9 am to 5 pm. Entry fee Rs 6, camera fee Rs 50.

Bottom of Amber Hill

There is an interesting 500-year-old temple called **Jagat Shiromani Temple,** dedicated to Sri Krishna, at the bottom of the hill. It has an intricately carved Garuda Shrine and a marble gate with elephant statues on either side. There are several other temples at the bottom of the hill. The ancient **Sanwalaji Ka Jain Temple,** is across the street from the Jagat Shiromani Temple. Nearby is the Ambika Swara Mahadeva Temple, Kalyauji ka Mandir, Sunghi Jhunta Ram Temple, and the Laksmi Narayanji ka Temple.

Where To Stay – Lower

The very popular *Ever Green Guest House* (363-446), Mumtaz Bagh, Chameliwala Market, is opposite the GPO. Double rooms with bath are Rs 80 to Rs 130, and rooms with bath and hot water are Rs 150 to Rs 250. Dorm beds are Rs 50. There are also A/C rooms. It has a nice garden and a tiny swimming pool. It is always full with foreigners.

The popular *Jaipur Inn* (316-157), B-17, Shiv Marg, Bani Park, has a selection of clean rooms ranging from Rs 90/ 130 up to Rs 250/300. The more expensive rooms have hot water. It also has a good dorm (Rs 40) and camping facility on the lawn (Rs 25). It is usually full of foreign travelers. It is very well-managed. It has a kitchen that guests can cook in.

The popular *Diggi Palace* (373-091), Shivaji Marg, Hospital Rd, is a 200-year-old former palace with a huge lawn. It is clean, well-managed, and has a peaceful atmosphere. There is a selection of rooms from Rs 100/150 for a room with common bath up to Rs 375/425 for an air-cooled room.

The *Swagatam Tourist Bungalow* (310-595), near the railway station, has rooms for Rs 100/150 and Rs 225/300 for an air-cooled room. Dorm beds are Rs 30. It is convenient if you have an early morning train to catch. It is not too noisy, and it has a good lawn. The *railway retiring rooms* are Rs 80/130 with bath, and Rs 225 with A/C, and Rs 30 for a dorm bed. Rooms with common bath are Rs 50/90. *City Centre Hotel,* near Sindi Camp Bus Station, is a good deal.

Where To Stay – Middle

On Banasthli Marg there are several modern mid-range hotels costing around Rs 350/450.

Aangam Travellers Home (370-880), 4 Park House Scheme, opposite AIR, just off MI Road by Station Road, has nice rooms in a quiet area for Rs 275/300 to Rs 400. It is a good place. Right next door is the *Atithi Guest House* (378-679), Motilal Atal Rd, between Station Rd and MI Rd, which is also good. It has very clean well-maintained rooms with bath and hot water for Rs 225/275 and Rs 350/375 for a deluxe room. It is very well managed by a nice family.

The *Kailash* (565-372), Johari Bazaar, is in the middle of the old city. Rooms with bath are Rs 150/175 to Rs 265/325. The rooms are a little small.

The *Madhuban Hotel* (319-033), Bani Park, is a family run place with rooms for Rs 200/250 and Rs 250/400 for a large room. It is a good value with a nice lawn and garden. This is a good place to stay. Near by is the *Marudhara Hotel*, behind the collectorate, which has rooms with common bath for Rs 70 and rooms with bath for Rs 100/150.

The *RTDC Teej* (74206), Collectorate Rd, Bani Park, is a well-managed clean government hotel with air-cooled rooms for Rs 200/250 and A/C rooms for Rs 300/350. Dorm beds are Rs 30.

Hotel Mangal (75126), Sansar Chandra Rd, off the main road near the bus stand, is a good place with rooms for Rs 275/300 and rooms with A/C for Rs 500/550. It has a vegetarian restaurant, health club, and sauna. It has 24 hour checkout facility as well.

The popular *Arya Niwas* (372-456, fax 364-376), just off Sansar Chandra Rd, (behind the Amber Cinema), is a recommended place with clean large rooms with bath from Rs 200/300 to Rs 350/450. It has a small book shop, a front lawn with chairs, money changing facilities, parking area, and hot water in the winter. It is a really good place. You should ask to see a few rooms, as some are better than others.

The *RTDC Ganguar Tourist Bungalow* (371-641), just off Sansar Chandra Rd, has comfortable rooms with bath and hot water for Rs 225/275 and Rs 400/500 with A/C. It has a nice lawn and is a pretty good value.

The well-managed *Hotel Megh Niwas* (32266, fax 321-018), Bani Park, is a very good place with rooms for Rs 400/500 and Rs 500/600 with A/C. It has a nice garden and a swimming pool.

Where To Stay – Higher

The *LMB*, (565-844), Johari Bazaar, costs Rs 775 for a standard double room and Rs 1175 for a luxury room. The rooms in the front are better than those in the back, so ask to see the rooms before you take one. The best thing about this place is its excellent restaurant. It is well-located—close to the temples, the palace, and the shopping areas.

The *Hotel Khasa Kothi* (375-151), south of the junction of MI Rd and Station Rd, was a former minor palace. It has a swimming pool and comfortable large rooms for Rs 600/700 to Rs 1500. This place has a big lawn and gardens.

The *Hotel Bissau Palace* (310-371), outside Chand Pole, dates from the 1920s and has a nice atmosphere, with comfortable rooms for Rs 495/660 and Rs 900/990 with A/C. Some of the rooms are very good, while others are not, so you have to see the rooms before you rent one. It has a swimming pool and tennis court.

The *Narain Niwas Palace Hotel* (561-291) is a former palace with rooms for Rs 845/1125 for a room with A/C. It is in a quiet location and has big gardens. The big rooms have classic antique furniture.

The *Samode Haveli* (42407), in a quiet location in northeast Jaipur, is a really nice place with rooms for Rs 1100/1400 and Rs 2100 for a suite. It is the

200-year-old house of the former prime minister of Jaipur. It has a nice patio area and a remarkably painted dinning room. It is popular with foreign tourist.

The *Hotel Meru Palace* (371-111), Sawai Ram Singh Road, has rooms with TV and hot water for Rs 1195/1400. It is not a good value, but has the first-class South Indian style restaurant, Woodlands.

Where To Stay – Luxury

The *Rambagh Palace* (381-919, fax 381-098) is one of the nicest places anywhere in the world. It formerly belonged to the Maharaja of Jaipur and is a very prestigious and superb place with a fountain garden. Because it is such a good place to stay, most of the time it is totally full. So it is best to reserve a room in advance. The cheapest room is $155/175 and the most expensive Royal Suite will run up to $625. If you stay in no other luxury place in India, this along with the Lake Palace Hotel in Udaipur are the places to stay in order to sample the classic comforts and atmospheric luxuries that were the norm during the times of the British Raj.

The *Jai Mahal Palace* (371-616, fax 365-237), corner of Ajmer Marg and Jacob Rd, south of the railway station, also used to belong to the Maharaja of Jaipur. It has rooms from $130/150 to $350 for a luxury suite. It has a majestic atmosphere, swimming pool and gardens. This and the Rambagh Palace are the two most luxurious places in town.

The *Rajmahal Palace* (381-757, fax 381-887), on Sardar Patel Marg, belonged to a former British ruler. It has opulent rooms for $75/95 and $275 for a suite.

The *Mansingh Hotel* (378-771), off Sansar Chandra Rd, is a modern place close to town center. It has opulent rooms

for $80/95. It has a swimming pool. The *Hotel Clarks Amer* (550-616, fax 550-013), Jawaharlal Nehru Marg, ten km from the center of the city, has rooms for $100/110. The *Jaipur Ashok* (320-091), Bani Park, has a pool and good rooms for Rs 1200/1800. It needs to be better maintained. The new *Holiday Inn* (45897), on the road between downtown and the Amber Fort has comfortable rooms for Rs 1800/2000.

The *Rajputana Sheraton* (360-011, fax 367-848), Palace Rd, near the railway station, is a well-designed deluxe hotel built around a swimming pool. Rooms are $125/150.

Where To Eat

LMB, Johari Bazaar, is one of the better restaurants in India. No onion or garlic is used in the cooking here. The Cordon Blues Sizzler is the house specialty and is excellent, as are the mango milkshakes. It is well known all over India for its famous Indian sweets. It is a highly recommended place.

Natraj on MI Road and next door the *Surya Mahal* are recommended higher class places.

Nearby *Annapurna*, behind Raj Mandir cinema, has good Gujarati dishes at economical prices.

Temptations (*370-129*), C-1 New Colony, off MI Road near Panch Batti, serves good pizza for India. It has a good international menu, including Mexican and Chinese dishes. *Woodlands*, Sawai Ram Singh Road, in the Hotel Meru Palace, is a first-class South Indian restaurant.

Canakya (376-161), on MI Road, is recommended by some as being the best restaurant in Jaipur. It is a fancy place with excellent food. The restaurant is very clean and the Marwari dishes cooked by the chefs there rival even those dishes prepared by the Marwari ladies at home. The Special Sizzler is excellent.

Lassiwala, across the street from the Surya Mahal restaurant on MI Rd, has *lassis* that many people recommend to be the best lassis in India. They are excellent. There is another *lassi* shop a few stores down from this famous shop. The original Lassiwala is on the corner, to the left of the other *lassi* shop and says Kishan Lal Agarwal on it.

There and Away

Air There are flights to Agra, Delhi, Bombay, Udaipur, Calcutta, Varanasi, Aurangabad, and Ahmedabad. The airport is 14 km out of town. The airport bus into town costs Rs 20 and a taxi costs Rs 100.

The Indian Airlines office (514-407) is at Nehru Place. There are some international airlines offices at the Jaipur Towers, MI Rd: Air India (365-559), Gulf Air (577202), Thai Airlines (70062), Delta Airlines (62525), Air France (77202), and Alitalia (69120). British Airways (70734) is on Park St, off MI Rd.

Rail The railway station is 1 km west of the old city by the main concentration of hotels. Trains are usually slower than buses from Jaipur because it is on a metre-gauge line.

The Pink City Express leaves **Delhi** at 5.50 am and arrives in Jaipur at 11.05 am. It continues to Ajmer (Pushkar) and Udaipur (10 hr). The Pink City Express to Delhi departs Jaipur 5 pm and arrives in Delhi at 10.15 pm. The Chetak Express leaves Delhi at 1 pm and arrives in Jaipur at 8.30 pm. The Ahmedabad Mail leaves Delhi at 10 pm and arrives in Jaipur at 4.30 am. The overnight Jaipur-Delhi Shekawati Express #9734 departs Jaipur

for Delhi at 5.15 pm (12 hr).

The superfast Jaipur-Agra Fort Express to **Agra** (5 hr) departs Jaipur at 6.10 am. It returns to Jaipur at 5 pm, arriving at 10 pm. This is a popular train and should be booked in advance.

You can connect with trains to south and western Gujarat by going to Ahmedabad. The best train to **Ahmedabad** is the 5.50 pm Ahmedabad Express #9903, which arrives the next morning after stopping at **Abu Rd** (by Mt. Abu) at 5 am. There are several express trains to **Ajmer** and **Abu Road**.

The convenient Chetak Express leaves Jaipur at 9 pm and arrives in **Udaipur** at 9.15 am. There is a fast daily Express #7569 train to **Hyderabad** (Secunderabad) which departs at 1.40 pm and arrives at 6.20 the next day.

The only train to **Mathura** is the Marudhar Exp #2464 (10.20 pm, Wed, Fri, Sun) which arrives in Mathura at 3.25 am. The Marudhar Exp #2463 departs Mathura at 11.05 pm (Tue, Thu, Sat), and arrives in Jaipur at 4.50 am.

Most trains should be booked a day in advance. The computerised booking office is open 8 am to 8 pm, Monday to Saturday, and 8 am to 2 pm, Sunday. If you have a problem getting a train here go to the station superintendent and ask for his assistance.

Bus Long-distance buses depart from the Interstate bus terminal on Station Road. Deluxe buses can and should be booked a day in advance at the Tourist Information Booth, platform 3, Sindhi Camp bus stand. Deluxe buses depart from platform 3, which is in the right rear corner of the bus station yard. Express buses can be booked at Ashok Travels by the ITDC Tourist Office.

There are five deluxe buses leaving

to **Agra** (4½ hr) daily.

There are also regular buses to and from Ajmer and a few direct buses to **Pushkar.** There are 8 deluxe buses to Ajmer (2½ hr) daily. There are three deluxe buses daily to Udaipur (10 hr) and 7 buses each day to Jodhpur.

From the **Vrindavana** bus station a local bus leaves daily to Jaipur at 5.45 am. The journey is about 6½ hr. From the New Bus Stand in **Mathura**, buses depart to Jaipur (6 hr, Rs 70) almost every hour. If you're going to Mathura you can take an express luxury bus to Bharatpur and take one of the regular local buses the rest of the way (1hr).

From **Delhi** (305 km, 5 hr) you can get deluxe coaches from the Interstate Bus Terminal. Also deluxe coaches leave from Bikaner House, the Rajasthan Tourist Office near Indian Gate, and from the ITDC Office. There are 20 deluxe buses daily from Jaipur to Delhi.

Private companies offer deluxe buses to many of these places. They can be arranged by the travel agents around town. The overnight deluxe video buses offered by private companies can be extremely noisy.

Car The easiest way to get to Jaipur from Delhi or Vrindavana is to take a taxi. It is expensive, but it is by far the most comfortable way to travel. Once in Jaipur you can continue to use the taxi for a daily fee. You should make sure the taxi driver knows Jaipur to some extent or you may find yourself very frustrated and taking rickshaws anyway.

The price from Vrindavana is Rs 1500 round trip in the same day and Rs 600 a day or Rs 3 a km (whichever is more) to use the taxi in Jaipur. From Delhi a taxi round trip to Jaipur should cost no more than Rs 2000.

KAROLI (KARAULI)

Karoli is about 182 km southeast of Jaipur and about 100 km southwest of Mathura. It is a small town which contains the important Madana Mohana Temple. Beside the temple, there is an interesting City Palace which has a good collection of stone sculptures and paintings.

Madana Mohana Temple

Madana Mohana means "one who can enchant even Cupid." In the temple there are three altars. On the center altar is Madana Mohana, with Sri Radha on His left and Lalita Devi on His right. On the left altar is Gopalaji Krishna with Radha and Lalita. The king of Karoli worshiped these Deities 100 years before Madana Mohana came to Karoli.

There is a midday offering of 56 dishes to the Deities. The preparations are mainly sweets such as *malpura*, sweet *samosas*, and various other items. Every morning about 300 people attend *mangala-arati* at 4.30 am.

These Deities were worshiped by Sanatana Goswami in Vrindavana in the Madana Mohana Temple. Madana-Mohana was brought to Jaipur from Vrindavana by Maharaja Jai Singh.

His brother-in-law Maharaja Gopal Singh had a dream in which Madana-Mohana came to him and said "Take Me to Karoli." He then told his brother-in-law Maharaja Jai Singh about the dream and asked permission to bring Madana-Mohana to Karoli. Maharaja Jai Singh told him if he could distinguish Madana-Mohana from Govinda and Gopinatha, the two other main Deities of Jaipur, while blindfolded, then he could take the Deity. When Gopal Singh was blindfolded he directly approached Madana-Mohana and touched His lotus feet.

Practicalities

For staying, there is the *Bhamivar Vilas Palace* (07464-20024) at Karoli. It has comfortable rooms and a pool in pleasant surroundings. You can reserve a room for there at Karauli House (07464-367-532), New Sanganer Rd, Sodala area in Jaipur.

If you are going from Bombay to Mathura or Delhi you could stop in the city of Gangapur, the train junction for Karoli, early in the morning. Gangapur is 50 km from Karoli.

Coming from Delhi or Mathura you can get down at the station in Hindaun. You can also get trains to Mathura or Delhi from this station. The bus from the train stations lets you off about two km from the temple.

The easiest way to get to Karoli from Vrindavana is to go by taxi on the way to Jaipur. It will take you an extra two hours out of the way. If you leave Vrindavana by 8 am in the morning, you should get to Karoli for the noon *arati*.

AJMER

Population: 400,000, STD Code 0145

The main reason to come here is that you have to travel through Ajmer to get to Pushkar. It is a fairly boring place, so most people would not want to spend much time here. It is 138 km southwest of Jaipur.

There is a richly decorated Jain temple here, with models depicting the Jain's conception of the universe and theology.

Information

The very helpful **tourist office** (Mon-Sat, 8 am to noon and 3 to 6 pm) is in the Khadim Tourist Bungalow near the bus stand. They can arrange tourist taxis and approved guides. There is an information counter in the railway station.

You can **change money** at the State Bank of Bikaner and Jaipur, on Station Rd, and the State Bank of Baroda, Pushkar Rd, opposite the GPO.

Where To Stay – Lower

The *Anand Hotel* (23099), Prithviraj Marg, has rooms with bath and hot water for Rs 80/110. The *Rajmahal Lodge* (21347), Prithviraj Marg, is a budget hotel by the GPO with rooms for Rs 70/90.

The *King Edward Memorial Rest House (KEM)* (20936), across the street from the railway station, has basic rooms for Rs 60/100 and Rs 90/150. It is a good value. You should ask to see some rooms, as many of them are different.

Popular with travelers is the *RTDC Khadim Tourist Bungalow* (20490), which is by the bus station and an eight minutes auto-rickshaw ride from the railway station. Rooms are Rs 150/200 and Rs 300/400 with A/C. There are dorm beds for Rs 40. It has a nice location, but is not so well maintained.

The *Hotel Samrat* (31805), Kutchery Rd, has rooms with TV for Rs 200/275 up to Rs 500. It is close to the private bus companies and is convenient for an early morning bus departure. It is overpriced.

The *Bhola Hotel* (23844), opposite the church at Agra Gate and not far from the train station, is the best value of the cheaper places. Rooms having bath and hot water are Rs 90/145. It has an added plus, the best vegetarian restaurant in town.

The *Nagpal Tourist Hotel* (21603), across the street from the railway station, has modern double rooms for Rs 300.

Where To Stay – Middle and High

The *Hotel Regency* (30296), Delhi Gate, has good modern rooms for Rs 480/500 and Rs 770/800 with A/C.

The *Mansingh Palace Hotel* (425-855), Ana Sagar Circular Rd, a few km northeast of town, is the only high-end hotel, but at Rs 1195/2000 for a room it is not a good value. It is a nice place and well-located, but not well-maintained.

Where To Eat

The restaurant in the *Bhola Hotel* is recommended. Not only is the food good, but it is cheap too. The *Jai Hind Restaurant*, behind the clock tower, across from the train station, is also a good place.

Travel

Train Ajmer is on the Delhi-Jaipur-Ahmedabad line, and most trains on this line stop here. The Pink City Express #2916 (1.50 pm) takes about 2½ hours to get to **Jaipur**. The Chetak Exp #9815 (3.35 pm, 8 hr) goes to **Udaipur**. The most convenient way to get to **Delhi** is the overnight Aravalli Exp #9932 (7 pm, 10½ hr).

The Ahmedabad Exp #9903 (9.50 pm, 12½ hr) and the Ahmedabad Mail #9901 (8.30 am, 12 hr) are two of the five trains daily to **Ahmedabad**. The Agra Fort Fast Passenger Exp #9706 (8 pm, 10½ hr) goes to **Agra**.

Bus The bus station is about 2 km southwest of the train station. There are deluxe buses to Delhi, Bombay, Jaipur (2½ hr), Udaipur (8 hr), Mt Abu, and Ahmedabad. If you book a ticket to one of these places in Pushkar with a travel agent, the ticket agent will provide a free jeep ride to Ajmer. Local buses depart every half hour to Jaipur.

Buses to **Pushkar** (Rs 4, return Rs 3) depart from outside Gandhi Bhawan, a few hundred metres from the railway station. There are also shared jeeps (Rs 5) to Pushkar.

PUSHKAR

Population: 11,000, STD Code 014581

Pushkar is a small, mellow town with no vehicle traffic on the main street. There are over 400 temples in Pushkar. Some of the important temples are dedicated to Brahma, Raghunath, Varaha, Savitri, and Gayatri. It is famous for the Camel Fair, which takes place here in Oct/Nov. Alcohol and meat are supposed to be banned here. Pushkar is on the edge of the Rajasthan desert, ten km northwest of Ajmer, 400 km southwest of Delhi, and 145 km southwest of Jaipur, .

It is said that Lord Brahma's lotus flower fell in three separate places in the Pushkar area, and water came from the ground at each place. They are located within a radius of six miles. Senior Pushkar, where the hotels are located, is considered the most holy place, because the lotus fell here first. Middle Pushkar is 3 km down the road and has a small Hanuman temple and a 200-year-old banyan tree. New (Junior) Pushkar, 3 km further north, has a small Krishna temple. As Brahma threw the *pushpa* (flower) with his *kar* (hand), so the place received the name Pushkar.

In the *Mahabharata,* concerning Pushkar, it is said: "The holy place of Lord Vishnu, Pushkar-tirtha, renowned in the three worlds, is situated on this earth. Fortunate souls can enter that place. O son of the Kuru dynasty, at Pushkar-tirtha billions of *tirthas* gather at daybreak and sunset. Sins of both men and women, including the sin that caused their birth, are destroyed simply by taking a bath at Pushkar-tirtha. As Madhusudana is the original God, so Pushkar is the original *tirtha*."

It is believed that to bathe in Pushkar Lake on Kartika Purnima (the full moon day in Oct/Nov) gives one salvation. The

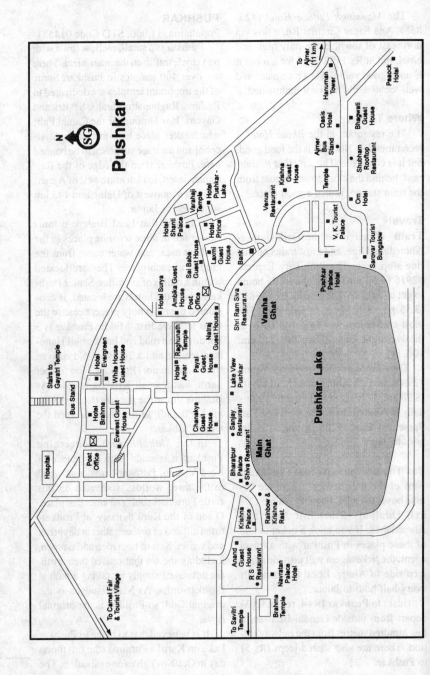

Pushkar

N

To Ajmer (11 km)

Peacok Hotel

Hanuman Tower

Oasis Hotel

Bhagwati Guest House

Ajmer Bus Stand

Shubham Rooftop Restaurant

Krishna Guest House

Temple

Om Hotel

Varahaji Temple

Hotel Pushkar Lake

Venus Restaurant

Sarovar Tourist Bungalow

Hotel Shanti Palace

Hotel Prince

V. K. Tourist Palace

Sai Baba Guest House

Laxmi Guest House

Bank

Hotel Surya

Ambika Guest House

Pushkar Palace Hotel

Post Office

Varaha Ghat

Shri Ram Siva Restaurant

Stairs to Gayatri Temple

Hotel Evergreen

Raghunath Temple

Natraj Guest House

Pushkar Lake

White House Guest House

Hotel Amar

Payal Guest House

Bus Stand

Hotel Brahma

Everest Guest House

Lake View Pushkar

Main Ghat

Chanakya Guest House

Sanjay Restaurant

Shiva Restaurant

Hospital

Post Office

Bharatpur Palace

Krishna Palace

Rainbow & Krishna Rest.

Anand Guest House

R S House

To Camel Fair & Tourist Village

Navratan Palace Hotel

Brahma Temple

To Savitri Temple

full benefit of taking bath in Pushkar Lake is said to be during the last five days of Kartika month. Those who take bath at this time are said to be relieved of all sins and promoted to heaven when they leave their bodies. It is said to be especially auspicious to do *parikrama* (walk around) of the three Pushkars (16 km) on the Kartika Purnima.

Gaya Kund, near Junior Pushkar, is where people do *puja* (worship) for the salvation of their ancestors.

Story of Pushkar

It is said that while Lord Brahma was passing this spot he dropped a lotus flower. From the spots where the petals fell, water sprang out and lakes were formed. There is a rectangular lake here surrounded by temples. According to the *Padma Purana*, Brahma, the lord of creation, killed a demon with a lotus flower here. He dropped the lotus at this place to kill the demon. Petals fell in three spots, where lakes emerged.

Brahma wanted to perform a *yajna* on the full moon day in Kartika (Oct/Nov). Lord Brahma, the creator, was in search of a suitable place to perform the *yajna*. The lotus from his hand fell down, rebounded, and fell at three places, from where water sprang. Thus Brahma decided to perform the *yajna* at Pushkar (*push*—lotus; *kar*—hand). But the *yajna* could not take place without his wife, Savitri, by his side, and she was late. Brahma therefore had to ask Indra to arrange a marriage for him, so that he could fulfill the religious obligations. So the priest manifested a daughter called Gayatri. Because she was an untouchable, to purify her, she was put into the mouth of a cow and removed from the other end, which totally purified her. When Savitri arrived, she saw Brahma married with-

out her permission. So she cursed Brahma that he would only be worshiped at Pushkar.

Enraged, Savitri went and established a temple at Rathkagir, on top of the hill a little south of Pushkar. It is said to be due to Savitri's resentment that Brahma is mainly only worshiped at Pushkar.

Information

There is an unofficial **curfew** at 11 pm. All the shops are supposed to be closed, and the police expect Westerners to be off the street at this time.

The owner of the Pushkar Hotel is full of information, which is a good reason to stay there.

The State Bank of Bikaner & Jaipur, in the main bazaar, is the only place to **change money** in Pushkar. But many people will ask you to change money on the black market.

The GPO post office is near the Marwar bus stand at the end of town. There is a small post office in Sadar Bazaar.

Ram's Camel Adventures, by Pushkar Palace Hotel, runs camel and jeep trips. You can get a camel ride for about Rs 100. You can rent a bicycle near the Pushkar Hotel.

Temples

The **Brahma Temple** has a red tower and a *hans* (swan), the carrier of Lord Brahma, over the doorway. In the temple there is a deity of four-headed Brahma with Gayatri on the left and Savitri on the right. There are also deities of Indra and Kubera, the god of wealth, in the temple.

The **Varaha Temple** has a beautiful two-foot-high white Deity of Lord Varaha. Lord Varaha is said to have appeared in Pushkar. The original temple here was built in the 12th century. Anyone can enter the temple. It is said that persons who visit the **Pap Mochini Temple**, north of town, become free from the sin of killing a Brahmin.

There are two Raghunath temples in Pushkar—the old and the new one. The Deities in the **New Raghunath Temple** are Vaikunthanath and Laksmi. The Deities in the **Old Raghunath Temple**, build in 1823, are Venugopal, Narasimha, and Laksmi. In India I saw many signs saying "non-Hindus not allowed" at temples, but these temples had signs that said "Foreigners not allowed."

The **Savitri Temple**, on top of a hill, a little outside of town, is dedicated to Brahma's wife. The temple dates back 2000 years. It is a tough hour climb up a 4th century stairway to reach this temple. From the top of the hill you have a great view of the surrounding countryside. On the other side of town by the Marwar Bus Stand is the **Gayatri Temple**, who is the wife that sat in on Lord Brahma's sacrifice when Savitri, his first wife, was late. To get to the Gayatri Temple, you start by walking to the temple right behind the bus stand. From there a path leads to the stairs to the top of the hill. Both of these temples are closed in the afternoon, so it is best to visit them in the morning before 12 noon.

Pushkar Lake

This sacred lake is said to have been created by Lord Brahma. It has 52 *ghats*. Varaha, Brahma, and Gau Ghats are the most important *ghats*. At Varaha Ghat, Lord Vishnu is supposed to have appeared in His boar incarnation. It is said that the River Saraswati restarts at Pushkar Lake, after it disappears at Vinasana near Kurukshetra. It is said that Lord Rama bathed in this lake. Photography is prohibited at the *ghats*, as is walking too close to the lake with your shoes on.

Nag (Yajna) Hill

It is said to be one of the oldest hills in the world. Its height is said to have been ten *crores yojanas* in Satya-yuga, ten lakhs *yojanas* in Treta-yuga, and ten thousand *yojanas* in Dwapura-yuga. In Kali-yuga its height is decreasing day by day because it is sinking into the earth. By the end of Kali Yuga it will almost disappear. It is said that if you visit this hill on your pilgrimage to Pushkar you will not have any interference or difficulties.

On this hill is **Nag Kund**. The story of this hill is that Rishi Chyavan cursed Vatu, the grandson of Brahma, to become a snake on the second day of the sacrifice performed by Brahma. Vatu was cursed because at the sacrifice he released a snake that coiled around Bhrigu Muni, the father of Rishi Chyavan. After Vatu begged for forgiveness, Brahma blessed him to live near this natural *kund* (lake) on Nag Hill. Vatu did austerities here. People who worship here on the 5th day in Krishna Paksha of Sravana (July/Aug) are said to get their desires fulfilled. Agastya Muni's residence is said to be a cave on Nag Hill. It is about 2 km from Senior Pushkar. You cross Nag Hill to go from Ajmer to Pushkar.

Camel Festival

This huge interesting festival takes place on the full moon day (*Purnima*) of Kartika in October or November. About 200,000 people come to the fair along with 50,000 camels, cows, and buffaloes. The reason why many of the people come during this time is because it is considered a very auspicious time to bath in the Pushkar Lake. They are not just coming to see the camels.

Women, by themselves, should be careful about going into crowded situations during the festival, as men have a bad habit of heavily groping (touching) women.

The dates of the Camel Fair are in 1996—November 22 to 25, 1997—November 11 to 14, and in 1998—November 1 to 4.

Shopping

Both Nathu Rama's Chilum and Swami Lilashah Cloth Store, by Gau Ghat, are good shops to get clothes and other items.

So-called silver in Pushkar is often 60% copper. Most of the times antique silver is only a month old and just made to look old. This does not mean you should not get the jewelry, but you should bargain accordingly.

Where To Stay – Lower

Hotel prices are greatly increased during the Camel Fair.

Rooms in the same hotel often vary considerably in design from each other, so it is best to ask to see an assortment of rooms. Rooms are usually pretty basic. Mosquitoes can also be a problem, especially with the hotels by the lake.

The *Hotel Om* has decent rooms for Rs 70/90. It has a pool about the size of a large bath-tub. The *Lake View Hotel* is a basic place with a good location, right off the main road by the lake, with rooms for Rs 45 to Rs 80. The *Payal Guest House*, in the middle of the main bazaar, has run-down rooms with bath for Rs 70/85 and with common bath for Rs 60.

The *Hotel White House* (2147), about a five minute walk from the Marwar bus stand, is a good place having very small rooms with a common bath for Rs 75/

100 and larger doubles with bath from Rs 150 to Rs 250. It is clean and the management is helpful. The restaurant here is good.

Across the street from the Marwar Bus Stand in the north of town is the *Hotel Brahma*, which has rooms for Rs 60/80 with common bath and Rs 145 with bath. It can be a little noisy, because it is on the main road.

The *Amar Hotel,* in the center of town away from the main road, is a good place with a garden. Rooms with common bath are Rs 60/70 and rooms with bath go for Rs 110. The double rooms in the back building, with bath, are one of the best deals in Pushkar. The *Everest Guest House* is a clean place having small basic rooms with bath for Rs 80/100 and rooms without bath for Rs 60/70. This place has hot water.

The *Hotel Navratan Palace* is a good value having rooms with bath for Rs 100/120. This hotel has a good-sized pool. The place is somewhat impersonal, but the rooms are good.

The *Krishna Palace Guest House* has basic rooms, but the price is good at Rs 70 a night. The *Oasis Hotel*, by the bus stand to Ajmer, has good rooms for Rs 90/110 with bath and Rs 60/80 without bath.

The *Peacock Hotel*, on the eastern outskirts of town, has rooms with bath for Rs 125 and with common bath for Rs 60/80. It has deluxe rooms for Rs 250 up to Rs 650. It has a pool and a shady courtyard. If you are not staying at the hotel you can use the pool for Rs 25.

Where To Stay – Middle

The *RTDC Sarovar Tourist Bungalow*, by the lake, has rooms with bath for Rs 110/175 and Rs 185/270. I could not see any difference between the two ranges of rooms. It is a recommended place in the middle range. It has rooms with A/C for 285/370. You are supposed to pay in hard currency, and you can rent a heater in the winter. It has a vegetarian restaurant in it. Part of the hotel was a palace for the Maharaja of Jaipur.

The *Pushkar Palace Hotel* (3401, fax 2226) is a nice place that has simple rooms with common bath for Rs 80/120. Good doubles with bath and hot water range from Rs 250 to Rs 450. A/C suites are Rs 650/750. Some of the cheaper rooms have an excellent view of the lake, and there is a small garden right next to the lake. It has a vegetarian restaurant. The cheaper rooms will be full later in the day, so if you arrive late, come the next day at 9 am. It is a nice place.

Tourist Village

During the camel festival a tented village is set up by the RTDC right next to the Camel Fair. A standard tent is Rs 1000/1300 and a hut is Rs 1500/1900. A double deluxe tent costs Rs 3200. A dorm bed is Rs 100.

The demand is high for these tents. To book a tent you have to phone the Rajasthan Tourist Corporation in Jaipur at 0141-310-586 (fax 0141-316-045). You are supposed to pay in full 45 days before the fair begins.

Where To Eat

All the restaurants in town are strictly vegetarian, not even eggs. Many of the places in town offer buffet lunches and dinners for Rs 35 for all you can eat. Basically they are *thalis* that you serve yourself. Many times the food is sitting all day, so it may be unhealthy. It is best to get food, especially in India, when it is freshly cooked.

Close to the bazaar post office, at the *Shri Ram Siva Restaurant*, you get an all you can eat breakfast for Rs 30. This includes cereal, fruit, brown bread with your choice of butter, peanut butter, jelly, or cheese, and other items. This meal is a real bargain and is recommended.

Most likely the best place in town for a regular meal is *Raju's Garden Restaurant*, which is in the center of the town off the main road. The spaghetti is very good, and for western food this is one of the better places in India. The *RS Restaurant*, by the Brahma Temple, is one of the better places in town.

Sunset Cafe in the Puskhar Inn, *Natraj Panoramic Roof Top Restaurant*, and the *Krishna Restaurant* are all decent places.

Travel

Air The closest airport is 131 km away in Jaipur.

Train The nearest railway station, in Ajmer (10 km), has trains to Jaipur, Delhi, Udaipur, and Ahmedabad. From Ahmedabad you can get a train to Bombay or Dwarka. You can have a travel agent in Pushkar arrange your train a day or two in advance for a Rs 30 charge, rather than going to Ajmer yourself. The best way to get to Delhi is to catch an overnight train from Ajmer. It is much better than taking an overnight bus, but it takes a little advance planning.

Bus There are two bus stands in Pushkar—the Marwar bus stand, in the north of town by the post office, which services some long distance places, and the Ajmer bus stand, east of town by the Pushkar Hotel, which has buses to Ajmer and Jaipur. There are regular buses from Pushkar to Ajmer (Rs 4). The buses from Ajmer to Pushkar depart every hour from 6 am to 10 pm from near the Ajmer railway station.

In Pushkar there are ticket agents that sell tickets for deluxe buses to cities all over this part of India. The buses depart from Ajmer, and the ticket agents usually arrange free jeep transport to Ajmer to get the bus.

One express bus leaves daily from the Marwar bus stand in Pushkar for Delhi. It departs at 10.15 am and arrives at 6.15 pm, but it is a noisy video bus. There is a deluxe bus that leaves from the Ajmer bus stand at 7.15 am for Delhi. There is a direct bus from Udaipur to Pushkar, stopping in Nathdwar, which takes about eight hours.

Car From Ajmer there are collective jeep taxis to Pushkar, which depart from the railway station. The jeep taxis from Pushkar to Ajmer leave from the main street in the bazaar and from the old bus stand.

NATHDWAR

Population: 20,000, STD Code 02953

This small town is famous as the home for Sri Nathji, one of the most popular Deities of Lord Krishna in India. The name of the town means doorway to Nathji. Nathdwar is very crowded on Janmastami and during Govardhana Puja.

Nathdwar is located 48 km northeast of Udaipur, in Rajasthan, on the right bank of the Banas River.

Sri Nathji Temple

Sri Nathji is an absolutely beautiful black marble Deity of Lord Krishna, standing with His hand upraised lifting Govardhana Hill.

The same Deity (known then as Gopala) was worshiped by Madhavendra Puri in Vrindavana, as described in the *Caitanya-caritamrita*. Sri Nathji was brought to Nathdwar by Rana Raj Singh

of Mewar in the 17th century. The temple of Sri Nathji is said to be the second richest in India, after the Balaji Temple in Tirupati.

Architecturally the temple is simple, but the devotees' enthusiasm is among the greatest in India. Every day Sri Gopala is offered large quantities of opulent foodstuffs cooked in ghee. The variety and quantity of food offered to the Deity is beyond estimation, and it's all of the highest quality. The *maha-prasada* is excellent and can be easily obtained in stalls outside the temple.

Mangala-arati begins at 5.30 am. After *mangala-arati*, *darshan* goes on. The *mukhiyajis*, as the priests here are known, close the curtain in front of the Deity, but everyone cries for more *darshan*. So the curtain is raised and lowered several times.

The Lord wears a large diamond beneath His lips, which is said to be a gift from the Muslim emperor Akbar. Many devotees who visit Nathdwar do service for the Deity, such as carry wood, cut vegetables, sweep the temple, or make garlands.

There is a story that Sri Nathji once tore His garment while rushing back to the temple to be on time for *darshan*. From that day on it has been a custom to blow the conch and then wait several minutes before opening the altar doors. In that way Sri Nathji may return leisurely to His temple from wherever He may be sporting.

The temple of Sri Nathji and other places of worship for the followers of Vallabhacarya are like houses. They are made to be like the Vrindavana house of Krishna's father, Nanda Maharaja. The temple, therefore, is also known as Nanda Bhavan or Nandalaya, "the house of Nanda Maharaja." On the top of the temple is a spire, or *kalasa*, as well as the disc of Lord Vishnu and seven flags.

The priests of the temple are followers of Vallabhacarya, who was born in 1479. His son Sri Vitthalanathji raised the worship of Sri Nathji to a very high standard. The temple is under the management of the main *acarya* (spiritual leader) of the Vallabha-sampradaya, called the Tilakayata. He is the head of the temple.

Once when Sri Vallabhacarya defeated a large group of impersonalist scholars at Vidyanagar, King Krishnadeva Raya gave him a gift of many gold coins. Sri Vallabhacarya gave most of these to the local *brahmanas* and kept only seven. Those seven coins were then made into an ornament for Sri Nathji. It is still worn by the Lord today.

The holdings of the temple include hundreds of shops and buildings and thousands of acres of land, including farms and cow pastures. The temple owns over 500 cows. One of the cows is called the "Sri Nathji's cow" and comes from a lineage that has served the Deity for generations. The milk from this cow goes only for Sri Nathji to drink. Milk from the other cows is made into various sweets for the Deity.

Many people go to each *arati*. It is extremely crowded and you have to constantly move. When you enter the actual temple room it is very crowded, and you may be pushed around, even sometimes out of the temple room. The pushing is not like when you normally get pushed in India. It is actually pleasurable to experience the devotees' extreme desire to see Sri Nathji.

There are eight offerings and six *aratis* each day. The Lord has His last *darshan* in the evening before taking rest. When He lifted Govardhana Hill He was just a young boy, so He takes rest early.

Mangala-arati is 5 am in the winter and 6 am in the summer. The last *arati* 6.30 pm in the winter and 7 pm in the summer. The temple is closed in the afternoon until 3.15 pm in the winter and 3.45 pm in the summer.

Non-Hindus are technically not allowed to enter the temple. If you are a foreigner and wish to enter, the guard will ask you to sign a piece of paper at the main entrance, which is written in Hindi. I believe it says you are a Hindu. You can then enter the temple.

Sri Nathji (Sri Gopala)

Sri Nathji is Lord Krishna in His pastime of lifting Govardhana Hill. The Lord's left hand is upraised. His right hand, closed in a fist, rests on His hip. It is said that the Lord waves His devotees towards Him with His left hand and keeps the nectar of devotion in His right. His eyes glance downward affectionately at His devotees. Sri Nathji is a very special and beautiful Deity.

The servitors of Sri Nathji say that the Deity is the original form of Sri Krishna, known as Nikunja Nayaka, "the Lord of the Celestial Bower." Since this form of Lord Krishna includes all others, His devotees see Him both as Sri Radhanath (the Lord of Radha) and as child Krishna. The Deity is, therefore, sometimes entertained with childish toys like spinning tops and silver animals and sometimes offered a herding stick meant for a cowherd boy.

The Deity appears in a large black stone from which His form emerges in bas-relief. The stone around the Deity bears several marks: two cows, a snake, a lion, two peacocks, a parrot by the Lord's head, two sages seated on His right side and a third on His left, and then below the sages is another snake. Around the Lord's neck is a flower garland, resembling a black snake.

Deity Story

Sri Nathji is the Deity of Krishna formerly known as Gopala, who stands as if holding up Govardhana Hill. This Deity was originally installed by Vajranabha, the great-grandson of Lord Krishna, 5000 years ago. Over 500 years ago the Deity was found by Madhavendra Puri in some bushes next to Govardhana Hill in Vrindavana, as described in *Caitanya-caritamrita*. Madhavendra Puri then established the worship of Sri Gopala in a temple on Govardhana Hill. Madhavendra Puri handed the service of the Deity to the son of Vallabhacarya named Vitthala.

Sri Nathdwar means "the gateway to Lord Sri Nathji." The town was built in the seventeenth century for Lord Nathji, after He was brought from Vrindavana. The Deity was brought to Rajasthan to protect Him from the destructive reign of the Muslim ruler Aurangzeb, who terrorized the Vrindavana area in 1665. When the devotees saw the Mogul army coming to Govardhana, where Nathji was staying, they showed the Muslims the titles and gifts given to the temple by previous Mogul kings. The army commander told them to move the Deity from Govardhana as soon as possible. For almost six months the Deity stayed in Agra, and then He was moved to Mewar. Wherever Sri Nathji went His devotees were enthusiastic to welcome Him. Thus the journey from Govardhana to Mewar took about 32 months to complete. The Lord arrived in Nathdwar around 1669.

Other Places

In Nathdwar there are also temples dedicated to **Madana Mohana** and **Naveet Priya**, which are connected to the main temple of Sri Nathji. *Naveet* mean "butter" and *priya* means "lover," so Naveet Priya means "one who is fond of butter." The Naveet Priya Temple is visited by most of the people that come to the Sri Nathji Temple. The Deity of Madana Mohana was presented to the temple by the wife of Maharana Fateh Singh of Udaipur.

Vitthalnath Temple is just opposite the entrance of the Sri Nathji Temple. This Deity used to be located at Gokula, in Braja. The **Banamali Temple** is a Krishna temple, located to the right of the main entrance of the Sri Nathji Temple.

About 15 km away in Kankroli there is a Deity of Lord Krishna called Dwarkadhish. The Deity was brought there from Mathura in 1676.

Festivals

The largest festival is known as **Annakuta**. It commemorates the pastime in which the people of Vrindavana worshiped Govardhana Hill. Many thousands of people come in special trains, and all the guesthouses are full. As part of the celebrations, a 2500-kilo hill of rice is offered to the Lord. Then the temple gates are closed. In the evening the gates are opened for *darshan* of Sri Nathji, and the people start looting the rice *prasada* from the Annakuta. **Diwali** is also an important festival here, mostly because it precedes the Annakuta festival by one day.

In April there is a **Rose festival**. In the summer the courtyard is filled with water and devotees have to walk knee-deep in water to get a close look at the Deities.

At the end of the summer is **Rathayatra**. The Lord is taken around on a silver chariot and 100,000 mangoes are offered. The swing festival, **Jhulana-yatra**, takes place in June-July. There are swings made of gold, silver, glass, and flowers. **Janmastami** (Aug/Sept), the appearance day of Lord Krishna, is a major festival.

Where To Stay

There are a few large dharamsalas about five minutes walk straight down the road from the temple. The *Vallabh Bhavan* is a large place with double rooms for Rs 80.

The *Hotel Rajshee*, right next to the bus stand, has decent rooms with common bath for Rs 100. The *Krishna Guest House*, a minute from the bus stand down a side road, is a nicer place having double rooms with bath for Rs 120. A little further down the road is the *Vandana Hotel* (02953/2162), which is a nice place with rooms for Rs 325 and Rs 575 with A/C.

On a side road close to the Sri Nathji Temple is the *Hotel Vrinda* (02953/2218), which has double rooms for Rs 225 up to Rs 425 for a room with A/C. It was full when I was there. One of the best places in town is the *Hotel Vallabh Darshan* (02953/30038), which is also down a side road about a two minute walk from the temple. It has double rooms from Rs 500 up to Rs 675. It has a 9 am checkout.

The *RTDC Gokul Tourist Bungalow*, which is inconveniently located 3 km outside of town in the middle of nowhere, has rooms for Rs 225/275. There are also dorm beds for Rs 50. The best place in town is the *Hotel Utsav* (2277), National Highway No 8, 1 km from the downtown, which has rooms for Rs 450/850 and Rs 650/1000 with A/C. You can also stay in Udaipur, 48 km south, where there are many places to stay.

Where To Eat

Outside the temple you can purchase excellent Lord Nathji *maha-prasada*. It is cheap and there are many different preparations, both sweet and salty. There is unlimited Sri Nathji *maha-prasada*, which is one of the things for which Nathdwar is famous for.

The *Hotel Vallabh Darshan* has a vegetarian restaurant.

Travel

Air The nearest airport is in Udaipur, 48 km south.

Train If you are coming from Gujarat or Maharashtra, you can get a train to Udaipur and from there take a bus to Nathdwar. About a five-minute walk straight down the road from the Nathji Temple there is a train reservation office where you can reserve a train north to Delhi and some other places. Nathdwar is 13 km from the Nathdwar railway station.

Bus The bus stand is a 15-minute walk from the temple. From Udaipur there are two express buses daily as well as many other buses that take about two hours to reach Nathdwar. There are express buses to and from Ahmedabad, Pushkar, Ajmer, Jaipur, and Delhi, which can be reserved from the travel agents next to the bus stand.

UDAIPUR

Population: 310,000, STD Code 0294

Udaipur has attractive landscaped gardens and beautiful lakes. The city is about 2000 feet (610 m) above sea level. The city palace, which is a popular tourist site, is located high over the waters of Lake Pichola. This city is one of the most popular cities in India with foreign tourists. The wall surrounding the old city has five gates with iron spikes on them to protect against elephant attacks.

Udaipur was named after Maharaja

Udai Singh, who founded the city in the middle of the sixteenth century. The Maharaja of Udaipur is the highest-ranked Rajput ruler. The Maharaja is known as the "Sun King" and has the emblem of the sun on his standard.

Udaipur is the closest major city to Nathdwar, where the Sri Nathji Deity is located.

Information and Tours

The old city is surrounded by a wall. The bus station and railway station are outside this wall in the southeast part of town. Most of the accommodations and the City Palace are near the Jagdish Temple, which is a landmark that all the rickshaw drivers know.

The **tourist office** (411-535) is in the northeast part of town, outside the city walls and about 1 km from the bus stand. It is open 10 am to 1.30 pm and 2 to 5 pm, Monday to Saturday. There are tourist information counters at the airport and railway station.

An afternoon Rajasthan Tourism tour goes to Nathdwar, Eklingji, and Haldi Ghati. It starts at the Kajri Tourist Bungalow at 2 pm and ends at 7 pm.

Bicycles can be hired next to the Hotel Keerti on Airport Rd.

City Palace

This is the largest palace in Rajasthan. Its upper balconies are the highest point in the area and give you a good view of Pichola Lake and the city. The palace has inner patios, courtyards, and marble balconies. The Peacock Courtyard has glass peacocks, made up of thousands of tiny colored glass slivers inserted into the wall.

Rooms have mirrored walls, ivory doors, colored glass windows, and much more. There is a room that is totally covered with painted miniatures. There are elephant stables that can hold 20 elephants.

Outside the main building there is a small interesting museum with some old sculptures. There is also the queen's palace near the entrance gate. It is not as interesting as the main palace, but it has a nice exhibit on the upper floor, on the right side of the complex. The palace is open from 9.30 am to 4 pm.

Jagdish (Jagannatha) Temple

This is a Vishnu temple that was built by Maharaja Jagat Singh I in 1652. It is nearly 80 feet high. There is a black stone Deity of Lord Vishnu as Jagannatha, Lord of the universe. It is located outside the City Palace near the cheaper hotels. The Jagannatha Temple has a large bronze statue of Garuda in it. This beautiful temple is the largest and finest temple in Udaipur.

Eklingji Temple

Eklingji is the patron deity of the royal family of Udaipur. Eklingji is known as "Kailashpuri," the abode of Lord Siva. The temple is said to have been built in 728. Inside the temple is a black marble image of Lord Siva with four faces. This temple is 24 km from Udaipur.

Ranakpur

This is one of the biggest and most important Jain pilgrimage centers. Most of the intricately carved temples here date from between the 12th and 15th centuries. The main temple, which is called Chaumukha, is dedicated to Adinath. It has 29 halls with 144 pillars of which no two are alike.

If you want to stay overnight, there are dharamshalas and the *Shilpi Tourist Bungalow*. Ranakpur is 96 km from

Udaipur. The nearest railway station is 35 km away at Falna.

Shopping

You can get excellent *picchwais*, colorful wall-hanging paintings, in Udaipur and Nathdwar. This art originated at Nathdwar as backdrops for the Nathji Temple. These painting are usually of Krishna's pastimes.

The Rajasthan Government Handicrafts Emporium is at Chetak Circle. Hathipol Market is a good general place for shopping. You can get handicrafts at Ganesh Handicraft Emporium and Shree-nath Emporium on City Palace Road and Chelawat Art Gallery on Jagdish Road.

Where To Stay

The Jagdish Temple area is the main tourist area of town and is a pleasant area. The hotel area by the bus station is both noisy and very polluted. The hotels in the bus station area could be used if you are just traveling through and need a quick place to sleep.

Lower – Jagdish Temple Area

Lalghat Guest House (525-301) is a good place with a courtyard. Rooms are Rs 75/100 to Rs 125/150, and dorm beds are Rs 40. There are better rooms with bath and a view of the lake for Rs 200. The rooftop has a great view of the lake. The *Lake Ghat Guest House* has rooms for Rs 70/90 with common bath and Rs 125/150 with bath. There is a good view from the terrace. Among the lower priced hotels, I believe these two places are about the best for atmosphere and location. Both places are popular and very close to the lake.

Next door is the *Evergreen Guest House* (527-823) which has rooms with common bath for Rs 80 and Rs 125 with bath. There is a nice terrace area. The management is friendly.

Nearby is the popular *Badi Haveli* (525-420), which is a nice 350-year-old place having rooms with common bath for Rs 80/120 and Rs 190 with bath. There is a courtyard and a good view of the lake from the roof. Next door is the *Lehar Guest House*, which has simple rooms, some with a lake view, for Rs 90/110. Nearby is the *Anjani Hotel* (527-670), which has rooms starting at Rs 100 with common bath.

The *Jheel Guest House* (28321), by the *ghat*, is in an old building with a nice atmosphere. Rooms are Rs 75/100 with common bath, Rs 125 for a room with a view, and Rs 200 for a room with a bath.

Lower – Lake Palace Road Area

The *Ranjit Niwas Hotel* (525-774), Lake Palace Rd, has rooms with bath for Rs 150, with common bath for Rs 100, and Rs 25 for a dorm bed. It is well located and has a courtyard with a garden.

The *Hotel Mahendra Prakash* (529-370), Lake Palace Rd, has singles for Rs 80 and Rs 150/250 for an air-cooled double with hot water. It has a good-sized garden and a central courtyard. Right next door is the *Hotel Shambhu Vilas* (28109), Lake Palace Rd, which has singles for Rs 80 and Rs 150/250 for an air-cooled double.

The *Monalisa* (26147), 104 Bhatiyani Chohatta, City Palace Road, down from the Jagdish Temple, is good bargain place run by a nice family. Rooms with bath range from Rs 60 to Rs 150. It is a good value and is quiet.

Lower – Bus Terminal Area

If you are passing through on your way to Nathdwar or other places, there are a good number of hotels by the bus stand. The *Hotel Apsara* (523-400) is a big place set back from the road, so it is fairly quiet. It has double rooms for Rs 100 and higher and also dorm beds. It is one of the best places in the area.

The conveniently located *Hotel Yatri* (527-251), which is across from the bus stand, has rooms for Rs 110/135 with hot water. Across the street, the *Hotel Welcome* (525-375) is a better place with good double rooms for Rs 110/135. Also near the bus stand is the *Gokul Palace Hotel* (27317), with good double rooms for Rs 150 and A/C rooms for Rs 225.

The *Pratap Country Inn*, Airport Rd, Titadhia Village, 7 km from city center, has comfortable rooms cost ranging from Rs 200 to Rs 600. They have a swimming pool and free two-hour horse rides daily, if you stay more than one night. It is a relaxing and beautiful place. You can arrange your stay at the Pratap Country Inn at the *Keerti Hotel*, on Airport Rd in Udaipur.

Where To Stay – Middle

The *Hotel Jagat Niwas* (529-728), Lal Ghat area, on the lake shore, has rooms for Rs 175 to Rs 325 with common bath and rooms with bath for Rs 450 to Rs 750. It is a recommended place. It has a quiet courtyard and a rooftop with a good view of the lake. The *Hotel Raj Palace* (523-092), Bhattiyani Chotta, down the road from the Jagdish Temple, is a good place with either air-cooled or A/C rooms for Rs 150 to Rs 450.

The *Hotel Sai Niwas* (524-909), 75 Navghat, near the City Palace by the *ghat*, has well decorated rooms with traditional furniture. Rooms are Rs 350 to Rs 600 with bath and hot water. The better rooms have a lake view. It has a good atmosphere and is well-managed.

The *Ratan Palace Guest House* (527-

935), near the Sai Niwas, has clean comfortable rooms for Rs 250 to Rs 400 for a double. There is a lake view from the terrace. This place is a good value.

The *Rang Niwas Palace Hotel* (253-891), Lake Palace Rd, is good place with large rooms with common bath for Rs 150/200 and Rs 300/350 with attached bath. It has A/C rooms with hot water for Rs 400 to Rs 600. Formerly a small palace, this relaxing and peaceful place has a large garden and a swimming pool. This place is a good value, but is away from the lake. It has a vegetarian restaurant.

The *Hotel Lake End* (523-841, fax 523-898), by Fateh Sagar, has a swimming pool with a garden by the lake. Modern rooms are Rs 500/700 and Rs 800/1100 with A/C.

The *Chandralok Hotel* (560-011), 123 Saheli Marg, is a good place that has A/C rooms for Rs 700/900.

Where To Stay – West side of Lake Pichola

Located in a peaceful area next to the lake and near the Lake Pichola Hotel is the *Lake Shore Hotel*. It has fairly basic rooms with a beautiful view overlooking the lake for Rs 120/130 to Rs 225. Out of the way, the peaceful *Natural Hotel* (527-879), near Raj Bridge, Rang Sagar, has basic, large clean rooms Rs 50/90 with common bath and Rs 85130 with bath. It is a fairly popular place.

Where To Stay – High

The *Lake Pichola Hotel* (529-387, fax 410-575), Chand Pol, on the other side of the bridge from the Jagdish Temple, is by far the best of the lower end high-range places. It is a well-managed place having well-maintained rooms with A/C, bath, and hot water. If you cannot get in the Lake Palace Hotel, this is a nice place to stay with rooms that overlook the *ghats* and the City Palace. Standard rooms are Rs 650/700, and rooms with a lake-side view are Rs 775/800. This place is an excellent value and is highly recommended.

Where To Stay – High Fateh Sagar

The four-star ITDC *Laxmi Vilas Palace Hotel* (529-711), between Fateh Sagar and Pichola Lake, is a luxurious place with a swimming pool and rooms for Rs 1500/2300 up to Rs 3000 for the Maharani Suite. This place was built as a royal guest house. It is best to book this place in advance, as it is often full. Next door is the *Hotel Anand Bhawan* (523-256, fax 523-247), which is a first-class place that has rooms with hot water for Rs 450/550 and deluxe rooms with a lake view for Rs 700/800. It is a very good value. The *Hilltop Palace* (28764, fax 525-106) is another high-class hotel above Fateh Sagar with rooms for Rs 1175/1600.

Where To Stay – Luxury

The famous *Lake Palace Hotel* (527-961, fax 527-974) is one of the best hotels in the world. It looks exactly as you would expect a Maharaja's Palace should look. It has a central swimming pool. Rooms start at $150/180 and go up to $550 for the top suite. It is in high demand, so it is advisable to reserve a room in advance. It can be booked for months in advance, because it is very popular with tour groups.

The grand *Shivniwas Palace Hotel* (528-016, fax 528-006), which is part of the City Palace, is also excellent and has rooms starting at $65. There are also rooms and suites that cost from $175 to $350. It has an excellent pool and was formerly a guest house for the Maharaja. It can be heavily booked like the Lake Palace Hotel, but there are sometimes cancellations. The *Hotel Fateh Prakash Palace* (28239), also part of the City Palace, is also an excellent place that has rooms with a view of the lake for $100 and suites for $150. Both of these places are excellent alternatives if you cannot stay at the *Lake Palace Hotel*. They were both full when I went there, but I was told that a room might be available if I came at 9 am in the morning.

Where To Eat

Shreeji Garden Cafe is a very good place with cheap prices. It is run by a *Brahmin* family—the wife cooks and the husband serves you. It is located a little down the road from the Rang Niwas Palace Hotel on a lawn next to the owner's house. It is a good setting for an evening meal, but it can be hot during the day. Further down the road, toward the bus stand, is the *Garden Hotel*, which serves *thalis* for Rs 30.

Opposite the Jagdish Temple, the *Mayur Cafe* serves South Indian food and some western preparations. It seems to be the best place in that area. Around the corner is the *Siva Restaurant*. The *Nataraj Restaurant*, by Suraj Pol, was suggested by the locals as a good place to get a Gujarati *thali*.

The *Hotel Natural* is supposed to have a good vegetarian restaurant.

Travel

Air The airport is about 25 km from the city. A taxi into town costs about Rs 150. The Indian Airlines office (410-999) is on Dhan Mandi, off Ashwani Rd, near Delhi Gate. There are flights to Delhi ($74), Jaipur ($51), Bombay ($88), Goa and Aurangabad (4 flights weekly, $84). The trip to Aurangabad by train or bus is a tedious trip that takes as much as 24 hours, so a plane trip is worth considering even for a budget traveler.

Train The Garib Nawaz Express #2916 (5.40 am) is the best train to **Delhi** (15½ hr). It goes via **Jaipur** (11 hr) and **Ajmer** (8 hr). The problem with this train is that it arrives in Delhi at 10.20 pm. The overnight Chetak Express #9616 (6.10 pm) takes 20 hours to reach Delhi, via Chittaurgarh (3½ hr), Ajmer, and Jaipur (12 hr). The Udaipur-Ahmedabad Express #9644 at 7 pm to **Ahmedabad** takes 10 hours.

Bus It is best to take an express bus for long distance trips, as the local buses take a long time. The buses operated by the private companies are best for long distance trips. Express buses go to Jaipur (10 hr), Ajmer (8 hr), Ahmedabad (7 hr), Bombay, Delhi (4 pm & 7 pm, 17 hr), Mt Abu (6 hr), Agra (15 hr), Mathura (15 hr), Vadodara (10 hr), and many other places. Most of the private bus companies have offices on Khangipur Rd, which is the road the bus station is on. You can arrange private buses to many places with the many travel agents in town or at your hotel.

There are many buses to Nathdwar (2 hr), including two express buses.

MOUNT ABU
Population: 17,000, STD Code 02974

Mt Abu is a quiet mellow town with no bike or auto-rickshaws allowed. It is a hill station 1200 metres above sea level in the southwest corner of Rajasthan, by the Gujarat border. To get here you can take a side trip from Udaipur (7 hr), or you can stop here while going to Dwarka or Bombay from Delhi.

This is a Jain pilgrimage site, because of the marble temples located at Dilwara,

which are covered with some of the most intricately carved sculptures in India.

There are no beggars and no pushy salesmen or commission agents, except for a few guys who want to help you find a hotel. Mount Abu is mainly visited by middle-class Indian tourists and honeymooners, with a small percentage of western tourists. Many budget travelers find Mt Abu expensive, especially during the busy season.

The best time to visit is March to June and September to November. It can be cold here in the winter because of its elevation. I was there at the end of February and you needed a sweater at night, but it was not uncomfortable. March to April is a quiet time with hotel rooms at half-price. You can see everything here in one day, but you may want to stay a few more days, as it is a pleasant place. The high season is April to June and September to October, when the room rates can be three times the rate of the other times of the year. The winter temperature is 7°C to 26°C and in the summer it is 17°C to 33°C.

Mount Abu is on a plateau, which at the top is about 22 km by 6 km and varies in height from 3500 to 5600 feet. The town of Mount Abu is flat, but everywhere else in the area is hilly. You have to make some steep climbs to see some of the sites.

Information

The **tourist office**, opposite the bus station, is open from 8 to 11 am and 4 to 8 pm.

The RTDC has **daily tours** of the main sites in the area. One tour starts at 8.30 am and ends at 1.30 pm, and the second tour goes from 1.30 to 6 pm and ends at Sunset point, if there is enough time. Both tours start at the tourist office.

The same tour is run by private companies.

There is a small booklet about Mt Abu and also a very detailed book called *Abu to Udaipur* by Jodh Singh Mehta.

You can **change money** at the Bank of Baroda, at the south end of the polo grounds, and at the Chacha Museum, a shop on Nakki Lake Rd.

If you have heavy luggage, you can hire a person with a push-cart to push your baggage to a hotel.

Vasistha Muni Ashram

It is said that Mount Abu used to be the home of Vasistha, Rama's guru. This place was called Nandivardhan after Nandini, the wish-fulfilling cow, who lived with Vasistha. One time Nandini was grazing by the lake here and she fell in. Vasistha then flew to the Himalayas to ask the gods to save her. They sent Arbuda, the celestial cobra, who brought a huge rock on his hood. Arbuda dropped the rock in the lake and it became the present Mount Abu. The water from the lake was displaced and Nandini saved. The spot is now known as Arbudachala, the hill of Arbuda.

Parasurama, an incarnation of Lord Vishnu, killed the *kshatriya* (warrior) caste 21 times to avenge the death of His father, who was murdered by some *kshatriyas*. It is said that the gods came to Mount Abu to ask Vasistha to restore the situation caused by the lack of *kshatriyas* on the earth. Vasistha performed a fire sacrifice and out of the flames came the four "fire-born" Rajput clans.

There is a temple at this place which is said to mark the place where Vasistha's *ashram* was located. It is said to have been built in 1337. Inside this temple are deities of Lord Rama, Laksman, Vasistha, and his wife, Arundhati. In front of the main shrine is the sacrificial fire-pit from which the Rajput clan is said to have come.

Dilwara Jain Temples

There are five magnificent temples here. The Adinatha Temple (Vimala Vasahi) and Neminatha Temple (Luna Vasahi) are the most notable. The Adinath Temple was built in the 11th century (1031) by Vimala Shah, a minister of the Solanki king, Bhima I. It is dedicated to the first Jain tirthankar, Adinatha. It is said to have cost 180 million rupees.

The **Adinatha Temple** (Vimala Vasahi) is built completely of white marble. It is covered with very superb carvings. It has intricate carvings of Narasimha and Krishna's pastimes. It is said that it took 1500 sculptures and 1200 laborers 14 years to complete. The bronze figure of Adinatha has a gem necklace and eyes made of precious jewels. In the ceiling of the 34th cell (old No. 29) is a beautiful sculpture of Krishna subduing the Kaliya snake. When you come off the street into the entrance of the temple complex, directly in front of you is the small Mahavir Temple and slightly to the right is this temple.

The **Neminath Temple** (Luna Vasahi) was built in 1231 by Vastupal and Tejapala, ministers of the King of Viradhaval in Gujarat. It is dedicated to the 22nd tirthankara, Neminath. The carvings on this temple are extremely intricate. Several full-time carvers are employed to maintain and restore the temple.

The **Chaumukha Temple** (Parsvanatha) was built around 1459 and is the tallest of the Dilwara temples. The unfinished **Sri Risha Deoji** has a huge 4.3 ton brass tirthankara statue made of *panchadhatu* (five metals)—gold, silver, brass, copper and zinc.

These temples are open from 12 noon to 6 pm for non-Jains. You cannot bring any leather objects into the temples, and this is very strictly enforced. Video cameras are also prohibited.

There is a sign at the entrance that says: "Entry of women on their monthly course is strictly prohibited." Women may be questioned about this. These temples are a one-hour walk from the downtown. Shared jeeps (Rs 3) come here.

There are four ruined temples to the northwest of the Jain temples including a **Vishnu temple** and the **Kanya Kumari temple.**

Trevor's Tank is about 50m from the Dilwara Jain temples. Crocodiles lie around on the bank of the tank. You can get a good view of the tank from the trails that lead through the park.

Nakki Lake

This is the nice lake right next to the downtown. Bathing in this lake is held to be as purifying as bathing in the Ganges. It is said to have been dug by a sage using only his nails (nakha). It is virtually in the center of Mt Abu. The 14th century Raghunathji Temple, which has Deities of Lord Rama, Laksman, and Sita, is right next to the lake. Southwest of the Raghunathji Temple is a famous huge rock that looks like a toad. By the lake is Ram Kund, which is a small well that never dries up.

Achalgarh

There is an ancient 9th century Siva temple and fort in Achalgarh, 11 km from town. The **Siva temple** has Siva's toe-print instead of a *linga*. Lord Siva is said to have stood on Abu Mountain to stop it from moving. Where the Siva-linga would normally be located, there is a deep hole that is supposed to go all the way down to Patala, the innermost core of the earth. In the temple compound there is a **Lakshmi Narayana temple**, which has figures of the ten incarnations of Vishnu.

There is a tank here called **Mandakini Kund** (near the temple) with three stone buffaloes and a king shooting them with a bow and arrow. The *kund* is now in ruins. It is said that the tank used to be filled with ghee. When three demons came every night in the form of buffaloes to steal the ghee, the king shot them. The Parmar Chief Dharavarsha is said to have killed these three buffaloes with one arrow.

There is a path that goes to a group of interesting Jain temples on the hill (10 minute climb).

Places To See

There is a small Vishnu **Dattatreya temple** at Guru Shikhar, 15 km out of town at 5,650 feet above sea level. There are 300 steps that lead to this temple on top of a hill. A little to the northwest is a temple dedicated to **Ahalya**, the mother of Dattatreya.

The **Adhar Devi Temple** is 3 km out of town. It is a 500-year-old Durga temple that you have to climb over 400 steps to reach. The temple is built in a small cave, and you have to bend over to get into the temple. You have a good view of Mt Abu from here.

It is traditional for tourists to go to **Sunset Point** (2 km out of town) to see the sunset. You can get there by renting a camel at the end of Sunset Road.

Shopping

The Rajasthan Handicraft Emporium, near the bus stand, and the Khadi Gramodyog Bhavan are two good shops. The Chacha Museum is a big old emporium with many interesting objects.

Where To Stay

The high season goes from mid-March to mid-November. The peak times are May 15 to June 15, Diwali time in November, and Christmas and New Years. During the high season, hotel owners raise their prices. During the off-season there can be up to a 50% discount off the hotel prices. The prices given are mainly for the off-season.

During the high season most of the hotels will be full. If you come during the peak time, the touts (commission agents) that meet you at the bus stations can actually help you get a room. They will know which hotels still have rooms left.

Where To Stay – Lower

The *Hotel Panghat* (3386) by the lake has rooms with hot water between 7 and 9 am. During the low season rooms are Rs 90 or Rs 130 with a view of the lake. The *Hotel Nakki Vihar*, close to the lake in a good location, has some rooms with a view of the lake. Rooms are Rs 125 to Rs 175 for a double with bath. There are also some cheaper rooms. The *Shree Ganesh Hotel* (3591), which is further up the hill from the Hotel Nakki Vihar, has clean rooms for Rs 90 during the low season. The price is so reasonable because of its out of the way location.

The *Hotel Lake View* (3659) has rooms with hot water between 6 and 11 am and a view of Nakki Lake for Rs 350. Single rooms are Rs 80 to Rs 150, and double rooms range from Rs 100 to Rs 350. Rooms are double to triple these prices during the high season. It is a popular place, so if you want to get a room here, it is best to come around 9 am in the morning. Later in the day it is usually full. It is not a very good place, but it has a good location and the best view in town.

At the far end of the polo grounds is the *Hotel Saraswati* (3237), which has clean rooms with bath and bucket hot water for Rs 70. It has other rooms for Rs 100 to Rs 250. The *Hotel Surya Darshan* (3165) has simple rooms for Rs 125 and bigger rooms with TV and hot water for Rs 200. They told me the same Rs 125 room would cost Rs 350 during the high season.

The *Hotel Natraj* (3532), which is reached by going up the right fork opposite the taxi stand, has reasonably priced rooms with a balcony and hot water for Rs 120/170. The *Tourist Guest House* (3200), by the Tourist Bungalow just off the main road, has run-down but clean rooms for Rs 75/90 up to Rs 120. Rooms have hot water in the morning. It has a small garden and a helpful manager. It is a good value, but is fairly basic. During the season the prices are much higher.

The *RTDC Shikar Tourist Bungalow* (3129), up a steep little hill off the main road, is a big place with 82 rooms. Rooms go for Rs 125/175 up to Rs 250/300. If you decide to stay here, ask to see some rooms before you choose one, as they range from horrible to good. From the reception desk, I had to walk almost ten minutes to see a room.

Where To Stay – Middle

The *Suruchi Hill Resort* (3577), at the bottom end of the backside of the polo ground, has rooms for Rs 450/650, with a 30% discount during the off-season. The *Hotel Sheratone* (3544), by the main road, has good big clean rooms with bath for Rs 500 during the off-season.

The *Hotel Vrindavan* (3147) is a nice place that has rooms with bath for Rs 250/350 and Rs 400 for a bigger room with a TV.

The *Samrat International* (3173) and

Hotel Navijan, which share the same check-in counter, have rooms from Rs 100 for a simple single to Rs 225 and higher for a nice double during the off-season. Across the street is the *Maharaja Hotel* (3161), which has good rooms with TV and a view of the polo grounds for Rs 175/250. Both of these places are a good choice.

The *Hotel Lake Palace* (3254) has a good location next to the lake. Double rooms with bath are Rs 550. A 30% discount is given during the off-season.

The well-managed *Hotel Sunset Inn* (3194) is a modern place with rooms for Rs 500. It has a 30% discount during the off-season.

Where To Stay—High

The *Hotel Connaught House* (3360) was owned by the former Maharaja of Jodhpur. It has rooms for Rs 850/1150. It has a beautiful garden and is a mellow place with rooms that have a good atmosphere.

The *Hotel Hilltone* (3112) is a good place with a swimming pool and sauna. It has rooms for Rs 850/950. On the weekends and during the high season it is best to book this place in advance. There is a 20% discount during the off-season. The *Hotel Hillock* (3277) is a good value with modern clean rooms for Rs 800/1000 during the off-season and Rs 990/1300 during the high season.

On a hill above the Hotel Hillock is the *Sunrise Palace Hotel* (3214), a former Maharaja's summer palace that has large luxurious rooms from Rs 550 to Rs 1000. With up to 30% discount during the off-season, it is a good value. The rooms are well-furnished and have a very good view. It is one of the best higher ranged places.

The *Palace Hotel* (3121), Bikaner House, Dilwara Road, was the summer palace of the Maharaja of Bikaner. It has rooms for Rs 800/950 and Rs 1150/1800 with A/C. It is a recommended place, but it is often full. The hotel is located well outside the city in a peaceful location and has its own lake and private lawns. During the season it is best to book this place in advance.

Where To Eat

King's Food and *Hencky Francky* are across the street from each other on the upper side of the polo ground going toward the lake. Both are fast-food places that are owned by the same people, and both have about the same menus, which include vegetable burgers, *dosas*, and not so good pizzas. Both are good places, and the owner was able to give me exactly what I asked, which is very unusual for India. *Haveli*, which is also owned by the same people, is back from the street next to King's Food. It is a good place with a bigger menu, mainly Punjabi food.

The *Kanak Dining Hall*, uphill from the bus stand, is a good cheap place with good South Indian dishes. Further up the hill at the bottom end of the polo grounds is the *Veena Restaurant*, which has good cheap Gujarati *thalis* and a "Super Special" *masala dosa*.

Travel

Air The closest airport is in Udaipur, six hours away by road.

Train The railhead for Mt Abu is at Abu Road, which is 27 km away. It is on the metre-gauge line between Ahmedabad and Delhi via Ajmer and Jaipur. It is about 765 miles north of Bombay. There are no direct trains to Bombay. You have to either get a bus or train to Ahmedabad and from there get a train to Bombay. You can book railway tickets and make reservations in Mt Abu by the service station near the Tourist Bungalow. The booking office is open daily from 9 am to 1 pm and 2 to 4 pm.

The Ashram Express #2906 (10.30 pm, 13½ hr) goes to **Delhi** via Jaipur (8 hr) and Ajmer (3 hr). There are other trains to Jaipur, Delhi and Ajmer. There are several trains to **Ahmedabad** (5 hr, 187 km). The Agra Fort Fast Passenger Exp #9706 takes 25 hr to reach **Agra**.

Bus There are many buses from here. Using one of the private buses can be much faster than going to Abu Road and taking a train. It takes 8 hours to get to Ajmer and 11 hours to Jaipur. There is an express bus to Ahmedabad (7 hr) that connects with the overnight Girnar Express to Veraval (Somnath) in Gujarat. There is private luxury day bus to Udaipur (6 hr).

There are regular buses between Abu Road (27 km, 45 min, Rs 10) and Mt Abu. As you enter Mt Abu there is a tollgate where passengers are charged Rs 5. Some state buses go to Mt Abu and others go to Abu Road, so make sure you get the correct bus.

Deshnok

Deshnok is located 30 km south of Bikaner. The reason to come here is to see the Karni Mata Temple that has rats running all over the floor and altar of the temple.

Karni Mata Temple

Karni Mata, who was born in 1387 near Phalodi, is said to be an incarnation of goddess Durga. This temple is famous because there are rats running all over the temple room floor.

The temple has a beautiful silver door and a wire mesh over the courtyard to protect the rats, who crawl all over the temple, from birds. The temple has an image of Karni Mata holding a *trishul* (trident), surrounded by rats. The rats are called *kabas*. If you injure a rat while you are in the temple you have to present a gold or silver replica to the temple or suffer misfortune. The rats eat from huge metal bowls full of milk, sweets, and grains donated by devotees. It is considered auspicious to see a white *kaba* near the image of Karni Mata.

The story of the temple is that a woman brought to Karni Mata the body of her recently dead son and asked her to restore the boy to life. Karni fell into a deep trance and encountered Yamaraja, the lord of death. He told her the boy had already taken another body and could not be recalled. Karni refused to accept this and said that her tribe of Charans would not be governed by Yamaraja. At death they would enter the bodies of *kabas*, or sacred rats, and when the rats died they would be reborn as Charans. This is the story behind the rats in the temple.

Practicalities

The RTDC *Yatri Niwas* (0151-65332) has rooms for Rs 140/160 and dorm beds for Rs 40.

There are hourly buses to and from Bikaner. A taxi will be at least Rs 200 to go to the temple, wait for an hour, and return to Bikaner.

CHAPTER TEN

North India

HARYANA

KURUKSHETRA

This is where the battle of Kuruk-shetra took place and where the *Bhaga-vad-gita* was spoken, as narrated in the *Mahabharata*. Kurukshetra is a very holy place. Kurukshetra is called Dharma-kse-tra in the *Bhagavad-gita*. It is believed that all the holy waters of India flow into the Kurukshetra tank at the time of an eclipse. At that time one million people come to bathe. Lord Krishna met the *go-pis* and the residents of Vrindavana here at the time of a full solar eclipse. It is said that those who visit this area, reside here, take bath in the tanks here, or die in Ku-rukshetra go to heaven after death.

Kurukshetra is 160 km north of Delhi. The Kurukshetra area covers a 100 mile area and there are many places of pilgrim-age related to *Mahabharata* here. The area includes Pehowa, Kalayat, Amin, Phalgu, Thanesar, Jyotisara, and Kuruk-shetra town.

Brahma, after a great *yajna*, created the Universe from here. It is said that **Manu** wrote *Manu-smriti* here, and the *Rig* and *Sama Veda* are said to be have been compiled here. This place is named after King Kuru, who performed a great sacrifice here.

Kurukshetra is mentioned in the *Ma-habharata,* the *Rig Veda,* and the *Padma*, *Narada*, *Matsya* and *Vamana Puranas*.

The *Mahabharata* says that one who dies here attains salvation. In the *Maha-bharata*, *Kurukshetra-mahatmya*, the great sage Pulastya says, "O Rajendra, please go to Kurukshetra, which fulfills all desires. By seeing that place all living entities are liberated from their sins. If the dust of Kurukshetra is raised by the wind and falls on the limbs of a sinner, that sinner will attain the highest abode."

Bhisma Kund is where Bhisma lay on a bed of arrows. Ban Ganga was created by Arjuna shooting an arrow into the earth there, and the now subterranean Saraswati once flowed there. King Prithu, son of Vena, is said to have performed *sraddha* here. The astronomical meri-dian goes through Kurukshetra, Mathura, and Ujjain.

Lord Buddha is said to have visited Kurukshetra. Srila Prabhupada came here in December, 1975.

Gita Jayanti is a major festival cel-ebrated here in December. This is the anniversary of when the *Bhagavad-gita* was spoken by Lord Krishna.

The university here is one of the best ones in the country.

Brahma Sarovara Tank

This is one of the holiest tanks in all of India. It is said that by bathing in this tank you get the benefit of performing an Ashvamedha-yajna. It is also said that if you bath here during a solar eclipse you are absolved from all sins. It consists of

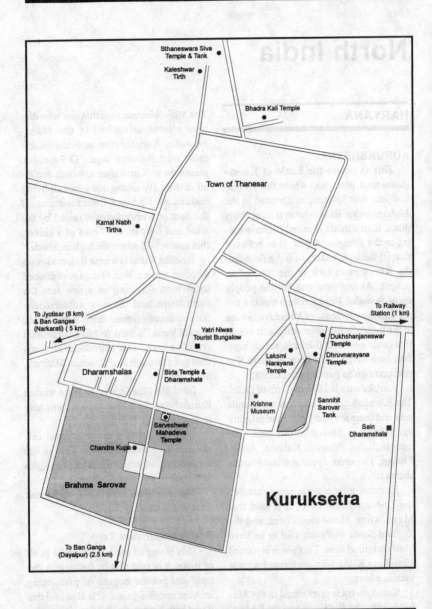

Sthaneswara Siva Temple & Tank

Kaleshwar Tirth

Bhadra Kali Temple

Town of Thanesar

Kamal Nabh Tirtha

To Jyotisar (8 km)
& Ban Ganges
(Narkarati) (5 km)

To Railway
Station (1 km)

Yatri Niwas
Tourist Bungalow

Dukhshanjaneswar
Temple

Laksmi
Narayana
Temple

Dhruvnarayana
Temple

Dharamshalas

Birla Temple &
Dharamshala

Krishna
Museum

Sannihit
Sarovar
Tank

Sain
Dharamshala

Sarveshwar
Mahadeva
Temple

Chandra Kupa

Kuruksetra

Brahma Sarovar

To Ban Ganga
(Dayalpur) (2.5 km)

a large lake about a half a km wide and a km long (3,600 by 1,500 feet). The water is very clean, and there are *ghats* for bathing at regular intervals. It is said that Lord Brahma created the earth here. Krishna, Balarama, and Subhadra came here to bathe during a solar eclipse. One million people come here to bathe at the time of an eclipse.

In the middle of the Sarovara there is a temple of Mahadeva (Siva) that is linked to the shore by a small bridge.

There is a well on the big island in the middle of the tank called Chandra Kupa, which is one of the four sacred wells in Kurukshetra. There is a temple near this well. After the battle of Kurukshetra, Yudhisthira is said to have erected a victory pillar here.

The area by this tank is very peaceful.

Sannihit Sarovara

This is a holy bathing tank 500m by 150m (1,500 by 450 feet), which is believed to be the meeting point of seven sacred Saraswatis. It is said that if you perform *sraddha* and take bath in this tank on the day of an eclipse all your sins are absolved and you receive the results of doing 1,000 Ashvamedha-yajnas. All the *tirthas* are said to assemble at this tank on the Amavasya day (new moon day).

This is also a place to do *pinda* for the deceased, especially if the death was unnatural. It is said that this is the place where Lord Krishna met the *gopis* and the residences of Vrindavana, and that He also bathed in this tank.

There is a temple dedicated to Dhruv Narayana with the deities of Lord Vishnu, Dhruv Bhagat, Hanuman, and goddess Durga on the bank of this tank. On the other side of the tank is a Laksmi Narayana temple.

Jyotisar

This is said to be the place where the *Gita* was spoken. There is a banyan (Vat) tree that marks the spot where Lord Krishna spoke the *Bhagavad-gita* and showed His universal form (Virata Rupa) to Arjuna. There is a marble chariot under the tree to mark the spot. The Jyotisar tank here is 325m by 165m (1,000 by 500 feet). There is an old Siva temple here, which also has a banyan tree over it.

Jyotisar is located about 8 km west of Brahma Sarovara on Pehowa Road. It is possible to stay here overnight at the Canal Rest House.

Bana Ganga Narkarati (Bhisma Kund)

Bana Ganga is 5 km from Brahma Sarovara on the way to Jyotisar. If you get an auto-rickshaw to Jyotisar, you can see both places at the same time. On the 11th day of the battle of Kurukshetra, Bhisma laid on a bed of arrows and asked for water. Arjuna is said to have pierced the earth with an arrow to quench the thirst of Bhisma.

It is said if you bathe in this tank you receive the benefits of bathing at all the *tirthas*. Bhisma rested on a bed of arrows until the end of the war, and he then instructed Yudhisthira Maharaja on the path of *dharma* (religious activities). There is a Deity of Lord Krishna in His Viswarupa form and a huge 26-foot-high Hanuman deity here.

Sri Krishna Museum

On the ground floor of this museum there are many interesting ancient stone carvings and Deities of Krishna or Vishnu. On the next two floors there are many nice paintings of Krishna from all over India. It is a recommended place to visit.

Ban Ganga (Dyalpur)

Arjuna is said to have shot an arrow in the ground here to get water for his horses when he was trying to kill Jayadratha. Jayadratha had helped to kill Arjuna's son Abhimanyu unfairly, so Arjuna had vowed to kill him before the sun set or kill himself. The Kauravas hid Jayadratha to stop Arjuna from fulfilling his vow, so he had to fight extremely hard. His horses were wounded in this battle and needed water. Lord Krishna then bathed the horses and gave them water to quench their thirst from this well. It is a tank 78 by 110 feet about 3 km south of Brahma Sarovara.

Sthaneswara Temple and Tank

It is said that at the Sthaneswara Mahadeva Temple the Pandavas prayed to Lord Siva to receive his blessings for victory in the battle at Kurukshetra. The water of the tank next to the temple is said to be very holy. A few drops from this tank are said to have cured King Ban of leprosy.

This temple is located a short distance north of Thanesar town. The Siva-linga here is ancient.

Other Places

Kamal Nabhi is a tank next to the town of Thanesara. It is said that Brahma was born out of a lotus from Lord Vishnu's navel here. There is a Vishnu and Brahma temple here.

It is said if you take bath in the small tank called Apaga Tirtha, located south of the University Campus, it is the same as taking bath at Gaya. People make offerings to their ancestors here.

The Bhadra Kali Temple is located near Sthanu Siva Temple on Jhansa Road. This is said to be the place where the right ankle of Sati fell when Lord Vishnu cut up Sati's body, which was being held by Lord Siva.

Birla Mandir is a nice temple by Brahma Sarovara.

Nine of the ten Sikh Gurus came to Kurukshetra. Gurdwara Sidhabati is said to be the place where Guru Nanak stayed when he came to Kurukshetra.

At Pehowa, 27 km west of Brahma Sarovara, King Prithu is said to have done sraddha for his father.

Amin is a large mound about 8 miles from Thanesar, where it is said Abhimanyu, the son of Arjuna, was trapped in the Chakra Vyuha.

Karna Vadha is a long trench where the wheels of Karna's chariot got stuck and where Karna was killed.

Soma Tirtha is a pool where Soma is said to have performed sacrifices.

In the towns of Jind and Safidon are several tirthas. At Ram Hridaya, near the Jind railway station, Parasurama is said to have performed a sacrifice. Varaha Tirtha, at Birhi Kalan near Jind, is believed to be where Varaha, Lord Vishnu in His boar incarnation, appeared to save the earth. Jamadagni, the father of Parasurama, is believed to have performed a sacrifice at Pushkar Tirtha, which is 5 km from Pindara. Sarp Damam, located in Safidon, is said to be where Janamejaya performed a yajna to destroy all the snakes on earth.

There is an ISKCON temple (01744-33529) in the town of Thanesar, which is a few km from Brahma Sarovara. It is a small center with helpful devotees, but there is no real guest facilities. It is a near a monument of a man riding a horse, in downtown Thanesar.

There is a libraray, between the university and Brahma Sarovara tank, which has an excellent collection of Vedic literature both in English and Sanskrit.

Where To Stay and Eat

The *Birla Dharamsala* has decent rooms for Rs 41 to Rs 61. There are several dharamsalas near Brahma Sarovara Tank, including the Aggarwal, Kali Kamli Wali, and Bharat Seva Sharan Dharamshalas. The *Ror Dharamsala*, right next to Brahma Sarovara, is free for pilgrims and seems to be a decent place. There is a nice clean asrama at the *Modi Mandir*, next to Brahma Sarovara Tank, in which pilgrims can stay free of charge for two days.

The well located *Neelkanthi Krishna Dham Yatri Niwas* (31615) is a few kilometres from the railway station and a five minute walk from Brahma Sarovara Tank. It has dorm beds for Rs 25, good double rooms for Rs 150, and A/C rooms for Rs 400. In the winter a room with a heater costs Rs 200. It also has a good vegetarian restaurant. This is recommended as the best place in town.

There are rooms at *Panchayat Bhavan* for Rs 200 to Rs 300 for a double. I do not know why anyone would stay there unless there is a huge festival, as it is totally out of the way.

At Jyotisar, where the *Bhagavad-gita* was spoken, by Bhakra Canal, there is a the *Canal Guest House*. It is surrounded by a nice garden and is very secluded. To stay there you contact the Kurukshetra Development Board Office, next to Brahma Sarovara Kund. There is also a new *Tourist Bungalow* with two rooms in Jyotisar. It has a small vegetarian restaurant.

At Pipli, five km from Kurukshetra on National Highway 1, is the *Parakeet Hotel* (30250), which has A/C rooms for Rs 600 to Rs 700.

Travel

The closest airports are in Delhi and Chandigarh.

There is a railway junction in the town of Kurukshetra. There are regular trains to and from Delhi (4 hr). There are direct trains to Bombay, Mathura, Agra, Vadodara, Chandigarh and Shimla. The Paschim Exp #2925 departs from Mathura at 7.35 am and arrives in Kurukshetra at 1.30 pm. The Jhelum Exp #1078 departs from Kurukshetra at 6.52 am and arrives in Delhi at 10.15 am and Mathura 12.45 pm.

There are regular buses to Haridwar (4 hr), Chandigarh, and Delhi.

JAMMU AND KASHMIR

AMARNATH

Amarnath is 145 km east of Srinagar in Kashmir. There is an ice Siva-linga here that changes size with the seasons, and also as the moon waxes and wanes it becomes bigger and smaller. On the full moon day the *linga* is about 6 ft high. Each year on the full moon day of July-August (Sravana) when the Siva-linga attains its maximum height there is a festival at this cave temple. It is said that Lord Siva first appeared on this day.

It is located in a glacial valley at 4,175m (13,700 ft). The cave is about 150 feet high and 90 feet long. Within the cave there are four or five ice formations that resemble the figures of different gods. The biggest figure is regarded as Siva (Amarnath). On the left side of the *linga* is an ice formation called Ganesh, and on the right side is one of Parvati and Bhairava.

The area is covered with snow from September to June. The cave opens only in July and August. This is the rainy season, so pilgrims have to brave the rain to get there.

You have to walk uphill for about 5 days to reach this cave temple. About 25,000 people make this pilgrimage each year. You can also hire ponies and dandies for the trip. It is very crowded during the annual Sravana festival. There is a yearly pilgrimage starting from Srinagar that is led by the **Chhari Saheb**, the holy scepter.

Amarnath is 46 km from Pahalgam, which is the place from which most people start their trek. From Pahalgam it is a tough three to five day trek. The *yatra* (pilgrimage) from here starts on the 11th day of the moon. Before entering the cave, pilgrims bathe in the Amaravati.

WARNING At the present time this is a very dangerous area and it is highly advised that foreign tourists do not go here because of Kashmiri militants. It is best to check the situation in advance. In early 1996 going to this area was totally banned for foreign tourists.

JAMMU

Population: 225,000, STD Code 0191

Jammu is the closest big town to the Vaishno Devi Temple. In the summer it is hot, but temperatures can go down to 4°C (39°F) in the winter. There have been problems here with militants, so it is best to check on the current situation of the area before you come here.

Information

The J & K tourist office (548-172) is at the Tourist Reception Centre on Vir Marg.

Raghunath & Rambireswar Temple

This temple, which has seven shrines, was built in 1835 by Maharaja Ranbir Singh. It is one of the largest temples in Northern India. The main Deity of the temple is **Lord Rama**. The interior is gold plated. Pilgrims usually visit this temple either before going to Vaishno Devi or after returning.

In this temple there are hundreds of Siva-lingas brought from the Narmada River in South India. This temple is in the center of the city.

The **Rambireswara Temple** (1883), opposite Dogra Art Gallery, is the largest Siva temple in North India. It has a 75m (225 ft) tower.

Museums

Dogra Art Gallery, Gandhi Bhawan, near the New Secretariat, has a good collection of sculptures, Pahari miniatures, manuscripts, and terracottas. It is open in the summer, 8 am to 1.30 pm, winter, 11 am to 5 pm, and closed on Mondays. It is free.

In the **Amar Mahal Museum** there is a portrait gallery, royal items, and Pahari paintings of scenes from the *Mahabharata*. It is open in the summer, 5 to 7 pm, winter, 10 am to 12 noon and 3 to 5 pm, Sun, 10 am to 12 noon, except Monday.

Where To Stay – Low

The *Tawi View Hotel* (547-301), Maheshi Gate, is a recommended place that has rooms with bath for Rs 80/100. The *Hotel Vimal Palace* is a good cheap place. The railway station has *retiring rooms* for Rs 75 and Rs 135 with A/C.

Where To Stay – Middle

The *Hotel Jewel's* (547-630), near the Jewel Cinema, has good clean rooms with TV for Rs 350/410 and Rs 425/510 with A/C.

The *Tourist Reception Centre* (549-554), Vir Marg, has rooms for Rs 175, Rs 275 with air-cooling, and Rs 325 with

A/C.

The *Hotel Asia Jammu Tawi* (535-756), between the railway and bus station, has rooms for Rs 1200/1350. The *Hotel Jammu Ashok* (543-127) is a higher end place for around the same price. The *Hari Niwas Palace Hotel* (543-303) is a good place with rooms for Rs 1000/1100.

Where To Eat

There is a vegetarian restaurant at the *Tourist Reception Centre* on Vir Marg. The *Rachna* on Shalimar Rd is vegetarian. Across from the Raghunath Temple is a nice vegetarian restaurant where they cook with pure ghee.

Travel

Air Indian Airlines has daily flights to Delhi and Srinagar. There are also flights to Bombay, Calcutta, Chandigarh, and Leh. The Indian Airlines office (542-735) is at the Tourist Reception Centre on Vir Marg.

Train The Shalimar Express departs from Delhi at 4.10 pm and arrives in Jammu at 7 am. There are other trains to and from Delhi. From Jammu there are direct trains to Bombay, Calcutta (Jammu Tawi Exp #3152, daily, 6.15 pm, 46½ hr), Madras, Gorakhpur, and Varanasi.

Bus There are regular buses to Katra (52 km) to make the trek to Vaishno Devi. There are many buses to Srinagar (10 to 12 hr). Most buses leave between 6 and 7 am, in order to arrive before night. A ticket to Srinagar should be booked in advance. There are buses to Delhi (14 hr), Amritsar (5 hr), and Pathankot (3 hr). From Pathankot you can get a bus to Dharamsala and Dalhousie. Deluxe buses depart from the railway station, usually between 6 and 7 am.

VAISHNO DEVI

This is an important cave temple where the three major goddesses are worshiped. It is dedicated to the goddesses **Laksmi, Kali, and Saraswati**. The goddess Durga is said to have killed the demon Bhairon here. Vaishno Devi is 61 km north of Jammu and 14 km from Katra, which has a population of 20,000. The cave is at an elevation of 1,700m (5,100 ft) and is 30m (93 ft) long and just 1.5m (5 ft) high.

Vaishno Devi is a hard four-hour (13 km) climb from Katra. The best time to come is March to July, as the rest of the time of the year it can be very cold. The main pilgrimage time is March-April and Sept-Oct. In 1986, 1.6 million people came here, or 15 to 20 thousand people a day. The cave ideally handles just 8 or 10 thousand people a day, as only 12 or 15 people are let into the cave at a time. On the full moon day in Kartika (Oct/Nov) the line to get into the cave can be four km long. It is believed that the arm of Sati fell at this place.

Tours

There is a tour to Vaishno Devi from Delhi for Rs 550. It departs from Delhi at 8.30 pm on Friday and returns on Monday morning. It is organized by the India Tourism Development Corporation (ITDC), L Block, Connaught Circus. This means two hard all-night bus rides, one each way.

Vaishno Devi Story

About 700 years ago there was a devotee of the goddess named Pt. Baba Shridar in the village of Hansali, about 2 km from Katra. He was busy arranging Kanya Puja at his home when a divine young girl appeared, asked him to arrange *bhandara* (a collective meal), and then disappeared.

He could not understand how he would be able to do this as he was very poor, but he went anyway to the villages in the area and invited people. Along the way, he met Guru Gorakhnath and his 360 disciples and he invited them too.

When all the guests arrived, the divine girl appeared and started serving all the guests from her Kamandal (vessel). Everyone got the food of their choice. Guru Gorakhnath and his disciple Bhairon wanted to harass her, so they asked for meat and wine. She told them that she could not give them meat and wine in a pious Vaishnava Brahmin's home. When the goddess started to go toward Trikuta Hill in the subtle form of air, Bhairon chased after her in great anger.

While being chased the girl entered a womb-like cave and meditated for nine months. This cave is at Ardh Kuwari and is called Garbh-Joon. Eventually Bhairon reached this cave and entered it. The goddess escaped from the end of the cave by using her trident. The girl then went to the peak of the mountain, and Bhairon followed her. She entered a cave at the peak, and Bhairon was killed by her.

Information

There is a good detailed book about going to Vaishno Devi called *Shri Mata Vaishno Devi Yatra Guide,* published by R Tandon.

You should bring only minimum baggage for the trip, as it is a hard climb. There is a cloak room at Katra where you can leave your bags.

Yatra Parchi Slip (Must Read)

Without this slip you cannot get past Ban Ganga, which is a checkpoint along the route from Katra to Vaishno Devi. You get this slip near the Katra Bus Stand.

After getting this slip you must reach Ban Ganga within six hours. At Ban Ganga you are issued another slip, and you get another slip at the Darbar Yatri Check Post. The slips are issued free of charge.

Bhumika Temple

At Darshani Darwaza, 1 km from Katra, the goddess disappeared. This place is called Darshani Darwaza because the Trikut mountain is visible from here. Trikuta Parvat is three high peaks that are the abodes of the goddess Vaishno Devi.

Ban Ganga Temple

After the goddess left the Bhumika Temple, she went to the Trikuta Hills passing through here. At this time, Langoor Vir (Veer Langur) felt thirsty. The goddess shot an arrow into the stone and a holy river was produced, now known as Ban Ganga. It is called Ban Ganga because the goddess washed her hair at this place. Most pilgrims take bath here. You must show the slip you got near the Bus Stand in Katra to pass this point. Ban Ganga is about 3 km from Katra.

Charan Paduka Temple

This is where the goddess stopped for some time while Bhairon was chasing her. Her footprints are supposed to be visible on a stone at this place. Charanpaduka means "holy footprints." It is about 1.5 km from Ban Ganga at 3,380 feet.

Ardh Kuwari

Ardh Kuwari is the halfway point, and some pilgrims stay here for the night. There is a 15-foot-long cave called **Garbha Joon** where the goddess hid herself for nine months and showed herself to a saint. The cave is narrow, and you have to almost crawl all the way though it. When Bhairon entered the cave, the goddess made a new opening with her trident and ran away. Ardh Kuwari is 4.5 km from Charan Paduka and 4,800 ft above sea level.

After Ardh Kuwari the path gets very steep for 2.5 km. This ascent is called **Hathi Matha** ascent, because the mountain is shaped like the forehead of an elephant. It is best to use the footpath rather than the stairs, as the climb will be easier. From here it is another 1500-ft climb to Sanjhi Chatt, and from there another 4 km to the cave

Vaishno Devi Darshan

The temple here is located in a cave. At the end of the cave are the three deities, consecrated as "Pindies" (rocks) of Maha-Laksmi (middle), Maha-Saraswati (on the left side), and Maha-Kali (on the right side). This cave is 5,200 feet above sea level. There is a lamp here that is always lit. This is the only temple in India where all three goddesses are worshipped in the same place. Before entering the cave, pilgrims take bath in the water coming out of the cave.

When the group number you receive at the parchi counter (Bhawan) is announced you stand in a queue at gate number 2.

You have to enter the cave by bending down for the first two yards. You cannot stand upright inside the cave. You have to walk in cold ankle deep water to see the deity. This water is called **Charan Ganga**.

On a busy festival you may have to wait several hours up to your knees in cold water. You walk about 100 ft in the knee deep water and then up four steps to see the *pindies*. If the wait is long, you may be able to find an official to take you around the back way.

The **Sri Ram Temple** is near Vaishno Devi cave. There is a Siva-linga in a cave 125 steps down from the Ram Temple.

The Bhairon (Bhairav) Temple

This temple is about 2.5 km from Vaishno Devi cave at about 6,700 feet. It is traditional to visit this temple after visiting the Vaishno Devi Temple. Bhairon (Bhairav) was absolved of all sins when Durga killed him.

When Bhairon was killed by the goddess his head flew to this place. There is a huge stone outside the cave that represents the body of Bhairon. After he was killed, he prayed to the goddess to forgive him. It is said that the goddess gave the benediction that the desires of her devotees who visit this place would be fulfilled.

Where To Stay and Eat

At Vaishno Devi there is a place to stay overnight that is run by the *Dharma Trust*. They serve vegetarian food. There are basic rooms at the half-way point.

There is only vegetarian food available on this pilgrimage.

Travel

Vaishno Devi is located 14 km from the town of Katra and 52 km north of Jammu. Katra is situated at 2,800 feet and takes about 2 hours to reach from Jammu by bus.

Air The nearest airport is in Jammu, which is 48 km from Katra. There is a helicopter service that departs from the airport at Sanjhi Chat in Jammu in the morning. The ride costs about Rs 2,000 one way (baggage 2 kg, 15 minute).

Train The nearest train station is in Jammu.

Bus There are regular buses leaving for the 52 km trip from the central bus stand in Jammu to where the road ends at Katra (2 hr).

Walking From Katra it is a steep 13 km walk. You can rent a horse or be carried up from Katra. You can go up to the cave and back in the same day. It takes about 4 hours to climb up and 3 hours to come down. Pilgrims must get a **Yatra-Slip** from the tourist reception center near the bus stand in Katra to get pass Ban Ganga. It is a hard climb to Vaishno Devi

Katra

You must pass through Katra to get to Vaishno Devi. It is where the road ends.

There is an **ISKCON temple** (01991-33047) in Katra. It is located at the **Kalka Mata Mandir**, opposite the petrol pump. The Kalka Mata Mandir is an ancient Siva and Kali temple which has been put under the care of ISKCON. The deities are said to be self-manifested. This temple is visited by many pilgrims. Construction has begun on a temple and large guest house here.

Where To Stay

There is the *Katra Yatri Niwas, Asia Vaishnodevi, Vishram Ghar Rest House, Ambica*, and the more simple *Tourist Lodge*.

Jammu & Kashmir Tourism runs the *Tourist Dak Bungalow and Retiring Center*. The *Shri Dhar Sabha Dharamshala* can house thousands of pilgrims.

The *Hotel Ambica* (01991-2062) has rooms with hot water for Rs 300/475 and Rs 450/750 with A/C. The *Hotel Asia Vaishnodevi* (01991-2061, fax 3344) has rooms for Rs 725/850 and Rs 850/1000 with A/C.

PUNJAB

AMRITSAR
Population: 750,000, STD Code 0183

Amritsar is the main Sikh center and the major city in Punjab state. Amritsar was founded by Ram Das, the fourth Sikh guru in 1577. **Amritsar**, or **Pool of Nectar**, (*amrit*–nectar, *sar*–pool) is the name of the sacred pool by the Golden Temple.

Amritsar is 450 km (280 miles) northwest of Delhi.

Information

The tourist office is one km east of the bus station, in the former youth hostel. Phone numbers are being changed now in Amritsar. If you want to get a new number you phone 550-197.

Sikh Religion

Sikhism was established by Guru Nanak (1469-1539) in 1497. He believed that God was one and could be reached by anyone. He emphasized three actions to understand God: meditating on God's name, giving charity, and bathing. He rejected the worship of the Deity form of God. The Sikh religion was originally intended to bring the Hindu and Islamic religions together. It is similar to Hinduism, but the Sikhs are opposed to caste distinctions and pilgrimage to holy rivers. They are not opposed to pilgrimage to holy sites.

The holy book of the Sikh religion is the *Granth Sahib*. Guru Nanak was the first of ten Gurus. The last Sikh Guru, Gobind Singh (1666-1708), did not name a successor, but said the *Granth Sahib* would be the Sikh Guru.

The Sikhs worship as a congregation in temples called Gurdwaras (gateway to the Guru). Many Sikh homes have a room with a copy of the *Granth Sahib* in it. Members of the household start the day with private meditation, and they recite verses written by Guru Nanak (*Japji*).

The Sikhs are supposed to have the following five symbols (*kakkars*): a sword, or *kripan*; a comb, or *kangh*; short drawers, or *kacha*; an iron ring on the right arm, or *kada;* and long hair, or *kesh*.

There are about 13 million Sikhs in India, and they mainly live in Punjab and Delhi.

Hari Mandir (Golden Temple)

This is the holiest temple of the Sikh religion. The Sikhs refer to this temple as **Hari Mandir** (the temple of the Lord), or **Darbar Sahib** (the court of the Lord). It is located in a large tank called **Amrita Sarovara** or "Pool of Nectar." The dome of the temple is covered with 100 kg (220 lb) of gold leaf. This is why the temple is called the golden temple. The interior of the temple is very elaborate.

The tank was established in 1577 by Guru Ram Das, the fourth of 10 gurus of the Sikh religion. His son, the fifth Guru, Arjun Dev, built a temple in the middle of a pool, purified its waters, and installed the *Granth Sahib*, the Sikhs' holy scripture, here in the late 16th century. The present temple was rebuilt by the Sikh Maharajah Ranjit Singh (1780-1839) in 1803.

Granth Sahib (Adi Granth)

Arjun, the fifth Guru, compiled a collection of verses by persons he considered great saints: Ramananda, Kabir, Namdev, Nanak, and others, including the Gurus. This is the Sikh scripture called the **Adi Granth, or Granth Sahib** (the original Holy Book), which was installed in the temple.

Gobind Singh, the tenth Sikh guru, revised the *Adi Granth*. He did not name a successor, but instead said that the Sikh guru would be the *Adi Granth* itself. From that time the *Adi Granth* has been known as **Guru the Granth Sahib** (the "Holy Book as Guru"). It contains nearly 3,500 verses.

While you walk around the temple complex you will hear the chanting of the *Adi Granth*. There are four booths around the *parikrama* where there are priests, or *granthis*, chanting verses from the *Adi Granth*. Professional singers (*ragis*) chant in three-hour shifts, and a continuous reading takes 48 hours. Chanting is done continuously from 4 am to 10 pm in the summer and 5 am to 11 pm in the winter.

At 4 am in the summer (5 am, winter) the *Adi Granth Sahib* is brought in a ceremonial procession from the Akal Takht to the Hari Mandir, where it is kept during the day. It is returned at 10 pm.

Parikrama

You enter the temple complex by the north gateway, the clock tower. Directly in front of you in the middle of the Amrita Sarovara tank is the Hari Mandir (Golden Temple). The *parikrama* path is always circled in a clockwise direction. Upstairs in the clock tower is a gallery of paintings that tell the story of the Sikhs and their martyrs.

The shrines at the east side of the tank are known as the 68 Holy Places. When the tank was built, Arjun Dev told his followers that a visit to these shrines was equal to visiting the equivalent 68 most important Hindu pilgrimage sites.

In the Guru-ka-Langar, a giant dining hall at the east end of the tank, free vegetarian food is given to anyone who comes to the temple. The 3rd Guru, Amar

Das (1552-1574), abolished the custom of eating only with persons of the same caste. The food distributed is usually *chapatis* and *dal* (beans). Thousands of people are fed each day. Meals are 11 am to 3 pm and 7 to 9 pm.

Next to the dining hall are the Guru Ram Das Sarai and the Guru Nanak Niwas gurdwaras (guest houses), which provide free lodging for all. Pilgrims can stay for up to three nights. Next to the garden, to the right, is the large impressive assembly hall. There is also a post office, bank, railway booking agent, and library.

On the southeast side of the temple tank is the shrine of Baba Deep Singh. When Ahmad Shah Durrani attacked Amritsar in 1758, Baba Deep Singh vowed to defend the temple with his life. Six km from the town he was mortally wounded, but he kept fighting. On his way back to the temple he died at this spot.

To the south of the temple compound are the temple gardens. They cover thirty acres. At its south end is the eight-storied **Baba-Atal Tower**. This tower is dedicated to Atal Rai, the son of the sixth guru, Hargobind.

In the northwest part of the *parikrama* is the Jubi Tree, under which the first temple High Priest, Baba Gujhaji, sat and supervised the construction of the temple 450 years ago. It is believed to have special powers. Barren women who want a son hang strips of cloth on its branches.

The **Akal Takhat** (throne of the timeless God) is directly opposite the main entrance of the temple. This is where the Shiroman Gurudwara Parbandhak committee, which is the religious governing body of the Sikh religion, meets. Each evening the *Adi Granth* is brought from the Hari Mandir to here. Housed here are some weapons, including Guru Gobind's sword. By the Akal Takhat is the shrine of Guru Gobind Singh, the tenth and last Guru, and the flagstaffs.

Hari Mandir

The three-story Hari Mandir was built by Arjun Singh to house the *Adi Granth*, which is located on an elaborate throne covered by a jeweled silk canopy on the ground floor of the temple. The bridge called "Guru's Bridge" joins the temple to the west bank of the Amrita Sarovara tank. You get to the temple via the Darshani Deorhi archway.

On the first (US second) floor of the temple, three respected Sikhs perform the Akhand Path (Unbroken-Reading). On the top floor is the Hall of Mirrors (Shish Mahal). The gurus used to sit here. This place is swept with brushes made from peacock feathers. The Golden Temple's architecture is a mixture of Hindu and Muslim styles.

Temple Information

Visitors should wash their feet before entering the temple. Socks cannot be worn. Visitors to the temple must keep their heads covered while in the temple. You cannot bring tobacco, alcohol, or drugs of any kind into the temple.

The best time to visit the temple is on a weekday morning before it is swamped with crowds. Photography is permitted on the *parikrama,* but not inside the shrines. English speaking guides are available at the information office near the clock tower.

Other Places

In the old city, in the center of a lake, is the **Laksmi Narayana Temple**, which is built like the Golden Temple. The 16th century **Durgiana Temple,** dedicated to the goddess Durga, is about a 15 minute walk from the Golden Temple.

Jallianwala Bagh park, about a five minute walk from the Golden Temple, is where 2,000 Indians were killed or wounded when they were indiscriminately shot by the British in 1919. This event was re-enacted in the movie *Gandhi*.

RAM TIRTHA SAVOVARA

About 11 km northwest of Amritsar is Ram Tirtha Savovara. It is said that *maha-rishi* Valmiki had his ashram here, and mother Sita gave birth to the sons of Ramacandra named Kush and Luv, at this place. There is a large sacred tank here that is said to have been dug by Hanuman. It is said that Rishi Chavan Prash cured Valmiki Rishi of leprosy here by having him bathe in this small pond. There is a big festival here in November every year.

Where To Stay – Lower

You can stay at the temple gurdwaras. The *Guru Ram Das Niwas* and *Sri Guru Nanak Niwas* temple guesthouses are free to pilgrims and tourists for three days, but you are expected to give a donation. You can also eat free. There is a large dorm. For a double room with bath at the Sri Guru Nanak Niwas it is a Rs 15 donation. By staying at a gurdwara you can get a good understanding of Sikh culture and experience their excellent hospitality. The *Sri Guru Hargobind Niwas* is a new guest house which is under construction. Rooms with attached bath are Rs 125.

Sita Niwas (43092), near the Golden Temple, has rooms for Rs 100 with common bath and Rs 150 with bath. The rooms can be a bit noisy.

The *railway retiring rooms* are Rs 100 and Rs 175 with A/C.

The popular *Tourist Guest House*, which is east of the railway station, is a good budget place with rooms starting at Rs 80/100. There are also rooms for Rs 150 and Rs 250 with A/C. The rooms in the back by the railway are noisy.

The *Hotel Pegasus-Palace* is one of the better budget places across from the station, but that's not saying much. It is actually two hotels owned by two brothers. Rooms at the Pegasus are Rs 110/130 and rooms at the Palace are Rs 90/110. On Station Link Rd, opposite the railway station, are several lower and middle range places.

The *Hotel Rosh* has rooms with bath for Rs 200 and Rs 350 with A/C.

Where To Stay – Middle

The *Hotel Blue Moon* (20416), Mall Rd, about a km from the railway station, is a good place with rooms for Rs 250/325 and Rs 400/450 with A/C.

The *Grand Hotel* (62977), Queen Rd, across from the railway station, is a good place with clean rooms for Rs 250/350 and rooms with A/C are Rs 450/550. Rooms are set around a garden and have a TV.

Mrs Bhandari's Guest House (222-390), 10 The Cantonment, is a recommended well-managed place in this class. Rooms are Rs 400/500 and Rs 600 with A/C. It is in a colonial house with 1950s furniture, a swimming pool, and a large garden.

The *PTDC Amritsar International* (31991), off Delhi Rd near the bus stand, is a modern government run hotel with spacious lawns. Rooms are Rs 450/500 and Rs 525/575 with A/C. The *Airlines Hotel* (64848), Queens Rd, by the train station, is a reliable mid-range hotel with rooms for Rs 300/350 and Rs 650/700 with A/C.

Where To Stay – High

The best hotel in town is the *Mohan International Hotel* (227-801, fax 226-520) on Albert Rd. It has rooms for Rs 950/1400. It has a swimming pool and air-con.

The *Hotel Ritz* (226-606), 45 The Mall, is a good place with A/C rooms for Rs 950/1200. It is in a quiet part of town and has a gym, pool (Rs 50 for non-guests), and some nice lawns.

Where To Eat

Sharma Vaishna Dhaba, near the temple, is a supposed to have good vegetarian food. Vegetarian meals are served at the *Guru ka Langar* at the Golden Temple.

Travel.

Air There are three Indian Airlines flights a week to Delhi and Srinagar. The Indian Airlines office (225-321) is at 16 The Mall, by the Ritz Hotel in the center of the city. Modiluft (226-606) has two flights a week to Bombay.

Rail The station is a 10 minute auto-rickshaw ride from the Golden Temple. There are several trains daily to **Delhi,** which take 8 to 11 hours. The Frontier Mail #2904 leaves Amritsar at 9.30 pm and arrives in Delhi the next morning at 7.20 am. The Amritsar-Howrah Mail #3006 (6.15 pm) is a direct train to **Calcutta** (39 hr), which stops at **Varanasi** (23 hr) and **Lucknow** (17 hr). The Tata/Hatia-Pathankot Exp # 8101 goes to **Pathankot** (2½) at 5.50 am.

Bus Taking a train from Delhi is more comfortable than taking a 10 hour bus. There are early morning buses to Dehra Dun (10 hr), Dharamsala, and Kullu (11 hr). Generally the best way to get to Ra-jasthan is to go through Delhi. There are frequent buses to Panthankot (3 hr), Jammu (5 hr), and Chandigarh (6 hr). Private bus companies, by the train station, also run express buses to Chandigarh and Jammu.

Bhrigu Reader in Hoshiarpur

There is a women who does Bhrigu reading called Sneha Amritananda in Hoshiarpur. Hoshiarpur is located about 100 km east of Amritsar in the Punjab. Her phone number is 1882-22122. You are supposed to call in advance and make an appointment, as sometimes she is not there. It is also suggested that you call her and give her your birth information so she can do a chart before seeing you. You can also contact Nalini Kantha (310-204-2162), PO Box 34966, Los Angeles, CA 90034 to have a chart done in advance. He is a highly experienced astrologer and has been to see her over 15 times and brought 50 people with him. He has a good deal of faith in this lady's abilities.

Bhrigu Muni is the authority on Vedic astrology. It is said that many years ago he wrote down the destiny of many living entities. A Bhrigu reading is when an experienced Bhrigu reader reads to you what was written. This lady is said to have a book written by Bhrigu Muni himself which includes the destiny of every living entity. She has a small Bhrigu temple in her home.

HIMACHAL PRADESH

DHARAMSALA

Population: 17,000, STD Code 01892

Many young foreign tourists come here, and the atmosphere is like Kathmandu. This is where the **Dalai Lama** lives with his followers. It is located at an attitude between 1200m and 1800m, so it is a good place to come in the summer, but the winters gets very cold here. It is a nice place to take a walk around the countryside.

The town is divided into a lower part and upper part, which is called **McLeod Ganj**. From the lower part of town to McLeod Ganj is a 30 minute bus ride. The buses run every hour and there are also Maruti van-taxis that make the trip. You can walk down the hill to the lower part of town in 30 to 40 minutes.

Information

The useful **tourist office** is close to the Dhauladhar Hotel and the bus stand, in the lower part of town.

The Bookworm is a good bookshop.

The TCV Handicrafts Centre, between McLeod Ganj and lower Dharamsala, has a good range of quality Tibetan products.

Potala Travels, Bhagsu Rd, opposite the Hotel Tibet, is a good travel agent.

Tours

Himachal Tourism has two luxury bus tours daily (during the season) from Dharamsala. One goes to McLeod Ganj, Jawalamukhi, Kangra Temple and the Fort in Kangra (10 am to 7 pm, Rs 100). The other tour goes to Bhagsunath, Dal Lake, Tapovan, Talnu, and Chamunda (9 am to 5 pm, Rs 60).

The Dalai Lama

Every year in March the Dalai Lama usually gives classes, which are open to the public. You may request to see His Holiness the Dalai Lama by contacting his office in McLeod Ganj. You are supposed to ask for an appointment at least four months in advance, because his schedule is so busy. Only a select few are granted a private audience. The Dalai Lama's secretary receives hundreds of requests every day.

Most people can only count on attending a public audience, where he greets up to three hundred people at one time. You have to ask in advance to come to one of these public audiences. I was told that the Dalai Lama personally greets each person at these meetings.

Nearby

Kangra has some old temples. The most famous is the one dedicated to the **goddess Vajreswari**. It is said a fortune of jewels, diamonds, and gold were plundered by Mahmud of Ghazni from this temple.

The **Jwalamukhi Temple**, 30 km from Kangra, has an eternally burning blue flame that comes from the rock sanctum.

At **Chamunda Devi Temple**, the goddess is believed to grant the desires of anyone who worships there. There is a cave behind the temple with a natural stone Siva-linga.

From **Dharmkot**, 11 km from Dharamshala, there is a good view of the Kangra valley. **Masrur**, 40 km from Dharamshala, has 15 intricately carved rock temples, like the ones in Ellora. There is a cave temple with a stalagmite dedicated to Lord Siva there.

Where To Stay

There are two areas to stay—the lower part and McLeod Ganj. The accommodations in the lower part are not so good, and the only reason to stay there is that you have an early morning bus or you arrive late. The busy season is from Oct to March, especially Feb/March during the Tibetan New Year.

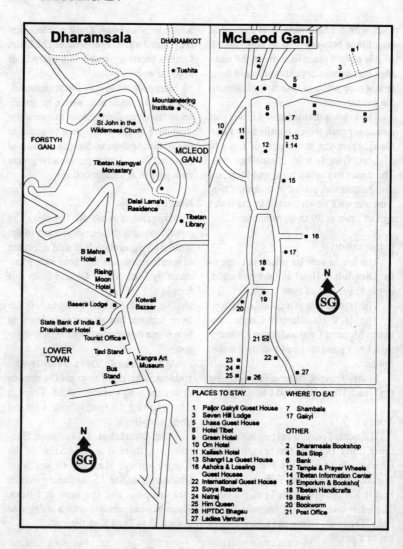

Dharamsala

DHARAMKOT

● Tushita

Mountaineering Institute ●

St John in the Wilderness Churh ●

FORSTYH GANJ

Tibetan Namgyal Monastery ●

MCLEOD GANJ

Dalai Lama's Residence

Tibetan Library

B Mehra Hotel ■

Rising Moon Hotel

Basera Lodge ■

State Bank of India & Dhauladhar Hotel ●

Tourist Office ●

LOWER TOWN

Taxi Stand

Kotwali Bazaar

Kangra Art Museum ●

Bus Stand

N SG

McLeod Ganj

N SG

PLACES TO STAY

1 Paljor Gakyil Guest House
3 Seven Hill Lodge
5 Lhasa Guest House
8 Hotel Tibet
9 Green Hotel
10 Om Hotel
11 Kailash Hotel
13 Shangri La Guest House
16 Ashoka & Loseling Guest Houses
22 International Guest House
23 Surya Resorts
24 Natraj
25 Him Queen
26 HPTDC Bhagsu
27 Ladies Venture

WHERE TO EAT

7 Shambala
17 Gakyi

OTHER

2 Dharamsala Bookshop
4 Bus Stop
6 Bank
12 Temple & Prayer Wheels
14 Tibetan Information Center
15 Emporium & Bookshol
18 Tibetan Handicrafts
19 Bank
20 Bookworm
21 Post Office

Where To Stay – Dharamsala

Most people stay in the lower part of Dharamsala only long enough to get a bus to McLeod Ganj.

The *Rising Moon Hotel* is a real basic place with rooms for Rs 65, some with bath.

The *B Mehra Hotel* and the *Tibet United Association Hotel* is about the

same. The *Basera Lodge* (2234), Kotwali Bazaar, is the best of the budget places with clean rooms with bath for Rs 95. The *Hotel Shimla* is a good place with rooms for Rs 125.

HPTDC Dhauladhar Hotel (2107), near the bus stand, has good sized double rooms with hot water and a good view from the balconies for Rs 550 to Rs 1000.

It has dorm bed for Rs 45. It is the best place in the lower part of town.

Where To Stay – McLeod Ganj

Most visitors stay here. It is very popular and many hotels are often full, especially in March when His Holiness the Dalai Lama gives classes.

The *Tibetan Ashoka Guest House* is a budget hotel that has rooms with common bath for Rs 55/65 and rooms with bath for Rs 175 to Rs 220. The *Om Hotel*, near the bus stand, is a popular quiet place that has rooms with common bath for Rs 45/80, but it is often full. It is not really such a good place.

The *Paljor Gakyil Guest House* (22571) is a recommended place that has clean rooms with bath for Rs 90/120. Rooms with hot water, a carpet and a great view are Rs 240. A popular cheap place is the *Green Hotel* which has rooms with common bath for Rs 40/70 and rooms with bath for Rs 120.

The *Lhasa Guest House* has good rooms with common bath for Rs 75 and Rs 175 with bath. The bus stand next door can make it noisy at times. The *Hotel Tibet* (22587) is a good place with comfortable rooms with bath and TV for Rs 350 to Rs 500.

The *Kalsang Guest House* (22609) has rooms with common bath for Rs 50/80. Rooms with bath and hot water are Rs 150 to Rs 250. There is a good view from the roof. The *Hotel Natraj* (22529) has nice rooms for Rs 275 to Rs 440. The front rooms and the roof have a good view.

The *Drepung Loseling Guest House* (23187) has good rooms with bath for Rs 125, Rs 165 for a room with hot water, and Rs 225 for a room with a good view. This is a good popular place. Also good is the *Ladies Venture Guest House* which has very clean rooms. Rooms with bathrooms shared between two rooms are Rs 135/185, and a room with a private bath is Rs 150/250. It is a well-managed place.

The well-managed *HPTDC Hotel Bhagsu* (3191) has comfortable rooms for Rs 450 to Rs 1000. Better than this place is the *Chonor House* (22006, fax 22010), at the south end of McLeod Ganj. It has double rooms with bath for Rs 800 and singles with bath shared between two rooms for Rs 600.

Where To Eat

The *Tsongkha Restaurant* has good vegetarian Tibetan food. The tofu dishes are good.

Travel

Air There is an airport at Gagal (15 km) with flights to Delhi (Tue, Thu, Sat) via Kullu.

Train The nearest broad gauge railway station is at Pathankot (4 hr). The Jhelum Exp #1077 departs from Delhi at 9.50 pm and arrives in Pathankot at 8.25 am, and from there you take a bus. You can also take the Jammu Tawi Mail #6031 (11.20 pm) from Delhi to Pathankot (12 hr).

Bus It takes 14 hours to get to Delhi and 10 hours to get to Shimla. The long distance bus station is in the lower part of town by the tourist office. There are buses to Kullu/Manali (13 hr) and Pathankot (4 hr). From Pathankot you can get a bus to Amritsar (3 hr).

The first bus down from McLeod Ganj to Dharamsala is at 4 am and takes about a half hour.

Kullu Valley

It is said that the great sages Vyasadeva, Vasistha, Kapila, Narada, Kanva,

Gautama, and Markandeya performed *tapasa* (austerities) in this valley. The Kullu Valley is known as the "Valley of the Gods."

It is referred to in the *Mahabharata* and *Ramayana*. The Pandavas are supposed to have visited this valley three times. The first time was supposed to be after the house of lac was burned. Arjuna is said to have received the famous Pasupati weapon here. It is also said that the Pandavas came through this valley when they went to the Himalayan mountains to leave this world.

MANALI
Population 3,000, STD Code 01901

Manali is a major tourist town and hill resort. It is located at an altitude of 1,829m (6,000 ft). In September the nights can be cold, and you definitely need some warm clothing. May and June is when most tourists come here. From November to the beginning of March it is very cold here.

Many young people come here to spend months or even years, as it is a very beautiful place. For some people it is a major stopping point on their trip to India.

There are also a few interesting spiritual places in the Kullu Valley. When the Pandavas were in exile they are said to have resided in the Manali area for a year.

Hadimba Temple (Dhoongri)
This temple was built in 1553 and is dedicated to Hadimba, the wife of Bhima. It is said that Bhima was married to Hadimba here, after he killed her man-eating brother, Hadimb. Bhima and Hadimba had a son named Ghatotkatch, who died a hero's death on the battlefield of Kurukshetra. It is in the Dhoongri area of Manali.

Manu Temple (Old Manali)
It is said that after the great deluge, Manu first stepped back onto land at this place and then lived here. Manali is supposed to be the changed name of "Manu-Alaya," or the "home of Manu." When the entire world was covered with water, the Lord took the form of a fish called Matsya and protected Vaivaswata Manu, keeping him on a boat. He also saved the *Vedas* from the flood.

This temple is located in the old Manali village, about 3 km from downtown Manali. It is most likely the only temple of Manu in India.

Where To Stay
The prices change according to the season. The high seasons are April to June and mid September to early November. At these times there are many Indian tourists. In July and August the prices of rooms are discounted by about 50%. The prices are even lower from December to February because it is very cold and there are no tourists. All hotels must display a tariff card. You can understand the maximum price by seeing this card. The main part of town is not such a nice place to stay. The rise on the western side of town is a nice area to stay. Many of the budget travelers stay in Old Manali.

Where To Stay – Lower
The lower priced places are mainly in Old Manali, where there are many family-run budget places. The price there for a double room ranges from Rs 70 to Rs 100. Some can be really run down and dirty, so it is a good idea to check out a bunch of places. If you plan to stay for a while, you can stay in the first decent place that you see. You could then ask and look around for a cheap place that suits your fancy.

The *Veer Guest House* is a nice place that has rooms with bath for Rs 80. It has a great view of the valley. The *Laxmi*, in Old Manali, is a good place that has large nice rooms with common bath. There are many other places like these two in Old Manali.

The *Rising Star*, by Rohtang Manalsu, is a good value. The *Saccharin Guest House*, in the main part of town, has double rooms for Rs 175 and dorm beds for Rs 25. The *HPTDC Yatri Niwas*, above the tourist office, has dorm beds. The *Hotel Kalpana*, northwest of the downtown, has big rooms for Rs 150 to Rs 200 with hot water. The *HPTDC Beas Hotel*, near the riverside, has rooms from Rs 210 to Rs 450.

Where To Stay – Middle

There are many middle class hotels between the main street and the rise on the western side of town. Rooms go for Rs 250 to Rs 450 normally, but the same rooms can be just Rs 200 during the low season. The *Samiru Hotel*, in the center of town by the Mayur Restaurant, has good rooms for Rs 450 or Rs 300 during the off-season.

The *Hotel Tourist* (2297), just off the road to Old Manali, has rooms with hot water and a balcony with a view of the valley for Rs 425 or just Rs 200 in the off-season. The nearby *Hotel Zarim* has modern high standard rooms from Rs 500 to Rs 900.

Down the road is the well-managed, good-valued, old guesthouse, *John Banon's Guesthouse* (2335). It is an older building with good facilities and a peaceful surrounding. Rooms are Rs 225/450. The *Sunshine Guest House*, on the same road, has a lawn and big rooms with a good view for Rs 275 to Rs 500. The *Pinewood*, off Old Manali Rd, is a good value.

Higher up on the hill, not far from the Hadimba Temple, is the *Hotel Rajhans,* which has rooms for Rs 450 or Rs 300 during the off-season. It is a new place in a nice area with a good view. The new *Hotel Chetna* is in a peaceful location and has a lawn and great views. It has good large rooms with hot water for Rs 450. It is closed during the off-season. The *Hotel Highland* is an older place with character. Rooms are Rs 350 to Rs 500.

The HPTDC has a few places out of the center of town. The *Hotel Rohtang Manalsu* has a nice garden with some decent views of the valley. The double rooms are Rs 450/550. The *Honeymoon Huts and Honeymoon Cottages* are huts with an attached bath for Rs 600. The *Hotel Hema*, in Old Manali, has overpriced rooms for Rs 350 during the season, but is a bargain at Rs 150 during the off-season.

Where To Stay – High

The *Hotel Ibex* (2440), main street, has rooms for Rs 860. The nearby *Hotel Piccadily* (2114) has rooms for Rs 600/1200.

The *Mayflower* (2104), The Mall, has large, well decorated suites with log fires. This place is well-managed and recommended.

The *HPTDC Log Huts* (2134), by the riverside, has fully equipped two bedroom cottages and good facilities, but is overpriced at Rs 3500.

The *ITDC Hotel Manali Ashok* (2331) has good double rooms for Rs 1000 up to Rs 1600 and a great view of the valley. It has a 50% discount during the off-season. The *Hotel Shingar Regency* (2251), high up on the western ridge, has rooms for Rs 1390.

Across the river, about 20 minutes from town, is the well-managed *Holiday*

Inn (2262, fax 3312) with rooms for $80 to $125. There is a 30% discount during the off-season. It is in a peaceful area with some good views of the valley.

Where To Eat

The *Mehak Restaurant*, on a side street off the main street in town, is a good Indian vegetarian place with a good selection of items. *Il Ferno*, on the road between the downtown and the bridge to Old Manali, is a good Italian restaurant, run by actual Italians. They have good pizzas and a good selection of salads.

Some restaurants have signs saying they are pure veg, but they will cook you up some eggs if you want. The *Out to Lunch Restaurant*, Dhoongri (Dhungri) area, is a small place run by a couple of westerners, so there is a good western touch to the food. They serve good salads, especially the potato salad. This place does serve eggs in the morning, so is not pure-veg. It also has a few decent double rooms.

Travel

Air There is an airport south of Kullu in Bhuntar (50 km) that has regular flights to Delhi ($120) and Chandigarh. Taxis are Rs 450 from there to Manali.

Bus There are deluxe buses to and from Delhi (16 hr, Rs 400). Buses depart from the road in front of the New Delhi train station and from the Inter-State bus stand in Old Delhi. Deluxe bus tickets can be purchased from travel agents in Paharganj or by the train station.

There are also deluxe buses to Shimla (10 hr) and semi-deluxe buses to Dharamshala (10 hr, Rs 300). The deluxe buses to Shimla and Delhi are booked and leave from the tourist office. During the season the demand is heavy for these buses,

so it is best to book as far in advance as possible.

There are local buses to Dharamsala (12 hr), Amritsar (16 hr), Jammu (16 hr), and Kullu (1½ to 2½ hr, every 15 min).

The trip by bus to Leh takes two days (28 hours actually driving). You may have to stay in a tent overnight. The Manali-Leh Highway is officially open from mid-June to Sept 15, when the state-run services stop. Some of the private companies keep operating into October.

Nearby Manali

Arjuna Gupha (Deotibba)

This is said to be the place where Arjuna, under the advice of Vyasadeva, performed austerities in a cave, called "Arjuna Gupha," in order to get the powerful Pashupata Astra weapon from Siva. Here he fought Lord Siva, who was disguised as a Kirata, and satisfied him, thus winning his grace and succeeded in getting the Pashupata Astra. This place is located about 5 km south of Manali, just before Jagsukh, in a small place called Prini by the Prini Cafe. It is a hard two-hour climb up to this place from the road, and there is really not much to see when you reach it. I have heard about two other places in India that are claimed to be the site of the same event.

Beas Kund

Vyasadeva is said to have performed austerities here during the Mahabharata period. It is the source of the Beas River by the Rohtang Pass.

Bhrigu Kund

Bhrigu Muni is said to have performed austerities here. It is a very hard 5 or 6 hour walk to get to this beautiful place.

Jagatsukh

Jagatsukh is 6 km south of Manali. There are two old temples here—one small Lord Siva temple and the ancient Sandhya Gayatri and Brahma Temple. The locals say that the Pandavas came to these temples.

Naggar

Naggar is about 13 km south of Manali, pass Jagatsukh. The **Naggar Castle**, which is an interesting building with a nice courtyard, has been converted into a hotel. Within the castle is the **Jagti Patt Temple**. Inside the temple there is a stone slab 5 ft by 8 ft by 6 inches. The story written on the side of this temple says that it was decided to make Naggar the celestial seat of all the gods. Therefore the gods were transformed into honey bees with herculean power. They cut a stone from Deotiba and carried it through the air to what is now the Naggar Castle.

In Naggar there are some interesting temples. To reach the **Krishna Temple** you have to make a hard twenty-minute climb. It is open in the morning until 12 noon and then opens later in the afternoon.

The **Lord Vishnu Temple** is right off the main road. There is a beautiful four-foot high Deity of Lord Vishnu in this temple. The **Tripura Sundri Temple** is a Durga temple. There is a **Siva temple** that has deities of Siva and Parvati.

Vashisth

It is a small town on the other side of the river from Manali. Many young foreign travelers stay here, some for long periods. There are a few interesting small temples here and some hot springs for bathing in. Vasistha is a nice, interesting place to visit.

Vasistha and Rama Temples

Vasistha was the spiritual master of Lord Rama and is said to have done austerities here. The place where his ashram is said to have been is called Tat Baba and is about a ten-minute walk away from the Vasistha Temple. There is one story in which Vasistha tied himself with ropes and flung himself into the river near Manali after his 100 sons were killed by the Rakshasa Kalmashped. The river is said to have released the Rishi from his bonds. The river got the name Vipasha, liberator from bondage, after this event.

There is an old Sita-Rama temple next to the Vasistha Temple.

Hot Springs

Vashisht is famous for its hot sulfur springs. Inside the grounds of the Vasistha Temple there are two hot spring pools that are free. There are also clean hot springs at a complex about a ten-minute walk from the downtown, going towards Manali. There are private baths here for Rs 35 a person. The springs are supposed to have good health benefits, and they certainly feel good.

Practicalities

Vashisht is about three km from Manali.

There are a number of basic guesthouses with rooms for Rs 50 to Rs 80. Many offer discounts for long-time stayers. The *Dharma* has basic rooms with common toilets for Rs 80. The *Sonam* is a popular place that is falling apart.

The *Bhrigu Hotel* (8240) has rooms with bath for Rs 300 (Rs 100 during the off-season). The west-facing rooms have great views from the balconies. The *Vishranti Resort* has large clean rooms and is the best valued middle class hotel.

The *Ambassador Resort* has rooms for Rs 2100.

Kullu

Population: 15,500, STD Code 01902

It is famous for its Dussehra festival and beautiful shawls. It is situated at 1,219m (4,000 ft).

Raghunathji (Rama) Temple

The **Sri Rama** Deity in this temple was originally brought here by Raja Jagat Singh from Ayodhya in 1651. This is the presiding Deity of the Kullu Valley. The temple is located on a hill overlooking the city. To get there, you go up the hill by following the small road opposite the Kailash Cinema, which is near the bus stand. The temple is behind the Kullu Raja's Rupi Palace. The temple is open in the morning and after 5 pm.

Bijli Mahadeva Temple

This temple is located eight km southeast of Kullu. When its 65-foot flagstaff attracts lighting, it is said to be an expression of divine blessing. When the flagstaff is struck by lighting, the Sivalinga inside the temple is broken to pieces. It is then put back together with *sattoo* (a paste of roasted gram and wheat powder) and butter. Located at 2,438m (8,000 ft), you reach it by a hard 6 km climb.

Other Temples

The **Vaishno Devi Temple** is 4 km from Kullu on the road to Manali. It is a small cave with a deity of the goddess Vaishno.

The **Jagannathi Devi Temple** is 3 km from Kullu in the village of Bhekhli. It is a hard climb, but there is a good view over the town from the temple.

The **Basheshar Mahadev Temple** is 15 km south of Kullu in Bajaura. It has fine stone sculptures.

Dussehra Festival

This festival is in October or early November. At this time, the Deity of Raghunathji (Lord Rama), the presiding Deity of the valley, is brought down to the valley from the mountains for a week. The other 200 or so gods in the valley are brought to Lord Raghunath to offer their worship to Him.

The Deity of Raghunathji is brought on a chariot from Rupi Palace to the middle of Dhalpur Maiden in a huge procession. The last day of the fair celebrates the defeat of Ravana by Lord Rama, who is also known as Raghunathji. Raghunathji is taken to the bank of the Beas River, where a huge pile of wood and grass are burnt to symbolize the burning of Lanka.

This festival begins on **Vijaya Dashami** and lasts for seven days. Vijaya Dashami is the day that Dussehra normally ends in the rest of India. As this is an extremely popular festival, you have to book accommodation as far in advance as possible.

Where To Stay

The *Madhu Chandrika* (2771), lower Dhalpur, is a good budget option with clean double rooms and dorm beds. The well-located *Hotel Bijleshwar View* (2677), behind the tourist office, is a good value. It has clean rooms with bath and fireplace for Rs 85/110. The same rooms are Rs 150 in the summer. A bucket of hot water is Rs 5. It is a recommended place.

The newly renovated *Hotel Daulat* (2358), Circuit House Rd, has rooms with balconies for Rs 200. Their rates are half that in the off-season. The *Hotel Rohtang*, by the maidan, is a good value with rooms for Rs 150/225. A good place is the well-managed *Hotel Siddhartha* (4243), which has clean double rooms with bath for Rs 200. This place is a good value.

The well-managed *HPTDC Hotel Savari* (2471), near the maidan, has double rooms for Rs 300, A/C rooms for Rs 500, and dorm beds for Rs 45. The *Shobla Hotel* (2800), Dhalpur, is the best place in town. It has a lawn and large comfortable rooms overlooking the river for Rs 400.

Travel

There is an airport in Bhuntar, 10 km south of Kullu. There are daily flights to Delhi ($125) and Bombay.

There are direct buses to Delhi (14 hr), Dharamsala, Chandigarh (270 km), and Shimla (235 km). There is a HPTDC A/C super-deluxe bus to and from Delhi.

There are regular buses between Kullu and Manali. Buses on the main road take less than two hours, but buses that go on the east side of the river, the Naggar side, can take three and a half hours.

Nirmund

Nirmund is about 90 km northeast of Simla, via Rampur. Parasurama is said to have performed austerities here. His father sent him off to atone for the killing of Sahasrabahu (Kartaviryarjuna). While Parasurama was gone, the sons of Sahasrabahu came to the ashram of Jamadagni (near Agra) and cut off his head. Parasurama's mother, Renuka, then beat her breast 21 times in anguish. When Parasurama returned, he made a vow to rid the earth of the *kshatriya* (warrior class) 21 times. The cave where Parasurama did austerities has a large silver Deity of Parasurama.

The ancient temple of **Devi Ambika** here is said to have been established by Parasurama. When Lord Vishnu cut up the body of Sati, her head is said to have fallen here.

Mount Kailash

This is the abode of Lord Siva and his consort, Parvati (Uma). It is located in Tibet. Mount Kailash is a mountain 50 km in circumference, which rises about 22,028 feet above sea level. Besides being worshipped by Hindus, it is also worshipped by the Buddhists and Jains. It takes two or three days to walk around Mount Kailash. It is believed that if you go around Mount Kailash 108 times you attain *nirvana* (liberation).

Mount Kailash is about 45 km north of the auspicious **Manasarovara Lake** (16,000 ft), which is also called Cho Mapan Lake. It takes four to six days to go around Manasarovara Lake (80 km). There are many swans swimming on this lake. There is another lake next to Manasarovara called **Rakshasa Tal**, where it is said that Ravana performed penance to please Lord Siva. It is said that Manasarovara is one of the 51 Sakti Peeths and that the right palm of Sati fell here.

It takes one and half months to do the entire *yatra* (pilgrimage) of Kailash and Manasarovara. It is considered an essential part of the pilgrimage to circumambulate (do *parikrama*) of Mount Kailash and Manasarovara Lake.

Travel

First you have to go to the Chinese Embassy in Delhi and get a month visa to go to Tibet.

Vishnu International Tours & Travels (725-0293), 334 Hakikat Nagar, Mall Rd, Delhi 110 009, has a tour to Mt. Kailash that takes 17 days for Rs 46,666. From Delhi you fly to Kathmandu, and from there you take a jeep to Mt. Kailash.

The best time to start this pilgrimage is the second week of June. Mount Kailash is a 330-mile trek from Kathmandu and double that by road. You can also fly to Tibet and from there take a jeep. Many people start their trek to Mt. Kailash from India.

There is no easy way to get to Mount Kailash. It is a long hard path. Pilgrims usually go via the Lipu Lekh pass, which is 16,750 ft high. They first go to Tonakpur, then Pithoragagh, Askot, Dharchula, and then Garbiang, which is the last town in India. After crossing the pass you come to Taklakot, which is a Buddhist center with about 300 monks. Manasarovara is about 60 km from here. It takes about two weeks to reach Mount Kailash from India.

One road by Vishnu Prayag, via the Niti Pass, leads to Mount Kailash. At Vishnu Prayag, which is between Haridwar and Badrinath, the Dhauli Ganga River meets the Alakananda River. You walk along the valley of the Dhauli Ganga and then go through the Niti pass. You can also go via Kathgodam, Kapkot, Milon, Kailash, and Manasarovara.

A fairly cheap way to get to Mt. Kailash is to start in Badrinath. The trip to Mt. Kailash from Badrinath takes 15 days each way. In Badrinath you have to find a guide to bring you to Mt. Kailash, as many people have died going there. One person told me they went with a guide named Kripa. By asking around in Badrinath for a few days he was able to find him. Many people say they can bring you there, but have never been there. Kripa has pictures to prove that he has been there and will show them to you. The guide cost Rs 200 a day. You also have to hire a pony or donkey to carry your gear.

You need a good set of boots, a good tent, and a sleeping bag, as it can be very cold, and many times you have to camp out in the middle of nowhere. You also have to bring your own food for the entire trip as there is often no place to get food. The trip for one person costs over Rs 10,000.

CHAPTER ELEVEN

Bihar

GAYA

Population: 300,000, STD Code 0631

Gaya is a fairly good size city between Varanasi and Calcutta. Besides the holy places in town, there is not much to see or do in Gaya. It is 456 km west of Calcutta and 91 km south of Patna. Gaya was included in the ancient kingdom of Magadha. Two or three hundred thousand pilgrims come here each year, many to do **Pinda** (offer funeral cakes) and the **Sraddha ceremonies** for their ancestors. Gaya is the train junction for Bodh Gaya (13 km).

The greatness of Gaya is described in the *Mahabharata*, and the *Padma*, *Naradiya*, *Varaha*, *Kurma*, *Garuda* and *Vayu Puranas*.

The main temple in Gaya is the **Vishnupada Temple**, where pilgrims worship the lotus footprint of Lord Vishnu and perform the *sraddha* ceremony to liberate their departed forefathers. Gaya is on the bank of the sacred **Phalgu** (Dry) **River**. So-called because its bed usually appears dry, but if you scoop with your hand you at once come to clear water.

It is said that Lord Ramacandra came here with Sita to perform ceremonies for His father. This is where Sri Caitanya Mahaprabhu was initiated by Iswara Puri.

The city is named after Gayasura, the son of Tripurasura. The history of Gaya is found in the *Gaya Mahatmya*, an appendix to the *Vayu Purana*, and in a shorter form in the *Agni* and *Garuda Puranas*. The *asura* Gaya acquired divine powers so that anyone who saw or touched him went straight to heaven. This intruded on the jurisdiction of Yamaraja, the god of death. So Lord Vishnu killed the demon, after granting him the boon that the ground covered by his body, some ten miles in extent, would become the holiest place on earth and be known as Gaya Ksetra. The ancestors of those who perform funeral ceremonies here are supposed to be sent straight to heaven.

There are 55 places in India to perform *sraddha* (*pinda* to one's ancestors to save them from hell). Of these, Gaya is the most important place, and the Ganges is the most important river. There are 45 places to offer *pinda* and perform *sraddha* ceremonies within the 35 square mile area of Gaya Ksetra.

Sraddha Ceremony

The idea is this: We all perform both pious and sinful acts, which in the next life (or lives after that) bring both good and bad results. This is the science of *karma*, you reap what you sow. Pious acts in this life give good results in the next; sinful acts give bad results. The laws of karma take all our acts into account, so even the most pious soul may sometimes get stuck with a bitter dose of fate. Therefore a pious son, to save his father from the possibility of hellish or ghostly life, goes to worship Lord Vishnu at Gaya.

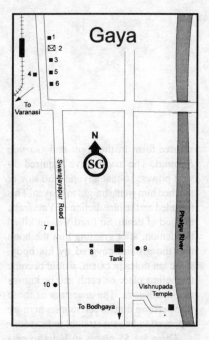

1	Ajatsatu Hotel
2	Post Office
3	Pal Rest House
4	Madras Hotel
5	Shanti Rest House
6	Siddharta International
7	Samrat Hotel
8	Hotel Surya
9	Bus and Auto-rickshaw Stand (for Bodhgaya)
10	Gandhi Maiden Bus Stand

Vishnu, or Krishna, the Supreme Lord, is supremely pure. He alone awards liberation from all material miseries. When a pious son makes an offering to Lord Vishnu and then by ritual and meditation gives the remnants of that offering to his departed father, the father is purified of sins, and if he is suffering from ghostly or hellish life, he is released.

To perform this offering is the traditional Vedic duty of a son. A pious son, therefore, is called *putra*, or "one who can deliver his father from hell."

Before leaving home to go to Gaya the pilgrim is supposed to walk 5 times around his village to call the souls of his ancestors to accompany him on the journey. There are many places where *sraddha pinda* is performed at Gaya. Within an area of 35 square miles there are 45 places where the pilgrims should offer funeral cakes, but they usually just visit

seven places, and many times only the three most important places. The three main places are bathing in the Phalgu River and visiting the Vishnupada Temple; Ramsila Hill, in the north part of town; and Pretsila, the Hill of Ghosts.

Vishnupada Temple

On behalf of their forefathers, the pilgrims pour water on the temple's main object of worship, a stone imprint, 40 cm long (16 inches) and 6 inches wide, of the lotus feet of Lord Vishnu in an octagonal basin, 4 ft in diameter. The footprint is imprinted in solid rock and is surrounded by a silver-plated basin. This temple has a 30 metre (93 ft) high tower. The temple was renovated by Ahalya Bai, queen of Indore, in 1787.

The temple is on the banks of the Phalgu River. The river is completely dry in the winter, but there is plenty of water in November.

Last rites are offered to the ancestor under the Akshaya-vat, or immortal banyan tree, which grows in the yard of the Vishnupada Temple. It is said that Buddha practiced meditation under this tree before going to Bodh Gaya to attain liberation.

There are other shrines near the

Top: Shore temple in Mallallapuram.

Bottom: Channakeshava Temple in Belur.

Rupa Raghunatha Dasa

Radha Shyamasundara (Krishna) at the Krishna Balarama Mandir
Vrindavana, UP.

Parathasarathi Temple in Madras.

Kusuma Sarovara near Radha Kunda, Vrindavana, UP.

Bahubali (Gomateshvara)
Sravanabelagola, Karnataka.

Badrinath Temple

Sun temple in Konark.

Gupta Godavari near Chitrakut in UP.

Sri Kurma Temple
Srikurman in Andhra Pradesh.

Being Blessed by temple elephant
after giving a donation.

Bathing Ghat in Varanasi as seen from boat on the Ganges in the early morning.

Ananda Nilayam above Sri Venkateswara in Tirumala.

Top Left: Hanuman at Srirangam Temple in Tamil Nadu.
Top Right: Lord Vishnu at Srirangam Temple.
Bottom: ISKCON Chandradoya Mandir in Mayapur, 130 km north of Calcutta.

Vishnupada Temple. There are Deities of Adi Gadadhar, Saksi Gopala, and Krishna Dwarka. There is an ancient carving of Lord Vishnu on Sesa-naga in back of the temple where Lord Vishnu's footprints are located.

Non-Hindus are not supposed to enter the temple, but ISKCON devotees or converted Hindus can enter the temple. I was welcomed with open arms.

Brahmayoni (Brahmajuni) Hill

Brahmayoni Hill is one km southwest of the Vishnupada Temple. There is a good view of the city from the top of the hill. You have to walk up 424 high stone steps to get to the top of the hill. It is a hard 40 minute to one hour climb. There are two narrow caves at the top of the hill called Brahmayoni and Matreyoni caves. It is said that if you pass through these caves you will not experience rebirth. There is a temple dedicated to Astabhujadevi and other goddesses at the top of the hill.

Other Places

Ramshila Hill is five km from the Vishnupada Temple. There is a Sita-Rama Laksman Temple and Paleswara Temple at the top of the hill. *Pinda* is offered at Ramkund. Pretshila Hill is located 3 km from Ramshila Hill. Pilgrims bath in the *kund* at the bottom of the hill and offer *pinda* there. They then climb the hill.

On the top of **Mangala Gauri hill** there is a *sakti* temple. This is where the breast of Sati is said to have fallen when Lord Siva was carrying her body.

On the way to Brahmayoni Hill is the **Akshya-vat**, or the immortal banyan tree. Pilgrims come here to complete their rituals for their departed ancestors. It is said that the tree existed since Treta-yuga,

when Sitadevi gave a boon that the tree would remain immortal.

There is a **Surya Temple** in Deo, 20 km away.

There is a small **archaeological museum** (10 am to 5 pm, closed on Mon) near the tank by where the buses depart to Bodh Gaya.

The **Barabar Caves** (the "Marabar" Caves of E. M. Forster's *Passage to India*) are located 35 km north of Gaya.

Where To Stay and Eat

There are many places to stay by the railway station. Some places are the *Pal Rest House, Madras Hotel,* and the *Shanti Rest House,* which all have rooms for about Rs 80. The *Hotel Siddarth* has rooms for Rs 50/70 with common bath and Rs 90 with bath.

There are clean *railway retiring rooms* for Rs 100/200. There are also dorm beds in the station for Rs 25.

The *Hotel Surya* (24254), about a km from the station, is a recommended place. Rooms are Rs 150 and Rs 150/175 with hot water and a TV. Noise from the road can be a little loud, so it is best to ask for a room in the back. The nearby *Samrat Hotel* (24004) has double rooms for Rs 150, which are not as good as the Hotel Surya, but this place is set back from the road and is quiet. The *Ajatsatu Hotel* (21514), directly across from the railway station, has decent rooms with bath for Rs 215 to Rs 375.

The *Hotel Siddhartha International* (21254) is the best hotel in town with rooms for Rs 700/800 to Rs 900/1100 with A/C.

I personally could not find any decent place to eat in this town. There is a very basic Gujarati *thali* place down the road from the railway station. All the vegetarian eating places in town are very basic.

Travel

Air The closest airport is located in Patna, four hours north. There are daily flights from there to Delhi, and three flights a week to Calcutta, Varanasi and Lucknow.

Train Many of the trains going between Delhi and Calcutta go through Gaya. There are direct trains to Varanasi (4-6 hr), Puri, and Patna (2½ hr). As the trains are extremely crowded between Varanasi and Gaya, it is best to book a ticket in advance. The New Delhi-Puri Exp #2616 (9.10 pm, 19 hr; Mon, Wed, Thu, Sat) and the Purushottam Exp #2802 (1.10 pm, 18½ hr; Mon, Tue, Thu, Fri, Sun) go to Puri.

The Poorva Express leaves Calcutta (Howrah Station) at 9.15 am (Wed, Thu, Sun) and arrives in Gaya at 3.50 pm. The night Doon Express leaves Calcutta at 8 pm, reaches Gaya at 6 am, and then continues on to Haridwar. The Rajdhani Express #2302 goes to Calcutta (4.41 am, Mon, Tues, Wed, Fri, Sat, 6½ hr). The Rajdhani Exp #2301 goes to Delhi (10.05 pm, 12 hr).

Bus Buses to Patna (100 km, 3 hr) and Ranchi leave from the Gandhi Maidan Bus Stand.

BODH GAYA

Population: 23,000

This is where Prince Gautama attained enlightenment under the sacred Asvatta tree (Bodhi tree) and became known as Lord Buddha. This is one of the four most sacred pilgrimage places for the Buddhists. The other three important places are his place of birth at Lumbini, Nepal; the site of his first lecture at Sarnath, near Varanasi; and the place where he left his body at Kushinagar, near Gorakhpur.

Buddhists from all over the world have built temples here in Bodh Gaya.

The Dalai Lama often spends time here. Tibetan pilgrims come here for the winter from Dharamsala. Bodh Gaya is located about 13 km from Gaya, 450 km west of Calcutta, and 90 km south of Patna.

Information

The **tourist office** is by the Mahabodhi Temple. It hires out guides. I personally got a good guide for Rs 30 at the entrance of the Mahabodhi Temple.

You can **change money** at the Bank of India near the Tourist Bungalow and at the State Bank of India in the shopping area.

Mahabodhi Temple

The Mahabodhi Temple is located at the place of Lord Buddha's enlightenment. The temple has a 50m (170 ft) tower. The present temple was restored around 1880. There have been several other temples on this site. A previous temple was destroyed by the Muslims in the 11th century. Parts of the intricately carved railings to the south and west of the temple are very old. Some of the railings are original and parts of the railings are reproductions.

In the inner sanctuary there is a huge Buddha. In the center of the temple there is also a Siva-linga that was installed about 860. This temple is also sacred to the Hindus because Lord Buddha is the ninth incarnation of Lord Vishnu.

The **Bodhi tree** here is said to be a descendent of the tree under which Buddha attained enlightenment. A sapling of the original *bodhi* tree that the Buddha sat under was carried by Emperor Ashoka's daughter (Sanghamitta) to Sri Lanka. That tree is at Anuradhapura in

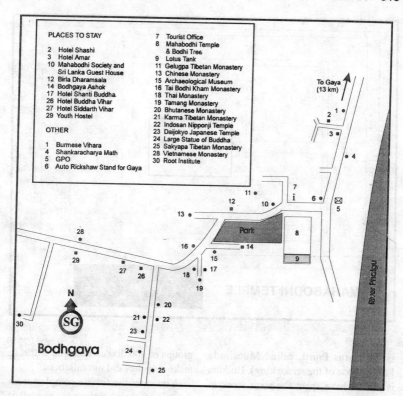

PLACES TO STAY

2 Hotel Shashi
3 Hotel Amar
10 Mahabodhi Society and
   Sri Lanka Guest House
12 Birla Dharamsala
14 Bodhgaya Ashok
17 Hotel Shanti Buddha
26 Hotel Buddha Vihar
27 Hotel Siddarth Vihar
29 Youth Hostel

OTHER

1 Burmese Vihara
4 Shankaracharya Math
5 GPO
6 Auto Rickshaw Stand for Gaya

7 Tourist Office
8 Mahabodhi Temple
   & Bodhi Tree
9 Lotus Tank
11 Gelugpa Tibetan Monastery
13 Chinese Monastery
15 Archaeological Museum
16 Tai Bodhi Kham Monastery
18 Thai Monastery
19 Tamang Monastery
20 Bhutanese Monastery
21 Karma Tibetan Monastery
22 Indosan Nipponji Temple
23 Daijokyo Japanese Temple
24 Large Statue of Buddha
25 Sakyapa Tibetan Monastery
28 Vietnamese Monastery
30 Root Institute

To Gaya
(13 km)

Park

River Phalgu

N

Bodhgaya

Sri Lanka. A cutting from that tree was planted in Bodh Gaya when the original tree died. Under the tree is a red sandstone slab that is said to be the **Vajrasana**, the diamond throne, that Buddha sat on and attained *nirvana*. The tree is located behind the temple and is about 80 feet high and about 115 years old.

After attaining enlightenment, Buddha spent seven weeks in the area of the Bodhi tree. The first week he spent under the Bodhi tree.

The second week he spent looking at the tree from the **Animeshlochana Stupa**, a spot now marked by a small white temple to your right as you enter the gate of the temple. *Animeshlochana*

means the place of unwinking gazing.

The **Jewel Walk (Chankramana Chaitya)** is a raised platform where Buddha walked up and down in meditation during the third week. The platform was originally built in the 1st century BC and is 3 ft high and 60 ft long. Carved stone lotuses mark the spots where he put his feet.

The **Ratanagraha Chaitya** is where he spend his fourth week in basic contemplation. It is said that red, blue, yellow, orange, and white rays emanated from his body when he meditated on the Patthana, or causal law.

It is said that Buddha spent the fifth week under the **Ajapala Nigrodha** tree. By the northern wall of the compound

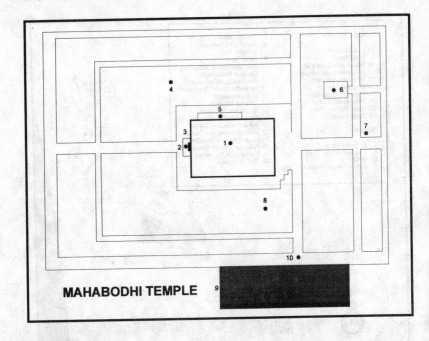

MAHABODHI TEMPLE

is the **Lotus Pond**, called Mucalinda Lake (abode of the snake king). Buddha is said to have spent the sixth week in meditation here. There is a life size Buddha covered by a cobra here. A cobra is said to have saved Buddha from drowning while he was in deep meditation. This pond is full of beautiful lotus flowers. In front of the pond are the remains of an **Asoka pillar,** which is now about 20 feet high.

The seventh week was spend at **Rajayatana,** which is a tree under which Lord Buddha sat. The exact location of where this tree was is not known, but a spot has been chosen to mark the place.

After the seventh week Lord Buddha went to Sarnath to teach five Brahmins there.

There are many people at this temple who have made vows to pay 400,000 obeisances at this temple. They do it in groups of 100,000 and then do extras to make sure they did not miscount.

You enter the temple complex from the east, off the main street to your left as you look at the temple from the road. The temple is open 6 am to noon and 2 to 6.30 pm.

Other Places

The **Mohanta's Monastery,** located right next to the Mahabodhi Temple, is a Shaivite monastery. It is said that **Adi Sankaracharya** spent days here in a heated debate with Buddhist philosophers.

At the **Tibetan Mahayana Monastery** (1938) there is a large Dharma Chakra, or wheel of law. It is believed that you will be freed of sin if you spin this wheel three times in succession from left to right. It is a 10m high metal drum painted gold and red.

1	Mahabodhi temple
2	Bodhi Tree
3	Adamantine Diamond Throne
4	Ratanagraha Chaitya
5	Bejewelled Walk
6	Animeshlochana Stupa
7	Ajapala Nigrodha Tree
8	Rajayatana Tree
9	Muchalinda Lake
10	Ashoka Pillar

Buddha bathed in the nearby **Niranjana** (now called Lilanjan) **River** after attaining enlightenment. The Niranjana River is about 250m east of the temple. Prince Siddharta crossed this river to reach the Bodhi tree.

It is said that Lord Buddha sent his begging bowl upstream in this river. He made a solemn declaration that if he was to become Buddha the bowl would float upstream and join those of the previous Buddhas. The bowl floated upstream as he desired.

The small **Bodh Gaya Site Museum** has a fine collection of exhibits collected from the local area. There are gold, bronze, and stone sculptures of Buddha here. It is open from 9 am to 5 pm daily.

In **Dungeswari**, 12 km from Bodh Gaya, there is a cave where Buddha meditated for some time and came to the conclusion that knowledge could not be gained through mortification of the flesh.

There are also Japanese, Burmese (1936), Bhutanese, Chinese, Sri Lankan, Vietnamese, Nepalese and Thai monasteries here.

There is a 25-metre Great Buddha Statue, which was unveiled by the Dalai Lama in 1989. It is across the street from the Sakya Tibetan Monastery.

Buddha Jayanti Festival

The Buddha Jayanti festival in May, celebrates the appearance day of Buddha, the day he got enlightenment, and the day he left his body. It is the biggest festival day here.

Where To Stay – Lower

Pilgrims can stay at the monasteries. Most of the rooms are as basic as they come. At the *Bhutanese monastery* you can get a room with common bath for Rs 40/60. The *Tibetan monastery* is more basic.

The *Burmese monastery* is very spartan, but popular. You can stay there for Rs 15 to Rs 30 a day. You have to follow the rules of the monastery, such as no smoking.

The *Hotel Amar* has good valued rooms, some with bath for Rs 100. This is good place to stay for the budget traveler, if you prefer not to stay in a monastery.

The *Hotel Buddha Vihar* has only dormitory beds for Rs 75. Next door, the *Hotel Siddharth Vihar* has rooms with bath for Rs 200 up to Rs 300. Both these places are government tourist bungalows. The *Sri Lanka Guest House* is run by the Mahabodhi Society and is a nice place, but often full. The rooms are Rs 125.

Where To Stay – High

The *Hotel Shanti Buddha* (063-81785), near the Thai Temple, has rooms for Rs 350/450 and Rs 700/850 with A/C. The rooms are good, but the place is really overpriced. The *ITDC Hotel Bodhgaya Ashok* (063-22708) has comfortable rooms for Rs 800/1200 to Rs 1195/1800 for a room with A/C. It may be possible to get a 30% discount here during the off-season from April to September.

Travel

Normally you would first go to the nearby city of Gaya, which is about 13 km from Bodh Gaya. Bodh Gaya is 243 km east of Varanasi.

Air Patna (125 km) is the closest airport. Calcutta (480 km) has an international airport.

Train The closest train station is located in Gaya. Gaya is on the main train line from Delhi to Calcutta.

Bus There are regular buses that go the 13 km between Gaya and Bodh Gaya. You can rent a motor rickshaw for Rs 90. A very crowded shared rickshaw is Rs 5 a seat. You get a shared auto-rickshaw or minibus (Rs 4) from Kacheri, in the center city area of Gaya. Several government buses leave from the railway station in Gaya.

It is supposed to be dangerous to travel at night from Gaya to Bodh Gaya, so this should be avoided.

PATNA

Population: 1.2 million, STD Code 0612

Patna, situated on the bank of the Ganges, is the capital of Bihar. There is not really much to do in this town. Travelers might have to come here on their way to and from Nepal or to visit some of the Buddhist sites in the area.

The **Patna Museum** is an interesting place with a collection of ancient stone and metal sculptures. It is open 10 am to 4.30 pm and is closed on Mondays.

Information

The useful **Government of India Tourist Office** (226-721), Beer Chand Patel Path, organizes a weekend tour that goes to sites in Patna, Nalanda, Pawapur,

and Rajgir. The **Bihar Tourist Office** is at the Hotel Kautilya on Frazer Rd. There are also counters at the airport and railway station.

You can **change money** at the State Bank of India on West Gandhi Maidan.

Ashok Travel & Tours, in the Hotel Pataliputra Ashok, and *Travel Corporation of India*, Maurya Patna Complex, are reliable travel agents.

Where To Stay – Lower

One of the best budget places is the *Hotel Shyama* (655-539), Exhibition Rd, which has rooms with bath for Rs 60/80. The *Rajkumar* (655-011) has rooms for Rs 70/110. There are *retiring rooms* in the station for Rs 100 and Rs 175 with A/C. A dorm bed is Rs 35. The *Indrasen* (226-872), Frazer Rd by the railway station, is a good value.

Where To Stay – Middle

The *Hotel Mayur* (224-149), on Frazer Rd, not far from the railway station, is a good place that has rooms with bath and hot water for Rs 140/170. The *Hotel Sheodar Sadan* has good clean rooms for Rs 135/165 and Rs 275 with A/C.

Hotel Republic (655-021), Exhibition Rd, is a good place with rooms for Rs 430/540 and Rs 600/700 for an A/C room. The *Hotel President* (220-600), on a side street off Frazer Rd, has rooms for Rs 260/300 and Rs 475/555 with A/C.

The *Tourist Bungalow* (225-411), R-Block on Beer Chand Patel Path, has impersonal rooms with bath and hot water for Rs 150/200 and dorm beds for Rs 60.

The *Hotel Samrat International* (220-560, fax 226-386) is a good place that has rooms with hot water for Rs 350/450 and Rs 600/700 with A/C. The *Satkar In-*

ternational Hotel (220-551, fax 220-556), Frazer Rd, has rooms for Rs 300/400 and Rs 475/575 with A/C.

Where To Stay – High

The three-star *Hotel Chanakya* (223-141, fax 220-598), by the Tourist Bungalow, has comfortable rooms for Rs 950/1250. It is popular with businessmen.

The luxury *Welcomegroup Maurya Patna* (222-061), well located near Gandhi Maiden, is the best hotel in town. It has a pool, and the rooms are Rs 1195/1800. The friendly *Pataliputra Ashok* (226-270), Bir Chand Patel Path, has rooms for Rs 1050/1300.

Where To Eat

The *Rajasthan Hotel*, Frazer Rd near the Bihar Tourist Office, has a good restaurant with good ice cream.

Travel

Air There are daily flights to Delhi and three flights a week to Calcutta, Varanasi and Lucknow. The Indian Airlines office (226-433) is on South Gandhi Maidan.

Train Patna Junction is on the Calcutta-Delhi line. There are trains to Calcutta (9 hr), Delhi (13 hr), Varanasi (5 hr), and Bombay. There is a daily train to Gaya (92 km, 3½ hr), but it leaves in the evening and arrives late at night. It is better to take a bus or taxi to Gaya. To get to Darjeeling there is a train to New Jalpaiguri (9.15 am, 12 hr) and from there you can take the "Toy Train" or a bus.

Bus The main bus station is at **Harding Park**, half a km west of the Patna Junction railway station. Buses to Gaya (3 hr), Varanasi, Siliguri, and Ranchi leave from here. Buses depart to Raxaul (6 hr) via Muzaffarpur from Gate 6. Many govern-

ment buses depart for places all over Bihar from the **Gandhi Maidan bus stand**.

To and From Nepal

The border crossing near Patna is a five-hour or six-hour drive north at **Raxaul/Birganj**. It is better to take a bus to the border than a train, as there are no direct trains. There are some direct buses to Raxaul (5 or 6 hr) from the main bus stand, and some others depart from the government bus stand. You can also get a bus to **Muzaffarpur** and from there get another bus to Raxaul, which is easily done. If you are coming from Delhi or Varanasi, it is better to cross the border at Gorakhpur/Sunauli.

You can buy a through ticket to Kathmandu from a travel agent in Patna that includes a bus to the border, a rickshaw for the border crossing, basic accommodation in Raxaul, and a bus from the Nepal border to Kathmandu. It is just as easy, much cheaper, and much more reliable to do it yourself. When you come out of the train station, if you ask a rickshaw driver to bring you to the bus to Nepal, there is a good chance you will be brought to one of these private operators, because the rickshaw drivers get a commission on your ticket. There is really no reason to deal with these characters. More than likely they will charge you two to three times the price of what you could have arranged yourself.

Nalanda

There was a great **Buddhist University,** dating back to the 5th century, in Nalanda. All that is left is the ruins of the impressive university, which had 1,500 teachers and 8,500 students. Buddhist and Brahminical scriptures, medicine, Sanskrit, and logic were taught at the university.

It once had a library with 9 million manuscripts. It was destroyed in 1199 by the Afghan Bhaktiar Khalji, who killed many of the teachers and students and burned and sacked the university. This place was visited by the Buddha and Mahavir.

The site of the university was hidden for centuries under a large hill and was rediscovered in 1860. Excavation of the site took 20 years starting in 1916. The site includes the ruins of temples and monasteries. Entry is Rs 5 to the site, which is open for 9 am to 5.30 pm. The Archaeological Survey's book on *Nalanda* gives a detailed description of this site.

In the Nalanda **Archaeological Museum** (10 am to 5 pm) there is a good collection of Buddhist and Hindu stone sculptures, terra-cottas, coins, and bronze. Many of the items date from the Gupta and Pala periods.

Practicalities

The best place in town is Bihar Tourism's *Gautam Vihar*. It is fairly ordinary, but it has some A/C rooms. The *Tathaghat Vihar* has simple rooms. *The Ajatashatru Vihar* has basic dorms only. There are also several other real basic places.

Nalanda is 90 km southeast of Patna and 15 km from Rajgir, which has a railway station.

Rajgir

Population: 25,000, STD Code 06119

The **first Buddhist Council** was held at Saptaparni Cave, about six months after the death of Buddha. At that time they then put down in writing the teachings of the Buddha for the first time. Buddha spent 12 years here. He used to preach at **Griddhakuta Hill** (Hill of Vultures), where he delivered many important sermons. At **Venuvana**, the bamboo grove, Buddha stayed for awhile. He bathed in **Karanda Tank**, which is now a small zoo.

Near Venuvana are some Hindu and Jain temples. Venuvana is the site of a monastery built by King Bimbisara for the Buddha. There is the interesting **Vishwa Shanti Stupa Temple**, on top of a hill, which was constructed by the Japanese. It is open 8.15 am to 1 pm and 1.30 to 5 pm daily.

Rajgir is also sacred to the Jains because **Mahavira** studied and meditated here. The 20th Tirthankara was also born here. There are Jain temples on many of the hilltops in the area.

Rajgir was once the capital of the kingdom of Magadha, which **King Jarasandha** is said to have ruled. It is said that at **Jarasandha-ka-Akhada**, Bhima fought with Jarasandha for 28 days before he killed Jarasandha by tearing his legs apart.

The 5th century **Ajatasatru Fort** and the 40 km wall that used to encircle the ancient city here are now in ruins.

Rajgir has a popular hot springs.

Practicalities

There are several basic *Jain Dharamshalas* near the station. The *Hotel Anand*, by the bus stand, has rooms upstairs for Rs 100 and dismal rooms downstairs for Rs 75. It has a basic vegetarian restaurant.

The Bihar Tourism *Tourist Hotel* has rooms for Rs 175 and Rs 275 with A/C. Dorm beds are Rs 45.

The *Hotel Rajgir* (5266) has decent rooms for Rs 85/175 with bath. It has a good garden.

The *Hotel Siddharth*, near the hot

springs, has rooms for Rs 80/135. The *Triptee's Hotel* has some good rooms with balconies for Rs 200.

There is the first-class five-star *Centaur Hokke Hotel* (5245), which is located 1 km from the bus station. Rooms are $70/110.

Travel

Rajgir is 19 km from Nalanda. There are shared jeeps to Nalanda (Rs 4). The closest railway station on a broad-gauge line is in Gaya (92 km), which is on the Delhi-Calcutta line. The nearest airport is located in Patna (90 km). There are regular buses to Gaya (2 hr) and Patna (3 hr).

Vaishali

Buddha preached his last sermon here and announced his coming *parinirvana*. Vaishali was visited three times by Lord Buddha in his lifetime. A century after the Buddha passed away, in 383 BC, the **second Buddhist Council** was held here. Ashoka erected one of his famous pillars here at Kolhua. The 18.3m high pillar is made of highly polished red sandstone, and has a life size lion carved on top. Vaishali is in the ancient land of Mithila.

There are two ancient Buddha *stupas* here, said to contain Buddha's ashes. **Ramkund** (Monkey Tank) is said to have been dug by monkeys who offered Buddha a bowl of honey. The water from the **Coronation Tank** (Kharauna Pokhar) was used to anoint the ruler of Vaishali at his coronation.

There is a temple at **Basarh** by Bavan Pokhar tank. The 4th century **Chaumukhi Mahadeva Temple** at Kamman Chapra has a four-faced Siva. The ruins of **Raja Vishala ka Garh** is surrounded by a wall about 1 km long. The Parliament House was large enough to hold over 7,000 representatives.

The Vaishali **Archaeological Museum** (10 am to 5 pm, closed Fri) has sculptures, terracottas, pottery, and coins.

Practicalities

Places to stay are the *Tourist Bungalow, PWD Rest House, Youth Hostel,* and a *Jain Dharamshala*.

Vaishali is 55 km from Patna, which is where the nearest airport is located. There are regular buses between here and Patna. The nearest railway junctions are Hajipur (35 km) and Muzaffarpur (36 km).

Jagannathpur

There is a famous Jagannath Temple on a hillside, built in the same style as the Jagannath Temple in Puri. There is a big cart festival, like in Puri, in June/July. Jagannathpur is 10 km southwest of Ranchi.

CHAPTER TWELVE

West Bengal

CALCUTTA

Population: 11 million, STD Code 033

Calcutta was mainly a British creation over the last 300 years. It was the capital of India under the British until they moved the capital to Delhi in 1931. It is the biggest city in India.

It is said that Calcutta got its name from when Sati killed herself after her father insulted her husband, Lord Siva. Lord Siva arrived after his wife's body was already burning. He tore the body from the fire and started his dance of cosmic destruction. All the other gods wanted him to stop, so they asked Lord Vishnu to help. In order to get Siva to stop, Lord Vishnu cut Sati into 51 pieces. Her toe is said to have fallen at **Kali Ghat** in the south part of Calcutta. Therefore the city was called Kalikata and later Calcutta.

Getting Your Bearings

The main part of the city lies along the eastern bank of the Hooghly River (a branch of the Ganges). Howrah, the main train station, is on the west side of the river. **BBD Bagh** (Dalhousie Square) is where the GPO, West Bengal Tourist Office, American Express, and railway booking offices are located. It is towards the north of the downtown, close to the river.

The **Maidan** is a large park in the center of the city that goes along the river, and the Chowringhee area is to the east

of it. The northern part of this area is where Sudder Street and the cheap hotels are located. There are several places where you can get cheap international tickets in the **Sudder Street area**. Along the Maiden is where many of the middle and higher class hotels, the airline offices, and the Indian Museum are located. It is a nice part of Calcutta and the main area that most tourists see. Kali Ghat is located in south Calcutta.

Information

The useful and helpful **Government of India Tourist Office** (242-1402) is located at 4 Shakespeare Sarani. They can give you a computerized printout of many places in India. There is also a Tourist Office counter at the airport, open when flights are arriving and departing. The **West Bengal Tourist Bureau** (248-8271) is at 3/2 BBD Bagh East. They also have counters at the airport and Howrah Station.

Some of the states that have tourist offices in Calcutta are **Bihar**, 26B Camac St (247-0821); **Himachal Pradesh**, 25 Camac St (2nd Flr); **Jammu & Kashmir**, 12 JL Nehru Rd; **Madhya Pradesh**, Chitrakoot Bldg, 6th Flr, Rm 7, 230 AJC Bose Rd (247-8543); **Orissa**, 55 Lenin Sarani (244-3653); **Rajasthan**, 2 Ganesh Ch Ave; and UP, 12 A Netaji Subhas Rd.

Money

American Express (248-4464, fax

248-8096), 21 Old Court House St, changes money quickly and efficiently. *Thomas Cook* (247-4560, fax 247-5854), Chitrakoot Bldg, 230 AJC Bose Rd, also changes money efficiently. Some of the main banks are *Grindlays Bank*, 41 Jawaharlal Nehru Rd & 19 Netaji Subhas Rd; *State Bank of India*, 1 Strand Rd & Jawaharlal Nehru Rd; *Bank of America*, 8 India Exchange; and *Citibank*, 43 Jawaharlal Nehru Rd. There is a 24-hour branch of the *State Bank of India* at the Calcutta airport.

RN Dutta, Stephen House, 4-5 BBD Bagh East and 5&7 Kidderpore Dock as well as *Maneek Lal Sen*, New Market, are licensed brokers who can change money outside banking hours.

Post and Phone

The GPO at BBD Bagh has an efficient poste restante. The New Market post office is right next to Sudder St. The Park St post office is efficient for mailing parcels.

The Central Telegraph Office is at 8 Red Cross Place. The Telephone Bhavan is at BBD Bagh. There is a fax place on Shakespeare Sarani and other places.

Foreigners Registration & Income Tax

The Foreigners Registration Office, 237 AJC Bose Rd (247-3301), is where you apply for a visa extension and a permit to visit the Andaman Islands. To get an income tax clearance you go to Room 11, Income Tax Building, Bentinck St.

Photography

Narain's Photo Cine Centre, 20H Park St; *Bombay Photo Stores*, 33-34 Park Mansions, Park St. *North East Colour Photo*, 14 Sudder St, by New Market, offers one hour processing.

Foreign Consulates

Bangladesh
  9 Circus Ave (247-5208)
  To get a visa to go to Bangladesh you have to go to Delhi, even though there is a consulate here.
Bhutan
  48 Tivoli Court, Pramothesh Baruna Sarani (241-301)
Denmark
  3 Netaji Subhas Rd (248-7478)
France
  26 Park St (290-978)
Germany
  1 Hasting Park Rd (479-1141)
Italy
  3 Raja Santosh Rd (479-2426)
Japan
  12 Pretoria St (242-2241)
Nepal
  19 Sterndale Rd (479-1003)
Netherlands
  18A Brabourne Rd (262-160)
Russia
  31 Shakespeare Sarani (247-2006)
Thailand
  18B Mandeville Gardens (760-836)
UK
  1 Ho Chi Minh Sarani (242-5171)
USA
  5/1 Ho Chi Minh Sarani (242-3611)

Travel Agents

Blue Sky Travels (244-0934) at 2/1 Sudder Street was recommended to me as a discount travel agent. They are efficient and cheap. *Crystal Travel*, Paragon Hotel off Sudder St, is supposed to be a good place for cheap tickets.

American Express (248-6181), 21 Old Court House St; *Sita World Travels* (292-174), 3B Camac St; as well as *Mercury Travels* (242-3535) and *Travel Corporation of India*, both at 46C Jawaharlal Nehru Rd, are reliable travel agents.

Places To Shop

New Market, Lindsay Street, is a large market that carries a wide range of items. It has more than 2,000 stalls. The Central Cottage Industries Emporium, 7 JL Nehru Rd, has a wide selection of items.

Bookstores

The Oxford Book Shop, Park St, and Cambridge Book Company, 20D Park St, are good book stores. Newman's is on the same block as the Great Eastern Hotel. The Bookmark is upstairs at 56D Mirza Ghalib St. Booklands, at the eastern end of Sudder St, has a good selection of tourist books. Many of the book stores along Mirza Ghalib Street have a good selection of books.

The Survey of India has a **Map Sales Office**, 13 Wood St, where they sell excellent maps of the major cities in India. There is a large book fair in the Maiden in December-January. It is like having hundreds of bookshops all in one place.

Medical and Opticians

The *Wockhardt Medical Centre* (475-4046), 2/7 Sarat Bose (Lansdowne) Rd, is open from 10 am to noon. *Dr Paes, Vital Medical Services* (242-5664), 6 Ho Chi Minh Sarani, is open from 8 to 10 am. There is also the *Centre for Tibetan Herbal Medicine*, 400 Jodhpur Park.

Some opticians are *Stephens*, 23 JL Nehru Rd; *Himalaya*, 25 Camac St; and *President*, 306 Bepin Behari Ganguly St (Lal Bazaar).

Indian Museum

This is the largest and one of the best museums in India. It is located at the intersection of Chowringhee Rd and Sudder Street. On the right side of the main entrance is the Archaeological Section, which contains a large collection of old deities. There is an interesting collection of stone railings with sculptures from the Buddhist site at Bharhut, Madhya Pradesh, dating from the second century BC. The museum is open daily, except Mondays, from 10 am to 5 pm and closes a half hour earlier between December and February.

Other Places

The extensive peaceful **Botanical Gardens**, on the west side of the river (the same side of the river as Howrah Station), claims to have the world's largest banyan tree. Despite losing its central trunk the banyan tree covers an area of over 10,000 square metres (400 metres in circumference). The gardens are 10 km south of Howrah. From the Chowringhee area you take the No 55 or 56 bus. A more pleasant way to go is by ferry, which you can get at Chandpal and Babu Ghats.

Victoria Memorial Hall, at the south end of the Maidan, is an interesting museum that has sculptures, paintings, and objects of arts. It is open daily, except Monday, from 10 am to 4.30 pm.

The **Zoo** has white tigers and is open from sunrise to sunset. It is located south of the Maiden. The **horticultural gardens** are located south of the zoo on Alipore Rd. It is open from 6 to 10 am and 2 to 5 pm.

ISKCON Temple

The ISKCON Temple (247-6025, fax 247-8575) is located at 3C Albert Road, in the center of the city, near the junction of Camac Street and Acharya J C Bose Road. If you get on Camac Street, people will know where the Hare Krishna Mandir is located. It is an old building with Gaura-Nitai, Jagannatha, and Radha-Govinda Deities. The devotees are enthusiastic to help guests. They have

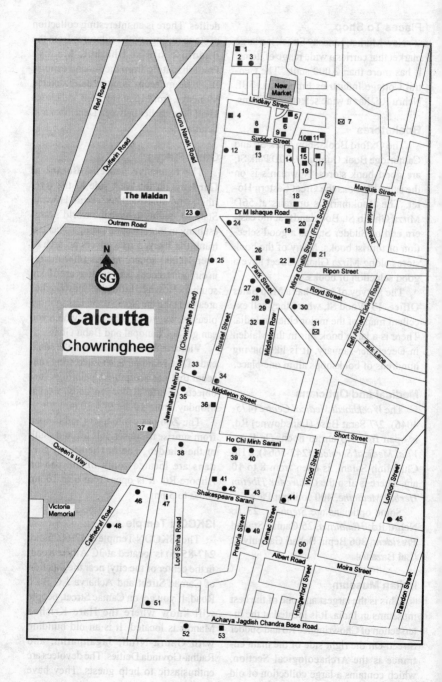

PLACES TO STAY		28	Junior Brothers
		34	Hare Krishna Bakery
1	Oberoi Grand Hotel	39	Jyoti Vihar
2	Carlton Hotel	42	Vineet
4	YMCA		
5	CKT Inn	**OTHER**	
6	Gujral Lodge & Lindsay		
	Guest House	7	New Market Post Office
8	Lytton Hotel	12	Indian Museum
9	Fairlawn Hotel	23	Park St Metro Station
10	Astoria Hotel	24	Bangladesh Biman Airlines
11	Centrepoint Guest House	25	State Bank of India
13	Salvation Army Guest	27	Singapore Airlines
	House	29	Thai International
15	Hotel Maria	30	French Consulate
16	Hotel Paragon	31	Park St Post Office
17	Modern Lodge	33	Air France, RNAC &
18	Neelam Lodge		British Aiways
19	East End Hotel	35	KLM & Cathay Pacific
20	Classic Hotel	37	Maiden Metro Station
21	Hotel VIP	38	British Consulate
22	Paramount	40	USA Consulate
26	Park Hotel	44	ANZ Grindlays
32	YWCA	45	CIS Consulate
36	Old Kenilworth	46	Birla Planetarium
41	New Kenilworth Hotel	47	Government of India
43	Astor Hotel		Tourist Office
53	Hotel Hindustan International	48	Air India
		49	Japanese Consulate
WHERE TO EAT		50	ISKCON
		51	Aeroflot
3	Friends Home	52	Foreigners' Registration
27	Magnolia Restaurant		Office

recently made some nice guest rooms in a new building behind the temple, but guests must follow ashram rules. There is an excellent bakery there.

Every year in June/July there is a Ratha-yatra (chariot) festival organized by the temple. It is said that well over a million people attend this interesting event.

There is a bus to Mayapur that leaves almost every day from the temple at 6 am and returns to Calcutta at 8 pm. It is a good idea to reserve the bus a day in advance. You can call 247-3757 or 247-6075 for reservations. The bus costs Rs 75 (one way) and is a very good way to go to Mayapur. The bus also stops at Gariahat at 6.30 am, then Prachi Cinema, Capital Electronics (Ultadanga), and Airport Hotel to pick up passengers.

Srila Prabhupada's Home

Calcutta is the birthplace of AC Bhaktivedanta Swami Srila Prabhupada, the Founder-Acarya of ISKCON, and is where he lived in his childhood. The house that he lived in as a child is in north Calcutta.

Kali Temple

This interesting temple is dedicated to Kali (*kali* means 'the black'), the patron goddess of Calcutta. She has blood dripping from her tongue, and she wears a garland of skulls. This temple is said to be where Sati's toe fell after her body was cut into 51 pieces by Lord Vishnu, when she was being carried by Lord Siva. The present temple here was built in 1809. It is said that they used to sacrifice humans at this temple. Now they have daily sacrifices of goats. Foreigners are allowed limited access in this temple. It is open from 3 am to 8 pm.

Where To Stay – Lower

Calcutta has a shortage of budget accommodations. Most of the budget places are around Sudder St, off Chowringhee Rd, by the Indian Museum. Sudder St is the hang-out street for the traveler's crowd.

Where To Stay – Sudder St Area

The *Salvation Army Red Shield Guest House* (245-0599), 2 Sudder St, is a popular budget place with clean rooms for Rs 150 and Rs 30 for a dorm bed. It is often booked, but if you can get in, it is a very good value. They will look after nonresident's baggage for Rs 10 a day. The popular *Hotel Maria* (245-0860), further down Sudder St, has rooms for Rs 100 to Rs 150 with bath. Dorm beds are Rs 40.

The *Hotel Paragon* (244-2445), 2 Stuart Lane, is a popular place on a quiet street. It has rooms for Rs 80/110 with common bath, Rs 150 with bath, and dorm beds for Rs 40. The upstairs rooms are much better than the gloomy ground floor rooms. It has a pleasant courtyard upstairs. The *Modern Lodge* (244-4960), 1 Stuart Lane, is a popular place that has rooms with common bath for Rs 75/100 and with bath for Rs 100/150. The best rooms are the ones with bath on the upper floor and roof. The manager here can help you get a cheap flight. Many budget travelers stay at these two places.

The *Hotel Plaza*, Sudder St, is a decent small place with double rooms for Rs 350 and Rs 350/450 with A/C. The *Tourist Inn* (243-732), 4/1 Sudder Street, is a clean place.

The *Hilson Hotel* (249-0864), 4 Sudder St, has rooms with common bath for Rs 110 and Rs 270 for a double with bath. Down the street and about the same is the *Shilton Hotel* (245-1512), which has rooms with bath for Rs 200/350. *Centrepoint Guest House* (244-2867), 20 Mirza Ghalib St (Free School St) by Sudder St, is a decent place that has rooms with bath for Rs 125/150 and Rs 275/325 with A/C.

The *Neelam Hotel* (298-582), Dr M Ishaque Rd, south of Sudder St, has big run-down rooms for Rs 125/200. Across the street is the *East End Hotel*, (298-921), Dr M Ishaque Rd, which is a decent place that has rooms with TV for Rs 200/320.

The *Classic Hotel* (297-390), down an alley off Mirza Ghalib St, has singles, some without windows, for Rs 115, doubles with bath and TV for Rs 205, and A/C rooms for Rs 375. The rooms are all right, but the paint-job is seriously bad. You can get buckets of hot water here. The *Khaja Habib Hotel* (293-305),

33 Mirza Ghalib St, has well-maintained clean rooms.

The *YMCA* (249-2192), 25 Jawaharlal Nehru Rd, near the Indian Museum, is a large gloomy building with rooms for Rs 275/375 and Rs 500/650 with A/C. This place is popular with Indian businessmen, so it is often full.

Where To Stay – Others

There are retiring rooms with bath at the Howrah Railway Station that cost Rs 70. The *Railway Yatri Nivas* (660-1742), next to the station, has rooms with attached bath for Rs 275 and with A/C for Rs 400. Dorm beds are Rs 75. You have to have a train ticket for 200 km or more to stay here.

About a five minute walk from Howrah Station, on the same road as the Howrah bridge, are a group of hotels. The *Hotel Meghdoot* (666-4018), P-3A Dobson Lane, has rooms for Rs 150 and Rs 390 with A/C.

Next door, the *Natraj* (666-2536) has rooms for Rs 200 and Rs 350 for a room with a TV. The *Hotel Saket* (666-4839), just off Dobson Lane, is a big place with rooms for Rs 180/200 and Rs 375 for an A/C room. The *Hotel Manish* (666-6317), P-1 Dobson Lane, is centrally air-conditioned and has rooms from Rs 500/600 up to Rs 900 for a suite.

The Calcutta Airport has *rest rooms* for Rs 175/250 with A/C. Dorm beds are Rs 40.

The *YMCA* (244-3814), 42 Surendra Nath Banerji Rd, has doubles for Rs 75 and dorm beds for Rs 30, plus a temporary membership fee of Rs 15. It is often full.

Where To Stay – Middle

The *Hotel Swagath* (475-6150), 37 Hazra Road, is good place to stay in south Calcutta. This is the closest nice place to the ISKCON Calcutta Temple. Rooms are Rs 400/450 to Rs 525/550 with A/C. Check-out time is 8 am. They also have a decent vegetarian restaurant. They are the suggested middle class place to stay if you want to stay by the temple or you have to catch the bus to Mayapur the next morning. It is a good idea to call them before you go there, because they are often full, especially in December or January.

The *Hotel Trimoorti* (475-6878), 24 Ray Street (off Elgin Road), is a good place that has rooms with TV for Rs 400/550 a night.

Hotel Circular (244-1533), 177A AJC Bose Road, is a good place that is centrally located. Rooms with hot water, air-con, and TV are Rs 495/595 up to Rs 625/775 with an 11% luxury tax. It is across the street from Mother Teresa's Missionaries.

The *Hotel Carlton*, 2 Chowringhee Place, is a good place with rooms for Rs 450.

Where To Stay – BBD Bagh

The *Hotel Embassy* (279-040), Princep St, has rooms with bath for Rs 200/275. The *Broadway Hotel* (263-930), a block east of Princep St, has rooms for Rs 150 for a single with common bath and Rs 220/300 with bath and a TV. It is often full.

The *Central Guest House* (274-876), Chittaranjan Ave and 18 Prafulla Sarkar St, is a recommended place with rooms for Rs 225/275 and Rs 300 with A/C. It is in a relatively quiet area. The hotel is on Chittaranjan Ave, but the entrance is down a back alley off Prafulla Sarkar St. The rooms in the back are quiet, while the rooms on Chittaranjan Ave can be noisy.

Where To Stay – Chowringhee

Hotel Lindsay (244-1374, fax 245-0310), 6th floor, 8A Lindsay St, opposite New Market, is a decent place that has rooms for Rs 350/450 and Rs 575/750 with A/C. *The Lodge* (440-620), by Sudder St, is a clean place with rooms for Rs 230/330 and Rs 450 with A/C. The *Lindsay Guest House* (244-8639), on the floor above, has fairly simple clean rooms that are a decent value. Rooms are Rs 350/450 and Rs 575/750 with A/C.

The Hotel Plaza (244-6411), 10 Sudder St, has recently renovated good rooms for Rs 275/375 and Rs 375/475 with A/C.

The *CKT Inn* (244-8246), 12 A Lindsay St, is a good place that has rooms with A/C and TV for Rs 500/635. This place is often full. The *Hotel VIP* (296-428), Mirza Ghalib St, has rooms, some without windows, for Rs 450 and Rs 600 with A/C. The *Astoria Hotel* (245-1514, fax 245-0190), 6/2 Sudder Street, has A/C rooms with TV for Rs 700/900.

Where To Stay – High

The *Fairlawn Hotel* (245-1510, Fax 244-1835), 13/A Sudder Street, is a classic example of a British Raj hotel and is recommended for its atmosphere. Rooms are $35/50, which includes meals. My friend was able to get a slightly cheaper price by telling them he would not eat the meals that are included in the price. It is run by Mr and Mrs Smith, who still run the hotel almost 50 years after Independence. After meeting Mrs Smith, I told her she was the nicest lady I had met in any hotel in India, and she was.

The *Tollygunge Club* (473-4741, fax 473-1903), 120 Deshapran Sasmal Rd, is a country club with a relaxing atmosphere in the southern part of Calcutta. Foreign guests are allowed to stay, as long

as they are tidy. But to stay here you have to write, fax, or call in advance. Rooms range from Rs 650/700 to Rs 1300/1400. It has an indoor and outdoor poor and many other facilities. It is a ten-minute walk from the Tollygunge metro station.

The *Lytton Hotel* (249-1872, fax 249-1872), 14 Sudder St, is a good centrally located place with rooms for Rs 1000/1400. You have to get a room here early, as it fills up. It is a recommended place. The *Old Kenilworth Hotel* (242-5325), 7 Little Russel St, has a lot of atmosphere and large rooms for Rs 700/800 and Rs 900/1000 with A/C. It is in an old colonial-style house, and the rooms have balconies. All rooms have bath, and the drinking water is thoroughly boiled.

The *Great Eastern Hotel* (248-2311, 248-0289), 1-3 Old Court House St, is a big old place with 200 rooms. It dates back to the British-Raj and has seen better days. It has rooms for Rs 500/700 and Rs 970/1350 with A/C. A suite is Rs 1690. It is very popular and is usually full by noon. The cheaper rooms are recommended. The *Kenilworth Hotel* (242-8394, fax 242-5136), 1 Little Russel St, has modern rooms with A/C for $60/70.

Where To Stay – Luxury

The *Oberoi Grand Hotel* (249-2323, fax 249-1217), 15 Jawaharlal Nehru Rd, is an excellent hotel with a great atmosphere. It is one of the best hotels I have every seen. It looks like nothing from the outside, but it has a beautiful courtyard surrounding a big pool. Rooms are $200/220. The *Taj Bengal* (248-3939), south end of the Maidan, is another excellent place with room for $190/210 to $400. This place has a swimming pool and health club.

The *Park Hotel* (297-336, fax 297-343), 17 Park St, is centrally located and has rooms for Rs 3950/4450. It has a pool. The five-star *ITDC Airport Ashok* (552-9111, fax 552-9137), by the airport, is good if you are taking a flight in the morning or arriving late at night. Rooms are Rs 2600/3000.

Where To Eat

The *Hare Krishna Bakery* (247-3757, 247-6075), 6 Russel Street, is a small place that serves excellent baked goods including pizza, cakes, and mango milkshakes. It is run by the Calcutta ISKCON Temple, so everything is *prasada*.

Junior Brothers, above Gupta Confectionery at 18B Park St, is a good place. Nearby is the *Magnolia Restaurant*, Park St, which is an expensive place with tasty food. *Vineet* (440-788), 1 Shakespeare Sarani, across from the Tourist Office and in the basement of the Air-Conditioned Market, is an expensive first-class place.

The *Anand Restaurant*, Chittaranjan Ave, is one of the best restaurants in town. It is a higher class South Indian place and is very popular. In the evening you may have to wait a half hour for a seat.

Jyoti Vihar, a few buildings down from the US Embassy on Ho Chi Minh Sarani, is a South Indian snack place. *Friends Home*, on a side road next to New Market, is a snack and juice place that is popular with the locals. *Vicky's*, Lindsay St, has good South Indian food and is a good value.

Ideal Vegetarian Refreshment, 26/4 Hindustan Park Rd, serves South Indian food and is open from 11 am to 9 pm. The *Hotel Swagath*, 37 Hazra Road, has a decent vegetarian restaurant, which is convenient if you stay there.

Getting Around

The **Metro** is a train service that goes underground from Esplanade to Tollygunge with eight stops. It operates every day but Sunday, from 8 am to 9.15 pm and is an efficient way to get around.

The black-and-yellow **cabs** can travel only in the city and the yellow cabs can make suburban journeys.

To get a local bus from Howrah Station to the Chowringhee (Sudder St) area is easy. There is a bus stand right next to the station. A landmark that everyone knows is New Market, which is a block from Sudder St. The bus costs Rs 2.

Travel

Air There are many international flights to Calcutta. GSA Jet Air (477-783), 230A Acharya J C Bose Rd., handles booking for several airlines such as Gulf Air, TWA, Philippine Airlines, and Kuwait Airways. From Calcutta you can fly to many cities in India.

Calcutta is a good place to get cheap tickets to other parts of Asia. You can get a cheap ticket to Kathmandu or Bangkok from here. Many times it will be 30% or 40% cheaper than from Delhi.

The Indian Airlines office, on Chittaranjan Rd, has a counter for tourists. This means you can finish your work quickly. It is open from 9 am to 9 pm, every day of the week.

If you are getting a taxi downtown from the airport, it is usually best to go to the prepaid taxi stand, as the fare will be cheaper. The price is about Rs 100 to the Sudder St area. The price will be about 25% higher on the ride back to the airport. There is an Indian Airlines bus that goes downtown to Chowringhee Rd. The airport is about a 30 minute ride north of the downtown.

From Calcutta there are flights to Bangalore (daily, $210), Bhubaneswara (5 weekly, $65), Bombay (5 daily, $175),

Delhi (5 daily, $151), Hyderabad (6 weekly, $170), Lucknow (3 weekly, $178), Madras (2 daily, $172), and Visakhapatnam (3 weekly, $107).

The Calcutta Airport has retiring rooms. You can change money in the international terminal.

Airlines Offices

Aeroflot
    58 JL Nehru Rd (242-9831)
Air Canada
    230A AJC Bose Rd (247-7783)
Air France
    41 JL Nehru Rd (290-011)
Air India
    50 JL Nehru Rd (242-2356)
Air Mauritius
    50 JL Nehru Rd (223-356)
Air Lanka
    230A AJC Bose Rd (247-7783)
Alitalia
    2/3 Chitrakoot Building, AJC Bose Rd (477-394)
American Airlines
    HHI, 235/1 AJC Bose Rd (472-394)
Bangladesh Biman
    1 Park St (293-709)
British Airways
    41 Chowringhee Rd (293-430)
Cathay Pacific
    1 Middleton St (403-2112)
Continental Airlines
    3C Camac St (292-092)
Delta
    42 J L Nehru Rd (247-5008)
Gulf Air
    230A AJC Bose Rd (447-7383)
Indian Airlines
    39 Chittranjan Avenue (263-390)
Iberia Airlines
    230A AJC Bose Rd (247-4495)
Japan Airlines
    35A Chowringhee Rd (298-370)
KLM

    1 Middleton St, (247-4593)
Kuwait Airlines
    230A AJC Bose Rd (247-7783)
Lufthansa
    30 A/B JL Nehru Rd (299-365)
Malaysian Airlines
    1 & 2 Russel St (292-092)
North West Airlines
    75C Park St (299-218)
Quantas
    Hotel Hindustan International 235/1 Lower Circular Rd (247-0718)
Royal Jordanian Airlines
    Vasundhara Building, 2/6 Sarat Bose Rd (475-1261)
Royal Nepal Airlines (RNAC)
    41 JL Nehru Rd (293-949)
SAS
    18G Park St (747-622)
Singapore Airlines
    18G Park St (299-293)
Swissair
    46C J Nehru Rd (242-4643)
Thai International
    18G Park St (299-846)
United Airlines
    2/7 Sarat Bose Rd (747-622)

Domestic Airlines

Indian Airlines
    39 Chittaranjan Ave (263-135)
Citylink Airways
    Suite 308, Park Hotel, 17 Park St (298-254)
Damania Airways
    2-5 Sarat Bose Rd (475-5660)
East West Airlines
    43 Park Mansions, Park St (290-667)
Modiluft Airlines
    2 Russel St (296-257)
Sahara Indian Airlines
    227/2 AJC Bose Rd, Mangal Jyoti (247-2795)

Train There are two train stations in Calcutta—**Howrah** and **Sealdah**. Most trains depart from Howrah, while some trains going north depart from Sealdah.

Tourist quota reservations are made at 6 Fairlie Place, near BBD Bagh. It is open Monday to Saturday from 9 am to 1 pm and 1.30 to 4 pm and on Sundays from 9 am to 2 pm. You can book from here trains that do not depart from Calcutta if you have a Indrail pass.

If you do not have a pass and need to book a train from another station, go to the other tourist quota office at 14 Strand Rd. You can purchase tickets from there that go to or from Bombay, Madras, and Delhi. You can book trains from there up to 60 days before departure, except for the Shatabdi Express, which can be booked only 15 days before departure.

There is another computerized booking office at Tollygunge metro station. The rail reservation office at the airport has a quota for air-travellers for same day and next day trains.

The fastest train to **Delhi** is the fully A/C Rajdhani Express #2305 (1.45 pm, 18 hr), which departs from Howrah daily, except Wednesday and Saturdays. The Poorva Express #2381 or #2303 (9.15 am) and the Kalka Mail #2311 (7.15 pm) are two good trains to Delhi. The Poorva Exp #2381 departing on Tuesdays, Wednesdays, and Saturdays at 9.15 am goes to **Varanasi** (12 hr) and then arrives in Delhi the next morning. The fastest train to **Bombay** is the Gitanjali Express #2860 (12.30 pm, 33 hr). For **Madras** the best train is the Coramandel Express #2841, which leaves Howrah at 2.05 pm, arrives at Bhubaneswara at 9.40 pm, and at Madras at 5.35 pm the next day. Trains can take much longer to get to Madras during the monsoon, as the railway can be severely flooded in Andhra Pradesh.

The Puri Exp #8007 (10.15 pm takes 10 hours to get to **Puri**. There are nine trains daily to Bhubaneswara. There are also trains to Ahmedabad, Nasik, Bombay, Haridwar, Lucknow, and Gaya.

Trains to **Krishnanagar** depart from Sealdah train station and trains to Navadvipa leave from **Howrah**. The **Darjeeling Mail** #3134 departs from Sealdah at 7 pm and arrives in **New Jalpalguri** at 8.30 am. From there you can then get the "Toy Train" or a bus (4 hr) to Darjeeling.

Howrah train station is one of the worst places in the world for pickpockets and other such people, so you should be totally alert. I know of at least three attempted thefts there, two of which were successful. One person had fiberglass dropped down his shirt. When he dropped his bags to try to get it out, his bags disappeared. Another person had his money belt cut off by a man who had a razor blade glued on his finger nail. He caught the guy.

Bus It is usually best to travel by train to and from Calcutta, as bus service is not very good. Long-distance public buses depart from the **Esplanade Bus Stand** on Chowringhee Rd, at the north end of the Maidan. Private bus companies have their own stands. You get long-distance buses to the south at **Babu Ghat Bus Stand**, by Fort William on the east bank of the river.

There is a direct bus to **Mayapur** at 7 am in the morning from the Esplanade Bus Stand. To **Vishnupur** (5 hr) there are three buses in the morning before 9 am and another one at 2.45 pm.

Ganga Sagara

This is where the Ganges flows into the Bay of Bengal. Sagara Island is 105 km from Calcutta and about 64 km (40 miles) from Diamond Harbour, at the confluence of the Bay of Bengal and the Ganges. At this point the Ganges is about 24 km wide. There is a temple here in which Kapiladeva resides with Ganga-mata (the goddess of the Ganges) on his right and Raja Sagara on his left. It is said that the great sage **Kapila Muni** resides here in trance for the deliverance of the conditioned souls.

Every year on **Makara-sankranti** (mid January), there is a large three-day festival here in which thousands of pilgrims come to bathe, hoping to be liberated from rebirth. The bathing festival literally has hundreds of thousands of people attending from all over India. This festival can be a very austere event. One person who went told me they slept just three hours in three days and did not eat at all.

To get to Ganga Sagara during the festival you have to share a boat with 100 people, although the boats are meant for 20, then take a bus, a rickshaw, and finally walk a good distance.

Where To Stay

There is a *Youth Hostel* here. The *Bharat Seva Sangha Dharamsala* is free for 3 days.

On the way you could stay at Diamond Harbour in the *Sagarika Tourist Lodge*, which has some A/C rooms and cheap dorms.

Travel

You can first go to Diamond Harbour by train. From Diamond Harbour you take either a bus or taxi to Harwood Point. You then take a 30 minute ferry crossing to Kochuberia Ghat (Sagar). From there you take a bus on the island to where the Ganges meets the sea. You can also go by vehicle up to Kaka Dwip and from there get a boat to the confluence.

VISHNUPUR (BISHNUPUR)

Population: 58,000, STD Code 031442

This peaceful place, situated 152 km west of Calcutta, has beautiful terracotta carved temples. There are over thirty brick and stone temples here dating from the 17th to 18th century, mostly dedicated to Radha and Krishna. Because there is no stone in the area, the temples were built from brick. There are eight large tanks, locally known as *bandhs*, which were mainly dug between 1657-1677. Many of the temples have beautiful scenes from the *Ramayana* on them.

Vishnupur rose to be an important place under the Malla ruler, Bir Hambir. He was at first considered a cruel ruler, but later he became a Vaishnava by the association of **Srinivasa Acarya**, a follower of Sri Caitanya. Bir Hambir introduced the worship of Madana Mohana and built the Rasa-mancha. This is a pyramidal structure in the center of town, where the Deities from all the temples are bought on the occasion of the *rasa* festival.

The **museum** here is interesting. The State Bank of India changes money.

Temples

On the outside of the temples, especially the brick ones, there are square panels of terra-cotta reliefs. Most of the temples are decorated with beautiful carvings on the walls and arches. There are many panels with scenes from Krishna's pastimes and the *Ramayana*.

Most of the major temples in Vishnupur, such as the Radha-Govinda Temple, Kalachand Temple, Madhava Temple, and the Nandalala Temple, are along the south bank of the Lal-bandh. The Patpur Temple is on the bank of the Krishna-bandh.

There are four distinct styles. The first

has a single tower. The second is a single tower resting on a square building with a curved roof. Examples of this are the Madana Mohana, Lalji, and Radheshyam Temples. The third type is seen in the Shyam Raya Temple, which has five towers. The fourth type resembles two huts joined by a small tower, as seen in the Krishna Raya Temple, built in 1726.

The **Lalgiri Temple** has a single tower and was built around 1658. The **Madana Mohana Temple** is brick and was built in 1694. It is one of the largest temples. The **Shyam Rai** (1643) and **Madana Gopal** (1665) are of the *pancha-yatana* style, temples with five towers. The **Syama Rai Temple**, dedicated to Radha-Krishna, is especially outstanding because of the carvings on its walls. This temple has some of the best examples of brick carvings. Another interesting temple is the **Jor Bangla Temple**.

Where To Stay

The best place to stay is the *Vishnupur Tourist Lodge* (03244/52013), 3 km from the railway station. It has rooms with bath from Rs 100/150 to Rs 350 and dorm beds Rs 50. There are also A/C rooms for Rs 250. It is next to a tank by the temples. There are cheaper places such as the basic *Tarama Lodge, Rangini Lodge, Bharat Boarding House,* and the *Lali Hotel,* Poka Bandh, North Side.

Travel

There are no direct trains from Calcutta to Vishnupur. First you have to get a train to Kharagpur and from there get another train or bus to Vishnupur. This trip takes over five hours. The trains from Calcutta to Kharagpur depart from Howrah Station. You can also get a train from Howrah Station to Tarakeshwar and get a bus from there.

From the Esplanade Bus Stand on Chowringhee Rd in Calcutta (5 hr) there are three buses in the morning before 9 am and another bus at 2.45 pm. From Calcutta it is quicker to go by bus than to go by train.

There are buses to Durgapur from Krishnanagar, and from there you can get another bus to Vishnupur. You can go to Vishnupur on one of the Government of West Bengal tours. The tour lasts for three days and goes to several other places.

Bankura

Population: 20,000

In this town there is an excellent carver of wooden Gaura-Nitai Deities, Suddhir Chana. Many wooden Gaura-Nitai Deities that you see in temples are carved by him. He does not speak English, so if you want something specific you will need a translator. To get to his house you go towards Rampura from the center of town and his house is by Chotta Kali Tala. Once you are in this area, many people there will know him.

This town is about six hours northwest of Calcutta, in the middle of West Bengal.

MAYAPUR

STD Code 3472

This is the birthplace of Lord Sri Chaitanya Mahaprabhu. He appeared in 1486 and then performed many of His early pastimes here. Mayapur is 130 km north of Calcutta and across the Ganges River from the city of Navadvipa. Navadvipa was the capital of Bengal in the 11th and 12th century.

The Mayapur area is one of the most holy and peaceful places in all of India. According to Gaudiya Vaishnavas, Lord Chaitanya Mahaprabhu is non-different from Lord Krishna. Because Mayapur is the site of Lord Chaitanya's appearance and childhood pastimes, it is understood that Mayapur Dhama is non-different from Vrindavana. It is an extremely important holy place. Over a half million pilgrims come here each year.

The world headquarters of ISKCON (International Society for Krishna Consciousness) is at Mayapur. This is a highly suggested place to visit, if just for its peacefulness and beautiful gardens.

On the auspicious appearance day of Lord Chaitanya Mahaprabhu (February/March full moon day) over two hundred thousand pilgrims come to Mayapur.

Orientation

Mayapur is across the river from the fairly large city of Navadvipa. It basically consists of several temples along Bhaktisiddhanta Road, which cuts between some rice fields. Nearby Mayapur is the confluence of the Ganges and Jalangi Rivers. The birthplace of Sri Chaitanya Mahaprabhu is marked by a temple, 1½ km from the ISKCON temple. In addition to the places in reference to Lord Chaitanya's pastimes, there are many other holy places in the area.

Gauda Mandala Area

Gauda Mandala is one hundred sixty-eight miles in circumference, with the Ganges running through the center. Gauda Mandala takes the form of a hundred-petaled lotus with Navadvipa in the center. Navadvipa consists of nine (nava) islands (dvipa), and the nine islands resemble an eight-petaled lotus flower. The circumference of the center of the flower, Antardvipa, is ten miles, and the circumference of the eight flower petals of Navadvipa is thirty miles. According to the scriptures, the diameter of Gauda Mandala is 56 miles and the radius is 28 miles.

The center point, situated within Navadvipa, is Yogapitha, the sacred place where Lord Chaitanya advented. The whole of Navadvipa is a spiritual manifestation, for at this holy place Sri Chaitanya performed His transcendental activities.

The area of Sri Navadvipa Dhama is divided into nine divisions, called islands. Within the central island of Antardvipa is Mayapur. This entire area is considered a holy place. Each one of these divisions represents one of the nine processes of devotional service. The nine divisions are: 1) Antardvipa, Sri Mayapur (surrendering everything); 2) Simantadvipa, Simuliya (hearing); 3) Godrumadvipa, Gadigaccha (chanting); 4) Madhyadvipa, Majdia (remembering); 5) Koladvipa, Navadvipa city (serving the lotus feet); 6) Ritudvipa, Ratupura (worshiping); 7) Jahnudvipa, Jannagara (praying); 8) Modadrumadvipa, Mamgachi (being a servant); and 9) Rudradvipa, Rudrapara (being a friend).

SRI CHAITANYA'S BIRTHPLACE (YOGAPITHA)

This is the place where Lord Chaitanya appeared underneath a neem tree. To mark the birthplace there is a small house with deities of Lord Chaitanya's father, Jagannath Misra; His mother, Sacidevi; and baby Nimai, which was Lord Chaitanya's name as a boy. He appeared on the evening of the full moon of the month of Phalguna (Feb/March) 1486.

When you walk in the gate, there is a temple dedicated to Srila Bhaktivinoda Thakur to your right. To your left is the main temple which has about a 100 foot high tower. The Deities on the left altar are Radha-Madhava with two Deities of Lord Chaitanya. The Deities on the center altar are Lord Chaitanya and His two wives—Vishnupriya and Laksmipriya.

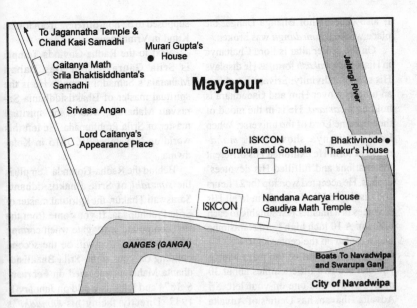

To Jagannatha Temple &
Chand Kasi Samadhi

Murari Gupta's
House

Caitanya Math
Srila Bhaktisiddhanta's
Samadhi

Mayapur

Srivasa Angan

Lord Caitanya's
Appearance Place

ISKCON
Gurukula and Goshala

Bhaktivinode
Thakur's House

Jalangi River

ISKCON

Nandana Acarya House
Gaudiya Math Temple

GANGES (GANGA)

Boats To Navadwipa
and Swarupa Ganj

City of Navadwipa

Also on this altar is a small four-armed Deity of Adhoksaja Vishnu, which was discovered during the temple excavation. Adhoksaja Vishnu was the worshipable Deity of Jagannath Misra. On the right altar is the Panca-tattva, which includes (left to right): Advaita Acarya, Lord Nityananda, Lord Chaitanya, Gadadhara, and Srivasa Thakur. In front of them is a Deity of Lord Jagannath.

In back of the main hall there are Laksmi Narasimha Deities, which are over 60 years old. There are also Gaura-Gadadhara Deities. Behind the birth-site is a Siva-linga called Vridha Siva or Ksetra-pala, the protector of the holy *dhama*.

Srila Bhaktivinoda Thakur personally went door to door to raise funds for the construction of the original temple memorialising Lord Chaitanya's birthplace. To get here you make a right when you come out of the ISKCON Temple gate and then go about 1½ km. A rickshaw costs Rs 6 to Rs 8.

Sri Srivasa Angan

This place is also called Khol Bhanga Danga—where the *mrdanga* was broken. When you enter the gate, in front and slightly to the right is a temple marking where Srivasa Thakur's house was located. On the left altar are Deities of Radha-Krishna. There is also Lord Chaitanya with His arms raised in the air. Lord Chaitanya and Lord Nityananda are on the right altar.

When you come out of the ISKCON temple gate you make a right. You then go about 1¾ km and this place is on your right less than a half kilometre past Lord Chaitanya's appearance place.

Srivasa Pandit was born in Sri Hatta, but he later moved to Navadvipa, near the residence of Sri Jagannath Misra, so he could render devotional service to Lord Chaitanya. Lord Chaitanya and His associates used to have *kirtana* here all night long. This is where Chand Kasi and his men broke the *mrdanga*. Therefore it is also called Khol Bhanga Danga, the place where the *mrdanga* was broken.

On the center altar is Lord Chaitanya in His *maha-prakash* form, as He displays His supreme divinity. Srivasa is holding an umbrella over Him and Gadadhara is holding a *camara*. He is in the mood of the Supreme Lord of the universe. When Lord Chaitanya showed His *maha-prakash* form He exhibited His different incarnations and fulfilled His devotees' desires. He accepted worship for 21 hours and displayed His divine form to all His devotees in a manner just suitable to each of them. A 10 inch high Lord Narasimha Deity is also on the center altar.

If you walk out of the main temple you can see two little temples about 30 metres away. The one on your left, Sri Advaita Bhavan, has Deities of Advaita Acarya sitting at the feet of Lord Chaitanya. The temple on your right is called Sri Gadadhara Angan and has Deities of Lord Chaitanya and Gadadhara. Advaita Acarya and Gadadhara were both associates of Sri Caitanya Mahaprabhu.

Sri Chaitanya Math

If you enter the main gate (the second gate of the Math when coming from the ISKCON temple) fifty feet ahead and to your right there is a temple dedicated to Radha-Govinda. On the altar to the right of Radha-Govinda are two Lord Chaitanya Deities, with Their right arms raised. When you walk around the Deities you will see four altars, one for each of the Vaisnavas acaryas—Sri Madhvacarya, Acarya Vishnuswami, Sri Nimbarka, and then Sri Ramanujacarya.

To your right after leaving the Radha-Govinda Temple is Govardhana Hill. There are hundreds of large Govardhana-shilas on it. Next to Govardhana Hill is a pond called Radha Kund. This pond is supposed to be non-different from Radha Kund in Vrindavana.

Next to the Radha-Govinda Temple is Srila Gaura Kishor Das Babaji Maharaja's Samadhi Temple. He is the spiritual master of Bhaktisiddhanta Sarasvati Maharaja, who is the spiritual master of Srila Prabhupada. He left this world on November 19, 1915 in Koladwipa.

Behind the Radha-Govinda Temple is the *samadhi* of Srila Bhaktisiddhanta Saraswati Thakur, the spiritual master of Srila Prabhupada. If you come from the first compound entry gate when coming from ISKCON, this will be the second building on your right. Srila Bhaktisiddhanta Maharaja appeared on February 6, 1874 and left this world on January 1, 1937. Directly facing his *samadhi* is Shyama Kund.

Srila Bhaktisiddhanta called the area of this compound Vraja Pattan, which means the place where Vrindavana is manifested. This is where the house of Candrasekhar was located. His wife, Malati, was the younger sister of Srimati Sacidevi. When Jagannath Misra left this world, Candrasekhar acted as the Lord's father, accepting Him as his son. He also accepted all responsibility for the welfare of Sacimata.

You can get some books in English by Bhaktisiddhanta Maharaja and Bhaktivinoda Thakur here.

Sri Chaitanya Math is about a kilometre past Lord Chaitanya's birthplace. There are two gates for this place, the main entrance (second gate) by the Radha-Govinda Temple and another entrance by Bhaktisiddhanta Maharaja's Samadhi, where there is a sign that says "Sri Chaitanya Math" to the left of a colorful gate. If you go by rickshaw you can have them drop you at one gate and pick you up at the other gate.

Murari Gupta's House

This temple is located just behind the Chaitanya Math, near the bank of Ballal Dighi and east of Yogapitha. To get there you walk out the exit by Bhaktisiddhanta Maharaja's Samadhi, and then walk about ten minutes through the rice fields on the left. You could ask the devotees at the Chaitanya Math how to get there. There is a small temple here with Deities of Sita, Rama, and Hanuman, said to have been worshiped by Murari Gupta. There is also a Narayana Deity, which was found when the temple was excavated, on the right side of Sita and Rama. The age of this Deity is unknown.

Chand Kazi's Samadhi (Tomb)

Chand Kazi was the chief magistrate of Navadvipa during the time of Sri Chaitanya Mahaprabhu. After initially trying to impede the Lord's *sankirtana* movement, he was converted and vowed that neither he nor his descendants would obstruct the chanting of Hare Krishna again. A champaka tree has sprung up from his tomb which is said to be around 500 years old. It grows along with a neem tree. This place is situated in Simantadvipa, the island of hearing, *sravanam*. It is a located about two kilometres past Lord Chaitanya's birthplace on the left side of the road, in the middle of a small village.

Jagannath Mandir (Sabara Danga)

There are beautiful Deities of Lord Jagannath, Lord Balarama, and Lady Subhadra situated in this temple which is about four kilometres from the main ISKCON Temple. When you enter the beautifully painted gate there are a series of dioramas (clay figures) that depict the

pastimes of how these Deities were made. Lord Jagannath daily receives a large food offering called Chapana Bhoga (56 preparations).

The story of the Deites here is that five hundred years ago, during the time of Lord Chaitanya, there lived a devotee named Jagadish Ganguli. He used to go every year to Jagannath Puri to see Lord Chaitanya and Lord Jagannath. In his old age he became blind and was unable to make the pilgrimage. Then one night Lord Jagannath appeared to him in a dream and told him on the following day when he took his bath in the Ganges, a log would touch his head and restore his vision. He was told to take that log to a certain devotee carpenter, to have him carve a Deity of Lord Jagannath. The Lord told him that the carpenter would at first refuse, because he had leprosy, and that the leprosy would be cured when he finished carving the Deity.

When the Deity was completed, the devotee-leper was cured. Lord Jagannath was carried to the site of the present temple, and His worship was established there. A few nights later, Jagadish had a dream in which Lord Jagannath instructed him to request the same carpenter to make Deities of Lady Subhadra and Lord Baladeva, which the carpenter did. After Jagadish left this mortal world, the Deities were gradually neglected and the temple collapsed.

Some centuries later a villager saw a beautiful blue flower on a termite hill. He went close to see it and was amazed to hear a voice calling "Please, please give Me some water. I'm so thirsty. Oh, please give Me some water." He quickly began digging and soon found Lord Jagannath in the hill. He was astonished to see that although the Deities were in a termite hill, Their wood was unharmed. This happened about 60 years ago. In 1978 the aging *pujari* of the temple offered the service of Their Lordships and Their property to ISKCON.

It is said in the scriptures that the holy *dhama* of Sri Ksetra, Jagannath Puri, is eternally manifest in this holy place. All the benefits one can attain by visiting Jagannath Puri may be achieved by visiting the Sri Jagannath Mandir in Sri Navadvipa Dhama.

Sridhar Angan

The former home of Kolaveca Sridhara is located just behind the ISKCON Jagannath Temple, in a field past the mango grove.

Nandana Acarya's House

This is where Lord Chaitanya and Lord Nityananda first met. There is a temple that marks the spot where the house used to be, on the way from the ISKCON Temple to the Navadvipa boat ghat.

Bhaktivinoda Thakur's House

While staying here Bhaktivinoda wrote the *Navadvipa Dhama Mahatmya*, which describes the glories of Navadvipa Dhama. Bhaktivinoda Thakur's Samadhi and Gaura Kishor Das Babaji's *bhajana kutir* are also here.

To get to this house you go to Hoolar Ghat and then get a boat across the Jalangi River to Swarupa Ganj, where Srila Bhaktivinoda Thakur's house is located. Hoolar Ghat is near where you get the boat to Navadvipa. When you get across the river all the rickshaw drivers know how to get there. A more pleasant way is to walk about five minutes past the ISKCON gurukula and goshala to the Jalangi River. During the *Gaura Purnima* festival a boat (Rs 1) will usually be there.

From here Bhaktivinoda's house is on the other side of the river, just across the street.

ISKCON CANDRADOYA MANDIR

This is the international headquarters of ISKCON. Plans are underway for construction of the largest temple built in India in the last 200 years, at a cost of over 100 million dollars. Surrounded by a Vedic city, the temple will include a Vedic planetarium. At the present time there is a temple, various guest house facilities, Srila Prabhupada's Puspa Samadhi, the rooms where Srila Prabhupada lived, a hut where Srila Prabhupada stayed, a gurukula school, a goshala (dairy), and beautiful gardens.

The main Deities are Sri Sri Radha-Madhava. The Deities are larger than life-size. There are also eight *gopis*, four on each side of Radha-Madhava. They are, from left to right, Srimati Tungavidya Devi, Srimati Chitra Devi, Srimati Champaklata Devi, Srimati Lalita Devi, Sri Sri Radha-Madhava, Srimati Visakha Devi, Srimati Indulekha Devi, Srimati Rangadevi, Srimati Sudevi. Also on the main altar is a small set of Radha-Krishna Deities.

On the left altar are Deities of the Panca-tattva—Advaita Acarya, Lord Nityananda, Lord Chaitanya, Gadadhara, and Srivasa Thakur. To the left of this altar is another altar with an impressive Deity of Lord Narasimha.

Temple Schedule

Mangala-arati, 4.30 am; Greeting the Deities, 7.15 am; Srila Prabhupada's *Guru-puja*, 7.30 am; *Bhagavatam* class, 8 am; *Bhoga-arati*, 12 noon; *Dhoop-arati*, 4 pm; *Sandhya-arati* 6.30 pm (6.00 pm in winter, Nov-March); *Bhagavad-gita* class 7.30 pm; and *Shayan-arati*,

8.15 pm. The temple is closed from 1 pm to 4 pm and 8.30 pm to 4.15 am.

Mangala-arati at 4.30 am is the most auspicious arati to attend. *Sandhya-arati* at 6.30 pm (6 pm in winter) is the most interesting *arati*, with at least 100 to 200 devotees chanting and dancing with enthusiasm.

Morning *Bhagavatam* class in English is usually given on the first floor of the lotus building (the building to the left of the temple), except during the Mayapur Gaura Purnima festival.

Communications

There is an STD, ISD phone and a photo-copy machine in the middle of the ground floor of the long building. In office 206 you can mail letters, purchase stamps, and make photo-copies. In office 207 you can send and receive com messages. In office 208 you can send and receive faxes.

Money

You can change money at the Indian Overseas Bank just outside the parking lot gate. An exchange certificate is Rs 20. They may only accept travellers' cheques.

Purchasing Needed Items

There is a supply store that has basic necessities just inside the front gate of the ISKCON property.

The closest vegetable markets to the ISKCON temple are in Navadvipa and in the village where Chand Kazi's Samadhi is located.

There is also a vegetable supplier who delivers vegetables and other items. He sets up by a tree in the middle of the apartments around 11 am. He may have some items to sell you immediately, but usually you have to make an order for the next day.

Main Gate Closure Time

The main gate closes at 8 pm. It is not really safe to be outside the gates after 8 pm.

Srila Prabhupada's Residences

As you enter the main gate, on your left is a simple hut where Srila Prabhupada stayed after ISKCON first got this property and before anything else was built. Also residing here are Nitai-Gaurasundara, the Deities that travelled from Dwarka to Kanniyakumari and then to Mayapur during Padayatra from 1984 to 1986.

After the Lotus Building was completed, Srila Prabhupada stayed on the second floor in 1976 and 1977. You can see here his sitting room, bedroom, and some personal items.

Srila Prabhupada's Puspa Samadhi

Installed here is a beautiful deity of Srila Prabhupada. Buried under this deity are some flowers (*puspa*) that Srila Prabhupada wore when he left his body in 1977. This is a memorial for him. There is an auditorium, a garden, a diorama exhibit, and small lake in front of the *samadhi*.

This is the largest *samadhi* in India. There are conducted tours of the *samadhi* that explain some facts about Srila Prabhupada's life.

Others

There is a **Padayatra Memorial** with 108 stone circles around it. People are trained there how to chant the Hare Krishna mantra properly. They chant the mantra once on each circle and then step to the next circle.

There is a small **zoo** with an elephant and other animals.

Out in the fields behind the temple is

a **goshala** (cow barn) where cows are protected. In Vedic culture, a cow should never be killed for any reason. Even better than this is to protect mother cow, so she will not come to any harm. The bull and cows are protected here even in their old age, so they can die a natural death.

Next to the goshala is a **gurukula**, or school of the guru, where students are taught in an ashram situation. Students are given both a spiritual and material education.

Drinking Water

You should not drink water from just any tap. The quality of the water largely depends on how deep the well is dug. Certain water is marked as drinking water. There are drinking taps on the outside wall of the middle stairway of the long building. There is also a tap in the basement of the Gada building and drinking taps in a small building by the temple. Drinking bad water is a major cause of disease in India.

Gaura Purnima Festival

Lord Chaitanya's appearance day (Gaura Purnima) is celebrated each year on the full moon day in Feb/March. It is at the same time as the Holi festival. During this time hundreds of thousands of people come to Mayapur.

For the occasion over a thousand ISKCON devotees from around the world come and associate together. Living space is at a premium with four people living in a room that would normally hold only two. Also room rates are increased by 50%.

Navadvipa Parikrama

Every year during the Gaura Purnima festival devotees from around the world walk to the nine islands of Navadvipa Dhama. Yearly 800 to 1200 devotees engage in this ecstatic event. The fee is around US$35, and the *parikrama* lasts for seven days. Many of the places associated with Lord Chaitanya and His devotees pastimes are visited. One would not normally have a chance to go to these places otherwise. Devotees stay in simple tents and have to rough it, but the *prasada*, *kirtanas*, and lectures make it well worth while.

Where To Stay – ISKCON

The *Long (Chakra) Building*'s rooms, with common bath, are simple and cost Rs 70 a night regardless of how many people are in the room. There are also some rooms with four beds and attached bath for Rs 265. Rooms in the *Lotus Building* are much nicer, but you have to use a common bathroom. Rooms in this building cost Rs 200.

The *Gada Building* is the newest building. It has simple but very clean rooms with attached bath for Rs 175 for a double and Rs 300 for a bigger room. There are also rooms with common bath for Rs 70/85. Rooms with common bath in the Gada Building are much better than the rooms in the long building, as there is more privacy. They are recommended, if you are on a budget. There are also dorm beds in the Gada Building for Rs 30.

The *Conch Building* has very nice rooms with attached bath and hot water for Rs 500. There are also four rooms with A/C for Rs 625. There are two smaller rooms, which are recommended, for Rs 300 a night. You have to ask about these two rooms.

The phone number in Mayapur is 91 (3472) 45213 or Fax 91 (3472) 45250 for guest reservation. Checkout time is 9 am. If you are leaving in the afternoon, you can pay an extra half-day and leave at 4 pm. On Saturdays and important holidays all the rooms here can be fully booked. During the Mayapur festival (Feb/March) there may be no rooms available for a few weeks.

You can book a room for the Mayapur Guest Houses at the Calcutta ISKCON Temple. They also have a regular bus service to Mayapur (Rs 75, leaving 6 am). The Calcutta temple is located at 3C Albert Road, about a quarter of a mile from the junction of Camac Road and Acharya Jagadish Chandra Bose Rd. You can call (33) 247-3757, 247-6075 or fax (33) 247-5815 for reservations.

Where To Stay – Other Places

If you come out of the main entrance of the ISKCON grounds and make a left, down the road about an eight-minute walk is the Janhbitirtha Hotel, which has rooms with private bath. I was told the bathrooms are not very clean, but it is a private place to stay during the Mayapur festival.

Where To Eat

Guest House prasada is served in the Gada Building at 1 pm and 8.30 pm. The lunch costs Rs 20 and consists of rice, dal, two subjis (vegetables), chapatis or puris, pakoras, and a sweet. Dinner is Rs 12. This is a recommended eating place. You pay for this meal at the inquiry room (room 111) in the long building, where you check-in.

There is *devotee prasada* at 9 am and 4.30 pm in the main *prasada* hall. This is simpler *prasada* which costs only Rs 8 a meal. You pay for this at the door when you enter. There is also *Sulam (Simple) prasada* at 1 pm for Rs 8 in the main *prasada* hall. You pay for this at a table set up by the front gate. Neither meal is

nearly as good as the Guest House *prasada*, although some people like them better, because these meals are not as rich.

There is a *restaurant* halfway between the main gate and the temple. It serves pizza, sandwiches, dosas, sweets, and other such things. It is not very good and most items are served cold, unless you ask to have them heated up. It is open from 7 am to 2 pm and 5 to 8 pm, except during the festival when it is open later.

You can purchase very nice cakes and sweets from the *maha-prasada* booth by the front door of the temple. In the morning around 8 am and in the evening at 8.20 pm there is a fresh supply of special cakes, pies, and cookies, which are quickly purchased.

You can also book the 12 pm Deity's **maha-prasada** plates. Radha-Madhava's plate and Lord Jagannath's *prasada* cost Rs 200 each. Srila Prabhupada's and Lord Narasimhadeva's plates cost Rs 100 each. It takes about five hungry people to eat the Rs 200 plate. You book the *maha-prasada* inside the temple with the devotee who sits on the platform to the right of the Deities. Bookings should be done as far in advance as possible.

To and From Calcutta

Train There is a crowded local train from Howrah train station to Navadvipa. From there you take a rickshaw to the boat crossing. You then cross the Ganges by boat (Rs 1) and get another rickshaw (Rs 6) on the other side for the last 2 km to the temple. Trains leave from Howrah station to go to Navadvipa at 6.30 am and at 1, 3, and 6 pm.

You can also take a very crowded passenger train from Sealdah station to Krishnanagar (2½ hr, Rs 15). You get a ticket for this train at counter 17, which is to the left of the entrance. Sealdah is a

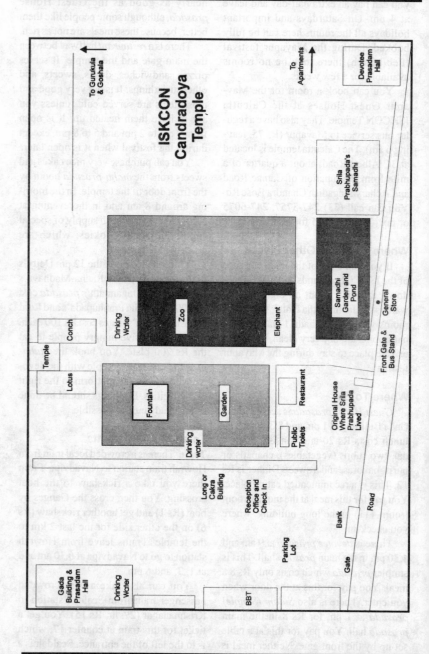

ISKCON Candradoya Temple

To Gurukula & Goshala

To Apartments

Devotee Prasadam Hall

Srila Prabhupada's Samadhi

Samadhi Garden and Pond

General Store

Front Gate & Bus Stand

Drinking Water

Zoo

Elephant

Conch

Temple

Lotus

Fountain

Garden

Drinking water

Restaurant

Public Toilets

Original House Where Srila Prabhupada Lived

Long or Cakra Building

Reception Office and Check In

Bank

Road

Gada Building & Prasadam Hall

Drinking Water

BBT

Parking Lot

Gate

Rs 40 taxi ride from Howrah train station or Rs 25 from the ISKCON Temple.

From the Krishnanagar bus stand there are regular buses to Mayapur (Rs 4) that take about 40 minutes. If you have a decent amount of luggage this is the advised way to go, as the bus stops directly in front of the ISKCON temple. You can also take a bus to Swarupa Ganj boat ghat (20 min), which is by Bhaktivinoda's house on the other side of the Jalangi River. From there you get one of the regular boats (Rs 1) across the river. Once you cross the river you get a rickshaw for Rs 6 to the ISKCON Temple. You can also get a shared rickshaw (Rs 15) or a tempo (Rs 6) from the train station in Krishnanagar to Swarupa Ganj. The tempos are very crowded, and most people would prefer the bus.

Bus There is a 7 am direct local bus to Mayapur that departs from the Esplanade bus stand on Chowringhee Rd at the north end of the Maidan. From the Esplanade bus stand you can also get one of the regular buses during the day to Krishnanagar and from there get another bus to Mayapur.

To get from Mayapur to Calcutta, there is a direct public bus to Calcutta that leaves at 6 am from the ISKCON front gate. This is the easiest way to go to Calcutta, except for taking the 4 pm ISKCON bus. You can also take a bus from outside the temple to Krishnanagar and from there get another bus to Calcutta.

ISKCON Temple Bus The Mayapur Bus departs daily from the ISKCON Calcutta temple at 6 am. The temple is located at 3C Albert Road, about a quarter of a mile from the junction of Camac Road and Acharya Jagadish Chandra Bose Rd. The bus costs Rs 75 and is a convenient cheap way to get to Mayapur from Calcutta. You can call (33) 247-3757, 247-6075 or fax (33) 247-5815 for reservations.

The bus picks up passengers at Gariahat at 6.30 am, then Prachi Cinema, Capital Electronics (Ultadanga), and Airport Hotel. You can also be dropped at these places on the return trip. You should arrange your bus ticket the night before you want to go to Mayapur, as this bus is often fully booked in advance.

The ISKCON temple bus usually departs daily from Mayapur at 4 pm. It arrives about 8 pm in Calcutta. To reserve the bus to Calcutta in advance (a good idea) it is best to meet the bus when it arrives in Mayapur at 11 am, or you have to look for the devotee who is in charge of the bus later, which may not be so easy. You can also arrange a seat the day before by talking to the devotee in charge of the bus at a little before 4 pm, when the bus is about to depart. Usually the bus is not full for the return trip and you can just get a seat, but it is still best to reserve it in advance.

Taxi A taxi from the Howrah train station to Mayapur costs from Rs 850 to Rs 1100. From Calcutta airport the price is Rs 800 to Rs 1050, as the airport is a half hour north of the train station. From other areas of Calcutta you may have to pay as much as Rs 1200. It is suggested that you travel during the day if possible, as this area of Bengal is not very safe at night. To get to Mayapur from Calcutta by car you drive north on National Highway 34 via Barasat to Krishnanagar. About 10 km past Krishnanagar you make a very sharp left when you see the signboard to Sri Mayapur. The drive takes about four hours.

A taxi from Mayapur to Calcutta costs

Rs 950. You should reserve the taxi a day in advance at the main desk in Room 111 of the long building.

Taxi Warning

If you arrange a taxi at the train station there is a good chance the taxi driver will tell you a real bargain price, say Rs 800. He then drives you to another taxi and tells you to change taxis. He tells the other taxi driver to bring you to Mayapur, which, he tells the other taxi driver, is a little pass Krishnanagar. He then asks you to pay him Rs 300 in advance and tells you to pay the other taxi driver Rs 500 when you arrive in Mayapur. Off you go.

When you reach Krishnanagar the second taxi driver drives a little pass Krishnanagar and wants to know where Mayapur is located, which you may not know if you have never been there. He then asks you to pay more for the taxi. It takes you another 40 minutes to reach Mayapur and the second driver feels really ripped off and demands Rs 700 or Rs 800 from you instead of the Rs 500 that you owe him. This has happened to me twice. This has also happened to me at other places too.

You can avoid this problem by insisting that the taxi driver at the train station has to drive you all the way to Mayapur and that you will refuse to take a second taxi.

If you are forced to take another taxi, you should insist to pay the first taxi driver nothing and just pay the second taxi driver on arrival in Mayapur. If you are in a taxi on the way to Mayapur and the taxi driver starts insisting that he wants more than the settled price, just agree, especially at night. When you arrive in Mayapur, take your bags out of the taxi and just pay the driver the price that you agreed to pay and walk away.

Mayapur to Navadvipa

From the ISKCON Temple you can either walk or take a rickshaw (Rs 6) to the boat ghat (2 km). Just before you come to the end of the road, you make a right and walk 200 feet to get the boat to Navadvipa. It costs just a rupee or two. It is a good idea to sit in the front of the boat as the exhaust coming from the engine is extremely bad. You can tell the front because the steering guide is in the back.

When you return to Mayapur, remember all the boats do not go to Mayapur, so you have to ask which boat to take.

Long Distance Travel

Air The closest airport is in Calcutta, 130 km south of Mayapur.

Train The closest railway stations on the broad-gauge line are in Calcutta and Burdwan (Barddhaman). Burdwan is about three hours west of Mayapur by road.

The fastest train from Delhi to Calcutta is the Rajdhani Express #2302 (5.15 pm, Mon, Wed, Thu, Sat, Sun) which takes just 17½ hours to arrive in Calcutta at 10.45 am. It has first class A/C, and two and three tier A/C. There is also a Rajdhani Express #2306 (5.15 pm, Tues, Fri) which goes via Patna which takes 19½ hours arriving at 12.50 pm.

The Rajdhani Exp #2301 (4.30 pm, Mon, Tue, Wed, Fri, Sat) departs from Calcutta to Delhi. The Rajdhani Exp (1.45 pm, Thu, Sun) goes from Calcutta via Patna to Delhi.

If you take the Kalka Mail from Delhi #2312 (7.30 am) or Tundla (11.05 am), you can get down at Burdwan (Barddhaman), which is about two hours before Calcutta, at 5 am.

The Poorva Express #2382 or #2304

departs Delhi at 4.30 pm and Tundla at 7.50 pm. It arrives in Burdwan at 2.36 pm and Calcutta at 4.15 pm. Both trains take 25 hours to go from Delhi to Calcutta, and from Tundla to Burdwan they take 20 hours.

From Burdwan you can then get a taxi or bus to Mayapur. From Burdwan a taxi costs Rs 750 to Rs 850. From Tundla to Vrindavana a taxi costs Rs 550 to Rs 600. From Burdwan you can get a bus to Navadvipa (2 hr) and from there get a rickshaw to the boat ghat (Rs 6), a boat across the river and another rickshaw to the ISKCON temple. Burdwan Station is also known as Barddhaman. On the ticket it says Burdwan, and the signs at the station say Barddhaman.

The Poorva Express departs from Calcutta at 9.15 am and arrives at Burdwan (Barddhaman) at 10.30 am. From there it takes 20 hours to reach Tundla arriving at 4.30 am. The Kalka Mail #231 departs from Calcutta at 7.15 pm, stops in Burdwan at 8.43 pm, and arrives in Tundla at 4 pm and Delhi at 7.30 pm the next day. Both these trains can be boarded at Burdwan instead of Calcutta.

From Mathura, the Toofan Express #3008 (11 am) going via Agra takes 36 hours to reach Calcutta. You can get off the train at Burdwan at 3.21 pm or at Bandel at 5.05 pm, which is a few km north of Hooghly and 43 km from Calcutta. From Bandel you can then get a crowded local train to Navadvipa. It is not safe to travel at night on this local train. The Toofan Express is a slow passenger train and it is very crowded. Most people who have taken this train said they would not take it a second time.

If you arrive at night in Calcutta it is best to stay overnight and travel the next day to Mayapur, because the area between Calcutta and Mayapur is not safe at night.

NAVADVIPA
Population: 120,000

Navadvipa is 130 km north of Calcutta, on the bank of the Ganges River. Across the Ganges River from this city is Mayapur. Navadvipa was the capital of Bengal in the 11th and 12th century. There are many temples here.

Devananda Gaudiya Math

This is where Sri Chaitanya forgave Devananda Pandit for his offences. Whoever comes here becomes free of all offenses. The Radha-Krishna Deities on the altar are named Radha-Vinod Bihari. There is a Varaha Deity on the left.

In Satya-yuga, Lord Varaha appeared before Vasudeva, one of His devotees, who lived in Navadvipa. He told him how He would advent Himself in Kali-yuga as Sri Chaitanya Mahaprabhu. Lord Chaitanya also showed His Varaha form in this area.

This is the Math of Bhakti Prajnan Kesava Gosvami Maharaja who gave *sannyasa* to Srila Prabhupada. His *samadhi* mandir is here.

This temple is on the island of Koladvipa, which is the place where all offences are forgiven. Devananda Pandit was a professional *Bhagavatam* reciter who offended Srivasa Thakur, but was later blessed by the Lord when he surrendered to Him and rendered service to Srivasa.

To get here you first have to get to Navadvipa. You then get a rickshaw. The sign over the gate says Sri Devananda Goudiya Math. There are statues of two elephants and lions fighting on the gate and devotees with folded hands.

Dhameswara Temple

This temple says on top of the entrance door "Dhameswara Sri Sri

Gauranga Mahaprabhu." The Deity of Lord Chaitanya in this temple has His two arms extended out towards the devotee. This Lord Chaitanya Deity was worshiped by Lord Chaitanya's wife, Srimati Vishnupriya, after the Lord took *sannyasa*. Visnupriya was 16 when Lord Chaitanya took *sannyasa*. She died when she was 96, so she worshipped this Deity for 80 years. This place is also called Mahaprabhu Bari.

There are wooden shoes here, which are said to have been worn by Lord Chaitanya. This temple is located about an eight-minute rickshaw ride from the boat ghat.

Kuliya Dharamshala

This is also called Srila Gaura Kishor Das Babaji ka Bhajana Sthala. To avoid disturbances to his worship of the Lord, Gaura Kishor Das Babaji took up residence in an old toilet just behind Kuliya Dharamshala.

Getting Around Navadvipa

If you want to go see the different places in Navadvipa you can rent a rickshaw by the hour. Make sure you make it clear where you want to go, as many times the rickshaw drivers will bring you to the wrong place.

PLACES IN THE AREA

Rasapur

This is a village on the outskirts of Vidyanagar where Nimai studied in the ashram of Ganga Das, who is nondifferent from Sandipani Muni.

Once Nimai planted His wooden pens in the ground and they grew into trees. Even today several unusual trees can be seen here. Botanists who studied them concluded that similar trees do not exist anywhere else.

Nearby is a temple with Vasudeva Datta's Deities. In the courtyard of the temple is a bakula tree under which Lord Chaitanya used to take rest. When the Lord saw that the tree was dying, He embraced it. The Madana Gopala Deity here was worshipped by Vasudeva Datta. Vasudeva's Datta original temple is close to this place.

Prithu Kund (Ballal Dighi)

Prithu Maharaja had a lake dug here. Later the Sena dynasty had their capital here. King Laksman Sena had this *kund* dug out and enlarged. He then renamed the *kund* after his father, King Ballal Sena.

Narasimha Palli (Deva Palli)

This is where Lord Narasimha rested after killing Hiranyakasipu. There is a lake here where Lord Narasimha washed Hiranyakasipu's blood off His hands.

There is a very ancient Deity of Narasimhadeva here, said to date back to Satya-yuga, with a decapitated Hiranyakasipu. Prahlada Maharaja is taking shelter directly under the foot of the Lord Narasimha. Lord Chaitanya and His associates used to come to this place.

Hari-Hara Ksetra and Area

There is a Deity here who is half Vishnu and half Siva. The Lord manifested Himself in this form to show how dear Lord Siva is to Him. It is on the bank of the Gandaki River.

Amghat (Amra ghat) is where Lord Chaitanya performed the miracle of planting a mango (*am*) seed, which immediately grew into a tree full with ripened mangoes. Daily after *kirtana* with Lord Chaitanya and Nityananda Prabhu, the devotees would hold a mango-eating festival. The tree would give mangoes all year without interruption. The fruits had neither seeds inside nor skins outside and were so sweet that by eating only one the devotee was satisfied.

Suvarnabihar

This is the site of the palace of Suvarna Sena, a fabulously wealthy king who lived during the Satya-yuga. During Chaitanya-lila he took birth here as Buddimanta Khan. It is in the island of Godrumadvipa.

Hamsa Vahana Siva Temple

At Hamsa Vahana in Madhyadvipa, the island of remembering (*smaranam*), there is a small temple dedicated to Lord Siva. The deity comes here only three days in a year. The rest of the time Lord Siva is kept underwater in a nearby lake to cool down his fiery anger. The name Hamsa Vahana refers to Lord Brahma's swan carrier.

Desiring to hear narrations about Lord Chaitanya, Lord Siva once quickly came here on Lord Brahma's swan carrier. Two large ancient banyan trees by the lake provide a good place to rest for awhile.

Belpukur

There is a Deity of Krishna here which was worshiped by Nilambhara Cakravarti Thakur, Lord Chaitanya's maternal grandfather.

Samudragarh

At the time of the Rajasuya sacrifice performed by King Yudhisthira, a devotee king named Samudra Sena lived here. He refused to pay his taxes and fought Bhima in order to oblige Krishna to appear here. The Lord fulfilled his desire and also showed him His form as Gauranga Mahaprabhu.

Campahatti

This place is named after the campaka trees that grow profusely in this area. There is a temple here dedicated to Gaura-Gadadhara. These Deities were worshiped by Vaninath Pandit, Gadadhara Pandit's brother. The Deities of Lord Caitanaya and Gadadhara are very large, and both of Them stand with palms outstretched.

Jayadeva Gosvami wrote *Gita-govinda* nearby.

Vrindavana Das Thakur's House

He lived and wrote the *Chaitanya-bhagavata* here. His personal Deities of Gauranga and Jagannath are worshipped here.

Vidya Nagara

Sarvabhauma Bhattacarya took birth here and lived here when he was young. Since the *Vedas*, which contain all *vidya*, or knowledge, were brought here during the universal devastation, this place is called Vidya Nagara.

EKACAKRA

This is the birthplace of Lord Nityananda. Ekacakra is located about 165 km from Mayapur. From Mayapur it takes about four and a half hours by car or bus. Lord Nityananda's father's name is Hadai Pandit, and His mother's name is Padmavati. Another name for Lord Nityananda is Nitai.

There is a small ISKCON temple here, and the local devotee can help show you the area. There is also a small guest house for pilgrims.

This town is very small and there are virtually no facilities here, not even a cold drink stand or a place that sells water. There are several places that have spiritual significance here.

Garbhavasa

This is the birthplace of Lord Nityananda. In the Janmasthan Mandir there is a Deity of Nitai (Nityananda). Hadai Pandit Bhavan is the site of the original house of Nityananda's father. The little white temple next to Nitai Kund is the exact spot where Lord Nityananda was born. There are two banyan trees by this temple that are said to have existed since the time of Nityananda.

In the center of the main altar of the temple is a Deity of Lord Nityananda, and to His left is Lord Chaitanya. On Nityananda's right is Advaita Acarya. The side altar has Deities of Radha-Radhakanta and Radha-Srikanta on the top, a large dancing Gauranga in the center, and ten brass *sakhis* at the bottom.

Padmavati Kund

This *kund* (tank) was dug by Lord Nityananda's grandfather for his daughter (Nityananda's mother), and he named it after her. It is located behind Lord Nityananda's birthplace. This *kund* is a nice place to bathe in.

Pandava Tala

This place is a five minute walk into the fields, southeast of Lord Nityananda's birthplace. It is surrounded by a group of Keli-kadamba trees. The Pandavas lived here with their mother, Kunti, when they were exiled to the forest. At that time, Bhima killed the Bakasura demon, who was eating the local residences.

Hantugada, or Jahnu Kund

This is a *kund* in which Nitai brought all the holy places to save the local residents from having to journey to the Ganges to take a sacred bath. You get here by walking east out of the village, past the birthplace of Lord Nityananda. It is a small *kund* surrounded by grass and a lone tree, which hangs over the water.

Other Places

Between the birthplace and Jahnu Kund is a young Bakula tree surrounded by a cement platform. This is the site of the original **Bakula tree** under which Nitai and His young friends used to perform their childhood pastimes. It is said that the umbilical cord of Nitai is buried underneath this tree. This area was formerly the large estate of Hadai Pandit, the father of Nitai.

Nitai used to bath in **Kundu Kund,** which is on the east side of the Yamuna. There is an old banyan tree on the bank of the Yamuna called **Nityananda Visram Tala**, which is said to have existed since the time of Lord Nityananda. The small temple of **Kadam Khandi** marks the spot where Lord Nityananda recovered the Bankim Raya Deity from the Yamuna River. In the rear of the temple is a small river and *ghat* (stairs) where Bankim Raya was found.

Virchandrapur Side

Bankim Raya Temple

On the altar of this temple is Krishna as Bankim Raya. On His left side is Srimati Radharani, and on His right is Jahnava Devi. It is said that Lord Nityananda left the planet by entering into this Deity. The temple was built under the direction of Virchandra Gosai, the son of Lord Nityananda.

To the right of the altar, out the gate, is another little temple dedicated to Madana Mohana (Krishna). On His left is His consort, Radha, and on His right is the *gopi* Candravali. On the right side is Radha-Vrindavana Candra. These Deities are supposed to have been worshipped for 13 generations and are over 450 years old. The priest says that he is a descendant of Lord Nityananda.

Other Places - Virchandrapur Side

North of the Bankim Raya Temple is a temple dedicated to **Lord Jagannath** and Sakshi Gopal. In this temple there is a deity of **Ekacakra Siva**, also known as Bhandiswara, who was worshiped by Hadai Pandit, the father of Lord Nityananda.

There is a small *kund* between the road and Bankim Raya Temple called **Sweta Ganga**. Its water is used to worship Bankim Raya. It was dug by 1200 *shaktas* of the Neradi-sampradaya who approached Jahnava Mata, the wife of Lord Nityananda, to test Her potency.

The local residents say that **Radha Kund**, also known as Raya Pukur, and **Syama Kund** (Syama Pukur) are located on the western side of the Virchandrapur village in some fields. The local residents have to point them out to you. The local residents also say that south of the Bankim Raya Temple, outside the village in the fields, lies **Govardhana Hill**, which is a small mound 1/5 acre in size. East from there, across the road, just past a bridge that crosses the Yamuna River, is **Kaliya Damana Ghat**. It is marked by a sole tree overhanging the Yamuna, on the northern bank of the river, close to the bridge.

Please Help Us

As the subject matter of this book is extremely complex and detailed it is very difficult to include everything relevant. So if you have some information that would be valuable to the readers of this book please send it to us, so they may be benefited.

Whatever you can tell about any temple, the story behind the Deity, what Deities are in a particular temple, or other interesting facts may be valuable information. Also of interest is your opinion on hotels, restaurants or dharamshalas, especially ones missed in this book. Travel information is also valuable. Please refer to the page number in this book in reference to the place that you are writing about.

Please give as detailed information as possible.

For temples or holy places please send:
Temple name, location, Deities' names
What is especially interesting about the temple or place
Story about the temple or Deities
Opening or closing hours
How to get there, what bus or train
Potential problems such as guides, hard climbs, or monkeys

For hotels and restaurants please send :
Name, address, phone number, opening hours of a restaurant
Tariff card or room rates
Location, distance from a land-mark either walking or by rickshaw.
How close to a railway or bus station.
How to get there and how much it cost.
Your comments on why this place stood out.
For a restaurant, any recommended preparations or things to be avoided

The writers of the ten best letters will receive an updated edition of this book.

Thank you very much for your help.

Write to

Spiritual Guides   Jada Bharata Dasa
Krishna Balarama Mandir
Bhaktivedanta Swami Marg
Vrindavana, Mathura Dist. UP, India

CHAPTER THIRTEEN

Orissa

Orissa is a tropical state located on the eastern coast of India, south of West Bengal. This state has a long and well renowned history and some of the most beautiful scenery in India. Its main holy place is Puri (Jagannatha Puri). Also prominent are Bhubaneswar, the state capital, and the famous Sun Temple at Konark.

Temple Design

The Orissan temples' architectural style is known as Nagara. As a rule, an Orissan temple consists of two essential parts: the *deul* and *jagmohana*. The tall, main structure (*deul* in Orissan) is a spiring elevated tower, crowned with a lotus-shape top. At the center of the *deul* is the inner sanctum where the temple deities are located. In front of the *deul* there is usually a porch structure (*jagmohana*) that is rectangular in shape.

There may also be a hall of dance (*nata-mandira*), a congregational hall (*bhoga-mandapa*), bathing tanks, and subsidiary shrines all enclosed by a wall.

PURI

Population: 125,000, STD Code 06752

Puri is located 60 km from Bhubaneswar on the coast of the Bay of Bengal. It is one of the four holy *dhamas* of India—Puri, Dwarka, Rameswaram, and Badarinatha—and it is considered that a pilgrimage of the temples of India is not complete without making the journey to Puri.

Puri is called Sri Purusottama Dham or Martya Vaikuntha, the abode of Lord Vishnu on earth. Other names are Sriksetra (best of all sacred centers), Purusottama Ksetra (the abode of the supreme being), Nilachal, Nalagiri, Sankha Ksetra, and Jagannatha Dhama. Puri is about 2 km wide and 4 km long.

The Jagannatha Temple here is one of the major temples in India. The worship of Lord Jagannatha is so ancient that there is no idea how long He has been worshiped. The Lord has had many temples before the present one we see today.

Sri Ramanuja visited Puri between 1107 and 1117 and stayed for some time. Vishnu Swami visited Puri in the second half of the 12th century and established a Matha near Markandeswar Tank, called Vishnuswami Matha. Nimbarka Acarya also made a pilgrimage to Puri, and Srila Prabhupada visited in January, 1977.

A major reason that Puri is so important to the Gaudiya Vaishnavas is because Lord Caitanya spent so much time here. Many of His pastimes with His most intimate associates took place at different sites in this area.

Non-Hindus (actually non-Indians) cannot enter the Jagannatha temple. This is strictly enforced.

Besides being an important holy town Puri also has one of the best beaches for swimming in India. It is one of the most visited places in India by young foreign tourist. It is a very pleasant place.

Getting Your Bearings

The Jagannatha Temple is in the middle of town at one end of Grand Rd, which is a wide road that runs to the Gundicha Temple, 3 km northeast. The Jagannatha Temple is about one km from the beach, where most of the hotels are located. Most of the foreign visitors stay at the eastern end of the beach, on or near Cakra Tirtha Rd. By the Puri Hotel there is another area of hotels, which is fairly crowded. The spiritual places in town are spread out and it is best to have some kind of transportation to get around.

Information

The **OTDC tourist office** (Mon-Sat, 10 am to 5 pm) is on Station Rd and there is a 24-hour tourist counter at the railway station. The **post office** is on Temple Rd; for poste restante, use the door on the left side of the building.

You can change money at the **State Bank of India** (Mon-Fri 10 am to 2 pm, Sat 10 am to noon, and Sun 11.30 am to 1.30 pm). Changing money here can take an hour or more.

Two good detailed books about Puri are *A Visit to Jagannatha Puri* by Satsvarupa dasa Goswami and *Sri Caitanya Mahaprabhu in Jagannatha Puri* compiled by Mahanidhi Swami.

You can rent a bike at different shops for about Rs 20 a day on Chakra Tirtha Road.

Weather

You will find a low of 17°C (62°F) in the winter and a high of up to 32°C (90°F) in the summer. You need light cotton clothing in the summer and light woolens for winter mornings. You can swim in the ocean or sun bathe all year round. It is comfortable to swim even in December, though less so in January. The gen-erally temperate weather is good all year round, which makes Puri an ideal place to visit most seasons. The Ratha-yatra in June/July is during the rainy season and it often rains very hard during the pulling of the carts.

Tours

There is a daily OTDC Luxury Coach that goes to Konark, Dhauligiri (Buddhist temple), the temples of Bhubaneswar (Lingaraja, etc.), Khandagiri, Udayagiri, Nandankanan Zoo, and Saksi Gopal Temple for Rs 105. It starts at 6.30 am and ends around 7 pm. It is a long trip (over 12 hours). This tour can be arranged by the many travel agents in Puri.

Tours go to Chilika Lake on Mon, Wed, and Fri (6.30 am to 6.30 pm) for Rs 120 by OTDC Luxury Coach. It is the biggest inland lake in the country and attracts a large number of migratory birds in the winter.

Lord Jagannatha Temple

The name Jagannatha literally means Lord of the Universe. It is said that the present temple was begun by King Chora Ganga Deva and finished by his descendant, Anangabhima Deva, in the 12th century.

The main temple structure is 65m (214 feet) high and is built on elevated ground, which makes it look even larger and adds to the imposing impression you get as you first come within sight of the temple. The temple complex comprises an area of 10.7 acres and is enclosed by two rectangular walls. The outer enclosure is called **Meghanada Prachira** (665 x 640 feet). The walls are 6 meters (20 feet) high. The inner wall is called **Kurmabedha** (420 x 315 feet). The walls were built during the 15th or 16th century.

This temple is said to have the largest

kitchen in the world and feeds thousands of devotees every day. The kitchen can prepare food for 100,000 people on a festival day and 25,000 is not unusual for a normal day. There are 36 traditional communities (Chatisha Niyaga) who render a specific hereditary service to the Deities. The temple has as many as 6,000 priests.

There is a wheel on top of the Jagannatha Temple made of an alloy of eight different metals known as asta-dhatu. It is known as the **Nila Chakra** (blue wheel). It is 11 feet 8 inches high and has a circumference of about 36 feet. A flag is tied every day on a mast attached to the Nila Chakra. On every Ekadasi day a lamp is lit on top of the temple near the wheel.

The main temple is surrounded by 30 different smaller temples. The **Narasimha temple** adjacent to the western side of the Mukti-mandapa is said to have been constructed before the present temple.

In front of the main gate is an 11m pillar, called Aruna Stambha, which used to be in front of the Sun Temple in Konark. It was brought to Puri during the 18th century. The figure on top of the pillar is Aruna, the charioteer of the sun-god. In the passage room of this gate is a Deity of Lord Jagannatha called **Patita Pavana** (Savior of the most fallen). This Deity is visible from the road, so non-Hindus can take *darshana* of the Lord.

There are four gates—the Eastern Singhadwara (Lion Gate), the Southern Ashwadwara (Horse Gate), the Western Vyaghradwara (Tiger Gate), and the Northern Hastidwara (Elephant Gate). There is a carving of each form by the entrance of each gate. The Lion Gate, which is the main gate, is located on Grand Road.

Lord Caitanya used to regularly visit the Jagannatha Temple. In front of the altar of Lord Jagannatha is a column on which the statue of Garuda is situated. It is called the Garuda Stambha and is very revered and worshiped, as Sri Caitanya Mahaprabhu usually saw Lord Jagannatha from a distance behind this column. Behind that column is a moat-like *kunda*, or ditch, which was sometimes filled with Lord Caitanya's tears. Also an impression of Lord Caitanya's own hand-print is found imbedded in the column.

"If one is not allowed to enter the temple, or if he thinks himself unfit to enter the temple, he can look at the cakra and wheel from outside, and that is as good as seeing the Deity." (Cc. M.11.195) Non-Hindus (non-Indians) cannot enter the temple. Also you should be careful if you have an Indian body and look too westernized. I know of at least one case of an Indian settled in America who was stopped for wearing western clothes. They will only speak in Hindi or Oriyan.

Lord Jagannatha & Other Deities

The main Deities in the temple are Lord Jagannatha, His brother, Baladeva, and His sister, Lady Subhadra. Lord Jagannatha is another name for Lord Krishna.

"Being absolute, Lord Jagannatha is identical with His name, form, picture, qualities, and pastimes. If one thinks that the form of Lord Jagannatha is an idol made of wood, he immediately brings ill fortune into his life. A pure devotee who knows the science of Krishna Consciousness makes no distinction between Lord Jagannatha and the actual form of the Lord. He knows that they are identical, just as Lord Krishna and His soul are one and the same." (Cc. Ant.5.146-152)

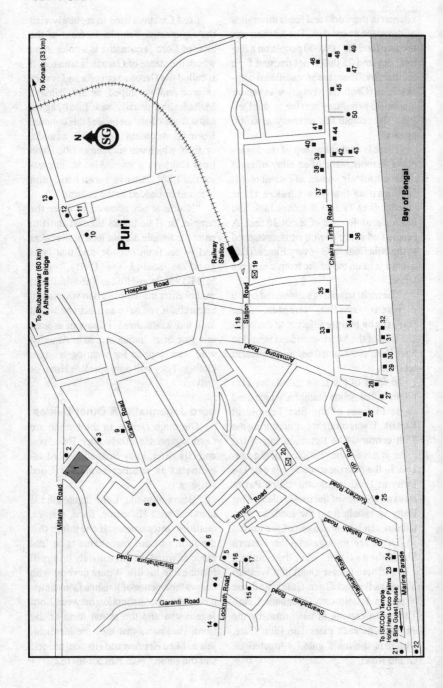

PLACES TO STAY

9	Hotel Subhadra
23	Victoria Club
24	Puri Hotel
26	Hotel Nilachal Ashok
27	Hotel Golden Palace
28	Panthanivas Tourist Bungalow
29	Hotel Repose
30	Mayfair
31	Hotel Vijoya International
32	Hotel Sumudra
33	Hotel Sealand
34	Youth Hostel
35	South-Eastern Railway Hotel
36	Hotel Holiday Resort
37	Bay View Hotel
38	Hotel Love & Life
39	Hotel Dreamland
40	Hotel Sea 'n Sand
41	Ghandara
42	Sea Foam Hotel
43	Hotel Shanker International
44	Holiday Inn
45	Z Hotel
46	Hotel Sri Balaji
47	Pink House
48	Satya Lodge
49	Sagar Saikate

HOLY PLACES

1	Narendra Sarovara
4	Lord Jagannatha Temple
6	Balagandhi
7	Jagannatha-vallabha Gardens
8	Bhaktisiddhanta's Appearance Place & Gaudiya Math Temple
11	Gundicha Temple
12	Narasimha Temple
13	Indradyumna Tank
14	Paramananda Puri's Well
15	Sarvabhauma Bhattacarya's House
16	Siddha Bakula
17	Gambhira
21	ISKCON Temple
22	Haridas Thakur's Samadhi
50	Chakra Tirtha Temple

OTHER

2	Bus to Alalanatha Temple
5	Raghunandan Library
10	Bus Station
18	Tourist Office
19	Post Office
20	GPO
25	State Bank of India

Some of the other temples within the walls of this temple house Deities of Satya Narayana, Lord Caitanya, Ramachandra, Gopala, Hanuman, Narasimha, Varaha and others.

Temple Compound Sites

1. **Baisipahacha**—Twenty-two steps that take one from Grand Road and connect the inner and outer wall. Great respect is given to these steps because many devotees pass here and the dust of their feet sanctifies the steps

2. **Kalpavata**—*Kalpa* means a thousand years and *vata* means banyan tree. It is towards the south side of the temple. It is supposed to be able to fulfill all desires.

3. **Mukti-mandapa**—It is a 16 pillar hall known as Brahmasava (divine assembly).

4. **Niladri Vihar**—Approached from the western gate, it is situated between the outer and inner enclosure. It is an art gal-

lery which shows the pastimes of Lord Jagannatha as well as the 12 incarnations of Lord Vishnu.

5. **Sona Kua** (golden well)—Near the northern gate. The water of this well is used to bath Lord Jagannatha during Snana-yatra.

6. **Koila Vaikuntha**—In the western portion of the temple between the outer and inner walls. It is approachable from the northern gate. During Nava-kalevara (new incarnation ceremony), when Lord Jagannatha, Baladeva, and Subhadra are newly carved, the old images are buried here.

7. After you come up the 22 steps by the Lion (main) Gate, on the right is **Ananda Bazaar**, where *maha-prasada* is purchased.

Main Temple

The main temple is the home of Their Lordships Balabhadra (white), Subhadra (yellow), and Jagannatha (black). They are seated on the Ratna Singhasan. Devotees can circumambulate the Deities between 8.30 and 9.30 am.

1. **Mukhasala**—Next to the main temple in a straight line is the hall of audience, which can be entered through 4 separate doors. The Kalaghata door leads to the sanctum sanctorum. The southern door leads out of the temple and the northern to the Ratna Bhandar (Treasury house).

2. **Nata Mandira**—This is a spacious hall, 21 metres (65 ft) in length and 20 metres (61 ft) wide. This is where the Garuda Stambha is located, where Lord Caitanya used to stand. It is believed that the potency of a devotee's prayers to the Lord becomes increased while he stands near this sacred pillar.

3. **Bhoga Mandap**—Next to Nata Mandira. It is a spacious hall, 18 metres

in length and 17 metres wide. There are sculptures and paintings about Lord Krishna's pastimes and other stories in this hall.

Temple Tours & Temple Pandas

When you first enter the viewing area to see Lord Jagannatha, Baladeva, and Lady Subhadra, you are a good distance from the Deities. With the help of a temple *Panda* (*Brahmin* guide) you can get a closer view of Lord Jagannatha. You get his help by giving a donation. It is best to work out a price in advance, but this may not be possible. When you get fairly close to the altar you will be approached for a donation for the Deities.

If you look like you have some money, when you enter the temple the temple *pandas* (*Brahmin* guides) will invariably approach you and offer to guide you around the temple. They can be extremely aggressive and will gladly bring you to see every Deity in the temple complex, where they will explain to you why it is important to give a large donation to help yourself, your family, your loved ones, and everyone else in the universe.

Giving Rs 100 to the *Brahmin* (*panda*) is a good donation for showing you around for an hour and most will be satisfied with this, although they may request more at first. However even Rs 50 for an hour tour is not unreasonable.

How To View The Temple

You can get a view of the temple from the Jaya Balia Lodge or the roof of the Raghunandan Library on Grand Rd, opposite the main entrance of the temple. You can also view some ancient leaf books in the library for a small donation. The library is open from 9 am to 12 noon and 4 to 8 pm. You can get a good photograph of the temple from the library.

Maha-Prasada

Lord Jagannatha's *maha-prasada* is pure vegetarian spiritual food offered to Lord Jagannatha. Just by honoring this *maha-prasada* one makes great spiritual advancement. Every day 56 varieties of *prasada* are offered to Lord Jagannatha. The main offering of the day becomes available anywhere from 3 to 5 pm (sometimes later). The offering times are not exact and change every day. *Maha-prasada* should ideally be eaten while sitting on the floor, rather than standing or sitting at a table.

To get *maha-prasada*, you can go to the main gate of the temple on Grand Road. There one of the local *pandas (Brahmins)* will come up to you and ask if you want some *maha-prasada*. You then ask him the price and he will tell you. You then give him the money and a few minutes later he will come back with it. You can usually request *maha-prasada* in the morning at the hotel you are staying and they can send someone to bring it for you. Of course, if you are Indian, you can enter the temple and purchase it yourself.

Unless you are very fond of rice, you should make it clear how much you want while ordering. Even if you say it ten times you will probably be brought way too much the first time. Normally *maha-prasada* means a few small pots of *subji* (vegetable), *dahl*, and a pot of rice ten times the size of the small *subji* pots.

There can be a wide selection of items, and many times it depends on the ability and connections of the person getting it for you. I have had as little as three preparations and at other times more than ten preparations.

Gundicha Mandir (Temple)

This temple is located at the end of Grand Road (the main road) about 3 km northeast of the Jagannatha Temple. At the time of the Ratha-yatra festival, Lord Jagannatha goes to the Gundicha Temple and stays there for one week. After one week He returns to His original temple.

It is said that the wife of Indradyumna, the king who originally established the temple of Jagannatha, was known as Gundicha. The cleansing of the Gundicha temple takes place the day before the Ratha-yatra festival as mentioned in *Caitanya-caritamrita*.

Non-Hindus can walk within the walls and see the beautiful garden, but they are not allowed in the temple building.

Narasimha Temple

This temple is located next to the Gundicha Temple. There are two Deities of Lord Narasimha, one behind the other. The Deity in front is called Santa Narasimha (sober). Anyone who see this Deity will be cooled down; all his anger, frustration and anxiety will vanish.

The Deity in the back is called Raga Narasimha (anger). He is the internal mood of Narasimha. When the Muslim Kalapahad attacked Puri and was breaking the Deities, he saw Santa Narasimhadeva and his anger subsided; hence he could not break the Deity as he had planned. Santa Narasimha's features are human-like. He has a sharp human nose, large, curly mustache, and an outstretched tongue.

Lord Caitanya took *darsana* here during His Gundicha pastimes. Lord Caitanya rested near this temple after cleaning the Gundicha Temple. Non-Hindus are not allowed in the temple, but you can see the Deities if you stand by the door. A generous donation (at least Rs 200) may be accepted by the *pujari* (priest) to be allowed to enter this temple.

Haridasa Thakura's Samadhi

The *samadhi* temple of Haridasa Thakura, the *nama-acarya* (teacher of the chanting the holy names) is located by the beach in the Swarga Dwara area near the Purusottama Gaudiya Math. If you are walking on the beach there is a sign for the Sea Hawk Hotel. It is right behind this hotel. Many rickshaw-walas know where it is located.

Within the temple, the chapel structure is Haridasa Thakura's *samadhi*. There is a very nice painting of Haridasa Thakura in the *samadhi*. On the center altar is a wooden Deity of Lord Caitanya; on the right altar, Lord Nityananda; and on the left, Advaita Acarya.

Sri Caitanya gave a benediction saying, "Anyone who has chanted and danced here at Haridasa Thakura's *samadhi* will achieve the favor of Krishna very soon. There is such wonderful power in seeing Haridasa Thakura."

Residence of Haridasa Thakura

Siddha Bakula is the *bhajan-kutir* of Haridasa Thakura, where he chanted 300,000 names of God daily. In order to provide shade for Thakura Haridasa, Sri Caitanya planted a toothpick used by Lord Jagannatha. All of a sudden it grew up and appeared as a great shade tree. Rupa Goswami recited *Lalita Madhava* and *Vidagdha Madhava* before Sri Caitanya and His followers under the tree here. During his stay in Puri, Sanatana Goswami lived here with Haridasa Thakura. This is considered a very holy spot for the Gaudiya Vaisnavas, as this is where Haridasa Thakura left his body and where, after his departure, Sri Caitanya carried his body while dancing in ecstasy.

In course of time, the then King of Orissa ordered his officers to cut down the tree here in order to construct Lord Jagannatha's Ratha-yatra cart. The next morning the royal officers found the tree hollow and returned without cutting it. The main branch of the tree is petrified, stone to the touch. This is the part that was transformed, so the king would not take it. People tie stones to this *kalpa-taru* (wish-fulfilling tree) and make their wishes.

About a hundred feet away in the same compound is the **Sri Haridasa-Sadbhuj Temple**. There is a Sadbhuj-murti (six-armed form) of Lord Caitanya on the altar. Beside this Deity is Lord Nityananda on one side and on the other side a shorter Advaita Acarya. A *murti* of Haridasa Thakura is in front, to the side of the main altar. There is also a Deity of Lord Narasimhadeva.

Gambhira

Gambhira is located close to Siddha Bakula. There is a sign over the door that says "Shri Shri Radhakanta Math, Gambhira." It is about half a km from the Lion Gate going toward Swarga Dwara or the ocean. On the left of the entrance is a small temple with Deities of Radhakanta (Krishna), and Lalita and Vishaka. Radhakanta were worshiped by Gopalaguru Goswami, the disciple of Vakreswara Pandita. On the far right is Lord Gauranga, and on the far left is Nityananda.

This is the former house of Kasi Misra. You can look through a small barred window into the room called **Sri Gambhira**. This is the room where Sri Caitanya lived. There is a lamp here that remains always lit and never goes out. You can see Sri Caitanya's original wooden sandals, His quilt, water pot, and bed. Sri Caitanya lived for 12 years in this room. On a marble throne, a *murti* of

Sri Caitanya is encircled by a cloth, so that just His face is visible. Upstairs there are dioramas of the life of Sri Caitanya.

Sarvabhauma Bhattacarya's House

This house is about one-half kilometre south of the Simha-dwara (main gate) of the Jagannatha Temple. If you walk out of the Jagannatha Temple, turn right and follow the road toward Swarga-dwara (the ocean). Go past the first right, which goes around the temple, and then walk about another 100 metres and make the next right to Sweta Ganga Tank. Sarvabhauma's house, better known as Gangamata Math, is on the left.

There are Radha-Krishna Deities called Radha-Rasikaraja in this house, which are said to have been worshiped by Sarvabhauma Bhattacarya. Inside there are paintings of devotional scenes all over the walls. The black wooden sandals are said to have belonged to Sarvabhauma. There is a hidden tunnel in the house which is said to lead in two directions—to the sea and to the Jagannatha Temple. It is said that this tunnel was used by Sri Caitanya.

Bhaktisiddhanta Saraswati Thakura's Birthplace

It is located about one km from the Jagannatha Temple on Grand Road. There is a Gaudiya Math temple here, with Jagannatha Deities and a *murti* of Bhaktisiddhanta Maharaja. There are also *murtis* of the heads of the four Vaishnava sampradayas—Vishnuswami, Madhvacarya, Nimbarka, and Ramanuja.

Jagannatha Vallabha Gardens

Sri Caitanya used to meet here with Ramananda Raya. Ramananda Raya used to train girls here to dance for the pleasure of Lord Jagannatha. There are three altars in the Jagannatha Vallabha temple. On one altar there are large Deities of Lord Jagannatha, Baladeva, and Lady Subhadra. On the middle altar there are Deities of Lord Caitanya (in saffron) and Ramananda Raya (in white). On the third altar are Radha-Krishna.

This place is about one km from the Jagannatha Temple on Grand Road. Non-Hindus cannot enter the temple, but can walk around some of the gardens. There is also a small lake here.

Tota Gopinatha Temple

Gaudiya Vaisnavas accept that Sri Caitanya Mahaprabhu ended His manifested pastimes in Jagannatha Puri by entering into the knee of the Tota Gopinatha Deity.

On the far left altar is Lord Balarama and His two wives, Revati and Varuni. On the middle altar is Tota Gopinatha, accompanied by black Deities of Radha and Lalita. Tota Gopinatha is in a sitting position. If you come in the morning around seven, you can give a donation to see the crack in His knee where Lord Caitanya entered the Deity and left this world. On the right altar are the Deities of Radha-Madana Mohan and Gaura Gadadhar. Sri Gadadhar used to worship Tota Gopinatha regularly as per Sri Caitanya's personal instructions.

This temple is located by a large white water tower in the Gaurbat Sahi area. It is five minutes walk from the Chatak Parbat Purushottam Gaudiya Math temple. The sign on the door says "Shree Tota Gopinathjee," and there are two stone lions by the door. It is a 15 minute walk from Haridasa Thakura's Samadhi.

Chatak Parbat Gaudiya Math

This temple is in the area where Sri Caitanya mistook the sand dune hills to be Govardhana Hill. The **bhajana-kutir** of **Srila Bhaktisiddhanta Maharaja** is here, as well as his bed. You will also find a *murti* of Veda-Vyasa in the *bhajana-kutir*.

This temple is by a big white water tower, about a 10-minute walk from Haridasa Thakura's *samadhi*. It is a 5-minute walk from Tota Gopinatha Temple.

Narendra Sarovara

This is a large tank. There is a small temple, on an island about a hundred feet into the tank, with Deities of Lord Jagannatha, Baladeva, and Subhadra. Directly behind Lord Jagannatha is a deity of Yasoda, the mother of Krishna. At the other end of the temple room is a Deity of Laksmi. Also on the island is a Siva-linga temple and a Deity of Bala Krishna.

This is where the boat festival called Chandana-yatra is held during which Lord Jagannatha goes for a boat ride. Since Lord Jagannatha is very heavy, the *vijaya vigraha* (festival Deity), known as Govinda, rides in the boat. Sri Caitanya and His devotees took part in this festival.

It is located off Grand Road, on the same side as the Jagannatha Temple. To take a picture of the temple in the middle of the tank here, you are expected to pay a Rs 5 fee. If you take a picture without paying the fee a priest will run up to you and demand insistently that you do so.

Paramananda Puri's Well

Sri Caitanya told all the devotees that this well water is the same as Ganges water, and a person who drinks it or bathes in it would certainly develop pure love of Godhead. It is a five minute walk behind the West gate of the Jagannatha Temple. It is located on Lokanatha Rasta, inside the gate of the Baselisahi Out Post

(policemen's residence).

Indradyumna Sarovara

This water tank is about a half km from the Gundicha Temple. Water to clean the Gundicha Temple is brought from this *kunda*. Sri Caitanya engaged in water sports with His intimate associates in this tank.

Balagandhi

This is the place where Lord Jagannatha stops His chariot to accept a massive *bhoga* offering. There is a temple on the right side of the main road marking the spot, about a km down from the Lion Gate (Main Gate) on the way to Gundicha Temple.

Alalanatha

Alalanatha is also known as Brahmagiri. It is about 25 km from Jagannatha Puri, close to the beach. There is a temple of Lord Jagannatha here and a large stone slab marked with the impression of Sri Caitanya's transcendental body. The stone melted while the Lord lay there in ecstasy. Anyone can view the stone, but non-Hindus cannot enter the temple.

Sri Caitanya would often come here during the two weeks when Lord Jagannatha remains in seclusion before the Ratha-yatra festival. At the rear of the dome of the temple is an inset sculpture of Narasimha, with Hiranyakasipu on His lap. There is also a sculpture of Lord Vamana piercing the outer shell of the universe.

When you come here you can also visit **Ramananda Raya's house** in a place called Benta Pura, which is a few km away, near a rice mill. It is in a small village on the way back to Puri. There is a Deity of Lord Caitanya with a shaven head, with Ramananda Raya seated beside Him in saffron robes. Many of the locals and the priest of the Alalanatha temple can tell you how to get there.

You can get to the Alalanatha temple by catching a mini-bus at the back of Narendra-Sarovara, to Brahmagiri. It takes about an hour to get there. To go there and back by taxi costs about Rs 550.

Atharanala Bridge

This bridge is at the entrance of Puri. It has 18 arches. *Athara* means 18. "When all the devotees coming from Bengal arrived at the bridge, Lord Caitanya sent two garlands with Govinda to offer to Lord Nityananda and Advaita Acarya." (Cc, Madhya-lila). This bridge is symbolic of the emotion of arriving or departing from Jagannatha Puri.

The present bridge is an addition, constructed directly on top of the original brick bridge. You can see the **temple cakra** from it.

Ratha-yatra (Cart) Festival

During this festival the Deities of Lord Jagannatha, Baladeva, and Lady Subhadra are carried out of the temple. It takes at least six big strongly built *pujaris* (priests) to carry these enormous forms of the Lord. The Deities are then placed upon three gigantic chariots, which are pulled with ropes by many thousands of devotees who come from all over India for this occasion.

This famous festival begins from the second day of the bright fortnight of Asadha during June/July. The Deities are pulled on Their huge carts along the entire distance of Grand Road from the Jagannatha Temple to the Gundicha Temple, a distance of about 3 km. The Deities stay at Gundicha temple for 9 days and return to the main temple on the 10th day. This is called Bahuda-yatra, return cart festival. The festivals—cart and return cart—are the only opportunities in the year that non-Hindus have to see the Deity of Lord Jagannatha.

The chariot of Lord Jagannatha, known as **Nandighosh**, is 45 feet (13.7 m) high and has 18 wheels. It is covered with brightly colored yellow and red fabric and a wheel rests on top of the car. The chariot of Lord Balarama is 44 feet (13.2 m) high and has 16 wheels. It is called **Taladwaja**, and the fabric on the roof is red and green. It is crowned with a Tala fruit. Lady Subhadra's cart is 43 feet (12.9 m) high and has 14 wheels. It is named **Padmadhwaj** or Darpadalan and is covered with red and black fabric. There are side deities on each of the carts. With the exception of the *kalasa* (the pinnacles on top of the chariots), the 14 side deities, and the wooden charioteers and horses, which are all reused, the carts are newly constructed each year according to strict and ancient specifications.

The **Pahandi**, or procession of the Deities from the temple to the carts, is the most colorful part of the festival. First Sudarsana Cakra is brought from the temple and put on the chariot of Lady Subhadra. Then Balabhadra, Subhadra, and finally Jagannatha are each placed on Their respective carts. The Deities are extremely heavy, and They take many strong men to move them, step by step. The king of Orissa then sweeps the street in front of the carts with a golden handled broom.

There is no steering system for the carts. If a cart does not reach the Gundicha Temple the first day by sundown, it continues its journey on the next day. This is what usually happens, as the streets are usually so crowded with devotees and pilgrims that each movement of the Deities takes longer than expected. The carts stop their movement at sundown and continue the next day. This is the Lord's merciful way of allowing devotees, even non-Hindus, to take Their *darshana*.

Annually, after the festival, the carts are broken up and the wood is made into sacred relics.

Other Festivals

Chandana-yatra (April) is when the processional Deities are taken for a boat ride in the Narendra Tank after They are bathed in sandalwood (chandan) scented water. The festival lasts 42 days. The first 21 days are called Baha Chandana. During these days Rama, Krishna, Madana Mohana, Laksmi, and Saraswati are taken on boat rides. The last 21 days are called Bhittara Chandana, and this festival takes place in the temple.

Snana-yatra is when the main Deities are bathed. This is done on Jyestha Purnima. The main Deities along with Sudarsana are bought to the *snana-mandapa* in a procession called Pahandi, and around mid-day 108 pots of water are poured on the Deities. The Deities go back into the temple in a procession and stay in seclusion for 15 days, as They are said to have caught a cold during this bathing ceremony and need the seclusion in order to recuperate.

The word Anavasara is used when Sri Jagannathaji cannot be seen in the temple. During His recovery and convalescence, He is removed to His private apartment and offered special healing foodstuffs. During the **Anavasara festival** it is said that Lord Jagannatha suffers from fever and is offered an infusion of "drugs" in the form of soups and fruit juices.

The body of Lord Jagannatha, having been washed, is in need of yearly re-painting. This is known as **Anga-raga**. It takes about two weeks to complete the repairs of Lord Jagannatha's body. The renovation festival is also called **Nava-yauvana**, which indicates that the Jagannatha Deity is being fully restored to youth.

Nava-kalevara is when Lord Jagannatha gets a new body. This takes place when ever a double Asarha occurs in a year. This usually happens every 8, 11, or 19 years (1996).

ISKCON

There are two ISKCON centers (06752-23740) in Jagannatha Puri. One is located in the Swarga Dwara area by Haridasa Thakura's *samadhi*. This is where Bhaktivinode Thakura's had his *bhajana kutir*. A temple and a guesthouse are being built there.

There is another ISKCON center, located about 5 km from the Swarga Dwara area past the Hans Coco Palms Hotel. The land itself is very nice, and Gaura-Nitai Deities are installed there. However, there are very few facilities available for pilgrims as of January, 1996.

Ticket Agents

Gandhara International (06752-3077) is located by the fishing village on Chakratirtha Road, by the hotel of the same name, in the eastern part of town. This is a discount ticket place and does a lot of business. They can arrange for tickets to most destinations in India and international tickets as well.

Heritage Tours (06752-3656), located at the Mayfair Hotel, is a reliable ticket agent that has been recommended to me by people who live in Puri, but their prices are higher than Gandhara.

Medical and Dentist

SCB Medical College is supposed to be the best in Orissa.

Dr S K Mahapatra, near the Rajalaxmi Medicine Store and Jaduani Library, Heragohiri Sahi area, was recommended to me as a good dentist. When I went to him, he was good at one repair and not so good at another, but in an emergency he will do.

Where to Shop

Sudarsana Das Mahapatra at *Goldie Photo Studio* on Temple Road, has nice photos of Lord Jagannatha. He is one of the head priests during the Ratha-yatra and takes the pictures himself. If you walk out of the main entrance of the Jagannatha Temple and continue to walk straight down Temple Road, his shop is about an eight minute walk on the right.

Sun Craft, run by Gajendra Maharana, has a good collection of Jagannatha Deities, stickers, and paintings. He can also help you get an excellent variety of Jagannatha *prasada*, if you arrange it a day in advance. It is located on Armstrong Road not far from the railroad station in the Tini Konia Bagicha area. Mr Maharana is an honest man and can help you get many different items made in Orissa. For items that he does not manufacture the prices can be above average, but the quality is guaranteed.

The small town of **Pipli** has many shops that sell applique works, including fancy colorful wall hangings and mirror work umbrellas. This is where most of the applique items you see all over Puri are made. It is located halfway between Puri and Bhubaneswara.

Raghurajpur, which is 14 km from Puri, is famous for Patta Chitra, or leaf paintings. You can get the paintings much cheaper here then anywhere else, but most likely you will need a translator.

Warning

The ocean current can be very strong in Puri and it is not unusual for people to drown here. So be careful when you go swimming. It is best not to swim alone.

Where To Stay

There are a few main areas where there are hotels along the beach. The northeast part, near the fishing village, on or just off Chakra Tirtha Rd, is where most of the budget hotels are located and is a popular area for western tourists. You have to be careful about swimming at this end of the beach because there is a canal that carries raw sewerage right into the ocean.

Another area is the main Indian tourist area, which is by the Puri Hotel, near Beach Sea Road. Most of the people staying in this area are Indians. It is very crowded with tourists and salesmen and therefore not too conducive for a peaceful and relaxing rest on the shore. Five salesmen may approach you (very aggressively) in the two-minute walk from your hotel to the beach.

There are also a few hotels in the southwest part of town. It is quiet there and the sea water is clean and rarely do you ever see a salesman, but there is no shortage of fisherman who like to use the beach as a toilet. So the beach is not very clean.

Where To Stay – Low End

Sree Chaitanya Saraswata Gaudiya Matha Temple in the Gourbar Sahi area has a nice little guesthouse. It has rooms with bath for Rs 90 a night. It is behind their temple by the Hotel Raj, on the road between the Birla Guesthouse and Tota Gopinatha temple. It is a suggested clean place. A very cheap place is the *Purushottama Gaudiya Math* in the Swarga

Dwara area by Haridasa Thakura's *samadhi*. It has very basic rooms with common bath for about Rs 20 a night. It is on the road a minute from the beach. Both these places are ashrams with a strict no smoking rule and other restrictions as far as no meat, alcohol, drugs, etc.

The *Bharatsevashram Sanga*, near Swarga Dwara, and the *Vagla Dharamsala* near the hospital on Grand Road are basic cheap dharamsalas.

Hotel Subhadra (3686), on Grand Road, is a decent low end place in the center of town.

Where To Stay – Chakra Tirtha Rd

Most of the budget hotels for travelers are at the end of Chakra Tirtha Road, by the fishing village. Most western tourists stay here.

Hotel Dreamland is a popular place for travelers with rooms for Rs 60/70. It has a pleasant garden and is located slightly back from the main road, so it affords a bit of peace. The *Bay View Hotel* is a good quiet place with rooms for Rs 65 to Rs 110, most of which have private baths.

Hotel Shankar International (23637) is a good place, right on the beach with an assortment of rooms from Rs 130 to Rs 350. It has a garden and is a popular place.

The well-managed *Z Hotel* (pronounced Zed) (22554) is an old former palace. This place has a good atmosphere and is recommended. It has rooms with common bath for Rs 85/160 and Rs 250 for a large room with a bath. It is very popular with travelers, therefore it is often full. It has large, breezy rooms, many of them with a seaview, and also a roof terrace with an agreeable view of the sea.

The *Santana Lodge*, at the end of the fishing village, is a recommended budget place that has rooms with common bath for Rs 50/70 and Rs 85 with bath. The *Hotel Sri Balaji* is a good place with rooms for Rs 60 to Rs 100.

Hotel Repose, on Chakra Tirtha Road, Sea Beach, is Rs 200 for a downstairs room and Rs 250 for an upstairs room. It is not such a good value. *Hotel Gandhara* (06752-4117), Chakra Tirtha Road by the fishing village has clean rooms for Rs 100/120 with bath. There is a good discount travel agent in front of the hotel.

Where To Stay – Middle

The *Birla Guest House*, Gourbar Sahi, located in a peaceful location in the southwest part of town, right next to the ocean, is one of the best values in town. You get a nice clean double room on the first floor for Rs 150. On the second floor there are rooms with hot water that have a private balcony with a great view of the ocean, and a living room and kitchen for Rs 375 to Rs 475. The food served at the hotel is 100% vegetarian and the manager is a friendly and helpful person. You can order special meals in advance. This place is highly recommended if you want to be away from the action. This place is used mainly by middle-class Indians. This place has a strict no drug policy and they are selective about who they allow to stay.

Hotel Raj, near the Birla Guest House, has nice rooms, which have a small balcony facing the ocean and private bathrooms with hot water for Rs 225/250. You could use this place as a backup if the Birla Guest House is full.

Vijoya International (22702), on Chakra Tirtha Road by the ocean, is a well appointed and recommended place. It is a good hotel with rooms for Rs 400 for a double and Rs 700 for a room with A/C. The rooms are nice and have hot water. Check out time is 8 am though. The *Ho-*

tel Samudra (22705), right next to the Vijoya International, is a good place on the beach with rooms from Rs 250/400 to Rs 555 with A/C. Both of these hotels are good places to stay, but they are right by the open sewage, a canal that flows into the ocean, so it is a bad place to swim. Nearby is the *OTDC Panthanivas Tourist Bungalow* (22562), which is right on the sea with doubles for Rs 230/290 and Rs 450 with A/C. It is a decent place to stay and each room has an ocean view from the balcony.

On Chakra Tirtha Rd is the *Holiday Inn* (23782), which has nice double with bath for Rs 200 or Rs 250 for a room on the second floor with a sea view.

The *Puri Hotel* (22114), on Marine Parade, is a six story place with rooms for Rs 150/180 upward. A double room with a balcony and an excellent view of the ocean is Rs 400. It is a good value, but it is located in a crowded area. It is popular with middle-class Indians. It has a free minibus that picks up people in the morning at the railway station. There is a 24-hour checkout. The *Sea Hawk Hotel*, at the other end of the road from the Puri Hotel, is a decent place right next to the sea, near Hari Dasa Thakur's samadhi.

Hotel Holiday Resort (22430), Chakra Tirtha Rd, is a nice place that has doubles with balconies overlooking the sea for Rs 430 and Rs 830 with A/C. There is a 10% service charge added. All rooms have balconies overlooking the sea, attached bath, TV, and telephone. Checkout time is 8 am. The *Hotel Golden Palace* (23192) is right on the beach and has rooms for Rs 200 on the ground floor and Rs 275 for a room on the second floor with a balcony.

Where To Stay – High End

The *Mayfair Beach Resort* (24041) is a beautiful newish hotel. It has 34 air-conditioned cottages, a private lawn, a swimming pool, and a health club. The manager was very friendly, and the service seemed excellent. The cottages are Rs 1200 and suites are Rs 1800, plus there is a 20% tax. It is the best place in town.

The *South Eastern Railway Hotel*, (22440), Chakra Tirtha Rd, is an old place with old-world atmosphere. It is a typical British Raj type place with a large verandah and a spacious lawn. Normal rooms are Rs 420/650 and A/C rooms are Rs 475/700.

The *Nilachal Ashok* (23639), Raj Bhavan, VIP Rd, is a comfortable place set back from the beach and road. It has rooms with A/C for Rs 500/750.

Hans Coco Palms (22638) is a high quality hotel with A/C rooms. To get there you may have to ask for the Prachi Hotel, which is its old name. It is modern, but some of the rooms are a little small. The best thing about the hotel is that it is in a good quiet area where the sea water is not polluted. Rooms are Rs 900/1100 and deluxe rooms are Rs 2200.

Sterling Resort (24857), by the Bhargavi River, 7 km from town, is a new high class place. It is not far from the ISKCON temple.

Places To Eat

There are few pure vegetarian places in Puri, as most of the residents are sustained by a diet of seafood.

At the *Birla Guest House* they serve vegetarian meals with no onion or garlic. It is a good place to stay and eat, but if you are going to eat there you have to let them know in advance so they can prepare everything properly.

You can also order meals in advance at some of the Gaudiya Math Temples for a donation.

Travel

Air The nearest airport is 62 km away at Bhubaneswar. There are Indian Airlines flights from there to Delhi, Calcutta, Hyderabad, Madras, and Bombay. **Indian Airlines**, Bhubaneswar City (400-533), Airport (401-084), Reservations (402-380).

Train Puri has direct train service to and from Calcutta, New Delhi, Ahmedabad Visakhapatnam, Vijayawada, and Tirupati. The Neelachal Express #8475 (9.15 am) and the Puri-New Delhi Exp #2815 (9.15 am), take 32 hours to reach **Delhi**, and the Utkal/Kalinga train takes 40 hours. Departing from New Delhi station the Puri-New Delhi Exp (6.30 am), Neelachal Exp (6.30 am), and the Purushottam Exp (10.30 pm) all take 32 hours. The once a week Rajasthani Express (Fri, 5 pm) takes 25 hours to go from Delhi to Bhubaneswar.

The Howrah-Puri Express is a good, fast train that departs from Howrah Station in **Calcutta** at 10 pm and arrives in Puri at 8.10 am. This train #8008 returns from Puri at 6 pm and arrives in Calcutta at 5.30 am. The Jagannath Express #8410 leaves Puri at 9.10 pm and arrives in Calcutta 11 hours later.

There are several trains to **Bhubaneswar**, but the buses are faster. The train takes two hours and the bus takes one and a half. If you are going to or from South India you can change trains at Bhubaneswar or at Khurda Road junction (44 km from Puri), which is south of Bhubaneswar on the Madras-Calcutta main line.

The Puri-Tirupati Exp #8479 (9.45 am, 33 hr) is a direct train to **Tirupati**.

Train to all over India can be gotten from Bhubaneswar. From Bhubaneswar there is a daily train to **Madras**, two trains a week to **Bangalore** (Wed, Thurs), four a week to **Kochi** (Fri, Sat, Sun, Mon) and on Tuesday the Guwahati-Trivandrum Express goes to **Thiruvananthapuram**. There are five trains a day to Balasore, near **Remuna**. There is a daily train to Agra and three trains a week to Varanasi. To get to **Bombay** you have to take the Delhi train to Kharagpur Junction, just north of the Orissan border, then wait five and a half hours, and then get the Bombay Mail #8002 (9.55 pm) coming from Calcutta. The total traveling time is about 47 hours.

You can make reservations for all class tickets at the station or for second class tickets only at the city booking office, opposite the police station on Grand Rd. Especially during the pilgrim season, trains should be booked as far in advance as possible. To get a tourist quota ticket I went to the station manager who referred me to the man in charge of ticket reservations.

Be prepared for the extremely aggressive taxi and rickshaw drivers when you arrive at the station. They will try to get at least three times the normal price. Whatever price you are quoted, offer one third that and you will still be over-paying.

Bus The bus stand is by the Gundicha Mandira on Grand Rd.

The Canter minibuses to and from Bhubaneswara are quicker than the larger buses. Minibuses from Bhubaneswara to Puri (1½ hr) leave regularly from the Baramunda (New) Bus Stand, the Old Bus Stand, and from by the petrol station opposite the Ashok Hotel from 5.30 am to 9.30 pm. To get to Bhubaneswara takes at least two hours by train, and only an hour and a half by bus. The non-stop buses, which stop once or twice, are the quickest.

There are regular hourly buses to Konark (1 hr). Some of the private buses leave from the junction of Grand Rd and Hospital Rd.

Saksi Gopala Temple

This is an important Krishna temple that is dedicated to Saksi Gopala. Saksi Gopala means the witness Gopala. This Deity was originally in Vrindavana.

The story of the Deity is that once there were two Vidyanagara Brahmin, one elderly and the other young. After touring many places of pilgrimage, the two Brahmins finally reached Vrinda-vana. In reciprocation for the service that the young Brahmin rendered, the older Brahmin offered him his daughter in marriage. He promised this before the Go-pala Deity in Vrindavana. Some time after they returned to Vidyanagara, the young Brahmin reminded the older Brah-min about the promise he made. Due to family considerations, the elderly Brah-min said he could not remember the promise. The younger Brahmin then re-turned to Vrindavana and told the whole story to Gopalaji. Being obliged by the young man's devotional service and atti-tude, Sri Gopala followed him to South India, where He bore witness of the prom-ise of the elderly Brahmin. Hence, by the grace of the Lord, the marriage was per-formed. The Deity was later moved to Cuttack, then to the Jagannatha temple and finally to its present location.

Both Sri Caitanya and Srila Prabhu-pada visited this temple. Although Srila Prabhupada was accompanied by a group of western disciples, the current strictly enforced temple policy is that non-Hin-dus are not allowed inside. So if you are not an Indian there is little hope of see-ing the Deity, which I have been told is very beautiful. This temple is 10 km west of Jagannatha Puri. You can take a train to this spot, as it is a stop on the Puri-Bhubaneswara line. You can also take a bus or a taxi.

KONARK

Population: 11,000, STD Code 06758

Konark, also known as Arka-Tirtha, is known for its temple of Lord Surya, the sun-god. It is situated on the seashore, 33 km north of Puri and 64 km from Bhubaneswar. It was constructed of black stone in the beginning of the 13th cen-tury, and it is considered one of the most vivid architectural showpieces of Hindu India. Despite the fact that the 'Black Pagoda' is in ruins, the remaining porch area and other structures of this temple complex remain as a crown jewel of Oris-san art work.

Mistaking the sea at Puri for the Ya-muna River, Sri Caitanya jumped in and was washed by the ocean 33 km north to the Konark area, where an astonished fisherman caught Him in his net.

Sun Temple

This temple was built in the 13th cen-tury by the Orissan King Raja Narasim-hadeva I. It took 1,200 workmen over 16 years to build. It is believed that the temple was no longer used from the early 17th century when the temple was des-ecrated by Muslim invaders. In 1904 the sand around the temple base was cleared.

The story of the temple is that Samba, the son of Krishna, was cursed to suffer from leprosy for 12 years. Because he was cured by Surya, the Sun God, he built a temple dedicated to Surya.

This impressive temple resembles a **huge chariot** with **24 huge wheels** be-ing pulled by **seven horses**. Great pairs of large intricately carved wheels were carved on both sides of the 4m high platform that the temple is on. There are two rows of 12 wheels on each side of the temple. Some say the wheels represent the 24 hours in a day and others say the 12 months. The seven horses are said to symbolize the seven days of the week. There is a dancing hall here, an audience hall and a high tower. The main tower, which has since collapsed, was 220 feet (70 m) high. The *jagmohana* (porch) is over 120 feet (39 m) high and is filled in and fortified with rocks to keep it from collapsing. Both the tower and porch were built on a high platform. The temple is covered with many intricately carved sculptures. This temple was once called the Black Pagoda by sailors because it was supposed to draw ships into the shore and cause shipwrecks.

There are three impressive chlorite **figures of Surya** facing different directions to catch the sun at dawn, noon and sunset. The three statues of Surya change their facial expressions from wakefulness in the morning (south) to weariness towards the end of the day (north). The main entrance has large statues of two stone lions crushing elephants. There is a small shrine dedicated to **Mayadevi**, the wife of Surya, in the southwest corner of the enclosure. At the north part of the enclosure, to the right of the entrance, are a group of elephants. At the south side is a group of horses rearing and trampling men. Between the entrance and the main part of the temple is an intricately carved dancing hall. All over the base, walls and roof of the temple are intricate carvings. You can climb down to the inner sanctum of the temple at the west side of the temple. All over the temple there are many erotic carvings likes the ones in Khajuraho.

There is also a temple containing the **nine planets**: Sun, Moon, Mars, Mercury, Jupiter, Venus, Saturn, Rahu and Ketu. It is located to the right of the main entrance, before you enter the complex. To visit this temple in its entirety takes about 2 hours.

Information

There is a small museum on the main road (10 am to 5 pm, closed Friday), which has many sculptures found during the temple excavation. You can purchase the Archaeological Survey of India's *Sun Temple-Konark* here for Rs 10. It is not sold at the temple itself.

Most evenings the temple is floodlit up to 9.30 pm.

The **Konark Dance Festival**, featuring classical Indian dancing, is in November. There is another similar dance festival in February.

Konark is a major tourist spot and fighting away the hawkers and vendors can be a tedious task. These people will charge you at least double, if not triple, the normal price for the items they sell, except the booklet about the place.

There is a nice **quiet beach** about 3 km from the temple. The currents can be strong here, so swimming can be dangerous. Not far from the beach is a pond where Krishna's son Samba is said to have been cured from leprosy. Every year during the full moon phase in the month of Magha (Jan/Feb) there is a festival called Magha Saptami mela. People bathe in the pond at night and then watch the sun rise over the sea the next morning.

Where To Stay

The *Labanya Lodge*, in a quiet area, is a popular place with travelers and has rooms with common bath for Rs 65 or Rs 80. The *Lodging Sunrise* is the cheapest place in the area.

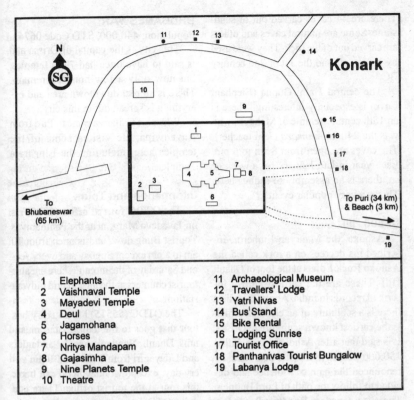

1	Elephants	11	Archaeological Museum
2	Vaishnaval Temple	12	Travellers' Lodge
3	Mayadevi Temple	13	Yatri Nivas
4	Deul	14	Bus Stand
5	Jagamohana	15	Bike Rental
6	Horses	16	Lodging Sunrise
7	Nritya Mandapam	17	Tourist Office
8	Gajasimha	18	Panthanivas Tourist Bungalow
9	Nine Planets Temple	19	Labanya Lodge
10	Theatre		

The *Yatri Niwas* is a good value with nice clean rooms for Rs 90. Orissa Tourism's *Travellers' Lodge* has A/C rooms for Rs 225; however, the rooms are not well-maintained.

The *OTDC Panthaniwas* (8831), opposite the main temple entrance, is in a good location and is a clean, well-maintained place that has rooms with hot water for Rs 150 for a double and Rs 300 for an A/C room.

How To Get There

Konark is located 65 km from Bhubaneswar and 35 km north of Puri on Marine Drive, right next to the ocean. There are regular buses to and from Puri that take about an hour. From Bhubaneswar, with a change of buses at Pipli, it takes from two to four hours. There is a direct tourist bus that leaves from the town bus stand in Bhubaneswar at 10 am. There is a daily tour bus that goes to Konark from Puri and a tour bus from Bhubaneswar (Tues to Sat). You can take a taxi from Puri for about Rs 400 round-trip.

PLACES AROUND BHUBANESWAR & PURI

Udayagiri and Khandagiri Caves

The caves here are ancient (over 2000 years old) Jain caves located about 7 km west of Bhubaneswar. There are two sets of caves carved into two opposite hills.

There are 44 caves carved out of sandstone. Some are natural caves and others are carved out of the rock. They were used by monks around the 1st or 2nd century BC.

The central Hathi Gupha (Elephant Cave) is especially interesting. There is an 18th century temple of Mahavir, who was the 24th *tirthankara* (Jain teacher). The caves are open from 8 am to 6 pm. Each year in late January for a week or so, there is an assembly of sadhus here. This is a very popular event.

Dhauli Hill

Ashoka, the Mauryan Emperor, inscribed his decrees on a rock called the **Ashoka Rock Edicts** at the foot of Dhauli Hill. These are the earliest known inscribed records in India. Above the edicts there is a sculpture of an elephant which is the earliest known sculpture in Orissa. It is said that after Ashoka's army killed 150,000 people in a battle near here, he renounced the path of violence and decided to follow the path of Lord Buddha. There is a Japanese Buddhist **Peace Pagoda** on top of this hill. The temple of Lord Dhaveleswar is at the top of the hill above the white-domed pagoda.

This hill is 8 km from Bhubaneswar. The OTDC organized tours are a convenient way to visit this spot. If you don't travel in your own vehicle, be prepared to walk about 2 km from where the public bus lets you off.

Nandankanan Zoo

This zoo has a lion safari, white tigers, and elephant rides. There is an exotic Botanical Garden. It is 20 km from Bhubaneswar, from where there are hourly buses to reach the zoo. The OTDC bus tours from Puri and Bhubaneswar come here as well.

BHUBANESWAR

Population: 440,000, STD Code 0674

This city is the capital of Orissa and is said to have once had 7000 temples, but now only a few hundred remain. There is no real downtown area and everything is spread out in this city.

When Sri Caitanya came to Puri from Navadwipa, He visited some of the temples here, including the Lingaraja Temple.

Information and Tours

The **OTDC tourist office** (50099) is on Jayadeva Marg, near the Panthanivas Tourist Bungalow, and is open from 10 am to 5 pm except Sunday and every second Saturday of the month. There are also tourist counters at the airport and railway station.

The OTDC (55515) has a luxury bus tour that goes to the temples and museums, Dhauli, Nandankanan, Khandagiri, and Udayagiri from 9 am to 5.30 pm every day, except Monday. You can book this tour at the tourist office. There is a daily OTDC tour to Puri and Konark, which stops at Pipli village for applique. It departs from the railway station at 8.30 am (9 am from the Panthanivas Hotel) and returns at 6 pm. It has a good guide.

The useful **Government of India tourist office** (412-203), BJB Nagar, around the corner from the Panthanivas Hotel, has an assortment of leaflets that can be helpful to plan your journey around the area.

General Information

The GPO is by the bus stand. Genesis Travel (56493), at the Jajati Hotel, is reputed to be a good and reliable travel agent.

You can **change money** at the State Bank of India on Raj Path, opposite New

Market. Most banks are closed on Monday.

Shopping

Most shops close from noon to 4 pm every day and Thursday all day.

The Modern Book Department, New Market, has a good selection of books on Orissa. You can get good fabrics at Handloom Weavers' Co-operative, Hall No. 2, West Market Building, which is closed on Sunday.

Utkalika, the Orissa State Emporium at East Tower Market Building, has a good selection of quality Orissan items, but may be a little more expensive than other shops. Most of the year, however, the government emporiums offer some discount, and the quality is guaranteed.

Bindu-sarovara Tank

It is said that Lord Siva established this tank as a place of pilgrimage by bringing water from all the holy places. Taking bath here and drinking the water of this lake is said to cure any disease of the stomach. Lord Caitanya took bath in this lake when He first came from Bengal to Puri. It is located right next to the Lingaraja Temple. A pilgrimage to Bhubaneswar is supposed to start with a bath here. On the eastern bank is the Ananta Vasudeva Temple, which is dedicated to Krishna and Balarama.

The Lingaraja deity is brought to the pavilion in the middle of the tank and ritually bathed during the annual Car Festival (Ashokastami). The best time to come here is around sunrise.

Temples

Most of the temples are located near the Bindu-sarovara Tank, which is about two km south of the city center. Lingaraja and Vital Duel Temples are located west of the tank. Parasumaresvara and Muktesvara temples are east of the tank. The Rajrani and Brahmesvara Temples are a ten to fifteen-minute walk east of the Muktesvara Temple.

Lingaraja Temple (11th century)

The presiding deity is the *svayambhu linga*, Hari-Hara Linga, which is half Siva and half Vishnu. He is also named Tribhuvaneswara, the Lord of the three worlds. The *linga* of Lingaraja, or Krittivasas, is an uncarved block of granite 8 feet in diameter raised 8 inches above the ground. The Siva linga is bathed daily with water, milk and *bhang*. There are many other deities in the temple. In the northeast corner of the temple there is a deity of Parvati.

The main tower is 55 metres (180 feet) high. The temple area is about 150 square metres. The present temple was built between 1090 to 1104, but parts of the temple are over 1400 years old. Tradition says that one should first visit this temple before going to Puri. Sri Caitanya Mahaprabhu came here before going to Puri.

There is a four-day chariot festival every Mar/April when Lingaraja is drawn on his chariot to the Ramesvara Temple.

Non-Hindus are not allowed in this temple, and this rule is strictly enforced. There is a 20 foot high **viewing platform** along the northern wall of the temple, and from this vantage point you can get a good view of the temple compound. You will be asked for a donation at the platform and shown a book to show that some people gave over Rs 1000, but Rs 5 should be more than enough. This temple is immediately south of Bindu Sagar.

Muktesvara Temple

Built in the 10th century, this small

elegant temple has been described as the most exquisitely ornamented temple in Bhubaneswar. It has an 11m (35 feet) high tower. The sandstone carvings are the most notable feature of this temple. It is also known for its ornamental gateway, carved dwarves, and intricate motif carvings of a smiling lion, adorned with beaded tassels in its mouth. Muktesvara means the Lord who bestows freedom through yoga. The **Siddeswara Temple** is on the same grounds and has a Ganesh deity.

The small **Marichi Kund**, between the Mukesvara Temple and the road, is known to cure infertility in women. It is a pleasant place to sit for awhile.

Parasurameswara Temple

This temple is the oldest Siva temple in Bhubaneswar, built in the late 7th century. There are many intricate carvings on this temple. It is close to the Bhubaneswar to Puri road, on the east side of Bindu-sarovara, northeast of the Lingaraja temple. It is the best preserved and most impressive of Bhubaneswar's early temples. It has interesting carvings of elephant and horse processions and intricately carved windows. In the corner of the courtyard is the **Sahasra-linga**, which is 1000 small *lingas* joined together.

Raj Rani Temple

The Raj Rani Temple (11th century), which is surrounded by a nice garden is no longer used for worship. This temple was dedicated to **Lord Brahma** and is known for its well-carved tower. It is about a km east of the main road. It is one of the later Bhubaneswar temples.

Around the temple are carvings of the eight *dikpalas* (temple guards), who protect the temple from the different directions. They are eight important demigods.

They are **Indra** (east) the head of the demigods, **Agni** (southeast) god of fire, **Yamaraja** (south) god of death, **Nirritti** (southwest), **Varuna** (west) god of water, **Vayu** (northwest) god of air, **Kubera** (north) god of wealth, and **Isana** (northeast).

Brahmeshwara Temple

This temple was built around 1050 and is a Siva-linga temple with active worship. It is known for its intricately carved sculptures. The main tower is over 18m high. It is about a km east of the main road, a good walk from the Raj Rani Temple. On the north wall of the porch is a carving of Laksmi.

Vaital Deul Temple

This interesting 8th century temple is dedicated to **Chamunda (Kali)**. She wears a necklace of skulls and is shown as the eight-armed slayer of the buffalo demon. Her necklace of skulls and the corpse she is sitting on are usually hidden by her robes. In her arms she holds a snake, a bow, a shield, a trident, a thunderbolt and an arrow with which she is piercing the neck of the demon, thus displaying the most terrifying aspect of the goddess Kali.

This temple is close to Bindu Sagar, and it has some intricate exterior carvings. To get a good view of the temple's interior, a flashlight (torch) is needed.

Orissa State Museum

This museum has a collection of religious sculptures, weapons, coins, and musical instruments. It also has a good collection of antique paintings and palmleaf manuscripts in a small room at the end of the corridor on the first floor.

It is located at the top of Gautam Nagar (Lewis Road), not far from the

Hotel Ashok. It is open Tues to Sun, 10 am to 1.30 pm and 2.30 to 5 pm.

ISKCON Temple

The beautifully built ISKCON temple (413-517) is located on National Highway No 5, Nayapali. The Deities in the temple are Krishna Balarama, Jagannatha, Baladeva and Subhadra, and Gaura-Nitai. There is also a new Radha-Krishna temple. Srila Prabhupada laid the cornerstone for this temple in February 1977, and it was finished in 1992.

There is a small guesthouse here with rooms that have attached bathrooms. These rooms are not always available, but they are quite nice if you can get one. To stay here you have to follow the ashram rules. There is a fairly basic vegetarian restaurant here.

Where To Stay – Lower

The *Yatri Niwas*, Cuttack Rd, has dorm beds for Rs 20 and is like a youth hostel. The *Venus Niwas*, Cuttack Rd, is a good place that has rooms with bath for Rs 60/70. It has 24 hour checkout time. *Hotel Janpath* is a recommended good valued place having rooms with bath for Rs 40/50.

The *Pushpak* (50896), Kalpana Square, is a decent value, having large rooms with bath for a reasonable price. *Bhagwat Niwas* (411-545), 9 Buddha Nagar, behind the Pushpak, is well managed. It has basic, but clean, economical rooms for Rs 60/90 and Rs 200 for an air-cooled room. The *Hotel Padma* (51198), Kalpana Square, is a new place that has rooms with bath for Rs 100/120.

The *Bhubaneswar Hotel* (51977), Cuttack Rd, on the east side of the railway station, is a popular place with nice clean rooms with hot water for Rs 90/140 and rooms with A/C for Rs 250/400.

Where To Stay – Middle

The popular *Tourist Guest House* (400-857) is a good place having comfortable rooms with bath for Rs 175/225. The *Hotel Natraj* (54842) has rooms for Rs 175/200 and Rs 3250/375 with A/C. The *OTDC Panthanivas Tourist Bungalow* (54515), Jayadev Nagar, is nicely located in close proximity to the ancient temples. It has rooms with bath and hot water for Rs 200 or R 400 with A/C, but there is an 8 am checkout time.

The *Hotel Anarkali,* Station Square, is a good place with good-valued, standard rooms. *Meghdoot* (55802), 5-B Sahid Nagar, has standard rooms, as well as fancy rooms with wall to wall carpeting and bathtubs. It is good value, but it is a bit out of the way.

Where To Stay – Higher

Hotel Keshari (408-593), 113 Station Square, has rooms with hot water and TV for Rs 450/520 and A/C rooms for Rs 675/800. It is a recommended place.

The five-star *New Kenilworth Hotel* (411-723, fax 456-147), 86/A-1 Gautam Nagar, in the center of town, is a recommended place with a swimming pool and book shop. Rooms are Rs 1075/1275.

The *Hotel Prachi Bhubaneswar* (402-366, fax 403-287) has rooms for Rs 850/1000 This hotel has good facilities, including a pool and tennis court. The ITDC *Hotel Kalinga Ashok* (53318) is a modern place with rooms for $20/40. The *Hotel Swosti* (404-178, fax 407-524), 100 Janpath, a five minute walk from the railway station, is a highly recommend place with rooms from Rs 1050/1550.

Where To Stay – Luxury

The five-star *Oberoi Bhubaneswar* (440-890, telex 6348, fax 440-890), CB-1 Nayapalli, located on over 12 acres of

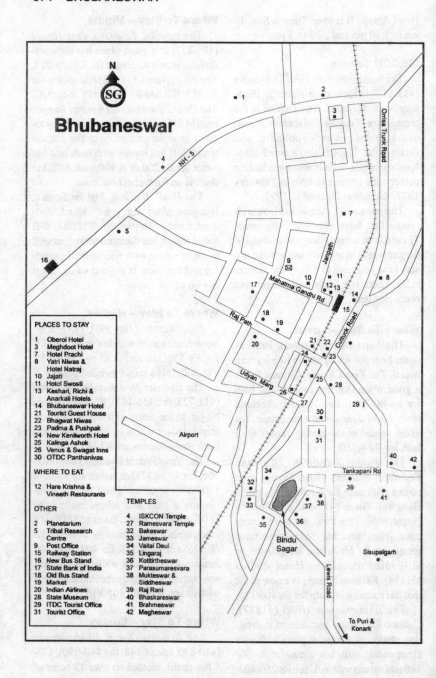

Bhubaneswar

N
SG

NH - 5

Orissa Trunk Road

Janpath

Mahatma Gandhi Rd

Cuttack Road

Raj Path

Udyan Marg

Airport

Tankapani Rd

Bindu
Sagar

Sisupalgarh

Lewis Road

To Puri &
Konark

PLACES TO STAY
1   Oberoi Hotel
3   Meghdoot Hotel
7   Hotel Prachi
8   Yatri Niwas &
     Hotel Natraj
10   Jajati
11   Hotel Swosti
13   Keshari, Richi &
     Anarkali Hotels
14   Bhubaneswar Hotel
21   Tourist Guest House
22   Bhagwat Niwas
23   Padma & Pushpak
24   New Kenilworth Hotel
25   Kalinga Ashok
26   Venus & Swagat Inns
30   OTDC Panthanivas

WHERE TO EAT
12   Hare Krishna &
     Vineeth Restaurants

OTHER
2   Planetarium
5   Tribal Research
     Centre
9   Post Office
15   Railway Station
16   New Bus Stand
17   State Bank of India
18   Old Bus Stand
19   Market
20   Indian Airlines
28   State Museum
29   ITDC Tourist Office
31   Tourist Office

TEMPLES
4   ISKCON Temple
27   Ramesvara Temple
32   Bakeswar
33   Jameswar
34   Vaital Deul
35   Lingaraj
36   Kotitirtheswar
37   Parasumaresvara
38   Mukteswar &
     Siddheswar
39   Raj Rani
40   Bhaskareswar
41   Brahmeswar
42   Megheswar

land, is a excellent hotel. Rooms are $85/95. It is 4 km from city center, but is close to the airport.

Where to Eat

The Hare Krishna Restaurant (407-186), Lal Chand Market Complex, Station Square, has excellent food, but is not cheap. It is the most highly recommended place in town. It is managed by initiated ISKCON devotees.

The *Venus Inn*, 217 Bapuji Nagar (2nd floor), is a good South Indian vegetarian restaurant. There is a vegetarian restaurant at the *ISKCON Temple*.

How To Get There

Air There are Indian Airlines (400-533) flights to Hyderabad (Wed, Fri, Sun), Nagpur, Calcutta (Tues-Fri, Sun), Delhi (daily), Varanasi, Bombay, and Madras (Tues, Thur). The airport is very close to town (Rs 70 by taxi). If you have an early morning flight, it is a good idea to have your hotel arrange a taxi the night before and pay a little more to avoid the morning inconvenience of finding a taxi at that time. The Indian Airline office (400-544/33, Reservations 402-380) is on Rajpath, by the bus stand.

Train Bhubaneswar is on the main Calcutta to Madras line so many trains stop here. The Coromandel Express leaves Calcutta at 2.30 pm and arrives in Bhubaneswar around 10 pm. The return train leaves about 4 am and arrives in Calcutta at 12 noon. The Howrah-Puri Express departs from Howrah at 10 pm and arrives in Bhubaneswara at 5.40 am the next morning and goes on to Puri, arriving there at 8.10 am. This train returns to Calcutta, leaving Puri at 6 pm, Bhubaneswar at 8.10 pm and arrives in Calcutta at 5.30 am the next morning. There

are other slower trains between Calcutta and Bhubaneswar.

The Howrah-Bangalore Mail #2611 (Wed, 6.30 am, 22 hr) and Guwahati Bangalore Exp #2674 (Mon, Thur, 6.30 am, 22 hr) go to Bangalore. The Coromandel Exp #2841 (daily, 10 pm, 20 hr) is a good train going to Madras.

There are direct trains to Delhi (25-42 hr), Agra (39 hr), Remuna (5 daily, 5 hr), and Varanasi (21 hr). The Rajdhani Express (5 pm, 25 hr) departs from Delhi one day a week on Friday to Bhubaneswar. The Puri-New Delhi Exp #2815 (Mon, Wed, Thur, Sat, 10.50 am, 30 hr) is a good train to Delhi.

Bus The best way to get from Bhubaneswar to Puri is on one of the Canter minibuses that leave from the old bus station in the center of town, the new bus stand, and from the petrol station opposite the Ashok Hotel. They take a little more than an hour to get to Puri. There are also larger buses that go Puri, but they are slower than the minibuses. It is best to get an express bus to Puri, which make only one stop en route. There is a direct bus to Konark at 10 am (1½ hr, City Bus Stand). If you don't get the direct bus, you can take a Puri buses to Pipli and from there get another bus to Konark.

Most of the long-distance buses depart from the new bus stand (Baramunda Bus Stand) which is about 5 km from downtown on the main road to Calcutta. There are buses to Calcutta, Cuttack (10 hr), and other places in Orissa. Buses to Puri also leave from this station.

REMUNA

The **Kshira Chora Gopinath Temple** is located in Remuna. It is a small town located nine km east of Balasore (Baleshwar), about halfway between Calcutta and Puri. The name "Remuna" is derived from the word "Ramaniya" which means very beautiful.

It is said that Sri Rama carved Gopinath with His arrow and that Sita worshiped this Deity in Citrakut. This Deity was brought to Remuna in the 13th century from Citrakut by King Langula Narasingha Dev, the king of Orissa. This king also arranged to have dug the two big tanks, Brajapokhari and Kutapokhari.

Gopinatha Temple

Sri Gopinatha is the Deity who stole sweet-rice for Madhavendra Puri. Being worshiped on the altar with Sri Gopinatha are Sri Madana Mohana, Sri Govinda, Radha-Rasabihari, and Caitanya Mahaprabhu with Lord Jagannatha on one side and numerous *shalagram-shilas* on the other side. Lord Gopinatha, flanked by Sri Govinda and Sri Madana Mohana, is made of black stone. Sri Gopinatha stands in bas-relief. Govinda and Madana Mohana, who were brought from Vrindavana in about 1938 by a devotee named Caitanya Dasa Babaji, are free standing.

You get delicious *kshira* here call *amrita-keli*. The Gopinatha *kshira* is a preparation of condensed milk, sugar, and cream, with a sprinkling of raisins. It comes in pots of various sizes which are personally tasted by Lord Gopinatha Himself. Sri Gopinatha is known as Kshira Chora Gopinatha because He stole and hid a pot of *kshira* out of love for Madhavendra Puri. *Chora* means thief.

The present temple was renovated by Rasikananda, after the prior temple built by King Gajapati Maharaja Langula Deva was destroyed by Muslim invaders. Rasikananda found the Gopinatha Deity in a pond 4 km from the temple, where Gopinatha was hidden to protect Him from being destroyed by the Muslim king. Rasikananda was the foremost disciple of Syamananda, who helped transport the important writings of the Goswamis from Vrindavana to Bengal. The *samadhi* tomb of Rasikananda Prabhu is near the temple.

In the temple room you will find many pictures of Caitanya Mahaprabhu's pastimes, as well as a picture of the Pancatattva over the main altar.

The *pujaris* every morning bathe and dress the Deities in full view of the congregated devotees. Each day a few hundred pilgrims come to this temple, and on Sundays up to a thousand people visit. The temple is located about a half a km from the village of Remuna. Western devotees are allowed in the temple.

During **Chandana-yatra**, the Deities are smeared with cooling sandalwood pulp *(chandana)*. The temple priests apply *chandana* to the chest of the temples' three Krishna Deities—Madana-Mohana, Govinda and Gopinatha. On **Aksaya-tritiya** the Deities' entire bodies are smeared with sandalwood.

Deity Story

Over 500 years ago Madhavendra Puri was going to Puri to get some scented sandalwood to bring to his Sri Gopal Deity in Vrindavana. When he stopped at Remuna and saw Sri Gopinath, his heart was filled with devotion and joy. When he saw the delicious *kshira* offered to the Deity he desired to taste some so he could offer the same preparation to Sri Gopal. Madhavendra Puri would only accept food that was offered to him. Because he was not offered any of the kshira he left the temple without tasting it.

After finishing the worship to Gopinath the *pujari* (priest) took rest. In a dream Gopinath told him to get up and take the pot of *kshira* that He had hidden under His garments and to give it to Madhavendra Puri. The *pujari* got up and found the sweet rice and brought it to Madhavendra Puri. The *pujari* told him "For you Sri Gopinath has stolen *kshira*. There is no other fortunate man like you." (Cc) This is how the Deity got the name Kshira Chora (thief) Gopinath.

Madhavendra Puri established an *Ashram* in Remuna and stayed there for some time. The wooden sandals of Madhavendra Puri are worshiped in this *Ashram*.

When Lord Caitanya came here, flowers from the body of the Deity fell down on His head. Sri Caitanya then danced in overwhelming joy.

In The Area

In the area is the *samadhi* of **Madhavendra Puri** (2 minutes from the temple), the *samadhi* of **Rasikananda Prabhu** (inside the Gopinatha Temple compound), and a Siva temple where Gargamuni is said to have had his *ashram*.

Near the Gopinatha temple there is a **Jagannatha temple** and a few other temples.

Where To Stay and Eat

Remuna is a very small village, so there are not many places to stay. There is a small guest house near the temple that has a few basic rooms with private bath for Rs 50. There is a guest house built by a religious lady with fairly nice facilities for those who want to stay overnight in Remuna to see the Deities.

There is a good assortment of hotels in the nearby towns of Balasore and Chandipur.

You can arrange *prasada* with the temple. There are two types of meals, one economical and the other is a little more expensive.

How To Get There

The nearest train junction to Remuna is at Balasore, which is the first major town in Orissa coming from Calcutta. You can get a night train from Calcutta that stops in Balasore in the early morning. From there you can get a taxi or bus to Remuna. If you arrive in Remuna in the morning, you can see the Deities and then catch a night train to Puri.

BALASORE AND CHANDIPUR

Balasore is the first major town in Orissa coming from Calcutta, about halfway between Calcutta and Puri. Chandipur, on the coast 16 km from Balasore, has one of the best beaches in Orissa. The tide recedes 5 km each day here. A spiritual reason to come here is that it is the nearest train junction to the Gopinatha Temple at Remuna.

You can get an **OTDC tour** from Chandipur that goes to the temples in the area. It is scheduled to leave twice daily, at 7.30 am and 1.30 pm.

Where To Stay

The *Deepak Lodging Tourist Bungalow* is a decent enough place. From the train station, go to the main road and turn left and it is on the right side, across from the cinema. There is also the *Hotel Moonlight* and *Hotel Sagarika*.

The *Hotel Swarnachuda* (06782/756001), Sahadevkhunta Rd, up from the bus stand, is a good well-managed place with rooms for Rs 150. The *Suraj* has only cheaper rooms. Top of the line is the *Hotel Torrento* (06782/63481), which is a comfortable place, three km out of town on NH5. It has large rooms, most having central A/C for Rs 375/550.

The *Panthanivas Tourist Bungalow*, in Chandipur, has rooms for Rs 240 and Rs 390 for A/C. The *Shubam Hotel* is clean and has a garden. The *Chandipur Hotel* is more basic. The *Yarica Yatri Niwas* (06782/72374) is a newish place with rooms centered around a courtyard for Rs 190 and Rs 350 with A/C. It also has dorm beds.

Where to Eat

Rainbow Restaurant is a good vegetarian place and is recommended

How To Get There

Balasore is on the Calcutta-Madras line. There are regular trains to Calcutta, Puri, and Bhubaneswar (5 daily). The railway station is just off the main street. It is a ten minute *rickshaw* ride from the railway station to the bus station.

There are regular buses to Remuna, Bhubaneswar, Calcutta, and Chandipur.

Jajpur

Jajpur is situated on the River Vaitarani. It is Navigaya Ksetra, where *pinda* is offered to the ancestors. It is also known as **Vaitarani-tirtha**. There is a temple of **Sveta Adi Varaha** (the white boar incarnation of Lord Vishnu) here. At the **Dasasvamedha Ghat** is a flight of steps leading to the Vaitarani River, where ten-horse sacrifices were performed in the past.

Lord Caitanya came here during His travels. Srila Bhaktisiddhanta Sarasvati Thakura built an elegant temple on the left of the Varaha temple and installed footprints of Lord Caitanya there.

Practicalities

You can stay at *Viraja Panthasala* or the *Inspection Bungalow*.

The nearest railway junction is at Jajpur Keonjhar Road on the Calcutta-Madras line. Jajpur is 92 km north of Cuttack.

Vyasa-sarovar

This small lake is named after Vyasadeva, the compiler of the *Vedas* and the *Mahabharata*. You will find a temple of Jagannatha, the hermitage of Vyasa, and Gupta Ganga on the bank of this tank that covers about 150 acres.

Sambalpur

Population 210,000, STD Code 0663

Sambalpur is in western Orissa, near the border of Madhya Pradesh. It is where many of the Orissan saris are made.

Where To Stay

The Indhrapuri Guest House (21712), by the bus stand, is a basic place with rooms for Rs 40/60. The Hotel Uphar (21558), near to the bus stand, has rooms with bath for Rs 200/250 and Rs 400/450 for a room with A/C and TV. They often give a 20% discount.

The OTDC Panthanivas Tourist Bungalow (21482), at the end of the main street on top of a hill, has decent rooms for Rs 125 with bath and Rs 250 with A/C.

Travel

There are trains to Bhubaneswar, Delhi, Madras, and Calcutta.

There are three direct buses daily to Puri. You can also get a bus to Cuttack and then get another bus to Puri. There are also night deluxe video buses to Puri and Bhubaneswar.

CHAPTER FOURTEEN

Madhya Pradesh

KHAJURAHO

Population: 7,000, STD Code 076861

This is one of the most popular places with foreign tourists in India, even though it is in the middle of nowhere. There are many ancient temples here built by the Chandela kings between 950 and 1050 AD. The Chandela were a dynasty that ruled this part of India for five centuries before being defeated by the Mughals. Only about 25 of the original 85 temples still exist. About 10% of the elaborate carvings on the temples are erotic sculptures, which are what the place is famous for.

The temples are divided into three main groups—the west, east, and south. The western group, especially the Laksman Temple, is the most interesting.

The Khajuraho Dance Festival is held every year in March for 10 days. Celebrated dancers from all over India come to pay tribute to the gods and goddesses enshrined in the temples of Khajuraho.

Most people stay here just one day. You can see all the temples in about 5 or 6 hours. It can be very hot here during the summer, going up to 42°C (108°C), and cold in the winter, going down to 4°C (39°F).

Information

The village of Khajuraho is by the western group of temples and contains hotels, restaurants, and shops. The old village of Khajuraho is about 1 km east of the bus stand. The **Government of India tourist office** is here. There are also tourist offices at the bus stand and airport. These offices can help you book hotels during the busy season.

You can hire an official guide at the tourist office. Guides charge Rs 80 for a two hour tour and Rs 150 for four hours. Unofficial guides and touts are not allowed in the western group of temples.

Western Group

This is the main group of temples and should be seen first if your time is limited. There is a free guided tour daily at 9 am and 2.30 pm except Fridays and holidays. There is a good Archaeological Survey of India booklet about the temples by Krishna Deva for Rs 5.

The **Laksman Temple** (950) is the best preserved of the temples. There are many carvings on the exterior. The sanctum doorway has a panel of incarnations of Lord Vishnu. There is also a panel of the 9 planets. There are carvings of Krishna on the walls. The *pancha-ratha* sanctum has a three-headed, four-armed form of Lord Vishnu. He is surrounded by 10 incarnations and 14 other forms of Lord Vishnu.

The **Varaha Temple** (10th century) is a temple dedicated to Vishnu in His boar incarnation. Varaha saved the earth by killing the demon, Hiranyaksha. It is a large temple with hundreds of sculptures on it.

Khajuraho

The **Kandariya Mahadeva Temple** (1025-1050) is a Lord Siva temple. It is the highest temple, soaring 31m (95 ft) high, and most developed temple. The temple has a marble *linga* in the inner sanctum. Beside the main *sikhara* (tower), there are 84 smaller subsidiary towers, which are replicas of the main tower. The **Jagadambi Temple** (early 11th century) has a standing Parvati deity in the sanctum, but this temple was originally a Vishnu temple. There are several beautiful carvings of Lord Vishnu on this temple.

The **Chitragupta Temple** (early 11th century) is dedicated to Surya, the sun-god. The **Vishvanantha Temple** (1002) is dedicated to Lord Siva. It has a Nandi Pavilion with a 2.2m high sandstone Nandi bull (Siva's carrier). The **Chausat Yogini Temple** (900) is dedicated to goddess Kali and is supposed to be the oldest temple.

Eastern Group

The eastern group is mainly Jain temples. There are three Jain temples within an enclosure wall. The **Parsvanath Temple** (mid 10th century) is the largest and one of the best. There are many beautiful Vaishnava Deities carved on the walls of this temple. The temple was originally dedicated to Adinath, but the image of Parsvanath was placed in the sanctum in 1860. Only the sanctum of the **Adinath Temple** (late 11th century) is original. The porch is modern. The **Santinath Temple**, with a 4.5m statue of Adinath, is the main place of worship. The temple has been renovated, but there is an inscription on one of the walls dated to 1027.

There are also some temples north of the Jain temples. There are some detailed carvings on the ruined **Ghantai Temple** (late 10th century). The **Javari Temple** (late 10th century) is dedicated to Lord Vishnu. The **Vamana Temple** (late 11th century), 200 metres north of the Javari Temple, is dedicated to Lord Vishnu in His dwarf incarnation. The **Brahma Temple** (early 10th century) has a sandstone *sikhara* on a granite structure.

Southern Group

The **Chaturbhuja Temple** (around 1100), 3 km south of the village, has an excellent sanctum which contains a 2.7m four-armed Dakshina-murti image of Lord Siva. The **Duladeo Temple** (early 12th century) was the last Chandela temple built in Khajuraho.

Archaeological Museum

This interesting museum has a good collection of deities and sculptures from the area. There is a Vaishnava Gallery that includes a beautiful Bhu Varaha sculpture. It is open from 9 am to 5 pm. It takes about 20 minutes to see everything.

The museum gives you an opportunity to see the sculptures of the temples from eye level. The artists of Khajuraho made adjustments to the figures to compensate for the angle and distance from which the viewer would see the sculptures. Therefore the sculptures may look slightly out of proportion when seen at eye level.

Where To Stay – Lower

The *Yadav Lodge* is a good place with rooms for Rs 60/70. The *Hotel Plaza* has rooms with bath for Rs 50. The *Yogi Lodge* (2158) is a recommended good-valued, clean, budget place with a courtyard. Rooms are Rs 60/80. During the slow hot season this place may be the only budget hotel with any people in it.

The *Jain Lodge* (2052) is a good place with a vegetarian restaurant. It has a selection of rooms that start at Rs 60/80. It is popular with travelers.

The *Hotel Harmony* (2135) is a nice place with large clean rooms for Rs 150/170. The rooms facing the nice garden are the best. It also has a vegetarian restaurant. Next door, the *Hotel Surya* (2145) is a good clean place with a small garden. Rooms with bath are Rs 100/125 and Rs 150 with an air-cooler. It is a good value.

The *Hotel Lakeside* (2120) has good clean rooms for Rs 150/200, rooms with bath for Rs 225/400, and dorm beds for Rs 35. The rooms are around a courtyard.

The *Tourist Village* (2128) is well located in a quiet place. It has rooms with bath for Rs 120/160. The *Temple Hotel* (2035), Airport Rd, is a nice Indian-style hotel that has rooms for Rs 150/200. The *Sunset View* (2077) is a good clean place with a garden. It is in a good location near the lake. It has a wide selection of rooms costing from Rs 70 to Rs 250. It is a decent value.

Where To Stay – Middle

MP Tourism's *Hotel Jhankar* (2063)

has comfortable rooms with bath and hot water for Rs 225/275 and Rs 440/490 with A/C. It is the best of the government run places. The popular *MP Tourist Bungalow* has a good location. Rooms with bath are Rs 200/250.

The *Hotel Payal* (2076) is a nice clean place with good-sized well-maintained rooms for Rs 225/275 and Rs 425/475 with A/C. It has a garden and a quiet location. For the price it is recommended.

Where To Stay – High

The *Hotel Chandela Taj* (2054, fax 2095) is the best hotel in town. The rooms are $70/80. It has a pool, health club, tennis court, chandeliers, and bathtubs in the attached bathrooms. It has a good bookshop and a pleasant garden.

The *Hotel Jass Oberoi* (2085, fax 2088) is a deluxe place with a swimming pool. It has a pool, a garden and first-class service. Rooms are $40/75.

The well-managed *Khajuraho Ashok* (2024) is a luxury place with a pool. Some rooms have a view of the temples. It has rooms for Rs 950/1150. It is not a very good value. The pool can be used by non-guest for Rs 50.

The *Holiday Inn* (2178) is a new well-managed place. It has comfortable rooms and a pool. Also new is the *Hotel Clarks Bundela* (2366), which is a first class place with rooms for $40/55. It is a good value.

Where To Eat

The *Jain Lodge* has a good vegetarian restaurant. The *Hotel Harmony* has a vegetarian restaurant. These two places are not open April till June. The *New Bharat*, downstairs from the Raya Hotel, is supposed to have good vegetarian food. *Jata Shankar*, by the Western temple group, has decent cheap *thalis*.

Getting Around

Bike-rickshaws are expensive (Rs 30 for a short ride). A good way to get around is to rent a bike for the day for Rs 15 or Rs 20. A taxi can be hired from MP Tourism or Khajuraho Tours.

Travel

Air There is a daily flight to Delhi via Agra that takes one and a half hours. There is a flight that goes to Varanasi and then continues on to Kathmandu. There are daily flights to Bombay and Calcutta. Flying is the best way to get to Khajuraho, because there is no nearby train station. The Indian Airlines office (2035) is at the Temple Hotel on Airport Rd. You can also book flights at the airport.

Rail The closest stations are Jhansi (176 km), if you are taking a train from Agra or Delhi; Satna (117 km), if you are coming from Allahabad, Varanasi, Calcutta, or Bombay; and Mahoba (51 km) if you are coming from Varanasi. It is usually better to get a train from Satna, because from Mahoba there are only a few slow trains daily with a small quota.

From Delhi the Shatabdi Express is the best train to Jhansi. It leaves Delhi at 6.15 am, arrives in Agra at 8.10 am, and arrives in Jhansi at 10.40 am. There is a deluxe bus that meets the train and takes about five hours to get from Jhansi to Khajuraho. The Shatabdi Express departs from Jhansi (5.50 pm) to Delhi (4½ hr). During the day there are also other much slower trains that go from Jhansi to Delhi.

There is no direct train connection to **Varanasi**. The closest train stations to Khajuraho are Satna (117 km east) or Mahoba (51 km). From Satna you can get an express bus (4 hr) or taxi to Khajuraho. From Satna there are trains to Bombay, Gorakhpur, Calcutta, and Varanasi.

If you are leaving Khajuraho for Varanasi (415 km northeast), you can take a bus to Mahoba (3 hr) and get the #1107 train to Varanasi at 8.50 pm. To get here from **Jaipur** you have to change trains at Agra and take another train to Jhansi.

Bus There is a bus from Agra (12 hr) and about 6 buses daily from Jhansi (6 hr). There is luxury bus that meets the Shatabdi Express at the Jhansi Railway Station. A luxury A/C bus to Jhansi departs from Khajuraho at 12 noon to meet the Shatabdi Express going to Agra and Delhi. It costs Rs 200 There are other cheaper and slower buses to Jhansi during the day. There are only uncomfortable local buses for the 10 to 12 hour ride to Varanasi or Allahabad.

Taxi A taxi from Jhansi to Khajuraho costs about Rs 1400 and takes about four hours.

JHANSI

Population: 375,000, STD Code 0517

The main reason most travelers come to Jhansi is because it is the closest train junction on the Delhi-Bombay line to Khajuraho. It is 5½ hours by bus to Khajuraho from Jhansi.

Jhansi is actually in Uttar Pradesh, but because it is close to Khajuraho which is in Madhya Pradesh it is included in the Madhya Pradesh chapter.

Places to See

There is a **fort** here that was built in 1613 by Maharaja Bir Singh Deo of Orchha. Near the fort is the **Rani Mahal** (10 am to 5 pm, daily except Mon), which was the Rani of Jhansi's palace. It is now a museum with 9th to 12th century sculptures.

Where to Stay

There are *retiring rooms* in the railway station for Rs 100 and Rs 180 with A/C. Dorm beds are Rs 20. The *Hotel Pujan* (1737), Gwalior Rd, is a cheap place which is a good value. The recommended *Hotel Samrat* (444-943), Chitra Chauraha near the railway station, is a new place with clean rooms.

UP Tourism's *Hotel Veerangana* (442-402), a 15-minute walk from the station, has rooms for Rs 75/100 and Rs 250/300 with A/C and also dorm beds for Rs 25. It is not so well-maintained.

The *Prakash Guest House* (443-133), Shri Sardari Lal Market, has good clean rooms with hot water for Rs 160 and Rs 300 with A/C. It is a recommended place. It has 24-hour checkout.

The *Jhansi Hotel* (443-360) is one of the best places in town. It has a big garden and verandas. It was a hotel during the British Raja. Rooms are Rs 250/375 and Rs 375/500 with A/C.

Close by is the Hotel Raj Palace (442-554), which has air-cooled modern rooms for Rs 180/225 and A/C rooms for Rs 300/350. It is a clean place.

The *Hotel Sita* (442-956), Shivpuri Rd near the station, is a new modern hotel with comfortable clean rooms. It is a well-maintained, recommended, mid-range place. Rooms cost Rs 350/425 with air-cooling and Rs 500/550 with A/C.

There are no high-range hotels in Jhansi.

Travel

Train Jhansi is on the main Delhi-Agra-Bhopal-Bombay line. The Shatabdi Express #2002 is the quickest train from **Delhi** (4½ hr, 6.15 am) to Jhansi. From Jhansi the Shatabdi Exp departs to **Bhopal** at 10.47 am and returns to Delhi at 5.58 pm via Agra (2½ hr).

There are trains to **Delhi** (5 daily, 4½ to 8 hr), Bombay (21½ hr), **Agra** (2½ to 3½ hr), **Indore** (10 hr), **Bhopal** (4 hr), and **Gwalior** (1½ hr). Other trains go to **Varanasi, Bangalore, Madras**, and **Lucknow**. The Bundelkhand Exp #1107 (5 pm, 17½ hr) goes to **Varanasi** and the Punjab Mail # 1038 (3 pm, 21½ hr) goes to **Bombay**.

Bus There are express buses to Khajuraho (5½ hr, Rs 175) that depart from the railway station at 6, 7, and 11 am. The MP Tourism counter on platform one of the railway station sells tickets for the express buses to Khajuraho. Slower state buses depart for Khajuraho from the bus stand on Kanpur Road, 5 km east of the railway station, in the morning and at 1.15 pm.

Satna

Population: 160,000, STD Code 07672

One may pass through Satna on the way to or from Khajuraho. Other than that, there is nothing in this town to see or do.

Where To Stay

The *Hotel India*, by the bus stand, is a good budget place that has rooms with bath for Rs 75/125. It also has a good cheap vegetarian restaurant. The *Hotel Park*, 1½ km from the railway station, has clean rooms for Rs 70/100 and Rs 200 with A/C. It also has a vegetarian restaurant.

MP Tourism's *Hotel Barhut* (2041) is a clean place with rooms for Rs 190/240 and Rs 275/325 with A/C.

Travel

The trains to Varanasi take 8 hours. There are also trains to Allahabad (4 hr), Bombay, Calcutta, and Madras. There are

6 am, 10 am, 2.30 pm, and 3.30 pm buses to Khajuraho.

INDORE

Population: 1,200,000, STD Code 0731

There is a chance that you may pass through here on the way to Ujjain, Omkareshwar, or Mandu.

Information

The helpful **MPTDC information office** (10 am to 5 pm) is behind the Ravindra Natya Griha Exhibition Hall on RN Tagore Rd. They can arrange a tourist taxi for you. They run a one-day tour to Omkareshwar and Maheshwar (Rs 250) and a two-day tour to Mandu (Rs 500).

The State Bank of Indore on Raj Wada (10 am to 2 pm, Mon to Fri, Sat 10 am to noon) **changes money**. As does the State Bank of India on AB Rd, next to the GPO.

Places to See

The **Central Museum** near the GPO has an interesting collection of sculptures and old deities. It is open daily 10 am to 5 pm except Monday.

The **Lal Bagh palace** (10 am to 5 pm, except Mon) is one of the most elaborate palaces in India. This extravagant palace, which took thirty years to complete, was the former home of the Maharaja.

Where To Stay – Lower

Most of the budget hotels are by the Sarwate Bus Stand and the railway station, which are only a few minutes apart. The mid-range hotels are a better value than the budget ones. The dorms at the railway station were recently renovated.

The *Janta Hotel* (name in Hindi), next to the Hotel Ashoka, is the cheapest place. The *Hotel Shalimar* is a good value with rooms with bath for Rs 60/80. The *Hotel*

Sagar International has a selection of large rooms for Rs 110/130. It is a good choice. It has 24 hour checkout.

The *Hotel Neelam* (466-001) has rooms with a TV for Rs 100/130. Rooms have hot water and are decently clean. Nearby, the *Hotel Ashoka* (465-991) has rooms for Rs 95/140. It has 24 hour checkout. Both these places are good values.

The *Hotel Payal* (463-202), 38 Chhoti Gwaltoli, is a recommended good place that has clean rooms with a TV for Rs 100/135. Bucket hot water is supplied for free. It is near the bus station.

Where To Stay – Middle To High

The *Samrat Hotel* (433-890), 18/5 MG Road, is a big, good-valued place that has nice rooms for Rs 250/300 and Rs 300/350 with A/C. The *Purva* (38554), 1-4 Dhenu Market, five minutes from the station, has clean rooms that are a good value.

The *Tourist Bungalow* (38888), RN Tagore Rd, has rooms for Rs 200/250 with A/C. It is a good place in a peaceful location.

The *Central Hotel* (538-547, 38541) is a popular older place, with large well-maintained rooms for Rs 175/250 and Rs 300/375 with A/C. They do not give commissions, so rickshaw drivers may tell you it is full. It is a good value. The front rooms are noisy.

The *Surya Hotel* (431-155), North Mandi Rd, is a recommended quiet place with modern rooms for Rs 300/425 and Rs 475/600 with A/C. The *Shreemaya Hotel* (431-942), near the railway station, is a good place with rooms for Rs 300/400 and Rs 450/550 with A/C. You can change money here. This place is recommended.

The *Hotel President* (433-156), 163 RNT Marg, with a turbaned doorman, has good rooms for Rs 475/625 and Rs 575/725 for an A/C rooms. There are also higher priced rooms. It has a sauna and health club. This is a recommended place. The vegetarian Woodlands Restaurant here is excellent.

The four-star *Indotels Manor* (537-301, fax 434-864), AB Rd, 4 km from the center of town, is one of the best places in town with rooms for Rs 700/900 up to Rs 2000 for the Maharaja Suite. The *Taj Residency* (557-700, fax 555-355), near Meghdoot Gardens, 5 km from the downtown, is a deluxe place with rooms for $75/85.

Where To Eat

The *Apsara*, at the Tagore Natya Griha Hall, in front of the Tourist Bungalow, is popular with the locals. It is a very good place and is recommended. The macaroni and vegetable pulao are very good. The *Woodlands Restaurant* at the Hotel President, 163 RNT Marg, is a high-class excellent South Indian place and is also recommended. These are two of the better places you will see in India.

The *Volga Restaurant*, Regal Theatre Premises on MG Road, is a high-class place. The *Status Restaurant*, 565 MG Road, is also a good place.

Travel

Air Indian Airlines (airport: 411-782) has flights on Mon, Tues, Thur, and Fri to Bombay and flights on the same days to Delhi via Bhopal and Gwalior. There is a daily flight to Bombay on Damania Airways. The Indian Airlines office (431-596) is on Race Course Rd. The airport is 9 km from the city.

Train Trains to Delhi go via two different routes. The daily Indore-Nizamuddin

Express #9301 departs 9 pm from Indore, goes via Ujjain and Bharatpur, and arrives in **Delhi** at 12.30 pm. The Malwa Express #4068 (3.05 pm) takes the other route—via Bhopal, Jhansi, Gwalior, and Agra—and arrives in **Delhi** at 9.35 am. The Shipra Exp #1172 goes Wed, Thur, and Fri to **Calcutta** (7.30 pm, 36½ hr). There are also trains to **Bombay** and Secunderabad (**Hyderabad**).

There are three trains daily that go to Chittaurgarh, Ajmer, and Jaipur in Rajasthan on a metre gauge line. The Meenakshi Exp #7570 (10.30, 15½ hr) is the fastest train to **Jaipur**. To get to Ajanta and Ellora involves getting to **Jalgaon**, 55 km north of Ajanta. To get there you have to change trains at both Khandwar and Bhusawal junctions.

Bus There are regular buses to **Ujjain** (1½ hrs) and a direct bus to **Ajanta** (5 am) from the Sarwate Bus Station. You can get overnight luxury buses to **Nasik** or **Aurangabad** from private companies. The buses leave around 9 pm and arrive about 12 hours later. These buses are painful, but still they are probably the best way to get to these places.

MP Tourism runs an air-conditioned express bus (Rs 175) to **Bhopal** at 8 am and 3.15 pm from the Tourist Bungalow. This bus meets the superfast Shatabdi Express to and from Delhi.

Vijayant Travels is a reliable travel agency that operates overnight luxury buses to Bombay, Nasik, Aurangabad, Nagpur, and other places. Also reliable are Royal Travels, 164 RNT Marg, and Multani Sona Travels.

UJJAIN

Population: 370,000, STD Code 0734

According to the *Aranya-parva* of the *Mahabharata*, Ujjain is one of the seven sacred cities in India known as *moksa-puris* or *sapta-puris*: Ayodhya, Mathura, Haridwar, Kasi (Varanasi), Kanchipuram, Avanti (Ujjain), and Dwarka. It is about 80 km north of Indore.

Ujjain is situated on the bank of the Shipra River, which is one of the western most tributaries of the Ganges. It is believed that those who take bath in this river will attain *moksa* (liberation). It is said that bathing in the Shipra will also cure you of fever. The river flows north around the western side of Ujjain, passing through Narasimha Ghat, Ram Ghat, Ganga Ghat, Mangal Ghat, and Siddhavat before reaching Gadhi and Rana Pratap Sagars. It then joins the Chambal River, which flows into the Yamuna, which flows into the Ganges River.

It is said that Siva killed the demon Tripura at Ujjain.

According to Indian Astrology, zero degrees begins in Ujjain, which is also situated on the Indian "Tropic of Cancer." Lord Nityananda visited Ujjain.

Information

There is a **MP tourist information counter** in the railway station. The State Bank of India is on Udwaria Rd, east of the main bazaar.

Sandipani Muni's Asrama

Ujjain is the where Sandipani Muni instructed Lord Krishna and Balarama. Ujjain was called Avantipura when Lord Krishna studied here. Nearby Sandipani Muni's *asrama* is **Gomati Kund**, where Krishna called all the holy rivers so His guru would not have to go on pilgrimage. Also nearby is **Ankapata**, where Krishna would wash His writing tablets. The numbers 1-100 are found here on a stone, believed to have been engraved by Sandipani Muni himself.

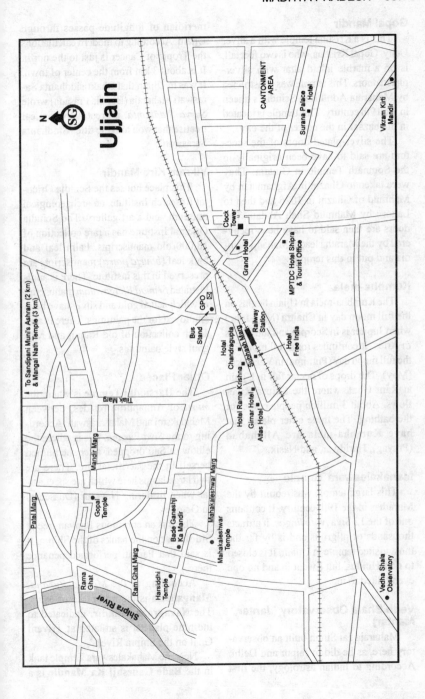

Ujjain

Gopal Mandir

This is a Krishna temple with a silver Deity. Gopal Krishna, who is two feet tall, is on a marble inlaid altar with silver-plated doors. This temple was constructed by Maharaja Adult Rao Scindia's queen in the 19th century. This temple is located in the bazaar in the center of the city.

The silver-plated doors of the sanctum are said to have been originally in the Somnath Temple in Gujarat. They were taken to Ghazni in Afghanistan by Mahmud of Ghazni in 1026 and then to Lahore by Mahmud Shah Abdati. The doors are then said to have been recovered by the Maratha leader Mahadji Scindia and put in this temple.

Kumbha-mela

The Kumbha-mela in Ujjain begins on the full moon day in Chaitra (May-June) when Jupiter is in Scorpio and the Sun is in Aries. It continues for a full month to the full moon day (Purnima) in Vaishakha (May). The drops of nectar fall in Ujjain at Ram Ghat, where the Shipra River flows. About 3 million people come for the bathing. The three other places that have Kumbha-mela are Allahabad (Prayag), Haridwar, and Nasik.

Mahakaleswara Temple

This large temple was rebuilt by the Marathas in the 19th century. It contains one of the 12 Siva *jyotirlingas*. It attracts thousands of pilgrims and is by far the most visited temple in Ujjain. It is closed to non-Hindus, but I went in and no one even talked to me.

Vedh Shala Observatory (Jantar Mantar)

Maharaja Jai Singh built an observatory here, as he did in Jaipur and Delhi. According to Indian astrology, the first meridian of longitude passes through Ujjain. According to modern calculations the Tropic of Cancer is just to the north. It is about 3 km from the center of town. It was in Ujjain that Bhaktisiddhanta Saraswati Maharaja (Bimala Prasada) wrote *Surya Siddhanta*, a great astronomical treatise that won him the title "Siddhanta Saraswati".

Vikram Kirti Mandir

This place houses the Scindia Oriental Research Institute, an archaeological museum, and a art gallery. The Scindia Oriental Institute has a rare collection of 18,000 old manuscripts. Palm leaf and bark leaf (*bhurja patra*) manuscripts are preserved in this institute. There is an illustrated *Srimad Bhagavatam* manuscript in which actual gold and silver have been employed for the paintings. There is also a rich collection of old Rajput and Moghul style paintings.

Other Places

The **Harsiddhi Temple** is where the *murti* of Annapurna resides, between Mahalaksmi and Mahasaraswati. According to the *Siva Purana*, this is where the elbow of Sati dropped, after she burned herself in the sacrificial fire. There are two large lamps here which are spectacular when lit during Navratri (Dussehra) in October.

There is an enormous Banyan tree at **Siddhavat** on the banks of the Shipra. It is said that Parvati performed penance there.

According to the *Matsya Purana*, **Mangalnath** is the birthplace of Mars. The **Navagraha Mandir**, dedicated to the nine planets, is situated at Triveni Ghat on the Shipra River.

Near the Mahakaleswara Temple tank in the **Bade Ganeshji Ka Mandir** is a very large deity of Ganesh called Chintaman Ganesh, who is manifested with his consorts Riddhi and Siddhi.

Where To Stay

Most of the hotels are by the railway station and for the most part reasonably priced. The *Vikram* (25780), opposite the railway station, is the cheapest place, but you should make sure it is decently clean. Rooms are Rs 60/85. The *Surya Hotel* next door has rooms from Rs 80/100 to Rs 175/225. The *Hotel Ajay* is also a decent budget choice.

The *Grand Hotel* is over the railway bridge. It has basic rooms with bath for Rs 125/175. It is best to get a front room. It looks like it was very grand at one time, but it is totally run down now.

The *Hotel Chandragupta* (25500) and the *Hotel Rama Krishna* (25912), across the street from the railway station, are both pretty good similar places. The Hotel Rama Krishna has rooms for Rs 125/150 with bath to Rs 200 for an A/C room. It also has some very basic rooms for Rs 50/60. The Chandragupta has rooms for Rs 80/100 to Rs 140/160. Both these hotels are a good value.

The *Girnar Hotel*, a ten minute walk from the railway station, has rooms for Rs 175/225 to Rs 325 with A/C. The *Hotel Free India* (52534), next to the railway station, has good large rooms with hot water for Rs 200.

The *Shirpra Hotel* (51496) has rooms with bath and hot water for Rs 300/350 and with A/C for Rs 450/500. It is one of the best places in town and is located in a quiet area. To get to this hotel from the railway station you exit at platform 7.

The *Surana Palace* (25474), 23 GDC Rd, is about the same as the Shipra Hotel. It has a nice lawn and large, comfortable rooms.

Where To Eat

The *Hotel Rama Krishna* and the *Hotel Chandragupta*, across from the railway station, both have better than average vegetarian restaurants. The *Chanakya* is a good place. The *New Raj Kumar*, 20 Bhaktawar Ganj, is a low priced place by the Surana Palace.

Travel

Train The Malwa Express #4067 (4.55 pm, 15½ hr) is the fastest train to **Delhi**. The Malwa Exp #4668 leaves Delhi at 7.15 pm and arrives in Ujjain at 10.35 am going via Mathura (8.18 pm). The Intercity Express leaves **Mathura** about 12 pm and arrives in Ujjain the next morning at 10 am. From **Bombay** you get down at Nagda and take a passenger train for another 1½ hours.

There are three trains daily to **Ahmedabad**. The Bhopal-Rajkot Exp #1270 (11.50, 9½ hr) goes to Ahmedabad. The Sabarmati Exp #9166 (8.50 pm) arrives in Ahmedabad at 7.20 am. The Sabarmati Exp #9165 returns to Ujjain from Ahmedabad at 8.15 pm and arrives at 5.40 am. At 6.05 am the Sabarmati Exp continues on to **Varanasi** (32½ hr) via **Lucknow** (22½ hr) and **Faizabad** (Ayodhya). There are also trains to **Agra**, **Jhansi** and **Calcutta**.

Bus There are a number of buses to Indore (1½ hr, 55 km) and two buses a day to Mandu and Bhopal (6 hr). A convenient way to get to Nasik is to go to Indore and from there get an overnight luxury bus at 9 pm.

OMKARESWARA

Omkareswara is on Mandhata Island, which is 2 km long and 1 km wide, at the confluence of the Narmada and Kaveri Rivers. It is 77 km south of Indore. On the island itself all the temples are dedicated to Siva. On the north side of the Narmada are a few old ruined temples dedicated to Lord Vishnu and some Jain temples. There is a temple dedicated to **Varaha** that has 24 figures of Vishnu carved in green stone. There is also an 18-foot long female figure of Chamundi that has 10 arms holding clubs and skulls.

There is a major festival here during Siva-ratri (Feb-March) and another during Kartika Purnima (Oct-Nov).

The island is reached by crossing a concrete footbridge or taking a boat across the river.

Omkareswara Mandhata Temple

One of the 12 *jyotirlingas* is located in this temple. The sculptures on this important Siva temple are extremely detailed. The main reason pilgrims come to Omkareswara is to visit this temple.

Around the Island

There is a traditional *parikrama* (circular tour) of the island that begins at the *ghats* below the Sri Mandhata Temple and goes clockwise around the island. It takes at least a couple of hours. It is a nice walk for the first half hour until you reach **Triveni Sangam** (three rivers confluence), where the Narmada and Kaveri meet. From here, the path climbs along the north shore until you reach the **Gauri-Somnath Temple**, which is surrounded by numerous sculptures. There is a huge Nandi carved of green stone in front of the Gauri-Somnath Temple. There is a large Siva-linga in this temple. From here you either go down a flight of stairs to the village or head east to the fortified town that was ransacked by the Muslims.

After going up a gully you come to the **Surajkund Gate**, with 9 ft high Arjuna and Bhima, the two Pandava brothers, on either side. Five minutes from here you come to the 10th century **Siddhnath Temple**, which is the oldest temple on the island and has elaborate carvings. From here there are two routes back to the village. One takes you along the top of the plateau, dropping sharply along a ruined temple and the Maharaja's palace, reaching the Sri Mandhata Temple. The other way takes you down a flight of steps to the riverbanks, then past some sadhu's caves to the main *ghats*.

Practicalities

There are mainly only dharamsalas to stay at here. The only hotel-type place is the basic *Yatraki Niwas*, behind the bus stand, which has some rooms with bath.

Most of the dharamsalas have windowless rooms with simple washing facilities. The cleanest places are the *Ahilya Bhai*, left of the main square, *Rewa Gauza*, near the Mamaleswara Temple, and the *Shri Tirole Kumbhi*, near the river. By the steps leading to the *ghats* from the village square, there is a building in which the owner rents out rooms to long staying western visitors.

You can get mineral water at Jain Cold Drinks, 100m from the bus stand. There are no money changing facilities here. There are only very basic eating places here.

Travel

Omkareswara Road, on the Ratlam-Indore-Khandwa line, is the closest railway station. It is 12 km from Omkareswara. Only slow passenger trains stop there.

There are local buses to Ujjain and Indore (77 km, 2½ hr) from here. There is a tour that comes here from Indore, which is a convenient way to come here.

Amarkantak

This is the source of the Narmada River. Some of the temples here date back to the 11th century. Amarkantak is located in eastern Madhya Pradesh. There is a temple and dharamsala here.

SANCHI

Sanchi has the best-preserved Buddhist Stupas in India. It is 68 km northeast of Bhopal. The Buddhist monuments and sculptures were made 'between the third century BC and the 13th century. The fine quality of the sculptured panels of Sanchi make them unique in the entire world. This place is not associated with Buddha's life.

The Archaeological Museum

This museum has a good collection of damaged sculptures from around the site. It has an interesting Asoka pillar topped with a "Lion Capital", which serves as the emblem of the Indian Republic. It is similar to the one found in Sarnath. There are some Hindu sculptures of Vishnu, Laksmi, Ganesh, and various others. It is open 9 am to 5 pm every day. There is a good guide book written by Debala Mitra and published by the Archaeological Survey.

The Great Stupa

The foundation of the Great Stupa was built by emperor Ashoka sometime in the third century BC. There are four elaborately carved gateways (*toranas*) dating to about 450 AD. Four statues of Buddha in meditation were installed, facing each gateway. The four entrances are staggered. This is supposed to keep out evil spirits, who are believed to be only able to go in a straight line.

Where To Stay

There are two good *retiring rooms* at the railway station. The *Sri Lanka Mahabodhi Society Guest House* has cell-like rooms for a Rs 30 donation.

The MPTDC *Tourist Lodge* (81223) has big clean rooms. It is the best place in town, but it is often full. It is best to reserve a room at least five days in advance at any MPTDC office or in Delhi.

Travel

Train Sanchi is on the Delhi-Bombay line, but mostly only slow passenger trains stop here. First-class passengers who have come at least 161 km can arrange to have the train make a special halt at Sanchi. The nearest mainline station is Vidisha (10 km northeast). There is a train that departs from Bhopal at 9.50 am that takes only 45 minutes to reach Sanchi.

Bus There are hourly buses from Bhopal taking two different routes, one takes an hour and a half and the other takes two and a half hours.

Please Help Us

As the subject matter of this book is extremely complex and detailed it is very difficult to include everything relevant. So if you have some information that would be valuable to the readers of this book please send it to us, so they may be benefited.

Whatever you can tell about any temple, the story behind the Deity, what Deities are in a particular temple, or other interesting facts may be valuable information. Also of interest is your opinion on hotels, restaurants or dharamshalas, especially ones missed in this book. Travel information is also valuable. Please refer to the page number in this book in reference to the place that you are writing about.

Please give as detailed information as possible.

For temples or holy places please send:
Temple name, location, Deities' names
What is especially interesting about the temple or place
Story about the temple or Deities
Opening or closing hours
How to get there, what bus or train
Potential problems such as guides, hard climbs, or monkeys

For hotels and restaurants please send :
Name, address, phone number, opening hours of a restaurant
Tariff card or room rates
Location, distance from a land-mark either walking or by rickshaw.
How close to a railway or bus station.
How to get there and how much it cost.
Your comments on why this place stood out.
For a restaurant, any recommended preparations or things to be avoided

The writers of the ten best letters will receive an updated edition of this book.

Thank you very much for your help.

Write to

Spiritual Guides   Jada Bharata Dasa
Krishna Balarama Mandir
Bhaktivedanta Swami Marg
Vrindavana, Mathura Dist. UP, India

CHAPTER FIFTEEN

Maharashtra

Population: 80 million

Maharashtra is the third largest state in India. The main language spoken is Marathi.

BOMBAY

Population 12.5 million, STD Code 022

The name Bombay is a Portuguese corruption of "Mumba" or "Mumbai," which is a name for Parvati, the wife of Lord Siva. Bombay is made up of a collection of seven islands connected by a reclamation from the sea.

It was taken over by the Portuguese in the early 16th century. They leased it to the British in 1668. When the British took over it was a very small town. The British then built it into an important port city.

Now Bombay is the most important city in India for business activities, having a good percentage of all the wealth in India. Over one-third of the income tax paid in India is from Bombay, and half the foreign trade is done from here. The best time to visit Bombay is in January. During the rainy season it has some of the heaviest rains in all of India.

Getting Your Bearings

The city is a long thin island running north to south. The downtown is in the south, at the thinnest point of the island. The old part of the city is by the Taj Mahal Hotel and Gateway of India. The cheap hotels are in this area, up to Victoria Terminus. This area is called Colaba, and many tourists never leave this area of Bombay.

Juhu Beach is in the northern part of Bombay, 20 km from the main downtown area. From the downtown it takes about 40 minutes to reach Juhu by train.

A while ago the city changed many of the street names. Some name changes were not accepted, so many people will know the old street name, but not the new one.

Information

The **Government of India Tourist Office** (203-2932) is across from Churchgate Station at 123 Maharishi Karve Rd. It is right next to the office where you buy tourist quota tickets for the train. They are efficient and helpful and have a lot of information to hand out. They are open from 8.30 am to 6 pm Monday to Friday and on every other Saturday from 8.30 am to 1.30 pm. They are closed on Sundays. There are also **tourist counters** at both the international (Sahar) and domestic airports.

The **Maharashtra Tourism Development Corporation office** (202-6713), CDO Hutments, Madame Cama Rd, conducts tours of Bombay and operates long distance bus services to places like Aurangabad. They also have a chain of hotels that they operate all over Maharashtra. You can book rooms for their hotels at this office.

State Tourist Offices

Delhi
> c/o MTDC, CDO Hutments, Madam Cama Rd, Nariman Point (285-5736)

Gujarat
> Dhanraj Mahal, PJ Ramchandani Marg (202-2945)

Himachal Pradesh
> World Trade Centre, Cuffe Parade (218-1123)

Jammu and Kashmir
> World Trade Centre, Cuffe Parade (218-6249)

Kerala
> c/o Kairali, Nirmal Building, Nariman Point (202-6817)

Madhya Pradesh
> World Trade Centre (218-7603)

Rajasthan
> 230 Dr DN Marg (204-4162)

Tamil Nadu
> c/o Peerless Hotels and Travel Ltd, Churchgate Chambers, New Marines Lines (262-4811)

Uttar Pradesh
> World Trade Centre (218-5458)

Tours

The **city tour** (2 to 6 pm) goes to the Gateway of India, the Aquarium, the Prince of Wales Museum, Hanging gardens, Kamla Nehru Park, and the Gandhi Museum. It costs Rs 55 and leaves from the MTDC Office on Madame Cama Rd (Opp LIC Office) at Nariman Point every day except Monday.

The **Suburban Tour** goes to the Hare Krishna Temple at Juhu Beach, the Kanheri Caves, the National Park, and the Lion Safari Park from 9.15 am to 6.15 pm for Rs 90.

There is a daily four day tour to **Aurangabad** run by ITDC that includes staying at the three-star Aurangabad Ashoka Hotel. The tour costs Rs 1600.

ITDC also runs an overnight bus that takes 12 hr to get to Aurangabad for Rs 130.

MTDC runs a one day overnight tour to **Nasik** for Rs 350. They also have a luxury bus that departs at 6.30 am to Nasik (6 hr) for Rs 92.

Visa Extension

The Foreigner's Registration Office (262-0446) is at Annexe 2, Office of the Commissioner of Police, Dadabhai Naoroji Rd, near Crawford Market. This is where you apply to extend your visa. I have been told that you are much more likely to receive a visa extension in Bombay than in Delhi.

Money

You can change money quickly at the American Express office (204-8278) at the Oriental Building, 364 Dr DN Rd, at the intersection of Colaba Causeway and Sivaji Marg. Equally efficient is Thomas Cook (204-8556) on Dr DN Rd between Flora Fountain and the Khadi Bhavan. The major banks downtown all change foreign currency. Bank of America, Express Towers, Nariman Point, accepts Mastercard; and the Andhra Bank, 18 Homi Modi St (near Flora Fountain), accepts Visa cards.

At Sahar airport you can change money at the State Bank of India's 24-hour counter, where the rates are standard. You can also change money quickly at the Air India Building at Nariman Point, which is open all night.

Be careful of changing money on the streets, as Bombay is known for rip-offs. You may be handed a wad of bills stapled together and just when you hand over the foreign money, you are suddenly told the police are coming and everyone disappears. When you go to count your money you find out the wad of bills you were handed has a few real bills on the top and bottom of the pile and the rest is just regular paper.

Foreign Consulates

Australia
Makers Tower, E Block, Cuffe Parade (218-1071)

Belgium
Morena, 11 M L Dahanukar Marg (492-9202)

Canada
41/42 Maker Chambers VI, Nariman Point (287-6028)

Denmark
L & T House, N Morarjee Marg, Ballard Estate (261-8181)

France
Data Prasad Bldg, N G Cross Rd, off G Deshmukh Rd (495-0918)

Germany
Hoechst House (10th Floor), Nariman Point (283-2422)

Ireland
2nd Floor, Thomas Cook Building, Dr D Naoroji Rd (285-0330)

Israel
Kailash, Peddar Rd (386-2794)

Italy
Kanchanjunga, 72 G Deshmukh Rd (387-2341)

Japan
1 Babasaheb Dahanukar Marg, Cumballa Hill (494-4310)

Mauritius
Dhanraj Mahal (3rd floor), Apollo Bunder (202-7244)

Netherlands
16 M Karve Rd (206-6840)

Philippines
116 Free Press House, Nariman Point (202-0375)

Singapore
Sakhar Bhavan, 230 Nariman Point (204-3209)

Spain
Ador House, 6 K Dubash Marg (287-4797)

Sri Lanka
Sri Lanka House, 34 Homi Mody St, Fort (204-5861)

Sweden
85 Sayani Rd (436-4093)

Switzerland
Manek Mahal, 90 Veer Nariman Rd (204-3550)

Thailand
Krishna Bagh, 43 Bhulabhai Desai Rd (363-1404)

UK
Maker Chambers IV, 2nd Floor, Cuffe Parade (283-3602)

USA
Lincoln House, 78 Bhulabhai Desai Rd (822-3611)

Travel Agencies

You can usually get international tickets cheaper in New Delhi or Calcutta than Bombay. You can get discount tickets from Travel Corner Ltd, Marine Drive, near the Ambassador Hotel.

For discounted tickets, Transway International (262-6066, fax 262-3518), Pantaky House, 8 Maruti Cross Lane (off Maruti St), Fort, is an recommended travel agent.

Space Travels (266-3397), Nanabhoy Mansion, Sir P Mehta Rd, is also a good discount travel agent.

Good travel agents are Mercury Travel (202-3663), 70 V B Gandhi Marg and the Oberoi Hotel; Sita World Travel (223-3155), 8 Atlanta Building, Nariman Point; American Express (204-6349), Majithia Chamber, Dadabhai Naoroji Rd; and Thomas Cook (204-6349), Cooks Building, Dadabhai Naoroji Rd.

Post and Phone

The GPO is off Nagar Chowk, near Victoria Terminus (VT). There are people outside the post office to pack and seal your packages. The parcel post office, open from 10 am to 4.30 pm, is in the back of the building, on the 1st floor.

There is a reliable **poste restante** service open Monday to Saturday from 9 am to 6 pm. They usually throw away letters after four weeks.

At Videsh Sanchar Bhavan, the government telecom building on MG Marg, you get low prices for calls and faxs. You can also make collect calls there and receive incoming calls for Rs 5.

Bookshops

The *Bookpoint* in the Ballard Estate and *Nalanda Bookshop* in the Taj Hotel are both good shops. The *Strand Book Stall*, 15 Dhannur, off Sir P.M. Road, Fort area, north of Flora Fountain, has a good selection of books. They give 20% discounts.

Bharatiya Vidya Bhavan, Kulapati, KM Munshi Marg by Chowpatty Beach, has a good selection of spiritual books. It is a well-known place, so many people know where it is located.

Dentist

Dr Arun S Shah (612-7688, Res: 615-0251), 1A Gul Manzil, Opp Gurudev Hotel, just off the street going to Vile Parle train station, is a recommended dentist. His hours are 9.30 am to 12 noon and 6 to 9 pm. You are supposed to make an appointment in advance. I know many people who have been going to him for years and are satisfied with his work.

Photography

The Javeri Colour Lab, opposite Regal Cinema in Colaba, has print and slide film. You can get Polaroid passport photographs at a stand behind the florists in Shakhari Bunder Market.

Prince of Wales Museum

This museum has some interesting paintings, sculptures, and historical exhibits. In the excellent weapon collection are the swords of the emperors Shah Jahan and Aurangzeb and the shield of Akbar. The museum is open from 10 am to 6 pm daily, except Monday.

Malabar Hill

The Pherozeshah Mehta Gardens (**Hanging Gardens**) were set out in 1880 and redone in 1921. The best time to visit is in the early evening, as the sun is not strong then and you can have a pleasant walk. It is on top of Malabar Hill.

The Parsee **Towers of Silence** are next to the gardens, but they are totally forbidden to visitors. The Parsees believe that a dead body should not be placed into the earth or burned. When someone dies their body is put on the Towers of Silence and vultures come and strip the flesh from the body. The bones are then purified by the sun and wind.

The **Walkeshwara** (Sand Lord) **Temple** is at the end of the peninsula. Lord Rama, on His way to rescue Sita from Ravana, is supposed to have stopped here. It is said that every night Laksmana would provide his brother with a Sivalinga from Varanasi to worship. On this night he did not arrive on time, so Rama stooped here and built a *linga* of sand. The current temple was built in 1715, but there has been a temple here for thousands of years. At one time the temple was very busy, but now hardly anyone comes here. There is the large sacred **Banganga** bathing tank next to the temple. It is said to have been created by an arrow from

Rama's bow shot into the ground. This temple is by the Raj Bhavan, the governor's residence.

Mahalaksmi Mandira

This temple is inside an alley off Bhulabhai Desai Rd, north of Malabar Hill, by the seashore. A temple has been here for a thousand years, but the present temple was built in the 18th century. In the 18th century, when this area of the city was a swamp, it was drained and a breach-wall constructed. It is said that Laksmi appeared to the contractor in a dream and told him that unless he installed in a temple the Deity of her that would appear from the sea, the breach-wall would not hold. The next day a Laksmi Deity was found by the workmen and was duly installed in the temple at this spot.

On weekends the queue (line) to see the Deity can be very long.

Elephanta Caves (Gharapuri)

These 1,000 year old caves are 10 km from Bombay on an island in the middle of the harbor. There are four rock-carved temples on the island that are said to have been carved between 450 and 750 AD.

There is a Siva temple here carved out of the western hill, about 250 feet above sea level. The three-headed Trimurti statue is carved out of a single rock and is considered to be one of the masterpieces of Indian sculpture. It is 20 feet high, and each head is six feet high.

Boats leave every 30 minutes from the Gateway of India until 2 pm. You purchase a ticket from the booth on the boat landing or just before you get on the boat. Luxury boats cost double the price of the regular boats. They both get you to the same place at the same time, but the luxury boat may have a guide on board

and not be as crowded. The boat trip takes about an hour and is quite interesting.

You have to go up steep stairs to reach the caves. A palanquins can be hired to be carried up. It takes about an hour to see everything at the top of the hill.

Kanheri Buddhist Cave Temples

They are 40 km north of Bombay. There are 109 caves, but only a few are interesting. The caves date from the 2nd to the 9th century. They are excavated on the face of a hill in the center of Salsette Island. The Great Chaitya Cave (No. 3) has two figures of Buddha 21 feet high. Caves 1, 2,10, 11, 14, 21, 34, 35, 66, and 67 are interesting, and from cave 35 there is a good view of the sea. The caves are open from 9 am to 5.30 pm. To get here you get a suburban train (50 min) from Churchgate station to Borivli Station. You then get an auto-rickshaw or taxi (8 km) to the caves. You should bring water with you as the stalls there sell only cold drinks.

There is a **Lion Safari Park** (Tues to Sun, 9 am to 5 pm) at Krishnagiri Upavan National Park near the caves. You have to get there by auto-rickshaw, either from the caves or the train station.

Hospitals

Breach Candy Hospital, Bhulabhai Desai Rd, is recommended by the foreign embassies. *Bombay Hospital* (286-3343), V Thackersey Marg, is a good private hospital in the downtown area.

P D Hinduja National Hospital (467-575) is one of the most modern and best hospitals in all of India.

Shipping

A good reliable shipper is Perfect Cargo Movers (287-3935), 56 Abdullabhai Currimjee Building, 4th Fl.,

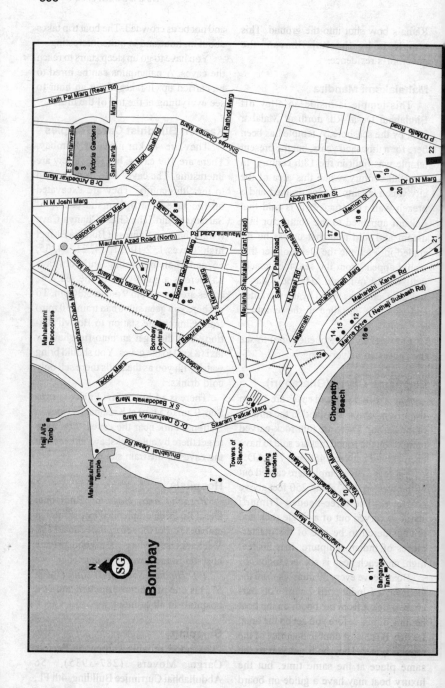

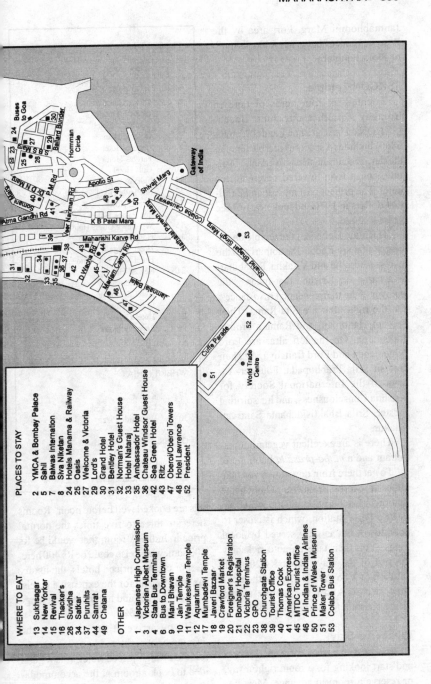

WHERE TO EAT

13 Sukhsagar
14 New Yorker
15 Revival
16 Thacker's
26 Suvidha
34 Satkar
37 Punjabi
44 Samrat
49 Chetana

PLACES TO STAY

2 YMCA & Bombay Palace
5 Sahil
7 Bajwas International
8 Siva Niketan
24 Hotels Manama & Railway
25 Oasis
27 Welcome & Victoria
29 Lord's
30 Grand Hotel
31 Bentley Hotel
32 Norman's Guest House
33 Hotel Nataraj
35 Ambassador Hotel
36 Chateau Windsor Guest House
42 Sea Green Hotel
43 Ritz
47 Oberoi/Oberoi Towers
48 Hotel Lawrence
52 President

OTHER

1 Japanese High Commission
3 Victorian Albert Museum
4 State Bus Terminal
6 Bus to Downtown
9 Mani Bhavan
10 Jain Temple
11 Walukeshwar Temple
12 Aquarium
17 Mumbadevi Temple
18 Javeri Bazaar
19 Crawford Market
20 Foreigner's Registration
21 Bombay Hospital
22 Victoria Terminus
23 GPO
38 Churchgate Station
39 Tourist Office
40 Thomas Cook
41 American Express
45 Air Indian & Indian Airlines
46 MTDC Tourist Office
50 Prince of Wales Museum
51 Maker Tower
53 Colaba Bus Station

Janmabhoomi Marg, Fort area by the Reserve Bank of India, a few blocks north of Flora Fountain.

ISKCON Temple

Located on four acres of land in Bombay's picturesque Juhu Beach, ISKCON's Hare Krishna Land (022-620-6860) includes a spacious marble temple, theater, restaurant, Bhaktivedanta Institute, and a twin-towered seven-storied hotel. The project cost more than $2 million dollars in 1976 and took nearly three years to build.

The main Deities of the temple on the center altar are Radha-Rasabihari and the two *gopis* Lalita and Visakha. Rasabihari is a name for Krishna that means "the enjoyer of the transcendental *rasa* dance". On the right altar are Sita-Rama, Their servant Hanuman, and Rama's brother Laksmana. On the left altar are Lord Nityananda and Lord Caitanya. At Their feet sit Srila Prabhupada, Founder-Acarya of the International Society for Krishna Consciousness, and his spiritual master, Srila Bhaktisiddhanta Sarasvati Thakur.

There is an excellent vegetarian restaurant and a *maha-prasada* booth here.

To get there from downtown you take either an express train from Churchgate Station to Andheri Station or a local train to Vile Parle Station, which is closer to downtown, but is only served by local trains. You then take an auto-rickshaw the rest of the way (about Rs 20 from Andheri or Vile Parle). Most of the rickshaw drivers know the temple as the "Hare Krishna Mandira, ISKCON".

Where To Stay

It is best to arrive early in Bombay and start looking for a room right away, or reserve a room in advance. Most ho-

PLACES TO STAY

1	Ascot Hotel
2	Apollo Guest House
3	Hotel Cowies
4	Oliver Guest House
5	Godwin Hotel
6	Bentley's Hotel
7	Hotel Kishan
8	Garden Hotel
9	Fariyas Hotel
10	Gulf Hotel
11	India & Sea Shore
12	Shelley's Hotel
13	Strand Hotel
14	Sea Palace Hotel
15	Whalley's Guest House
16	Hotel Prosser's
18	Hotel Volga II
20	Hotel Moti International
21	Regent Hotel
22	Salvation Army Hostel
23	Hotel Diplomat
24	Carlton Hotel
25	Hotel Crystal
26	Regency Hotel
27	Suba Guest House
31	YWCA

WHERE TO EAT

17	Kamat
19	Dipti's Pure Drinks
30	Woodside Pizza

OTHER

28	Central Cottage Emporium
29	American Express

tels are booked well before noon. Rooms here are three to five times the normal price in India. A room that would be Rs 100 somewhere else could be Rs 400 here.

For cheaper priced hotels, the luxury tax is 10%, and for the expensive hotels, service charges and luxury tax can range from 30% to 42%.

If you arrive at the airport in the evening or at night and you plan to get a middle or high priced hotel, it is a good idea to book a room at the accommodation booking desk in the lobby of the air-

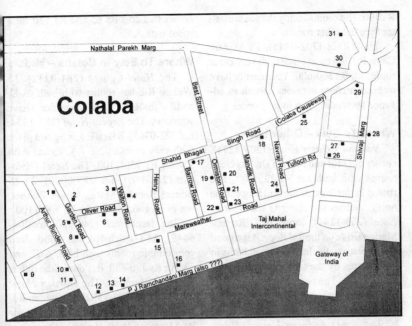

Colaba

port. By this time most of the hotels will be full. If you go to the Colaba area to get a cheap room in the afternoon you may want to engage a tout (commission agent) to find you a room, as it can be very difficult to find a room at this time. They know what hotels have rooms available. One person told me she went around to five places, all full, before hiring a tout.

Where To Stay In Colaba – Lower

The *Hotel Lawrence* (243-618), 3rd floor, Rope Walk Lane, at the back of the Prince of Wales Museum, is a small recommended place with clean rooms for Rs 125/225. It is a good-value and is usually full.

The *Bentley's Hotel* (284-1474, 287-1846), 17 Oliver Rd, has rooms with common bath for Rs 300/400 to Rs 600. The *Salvation Army Red Shield Hotel* (241-824), 30 Mereweather Rd, behind the Taj, has rooms for Rs 300 and dorm beds for Rs 75. It is the least expensive

place in town. Checkout time is 9 am.

The popular *Whalley's Guest House* (283-1802, fax 283-4206), 41 Mereweather Rd, on the third floor, has big rooms with nice verandas for Rs 300/450 and Rs 400/600 with A/C. The rooms on the top floor overlooking the street are the best. Many backpackers like the *Rex-Stiffles*, by the Taj Hotel, which has rooms for Rs 250. The *Hotel Volga II* (287-3436), Navraji Rd, upstairs next door to the Leopold Restaurant, has rooms with common bath for Rs 250/350 and a room with a bath for Rs 350/400. There is no sign for this place.

The *Carlton* (202-0259), 12 Mereweather Rd, is a decent value, but run-down. Single rooms are Rs 150 and double rooms are Rs 225 to Rs 275. The *Hotel India*, 4th Floor, 1/39 Kamal Mansion, Arthur Bunder Rd, has partitioned rooms with no windows. It is one of the cheaper places. The *Sea Shore*, above the India, is a decent value with rooms for

Rs 300. The rooms facing the sea are better then the other rooms.

The *YWCA* (202-0445), 18 Madam Cama Rd, is a quiet place with very clean rooms for Rs 300/600. You usually have to book a room here one month in advance by sending in a money order.

Where To Stay – Other Lower

Norman's Guest House (203-4234), corner of D Rd and Marine Dr, has clean rooms with bath for Rs 225/300. The rooms in the front of the building can be noisy. Across the street is the *Bentley Hotel* (203-1244), corner of D Rd and Marine Drive on the 3rd floor. It is a good cheap place with clean common baths in a quiet area by the seashore. Rooms are Rs 300/350. The two rooms in the back of the hotel are much better than the rest of the rooms.

The *Jones Lodging House*, Abbas Building, 35 Mereweather Rd, is a very basic place, but a good value for the price.

There are a number of cheaper places by Victoria Terminus. The *Railway Hotel* (266-705), 249 P D'Mello Rd, is better than average, with rooms for Rs 420/550. The *Rupam Hotel* (411-4741), 239 P D'Mello Rd is a good clean place with rooms for Rs 450/525 and Rs 575/675 with A/C.

Lord Hotel, 301 Mangalore St, off P D'Mello Rd, is a good place. The *Oasis* (261-7886), 272 SBS Marg, is a good value with well-maintained rooms. The *City Lodge* (265-515), City Terrace, W H Marg, opposite Victoria Terminus, has rooftop rooms with a good view of the city.

The *Bombay Palace* (308-6118), Syed Villa, off YMCA Rd, near Bombay Central, is a mid-priced place with good-sized comfortable A/C rooms. Bombay Central and Victoria Terminus have *retiring*

rooms that cost Rs 65 and Rs 130 for a room with A/C.

Where To Stay In Colaba – Middle

The *Hotel Cowies* (284-0232), 15 Walton Rd, has rooms with bath, A/C, and TV for Rs 715. The rooms don't have windows. The *Regent Hotel* (287-1854, fax 202-0363), 8 Best Rd, is a good place with very comfortable A/C rooms with TV for Rs 750/1100. The *Hotel Diplomat* (202-1661, fax 283-0000), 24-26 Boman Behram Marg, Apollo Bunder, has quiet good rooms for Rs 900/1100.

The *Ascot Hotel* (240-020, fax 204-6449), 38 Garden Rd, has good-sized comfortable rooms with bath, A/C, and TV for Rs 390/680. It is one of the oldest hotels in Bombay. The *Garden Hotel* (241-476, fax 287-1592), 42 Garden Rd, has double rooms with bath and TV for Rs 850 to Rs 1050. It also has more expensive rooms.

The *Godwin Hotel* (287-2050, fax 287-1592), 41 Garden Rd, has rooms for Rs 1090/1400. It is a recommended clean, well-managed hotel. The rooms on the upper floors have better views.

The *Strand* (241-624, fax 287-1441), 5 Apollo Bunder, and the *Regency* (202-0292, 287-3371), behind Regal Cinema, both have comfortable rooms. Rooms at the Regency are Rs 500/720 and rooms at the Strand are Rs 500/600 and Rs 600/800 with A/C. For both places it is best to see the rooms, as they have quite a variety. The *Hotel Apollo* (202-0223, fax 287-4900), Lansdowne Rd, behind Regal Theatre, is a good place with rooms for Rs 900/1100. The rooms with a sea view are the best.

Where To Stay – VT Station Area

The *Grand Hotel* (261-8211), 17 Sprott Rd, Ballard Estate, is a large place built around a central courtyard. It has comfortable rooms with bath, a small balcony, and TV for Rs 950/1100.

Where To Stay – Marine Drive

The *Sea Green Hotel* (282-2294, fax 282-2294), 145 Marine Drive, has clean rooms with A/C and TV for Rs 725/850. It has 24 hour checkout. The *Sea Green South* (221-613), next door, is about the same.

The *Chateau Windsor Guest House* (204-3376, fax 285-1415), 86 Veer Nariman Rd, is a popular place with a selection of clean rooms. Rooms are Rs 600/800 and Rs 800/1000 for an A/C room. As there are a variety of rooms it is best to look at a few rooms.

Middle – Juhu Beach

The *ISKCON* (620-6860, 620-0870), Juhu Beach, is attached to the Hare Krishna Temple. A donation is asked to stay in the rooms here of Rs 600/700 and Rs 640/800 with A/C and hot water. This is a really good price for the quality and location. There are also beds for Rs 150 a night, with the bath in the hall. The guesthouse for ISKCON Life Patrons is usually booked months in advance. There are also rooms for Rs 400 in another building, which should also be booked in advance. ISKCON Life Patrons should book a room here at least two months in advance. Smoking and drinking are not allowed on the premises.

The *Anand Guest House* (620-2234) is located just down the road from the ISKCON Temple, going towards the beach. It is a nice clean place with rooms for Rs 700/750. It has an 8 am checkout time. It is best to reserve a room in advance or book a room early in the morning. A couple blocks away is *Hotel King's* (614-9775), 5 Juhu Tara Rd, which has overpriced rooms for Rs 800/900.

The *Sea Side Hotel* (620-0293), 39/2 Juhu Rd, has A/C rooms with bath for Rs 750/900. The *South End Hotel*, 11 Juhu Tara Rd, has rooms for Rs 500 to Rs 600.

The *Golden Manor* has a pool and A/C rooms from Rs 900 to Rs 1200. It is a nice place. The *Sea View Hotel*, Juhu Beach, has rooms with a good view of the sea for about Rs 700.

Where To Stay – Airport

There are some cheaper hotels about a ten-minute walk from the airport. The *Hotel Shangri-la* at NP Rd, off Nehru Rd, Vile Parle, ten minutes from the airport, is the cheapest place in the area. The *Hotel Aircraft*, 179 Dayaldas Rd, opposite Western Express Highway, is one of the cheapest hotels in the area with rooms for Rs 475/525 and Rs 550/625 with A/C. The *Highway Inn* (832-0021), Vishal Shopping Center, Andheri Kurla Rd, 3 km from Sahar by the Andheri railway station, has a selection of inexpensive clean rooms that are a good value. The *Hotel Airways* (514-9855), near Sarvodaya Hospital, 5 km from the airport, has rooms for Rs 250/300 and Rs 500/600 with A/C.

The hotels by the airport are mainly high-priced. Behind the Centaur is a group of fairly high-priced good hotels. The modern *Hotel Airport International* (612-2883, fax 614-1773) has comfortable clean rooms for Rs 900/1100. The *Hotel BAWA* (611-3636) has rooms for Rs 1190/1900. The *Avion Hotel* (612-3902), Nehru Road, has rooms for Rs 990/1190.

The *Hotel Atithi* (611-6124, fax 611-1998), near the domestic terminal, is a popular place with rooms for Rs 1350/1800. It is heavily booked, so it must be reserved in advance. The five-star *Centaur Hotel* (612-6660, fax 611-3535), directly across from the Indian Air Terminal, has rooms for $90/100. The best place near the airports is the excellent *Leela Kempinski* (836-3636, fax 836-3636), near the international terminal, which has rooms for $250/275.

You can get a room at the domestic airport if you are departing on a flight within 24 hours. To get a room you ask at the airport manager's office.

Where To Stay – High

Colaba and Downtown

The *West End Hotel* (203-9121, fax 205-7506), 45 New Marine Lines, is a well managed recommended place with comfortable rooms for Rs 1090/1800. It is a good value for what you get. The *Fariyas Hotel* (204-2911, fax 283-4992), west of Arthur Bunder Rd, near the Taj, has very good rooms with A/C for Rs 2400/2800. It has a swimming pool.

The *Taj Mahal Intercontinental* (202-3366, fax 287-2711), next to the Gateway of India, is considered one of the best hotels in the world. It has a good bookshop and a good swimming pool. The opulent rooms cost $275/295 and the Presidential suite is $650. This hotel has a new and an old wing. The five-star Taj Group's *Hotel President* (215-0808, fax 215-0808), 90 Cuffe Parade, Colaba, is a luxurious place with rooms starting at $195/215.

The four-star *Ambassador Hotel* (204-1131, fax 204-0004) is a luxury place with a revolving rooftop restaurant. Rooms are $120/140. The *Oberoi/Oberoi Towers* (202-4343, fax 204-1505) is the most expensive hotel in India with rooms starting at $225, going to well over a $1,000. It competes with the Taj for be-

ing the most luxurious hotel in Bombay.

High – Juhu Beach

Most of the hotels in Juhu Beach are expensive. The *Centaur Hotel* (611-3040, fax 611-6343), Juhu Beach, is one of the best hotels in India. Rooms range from $150 to $400. There is a reservation office here for Indian Airlines and Air India. The four-star *Hotel Sands* (620-4512, fax 620-5268), 39/2 Juhu Beach, has rooms for Rs 1100/1500 and suites for Rs 2500.

The five-star *Hotel Sea Princess* (612-2661, fax 611-3973); *Hotel Horizon* (614-4512, fax 611-6715), 37 Juhu Beach; and *Sun-n-Sand Hotel* (620-1811, fax 620-2170) are all first-class places with rooms for around Rs 2500/3000.

The *Holiday Inn* (620-4444, 620-4452), Balraj Sahani Marg, has rooms for $155/200 up to $300. The *Ramada Inn Palm Grove* (611-2323, fax 611-3682), Juhu Beach, has rooms from $120/150 to $225 for a suite.

Where To Eat

Bombay has some of the best eating places in all of India. They also have their own excellent brand of ice cream called *Yankee Doodle*, which is available in a shop of the same name on Marine Drive and other places.

Juhu Beach

The *ISKCON Temple* has a good restaurant that serves buffet style *thalis* for Rs 90 for all you can eat during lunch and dinner. The Special *thali* for Rs 120 includes a curd *subji* and a few extra fancy preparations. At other times they serve snacks, including pizza and vegi-burgers. There is a new menu every day. There is also a popular *maha-prasada* booth at the temple. The temple *prasada* is also good.

Natural Ice Cream located behind the ISKCON Temple, has many different varieties of homemade ice cream. They say that they only use cow milk. It is a recommended place. *Woodland's Garden Cafe*, Juhu Scheme, Vaikuntlal Mehta Rd, near Juhu Beach, is a recommended South Indian place, which also serves pizza and tasty *thalis*. It has some of the best food in town, but it has a fairly limited menu. Next to Woodlands is the *Utsav Restaurant*, which is a fancy high priced place.

Downtown

Samrat, Prem Court, J Tata Road, near Churchgate Station, is a recommended place that serves good Gujarati food and other items. It has good service and is one of the best restaurants in India. *Woodlands*, Mittal Chambers, Nariman Pt, near Oberoi Towers, has excellent South Indian food and good *thalis*. It is a recommended place.

Purohits, Vir Nariman Road, a couple of blocks from Churchgate station, is a good place. It is one of the most famous places in town with reasonably priced *thalis* (Rs 45) during lunch and dinner and snacks at other times. *Satkar*, in the Indian Express Building, right next to Churchgate Station, is a crowded place during lunch. It has good food and some of the best prices in Bombay. Near Satkar, is the *Suryodaya* store, which is like a small supermarket with a good selection of food items.

Suvidha, which is located between Victoria Station and Handloom House, has nice food including a special suggested preparation called *raiva idli*. *Chetana*, 34 K Dubash Marg by the Prince of Wales Museum, is a very good place. *Kamats Restaurant*, Navrose Mansion, Tardeo Rd, Colaba area, has good

ice cream and snacks and is economically priced.

If you are getting a train from Central Station and need a place to eat, you can go to the *Shagun Restaurant*, which is across the street and to your right when you walk out of the station. Around the corner is the *Annaleela Udipi Restaurant*.

Chowpatty Beach

Across from Chowpatty Beach, the *New Yorker* has good pizza, Mexican food, and baked potatoes. The Nachos are very good, with real cheese like you would get in the West. It is the best place in town and maybe in India, if you want this type of food. *Sukhsagar* by Chowpatty Beach, is like a road-stand with good *idlis* and a juice bar.

Revival, Chowpatty Sea Face, above the London Pub, is a good, but high priced place. It has many imaginative preparations, but I believe it is best to stick to the Indian items. Across the street, *Thacker's*, 116/118 First Marine St, by Marine Lines railway station, is a famous well-established place.

Local Trains

Bombay has a good local train system with 28 stations. They are very crowded most of the day and especially during rush hour. Most trains have ladies only compartments, which are very advisable for ladies, especially during rush hour, because in a crowded situation the men love to grope (touch) the women. You should be very careful getting on and off the trains because they are not like in the West where they try to make sure people will not get hurt. Someone I know tried to get on one of these trains as it was taking off and broke one of his legs.

There are both first-class and second-class compartments. First-class is about

10 times the price and often much less crowded, except during heavy rush hour. If you have a second-class ticket and are caught on a first-class compartment you may be arrested and fined. They do catch people and consider ignorance no excuse, even if you are a foreigner.

Taxis and Auto-Rickshaws

I found that most of the time the taxi drivers use the meter. They have a fare adjustment chart, and you must pay 9 times the meter for taxis and 5.5 times the meter for auto-rickshaws.

To hire a car for the day (8 hr or 80 km) cost: Rs 800 for A/C Luxury, Rs 600 for non-A/C; Rs 500 for an Ambassador. You can hire a car from Makson Auto Hirers (812-1701), Sagar Kunj, L Jagmohanda Marg; Bhuta Travels (632-5334), Nagardas Park, Old Nagardas Rd, Andheri; or Budget (494-2644).

Arrival by Air

The downtown can be an hour (sometimes 2 hr) drive from the airport during rush hour. If you arrive at night you may want to pay in advance at the pre-paid taxi stand, which is slightly higher than the meter charge. At least you will be brought by the most direct route. Taxi drivers will try to get you to go to the hotel of their choice. It is usually best to not agree with their suggestions, as their commission will be added to the price of the room. Later in the day, however, it may be difficult to find a hotel at any price, so they may be helpful at that time.

You should not get an auto-rickshaw at the airport to go downtown, as they are not allowed downtown. They may leave you with an unscrupulous taxi driver at Mahim Creek, which is as far south as they can go.

The EAT bus (Rs 40) leaves hourly from Sahar airport. It is a cheap and easy way to get downtown. Most of the higher priced hotels, especially the ones by the airport, send courtesy coaches to pick up people at the airport.

To get downtown you can take an auto-rickshaw to the suburban train, which is very cheap into the city. From Sahar international airport you go to Andheri station, and from Santa Cruz domestic airport you go to Vile Parle station. It is a much better to take a train downtown than to go by public bus. It takes about 45 minutes to get downtown by train. If you have heavy bags this will be a difficult trip during rush hour.

Travel

Air The Bombay airport is the busiest airport in India. Most of the major international airlines fly into Bombay. Many times you can fly into Bombay and out from Delhi for the same price. There are several flights a day to the major cities in India.

There are two airports in Bombay— the domestic airport, called **Santa Cruz**, and the international airport, named **Sahar**. When taking a flight you should make sure you go to the correct airport. Many people make this mistake. Both airports are north of the downtown, about 26 km from the center city. Every 15 minutes there are shuttle buses between the two airports. There are airport buses every half hour to the airport from the Air India building at Nariman Point. Taxis from downtown can take two hours to reach the airport, but usually take 45 minutes (Rs 200). From Juhu Beach it takes about a half hour to get to the airport. The Air India office at Nariman Point can be very crowded.

Some flights from Bombay are: Ahmedabad (6 daily, $61), Aurangabad

(2 daily, $52), Bangalore (8 daily, $115), Calcutta (5 daily, $157), Delhi (15 daily, $165), Madras (6 daily, $110), Madurai (daily, $121), Mangalore (daily, $110), Trivandrum (daily, $165), Udaipur (daily, $65), Varanasi (9 weekly, $225), and Vishakapatnam (daily, $159).

There are clean comfortable **retiring rooms** at the Domestic terminal for Rs 440 for a double room and Rs 165 for a dorm bed.

International Airlines

Aeroflot
   241/242 Nirmal, Nariman Point
   (221-1682)
Air France
   Maker Chambers VI, 220 Nariman
   Point (202-4818)
Air India
   Air India Building, Nariman Point
   (202-4142)
   Reservation office at the Centaur
   Hotel, Juhu Beach
Air Lanka
   Mittal Towers (C Wing) Nariman
   Point (223-299)
Air Mauritius
   Air India Building, Nariman Point
   (202-8474)
Alitalia
   Veer Nariman Rd, Churchgate
   (222-144)
American Airline
   222 Maker Chambers, 221 Nariman
   Point (232-438)
Bangladesh Biman
   199 J Tata Rd, Churchgate (224-659)
British Airways
   Valcan Insurance Building, 202 B
   Veer Nariman Rd (220-888)
Canadian Airlines
   Podar House, 10 Marine Dr
   (204-2174)
Cathay Pacific Airways

Taj Mahal Hotel, Apollo Bunder
   Colaba (202-9112)
Continental Airlines
   Ground Fl, 6 Maker Arcade, Cuffe
   Parade (218-1440)
Delta
   505 Raheja Chambers, Nariman
   Point (204-2703)
Emirates
   Mittal Chambers, 228 Nariman Point
   (287-1650)
Ethiopian Airways
   Taj Mahal Hotel, Apollo Bunder,
   Colaba (202-8787)
Gulf Air
   Maker Chamber V, Nariman Point
   (202-4065)
Japan Air Lines
   2 Raheja Centre, Nariman Point
   (287-4036)
Kenya Airways
   199 J Tata Rd (220-064)
KLM
   Khaitan Bhavan, 198 J Tata Rd
   (283-3338)
Kuwait Airlines
   86 Veer Nariman Rd (204-5351)
LOT (Polish Airways)
   6 Maker Arcade, Cuffe Parade
   (218-5494)
Malaysia Airlines
   6 Maker Arcade, Cuffe Parade
   (218-1431)
Lufthansa
   Express Towers, Nariman Point
   (202-3430)
Pakistan International Airlines
   Nariman Bhavan, Nariman Point
   (202-1598)
Qantas
   42 Sakhar Bhavan, Nariman Point
   (202-0343)
Royal Jordanian Airlines
   B-1 Amarchand Msn, Madame
   Camma Rd (223-080)

Royal Nepal Airlines
   6 Maker Arcade, Cuffe Parade (211-440)
Sabena
   Nirmal, Nariman Point (202-3240)
Saudia Arabian Airlines
   Express Towers, Nariman Point (287-0656)
Scandinavian Airlines (SAS)
   Podar House, 10 Marine Drive (202-7083)
Singapore Airlines
   Taj Mahal Hotel, Apollo Bunder (287-0986)
Swissair
   Maker Chambers VI, 220 Nariman Point (287-2210)
Syrian Arab Airlines
   7 Barbourne Stadium, Nariman Point (224-375)
Thai International
   Podar House, 10 Marine Drive (202-3284)
United Airlines
   1 Brabourne Stadium, Churchgate

Domestic Airlines
Indian Airlines
   Air India Building, Nariman Point (202-3031)
   Reservation desks in the Taj Mahal Hotel and the Centaur Hotel, Juhu Beach
Damania
   17 Nehru Road Vakola, Santa Cruz (610-2525)
East West Airlines
   Sophia, 18 New Kantwadi Rd, off Perry Cross Rd, Bandra (643-6678)
Jet Airways
   41-42 Maker Chamber-III, Nariman Point (838-6111)
Modiluft
   89 Bhulabhai Desai Rd (363-1921)
Sahara India

G-6 Maker Chamber-V, Nariman Point (283-2446)

Rail There are three different long-distance train stations in Bombay. Central Railway trains depart from **Victoria Terminus** (Bombay VT), in the center of the city, for the east and south. A few trains also depart to northern Rajasthan and Delhi from here. It is a 15-minute ride from the Colaba area. Victoria station has a very good Foreign Tourist Bureau from which you can get tourist quota tickets. They are very helpful in making an itinerary and providing good information. You have to first get an authorization slip from the tourist information booth on the main railway station concourse and then go to the tourist counter in the Computerised Reservations System Building office (9 am to 1 pm and 1 to 4 pm, daily). You can make a reservation for any train leaving from any of the Bombay stations. Counters 1 and 2 are set aside specifically for foreign tourists. They also sell Indrail passes here.

Bombay Central Station is the headquarters of Western Railways. It is a few km north of the center of the city. You can get trains here that go north to Gujarat, Rajasthan, and Delhi. You can take a local train from Churchgate Station to get here.

The third long-distance station is **Dadar**, in the northern part of the city. Some of the Central and Western Railway trains stop here. You can get a local train from here to the downtown. Some trains to Calcutta leave from **Kurla station**, near the airport. Getting to these stations with luggage can be difficult by public transportation.

Churchgate Station, near the center of the downtown, is mainly a commuter station. The Foreign Tourist Bureau and foreign reservation counters are on the mezzanine floor in the CRS building next to this station, next to the Government of India Tourist Office. This office is open from 9.30 am to 4.30 pm, Mon to Fri, and 9.30 am to 2.30 pm on Saturdays. To reserve a train here you first get a slip from the man sitting in the back of the room, and then purchase your ticket. If you want to take a night train, you usually have to purchase the ticket on the morning the train departs. If you are taking a morning train, you come and purchase the ticket one day before. You cannot usually purchase a tourist quota ticket a few days in advance. If you get off one of the trains at Churchgate Station, coming into the city, the CRS building is to your left as your head toward the main entrance. You must pay for your ticket in foreign currency or show a recent encashment certificate.

There are many trains coming in and out of Bombay every day. The superfast Rajdhani Express #2951 (5 pm, 16½, daily except Mon) from Bombay Central goes to **Delhi**. The Frontier Mail #2903 (9.15 pm, 22 hr) to Delhi is also fast. The Dadar-Madras Express #6063 (7.50 pm, 24½ hr, Dadar Station) and Bombay-Madras Mail #6511 (2.25 pm, 25½ hr, VT Station) are the fastest trains to **Madras**. If you want to go north to **Mount Abu** or **Udaipur**, you have to take a train to Ahmedabad and from there get a train or bus to these places. The Saurashtra Mail #9005 (8.10 pm, 21 hr, Bombay Central) departs to **Dwarka** via Vadodara (5 hr) and Ahmedabad (9½ hr). The Punjab Mail #1037 (4.15 pm, 24 hr) departs daily to **Agra**. The Jalna Exp #1003 (10.30 pm, 10 hr) is a direct train to **Aurangabad**. The Gitanjali Exp #2859 (6.05 am, 32½ hr) and Calcutta Mail #8001 (7.10 pm, 36 hr) depart to **Cal-**

cutta. To **Bangalore** is the Udyan Exp #6529 (7.55 am, 24½ hr). For **Guntakal** (for Hampi) is the Madras Mail #7009 (11.15 pm, 19½ hr). The Kanniyakumari Exp #1081 (3.30 pm, 45 hr) goes to **Thiruvananthapuram**. The Mahanagiri Exp #1093 (11.55 pm) departs daily to **Varanasi** (28 hr) via **Allahabad** (24 hr) and the Bombay-Varanasi-Ratnagiri Exp #2165 (5 am) departs to Varanasi (27½) via Allahabad (24½ hr) on Mon, Wed, and Thu.

There is a rail reservation counter at Bombay's international airport, open from 11 pm to 7 am in the morning, to coincide with international flight arrivals.

There are trains to Agra (2 daily, 24 to 27 hr), Ahmedabad (7 daily, 9 to 11 hr), Aurangabad (1 daily, 10 hr), Bangalore (2 daily, 24½ hr), Calcutta (4 daily, 33 to 40 hr), Delhi (7 daily, 17 to 33 hr), Hyderabad (2 daily, 15 to 18 hr), Jaipur (1 daily, 23 hr), Madras (3 daily, 24 to 31 hr), Mangalore (1 or 2 daily, 40 to 46 hr), Nasik (14 daily, 4 hr), Pune (15 daily, 4 hr) Ujjain (1, daily, 14 hr), Trivandrum (1 daily, 45 hr), and Varanasi (4 daily, 28 to 31 hr).

Bus The Long Distance Bus Station is opposite Bombay Central Train Station. The State bus companies' offices for Maharashtra, Gujarat, Madhya Pradesh, and Karnataka are here. The MTDC luxury buses are the best buses. You can make advance reservation for some luxury buses. The booking office is open from 8 am to 11 pm. It is a very hectic place, so you should arrive for your bus as early as possible. To make a reservation can take a couple of hours.

Most Maharashtrian state buses depart and arrive at the ASIAD bus stand, beside the main street in Dadar. It is a thirty-

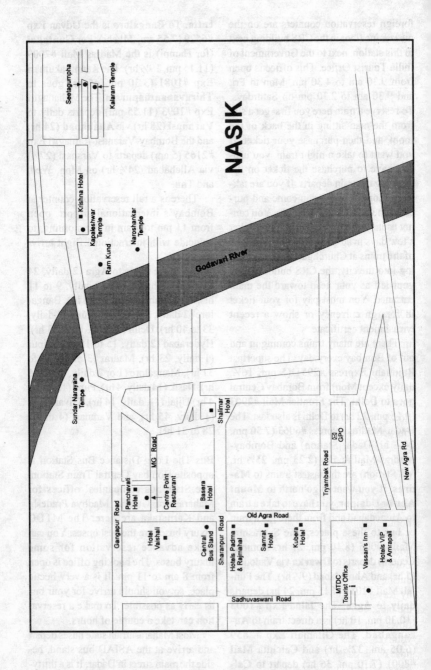

NASIK

Godavari River

Seetagumpha

Kalaram Temple

Krishna Hotel

Kapaleshwar Temple

Naroshankar Temple

Ram Kund

Sundar Narayana Tempe

MG Road

Shalimar Hotel

GPO

Tryambak Road

New Agra Rd

Gangapur Road

Panchavati Hotel

Centre Point Restaurant

Basera Hotel

Hotel Vaishali

Central Bus Stand

Sharanpur Road

Old Agra Road

Hotels Padma & Rajmahal

Samrat Hotel

Kubera Hotel

Vassan's Inn

Hotels VIP & Amrapali

MTDC Tourist Office

Sadhuvaswani Road

minute, to one hour taxi ride from the downtown. You can get a local train downtown from the Dadar railway station. To get to this station you walk over Tilak Marg bridge.

Most of the private bus companies operate out of Ballard Pier in the Fort area.

You can book MTDC buses at the MTDC office on Madame Cama Rd. You can book morning buses to Nasik and Mahabaleswara at the India Government tourist office, 123 M Karve Rd, Churchgate. It is usually best to leave Bombay by train.

Karla (Karli)

In Karla is the largest and best preserved Buddhist cave *chaitya* (temple) in India. The caves here were carved around 80 BC. You may want to come here if you cannot go to Ajanta or Ellora. Not many foreign tourists visit here.

Karla is about 126 km southeast of Bombay. You can get here by taking a train (2 hr) from Bombay to Lonavala. From Lonavala, it is a 14 km bus or taxi ride to the foot of the hill. The *Peshwa Holiday Resorts*, near the caves, is a decent place to stay with rooms from Rs 125/225 up to Rs 500 for an A/C cottage.

NASIK

Population: 790,000, STD Code 0253

Nasik is a holy city located about five hours northeast of Bombay (187 km). Lord Rama stayed here for some time during His exile, and Sita was carried off by Ravana from this place. Nasik is on the banks of the Godavari River, which flows to the Bay of Bengal. Laksman, the younger brother of Lord Rama cut off the nose of Surpanaka, the younger sister of Ravana, here. That is why this place has

the name Nasik. Kumbha-mela takes place here every 12 years. Sri Caitanya visited here.

This place was known as Padmanagar in Satya-yuga, Trikantaka in Treta-yuga, Janasthana in Dwapara-yuga, and Nasik in the present Kali-yuga.

Nasik is a fairly large city, though it does not seem to be. Not many foreign tourists come here, and it is a relatively hassle free place. Coming from Bombay, you can easily stop here on the way to the Ellora and Ajanta Caves or while traveling on some of the trains that go between Delhi and Bombay.

Information

The **Maharashtra Tourism office** (70059) is near the Golf Club on Old Agra Rd.

You can **change money** at the State Bank of India, on Swami Vivekananda Road, by the City Bus Stand (Mon-Fri, 10 am to 2 pm, Sat 10 am to noon).

Nasik Darshan Tour

There is a daily "Darshan Tour" (7.30 am to 5 pm, Rs 40), which is a good way to see some of the sites in the Nasik area. It is an all-day tour that goes to the Pandava Lena caves, Sita Gupha, Kala Rama Mandira, Tapovan, Trimbakeswara Temple, and other sites. It is a good value. You find the bus by asking for the "Darshan Tour" bus. You should book this tour at the City Bus Stand in advance as it is quite popular. The counter to book your ticket is to your right as you enter the station.

Ram-kund Area

This interesting area by the Godavari River is the main pilgrimage place in Nasik. Ram-kund is where Rama and Sita used to bathe, so this tank is considered especially sacred. It is also called Asthi Vilaya Tirtha (Bone Immersion Tank), because bones dropped in here, dissolve. In recent years the following people's bones were dropped in the Asthi Vilaya Tirtha after they died: Mahatma Gandhi, Jawaharlal Nehru, Indira Gandhi, her son Rajiv Gandhi, Dr Rajendra Prasad, and many other famous people. Lord Rama is also said to have performed funeral rites here in memory of His father, King Dasaratha. It is surrounded by a concrete viewing tower.

An architecturally interesting temple to see is the **Sundara Narayana Temple**, built in 1756, which contains 3-foot-tall Vishnu and Lakshmi Deities. This temple is across the river from Ram-kund by the bridge.

The **Naro Sankara Mandir** is a Siva temple built by the Marathas in the 18th century. It is also known as the Rameswara Mandir. It has an enormous church bell taken from the Portuguese at the battle of Vasai (Bassein) in 1739.

Near Ram-kund is the 600 year old **Kapileswara Temple**, "God of the Skull", which is dedicated to Lord Siva. You have to climb up 50 steps to reach it.

Kumbha-mela

Kumbha-mela is held in Nasik every 12 years. It also takes place at Allahabad, Haridwar and Ujjain. This is one of the places that the drops of nectar fell when the demigods and demons fought over it. It is said that if one takes bath in the Godavari River while the nectar is falling, one accumulates merit equal to bathing in the Ganges for 60,000 years. About three and a half million people came here to the Kumbha-mela in 1991. The next Kumbha-mela is August-September, 2003.

Sita Gumpha & Kala Rama Temple

Sita Gupha is said to be the place from where Ravana abducted Sita to take her to the island of Lanka. It is a small cave by the Kala Rama Temple. You have to crawl into the cave to see the Deities of Sita, Rama, and Laksmana. Nearby is the Kala Rama Temple, or Black Rama. The Kala Rama Temple (1782) has jet-black Deities of Sita, Rama, and Laksmana. The tower over the temple is 25m (83 ft) high. There is no restriction on who can enter this temple.

Tapovana

It is said that at Tapovana, Laksmana cut off the nose of Ravana's sister, Surpanakha. Ramacandra lived here during His exile. Great sages and *rishis* used to practice austerities at this place which was part of the Dandakaranya forest. It is fairly close to Sita Gupha.

Pandava Lena Caves

These Hinayana Buddhist rock-cut monasteries and temples, built in the 1st century AD, are located ten km from Nasik on the road to Bombay. They are like the Ajanta Caves. There are 24 Buddhist caves, the most interesting caves being numbers 3, 8, and 15. The most straight-forward way to gets to the caves is by auto-rickshaw or by the Nasik Darshan tour bus. There are infrequent and crowded buses that pass the caves. It is a steep ten-minute walk to reach the caves and some people find it difficult to make the climb.

Where To Stay – Central Bus Stand Area

Most of the hotels in town are in the middle level, so it is not easy to find a decent budget hotel here. The budget places are by the Central Bus Stand and fill up early. I found the hotels here to be more expensive than average.

The *Raj Mahal Lodge* (572-880), Sharampur Rd, near the central bus station, has rooms with hot water and TV for Rs 140/170 up to Rs 180/230, but it fills up early. It is about the best valued budget place.

The *Padma* (576-837), Sharampur Rd, opposite the Central Bus Stand, is clean and convenient and has rooms with hot water. The *Basera* (575-616), Sivaji Rd by the Central Bus Stand, is a good value. It has rooms with bath and hot water and some rooms have A/C. The *Holiday Plaza* (573-521) is a popular place with Indian businessmen. It has rooms for Rs 310/430 and Rs 500/600 with A/C. It has a vegetarian restaurant.

The *Hotel Midtown*, by the Central Bus Stand, has small singles without baths for Rs 160 and good clean doubles for Rs 275. The *Hotel Samrat* (578-211), Old Agra Road, near the Central Bus Stand, is a good small place that is centrally located. Rooms with TV and hot water go for Rs 250/375 and Rs 375/450 with A/C. I would recommend it, but it is slightly overpriced.

The *Hotel Panchavati Yatri* (571-273), which is just behind the Hotel Panchavati, has rooms with bath for Rs 225/350 and Rs 400/500 with A/C. It is an older version of the hotel in front of it, and at this level is a recommended place.

The two-star *Hotel Panchavati* (575-771), 430 Vakilwadi, has A/C rooms for Rs 550/750 and other rooms for Rs 350/550. It is one of the best places in town.

Where To Stay – Other Places

The *Hotel Krishna*, near the Ahilyabai Holkar Bridge, by Ram-kund, is a nice place with hot water for Rs 150/275. The *Greenview* (572-231), 1363 Trimbaka Road, is a modern place with rooms for Rs 375 and Rs 475 with A/C. It has a nice garden. The *Hotel Dwaraka Tourist*, Deolali Naka, is a western style hotel.

The *VIP*, on Old Agra Road, has modern rooms for Rs 225/300 and Rs 375 with A/C. The *Hotel Sachin*, on the Bombay-Agra highway 3 km outside of Nasik, is a good place to stay, but it is inconveniently located.

The *Hotel Siddharth* (573-288), on the Nasik-Pune Road by the airport, is a good place. The good-sized well-maintained rooms are Rs 135/175 and Rs 250/275 with A/C. The two-star *Wasan's Hotel* (577-881), Old Agra Rd, is a good place with rooms for Rs 350/475 and Rs 525/650 with A/C.

Where To Eat

The best place in town is the *Woodlands Restaurant*, which is across the road from the Hotel Siddharth. It serves excellent South Indian meals and *thalis*. The service is also good, and it is reasonably priced.

The *Centre Point Restaurant*, on the main road near Hotel Panchavati, is a good high-class place which serves good Macaroni with cheese and Vegetable Biryani. It is a suggested place, but it is not cheap. There is a pure-veg restaurant with reasonable prices in the *Hotel Panchavati*. The *Hotel Holiday Plaza*, Shivaji Rd, Shalimar Chowk, has a pure vegetarian restaurant.

Travel

Air The nearest airport is in Bombay, 182 km away.

Train The train station is at Nasik Road

(8 km southeast of town). It is on the main Bombay-Delhi and Bombay-Calcutta line of the Central Railway. You can book train tickets at the city booking counter off MG Road (Mon-Fri, 10 am to 5 pm).

There are regular trains to **Bombay** (12 daily) that take about 5 hours. The Panchavati Express departs at about 7.20 am and takes just 4 hours. It is best to reserve this train in advance. The Punjab Mail #1037 (10.30 pm) is the best train to **Delhi** (21 hrs) and Agra (17½ hours). There are also trains to **Calcutta** and **Varanasi**. The only train to **Aurangabad** departs at about 3 am in the morning.

Bus You get the bus to Aurangabad (5 hrs) and the Nasik Darshan Bus at the City Bus Stand in the center of town. This bus station is close to the hotels and restaurants.

You get buses to **Bombay** at the Mahamarga Bus Stand, which is a ten-minute auto-rickshaw ride from the center of town. There are four luxury buses a day to Bombay which take four hours to reach Dadar Station. You must book tickets for these buses in advance at the reservation counter at the City Bus Stand.

Trimbak

Population 8,000

The town of Trimbak (three eyes) is 30 km west of Nasik. One of the 12 *jyotirlingas* is here, and close by is the source of the Godavari River. There is also an impressive Maratha Fort on the nearby hill.

Trimbakeshwara Temple

The three *lingas* in this 18th century temple dedicated to Trimbakeswara are eye-shaped. *Tri* means "three," and *Ambak* means "eye," thus *trimbaka*

means the "three-eyed one," who is Lord Siva. Trimbakeshwara is one of the twelve *jyotirlingas*. This temple was visited by Lord Caitanya.

This interesting temple was built in 1730 by Baji Rao Peshwa, costing almost a million rupees. There is a large tower over the sanctuary.

Non-Hindus are not supposed to enter the temple, but they can go up to the steps and look inside. I went inside and no one said anything to me.

Source of Godavari River

Trimbak is the source of the Godavari, which is one of the most important holy rivers in India. This river flows almost 1000 km east to the Bay of Bengal. It is said that this is the exact spot where the drop of nectar fell from the Kumbha vessel, for which Kumbha-mela is famous. You have to walk up a flight of 690 stairs to reach Gangasagar, a tank of water fed by the Godavari's source. It is said that the Ganges and Godavari emanate from the same source by an underground passage. Bathing here is said to cleanse you of the worst sins.

The round-trip climb to Brahmagiri, the source of the Godavari, takes two or three hours and is best done in the morning. It is a hard climb, so you should bring water with you. On the way you pass a temple dedicated to the goddess Ganga, a cave that has 108 Siva-lingas, a temple dedicated to the sage Gautama Rsi, whose *asrama* was said to be here, and the remains of the Anjeri Fort. About twenty minutes from the Anjeri Fort is the Gaumukha (Mouth of the Cow) Temple, where the source of the Godavari is located.

Kushawarth Tirtha

A few minutes' walk from the

Trimbakeshwara Temple is Kushawarth Tirtha, a bathing tank which is said to contain Ganges water. It is mentioned in the *Puranas*. It is said to have gotten its name because *kusha* grass used to grow in profusion around it.

Practicalities

Trimbak is a nice peaceful place, so you may want to stay here overnight. The *MTDC Tourist Bungalow* is the best place to stay at, but it is not much. All the eating places are basic.

There are hourly buses from Nasik that take about 45 min from the City Bus Stand. You can get a bus back to Nasik or one of the shared taxis that wait outside the bus stand.

AURANGABAD

Population: 600,000, STD Code 0240

This is a convenient city to use as a base to go to the Ajanta and Ellora Caves.

The caves at Ellora and Ajanta are off the railway lines and in the middle of nowhere. Usually they are visited from Aurangabad (Ellora 30 km northwest, Ajanta 106 km north) or from Jalgaon (59 km north of Ajanta). Jalgaon is on the main railway line from Bombay to Allahabad. Aurangabad is off the main line and there is just one direct train from Bombay daily.

Orientation

Aurangabad is spread out. The tourist offices, cheaper hotels, and railway station are in the southwest part of town. It is a good distance to the older part of town, which is in the center of the city.

The higher class hotels are located on the road going towards the airport, in the east part of town, and in the area between the railway station and the old part of town.

Tourist Offices and Information

The **Government of India Tourist Office** (331-217), Station Rd, is open from 8.30 am to 6 pm weekdays and from 8.30 am to 12.30 pm on Saturdays.

The **Maharashtra Tourism Development Corporation** (331-513) is at the Holiday Resort Hotel on Station Road (open daily, 10 pm to 5 pm). MTDC also has tourist information counters at the railway station and the airport (open at the time of flights only).

The GPO and poste restante counter are at Juna Bazaar Chowk, in the north part of town. Outside the post office there is someone to sew and seal packages.

The State Bank of India is at Kranti Chowk. The Ashok Hotel has money changing facilities for non-residents between 5 and 10 pm.

Tours

Tours are arranged by the MTDC, the ITDC, and the State Transport Company. You can be picked up at your hotel if it is conveniently located. The ITDC tour and State Transport tour are cheaper than the MTDC tour. I was satisfied with the MTDC tour to Ajanta. The tour guide spoke good English and explained everything I wanted to know. I was also given enough time to see everything, but for some people it would be too rushed. This tour is a good value and is recommended.

I also took the MTDC tour to the Ellora Caves, which includes Daulatabad. None of the guides spoke English. At the Ellora Caves they rush you around like there was a fire, and for some reason or other they really believed I understood Hindi. I really question the intelligence of the organizer of this tour. If you don't mind being rushed around it is not such a bad value.

The State Transport Corporation tours

start at the railway station, and you book tours at Window 1 at the city bus stand. You get the ITDC tour tickets at the Hotel Aurangabad Ashok (24143).

Maharashtra Tourism Development Corporation (24713) tours start from the Holiday Resort Hotel, Station Road, but you can also be picked up at your hotel.
Ajanta Caves – Daily from 8 am to 5 pm.
Ellora Caves and City Tour – Daily from 9.30 am to 5.30 pm.

India Tourism Development Corporation tours start at the Hotel Aurangabad Ashok (24143). You arrange the tour in advance at the tourist office on Station Rd or at Ashok Tours and Travel in the hotel lobby.
Ajanta Caves – 8 am to 5 pm.
Ellora Caves – 9.30 am to 5.30 pm .

When to Visit

The best time to visit is October and November, and the second best time is from December to March. By April and May the weather is extremely hot, and this is one of the hottest areas in India.

Aurangabad Caves

The caves are mainly Buddhist, but there are some Hindu caves too. They are located 3 km north of Aurangabad. These caves are interesting, but not as good as Ellora and Ajanta. There are two groups of caves: caves 1-5 and caves 6-9, which are about a 2 km walk apart. The caves are said to date from the 4th to the 8th century, except Cave 4, which dates back to the first century. You can drive up to Caves 6 and 7, which are the most interesting.

You have to negotiate in advance for waiting time for an auto-rickshaw or taxi. These caves are not visited by many people. There is a book you can get about the caves by Carmel Berkson called *The Caves at Aurangabad.*

Where To Stay – Lower

Most of the cheap places are by the railway station. The clean well-managed *Youth Hostel* (334-892), between the main section of town and the railway station, is a recommended place for the budget traveller. It has a few clean double rooms and dorm beds for Rs 30. Check-in times are 7 to 11 am and 4 to 8 pm. Checkout time is 9 am. The *Hotel Panchavati* (25204), next to the Youth Hostel, has rooms with bath and hot water in the morning for Rs 90/110.

The *Hotel Natraj*, Station Rd, is one of the best cheap places, having rooms with bath for Rs 60/80. *Tourist's Home*, Station Rd, is a clean basic place having rooms with common bath for Rs 70 and rooms with bath for Rs 90. It is one of the better cheap places.

The *MTDC Holiday Resort* (334-259), close to the railway station, is a good value with rooms for Rs 150/200 and Rs 300/350 with A/C. Checkout time is 8 am.

The *Hotel Printravel* (29707), Dr Ambedkar Rd, between the bus and railway stations, is a recommended place with rooms for Rs 110/160 with bath and hot water. The rooms are fairly basic. It is a big quiet place. There is a good vegetarian restaurant in front of the hotel. The *Hotel Ira*, in the Samartha Nagar area by the bus stand, is a good place with rooms for Rs 200.

Where To Stay – Middle

The *Hotel Rajdhani* (336-553), Station Rd, is clean and new. It has rooms for Rs 325/400 and Rs 375/425 with A/C. The *Hotel Nandavan* (336-314),

Station Rd, has big decent rooms with hot water and TV for Rs 150/200 and Rs 300 with A/C. It also has a vegetarian restaurant.

The *Hotel Ravi Raj* (27501), Dr Rajendra Prasad Marg, by Station Rd, has a good location. It has decent rooms, but they are not a very good value. Rooms go for Rs 350/425 and Rs 400/450 for the A/C rooms.

The *Great Punjab* (25598), Station Rd, near the train station, is a new business type hotel with good-valued rooms for Rs 200/225 and Rs 300/350 with A/C. This is the best middle-class hotel by the station.

The *Ashiyana* (29322), Bansilal Nagar, off Station Rd by the tourist office, is a new hotel with good-valued clean quiet rooms. Rooms are Rs 125/175.

Where To Stay – Higher

Quality Inn Vedant (337-412), Station Rd, is a new place with rooms for Rs 1295/1500. The *Aurangabad Ashok* (332-492) on Dr Rajendra Prasad Marg has A/C room for Rs 900/1200. It has a pool and its own garden. It is not so well maintained.

The *Ajanta Ambassador Hotel* (485-211, fax 484-367), Chikal Thana, is a five-star hotel with rooms for Rs 1200/2250 and suites that cost up to Rs 3000. It is a well-managed place with a good pool and quiet gardens.

The *Welcomegroup Rama International* (84441, fax 84768), R-3 Chikal Thana, is a first-class marble luxury place with rooms for $40/75 and suites for up to $125. It is well located with large gardens.

The new *Taj Residency* (333-501, fax 331-223), 8N-12, CIDCO, has impressive gardens and is well located. Very comfortable rooms are $40/50. This place is recommended.

Where To Eat

The restaurant in front of the *Printravel Hotel* on Dr Ambedkar Road is a good place. It is open from 11.30 am to 3 pm and 7 to 11 pm for full meals, and snacks are served the rest of the time. The *Radhika Restaurant*, at Hotel Nandanvan (23315) on Station Rd, has a very reasonably priced vegetarian restaurant.

The *Woodlands Restaurant* (82822), on Jaina Road near the Cidco Bus Stand and the Rama International Hotel, is by far the best place in town. It is popular with the locals. It is about a twenty-minute auto-rickshaw ride from the train station. It has above average prices.

Local Transport

To go by taxi to the Ellora Caves via Daulatabad Fort costs about Rs 500. This includes waiting time. Local taxis are Rs 250 for 4 hours (40 km) and Rs 350 for eight hours (80 km). Regular buses from the Central Bus Stand go to Daulatabad, Ellora, Ajanta (3 hr) and Jalgaon (4½ hr). There are two stalls by the bus stand that rent out good bikes.

Travel

Air You can get a flight to and from Bombay, Delhi, Jaipur, and Udaipur. The Indian Airlines office (485-421) is on Airport Rd (Jalna Rd). It is open daily 10 am to 5 pm, except Sundays. The flights are usually overbooked way in advance, so it is best to book your flight at least a week in advance, if not more. The airport is about 10 km from the center of town. To fly to Udaipur takes just a half hour, but to travel there by train or bus can take almost 24 hours.

Train At 7.30 pm the Devagiri Exp #1004 departs to **Bombay** (10½ hr). From Bombay the Jalna Exp #1003 (10.30 pm, 10 hr) is a direct train to Aurangabad. From Bombay you can also get a train to Manmad and from there get another train for the uncomfortable 110 km ride to Aurangabad. This trip takes about 8 hours.

You can also take a train to Jalgaon and take a bus to either Ajanta or Aurangabad. If you are coming from Bombay and then heading north, you can see the Ellora caves first, then go to Ajanta, and then get a train from Jalgaon. Trains from Jalgaon go to Delhi, Agra, Udaipur, Calcutta, Madras, and Varanasi.

To get to **Delhi** you can take a train to Manmad (2½ hr) and from there get another train. You should be able to book the train departing from Manmad to Delhi in Aurangabad.

A direct day train to **Hyderabad** takes 12 hours. You can also travel to Hyderabad overnight by taking a 5.30 pm train to Pune and then from there getting another train to Hyderabad at 10.30 pm, all booked on the same ticket. The train from Pune will not depart until the train from Aurangabad arrives.

Bus There are bus connections to Pune (7 daily, 5 hr), Indore (12 hr), Nasik (5 daily, 5 hr), and Bombay. MTDC operates a daily luxury bus from Bombay (8.30 pm, 10 hr). The MTDC (202-6713) office in Bombay is opposite the LIC Bldg, Madame Cama Road. You book tickets at the MTDC Holiday Resort for the deluxe night bus from Aurangabad to Bombay. There is a four-day tour out of Bombay run by MTDC. The ticket price includes accommodation at the Aurangabad Ashok.

TPH Tours and Travels at the Hotel Rajdhani, Station Rd, books luxury buses to Bombay.

To get to Udaipur from here you either have to take a bus to Indore (12 hr) and another 12 hour bus from there, or take a bus to Ahmedabad and from there take another bus to Udaipur.

From Bombay you could hire a car and driver. The trip will take four days, two days actually seeing the caves.

Daulatabad Fort

Nine miles northwest of Aurangabad on the road to Ellora is the Daulatabad Fort. It was constructed by the Yadava dynasty's Bhilama Raja in the 12th century. Daulatabad means "City of Fortune". In 1327 the Delhi Sultan, Mohammed Tughlaq (who was known to be crazy), seized Daulatabad and decided to make it his capital. He marched the residents of Delhi here and 17 years later marched them back. Many of the residents died on the 1100 km (690 mile) march.

Until recently the only entrance was a pitch-black underground tunnel 640 feet long. No attacker ever made it to the top, but it was captured by siege. The water supply ran out.

The Fort is built on volcanic lava rock, 250 metres above the rest of the area. It has three walls around it and was surrounded by a moat with crocodiles in it. You have to go up a long tortuous tunnel, which at one point divides and meets, so attackers may attack each other in the dark. Hot coal can be throw into the tunnel and it can be filled with toxic gas. Then at the end of the tunnel one is forced to crawl the last few metres, so one could be attacked while he was bent over.

You can stop here on the way to the Ellora caves, which the tour buses do. But they do not stop long enough to get a good look at the place. The resident guides who bring you to the top of the fort with the help of a torch do a good job. Without a good torch you cannot see a thing in the passageways. There is a good view from the top of the hill and a huge (6m) cannon. The fort has huge spiked gates to deter elephant charges.

ELLORA

There are 34 elaborately carved caves at Ellora, 30 km northwest of Aurangabad. The 12 southern caves are Buddhist, the 17 caves in the center are Hindu, and the 5 northern caves are Jain. They were built in that order (Buddhist, Hindu, then Jain), from the 7th to the 13th centuries AD. They extend for about 2 km. The carvings and sculptures are impressive. The main site is cave 16, the Kailash Temple, which is one of the most magnificent structures in the world. It is open from 9.30 am to 5.30 pm and is best viewed in the late afternoon. The other caves are open from sunrise to sunset.

The caves are numbered consecutively from south to north. But they were not built in that order. It is believed that carving on the Hindu caves began before all the Buddhist caves were finished. Caves 1, 5, 10, and 12 are good examples of Buddhist caves. Cave 16, the Kailash Temple, is the best example of cave architecture in India. Cave 32 is a good example of Jain sculptural art. These caves give a good overview of all the caves.

The caves here were dug out of a slope in the hill, in a north-south direction. They face west, so they get the light of the setting sun. These cave temples were carved from the top down so they did not need scaffolding. The carvers started at the roof and worked their way down.

For some unknown reason Ajanta was abandoned around the 7th century, and the people making the caves there moved to Ellora, 100 km south.

You can arrange for a guide to show you the caves through the Tourist Office in Aurangabad. You can also hire guides at the site.

Buddhists Caves

Caves 1 to 12 are Buddhist caves. Only cave 10 is a *chaitya* (temple). All the other Buddhists caves are *viharas* (monasteries). These caves are not as architecturally as interesting as the Hindu caves.

Cave 2 has well-carved pillars and figures of Buddha. In the middle of the back wall is a 3m (9 ft) high seated Buddha and two standing Buddhas. Cave 3 is similar with a Buddha sitting on a lotus at the end of the cave. Cave 5 is the biggest Buddhist cave and seems to have been an assembly or dining hall. On the first pillar to the left there are some impressive carvings. Buddha is seated at the back of the cave on a chair.

Cave 6 has a large seated Buddha and a statue of Saraswati, the goddess of learning, surrounded by Buddhist figures. Cave 10 is called Viswakarma or the "Carpenter Cave." This cave is named after Viswakarma, the architect of the demigods. It is the only *chaitya* (chapel) cave in Ellora. There is a beautiful 4.5m image of Lord Buddha in the cave. Light comes into the cave through a horseshoe window. This cave has a second story reached by a flight of stairs inside the cave.

Cave 11 has three stories. At first this cave was believed to have just two stories, but it was later discovered to have a third story. Cave 12 has three stories (both caves are 8th century). The three-storyed Cave 12 is a monastery with a row of seven Buddhas and an open courtyard in front.

Hindu Temples

Caves 14 and 15

In **Cave 14** (7th century) there are carvings of Varaha, Lakshmi, and Siva. This cave is called Rava Kakhai. Most of the carvings are of Lord Siva and his pastimes. **Cave 15** (mid 8th century) is called the Dasa Avatara Cave. It is one of the more impressive caves. There is a Nandi bull here and many sculptures of Lord Siva. There are various carvings including Lord Narasimha and Lord Vishnu rescuing Gajendra the elephant. It is reached by going up a flight of steps.

Kailash Temple Cave 16

The Kailash Temple is a Siva temple with a huge *linga* in the shrine. It is the largest and most magnificent rock cut temple in the world. It is considered one of the wonders of India. Three million cubic feet of rock was chiselled away to complete the temple buildings, life-size elephants, and sculptures. It is estimated that to carve the Kailash Temple 200,000 tons of rock had to be removed by thousands of workers for over 150 years. Archaeologists estimate it took thousands of skilled stone cutters seven to eight generations to make this temple. This temple is comparable to the Pyramids. It is twice the size of the Parthenon of Athens and 1½ times as high. It is 81m long, 47m wide, and 33m high. It is carved out of the side of a hill from the top down.

On the south side of the *mandapa* (hall) is a remarkable sculpture that shows Ravana being crushed underfoot by Lord Siva. He did this because Ravana desired to lift Siva's Kailash mountain and shake it. Other impressive carvings are the Ra-

vana-ki-Khai, or Abode of Ravana, and the Dasavatara, or ten incarnations of Vishnu. There are also carvings telling the stories of the *Ramayana* and *Mahabharata* on the walls of the temple.

Other Caves

The rest of the Hindu caves are not nearly as interesting as the Kailash Temple.

Cave 21, the Rameswara (late 6th century), has a carving of Siva dancing and Durga killing the buffalo demon. It has an inner sanctum and is one of the more interesting caves. It has a courtyard with a Siva-linga and a Nandi bull in the middle. The large **Cave 29** is also worth seeing. It has carvings of Lord Siva's pastimes as the destroyer.

Caves 30 to 34 are Jain caves. Of these, **Cave 32**, the Assembly Hall of Indra, is the most impressive. It is dedicated to Mahavira. The Jain caves are not as dynamic as the Hindu caves.

Ghrisneswara Temple

Close by is the important 18th century Ghrisneswara Siva Temple in the village of Verul, about a km from the Ellora caves. This is an important Siva temple because it contains one of the 12 *jyotirlingas*.

Where To Stay

Close to the caves is the *Hotel Kailash* (02347-41063), which has nice rooms with attached baths for Rs 250/350 and Rs 500/700. The more expensive rooms have a view of the caves and A/C. There are also more basic rooms for Rs 150. Most people stay in Aurangabad.

Travel

There is an airport and railway station 29 km away at Aurangabad. From

Aurangabad there are daily MTDC or ITDC buses. There are local buses that leave every half hour from Aurangabad for the Caves. From Aurangabad a taxi costs Rs 500 round-trip to go to both Daulatabad Fort and the Ellora caves.

AJANTA

This is the location of the beautiful Buddhist rock-cut caves, which have carvings and beautiful specimens of Indian mural paintings on the walls. Ajanta is located 420 km northeast of Bombay and 1120 km southwest of Delhi. This is one of the major tourist places in India. For years the caves were hidden underground, until they were re-discovered by a small group of British officers, who were out hunting in 1819. When you arrive at the caves you can expect to be harrassed by the extremely aggressive salesmen trying to sell you things.

There are 30 caves in all, created from 200 BC to 650 AD. The most interesting ones are 1, 2, 9, 10, 12, 16, 17, 19, and 26. The caves here are famous both for their intricate carvings and for their ancient murals. The caves are numbered consecutively from the western side, but their numbers bear no relation to when they were built. An order to view the caves could be 10, 9, 12, 19, 24, 26, 2, 1 which show the development of Buddhist rock-cut architecture.

Cave 1 has both intricate carvings and paintings. It is the best and most recent of the caves. Cave 4 is a *vihara* cave, or monastery, which was used mainly for living. It has some elaborate sculptures. Caves 2, 16, 17, and 19 have the best paintings. Caves 17, 19, and 26 have the best sculptures. Cave 10 is the oldest and also the first that was discovered. Caves 9, 10, 19, 26, and 29 are *chaityas*, or Buddhist temples, and were used for worship. The other 25 caves are *viharas*.

Information

Beside the entry charge, you have to get a lighting ticket so one of the guards will light up the caves for you, otherwise you cannot see anything.

You should carry a good flashlight (torch). Our tour guide did not have a torch and had to borrow one from one of the people taking the tour. Even with the lights on in the cave many paintings are still hard to see, as they are very old. You are not allowed to take flash photographs of the paintings anymore, as the flash ruins the paintings. As the light is very dim, even with the lights on, if you want to get a decent photo you should have extremely fast speed film in your camera.

You can get Mitra's cheap guide book of *Ajanta* at the ticket office for a detailed explanation of the caves. At the Archaeological Survey you can get a good booklet on Ajanta. ASI publishes a photo book on the caves.

Near Cave 16, by the carved elephant, there are steps that lead down to the river where there is a nice walk by a waterfall and a nice forest area. From the garden along the riverbank is a path that leads to the "view point," which is across the ravine. From there you get a good view of the caves and the surrounding areas. To reach the view point is a hard 30 or 40 minute climb.

The caves are open from 9 am to 5.30 pm. It is best to avoid coming here on a public holiday or weekend when it is extremely crowded. Ajanta is a popular tourist spot.

Mahayana Group

Cave 1 (late 5th century), which is a *vihara* (monastery), has several outstanding murals on its wall. In the center of the cave is a large shrine of Buddha supported by Indra. Above the verandah there are friezes of a sick man, an old man, a corpse, and a saintly person. When Buddha saw such persons he realized the miseries of material existence. There are panels of groups of foreigners in the four corners. The Mahajanaka Jataka, on the left wall, depicts when the Buddha took the form of an able and just ruler. There is also a scene of him being enticed by beautiful women.

On either side of the shrine room are two of the most famous paintings at Ajanta. On the left is the **Bodhisattva Padmapani**, holding a blue lotus, and to the right is the **Boddhisattva Avalokiteswara**. Inside the shrine, Buddha is seated in the teaching position. When the guard shines a light on the left side of Buddha's face, his facial expression is one of solemn contemplation. When the light is shined from the right side of the face, you see a smile of joy on the Buddha's face.

Cave 2 (6th century) is a *vihara* hall. On the left wall is a painting of the Birth of Buddha and also a painting of the Thousand Buddhas. This shows when the Buddha multiplied himself to confuse a non-believer. The ceiling is painted like a draped cloth canopy. On the right of the main shrine is the Hariti Shrine, which shows an ogress who would eat children. **Cave 3 to 7** were carved in the late 5th century.

Hinayana Group

The Hinayana Group is Caves 6-10 and 12,13, and 15. These caves date from the 2nd century BC. **Cave 8** is a small *vihara* and **Cave 9** is a *chaitya* (temple). There are some ancient paintings in **Cave 10**. One of the oldest paintings, on the

rear wall, depicts the King and Queen approaching the sacred Bodhi tree.

Later Mahayana Period

At the entrance of **Cave 16** is a kneeling elephant. In this cave Buddha is seated on a lion throne. The "Dying Princess" depicts Nanda's new bride being told that her husband became a monk. Her misery is shared by everyone around her. **Cave 17** has the most murals of all the caves.

Cave 19 is a *chaitya* hall that has paintings all over it. The later caves have a separate design. Of them, just Cave 26 is really interesting. **Cave 26** is a large *chaitya* hall with a 9m reclining Buddha on one of the walls.

Where To Stay

The *MTDC Holiday Resort*, about five km away in the town of Fardapur, has decent rooms for Rs 200. It also has dorm beds for Rs 40. The *MTDC Travellers' Lodge*, by the entrance to the caves has basic rooms for Rs 100/150 and dorm beds for Rs 40. Checkout time is 9 am.

Travel

Most people stay in Aurangabad and come up to the caves for a day trip.

Air The closest airport is in Aurangabad, which is 106 km south.

Train The closest railway stations are Jalgaon (58 km north) or Aurangabad. From these two places you either get a bus or taxi to the caves. From Bombay to Jalgaon takes 8 hours by train.

Road From Aurangabad to Ajanta takes about 3 hours by bus. From Jalgaon, which is north of Ajanta, it takes about 2 hours by bus. From Ajanta, the last bus to Aurangabad departs at 5.40 pm and the last bus to Jalgaon departs at 6.50 pm.

There are daily MTDC (Rs 125) or ITDC (Rs 110) conducted bus tours from Aurangabad. I took the MTDC tour and thought it was good. It was a nice bus, the tour guide spoke good English, it was economical but not painful, and it is not hurried. Your total time at the caves on a conducted tour is about two hours; many people will consider this rushed. The tour bus departs at 8 am and returns at 6 pm.

There is a cloakroom at the Ajanta Caves where you can leave you bags. So you can arrive in Jalgaon in the morning, go to the Ajanta Caves, and then go to Aurangabad in the evening.

A taxi from Aurangabad costs about Rs 1000 round-trip.

Jalgaon

Population 250,000, STD Code 0257

To get to the Ajanta Caves (58 km south, 1¾ hr) you may have to stop here. Other than that there is nothing to do in this town.

Where To Stay

The *PWD Rest House* (29702) is a good place with rooms for Rs 85 a person. The *railway retiring rooms* are a good value.

The *Tourist Hotel* (25192), a half km from the railway station, has rooms for Rs 125/150 and deluxe rooms for Rs 225/250. The nearby *Hotel Morako* (26621) is about the same in both price and quality.

The *Amram Guest House*, by the station, is one of the better budget places. The new *Hotel Plaza* (24854), Station Rd, is the best mid-range place. It has clean rooms with bathrooms and TV for Rs 125/150. It has 24 hour checkout.

A good place to eat is the Gujarati restaurant at the *Hotel Anjali*, right outside the station to the right.

Travel

The railway station is on the main Delhi-Bombay line, so several trains a day depart from here to Bombay (8 hr) and to Delhi. Trains also go to Bhopal (8 hr) and Nagpur.

There is an hourly bus to Ajanta which continues on to Aurangabad (4 hr). You should confirm that the bus stops at the caves, as some buses only stop at Fardapur, which is 15 minutes north of Ajanta.

Kaundanyapur (Kundina)

This is the birthplace of Rukmini, the main wife of Lord Krishna.

Nearby Amravati was known five thousand years ago as Bhojakata. This is where Rukmini's eldest brother, Rukmi, stayed after being defeated by Lord Krishna.

PANDHARPUR

Population: 70,000

Pandharpur is known as Bhu-Vaikuntha, the spiritual world on earth. It is also called Daksina Dwarka, the Dwarka of the south. It is located on the western bank of the Bhima River, which is locally called the Chandrabhaga (crescent moon). For devotees of Vitthala, this river is as holy as the Ganges. Along the riverbank are fourteen important *ghats*, or bathing places.

Lord Caitanya Mahaprabhu stayed in Pandharpur for 11 days. He took *darshan* of Lord Vitthala and bathed in the Chandrabhaga River. Upon meeting Sri Ranga Puri, one of Madhavendra Puri's disciples, He discovered that His brother, Viswarupa, had passed away and attained samadhi in Pandharpur.

Vitthala Temple

Sri Vitthala is a form of Lord Krishna. The Deity is also called Vithobha or Panduranga. The Deity is a five thousand year old, self-manifest Deity. Parts of this temple date to the 12th and 13th century, but most of the temple was built in the 17th century and later.

According to Maharastrian tradition, when Lord Krishna was performing His Dwarka pastimes, He came to Maharashtra upon the request of His devotee Pundalika. When the Lord arrived, Pundalika was so busily engaged serving his parents that he asked the Lord to wait on the top of a brick platform. Thus the Lord is named Vitthala, which means "one who stands on a brick" (in a waiting posture).

When you enter the main door of the temple, you see a deity of Sri Ganesh, who is prayed to for removing all obstacles in the worship of Sri Vitthala. On either side of the Deity room are huge four-armed statues of Jaya and Vijaya, the doorkeepers of Vaikuntha, the spiritual world.

Sri Vitthala is a slightly smiling, blackish complexioned, three-and-a-half-foot Deity. His hands rest on His hips, and He wears a Vaijayanti garland and *tulasi* garland. His right hand holds a lotus flower, and His left holds a conchshell. On His forehead beneath His crown is a broad mark of *tilaka*. Everyone is allowed to go up to the altar and touch the lotus feet of the Deity. Some pilgrims rest their head upon His feet.

Lord Vitthala is bathed in public view after the 4 am *mangala-arati*. At some point the bathing is interrupted so that the Lord may be fed butter mixed with sugar candy. A big lump of butter is literally put into His mouth. Then a short *arati* is offered, and the bathing resumes. The last *arati* is at 11 pm.

Behind Lord Vitthala's shrine stands the shrine of Srimati Rukmini Devi, the consort of the Lord. Shivaji, the great Maratha general, was a devotee of Sri Vitthala.

Deity Story

The *Padma Purana* and *Skanda Purana* explain why Lord Krishna went to Pandharpur and why He stays there in this form. Once Srimati Radharani, Lord Krishna's consort in Vrindavana, visited Dwarka. At that time, Rukmini Devi, Lord Krishna's Queen, noticed that Krishna was dealing more intimately with Radharani than He had ever done with her. Upset, she departed for the forest of Dindirvana, near Pandharpur.

Lord Krishna followed Rukmini to apologize, but His apology left her unmoved. So the Lord moved on to Pandharpur to visit one of His devotees, Bhakta Pundarika (also known as Pundalika). When the Lord reached Pundarika's *asrama*, Pundarika was serving his elderly parents. So Pundarika gave the Lord a brick to stand on and asked the Lord to wait. The Lord did as He was told. He stood, hands on His hips, waiting for Pundarika to return.

While He was waiting, Rukmini, having forgotten her distress, came from Dindirvana and rejoined Him. Both of Them stayed in Pandharpur in Deity form. To this day the Lord stands on the same brick.

Temple Complex

The chief entrance to the temple courtyard on the northern side of the temple is called the Namdev gate after a famous 13-century devotional poet who was a friend of Jnaneswara. Close to the first step is a brass bust of Namdev. The step where this bust is located is called the Namdev step and no one steps on it. It is stated that Namdev requested to be able to remain at the steps of the temple so he would receive the dust from the feet of Vitthala's devotees.

When you enter the Namdev gate you come to a narrow passage that leads to a spacious hall (120 ft by 60 ft). From here you go up six steps to a narrow *mandapa* (50 ft by 10 ft). There are three gates on the northern wall. On either side are the *dwarapalas* (guards) Jaya and Vijaya. To the left of the gateway is a deity of Ganesh and to the right is the goddess Saraswati. From the center door you enter the *Solkhamba mandapa,* or hall with sixteen pillars. There are scenes from Krishna's pastimes and the *Dasa-avatars* depicted in the ceiling. Around the hall are shrines dedicated to Rama and Laksman, Kashi Viswanatha and Kal Bhairava. The central door in the back wall of this hall leads to the Chaukhamba hall. You then come to the main altar which contains the Deity of Vitthala.

There is a temple dedicated to Rukmini, the wife of Lord Krishna behind the Vitthala temple. Near this deity are shrines for Radha and Satyabhama (another wife of Lord Krishna).

Pundalika Temple

The Pundalika Temple is about a half km from the Vitthala Temple. This temple marks the spot where Pundalika, the Lord's devotee, spent the last years of his life. It is in the middle of the riverbank.

Vishnupada Temple

The Vishnupada Temple is about a kilometre south of the Pundalika temple. The Vishnupada Temple is in the middle of the river connected by a causeway to the shore. During the rainy season this temple is under water for about three months.

In the middle of this temple is a square five feet by five feet. There are three rocks in this square that have the foot-prints of Lord Krishna and of a cow embedded in them. Krishna's footprints are in two positions. In one position He is standing on both feet, and in the other position He is standing on His left foot with His right foot crossed and resting on His toes. There are footprints of a cow at each corner of the square.

On the first day of the month of Margashirsha the sandals of Vitthala are taken to this temple. On the last day of the same month the chariot of Vitthala is brought to this temple in a grand procession. *Sraddha* is performed at this temple. Pilgrims perform funeral rites here for their departed ancestors.

ISKCON Center

ISKCON has a small center located across the Chandrabhaga River from the Vitthala Temple.

Dindi

Every year for the past 700 years, anywhere from 200,000 to 300,000 devotees of Lord Vitthala (Lord Krishna) go on a walking pilgrimage from Alandi (Pune area) to Pandharpur (230 km away). Although the main procession comes from Alandi, other processions come from all over Maharashtra. They begin their journey 18 days before Sayani Ekadasi. They are divided into hundreds of groups, ranging from 50 to 250 devotees in each group. There is continuous dancing and chanting "Jaya Jaya Rama, Krishna Hari" and other Marathi prayers, and sometimes the Hare Krishna *maha-mantra*. People who take part in this walk are called

Varkaris.

The devotees reach Pandharpur in time for the **Sayani Ekadasi festival** which draws a total crowd of 700,000 people. It falls during the month of Asadha (July/Aug) and marks the beginning of Caturmasya. According to the *Padma Purana* the Lord goes to sleep for four months on that day.

About 700 years ago, one devotee of Lord Vitthala by the name of Jnaneswara appeared in Maharashtra. At the age of 16, he became famous for writing *Bhagavad-gita* purports so simple that common people (farmers, merchants, women, etc.) could understand them. Out of his love for the Lord, he began this walking pilgrimage, which has been performed every year since without fail. He passed away at the age of 21.

Tukurama, another great devotee of the Lord, became very popular in Maharashtra, and he attended Dindi every year. He is the main force behind the continuous *kirtanas* and *bhajanas* that are so sweetly performed during the entire Dindi. He lived during the 16th century and was initiated by Lord Caitanya when the Lord visited Pandharpur.

When Dindi arrives in Pandharpur the lines to see Lord Vitthala are 5 km long. During this time the Deity *darshan* is only a few seconds, after a long wait. *Darshan* goes on 24 hours continuously, for days and nights. The Lord mercifully reduces His resting time to allow everyone to approach Him. His bathing and dressing ceremonies are all in public.

After Sayana Ekadasi, Caturmasya begins and Lord Vitthala sleeps for four months. Again, when He wakes up at the end of Kartika (November), a flow of pilgrims will come to greet Him on **Utthana Ekadasi**. The Lord's pastime of resting for four months during Caturmasya has been explained in the *Padma Purana*.

Practicalities

The *MTDC Guest House* has rooms for Rs 100 and dormitories facilities for Rs 10/30.

Pandharpur is located 386 km southeast of Bombay. The nearest airport is 204 km away at Pune. It is on the Kurduwadi-Miraj line of the South Central Railway. A convenient train junction for trains on a broad-gauge line is Solapur, 74 km away.

Mahabaleswara

Population: 10,600, STD Code 02168

Mahabaleswara is located about 250 km southeast of Bombay. The **Mahabaleswara Temple**, dedicated to Lord Siva, houses one of the 12 *jyotirlingas*. There is a room in the temple containing a bed, which each morning is supposed to show signs of having been slept in, although the doors are locked.

Beside the famous Mahabaleswara Temple there is the Atibaleswara Temple. There are several old temples dating back to the 13th century near the old village, about 5 km from the main post office. In the old town there are three temples—the Krishnabai, Rama, and Hanuman temples. Panch-ganga is said to have five rivers flowing from it, including the Krishna River.

Mahabaleswara is also a popular hill station being at an altitude of 1370 metres (4000 ft). It is in the Sahyadri range, which is the source of the holy Krishna River, one of India's seven holy rivers.

Information

There is a Tourist Information center at Kedar Complex, Station Rd. The MTDC has conducted tours that last for

4 hours, bookable through their Holiday Resort. You can get a map of the area from Treacher & Co in the main bazaar.

October to May are good months to visit here. During the monsoon season it rains heavily here.

Where To Stay and Eat

Room prices go up in the high season from mid-April to mid-June and November to January. Many of the hotels are closed during the monsoon.

Vyankatesh Lodge (60397), Main Rd, is a budget place. The *Hotel Saraswati*, Mari Peth, has rooms with hot water for Rs 80/100. During the high season double rooms are Rs 250

The *Ripon* (60291), opposite IOC Holiday Home, is a family run place with a lake view. Rooms are Rs 325 during the low season and Rs 525 in the high season.

The *Grand Hotel* (60310), Woodlawn Rd, is a decent mid-range place with a veranda and garden. The *Dreamland* (60060), behind the bus stand, is a mid-range place with rooms for Rs 300/600. It has an outdoor vegetarian restaurant with Mexican food.

The MTDC *Holiday Camp* (60318) has a wide range of reasonably priced rooms as well as a dorm and large cottages. Rooms range from Rs 150 to Rs 550. You can book rooms at this hotel at the MTDC office in Bombay. The *Fountain Hotel* (60227), opposite Koyna Valley near the downtown, is a good-sized mid-range place with a vegetarian restaurant. Rooms range from Rs 700 to Rs 1800.

The *Brightland Holiday Village* (60353), Nakhinda Village, has a pool and is the best place in town. It is 4 km from city center. The Hotel Anarkali (60336), Kasam Sajan Rd, has good rooms for Rs 1200/1800.

The *Krishna Hotel*, opposite Holiday Camp, is supposed to have a vegetarian restaurant. The *Shreyas* is a vegetarian restaurant by the bus stand.

Travel

The nearest airport and railway stations are in Pune, 122 km away.

MTDC has a direct luxury bus departing from Bombay (7 hr, Rs 125) at 7 am. You book this bus in Bombay at the MTDC office, CDO Hutment, Madame Cama Road. The MTDC deluxe bus departs to Bombay at 3 pm.

The closest railway station is in Pune. There are regular buses between Pune and Mahabaleswara (3 hr, Rs 25).

PUNE (POONA)

Population: 2,485,000, STD Code 0212

Pune was the early home of Shivaji, and it became the Maratha capital in 1750. It came under the control of the British in 1817 and was used as the capital of the region during the monsoon season. It is a major industrial town.

The Osho Commune International (formally Rajneesh Ashram), established by Bhagwan Rajneeh (Osho) is in Koregaon Park. Rajneesh died in January, 1990, but the ashram is still popular and attracts thousands of people.

Mahatma Gandhi was placed under house arrest in the Palace of the Aga Khan, which is now the Gandhi National Memorial. Gandhi's wife, Kasturba Gandhi, died here while interned. It is across the river in Yeravda and is open from 9 am to 4.45 pm, daily.

Where To Stay – Lower

Most of the cheap places are opposite the railway station in the area known as Wilson Garden.

The *National Hotel* (625-054), 14 Sassoon Rd, opposite the railway station, is an old mansion with verandahs and high ceilings. It is popular and the best of the cheaper places. There are ten cottages in the back that are quiet. A single with common bath is Rs 85 and a room with bath is Rs 160/240. Also popular is the *Ritz Hotel*, Connaught Rd, which is to the left as you come out of the station then down the first main road on the right. It has large clean rooms for Rs 100/150. It has hot water in the morning.

The *Hotel Jinna Mansion* (667-158), Wilson Gardens, is a popular place that has clean rooms with good bathrooms. There is hot water from 7 to 9.30 am. The *Grand Hotel*, MG Rd, north of Moledina Rd, is an older place on its own grounds with rooms for Rs 90/150. The rooms are clean, but a bit run-down. There is hot water in the morning. The *Hotel Avanti* (445-975), near the Swargate bus station, is a good value that has clean rooms with hot water. The retiring rooms at the station are good.

Places To Stay – Middle

The *Hotel Woodland* (626-161, fax 623-131), off Sadhu Vaswani Circle, has a selection of nice well-maintained rooms for Rs 400/500 and Rs 800 for a suite. It has a good vegetarian restaurant. The *Hotel Gulmohr* (661-773), 15 A/1 Connaught Rd, close to the railway station, has rooms with hot water for Rs 180/270 and Rs 325/400 with A/C.

Hotel Ashirwad (628-585), 16 Connaught Rd, has large rooms with balconies for Rs 350/450 and Rs 500/650 with A/C. It has a good vegetarian restaurant with good *thalis*. Also good is the *Hotel Amir* (661-840, fax 477-902), 15 Connaught Rd, which has rooms for Rs 400/500 and Rs 850/1000 for a deluxe room.

It is a popular place with flexible checkout, a health club, and exchange facilities.

Places To Stay – High

Hotel Sagar Plaza (622-622, fax 622-633), 1 Bund Garden Rd, has comfortable rooms for Rs 1100/1300. It has a small pool and a bookshop. *Aurora Towers* (641-818, fax 631-826), 9 Moledina Rd, is centrally air-conditioned and has a pool. Rooms here start at Rs 1075.

The five-star *Pride Executive* (324-567, fax 323-228), 5 University Rd, is a good place with clean comfortable rooms for Rs 1195/1495. It has many facilities.

The five-star *Blue Diamond Hotel* (625-555, fax 627-755), 11 Koregaon Rd, is a modern place, 2 km northeast of the railway station. It has a pool, a health club, and 24 hour checkout. Rooms are Rs 1300/1600 and Rs 2500 for a deluxe room.

Where To Eat

Woodlands Hotel has a good restaurant. *Shabree*, near Ferguson College, makes good vegetarian Maharastrian food. *Shri Krishna Palace*, Wilson Gardens near the railway station, is a busy economical South Indian place.

The *Hotel Sunderban*, 19 Koregaon Park, next to Osho Commune; the *Vandana Hotel*, opposite Sambhaji Park; and the *Dreamland Hotel* 2/14 Connaught Rd, opposite the railway station, have vegetarian restaurants.

Getting Around

The No 4 bus goes from the Railway bus stand to Swargate via the Shivaji Nagar bus station. About half the auto rickshaw drivers will use their meter. The ones who refuse to use the meter will usually ask you for double the meter price. You can rent a bike by the entrance of the National Hotel.

Travel

Air The are three flights a week (Mon, Wed, Fri) to Bangalore and Madras. There is a daily flight to Delhi and to Bombay. The Indian Airlines office (659-639) is on Connaught Rd, next to the Hotel Amir. Air India (640-862) is on Moledina Rd. There is an Ex-Servicemen bus into town (8 km).

Train Because many of the trains going to and from **Bombay** stop here it is a busy station. As you leave the station the computerised booking office is to the right. There are many trains daily to Bombay. Good trains to Bombay (3½ to 4½ hr) are the Deccan Queen Express (7.15 am), Pragati Express (7.30 am), and Sahyadri Express (7.35 am). Some of the trains going to Bombay go to Dadar station.

There are daily trains to New Delhi, Bangalore (31 hr), Madras (40 hr), Hyderabad, and Thiruvananthapuram. The Sahyadri Express (10.42 pm) and the Udyan Express (12.10 pm) are two good trains heading southeast. The daily Goa Express #2702 (3 pm), goes to to Vasco da Gama via Miraj.

Bus There are three bus stations in Pune. The bus stand next to the station has buses to points south such as Mahabaleswara (3 hr), Goa (15 hr), and Kolhapur. Asiad buses to Bombay (4 hr) depart every 30 minutes. They must be booked in advance.

The MTDC operates a deluxe bus to Mahabaleswara. You make reservations at the tourist information counter in the railway station.

Buses depart from the Shivaji Nagar bus stand to points north and northeast. There are regular buses from the Shivaji Nagar bus stand to Aurangabad (6 hr). There are also buses to Nasik (20 a day), Ahmedabad, and Nagpur.

Bright Star Tours & Travels (669-647), 13 Connaught Rd, operates private luxury buses to Bangalore, Hyderabad, Aurangabad, Ahmedabad, Mangalore, and Goa. *Karan Travels* (663-850), 7 Konark Park, operates buses to Indore, Ahmedabad, Vadodara, and Goa.

You should be careful of agents by the railway station who may charge you a 50% commission for a bus ticket, promising you a deluxe bus, and then they put you on a regular state bus. You can get a taxi from Dadar station in Bombay to Pune.

Please Help Us

As the subject matter of this book is extremely complex and detailed it is very difficult to include everything relevant. So if you have some information that would be valuable to the readers of this book please send it to us, so they may be benefited.

Whatever you can tell about any temple, the story behind the Deity, what Deities are in a particular temple, or other interesting facts may be valuable information. Also of interest is your opinion on hotels, restaurants or dharamshalas, especially ones missed in this book. Travel information is also valuable. Please refer to the page number in this book in reference to the place that you are writing about.

Please give as detailed information as possible.

For temples or holy places please send:
Temple name, location, Deities' names
What is especially interesting about the temple or place
Story about the temple or Deities
Opening or closing hours
How to get there, what bus or train
Potential problems such as guides, hard climbs, or monkeys

For hotels and restaurants please send :
Name, address, phone number, opening hours of a restaurant
Tariff card or room rates
Location, distance from a land-mark either walking or by rickshaw.
How close to a railway or bus station.
How to get there and how much it cost.
Your comments on why this place stood out.
For a restaurant, any recommended preparations or things to be avoided

The writers of the ten best letters will receive an updated edition of this book.

Thank you very much for your help.

Write to

Spiritual Guides   Jada Bharata Dasa
Krishna Balarama Mandir
Bhaktivedanta Swami Marg
Vrindavana, Mathura Dist. UP, India

CHAPTER SIXTEEN

Gujarat

Population: 44.5 million

Gujarat has a few important holy places and temples. Dwarka, which is on the coast is where Lord Krishna lived after leaving Mathura. Somnath is where He left His body. Also in Somnath is an important Siva temple which contains one of the *jyotilingas*. There is an interesting Krishna temple in Dakor called the Ranchorji Temple.

AHMEDABAD

Population: 3,500,000, STD Code 079

If you are going to Dwarka or traveling between Bombay and Rajasthan, there is a good chance that you will have to come here as a stopover. You may also stop here if you are going to the Ranchorji Temple in Dakor, which is a couple of hours away.

Information and Tours

The **Gujarati Tourist Office** (449-683) is across the river from the downtown, just off Sri RC Rd. It is open from 10.30 am to 1.30 pm and 2 to 5.30 pm. There are tourist counters at the railway station and airport. There is a **city tour** from 9.30 am to 1.30 pm and 2 to 6 pm.

The tourist office runs a five-day tour of **Western Gujarat**, which includes Dwarka, Somnath, Sasan Gir, Junagadh, Girnar, and Palitana for Rs 1850. The tour leaves every Friday.

On Saturdays a five-day tour leaves for **North Gujarat and Rajasthan**. The tour costs Rs 1650 and includes Udaipur,

Mt Abu, Chittorgarh, and Modhera.

The **Royal Orient train** goes on a luxury tour of Rajasthan and Gujarat for $150 a day between April and Sept and $200 a day between Oct and March. It stops in Chittorgarh, Udaipur, Palitana, Somnath, Diu, Sasangir, Junagadh, Ahmedabad, and Jaipur. You can book the tour from the Gujarat Tourism Office in Delhi or the office in Ahmedabad.

You can **change money** at the Bank of India, Bhadra; Bank of Baroda, Relief Rd; and Central Bank of India, Lal Darwaja, which are all open 11 am to 3 pm, Mon-Fri, and 11 am to 1 pm, Sat.

The *Choice Is Yours* publication has information about the city and a fare conversion table for rickshaw meters. The Ahmedabad edition of the Times of India has the lastest flight and train information on the second page.

Modhera Sun Temple

This partially ruined temple is located about 106 km northwest of Ahmedabad. The temple was built by King Bhimdev in 1026, and it is one of the finest ancient Hindu temples in Gujarat. There are some excellent carvings on this temple. Modhera is far off the normal tourist route. There are direct buses from Ahmedabad to here.

ISKCON Temple

This newly built temple (449-945) is located at Sattelite Rd, Gandhinagar Highway Crossing.

Where To Stay

When I arrived at the train station, the rickshaw drivers insisted that the two hotels I wanted to go to were closed. Of course they weren't. They did know a few really good places that I could go to that were open.

Where To Stay – Lower

Most of the budget hotels are by the railway station or close to Tilak Road. The ones by the station can be really noisy. There are *retiring rooms* at the railway station that cost Rs 50 per person and Rs 100/150 for a room with A/C and a private bath. Dorm beds cost Rs 30. The *A-One Guest House* (349-823), opposite the station, has basic unclean rooms with common bath for Rs 65/80, decent double for Rs 140/200, and dorm beds for Rs 35. Get an outer room, as the inner rooms are rather dismal.

The *Hotel Esquire*, opposite Sidi Saiyad Mosque and off the road, has clean rooms for Rs 125 a person, but it is often full. The *Hotel Bombay* (351-746), just north of Sidi Saiyad Mosque on the third floor of the KB Commercial Centre, has rooms for Rs 75/120 with common bath and no window. It is Rs 150/200 for rooms with bath and hot water. Checkout time is 24 hours.

The *Ashiana* (351-114), Salapose Rd by the GPO, has rooms with common bath for Rs 90/110 and Rs 100/120 with bath. Checkout time is 24 hours. The Hotel *Naigra* (384-977), near Tilak Rd, has rooms for Rs 75 with common bath, Rs 125/200 with bath, and Rs 250 with A/C. Checkout time is 24 hours.

The *Hotel Relax* (354-301), down an alley across from the Advance Cinema, is a popular clean place and a good value. Rooms with hot water are Rs 90/140 and Rs 175/225 with A/C.

The *Hotel Natraj* (350-048), Dada Mavlankar Rd, near the Lal Darwaja local bus stand, is in a quiet area. It has good rooms, some with balconies, for Rs 85/150. The *Hotel Cadillac* (351-481), Dr Tankaria Rd, Lal Darwaja, has cheap rooms, some with bath, and a dorm for men.

Where To Stay – Middle

The *Metropole* (354-988), opposite Electric House, Relief Rd, has rooms that are a pretty good value for Rs 200/275 to Rs 350 and Rs 350/450 with A/C. The *Hotel Mehul* (352-862) has cheaper rooms that are not quite as nice, but are still good for Rs 150/200. Both of these hotels are located down a side street near the end of Tilak Rd.

The *Hotel Good Night* (351-997), Dr Tankaria Rd, has good well-maintained rooms with TV for Rs 225/300 and Rs 300/375. It is a little off the road, so it is fairly quiet. Next to the Hotel Relax by the Advance Cinema, is the *Hotel Sahil* (354-181), Dr Tankaria Rd, which has good rooms for Rs 125/275 and Rs 375 with A/C.

The *Hotel Embassy* (535-8464), Lal Darwaja, has rooms for Rs 225/350 and Rs 475/575 with A/C. Rooms here are a good value. The *Hotel Gujarat*, third floor of Sneha complex, Dr Tankaria Rd, is a modern clean place with a roof terrace.

The *Hotel Ambassador* (550-2490), on Lady Vidyagauri Rd, near the end of Tilak Rd by the river, is a good large place that has clean rooms with hot water. Rooms are Rs 225/300 and Rs 325/400 with A/C. The *Hotel Kingsway* (550-1215), Ramanlal Sheth Rd, close to Tilak Rd and the GPO, is a nice place with rooms for Rs 275/400 and Rs 375/525 with A/C. All rooms have hot water and a color TV.

By the railway station and just off Station Rd is the *Hotel Shakunt* (344-615), which has rooms for Rs 225/250 and Rs 400/450 with A/C. All rooms have hot water, phone, and TV. A problem with this place is the rooms do not have exterior windows, but as the area is very noisy, this may not be so bad. The *Moti Mahal Guest House* (339-091), Kapasia Bazaar, by the railway station, is a well-maintained place having clean rooms with bath and TV.

Across the river is the *Stay Inn* (354-127), Lady Vidyagauri Rd, and *Alif International* (359-440), opposite Bombay Mercantile Bank. Both are good clean comfortable places. The Hotel Alif has rooms for Rs 275/325 and Rs 325/450 with A/C.

Where To Stay – High

The *Hotel Capri* (354-643), has poorly maintained clean rooms for Rs 325/375 to Rs 375/475. For the price, it is not so bad. The *Rivera Hotel* (550-4201), Khanpur, has clean comfortable rooms for Rs 600/800. It has a lawn. It is a good value and is recommended.

The Hotel Mascot (359-547) is a new hotel with modern rooms for Rs 600/800. It is a good place.

The four-star *Cama Hotel* (550-5281), Lady Vidyagauri Rd, along the river, has a pool, garden terrace, bookshop, and currency exchange. Its opulent rooms are $40/45 and there are more expensive rooms. Checkout time is 9 am. It is a recommended place.

Across the river on Ashram Rd is the four-star *Hotel Nataraj* (448-747), which has A/C rooms. The *Holiday Inn* (550-5505), near Nehru Bridge, has A/C rooms for 1800/2000. It has a pool, health club and other facilities. It is the best place in

town. Checkout time is 9 am.

Where To Eat

Kalapi, Dr Tankaria Rd opposite the Advance Cinema, is the best restaurant in the Bhadra area. The *Advance Restaurant*, almost right next door, is cheaper.

Chetna Dining Hall, Relief Rd, is considered a good Gujarati *thali* place. They also serve South Indian dishes.

Woodlands is a first-class South Indian restaurant on the other side of the river, near Navrangpura Municipal Market on CG Road. The *Sankalp Restaurant*, also across the river, off Ashram Rd, not far from the tourist office, is a good South Indian restaurant. It has the longest dosas in India, over 4 feet long, costing Rs 151. They also have the highest stack of napkins at your table, about two feet high.

Gopi Dining Hall (76388), Pritamrai Rd, on the west side of Ellis Bridge, is a very popular good place. It is closed from 3 to 6 pm.

Travel

Air The airport (67195) is 10 km south of the city. From the airport a rickshaw costs Rs 150 to the city center. There are also local buses that go to Lal Darwaja, the local bus stand in town. The **Indian Airlines** office (305-599) is near the High Court, close to Nehru Bridge. Indian Airlines flies twice daily to Bombay and Delhi. There are also flights to Vadodara (daily), Agra (daily except Sun), Calcutta (daily), Jaipur (daily except Wed), Khajuraho (daily except Sun), Varanasi (daily except Sun), Goa (twice weekly), Bangalore (Wed, Fri, Sun), Madras (Wed, Fri, Sun), and Pune (daily).

The **Air India** office (448-853) is west of the river, in the Premchand House Building on Ashram Rd, near the High

Court. Air India has direct flights to the USA and UK.

Train Ahmedabad in not on the broadgauge line between Delhi and Bombay. There is, however, a separate broadgauge line that goes between Ahmedabad and Bombay. There is a metre-gauge line that goes north to Delhi, passing through some major towns in Rajasthan on the way.

There are eight trains a day to **Bombay** that take between 9 and 15 hours. There are five trains daily to **Delhi**. The trip to Delhi on the #2906 Ashram Express (5 pm) takes 17 hours. Some of the Delhi trains stop at Abu Road (6 hr), Ajmer (14 hr), and Jaipur (17 hr). The Delhi Express #9904 (6 pm) is the quickest train to **Jaipur** (16 hr 20 min). There is a train to **Madras** (35 hr) four times a week. The Ahmedabad-Udaipur Exp #9644 (11.15 pm, 9 hr) departs daily to **Udaipur**. There are two trains daily to **Ujjain** (9½ hr). There are several daily trains to **Mount Abu** (3½ to 6 hr)

The Saurashtra Mail #9005 (6.15 am) departs daily to **Dwarka** (10 hr) via Rajkot (3½ hr). The overnight Girnar Express #9846 (9.10 pm) goes to **Veraval** (11 hr) via **Junagadh** (9½ hr). The Somnath Mail #9924 (11 pm, 12 hr) goes to Veraval via Junagadh.

Outside the main station is a computerised booking office that is open Mon-Sat from 8 am to 8 pm and on Sunday from 8 am to 2 pm. Counter No 2 efficiently deals with tourist quota tickets. If you do not have a reservation a berth on some trains can be reserved at a temporary counter on the platform just before the train departs.

Bus The Central Bus Stand is southeast of the old city, a few km from any accommodations. Buses to all over Gujarat and the neighboring states leave from here. For long distances the private minibuses are slightly more expensive, but quicker.

There are regular buses to Bombay (11 hr), Ujjain, Udaipur (7 hr), and Mt Abu (7 hr). It is usually quicker and more convenient to take a bus to Mt Abu than to take a train to Abu Road and a bus from there to Mt Abu.

There are many travel agents that run private luxury buses to the major cities and tourist towns in Rajasthan, Gujarat, and Maharashtra. I was told by the tourist office that Punjab Travels was a good travel agent. They are located around the corner from the tourist office by the Sankalp Restaurant at Embassy Market. They also have an office at Delhi Gate, Shahpur Rd (23111).

VADODARA (BARODA)
Population: 1,200,000, STD Code 0265

Vadodara is a city that you might stop at to get to the western coast of Gujarat. Vadodara is 390 km north of Bombay (7 hr) and 100 km south of Ahmedabad (2 hr). The Ranchorji Temple in Dakor is a two-hour bus ride north of here.

Information
The railway station, cheap hotels, and bus stand are all in the same area of town.

The **Tourist Office** is across the street from the railway station and to the left. The **State Bank of India**, near the Kirti Mandir, is open Mon-Fri from 11 am to 3 pm and on Saturdays from 11 am to 1 pm.

Places To See
Sayaji Bagh is a large park with a mini-railway around it. The **Vadodara Museum** and Art Gallery (9.30 am to

4.45 pm daily) is in the park. The **Maharaja Fateh Singh Museum** is an art museum open from 9 am to noon and 3 to 6 pm from July to March, and between April and June it is open 4 to 7 pm. It is closed on Mondays.

ISKCON Temple

The **ISKCON Temple** (326-299) is in a peaceful area on Gotri Rd, about two km from the railway station. There is a new temple presently under construction.

Where To Stay – Lower

Many of the cheaper hotels are within walking distance of the train station.

The *Jagdish Hindu Lodge* is on the third road to your right, as you come straight out of the train station. It is very basic, but perhaps the best cheap place, with rooms for Rs 70. On the same road is the *Hotel Vikram* (327-737), which has rooms for Rs 80/125 and Rs 140/180 with A/C.

The *Green Hotel* (63111), R C Dutt Rd, is a quiet clean well-kept place with rooms for Rs 75 a person. It is the best budget option. The *Delux* (329-604), Kadak Bazaar, is a clean budget hotel, just south of the station.

The large *Ambassador Hotel* (327-417), on the right from the station, is a good mid-range choice with big quiet rooms for Rs 175/290 and Rs 350/400 with A/C. They have a few dumpy rooms on the ground floor, so get a room upstairs. They have a 24 hour checkout time. In the next street over is the *Apsara Hotel* (328-251), which is a well-maintained place with good rooms for Rs 100/140.

Where To Stay – Middle and High

The *Hotel Surya* (365-500), opposite the Ambassador Hotel, is a modern place with rooms for Rs 325/450 and Rs 550/750 with A/C. Across the street is the brand new *Rama Inn* (330-131), which has first-class facilities such as a swimming pool and cable TV. It is a very good value and checkout time is 24 hours. Rooms are Rs 375/525 and Rs 600/825.

The four-star *Express Hotel* (330-750), RC Dutt Rd, one km from the railway station, has A/C rooms for Rs 900/1100.

The *Welcomgroup Vadodara* (330-033), R C Dutt Rd, is a five-star hotel with luxury rooms ranging from $60/70 to $130/140.

Where To Eat

The best place in town is the South Indian *Woodlands Restaurant* on Race Course Road, by the circle.

Kansaar, 101 Unique Trade Centre, Sayajigunj, is a Gujarati *thali* place, about a five minute walk, to your right, from the railway station.

Travel

Air There are flights to Bombay (two daily), Delhi (Mon, Tue, Fri, Sun), and Pune (daily). The Indian Airlines office (329-668) is on University Rd, Fateh Ganj.

Train Vadodara is on the main Delhi–Bombay line. There are many trains to both Bombay and Ahmedabad. The Saurashtra Mail #9005 (3.50 am, 13 hr) departs to Dwarka via Ahmedabad. There are five trains daily to and from Mathura and Delhi. The Paschim Exp #2925 (5.50 pm) is a good train to Delhi (18 hr) via Mathura (15½ hr). The Rajdhani Exp #2951 (5.30 pm, 12 hr) departs daily to Delhi.

Yogikrupa Travel Service, opposite the station, can purchase a train ticket for you, so you don't have to wait in the long lines yourself.

Bus The long distance bus station is half a km north of the railway station. From here there are buses to all over Gujarat, northern Maharashtra, and western Madhya Pradesh. The private bus companies have their offices by the bus station.

DAKOR

Ranchorji Temple

This is Gujarat's most beloved Deity of Krishna. Ranchor is the name given to Lord Krishna because He fled from the battlefield in Mathura, while fighting against the armies of King Jarasandha. Ranchor literally means "one who gave up the battlefield".

This Deity was installed and worshiped in Dwarka up to 800 years ago. The present temple was built in 1772, about 200 years ago.

The Deity of Sri Ranchorji is similar to the Deity of Dwarkadish in Dwarka, both being made from black stone. Devotees are allowed to touch the feet of the Deity. Every full moon day a large numbers of devotees come to this temple.

After the death of Kamsa, Mathura was besieged by the soldiers of Kalayavana and Jarasandha. At that time Krishna fled from the city, and thus He is known as Ranchor, or one who fled from fighting. In order to prevent further killing of soldiers and to attend to other important business, Lord Krishna left the battlefield without fighting. Krishna, the Ranchorji, did not leave the battlefield because He was afraid, but because He had some other purpose. The purpose was to attend to a confidential letter sent by Rukmini, His future first wife.

The act of Krishna's leaving the battlefield is a display of one of His six opulences. Krishna is the supreme powerful, the supreme wealthy, the supreme famous, the supreme wise, the supreme beautiful, and the supreme renouncer. His leaving the battlefield is an example of His super-most opulence of renunciation.

Mangala-arati is every morning at 6.45 am. Ranchorji is dressed and decorated in full view of the public. Ranchorji is especially fond of *moga laddus*. Saffron-flavored milk that has been cooked overnight in silver pots by a process of slow combustion of cow dung is offered in the morning.

There are 5 *aratis* a day—three in the morning and two in the afternoon—and eight *darshans*. There is a big festival on Sharad Purnima day, the full-moon day of Sharad season (Sept-Oct). The temple is closed in the afternoon.

Travel

There are direct buses from either Ahmedabad or Vadodara (Baroda) that take about two hours. Dakor is located 50 km north of Vadodara and 50 km southeast of Ahmedabad.

DWARKA

Population: 30,000, STD Code 02892

Dwarka was Lord Krishna's capital 5000 years ago, after He left Mathura. Lord Krishna spent 100 years here. Modern day Dwarka is a small city located at the western tip of the Gujarat peninsula on the Arabian Sea. Dwarka has a climate that is very nice in the winter and not too hot in the summer. It is a good place to stay for a few days, as it is peaceful and hassle free.

Dwarka is one of the Saptapuris, seven holy cities, of India, which include Ayodhya, Mathura, Haridwar, Kashi (Varanasi), Ujjain, Kanchipuram, and Dwarka.

It is also one of the four holy *dhamas* in India, the others being Rameswaram, Puri, and Badrinath.

The Dwarkadhish Deity is that of Lord Trivikrama. It is said that "Sri Krishna placed all His arts, achievements, properties, and His ownness into Lord Trivikrama." Sanaka Rsi, Marici, Atri, Angira, and other sages are said to have performed penances here.

Archaeological excavations indicate that Dwarka is built on four (some say five) former cities. Much of the present town was submerged by the rising sea levels. Marine archaeologist SR Rao discovered a 250 kg anchor, which indicates that a 120-ton ship may have used the port. There is evidence to suggest that this city was a large port at least as far back as the 15th century BC.

If you are just coming for the day to Dwarka, you could visit the Dwarkadhish temple, take a bath in the ocean where it meets the Gomati River, go see the Rukmini Temple, and then take lunch. You could then go to Bet Dwarka to see the temple there, which opens at 5 pm.

Dwarka means door. One of the four original *mutts* founded by Shankaracarya is in Dwarka. Both Ramanujacarya and Madhvacarya came here for pilgrimage.

Tours

There is a tour bus run by the Dwarka Darshan office that goes to the various pilgrimage sites outside the city of Dwarka including Nageshwar Temple, Patrani Temple, Bet Dwarka and Gopitallava. There are two tours daily at 8 am and 2 pm. The tour takes about five hours (can take 7 hr).

Tickets can be booked at the Dwarka Darshan office or from a local travel agent. You should book the morning tour the day before.

Description of Dwarka 5000 Years Ago

In the *Srimad Bhagavatam* there is the following description of Dwarka, when Narada came to visit Lord Krishna:

When Narada arrived in Dwarka, he saw that the gardens and parks were full of various flowers of different colors and the orchards were overloaded with a variety of fruits. In the city there were as many as 900,000 great palaces built of first-class marble with gates and doors made of silver. The posts of the houses and palaces were bedecked with jewels such as touchstone, sapphires, and emeralds, and the floors gave off a beautiful luster. The big avenues, crossings, lanes, streets, and also the thresholds of every residential house, were very clean. At regular intervals there were large trees that shaded the avenues so that the sunshine would not bother the passersby.

In this greatly beautiful city of Dwarka, Lord Krishna, the Supreme Personality of Godhead, had many residential quarters. The architectural plans were made personally by Visvakarma, the engineer of the demigods, and in the construction of the palaces he exhibited all of his talents and ingenuity. These residential quarters numbered more than 16,000, and a different queen of Lord Krishna resided in each of them. The pillars were made of coral and the ceilings were bedecked with jewels. The walls as well as the arches between the pillars glowed from the decorations of different kinds of sapphires. Throughout the palace there were many canopies made by Visvakarma that were decorated with strings of pearls. The chairs and other furniture were made of ivory, bedecked with gold and diamonds, and jeweled lamps dissipated the darkness within the palace.

Dwarkadhish Temple

In the middle of the town is the Dwarkadish Temple, which was built in the 16th century. Dwarkadish is another name of Lord Krishna that means the "Lord of Dwarka". The five-story high temple is built on seventy-two pillars. The temple spire is 78.3m (235 feet) high. From the temple dome waves an eighty-four foot long multicolored flag decorated with the symbols of the sun and moon. Lord Krishna's grandson, Vajranabha, is said to have built the original temple of Dwarkadhish over the *hari-griha* (Lord Krishna's residential place).

The sanctum of the temple is formed by the Jagat Mandir, or Nija Mandir, which dates back at least 2500 years. The Jagat Mandir has a tall tower and a hall of audience.

There are two entrances to the temple. The main entrance (north entrance) is called "Moksa Dwara" (Door to Salvation). This entrance leads to the main market. The south entrance is called "Swarga Dwara" (Gate to Heaven). Outside this doorway are 56 steps that lead to the Gomati River. The audience hall has both ancient and fairly modern sculptures.

The main Deity in this temple is Lord Dwarkadhish, who is on the center altar. The Deity represents the four-armed form of Vishnu called Trivikrama. There is a temple to the right of the main Deity that contains the Deity of Lord Baladevaji (Balarama), who is the older brother of Lord Krishna. The temple to the left of the main Deity contains a big Deity of Pradyumna and a small Deity of Aniruddha. They are the son and grandson of Lord Krishna. Opposite this shrine is the shrine of Purusottama (Vishnu). Next to this shrine is a shrine dedicated to Kuseswara Mahadeva (Siva).

The shrine that is across from Lord Dwarkadhish contains the deity of Devaki, the mother of Lord Krishna. Next to this shrine is a temple dedicated to Veni-madhava (Lord Vishnu). In back of the main temple in the eastern part of the temple compound are shrines of Radhikaji, Jambavati, Satyabhama and Lakshmi. There are also shrines of Sarasvati and Lakshmi-Narayana.

This temple is a very interesting place where the extreme devotion of the pilgrims can be observed. The temple is open 6 am to 12.30 pm and 5 to 9 pm. Non-Hindus are not normally allowed in the temple. Non-Indians can request to fill out a form saying that they believe in the Hindu religion and can then enter the temple.

Rukmini Devi Temple

This small temple, which is 1.5 km north of town, is an architectural masterpiece. Rukmini is the most important of Krishna's 16,108 wives. The temple walls are decorated with beautiful paintings depicting the pastimes of Rukmini and Krishna. This temple is said to date back to the 12th century.

The story behind this temple is that one day Durvasa Muni, who is easily angered, invited Lord Krishna and His wife Rukmini to dinner. When a person is invited to dinner, etiquette is that he is not allowed to eat or drink until served by his host. On the way to take dinner Rukmini became very thirsty, and she asked Krishna for help. Krishna then put His foot in the ground and the waters of the Ganges came from the earth while Durvasa was not looking. But, as Rukmini was drinking the water, Durvasa turned and saw her drinking without his permission. He became very angry and He cursed her to live separate from Lord

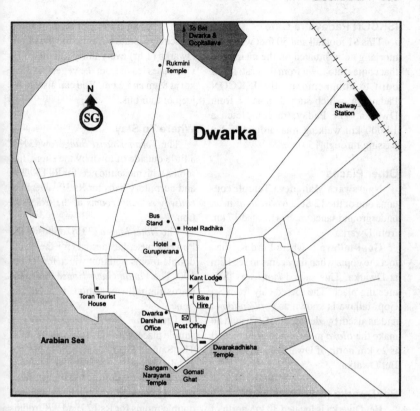

Map labels: To Bet Dwarka & Gopitallava; Rukmini Temple; N; SG; Dwarka; Railway Station; Bus Stand; Hotel Radhika; Hotel Guruprerana; Kant Lodge; Toran Tourist House; Bike Hire; Dwarka Darshan Office; Post Office; Dwarakadhisha Temple; Arabian Sea; Sangam Narayana Temple; Gomati Ghat

Krishna. That is why Krishna's temple is in the town and her temple is located just outside the town.

Gomati Ghat Temples

If you go out the back entrance of the Dwarkadish Temple, you can see the Gomati River. The temple is located almost at the spot where the Gomati meets the ocean.

Gomati, the descended Ganges, meets the sea at **Chakra-tirtha Ghat**. To take bath where the Gomati meets the ocean is supposed to give liberation to a devotee.

The **Samudra Narayana Temple** (Sangam Narayana) is an imposing temple at the confluence of the Gomati River and the sea. **Panchanada Tirtha** is five sweet water wells surrounded by sea water.

At **Chakra Narayana**, Lord Vishnu was manifested as a stone marked with a chakra on the seashore. The **Gomatiji Temple** has an image of the Gomati River in it said to have been brought down from heaven by Vasistha Muni.

Lighthouse

You can get a good view of Dwarka and the surrounding area from on top of the lighthouse. It is open from 4 to 6 pm or 1 hour before sunset, whichever is earlier.

ISKCON Padayatra Gate

This 61 foot tall and 50 foot wide memorial gate is situated on the main road that comes into town from the east. It was built to commemorate the ISKCON Padayatra, which started in 1984 from Dwarka. The Padayatra completed a 14,000 km walking tour around India, passing through 15 states.

Other Places

Nageswara Mahadeva Temple contains one of the 12 Siva *jyotirlingas* in an underground sanctum. It is located 17 km from Dwarka.

Gopi-tallava is where Lord Krishna met the gopis when they came to see Him at Dwarka. This sacred *kund* was their meeting place. The sacred clay from Sri Gopi-tallava is known as *gopi-candana* and is used by devotees of Krishna to make the *tilaka* marks on their bodies. It is 23 km north of Dwarka on the way to Bet Dwarka.

Bet Dwarka (Dwarka Island)

Bet Dwarka is located 30 km north of Dwarka on an island in the middle of the Arabian Sea, next to the coastal town of Okha. You take a 20 minute boat ride to reach the island. Bet Dwarka is said to be the remains of the 12 *yojanas* (96 square miles) of land borrowed from the ocean to build the original city of Dwarka.

The Dwarkadhish Temple here has some very beautiful Deities. The temple is open in the morning and again at 5 pm. When the temple opens at 5 pm there is a mad rush to see the Deity. There is also a Balarama Temple (Dauji) here. Bet Dwarka is where Sudama Brahmana is supposed to have met Lord Krishna.

The entire trip to the island from the town of Dwarka will take at least four hours. The boats usually depart only when full, and they can take a hundred passengers. State buses go to Okha from Dwarka (1 hr) every thirty minutes. Private buses leave from the vegetable market at 8 am and 2 pm. You can also go by jeep or tour bus.

Where To Stay

The *Toran Tourist Bungalow* (313), a little outside of town by the shore, has rooms with mosquito nets for Rs 150/200 and dormitory beds for Rs 30. There are *railway retiring rooms* at the train station.

The *Hotel Meera* (331), opposite the Power House, has decent (for the price) double rooms with hot water for Rs 60/100. The *Vanda Guest House* (440), towards the railway station, is about the same.

The *Uttam Guest House* (234) is a simple place by the Dwarkadish Temple. The Satnam Wadi Guest House has basic clean rooms for Rs 90/110.

The *Hotel Radhika* (754), a little outside of town opposite the bus stand, has double rooms for Rs 175 and A/C rooms for Rs 375. Nearby is the *Hotel Guru-prerana* (385), which is a little closer to the center of town, with rooms for Rs 250 and Rs 500. *Hotel Gokul* (554), in the same area, by the main post office, has rooms with bath for Rs 175. All these places are about the same.

Where To Eat

The only type of eating places I saw here were basic Gujarati *thali* places. There is a good place at the *Hotel Meera* with all-you-can-eat *thalis* for Rs 25. There is another place with spicy food at the *Hotel Radhika* for Rs 35 a *thali*. The *Kant Lodge* (sign in Gujarati), Teen Batti Chowk, serves inexpensive *thalis*, some North India items and *masala dosas*.

Travel

Air and Train The nearest airport is located in Jamnagar (145 km). Dwarka is 378 km west of Ahmedabad on the coast. The Saurashtra Mail #9006 (12.05 pm) goes to Bombay (20 hr) via Rajkot (5 hr), Ahmedabad (10 hr), and Vadodara (12½ hr). From Bombay Central the Saurashtra Mail #9005 departs daily to Dwarka at 8.10 pm (20 hr). If you are coming here from Mathura, you first go to either Ahmedabad or Vadodara and from there get the Saurashtra Mail to Dwarka. The Saurashtra Mail for Dwarka departs from Ahmedabad at 6.15 am and from Vadodara at 3.50 am.

Bus The long-distance bus stand is about a 15-minute walk from MG Road. There are buses from here departing to cities all over Gujarat. There are regular buses to Veraval (7 hr, for Somnath), several daily buses to Porbandar (3 hrs), and four buses daily to Junagadh.

Mul Dwarkadish (Visavada)

Mul Dwarkadish is about 25 km north of Porbandar on the way to Dwarka. Located here is the Mul Dwarkadish Temple and a well that is said to be as sacred as the Ganges. The temple of Ranachodji faces a Siva temple here. Lord Krishna is said to have stopped here on His way to Dwarka. Despite being in the middle of nowhere it is a very visited temple with a beautiful Deity of Krishna.

Porbandar

Population 160,000, STD Code 0286

Porbandar is on the seashore between Dwarka and Somnath. It is said to have been the home of **Sudama Brahman**, who studied with Krishna in the ashram of Sandipani Muni. Porbandar used to be called Sudama Puri, and there is a Sudama Temple in the center of town.

Almost every Indian knows this town as the birthplace of **Mahatma Gandhi**. The house where he was born, in October 1869, is a popular tourist spot in the middle of town. Gandhi's family left the house in 1881. There is a *swastika* in the house that marks the spot where Gandhi was born. There is a photo exhibit and a small bookshop in the building next door.

Where To Stay and Eat

The *Rajkamal Guest House*, MG Road; the *Nilam Guest House*; and the *Darami Guest House* are all decent basic places for around Rs 50.

The *Toran Tourist Bungalow* (22745), Chowpatty, has a good location by the sea. The large, clean rooms are Rs 250 and Rs 300 with A/C. The good dorm beds are Rs 30.

The *New Oceanic Hotel* (20217), Chowpatty seaface, is a small villa with rooms for Rs 400 and Rs 600 with A/C. The *Sheetal Hotel* (41821), opposite the GPO, has rooms for Rs 150 and Rs 350 with A/C. Many of the rooms do not have windows, so it is best to see a few rooms before selecting one.

The *Hotel Flamingo* (23123), MG Road, is a clean place with a good manager. It is a decent value with rooms for Rs 200 with bath and Rs 450 for a fancy A/C room. Some rooms don't have windows.

The *Aadarsh Restaurant* and *Samrat* are good eating places on the MG Rd.

Travel

There are flights to Bombay (Tue, Sun, $70). The Saurashtra Express #9216 (8 pm, 25 hr) goes to Bombay via Rajkot (4½ hr), Ahmedabad (10 hr), and Vadodara. The long-distance bus stand is about a 15-minute walk from MG Road. There

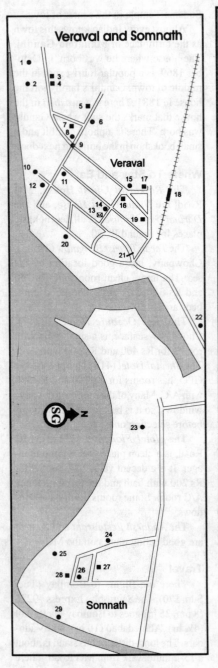

Veraval and Somnath

PLACES TO STAY

3	Toran Tourist Bungalow
4	Circuit House
5	Ajanta Hotel
7	Satkar Hotel
16	Sri Niwas Guest House
17	Chandrani Guest House
19	Hotel Supreme
27	Hotel Sivam
28	Hotel Mayuram

WHERE TO EAT

8	Sagar Restaurant
15	New Apsara

OTHER

1	Temple
2	Lighthouse
6	Bus Stand
9	Clock Tower
10	Temple
11	Bank
12	Fruit & Vegetable Market
13	GPO
14	Bank
18	Railway Station
20	Bank
21	Junagadh Gate
22	Bhalka Tirtha Temple
23	Temple
24	Museum
25	Somnath Temple
26	Bus Stand
29	Triveni Tirtha

are regular buses to Dwarka, Veraval (3 hr), Junagadh, and Rajkot.

Veraval

Population: 105,000, STD Code 02876

This is the city next to Somnath and Prabhas Patan. You would normally use this town as a base if you are visiting the pilgrimage town of Somnath, as Somnath is a very small town.

Information

The State Bank of India near the railway station just changes cash. No banks here will change travellers' cheques.

The ancient Junagadh Gate was broken by Mahmud of Ghazni when he entered the town to loot the temple. About a kilometre from the gate is the ancient Mai Puri, which was previously a sun temple and has now been converted into a mosque.

Where To Stay – Veraval

The *Satkar Hotel* (20120), near the bus stand, is a good place to stay. It has well-maintained clean rooms for Rs 100/150 up to Rs 275/375 with A/C. It has hot water in the morning and dorm beds for Rs 50. It is on a side street so it is not noisy at night. The *Hotel Ajanta*, across from the bus stand, is a good place that has rooms with bath for Rs 125 and Rs 175 for a deluxe room with TV. Also near the bus stand is the *Hotel Kasturi* (20488) It has good-sized rooms with hot water for Rs 100/175 and Rs 250/275 with A/C.

The *Toran Tourist Bungalow* (20-488), College Rd, near the seashore and lighthouse, has rooms for Rs 150/200. It is inconveniently located and checkout time is 9 am.

There are *railway retiring rooms* at the station with rooms for Rs 60/70. Dorm beds are Rs 30. The *New Oceanic* and *Circuit House* are also near the lighthouse. Both places have a nice view of the sea.

Where To Stay – Chorwad

At Chorwad, 20 km from Veraval, there is a former summer palace of the nawabs of Chorwad that has been converted into the *Palace Beach Resort* (0287688 557). Rooms in the cottages are Rs 375. Rooms in the annex are Rs 200 and Rs 500 with A/C. This place can be booked ahead at a Gujarat tourist office. It is a pleasant place with a nice garden. This place is very badly maintained and is starting to fall apart.

Where To Eat

The *Sagar Restaurant*, Riddhi Siddhi Complex, Depot Road, not far from the bus stand, is a good A/C place. It is recommended. It is between the bus stand and the clock tower. The *New Apsara*, near the railway station, is supposed to serve good vegetarian food.

Travel

Air There is an airport in Keshod, 47 km away. There are daily flights to Bombay. There is no Indian Airlines office in Veraval, but Somnath Travels, Satta Bazaar, can get tickets.

Rail The Girnar Express #9845 (7.30 pm, 10 hr) and the Somnath Mail #9923 (5.05 pm, 9½ hr) go to Ahmedabad via Junagadh (2 hr). To get to Bombay you can take the Veraval-Rajkot Mail #9837 (11.25 am, 5 hr) to Rajkot and from there get the Saurashtra Mail #9006 (5.20 pm, 13 hr) to Bombay Central via Ahmedabad.

Bus Buses depart from here to all over Gujarat. There are buses to Dwarka (7 hrs), Junagadh, and Porbandar. Mayur Travels is an agent for the private bus companies.

Veraval to Somnath

Between Veraval and Somnath there are buses that depart from the bus stands every 15 minutes for a few rupees. It costs about Rs 20 by rickshaw. You can also hire a rickshaw to bring you to the Somnath Temple, stopping on the way at Bhalka Tirtha and then Triveni Tirtha. You can hire a bike opposite the bus or railway stations, and this is a good way to get around.

The road from Veraval to Somnath is in bad condition.

SOMNATH

Somnath is famous as the place where Lord Krishna was shot in the foot by a hunter. It is also known as Prabhas Patan. This is where the Yadavas, the relatives of Lord Krishna, fought between themselves by the will of the Lord. The explanation is that after Krishna finished His mission on earth, He wanted to recall His eternal associates, the Yadavas. They were, however, too powerful to be vanquished by anyone, so by the will of the Lord they were cursed, and as a result of intoxication they fought among themselves.

One of the 12 *jyotirlingas* is at the Somnath Temple.

Somnath is on the extreme southwest coast of Gujarat on the Arabian Sea about 300 km southwest of Ahmedabad. The town of Somnath consists of a few streets near the temple and bus stand. There is a nice beach by the temple.

Somnath Temple

The temple is on the shore of the Arabian Sea, 6 km south of Veraval. In this temple is one of the 12 Siva *jyotirlingas*. A Lord Siva temple has been at this place since ancient times. The temple was destroyed and raided by the Muslims several times, first by Mahmud of Ghazni in 1026.

It is said that this temple was origi-

nally built by Soma, the moon-god, to atone for the curse Daksha put on him. It is said that Soma was cursed by Daksha because he showed partiality to Rohini over his other wives, who were also daughters of Daksha. Because of the curse the moon began to wane. Daksha advised Soma to go to Prabhasa to get rid of the curse. The moon bathes here on *amavasya*, the new moon day, before regaining light. Because the moon regained light here this place is known as Prabhasa. Somnath means the "lord of the moon".

Somnath is said to be located where the River Saraswati flows into the sea.

This temple is said to have been built by the moon-god out of gold, then rebuilt by Ravana out of silver, then by Lord Krishna out of wood, and later by Bhima (one of the Pandava brothers) from stone. Two thousand *brahmanas* are supposed to have served in this temple. The temple was also supposed to have once had 300 barbers, 500 dancing girls, and 300 musicians.

The temple was raided and destroyed by Mahmud of Ghazni in 1026. He removed a solid silver gate at that time and brought it back to his homeland. The temple was also destroyed in 1297, 1394, and for the last time in 1706 by Aurangzeb, just before he died.

The present temple was rebuilt in 1950. It is big, but not very artistic. The present temple has a tower over 50m (165 ft) high over the main sanctum (altar). It was constructed on the exact spot where the original temple was situated. You can see remains of an ancient temple right next to the present temple.

The main *aratis* are at 7 am, noon, and 7 pm. It is a very popular temple that non-Hindus can also enter. This is a popular temple.

Prabhas Patan Museum

This interesting museum has remains of the magnificence old temples in it. It is located about a five-minute walk down a small road to the right of the temple entrance. The entrance to the museum is on the left and is a little hard to find. The person who runs the museum is a good source of information about the area. It is open daily 9 am to noon and 3 to 6 pm, except Wednesday.

Prabhas Patan (Bhalka Tirtha)

"Bhalka" is the name of the village, and "Tirtha" indicates that it is a holy place. After the destruction of the Yadu and Bhoja dynasties in Dwarka, Lord Krishna left His palaces and came to this area called Prabhasaksetra. He was accompanied by Uddhava. When He was absorbed in deep thought, a hunter named Jara shot an arrow that accidentally hit Krishna's foot, apparently wounding Him. There is a temple built by the tree that is said to be the same tree under which the Lord was sitting. On the altar there is a beautiful white Deity of Krishna sitting. One can see the bottom of Krishna's foot, pink colored with different auspicious symbols. Nearby is the hunter, Jara, with folded hands and one knee on the floor. This place is a few km east of Veraval on the road to Somnath.

Near Prabhasa, the Yadavas became intoxicated and fought with each other. Arjuna also came to Prabhasa.

The **Gita Mandir** is located at the confluence of three rivers, called Triveni Tirtha, about a kilometre south of the Somnath Temple by the sea. It is said that Lord Krishna walked about 4 km, from Bhalka Tirtha to this place, after He was shot in the foot by the hunter, and left the planet at this point. There are a few other temples here and the place where Lord Balarama is said to have left the planet.

The ancient Suraja Mandir, which is a temple dedicated to the sun god, was half broken by Mahmud of Ghazni.

Where To Stay – Somnath

The *Sri Somnath Temple Trust Guest House* has very basic rooms for Rs 40/60. It is close to the temple. The *Hotel Mayur*, across from the bus stand, is clean but basic. Rooms are Rs 100. The *Hotel Sivam*, not far from the temple, has double rooms with bath for Rs 125 and Rs 275 with A/C.

JUNAGADH

Population: 167,000, STD Code 0285

Junagadh was the capital of Gujarat under the Kshattrapa rulers from the 2nd to 4th centuries. The Chadva Rajputs ruled from Junagadh from 875 AD. The city is surrounded by an old wall, much of which is now missing.

Mount Girnar

It is said that Mount Girnar was once a flying mountain. The mountain is about 1100m (3400 ft) high.

On the plateau, about 600 feet from the top of the hill, is a group of Jain temples built between 1128 and 1500. Neminath, the 22th tirthankara, is said to have died on Mount Girnar after living there 700 years. There is special temple dedicated to him here.

On top of the hill is a small Vishnu temple dedicated to Dattatreya. There is also a temple dedicated to the goddess Amba Mata, which dates back to the 12th century.

The steps go down and up again to Gorakhnath Peak at 3666 ft, where there are footprints of the pilgrim Gorakhnath. There is another peak where there are footprints of Neminath. Further on is a goddess Kalika shrine.

To reach the top of the hill is about 5500 steps, so it is best to start early in the morning. It is a tough steady two-hour climb. Hundreds of people each day climb this hill. There are many stalls selling cold drinks, but none selling bottled water, so bring your own.

You are allowed to wear shoes to walk up the hill. There are regular buses from downtown to the foot of the hill, or you can take a rickshaw for Rs 25.

Damodara Kund

This *kund* is about a kilometre before the bottom of Girnar Hill. It is a sacred bathing tank. Close to Damodara Kund is **Revati Kund**. It is said that Revata left Dwarka and moved near Girnar Hill after his daughter, Revati, married Lord Balarama.

Near Aswatthama Hill, which is north of Damodara Kund, is the **Damodarji Temple**, which is said to have been built by Vajranabha, the great-grandson of Sri Krishna.

Uperkot and Ashokan Edicts

Uperkot is an impressive peaceful fort area, open daily 6 am to 7 pm. Some parts of the walls of the fort are 20 metres high. There are some old Buddhist Caves down the road from the main gate that are said to be 1500 years old. There is a huge 15 foot-long cannon made in Egypt in 1531. There are two interesting large step wells here. There is also a nice garden up the stairs to your right from the main gate.

About two km east of Junagadh and 6 km from the foot of Girnar Hill, between the two places, is an **edict of Emperor Asoka** inscribed on a rock. It is in a small building to your right, on the way to Girnar Hill.

Other Places

Durbar Hall & Museum (9 am to 12.15 pm and 3 to 6 pm, closed on Wednesdays, public holidays, and the 2nd and 4th Sundays of each month) has a collection of weapons, thrones, and palanquins, etc.

The **Junagadh Zoo** at Sakar Bagh has Gir lions, tigers, leopards, and some other animals.

Where To Stay

The *Hotel Relief* (20280), Chittakhana Chowk, is a nice clean place with a good manager. Rooms are Rs 100 with common bath and Rs 150 to Rs 200 for a double with bath. Rooms with A/C are Rs 300/400. All rooms have hot water. It is a good place, but the front rooms can be extremely noisy, to the point where you cannot sleep. I believe the price is higher than it should be.

Also good is the *Hotel National* (27891), Kalwa Chowk, which has simple rooms for Rs 90/120, good clean double rooms for Rs 150, and A/C rooms for Rs 200/300. This place has hot water and is recommended.

Also good is the *Hotel Ashiyana* (20706), which has rooms for Rs 100/150 and Rs 200/300 with A/C.

The *Capital Guest House*, Kalwa Chowk, is a basic budget place with rooms for Rs 35/50. The nearby *Lake* and *Jai Shree Guest Houses* are about the same.

The *Hotel Anand* (22657) is a clean newer place with rooms for Rs 100/150 and Rs 400 with A/C, phone, and TV. The rooms in the front are noisy. It is not such a good value. The GTDC state-run *Girnar* (21201), Mejwadi Gate, is in a quiet, inconveniently located area of town. Rooms are Rs 200/250 and Rs 300 with A/C. Dorm beds are Rs 35.

The *President* (25661) is a mid-range place with all rooms having hot water and TV. The front rooms are on a busy road and are noisy.

Where To Eat

The *Santoor Restaurant*, Mahatma Gandhi Rd, south of Chittakhana Chowk, has good Punjabi and South Indian food. Also good is the *Swati Restaurant*, Jayshree Talkies Rd.

Travel

Train The Girnar Express #9845 (9.10 pm, 10 hr) and the Somnath Mail #9923 (7.02 pm, 9½ hr) go to Ahmedabad. There are three trains daily to Veraval (2 hr).

To get to Bombay you take the Veraval-Rajkot Mail #9837 (1.18 pm, 3¼ hr) to Rajkot and from there get the Saurashtra Mail #9006 (5.20 pm, 13 hr) to Bombay Central via Ahmedabad. Both trains can be reserved on the same ticket.

Bus The Central bus stand is just west of Chittakhana Chowk. Buses go to Veraval (Somnath), Porbandhar, and Rajkot (2 hr)

Palitana

Population: 46,000, STD Code 02848

This is the base to visit the nearby Jain temples on Shatrunjaya Hill. Palitana is 51 km southwest of Bhavnagar and 277 km from Ahmedabad.

Shatrunjaya Hill

Nearby Palitana is the holy mountain of Shatrunjaya, which has 863 Jain temples on it, many intricately carved in marble. Construction took 900 years, but the temples are not as intricate as Dilwara (Mt Abu). The oldest temples date back to the 11th century. It takes about two hours to climb the 3950 steps (4 km)

1800-plus feet (600m) high. It is a hard climb.

There are two groups of temples along the two ridges of the hill and several temples between these two groups. You may be able to see the fabulous temple jewels here at the Adiswara Temple, which is one of the most interesting temples. The Chaumukha Adinath Temple (four-faced), built in 1618, has an image of Adinath facing the four cardinal directions. Other important temples are Vimal Shah, Sampriti Raj, Ramaji Gandharia (16th century), Bhulavani, and Kumar Pal. The Vallabhai Temple and Motisah Temple are between the two groups of temples.

Adinath, the first Tirthankara, visited this hill several times, and the first temple was built by his son. Jains believe that Pundarika, who was the main disciple of Adinath, attained **nirvana** here.

Shatrunjaya Hill is 3 km southwest of Palitana. No one is allowed to stay on the hill overnight, not even the priests. The temples are open from 7 am to 7 pm. Photography is allowed, but you must get a permit at the Anandji Kalyanji Pedhi, on the way up the hill, or you can enquire at your hotel. You cannot carry any leather items up the hill. You should carry your own water with you and you are not supposed to carry any food. You can be carried up the hill by *dhooli* (rope chair) for Rs 100.

Places To Stay

There are 150 dharamshalas. Most of the places are only for Jain pilgrims, but some allow non-Jains. The Gujarati Tourism *Hotel Sumeru*, (2327), Station Rd, is a recommended place with rooms for Rs 275/325 and Rs 400/425 for an A/C room, and Rs 20 for a dorm bed. For the price, this is the best place in town.

The *Hotel Shravak* (2428), opposite the bus station, has rooms for Rs 125/200 and also more expensive A/C rooms. Dorm beds are Rs 25. Checkout is 24 hours.

Where To Eat

Vaishali, Main Bazaar, has Gujarati thalis and South India food. The *Siddhgiri Bhojanalaya*, Taleti Rd, has Gujarati thalis.

Travel

Air and Train The nearest airport is in Bhavnagar (50 km NE). Palitana is on a metre gauge line. From Ahmedabad (277 km) it takes 9 to 11 hours with a change at Sihor, which is close to Palitana. There are local trains to Bhavnagar (1½).

Bus Ahmedabad is 215 km away by road, and an express bus takes 4½ hours, which is an hour less than the normal buses. Private bus companies operate to Bombay and Surat via Vadodara. There are also state transport buses to Bhavnagar (1½), Vadodara, Jamnagar, and Rajkot.

CHAPTER SEVENTEEN

Andhra Pradesh

Population: 66 million

Andhra Pradesh is located on the eastern coast of India. It is bordered by Maharashtra on the west, Orissa to the north, and Tamil Nadu to the south. The presiding Deity of Andhra Pradesh is Lord Narasimha, the half-man and half-lion incarnation of Lord Vishnu.

HYDERABAD

Population: 4,700,000, STD Code 040

Hyderabad is the capital city of Andhra Pradesh. Its twin city, Secunderabad, is located 10 km north, and the large Golconda Fort is located about 8 km west. Hyderabad was formerly a state about the size of France. Between the 15th and 19th centuries it was ruled by Muslim leaders known as Nizams , even though the Hindu population was predominant.

At that time Hyderabad was a center for some of the greatest jewelry design and art work in all of India. Hyderabad is still world famous for its art, jewelry, poetry, and architecture. The wealth and grandeur of the collections in Hyderabad's museums can easily rival or even outclass some of the greatest museum collections in Europe.

Information

The Government of India Tourist Office (630-037) is located in the Sendozi Building, 26 Himayatnagar Rd. It is open 9.15 am to 5.45 pm, Monday to Friday, and Saturdays 9.15 am to 1 pm. There are tourist counters at the Hyderabad and Secunderabad railway stations.

The **Andhra Pradesh Travel and Tourist Development Corporation (APTTDC)** has two offices. One is in Hyderabad (557-530) at Gangan Vihar, 5th floor, Mukarramjahi Rd (10.30 am to 5 pm, Monday to Saturday). The other office (843-931) is on Sardar Patel Rd in Secunderabad (9 am to 7 pm). There is also a tourist counter at the airport.

Tours

Andhra Pradesh Tourism operates tours around South India. One popular tour that leaves on Friday afternoon and returns on Monday night provides a nice weekend excursion to **Tirupati**, Kalahasti, Mangapuram, and Tiruchenur. The bus trip to Tirupati takes 14 hours.

Another tour goes to **Srisailam**, six hours each way. It departs at noon on Saturday and returns at 9 pm Sunday.

There is a **7-day pilgrimage tour** that goes to Bhadrachalam, Simhachalam, Vijayawada, Tirupati, Kanchipuram, and Srisailam. However, these long-distance tours can be grueling.

For those who are determined to see as much as possible and have the energy to do so, there is a **15-day tour** that leaves on the second Saturday of each month. On this tour you can visit 30 places in South India including Tirupati, Mamallapuram, Rameswaram, Guruvayur, and Srirangam. Though such intense bus travel can be somewhat laborious, this tour allows you to see the most for your money.

Foreign Exchange

Thomas Cook (231-988), Nasir Arcade, Secretariat Rd changes money quickly and efficiently. They are open Monday to Saturday from 9.30 am to 5.30 pm.

The State Bank of India (10.30 am to 2.30 pm, Saturday until 11.30 am), Mahipatram Rd, and the Bank of Baroda by Abids Circle both offer foreign exchange services.

Post and Phone

The **main post office** is just south of Sadar Patel Rd, Secunderabad. The **GPO** is at Abids Circle, Hyderabad.

Doorshanchar Bhavan, Station Rd, by the Annapurna Hotel, is a good place to make international calls. It is open Monday to Saturday from 8 am to 8 pm.

Book Shops

A A Hussain & Co, Abids Rd, and *Ashah Books*, off Mahatma Gandhi Rd, near the Hotel Emerald, are two of the best book shops in town, but their selections are nothing special.

Travel Agents

Two travel agents are Sheriff Travels (237-904), Basheer Bagh, and Sita World Travels (233-638), Hyderguda and Chapel Rd.

Venkateswara (Balaji) Temple

This is a beautiful marble-carved temple built by the Birla foundation. It is located on the highest point in Hyderabad, and it is worth the trip just for the spectacular view. It is open from 4 am to 9 pm on weekdays and from 7.30 to 11 am and 3 to 7.30 pm on weekends.

Salar Jang Museum

This museum has over 35,000 exhibits from all over the world. It has an incredible collection of weapons, metalwares, textiles, ivory, and jade. It is open daily from 10 am to 5 pm except Fridays and government holidays. Sundays are best avoided because of heavy crowds.

For those particularly interested in art, precious artifacts, and architecture, some other places of interest are **Falaknuma Palace** and **Purani Haveli**. These collections are housed in grand old palaces and mansions, and prior permission is required to visit.

Golconda Fort

This fort is 8 km west of Hyderabad and was the capital of the seven Qutb Shahi kings from 1518 to the end of the 16th century, when the capital moved to Hyderabad. Its outer walls are as high as 18m, and it has 8 huge gates with elephant spikes. It covers 40 square kilometres and can take all day to see. The perimeter of the fort is over 8 km.

Golconda is famous as the market for the neighboring diamond mines. Some of the famous diamonds that came from here are the Orloff Diamond (Catherine the Great), the Hope Diamond, Kohinoor (British Crown), and the diamonds on the Peacock Throne (Shah of Persia). You can get buses #119 and #80R from Nampally, just near the railway station in Hyderabad, to Golconda Fort.

ISKCON Temple

The ISKCON temple (552-924) is on Nampally Station Rd, not far from the railway station. The Deities in the temple

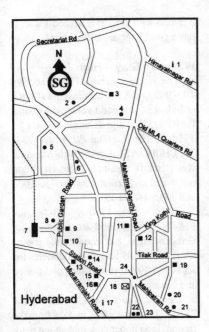

Hyderabad

are Sri Sri Gaura-Nitai, Sri Sri Radha Madana-mohana, and Sri Sri Jagannatha-Baladeva-Subhadra.

Where To Stay – Lower

The budget hotels are in the Abids area between Hyderabad railway station and Abids Circle. The average price range is between Rs 60 to Rs 110 with attached bath, and hot water is usually available in the morning.

The *Royal Lodge* and *Gee Royal Lodge*, opposite the train station, are nothing fancy, but provide the basic necessities with attached bathrooms. These places cost about Rs 55/100.

The *Hotel Rajmata* (201-020), opposite the station, has rooms for Rs 55/75 with common bath and Rs 70/90 with bath. It has deluxe rooms for Rs 240/290. The cheaper rooms are in the rear building and are rather dumpy. I had to climb over someone to get to the room. The

newer building in the front, however, has deluxe rooms that are fairly reasonable and comfortable.

The *Hotel Imperial*, on the corner of Station Rd and Public Gardens Rd (Nampally High Road), has basic rooms for Rs 90/120. The *Apsara Hotel*, Station Rd, has rooms with bath and hot water delivered in buckets in the morning for Rs 100/140.

The *Hotel Suhail* (590-386) is a good value, having rooms with bath and hot water for Rs 120/140 up to Rs 200/230. This hotel is behind the GPO. The sheets were slightly dirty when I was there, but the rooms were good.

Where To Stay – Middle

The *Hotel Saptagiri* (503-601), just off Station Rd, around the corner from the Annapurna Hotel, is a recommended place. The rooms have a balcony and attached bath with hot water, and the cost is Rs 140/175 and Rs 300 with A/C. Being on a side road it is not too noisy. Most rickshaw drivers do not know it, so ask for the Annapurna Hotel and find your way from there.

The *Hotel Jaya International* (232-929), just off Bank St, has good rooms for Rs 140/200 and A/C rooms for Rs 300/375. The *Hotel Siddhartha* (557-421), Bank St, is a really nice place with rooms for Rs 185/230 and Rs 275/325 with A/C.

The *Hotel Aahwaanam* (590-301), by J N Rd, near the Ramakrishan Cinema, has good rooms. Rooms with attached bath and hot water are Rs 175/210 and Rs 280/310 with A/C.

The *Taj Mahal Hotel* (237-988), at the junction of King Kothi Rd and Mahatma Gandhi Rd (Abids Rd), is a grand old place with a pleasant atmosphere. It has large clean rooms with bath and hot water for Rs 225/300 and Rs 300/400 with A/C.

The *Annapurna Hotel* (557-931), Nampally Station Rd, is an Indian-style hotel with very big rooms for Rs 185/250 and Rs 280/380 with A/C. The maintenance of this hotel leaves something to be desired.

The popular *Hotel Sai Prakash* (511-726), Nampally Station Rd, near the railway station, is a nice place with comfortable rooms for Rs 425/525 and Rs

525/625 with A/C. It is a good value. It has a good vegetarian restaurant.

Where To Stay – High

The *Hotel Emerald* (202-836, fax 203-902), off Mahatma Gandhi Rd (Abids Rd), is a good value with rooms for Rs 425/525 and deluxe rooms for Rs 475/600. The four-star *Ritz Hotel* (233-571), Hill Fort St, near the Birla Mandira, was formerly a palace. It has charming old world style rooms for Rs 750/1000 and suites for Rs 1500.

The new *Hotel Viceroy* (618-383, fax 618-797), Tankbund Rd overlooking Hussain Sagar, has comfortable rooms for Rs 895/1195 and deluxe doubles for Rs 1195/1495. It is fully air-conditioned and has a pool.

Central Court Hotel (233-262, fax 232-737), Lakdi-ka-Pul, two km from the station, is an upper end, mid-range hotel with rooms for Rs 700/900, which provide reasonable comfort for the price.

The *Holiday Inn Krishna* (393-939, fax 392-684), Banjara Hills, has luxury rooms for $80/100. The *Taj Residency* (399-999, fax 392-218), Banjara Hills, is a first-class place with rooms for $70/90.

The five-star *Krishna Oberoi* (392-323, fax 223-079), Road No 1, Banjara Hills, has rooms for $100/110. A stay here, nestled amongst nine acres of beautiful gardens, is indeed a relaxing and pleasurable experience.

Where To Eat

There is a good restaurant at the *Hotel Annapurna*, Nampally Station Road, Abids area. It is well known for good ice cream. The *Kamat Hotel*, a famous South Indian restaurant chain known for reasonable prices and good food, can be found on Nampally Station Road. There are also branches near the public gardens and in Secunderabad.

There is a restaurant at the *Taj Mahal Hotel*, but I could not get anything without onions. When ordering food without onions the easiest way to ask for it, by the way, is to inquire whether they serve Jain meals.

The best place I found, by far, was the *Woodlands Restaurant* at the Hotel Sai Prakash, not far from the railway station. This is a well known name in South Indian restaurants, and they also have branches throughout India.

Getting Around

I found the rickshaw drivers to be difficult to deal with. You can hire a tourist taxi from AP Tourism (557-531), Gagan Vihar, 1st Flr, MG Rd, and Ashok Travels (230-766), Lal Bahadur Stadium.

Travel

Air There are Indian Airlines flights from Hyderabad to points all over India. Other domestic airlines are East West (815-881), Modiluft (243-783), and Jet (840-382). The Air India office (232-747) is on Secretariat Rd. Indian Airlines (236-902) is near the Secretariat building. There are flights to Bombay (6 daily), Calcutta (2 daily), Delhi (3 daily), Madras (2 daily), Bangalore (daily), and three flights a week to Bhubaneswara. East West Airlines has a daily flight (except Sun) to Visakhapatnam. East West has four flights a week to Tirupati.

The airport is at Begumpet, Secunderabad. By the meter it costs about Rs 40 to the airport by auto-rickshaw, but most drivers will not use the meter. There are prepaid taxis at the airport.

Train There are two train stations— Hyderabad Railway Station (also called Nampally) and Secunderabad. Trains leave daily from both stations for almost all parts of India.

Some trains from Hyderabad Railway Station are the daily Charminar Express #6060 to Madras (6.30 pm, 15 hr), the Hyderabad Express #7085 to Bangalore (5.30 pm, 17 hr), the Hyderabad-Bombay Express #7032 (7.30 pm, 17 hr), the Godavari Express to Vijayawada #7008 (5.15 pm, 6½ hr), and the Nizamuddin-Hyderabad Express to Delhi (33½ hr), The fastest way from Calcutta to Hyderabad is to take the Coromandel Express to Vijayawada and then get another train from there (total travel time is at least 32 hr).

From the Hyderabad station the Rayasaleena Express #7429 (5 pm, 16½ hr) goes to **Tirupati**. From Secunderabad the Venkatadri #7597 (3.30 pm, 18 hr) goes to Tirupati.

From Secunderabad to **Aurangabad** there is the Ajanta Express #7551 (6 pm, 12½ hr). There is a day train from Aurangabad to Hyderabad. If you want to travel at night from Aurangabad to Hyderabad you can get a 5.30 pm train to Pune and connect with another train at about 10.30 pm to Secunderabad. The train leaving Pune can be reserved at the Aurangabad train station and will not leave until the Aurangabad train arrives. The Andhra Pradesh Express #2723 goes to **New Delhi** (6.30 am, 26 hr). It takes 39 hrs to reach Ajmer from Secunderabad. To get to Hospet and **Hampi** you take the Venkatadri Exp #7598 to Guntakal (3.30 pm, 9 hr) and then connect with the Vasco Exp #7829 (3 am, 2½ hr).

You can book train tickets at the Hyderabad Station for trains leaving from the Secunderabad Station as well. When you purchase a train ticket you have to ask what station the train departs from, as the two stations are about a half hour apart and this can sometimes cause confusion.

The booking office is open 8 am to 2 pm and 2.15 to 8 pm, Monday through Saturday, and on Sunday from 8 am to 2 pm. Both stations have tourist quotas. The Reservation Office is to the left as you enter the station. Counter #123, next to enquiry, is for tourist reservations (also lost and group tickets). Foreign tourists can book their tickets with the Chief Reservation Inspector's Office on platform 1, daily from 9 am to 5 pm.

Bus   The APSRIC bus station, Gowliguda, has buses going all over the state. You can get semi-deluxe and super-deluxe buses from here. There is a computerized booking office open daily from 8 am to 9 pm. There are two bus stations—the old and the new. More than likely you will want to go to the new bus station, and you should make this clear to the rickshaw driver as it is further than the old bus stand. Otherwise they will drive you to the old bus stand and then ask for more money to get you to the new bus station.

There are buses departing to Tirupati (10 daily, 9 hr), Vijayawada, Aurangabad, Madras (1 daily, 16 hr), Bombay (8 daily, 17 hr), Bangalore (10 daily, 13 hr), and many other places. There is a 10 am luxury bus to Srisailam, which cannot be booked in advance.

There are **private bus companies** that have super-deluxe video buses to major cities like Bombay, Bangalore, Tirupati, and Madras. Their main offices are on Nampally High Rd (Public Gardens Rd) by the railway station. Noble Travels (201-275) and Asian Travels (202-128) both seem to be reliable ticket outlets. Most of these buses leave in the late afternoon and travel overnight.

YADAGIRI-GUTTA

It is 60 km north of Hyderabad. This place was named after a sage named Yadava, who performed intense austerities to see Lord Vishnu in His form of Lord Narasimha. Being pleased with him, Lord Vishnu gave him *darsana* (sight) of His form as Jwala Narasimha, Gandabheranda Narasimha, and Yogananda Narasimha. He begged the Lord to permanently remain on the hill in these three forms. Yadagiri is the corrupted form of the original name, Yadavagiri. The temple here is on top of a hill.

Laksmi Narasimhadeva Temple

There are three forms of **Lord Narasimha** in this temple—Jwala Narasimha, Gandabheranda Narasimha, and Yogananda Narasimha—each embedded in stone. The oil lamps here are kept burning 24 hours a day. Many people visit this temple.

If you come through the main door (*simhadwara*) of the temple from the town square, not the road after getting off the bus, then you will see a Hanuman temple to the right. Just beneath Hanuman is a horizontal gap in the rock, 10 inches wide and about 60 square feet in area. The narrow cave is said to be the place where the Lord manifested Himself in the form of **Gandabheranda Narasimha**.

You then go down the stairs and come to the main hall, and behind you to the left is a temple. If you enter the hall by the entrance where the bus lets you off, this temple will be directly in front of you. Close to the rear pillar is a natural cave about 12 feet wide and 30 feet in length. This cave is under a huge rock that forms a sloping roof, which is about 5 feet high in the middle of the passage.

At the end of the cave are the forms of Lord Narasimha. There are two rocks fastened to each other. On one of the rocks there is an image in the shape of a serpent. This is the form of **Jwala Narasimha**. On the other rock is an image of a figure seated in meditation that is said to be the image of **Yogananda Narasimha**. There are also silver Deities of Laksmi and Narasimha. To the left of the front pillar there is a shrine dedicated to the goddess Andalamma.

This temple is a very sacred place, and it is said that whatever a sincere devotee prays for here will not go unfulfilled—no pilgrimage to this place is made in vain. It is also stated that even incurable diseases will be cured here if one worships the Lord for a week or two, or even better for forty days, with full faith and determination.

This temple is located upon a 300 foot hill. At the foot of this hill is a gateway with a *gopuram* over it that is called **Vaikuntha-dwara**, or gateway to Vaikuntha, the spiritual world. Saturday morning is crowded, and you may have to wait two hours in a queue (line) for a one second *darsana*. I went later in the day and there was just a small line and I was able to view the Deities as long as I liked. There was a Deity procession outside the temple the Saturday night that a was there.

Where To Stay

If you want to stay here overnight there are some basic *dharamasalas* at the top of the hill and a few basic, though not too economical, hotels at the bottom of the hill. There are only basic eating places here. At the base of the hill you will find the run-down *Siva Hotel* with rooms for Rs 90/110 and a deluxe room, if you can call it that, for Rs 275. This is supposed to be the best place in town. Bring your own sheets and it is tolerable.

Travel

From Hyderabad (2 hrs) there are regular buses that leave from platform 48 or 50, from the new APSRIC bus station, Gowliguda, about every half hour. There is a big picture of Narasimha at the platform. There is another town called Yadgir, so don't get on the wrong bus, a mistake I made myself. The rickshaw drivers will try to bring you to the old bus stand, as it is closer. Tell them in advance you want to go to the new bus stand, which is a very big, new looking place. Once you get to Yadagiri-gutta, which is the last stop, you can either walk up, get another very crowded bus, or an auto-rickshaw to the top of the hill. It takes about a half hour to walk up.

SRISAILAM

Population: 21,000, STD Code 085195

It is located on Rishabhagiri Hill, on the bank of the sacred river Krishna, about a 6-hour bus ride south of Hyderabad (200 km). Srisailam is also called Sri Sailam or Sriparvata. It is a very ancient place and is mentioned in the *Mahabharata* and the *Puranas*. On top of the Srisailam Hill is the famous Mallikarjuna Temple, dedicated to Lord Siva. It is one of the most visited temples in Andhra Pradesh.

It is considered to be a necessary part of Srisailam pilgrimage to bathe in the **Pathalaganga River**, which is the local name for the **Krishna River**. It is located about 3 km east of the Mallikarjuna Temple. From the temple, there are steps leading down the hill to the river. **Siva-**

linga stones are collected from the banks of this holy Krishna River.

The **Uma-maheswara Temple**, about 3 km northwest of the Mallikarjuna Temple on the way to Pathalaganga, is a very ornate temple. In Basar is a temple dedicated to **Saraswati**. This is one of the only Saraswati temples in India, except for one in Kashmir.

You can get a small book about the temple called *The Holy History of Srisailam* for Rs 15 from salesmen in front of the temple or at the bus stand.

Mallikarjuna Temple

This temple, dedicated to Lord Siva, is nestled in the Rishabagiri Hills on the south bank of the Krishna River. It is also called Sriparvata. The Mallikarjuna Swami Temple is one of the **12** *jyotirlinga* Siva temples, or main Siva temples in the country. The main temple has four lofty towers and was built by King Harihara Raya (1404-1405). The temple is surrounded by an 8.5m high wall. As you enter this temple you will first notice a well-carved *mukha-mandapa* (hall) with a huge carved stone Nandi (bull). The Lord's consort is known as Bhramarambika.

Anyone who comes here is allowed to touch the Lord or bow and touch their heads to the *linga*. There are also smaller shrines dedicated to Panchapandavas, Vata Vriksha, and Sahasra-linga in this temple.

To the right of the main temple is the Old or **Vriddha Mallikarjuna** Sivalinga (7th century), which is the original Siva-linga that was installed in this temple. It is said that because this Siva-linga was originally worshiped with jasmine, or *mallika* flowers, it was given the name Mallikarjuna. The interesting **Mirror Hall** directly to your right as you

enter the main gate is where the Lord takes rest at night.

Lord Caitanya visited this temple, and Sankaracarya also stayed at Srisailam for some time. The Maratha General Shivaji came here in 1674. It is said that this temple was visited by Prahlada Maharaja and also by Lord Rama, after He returned from Lanka. Lord Rama is said to have personally installed the Sahasralinga here. This **Sahasra-linga** is surrounded by a three-headed Naga and consists of 1001 miniature *lingas*. There are five *lingas* in the inner courtyard that are said to have been installed by the Pandavas called the **Panchapandavas**.

Behind the main temple and up a flight of stairs is the temple of the goddess **Bhramarambika** (Parvati), who is said to have assumed the form of a bee to kill the demon Mahisasura. If you press your ear to a tiny hole on the exterior back wall of the sanctum, you can hear the buzzing of a bee.

The outer enclosure walls of the Mallikarjuna Temple have five regular rows of sculptures on the eastern, southern, and northern walls. At 5.30 pm there is a **special** *arati* that costs 5 rupees, and then right after that a special *arati* at the Bhramarambika (Parvati) Temple. The Sivaratri festival here in February-March is huge, being the high point of the year. Non-Hindus are allowed to enter this temple.

Where To Stay

There are cottages and choultries run by the temple as well as an APTDC *Sailamvihar Tourist Rest House*. There are many basic dharamshalas here as it is a very visited place. A basic room with bath is about Rs 70. They do not see many foreigners here, so it may be difficult to find a place that has foreigner registration forms. There are only basic eating places here. To come here you should be prepared to rough it a bit.

Travel

It is due west of Vijayawada, 170 km east of Kurnool and 110 km north of Nandyal.

Air The nearest airport is in Hyderabad (200 km).

Rail The closest railway station is Markapur Road, on the Guntur-Hublim metre gauge line that heads west from Vijayawada. Srisailam can also be reached from Nandyal (110 km) and Kurnool stations.

Bus By bus it is 200 km southeast of Hyderabad (6 hrs) and 260 km southwest of Vijayawada. There are several buses coming here from **Hyderabad**, but the 10 am luxury bus is the easiest and most pleasant. Get there early for this bus, as I was told it is not possible to book this bus in advance.

There are directs buses to Kurnool (1.15 pm), Tirupati (7.30 am), and Madras (6 pm). To get to Ahovalam from Srisailam (starting with a 6 am bus) takes about 10 hours and you need to change buses three times. I was told that there is also a direct bus to Ahovalam that leaves in the afternoon.

AHOVALAM (AHOBALAM)

Ahovalam is said to be the place where Lord Vishnu took the half-man, half-lion form of **Lord Narasimha** in order to defeat the great demon Hiranyakasipu. Ahovalam, 49 km south of Nandyal Railway Station and about 300 km south of Hyderabad, is 2,800 feet above sea level. It is also known as Singavel Kundram.

Ahovalam is the only place in India where all nine forms of Lord Narasimha, **Nava Narasimha**, are worshiped. The nine (*nava*) forms of Narasimha are: 1) Prahlada-varada Narasimha or Laksmi Narasimha, 2) Chatravata Narasimha, 3) Yogananda Narasimha, 4) Karanda Narasimha, 5) Krodha Narasimha, 6) Guha Narasimha, 7) Jwala Narasimha, 8) Malola Narasimha, and 9) Pavana Narasimha. The Narasimhadeva Deity in the Ugra Narasimha Temple in Upper Ahovalam is said to be self-manifested (*swayambhu*). This place of pilgrimage was visited by Lord Caitanya.

Ahovalam is a very small town and not many foreigners come here, because it is really out of the way. If you are not an Indian you can expect to be stared at a lot.

Information and Guides

To fully explore both Upper and Lower Ahovalam takes about two days. To reach Upper Ahovalam (8 km) there are regular buses (20 min) from Lower Ahovalam.

In Upper Ahovalam there are many natural caves, some of which are also used as temples. If you want to see the pillar from which Lord Narasimha appeared, it is best to have a guide, as it is very difficult to get there without one. You can hire a guide at the small tea stall next to the entrance of the Ugra Narasimha Temple.

Some of the priests in the temple are very knowledgeable and can be very helpful.

The Prahlada-varada Narasimha Temple in Lower Ahovalam and the Ugra Narasimha Temple in Upper Ahovalam are major temples with formal worship. The other temples in the area may have very little formal worship and few visitors. Some are difficult to reach.

Lower Ahovalam

The impressive and beautiful 800 year old **Prahlada-varada Narasimha Temple** is in the town of Lower Ahovalam, near the bus stand. This temple is dedicated to the aspect of Lord Narasimha blessing Prahlada. To your right when you enter the temple are eight pillars, each intricately carved with one of the nine forms of Narasimhadeva. The priests in this temple are very friendly.

The temple dedicated to **Chatravala Narasimha** is about two km from the bus stand under a *pippal* tree. About 4 km up the hill to Upper Ahovalam are the **Karanda Narasimha** and **Yogananda Narasimha** Temples. It is said that Lord Narasimha taught Prahlada several yogic postures here, that is why the Lord is known here as Yogananda Narasimha. It is best to have a guide to reach these temples.

Upper Ahovalam

The elaborately decorated temple that contains the fierce form of **Ugra Narasimha** is located near the bus stand in Upper Ahovalam. This temple is dedicated to the form of Sri Narahari, who emerged from the pillar to kill Hiranyakasipu. This temple has a *mandapa* (hall) and *gopuram*. Several feet from the Ugra Narasimha Deity is **Guha Narasimha**, who is in a little cave. *Guha* means cave. There is also a Sudarsana Yantra to the right of the Deity in another room. There is a small *darsana* fee charged at this temple.

If you leave from the back entrance of this temple and walk ten minutes, you come to the **Krodha Narasimha** Temple, where the Lord is worshiped in His boar

form. There is a temple cave of Varaha Narasimha here. The main temple room is completely carved into the stone wall of the mountain side. The Deity of Varaha Narasimha is standing majestically on a raised stone platform. Varaha, the boar incarnation of Lord Krishna, killed Hiranyakasipu's younger brother, Hiranyaksa, thus incurring the wrath and hatred of Hiranyakasipu. Thus the two incarnations, Narasimha and Varaha, responsible for destroying the two demon brothers, have been installed together in this temple and worshiped for thousands of years.

The **Malola Narasimha** Temple is about 2 km from here. The Deity here is said to be in *santa-rupa*, always in sport with Laksmidevi. Both this temple and the Varaha Narasimha Temple are small and not very well kept. More than likely no one will be there to assist you. They are, however, well worth the visit, and you can get to both of these temples without the assistance of a guide.

About a half hour walk up the hill on the way to the pillar, is the **Jwala Narasimha** Temple, where the Ugrakala form of the Lord is found. This is said to be the actual spot where Lord Narasimha tore apart Hiranyakasipu. This Deity is located in a cave overlooking a steep cliff. You need a guide to reach this place, which is at the end of a hard, exciting climb.

Looming fifteen stories into the sky over Ahovalam is the **ugra-stambha**, the pillar from which Lord Narasimhadeva appeared. You get your first sight of the pillar after walking about a half hour from where the bus lets you off in Upper Ahovalam. You will need the help of a guide to reach the pillar, as the trek takes about two hours. It is a hard climb directly up the mountain's side. Even if you have to stop every five or ten minutes to rest, the feeling of exhilaration upon arrival at this very sacred spot is adequate and rewarding compensation for the effort.

To see the **Pavana Narasimha** temple, where the Shakta form of worship of the Lord is done, also requires the services of a guide. It is a couple hours walk (8 km) from the main Ugra Narasimha Temple, in a different direction from the other temples.

Other Places

It is said that at **Rakta-kunda**, Lord Narasimha washed His hands after killing the demon Hiranyakasipu and interestingly, the water is still red as a result of this pastime. The **Rama-tirtha tank** is eight km from Lower Ahovalam.

Where To Stay and Eat

There is a small basic *Government Tourist Rest House* with rooms for Rs 40/50. It is near the bus stand in Lower Ahovalam. During the day there may not be anyone there, but a man in the small house to the right of the Rest House has a key and can let you in. The manager of the Rest House will show up later in the day. There are a few basic guesthouses near the temple in Lower Ahovalam with rooms for Rs 40/50. There is also a larger basic **Rest House** where the bus lets you off at Upper Ahovalam.

There is a small basic restaurant by the bus stand. It is much preferable to bring your own food or cooking equipment, as there is not much in the way of food or drink for sale in this town. Bottled water is not available and the only fruit I saw was bananas.

Travel

Ahovalam is located halfway between Madras and Hyderabad. It is not an easy place to get to, as it is totally in the middle of nowhere. The closest big city is Kurnool in Andhra Pradesh. To get to Ahovalam you usually first have to go to Allagudda. There is a small road that goes northeast from there to Ahovalam (40 km).

Rail There is a station at Nandyal, about 6 hours south of Hyderabad. From there you can get a bus to Allagudda and from there another bus to Ahovalam (1 hr).

You can also go to the railway station at Cuddapah, which is an important stop on the Madras-Bombay route. From there you get a bus to Allagudda about 60 km north and then get another bus to Ahovalam.

There is also a railway station at Dhone. From there you take a bus to Ahovalam via the towns of Banganapalli and Koilkuntla.

Bus To get a bus to Ahovalam, generally you have to first get a bus to **Allagudda,** which is on the main road halfway between Hyderabad and Madras (Tirupati). From Allagudda to Ahovalam takes about an hour.

To get to Ahovalam from Srisailam (starting with a 6 am bus) takes about 10 hours and you need to change buses three times. There is one direct bus to Ahovalam that leaves in the afternoon from Srisailam. There is a fast luxury bus from Tirupati to Allagudda. You can also get a bus from Kurnool to Allagudda. To get to Hampi from here you have to take three or four buses and the trip takes about 12 hours. There is a direct bus to Tirupati (7 hr) and Madras (11 hr) that departs around 5.30 pm from Lower Ahovalam.

Nandyal

The **Mahanandi Temple** is 16 km

from Nandyal and about 280 km south of Hyderabad. It is an ancient temple dedicated to Lord Siva. The *linga* is unique because it is like a rough uncut rock, with two cavities. The priests here allow you to touch the Lord. There is a huge Nandi in front of the main shrine. Many people include this temple in a visit to Srisailam.

This temple is unique for South India because the *vimana* (tower) over the *linga* is built in the North Indian style. The main gate of the temple faces west. There is a tank here, 60 foot square, which is always 5 ft deep. The mystery is that no one knows how the water enters the tank—only that it is always the same level and completely crystal clear.

There is a railway station in Nandyal. To get to Ahovalam you can get a train to here, then get a bus to Allagudda, and from there get another bus to Ahovalam.

Tadpatri (Tadapatri)
Population: 71,000, STD Code 08558

There are two interesting temples here built by the Vijayanagar kings. The **Venkataramana Temple** (mid-16th century) is dedicated to Lord Vishnu. It has an impressive *gopuram* and beautiful sculptures of the pastimes of Krishna and Rama. This temple is about 1 km northeast of the bus station.

One km north of this temple is the **Ramalingeswara Temple**. This temple, on the south bank of the Pennar River has two impressive *gopurams*. It has outstanding sculptures and pilastered walls that are encrusted with friezes of jewels, petals and miniature scrollwork. The main shrine of this temple is dedicated to Lord Siva. There is a Siva-linga here whose stand is filled with water. There are also two other shrines—one dedicated to Parvati and the other to Rama, Laks-

mana and Sita.

Tadpatri is about halfway between Hyderabad and Bangalore. It is about 120 km southwest of Ahovalam.

SRIKURMAN (KURMA-KSETRA)

There is a temple here dedicated to Kurmadeva. In the *Prapannamrta*, it is said that one night Lord Jagannatha threw Sri Ramanujacarya from Jagannatha Puri to Kurma-ksetra. At that time Ramanuja thought the Deity of Kurma was Lord Siva. Later, when he understood that the Kurma-murti was another form of Lord Vishnu, he instituted gorgeous worship here. Thus this holy place of Kurma-ksetra or Srikurman, was reestablished by Sripada Ramanujacarya under the influence of Lord Jagannatha. Sri Caitanya Mahaprabhu came here on His South India tour.

Srikurman is located 100 km northeast of Visakhapatnam and 200 km southwest of Puri, on the shore of the Bay of Bengal, 15 km east of the town of Srikakulam. Srikakulam is a fairly large town which has decently good facilities. Srikurman is a very small town with virtually no facilities, so it is best to stay in Srikakulam and travel to the Sri Kurma Temple during the day. This is an area where few foreigners visit.

Kurma Temple

This temple is said to be the only temple of the tortoise incarnation on the planet. The present temple is at least 700 years old. The original temple was supposedly built in 200 AD.

Sri Kurma, a Deity of Lord Vishnu in the form of a *kurma*, or a tortoise, is one of the ten incarnations of Vishnu, who are collectively known as the Dasavatara. The Deity consists of two stones, about two feet long, coming out from the ground, which represent the head and body of Sri Kurma.

As you enter the inner sanctum of the temple, the Deities of **Lord Rama, Laksmana**, and **Sita** are on one side and the Deities of **Govindadeva** (Krishna) and His *sakhis* are opposite. The temple is located on the shore of Swatha Puskarini Lake.

While the temple faces east, the presiding Deity, Kurmadeva, faces the opposite direction, with His back to the entrance. According to traditional understanding, **Bilvamangala Thakura**, the author of *Krishna-karnamrita,* prayed to the back of the Deity with such extreme humility and sincere devotion that Sri Kurma graciously turned around to face His worshiper. To the left of the main temple is a small temple dedicated to the four-armed form of Bilvamangala. It is said that Bilvamangala's body is buried below this temple.

This temple has a devotional atmosphere and is architecturally beautiful to look at. There is a big festival in February, at which time many thousands of people come to bathe in the **Swatha Puskarini Lake**. The temple priests here are helpful and friendly. This temple sees few foreign visitors.

The *Caitanya-caritamrita* describes that when Sri Caitanya came to Kurmaksetra, He stayed in the house of a local *Brahmin.* When the Lord was preparing to leave, the *Brahmin* wanted to take *sannyasa* and travel with Him, but Sri Caitanya forbade him to do so. Rather, the Lord instructed the *Brahmin* to remain at home and always chant the holy name of Krishna. In this way, the process of transforming one's residence into a holy place by chanting the holy names of Krishna was introduced and passed down through the Vaishnava line. Perched on a hill in

Kurma-ksetra is a small shrine that houses the footprints of Sri Caitanya Mahaprabhu, who visited Kurma-ksetra in 1512. These footprints were established here in December, 1930 by Bhaktisiddhanta Gosvami.

Nearby

At **Arasavalli**, one and a half km from Srikakulam, there is a famous temple dedicated to **Surya,** the sun god. It is said that this temple was originally established by Lord Indra. The deity is carved from black granite stone.

Aruna, the charioteer of the sun-god, is the older brother of Garuda, the carrier of Lord Vishnu. The present temple was reconstructed in 1778 by Yelamanchili Pullaji Panthulu.

This place is between Srikakulam and the Kurma Temple, and it is convenient to stop and visit this temple on the way to the Kurma Temple.

Where To Stay and Eat

Right next to the railway station, 15 km from Srikakulam and 30 km from Srikurman, is the *Raja Lodge*, which is a basic place with rooms for Rs 50/70. It can be really tough to face the bathrooms here.

The decent places to stay are located in Srikakulam about 15 km west of Srikurman. The *Lodge Priyadarshini* (22770), Krishna Park Junction, Palakonda Rd, has good rooms for Rs 70/90 with bath, Rs 120/150 for deluxe rooms, and Rs 225 for a room with A/C. This is one of the best values in town. The nearby *Lodge Rajkamal* (22164), Palakonda Rd, has rooms for Rs 65/95, Rs 120 for a deluxe room, and Rs 225 with A/C.

The *Lodge Kinnera* (22392), Palakonda Rd, is not as good as some of the other places for the same price. It has rooms for Rs 75/100 and Rs 225 for a deluxe room. You can be shown a room with a balcony, with a view of the wall of the next building, five feet away.

The best place in town is the *Hotel Nagavali* (22956), Ring Rd. Rooms are Rs 150 up to Rs 350 for rooms with A/C, with an extra 10% luxury tax. It also has a decent vegetarian restaurant, which says in its handout sheet that it has a wide selection of dishes, but I did not find this to be true. When I ordered french fries (chips) I received with a smile 5 slices of potato about an eighth of an inch thick. All for 10 rupees. Still, it seems to be the best place in town to eat.

Travel

Train The closest train station to Srikurman, where the temple is located, is called Srikakulam Railway Station. It is located about 15 km west of the city of Srikakulam. From the railway station it is about 30 km to the Sri Kurma Temple. This station is on the main Madras-Calcutta route, so many trains stop here.

Road There are regular buses from Vijayawada (3 hr) to Srikakulam.

You can get a motor rickshaw to bring you from the bus stand in Srikakulam to the Kurma Temple and back, stopping on the way at the Sun temple at Arasavalli, for Rs 150. There are buses to the Kurma Temple from the bus station in Srikakulam. Since Srikurman is a very small town, taking an auto-rickshaw is more convenient than taking a bus, because you may have to wait a long time to get back to Srikakulam if you use the bus system.

It is Rs 80 to take an auto-rickshaw (20 min) from the train station to the bus stand. There are also very crowded regular buses between the train and bus stations.

VISAKHAPATNAM & WALTAIR

Population: 1,100,000, STD Code 0891

Visakhapatnam is called Viraz for short. The main spiritual reason to come here is to go the Varaha Narasimha temple at Simhachalam, 16 km north of Visakhapatnam.

There are a couple of nice beaches in this city, with crystal clear warm ocean water. Two beaches are Mission Beach, about 3 km from downtown, and Lawson Beach, 6 km away. Ramakrishna Beach, along Lawson's Bay, is a good beach. Because of the strong current, swimming can be dangerous here. Swimming at the harbor end of the beach is not recommended.

Information

The State Tourist office is on the 1st Floor of the Nehru Nagar Complex and is open from 10 am to 5 pm Monday to Saturday. There is also a tourist office at the railway station.

Where To Stay – Lower

The retiring rooms at the *bus stand* are well maintained and a good value. At the *railway station* there are also large, good standard retiring rooms for Rs 175, as well as cheaper dorm beds.

The *Hotel Poorna* (62344), Main Rd, has rooms with bath for Rs 60/80. The *Hotel Prasanth* (65282), Main Rd, has clean rooms with bath for Rs 70/110. The *Hotel Karanths* (69347), 33 Patel Marg, is a good reasonably priced place that has clean rooms with bath.

Where To Stay – Middle To High

The *Meghalaya* (555-141, fax 555-824), Asilametta Jn, is a good place with rooms for Rs 210/250 and Rs 310/350 with A/C. It is a five minute walk from the bus stand. The two-star *Ocean View Inn* (54828), at the northern end of the beach, is a good place to stay. Rooms are Rs 200/350 and Rs 275/400 for an A/C room. The *Palm Beach Hotel* (54026), Beach Rd, Waltair, has a good location, but is a little run down. It is a good choice for a cheaper middle-class place near the beach. Rooms are Rs 300/400 and Rs 350/400 with A/C.

The three-star *Hotel Daspalla* (564-825), Suryabagh, in the center of town, has rooms for Rs 250/280 and Rs 325/360 with A/C. It is a very good place with two good vegetarian restaurants. Also in the center of town is the recommended four-star *Dolphin Hotel* (567-000), Dadagardens, which has a swimming pool and rooms for Rs 595/795 up to Rs 1395.

The three-star *Hotel Apsara* (64861), Waltair Main Rd, costs Rs 400/450 for a room with A/C.

One of the best places in town is the *Park Hotel* (554-488), Beach Rd, right next to the beach, which has A/C rooms for Rs 1150/1950 and suites for Rs 3000. It has a book shop and a clean swimming pool.

About the same price is the *Taj Residency Visakhapatnam* (567-756), Beach Rd, which is recently refurbished and has sea-facing rooms for $55/65.

Where To Eat

There are two good restaurants at the *Hotel Daspalla*, one *South Indian* and the *Vaisakhi Restaurant*, which serves North Indian cuisine and is open to 10.30 pm.

Travel

Air There are daily flights to Hyderabad and Bombay. There are also flights to Calcutta (Mon, Thu, Sat), Madras (Mon, Tue, Thu, Sat), and Bhubaneswar (Wed, Fri). The airport is 12 miles from the city center.

Train Visakhapatnam is on the main route between Calcutta and Madras. It takes 13 hours to get to Calcutta on the Coromandel Express and 17 hours on the Howrah-Madras Mail #6004 (2 pm). To get to Hyderabad (700 km) takes 12 hours on either the Godavari Express or the Konark Express. The Konark Express also goes to Bhubaneswara. There are also trains to Tirupati, Madras, Trivandrum, Bangalore, and Puri via Bhubaneswara. You can connect for a train to Bombay from Hyderabad or Nagpur.

Trains are often delayed, especially during the rainy season. It is a good idea to phone the train station in advance to get information about the departure of your train. The phone number is 69421.

Bus You can get buses to all over the state from here and Puri in Orissa. It is convenient to take a bus to Srikakulam (3 hr) from here, as the train station in Srikakulam is 15 km out of the way.

Simhachalam

Simhachalam is about 16 km north of Visakhapatnam. *Simha* means "lion" and *chalam* means "hill." So Simhachalam means lion's hill. It is also known as Jiyada-Narasimha, Sri Singachalam, and Simhagiri. There is the famous Varaha Narasimha Temple here.

Near the foot of the hill is the sacred **Pushkarini bathing tank**. There is a perpetual spring called **Gangadhara** by the Varaha Narasimha temple that is said to have medicinal properties. To get to Gangadhara, if you are standing facing the temple entrance, you proceed to the left until the end of the road and then turn right and again go to the end of the road.

Varaha Narasimha Temple (Jiyada-Narasimha)

This temple, whose Deity is known as Varaha Narasimha Swami, is perched atop an 800-foot hill. In the Sanskrit language He is known as Simhadri Natha, and in the Telegu language as Simhadri Appanna (the Lion Lord of the Hill). This Deity is about 2½ feet high. He presents Himself in an enchanting two-armed, threefold-bending human form, but He has the head of a boar and tail of a lion, thus making Him a very unique Deity. Simhachalam is one of the 108 Divya Desam temples. It is one of the major Vishnu temples in India.

The *pujaris* daily apply layer upon layer of *candana* (**sandalwood paste**) on the Lord's body to cool His great anger. Srila Prabhupada commented that the sandalwood was to keep the Deity "cool-headed." The sandalwood is removed only once a year during the Vaishaka period (April/May), bringing thousands of pilgrims on that day to see the Lord's form. The Deity faces west, while the temple building faces east. The original Deity is situated within the depths of the temple, but another Deity known as *vijaya-murti* stands on the altar. There are two forms of the Lord: *nitya-rupa*, the form that you see covered with sandalwood, and *nija-rupa*, His actual form. When you come close for *darsana*, what you actually see is the Lord covered by a mound of dried sandalwood paste.

The temple of Lord Narasimhadeva known as Simhachalam is the most attractive and interesting temple in the vicinity of Visakhapatnam. It is a very affluent and well-kept temple and is a showcase example of the area's architec-

ture. Inscribed on a stone tablet is mentioned that a queen formerly donated enough gold plating to cover the entire body of the Lord. The original Deity is situated in the inner sanctum of the temple, but there is another Deity, a duplicate, known as the *vijaya-murti*. This smaller Deity can be moved from the temple and taken on public processions. Priests, who generally belong to the Ramanuja-sampradaya (Sri-sampradaya), are in charge of the Deity worship, and this *sampradaya* is well known for its opulence and cleanliness.

When Lord Caitanya came here on His South India tour, He chanted verses to Lord Narasimha. Then Lord Narasimhadeva's priest brought garlands and the remnants of the Lord's food and offered them to Lord Caitanya. Bhaktisiddhanta Goswami installed the footprints of Sri Caitanya in December, 1930, close to the main temple as a memorial of Lord Caitanya's visit. Srila Prabhupada came here in February, 1972. Ramanuja visited here in the 11th century.

As you approach the temple, the view of the high *gopurams* and elaborate carvings is very impressive. The temple was mainly built in the 13th century by a military commander of Narasimha I, who built the Konark temple near Puri. It is a combination of Orissan and Chalukyan styles of architecture. The temple buildings are black granite, and carved into the rock are the forms and pastimes of Vishnu, especially in His incarnation of Lord Narasimha. The temple has two perimeter walls around it. In the center of the outer enclosure walls are Deities of **Varaha** (north), **Trivikrama** (south), and **Narasimha** (east).

According to the priests, a visit to this temple will benedict barren persons to be blessed with offspring. Just outside the

Deity room, in the *mukha-mandapa* (hall) of the temple, is a pillar named **Kappam Stambham**, which is decorated with cloth and surrounded by silver plates and flower garlands. Women can be seen embracing this pillar and praying with great devotion, asking the Lord to fulfill their desire for a child.

North of the temple, outside the enclosure is the **Kalyana-mandapa**, which has 96 intricately carved pillars. Here there are many sculptures of Lord Narasimha and other Vishnu incarnations such as Matsya and Dhanvantari.

Saturday is a crowded day and there can be a long queue (line) to see the Deity in the morning, but it is usually not very crowded later in the day.

Temple Story

The temple story is that Hiranyakasipu told his servants to throw his son **Prahlada** into the sea here and place a huge mountain over him. Lord Vishnu jumped over the hill and lifted Prahlada from the sea, thus rescuing Prahlada again from his demoniac father Hiranyakasipu's attempt to kill him. The Lord is said to have tilted the hill a bit so Prahlada could escape from underneath.

On Prahlada's request, the Lord then assumed the form of the Varaha-Narasimha Deity, so that Prahlada could see both of the Lord's aspects—the one by which He had already killed Hiranyaksa and the one by which He would soon kill Hiranyakasipu. After he was granted this *darsana* (sight) Prahlada is said to have built a temple around the Deity. After thousands of years the temple deteriorated and was later found by **Pururava**, who is mentioned in the Ninth Canto of the *Srimad Bhagavatam*. Upon discovery, Pururava heard a voice from the sky telling him to cover the Deity with sandal paste and expose Him only once a year, on the day of Candana-yatra, the Vaishaka (trtiya) day in April or May. Pururava covered the Deity with sandal paste and rebuilt the temple, which has flourished ever since.

Festivals

On the day of **Candana-yatra**, the priests break the *candana* (sandalwood) covering of the Deity and the Lord can be seen directly. This event takes place on Aksaya-trtiya, the third day of the first half of the month of Vaishaka (April-May). The sandalwood covering is taken off and the Deity is then ceremonially bathed. In the evening the Deity is again covered with sandalwood.

The **Kalyanotsava Festival** celebrates the marriage of the Lord to His eternal consort, Laksmi. It is performed with all the rituals and fire sacrifices of a traditional Hindu wedding. It begins on the 11th day (Ekadasi) in the first half of the lunar month of Chaitra (March-April) and continues for five days till Purnima, the full moon day.

Practicalities

There are simple guesthouses by the temple.

The beautiful Simhachalam (Jiyada-Narasimha) temple is situated on top of a hill about 16 km northeast of **Visakhapatnam**. Adivivaram, the village at the foot of the hill, is 4 km from the Simhachalam Railway Station.

From Visakhapatnam the 6A bus goes to Simhachalam. You get this bus at the side of the RTC bus stand and you get off at the last stop. Once you get to the Simhacalam station, walk out of the station, turn right, and walk a few minutes to get to the bus that goes to the top of the hill. You can also approach the temple by climbing the hill, which has about 800 six-inch steps. Once you are on top of the hill you are directed to enter the temple through a side entrance. After walking through some passageways, you come into a hallway with large black pillars leading to the main altar.

Kovvur (Vidyanagara)

Sri Caitanya met Ramananda Raya for the first time here at Goshpada-ghata. Ramananda Gaudiya Math is near this spot, and in the rear corner of this temple Bhaktisiddhanta Maharaja installed Lord Caitanya's footprints. There are beautiful deities of Ramananda Raya speaking with Lord Caitanya. It may be possible to stay here at the Ramananda Gaudiya Math temple. The present town of Kovvur used to be called Vidyanagara and is located halfway between Visakhapatnam and Vijayawada on the bank of the Godavari River.

Nagalapuram

In the Veda Narayana temple here, the presiding Deity is Lord Matsya. This temple is reputed to be the only Matsya temple in India. The Deity has the head and torso of Lord Vishnu and golden human-like feet, but when the *pujari* moves the golden feet aside you can see the Lord's fish tail.

Bhadrachalam

Bhadrachalam is located on the bank of the Godavari River, 180 km due west of Visakhapatnam. There is the important **Sri Rama temple** here. Rama and Sita are said to have lived here before Sita was carried away by Ravana. It is said that the temple is located near the point where Rama crossed the Godavari on His journey to Lanka to find Sita. Staying here at that time was a sage

named **Bhadra**, and Lord Rama came here just to give him *darsana*. Hence, this temple is named Bhadrachalam after this sage.

The main Deity is the four-armed form of Lord Rama. In two hands He holds a bow and arrow, and in the other two hands He holds a conch shell and disc. The Deity is called **Chaturbhuja Rama**. The *utsava-vigraha* Deities here of Lord Rama, Sita, and Laksmana are so exquisitely beautiful that many pilgrims visit despite the difficulty getting here. The main festival is Rama-navami (the appearance day of Lord Rama) in April.

Travel

You can go to Burgampad and from there take a boat to Bhadrachalam. You can also take a train to Rajahmundry, which is on the Madras-Calcutta line. From there you take a boat about 70 km up the Godavari River. It is not an easily accessible place of pilgrimage.

VIJAYAWADA

Population: 845,000, STD Code 0866

Vijayawada is on the banks of the Krishna River, about 70 km from the sea. One of the main reasons for going to Vijayawada is to visit the Pana Narasimha temple in Mangalagiri. There are also several other ancient temples in the area and an ancient Hindu cave temple. If you are interested in visiting the famous Buddhist site, Amaravati, this is a good starting point.

Information

There is a **tourist office** on Gopal Reddy Rd, opposite the Old Bus Stand (6 am to 8 pm). They run a full day tour of the area. There is an **AP Tourism** counter at the RTC Bus Stand.

You can hire a **tourist taxi** from AP Tourism (75382), Krishnaveni Motel, Seethanagaram. You can **change money** at the State Bank of India on Babu Rajendra Prasad Rd.

Places To See

There is a 5th-century five-story-high cave temple at **Undavali**, which is close to the village of Sitanagaram. It was discovered in 1797. On the third story is a hall with a figure of Vishnu on the snake Ananta. There are several other interesting carvings of Lord Vishnu in this temple. It is about 4 km south of Vijayawada.

There are several temples carved in stone at **Indrakila**, which is said to be the place where Arjuna got the Pasupathastra weapon from Lord Siva.

There are three ancient temples in Vijayawada—the Vijayeswara Swami temple, Kanaka Durga temple, and the Malleswara Swami temple (Mallikarjuna temple). The **Malleswara temple** is reputed to have been originally installed by Yudhisthira, the oldest of the Pandava brothers, to celebrate their victory in the south. The present temple was built by the Chalukya King, Tribhuvana Malla, in the 10th century. The **Vijayeswara temple** is said to have been installed by Arjuna, the younger brother of Yudhisthira.

The deity in the **Kanaka Durga temple** is regarded as *swayambhu,* or self-manifested. The deity depicts the manifestation of Chandi as the destroyer of the demon Durgama. This deity is said to have been worshiped by Agastya, Markandeya, and the Pandavas. Many people come to this temple, which is especially crowded on Fridays.

The **Victoria Jubilee Museum** (10.30 am to 5 pm, except Fri), Bander Rd, has a collection of paintings and sculptures that includes a huge granite statue of Buddha.

Nearby Vijayawada

At **Akiripalli** there is a temple dedicated to **Vyaghra Narasimha,** called Sobhanachala Swami, on top of a hill. Also on top of the hill is a Siva temple called **Malleswara-swami temple**. Lord Vishnu as Vyaghra Narasimha is said to have incarnated in a cave on top of the hill here. There are also temples dedicated to Sri Venkatachala Swami, Sri Venu Gopala Swami, Rajya Lakshmi and the Alwars. There is a large *gopuram* at the bottom of the hill.

There is a huge tank here called **Varahapushkarini**, almost a hundred acres, which is said to have been dug by Varahadeva, Lord Vishnu in His boar incarnation. To get to Akiripalli you can take a bus from Vijayawada.

Where To Stay and Eat

The best cheap place to stay is the *Hotel Swapna Lodge* (65386), which is a clean place with rooms for Rs 65/85. It has some A/C rooms as well. It is on a quiet street. The *Shree Laksmi Vilas Modern Cafe* (62525), Besant Rd, about a km from the railway station, has rooms with attached bath for Rs 60/100 and with common bath for Rs 60/70. This place has a vegetarian restaurant.

The *Hotel Manorama* (77220), 27-38-61 Bunder Rd, has rooms with bath for Rs 200/275 and Rs 275/375 with A/C. The *Hotel Raj Towers* (61311), Congress Office Rd, has rooms with bath for Rs 180/250 and Rs 285/350 with A/C.

The best hotel in town is the fully air-conditioned three-star *Hotel Kandhari International* (471-311), M G Rd. Rooms here are Rs 315/440.

Where To Eat

The *Sri Durga Bhavan,* the *Hotel Nandini,* and the *Tilotthama Hotel*, near the bus stand, have vegetarian restaurants. The *Chaya Hotel,* Governorpet, has South Indian food.

Travel

Vijayawada is 445 km north of Madras, 380 km north of Tirupati, and 365 km south of Visakhapatnam.

Air There are three flights a week to Madras. The Indian Airlines office (472-218) is opposite the Old RTO Office, Bandar Rd. A taxi from the airport (20 km) costs Rs 150.

Train Vijayawada is on the main Madras-Delhi and Madras-Calcutta lines. The Tirupati Express goes to **Puri** and Tirupati.

The Coromandel Express #2842 (3.20 pm) takes 21 hours to get to **Calcutta** via **Bhubaneswar** (13 hr). The Konark Express #1019 (10 noon, 14 hr) also goes to Bhubaneswar. The Coromandel Exp #2841 (10.45 am) takes 7 hours to go the 432 km trip to **Madras**.

The Tamil Nadu Express #2621 goes to **Delhi** (3.50 am, 28 hours, 1761 km). The Konark Express #1020 goes to **Secunderabad** (2.40 am, 7 hr) and the East Coast Exp #8045 goes to **Hyderabad** (12.10 pm, 9 hr). There are direct trains to Varanasi, Bangalore, and Thiruvananthapuram (Trivandrum).

There are several trains a day to Visakhapatnam and Srikakulam Road.

Bus Buses are available for travel over the entire Andhra Pradesh and Madras area. The large new bus terminal is 1.5 km from the railway station. It has waiting rooms and dormitories. There are regular buses to Hyderabad (6 hr), Visakhapatnam (7 daily, 10 hr), and Madras (2 daily, 10 hr)

MANGALAGIRI

Mangalagiri is situated about 12 km south of Vijayawada. There is a major Lord Narasimha temple here. The Deity is called **Pana Narasimha** (Panakala Narasimha), because He is believed to drink half the quantity of *pana,* or cold drink, offered by worshipers. It is said that when the Lord is offered sugar syrup here, He does not take more than half. The temple is built around this self-manifest mouth of Lord Narasimhadeva. Over the mouth, completing the face of the Lord, is a brass mask with an angry expression. A chakra and club are also self-manifested in the stone.

The temple is on a hill and is approached by ascending 600 steps. This temple has the highest *gopuram* in the state of Andhra Pradesh. Inside this temple there is a conch shell presented by the late king of Tanjor, and this shell, according to the locals, was used by Lord Krishna Himself.

The *pujari* of the temple takes a pot of sweet drink called **jaggery water** and pours half of the drink with a conchshell into the Lord's mouth. The jaggery water drink is made of gur-water (sugar), camphor, black pepper, and cardamom. Half of whatever quantity of jaggery water prepared is offered to the Lord and the rest is returned to the offerer as *mahaprasad.* While the water is being poured into the mouth of the Lord you will hear a gurgling sound, as someone might make while drinking. Even though there is so much sugar water offered here, there is not a single ant seen on the hill. This is the reason the temple has the name **Panakala Narasimha**.

It is said that Lord Narasimha rested here after killing Hiranyakasipu, and Laksmi Devi then gave Him some nice drink to quench His thirst. At the bottom of the hill there is a very old **Laksmi Narasimha temple**. Mangalagiri is mentioned as a very holy place in the *Skanda* and *Brahma-vaivarta Puranas*.

Lord Caitanya came here in 1512. There is an imprint of His feet here and a verse dedicated to Him in the temple. During the month of March, a large festival takes place in this temple.

Travel

The best way to get here is to first go to Vijayawada or Guntur, and from either of these places there are frequent buses. There is a railway station at Mangalagiri on the Guntur-Vijayawada line.

Amaravati

Amaravati is a small village 30 km west of Vijayawada on the bank of the Krishna River. It is the site of an ancient Buddhist center. There are the remains of a **Great Buddhist Stupa** here that is believed to have been as large of the one in Sanchi. There is also a small interesting Archaeological museum (9 am to 5 pm, except Fri) which has some ancient Buddhist carvings and other items.

To get here from Vijayawada you take a bus to Guntur (30 min, every half hour) and from there take a bus to Amaravati (1½ hr).

LEPAKSHI

This is a small village located 17 km east of Hindupur. Hindupur is on the Hyderabad-Bangalore train line, about 100 km due north of Bangalore in Andhra Pradesh. It is said that Jatayu fell here after fighting with Ravana.

There is the famous **Veerabhadra Temple** here which has some of the best mural paintings from the period of the Vijayanagar kings. The temple is built on a low hill called Kurma Sailam, because it has the shape of a tortoise. **Lord Rama, Lord Papanaseswara** (Siva), **Veerabhadra**, and **Durga** are all worshiped here. There is also a Deity of **Gopala Swami** (Krishna). In the *Skanda Purana*, Lepakshi is said to be one of the 108 important pilgrimage sites dedicated to Lord Siva. Narrative reliefs on the south wall depict the pastimes of Lord Siva, including Arjuna's penance.

In the temple, the shrine of Lord Vishnu faces Lord Siva with Veerabhadra in the center. The pillars in the *Natya-mandapa* are intricately carved. The biggest **Nandi** in India is located 200 metres east of the temple. It is carved out of a monolithic rock and is 20 feet high and 30 feet in length. Apart from being famous for this huge Nandi, the temple is well known for its intricate sculptures and excellent murals that include Lord Krishna's and Lord Rama's pastimes. These murals have elegant line-work and vibrant natural colors and the costumes and facial expressions are most outstanding in their detail.

The treasurer to the king of Vijayanagar used taxes collected on the king's behalf to build the temple, while the king was away in Vijayanagar. When the king returned and found his treasury empty, he ordered the treasurer to be blinded as punishment. The treasurer blinded himself and dashed his eyes against the wall of the temple. There is a wall near the *Kalyana-mandapa* that has two dark stains said to be from his eyes. That is why the village is called "Lepa-akshi" (Lepakshi), "the village of the blinded eye".

Opposite the temple is the very basic *Rest House* (2 rooms only). You can also stay in Hindupur where there are several hotels by the State Bus Stand.

NELLORE

Nellore is situated three and a half hours by train north of Madras.

Ranganatha Temple

The main Deity, Garbhodakasayi Vishnu reclining on His couch of Ananta Sesa, is ten feet long. Laksmi is sitting on a lotus flower on His chest. Lord Brahma sits on a lotus rising from the Lord's navel. At the Lord's feet are 26" high deities of Sridevi and Bhudevi. In front of the main Deity are the *utsava-murtis* (festival Deities) of Ranganatha Swami. There is also a four-handed seated Deity of Laksmidevi called Ranga-nayaki-devi.

This temple was built about 1070. It is on the bank of the River Pennar, or Penarkini. The temple has a 110 year old 95 foot high *gopuram* covered with hundreds of forms of Lord Vishnu.

Where To Stay

The *Hotel Simhapuri* (27041), Railway Station Road, has rooms with hot water for Rs 130/200 and Rs 340 with A/C. The *Hotel Shivam* International (27181), 18/1 Achari St, has rooms with hot water for Rs 125/200 and Rs 300 with A/C.

TIRUPATI

Population: 190,000, STD Code 08574

Tirupati is 170 km northwest of Madras in Andhra Pradesh near the Tamil Nadu border, at the bottom of the Tirumala Hill. In Tirupati there is the important Sri Govindaraja Swami temple, Kothanda Rama Swami temple and the famous Kapileswara temple, which is dedicated to Lord Siva. In Tiruchanur, five km from Tirupati, is the Padmavathi temple, dedicated to the consort of Lord Venkateswara (Balaji).

The temple of Sri Venkateswara or Tirupati Balaji is situated above the actual city of Tirupati in the hilltop town of Tirumala. There is a steep staircase up the hill to Tirumala, used by pilgrims wishing to show their devotion by making the climb; otherwise standard transportation is readily available.

Information

The **AP State Tourist Office** (4818) is located on Govindaraja Car Street, near the Bhima Deluxe Hotel. There is also the **AP Tourism Regional** (23208), TP Area, near III Choultry. There are tourist counters at the railway station and airport. The **TTD Information Centre** (22777) is at 1 New Choultry.

Two helpful books that have good practical information about Tirupati and the local temples are the *TKT History of Tirupati*, by Viruraghava Charya, and the *Tirupati Yatra Guide*.

Heavy rains can be expected in October.

Tours

There is a four-hour bus **tour of the local temples**, available twice daily, at 10 am and 3 pm. It leaves from the Govinda Raja Swamy Choultry, which is located on the opposite side of the tracks from the station. This tour includes the Padmavathi temple and Govindaraja temple.

There is a **Local sightseeing tour** from the APSRTC Central Bus Stand (10 am to 5 pm) that goes to Sri Kalahasti, Padmavati temple, ISKCON (Hare Rama Hare Krishna), Govindarajaswami temple, Chandragiri Fort, Kapila-teertham, and Sri Venkateswara temple.

There are two daily tours to Tirupati (Tirumala) **from Madras**, one run by the Tamil Nadu Tourist Development Corporation and the other by ITDC. The tours lasts at least 15 hours, much of it traveling to and from Madras. The tour allows for a two-hour wait for special *darsana*, which on weekends and holidays can take much longer. This means the tour, which is supposed to last from 6 am to 9 pm, may not return until midnight or later. The fare includes breakfast, lunch, and the Rs 30 'special *darsana*' fee.

APTDC has a weekend tour to Tirupati **from Hyderabad**. The tour leaves at 4 pm on Friday and returns on Monday at 7 am. The tour includes 'special *darsana*' and accommodation. If you like, you can take the bus one way only.

Govindaraja Temple

In this temple there are two main shrines. In the northern shrine is Sri Govindaraja, who is Lord Vishnu lying on Ananta. He is considered to be Lord Venkateswara's brother. The other main shrine has Deities of Sri Parthasarathi (Krishna as the charioteer of Arjuna), Rukmini, and Satyabhama (Krishna's wives).

Parts of the inner shrine date back to the 9th and 10th centuries. The original temple had Sri Parthasarathi on the main altar. The Sri Govindaraja Deity was added around 1130 by Sri Ramanuja.

To your left as you enter the first gopuram (gate) of the temple is a temple dedicated to Laksmi (also called Salainachiyar or Pundarikavalli). She is seated on a lotus in her four-armed form, holding a lotus in each of her upper hands, while her other two hands are in poses of *abhaya*, fearlessness, and *varada*, benediction. Situated above the door of this temple there is a carving of Laksmi holding a lotus in her hand.

Near the first gopuram there is a shrine dedicated to Vedanta Desika. There is also a memorial for three of the Alwar devotees—Tirumallisai Alwar, Namm Alwar, and Kurattalwar—near the *Vahana-mandapa*, and another nearby shrine is dedicated to Sri Ramanuja. On the left of the second entrance is a Kurma Deity, Lord Vishnu as a tortoise.

This is a big temple. It has a seven story *gopuram*, built in 1628. There are carvings depicting the *Ramayana* and Lord Krishna's pastimes on the second *gopuram*. This temple is located just off the main road, near the Bhima Hotel and the Tirupati train station. The temple tower is hard to miss, but the rest of the temple is set back from the road.

Sri Venkateswara Museum

There is a great museum right next to the Govindaraja temple. It has many sculptures, Deities of Krishna, and other interesting displays. There is also a photo exhibit of the 108 Divya Desam temples, the 108 important Vishnu temples, that were immortalized in songs by the Alwar devotees. This exhibit has a picture and the name of each of the temples along with the names of the Deities and their locations. This museum is open from 8 am to 8 pm.

Kothanda Rama Swami Temple

About two km from Sri Govindaraja temple is the famous Kothanda Rama Swami temple built in 1480-1481. Lord Caitanya had *darsana* of Lord Sri Ramacandra Swami. The main festival of the year is in March-April, for Lord Rama's appearance day.

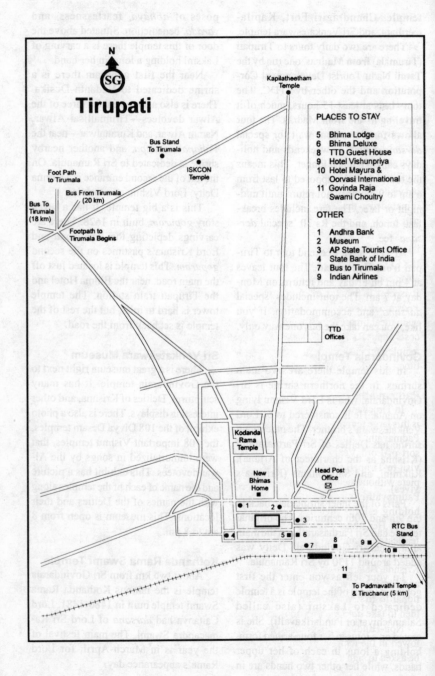

Tirupati

Bus Stand
To Tirumala

ISKCON
Temple

Kapilatheetham
Temple

Foot Path
to Tirumala

Bus From Tirumala
(20 km)

Bus To
Tirumala
(18 km)

Footpath to
Tirumala Begins

TTD
Offices

Kodanda
Rama
Temple

New
Bhimas
Home

Head Post
Office

RTC Bus
Stand

To Padmavathi Temple
& Tiruchanur (5 km)

PLACES TO STAY

5   Bhima Lodge
6   Bhima Deluxe
8   TTD Guest House
9   Hotel Vishunpriya
10 Hotel Mayura &
    Oorvasi International
11 Govinda Raja
    Swami Choultry

OTHER

1   Andhra Bank
2   Museum
3   AP State Tourist Office
4   State Bank of India
7   Bus to Tirumala
9   Indian Airlines

ISKCON (Hare Krishna) Temple

The ISKCON temple (08574-20114), Vinayaka Nagar (Driver's Quarters), is located at the foot of Tirumala Hill, on a piece of land given by the TTD. The Deities here are **Sri Sri Radha-Govinda**. The temple has a beautiful small garden with many different types of flowers and attractive plants. The Deities' doors are closed between 1 and 4.15 pm. Even though the temple seems to be in the middle of nowhere, there are many regular visitors during the day. This temple is included in the daily bus tours of Tirupati.

There is a good guest house next to the temple, mainly for life members of ISKCON and devotees. It has very nice clean rooms with hot water for Rs 150. It is best to book a room in advance. *Prasadam* is usually available during main meal times. From the downtown it costs about Rs 75 to go to the ISKCON temple and back, with an hour waiting time.

Padmavathi Temple

In Tiruchanur, five km from Tirupati, is this large temple dedicated to goddess Padmavathi (Alamelumanga), the consort of Lord Venkateswara (Balaji). A visit to Tirupati is not considered complete without seeing Sri Padmavathi. Sri Padmavathi is seated in Padmasana, holding a lotus in both of her upper hands. Her lower hands are in *abhaya,* fearlessness, and *varada,* benediction. Also in this temple are the Deities of Sri Krishna, Balarama, Sundararaja Swami, and Surya-narayana Swami. It is traditional to first worship Sri Krishna and then to take *darsana* of Sri Padmavathi.

Non-Hindus are technically not allowed in the temple. To enter you may be asked to sign a paper testifying to being a Hindu. There is a short wait to see the Deity, or for Rs 5 you can enter a special *darsana* line.

Once a year there is a large festival that celebrates the marriage of Lord Venkateswara to Padmavati Devi. The festivities attract tourists from all over India. If you visit during this festival it is definitely worth following the crowds to see the splendor as the wedding takes place. Padmavati Devi arrives at Tirumala on the back of a splendid elephant decorated with *tilaka* of solid gold as Lord Sri Venkateswara comes out to meet Her. This is one occasion among many during the year when this temple displays the splendor and pageantry of its worship.

The main festival, Brahmotsavam, is in Nov/Dec. The ninth day of this festival is the birthday of Sri Padmavathi. On this day Lord Sri Venkateswara presents His consort birthday gifts, which are brought from Tirumala on a magnificently decorated elephant, covered with jewels and pearls.

In The Area

At **Kapila-teertham**, a sacred tank two km from Tirupati, is the **Kapileswara Siva temple** where the sage Kapila was granted *darsana* of Lord Siva and his consort. Bathing in Kapila-teertham is supposed to extinguish all sins. This temple is situated in an attractive surrounding.

At **Narayanavanam**, 36 km from Tirupati on the road to Madras, is a temple dedicated to **Lord Kalyana Venkateswara Swami**. It is believed to be the place where the marriage of Lord Venkateswara and the goddess Padmavathi originally took place. After marrying Sri Padmavathi, Sri Venkateswara stayed here for a while before going to Tirumala.

Chandragiri Fort, 11 km southwest of Tirupati, is where the third Vijayanagar capital was located in the 16th century. There is a small museum here which contains weapons and sculptures. It is open from 10 am to 5 pm, daily except Friday.

Where To Stay

The *Gopi Krishna Deluxe*, by the railway station, has rooms with attached bath for Rs 50/70. The *Vasantha Vihar Lodge* (20460), about a minute walk from the railway station, has basic rooms for Rs 50/70.

The *New Bhimas Home* is a decent place with rooms for Rs 130. If the other places in town are full, there is a good chance there will be a room here.

The *Bhimas Hotel* (25747) is a suggested place with rooms for Rs 70/140, deluxe rooms for Rs 200, and A/C rooms for Rs 375. The two-star *Bhimas Deluxe Hotel* (25521, fax 25471), 34/38 G Car St, has comfortable and clean rooms for Rs 200/225 and Rs 425/450 with A/C, plus a 10% tax. Both these places are a five minute walk from the railway station and have vegetarian meals available.

There is also the more expensive new *Bhima's Paradise* (25747, fax 25568), Renigunta Rd, a little out of town, which has a swimming pool, TV, and is spotlessly clean. Rooms are Rs 300 and Rs 475/700 with A/C.

The *Hotel Vishnu Priya* (20300), opposite the Central Bus Stand, is a large middle-class place.

The three-star *Hotel Mayura* (25925, fax 25911), T P Area, 1 km from the railway station, is the best place in town. It has rooms with bath for Rs 375 and Rs 550/600 for an A/C room. Near by is the *Oorvasi International Hotel* (20202),

Renigunta Rd, which has rooms for about the same price. It has a good vegetarian restaurant.

Dharamshalas

There is free accommodation at two dharamshalas (unfurnished rooms) connected with the two main temples in Tirupati—Sri Govindaraja temple and Sri Kodanda Rama temple. There are furnished rooms at Sri Venkateswara Dharamshala, S.V. Guest House, Sri Padmavathi Guest House, and the TTD (Alipiri) Guest House for Rs 30 to Rs 150 a night.

Where To Eat

The *Laksmi Narayana Bhavan*, across from the bus stand, is a good place, as is the *Bhimas Hotel* at 42 G Car St. The *Konark* on Railway Station Rd, New Triveni, and the *Dwarka*, by the bus stand, are vegetarian restaurants. The *Sri Oorvasi International* has a high-class recommended vegetarian restaurant. The *Bharani Restaurant*, at the Bhima's Paradise, Renigunta Rd, has South Indian snacks and North Indian preparations.

Travel

Air The Indian Airlines office (22349) is at the Hotel Vishnupriya, opposite the Central Bus Stand. The airport is 15 km from the city center. East West Airlines has four flights a week to Hyderabad ($61, 8.45 am, Tue, Thu, Sat, Sun) and other flights to and from Madras ($50).

Train There are two express trains going to **Madras**—the Saptagiri Express #6054 (6.10 pm, 3½ hr) and the Tirupati-Madras Mail #6054 (10.25 am, 3¼ hr). The Saptagiri Express departs from Madras at 6.25 am and arrives 3½ hours later. The Madras-Tirupati Mail #6053 (3 hr)

departs from Madras at 1.50 pm.

As Tirupati is a popular pilgrimage place, you can find express trains that go to many locations in India, especially in the South. To get to **Bombay** you first take the Saptagiri Express to Madras (wait 45 minutes) and then take the Madras-Bombay Exp #6010 (10.20 pm, 30½). The total travel time is 35 hours. The Tirupati-Mysore Exp (10 pm) takes 12 hours to reach **Mysore**. The daily Rayalaseema Express #7430 goes to **Hyderabad** (3.30 pm, 16½ hrs, daily). The Tirupati-Puri Express #8480 (9.45 am) goes to **Puri** (22½ hr) via **Vijayawada** (11 hr) and **Visakhapatnam**. There are two other trains daily to Vijayawada. There is one train a day to Madurai (19 hr) and Tiruchirappalli, and two trains daily to Chidambaram. The Tirupati-Madurai Exp #6799 (3.40 pm) goes to **Madurai** (19 hr) via **Tiruchirappalli** (14 hr), **Thanjavur** (12 hr), and **Chidambaram** (9½ hr). The Cochin-Varanasi Exp #7489 (1.45 pm) goes to **Varanasi** (38 hr) via **Allahabad** (35 hr).

Bus The APSRTC Central bus station (22333) is about 2 km from the railway station on the same road. Express buses from Tirupati to Madras depart at 9.45 and 11.15 am, 12.15, 2.45, 3.10 and 8.30 pm.

There are express buses (route No 802) from the Thiruvalluvar Bus Station in **Madras** (4 hr) at 8.15 am, 3.30 pm, and 8.30 pm. The express buses can be booked in advance. There are many other local buses, which can take a long time. The train from Madras is much more comfortable. There are daily tour buses from Madras that go and come in the same day.

You can take direct buses to Hyderabad (14 hr, 10 daily), Tiruchirappalli via

Vellore (9½ hr, 4 daily), Madurai (5 daily), Vijayawada (hourly), and Bangalore. It is better to take a train to Hyderabad.

There are some direct buses to **Kanchipuram** (3 hr). There are also regular buses that go to a small town by Tirupati (20 min), from where you change to another bus to Kanchipuram.

TIRUMALA
Population: 17,000, STD Code 98577

Tirumala is where the **Venkateswara (Sri Balaji) temple** is located. Tirumala is located on Vyenkata Hill at an altitude of 2,800 feet. Vyenkateswara means "the Lord of Vyenkatachala." Vyenkatachala is a chain of hills. The temple is situated on the top of seven adjoining hills, also called Seshachalam Hills, which are said to be an incarnation of Ananta Sesa. Once Vayu and Sesa entered into a disagreement over who was stronger. Sesa wrapped his long body around Mount Meru and challenged Vayu to move it. Vayu tried but failed. Vayu pretended to be exhausted and stopped blowing. Then Sesa opened his mouth to breathe. At that moment, Vayu blew off part of the hill. After the hill had traveled a great distance, Mount Meru asked Vayu to leave it there. Ashamed of his defeat, Sesa did penance, meditating on Lord Vishnu. When Lord Vishnu appeared and offered a boon, Sesa assumed the shape of the hill and requested the Lord to stay on his head. This hill is called Sesachalam. It is said that when Ramanuja visited here, he walked up the hill on his knees to avoid stepping on Sesa Naga.

The Lord's appearance in Tirumala is mentioned in about 12 different *Puranas*. According to the *Brahma-Purana*, Lord Vishnu wanted a change from Vaikuntha, so He inquired from

Narada Muni about a place on earth for diversion and sport. Narada suggested Sesachala (the head of Ananta Sesa).

All the property at the top of the hill at Tirumala belongs to the Tirumala-Tirupati Devasthanam (TTD), well known for its excellent management even with crowds that can run to hundreds of thousands on special festival days. The TTD is recycling much of its wealth to such humanitarian works as schools, orphanages, and hospitals.

Tirumala is an unusual place for India in that the streets are totally clean of trash. Also beggars are totally banned from on top of the hill.

Sri Venkateswara (Balaji) Temple

This temple is one of the most important Vishnu temples in India and is also the richest. It is the most visited temple in India and is one of the most visited religious places in the world. This magnificent temple is located 20 km up a hill from Tirupati. It is a very peaceful place and coming to this temple is a very awe-inspiring and devotional experience. On a spiritual tour of South India it is an absolute must, as it is the crown jewel of all the temples in the South.

Some pilgrims walk from all parts of India just for a few-seconds glance at Sri Balaji, whose eyes are covered with the wide Ramanuja *tilaka*. Many people consider that one's life is not successful without visiting this temple at least once. Over 25,000 people visit daily on an average and on festival days it can run to over 100,000. In 1989 over 11 and a half million people made their pilgrimage here.

As you enter the inner sanctum the chanting becomes more and more intense—"Om Namo Venkateswara, Om Namo Venkateswara." On special days when the Deity is in "full dress" His entire outfit (His skirt) spreads from one end of the altar room to the other and all the jewels of the dress are real—gold coins, emeralds, diamonds, platinum. He is approximately 2 metres high and the dress which is entirely covered with jewels has a width of at least 5 metres.

It is said that at Tirumala, Lord Vishnu grants the wish of anyone who offers Him their weight in something, be it gold, fruit, cloth, or whatever. Pilgrims who make such an offering and ask a boon or blessing generally return (after achieving their desire) and make another offering to the Lord, acknowledging His kindness.

The worship in the temple is performed by Sri-sampradaya Vaishnava *Brahmins*, in the line of Ramanujacarya. Except for a shrine for Sri Ramanuja, there are no other shrines for Vaishnava saints, the Alwars, or the Acaryas.

The Venkateswara temple is 126.5m (414 ft) long, 80m (263 ft) wide, and covers an area of 2.2 acres. Because of the large number of people and everything that is happening there the temple can seem much smaller than it is. The temple itself is unusual in that nothing can be seen from the outside. It is only when you get inside the complex that you see everything. What is particularly stunning is the *vimana* (dome), called Ananda Nilayam, above the Deity's main room. It is covered in hammered solid gold. The flag-pole (*dwajasthamba*) is gold-plated, and the gates that guard the inner sanctum are also covered with gold.

Every day 100,000 luglus are made. The demand is much more, but the tradition is that all the luglus must be cooked in the temple kitchens. The cooks receive 52 luglus for every 1000 they make, as payment for their services.

The average income of the temple is

$30,000 (10 lakhs) a day. It has an annual income of 5 billion rupees (145 million dollars) a year. The TTD banks Rs 40 to 50 crores (12 million dollars) yearly. The Hundi (Deity box) collection is over 5 million dollars yearly. It is not unusual when they open this box at the end of the day to find gold and platinum coins and bricks inside.

The Deity's gold and silver palanquins and other sacred paraphernalia are on display. There is a temple staff of over 6,000.

It is said that Sankaracarya established the Dhanakarshana Yantra at this temple to attract people to visit the temple. Lord Caitanya came here on His tour of South India.

Sri Venkateswara (Sri Balaji)

Lord Venkateswara is an impressive 2 metre (6 feet) high Deity, who stands on a lotus that is placed directly on the ground. The Deity is known as Venkateswara, Venkatanathan, Srinivasa, Govinda, Perumal, or Balaji. Lord Venkateswara is a self-manifested Deity. Balaji is made of a jet-black stone. His diamond crown, made in Antwerp, the diamond capital of the world, is said to be the single most valuable piece of jewelry in the world.

His two upper arms hold a conchshell (*sankha*) and disk (cakra). The palm of His lower right hand is turned outward offering benediction (*varada*), while His lower left hand is turned inward (*katyavalambita*). Alarmelmangai-Nachchiyar (Laksmi), seated on a lotus, is carved on the right side of Sri Venkateswara's chest. She enjoys all the worship that is accepted by the Lord. Lord Ramacandra's marks are found on Venkateswara near the armpits: the bow and quiver (arrows).

The Lord's lotus eyes are covered by a large tilak like "V" made of camphor. For it is said that Lord Venkateswara's lotus-like eyes are so beautiful that if they were uncovered, then pilgrims would not want to leave. This form of the Lord is known for fulfilling any desire a devotee may express to Him. It is also said that His eyes are covered because His gaze would scorch the entire world.

The Deity wears very precious jewelry. He wears a garland of big solid-gold coins. His two hands, opened in benediction, are covered first with silver and then diamonds and rubies. He wears different big crowns made of solid gold covered in diamonds, rubies, and other precious gems. The Lord wears a big emerald called "Meru Pacha", which is 3 inches in diameter and is considered to be the biggest emerald in the world. All the jewelry is real gold. The Lord possesses over 250 crores (70 million dollars) worth of gems and 640 kgs of gold.

Temple Program

At 3 am is *suprabhatam*, the awakening prayers. Between 3 am and 5 am is *thomala-seva*, or the renewal of flowers for the Lord, which can be attended by purchasing a ticket. From 6 am to 11 am is *sarva-darsana,* or general *darsana* (viewing) of the Lord. The Lord takes rest for just two hours a day, from 1 to 3 am.

There is an hour break between 11 am and noon for cleaning and worship. There is *darsana* from 12 noon till 7 pm and then again from 8 to 10 pm. At 10.30 pm is *ekanta-seva*, or putting the Lord in a cradle.

The *padmaradhana*, or worship with 108 golden lotus flowers, is a popular *abisheka* done every Tuesday. Tickets are booked a year in advance.

Abhisheka, or the bathing of Sri Venkateswara, is done every Friday morning between 4.30 and 5.30 am. The articles used for the *abhisheka* are carried in a procession around the sanctum. This *abhisheka* can be viewed by paying a donation and should be arranged as far in advance as possible.

Srila Prabhupada At Tirupati

Srila Prabhupada went to Tirupati in April, 1972. He was asked why the Deity was called Balaji. "Balaji," Prabhupada said, "means child Krishna as a cowherd boy, not in His Vaikuntha aspect." During his two days in Tirupati, Prabhupada went three or four times a day to see the Deity of Balaji. Whenever he went, the *pujaris* would clear the inner sanctum of all other visitors and allow him a private *darsana* for as long as he liked.

Srila Prabhupada expressed admiration of the TTD for their efficiency and cited them as an example of excellent management and attention to detail.

Sri Ramanuja At Tirupati

Traditionally, a Deity of Lord Vishnu will bear in His hands certain distinguishing symbols: a lotus, a conchshell, a discus, and a club. During the time of Ramanuja, however, in the eleventh century, Lord Venkateswara's two upper hands were empty. No one knew why. It was not possible to verify the true identity of the Deity. Was this a form of the Supreme Personality of Godhead, Lord Vishnu, or a form of a demigod? To further complicate matters, some figures of snakes, symbols of Lord Siva, are on the body of the Deity. A dispute developed in which some people claimed the Deity was Lord Siva, while other insisted He was Lord Vishnu. The Saivaites insisted

He was Lord Siva, and the Vaisnavas insisted He was Lord Vishnu.

In the midst of this feud, Ramanuja came to Tirumala on pilgrimage. Both factions called on him to settle their dispute. He proposed that the paraphernalia of both Siva and Vishnu be left inside the Deity room overnight to let the Lord choose, while both parties waited outside the locked doors. They accepted this proposal. Sri Ramanuja locked the symbols of Lord Vishnu and Lord Siva in the Deity's room overnight. Next morning, all were astonished to find Lord Vishnu's symbols, the conch and discus, in the Deity's hands. Since that day Lord Venkateswara's identity as Lord Krishna has never been questioned.

Ramanujacarya established the Deity worship system that is used in this temple. There is a shrine dedicated to Ramanuja in the Venkateswara temple.

Other Deities In the Temple

Immediately to the left of the second *gopuram* entrance is a small temple dedicated to *Sri Varadaraja Swami*. You will be led past this deity to get to the inner altar, and it is traditional to offer worship to Varadaraja first.

As you come into the second *gopuram* (entrance), to your right is a Deity of *Lord Narasimha* in his form of Yoga Narasimha. He is sitting in a cross-legged yogic position, with His two lower hands resting on His knees.

Facing west near Lord Narasimha is a deity of *Sri Ramanuja*, the Sri Vaishnava Acarya. A part of the *prasadam* offered to Sri Venkateswara is offered to Sri Ramanuja. On certain festival days special honors are shown to Sri Ramanuja, because he established the day-to-day procedure of worship in this temple.

Deities On Main Altar (Sanctum)

Bhoga Srinivasa, who is a silver replica of the *mula-vigraha* of Lord Sri Venkateswara, is always near Sri Venkateswara and connected to the main Deity by a silk cord. This Deity receives the daily *abhisheka* (bathing ceremonies), whereas the main Deity is only bathed on Friday.

This Deity is said to have a *yantra* installed in Him and is said to grant material prosperity to His devotees. When the Deity is brought outside the inner sanctum for festivals, a gold link and silk cord still attach the Deity of Bhogasrinivasa to Sri Venkateswara.

Sri Malai Kuniya Nenran Perumal (Sri Malayappan) is the 3-foot-tall processional Deity (*utsava-murti*). The Deity wears precious jewels set in platinum and gold. Sridevi is to the right of this Deity and Bhudevi is also near by.

Ugra Srinivasa (Venkatatturaivar), who is about 1½ feet tall, is the previous processional Deity. *Ugra* means angry. The Deity is holding a *chakra* in a slightly tilted way, as if it could be used immediately. It is said that if the rays of the sun would ever touch this Deity it would do incalculable harm to the world, therefore He is amply provided with jewel-encrusted umbrellas.

Koluvu Srinivasa is brought daily after the morning *thomala-seva* (worship) and seated on a silver chair. He is the guardian Deity and supervises the temple affairs. The calendar of the day (*panchangam*) and the accounts of the temple are read to Him every day. He officiates for the main Deity.

There is also a set of Rukmini-Krishna Deities and Deities of Sita-Rama, Laksmana, and Sugriva.

There is also a deity of **Chakra Alwar** (Sudarsana cakra), the disc of the Lord, who always proceeds the *utsava-murti* (processional Deity) during processions.

Temple Complex

You enter the temple through the eastern entrance. As you enter the temple there is a small hall with two wings to your right and left. The one to your right (the northern side) has three metal statues of Krishnadeva Raya and his two queens, Tirumaladevi and Chinnadevi. In the southern wing (to your left) are metal statues of King Achyuta Raya and his two queens. These kings were important supporters of the temple.

To your right as you enter (southeast corner) is the *Ranga-mandapa,* where different festival events are held. To the west of this hall are the Annaunjal Hall and Tiurmalaraya Hall, which are also used for different festival events. In the north part of the courtyard is a hall called Aina-mahal (mirror hall). In the west of the courtyard, by the next entrance, is a *mandapa* that has the *dwajasthamba* (flagstaff) and *balipita* (platform of sacrifice).

The second enclosure area is called Sampangi Prakara. The wall that surrounds the inner sanctum and other structures is called the Vimana Pradakshina. It contains the altars of Sri Varadaraja, Sri Narasimha, and Ramanujacarya.

On either side of the entrance to the inner sanctum are the two *dvarapalas* (guards), Jaya and Vijaya. The Mukkoti Pradakshina is a path that encircles the inner sanctum. It is normally closed and is open only on Vaikuntha Ekadasi. One who goes through the special gate that circumambulates the inner sanctum of Sri Venkateswara is considered to gain liberation from this material world upon leaving this body.

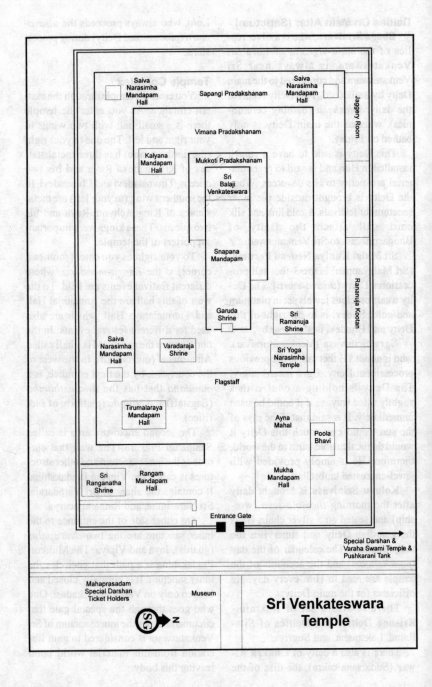

Saiva Narasimha Mandapam Hall

Sapangi Pradakshanam

Saiva Narasimha Mandapam Hall

Jaggery Room

Temple Complex

Vimana Pradakshanam

Kalyana Mandapam Hall

Mukkoti Pradakshanam

Sri Balaji Venkateswara

Snapana Mandapam

Garuda Shrine

Sri Ramanuja Shrine

Saiva Narasimha Mandapam Hall

Varadaraja Shrine

Sri Yoga Narasimha Temple

Flagstaff

Rananuja Kootan

Tirumalaraya Mandapam Hall

Ayna Mahal

Poola Bhavi

Sri Ranganatha Shrine

Rangam Mandapam Hall

Mukha Mandapam Hall

Entrance Gate

Special Darshan & Varaha Swami Temple & Pushkarani Tank

Mahaprasadam Special Darshan Ticket Holders

Museum

Sri Venkateswara Temple

N

Useful Information

No cameras are allowed, but if you have one, there is a good chance you will be allowed to bring it in as long as you do not use it. There are free cloak and shoe rooms outside the temple where you can leave your things.

The inner shrines of the temple are not officially open to non-Hindus. Foreigners may be asked to sign a paper saying they are Hindu. If they sign the paper, they can enter the temple.

Every pilgrim is entitled to free food, accommodation (very basic), and medical treatment.

Tirumala is a magnificent complex that consists of many buildings besides the main temple. There are buildings for religious ceremonies, administration, feeding, and sheltering the pilgrims. The entire administration of Tirumala is run by the Tirupati Tirumala Devasthanam (TTD). They not only maintain the temple and distribute the donated wealth to charities, but also ensure that the millions who visit are all sheltered and fed.

You can use your Rs 30 "special darshana" ticket to go to a special booth, to your right as you leave the temple, to purchase a large **prasadam luglu**. The normal *luglu* queue (line) may take an hour or more and this special line is almost immediate. The *luglus* are fantastic.

Mondays and Tuesdays are not very crowded days. At 7 am on Monday it may only be an hour waiting time in the special darshan line. Weekends and festivals days are the most crowded days to come.

How to Get in the Temple

There is a board by the temple entrance that tells you how long you will have to wait to see the Deities.

There are two queues available to the public for viewing the Deity. One is a free *sarva-darsana* line, which has a number of good-sized auditoriums with marble steps to sit on. When the auditorium next to yours empties you move to the next one and the gates are locked behind you. This queue usually takes between 8 to 12 hours and during festival times can take much longer. It is not advised to take this route.

For a 30 rupee fee, you enter the "special *darshana*" line that cuts your waiting time by 75% (3 hours instead of 12). There are also special *darshans* including one for Rs 5000, and sometimes if one is very fortunate one can get in for the bathing *darshans*, but special connections are required for this.

As you approach the main Deity room there is a flurry of activity with guards and officials milling about and *pujaris* (priests) carrying huge brass trays of *bhoga/prasadam* in and out. Once inside the Deity room the movement of the line picks up speed as there are officials on either side of the Deity pushing the pilgrims to move on. It is set up like a "U" turn, where you enter on the right side of the Deity, pass in front of Balaji, and exit out the left. If you keep to the extreme right when you enter, you may be able to stay in the corner and get an extra few seconds *darshana*. The average viewing time is five seconds, but if you are a foreigner sometimes the *pujaris* may give you a few extra minutes or seconds.

Once your *darsana* is finished, you continue to follow the queue outside the premises. Outside the temple you can purchase delicious round **luglus** made of dried fruits and nuts to take home, as they keep for long periods. Demand for these sweets are high and you'll have to battle your way to the counter through many pilgrims. If you have a special *darsana* ticket you can purchase a large *luglu* from the booth to your right as you leave the temple. This booth is up some stairs in a building across from the temple. You are limited to just one *luglu* per special *darsana* ticket in this line.

Around the Temple

There is a large water tank next to this temple called **Swami Pushkarini tank**, where pilgrims take bath before their *darsana*. The *Varaha Purana* says Swami Pushkarini was a pond used by Lord Vishnu in Vaikuntha for recreation. Tradition says that this tank was put here by Garuda.

Next to the tank is the **Varaha Swami temple**. It is stated in the *Puranas* that Lord Varaha was on Sesachala before Sri Venkateswara, and He granted space to Venkateswara to live on Sesachala Hill. It is a tradition to visit this temple before going into the main temple.

There is a small museum called the **Hall of Antiquities** (opened daily from 8 am to 8 pm), which is located opposite the temple entrance.

Akasa Ganga is a sacred waterfall 5 km south of the temple. Water is brought from here for Lord Venkateswara's *abhiseka* (bathing). On the way to Akasa Ganga is **Papavinasha Tirtha**.

After *darsana*, there are a number a things to do. Tirumala is more like a city than a temple, and one could easily spend a whole day just walking around. There are many sacred water tanks and smaller temples that house various paraphernalia, such as the chariot to carry the small processional Deities (*utsava* Deity) during festivals.

You can also visit the huge head-shaving center, which looks something

like a South Indian temple. Instead of the usual *murtis* of demigods, it has statues of barbers shaving the pilgrims. Devotees offer their hair in expectation of pleasing the Lord. Head shaving (tonsuring) is done by many people (many of them women). The hair is sold for wig making, and these proceeds are also used for increasing the prosperity of the Deities and the upkeep of the town, etc. Three or four crore rupees (over a million dollars) is raised from this process each year.

There are also other significant temples in the area and some beautiful waterfalls beyond Tirumala in the higher hills.

Festivals

Brahmotsavam (Aug/Sept), which lasts for 11 days, is the main festival. According to the *Bhavishottara* and *Varaha Puranas*, this festival has the name Brahmotsavam because Lord Brahma came to earth with all the gods to perform *utsavam*, or worship of the Lord.

The main day of Brahmotsavam is the cart procession (**Rathotsava**) on the eighth day. The processional Deity is led around the four streets surrounding the temple on a beautifully decorated cart. The Makarakanti ornament and the Laksmiharam (of the main Deity) are used to decorate the processional Deity on this day. This is the only day that these valuable ornaments are allowed to leave the temple. The fifth and eleventh days are also important. On the eleventh day the processional Deity is taken to the Swami Pushkarini, the tank by the temple.

The Tiruppaliodam Tirunal (**Float Festival**) is usually five days.

There is a major festival in reference

to the **Swami Pushkarini** tank (Dec/ Jan). A million sacred bathing places are said to flow into the tank at this time. The Chakra of Lord Vishnu (Chakara Alvar) is taken in procession through the streets and then bathed in the tank. This is considered to be an especially auspicious time to bathe in this tank.

It is said that **Kubera**, the god of wealth, lent Sri Balaji some money. Each year there is a ceremony, in which the descendants of Kubera seek to collect the loan. The Deity is put behind gold bars. On that day the offerings to the Deity are colossal, as people rush to bail out Balaji.

Pushpayagam is when flower worship is performed to Lord Sri Venkateswara to save the world from natural calamities like floods and droughts. More than 30 types of flowers weighting over two tons (2000 kilos) are offered to the feet of the *utsava-murti*.

Where To Stay and Eat

The Tirumala management runs many dharamshalas, cottages, and guesthouses which can house about 20,000 people. You can stay for free in very basic dorms. There are nice rooms with two beds and hot water for Rs 75. You can also get a luxury suite and good cottages.

To get a room you go to the Central Reservation Office, near the bus stand. You can book rooms 30 days in advance by writing the Reception Office, TTD, Tirumala and sending a Rs 100 demand draft drawn on a national bank in favor of the TTD, Tirumala.

The Tamil Nadu Tourist Development Corporation rents out cottages. You rent a room at cottage No 304 by the bus station, or rooms can be booked in their office in Madras.

The *Tirupati-Tirumala Devasthanam Trust* (TTD) serves vegetarian meals for free. The temple serves over 3000 full meals a day. They may contain onions. *Woodlands Restaurant*, a five-minute walk from the main area, is a popular *thali* place.

Tirupati to Tirumala By Road

You get a Tirumala Link bus to go up the hill at either the Central Bus Stand, two km from the railway station, or the Padmavati Bus Stand in the center of Tirupati, opposite the railway station. Buses leave every three minutes starting at 3.30 in the morning, and the trip takes 45 minutes. You may have to wait in line for up to two hours to get a bus on weekends and during festivals. The main rush is in the morning. It is a good idea to buy a return ticket so you do not have to wait in line to purchase a ticket at the top of the hill. It costs Rs 25 for a round-trip bus trip up and down the hill. You arrive in Tirumala at the Kesavanagar Bus Stand, near the Central Reception area, about a half km from the temple. You depart from the Rose Garden Bus Stand, east of the temple.

A shared taxi to the top of the hill is about Rs 35 a seat. There are 10 person jeeps up the hill for Rs 10 a person. A taxi costs Rs 250.

Walking Up the Hill

Many pilgrims walk the 16 km (24 km by bus) up the hill. The path begins at the bottom of the hill, not far from the ISKCON temple. You can't miss the beginning, as there is a huge *gopuram* (tower) with bright lights and a big statue of Hanuman. It is best to go in the early morning to beat the sun and crowds. Almost the entire way there is an overhead shelter with lights so you can walk at night or in the rain.

Before climbing the hill it is customary to circle three times the temple that contains a pair of brass slippers, at the base of the hill . The beauty of the mountain area has to be experienced to be believed. You pass nice forests, gardens, and a zoo. You should be a little bit of an experienced walker as it is mostly uphill, but not much of an incline. There are refreshment stands on the way. On the way up the hill is a small temple dedicated to Ramanujacarya.

The walk up the hill is about 4,047 steps, which takes two to four hours of steady climbing and is hard work. If you walk up the hill and want to stay overnight in Tirumala, you can leave your luggage at the baggage stand at the toll gate at the bottom of the hill. It will be transported up the hill free of charge, and you pick it up at the cloak room near the Central Reception Office at the top of the hill.

KALAHASTI

There is an important Siva temple here. It is on the right bank of the Suvarnamukhi River, 27 km northeast of Tirupati. It is between the two hills Sripuram and Mummudicholapuram, which form part of the Sesha Sailam hills.

Kalahastiswara Temple

This is an important temple dedicated to Lord Siva. This temple has one of the elemental *lingas*, the *vayu* (air) *linga*. There is a lamp inside the inner sanctum that is constantly flickering despite the lack of air movement inside. The air-linga can be observed to move even when the *pujaris* close off the entrance to the main Deity room, which does not have any windows. You can see the flames on several ghee lamps flicker as if blown by moving air. The *linga* is white and is considered Swayambhu, or self-manifested.

The main *linga* is untouched by human hands, even by the priest. *Abhisheka* (bathing) is done by pouring a mixture of water, milk, camphor, and *panchamrita*. Sandal paste, flowers, and the sacred thread are offered to the *utsava-murti*, not the main *linga*.

This temple is one of the most impressive Siva temples in India. It features an enormous, ancient *gopuram* (tower) over the main gate. The tower is 36.5m (120 feet) high. The entire temple is carved out of the side of a huge stone hill. It was built in 1516 by King Krishnadeva Raya.

The temple is run by neatly dressed Saivite *Brahmins*, who conduct the worship of the various deities inside. Inside the temple you will find the tremendously ornate and splendid architecture that South India is famous for. Elaborately designed pillars, altars, and paraphernalia abound.

The main entrance of the temple is from the south, but the deity faces west. There is an interesting underground temple for Lord Ganapathi, named Patala Vinayaka, which is 30 feet beneath the ground. The goddess here is called Jnana Prasannambha and is said to be the sister of Lord Venkateswara at the Tirumala temple. She is said to give supreme knowledge (*jnana*) to those who worship her.

The Suvarnamukhi River is a sacred river, said to have been brought to the earth by Agastya Muni. It is also called Uttara Vahini, because at this place it flows south to north, which is unusual. It is dry most of the year. You can climb to the top of the nearby Nagor Hill (1040 m) and get a good view of the area. Lord

Caitanya sanctified this spot with His visit.

By purchasing a special *darshan* ticket (Rs 10) you wait about 10 minutes instead of an hour on a normal day.

Temple Story

The main *linga* is in the shape of an elephant trunk, with tusks on each side and a figure of a spider at the bottom. If you look at the *linga* from the top it looks like a snake with five hoods. The spider is call "Sri," the snake "Kala," and the elephant "Hasti." The three names combine together in the name Srikalahasti.

It is said that the spider wove a web above the *linga* to protect it from the sun and rain. The elephant would get water with its trunk and bath the linga (perform *abhisheka*) and the snake would also worship the Lord. The snake was not aware that the elephant and spider were also worshiping the Lord. One day the snake found some *bilva* leaves and water near the Lord. He thought that someone was trying to harm the Lord, so he surrounded the Lord to protect him. When the elephant came the next day to worship the Lord the snake thought he was trying to harm the Lord so he got into his trunk. Unable to handle the pain, the elephant dashed his trunk against the *linga* killing both the snake and the spider. The elephant also died at this time. Lord Siva being satisfied by their devotion, gave liberation to his three devotees.

Nearby

Kalahasti is surrounded by two sacred hills. The **Durgamba temple** is on the northern hill. On the south hill there is the shrine of **Kannabeswara**, in memory of the Sage Kannappa, who offered an eye to the Lord. When he tried to offer his other eye as well, the Lord mercifully stopped him. There is also a temple dedicated to **Subramanya** on one of the surrounding hills.

Practicalities

There is the very basic *Devasthanam Guest House* and the *Hotel Madhu*.

You can visit Kalahasti while on an organized tour that goes to the temples in the Tirupati area.

There is a train station at Gudur on the Madras-Vijayawada line. It is easy to make a day trip from Tirupati to here. There are regular buses to and from Tirupati. From Tirupati you get the bus to Kalahasti from the Central Bus Stand, which is a few km from the railway station.

CHAPTER EIGHTEEN

Karnataka

Population: 45 million

Karnataka has several important temples and temple towns. Udupi, on the coast near Mangalore, has the famous Sri Krishna Temple. This temple was established by the important Vaishnava acarya Madhvacarya. Further up the coast is an important Siva temple at Gokarna called the Mahaballeswara Temple.

Three hours southwest of Bangalore is the interesting city of Mysore, the most popular city for foreign tourists in South India. There is a fascinating city palace in Mysore. Between Mysore and Bangalore is the important Sri Ranganatha Vishnu Temple at Srirangapatnam. North of Mysore are interesting temples in the towns of Belur and Halebid. Further north is the all but deserted city of Hampi, which at one time had a population of over a half a million people. In the extreme north of Karnataka are Badami, Pattadakal, and Aihole all of which have many ancient temples in them.

BANGALORE

Population: 4,000,000, STD Code 080

Bangalore is the capital city of Karnataka. Because it is 3000 feet above sea level it has a pleasurable climate even in the summer time. It was founded by Kempe Gowda in 1537. It is said that he had four bullock carts plow their way, with plowshares, in the four directions. When they stopped from exhaustion he had four towers built. They still stand today, as a reminder of how big Gowda expected his city to grow.

Bangalore is more Westernized than most Indian cities, but there is really not much to see. The nearby city of Mysore is a much nicer place.

Getting Your Bearings

Cubbon Park is the geographic center of Bangalore. About 2 km west of the park, past the race course, are the railway and bus stations. The area between the park and the railway station is a busy shopping area, where many of the cheap hotels and restaurants are also located. This is a convenient place to stay. East of the park is Mahatma Gandhi Rd (MG Road), Brigade Rd, and St Mark's Rd. This is where the tourist offices, airline offices, bookshops, GPO, the government emporiums, and the better hotels are located. This is where the action is in Bangalore. The old section of the city is in the south. The cantonment area was developed by the British in the beginning of the 18th century.

Tourist Offices

The **Government of India Tourist Office** (558-5917) is at KFC Building, 48 Church St. It is open weekdays from 10 am to 6 pm and Saturday from 9 am to 1 pm.

The **Karnataka State Tourism Development Corp.** (KSTDC) has its head office (221-2901) at 10/4 Kasturba Road, opposite the Aquarium. It is open from 10 am to 5.30 pm daily except Sunday. There are also counters at the airport (open 6.30 am to 8.30 pm), railway station (open 6.30 am to 8.30 pm), and Badami House, Narasimharaja Square.

The **Tirumala Tirupati Information Center** is at Vyalikaval, 16th Cross (near Chowdiah Memorial Hall). You can reserve rooms here for accommodation on Tirumala hill by Tirupati.

Other Information

The General Post Office is on Raj Bhawan Road. There are also post offices on Brigade Road and Museum Road.

Bangalore This Fortnight is a good magazine with information about what is happening in Bangalore.

The **Government Museum**, on the Kasturba Rd side of Cubbon Park, has 18 departments. It is open daily 9.30 am to 4.30 pm, except Wednesday.

Money

At Thomas Cook (558-6742), 55 MG Rd, you can change money quickly. It is open from 9.30 am to 6 pm, Monday to Saturday. The State Bank of India is on St Mark's Rd (by MG Rd).

Visa Extension

Extensions are issued at the office of the Commissioner of Police (236-6242), Infantry Rd, 10 minutes from the GPO. It is open Monday to Saturday from 10 am to 5 pm.

Shopping

Bangalore is known for its silks and handicrafts such as sandalwood and rosewood carvings, ceramics, and gold jewelry.

The **Karnataka Arts & Crafts Emporium,** on MG Road, has a good selec-

tion of arts and crafts. Things are very expensive here, but they have an interesting selection of items so it is worth coming here to just see the place. The major shopping areas are MG Road, Brigade Road, and Kempegowda Road. There is also the Jayanagar and Shrungar Shopping Centres. **Spencer Department Store**, on MG Road, is as close to a Western department store as you will get in India. It has a good selection of foods and many other items.

The *Book Cellar*, *Higginbotham*, 66 MG Road, and *Gangarams*, 72 MG Road, are some of the best bookshops in India. *Higginbotham* has one of the best selection of spiritual and travel books in India. *Premier Bookshop*, 46/1 Church St, round the corner from Berrys Hotel, has an excellent selection of books. You can get second-hand books in the cantonment area. *Morris's Guide to Bangalore* and *TTK Bangalore Guide* are good guidebooks of the city. At No 6 St Marks Road there is a *Motilal Banarsidass Book Shop*, which has a good selection of spiritual books.

Tours

Tours can be booked at the KSTDC office (221-5869), Badami House, N R Square, from 7.30 am to 1.30 pm and 2 to 7.30 pm daily.

There is a daily half-day Bangalore tour to Tipu's Palace, the Bull Temple, the Museum, Govt. Emporiums, the Soap Factory, and Vidhan Soudha (7.30 am to 1.30 pm or 2 to 7.30 pm).

Srirangapatnam, Mysore and Brindavan Gardens

This tour includes Ranganathaswami Temple, the Fort in Srirangapatnam, Chamundi Hill, the Palace, the Art Gallery, the zoo, and Cauvery Arts & Crafts

Emporium at Mysore. It costs Rs 120, which includes entrance fees. It is an interesting tour.

Belur, Sravanabelagola and Halebid

There is a daily tour, during the season, that leaves at 7.30 am and returns at 9 pm. It costs Rs 150.

ISKCON Temple

This newly built beautiful temple is located at Hare Krishna Hill, 1 'R' Block, Chord Rd, Rajaji Nagar. The telephone number is 321-956. The Deities in this temple are Krishna-Balarama and Gaura-Nitai. There are some guest facilities at the temple, but guests must follow ashram rules.

Bull Temple (Basavanagudi Mandir)

This temple is at the end of Bull Temple Rd, in the southwest part of the city, on Bugle Hill. It was built by Kempe Gowda, the founder of Bangalore. There is a huge Nandi bull here, 15 feet high and 20 feet long, carved from a single stone. The bull has a small iron plate on its head to prevent it, as tradition says, from growing.

Also there is a Ganesh temple, with a large deity made of 110 kilos of butter. The deity of butter is broken up and distributed every four years.

Gavi Gangadhareswara Temple

On January 14 (Makara Sankranti), between 5 and 6 pm, as the sun sets, its rays pass through the window and the horns of Nandi to strike the Siva-linga in this temple. There is an Agni deity, the god of fire, here. It is by the Kempambudi Tank, in the southwest part of the city. It was built by Kempe Gowda in the 16th century.

Where To Stay – Lower

The *Rainbow Hotel* (602-235), Sri Narasimharaja Rd, by City Market bus stand, has rooms for Rs 40/60 and A/C rooms for Rs 100. It is one of the best values in town. *Hotel Amar*, 5-6 Ayurvedic Hospital Rd, is a good value with rooms having attached bath.

The *Hotel Prashanth*, 21 E Tank Bund Rd, is a popular place with rooms that are a good value.

Where To Stay – Bus Station Area

The cheaper hotels are around the bus station, south of the railway station. The *Janata Lodge* is a good clean place having rooms with bath for Rs 85/100.

The *Hotel Tourist* (226-2381), Race Course Rd, is a good place that has rooms with bath and hot water in the morning for Rs 60/100.

The *Royal Lodge* (226-6951), 251 Subedar Chatram Rd, has clean rooms for Rs 70 with common bath and rooms with bath and hot water in the morning for Rs 120. The *Hotel Adora* (287-2280), 47 Subedar Chatram Rd, has decent rooms with hot water in the morning for Rs 100/165.

The popular *Ramakrishna Lodge*, Subedar Chatram Rd, is a good clean place. The KSTDC *Hotel Mayura Kempegowda*, Dhanavanthri Rd, has rooms with bath that are a good value for Rs 200/225. The *Janardhana Hotel* (264-4444), Kumara Krupa Rd, High Grounds, has big rooms with a balcony, bath, and hot water for Rs 150/200 and deluxe rooms for Rs 275.

Opposite the bus station is the *Hotel Mahaveer* (287-0774, fax 226-9843), 9 Tank Bund Rd, which is a modern clean place with rooms for Rs 150/250 and Rs 380 for an A/C room. The cheaper rooms in the front of the building can be noisy.

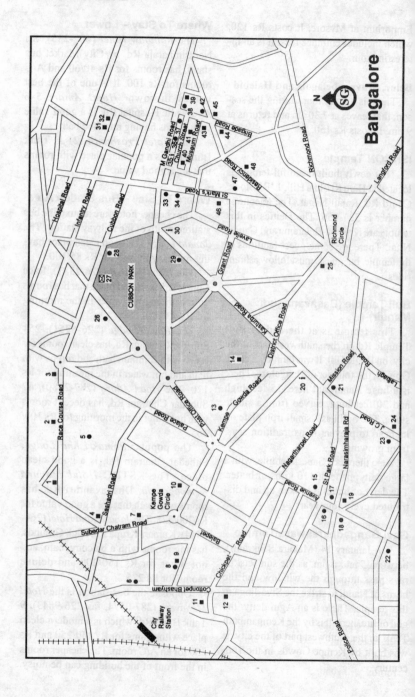

PLACES TO STAY

1	Bangalore International
2	West End Hotel
3	Chalukya Hotel
4	Hotel Tourist
7	Royal & Sri Ramakrishna Lodges
9	KTDC Mayura Kempe Gowda
10	Gupta Lodge
11	Sri Ganesha Lodge
12	Sudha Lodge
14	YMCA
19	Rainbow Hotel
24	Minerva
25	Woodlands
31	New Central Lodge
32	YWCA Guest House
39	Brindavana
40	Berrys Hotel
41	Hotel Gautam
43	Nilgiris Nest Hotel
44	Hotel Imperial & Shansug Hotel
45	Victoria
46	Nagar Heritage
48	Gateway

WHERE TO EAT

3	Chalukya
23	Kamat
25	Woodlands
40	KC Das

OTHER

5	Racecourse
6	City Bus Stand
8	Central Bus Stand
13	Indian Airlines
15	Chandra Vihar
16	City Market
17	City Market Bus Stand
18	Fort
20	Badami House
21	Air India
22	Tipu Sultan's Palace
26	Vidhana Soudha
27	GPO
28	Central Telegraph Office
29	Government Museum & Technological Museum
30	KSTDC Head Office
33	Motilal Banarsidass
34	British Library
35	Govt of India Tourist Office
36	Higginbothams Book Store & Gangaram's
37	Thomas Cook
38	Cauvery Arts Emporium
40	Premier Book Shop
42	Bus from Station
47	Air France

The more spacious deluxe rooms in the back are quiet and a good value.

Where To Stay – MG Rd Area

Hotels in this area fill up early. I went to five hotels in this area before I found a place that wasn't full.

The *Sunflower Lodge*, 129 Brigade Rd, has rooms for Rs 200. The *Hotel Gautam* (558-8461), 17 Museum Rd, has rooms with bath for Rs 250/350. The popular *Brindavan Hotel* (558-4000), 108 MG Rd, has rooms with bath for Rs 175/250 and A/C rooms for Rs 300/450. It is a good value and is recommended, but is almost always full, being booked in advance.

New Central Lodge (559-2395), 56 Infantry Rd, has clean rooms for Rs 100/175 to Rs 275. It has hot water between 6 and 9 am. It doesn't look so good, but is all right for the center of Bangalore. If all the lower-priced places in the MG Road area are full, there is a good chance this place will still have a room. Similarly priced is the *Hotel Vellara* (556-5684), 283 Brigade Rd, 1 km from MG Road. This hotel is centrally located and is a good value.

The *Airlines Hotel* (227-3783), No 4 Madras Bank Rd, has rooms for Rs 215/315 and Rs 600 with A/C. *Berrys Hotel* (558-7211), 48 Church Street, has rooms for Rs 300/350 and Rs 450/500 with A/C. It is a large place that is popular, mainly because of its location.

Where To Stay – Middle

Woodlands Hotel (222-5111), 5 Sampangi Tank Rd (Raja Rammohan Roy Rd), is a recommended place in a quiet area with nice gardens. It has two excellent vegetarian restaurants, one South Indian and the other continental. Rooms are Rs 275/550 and Rs 700 with A/C. There are also more expensive suites. It is a good value. It has an old and a new building.

The *Ashraya International* (261-921), 149 Infancy Rd, has rooms for Rs 400/600.

The *Hotel Nilgiris Nest* (558-8401), 171 Brigade Rd, has clean comfortable rooms for Rs 350/450 and rooms with A/C for Rs 450/550. It is centrally located and is a good value. The new *Hotel Highgate* (559-7172), centrally located at 33 Church St by MG Rd, is a modern place with central A/C and rooms that are a good value. Rooms are Rs 850/1000

The *Hotel Raceview* (266-147), 25 Race Course Rd, is close to the railway station and has rooms for Rs 300 and Rs 375 with A/C. The *Hotel Rama* (221-3311), Lavelle Rd, has nice clean rooms for Rs 575/675 and Rs 675/800 with A/C.

The *New Victoria Hotel* (558-4077, fax 558-4945), 47 Residency Rd, has its own garden with many trees. It has real character, it is clean, and it is a good value. You have to make a reservation in advance as it is heavily booked. The rooms here cost Rs 250/630 up to Rs 750 for a suite. It is a very good mid-range choice and is recommended.

Hotel Luciya (222-4148), 6 OTC Rd, has rooms for Rs 275/325 and Rs 325/405 with A/C. The *Hotel Bangalore International* (226-8011), 2A/2B Crescent Rd, High Grounds by the Race Course Rd area, has rooms with TV for Rs 350/395 up to Rs 675 for a deluxe A/C room.

The three-star *Hotel Abhishek* (262-713), 19/2 Kumara Krupa Rd, High Grounds, has rooms for Rs 475/525 and Rs 550/625 with A/C. It has two vegetarian restaurants.

Where To Stay – Higher MG area

Curzon Court (558-2997), 10 Brigade Rd, has rooms for Rs 500/650 up to Rs 800.

The *Cauvery Continental* (226-6966), 11-37 Cunningham Rd, has rooms for Rs 480/600 and Rs 600/800 with A/C. The four-star *Gateway Hotel* (558-4545, fax 558-4030), 66 Residency Rd, is a modern place with a swimming pool and rooms for $60/70. The *Ramanashree Comforts* (222-5152), 16 Raja Rammohan Roy Rd, has rooms for Rs 1195/1495 and is a good value.

Where To Stay – Luxury

The *Taj West End Hotel* (225-5055, fax 220-0010), Race Course Rd, is a recommended three-star hotel with a pool and a nice spacious garden covering 20 acres. Rooms with A/C are $155/165. Part of the hotel dates back to 1887. The nicest rooms are in the old part of the hotel. You should ask to see some rooms before you choose one.

Taj Residency (584-4444, fax 558-4748), 41/3 MG Rd, has rooms for $90/100. Non-residents can use the pool and health club facilities for Rs 175 a day. The *Ashok Radisson Hotel* (226-9462, fax 226-7676), Kumara Krupa Rd, High Grounds, has rooms starting at Rs 2200/2600. The pool can be used by non-guests for Rs 90.

Rooms at the *Holiday Inn* (267-2233, fax 226-7676), 28 Sankey Road, are $90/100. The *Oberoi Bangalore* (558-5858, fax 558-5960), 37-39 MG Road, has luxurious room for $175/190. The Oberoi has a landscaped Japanese garden and a pool. The five-star *Welcomegroup Windsor Manor Sheraton* (266-9898, fax 226-4941), 25 Sankey Rd, has rooms for $110/120 up to $700 for the top of the line suite. This hotel is in a beautiful old building.

Where To Eat

The *Kamat Hotel*, Subedar Chatram Rd, by the bus station, is a cheap place that serves South Indian snacks and some North Indian items. The *Hotel Abhishek*, 19/2 Kumara Krupa Rd, High Grounds, has two vegetarian restaurants. *Suvana Mandir*, 76 Mission Rd, serves South Indian food, *bhelpuri, samosas*, and other snacks. It is a good value.

The *Woodlands Hotel*, 5 Sampangi Tank Rd, has an outside South Indian restaurant and inside the excellent continental *Sunheri Restaurant*, which serves a good selection of Western and Indian items. It is open from 11.30 am to 3.30 pm and 7 to 11 pm. *Woods* at 177-178 Commercial Street is a good place open from 8 am to 11 pm. It has *thalis* from 11.30 to 3 pm and 7.30 to 9.45 pm.

Chalukya Hotel, Race Course Road, near the West End Hotel, has a very good South Indian restaurant. You can get a good selection of fruits in Bangalore, including avocados.

Travel

Air The airport is about 13 km north of the city center. There is a prepaid taxi counter at the airport that charges Rs 150 for a taxi and Rs 70 for an auto-rickshaw to downtown. There is also a KSRTC bus that goes downtown. There is a sign in the airport that tells you the taxi rates for various hotels.

There are special buses to the airport which depart from Sivajinagar Stop (near Hotel Harsha). At the airport you can **change money** at the State Bank of Mysore (8 am to 7 pm) and Vijaya Bank (8.30 am to 12.30 pm).

There are flights to most major cities in India including Bombay (6 daily), Delhi (3 daily), Calcutta, Madras (2 to 5 daily), Thiruvananthapuram (Trivandrum), Goa, Hyderabad, Mangalore, Ahmedabad, Cochin, and Coimbatore.

Air India (224-143, airport 222-4143) is in the Unity Building, Jayachamaraja Road. Indian Airlines (221-1914) is at Cauvery Bhavan, Kempegowda Rd.

Rail Most trains depart from Bangalore City Railway Station on the west edge of the city center. There are trains to every part of India from here, including several daily trains to Mysore. The Kaveri Exp #6222 (8 pm, 2½ hr), going via Srirangapatnam, and the A/C Shatabdi Exp (10.55, daily except Tues, 1¾ hr) are good trains to **Mysore**.

Many of the long-distance trains are slow, and you may have to change trains. It takes 24 hours to get to **Bombay** on the Udyan Exp #6530 (8.30 pm), 25 hours to get to **Calcutta** on the Bangalore-

Guwahati #2674 (11.30 pm), and 42 hours to get to **Delhi** on the Karnataka Exp #2627 (6.20 pm).

There is a prepaid taxi stand at the station. An auto-rickshaw to the MG Rd area is Rs 20.

Bangalore is one of the more difficult places in India to book a ticket from. However, the bus service is good out of Bangalore. There are no tourist quotas on any trains and many trains are hard to book. It is usually possible to use the emergency quota to get on many trains.

There is a tourist booking counter in the computerised booking center, just outside the main station, which is open from 7 am to 1 pm and 1.30 to 7 pm. Counter #14, the first one to the right as you enter, has a sign that says "the Disabled and Freedom Fighters Only". It is also for foreign tourists. Other counters will not handle foreign booking. If you have an Indrail pass, go to the Chief Reservation Supervisor's office on the first floor and your reservation is guaranteed.

The best train to **Hyderabad** is the Bangalore-Hyderabad Exp #7086 (5.15 pm, 16 hr). The **Hampi** Express departs at 9.40 pm and arrives in Hospet (near Hampi) about 6 am in the morning. The Bangalore-Madras Express #6024 (7.25 am, 7 hr), Brindhavan Express #2640 (1.55 pm, 6 hr), and the Shatabdi Express (4.30 pm, daily except Tues, 4 hr) are the best trains to **Madras**. The Kanniyakumari Express (7 pm) takes 18 hours to get to **Trivandrum**. To Vasco-da-Gama in **Goa** there is the #6201 Mail (5.10 pm, 20 hr).

Bus All long-distance buses leave from the Central (KSRTC) Bus Station, directly across from the City Railway Station, in the west part of town. There are buses to Mysore (3 hr, every 15 minutes),

Hassan (5 hr, 8 daily), Hospet (11 hr, 20 daily), Mangalore (8 hr, 4 daily), Madras (9 hr, 20 daily), Hyderabad (16 hr, 10 daily), and Madurai (15 hr, 15 daily). There are two direct buses to Hampi. The bus trip to Hospet is a tough trip, so it is better to take the train.

The interstate bus companies' offices are at Stand 13, in the Central Bus Station. You can do computerised advance booking here for KSRTC express and deluxe buses. You can also make advance bookings for buses operated by other state bus companies here. It is best to book in advance for all long-distance journeys.

Besides state buses, private bus companies also have buses between Bangalore and other cities. They have higher prices, but also better buses with more leg room. You can book these buses with travel agents around the railway or bus stations. The video buses are extremely loud and should be avoided.

MYSORE

Population: 700,000, STD Code 0821

Mysore is 139 km southwest of Bangalore and is called the Sandalwood City, because it has many sandalwood, rose, jasmine, and other flowering trees. This is where much of the incense and sandalwood oil in India is made. Also many carved products made of ivory, sandalwood, rosewood, and teakwood are made here.

Nearby, at Srirangapatnam, there is an important Vishnu temple. At Somnathpur there is an ancient beautifully carved temple dedicated to Krishna called the Channakesava Temple.

Mysore is an old city that was almost always ruled by Hindu rulers—in succession by the Cholas, Hoysalas, Vijayanagar, and Wodeyar dynasties. In 1759 the Hindu Wodeyar were overthrown by one of their Muslim generals, Hyder Ali. After overthrowing and killing Hyder Ali's son, Tipu Sultan, the British reinstated the Wodeyars. Mysore is a city of palatial buildings including 17 palaces.

The city gets its name from **Mahishasura**, a demon who caused trouble to the people in the area, until goddess **Chamundi** killed him.

The city is at an altitude of 770m, so the climate is nice all year around. The weather is best between September and January, but is still good up to April. September and October are the best months to come. This is when the **Dussehra festival** takes place. There is a victory procession to celebrate the killing of Mahishasura by Chamundi on the tenth day of this festival with elephants, horses, bands, floats, and real gold and silver coaches.

This is the most popular city in South India for foreign tourists. This is because there are some interesting places to visit in Mysore and the surrounding area. Plus it is a pleasant city, with relatively cheap and good accommodations.

Information

The Regional Tourist Office (22096) is at the Old Exhibition Building, Irwin Road. The Karnataka State Tourist Office (570-005) is at the Hotel Mayura Hoysala, 2 Jhansi Lakshmi Bai Rd.

Tours

The KSTDC **Belur, Halebid, and Sravanabelagola tour** runs daily in season (April to June and September to November) and three times a week the rest of the year. There are also tours run by private operators that leave almost every day. It is better to use the KSTDC tour if possible, as they use a luxury four seats across bus and the private companies use small, very bumpy (especially if you are in the back, I was) mini-buses. Both the private companies and the KSTDC tours pick you up at your hotel. This is a good way to see these places as they are difficult to reach by public transportation. Also not much time is needed to see these spots, so you do not really feel too hurried on this tour.

There is also a KSTDC **Mysore tour** that includes the Mysore Palace, Chamundi Hill, Srirangapatnam, Vrindavana Gardens, and Somnathpur. The tour runs daily in season (June to Sept). Private companies also do this tour. You book the KSTDC tours at their office at the Tourist Offices (22096), Irwin Road, or the Hotel Mayura Hoysala, which is where the tour begins. The tours run by the private companies are booked at one of the many travel agents in town.

Chamundi Hill

On top of Chamundi Hill is the **Shri Chamundeswari Temple**, dedicated to the consort of Lord Siva. The temple has a jewel Nakshatra-Malike with 30 Sanskrit *slokas* inscribed on it. The tower of the temple is 300 years old, but the foundation is 2000 years old. Halfway up the hill, along the road, is a 16 foot high and 25 feet long **Nandi bull** carved out of a large boulder. The temple has a seven story, 40m high *gopuram* covered with intricate carvings. The deity of the goddess **Chamundi** is solid gold. The temple is open from 9 am to noon and 5 to 9 pm.

There is a 16-foot-high statue of the demon **Mahishasura** near the temple. Mahishasura was slain by the goddess Chamundeswari (Durga or Parvati) to protect the area. Chamundi means terrible, and this is another name for Parvati, who is in an angry mood to slay the demon.

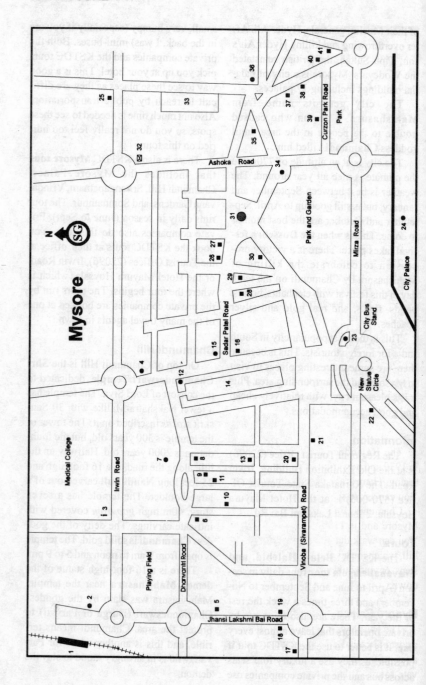

PLACES TO STAY

5	Hotel Mayura Hoysal
6	New Gayathri Bhavan
8	Hotel Indra Bhavan
9	Agrawal Lodge
10	Hotel Aashraya
11	Hotel Sangeeth
13	Hotel Chalukya
16	Hotel Anugraha
17	Southern Star Mysore
18	Hotel Metropole
19	Kings Kourt Hotel
20	Lakshmi Lodge
21	Sri Ram Lodge
22	Hotel Calinga
25	Sri Nandini Hotel
26	Hotel Dasaprakash
27	Hotel Durbar
28	Hotel Maurya
29	Hotel Mona
30	Hotel Srikanth
35	Hotel Mannars
37	Ritz Hotel
38	Mysore Hotel Complex
39	Hotel Park Lane
40	Hotel Roopa

WHERE TO EAT

26	Dasaprakash Restaurant
41	Hotel Siddhartha

OTHER

1	Railway Station
2	Commercial Superintendent's Office (Tourist Quota)
3	Tourist Office
4	Cauvery Arts Emporium
5	Indian Airlines
7	Hospitals
12	Book Shop
14	Devaraja Market
15	State Bank of Mysore
23	Geetha Book House
24	Maharaja's Palace
31	Gandhi Square
32	GPO
33	Central Bus Station
34	Clock Tower
36	Bus to Somnathpur

The **Rajendrah Vilas Palace,** built in 1939 and now used as a hotel, is worth seeing. There is a red velvet dining room. You can ask to see the royal bedrooms.

Chamundi Hill is 10 km by road from Mysore and is 1100 m (3,489 ft) high. You can walk the 4 km to the top of the hill, which means climbing about a 1000 steps, or you could take a bus up and walk down.

Mysore Palace

The palace was built in 1911-1912 at a cost of nearly Rs 42 lakhs. You can see a few of the royal Wodeyar family's private rooms. It has a remarkable Durbar Hall, which has a 200 kg **solid gold throne,** which is usually only seen during Dussehra. The rest of the time the silver throne is on display. The **durbar hall's** floor is inlaid with precious stones. The palace has a carved silver door, a magnificent **stained glass ceiling,** and an excellent **painting gallery**. There are paintings of the *Ramayana* and *Mahabharata* done by Raja Ravi Varma, one of India's most famous artists. The family **jewel collection** is on display. On Sunday evenings between 7 and 8 pm and also on festival days the building is illuminated with about **50,000 light bulbs**.

In another building on the palace

grounds there is a **museum** that contains many interesting items. Besides temples, this palace was definitely the most interesting building that I saw in India. It reminded me of Buckingham Palace. The former Maharaja still lives in a part of the palace, which is not open to the public.

Shopping

Some good book stores are the *Ashok Book Centre*, Dhanvantri Rd near Sayaji Rao Rd; *Geetha Book House*, New Statue Square, at the end of Sayaji Rao Rd and the *Premier Book House*, Anand Vihar, Makkaji Chowk.

The **Cauvery Arts and Crafts Emporium**, on the corner of Sayaji Rao Rd and Irwin Rd, is a recommended place that is open 10 am to 2 pm and 3.30 to 7.30 pm. It is closed on Thursdays. It does not have the cheapest prices, but the quality is excellent. They accept credit cards and will send your purchases home for you.

The **Sandalwood Oil Factory** (22856), just off Ambedkar Rd, is where about half the sandalwood oil in India is produced. You can phone and arrange a tour of the factory, which includes an explanation of how the oil is extracted and incense is made. It is open 9 to 11 am and 2 to 4 pm, Monday to Friday.

The **Karnataka Silk Industry Factory** (21803), on Mananthody Rd, is about 3 km from the downtown. You can call ahead to arrange a tour of the factory. It is open 7.30 to 11.30 am and 12.30 to 4.30 pm, Monday to Saturday.

Mysore is considered to be one of the best places to buy incense and sandalwood products in India. You have to be careful, however, about purchasing sandalwood products. Sandalwood oil is often put on other woods which are then sold as real sandalwood. Real sandalwood is very expensive.

Dussehra Festival

The Dussehra Festival, at the end of September or early October, is the most important festival. It lasts for ten days, and the highlight of the festival is when the Maharaja goes through the streets in a grand procession with elephants and camels.

Where To Stay – Lower

Mysore is a very popular tourist spot with many reasonably priced and often full hotels. The main areas for the budget hotels are Vinoba Rd, Dhanvantri Rd, and Gandhi Square.

The *Hotel Sangeeth* (24693), 1966 Narayana Shastry Rd, is a clean budget place that has rooms with bath and hot water for Rs 100/135. Nearby, the *Gayatri Bhavan* (21224), Dhanvantri Rd, has rooms with common bath for Rs 40/65 and double rooms from Rs 75 to Rs 105. The *Agrawal Lodge* (22730), just off Dhanvantri Rd, has rooms with bath for Rs 85/110.

The *Hotel Aashraya Mysore* (27088) has rooms with bath for Rs 150/350. The *Hotel Anugraha* (20768), at the junction of Sardar Patel Rd and Sayaji Rao Rd, is a good value. Rooms with bath are Rs 100/150. It also has rooms with TV for Rs 100. The *Hotel Mannars* (35060), by Gandhi Square, is a good clean place, in a relatively quiet area. Rooms with bath are Rs 110/150.

The *Hotel Dasaprakash* (24444), Gandhi Square, is popular with middle-class Indians. It has clean rooms for Rs 90/185 to Rs 135/250 and Rs 370 for a family room. It has a good vegetarian (*thali* only) restaurant.

The popular *Hotel Park Lane* (30400),

2720 Sri Harsha Rd, has rooms with bath for Rs 110/140 to Rs 180/210. It is a clean pleasant place, located next to a small park in a quiet location. The *Hotel Calinga* (31310), 23 KR Circle, opposite the City Bus Stand in the southern part of town, has rooms with hot water for Rs 180/260 and Rs 200/300 for a room with a TV. It is a good recommended place.

Where To Stay – Middle

KSTDC *Hotel Mayura Hoysala* (25349), 2 Jhansi Lakshmi Bai Rd, by the railway station, has good-sized rooms with bath for Rs 150/225 and suites for Rs 300. It has a garden. The bus tours run by KSTDC start here, and Indian Airlines have their office in this hotel.

The *Mysore Hotel Complex* (26217), near the bus stand, is a big place that has rooms with bath and hot water for Rs 200 to Rs 550. The more expensive rooms have A/C and a TV. It is built like an American motel, and is recommended, if you don't mind the impersonal design. It is mainly used by middle class Indians.

The *Hotel Sreekrishna Continental* (37042), Sri Madhvesha Complex, 73 Nazarbad Main Rd, has rooms for Rs 250, and rooms with A/C are Rs 400.

The *Ritz Hotel* (22668), Nilgiri Road, has good British-Raj style rooms with a nice atmosphere for Rs 250 to Rs 375. It is a very small place and is usually booked. To stay here you have to call and make a reservation at least a month in advance.

The *Hotel Roopa* (33770), Bangalore-Nilgiri Rd, has rooms for Rs 250/300 up to Rs 400 for rooms with a TV. The *Hotel Siddharta* (26869), 73/1 Government Guest House Rd, near the long-distance Central Bus Station, is a good centrally located place with a vegetarian restaurant. It has rooms for Rs 200/275 and Rs 250/ 350 with A/C.

The *Hotel Palace Plaza* (30875, Fax 520-639), 2716 Sri Harsha Rd, has large clean comfortable rooms from Rs 200 to Rs 525. It is a recommended popular place, so it is best to reserve a room in advance. *Dasaprakash Paradise* (515-565), 105 Vivekananda Rd, a few km from the downtown, is a recommended place with clean rooms for Rs 500/600 and Rs 600/700 with A/C. The vegetarian restaurant here is the best in town.

Where To Stay – Higher

Kings Kourt Hotel (25250), at the junction of Vinoba Rd and Jhansi Lakshmi Bhai Rd, is a really nice place with A/C rooms for Rs 690/890. It has more expensive rooms and is very popular.

Lalitha Mahal Palace Hotel (26316, 27650), T Narasipur Rd, is a recommended place about 8 km from the center of town. It is such a nice place that it is worth going to see as a tourist site. It was built as a guest house by the Maharaja. Rooms go for Rs 3000/3300 all the way up to Rs 15,000 for the Viceroy Suite. The name of the hotel means "beautiful building."

The *Southern Star Mysore* (27217), 13-14 Vinoba Rd, has comfortable rooms from Rs 1300/1900 up to Rs 4300. It has bookshop and a swimming pool.

The *Hotel Metropole* (520-681), 5 Jhansi Lakshmi Bai Rd, by Vinoba Rd, has comfortable rooms for Rs 595/690 to Rs 690/800 for an A/C room and Rs 1200 for the Deluxe Suite. It was once the Maharaja's guest house, so it is a fancy place with old-world charm, and at this level it is the recommended place. It has a well-kept garden and a nice veranda.

The *Hotel Rajendravilas Imperial* (520-690) is on top of Chamundi Hill,

14 km from town. The Maharaja of Mysore once went here for the weekends. It is a splendid-looking place with a good view of the city. Rooms are Rs 250/400 and Rs 300/500 with A/C.

Where To Eat

You can get a good *thali* in the clean *Akshaya Restaurant*, in the Dasaprakash Hotel, Gandhi Square. The *Dasaprakash Paradise*, about 5 km out of the city center, is the best restaurant in town and has good ice cream.

Hotel Siddhartha, 73/1 Guest House Rd, about a half km from the long-distance bus station has a good vegetarian restaurant. One part of the restaurant serves *thalis*, and the other part serves North Indian side orders. It is the best place I could find in the center of town, but it was nothing outstanding. It is very popular.

There is also the *Sujata, Modern Hindu Hotel, Indra Bhavan,* and *Chandra Vihar*.

Travel

Air The closest airport is in Bangalore, 138 km away. The Indian Airlines office (516-9432) is in the Hotel Mayur and is open Mon-Sat, 10 am to 1.30 pm and 2.15 to 5 pm.

Train There are several daily trains to Bangalore (138 km). The Tipu Exp #6205 (10.20 am, 2¾ hr) and the A/C Shatabdi Exp (2.20 pm, 1¾ hr) are the fastest trains to Bangalore. Other express trains take about 3½ hr. The Shatabdi Exp continues to Madras (7½ hr).

There is a slow train that goes north to Belur and Halebid, via Hassan. There is also a train to Mangalore. There is a new broad gauge line to Mysore, so new trains will be added to the schedule.

The City Railway Station, just off Irwin Road, is close to the center of town. The Advance Reservations counters, off the main lobby, take care of tourist enquiries and bookings. The Commercial Superintendent's Office, across the street, deals with tourist quota reservations.

Bus There are three bus stations in Mysore—Central Bus Stand on Irwin Rd, mainly for long distance buses; City Bus Stand, for local buses; and a suburban bus stand, for private buses and buses to Somnathpur (1 hr direct or longer via Bannur or Narasipur). There is a cloak-room at the Central Bus Station, where you can leave your bags if you are only visiting Mysore for the day.

Buses from Mysore go to Bangalore (3 hr, every 15 min, nonstop), Mangalore (7 hr, 8 daily), Hassan (2½ hr, 12 daily), Hospet (12 hr, 3 daily), Kochi (7 hr, 8 daily), Thrissur (8 hr, 2 daily) via Guruvayur (7 hr), Tirupati, and Madurai.

There are frequent buses from the Central Bus Stand to Srirangapatnam. The #125 bus from the City Bus Stand, which is northwest of the Palace, goes to Srirangapatnam.

You can get private luxury buses to Hassan and Ooty.

Around Mysore

SRIRANGAPATNAM

Population: 20,000

Srirangapatnam is on an island in the Kaveri River, 16 km north of Mysore and 140 km from Bangalore. Srirangapatnam was the capital city of Hyder Ali and Tipu Sultan. There is the important **Sri Ranganath Vishnu Temple** here. Hyder Ali helped to build the temple here, even though he was a Muslim. Besides the temple, there are the remains of a large fort here. There is also a **Narasimha Temple** and the **Gangadhareswara Temple,** which is northeast of the palace harem enclosure. Tipu Sultan was defeated and killed here by the British. The British army was commanded by Colonel Arthur Wellesley, also known as the Duke of Wellington.

Due north of the Ranganath Temple are dungeons that held British prisoners captured by Hyder Ali and Tipu Sultan. It is said that the prisoners stood in water with their arms crossed and chained for years.

Sri Ranganath Temple

This impressive temple dates back to the 10th century. **Sri Ranganath** is a black stone Deity of Lord Vishnu reclining on Adi Sesa. Gautama Rishi and the river goddess Kaveri are at His feet. There is a Deity of **Lakshmi** as Ranganayaki and a **Gopala Krishna Deity** in the west shrine. There are also shrines dedicated to Ramanuja, Desikar, and all the Alwars.

Ramanujacarya spent time here in 1133, when he came to avoid the Cholas king's repression. Sri Ranganath is said to have been worshiped by Agastya Rishi. Non-Hindus can go inside the temple, but not the inner sanctum. This temple is a hundred yards behind the railway station.

Practicalities

You can get a nice cottage for Rs 300 at the *Hotel Mayura River View* (52114), which is a few km from the railway station and bus stand. The *Amblee Holiday Resort* (08236/52326), on the Kaveri River, has a swimming pool, health club, and a hotel lake. Rooms are Rs 700/800 and Rs 900/1000 with A/C.

It is convenient to come here with a Mysore city tour. There are frequent buses from Mysore Central bus stand, and any Mysore to Bangalore train stops here. To get here from Mysore, you can take the #125 bus from the City bus stand, which is northwest of the Palace.

Brindavana Gardens

These are terraced gardens named after the original Vrindavana, where Lord Krishna appeared and had His pastimes. There is a large artificial lake here and a number of fountains that are floodlit with multi-colored lights. One of the fountains on the other side of the artificial lake is musical. It is a popular place, especially on the weekends. In April-May up to 400 tour buses a day come to this place. It is located about 20 minutes by train from Mysore Junction. The fountains are lit up: Summer weekdays 7 to 7.55 pm, Summer holidays 7 to 8.55 pm; Winter weekdays 6.30 to 7.30 pm, and Winter holidays 6.30 to 8.30 pm. There is a huge rush to this place in the evening.

There is the nice western-style *Hotel Krishnarajasagar* (08236/57222) here with rooms for Rs 500/600 and Rs 600/700 with A/C. There is also the more simple *Tourist Home*, which has rooms with attached baths.

SOMNATHPUR

This is where the 13th century intricately carved Hoysala Sri Channakesava Temple is located. Somnathpur is 35 km east of Mysore and 138 km west of Bangalore.

Sri Channakesava Temple

This temple has some of the most magnificent carvings that you will find in India. On this beautiful temple there are excellent sculptures of scenes from the *Mahabharata* and *Ramayana*. This temple was built in 1268 by the Hoysala general Somnath, who served under Narasimha III.

There is of a life-size (6½ ft) bronze Deity of Lord Krishna as 'Prasanna Channa Kesava' on the south altar and a Deity of Janardhana (another name for Vishnu) on the north altar. There is also a more recent Deity of Venugopala in the west shrine. North of the temple is a 30-foot-high stone pillar. This temple has beautiful domed ceilings and intricate carvings all over the buildings, including many sculptures of Lord Vishnu and His incarnations. The temple is open from 9 am to 5.30 pm.

Practicalities

The temple takes about an hour to see. To get to Somnathpur by public bus from Mysore you have to go either to Bannur or Narsipur (1 hr) and change buses to get to Somnathpur (20 min).

Next to the temple is the KSTDC *Hotel Mayura Keshava* (7017), which has good rooms with bath for Rs 40/70.

Halebid, Belur, Sravanabelagola

To see all three places in one day you have to either take the conducted tour from Mysore or Bangalore or come here by private car (at least Rs 1000). It takes two days to see these three places by public bus, because Sravanabelagola is in the opposite direction of Belur and Halebid. It is convenient to come here with a tour bus from Mysore.

If you are staying in Hassan, it is best to get the first of the ten buses to Halebid (1 hr, 8 am) and then go to Belur (30 min). From Belur, there are frequent buses back to Hassan (1½ hr, last bus 6.15 pm).

SRAVANABELAGOLA

Population: 4,000, STD Code 08176

Sravanabelagola is one of the most important and visited Jain pilgrimage sites. Chandragupta Maurya came here with his guru, Bhadrabahu, in the 3rd century BC. It is 51 km southeast of Hassan, 95 km north of Mysore, and 158 km west of Bangalore

The main reason to come here is to see the 17 meter (58 feet) high statue of the Jain sage Gomateswara (Lord Bahubali), which is on top of the Vindhyagiri Hill (also called Indragiri Hill). This statue can be seen from 24 km away. It is said to be the world's largest monolith statue. The statue was completed in 981 and named "Gommata" the handsome one. It represents Bahubali, who is the son of the first *tirthankara*. He renounced the world and sought enlightenment after he defeated his brother in a battle for the right to their father's kingdom. Realizing the futility of it, he gave the kingdom to his defeated brother. The depth of his meditation is shown by the creepers growing up his legs and arms.

You have to climb about 600 steps to go the 470 feet to the top of Vindhyagiri Hill. You have to leave your shoes at the bottom of the hill. If it is hot it is a good idea to bring socks with you, because the steps can get extremely hot. For those unable to make the climb, it is possible to be carried up the hill.

Every 12 years, thousands of people come here for the Mahamastakabhisheka. This is when the 1,800-year-old statue is bathed with precious stones, milk, ghee, yogurt, saffron, and gold coins. The next *abhiseka* (bathing) festival is in 2005. During the last festival, Gomateswara was bathed in 1000 litres of milk, 1008 containers of water, 150 litres of sugarcane juice, saffron, sandalwood, and a lot more.

There are many other Jain shrines on the way up Indragiri Hill. In the town at the bottom of the hill is the **Bhandari Basti** (1159), which has images of the 24 *tirthankaras*. There are also some Jain temples on the top of the nearby Chandragiri Hill.

Practicalities

There is a friendly **Karnataka State Tourist Office** opened daily from 10 am to 1 pm and 3 to 5.30 pm).

There are limited accommodations here, which include a few basic pilgrims lodges. *The Tourist Canteen and Rest House* is basic and cheap. The *Shriyans Prasad Guest House*, at the foot of the hill, is even more basic. It has dormitories and double rooms for Rs 60. The new *Yatri Nivas* has rooms with bath for Rs 100. The *Hotel Raghu* (7238) has rooms for Rs 70/85.

There are morning buses to here from Mysore. To get here from Hassan, you take a bus to Channarayapatna (1 hr, first bus 6.30 am) and from there get another bus to Sravanabelagola (30 min).

BELUR

Population: 17,000, STD Code 08233

Belur was the capital of the Hoysalas before they moved it to Halebid. The fifth king of the Hoysalas dynasty, Bittadeva, is said to have changed his name to Vishnuvardhana (1108-1042) when he was converted from Jainism to Vaishnavism under the influence of **Ramanujacarya**. Most of the temples in Belur and Halebid were built during his reign.

The reason to come to this town is to see the impressive **Channakeshava Temple** which has some of the most intricate and beautiful carvings of any temple in India. Beside this beautiful temple there are two other temples to see—the Viranarayana Temple and Channiga Raya Temple.

Channakeshava Temple

This temple is an excellent example of Hoysala architecture. It is very photogenic. It is named after the beautiful (*chenna*) long-haired (*keshava*) form of **Lord Krishna**. The 6-foot Deity is standing on a three-foot stand. The two upper hands hold a disc and conch, and the two lower ones hold a lotus and club. Construction of this temple was started in **1116 AD** and it took 103 years to complete. Built of grey-green chlorite, this temple is covered with intricate sculptures, which include many scenes from the *Ramayana* and *Mahabharata*.

To the left of the main shrine is a shrine dedicated to Kappe Chenniga Raya. There are two altars in this temple. The shrine facing east houses Kappe Chenniga Raya, and the one facing north houses Venugopala. Kappe Chenniga Raya received this name because a frog was found in a cavity in this Deity, after it was completed. This Deity was meant to be the main Deity of the temple, but because it had a cavity another Deity was brought from Bababuden Hill. There is another shrine dedicated to Soma-nayaki that has a tower (*vimana*) over it. To the west of the main temple is a shrine dedicated to Lord Vishnu called Viranarayana.

The temple walls are 443 by 396 feet. The temple itself is 178 feet by 156 feet. There is a five story *gopuram* over the main entrance. On either side of the main door are seven-foot sculptures of Jaya and Vijaya. A tall stone pillar in the temple courtyard is balanced only by its center of gravity. Inside the temple hall, to the left of the main entrance, is an intricately carved pillar with many small carvings of Lord Narasimha. This pillar used to rotate. There is one panel left blank on the pillar. It is said that the carver wanted to challenge anyone to carve a more beautiful image of Lord Narasimha than what was already on the pillar.

There are ten perforated screens on either side of the eastern entrance of the assembly hall. The screens to the right include the story of Vamana (Trivikrama) and Bali, the killing of Hiranyakasipu by Narasimha, and the killing of Kamsa by Krishna. The panels on the left hand side depict the churning of the ocean by the demigods and demons and Krishna's pastimes (fighting with the wrestler Canura, killing the elephant Kuvalayapida, and slaying Kamsa). Other scenes depicted are from the *Mahabharata* and *Ramayana.*

There is an inscription recording the date of erection of this temple in commemoration of **Vishnuvardhana's** victory over the Chola viceroy of Talkad. It is said that about this time, Vishnuvardhana was converted from Jainism into Vaishnavism by Sri **Ramanujacarya**. Behind the main temple is a temple dedicated to the goddess Lakshmi, the consort of Lord Channa Kesava

This temple is still used for worship, but non-Hindus can go inside. You can also take photos of the Deity. This temple is totally impressive.

Practicalities

The *Hotel Mayura Velapuri* is cheap and clean, but fairly basic, with rooms for Rs 60/80. It is about 200 metres from the temple. The *Hotel Vishnu Prasad* and *New Gayatri Hotel* on Main Rd are budget places.

Banks Hotel, on Temple Rd, is really basic, with rooms for Rs 35. The *Shri Praghavendra Tourist Home*, to the right of the temple, is even more basic, with rooms for Rs 25 with bath.

Belur is 222 km west of Bangalore,

16 km from Halebid, and 38 km from Hassan. It takes about 1½ hours to get to Belur by bus from Hassan.

From Mysore, the KSTDC **Belur, Halebid, and Sravanabelagola tour** runs daily in season (April to June and September to November) and three times a week the rest of the year. There are also tours run by private operators that leave almost every day. It is better to use the KSTDC tour if possible, as they use a luxury four seats across bus and the private companies use small, very bumpy (especially if you are in the back) minibuses. Both the private companies and the KSTDC tours pick you up at your hotel. This is a good way to see these places as they are difficult to reach by public transportation. There are also regular tours from Bangalore.

HALEBID

This town was the capital of the Hoysalas. It was known then as Dvarasamudra and was founded in the 11th century. Halebid was sacked by the Delhi Sultanate in 1311 and 1327. It is now a small village. There are several large tanks here.

Hoysaleswara Temple

The Hoysaleswara Temple, dedicated to Lord Siva, was started in the **mid-12th century** and is covered with some of the most intricately carved sculptures in India. Even after 87 years of building, it was never completed. This star-shaped temple is actually a pair of two identical temples with separate sanctuaries (altars) and *mandapams* (halls) right next to each other. One of the temples has active worship and the other does not. There are also two **Nandi bulls**. One of them is 16 feet long and is said to be the seventh largest in India.

The base of the temple has the emblem of lions and elephants carved around it, seemingly supporting the temple and signifying stability. There are 1,200 elephants carved on the outer walls and none of them are alike. There are carvings of Lord Krishna and Vishnu on this temple. There are scenes from the *Ramayana* and *Mahabharata* carved on the walls in intricate detail. There are about 20,000 sculptures on this temple. There is an interesting carving of **Lord Narayana** in the back right corner.

Other Places

The **Kedareswara Temple** nearby houses a Siva-linga named after Lord Siva who is worshiped at Kedarnath. Non-Hindus can enter the temple. There are a dozen or so other smaller temples in the area.

The **Archaeological Museum**, next to the temple, has a good collection of ancient sculptures.

Practicalities

Halebid is 216 km from Bangalore, 27 km north of Hassan, and 17 km east of Belur.

The *KSTDC Tourist Cottages and Bungalow,* by the Inspection Bungalow, is simple and clean.

Hassan

Population: 110,000, STD Code 08172

This is a good place to use as a base to see Sravanabelagola, Belur, and Halebid. The *Cauvery Tourist Centre* (8026), on Race Course Road, arranges tours of the local sights.

Where To Stay – Lower

The KSTDC *Tourist Lodge* has cottages and dormitories. *Vaishnavi Lodging* (67413), Harsha Mahal Rd, just north

of the bus station, is a cheap clean place with rooms for Rs 70/100. It has a vegetarian restaurant. The *Satyaprakash Lodge* (68521), Bus Stand Rd, is a good value. A basic room with a bathroom is Rs 40/60.

The *Mahaveer Hotel* (68885), B M Rd, near Narsimharaja Circle, has rooms with mosquito nets and a vegetarian restaurant.

Where To Stay – Middle & Higher

Hassan Ashok (68731, fax 67154), Bangalore-Mangalore Rd, in the center of town, has good facilities and is the best place in town. Rooms with a TV are Rs 800/950 and Rs 1050/1300 with A/C. The *Abiruchi Hotel*, BM Rd, west of City Circle, has a veg restaurant in it.

The *Hotel Amblee Palika* (66310), Race Course Rd, has good facilities and is a good value, but it fills up early. Comfortable rooms are Rs 225/275. It is clean and well-maintained. The *Kothari Residency* (67285), BM Rd, by the railway station, is a new place with spotless rooms.

Where To Eat

Vaishnavi Lodging, Harsha Mahal Rd, east of the bus station, has a good vegetarian restaurant. So does the *Hotel Mahaveer.*

Travel

Air The closest airport is in Bangalore.

Rail There are three trains a day going to Mysore (4½ hrs, 115 km). There are several trains a day to Mangalore. The night Mahalaxmi Express takes 6½ hours to get to Mangalore. To get to Bangalore you first take a train to Arsikere (1½ hrs) and from there get another train to Bangalore.

Bus There are many buses each day to Mysore, Bangalore, and Mangalore.

Arsikere

Population: 40,000, STD Code 08135

This is a good base to see the temples in Halebid and Belur and the Jain temples in Sravanabelagola.

In this town there is also a major Hoysala temple, which is on the main road.

Where To Stay and Eat

The *Geetha Lodge*, by the railway station, has clean rooms with bath for Rs 30/60 .

The *Janata Hotel*, opposite the bus station, has cheap rooms for Rs 30/50. The *Hotel Mayura*, by the bus station, has decent rooms for Rs 45/65. The *Janata Hotel* seems to have a vegetarian restaurant.

Travel

Train Arsikere is 156 km from Bangalore by train. From Arsikere to Hassan and **Mysore** there are three daily trains at 3.50 and 8 am and 2.15 pm. It takes 1½ hours to get to Hassan and 6 hours to get to Mysore.

The express trains between Bangalore and Bombay stop in Arsikere. For most trains to **Bombay**, you have to change trains at Miraj. The Udyan Express is the fastest train. There are no sleeping quotas for any of these trains. They have to be arranged at either Bangalore or Mysore. The Vasco Mail, departing at 9.10 pm, goes to Vasco da Gama in **Goa** (16 hrs).

To get to Hampi (Vijayanagar), you take a train to Hospet. You have to change trains at Hubli and maybe Gadag. You could also take a train to Harihar and from there get a bus to Hospet.

Bus There are frequent buses to Belur (1½ hr) and Halebid. A bus to Sringeri takes four hours.

North Karnataka

GOKARNA

Gokarna is about 200 km north of Mangalore and 56 km from Karwar on the seashore. According to the *Gokarna Purana,* "By mere entrance into this Ksetra, one becomes liberated from hundreds of sins, including even *brahma-hatya* (the killing of a *brahmin*)." Moreover, it is said that one becomes free from rebirth by just looking at the **Atma-linga**, by hearing the roar of the sea, or taking birth in Koti-tirtha.

Many long-term foreign visitors stay in Gokarna as there are nice secluded beaches here. A half hour walk from Gokarna is Om Beach, which is a good secluded beach popular with long-term travelers.

Mahaballeswara Temple

This Siva temple is said to be next in sanctity only to the Vishwanath Siva Temple in Varanasi. It is often called the Kashi of the South. Hindus come here to perform the death rites of their departed ancestors. Lord Caitanya came here and visited the temple of Lord Siva.

The story of this place is **Lord Rudra** (another name of Lord Siva) was sent to Patalaloka by Lord Brahma to undergo penance. He eventually came up through the ear of mother Earth and blessed her with the name of Gokarna—*go* (cow) and *karna* (ear). Thus, this place served Rudra as a womb. It is also known as *Rudra Yoni* and *Adi Gokarna*. As time passed, Rudra collected the essence (*sakti*) of all Brahma's creations as well as His own, and created a golden deer having four legs, three eyes, and three horns. Eventually the three horns (representing the three *guna-avataras*) were placed at Puskhar (Brahma), Saligram (Vishnu), and Gokarna (Siva). These places are known as Siddhi Ksetras.

Ravana desired to possess Siva's powerful horn-linga, also known as Pranalinga or Atma-linga. So Ravana performed great penance and received the *linga* in a box at Mount Kailasa. He then headed south with the powerful *linga* on the condition that wherever he placed the *linga* on the ground, it would remain permanently rooted.

Upon the request of the demigods, Lord Vishnu contrived a means to trick Ravana through Ganesh, disguised as a *brahmacari*. Eventually the Atma-linga was placed at Gokarna, rooted all the way through to Sapta Patala and became known as **Mahaballeswara** (*maha*— great and *bal*—strength).

Other Places in the Area

Koti-tirtha Kund is said to have been created by Garuda. There is a **Krishna Temple** here which is said to be where the Lord went to perform penance after killing Banasura. There is also a temple dedicated to **Sri Venkateswara** (Balaji).

Ram-tirtha, is said to be where Rama, Sita, and Laksman visited after leaving Lanka. Lord Rama and His brother Bharata are said to have performed penance here. There is a beautiful temple on the hill overlooking the sea at this spot.

Practicalities

There is a *Karnataka Tourism Tourist Home*, which is on a hill overlooking the sea.

There is a direct bus that leaves from Mangalore (252 km) at 1.30 pm that comes here without having to change buses. There is a bus from Bangalore at 9 pm and from Mysore at 6 am. There are regular buses to Goa from here.

HAMPI (VIJAYANAGAR)

Population: 1,000

Hampi was once the capital of the powerful Vijayanagar Empire, which for two centuries was one of the most powerful empires in Indian history. It is 360 km north of Bangalore. Vijayanagar means "the **city of victory**." It was considered at one time greater than Rome and "the best provided city in the world." At its height, half a million people lived in the city, and the Vijayanagar Empire had an army of over a million. Now only about 1000 people live here. It is a big tourist spot and is especially frequented by young travelers. If it weren't so difficult to get to, it would definitely be one of the top five most visited tourist sites in India, as it is an extremely interesting place. I never knew a place like it existed on earth.

The city dates back to 1343 when it was founded by two Telugu princes, Harihaka and Bukka. They were captured by the Delhi Sultanate and converted to become Muslims. Later they were sent back to rule the area, but they immediately broke away to set up their own kingdom. The city was destroyed in 1565 when the five Muslim kingdoms of the Deccan (South India) joined together to invade the city. The Vijayanagar emperor fled the city and over 100,000 people were massacred. Most of the city was destroyed at this time.

This place is said to be where Lord Rama first met Hanuman. It is also said to be the spot where Parvati (known locally as Hampi) met and married Lord Siva.

The ruins are spread over a 26 sq km area and there are over 500 monuments. For a one-day trip, you could see the Virupaksha complex in the morning and the royal area in the afternoon. If you go very quickly, you can see everything by walking in one day. The sights are spread out, and you should bring a good pair of walking shoes. Local transportation is negligible. You can hire a bicycle to get around.

A good place to start is the site museum, where you can purchase D Devakunjari's authoritative *Hampi* (1983). It has a good map and a good description of each monument.

The Virupaksha Temple and the Vitthala Temple are the two most interesting temples to see. The Vitthala Temple has 56 pillars that produce different musical tones when tapped.

It is a good idea to be especially careful of mosquitoes here, as Hampi is in a malaria zone.

Getting Around

Most people take a bus to **Hampi Bazaar** from Hospet, then walk to the Vitthala Temple. They then walk south to the Palace complex and then either walk back to Hampi Bazaar or to the village of Kamalapuram. You could also get off the bus at Kamalapuram and visit the site museum first, then the palace area, and then head north to Hampi Bazaar, and then walk to the Vitthala Temple. I would do it this way, if I were to do it a second time.

You can see all the sites in one day. Many people take a bus to Kamalapuram and hire a cycle. They ride to Hampi Bazaar, stopping at the Palace Complex on the way. They then walk along the river to the Vitthala Temple (leaving their bike at the bazaar). They then ride their bikes back to Kamalapuram, stopping at the shrine of Ugra Narasimha on the way.

Kishkindha

The town of Anegundi, about 5 km from Hampi, is situated on the north bank of the Tungabhadra River. Local people believe that this is the ancient place known as Kishkindha, where **Rama** met **Sugriva** and **Hanuman**. Also by Hampi is the **Rsimukha Mountain**, which is mentioned in the *Ramayana*.

The ancient place, Kishkindha, was ruled by the monkey-chiefs—two brothers, Sugriva and Vali. After a quarrel with Vali, Sugriva along with Hanuman were driven out. They then went to stay at **Matanga-parvata Hill**. You can get a good view of the surrounding area from the top of this hill. While searching for Sita, who had been kidnapped by Ravana, Rama and Laksman came south and met Sugriva and Hanuman. Rama killed Vali and restored the kingdom to Sugriva. While Hanuman went to search for Sita, it is said that Rama stayed at **Malyavanta Hill**, which is on the road to Kampili, about 6 km east of the Virupaksha Temple. There is a **Raghunath Temple** there with a large Deity of Rama.

On the way between the Virupaksha Temple and the Vitthala Temple there is a cave on the bank of the Tungabhadra where Sugriva is said to have hidden Sita's jewels for safety. There are marks and streaks on the rocks that are said to have been made by Sita's garments.

There is a huge mound of scorched ash in the nearby village of Nimbapuram that is said to be the cremated remains of Vali. The birthplace of Hanuman is said to be a little to the northwest.

Information

The Archaeological Survey of India,

in Kamalapuram, publishes a good booklet about Hampi, which has a map of the site. They also have a small museum. It is open from 10 am to 5 pm, except Friday. It sells the ASI booklet on Hampi.

There are **tourist information counters** at both Hospet at Rotary Circle (Taluk Office Circle) and Hampi Bazaar. The useful Michell and Fritz's *Hampi* is given away for free at the tourist office. They can arrange a tour or help you hire a private guide. The KSTDC tour lasts all day, but only the morning is spent at Hampi, which is not enough time to see everything. The tour guide spoke good English and was very informative. You could take the tour in the morning and stay at Hampi after the tour leaves.

There is a good bookshop at the end of Hampi Bazaar by the Virupaksha Temple. It has a good selection of books. You can get Longhurst's useful *Hampi Ruins* and R Sewell's *Forgotten Empire* here, if they are in print.

Royal Palace Complex and Archaeological Museum

The **Palace Complex** is in the extreme southern part of the ruins by Kamalapuram village. It is the first thing you see when you enter the Hampi area coming from Hospet.

The **Archaeological Museum** (daily except Fri, 10 am to 5 pm) is in the village of Kamalapuram. You turn right out of the bus station and then right again and walk about five minutes and the museum is on your left. In the museum are some interesting sculptures and a scale-model of the city.

To get from the museum to the Palace Complex you go back to the main road and take the turn marked "Hampi 4 km." After 200m you reach the inner city wall, which goes 32 km around the city.

You then reach the **Queen's Bath**, which is open to the sky and has a corridor around it with 24 different domes. To your right, further east, is a 14th century **Jain temple**. Beyond it is **Bhima's Gate**, which used to be one of the main entrances to the city. There are bas-reliefs of Bhima avenging the attempt to take off Draupadi's clothes, by killing Kichaka. Draupadi vowed not to put up her hair until Kichaka was killed. There is a panel showing her tying up her hair after Kichaka was killed.

Going northwest you come to **Mahanavami Dibba,** or the "House of Victory", built to celebrate a successful victory in Orissa. It is said that the king would give and receive gifts while sitting here. To the west of is what is believed to be the basement of the **King's Audience Hall**, which has 100 pillars. It was the highest building in the city.

North of here is the **Lotus Mahal**, part of the Zenana Enclosure, or women's quarters. The pavilion is open on the ground floor, and the upper floor has windows and a balcony. There is a moat around the building that is supposed to have cooled the place in the summer. It was built for Krishna Deva Raya's queen to relax in.

Beyond this is the **elephant stable,** which has ten-domed chambers. It is in the northern part of the complex. The elephants were chained by each foot and by their back and neck to beams in the ceiling.

As you walk west from here on the way to the main road to Hampi village, you come to the **Hazara Rama Temple** (one thousand Ramas). This temple is believed to have been a private temple for the royal family and was originally called Hajana Rama, which in Telugu means the palace temple. It was originally dedicated

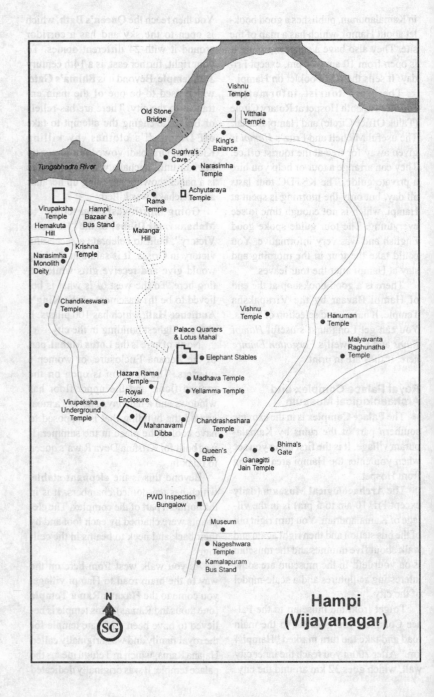

**Hampi
(Vijayanagar)**

to Sri Rama in the 15th century and contains many interesting sculptures of scenes from the *Ramayana* on the walls. It is no longer an active temple.

If you proceed west you then reach the Prasanna Virupaksha **Underground Temple**, which lies below ground level. The Underground Temple is on the main road. You turn right here and after about 1 km you reach Hemakuta Hill, next to Hampi Bazaar.

Palace Complex To Hampi Bazaar

Coming up the road from the south you come to two temples facing each other. In the **Virabhadra (1545) Siva Temple,** active worship still takes place. The other temple, **Chandikeswara**, is partly ruined.

By the Hemakuta Hill is a carving of a huge seated **Narasimha**, who is the incarnation of Lord Vishnu as half-man and half-lion, carved out of a single **7m (22 feet) high** boulder. Nearby this is **Badavi-linga,** a huge Siva-linga within a chamber that is fed from water from a nearby stream.

North of Narasimha is the **Krishna Temple**, built in 1513. This temple used to have a Deity of Balakrishna on the altar. There is a pillar in the temple that has a carving of all **ten avataras**.

On **Hemakuta Hill**, overlooking Hampi Bazaar, there is a group of pre-Vijayanagar temples, dating to around the 9th to 11th century. On the southeast slope of Hemakuta Hill are two large monolithic **Ganesh statues**. The smaller one is 2.5m (8 ft) high, and the larger one is about twice this size.

Virupaksha Temple or Pampapati

This temple is located at the end of Hampi Bazaar. It is dedicated to Virupaksha (Siva). Pampapati mean Siva as the husband of the local river goddess Pampa. It was mainly built in the 15th and 16th centuries. The Bristappaiah Gopuram, over the main gate, is 10 stories or 52m (165 feet) high. There is a large tank next to the temple. This temple is still used for worship. Worship has been going on here for at least 500 years. It is open from 6.30 am to 12.30 pm and 3 to 6.30 pm daily.

Hampi Bazaar to Vitthala Temple

From the Virupaksha Temple, you walk east the length of Hampi Bazaar. At the end of the bazaar, there is a path that goes to your left roughly following the riverbank.

There is a natural cavern marked with painted stripes where Sugriva is said to have hidden the jewels that **Sita** dropped after Ravana abducted her. The nearby pool is also supposed to have something to do with Sita.

On your way, you pass the deserted **Sule Bazaar**. At the southern end is the **Achyutaraya Temple**, which has musical pillars.

At the **Kodandaram** (bow-bearing Rama) **Temple** there are large Deities of Sita, Rama, and Laksman. It is opposite the bathing *ghat*. This is said to be the place where Rama crowned Sugriva as the monkey king. There is a temple cart in the Sri Ranganath Temple complex.

The **King's Balance** (Tula Purushadana) is a granite arch, 15 feet high and 12 feet across, which was built as a scale. On certain festival days the king would weigh himself and then distribute his weight in gold and jewels to the Brahmins. This is located close to the Vitthala Temple.

Vitthala Temple

This very ornate 16th century temple

is dedicated to Lord Vitthala, after the Deity in Pandharpur. It is on the southern bank of the Tungabhadra. It has musical pillars, which make different sounds when struck. On this temple there are sculptures of Varaha and other incarnations of Lord Vishnu. In the hall there are pillars decorated with various carved forms of Narasimha. It is considered to be the most outstanding temple in Hampi. It was never finished because the city was destroyed in 1565, before it could be completed. This temple is a *World Heritage Monument* (one of three in South India).

Other Places

The **Virabhadra Temple** is at Matanga Hill, where Lord Rama is said to have stayed. From on top of Matanga Hill you have a good view of the area.

In the village of **Anantashayangudi**, 1.6 km from Hospet on the way to Kamalapuram, there is a large Vishnu temple built around 1524. The main *vimana* (tower over the Deity) is about 24 meters high.

Places To Stay

There are only basic places to stay at in Hampi. To get a decent place you have to stay in Hospet. Many backpackers stay in Hampi for long periods, many of them going or coming from Goa. It has a good peaceful atmosphere. The decent places here are usually full, so it is usually best to stay in Hospet about 13 km away, unless you are going to be staying for more than a few days.

The *Shanthi Guest House* at Hampi Bazaar has very basic rooms for Rs 60. Also basic is the *Rahul Guest House,* which is on the left as you enter Hampi Bazaar from Hospet.

Besides these places, many people will offer you rooms in their homes. These are usually very basic and may be just a small room with a mattress on the floor and bathroom shared with the owner of the house. The Virupaksha Temple rents out a few unfurnished rooms and dormitory space.

The *Inspection Bungalow* (Power House Guest House) is at the southern part of the ruins at Kamalapuram, about 3 km from Hampi Bazaar.

Mayura Vijayanagara Hotel, at Tungabhadra Dam, 17 km from Hampi, is a good place, but is very inconveniently located.

Travel

Bus or Car There are buses every hour between 6 am and 8 pm that take about 30 minutes to go from Hospet to Hampi. They start at the bus stand in Hospet and can drop you off at Kamalapuram village or Hampi Bazaar, beside the river. You can also take a motor rickshaw or taxi. You can rent a taxi at the Malligi Tourist Home in Hospet.

HOSPET

Population: 140,000, STD Code 08394

Hospet is used by most people as a base to go see Hampi, the Vijayanagar ruins. There is really nothing to see or do in this town. It is a boring place. Hampi is 13 km away.

Information

The **KSTDC Tourist Office,** at Rotary Circle, behind the Hospet Bus Stand, is open 10 am to 1 pm and 2 to 5 pm daily. They have a free map of the Hampi site. At Malligi Tourist Home they can give you good information about the area. There is also a travel agent there who can help you with travel arrangements and getting a tour.

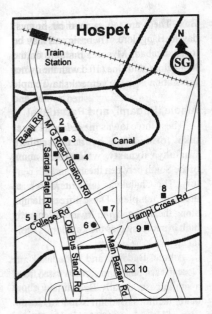

1	Shalini Lodging
2	Hotel Sandarshan
3	State Bank of India
4	Hotel Priyadarshini
5	Tourist Office
6	Bus Stand
7	Hotel Vishwa
8	Prabhu Hotel
9	Malligi Tourist Home
10	Post Office

Where To Stay

In December and January the middle class hotels will most likely be full later in the day. There are no high class hotels in Hospet, but the middle range hotels are good.

Where To Stay – Lower

The *Hotel Vishwa* (7171), Station Road, opposite the bus station, has good clean rooms with bath for Rs 70/125. It is a good value, but is often full. It can also be noisy, as it is on the main road. The *Hotel Sandarshan* (/8128), Station Rd between the bus and railway stations, has singles with common bath for Rs 40/60 and doubles for Rs 60/85.

The *Hotel Shalini Lodging*, MG Rd, is really cheap and has very basic rooms with common bath for Rs 40/60 and rooms with bath for Rs 50/85.

Where To Stay – Middle

The *Malligi Tourist Home* (08394/8101), Jambunath Rd off Hampi Road, by the canal, is a large, recommended place to stay. It has well-maintained rooms for Rs 150/200 to Rs 450. Deluxe A/C rooms are Rs 600/700. There are also suites for Rs 1500. The rooms have bath with hot water till 10 am. The service here is almost unbelievable, to the point of

The **State Bank of Mysore** by the Hospet tourist office changes travellers' checks. The **State Bank of India** changes only currency.

Tours

The KSTDC operates a daily tour from 9.30 am to 5.30 pm for Rs 60 to Hampi. In the morning it goes to the three main places in Hampi—Hampi Bazaar, the Royal Enclosure and Zenana Enclosure, and the Vitthala Temple. In the afternoon it goes to the Tungabhadra Dam. They bring you around to all the sites at a quick pace.

You may like to leave the tour at the Vitthala Temple and stay in Hampi instead of going to the Tungabhadra Dam. You can book this tour at the tourist office, Malligi Tourist Home, or the Hotel Priyardarshini.

The tourist guide speaks in both English and Hindi, and he is actually very informative.

overdoing it. They may ask if you need any help ten times in one day. Despite its size, there is a good chance it will be full.

The *Hotel Priyardarshini* (08394/ 8838), 45 Station Road, about a five minute walk from the bus stand, has singles for Rs 100, doubles for Rs 140 to Rs 250, and A/C rooms Rs 325/375. It is a recommended nice clean place. It has a 24 hour checkout, and the rooms have hot water.

Where To Eat

The *Shanthi Restaurant* is at the Hotel Vishwa, across from the bus stand. The *Amruth Garden* at the Malligi Tourist Home is a good place.

The *Hotel Priyadarshini* has a good restaurant with good service. It is most likely the best place in town.

Travel

Air The closest airport is located at Bellary (74 km east).

Train The closest train station to Hampi is in Hospet. The Hampi Express #6591 leaves **Bangalore** at 9.30 pm and arrives in Hospet at 6.20 am. The same train leaves Hospet at 9 pm daily and reaches Bangalore at 8 am the next morning. There are no other direct trains to Bangalore, but there are passenger trains, which require a change at either Guntakal or Gadag.

The Guntakal Vasco Express to **Goa** departs at 5.30 am. There is a direct train to **Badami** at 12.30 pm that takes six hours.

To get to Secunderabad (**Hyderabad**) takes a total of at least 14½ hours. First you take the daily Tungabhadra Exp #7508 (8.15 pm, 2¾ hr) to Guntakal and then wait 1½ hours. You then get the Venkatadri Exp #7598 at 12.30 am (9 hr).

Bus There are ten express buses each day to Bangalore. There are also buses to Hyderabad, Mysore, Badami (6 hr), Mangalore, and Goa (10 hard hours). The bus station is in the center of town.

Aihole, Badami, and Pattadakal

These three towns in northern Karnataka formed the heartland of the **Chalukya dynasty**, which ruled much of the South between the 4th and 8th century. The Chalukyas built literally hundreds of temples. These three villages along the *Malaprabha River valley* were built in succession as the kingdom's capital city.

Aihole, Badami, and Pattadakal are close to each other and can be visited from a single base, usually Badami, as it has better facilities. Badami is 189 km northwest of Hampi and 499 km north of Bangalore. Badami is 200 km due east of Belgaum in northern Karnataka.

Aihole was built around 450 AD. It was originally called "Arya-Hole" or "City of the Aryans." Badami, 46 km away, was built next, in about 550 AD. Pattadakal, 29 km from Badami and 17 km from Aihole, was founded in the 8th century. The Chalukya dynasty was destroyed in 753 AD, when they were defeated by the Rashtrakutas.

Badami is a town of 16,000, Aihole has about 3000, and Pattadakal has even less.

Getting Around

If you only go to the major places, you can go to all three towns in one day. You can get one of the regular local buses run by the KSRTC between all three towns. Both Aihole and Pattadakal are small enough to just walk around and see everything.

There are no organized tours, but you

can get information at the **tourist offices** at the Hotel Mayura Chalukya in Badami or the Tourist Home in Aihole. They can also arrange a trained guide.

BADAMI
Population: 17,000, STD Code 08357

This town used to be called Vatapi and was the capital of the early Chalukya rulers in the 6th and 8th centuries. The Agastya-tirtha tank, an artificial lake east of the village, was built in the fifth century. The rock-cut temples are famous. *The Cave Temples of Badami* is a good book to get for detailed information about the caves. You can get this at the first cave temple. Badami is a convenient base to use to visit Aihole and Pattadakal.

Five km from Badami is **Mahakuta**, which has two dozen Chalukyan shrines dedicated to Lord Siva. These temples, dating from the late 7th century, have both northern and southern influences in their design. The *Mahakuteswara and Mallikarjuna Temples* are especially interesting. The *Naganatha Temple* (2 km away) is also worth a visit.

You can **hire a car** for Rs 500 a day at the Hotel Mayura Chalukya to go to Pattadakal and Aihole.

There are many monkeys around the sites in Badami, and they can become aggressive if they see food.

Cave Temples
There are five elaborately carved cave temples, one of which is natural. You have to walk up about 200 steps to get to them, because they are part-way up a cliff.

Cave 1, late 6th century, is dedicated to Lord Siva and has an excellent sculpture of Nataraja, dancing Siva. There are also sculptures of Harihara, Lakshmi, Vishnu, and Ganesh.

Cave 2, late 6th century, is dedicated to Lord Vishnu. There are sculptures of Varaha, Vamana, Lord Krishna, and Vishnu riding on Garuda.

Cave 3, 578 AD, has sculptures of Vishnu, Narasimha, Harihara, Trivikrama, and many other scenes. Some of the sculptures are about 10 feet high.

Cave 4 is a Jain cave and has a statue of seated Parsvanath. **Cave 5**, which is a Buddhist temple, is a natural cave. It is near the Agasthya Lake.

Other Places
You have to go up a long stairway to get to the **north fort**, where there is another set of temples. There is a cannon at the south end of the fort, put there by Tipu Sultan. You can also get a good view of Badami from here. There is a temple called **Malegitti Shivalaya** (late 7th century), which is worth seeing. There are statues of Vishnu and Siva on the outer walls of this temple.

The **Bhutanath Temples** are several interesting temples near the eastern bank of the ancient **Agastya-tirtha Tank** (Bhutanath Lake). Behind the Bhutanath group of temples is a cavern with a sculpture of Lord Vishnu sleeping on Ananta and attended by Lakshmi.

Within the town is the **Jambulinga Temple** (699 AD), which was originally dedicated to Siva, Vishnu, and Brahma. The **Yellamma Temple** (11th century) is the best late Chalukya temple in the town.

There is an **Archaeological Museum** that has a collection of sculptures from Badami, Aihole, Pattadakal, and other sights in the area. It is open daily from 10 am to 5 pm, except Friday.

Where To Stay
The clean but basic *PWD Inspection*

Bungalow is a good choice if you can get in.

Hotel Mayura Chalukya, Ramdurg Rd, is one of the best places to stay in the area, but it is in need of repair. It is about a half km from the center of town. It has hot water, a quiet garden, and clean rooms. The rooms are Rs 120/145.

Your next choice is the *Sri Mahkuteswar Lodge*. The *Hotel Makambi* and *Hotel Chalukya* are on the main street. The *Shri Laxmi Vilas* has very basic double rooms for about Rs 100. The *Hotel Satkar* is clean and has hot water in the morning. The rooms are Rs 150. The best place in town is the new *Badami Court Hotel*, Station Rd, 2 km from town, which has comfortable mid-range rooms.

The closest town with good accommodation is Bagalkot, about 70 km away. The *Laxmi Vilas* has good veg meals.

Travel

Air The closest airport is at Belgaum, about 200 km west of Badami. This is about a five-hour trip by road.

Train Badami is on the Solapur-Hubli metre gauge line. The only trains to stop here are very slow, 2nd class only, passenger trains. There are six trains daily from Badami to Bijapur. Three trains terminate at Bijapur and the other three continue on to Solapur. To go north on a long-distance trip it is best to get a train to Solapur, which is on a broad-gauge line. From Solapur you can get trains to Vijayawada, Hyderabad, and Bombay.

If you are going south, you can get a passenger train to the railway junctions of Gadag, Guntakal, or Hubli. Hubli is on the broad-gauge line. There are five trains going south daily. There is a direct passenger train daily to Hospet and Hampi (6 hr) via Gadag. It is not on the station timetable, so you have to ask about this train.

Bus There are buses to and from Hospet (7 hr), Bangalore, Bagalkot, Belgaum, and Bijapur as well as frequent buses to Aihole and Pattadakal.

AIHOLE

Population: 3000

Aihole has around 100 temples, 50 within the city limit and 50 outside. Thirty temples are in a single enclosure. The temples here were built between the 6th to 12th centuries by the Chalukya and Rashtrakuta kings.

Most of the temples were originally dedicated to Lord Vishnu, but were later converted into Siva temples. Aihole used to be a big commercial center, but now it is just a small town with a lot of old temples to see. Aihole is 131 km north of Hampi on the banks of the Malaprabha River.

You can see the remains of the massive city walls and gates. Half the temples are within the fort, and the other half outside the fort.

Central Complex

The central complex is near the bus stand and is enclosed by a wall. The main temple here is the Durga Temple. The temples are open from sunrise to sunset. Flash photography is prohibited.

Within the town there are many temples, including the **Lad Khan Temple,** which was originally a marriage *mandapa* (hall) and a royal assembly hall built in the 7th century. It got this name because a Muslim prince, Lad Khan, used it as his home. A stone ladder leads to a shrine with sculptures of Vishnu, Siva, and Surya on its walls.

The **Durga Temple**, which is dedicated to Lord Vishnu, dates back to the late 7th century. It gets its name from the Kannada word "*durgadagadi*" or "temple near the fort." The temple has many excellent sculptures, including Narasimha, Vishnu with Garuda, Harihara, and Varaha. It has relief panels depicting scenes from the *Ramayana* and *Mahabharata*.

The Gaudar Gudi, Chakra Gudi, Kunti Group, Hucchappayya Matha, and Hallibasappa are all within the town and date from the 7th to 10th century.

Northeast Temples

As you leave the enclosed area of temples and you turn right, you come to the Chikki Temple, which has particularly well-carved pillars.

If you turn left from the main entrance, you come to the **Ravana Phadi Temple** (300m from the village), which is a 6th century cave temple located southeast of the Huchimalli Temple. It has some exceptionally fine sculptures including Nataraja, or dancing Siva, Ganesh, and Ardhanari. It also has a highly decorated ceiling.

The Huchimalli Gudi and Mallikarjuna Group, dating from the 7th to 11th century, are located northeast of town.

South Temples

There is an ancient **Jain cave** and the **Hucchappayya Gudi Temple** (7th century) south of town. On the hill in the southeast part of town is the partly rock-cut two-story **Buddhist Temple** and the **Meguti Jain Temple,** both dating from the 7th century.

There is an **Archaeological Museum** with a collection of 7th and 8th century Chalukyan sculptures. It is open daily 10 am to 5 pm except Fridays.

Practicalities

The *Glorious Aihole* booklet has a map showing the 24 main sights.

The KSTDC *Tourist Rest House* is a small, clean, passable place to stay and eat with rooms with bath for Rs 35/50.

There are regular buses to Badami (2 hr) and Pattadakal (30 min). The closest railway stations are in Badami or Bagalkot, which are on the Hubli-Solapur metre-gauge line.

PATTADAKAL
Population: 2000

Pattadakal was the second capital of the Chalukyan kings, between the 7th and 8th centuries. This is where the king was crowned. It is a small village 17 km from Aihole.

It has about ten temples that represent the ultimate in the early Chalukyan architecture. The Virupaksha, Papanath, and Mallikarjuna Temples were intricately carved in the 7th and 8th century. For construction of these temples they used sandstone that glows with a pink tinge in the sunset. The **Sanghameswara Temple** is the oldest temple. The **Papanath Temple** is a northern style temple with impressive carvings on the ceiling and pillars. This is a unique town due to the temples here that are built using the architecture of both North and South India.

The *Malprabha River* flows next to the town. There are no facilities in this town but a few tea stalls and coconut stands. Badami is an hour and a half away and Aihole is 30 minutes.

Temple Area

It contains six important temples and a small **sculpture gallery** that is open from 10 am to 5 pm on weekdays.

Virupaksa, the largest of the temples,

has sculptures depicting scenes from the *Ramayana* and *Mahabharata*. In front of the Virupaksha Temple there is a 2.6m high Nandi bull made of a deep green stone which is covered by a red cape. The interior pillars of the Virupaksha Temple are carved with scenes from the *Ramayana* and the *Mahabharata*. It is the largest temple in the village. This temple was built by Queen Lokamahadevi, the wife of King Vikramaditya II. There is a sculpture in this temple that looks like a buffalo on one side and an elephant on the other.

The **Mallikarjuna Temple** is small. It was built by King Vikramaditya II's second wife, Trailokyamahadevi. This temple has pillars with carvings depicting Lord Krishna's birth and activities.

There are other smaller 8th century temples, including the Kadasiddheswara, Jambulinga, Galaganath, Sangameswara, and Kashivishvanath Temples.

SRINGERI

Sringeri was the headquarters of Sri Sankaracarya. He established four main maths—in Joshimath, Dwarka, Puri and Sringeri. He spent 12 years of his 32 year life here. Lord Caitanya came here. This small town is near the source of the Tunga River.

Sringeri Math

Sankaracarya established the **Sri Sharada Devi Temple**. The deity installed in the temple stands on a Sri Chankra (yantra). Installed here is one of the **Sphatika-lingas** that was said to have been given to Sankaracarya by Lord Siva in the Himalayas. This temple is on the bank of the Tunga River.

There is also the exquisitely sculptured **Vidyasankara Temple** (1338) which houses the Vidyatirtha-linga. This temple combines both Dravidian and Hoysala temple architecture. There are **12 zodiac pillars** that are arranged so that the rays of the sun fall on the pillar corresponding to the month. In front of the temple are stone lions with stone balls inside their mouths that can be rotated.

Other Places

The **Janardana Temple** (Vishnu) was first built in the 9th century. There are four guardian Deities of Sringeri—Kali Kamba, Hanuman, Durga, and Kala Bhairava. There is an ancient Brahma temple here.

Practicalities

You can get a simple room for Rs 20 by going to the office in the temple. There is also a government guest house.

Sringeri is 85 km east of Udupi and northeast of Mangalore. It is 335 km from Bangalore. There are buses going to and from Mysore, Hassan, and Bangalore.

MANGALORE

Population: 450,000, STD Code 0824

There is not much to see in Mangalore. If you are going to one of the places in the area of Mangalore there is a good chance that you will have to stop here. Udupi is 60 km north of Mangalore. At Karkala, 53 km away, are several temples and a 13 metre high statue of Lord Bahu Bali, completed in 1432. At Moodabidri, 35 km away, there are 18 Jain temples. The oldest of them, the Chandranath Temple, has thousands of intricately carved pillars. Dharmasthala, 74 northeast of Mangalore, has some interesting Jain temples, including the Manjunath Temple.

Mangalore is on the coast about 990 km south of Bombay, almost due west of Bangalore.

Information

The **tourist office** (21692) is at the Hotel Indraprastha, in the center of town. KSRTC, the state bus company, has an office in the same hotel.

You can **change money** at the State Bank of India, KS Rao Rd.

Sri Manjunath Temple

This important Siva temple (1068 A D) is located at Kadri, about 3 km from the city center. There are Buddhist sculptures in the temple and a 5 foot high bronze image of Lokeswara. This temple is surrounded by attractive gardens.

Where To Stay – Lower

Most of the hotels are along KS Rao Rd in the center of town.

The *Hotel Vishnu Bhavan* (24622) has rooms with bath for Rs 85. The rooms in the front are noisy and very basic. The *Panchami Boarding & Lodging*, right next to the bus station, has rooms for Rs 80/120. It has hot water in the early morning.

The *Hotel Roopa* (21271), Light House Hill Rd, has rooms for Rs 70/100 and Rs 140/170 with A/C. The *Hotel Vasanth* (22311), KS Rao Rd, has rooms for Rs 75/95. The *Hotel KSTDC Mayura Nethravathi* (411-192), near the bus stand, has rooms with hot water and views of the ocean for Rs 90/110. The rooms are a good value.

Where To Stay – Middle

The *Hotel Navaratna Palace* (33781), KS Rao Rd, is newly built and has comfortable rooms for Rs 125/175 and Rs 250/275 with A/C. It is a good value and is recommended.

The *Indraprastha* (33756), Light House Hill Rd, has big rooms with bath and hot water for Rs 85/125. The rooms

in the back are quiet.

Where To Stay – Higher

The *Summer Sands Beach Resort* (0832/467-690), in Ullal, 10 km out of town, is a recommended place to stay with rooms for Rs 250/350 and Rs 380/500 with A/C. It has a swimming pool and some bungalows with two bedrooms, a living room, porch, and kitchen. Bus #44A takes you there.

The Poonja International (440-171, Fax 441-101), KS Rao Rd, is a new place with central A/C. It has clean rooms for Rs 250/350 and Rs 500/600 with A/C. The rooms here are a good value.

The three-star *Moti Mahal Hotel* (441-411), Falnir Road, has a swimming pool. Rooms are Rs 325/350 and Rs 350/425 with A/C. They also have suites. It is a recommended place. It has a veg restaurant. The *Hotel Srinivas* (440-061), GHS Rd, is about the same and has rooms for Rs 170/200 and Rs 275/325 with A/C.

The *Manjarun* (425-525), Bunder (Old Port) Rd, 2 km from the railway station, is a centrally air-conditioned place with all the facilities. Rooms are Rs 1050/1200, some with a seaview.

Where To Eat

Palimar, at the Navaratma Palace on KS Rao Rd, has both good food and good service. The *Kamadhenu Vegetarian Restaurant* is in the Roopa Hotel.

The *Taj Mahal* and *Navaratna* by the bus stand serve vegetarian food. The Moti Mahal, Falnir Rd, has the *Madhuvan* veg restaurant.

The popular *Dhanyavad*, at the intersection of Lighthouse Hill Rd and K S Rao Rd has cheap meals.

Travel

Air There are Indian Airlines flights

daily to Bombay and four flights a week to Bangalore and Madras. The Air Indian (414-300) and Indian Airlines offices are on Hathill Rd in the Lalbagh area four km out of town. Indian Airlines also has an office in the Hotel Moti Mahal. The bus to the airport leaves for the 20 km trip from here. The few flights a day are usually overbooked.

Train   There are daily trains to Hassan, including the Mahalaxmi Express, which departs at 11 pm, and a passenger train, which leaves at 6:10 pm and takes 6½ hours. It takes 18 hours to get to Madras on the Mangalore Mail #6002 and 17 hours to get to Thiruvananthapuram (Trivandrum). The twice-weekly fast passenger train to Bangalore takes 16 hours.

Bus   The bus station is three km north of the city center. The buses heading north and east are usually much quicker than the train. The buses are three different categories: red – ordinary; blue – semi-deluxe; and green – super-deluxe. There are daily buses to Hospet, Mysore, Bangalore, Hassan, Madras, Goa, and Bombay.

UDUPI

Population: 120,000, STD Code 08252

Udupi is located about 60 km north of Mangalore on the seashore. Madhvacarya took his birth in a small village near Udupi around the year 1200 and established the famous Udupi Krishna Temple here. There are several places in the Udupi area to see in reference to his pastimes. Lord Caitanya came here.

Information

You can get a small book called *Udupi, An Introduction* that gives a detailed explanation of the spiritual places here.

You can **change money** at the State Bank of India, opposite Affan Complex.

The **museum** at MGM College, 5 km from Udupi, has a collection of bronze sculptures.

Sri Krishna Mutt

The Lord Krishna Deity here called **Bala Krishna** is extremely beautiful. The temple has an energy charged atmosphere and is one of the most important Krishna temples in India.

Sri Krishna Matha was founded by **Srila Madhvacarya** (AD 1238-1317). There is a **lamp** beside the Deity of Sri Krishna that is supposed to have been lit by Madhvacarya himself and has never gone out since.

In order to display different pastimes for His devotees, Udupi Krishna has over 50 different dresses such as Cowherd Boy, Mohini Murti, Lakshmi and Durga. He was recently offered a **diamond crown** worth over one crore rupees ($350,000). Sometimes Krishna is dressed with a diamond dress.

You look at the Deity through a window called "**Navagraha**". You usually have about 10 to 20 seconds to see the Deity before you get pushed on. There are stands to purchase *maha-prasada* and beautiful pictures of the Deities.

The temple is small with black granite walls, sculptures, and silver carvings around the temple. Lord Krishna was originally installed facing east, but He turned west to see His devotee, **Kanaka das**, who wasn't allowed inside the temple. One can have *darsana* from outside the temple from the same spot where Kanaka did, through the crack/window on the western wall. Garuda and Hanuman reside on each side of the temple's interior. They were brought from Ayodhya and installed by Vadiraja Tirtha.

Delicious *prasada* is served twice daily. If you want to take temple *prasada,* you can make arrangements with the priest. There is worship (*puja*) in the temple from 5.30 am to 8.45 pm.

Deity's Story

The Udupi Krishna Deity was made from a *shalagram-shila* by Lord Krishna Himself, with the help of Visvakarma. It is said that the Deity was worshiped by Rukmini in Dwarka. He is Lord Krishna in His child form. The Deity was worshiped by and eventually given to Arjuna, who hid the Deity. After a lapse of time, the Deity became covered in *gopi-candana* (clay).

A sailor loaded the lump of *candana* in his boat as a ballast (counterbalance). Upon reaching Vadabhandeswara (5 km west of Udupi on the coast), the ship got into trouble and was almost totally lost. Sri Madhvacarya made some signals by waving his cloth so the boat could approach the shore, and it was saved. The ship captain came to Madhvacarya and requested him to take anything as a gift, as he was sure that by the grace of this holy man his ship was saved. Madhvacarya requested the *gopi-candana* as a gift. Upon breaking the clay, Madhvacarya discovered the beautiful *murti* of Krishna. Madhvacarya carried the Deity to Udupi and commenced worship, which has been carried on since that time by his disciples.

Cart Procession

The small processional Deities are taken out nearly every night on a parade around Car Street. The procession is replete with a decorated elephant and a musical band, and they stop at intervals along the route while the Lord is entertained by fireworks or worshiped by offerings from His many devotees. The parades start around **8 pm** and are usually over by 9.30.

The cart normally used is about 50 feet tall. The Cart festival goes around the small square in front of the temple known as **Car Street**. According to the significance of the festival being observed, sometimes one cart and sometimes three carts are used. A fourth cart, completely covered in silver, is used for special festivals. When I was there the Deities were taken out in the extremely beautiful golden cart because someone had given a large donation. I was told that this cart is used only two or three times a year.

Madhva Sarovar

The holy bathing tank called Madhva Sarovar is said to be fed by the Ganges every 12 years. It is located just to the right of the main entrance of the temple. Madhvacarya is said to have washed the Deity in this tank before the installation. Water from this tank is used for the daily worship.

Ananthasana Temple

The Ananthasana (Ananteswara) Temple, located in the middle of the temple square, is a temple dedicated to Lord Siva and Lord Vishnu. Lord Vishnu and His personal expansion Ananta Sesa are said to reside within the *linga. Ananta* means the serpent Ananta Sesa. One who is seated on Ananta is known as Ananthasana. Because He is the Lord of Ananta, He is known as Ananteswara.

The place where Sri Madhvacarya left his body while speaking to his disciples is north of the central *mandapam* (hall), just after you enter the sanctum.

Candramauleswara Temple

Sri Candramauleswara Temple is a

Lord Siva temple directly across the street from the Krishna Temple. Lord Siva has this name because he carries a crescent moon (*candra*) on his head. The temple of Candramauleswara faces the Sri Ananthasana Temple. Both are ancient temples.

Madhvacarya (1239-1319)

Madhvacarya was born in 1239 at Pajakaksetra of a pious Sivalli Brahmin couple, Madhyageha Bhatta and his wife, Vedavati. His parents named him Vasudeva, but he later received the name Madhva when he took *sannyasa* from Achyuta Preksha Tirtha. He was also known as Ananda Tirtha, Sarvajna, and Purnaprajna. Madhvacarya founded the Dwaita system of philosophy and preached it vigorously across the country.

He was a Vaishnava, or a devotee of Lord Vishnu. The basic tenet of Madhvacarya's philosophy is that Vishnu is supreme, omniscient, and infinite. He taught that there is the Supreme Lord, the individual souls, and the material world, and that they are all different. He taught that the individual souls are superior to matter and are distinct from God, being His servants.

He possessed an unusually strong body and extraordinary intellectual power. He went to almost every sacred place of pilgrimage, where he defeated scholars of rival schools and won them over to his faith.

He wrote 37 works, collectively known as the *Sarvamula-granthas*. Madhvacarya installed the Deity of Sri Krishna in the Sri Krishna Matha in Udupi. He gave *sannyasa* to eight of his disciples who were the first heads of the eight Maths located on Car Street. He disappeared from this world while preaching to his disciples in the Sri Ananthasana Temple.

Madhvacarya Pastimes Places

At **Vadabhandeswara**, six km west of Udupi, there is a Balarama temple where Madhvacarya received the Deity of Sri Krishna covered in *gopi-candana*.

Danda Teetha, 11 km south of Udupi, is a tank built by Madhvacarya. He made water from this tank flow into the field of his boyhood teacher by cutting a ditch with his *danda*. A *danda* is the staff (stick) carried by a *sannyasi*. There is a Krishna temple here.

Nadyantadi, halfway between Udupi and Subrahmanya, is where Madhvacarya would stay on the way from Udupi to Subrahmanya. There is a Math here that marks the place where He would take rest and two bathing tanks called Gada Tirtha and Gautama Kund. This place is between Mangalore and Charmadi. To get here you first go to Kavalkatte, and then you have to walk a few km to this place.

At **Kanva Tirtha** (now called Manjeswara), near Mangalore, is where Madhvacarya spent four months during *caturmasya*. Under a pipal tree here, he gave *sannyasa* to eight of his disciples who became the original pontiffs (leaders) of the eight Udupi Maths. There is a temple here.

At **Kadtila** (Sethu Tila), Madhvacarya buried his *Sarvamula-granthas*, which were written on copper plates. He then installed the Deity of Gopala Krishna over them.

Eight Sannyasi's Maths

Madhvacarya appointed eight *sannyasi* disciples to take charge of the worship of the Sri Krishna Matha. The responsibility of the worship is rotated in two year periods, called **paryaya**, among the eight *sannyasis* in disciplic succession from the original eight disciples of Madhvacarya. The **Paryaya Mahotsava** or "Handing Over Festival" occurs in even-numbered years on January 17 or 18. The incoming *sannyasi* goes on pilgrimage two months before Paryaya and comes back about a week beforehand. He is greeted on the outskirts of the city and brought in a procession to Car Street. He then pays respects to the Deities of Chandreswara, Ananthasana, and Sri Krishna.

The eight main *mathas* founded by Madhvacarya's disciples are located on Car Street, the road that circles the Candramauleswara and Ananthasan Temples and runs past the main entrance to Sri Krishna Matha. The eight *mathas* and the Deities worshiped in the *mathas* are the Sode (Bhu-varaha), Puthige (Vitthala Krishna), and Adamar (Kaliya Mardana Krishna) on the southern side; the Pejawar (Vitthala Krishna) and Palimar (Sri Rama, who was presented by Sri Madhvacarya to the first leader of the *matha*) on the western; the Krishnapur (Kaliya Mardana Krishna) and Shirur (Vitthala Krishna) on the northern; and the Kaniyur (Narasimha) on the eastern.

Festivals

The main festival of the year is the **Saptotsava** (seven *utsavas*) festival celebrated around the middle of January. On the first day of the festival the Deity of Sri Krishna is taken out on a boat in Madhva Sarovara. This is known as **Teppotsava**, or the float festival. Then there is a huge chariot festival. For the first five days of the festival two chariots are drawn each day.

On the sixth day, three chariots are drawn around the square. This is the day that Madhvacarya installed the Deity of Sri Krishna. On the biggest chariot (Brahma Ratha) is the Deity of Sri Krishna, and on the smallest chariot is the Deity of Mukyaprana. On the medium chariot are the deities of Anantheswara and Chandreswara. This is the only day of the year that three chariots are taken around the square. On the seventh day, the Deity is taken to Madhva Sarovar and given a bath. Everyone else takes bath at the same time, as it is considered especially auspicious.

Sri Madhva Navami (Feb) celebrates the disappearance day of Madhvacarya. There is a special *puja* (worship) done at the spot where he left his body in the Ananthasana Temple.

Deities of Ramacandra and Sita

During Lord Ramacandra's time, there was a Brahmin who took a vow to eat only after he saw Lord Ramacandra. Sometimes, due to business, Lord Ramacandra left His capital for a full week and could not be seen during that time. Because of his vow, the Brahmin would not drink even a drop of water during that time. Later, after eight or nine days, when the Brahmin could see Lord Ramacandra again, he would break his fast. Upon observing the Brahmin's rigid vow Lord Ramacandra told Laksmana, His younger brother, to give Sita-Rama Deities to the Brahmin. The Brahmin faithfully worshiped the Deities as long as he lived.

Before he died, the Brahmin gave the Deities to Hanuman, who for many years hung Them around his neck and served Them with devotion. After many years, when Hanuman departed, he gave the Deities to Bhima, one of the Pandava brothers, and Bhima brought Them to his palace, where he worshiped them. The last king of the Pandavas, Ksemakanta, worshiped the Deities in that palace.

The Deities eventually were worshiped by the kings of Orissa. One of the *acaryas*, Narahari Tirtha, who was in the disciplic succession of Madhvacarya, was given these Deities by the King of Orissa.

These particular Deities of Rama and Sita have been worshiped from the time of King Iksvaku. They were worshiped even before the appearance of Lord Ramacandra.

It is said that just three months before his disappearance, Sri Madhvacarya received these Deities and installed them in the Udupi Temple. Since then the Deities have been worshiped by the Madhvacarya-sampradaya at one of their monasteries.

Where To Stay – Lower

There are several simple dharamshalas here. There is one located across the street from the Woodlands Restaurant, about a five minute walk from Car Street.

The *Bhasker Vihar* is a simple place near the bus stand with rooms for Rs 65/90. *The Hotel Shaan* is a good value with rooms for Rs 70/90.

The *Tourist Hotel*, across the street, is similar with rooms for Rs 100. The *Kalpana Lodge,* by the bus stand, is a real dump, but rooms are only Rs 45/60. *The Hotel Shaan* is a good value with rooms for Rs 70/90.

Middle

Hotel Janardana (23880), conveniently located by the bus stand, is a good place with rooms for Rs 110/150 and Rs 275 with A/C and a TV.

The *Shri Rama Krishna Hotel* (23-189), about a five-minute walk from the temple, is a good value with rooms for Rs 110/150 and Rs 300 with A/C. It is a recommended place.

The *Hotel Mallika* (21121), KM Marg, has rooms for Rs 125 up to Rs 350 with A/C.

The *Kediyoor* (22381), about a five-minute walk from the bus stand, is the best place in town with clean modern rooms for Rs 150/175 and Rs 350/450 with A/C. Also good is the *Sharada International* (22912), which is outside the center of town, three km from the bus stand. It has rooms for Rs 350 up to Rs 650.

Where To Eat

The *Woodlands Restaurant*, about a three-minute walk from the Sri Krishna Temple, is what I consider to be one of the best restaurants in India. There is a Brahmin cook, and it is run by an Udupi Brahmin family, who own the Woodlands chain of restaurants all over India and overseas. The *thali* is both an excellent value and excellent tasting. The vegetable pulao, Vegetable Imperial, and macaroni are all great. The owner personally made sure everything was done perfectly. It is a highly suggested place.

Dwarike, Car St, facing Temple Square, is a good place that serves Western and South Indian food and ice cream. There is a vegetarian restaurant at the *Kediyoor Hotel*.

Travel

Air and Train The closest airport is in Mangalore, 60 km south. You can get a train to Mangalore, but not to anywhere else.

Bus Because Udupi does not have a long distance train station, it has a busy bus station. You can get an all-night luxury bus to **Bangalore** (10 hr overnight) and many other destinations in the South. There are about six buses to **Mysore** and 12 to **Bangalore**, not counting the luxury buses.

There are also two buses to **Panaji** in Goa. Buses to **Mangalore** (1½ hr) depart every 15 minutes. There are four daily buses to **Bombay** (11 am, 3.20 pm, 5 pm, 7.20 pm). There are frequent buses to **Dharmasthala** and **Hubli**.

Pajakaksetra

Sri Madhvacarya took birth here in 1239. It is 12 km southeast of Udupi. There is a large *shalagram-murti* of Madhvacarya, which is covered with a silver face and has copper feet. Nearby is the house temple where he grew up called **Moodu Matha**. Inside the house are his worshipable Deities, Lakshmi-Narasimha and Sri Anantapadmanabha, on a golden altar. Next to his home is a tank called **Vasudeva Teertha**, which was built by Madhvacarya for his mother.

There is a spot here that bears the marks of Madhvacarya's feet, when he jumped from the Durga Hill when his mother called him.

You can get a bus to here from the City bus stand, but it is better to take an auto-rickshaw or taxi as you may have to take two buses and wait a long time. It takes about a half hour to see everything here. About one km away on top of Kunjaru Hill is a famous **Durga Temple**. Pajakaksetra is a very small village with no facilities in it.

Sri Mookambika (Sri Kollur)

This small town is about a four hour bus ride northeast of Mangalore. This place is an ancient sacred place. The sacred **Sauparnika River** flows through this town.

There is a temple here dedicated to the goddesses Maha-Lakshmi, Saraswati, and Durga, combined as Mookambika to represent the full *shakti* of Sri Vishnu and His *guna-avataras*. **Sri Devi Mookambika** destroyed the powerful demon Mookasura and established this place as her eternal sporting ground, or Ambavana. There are several other deities in the temple. There is a temple dedicated to **Lord Krishna** here.

There is a beautiful **ISKCON farm** about 15 km from this town which has Gaura-Nitai Deities. It is located at the foot of Kutakacala Hill where it is said that Durga had some pastimes and where it is believed that Lord Rsabhadeva gave up His body in a forest fire. There are six rooms on the farm where single guests and families can stay. You can get to the farm by going to the ISKCON center in the town of Mookambika.

The ISKCON center in Mookambika is on a half-acre of land, just next to the place where people take bath in the Sauparnika River. On the property is **Garuda Guha,** a cave where Garuda is said to have performed austerities.

There are direct buses to Mookambika from Udupi and Mangalore.

Sri Varaha Vana Ashram

This ashram is located at Nooral Bettu, Karkal Takuk, about a two-hour bus ride northeast of Mangalore. This is a farm community run by some ISKCON devotees. Not far from this farm is Sri Varaha Tirtha, where Varaha, Lord Vishnu in His boar incarnation, is said to have lifted the earth with His effulgent tusk. For further information about this place you can write to Narasimha Das Vanachari, Sri Varaha Vana Ashram, P.O. Nooral Bettu (D.K.), Karkal Tq., 574 107.

Subrahmanya

In the *Skanda Purana* it is stated that Lord Subrahmanya washed the blade of his weapon "Shakti" in the Dhara (Kumaradhara) River here after killing the demon Tarakasura and his brothers. It is said in the *Skanda Purana* that Samba, the son of Sri Krishna, was cured of leprosy in Subrahmanya.

There is a major **Subrahmanya Temple** here. In the main shrine of this temple are the deities of Subrahmanya, Vasuki, and Sesa. There are also many other deities in this temple. In the southeast part of this temple there is a **Narasimha Deity** and a **Narasimha shalagram,** called Vedavyasa Samputa Narasimha Devaru, which were worshiped personally by **Madhvacarya**. This Deity is said to have been given to him by Vedavyasa.

The **Adi-Subrahmanya Temple** is about 250m north of the outer wall of the Subrahmanya Temple. It is believed that you have to visit this temple to get the benefit of pilgrimage to Subrahmanya. The **Kumaradhara River** is a sacred river. Skin diseases are supposed to be cured by bathing in this river.

On the way from the temple to the Kumaradhara River there is a cave called **Biladwara** where the serpent Vasuki is said to be hiding so he will not fall prey to Garuda. There is a south and north path into the cave. Everyone enters the cave from the south tunnel, but it is inaccessible during the rainy season. No one goes through the north tunnel because it is infested with bats.

Southeast of the Subrahmanya Temple is an ashram called **Subrahmanya Math** established by Madhvacarya. Madhvacarya's brother, Vishnu Tirtha, preached here. Sri Madhvacarya is stated to have received this Math from Bhatta Sannyasi, whom he defeated in a philosophical debate. This Math and the Deities of Vyasa, Vitthala and Samputa

Narasimha were given to Sri Vishnu Tirtha, the brother of Madhvacarya.

Sankaracarya also visited here. There is a **Sringeri Mutt** northeast of the Subrahmanya Temple. The deity in this temple is Candramauleswara.

There is a detailed book about the Subrahmanya Temple, the holy places, and other temples in the area called *Sri Subrahmanya Kshetra*. Subrahmanya is 105 km southeast of Mangalore (3 hr bus trip), 120 km west of Hassan (3¼ hr bus trip), and 55 km east of Puttur. The usual way to get here is from Mangalore, which is where the closest railway station is located.

Dharmasthala

Dharmasthala is 75 km northeast of Mangalore. This town is known for the **Manjunath Temple**, which is a Siva temple that is served by Madhvacarya priests and administered by a Jain trustee. A 12m high monolithic statue of **Bahubali** has recently been installed by the Jains. The temple distributes free meals to everyone who comes. The temple is open from 6.30 am to 1 pm for visitors. *Darsana* and *maha-puja* are between 7 and 8 pm. During the Laksha Deepotsava festival 100,000 lamps are lit. Pilgrims bath in the Netravati River, three km away.

Mudabidri

Population: 25,000

There are 18 Jain temples in this town. The 1000-pillar **Chandranath Basti** was dedicated in 1431. The outstanding monolithic columns in this temple have been intricately carved to the finest detail. There is a *Karnataka Tourist Cottage* here that has eight rooms. From Mangalore, Mudabidri is about an hour bus ride northeast.

CHAPTER NINETEEN

Tamil Nadu

Population: 61 million

Tamil Nadu is located at the southeast edge of India. Karnataka and Kerala are to the west and Andhra Pradesh is to the north. The main attraction of Tamil Nadu is its magnificent temples. In Tamil Nadu there are more than 30,000 temples, which have earned it the name "Land of Temples."

Most of the Vishnu temples in Tamil Nadu are dedicated directly to Lord Vishnu, not His expansions (incarnations). Some of the most important Vishnu temples in Tamil Nadu are Ranganatha Swami in Srirangam, Varadaraja Perumal in Kanchipuram, Lord Sarangapani at Kumbakonam, and Alagar Koil near Madurai.

Lord Siva is worshiped as five elements—sky or space in Chidambaram, water in Tiruvanaikkaval, fire in Tiruvannamalai, earth in Kanchipuram, and air in Sri Kalahasti, Andhra Pradesh. The Nataraja Temple in Chidambaram is one of the most important Siva temples in India.

The most important Parvati temples are Meenakshi at Madurai and Kamakshi in Kanchipuram.

Subrahmanya (Kartikeya), the son of Lord Siva and brother of Ganesh, has some opulent temples dedicated to him. There are six main temples of Subrahmanya located at Tiruttani, Swamimalai, Palani, Thiruparankunram, Parlamudircholai, and Tiruchendur.

People greet each other in Tamil Nadu by saying *vanakkam,* which means *namaste,* or "respectful greetings." The northeast monsoon brings plenty of rain from October to December.

MADRAS

Population: 6 million, STD Code 044

The city of Madras was built up by the British starting in 1639. It was the site of their first settlement in India. The East India Company came here in 1639 and constructed Fort St George by 1641. The Mylapore, Triplicane, and Tiruvottiyur areas of Madras, where the Parthasarathi and Kapaliswara Temples are located, are ancient.

There are two monsoon seasons here, June to August and September to November. Sometimes it may also rain heavily in early December. It is hot all year around here, so December to February is the best time to visit.

Information

The **Government of India Tourist Office** (869-685), 154 Anna Salai Rd, is open Monday to Friday from 9 am to 6 pm and on Saturdays from 9 am to 1 pm. There is also a tourist office at the airport. The **India Tourism Development Corporation** (ITDC, 478-884), 29 Victoria Crescent, is open weekdays from 6 am to 8 pm and Saturday and Sundays from 6 am to 2 pm. They arrange city tours and can book ITDC hotels in other cities.

The **Tamil Nadu Tourist Office** (830-390), 143 Anna Salai, is open weekdays 10 am to 5.30 pm. The **Tamil Nadu Tourism Development Corp** (TTDC, 830-390), 143 Anna Salai Rd and at the Central Railway Station, arranges tours and travel. Other state tourist offices—**Kerala, Rajasthan, Uttar Pradesh**, and **Himachal Pradesh**—are at 28 C-in-C Rd and are open 10 am to 5 pm, Mon to Fri. The **Orissa** tourist office is at Gee Gee Bldg, 2nd Fl (near Anna Theatre), and the **W Bengal** office is at 787 Anna Salai.

Hello Madras and *Aside* are two widely available publications that have good information about what's happening in Madras.

You can get a good view of the city from on top of **Tarapore Tower**.

Tours

There is a daily tour to **Tirupati** (Tirumala) run by the Tamil Nadu Tourist Development Corporation and by ITDC. The tour takes at least 15 hours, much of it traveling to and from Tirupati. The tour allows for a two-hour wait for special *darsana*, but on weekends and other special days it can be much more. So even though the tour is scheduled from 6 am to 9 pm, the bus may sometimes return after midnight. The fare includes breakfast, lunch and the Rs 30 "special *darsana*" fee.

There is a **seven-day tour** that goes to Bangalore, Sravanabelagola, Belur, Halebid, Mysore, Srirangapatna, and other places.

There are also tours operated by both ITDC and TTDC to **Kanchipuram**, **Thirukkazhukundram**, and **Mamallapuram**. It departs at 7.30 am and returns at 6.00 pm. This is a very rushed tour, as both Kanchipuram and Mamallapuram can easily take a day each just to see the sites.

There is another **seven-day tour** conducted by the TTDC. It includes Tiruchirappalli, Srirangam, Kodaikanal, Madurai, Kanniyakumari, Suchindrum, Tiruchendur, Rameswaram, Thanjavur, and back to Madras. It starts 7 am Saturday and ends around 6.30 pm on Friday.

Money

Thomas Cook (827-4941) has an office in the Eldorado Building, 112 Nungambakkam High Rd, that changes travellers' cheques efficiently and quickly. They also have an office in Egmore (825-8417), 45 Ceebros Centres, Monteth Rd and in George Town (534-0994), 20 Rajaji Salai. American Express (852-3638) is at G-17 Spencer Plaza, 769 Anna Salai.

There are branches of the State Bank of India on North Beach Rd and on Anna Salai Rd. They also have branches at the international and domestic airport terminals. There is a branch of Bank of America at 748 Anna Salai Rd and a Grindlays Bank at 768 Anna Salai Rd.

Post and phone

There is a poste restante service at the Mount Road Post Office in the Egmore area, at the northern end of Anna Salai Rd. The address is Poste Restante, Mount Road Post Office, Anna Salai Rd, Madras, 600002. This post office is a good place to post packages. It has an efficient packing service inside.

Visa Extensions, Permits, and Tax Clearance

The Foreigners Registration Office (827-8210), Shashtri Bhavan annex, 26 Haddows Rd, usually takes a few days to issue a visa extension. You must have four identical passport photos.

You get income tax clearance certificates at the Foreign Section, Office of the Collector of Taxes (827-2011), 121 Nungambakkam High Rd. This takes about three hours.

Shopping and Books

The city's main shopping areas include Parry's Corner, Mount Road (Anna Salai), Panagal Park, and Pondy Bazaar. For handicrafts, there are the Poompuhar showrooms of the Handicraft Development Co and Victoria Technical Institute on Anna Salai Road. You can get hand-embroidered linen and wall hangings at the reliable Victoria Technical Institute.

Spencer's Department Store, 769 Anna Salai, is a store where you find many different items in the same shop. You can get clothes, utensils, handicrafts, imported food, etc. It is an Indian attempt at a department store.

You can get Kanchipuram cottons at the Tamil Nadu Handloom Weavers' Co-Operative. Two good stores to get jewelry at are Bapalal, 24/1 Cathedral Road, and Vummidi Bangaru, 603 Anna Salai Road.

Higginbothams, 814 Anna Salai (Mount) Rd, is a good book store with one of the better selection of spiritual and travel books I have seen. Landmark Books in the basement of Apex Plaza, 3 Nungambakkam High Rd, has an excellent selection and is one of the best book shops in India.

Foreign Consulates Include:

France
16 Haddows Rd (827-0469)
Germany
22 C-in-C Rd (827-1747)
Japan
60 Spur Tank Rd, Chetput (826-5594)
Malaysia
6 Sri Ram Nagar, Alwarpet (434-3048)
Netherlands
64 Armenian St
Singapore
Apex Plaza (2nd Floor), 3 Nungambakkam High Rd (827-3795)
Sri Lanka
9-D Nawab Habibullah Ave, Anderson Rd (827-2270)
Russia
14 San Thome High Rd
UK
24 Anderson Rd (827-2270)
USA
Gemini Circle, 220 Anna Salai Rd (827-3040)

Travel Agents

Sita World Travel (478-861), 26 Commander-in-Chief Rd; Trade Wings (864-961), 752 Anna Salai Rd; and Travel Corporation India (868-813), 734 Anna Salai Rd; American Express (825-7640), G-17 Spencer Plaza; and Thomas Cook (827-4941), 112/G/4 Nungambakkam High Rd are reputable travel agents.

Sri Parthasarathi Temple

The Parthasarathi Temple was built in the 8th century by the Pallava kings. Additions were later made by the Chola kings and later by the Vijayanagara kings in the 16th century. This temple is one of the 108 main Vishnu Divya Desam temples.

The presiding Deity, Parthasarathi, is a form of Lord Krishna. During the battle of Kurukshetra, when the *Bhagavad-gita* was spoken, Lord Krishna became the chariot driver (*sarathi*) of Arjuna (Partha). The Deity here is named after that form of Krishna. There is also a deity of Vedavalli Ammai, the consort of Parthasarathi.

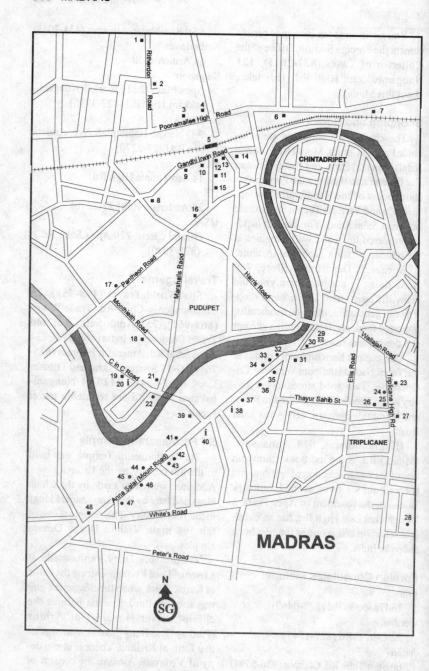

MADRAS

PLACES TO STAY

1	YMCA Youth Centre
2	Salvation Army Guest House
3	YWCA Guest House
4	Hotel Peacock
6	Everest Boarding & Lodging
7	TTDC Youth Hostel
8	Udipi Home
9	Tourist Home
10	Hotel Impala Continental
11	Hotel New Victoria
12	Hotel Imperial
13	People's Lodge
14	Vagai Hotel
15	Hotel Pandian
16	Dayal De Lodge
18	Hotel Ambasssador Pallava
19	Hotel Kanchi
23	Wheat Hotel
25	Hotel Comfort
26	Broadlands
27	Himalaya Hotel
31	Hotel Sangam
39	Hotel Connemara
48	Madras International Hotel

WHERE TO EAT

24	Maharaja Restaurant
30	Woodlands Restaurant
34	House of Dasaprakash
48	Yamuna Restaurant

OTHER

5	Egmore Railway Station
17	Government Museum & Art Gallery
20	Indian Tourism Development Corporation (ITDC) Office
21	Indian Airlines & Air India
22	British Airways
28	Parthasarathi Temple
29	Anna Road Post Office
30	Tarapore Tower
32	Poompuhar Handicrafts
33	Higginbothams
35	Railways Booking Office
36	Binny's Travel Service (American Express)
37	State Bank of India
38	Tamil Nadu Tourist Office
40	Government of India Tourist Office
41	Spencer Shopping Complex
42	Grindlays Bank
43	Lufthansa & Singapore Airlines
44	Bank of America
45	British Council Library
46	Automobile Association
47	Malaysian Airlines

The presiding Deity of the temple, Sri Parthasarathi (Venkatakrishna Swami), is also known as Gitacarya. Sri Parthasarathi holds a conch in His right hand and His left hand is in *jnana-mudra*. Sri Rukmini is on His right, and Satyaki is on His left. Balarama is to the right of Rukmini. Krishna's son Pradyumna and His grandson Aniruddha are on the northern side of the altar, facing south. There is a sword on the left side of the Deity

that represents the sword of knowledge. The processional (utsava) Deity of Parthasarathi has arrow marks on His face which represent the wounds caused by Bhisma in the battle of Kurukshetra. The impressive *vimana* (tower) over the central shrine is partially covered with gold and is called Ananda Vimana.

There is a separate shrine for Sri Ranganatha, who is lying on Adi Sesa facing east with Lord Brahma on a lotus coming out from His naval. Lord Ranganatha is also known as Lord Mannatha, which was the name given to Him by His divine consort, Vedavalli Thayar (Mahalaksmi). In the same shrine are Deities of Sri Narasimha and Sri Varaha.

There are Deities of Yoga Narasimha and the *utsava* Narasimha Deity, worshiped as Alagia Singar (beautiful lion), in the western part of the temple. There is an altar dedicated to Sri Rama (Sri Rama Sannidhi), Sita, Bharata, Satrughna, and Laksmana. There is also a Deity of Sri Varaha in the temple and a shrine dedicated to Sri Andal.

There is an altar dedicated to Sri Gajendra Varadar, the form of Vishnu who rescued Gajendra the elephant when his leg was caught by a crocodile. The Deity holds a *sankha* (conch) and cakra (disc) and is ever ready to assist His sincere devotee.

It is said that taking bath in the temple tank known as Karveni will give all happiness and prosperity. There is a festival called Teppam in February-March in which the Deities are seated on a beautifully decorated illuminated *teppan* (boat) and taken round the temple tank.

Non-Hindus are not allowed in the temple, but ISKCON devotees and converted Hindus can enter. Waiting in line to see the Deity takes about a half hour on a normal day. You can, however, buy a special *darsana* ticket for Rs 10 to bypass the line. This temple has good *mahaprasada*. The temple is open from 6 am to 12 noon and 4 to 10 pm.

The temple is located in the Triplicane area of town. It's a little hard to find. Most people know where it is, but even three blocks away they cannot easily explain how to get there. It is about three blocks east of Triplicane High Rd near Besant Rd.

Kapaliswaram Temple

Kapaliswaram Temple is an ancient Siva temple with an intricately carved towering gopuram in the Mylapore area. The temple has a large Siva-linga and a deity of Subrahmanya (Kartikeya).

In the courtyard of the temple is a shrine dedicated to the consort of Lord Siva, Parvati, in the form of a peahen worshipping a *linga*. This commemorates when Parvati allowed her attention to be distracted from Siva when she saw a peacock dancing beautifully at a distance. Siva became angry because of this and cursed her to become a peahen. Parvati became a peahen and came to Kapalinagar (present day Mylapore) and started to do rigorous austerities to please Lord Siva in the form of a *mayil* (peahen). After many years she became successful and rejoined Lord Siva. Thereafter this area became known as Mayilapore or Mylapore.

In 1566 the original temple was destroyed by the Portuguese. The present temple was built in the 16th century by the Vijayanagara kings. The gopuram (tower) is 37m (120 ft) high. Non-Hindus are not allowed in the inner sanctum. Important festivals are the boat festival called Tai Pusham (Jan/Feb) and Brahmotsava (March/April), which celebrates the marriage of Siva and Parvati.

The temple is located in the southern suburb of Madras off Kutchery Rd in the Mylapore area.

Government Museum

This museum is on Pantheon Rd, near Egmore Station. It has a large collection of antiquities from sites all over South India. It has an Archaeological section (stone sculptures), an art gallery, and a bronze gallery with the largest collection of South Indian bronze statues in the country. It has an impressive set of large standing Deities of Rama, Sita, and Laksmana from Vadakkuppanaiyur. On one side of the bronze gallery the deities are related to Lord Vishnu and on the other to Lord Siva. There are many sculptures of Nataraja, a dancing Lord Siva. There are also many other gods represented. The museum is open 9 am to 5 pm, daily except Friday.

ISKCON Temple

It is located at Burkit Road, T. Nagar (434-3266). The Deities here are Rukmini-Krishna. Satyabhama, one of the eight main wives of Krishna, is also on the altar. There are also Deities of Jagannatha, Baladeva and Lady Subhadra, and Gaura-Nitai. It is a small place with no overnight guest facilities. Meals are 9 to 10 am and 4.45 to 6 pm, and there is a Sunday feast program.

To get to the ISKCON temple you can get the 11A bus from Mount Road or any bus to Nagar Terminal in the south-central part of the city. The temple is a ten minute walk from the bus station on Burkit Rd. Once you are in the area most people know where the Hare Krishna temple is located. It is near the Sharadha Vidyalaya Girls School.

Fort St George

Fort St George is an interesting place with some old ruins and a scale model of how the fort used to look. It was huge. Inside the Fort is St Mary's Church which is the oldest British building still standing in India.

Getting Around

There is a 25 % over the meter charge for auto rickshaws. There is a suburban railway that can be used to get around town.

Taxi Warning

In Madras the taxi drivers can take advantage of tourists. They often refuse to use the meter and will then ask 4 or 5 times the normal fare. The rickshaw drivers can be tough to deal with in Madras.

Where To Stay

Around Egmore Station and on Poonamallee High Rd, between Central and Egmore Stations, there is a good selection of mid-range and a few budget places. The cheapest hotels are in the George Town area, between North Beach Rd, NSC Bose Rd, and Mint Rd. The high- range hotels are mostly on Mount Rd (Anna Salai) and the roads that run off it. Sometimes it can be difficult to find a room in Madras, especially in December and January.

Lower – Anna Salai (Mount) Rd

Broadlands (845-573), 16 Vallabha Agraharam St, by the Star Cinema and Triplicane High Rd, is a very popular place with backpackers. Rooms are Rs 110/200 with common bath and Rs 270 with bath. It has dorm beds for Rs 40. It is usually full with budget travelers and is a good place to meet people. The rooms are very clean. It has a few nice courtyards, and they have bike rentals. A prepaid taxi to Broadlands is about Rs 25 from Egmore station. This is the type of place you immediately like or don't like. Unless you are a backpacker you most likely won't like it.

Sam Mansions, 29 Triplicane High Road, not far from the Broadlands Hotel, has rooms with bath for Rs 180. The rooms are better than those is the Broadlands. The *Hotel Himalaya* (847-522), 54 Triplicane High Rd, is a good clean place that has rooms with hot water for Rs 185/ 255. It is well-managed and the rooms have balconies. The *Hotel Comfort* (845-117), 22 Vallabha Agraharam St, near Broadlands, has rooms for Rs 205/250. The rooms on the ground floor can be very loud, as noise carries down the hall from the lobby.

The *TTDC Youth Hostel* (589-132), by Central Station on Poonamallee High Rd, has poorly maintained rooms with attached bath for Rs 200 and dorm beds for Rs 50. It can be a little noisy.

Lower – Egmore & George Town

It is best to get a hotel as early as possible in this area. By the afternoon it can be very difficult to find a room.

The *Salvation Army Guest House* (532-1821), 15 Ritherdon Rd, has clean quiet rooms for Rs 100/160 and dorm beds for Rs 25. Checkout time is 9 am. The *Dayal De Lodge* (825-1159), 486 Pantheon Rd, has rooms with bath and hot water for Rs 110/200.

The *Sri Laxmi Lodge* (825-4576), 16 Kennet's Lane, has good rooms with bath, around a courtyard, for Rs 120/150. The *Alarmel Lodge*, 17-18 Gandhi Irwin Rd, just opposite Egmore Station, has rooms with common bath for Rs 60/85. The *Hotel Majestic*, Kennet's Lane, has rooms with common bath for Rs 80/110 and Rs 90/140 with attached bath.

Where To Stay – Middle

The *Kanchi Hotel* (471-100), 28 C-in-C Rd, is a recommended place that has rooms with hot water for Rs 350 and Rs 475 with A/C. The rooms are a good value. The rooms are built around a courtyard. This hotel has two vegetarian restaurant, one North and the other South Indian. The *Hotel Pandian* (825-2901, fax 825-8459), 9 Kennet Lane, is a good value with rooms for Rs 325/450 and Rs 550/600 with A/C. It is a popular place.

The large *Hotel Impala Continental* (825-0484), 12 Gandhi Irwin Rd, by Egmore Station, has rooms with bath and hot water for Rs 140/190 and Rs 350/375 with A/C. It is a good value and is often full. The *Hotel Vagai* (834-959), 3 Gandhi Irwin Rd, has rooms for Rs 215/275 and Rs 400 with A/C. It has a vegetarian restaurant.

The *YWCA Guest House* (532-4234), 1086 Poonamallee High Rd, has clean good-sized rooms for Rs 325/375 and Rs 500 with A/C. It takes both men and women, and is a good value, so it should be booked early. The *Dasaprakash Hotel* (825-5111), 100 Poonamallee High Rd by Central Railway, is a recommended place with rooms for Rs 200/300 and Rs 300/400 with A/C. It has a quiet roof garden and *Bhagavad-gitas* in the rooms. It also has a good vegetarian restaurant that packs lunches for you.

The *Hotel Ranjith* (827-0521), 9 Nungambakkam High Rd, is a good place by the consulates and airline offices. It has very clean rooms for Rs 500/650 and Rs 700/850 with A/C. The *Hotel Palm Grove* (827-1881), 5 Kodambakkam High Rd, is a good place with clean rooms for Rs 275/300 and Rs 375/500 with A/C.

The popular *Tourist Home* (825-0079), 21 Gandhi Irwin Rd, opposite the railway station, is a recommended place with good rooms with attached bathrooms for Rs 190/240 and Rs 325 with A/C. It is often full. *Udipi Home* (825-1515) is a well-managed place with clean rooms for Rs 260/370 and Rs 400/480 with A/C.

The *New Woodlands Hotel* (827-3111), 72/75 Dr Radhakrishnan Rd, Mylapore, is a recommended place with a swimming pool. Rooms with A/C are Rs 375/500. It has a good vegetarian restaurant.

Where To Stay – High

The *Hotel New Victoria* (825-3638), 3 Kennet's Lane, close to Egmore Station, has rooms for Rs 700/900. It is clean and quiet. The *Madras International Hotel* (852-4111, fax 852-3412), 693 Anna Salai Rd, is a good place with comfortable rooms for Rs 1120/1400. It is clean and quiet.

The *Hotel President* (832-211, fax 832-299), 16 Dr Radhakrishnan Rd, Mylapore, is a large place with good-sized rooms for Rs 590/790. Nearby the modern *Hotel Savera* (827-4700, fax 827-3475), 69 Dr Radhakrishnan Rd, has comfortable rooms for Rs 1250/1700. This place has a swimming pool.

Where To Stay – Luxury

The *Hotel Taj Coromandel* (827-2827, fax 825-7104), 17 Nungambakkam High Rd, has excellent rooms for $160/170. It has a convenient location and a good pool. *Connemara* (852-0123, Fax 852-3361), Binny Rd by Mount Rd, is a first-class luxury hotel with comfortable rooms for $100/110. It has a swimming pool and a good book shop. It is heavily booked from December to March.

The Welcomegroup Chola Sheraton (828-0101, fax 827-8779), 10 Cathedral Rd, has rooms for $100/120 to $375. The *Park Sheraton Hotel & Tower* (499-4101), 132 TTK Rd, is a very luxurious place with rooms for $110/120 to $190/200. The *Holiday Inn Crowne Plaza* (234-8976), 1 GST Road, has rooms for $120/130.

Away from the downtown is the five-star *Trident Oberoi* (234-4747, fax 234-6699), 1/24 GST Rd, which has pleasant gardens and a pool. It is convenient for the airport, which is 4 km away. Rooms are $110/120. It has a convenient 12-hour rate.

Where To Eat

The *Mathura Restaurant* (831-777), Tarapore Towers on Anna Salai Rd, is one of the best restaurants in India. It is a big and very popular place and is highly recommended. The Vegetable-pulau, Vegetable Imperial, and Macaroni are all very good.

Woodlands (827-1981), Cathedral Road, 6 am to 9 pm, is one of the best places in town and has been recommended by a few friends of mine. *Woodland's Drive-In* (471-981), 29/30 Cathedral Rd, serves excellent food and is a recommended place. Also recommended is the *New Woodlands Hotel* (827-3111), 72/75 Dr Radhakrishnan Road, which serves good thalis. The *Balaaji Woodlands* in the Vee Yes Hotel is a good restaurant.

The *Yamuna Restaurant*, at the lower end of Anna Salai Rd, is a good place. It is clean with good prices, and tasty food, good lassi and ice cream. The *Hotel New Maharaja*, 307 Triplicane High Rd by Broadlands, has cheap meals. The "limited meal" (not on the menu and only during lunch) is dirt cheap. It also has good ice cream and sweets.

Hotel Dasaprakash (825-5111), 100 Poonamallee High Road, (9 am to 6 pm) and *AVM Dasa* (House of Dasaprakash Ice Cream), 806 Anna Salai, are good places.

Saravana Bhavan, 77 Usman Rd, T Nagar near Ranganathan Street Market (Mambalam Station), is a very good popular place that serves cheap South Indian food. They have a deluxe "Tamil Nadu meal." On the ground floor they serve snacks, and on the upper floor they have an A/C restaurant. The *Matsya Restaurant*, at Udipi Home Hotel (825-1515), 1 Hall Road, Egmore (7.30 am to 12 midnight), is a recommended A/C place with a wide range of preparations available.

Other vegetarian restaurants are the *Lotus*, at Hotel Peninsula (825-2770), 26 G.N. Road, T Nagar; *Karpagam Restaurant*, at Hotel Atlantic (826-0461), 2 Montienth Road, 6.30 am to 10.30 pm; *Fairlands*, Kamarajar Salai; *Hotel Guru*, at 69 Marshalls Road; *Hotel Kanchi*, 28 C-in-C Road; *Hotel Palmgrove* (827-7161), 5 Kodambakkam High Road; and the *Hotel Sornam International*, 7 Stringer Street; Hotel Mallika, near Casino Theatre on Mount Road.

Travel

Air From Madras there are direct international flights to and from New York, London, Kuala Lumpur, and Singapore. There are also flights all over India. At Meenambakkam Airport, 17 km southwest of the city center, there are two terminals—one international and the other domestic, about a minute walk apart.

There are pre-paid taxis at the airport that cost about Rs 175 to most of the bigger hotels and Rs 200 to the railway station. A taxi to Mamallapuram costs Rs 650 from the airport. There is also an airport bus (Rs 60) that goes to the major hotels ending at Egmore Station. The suburban train from Egmore Station stops at Trisulam station, which is about half a km from the airport. This train is often packed.

Air India flies to New York, London, Singapore, Kuwait and Kuala Lumpur; British Airways flies to London; Singapore Airlines to Singapore; and Malaysian Airlines to Kuala Lumpur.

There are several daily flights to Bombay and Delhi, and a few flights daily to Bangalore, Calcutta, Coimbatore, and Hyderabad. There are daily flights to Tiruchirappalli (Srirangam), Madurai,

and Thiruvananthapuram (Trivandrum). There are three flights weekly to Pune, Visakapatnam and Mangalore, and two flights weekly to Bhubaneshwar.

Airlines Offices In Madras

Air India
    19 Marshalls Rd, Egmore (827-4477)
Air Lanka
    Mount Chambers, 758 Anna Salai (826-2301)
British Airways
    Khalili Centre, Montieth Rd, Egmore (827-4272)
East-West Airlines
    Mootha Centre, 9 Kodambakkam High Rd (827-7007)
Gulf Air
    52 Montieth Rd
Indian Airlines
    19 Marshalls Rd, Egmore (825-1677, fax 827-7675)
Kuwait Airways
    55 Montieth Rd, Egmore (826-1331)
Lufthansa
    167 Anna Salai (852-5095)
Malaysian Airlines
    498 Anna Salai (456-651)
Modiluft
    Prestige Point, 16 Haddows Rd (826-0048)
Qantas
    Eldorado Building, 112 Nungambakkam High Rd (827-8680)
Singapore Airlines
    167 Anna Salai Rd (852-1872)
Thai International
    198 Anna Salai (450-440)

Rail There are two train stations in Madras. Madras Central is bigger and is connected with most of the major cities in India from the north, east, west, and a few southern cities. From Madras Egmore, metre gauge trains depart to cities all over the south. Both stations are on Periyar EVR High Rd.

The reservation office at Madras Central is on the upper floor of the building next to the station. There is a "Tourist Cell" that handles tourist quota bookings and Indrail Passes. It is a useful office, but you must purchase tickets with foreign currency. It sells tickets for trains that depart from either station. In this same reservation office you can make reservations for trains that originate in Calcutta, Delhi, Jaipur, Bombay, Ahmedabad, and many other places (at different counters). This office is open 7.30 am to 1 pm and 1.30 to 7.30 pm, Monday to Saturday and 7.30 am to 1 pm on Sunday. The booking office at Egmore Station, up the stairs from the main entrance, has no tourist counter. There is a Railway Booking Counter at the airport.

Madras has very good rail connections. From Egmore, the Rameswaram Express #6101 (10.20 pm, 17 hr) goes to Rameswaram via Tiruchirappalli (10 hr). The overnight Sethu Express goes to Rameswaram in 15½ hours. To Madurai, the Mail goes overnight in 11½ hours and the fast Vaigai Express #2635 (12.25 pm) takes eight hours via Tiruchirappalli. Trains also depart from Egmore to go to Thanjavur (9 hr) and Chidambaram (6 hr).

Most other trains leave from Central. There are two express trains a day to Delhi—the Tamil Nadu Exp #2621 (9 pm, daily, 34 hr) and the Grand Trunk Exp #2615 (9.15 pm, 37 hr). The Dadar Madras Exp #6512 (9.15 am) goes to Bombay in 27 hours. The Coromandel Exp #2842 goes to Calcutta in 28 hr. The Ganga Kaveri Exp goes to Varanasi in 39 hours. The Trivandrum Mail #6319 (6.55 pm) goes to Thiruvananthapuram (Trivandrum) in 17 hours. The Lalbagh

Exp #2607 and Brindavan Exp #2639 (7.15) go to Bangalore in about 6 hours. The fully A/C Shatabdi Exp #2007 (6 am) takes just five hours to get to Bangalore. The Charminar Exp #7059 (6.10 pm, 13 hr) goes to Hyderabad. The fast Shatabdi Exp goes to Mysore daily except Tuesday.

There are two trains a day to Tirupati—the Saptagiri Exp #6057 (6.25 am, 3 hr) and the Madras Tirupati Exp #6053 (1.50 pm, 3 hr). Sometimes in the busy season the tourist quotas can be totally used up for a train to Calcutta from Madras and you may not be able to get a train for a week. You could take a train to Tirupati and book a train for the next day, as there is a direct train from there to Bhubaneswara and Calcutta.

Bus There are two long-distance bus stations in Madras—Thiruvalluvar and Broadway—opposite each other, in George Town, by the High Court building off NSC Bose Rd. The Tamil Nadu state bus company, also called the Thiruvalluvar Transport Corporation (TTC), has a reservation office (534-1835) upstairs where you can book in advance for most places. The booking office is open from 7 am to 9 pm daily. You can get the Bus Route Guide & Map at the enquiry office downstairs for Rs 5. It has a good map of Tamil Nadu and a detailed schedule of the Thiruvalluvar bus routes.

Thiruvalluvar mainly serves just Tamil Nadu. Broadway station has buses to Karnataka, Tamil Nadu, and Andhra Pradesh. You can also get a direct bus from Madras to Ahovalam (12 hr) via Tirupati from here. The terminal is chaotic, but there are young boys here that will help you get on your bus for a few rupees. You can purchase tickets for some buses at the TNTDC tourist office.

State buses to **Mamallapuram** (2½ hr, 60 km) leave from Broadway station. The #188, #188 A/B/D and K are faster buses and the #19C and #119A take a little longer. If you take the #19 and #119A along the coast you can get off the bus at the hotels just north of Mamallapuram. From the Mofussil bus stand near Esplanade you take the #19A, #19C, and #68 buses to get to Mamallapuram.

Public buses to **Kanchipuram** leave from Parry's Corner by the Law Courts where the Esplanade meets First Line Beach. Buses #41 and #76B take two hours. Express buses to Tirupati (#802, 4 hr) depart from the Thiruvalluvar bus station at 8.15 am, 3.30 pm and 8.30. There are many regulars buses, but they are slow, taking round about routes

There are private bus companies that have deluxe video buses that go to Madurai, Bangalore, Tiruchirappalli, and other places. They charge about the same price as the state buses, but are more comfortable, except for the noisy video. Their offices are mainly in the Egmore area.

Buses From Madras To:

Bangalore	9-11 hr	30 daily
Chidambaram	5-7 hr	20 daily
Hyderabad	18-20 hr	4 daily
Kanchipuram	2 hr	45 daily
Kanniyakumari	16-18 hr	6 daily
Kumbakonam	7-8 hr	5 daily
Madurai	10 hr	15 daily
Mamallapuram	2-3 hr	50 daily
Mysore	16 hr	1 daily
Pondicherry	5 hr	60 daily
Rameswaram	14 hr	1 daily
Thanjavur	11 hr	13 daily
Tiruchirappalli	8-9 hr	30 daily
Tirupati	3-4 hr	20 daily
Tiruvannamalai	5-6 hr	20 daily
Trivandrum	17 hr	4 daily

Nearby Madras

Tiruneermalai

There is a Divya Desam temple here called the **Sri Ranganatha Perumal Temple**. *Brahmanda Purana* recognizes this place as one of the eight *svayam vyakta ksetras,* or holy places where Lord Vishnu manifested Himself. The Lord is seen in four postures here: Neervannan—standing, Lord Narasimha—sitting, Lord Ranganatha—lying down, and Lord Trivikrama—walking.

Lord Ranganatha, Lord Narasimha (Sri Santa Narasimha), and Lord Trivikrama (Ulagalanda Perumal) are all in the temple at the top of the hill. You have to climb 250 steps to reach this temple. The main Deity at the top of the hill is Sri Ranganatha, who is lying on Adi Sesa. His consort is Ranganayaki Thayar.

The **Neervanna Perumal Temple** is at the foot of the hill. The *utsava vigraha* of Sri Ranganatha is in the Neervanna Temple. There is a shrine for Valmiki on the hillside.

Tiruneermalai is about 10 km from Madras.

Tiruvallur

There is a Vishnu Divya Desam temple here called **Sri Veeraraghava Swami Temple**. The Deity of Veeraraghava is Lord Vishnu lying on Adi Sesa, with Lord Brahma coming from His navel. The temple has a huge intricately carved *gopuram.* This temple is about 5 km north of the railway station.

It is believed that Lord Vishnu killed the demons Madhu and Kaitabha here at **Veeksharanya Ksetram**. This place is known as Punya-vrata Ksetram because it is believed whatever *punya* (good deeds) one does here is multiplied many times.

There is a bathing tank here called Hridaya-tapa-nasini-tirtham, which is said to cure all one's illnesses. The waters of the Ganges are supposed to flow into this tank on Amavasya, the new moon day in the month of January.

Tiruvallur is 42 km from Madras, on the railway line between Madras and Arkonam (Arakkonam).

Tiruttani

There is a hilltop temple here dedicated to **Subramanya** which is reached by climbing 365 steps. It is said to be the place where Subramanya married Valli, one of his two consorts. There are over 100 dharamsalas for pilgrims here, as this temple is popular. Tiruttani is on the way between Madras and Tirupati, 70 km from Madras.

Thiruvidaventhai (Tiruvadantai)

One of the Divya Desam temples dedicated to Lord Vishnu, Sri Nritya Kalyana Perumal, is here. The main Deity is nine feet tall and is called **Sri Laksmi Adi Varaha**. The left foot of Varaha is raised up to the knee and is placed on the head of Adi Sesa. The Lord's consort, Bhumidevi, is on the Lord's thigh. Lord Varaha wears a garland made from 108 *shalagram-shilas*. There is a big festival here on Vaikuntha Ekadasi. This temple is about 40 km south of Madras, going towards Mahabalipuram (10 km north).

VELLORE

Population: 300,000, STD Code 0416

Vellore is 145 km west of Madras. The Jalakanteswara Temple and Vijayanagar Fort are the interesting places to see here. This is not a major place to visit, but it is worth seeing if you are passing through the area. The **Christian Medical College Hospital** is one of the best tropical disease hospitals in India.

The **Vellamalai Temple** is 25 km away and is dedicated to Subramanya (Murugan in Tamil). The main temple is at the top of a hill and is carved from a giant stone.

Jalakanteswara Temple

This impressive large Siva temple was built around 1566 in the Vijayanagar style. This ancient temple is named after Jalakanteswara, or "Lord Siva residing in the water." The temple has a Nataraja Siva deity on the north altar, and on the west altar is a Siva-linga. This temple has just recently been reestablished as a place of worship. The temple is famous for its magnificent sculptures. There is a 100-foot-high, seven story *gopuram* of blue granite flanked by two carved *dwarpals* (guards). This temple is located in the Vellore Fort.

Vellore Fort

This large fort was built in the 16th century by Vijayanagar kings. There is a big moat around the fort that is still filled with water. There is a museum here that is open daily 8 am to 8 pm.

Where To Stay and Eat

The cheap hotels are on Babu Rao St and Ida Scudder St, near the hospital and bus stand. The *Mayura Lodge* (25488), Babu Rao St, is the recommended budget place with clean rooms for Rs 45/65. The *Hotel Solei* (22996) has rooms for Rs 60/90. It is decent, but some rooms do not have windows. The new Nagha International Lodge (26731), K V S Chetty St has rooms that are a good value for Rs 60/90.

The *Hotel River View* (25568), 1 km north of Vellore, is a recommended place with clean rooms for Rs 225/275 and Rs 350/400 with A/C.

The *Raj Cafe*, in the India Lodge across from the bazaar, is a good veg-restaurant. The *Hotel Geetha*, Ida Scudder Rd, may also have a vegetarian restaurant. One of the best vegetarian place in town is the *Simla Ice Cream Bar*, 88 Ida Scudder St, which has good naans.

Travel

Train Vellore has two metre-gauge train stations. Trains go to Tirupati and Tiruvannamalai from here. The broad-gauge railway station is at Katpadi (2 km from Vellore), on the Madras-Bangalore line. A bus from Vellore to Katpadi takes 20 minutes. It takes four hours to get to Bangalore from here and two hours to get to Madras.

Bus Thiruvalluvar Transport Corporation buses that go to Tiruchirappalli, Madurai, and Tiruvannamalai that begin in Vellore and can be booked in advance. There are also buses to Bangalore (3 hr), Tirupati, Thanjavur, and Madras. PATC has buses to Madras (3 hr), Bangalore, and Kanchipuram. The bus station here is not user friendly.

MAMALLAPURAM-Mahabalipuram

Population: 12,000, STD Code 04113

Mamallapuram, located on the Bay of Bengal, means "the town of Mamalla, the great wrestler." Mamalla is the title given to the Pallava ruler Narasimha Varman I, who built many of the temples here. The name Mahabalipuram means "the town of the great king Bali," from whom Lord Vamana begged three paces of land. This town was an ancient port of the Pallavas kings in the 7th century.

The rock carvings here are divided into three zones: the main group of carvings on the slopes of the hill, the Shore temple to the east, and the Pancha Ratha (Five Chariots) temples to the south. The temples here are among the earliest examples of monumental architecture temples in South India. They were made mostly between the 5th and 8th centuries. Most of the cave temples are carved out of a granite hill that is close to the sea. The Five Rathas are located south of this area. The Shore temple is located right next to the sea.

Besides the famous Shore temple there are 14 cave temples, 8 monolithic rathas, and many other small rock sculptures. The monuments are floodlit at night. There is a dance festival here during January and February.

Mamallapuram is one of the more visited places by foreign tourists in South India. It is a very peaceful town with a good atmosphere and is a good place to stay for a few days or more just to relax. It is located on the seashore, but I did not see anyone swimming there, as the water was very rough and appeared extremely dangerous.

Getting Your Bearings

East and West Raja Streets are the main streets in town and run north-south. The bus station is between the two streets. The carved cave temples are to the west of the village away from the sea. The Five Ratha temples are to the south of the village and the Shore temple is to the east of the village, right next to the ocean.

You can get a good view of the area from the lighthouse, which is open from 2 to 4 pm, or you can just climb to the top of the hill.

Information

The **tourist office** is one of the first buildings you see when you come from

Madras. It is located at the beginning of the village and is open from 10 am to 5.45 pm. Besides doing a good job of helping you with the local sites, they can also help you with information about your transportation needs.

You can change travellers' cheques at the Canara Bank, Indian Overseas Bank, or at the larger hotels. You can hire a bike on the main road by the bus station.

You can get a guide from the **Archaeological Survey Office** on East Raja Street, south of the bus station. They publish a guidebook that gives a good explanation of the sites.

Tours

There are tours operated by both ITDC and TTDC conducted from Madras covering Mamallapuram, Kanchipuram, and Thirukkazhukundram. It leaves at 7.30 am and returns at 6.00 pm. This is a quick way of visiting these places, as you could easily spend at least a day in both Mamallapuram and Kanchipuram.

Mamallapuram Dance Festival

The festival runs from the beginning of January till the beginning of February. Except for one continuous week of daily dances, there are classical Indian dances on Fridays, Saturdays, and Sundays. You can ask for information about the festival from the Tamil Nadu Tourist Office in Madras or other major cities.

CAUTION The current by the Shore temple is very dangerous and many people have drowned there.

Talasayana (Sthala Sayana) Perumal Temple

The Sthala Sayana Perumal Temple is one of the Vishnu Divya Desam temples. It has a good size gopuram (en-

trance tower). The goddess is called Nilamangai Naachiar. This temple is not far from the bus stand, in the center of town.

Arjuna's Penance (The Descent of the Ganges)

This is considered one of the great works of art in India. It is an artistic masterpiece with massive elephants, one being 17 ft long. It covers a rock wall 96 feet by 40 feet and has over 100 figures carved on it. It is next to the Talasayana Temple.

There are two schools of thought about this sculpture. One school says the sculpture depicts the story of Arjuna undertaking penance to get from Lord Siva a powerful weapon to destroy his enemies. To witness this, visitors rushed from the heavens and earth.

Another school says that the scene depicts the penance of Bhagiratha, to save the souls of his ancestors. After a long penance he brought the Ganges to come down to earth. The cleft in the rock depicts the Ganges descending into the world. There is an interesting relief of a cat meditating, while rats freely play around it. To take a photo the light is best in the morning.

Hill Area

To the left of Arjuna's Penance is **Krishna Mandapa**. It shows Krishna lifting Govardhana Hill in order to protect the people of Braj (Vrindavana) from the fury of Indra.

On top of the hill is a peaceful place with a good view of the countryside. Up the hill behind Arjuna's Penance is a good place to just wander around and see the other cave temples and carvings. When you come to the top of the hill, if you make a left, you come to the interesting

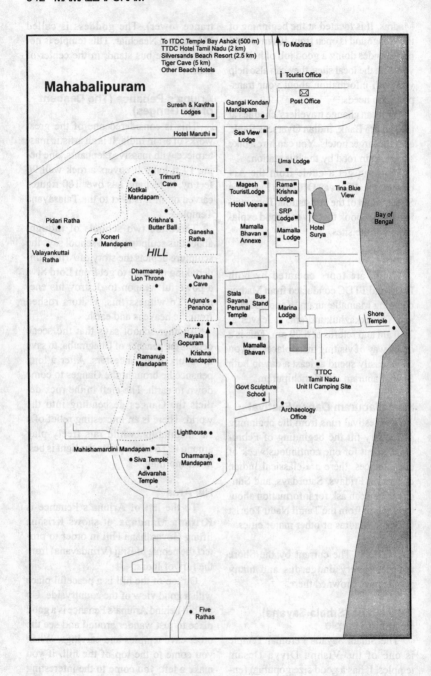

Mahabalipuram

To ITDC Temple Bay Ashok (500 m)
TTDC Hotel Tamil Nadu (2 km)
Silversands Beach Resort (2.5 km)
Tiger Cave (5 km)
Other Beach Hotels

To Madras

i Tourist Office

Post Office

Suresh & Kavitha Lodges

Gangai Kondan Mandapam

Hotel Maruthi

Sea View Lodge

Uma Lodge

Trimurti Cave

Kotikai Mandapam

Krishna's Butter Ball

Ganesha Ratha

Pidari Ratha

Koneri Mandapam

Valayankuttai Ratha

HILL

Dharmaraja Lion Throne

Varaha Cave

Arjuna's Penance

Magesh Tourist Lodge

Hotel Veera

Mamalla Bhavan Annexe

Rama Krishna Lodge

SRP Lodge

Mamalla Lodge

Hotel Surya

Tina Blue View

Bay of Bengal

Stala Sayana Perumal Temple

Bus Stand

Marina Lodge

Shore Temple

Rayala Gopuram

Krishna Mandapam

Ramanuja Mandapam

Mamalla Bhavan

Govt Sculpture School

TTDC Tamil Nadu Unit II Camping Site

Archaeology Office

Lighthouse

Mahishamardini Mandapam

Siva Temple

Dharmaraja Mandapam

Adivaraha Temple

Five Rathas

Varaha Cave temple. The Varaha sculpture shows Lord Vishnu taking the form of a boar to rescue the earth. The Lord is coming out of the ocean holding the earth. There is a sculpture of Vamana (Trivikrama), Lord Vishnu as the dwarf brahmin incarnation, on the southern wall of the cave.

If you continue to your left you come to the **Rayala Gopuram**, and a little further is the **Ramanuja Mandapa**.

If you make a right when you come up the hill from Arjuna's Penance you come to the **Ganesh Ratha**, a monolithic temple that is 11 ft by 19 ft and 28 ft high. If you keep walking up the hill you come to **Krishna's Butter Ball**, which is a huge almost totally circular boulder, that stays balanced on top of the hill. A little further is the **Trimurti Cave**, which contains bas-reliefs of the trinity—Brahma, Vishnu, and Siva.

South of Arjuna's Penance, at the highest point of the hill, is the **Olakaneswara cave temple,** or God of the Flaming Eye. It used to be used as a lighthouse until the beginning of the 20th century. Close by is the new lighthouse (open 2 to 4 pm), from which you can get a good view of the area.

Below the old lighthouse is the **Mahisasura-mardhini Mandapa** (Durga Cave). There is a sculpture in this cave that shows the goddess Durga fighting with the buffalo-headed demon. There is another sculpture of Lord Vishnu lying on Sesa Naga in His cosmic sleep.

The Pancha Rathas (Five Chariots)

The Five Rathas are named after the five Pandava brothers and their wife Draupadi. They do not have anything to do with the Pandavas and are not really chariots. Actually they are unfinished monolithic temples carved from large granite boulders. They are located about one km from the center of town, pass the lighthouse.

The Dharmaraja Ratha is shaped like a pyramid and is 35 by 29 by 35 feet. It has many detailed carvings on it. The Bhima Ratha has a wagon-shaped roof and is north of the Dharmaraja Ratha. It is 26 by 25 by 48 feet. Its bottom level is incomplete, except for the lions. The Arjuna Ratha contains Vishnu and His carrier, Garuda. It is 27 by 29 by 35 feet high and is four stories. It also has carvings of Indra with his elephant. The Draupadi Ratha, which is dedicated to Durga, and the Sahadeva Ratha are the smallest temples.

Shore Temples

The beautiful Shore temple is a two-towered structure built in the 7th century. There are actually two temples, one facing east and one facing west. The one facing east is a Lord Siva temple with a Siva-linga. The other temple is a Vishnu temple with a 2.5 metres Maha-Vishnu sleeping on Ananta Sesa carved onto a granite boulder, facing east. Lord Vishnu's pastimes are carved on the outer wall of the Vishnu temple. A wall has been built around these temples to protect them from the ocean. These temples are one kilometre from town, right next to the ocean.

North of Town

North of the main sites is the Tiger Cave (8th century), the Mukundanayanar Temple, and the Atiranachanda Mandapa. The Tiger Cave is in a peaceful area about 5 km north of town. You can get there by taking a Madras bus or by renting a bike. There is a sign posted on the right side of the road, but if you're coming via the beach there is no sign.

Kapaleswara-tirtha is located at the foot of a hill, about 2 km north of town. There is a *linga* called Kapaleswara and also a pond.

School of Sculpture & the Museum

There is an official state school of sculpture on East Raja Street. The school is open from 9 am to 1 pm and 2 to 6 pm. The Government College of Sculpture (2261) is 3 km away on Covelong Rd. You can visit the school, but you should first make an appointment.

Local carvers give lessons to people on how to make stone carvings. People stay a week or two and learn how to make their own masterpieces. It looked quite relaxing.

The Archaeological Museum, on W Raja St by the lighthouse (9 am to 1 pm and 2 to 5 pm, daily), has a collection of Pallava sculptures that were found in the area. They also sell good postcards at a reasonable price.

Where To Stay – Lower

The room rates here are very reasonable.

The *Tina Blue View Lodge* (42319), a 10 minute walk from the bus stand, is a good place with single rooms for Rs 70 and doubles for Rs 110 to Rs 170. Close by, near the beach, is the popular *Lakshmi Lodge* (42463), which has good rooms for Rs 140 to Rs 225. A little down the road is the *Ramakrishna Lodge*, No 8 Othavadi Street. It is a good place with rooms with bath for Rs 100/175. The problem with both these places is that there is a nearby temple that blasts extremely loud music from 4.30 till about 7.30 in the morning and again at other times in the day. It is hard to believe that everyone on the street is not totally deaf.

The *Uma Lodge* (42322), has clean rooms with bath for Rs 110 and without bath for Rs 80. The upstairs rooms are better.

The *Mamalla Lodge* (42250), on the main street right next to the bus station, has Indian style rooms with common bath for Rs 50 and rooms with attached bath for Rs 80. It is a good cheap place and is quiet at night.

The new *Selva Vinayaga* (42445), near the hospital, has very good cottages with private bath for Rs 150 to Rs 175.

The *TTDC Hotel Tamil Nadu Unit II Camping Site*, by the Shore temple is a good place with rooms from Rs 170 to Rs 240 and dorm beds for Rs 25. The *SRP Lodge*, 50 Thirukkula St, is a recommended place having rooms with bath for Rs 130 and other rooms for Rs 70.

Where To Stay—Middle In Village

Mamalla Bhavan Annexe (42260), on the main street, is a really good value with rooms with bath for Rs 175 and Rs 275 with A/C. It has a good vegetarian restaurant. It is a recommended place.

The *Hotel Veeras* (42288), which is right next door, has comfortable rooms for Rs 250 and Rs 375 with A/C. It also has a vegetarian restaurant. Both these places are about the same.

Where To Stay – Middle By Beach

There are a group of good hotels north of town along the beach. Some of these places are very good values for what you pay.

The *Ideal Beach Resort* (42240, fax 42243), about 3 km from the town, along the highway parallel with the sea, is a really nice place and is highly recommended. It has cottages and normal rooms for Rs 400/500 and A/C cottages for Rs 450/550. It is popular with foreigners.

The *Golden Sun* (42245) is an excellent place with rooms for Rs 350/400 and A/C rooms for Rs 500/600. It has deluxe rooms and a swimming pool in a nice garden. The rooms facing the sea are the best value.

The *TTDC Hotel Tamil Nadu Beach Resort Complex* (42235), 1.5 km from town, is an excellent value with a really good swimming pool. Rooms cost Rs 350 and Rs 450 with A/C and hot water. This is a very good choice. It is two km out of town.

The *Mamalla Beach Cottages* (42375) has rooms for Rs 200/250 and A/C rooms upstairs for Rs 350. All rooms have hot water.

Where To Stay – High

Just 500 yards from Mamallapuram is the well-located *ITDC Temple Bay Ashok Beach Resort* (42251), on the beach by the village. It has a view of the Shore temple and a nice garden and swimming pool. It has nine luxurious stone cottages with kitchenettes on the beach for Rs 1300/1600 with seafacing balconies and also 34 A/C rooms in the main building.

The *Taj Group's Fisherman's Cove* (04113-44304, Madras 474-849) is 12 km north at Covelong Beach. It has a beautiful location and a good pool. Rooms are $90.

Where To Eat

The *Mamalla Bhavan*, by the bus stand, is a cheap *thali* place that also has South Indian dishes.

The *Mamalla Bhavan Annexe* (2260), on the main street, has a good vegetarian restaurant. They often have live classical Indian music outside in the courtyard in the evening. It is a recommended place. The *Hotel Veera*, which is next door, has a good vegetarian restaurant.

Travel

Air The nearest airport is in Madras.

Rail The nearest railway station is in Chengalpattu (Chingleput), 29 km west of Mamallapuram and 60 km south of Madras. From there you can get a bus or taxi to Mamallapuram. If you're coming from Madras, it is best to take a bus to Mamallapuram.

Bus From Madras (2½ hr, 60 km) private buses leave from Parry's corner (next to the High Court Building) at the intersection of NSC Bose Road and Popham's Broadway. State buses to Mamallapuram (2½ hr) leave from Broadway station. The #188, #188 A/B/D and K are faster buses, while the #19, #108B, and #119A take a little longer. Young boys hang around the bus stand to help you get on the right bus for a rupee or two. From the Mofussil bus stand, near Esplanade in Madras, you take #19A, #19C, and #68 buses to get to Mamallapuram.

There are regular buses to Kanchipuram (2 hr) via Tirukkalikundram, Chengalpattu, and Pondicherry (2½ hr).

Taxi By taxi it takes an hour and a half to get from Madras to Mamallapuram. The cost is about Rs 650. To take a day excursion from Madras to here costs about Rs 1000 for the day. You can get a taxi from the bus stand in Mamallapuram for a long distance trip, but the prices are inflated and you really have to work to get a decent price.

KANCHIPURAM

Population: 170,000, STD Code 04112

Kanchipuram is known as the "Golden City of Temples". It is considered one of the seven main sacred cities of India. It has over a hundred temples

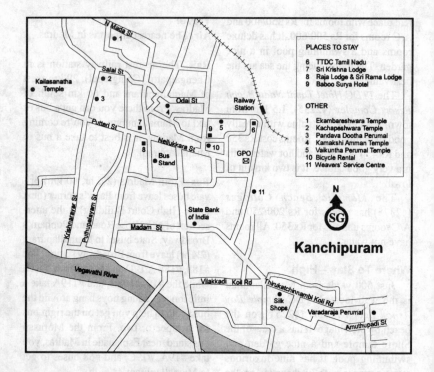

PLACES TO STAY

6 TTDC Tamil Nadu
7 Sri Krishna Lodge
8 Raja Lodge & Sri Rama Lodge
9 Baboo Surya Hotel

OTHER

1 Ekambareshwara Temple
2 Kachapeshwara Temple
3 Pandava Dootha Perumal
4 Kamakshi Amman Temple
5 Vaikuntha Perumal Temple
10 Bicycle Rental
11 Weavers' Service Centre

N

Kanchipuram

now, but at one time it is said to have had about one thousand. Kanchipuram is believed to give eternal happiness to one who goes there. Ramanujacarya lived in Kanchipuram during his youth, and Sri Caitanya visited here. Four of the Alwars—Pey Alwar, Poygai Alwar, Bhutatt Alwar, and Thirumalisai—were born within 50 miles of Kanchipuram. It is said that "Ka" (Brahma) "anchi" (worshiped) Lord Vishnu at this place and that is why the city was given the name Kanchipuram. *Puram* means "city." Kanchipuram is 71 km (45 miles) southwest of Madras on the Vegavati River and 64 km west of Mamallapuram.

Kanchipuram was the capital of the Pallavas rulers from the 7th to 9th centuries. It was also important during the Chola, Vijayanagar, and Nayaka periods.

It is an ancient place. It was mentioned in the *Mahabhasya,* written by Patanjali in the 2nd century BC.

The city is divided into two main parts—Sivakanchi, which is the northern suburb, and Vishnukanchi, which is the extreme east section of town. There is a group of Jain temples south, across the river. Kailasanatha and Vaikuntha Perumal temples were the most important temples built by the Pallavas. Varadaraja, Kamakshi, and Ekambareswara temples were originally built by the Cholas, but were added onto by the Vijayanagar and Nayaka rulers. Most of the temples are open from sunrise to 12.30 pm and from 4 pm to sunset. Many temples restrict entry to Hindus only.

There are thirteen Divya Desam temples in the area of Kanchipuram namely, Sri Vaikunthaperumal Temple, Sri Varadaraja Swami Temple, Sri Adi Varaha Perumal Temple, Pandavadootha Perumal Temple, Sri Deepaprakash Temple, Sri Yathoktakari Temple, Sri Alagiyasingar Temple, Sri Nilathingal Thundathan Perumal Temple in the Ekambareswara Temple, Sri Ashtabhuja Perumal Temple, Sri Pavalavannar Temple, Sri Ulagalanda Perumal Temple, and Sri Vijaya Raghava Perumal Temple (7 km away). The Sri Ulagalanda Perumal Temple has four Divya Desams temples in it—Peragam and Ooragam (always mentioned together), Neeragham, Karagham, and Karvannam. If you visit these temples you should take into consideration that some of the less popular temples may have the same priest doing the worship at a few temples. This means that you may come to one of these temples and it may be closed. If possible it is best to try to find a rickshaw driver who knows what time each temple is open.

Kanchipuram is famous for its handwoven silk fabrics and saris. The weavers use the highest quality silk and pure gold thread. This place is known to be the best source of high quality handwoven silk items, and Varanasi is known to be the best place for machine made silk items.

Getting Your Bearings

The city of Kanchipuram is on the north bank of the Vegavati River. The bus stand is in the center of town. The railway station is in the eastern part of the town, about 2½ km from the river. The temples and hotels are scattered within about 3 km of the bus station, in the center of town. Siva Kanchipuram is west of the railway station, and Vishnu Kanchipuram is about 3 km southeast.

Information

The temples are well spread out across the city and you need at least five hours to see the major ones. You can have a cycle rickshaw driver take you around to the temples for Rs 50 to Rs 100, depending on how many temples you go to see. You have to visit the temple either in the morning or late afternoon, as they are closed in the early afternoon (between 12.30 and 4 pm).

The **tourist office** is at the Hotel Tamil Nadu. The Archaeological Survey of India office is helpful and is located opposite the Kailasanatha Temple.

The State Bank of India is on Gandhi Rd. The post office is on Kossa St. In the summer the temperature is between 21°C (70°F) and 37°C (98°F), and in the winter the range is 20°C (68°F) to 29°C (84°F).

Brahma's Yajna

Kanchipuram is also known as Satyavrata Ksetra, due to the Aswamedha sacrifice performed here by Lord Brahma, who knew that good deeds performed here give a hundred-fold result. It is said that once Saraswati asked her husband, Lord Brahma: "Who is greater, Lakshmi or I?" Brahma replied that Lakshmi was definitely better. Hearing this reply made Saraswati leave her husband.

At this time Brahma was preparing to do a big sacrifice. When his consort, Saraswati, refused to participate in the sacrifice, Brahma began the sacrifice alone. Then in great anger Saraswati transformed herself into the fast-flowing Vegavati River and came rushing towards the *yajna* (sacrifice) area. Upon Brahma's appeal for help, Lord Vishnu laid Himself across the river's path—once at Pallikonda and again at Tiruvehka in Kanchi—and foiled goddess Saraswati's efforts. She also tried to stop the *yajna* in various other ways. At the end of the *yajna*, Sri Varadaraja came out of the *yajna-kundam* on a Sunday corresponding to Chaitra Sukla Caturdasi, Hastha Nakshatram. At Brahma's request Lord Varadaraja agreed to stay in Kanchipuram in that form and give *darsana* to His devotees.

Sri Varadaraja Temple

This is a major Vishnu temple built by the Vijayanagar kings in the 12th century. It is counted along with Tirupati and Sri Ranganatha (in Srirangam) as one of the major Vaishnava temples in South India. *Varada* means the bestower of benedictions, and *raja* means king. Thus, Varadaraja means the king of those who give benedictions. It is said that Brahma made a fire sacrifice to manifest Vishnu on an altar here. The present temple is said to reflect that same altar. The Deity is also called Devaraja Swami and Arulalar, which mean the source of all grace and one who bestows all boons. The Lord is also named Hastigirinatha, the Lord of Hastigiri (elephant hill). Other names of the Deity are Devaki Devarajan, Kari Varadan, Pranatar-tiharan, and Manicka Varadan.

Lord Varadaraja is standing facing west. He is large, and His four hands which hold a *sankha* (conch), *cakra* (disc), *gada* (club), and *padma* (lotus). He wears costly jewels. His consort is Sri Perundevi Thayar (Laksmi), who has her own temple to the right of the main temple. There is a beautiful garden inside the walls of the temple. Sri Perundevi Thayar goes every Friday to this garden and there is a festival there. There is a Lord Narasimhadeva Deity when you first enter the main temple area called Yoga Narasimha Swami.

This temple has a 30m (90 ft) high *gopuram* and a 96 pillar *mandapa,* with exquisite sculptures, that is one of the beauties of India. Mainly avatars of Vishnu and scenes from the *Mahabharata* and *Ramayana* are carved on the pillars.

Its main hall is supported by giant pillars, each carved from a different rock. There are also riders on horseback, beautiful figures of Rathi and Manmatha, and a massive chain carved out of a single stone.

The temple is on top of Hastigiri, or Elephant Hill, which is an elephant-shaped rock. It is said that Gajendra the elephant worshiped here in Treta-yuga. This hill is known as Hastigiri because the *hasti* (elephant) Gajendra, worshiped the Lord on this *giri*, or hill. The temple covers about 23 acres, which is one of the biggest areas covered by a temple in India. The temple's outer walls are 1200 by 1800 feet. Ananta-tirtham, the temple tank, is north of the 100 pillar *mandapa* hall. The temple *ratha* (cart) is 60 feet high and is a veritable temple on wheels. It is beautifully carved and very old.

The temple has an exquisite collection of temple jewelry that may be seen if you give a donation. One of the necklaces is said to have been given by Clive, the British Governor of the Madras Presidency. It is said that Clive came on the day of the Garuda-seva of Lord Varadaraja and that he presented his wife's necklace to the priest to adorn the Lord. The necklace is known as Clive Makarakandi and is used to decorate Lord Varadaraja on the Garudotsavam day.

The original Deity of Lord Varadaraja (Atti Varadar), who is said to have been installed by Lord Brahma himself, is in a silver casket inside the temple tank. The Deity is taken out every forty to fifty years for 45 to 48 days (some say 10 days). The last occasion was in 1979 and the next will be around 2019. The story is that Lord Brahma had Visvakarma, the architect of the demigods, make a wooden Deity of Lord Varadaraja. The *utsavamurti* is said to have emerged from Lord Brahma's sacrificial fire. The wooden Deity was known as Adi Hastigirinatha. It was felt that the wooden Deity would be ruined if constantly exposed and worshiped. Therefore the Deity was immersed in the temple tank, and a granite Deity was installed in its place.

Ramanujacarya used to regularly come to this temple in his youth. Sri Ramanuja is said to have met the great Vaishnava *acarya* Alavandar for the first time in the courtyard of this temple.

The main festival is the Brahmotsava festival, in May-June, which is attended by hundreds of thousands of people. During this festival the Deity is carried in procession. The main event is the Garudotsavam that draws thousands of devotees.

The main Deity is located up a flight of stairs in the back of the main temple and is a little hard to find. Non-Hindus are not allowed in the temple, which means not into the second court. ISKCON devotees and converted Hindus can enter, but are expected to wear traditional dress and *tilaka*. This temple is at the southeast end of the city, near the river, just off Thirukatchinambi Koil Road. There is a Rs 10 camera and Rs 50 video fee.

Sri Vaikuntha Perumal Temple

This Lord Vishnu temple was built in the late 8th century. It has three sanctums, one above the other, where Lord Vishnu is standing, sitting, and reclining. The goddess's name is Sri Vaikunthavalli Thayar.

This temple has a 20m-high tower, a pillar hall, and paintings on the walls. Its sculptures depict the wars fought between the Pallavas and the Chalukyas. The temple was built by Nandivarma Pallavamalla. The outer wall has lion pillars.

This temple is not very big. It is near the corner of East Raja Street and Kamakshi Amman Sannathi Street, in the center of the town by the railway station.

Sri Ulagalandar Temple

This temple is dedicated to Trivikrama (Vamana), who is called Sri Ulagalandar in this temple. The main Deity is called Ulagalanda Perumal (also called Peragathan or Peragam), the Lord who measured the world with His three steps. This Deity is nearly 35 feet in height. Trivikrama is another name for Lord Vamana, who begged from Bali Maharaja the amount of land that He could cover in three steps. The right foot of the Deity is in a lifted position, indicating that the Lord has already covered the earth and heaven. His left foot is pressed on the head of Bali Maharaja. A lamp, fixed to a big stick, is used to enable one to get a full view of the Deity. The consort of Ulagalanda Perumal is called Amrithavalli Thayar.

This temple has four Divya Desams shrines in it—Peragathan (Sri Ulagalandar) and Ooragam (always referred together), Neeragham, Karagham, and Karvannam shrines. The shrine of Adi Sesa, called Ooragam, is next to Ulagalanda Perumal. Ooragam means snake. Adi Sesa is the divine snake used as a couch by the Lord. Peragathan (Trivikrama) and Ooragam (Adi Sesa) are together referred to as one Divya Desam shrine.

Behind a beautiful 16 pillars *mandapa*

in the second *prakaram* is the shrine of Neeragathan, who is also called Jagadeeswara Perumal. It is said that the Lord gave *darsana* to Markandeya Muni here. Only the *utsava* (processional) Deity is now worshiped. This shrine is located on the north side of the temple.

In the third *prakaram* of the temple is the Divya Desam shrine of Karunakara Perumal. His consort is known as Padmamani Thayar.

The fourth Divya Desam shrine in the temple is Karvannam, who is also known as Navaneeta Chora. His consort is called Komalavalli Thayar.

There is an annual festival here in Jan/Feb.

Sri Vijaya Raghava Temple

This Divya Desam temple is seven km from Kanchipuram in the town of Thiruputkuli. The Lord is known here as Vijaya Raghava, which means literally "Rama the winner".

The goddess of the temple is known as Maragathavalli Thayar. In front of the temple is a bathing tank called Jatayu-pushkarini. On a hill to the east of the tank is a temple dedicated to Jatayu. The *Vamana Purana* says that Jatayu, who was killed by Ravana, was cremated at Thiruputkuli.

Sri Ramanuja studied under Yadava Prakasa in Thiruputkuli. There is a *mandapa* here where Ramanujacarya studied the *advaita* philosophy from Yadhava Prakash, in order to master it so he could defeat it. Since Ramanuja kept refuting the *advaita* philosophy taught by Yadhava Prakash he was expelled from the ashram.

Sri Ashtabhujam Perumal Temple

Lord Vishnu has eight hands in this temple. *Ashta* means "eight" and *bhuja*

means "hands." The four right arms of Lord Vishnu are holding a *cakra* (disc), sword, lotus flower, and arrow. The four left hands hold a conch, bow, shield, and club. It is said that goddess Saraswati let loose an army of demons to ruin the sacrifice performed by Brahma. These demons were all killed by Lord Vishnu. She then sent Sarabha, an unnatural type of ferocious beast with eight legs. To defeat this beast Lord Vishnu assumed this form with eight arms equipped with eight weapons.

It is also said that the crocodile caught hold of the leg of **Gajendra** the elephant in the temple tank here. When Gajendra cried out in despair to the Lord, Vishnu came and killed the crocodile with His *cakra* (disc).

The goddess is known as Puspa-kavalli Thayur. It is traditional here to worship the goddess first before worshipping the Lord.

There is also a Deity of Varahadeva, Lord Vishnu in His boar incarnation, in this temple. This is a Divya Desam temple. This temple is opposite the Yathoktakari Temple, about 1½ km from the Varadaraja Temple.

Pandava Dootha Perumal

The Pandava Dootha Perumal Temple is a Divya Desam Vishnu temple located by the Ekambareswara Temple. The main Vishnu Deity is in a sitting posture, facing east. The huge Deity is 25 feet high, to signify the Viswarupa (universal) form of the Lord. The consorts of Lord Vishnu are Rukmini Devi and Satyabhama.

It is said that Janamejaya, the great-grandson of Arjuna, performed penance here to get the *darsana* of Lord Krishna in His form as an envoy (representative) of the Pandavas to the Kauravas, before the Kurukshetra war.

Sri Deepa Prakasa Temple

In this temple the presiding Deity of Lord Vishnu is named Sri Deepa Prakasa, which means the "luster of the lamp". His consorts are Sri Devi and Bhu Devi. The name of Lord Vishnu's consort is Marakata Valli Thayar. The temple is also known as Vilokkoli Koil.

This is the birthplace of Sri Vedanta Desika, a great *acarya* and author in the Ramanuja-sampradaya. By the shrine of Deepa Prakasa, there is a shrine dedicated to Sri Desika, near the place where he was born.

It is said that Lord Vishnu is known as Deepa Prakasa because He intercepted and made a lamp out of the fire that goddess Saraswati started in order to burn the sacrificial site where Lord Brahma was performing an Asvamedha-yajna. Goddess Saraswati, Lord Brahma's wife, was said to have been annoyed because Lord Brahma had started the *yajna* without her. Another story says that Lord Vishnu appeared as a big light to dispel the darkness that Saraswati created to spoil the *yajna*. Saraswati then realized that if the omnipotent light of Lord Vishnu is present, there can be no darkness.

This temple is located about half a km west of the Yadhoktakari Temple of Lord Bhujagasayana and a half km west of Sri Ashtabhujam Perumal Temple.

Sri Yathoktakari Temple

In this temple, Lord Vishnu, called Lord Bhujagasayana, is in a lying posture. The main Deity is known as Lord Yathoktakari because he accepted the request of Tirumalisai Alwar, His devotee, to get up, follow him out of Kanchipuram, and to again return and lie down. *Yathokta* means "as requested" and *kari* means "a person who did it." The

consort of Lord Yathoktakari is known as Komalavalli.

It is said that when goddess Saraswati tried to stop Lord Brahma's *yajna*, she took the form of the Vegavati River and rushed towards the sacrificial site to wash away the place. Lord Vishnu is said to have laid down across the path of the river. On seeing Lord Vishnu, goddess Saraswati gave up her plan and went underground.

Sri Alagiyasingar Temple

Lord Vishnu is known here as Mukunda Nayaka. It is said that Lord Vishnu took the form of Narasimha and fought with the demon Kapalika to save Brahma's *yajna*. This temple is about ¾ km from the Deepaprakasa Temple.

Sri Pavalavannar Temple

The presiding Deity of Lord Vishnu here is in a sitting posture on the divine couch of the five-headed Adi Sesa. This Divya Desam temple is near the railway station ¾ km northeast of the Kamakshi Amman Temple. The consort of Pavalavannar is Pavalavalli Thayar. Opposite this temple is the Pachivannar Temple, which is also important.

Kailasanatha Temple

This sandstone temple, dedicated to Lord Siva, was built by Rajasimha Pallava in the 7th century. Mahendra Varman III added the front later. It is one of the earliest examples of Dravidian architecture and is one of the most beautiful temples in Kanchipuram. Kailasanatha means Lord of Mount Kailasa. It is famous for its sculptures. Most famous of these is the sculpture of Ardhanariswara, who has a vina in her hand. There are fresco style paintings on the inner walls of the shrine. The outer wall of the temple has 58 small shrines showing different aspects of Siva. The architecture resembles that of the Shore temple in Mamallapuram.

It is open between 8 am to 12 noon and from 4 pm to 6 pm. It is on Putteri Street in the western part of the city, about a km from the bus station.

Sri Ekambaranatha Temple

This temple dedicated to Lord Siva is the largest temple in Kanchipuram. This temple is also known as the Ekambareswara Temple. Parts of the main temple were built by the Pallava kings, but the rest of the temple complex was mainly built in the 16th and 17th centuries. It has a towering 60 metre (188 ft) high *gopuram* (tower) built by Krishna Devaraja of the Vijayanagar empire in 1509. No two towers of the temple are opposite each other, nor are the walls of the temple parallel to each other. There are almost no right angles in the temple. It has a 1000 pillar hall (actually 540). Most of the pillars are intricately and beautifully carved.

There is a **mango tree** behind the inner sanctum (main temple) that is said to be 3,500 years old. It has four branches, said to represent the four *Vedas*. Each leaf of this tree is a different shape. The name of the deity itself is believed to have been derived thus: Eka-Amra-Natha, meaning the Lord of the Mango Tree. The fruit from each branch has a different taste. In the path around the tree is a Siva-linga made of 108 small *lingas* and another one made up of 1008 *lingas*. You should circle around the tree clockwise. The other way is considered inauspicious.

The huge *linga* is known as the Prithvi-linga, or **earth *linga***, one of the five element *lingas* of South India. The other four are the Agni-linga (fire) at Thiruvannamalai, the Appu-linga (water) at Jambukeswara, the Vayu-linga (air) at Kalahasti, and the Akasha-linga (ether) at Chidambaram.

The story of the temple is that while Lord Siva was meditating Parvati playfully covered his eyes for a moment. This resulted in the earth being covered with darkness for years. This angered Siva who cursed Parvati to go to earth and do severe penances. She went to the earth and created the earth *linga* and worshiped it under a single (*eka*) mango tree in Kanchipuram. Siva sent different obstacles to test Parvati's sincerity. When he sent a flood, she clasped to the *linga* so tightly that imprints were made on it.

With the permission of a temple priest you can climb to the top of one of the gopurams and get a view of the area. It is believed that if a woman seeking a child worships here, her desire will be fulfilled. Non-Hindus are not allowed in the inner sanctum. This temple is between North Made and West Made Streets in the northwest part of the city.

There is a Vishnu temple within the temple complex, which is one of the Divya Desams shrines. The Deity is named **Nilathingal Thundatthan Vishnu**.

Sri Kamakshi Amman Temple

This temple is dedicated to goddess Kamakshi (Parvati), the love-eyed goddess. *Kamakshi* means one who has eyes full of love. Just in front of Sri Kamakshi is the **Sri Chakra**. All worship and sacrifices are offered to the Sri Chakra. Sri Kamakshi Amman Temple is one of the three main holy places of Sakti worship in India, the other two being Varanasi and Madurai. This temple has a golden *gopuram* and some fine carvings. It was built by the Cholas in the 14th century.

The Sri **Adi Varaha Perumal Temple**, one of the Divya Desam temples, is located within the temple's walls. This shrine is located to the left of the entrance to the inner sanctum (altar) of Kamakshi Amman. In the northeast part of the Pancha-ganga temple tank there is a shrine with three floors, each having a Vishnu Deity in a different posture: standing, sitting, and reclining.

An annual car festival is held on the ninth lunar day in February-March and draws a large crowd of about 25,000 people. The deity is taken on procession in a magnificent wooden temple cart.

On Tuesdays and Fridays at around 8 pm there is an elephant procession with fireworks and music. This temple is considered to be auspicious for marriage blessings. This temple is just off Odai Street, in the center of town.

Shopping

Kamatchi Co-optex, 182 Gandhi Rd; *Srinivas and Co*, 135 Thirukatchi Nambi St; *Thiruvallur Co-operative Society*, 207 Gandhi Rd; and *Murudan*, on Railway Rd have good names for silk items. The *Handlooms Weavers Service Centre*, at 20 Railway Rd, by the post office, can give you good shopping advice. It is open only on weekdays.

Where To Stay

The *Ashok Travellers Lodge*, near the railway station, is a basic cheap place. There is also the basic *Sri Krishna Lodge* (22831) 68-A Nellukkara St, and the *Rajam Lodge*, which has rooms with bath for Rs 55.

Raja's Lodge, 20 Nellukkara St, near the bus station, has real basic rooms for Rs 55/75. Next door, the *Sri Rama Lodge* (22435), 21 Nellukkara St, has basic rooms with hot water for Rs 100/110 and

Rs 250/300 for a room with A/C. It is better than the other budget places. It is not such a bad place, and it has a vegetarian restaurant. Across the street is the *Sri Krishna Lodge* (22831), which is about the same as the Raja's Lodge.

A good place to stay is the *Hotel Tamil Nadu* (22553), Kamatchi Sannathi St, near the railway station. Normal rooms are Rs 175 and comfortable A/C rooms cost Rs 300 and Rs 375. The rooms have hot water. It is full most of the time, so it is best to book a room in advance at a Hotel Tamil Nadu in another city.

The best place in town is the *Hotel Baboo Soorya* (22555), 85 East Raja Veethi, which has comfortable rooms for Rs 250/300 and Rs 350/400 with a 20% luxury tax. It is a recommended place with a good vegetarian restaurant.

Where To Eat

The best place in town is the restaurant at the *Hotel Baboo Soorya,* 85 East Raja St. The *Rama Lodge* has a cheap vegetarian restaurant with good *dosas*.

Travel

Air The nearest airport is in Madras, 71 km northeast.

Rail From Madras Beach Station one has to go via Chingleput (Chengalpattu). The two trains that go to Kanchipuram leave from Madras between 5 and 7 pm and take about three hours. The trains going back to Madras leave Kanchi between 6 and 7 in the morning. The train takes about twice as long as the bus. You can go to Kanchipuram via Arakkonam (Arakonam) from Madras Egmore Station. There are only two connections between Arakkonam to Kanchipuram—at 7.50 am and 5.20 pm and in the opposite direction at 9.25 am and 6.45 pm.

Bus There are regular buses to and from Madras (No 828, 2 hr), Tirupati (3 hr), Tiruttani, and Vellore (2½ hr). There are five direct buses a day to Mamallapuram (2 hr). There are many buses to Chengalpattu (Chingleput, 1 hr), and from there you can get another bus to Mamallapuram. There are direct buses to Bangalore (No 828), Tiruchirappalli (No 122, Srirangam, 7 hr), and Pondicherry (No 804, 3 hr). There are some buses that go direct to Tirupati. There are also buses to a small town near Tirupati, and then you have to get another bus for 20 minutes.

The bus stand is on the corner of Nellukkara St and Kossa St, in the center of town. Public buses for Madras leave from Parry's Corner by the Law Courts, where the Esplanade meets First Line Beach. Bus No 141 takes two hours to get here.

Others A convenient way to get around is to get a tourist taxi from Madras. Both ITDC and TTDC operate conducted tours from Madras to Tirukkalikundram, Kanchipuram, and Mamallapuram daily. This tour is very rushed.

TIRUKKALIKUNDRAM (Paksitirtha)

Tirukkalikundram means the "Hill of the Sacred Kite" (tiru—sacred, kaliki—kites, kundram—hill). It is 14 km west of Mamallapuram, 60 km southwest of Madras, and 65 km east of Kanchipuram. This place is famous because of two birds that have come here to eat almost every day for hundreds of years. Lord Caitanya came here.

There is an interesting fairly large Siva temple at the base of the hill with huge gopurams. There is a tank called **Sangutirtha** (sangu means conch) at the southeast end of the village. Every 12 years there is a Valampiri (right-turned) conch found in it that is then displayed in the Siva temple in the village. To have possession of a right-turned conch is considered good luck, and it is considered auspicious to just look at such a conch.

Bhaktavatsleeswara Temple

Bhaktavatsleeswara Temple is a Siva temple on top of the Vedagiri Hill. This hill has a five hundred foot elevation. The deity is known as Vedagiriswara. It is said that two birds have come here daily, since time immemorial, to receive food from the temple priest. It is said that these two birds are two sages who were cursed by Lord Siva. It is believed that they have their bath at Varanasi, their food at Paksitirtham, their rest at Chidambaram, and they worship at Rameswaram. You have to climb hundreds of steps to the top of the hill. As it is a fairly tough climb, it is possible to be carried up.

The priests prepare food and offer it to the Siva-linga. The priest then puts the rice in two silver pots and the birds come and eat it. The birds are seen for about 15 minutes, after which they fly away. Sometimes the birds eat out of the priest's hand. The birds usually arrive punctually every day between noon and 1 pm. When I was there the priest came out around 12 noon, but the birds did not come to eat that day and everyone left disappointed. At least I did. I was told that the birds had come regularly the month before, but had not come to eat in about two weeks.

Academic scholars accept evidence found recorded on the temple at the bottom of the hill that these birds have come almost daily for at least a thousand years.

Getting Here

The is no place to stay here. There are a few small shops where you can get cold drinks in the village. This place would normally be visited on a day trip from Mamallapuram, Kanchipuram, or Madras. The closest railway station is 9 km southwest at Chingleput.

There are regular buses from Mamallapuram (14 km, half hour). You can also stop here on the way from Kanchipuram to Mamallapuram by bus. There is a tour bus from Madras that goes to Mamallapuram, then here, and then to Kanchipuram, all in the same day. This tour is not usually on time to see the birds, which is the main reason to come here.

You can ride a bike here from Mamallapuram. It is a beautiful ride. You can also get an auto-rickshaw or taxi from Mamallapuram.

Sriperumbudur

Population: 13,000

This is the **birthplace of Ramanujacarya**. Sriperumbudur is 40 km southwest of Madras, halfway between Madras and Kanchipuram. There is the large **Adi Kesava Vishnu Temple** here. There is also a *murti* (statue) of Ramanujacarya that he personally embraced out of appreciation of its exact likeness of him. It is one of three Ramanuja deities installed during his lifetime. The deity is always decorated with an opulent crown, necklaces, earrings, and other ornaments of diamonds and gold.

There are regular buses to here from Madras and Kanchipuram.

Madurantakam

Population: 27,000

There is a beautiful important **Sita-Rama temple** here, wherein Sita and Rama are holding hands. It is said that while Rama was in the forest for 14 years he came to this place. As he was leaving, the sage Vibhandaka requested him to

visit this place on His way back to Ayodhya. When Sri Rama, Laksmana and Sita were returning to Ayodhya, after Rama killed Ravana, the Pushpaka Vimana (flower airplane) that was carrying them would not move when it reached this place. Sri Rama held Sita's hand to help her get down the steps of the Pushpaka Vimana. The Deity of Rama in this temple is called Erikatha Raman. There is also a Deity of Sri Karunakaramurthi in this temple.

Sri Ramanuja met one of his gurus, Maha Purna (Peria Nambi), in Madurantakam and was initiated under the Bakula tree in the Rama temple. In the temple there are a cakra and a conch that are said to have been used at the initiation ceremony of Ramanuja. The *panchasamskara* molds are in the shrine for Peria Nambi and Ramanuja, which is north of the flagstaff in the temple.

Madurantakam is 90 km south of Madras between Chingleput and Villupuram. Trains heading south from Madras stop here. There are regular buses from Madras and Chingleput.

Sholingur

There is a Divya Desam temple on a hill here called **Sri Yoga Narasimha Swami Temple**. You have to walk up about 1000 steps to reach this temple. The goddess of the temple is Amritavalli Thayar. There is another temple on a hill about 200 feet high nearby, where Lord Anjaneya (Hanuman) presides.

It is said that a person who is mentally deranged can be cured by first taking bath here in **Hanumath-tirtha**, then climbing the small hill and entering the Anjaneya (Hanuman) Temple and Yoga Narasimha Temple. Many other types of diseases are also said to be cured here.

Sholingur, which is also known as

Ghatikachalam is on the Madras Banga-lore Road. It is 27 km west of Arkonam (Arakkonam). There is a passenger train that stops here. The temple is 9 km from the station. There are buses to and from Madras.

Tiruninravur (Tiruninravoor)

There is a Divya Desam temple here called the **Sri Bhaktavatsala Perumal Temple**. The Deity is also called Pattha-ravi Perumal, which means that he is the very life of his devotees. The goddess is called Ennai Petra Thayar.

Tiruninravur is about 30 km from Madras, between Madras and Arkonam.

Tiruvannamalai
Population: 120,000, STD Code 04175

There are over 100 temples in this town. The most famous temple is the Arunachaleswara Temple, dedicated to Lord Siva and Parvati.

Arunachaleswara Temple

It has a 60m, or 13 story, high sculp-tured *gopuram*. It is at the foot of Arunachala Hill and is one of the largest temples in all of India. The Vijayanagar ruler Krishnadeva Raya (1502-29) built the temple, but the inner part of the temple dates back to the 11th century. In this temple is one of the five element *lingas,* god incarnate as Fire. This temple has a thousand pillared hall. There are also temples dedicated to Subrahmanya and Parvati on the temple premises. Thou-sands of visitors come during the **Kar-tika Deepam** celebration, in November/ December, during which a huge bonfire is lit on top of the hill. The fire can be seen for miles and burns for many days.

Where To Stay

The *Aruna Lodge*, 82 Kosamadam St,

is a basic place about 200m east of the temple entrance. The *Udipi Brindhavan Hotel* (22693), 57 Anna Salai, has very basic rooms with bath for Rs 60 and A/C rooms for Rs 200. It has a good cheap *thali* place. The *Park Hotel* is a clean place with rooms for Rs 40/60. The *Ho-tel Trishul* (22219), 3 minutes from the temple, has rooms for Rs 275/325 and Rs 500/550 with A/C.

Travel

Tiruvannamalai is over 100 km south of Kanchipuram and 185 km southwest of Madras. It takes about two or three hours to get here by train from Vellore, which is due north. The train station is on the line between Madurai and Tiru-pati, and there is a daily train in each di-rection. The Madurai-Tirupati Exp #6800 departs daily to Tirupati (10.55 pm, 6 hr). The Tirupati-Madurai Exp #6799 goes to Madurai (9.25 pm, 13 hr) via Chidam-baram, Thanjavur, and Trichy. Most people arrive by bus at the bus stand, about 2 km north of the temple.

PONDICHERRY
Population: 560,000, STD Code 0413

Pondicherry is 160 km south of Ma-dras. It is said that Agastya Muni had his Ashram here. The French ruled it from 1816 to 1954.

Pondicherry is famous as the location of the **Sri Aurobindo Ashram**, founded in 1920 by Sri Aurobindo. The main building of the Ashram is on Rue de la Marine. After Aurobindo left his body, one of his disciples a French woman called The Mother, became in charge of the Ashram, until her death in 1973 at the age of 97.

The **Varadaraja Temple** (12th cen-tury) is the most important Vishnu temple in town and is located just west of Gandhi Road, off Thyagaraja Street.

Auroville is about 10 km north of Pondicherry. This project has about 900 residents spread over 20 km. About two thirds are foreigners.

Information

The Vak Bookshops on Rue Nehru has a good selection of religious books. There is a Higginbothams Bookshop on Gingy St, on the other side of the canal.

The Post Office is by the canal in the center of town. You can hire a bike from shops on MG Rd and Mission St. You can **change money** at the Indian Overseas Bank, inside the Hotel de Ville, Goubert Salai, and at the branch on Nehru St.

Where To Stay – Lower

The *Aristo Guest House* (26728), 50-A Mission St, is a recommended place with rooms with bath for Rs 80/100 and Rs 300 with A/C. The *Hotel Ellora* has rooms for Rs 60/80 up to Rs 250 for a room with A/C. The *Hotel Kanchi* (35540), Mission St, has clean rooms for Rs 75/100. It is one of the better cheap places

Where To Stay – Middle

The *Aurobindo Ashram-run Guesthouses* are the best places to stay in town. You book them from the Ashram reception office on Marine Street, north of Government Square. They have a 10.30 pm curfew. Smoking and alcohol are banned in the Ashram guest houses.

The *Park Guest House* (34412), at the south end of Goubert Salai, is a recommended place that has rooms with balconies that face the sea. Rooms are Rs 150/200 and Rs 250/300 for deluxe rooms. It has a vegetarian restaurant. Your second choice is the *International Guest House*

(36699), Gingy St, which has clean rooms with bath starting at Rs 60/80 and A/C rooms for Rs 275.

The *Sea Side Guest House* (26494), 10 Goubert Salai, is a small place that has rooms with bath and hot water for Rs 125 to Rs 150 and Rs 250 to Rs 350 with A/C. The *Ajantha Guest House* (38898), 22 Goubert Salai, is a good middle-class place with rooms for Rs 150 and Rs 250 with A/C. *Anandha Inn* (30711), 154 S V Patel Road is one of the best places in town, with rooms for Rs 700/850.

The *Hotel Mass* (37221), between the state and TTC bus stands, has comfortable rooms for Rs 375/475 and a deluxe room for Rs 450/500. All rooms have hot water, A/C and a TV.

Where To Eat

The *Ashram Dining Room* has non-oily and non-spicy food. The *Seaside Guest House*, Goubert Salai, near the light house, has a vegetarian restaurant. *Picnic*, Kamaraj Salai, is a vegetarian place. There is a vegetarian restaurant in the *Park Guest House*, at the south end of Goubert Salai.

Travel

Air There is an airport in Pondicherry, but at the present time there are no flights there.

Train The closest railway junction is Villupuram (38 km), which is on the main Madras-Madurai line. Many express trains run in both directions. From Pondicherry you can get one of two local trains (8.05 am, 9 pm), which take about two hours, or a bus to Villupuram.

Bus There are two bus stations. The Thiruvalluvar (TTC) bus station is on Maraimalai Adigal Salai, an extension of

Lal Bahadur St, at the junction with Anna Salai. It is an easy place to deal with. From here there are many buses to Madras (5 hr, 60 daily) and Chidambaram. There are also regular buses to Bangalore (8 hr, 4 daily), Madurai (8 hr, 1 daily), and Tiruvannamalai.

The hectic state bus stand, about half a km away, has buses to Kanchipuram, Thanjavur (6 hr, 2 daily), Kumbakonam, Mamallapuram (2½ hr, 9 daily), Kanchipuram (3 hr, 5 daily), Tiruchirappalli (6 hr, 6 daily), Vellore, Bangalore, and Madras.

Tirunallar

There is the **Tyagaraja Siva temple** here. In this temple is a shrine dedicated to the nine planets (*nava-graha*). The planet **Saturn** has an altar inside the outer wall of this Siva temple. Saturn's blessings are overwhelming, but its wrath can cause great misery. Saturn was made powerless when King Nala took shelter of Lord Siva here. This is the most famous Saturn temple in South India.

A big festival is held here every time Saturn moves from one sign of the Zodiac to another. It celebrates the release of King Nala from the clutches of Saturn. Tirunallar is 8 km south of Karaikal (which is in the Union Territory of Pondicherry), near the seashore and 160 km east of Tiruchirappalli.

CHIDAMBARAM

Population: 69,000, STD Code 04144

The name Chidambaram comes from *chid*–human thinking, consciousness, and *ambaram*–the expanse of the skies or heaven, or "expanding consciousness". It is near the coast, 68 km south of Pondicherry on the way to Thanjavur. It is the home of the famous Sabhanayaka Nataraja Temple, which was built by Vira

Chola Raja in the 10th century.

Information

The **tourist office** is at the Hotel Tamil Nadu. You can **change money** at the Indian Bank, 64 S Car St; State Bank of India, Pava Mudali St; and Central Bank, 62 Bazaar St.

Sabhanayaka Nataraja Temple

This is the original temple dedicated to the Nataraja form of Lord Siva, where Lord Siva is found in his famous dancing pose, with one leg in the air and four arms. This temple is dedicated to Lord Siva in his aspect of Nataraja (the Celestial Dancer). Lord Siva is in the Ananda Tandavam dancing posture. He defeated goddess Kali in a dance contest. The Nataraja deity here has been the model for innumerable bronze statues of Siva performing this dance.

It is a 10th century temple, built during the reign of Vira Chola Raja. Raja Krishnadeva Raya of Vijayanagar reconstructed the temple in 1520. The outer wall is 1800 ft long and 1480 ft east to west.

The temple is spectacular with four huge *gopurams* towering 50m (150 ft) high. The north and south *gopurams* are 49 metres high. The east and west temple *gopurams* are elaborately carved with the 108 classical dancing postures of Nataraja. Siva is believed to have invented 108 different dances out of which the most famous is the "Tandava."

Non-Hindus are not technically allowed in the inner sanctum. The local *brahmanas*, known as Dikshitars, act as the guides for the temple. It may be a good idea to hire one because they can enable you to bypass the ban on temple entry. Without a guide non-Hindus are not supposed to go in the inner sanctum

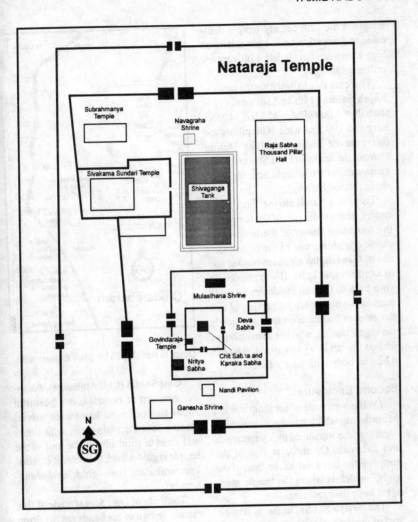

Nataraja Temple

Subrahmanya Temple

Navagraha Shrine

Raja Sabha Thousand Pillar Hall

Sivakama Sundari Temple

Shivaganga Tank

Mulasthana Shrine

Deva Sabha

Govindaraja Temple

Chit Sabha and Kanaka Sabha

Nritya Sabha

Nandi Pavilion

Ganesha Shrine

N

SG

of the temple.

The temple is in the northern part of the city. It takes at least an hour to see the temple. The temple is open from 4 am to 12 noon and 4.30 pm to 9 pm. The evening 6 pm *puja* is the most interesting. On Friday, before the temple closes, Nataraja is carried on a palanquin in procession, with priests triumphantly carrying tridents and torches.

Third Enclosure

If you enter the western *gopurams* and turn left, you come to the Siva-ganga tank, which measures 315 feet by 170 feet.

In front of the northern *gopuram* is a shrine dedicated to the **nine planets**. There is a 13th century temple dedicated to **Subrahmanya** (Kartikeya) in the northwest part of the temple. South of this temple is the 12th century temple dedicated to **Parvati**, who is known here as Siva-kama-sundari. It has 17th century ceiling paintings.

There are five halls within the temple. **Rajah Sabha** (14th to 15th century) is the hall of 1,000 pillars, which is 340 feet long and 190 feet wide. The pillars are finely carved granite monoliths. During festivals the deities of Lord Siva and Siva-kama-sundari are brought here for *abhisheka* (sacred bathing).

There is a **Nandi shrine**, Siva's bull carrier, in the south part of the temple. In the southwest corner of the temple is a shrine containing one of the largest deities of **Ganesh**, the elephant-headed son of Lord Siva, in India. If you stand with your back to Ganesh inside the entrance *mandapa*, you can see the carving of two devotees of Nataraja: on the right side is the sage Patanjali, who has a snake body, and on the left is Vyaghrapada, who has a human body with tiger's feet.

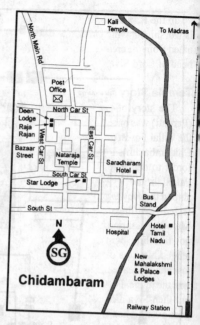

Second Enclosure

On the north side of the temple is the **Mulathana**, which has the *svayambhu-linga* that was worshiped by Vyaghrapada and Patanjali. On the east side of the temple is the **Deva Sabha,** or "hall of the gods," which is where the temple managers have their meetings.

The **Nritya Sabha**, in the southwest part of the temple, marks the place where Lord Siva out-danced Kali. It is carved like a giant chariot.

Inner Enclosure

What is unique about this Siva temple is that within its compound there is also a major Divya Desam Vishnu temple dating to the 14th century. This shrine is dedicated to **Govindaraja**, Lord Vishnu, who is reclining on Ananta Sesa. The Deity is worshiped by Sri Vaishnava *pujaris*.

Chit Sabha (Chit Ambalam), the inner sanctum of Nataraja, is a beautiful room covered with hammered silver, leading into the main altar, with doors and steps of solid silver. The roof of the temple is gold-plated, therefore it is called Ponnambalam (*pon*–gold, *ambalam*–temple).

The deity of Lord Siva is made of five metals. In two of his hands are the drum of creation and the flame of destruction. The Lord is worshiped here in two forms —Nataraja, the Lord of Dance, and as the Akasha-linga. To the left of Nataraja is a curtain with a string of golden bilva leaves in front of it. Behind this curtain is the **Akasha-linga**, know as the Rahasya or "secret", which is made of the most subtle element, ether (*akasha),* or space. This *linga* is one of the five element *lingas* and is invisible.

In the **Kanaka Sabha** a crystal *linga* is worshiped, which is said to have emanated from the crescent moon on the forehead of Lord Siva.

Temple Story

The story of the temple is that Kali (Parvati) was once the patron goddess of the Tillai Forest (what is now the city of Chidambaram). Lord Siva came to this forest to dance for two of his devotees Patanjali and Vyaghrapada. They worshiped the *svayambhu-linga*, a self manifested Siva-linga, which is now in the Mulasthana shrine of the temple. Kali did not like him being there, so she challenged him to a dancing contest and the loser had to leave the forest. Lord Vishnu was the judge. For a while they were tied, but then Siva did a dance where his leg goes over his head, the Ananda Tandava. At this point Kali knew she could not compete and left.

Festivals

There are two main festivals, one in May/June and the other in Dec/Jan. Both are ten day festivals ending with a cart festival on the ninth day and an *abhisheka*, bathing of the deities, on the tenth day. The best time to come, however, is for the **Natyanjali Festival** in February or March. During the last five days of the festival, dancers come from all over India to pay homage to the Lord of Dance. These festivals are popular, so you have to arrange accommodation in advance.

Where To Stay

One of the better basic places is the good valued *Star Lodge*, South Car St, which has rooms for Rs 55/60. The *Hotel Raja Rajan* (22690), 162 W Car St, has clean small rooms with bath for Rs 45/80. There is also the *Deen Lodge*

(22602), which has rooms for Rs 50/65.

The *Ramyas Deluxe* (23011), 46 South Car St, is one of the best cheaper places. Rooms are Rs 40/75 and a deluxe double is Rs 175.

The *Hotel Saradharam* (22966), 19 VGP St, opposite the bus stand, has large clean rooms for Rs 150/175 or Rs 250 with A/C. The *PM Lodge*, 15 S Sanathi, has basic cheap rooms.

The reasonably priced *Hotel Tamil Nadu* (22323), on Railway Feeder Rd, is the nicest place in town and has both air-conditioned rooms for Rs 275 and normal rooms for Rs 100/165. Check the room before you take one, as some of the rooms have seen better days.

The *Akshaya* (22181), 17/18 E Car St, is a modern hotel by the temple with 30 rooms. It has a rooftop veg restaurant.

The *Railway Retiring Rooms* are a good value with large clean rooms, but the bathrooms are a little run down.

Where To Eat

The *Babu Restaurant* in the Star Lodge serves good food and is crowded. There are also restaurants at the *Hotel Mahalakshmi* and *Udipi Hotel*. The *Akshaya Hotel* (22181), 17/18 E Car St, has a rooftop vegetarian restaurant open in the evening, with a view of the temple's *gopurams*.

Travel

Air The nearest airport is in Tiruchirappalli, 167 km southwest.

Train Chidambaram is on the main line of the Southern Railway, from Madras Egmore to Rameswaram. There are trains to Madras (243 km, 5½ hr, 4 daily), Kumbakonam (2 hr, 4 daily), Thanjavur (3 hr), and Trichy (4 hr). There are two direct trains daily to Tirupati and one train to

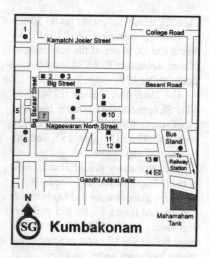

1	Sri Chakrapani Temple
2	VPR Lodge & Hotel Siva
3	State Bank of India
4	Hotel AAR
5	Kumbeshwara Temple
6	Ramaswami Temple
7	Poothamari Tank
8	Sarangapani Temple
9	Pandiyan Lodge
10	Arul Restaurant
11	New Diamond Lodge
12	Nageshwara Temple
13	PRV Lodge & Hotel Raya's
14	GPO & Clock Tower

Rameswaram (11 hr). From the temple to the train station is a twenty-minute walk or a Rs 5 cycle-rickshaw. There are railway retiring rooms and a post office on platform one.

Bus There are buses to Thanjavur (9 hr, 3 daily), Pondicherry (60 km), Madras (5-7 hr, 20 daily), Mamallapuram, Tiruchirappalli (Trichy), Kumbakonam, and Madurai. The bus station is about three blocks east of the temple, in the center of town.

Sri Mushnam

There is an impressive stone temple here that houses the beautiful Deity of **Lord Varaha** who is named Vrid-dhakola (Bhuvaraha). This Deity is said to have manifested from a *shalagram-shila*. The Lord looks very proud wearing silver armor with His hands on His waist and head held in an air of victory. It is said that this Deity was manifest when Lord Varaha rested here, after killing Hiranyaksa. Sri Mushnam is about 40 km west of Chidambaram.

Tirukkadaiyur

There is a Siva-linga in the **Amrita-ghateswara Temple** here. It is believed that anyone that visits this temple will not meet Yamaraja at the time of death. A visit to this place is supposed to be equal to performing 100 Aswamedha-yajnas (horse sacrifices). This beautiful huge temple has some of the most intricately carved sculptures in all of India.

The story of the temple is that when Yamaraja (the god of death) came to take Markandeya away, Markandeya clasped onto the Siva-*linga* to save himself from Yamaraja's shackles. Yamaraja threw a noose to catch hold of Markandeya, which also encircled the Siva-linga. Lord Siva is said to have then come out of the *linga* and killed Yamaraja. The clasp marks and the mark of Yamaraja's rope are still on the *linga*.

Tirukkadaiyur is about 40 northeast of Kumbakonam, between Mayuram and Tranquebar.

Gangaikondacholapuram

Gangaikondacholapuram was established as a capital city by the Chola ruler Rajendra I (1012-44). The reason to come here is to see the magnificent Brihadiswara Temple. The name of this town means "the town of the Chola who conquered the Ganga." There is a huge temple tank that had pots of water from the Ganges emptied into it by subservient kings to the Chola court.

Beside the Brihadiswara temple, there is not much to see, except a few ruins and the Archaeological Museum, two minutes east along the main road. The temple is closed between 12 and 4 pm, and there is nothing in the town other than a few cold drink stands.

Gangaikondacholapuram is 61 km northeast of Thanjavur (Tanjore) and 35 km northeast of Kumbakonam. There are regular buses to Kumbakonam and a few to Tiruchirappalli (Trichy) and Chidambaram. It is a good idea to bring a torch (flashlight) with you, as parts of the temple can be dark.

Brihadiswara Temple

Brihadiswara Temple is a large Siva temple that can be seen from a distance because of its enormous 55m high *vimana* (tower over the altar). This temple was built by Rajendra Chola in 1025 to celebrate his victorious expedition to the River Ganges. This magnificent temple was built in the same design as the Brihadiswara Temple in Thanjavur, which was built by his father. It has a massive Siva-linga enshrined in it, but the temple is no longer used for worship. There are shrines that house Kailasanatha and Ganesh. The temple has a huge wall resembling a fort and an assembly hall containing over 150 pillars. It has many detailed sculptures on it.

KUMBAKONAM & DARASURAM

Population 150,000, STD Code 0435

There are about fifteen temples in the town center dedicated to Lord Vishnu and Lord Siva. There is also a rare Brahma temple here. Kumbakonam is one of the oldest places in South India and was the capital of the Chola kings in the 7th century. It is 350 km south of Madras and about 70 km southwest of Chidambaram. The Sarangapani Temple is one of the most important Vishnu temples in South India. Kumbakonam is named after Kumbakarna, the brother of Ravana.

Information

The Indian Bank and State Bank are opposite each other on TSR Big St. There is a place to hire a bicycle opposite the New Diamond Lodge, Nagesvaran North St.

The town is a little spread out, but most of the temples are within walking distance of each other. The rivers Kaveri and Arasalar flow on the two sides of Kumbakonam.

All the temples in Kumbakonam are closed between noon and 4.30 pm.

Sarangapani Temple

This temple is considered to be one of the most important Vishnu temples in South India, along with Srirangam and Tirupati. Seven of the Alwars sang the glories of this temple. Lord Sarangapani is the presiding Deity of the temple. Most of the temple was built by the Nayak kings between the 13th and 17th centuries, but the central shrine dates to the end of the Chola period. It is the largest Vishnu temple in Kumbakonam, and it has a *gopuram* 44m (146 ft) high that is 90 feet by 50 feet at the base.

There are two entrances for entering the central shrine of the temple. You enter the southern entrance during the *dakshinayana* period, when the sun is in the southern hemisphere, and the northern entrance during the period of *uttarayana*, when the sun is in the northern hemisphere. There are many Deities in the temple, including Pathala Srinivasa (Vishnu). The Lord's consort is Sri Komalavalli (Lakshmi), whose shrine is located in the north part of the temple, to your right as you enter the temple.

Bathing in the Hema Pushkarani Tank next to the temple is considered very auspicious. The main central shrine resembles a chariot, with elephants and horses carved on the basement. There are many carvings on the walls of this shrine.

The temple has two big carts. It also has a silver cart for special occasions, such as the first day of Tai (January-February). On Vaikuntha Ekadasi there is a big festival in the temple. Another big festival is Mattai Adi in January-February.

Kumbeswara Temple

This is the largest and oldest Siva temple in town. It is located in the center of town. Its main *gopuram* is 128 feet high and has many intricately carved sculptures on it.

There is an excellent collection of silver *vahanas* (palanquins) used to carry the deities at festival times. There is a shrine dedicated to Adi Vinayaka (Ganesh). It is said that Vinayaka came to this place before Lord Siva.

Rama Swami Temple

This temple was built in the 16th and 17th century by the Nayak King Raghunatha. This temple has Deities of Lord Rama and His three brothers. As you enter the temple there are several exquisite pillars with sculptures of pastimes from the *Ramayana*. On the walls around the temples are beautiful murals of the *Ramayana* pastimes.

Nageswara Temple

This is a Siva temple that dates to 886 AD. The sculptures in this temple are said to be some of the best of the Chola period. Statues of Dakshina-murti (south wall), Brahma (north), and Ardanariswara (west) are on the outside wall of the inner shrine. The rays of the sun enter the inner sanctum through the openings in the gopuram three times a year. The rays of the sun fall right on the Siva-linga, and this is considered to be worship by Surya, the Sun god.

Sri Cakrapani Temple

This is an important temple dedicated to the all-powerful disc of Lord Vishnu. The *cakra* (disc) of Lord Vishnu is called Sudarsana, which means "auspicious vision." The disc of the Lord is called Sudarsana because he does not discriminate between high and low criminals or demons. The Sudarsana cakra is always concerned with annihilating the demons. The illuminating principles in this world such as the sun, the moon, and fire emanate from the effulgence of Sudarsana. Similarly, illumination by knowledge also comes from Sudarsana, because with the illumination of Sudarsana one can distinguish one thing from another, the superior from the inferior.

Mahamaham Tank

A major festival is held here at the Mahamaham Sacred Tank once every 12 years, on the full moon day in the month of Magha (Jan/Feb), when Jupiter passes over Leo. At this time the waters of the Ganges, Yamuna, and seven other sacred rivers are supposed to flow into the tank. Every year there is a smaller festival in the month of Magha, when the image of Lord Kumbeswara is taken on procession. As many as 2 million people came in

February, 1992. The next scheduled major festival is in 2004. The tank covers an area of 20 acres. This tank is by the railway station.

Airavateswara Temple

This temple is located across the Arasalar River in Dharasuram, 5 km southwest of Kumbakonam. Architecturally it is one of the finest temples amongst those built during the Chola period. This Siva temple was built by Raja II in the 12th century. In front of the temple are columns with detailed small sculptures. You can rent a bicycle in Kumbakonam and ride here.

Temples In The Area

A temple dedicated to **Lord Subrahmanya** is in Swamimalai, 6 km from Kumbakonam. The **Kampahareswara Siva Temple** at Thirubuvanam is 8 km away.

Where To Stay – Lower

The *New Diamond Lodge* (20870), 93 Nageswaran North St, has clean rooms for Rs 45/60 with bath. Not far away is the new *Chellam Lodge* (23896), 57 Ayikulam Rd, which has clean rooms for Rs 50/85. The *Pandiyan Lodge* (20397), 52 Sarangapani East St, has clean rooms with bath for Rs 70/90 and is a good value. In the same price range is the *PRV Lodge*, 32 Head Post Office Rd.

Kasi Towers, 140 TSR Big Street, by the Hotel AAR, has basic rooms for Rs 70/90 and rooms with A/C for Rs 200.

Where To Stay – Middle

There are no upper-class hotels in Kumbakonam

The *Hotel ARR*, (21234), 21 TSR Big Street, is a decent place with rooms for Rs 175/225 and Rs 300/350 with A/C,

plus a 15% sale tax. This is a recommend place.

VPR Lodge/Hotel Siva (21045), 21 Big St, has rooms with hot water for Rs 160 and Rs 275 with A/C. The *Hotel Siva* has large but featureless rooms. The rooms are really impersonal.

The best place in town is the *Hotel Raya's* (22545), 28-29 Head Post Office Rd, near the Mahamaham Tank, which has clean smallish rooms for Rs 300/400 and Rs 400/450 with A/C. However, you can get almost the exact same rooms at the Hotel ARR, which is also more centrally located by the temples, for a cheaper price.

The *Hotel Athitya* (24827), 11-12 Thanjavur Main Road, is in a quiet part of town and has rooms that are a good value for Rs 225/250 with bath and Rs 375 with A/C. This place is new, and the price will go up once it becomes more established.

Where To Eat

The *Arul Restaurant*, Sarangapani East St, opposite the Pandiyan Lodge, is most likely the best place in town. It is a five-minute walk from the Hotel ARR. There are good restaurants at the *PRV Lodge* at 52 Sarangapani East St and at the *Hotel Raya's* right next to it. The Hotel ARR has a vegetarian restaurant along with a non-vegetarian restaurant, so they may cook both veg and non-veg in the same kitchen.

Travel

Kumbakonam is on the bank of the Kaveri River, 68 km southwest of Chidambaram and 311 km south of Madras.

Train The railway station is just east of the Mahamaham Tank, about 2 km from the main temple area. There are trains to Madras (8 hr), Chengalpattu (6½ hr), Trichy, Chidambaram, and Thanjavur. There is a good train to Madras about 8.30 am which takes about 8 hours.

Bus There are regular buses to Chidambaram, Tiruchirappalli (4 hrs), Madras (7½ hrs, 4 daily), Thanjavur (Tanjore, ½ hr), and Bangalore. The bus station is north of the Mahamaham Tank, southeast of the center of town, about a ten minute motor rickshaw ride from the main temple area. Buses depart to Thanjavur and Gangaikondacholapuram every few minutes.

Kumbakonam Area Divya Desam Temples

Divya Desam temples are 108 important Vishnu temples in India sung about by the Alwar devotees.

The **Uppiliappan Temple** is 6 km from Kumbakonam. There is a shrine dedicated to Markandeya, who is installed as if performing the marriage rites of his daughter. Markandeya got a boon to have Laksmi as his daughter, whom he found as a baby beneath a Tulasi plant. When she grew up, he offered her in marriage to Lord Vishnu.

In this temple is a beautiful Deity of baby Krishna, holding the toe of His right foot and lying on Adisesha. This temple has five processional Deities (*utsava-vigrahas*). The goddess of the temple is Bhumi Devi (Laksmi). There is a sacred tank here called Ahoratra Pushkarani.

Saranathan Temple is 11 km southeast of the railway station at Tiruccherai. It is also called Pancha Saraksetram, and it is considered one of the most important Divya Desam temples. It is on the bank of the Kaveri River.

Amaruviyappan Temple is located between Kumbakonam and Mayuram. The Deity in the temple, Lord Amaruviyappan, is ten feet tall.

Narayur Ninra Nambi Temple at Thirunarayoor (Nacchiarkoil) is 10 km from Kumbakonam, on the bus route to Tiruvarur. The temple has a Garuda made of stone, which is used to carry Lord Nambi (Vishnu) twice a year during festivals. The goddess in this temple is Nambikai Nacchiar. She proceeds Lord Nambi during all festival processions.

Five km southwest of Kumbakonam is the **Vinnaghra Perumal Temple** at Nandipura Vinnagaram (Nathan Koil).

Parimala Rangan Temple is 5 km northeast of the Mayavaram railway station.

The **Kolavilli Raman** and **Sringara Sundaran Temples** are located 5 km east of the Mayavaram railway station.

Mayuram

There are a few Divya Vishnu Desam temples near this town. Mayuram is northeast of Kumbakonam, between Kumbakonam and Chidambaram.

The **Arumakadal Temple** is located 12 km from the Mayuram Railway Station and 3 km from Kollumangudi.

Naanmadeeya Perumal Temple is located 20 km from Mayuram in Tiruttalaichhanganammathiam. It can be reached from the Sembanarkoil railway station. This is a small temple in a solitary place in the forest.

Sirkazhi (Shiyali)

By the town of Sirkazhi there is a group of Divya Desam Vishnu temples called the Tirunangoor Tirupati Shrines, which can all be visited in a day or two. Sirkazhi is located about 50 northeast of Kumbakonam on the way to Chidambaram.

The **Taadaalan Temple** has a Deity of Trivikrama with His left leg raised. The goddess's name is Mattavizhum Kuzhali Nacchiar. This temple is 1 km from the railway station.

Five km east of the Sirkazhi railway station is the **Senganmal Temple** and **Manikkooda Temple**.

Ten km east of the station is the **Gopala Krishna Temple** at Thirukkavallambadi. Worship at this temple is conducted only once at about 10 am daily. About one and half km from the temple is the birthplace of Tirumangai Alwar.

Eleven km southeast of Sirkazhi is the **Kannan Narayana Temple** at Tiruvellakkulam (Annankoil). The **Vayalali Manavalan Temple** is at Thiruvaali, which is 10 km southeast of Sirkazhi railway station.

The **Taamaraiyaal Kelwan Temple** is 15 km from the Sirkazhi railway station. This temple has Deities of Parthasarathi, Rukmini, Satyabhama, and Rama with four hands.

The **Narayana Koil** (Nandavilakku Perumal) **Temple** is 8 km east of Sirkazhi station. On the Amavasya day the Deities of all the eleven Tirunangoor temples visit this temple and stay for the evening. The **Kudamaadu Koothan** Temple is near the Narayanar Koil Temple.

Vaikunthanatha Temple is 8 km east of Sirkazhi. The **Purushottam Temple** at Tiruvanpurudottam is 8 km southeast of Sirkazhi, and the **Perarulaalar Temple** at Tiruchembonsey Koil is 8 km east of Sirkazhi.

The **Daivanaayaka Perumal Temple** is 8 km from Sirkazhi at Tiruttevanarthogai.

THANJAVUR (TANJORE)

Population: 200,000, STD Code 04362

Thanjavur was the capital of the Chola Empire from the 8th to the 13th century. The Chola dynasty controlled a good part of South India and Sri Lanka. They celebrated many of their victories by constructing a temple, financed by the defeated party. There are over 70 temples in Thanjavur, the most important being the famous Brihadeeswara Temple. Thanjavur is situated halfway between Tiruchirappalli (60 km) and the coast. It is 114 km south of Chidambaram and 334 km south of Madras.

At Tirukandiyur, 10 km from Thanjavur, is a temple dedicated to Lord Brahma.

Getting Your Bearings

The old city is between the Grand Anicut Canal in the south and the Vadavar River in the north. The Brihadeeswara Temple is in the southwest part of the city, by the canal. The palace is in the center of the city. Most of the hotels, souvenir shops, and the tourist office, which is beside the Hotel Tamil Nadu, are on Gandhiji Road. The railway station is south of the canal on the southern part of Gandhiji Road (Railway Station Road). The bus station is south by the canal.

Information

There is a **Tamil Nadu Tourist Bureau** in Shop 3, next to the Hotel Tamil Nadu on Gandhiji Rd, open from 8 to 11 am and 4 to 8 pm, Wednesday to Saturday and 8 am to 8 pm, Sunday to Tuesday.

The Canara Bank on South Main Rd is a good place to change travellers' cheques. The State Bank of India, Hospital Rd, and the Hotel Parishutham also change money.

Brihadeeswara Temple

This is a magnificent Siva temple built

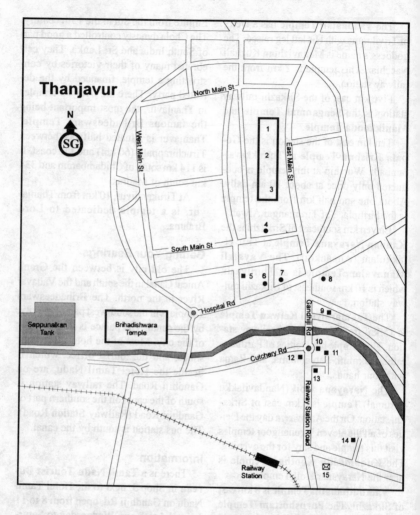

Thanjavur

in 1003 AD by King Rajaraja I, the Chola King. It is considered one of the grandest temples in India. The main shrine is dedicated to Lord Siva. This temple is unique because the *vimana* (the tower over the altar) soars into the sky, while the *gopurams* (the towers over the entrance) are small. The tower of the temple is 64.8 metres (216 ft) high with 14 stories, making it the tallest temple in South India. There has been continuous wor-

ship at the temple for more than 1000 years.

The temple is capped by a single 80 ton monolithic solid granite block. This enormous stone is said to have been moved up an incline that started 6 km from the temple. The *sikhara*, a spherical dome, is octagonal and rests on top of this granite block. The shadow of the *sikhara* never falls on the ground.

In the inner sanctum is the gigantic

PLACES TO STAY

5	Hotel Karthik
9	Hotel Parishutham
10	Rajarajan Lodge
11	Raja Rest House
12	Pandiyar Residency
13	Hotel Tamil Nadu
14	Hotel Valli

WHERE TO EAT

5	Karthik
8	Golden Restaurant

OTHER

1	Raja's Palace & Art Gallery
2	Entrance
3	Tamil University Museum
4	Canara Bank
6	Thiruvalluvar Bus Stand
7	State Bus Stand
13	Tourist Office
15	Post Office

Maha-linga, 3.5 metres (10½ feet) high and 7½ m (23 ft) in circumference. The *linga* is from the Narmada River. It is said that when the *linga* was taken out of the water, it kept increasing in size; which is why the *linga* is known as Brihadeeswara. There are over 250 *lingas* in the temple.

The giant **Nandi** (bull of Lord Siva), which is carved out of a single stone, is considered to be the second largest in India, next to the one at Lepakshi. It is 3.7 metres high (13 feet), 6 metres long (16 feet), 2.5 metres wide, and weighs about 25 tons. It is said that it grew in size every day, until a nail was driven in its back to keep it from growing.

The name of the goddess is Brihan-nayaki. There is a deity in this temple of **Jwarahareswara** who controls fever. It is believed if a person has a chronic fever, that it will subside if they offer sandal paste to this deity. This has been experienced by many people. There is a 55-foot-high temple dedicated to Lord Subrahmanya that is considered to have some of the best carvings in South India on it. There are many Vaishnava sculptures on the *gopurams*.

Beyond the western wall of the temple is the giant Seppunaikan Tank. The Sivaganga Tank is a sacred tank in the temple courtyard, within a 100-pillar *mandapa* (hall).

This temple is open from 6 am to noon and 4 to 9 pm. Unless you get special permission from the Archaeological Department of Madras, you cannot enter the inner sanction. Non-Hindus can go everywhere in the enclosure except the room where the Siva-linga is located and the halls that approach it.

By the courtyard is the interesting **Archaeological Museum**, which has exhibits that give a good history of the temple's restoration and the Chola empire. There is also a good collection of sculptures. The museum is open 9 am to noon and 4 to 8 pm daily.

Thanjavur Palace

This interesting palace was build partly by the Nayaks around 1550 AD and partly by the Marathas. The **Sangitha Mahal** (Durbar Hall or Hall of Music) on the first floor has a fine auditorium with excellent acoustics. The former armory is 190 feet high and was used as a lookout. From the top of the tower there is a good view of the area.

The Palace also contains the **Saraswati Mahal Library,** which dates back to 1700. The library has 30,000 volumes in Sanskrit, Tamil, Marathi, and English. The volumes are mostly paper manuscripts or on palm leaves. The library is open daily from 10 am to 1 pm and 2 to 5 pm, except Wednesday.

The **Art Gallery** has an excellent collection of bronze deities and statues. There are 113 granite and 250 bronze statues from the Chola period, dating from the 9th to the 12th century. There is also a collection of Tanjore glass paintings. It is open daily from 9 am to 1 pm and 2 to 5 pm, except government holidays.

Next to the palace is the **Tamil University Museum,** which has a stringed musical instrument collection and a good coin collection.

Divya Desam Temples

In Tiruttanjai, about 4 km north of Thanjavur railway station are three temples adjacent to each other which are Divya Desam temples. They are **Thanja Mamanikkoil, Tanjaiyali-koil,** and **Manikkunra Perumal**.

The **Aran Saapa Temple** is located in Thirukandiyur, which is 10 km from Thanjavur on the way to Tiruvaiyaru.

Where To Stay – Lower

Most of the hotels are on Gandhiji Rd, between the railway and bus stations, or on Trichy Rd, behind the railway station. There are six big clean *railway retiring rooms* at the station.

The *Raja Rest House* (20515), by the Hotel Tamil Nadu, has rooms with bath for Rs 55/80. It is a very good value and is the recommended budget place.

The *Ashoka Lodge*, 93 Abraham Pandithar St, has nicer rooms on the second floor than the first, but it isn't such a good place. The *Sri Mahalakshmi* is centrally located.

The *Hotel Anand*, 1 Racquet Court Lane, and *Hotel Arun*, 24 State Bank Road, are both nice places.

Where To Stay – Middle & Higher

The *Hotel Tamil Nadu*, (21421), Gandhiji Road, is the best place to stay in town. It has both Indian style and western style bathrooms with hot water in the morning. Most rooms have balconies, set around a courtyard. The problem with this hotel is that it is usually heavily booked, so you most likely cannot stay here. You can book in advance at a Tamil Nadu Tourist Office or another Tamil Nadu hotel in another city. It was once a Raja's guest house and is a good value with good service. It has comfortable clean rooms for Rs 150/175 and Rs 400 with A/C. The *Hotel Tamil Nadu II* (20365) is run down. Rooms are Rs 175/275.

The *Hotel Valli* (21584), 2948 MKM Rd, has rooms for Rs 100/120 and Rs 250 with A/C. It has a vegetarian restaurant.

The *Hotel Sangam* (25151), Trichy Rd, has A/C rooms for $37/42. The *Oriental Towers* (21467), 2889 Srinivasam Pillai Rd, has rooms for $32/42. Both these hotels have good facilities.

The *Pandiyar Residency*, Cutchery Rd, is a new place. All rooms have a TV, and the deluxe rooms have a view of the temple. The *Hotel Parisuthan* (21601, fax 22318), 55 Grand Anicut Canal Rd, is the best hotel in town, and everything looks neat and clean. It has a pool and comfortable rooms for Rs 600/900 and rooms with A/C are Rs 1300/1800. It also has deluxe rooms and suites.

Where To Eat

The *Padma Hotel*, Ananda Bhavan, Gandhiji Rd, opposite the Hotel Tamil Nadu, has a simple vegetarian place. The restaurant on the ground floor in the *Hotel Karthik* is popular. The *Hotel Valli* is supposed to have a vegetarian restaurant.

The rooftop *Golden Restaurant*, Hospital Rd, is a good place. The *Hotel Parisutham* has the fancy Geetham Restaurant in it.

Travel

Air The nearest airport is in Tiruchirappalli (Trichy), 60 km away. It is a small airport with flights to Madras and Madurai.

Train You can get a train to and from Madras (9 hrs, 3 daily), Chidambaram (3 hr, 4 daily), Rameswaram, Madurai (6 hr, 2 daily), Tirupati, and Tiruchirappalli (2 hr, 4 daily). The train station is south of the Anicut Canal, about 2½ km from the center of town. To **Madras** are the Cholan Exp #6154 (8.45 am, 9 hr) and the Rame-svaram Exp #6102 (8.40 pm, 9½ hr).

Bus There are two bus stations in the south of town, off Hospital Road—TTC Bus Stand and the Municipal (State) Bus Stand. The buses for Kumbakonam (1 hr, bays 7 or 8) and some of the buses to Tiruchirappalli (bays 9 or 10) leave from the local Municipal Bus Stand. From the long distance Thiruvalluvar (TTC) bus stand, frequent buses go to Madurai (8 hr, 9 daily) and Tiruchirappalli (1½ hr, 10 daily). There are also buses to Madras (9 hr, 12 daily), Tirupati, Chidambaram (9 hr), and Pondicherry (6 hr, 2 daily). There is a computerised booking office (7 am to 9 pm).

Nagappattinam

There is a temple here with three full-sized Deities of Lord Vishnu standing, sitting, and lying on Ananta Sesa. This temple is one of the 108 important Vaishnava temples. **Sundaryarajan**, the main

Deity, stands over 15 feet high. His upper body is made of shiny black stone, but His weapons and body are covered with solid silver. He is a truly spectacular Deity with gorgeous lotus eyes.

Nagappattinam is about 70 km east of Thanjavur (Tanjore) on the seashore. There is the TTDC Tamil Nadu Hotel (2389), Thonitturai Salai, near the railway station, which has rooms that are a good value for Rs 150 and Rs 250 with A/C.

Tiruvarur (Tiruvalar)

Tiruvarur is locate about 55 km from Thanjavur, going due east towards Nagappattinam.

Tyagaraja Siva Temple

This beautiful temple dedicated to Lord Tyagaraja was built between the 13th and 17th century. The outer walls of this massive temple are 846 feet long and 666 feet wide. It is one of the largest temples in South India. On each side of the temple is a huge *gopuram*. There is a bathing tank called Kamalalayam, where there is a temple dedicated to Sri Kamala (Laksmi) in the middle. It is considered to be one of the biggest tanks in all of India.

King Muchukunda is said to have installed the Siva-linga, which is called Achaleeswara. Achaleeswara means "the immovable Lord." The story of the temple is that there was a king named Samatkara who performed austerities here. When Lord Siva appeared before him, he begged Lord Siva to be present forever at this site. Lord Siva said he would remain here forever immovable and that even his shadow would not move. The shadow of the Achaleeswara-linga never moves and can be seen only in the eastern direction. It is said that the

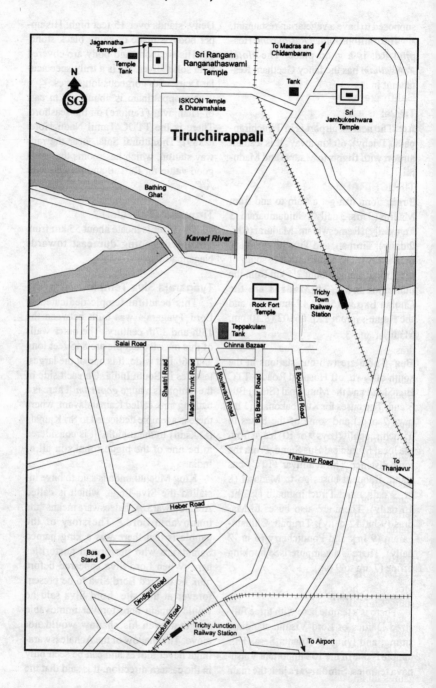

shadow of the *linga* will not be seen by someone who is about to die within six months.

Bakthavatsala Perumal Temple

This is a Divya Desam temple 6 km from Tiruvarur station towards Kumbakonam. The standing Vishnu Deity is known for His larger-than-normal size.

TIRUCHIRAPPALLI (TRICHY)

Population: 700,000, STD Code 0431

This city is famous for the Srirangam Temple in the middle of the Kaveri and the Rock Fort temple. Along with Tirupati, the Srirangam Temple is one of the most important Vishnu temples in South India. It is an important stop for a spiritual tour of South India.

Tiruchirappalli is 145 km northeast of Madurai and 320 km southwest of Madras.

Trichy is at the confluence of two major rivers—the Kaveri River and the Cooleron. Tiruchirappalli means "city of the three-headed demon." The city was supposed to be named in memory of a fight Lord Siva had with a three-headed demon named Trisiras.

The Pallavas and Pandyas fought over this town. In the 10th century the Chola gained control. When the Chola dynasty fell, the Vijayanagara kingdom from Hampi took over.

Getting Your Bearings

Trichy is spread over a wide area. Most of the hotels, the tourist office, bus stand, and railway station are all in the Cantonment (Junction Rd) area in the south of the city.

The Rock Fort temple is 1½ km north of this area by the Kaveri River. Srirangam is on an island in the middle of the Kaveri River, 1½ km north of the Rock Fort. Sri Jambukeswara Temple is about 2 km east of the Srirangam temple, on the same island.

Information

The **tourist office** is at the Hotel Tamil Nadu, opposite the bus station. It is open between 10.30 am and 5.30 pm. You can get a good map of the Trichy area for Rs 3. There are also tourist counters at the airport and at the Tiruchirappalli Railway Station (7 am to 9 pm).

The No 1 bus, which departs from the road next to the Central Bus Stand, goes to the Srirangam Temple, passing the Jambukeswara Temple and the Rock Fort temple on the way. Some of the No 1 buses do not go to Srirangam. The bus takes about a half hour.

There is a low-stocked Higginbothams Book Shop by the Rock Fort temple. You can rent a bicycle for Rs 15 a day at a few places by Junction Rd. You can **change money** at the State Bank of India on Dindigul Rd, north of Jenney's Residency.

SRIRANGAM

Sri Ranganathaswami Temple

Srirangam is the foremost of the eight self-manifested shrines of Lord Vishnu (Swayam Vyakta Ksetras). It is also considered the most important of the 108 main Vishnu temples (Divya Desams). This temple is a highly recommended place to visit. It was sung about by all the Alwars (the Tamil Vaishnava saints), except Madhurakavi. This temple is also known as Tiruvarangattirupathi, Periya Koil, Bhooloka Vaikuntham, and Bhogamandapa.

Srirangam is located 2 km north of Tiruchirappalli.

Sri Ramanujacarya made the Srirangam Temple his headquarters to preach Visistadvaita philosophy. His *samadhi* is within the premises of the Srirangam Temple. Sri Caitanya, Sri Vallabhacarya, and the Dalai Lama visited this temple. Many celebrated kings like Kulasekhara and Alabandaru resided in the temple of Srirangam. Sri Yamunacarya, Sri Ramanuja, and Sudarsanacarya supervised this temple.

The Srirangam Temple is the largest temple in India. It is on a 600 acre island surrounded by the rivers Kaveri and Kolladam (Coleroon). After Tirupati, this is the second most visited Vaishnava temple in South India.

The temple complex covers 2½ sq km or 155½ acres. It is known as "Koil" or "the temple." Over the roof is the Sriranga *vimana*, which is gold-plated. The temple has a great collection of jewelry.

Each morning at 6.45 am, a cow with her head facing away from Lord Ranganatha and an elephant facing her are brought before the altar. Thus when the Deity's doors are opened the first thing that Lord Ranganatha sees is the rear end of a cow and the head of an elephant, which are both considered very auspicious. I was told that instead of a conch shell being blown, the elephant blows his trunk. This is the most auspicious time to see Lord Ranganatha.

The *puja* of the temple is done according to the regulations of the Ramanuja-sampradaya. It is a traditional belief that Adi Sankara installed the Janakarsana Yatra at Srirangam and Dhanakarsana Yatra at Tirupati to attract pilgrims.

On a normal day you may have to wait about a half hour to see Lord Ranganatha, but it is worth waiting a lifetime.

There are many other shrines in the temple. There are shines for Sri Rama, Narasimha, Chakrathalwar, Garuda, etc.

There are also shrines dedicated to Vedanta Desika and all the Alwars.

The major festival in this temple is on Vaikuntha Ekadasi in December. At that time Lord Ranganatha is brought into the "Thousand Pillar Hall" under a golden dome.

Information

The **maha-prasada booth** is next to the Garuda Mandapa Hall, near the entrance of the fourth enclosure. There is very nice *maha-prasada* lemon rice and sweets. There is a ten-rupee camera fee. It is a good idea to engage a guide, as the temple is very large and there are many temples in the complex. The temple is open from 6.15 am to 1 pm and 3.15 to 8.45 pm.

There are many temples and places to see here beside the main shrine dedicated to Sri Ranganatha. Non-Hindus are not allowed in any of these temples, but ISKCON devotees and converted Hindus may enter. It is a huge place and can easily take four hours to see everything.

Temple Design

There are seven walls (*prakaras*) around the temple. The temple has 21 *gopurams* (towers). The main southern entrance *gopuram*, called Raja-gopuram, is the largest in India. It was finished in 1987 and is 72m (235 feet) high with 13 stories. You can climb a flight of stairs to the top of this *gopuram* and get a great view of the area. The passage under this tower is about 100 feet long. The other *gopurams* were built between the 14th and 17th century. The temple tank is outside the temple, west of the seventh enclosure.

The second enclosure surrounding Lord Ranganatha is called Rajamahendran Thiruveedhi, the third Kulasekaram

Thiruveedhi, the fourth Alinandan Thiruveedhi, and the fifth Ahalankan Thiruveedhi.

Seventh Enclosure (Chittai)

Inside the outermost walls, which are 2880 by 2475 feet, there are houses and a bazaar. In the seventh enclosure, by the southern *gopuram*, is a **Lord Vamana** (Lord Vishnu as a dwarf brahmin) **temple**. In the southwest corner of the seventh enclosure there is a fairly large temple dedicated to **Sri Andal**.

Sixth Enclosure

The **Jagannatha Temple** that marks the spot where Sri Caitanya stayed while in Srirangam is inside the northwest part of the sixth enclosure. Also within the sixth wall are the houses of the Brahmins who serve in the temple. Within this enclosure are the temple's processional carts.

In the southeast corner of the sixth enclosure there is a temple dedicated to **Manavala Mamunigal**, the daughter of the Sultan of Delhi, who became very devoted to Sri Ranganatha. There is a painting of the Princess hanging on the wall of this shrine.

The Muslim Sultan, after attacking the Srirangam temple, carried away the processional Deity of Sri Ranganatha, Sri Manavala Perumal. The daughter of the Sultan considered the Deity so beautiful that she fell in love with Him. She kept the Deity in her bedroom. When the priests of the Srirangam temple pleaded with the Sultan to return the Deity, his daughter objected. Then while she was sleeping, the Sultan returned the Deity to the priest. When she woke and found the Deity missing, she became so disturbed that she immediately left for Srirangam to see the Deity.

Fifth Enclosure (Ahalankan Thiruveedhi)

Before you enter the fifth enclosure (some say fourth enclosure) you have to remove your shoes. The **Rangavilas Mandapa** hall is directly in front of the southern gate. Next to this (to your left as you enter the southern gate) is the small, intricately carved Venugopala Temple. Inside the porch of the **Venugopala Temple** there are paintings which show Krishna having pastimes with the *gopis* (cowherd-girls). Near this temple there are stairs that lead up to the roof of a nearby building. From there you can get a good view of the *gopurams* and temple area. You have to get a ticket to go on the roof at the information booth in front of the Venugopala temple. From a platform on the roof, you can get some really nice photos of the gold-plated Sriranga *vimana* and the *gopurams*.

To the left (west) of the south gate is the Vasantha Mandapa hall and the **Chakrathalwar Temple**, which is dedicated to the Sudarsana Cakra of Lord Vishnu. To the left of the Venugopala Krishna Temple is a shrine dedicated to Andal.

Directly to the right of the south entrance are shrines dedicated to Vitthala Krishna, Koorathalwar, Thondaradippadi Alwar and Tiruppan Alwar.

There is an interesting **museum** with bronze and stone sculptures a short walk to the right of the southern gate. The museum is open from 10 am to noon and 3 to 5 pm. Next to the museum is the *samadhi* shrine of **Ramanujacarya**, where you can see his actual body. Srirangam was the preaching headquarters of Sri Ramanujacarya, who spent a good part of his life here.

The **Sesaraya Mandapa** (Horsecourt Hall) is on the east side of the temple. It

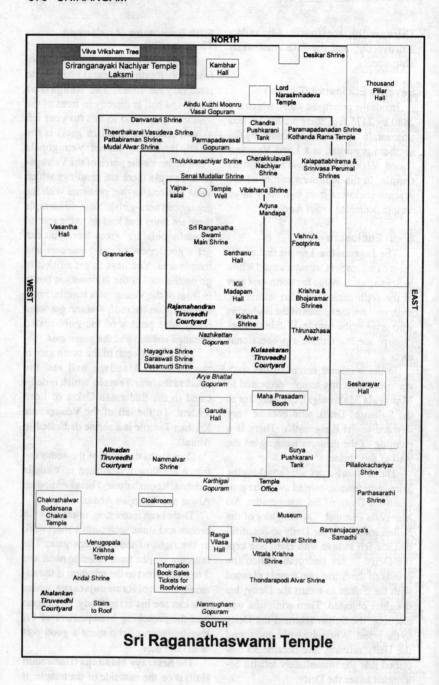

NORTH

Vilva Vriksham Tree

Sriranganayaki Nachiyar Temple
Laksmi

Kambhar Hall

Desikar Shrine

Thousand Pillar Hall

Lord Narasimhadeva Temple

Aindu Kuzhi Moonru Vasal Gopuram

Danvantari Shrine

Chandra Pushkarani Tank

Paramapadanadan Shrine
Kothanda Rama Temple

Theerthakarai Vasudeva Shrine
Pattabiraman Shrine.
Mudal Alwar Shrine

Parmapadavasal Gopuram

Kalapattabhirama & Srinivasa Perumal Shrines

Thulukkanachiyar Shrine

Cherakkulavalli Nachiyar Shrine

Senai Mudaliar Shrine

Yajna-salai

Temple Well

Vibhishana Shrine

Arjuna Mandapa

Vasantha Hall

Sri Ranganatha Swami Main Shrine

Vishnu's Footprints

Grannaries

Senthanu Hall

WEST

Kili Madapam Hall

Krishna & Bhojaramar Shrines

EAST

Rajamahendran Tiruveedhi Courtyard

Krishna Shrine

Thirunazhasa Alvar

Nazhikettan Gopuram

Hayagriva Shrine
Saraswati Shrine
Dasamurti Shrine

Kulasekaran Tiruveedhi Courtyard

Arya Bhattal Gopuram

Sesharayar Hall

Maha Prasadam Booth

Garuda Hall

Allnadan Tiruveedhi Courtyard

Nammalvar Shrine

Surya Pushkarani Tank

Pillailokachariyar Shrine

Karthigai Gopuram

Temple Office

Parthasarathi Shrine

Chakrathalwar Sudarsana Chakra Temple

Cloakroom

Museum

Venugopala Krishna Temple

Ranga Vilasa Hall

Thiruppan Alvar Shrine

Ramanujacarya's Samadhi

Andal Shrine

Vittala Krishna Shrine

Information Book Sales Tickets for Roofview

Thondarapodi Alvar Shrine

Ahalankan Tiruveedhi Courtyard

Stairs to Roof

Nanmugham Gopuram

SOUTH

Sri Raganathaswami Temple

has 8 intricately carved monolithic pillars of men on rearing horses.

On the same side of the temple (north-east side) is the impressive "**Hall of a Thousand Pillars**." Each of the 18-foot granite pillars is intricately carved. This hall actually has only 953 pillars. In the center of the hall is a pedestal shaped like a processional car. During Vaikuntha Ekadasi, the processional Deity is brought to this pedestal before going on procession.

You can keep proceeding around the temple to the Ranga Nachiyar Laksmi Temple.

To get to the Sri Ranga Nachiyar Temple from the inner enclosure (inner sanctum), you have to retrace your steps to the 3rd courtyard, because the **Paramapada Vasal Gopuram** (gate of salvation) on the north side of the third enclosure is always closed except during the last 10 days of the 20 day Vaikuntha Ekadasi festival. At this time the Lord passes out this opened gate. So you have to proceed out the south gate of the third enclosure until you reach the Garuda Hall, and then you can proceed around the temple (north). You then exit out the north gate and reach the **Sri Ranga Nachiyar Laksmi Temple**, on your left. Inside this temple there is the sacred Bilwa tree along the north wall. When Malik Kafur invaded the temple, the original Laksmi Deity in this temple was buried under the Bilwa tree, and after 80 years the Deity was found and restored to its original place.

Along the northeast wall near the Sri Ranga Nachiyar Temple is a shrine dedicated to Vedanta Desika, a famous Tamil Nadu Vaishnava devotee. There is also a temple dedicated to Lord Narasimha by the entrance of the Sri Ranga Nachiyar Temple.

Fourth Enclosure (Alanadan)

As you enter the southern **Karthigai Gopuram** to the fourth enclosure, the Namm Alwar shrine is on the left and the Tirukkachi Nambi shrine is on the right.

Within the fourth enclosure is a huge Garuda and the Garuda Mandapa Hall, which is a beautiful hall with intricately carved pillars. The **Garuda Mandapa Hall** has 12 rows of 16 pillars plus two center rows that have 10 pillars, for a total of 212 pillars. It is considered to be one of the most beautiful halls in the temple. Next to the Garuda Mandapa (to the right of the entrance gate) is the **Surya Pushkarani tank**, which is named after the sun-god.

In the northeast corner of this enclosure is the **Chandra Pushkarani tank**, the moon-pond, where Vibhishana first placed the Deity of Sri Ranganatha when he brought the Deity here. Next to this tank are shrines dedicated to Lord Rama, Krishna, and Vishnu lying on the serpent Ananta Sesa. A little south of these shrines are two shrines dedicated to Kilapattabhiraman and Srinivasa Perumal. Along the wall of the northwest corner of this enclosure are shrines dedicated to Pattabiraman, Mudal Alwar, Teertha Karai Vasudeva (Vishnu), and Dhanvantari (god of medicine).

The western wing has five old storehouses. Toward the southeast corner of this enclosure is a storage area for the sacred vehicles (*vahanas*) of the Deities, which are used for processions.

Third Enclosures (Kulasekharan)

To get to the third enclosure you go through the southern **Aryabhattal Gopuram**. The *dwajasthamba* (flag staff) and bali-peetam (sacrificial altar), both gold-plated, are in front of the inner sanctum. To the left of the entrance gate are shrines dedicated to Lord Vishnu Dasamurti, Lord Hayagriva, and goddess Saraswati (goddess of learning).

Second and First Enclosure (Raja Mahendran Prakara)

After passing through the **Nazihiketan Vasal Gopuram**, you have entered the last enclosure. As you enter, there is a Deity of Krishna to your right. Large mirrors have been put in the corners to reflect the Lord when He issues from the sanctuary (altar).

In the southwest corner is the storeroom of the temple's treasures. Amongst the large amount of golden items owned by the temple is a gold vessel given by King Edward VII of England in 1875. Behind the Deity (north side) is the Tiruvannazhi, the sacred well, and in the northwest corner behind the Deity is the Yajnasalai. In the northeast corner is the shrine of Vibhishana and the Senai Mudaliar Sannadhi.

In the east part of the east corridor, up some stairs, is the **Arjuna Mandapa**. From there you reach the Nachiyar and Serakulavalli Nachiyar shrines. To the south, at a lower level, is the **Kili Mandapa**. *Kili* means parrot. There is a parrot in a cage here that chants the glories of Sri Ranganatha.

The innermost enclosure is the sanctum of Sri Ranganatha. It is square inside, but circular outside. The steps of the sanctum are named after Kulasekhara Alwar. Immediately around the altar for Sri Ranganatha is a circumambulatory corridor that is used strictly for ritual purposes. There is a stone moat-like structure around the sanctuary that can be filled with water to keep the sanctuary cool in the summer. On the upper parts of the walls are some paintings that are about three centuries old. They depict the

108 important Vaishnava Divya Desam temples.

Above the main altar is the **Ranga** *vimana* (golden tower). On the four sides of the Ranga *vimana* are carvings of four forms of Lord Vishnu. On the side south is Paravasudeva, on the west is Acyuta, on the north Ananda, and on the east Govinda.

Deities on the Main Altar

The main Deity is Lord Ranganatha, or Lord Vishnu, reclining on Sesa Naga. He is 6.4 m (21 ft) long. Lord Ranganatha is in a recumbent pose with His right shoulder facing south. He is on a conch provided by the coils of the celestial serpent Adi Sesa, who has five raised and wide-open hoods. Near His feet are seated His two consorts, Sri Bhu and Sri Neela. In front of Lord Ranganatha is the effulgent *utsava-murti* of Lord Vishnu, called Sri Manavala Perumal. This Deity is taken out of the temple for processions. Along side Lord Ranganatha is Tiruvaranga, who was worshiped as a substitute during the Muslim period, when the original could not be found. At the feet of the Lord is Vibhishana, the brother of Ravana.

Story of the Deity

The Deity of Sri Ranganatha was first worshiped by Lord Brahma. The Deity was later given to King Ikshvaku to worship, and he brought the Deity to his capital, Ayodhya. Eventually Lord Rama worshiped the Deity. When Vibhishana, the brother of Ravana, came to Ayodhya, he requested permission to take the Deity of Sri Ranganatha to his capital in Lanka to worship. He was allowed to do so on the condition that if he placed the Deity on the ground, he would not be able to move the Deity from that spot. Vibhishana agreed and proceeded to carry the Deity south to Sri Lanka. On his way he placed the Deity on the ground at Srirangam, on the bank of the Chandra Pushkarani tank. Since that time Sri Ranganatha has stayed at Srirangam.

It is said that the Deity faces south, instead of the traditional east, so as to face Vibhishana in Sri Lanka, to grace him and his kingdom. The sanctum (altar) faces south and the main entrance is also from the south (normally it is from the east). It is believed that Vibhishana goes to Srirangam every 12 years to worship the Lord.

Sri Caitanya in Srirangam

In *Caitanya-caritamrita* (Madhya Ch 9.79-81) Sri Caitanya's visit is mentioned as follows: "Sri Caitanya Mahaprabhu finally reached Sri Ranga-ksetra. After bathing in the River Kaveri, Sri Caitanya Mahaprabhu saw the temple of Ranganatha and offered His ardent prayers and obeisances. Thus He felt Himself successful. In the temple of Ranganatha, Sri Caitanya Mahaprabhu chanted and danced in ecstatic love of Godhead. Seeing His performance, everyone was struck with wonder."

"Vyenkata Bhatta submitted that the period of Caturmasya had already arrived. He said 'Please be merciful to me and stay at my house during Caturmasya. Speak about Lord Krishna's pastimes and kindly deliver me by Your mercy," (Madhya Ch 9.84-86). Sri Caitanya Mahaprabhu remained at the house of Sri Vyenkata Bhatta in Srirangam for four continuous months.

The son of Vyenkata Bhatta was later known as Gopala Bhatta, one of the six Goswamis of Vrindavana. He established the Radha-Ramana Temple in Vrindavana.

While in Srirangam Lord Caitanya met the illiterate *brahmana* who used to visit the temple daily and recite the entire text of the *Bhagavad-gita*.

Festivals

Mohini Arangam, Vaikuntha Ekadasi, Garuda Sevai, the Flower Festival, and the Car Festival during the last week of December and first week of January are all important festivals.

Vaikuntha Ekadasi is celebrated for 20 days in Dec/Jan on the Sukla Ekadasi day of the Tamil month of Margazhi. The first ten days are called Pagal Pattu, and the second ten days are called Era Pattu. On Vaikuntha Ekadasi day, Lord Ranganatha, wearing a garment of rubies, goes out of the temple in a magnificent procession through the Parampada Vasal gate (gateway to salvation) and goes to the 1000-pillared hall. After Vaikuntha Ekadasi, there is a 10-day festival for **Sri Ranga Nachiyar**, the goddess Lakshmi, who is brought onto the streets in procession.

In January and April the Lord is taken out of the temple on His processional car. In March there is a **water festival** at the temple tank, which is outside the temple and west of the seventh enclosure. The Lord and His consort are put on an illuminated boat at night and taken to the stone pavilion in the middle of the tank and offered worship there.

During a nine-day festival in March/April the Lord goes to the temple of **Sri Nachiyar**, at Woraiyur, to meet His consorts. This festival includes several processions, an *abhisheka* (sacred bathing), and a quarrel between the Lord and His consort.

Bath in the Kaveri River

To take bath in the Kaveri, you walk

out of the main (south) gate and continue down the road for about a kilometre. There is a bathing ghat at the end of this road which has chains for people to hold onto so they are not swept away by the extremely strong current. It is a good idea to bathe here instead of trying to find a more secluded place, unless you are willing to walk around for a while, because the river is dangerous to swim in and it is hard to find a secluded spot.

Jagannatha Mutt & Sri Caitanya's Footprints

Jagannatha Mutt is a beautiful little temple, that marks the place where Lord Caitanya spent the four months of the rainy season in 1510. The house of Vyenkata Bhatta used to be at this place. The temple has many paintings depicting Lord Caitanya's pastimes at Srirangam. In the center hall of the temple there is a diorama of Lord Caitanya and a Deity of Lord Jagannatha. The family descendants of Vyenkata Bhatta still live in Srirangam.

This temple is a ten-minute walk around the temple from the main entrance of the Srirangam Temple, within the sixth enclosure of the temple. It is in the northwest corner of the sixth enclosure.

There is a small temple that contains the footprints of **Sri Caitanya Mahaprabhu** about 100 metres from the south gopuram of the Srirangam Temple. The temple has an inscription that says **Sri Caitanya** stayed in Srirangam for four months in 1510.

ISKCON Temple

It is a small temple with a few devotees. There are no guest facilities, but the devotees are helpful. The address is 6-A EVS Road, Renganagar, Srirangam. It is near the Srirangam bus stand and the

main entrance gate to the temple, on the same road as where most of the dharamsalas are located.

Sri Jambukeswara Temple (Thiruvaanaikkaval)

This temple is an important Siva temple which is architecturally interesting. It has elaborate carvings. In this temple is the **Appu-linga** (water), one of the five element Siva-lingas. The base of the Appu-linga is submerged in water coming from a spring in the inner sanctum. The *linga* is under a holy **Jambu tree**. *Jambu* is a guava tree, and *iswara* means "the Lord."

It is said that Lord Rama came here after killing Ravana and Kumbhakarna. It is also said that an elephant once worshiped this *linga*. Hence the Tamil name Thiruvaanaikkaval (*aanai* in Tamil means elephant). The goddess in the temple is Akhilandeswari.

This temple has seven *gopurams* and five surrounding walls. The fourth wall is 35 feet high, 6 feet thick, and about 2500 by 1500 feet long. Inside this wall is a *mandapa* (hall) with 800 pillars and a tank fed by a perpetual spring. There are many deities and beautiful sculptures in this impressive temple.

The temple is open from 6 am to 1 pm and 4 to 9.30 pm. It is located two km east of Srirangam temple, on the same island in the middle of the Kaveri. The No 1 bus passes it on the way to the Srirangam Temple. Non-Hindus cannot enter the inner sanctum.

Rock Fort Temple

It is on a huge 83 metre (273 feet) high rock, said to be one of the oldest rocks in the world, over 3.8 billion years old. There is not much of the fort left. The thousand pillars hall, which you can see as you walk up the stairs, was mainly destroyed by an explosion in 1772. From the top of the hill you have a great view of the city and the Kaveri River.

You can also see the Srirangam Temple on the other side of the river. There is a hall with a bell weighing about 2½ tons, which has a diameter of 4 feet at the base.

It is said that this rock is one of three pieces blown off **Mount Meru** by Vayu. One time Vayu challenged Adi Sesa to a show of strength. So Adi Sesa coiled around Mount Meru, and Vayu tried to loosen His grip. Because of their fight, the whole world had unprecedented hurricanes and storms. In spite of this, the wind-god could not loosen the grip of Adi Sesa. Lord Siva then asked Adi Sesa to loosen His grip, which He did. It is said that at this time Mount Meru broke into three pieces. One chip is said to have fallen at the site of the Rock Fort, one at Kalahasti, and another at Sri Lanka.

You walk up about 430 steps cut into a tunnel through the rock to get to the **Ganesh temple** (known as Ucchipillayar Koil in Tamil) at the top of the hill. It is not a hard climb. There are also some cave temples with beautiful sculptures of the Pallava era (7th century). Halfway up, there is the **Sri Thayumana Swami Temple** dedicated to Lord Siva. The *linga* is a projection of the rock. Non-Hindus cannot enter the inner sanctum of this temple.

There is small fee to go to the top of the hill and a Rs 10 camera fee. The Fort is open from 6 am to 8 pm.

Alagia Manavalan Temple

This is one of the Divya Desam Vishnu temples. It is the birthplace of Tiruppaana Alwar. It is about 2 km northwest of Trichy Fort Railway Station.

Area Divya Desam Temples

All the following temples are Divya Desam Vishnu temples and can be visited on the same trip by taxi. There is the **Tiruvadivlagia Nambi Temple** in Tiruanbil, which is 8 km east of the Lalgudi railway station. Lalgudi is 15 km northeast of Srirangam on the train line to Madras.

The **Uttamar Koil Temple** is at Karambanoor, which is 5 km north of Srirangam. The Vishnu Deity is called Purushottaman, and the goddess is Purvadevi. The Trinity—Lord Vishnu, Siva, and Brahma—are all worshiped in this temple. There are also several other Deities worshiped in this temple. It is said that Kadamba Maharishi, Markandeya, and Garuda performed penance here.

The **Pundareekaksha Temple** is located in Tiruvellarai, which is 16 km north of Srirangam, passing Uttamar Koil on the way. The goddess's name is Pangayacchelvi. It is on the bus route between Trichy and Salem or Trichy and Turaiyur.

The **Valvilli Raman Temple** is at Pullam Poothankudi, which is 4 km from Swamimalai railway station, on the main line between Trichy and Madras or between Kumbakonam and Swamimalai. Rama holds a bow. The *utsava-murti* (small Deity) of Lord Rama has four arms, which is not usually seen. This is said to be the place where Jatayu received liberation.

The **Appakudathan Temple** is located in Tiruppernagar (Tirupper), 24 km northeast of Srirangam. The goddess is named Indira Devi. Both Namm Alwar and Tirumangai Alwar said that whoever worships the Deity here would attain liberation. They said Krishna would attract the mind of anyone who worships here and He would always reside in their heart.

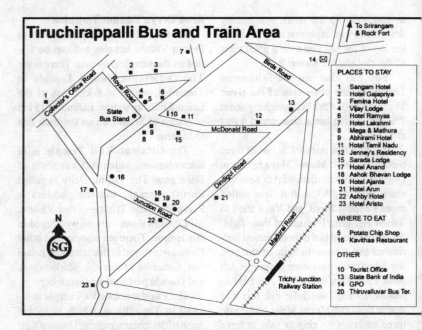

Tiruchirappalli Bus and Train Area

To Srirangam
& Rock Fort

PLACES TO STAY

1 Sangam Hotel
2 Hotel Gajapriya
3 Femina Hotel
4 Vijay Lodge
6 Hotel Ramyas
7 Hotel Lakshmi
8 Mega & Mathura
9 Abhirami Hotel
11 Hotel Tamil Nadu
12 Jenney's Residency
15 Sarada Lodge
17 Hotel Anand
18 Ashok Bhavan Lodge
19 Hotel Ajanta
21 Hotel Arun
22 Ashby Hotel
23 Hotel Aristo

WHERE TO EAT

5 Potato Chip Shop
16 Kavithaa Restaurant

OTHER

10 Tourist Office
13 State Bank of India
14 GPO
20 Thiruvalluvar Bus Ter.

Collector's Office Road

Royal Road

State
Bus Stand

Birds Road

McDonald Road

Dindigul Road

Junction Road

Madurai Road

N

SG

Trichy Junction
Railway Station

The **Andalakkumaiyan Vishnu Temple** is at Aadanoor, 3 km from Swamimalai railway station. The goddess's name is Ranganayakiyar. There is a deity of Tirumangai Alwar in the inner sanctum.

Where To Stay—Lower

Most of the cheap hotels are located in the Cantonment, the new part of town by the bus stand and railway station. There are cheap basic dharamshalas by the Srirangam Temple for the many pilgrims that visit the temple.

The *Guru Hotel* (461-881), 13-A Royal Rd, and the *Vijay Lodge*, 13-B Royal Rd, are both decent cheap places with rooms for around Rs 90/130. It is best to get a room in the back, as the restaurant is very noisy.

Hotel Lakshmi (460-098), 3-A Alexandria Rd, is a recommended place with good rooms with bath for Rs 100/138.

The *Hotel Aanand*, 1 Racquet Court Lane, is a good place that has rooms with bath for Rs 160/200 and A/C rooms for Rs 330/360.

The *Hotel Arun* (461-421), 24 State Bank Rd, has rooms for Rs 120/150 and with A/C for Rs 200/225. The *Hotel Ajanta* (40501), Junction Rd, has rooms for Rs 100/140 and with A/C for Rs 200/ 275.

The old *Hotel Aristo* (461-818), 2 Dindigul Rd, Cantonment, has rooms for Rs 85/110 and Rs 150/185 with A/C. It has cottages with A/C for Rs 200/300. The railway retiring rooms go for Rs 60 and Rs 100 with A/C. Dorm beds are Rs 15.

Where To Stay—Middle

Most of the middle-class hotels are by the Central Bus Stand. Most add a 15% sales tax onto the price of the room. The bus stand is a thirty-minute bus ride from the Srirangam Temple.

The *Hotel Ashby* (460-652), 17A Junction Rd, is an old British Raj style place, which is showing its age. The place has a veranda, a courtyard, and large rooms for Rs 150/175 and 300/400 with A/C. The *Hotel Tamil Nadu* (40383), McDonald Rd, Cantonment, is a better than average place with rooms for Rs 150/250 and Rs 250/450 with A/C.

The *Hotel Ramyas* (461-128), across from the bus stand, is a recommended well-managed place having modern rooms with bath for Rs 250/310 or Rs 420/510 with A/C. The *Hotel Abhirami* (460-001), 10 McDonald Rd, is one of the best values in the area. It has good rooms with a TV for Rs 220 and Rs 340 with A/C. I would recommend this place too.

The *Hotel Gajapriya* (461-144), 2 Royal Rd, has rooms with bath for Rs 175/225 and Rs 425 with A/C. The *Hotel Mega* (463-092), 8-B Rockins Rd, is a good place having rooms with bath for Rs 175/225 and Rs 300/350 with A/C. The *Hotel Mathura*, right next door, on Rockins Rd, has rooms for Rs 175/225 and Rs 300/350.

The *Femina Hotel* (461-551, fax 460-615), 14 C Williams Rd, is a three-star hotel with rooms for Rs 225/300 and Rs 450/600 with A/C. It also has deluxe rooms and suites.

Where To Stay—Higher

Hotel Sangam (464-700, fax 461-779), Collector's Office Rd, is a western style hotel with rooms for $30/40 to $40/55. It is not so well maintained and therefore not such a good value.

Jenney's Residence (461-301, fax 461-451), 3/14 McDonald Rd, is a western style hotel with 24 hour checkout. Room are Rs 650 and Rs 750/900 with A/C. This doesn't include the 20% sales tax and other taxes, which can add up to a total of 40% in taxes. It is, however, the best place in town, and it is in a quiet location. The rooms on the 4th and 5th floor are new.

Where To Eat

The *Kavithaa Restaurant*, located down the road from the Central Bus Stand, is a well known cheap *thali* place.

The *Vasantham Bhavan Restaurant* in the Abhirama Hotel, by the Central Bus Stand, is very popular. It may be difficult to get anything without onions at this place. The *Hotel Mega*, 8-B Rockins Rd, has a decent restaurant where you can get what you ask for. Next door is the veg-restaurant at the *Hotel Mathura*. There is a good *potato chip place* next to the Central Bus Stand, which makes a wide variety of fresh potato chips.

The *Vasanta Bhavan* Sweet Stall and Vegetarian Restaurant is a simple place near the Rock Fort that serves snacks and *dosas*. *Skylord*, Municipal Office Rd, in Chinese Bazaar by the Rock Fort, is a good cheap Indian vegetarian place.

The *maha-prasada* at the Srirangam Temple is good.

Travel

Air The airport is 8 km from the center of town. There are three Indian Airline flights weekly to **Madras** (11.45 am). There is a daily flight, except Sunday, to **Madurai**. The Indian Airlines office (43930) is at the Railway Co-operative Mansion, Dindigul Rd opposite the Aristo Hotel. There are two flights a week to Sri Lanka on Air Lanka. The Air Lanka office (27952) is located at the Hotel Lakshmi, 3A Alexandria Rd.

Rail There are trains to Madras (6-11

hr, 10 daily), Rameswaram (7 hr), Chidambaram (4 hr, 4 daily), Thanjavur (2 hr, 4 daily), Madurai (2½ to 7 hr, 7 daily), and Tirunelveli. The Rock Fort Express and Cholan Express from Madras Egmore to Tiruchirappalli take about six hours. To **Madras** are the Vaigai Exp #2636 (9.10 am, 5¼ hr) and Pallavan Exp #2606 (6.15 am, 5¼ hr). The Vaigai Express #2635 (5.45 pm) to **Madurai** takes 2½ hours. To **Bangalore** there is the Bangalore Exp #6531 (9.45 pm, 11½ hr). To **Ramesvaram** there is the Madras-Ramesvaram Exp #6101 (7 am, 6½ hr), and to **Mangalore** there is the #6531 Express (9.45 pm, 16½ hr).

To get from **Tirupati** to Tiruchirappalli you can get the Tirupati to Madurai Express #6799 (3.40 pm), which arrives at 5.50 am the next morning.

Bus There are two bus stands right next to each other, the **State Bus Stand** and the **Thiruvalluvar Bus Stand** (23680). At the State Bus Stand you buy your ticket from the conductor when the bus arrives. Express buses say "Fast" (in English) on the front of the bus. There are frequent buses to **Thanjavur** (1½ hr, every 15 min) and **Madurai** (3 or 4 hr, 15 daily). Bus No 1 brings you to the **Srirangam Temple** and the **Red Fort**.

The Thiruvalluvar buses, originating in Tiruchirappalli, can be booked in advance. There are buses to **Nagercoil** (8 daily), **Kanchipuram** (7 hr, 3 daily), **Tirupati** (9½ hr, 4 daily) via **Vellore**, **Madras** (8 hr, 20 daily), and **Bangalore** (3 daily). There are four super-deluxe buses to **Madras** from the Thiruvalluvar station.

You can also get private super-deluxe buses to **Madras** (7 hr). Both KPN/RR Travels, outside the Hotel Anand, and AKM Travels, opposite the Hotel Tamil

Nadu, offer this service.

Palani
Population: 76,000, STD Code 04545

Located here is one of the six major **Lord Subrahmanya** (Muruga) temples, dedicated to his form as **Sri Dandayudhapani**. Subrahmanya is standing with a stick in his right hand. *Dandam* means stick and *dandayudhapani* means "having a stick as a weapon in his hand." Here Subrahmanya is a sage who has renounced all connections with the world. This temple is on a 450 foot high hill. Each day hundreds and on Sunday over a thousand pilgrims climb up the 659 steps to the temple. Large numbers of pilgrims come during the festivals. Around 200,000 people come to the Tai Pusam Festival in January. The 10-day **Panguni Uttaram festival** in April draws large crowds of people. Also popular is Visakhan in June. The main festival is in Jan/Feb when pilgrims walk 80 km to reach this temple. This is a rich temple.

Palani is 119 km from Madurai on the railway line between Dindigul and Coimbatore. There are well-furnished dharamshalas here. Some places to stay at here are the basic *Devasthanam Rest House* and *Sri Venkatewaram Lodge*. The best place in town is *Ganpat Palani* (42294), 103 Poonga Rd, which is fairly basic. Rooms are Rs 110/150 and Rs 250 with A/C.

MADURAI
Population: 1,100,000, STD Code 0452

Madurai is the second largest city in Tamil Nadu, next to Madras. This interesting city was the capital of the Pandyan empire till the 14th century and is one of the oldest cities in India. Madurai is situated on the banks of the Vaigai River. The Meenakshi Temple is in the center of the old town and is the main reason why people come here. An average of 10,000 people a day go to the Meenakshi Temple. The foundation of the town and temple were built by the Pandyan king, Kulasekhara. It is a place of pilgrimage specifically meant for the devotees of Lord Siva, therefore it is called Saivaksetra, the place where Lord Siva is worshiped. Lord Caitanya came here on His South India tour.

Getting Your Bearings

Madurai is situated on both banks of the Vaigai River. The old city is surrounded by four streets—North, East, West, and South Veli Streets—which were made by the British when they filled in the moat that surrounded the city. The main shops, important offices, bus, and railway stations are on West Veli Street. The temple is in the center of the old city, as are many of the lower-priced hotels. The Anna Bus Stand, museum, and higher-class hotels are north of the river.

Information

The **tourist office** at 180 West Veli St provides a free map of Madurai and information about the city. The office is open from 10 am to 5.30 pm, Monday to Saturday, and between 10 am to 1 pm on Sunday. They also have offices at the airport and train station.

There is a daily **tour to Rameswaram** that departs at 7.30 am and returns around 6 pm. It goes to most of the major places there and is a convenient way to visit Rameswaram. You can arrange this tour with local travel agents. The tour bus picks you up at your hotel.

You can **change money** at the State Bank of India, 6 W Veli St, across from the train station and at the Central Bank of India, 15 Meenakshi Rd. At the Andhra Bank, on W Chitrai St, they accept Visa and Mastercard, but not currency.

You can hire a bicycle near the Uma Lodge on W Perumal Maistry Street. The **GPO** is at the corner of N Veli St and Scott Rd. There are good bookstores on West Veli St.

Meenakshi Temple

This 17th century temple has two sanctuaries, one dedicated to Lord Siva as **Sundareswara** ("Lord of Beauty") and the other to **Meenakshi**, his wife. Meenakshi holds a parrot and a bouquet. It is a huge temple, in which you can get lost. The present temple was built in the early 17th century by Tirumala Nayak, but its history goes back to the Pandya kings, 2000 years ago.

The temple has a hall with a thousand pillars (actually 985). There is an interesting art gallery and museum in this hall with some fascinating deities. The museum can be visited while the temple is closed in the afternoon, between 1 and 4 pm.

The temple is open daily from 5 am to 12.30 pm and 4 to 9.30 pm. Outside the Meenakshi Amman Shrine there is temple music between 6 and 7.30 pm and 9 and 10 pm. Every night at around 9.30 pm there is a dramatic ceremony during which Lord Siva is carried into the bedroom of Parvati. He is taken back to his temple around 6 am each morning.

The inner sanctums are restricted to Hindus only, but anyone can go anywhere else on the temple grounds. It is interesting to visit the temple both in the day and at night, as the dark corridors, with lamps burning here and there, are very impressive.

You can climb up to the top of the southern *gopuram* and get a great view of Madurai.

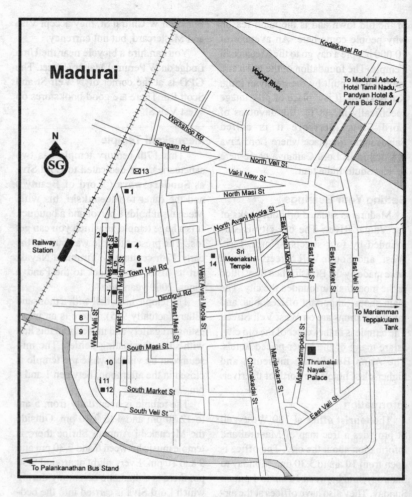

Madurai

Kodaikanal Rd

Vaigai River

To Madurai Ashok,
Hotel Tamil Nadu,
Pandyan Hotel &
Anna Bus Stand

Workshop Rd

Sangam Rd

N

SG

North Veli St

Vakil New St

⌧13

North Masi St

■1

North Avani Moola St

East Avani Moola St

East Masi St

East Market St

East Veli St

2●   ■3

Railway
Station

West Masi St

■4

West Perumal Maistry St

5   ■6

Sri
Meenakshi
Temple

■14

Town Hall Rd

7

Dindigul Rd

West Avani Moola St

West Masi St

To Mariamman
Teppakulam
Tank

8

9

West Veli St

South Masi St

Mahliyadampokki St

Manjankara St

Chinnakadai St

10   ■

Thrumalai
Nayak
Palace

i 11
■12

South Market St

East Vali St

South Veli St

← To Palankanathan Bus Stand

Temple Story

The story of the deities is that
Meenakshi was born, with three breasts,
out of the *yajna* fire that the Pandyan
king, Malayadhwaja, was performing to
get a son. The king was told that one of
the breasts would disappear when she met
the man she would marry. This happened
when she met Lord Siva on Mt Kailash.
Lord Siva told her to return to Madurai,
and eight days later he arrived in the form
of Lord Sundareswara to marry her.

Meenaksi means "one who has eyes
like a fish." Just as a mother fish has to
just glance on her spawn to develop life
in them, so in the same way her
worshiper's spiritual life comes alive
when goddess Meenakshi glances at
them.

Temple Information

There is a good detailed explanation
of the temple called *History and Description of Sri Meenakshi Temple*, which you

PLACES TO STAY

1	Duke Hotel
3	Supreme, Prem Nivas
4	Hotel Keerthi, Hotel International, Central & TM Lodges
5	New College House
6	Santhanam Lodge
7	Ruby Lodge
10	Hotel Aarathy
12	TTDC Tamil Nadu
14	Sree Devi

OTHER

2	State Bank of India & Indian Airlines
8	State Bus Stand (Periyar Bus Stand)
9	Thiruvalluvar Bus Stand
11	Tourist Office
13	GPO

can purchase at stalls inside the temple.

There is a Rs 25 camera fee payable at the temple office inside the southern gate, to the left as you enter. After taking a few pictures, I was asked by a regular-looking guy whether I had my camera ticket, so it is best to pay in advance. I know of another person who was asked whether he paid the camera fee a few seconds after taking his first picture.

The main section of the temple is closed between 1 and 4 pm, even for taking pictures. But the halls in the eastern part of the temple, including the 1000 Pillar Hall and the Ashta Shakti Mandapa, are open during this time.

Non-Hindus are not allowed in the inner sanctum. There is a jewel house next to where the vehicles of Meenakshi and Sundareswar are kept. The jewels can be seen for a donation.

Temple Complex

The outer wall of the complex is 259m by 221m (847 by 792 ft). It is estimated that there are **33 million carvings** in the temple. This temple has some of the most interesting architecture in India.

The temple has 12 large *gopurams,* or gates. There are four huge *gopurams* with colored statues on the outer wall. The **southern tower**, built in the 16th century, is the largest one and is 48.8 metres (170 ft) high with a 108 by 67 foot base. It has over 1500 sculptures on it. There are two huge *yalis*, which are like a combined lion and elephant, on both sides of the tower. The diameter of their eyes are two and a half feet, which gives an indication of the size of their bodies. The west tower, which is the first tower to be seen if you are coming from the railway station, is 154 feet high and has 1124 sculptures on it. The north tower is 152 feet high and has 404 sculptures on it.

The **eastern gopuram,** built in the 13th century by Maravarman Sundara Pandyan, is the oldest tower. The eastern gate, which in most temples is the main gate, is never used. The reason for this is that one of the priests of the temple jumped off this *gopuram* when the Palace officials levied taxes on the temple servants. After this incident the tax was immediately stopped. The gate is supposed to be haunted by his ghost.

People instead enter to the left of the eastern tower directly in line with the entrance to the Meenakshi Temple. There are beautiful sculptures of Ganesh and Subrahmanya on the sides of this entrance. There is also a scene of Sri Meenakshi's wedding. This entrance leads to the **Ashta Shakti Mandapa** (Eight Goddess Hall), where there is an interesting market. There are sculptured

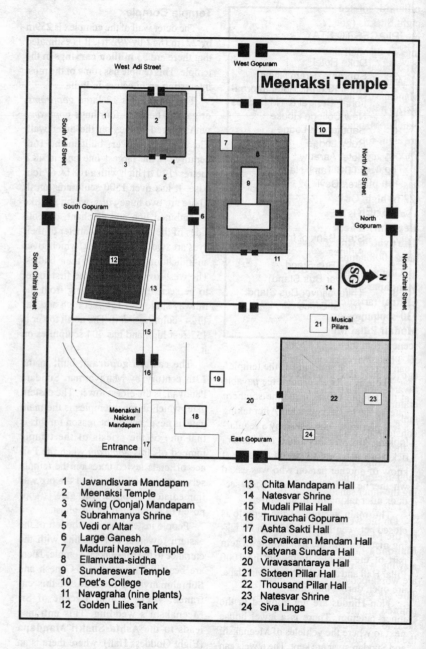

West Adi Street

West Gopuram

Meenaksi Temple

South Adi Street

North Adi Street

South Gopuram

North Gopuram

South Chitral Street

North Chitral Street

SG

N

Musical Pillars

Meenakshi Naicker Mandapam

East Gopuram

Entrance

1	Javandisvara Mandapam	13	Chita Mandapam Hall
2	Meenaksi Temple	14	Natesvar Shrine
3	Swing (Oonjal) Mandapam	15	Mudali Pillai Hall
4	Subrahmanya Shrine	16	Tiruvachai Gopuram
5	Vedi or Altar	17	Ashta Sakti Hall
6	Large Ganesh	18	Servaikaran Mandam Hall
7	Madurai Nayaka Temple	19	Katyana Sundara Hall
8	Ellamvatta-siddha	20	Viravasantaraya Hall
9	Sundareswar Temple	21	Sixteen Pillar Hall
10	Poet's College	22	Thousand Pillar Hall
11	Navagraha (nine plants)	23	Natesvar Shrine
12	Golden Lilies Tank	24	Siva Linga

pillars decorated with carvings of the eight Shaktis (goddesses) and Siva's 64 miracles at Madurai. There are also paintings in this hall that depict the birth of Sri Meenaksi.

A small hall connects the Ashta Shakti Mandapa to a large hall (43 m by 33.5 m, or 160 ft by 110 ft) called the Meenakshi Naicker Mandapa. In the small hall there are eight-foot-tall statues of a hunter and Parvati.

The **Meenakshi Naicker Mandapa** has 110 pillars, each of which is 6.7 m (22 ft) high. On each pillar is a figure of a *yali*, which is like a combined lion and elephant. There is a 25 foot high **Thiruvatchi** (frame of lamps) that contains 1008 lamps.

Going straight from the Ashta Shakti Mandapa, you enter the seven-story **Chitrai** (artistic) **gopuram**, which has 730 sculptures on it. This leads to the **Mudali Pillai Mandapa**. This hall has scenes from the *Puranas* on its walls.

The **Portramaraikulam tank (golden lotus tank),** also called Swarnapushpakarini, is where Tamil literature was presented and then put in the tank. The manuscripts that floated were considered great works of literature, and if they sank, they were dismissed. Pilgrims either bathe in the tank or wash their feet and hands there before entering the inner sanctum. The tank is 165 ft by 120 ft.

On the west side of the golden tank by the Meenakshi shrine is the **Oonjal Mandapa,** or Swing Mandapa, which has a swing where the two presiding deities are worshiped every Friday (6 to 7 pm). The six shrines of Subrahmanya are painted on the walls of this Mandapa. Next to this is the **Kilikootu Mandapa,** the hall of parrots. There used to be parrots here that chanted the name of Meenakshi, but there are no parrots in this hall now. It has some beautiful sculptures of the Pandavas, Vali, and Sugreeva, the king of the monkeys. There is a **Yali** here that has a stone ball that revolves in its mouth.

Next to the Kilikootu Mandapa is the main entrance to the **Meenakshi shrine**, also known as Amman Koyil, or "mother temple." The roof of the main shrine is covered with gold.

Across the corridor and next to the tank is the small **Rani Mangammal Mandapa,** which has an 18th century painting showing the marriage of Meenakshi and Sundara. In the hallway there are also sculptures from the *Ramayana* and *Mahabharata*.

Walking north from the Meenakshi shrine brings you to the Sundareswara shrine. By the doorway between these two shrines is a huge eight-foot tall monolithic **Ganesh**, said to have been found when the Mariamman Teppakkulam tank was excavated.

In front of the Sundareswara shrine are carvings of the **Navagrahas (nine planets)**. Next to this is the **Kambathadi Mandapa**, where there are carvings of the ten incarnations of Vishnu and the wedding of Meenakshi.

At the entrance of the **Sundareswara Temple** are 12 feet tall *dwarapalakas* (guards). In the southern part of this temple are shrines dedicated to **Saraswati** (goddess of learning) and the **63 Nayanmars** (important devotees of Siva). In the southwest corner is the *utsava-murti* (the deity taken out of the temple for processions). In the north section one can see **Durga, Siddhi** and **Laksmi** (goddess of wealth), as well as an ancient Kadamba tree and a well. In the northwest corner is **Kasi Visvanatha**. There is a tunnel in this enclosure which is said to have once been connected to the Thirumalai Nayak Palace. In the next enclosure is a **Lord Nataraja** shrine, called Velliambam or Rajatha Sabha, where Lord Siva is dancing with his right foot raised. You then enter the inner sanctum.

If after leaving the Sundareswar Temple you go straight (east) you come to the **Vira Vasantharayar Mandapa**, which has 46 pillars and a large Nandi, the bull carrier of Lord Siva. There is a large arch of lights in this *mandapa*.

The **Thousand Pillar Mandapa** was built in the 16th century. Each pillar is intricately carved. It is a huge hall, 250 by 240 feet, which is open all day. There is a large deity of **Nataraja** (dancing Lord Siva) at the far end of the hall. There is an interesting **museum** and some **musical pillars** in this hall. The musical pillars are just inside the entrance to the right. The museum is open 8 am to 8 pm.

When you exit out of this hall you come to the **Thirukkalyana Mandapa**. This is where the marriage ceremony of Sri Meenakshi is performed each year in April/May.

Between the north *gopuram* and the Thousand Pillar Hall on North Adi Street there are five **musical pillars**, each made of 22 rods carved out of a single block of granite. Each of the rods of the pillars produces a different note when struck. Near the pillars is a *mandapa* with 16 pillars called **Tattu Chutur Mandapa**, built in 1172.

Festivals

The **Chithirai festival** in April-May is the most important festival. It celebrates the **marriage of Meenakshi** (Parvati) with **Sundareswara** (Lord Siva). The two deities, riding on a golden bull and wearing pearl crowns, are brought on a spectacular procession around the town. **Lord Alagar's** (Vishnu) procession to the bank of the Vaigai River on the full moon day is one of the most interesting events of the festival. Lord Vishnu rides on a real-gold horse chariot to His sister's wedding. Meenakshi is considered to be the sister of Lord Alagar.

For several days in January or early February there is the **Teppam (Float) Festival**, where Sri Meenakshi and Lord Sundareswara ride on decorated boats (Floats) in the Mariamman Teppakkulam Tank. It is a very popular festival. During the **Avanimoola Festival** (Aug/Sept) temple carts are pulled around the streets of the city.

Koodal Alagar Temple

This is a Vishnu temple located 2 km west of the city. There are three altars, one on top of the other, in which Lord Vishnu is in three different poses: sitting, standing, and reclining. The main Deity of the temple is Koodal Alagar, who is in a sitting posture. Above the shrine of this Deity are the altars of Sri Ranganatha, in a reclining pose, and Sri Suryanarayan Perumal, in a standing pose. There are intricate woodcarvings here, including one of Lord Rama's coronation. This is one of the 108 Divya Desam temples. There is a Navagraha (nine planets) enclosure in this temple.

Mariamman Teppakkulam Tank

This huge tank, 1000 feet by 950 feet, is located 5 km east of the Meenakshi Temple. This is where the Float Festival takes place, during which the deities are taken out on decorated boats. The tank is fed water from the Vaigai River through underground channels and therefore never dries up. While digging up the earth here a huge Ganesh was found, which is now installed at the entrance of the Sundareswara sanctum. From the PRC bus stand, you catch bus No 4 to get here.

Thirumalai Nayak Mahal Palace.

This interesting palace is about 2 km southeast of the Meenakshi Temple. It was built in 1523 by the Nayak rulers. It has excellent stucco work on its domes and arches. The audience hall is known as Swarga Vilasam (Celestial Pavilion). It has a 20m-high dome without a single girder or rafter support. Architecturally, it is one of the best palaces in India.

There is a sound and light show on the life of Thirumalai Nayak in the evening. There is a museum in the palace dealing with the history of Madurai. It has a beautiful sculpture of Narasimha and a Deity of Lord Vishnu, both dating from around the 9th century. It is open from 9 am to 1 pm and 2 to 5 pm.

Gandhi Museum

This museum is located in the old Mangammal palace. It contains the blood-stained dhoti worn by Gandhi when he was assassinated. It also has an interesting "History of India" display.

By Madurai

ALAGAR KOIL TEMPLE

Alagar Koil is an important Vishnu temple, 18 km northeast of Madurai at Alagar Hill. Around the temple are ruins of an ancient fortified town. The presiding Deity is Alagar (the beautiful), who is also known as Sundararaja Perumal. The Deity is also known as Kallalagar, as He is the Deity of the Kallas people. The gopurams of this temple have recently been repainted, giving them an outstanding effect.

Alagar, who is Meenakshi's brother, was supposed to give her away in marriage to Sundareswara, but He arrived late for the wedding. This pastime is replayed at the Chitrai Festival. The panels in the Meenakshi Temple show carvings of Vishnu giving Meenakshi away in marriage, telling a different story.

Alagar Koil is one of the most ancient temples in India. All the twelve Alwars visited this place. It is stated in the *Mahabharata* that both Yudhisthira and Arjuna came here. It is said that Koorattalwar, the chief disciple of Ramanuja, got back his eyesight by worshipping the Deity here.

The processional Deity, Sundararaja, is a made of very valuable gold called Aparanji gold. There is a shrine dedicated to Lord Narasimha, known as Jwala Narasimha, located behind the inner sanctum. Every day He is bathed with milk, curd, and other items to cool down His anger. There is a big opening in the ceiling, just above His head, through which His anger and fury can pass out. There is a Deity of Sudarsana-cakra said to be 2,000 years old in this temple.

There are also deities of Parthasarathi, Ashtabhuja Krishna, Nartana Krishna, Saraswati, and Ramanujacarya. The temple is said to be perpetually guarded by Karuppanna Swami, a local Tamil deity. He has no image, but two large wooden doors of the entrance to the *gopuram*, at the 18th step, are dedicated to him. The keys to the treasury of the temple are entrusted to Karuppanna Swami every night.

There are temples on the hill dedicated to Siva, Bhairava, Subrahmanya, and Vinayaka (Ganesh). This place is one of the places dear to Subrahmanya. Water for the daily *abhisheka* is taken from a spring three km uphill called Noopura

Ganga, because any other water is said to blacken the Deity. The source of the Noopura Ganga is unknown.

On the fourth day of the nine-day **Chitrai Festival** Lord Alagar goes to Madurai to attend his sister Meenakshi's wedding. This is a grand event and hundreds of thousands of people attend this festival.

Non-Hindus are not allowed in the temple, but ISKCON devotees and converted Hindus can enter the temple. You take the No 44 bus from the state bus stand on West Veli St to get here.

Thirupparankunram

At this place is a temple dedicated to Lord Subrahmanya (Kartikeya), which celebrates his marriage to Indra's daughter, Devayanai. The temple was carved out of a mountain. This temple is one of Subrahmanya's six sacred abodes. Thirupparankunram is eight km southeast of Madurai, on the main railway line. From Madurai the No 5 bus from the PRC bus stand comes here. It is open from 5 am to 12.30 pm and 4 to 10 pm.

Kalamegha Perumal and Uramellaneyan Temples

Kalamegha Perumal Temple, one of the Divya Desam temples, is located 12 km southeast of Madurai, at Tirumogur, on the bus route to Melur.

The **Uramellaneyan Temple** is in Tirukkottiyur, 10 km south of Tirupattur, which is 50 km east of Madurai. There are two Deities of Lord Narasimha here. One shows Him chasing Hiranyakasipu, who is trying to elude His grip, and the other shows Him tearing the body of Hiranyakasipu to shreds. This place is the birthplace of Tirukkottiyur Nambi (Goshtipurna), one of Ramanuja's five gurus. He initiated Ramanuja into the import of the sacred mantra. It is said that Ramanuja got the sacred mantra from Tirukkottiyur Nambi after 18 visits. Sri Ramanuja then publicly explained the inner meaning of the mantra from the temple tower to all the Vaishnavas who had assembled there.

Where To Stay—Lower

Most of the cheaper places are along Town Hall Rd and West Perumal Maistry St, not far from the railway station.

New College House (24311), on 2 Town Hall Rd, is a good cheap place with a variety of rooms for Rs 90/150. It is best to see a few rooms here before choosing one. The *Natraj Lodge*, between the temple and railway station, is a good place with a view of the temple for Rs 85.

The *Ruby Lodge* (33633), 92 West Perumal Maistry St, has doubles with bath for Rs 60.

The *Hotel Ragu* (34566), 23 Town Hall Rd, is a good value having rooms with bath for Rs 55/75. *Thilaga* (30762), 111 W Perumal Maistry St, is a new place with clean rooms. There are big clean *railway retiring rooms*, which are usually full.

The brand new *Hotel Dhanamani* (24817), 20 Sunnambukara St, has rooms with an attached bath with a bucket shower for Rs 90/135 and a double with a bathroom with a shower is Rs 170. Rooms here are a good value.

Sree Devi (36743), 20 W Avani Moola St, is a good value with a great view of the Meenaksi Temple from the roof. It has good double rooms for Rs 138.

Where To Stay—Middle

A recommended place is the *Hotel Aarathy* (31571), 9 Perumal Kovil West

Mada St, by the bus stations. It has clean rooms with hot water for Rs 150/250 and A/C rooms for Rs 250/350. The temple elephant from the Meenakshi Temple comes to the restaurant out front and hangs around for a while at about 7.15 am.

Also recommended is the *Hotel Supreme* (36331), 110 West Perumal Maistry St, which has good sized rooms for Rs 270 up to Rs 595 for an A/C room. It is a nice place to stay and has a very good vegetarian restaurant. Also recommended is the *Arya Bhajann Hotel*.

There are two *TTDC Hotel Tamil Nadu hotels* in town. The one at West Veli St (37470) is centrally located and has rooms for Rs 120/190 and Rs 200/300 with A/C. The *Tamil Nadu Star* (42461), opposite the Pandyan Hotel, across the Vaigai River on Alagarkoil Rd in a quiet location, costs Rs 200/230 for a regular room and Rs 225/300 for an A/C room. The *Tamil Nadu Hotel* across the river is better, and all rooms there have a bath with hot water, but it is not conveniently located.

The *Hotel Prem Nivas* (37531), 102 West Perumal Maistry St, is a good place with rooms for Rs 135/225 and air-con rooms for Rs 325. It is popular with budget travelers. It also has a good vegetarian restaurant. This is a recommended place. Also good is the *Hotel Keerthi* (31501), across the street at 40 West Perumal Maistry St, which has rooms with hot water for Rs 135/175 and A/C rooms for Rs 275 up to Rs 400.

The *Duke Hotel* (26314), 6 N Veli St near W Veli St, is a clean place having rooms with hot water and TV. The non A/C rooms are a better value.

Where To Stay—High

The *Pandyan Hotel* (42471, fax 42020), across the river on Alagarkoil Rd, has central air-conditioning and is excellent. Rooms cost Rs 1000/1200, with 35% added on for sales tax and luxury tax. It has a good garden and a book store. You should ask to see some rooms, as some are good and others are run down.

The comfortable *Hotel Madurai Ashok* (42531), also across the river on Alagarkoil Rd, has rooms for US $25/45. It is also good and has central air-conditioning, a pool, and a good book store.

The luxury *Taj Garden Retreat* (601-020), Pasumalai Hills, 5 km from the city, on a hills overlooking the city, is the best place in town. It is an old colonial house with 15 rooms. It has a pool and gardens. Rooms are $80/95. There are also deluxe cottages with private terrraces. An auto rickshaw here costs about Rs 45.

Where To Eat

The A/C *Priya Restaurant* at the Hotel Prem Nivas, 102 W Perumal Maistry St, is a good place.

New College House has a basic *thali* type restaurant.

The best place in town is the recommended *Surya Restaurant* at the Hotel Supreme. It has an A/C restaurant on the ground floor that is open from 6 am to 11 pm. There is also a Roof Top restaurant, which is very popular with foreigners, and therefore the spicing is very mild and good. The rooftop restaurant is open from 5 pm to 12 pm.

Local Buses

The No 44 goes to Alagar Koil Vishnu Temple. The No 4 goes to Mariammam Teppakkulam Tank, No 1 and 2 go to the Gandhi Museum and Hotel Tamil Nadu, No 3 to the Anna bus stand, and No 5 to the Tiruparankundram rock-cut temple. You get these buses at the State bus stand.

Travel

Air There are a few flights daily to Madras. East West Airlines has a daily flight to Bombay via Thiruvananthapuram. The airport is six km south of the downtown.

The Indian Airlines Office (34495, Airport 35433) is at the TVS Building, 7A West Veli St. Air India is opposite the railway station on West Veli St. East West Airlines (42471) is at Office 119, 1st Flr, W Perumal Maistry Rd.

Rail Madurai Junction Railway Station is a 20-minute walk west of the Meenakshi temple on West Veli Street and just a few minutes from the main hotel area. There are trains to **Madras** (8-15 hr, 6 daily), **Rameswaram** (7 hr, 5 daily), **Kanniyakumari** (6 hr, 4.10 am), **Tirupati** (Madurai-Tirupati Exp #6800, 10.30 am, 19 hr), **Tiruchirappalli** (145 km, 2½ to 8 hr, 8 daily), and **Bangalore** (12½ hr, Madurai-Bangalore Exp. #6531, 8.10 pm). The Rameswaram-Madras Exp #6102 (3.20 pm) goes to Madras (14 hr) and stops at Thanjavur (5 hr), Chidambaram (8 hr), and Chengalpattu (13 hr) on the way. The Madurai-Quilon Express (10.25 pm) goes direct to **Thiruvananthapuram**, arriving the next morning at 5.30 am.

The Vaigai Express #2635 (12.45 pm) from Egmore Station in Madras takes 9 hours to get to Madurai stopping at Tiruchirappalli (Trichy) on the way. To Rameswaram there are three trains a day that take 5 or 6 hours. It is quicker to go by bus, which only takes 4½ hours. The Tirupati-Ramesvaram Exp #6799 (10.30 am, 5 hr) is the quickest train to Rameswaram. There are no direct trains to Delhi or Bombay from Madurai.

To get a tourist quota ticket you have to go to the Rail Tourist Information Counter in the main lobby. It is open 6 am to 8.30 pm. With a member of their staff you can jump to the front of the long queue (line) upstairs. The tourist quota reservation office on the ground floor is very helpful. They take you inside the office and arrange your ticket in a hassle free atmosphere. They can also arrange tickets that depart from other cities from here, and they will gladly help you do this. This is a good place to arrange your train tickets. Upper Class booking is to the right and is open 9.30 am to 1 pm and 2 to 5 pm.

Bus There is good bus service from Madurai to all parts of the South. There are four bus stands in Madurai. Most long-distance buses leave from the **State Bus Stand** (Periyar Bus Stand) and the **Thiruvalluvar Bus Stand** (TTC stand), which are both at the southern end of West Veli Street, not far from the railway station and most of the accommodations. From here there are buses to Madras (11 hr, 20 daily), Bangalore (9 hr, 20 daily), Tirupati (14 hr, 5 daily), Mysore (1 daily), Pondicherry (8 hr), and Mangalore. There are hourly buses to Madras and 12 super-deluxe buses go there daily.

You can book seats in advance for the Thiruvalluvar buses at the main bus stand or the relief stand across the street.

Buses to Thanjavur (6 hr), Kumbakonam, Rameswaram (4 hr), and Tiruchirappalli (3 hr) leave from the **Anna Bus Stand**, 5 km northeast of the temple and north of the Vaigai River. The No 3 bus from the Anna Bus Stand takes you to the State Bus Stand. From the **Arapalayam Bus Stand** buses depart to some destinations within Tamil Nadu and some places in Kerala. There are many buses to Coimbatore. There are nine buses a day to Kodaikanal (4 hr, Rs 100) from the Arapalayam Bus Stand.

The **Palankanathan Bus Stand**, in the southwest part of the city, 5 km from the center of town, serves cities in South Tamil Nadu and South Kerala, such as Kanniyakumari and Thiruvananthapuram (7 hr, 10 daily).

You can book super-deluxe video buses to Madras and Bangalore from private bus companies. They may also try to sell you a ticket to other destinations promising a super-deluxe bus and instead they will sell you a ticket on a state bus for double the normal price. This is a normal thing that the travel agents in Madurai do. Be careful of hustlers at the bus stands. They may help you get a bus ticket at an inflated price.

SRIVILLIPUTTUR
Population: 70,000, STD Code 04568

Srivilliputtur is 70 km southwest of Madurai by rail, going towards Trivandrum. There are two major temples in this town: the Vatapatrasayee Temple and the Sri Andal Temple. Srivilliputtur is the birthplace of Peria Alwar and Sri Andal.

In the southwest part of town there is a small Krishna, Rukmini, and Satyabhama temple. Four km north of town is the Tirupati Srinivasa Temple on top of a 100-foot hill. Southwest of town there is a large Siva temple. Srivilliputtur is a fairly large town.

Vatapatrasayee Temple

The main Deity in this temple, Sri Vatapatrasayee, is a light-blue Lord Vishnu Deity reclining on His couch of Adi Sesa. Sri Devi and Bhu Devi are at His feet. Bhrigu Muni is by His head and Markandeya is near His feet. The Deity is so large, He is viewed from three doorways. The altar is on an upper floor. This temple is also called Vadabadrasaikoil.

On the side of the temple is the original *tulasi* garden that was cared for by Vishnu Chitta (Peria Alwar), the father of Andal. He used to make flower garlands for Lord Vishnu with the flowers grown in this garden.

Sri Andal Temple

Next to the Vatapatrasayee Temple is a temple dedicated to Sri Andal, who was said to have merged into the body of Lord Ranganatha at Srirangam. Sri Andal, also known as Godadevi, is considered to be an incarnation of the goddess of fortune who was married to the Deity, Sri Ranganatha. She wrote two works *Tiruppavai* and *Nachiar Tirumozhi*, which express her burning love of God.

She was the daughter of one of the 12 Alwars named Peria Alwar, who was also called Vishnu Cittar. According to tradition, Peria Alwar used to take care of the flower and *tulasi* garden of the Vishnu temple in Srivilliputtur around the 8th century.

While tending the garden he found Andal as a baby and then brought her up. When her foster father tried to find a husband for her she refused any mortal man and said that she would only marry the Lord. Peria Alwar had a dream in which Lord Vishnu requested him to bring Andal to Srirangam so He could marry her. When she saw the image of Sri Ranganatha she merged with Him.

The Vishnu Deity's name in the Sri Andal Temple is Rangamannar. The *gopuram* of the Sri Andal Temple is 192 feet high and has 12 stories. This is the second highest temple tower in Tamil Nadu, the first biggest being at Srirangam. Peria Alwar is said to have built this tower with gold that he won in religious debates held in Vallabhadeva Pandya's court at Madurai.

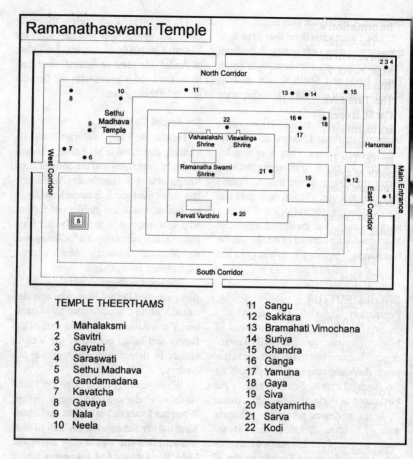

Ramanathaswami Temple

North Corridor

Sethu Madhava Temple

Vishaslakshi Shrine   Viswalinga Shrine

Ramanatha Swami Shrine

Parvati Vardhini

West Corridor

East Corridor

Main Entrance

Hanuman

South Corridor

TEMPLE THEERTHAMS

1 Mahalaksmi
2 Savitri
3 Gayatri
4 Saraswati
5 Sethu Madhava
6 Gandamadana
7 Kavatcha
8 Gavaya
9 Nala
10 Neela

11 Sangu
12 Sakkara
13 Bramahati Vimochana
14 Suriya
15 Chandra
16 Ganga
17 Yamuna
18 Gaya
19 Siva
20 Satyamirtha
21 Sarva
22 Kodi

For festivals, the temple has a wooden cart that has 9 gigantic wheels. It is said to be the biggest temple cart in India. The cart is over a hundred years old and takes 3,000 people to pull. There is a shrine dedicated to Peria Alwar next to the *tulasi* garden, south of the main shrine.

RAMESWARAM
Population: 35,000, STD Code 04573

There are four *dhamas*, or kingdoms of God, which are Badrinath, Rameswaram, and Dwarka. Rameswaram is located at the southeastern end of the Indian Peninsula. Rameswaram is on an island, which is the shape of a conch shell, 55 km by 12 km, in the Gulf of Mannar. The island is sanctified by the footprints of Lord Rama. It is said that Lord Rama bathed at Dhanushkodi, where the bay of Bengal and the Indian Ocean meet.

There a major Lord Siva temple here called the Ramanathaswami Temple. This name indicates that Lord Siva is a great personality, whose worshipable Deity is Lord Rama. This temple is very popular. Lord Caitanya came here.

Information and Bearings

The temple is in the center of town, right next to the sea. It is surrounded by West, North, East, and South Car Streets. This is where the shopping area is located. The **Tamil Nadu Tourist Office**, 14 E Car St, is open from 10 am to 5 pm. There is a tourist information counter at the railway station, which is open when trains arrive. The Hotel Tamil Nadu is a little north of town. Rameswaram is a small town and except for the holy places, there is not much to see or do.

You can **change money** at the State Bank of India, N Car St, and the Indian Bank, W Car St.

The post office and telegraph office are on Mela Street. Bicycles can be rented at a shop by the temple entrance or at the Hotel Tamil Nadu for about Rs 20 a day or Rs 3 an hour. This is a good way to get around town, as some of the places are a good distance from the center of town.

Tours

There is a bus tour that departs from Madurai at 6.30 am and returns at 7 pm. It goes to the Ramanathaswami Temple, Gandhamadhana Parvatham, Lakshman Teertham, Agni Teertham, a temple where there is a floating rock, and Indira Gandhi Bridge. It does not go to all the places in the area, but I considered it a good tour. You can arrange it at many of the travel agents in Madurai. You are picked up and dropped off at your hotel. The only problem with this tour is it goes in a mini-bus, which can be very uncomfortable if you sit in the back.

Sri Ramananthaswami Temple

This is one of the major Lord Siva temples in India. The name of the Deity, Ramananthaswami, indicates that Lord Siva is a great personality whose worshipable Deity is Lord Rama. Parts of the present temple were built in the 12th century. Many additions have been added over the years. The temple covers a 15-acre area. The eastern *gopuram* is 53m (160 ft) high.

This temple is about 200m from the sea, facing east. The temple is open from 4 am to 1 pm and 3 to 9 pm. Non-Hindus are not allowed into the inner sanctum to see the deities, but can walk around the rest of the temple. ISKCON devotees can enter. You have to wait in line about half an hour on a normal day to get a close view of the Ramanantha-linga.

The important festivals are during Maha Siva-ratri (ten days during Feb/March), Brahmotsavam (ten days during March/April), and Thirukalyanam (July/Aug), which celebrates the marriage of Siva and Parvati.

The sea at **Agni Teertham**, about 200m from the temple, is a sacred bathing place. It is said that if you take bath here all your sins are washed away. It is traditional to take bath at Agni Teertham before entering the Ramananthaswami Temple.

Temple Story

It is said that the *Siva-linga* in the Ramananthaswami Temple was installed by Sri Rama on His return to the mainland from the island of Lanka, after killing Ravana. Rama wanted to install a Siva-linga in Rameswaram to absolve Himself of the sin of killing Ravana, who was a Brahmin. Rama sent Hanuman to Mount Kailash to get the *linga*. Since Hanuman was late when the auspicious time for installation neared, Sita made a Siva-linga out of sand. This *linga* was then installed by Rama and is known as the Rama-linga, because it was installed

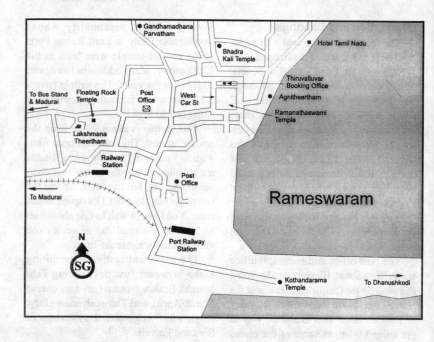

by Lord Rama.

At that time Hanuman came with the Siva-linga from Kailash. He was disappointed to find a *linga* already installed. Ram told Hanuman that he could remove the *linga* made by Sita and install the one that he brought in its place. Hanuman took hold of the *linga* with his hands and could not move it. He then wrapped his tail around it and tried to pull the *linga* out, but it did not move. The *linga* is said to still have the marks of Hanuman's tail on it. To pacify Hanuman, Rama had the *linga* that he brought, the Viswa-linga, installed alongside the Rama-linga. He ordered that *puja* (worship) be performed first to the Viswa-linga, which is still being done today.

Temple Complex

As you enter the main eastern entrance there is a deity of Hanuman trying to re-

move the sand Ramanatha Siva-linga. There is a 1,220m (3,700 feet) long beautiful corridor, which goes around the temple, with large sculptured pillars that are elaborately designed and carved. It is the **longest temple corridor** in India. The corridor is 9m high and 17 to 21 feet wide. There are 1212 pillars in the north and south corridors. These temple corridors are an impressive sight.

If you proceed straight from the east entrance you come to the huge bull carrier of Lord Siva, **Nandi**, who is 5m long and 3m high (15 ft by 8 ft by 9 ft). You then come to the **Ramanathaswami Siva shrine**. In the principal sanctum (altar) is the *linga* of Sri Ramanatha. This is the *linga* that Sita made and Sri Rama sanctified.

The **Viswa-linga**, installed by Hanuman, is to the right of the Ramanatha-linga, on an altar along the north wall.

Worship is first offered to this *linga*. Vishalakshi, his consort, is next to him on another altar.

The shrine of **Parvathavardhini**, the consort of Sri Ramanatha, is left of the Rama-linga. You can enter this shrine through a corridor to the left of the main altar.

Behind the Sri Ramanatha shrine, between the second and third walls, is a shrine dedicated to Lord Vishnu called **Setu Madhava**. Tradition says that if you bathe in the tank near this shrine and offer worship to this Lord Vishnu Deity you receive all the benefits of bathing in Setu.

Temple Teerthams–Bathing Tanks

There are 22 *teerthams* (tanks) in the temple in which pilgrims traditionally bathe in before seeing the deities. Each tank is said to give a different benefit. Many pilgrims bathe in all 22 tanks before seeing the deity.

These bathing tanks are 1) **Maha-Lakshmi**, Dhararaja bathed here and got wealth; 2) **Savitri**, King Kasibar got rid of a curse; 3) **Gayatri**, King Kasibar got rid of a curse; 4) **Saraswati**, King Kasibar got rid of a curse; 5) **Setu Madhava**, will receive the blessing of Lakshmideva and purification of heart; 6) **Gandamadana**, will receive wealth and sins will be absolved; 7) **Kavatcha**, you will not go to hell; 8) **Gavaya**, will receive shelter under Karpaga Virutchaga tree; 9) **Nala**, one will go to heaven and get Surya tejas; 10) **Neela**, one will receive the benefit of Samastha yajna; 11) **Sankha**, Vatsanaba got rid of the sin of ingratitude; 12) **Sakra**, Sun got hand turned golden; 13) **Brahmahatya Vimochana**, Brahma was absolved from his sins; 14) **Surya**, you will get knowledge of past, present, and future; 15) **Chandra**, you will get knowledge of past, present, and future; 16)

Ganga, Ganasuruthi Raja attained wisdom; 17) **Yamuna**, Ganasuruthi Raja attained wisdom; 18) **Gaya**; 19) **Siva**, completion of Bhaira Brahmahathi; 20 **Satyamrita**, Emperor Bururoonu got rid of a curse; 21) **Sarva**, Sutharishna got rid of old age and blindness (from birth) and then prospered; and 22) **Kodi**.

Gandhamadhana Parvatham

This two-story temple is on a small hilltop, about 2.5 km northwest of the Ramananthaswami Temple. There is a set of **Lord Rama's footprints** on a Chakra here and the small **Ramjharoka Temple**. There is a good view of the island from here. The place is called Vedaranyam. It is said that **Hanuman** made his great leap to Lanka from here. It is open 6 to 11 am and 3.30 to 6.30 pm.

Kothandaramasvami Temple

There are deities of Sri Rama, Sita, Laksmana, Hanuman, and Vibhishana here. It is said that Vibhishana, Ravana's brother, surrendered to Lord Rama at this place. A series of paintings inside the temple tells the story. In 1964 a cyclone wiped out everything in the surrounding area. The only thing left standing was this temple. It is located about 8 km from Rameswaram, or about 6 km from the southernmost tip of the island going toward Dhanushkodi.

Dhanushkodi

This is the place where the bay meets the ocean. Pilgrims are supposed to bathe in the small lagoon here called Ratnakara. This is a place to offer *sraddha* to the ancestors. It is said to be especially auspicious to bathe here in May.

Dhanushkodi is about 20 km southeast of Rameswaram. It is said that Lord Ramacandra destroyed a small bridge with His bow here due to the request of Vibhishana, the younger brother of Ravana. To get to Dhanushkodi you can share a four-wheel drive vehicle as far as the road goes, which is about 2 km from the end of the island. From there you have to walk the rest of the way into what seems like the middle of nowhere, as there is no road. It is a tough place to get to.

Darbha Sayanam & Adi Jagannatha Temple

Darbha Sayanam (Tirupallani, Pullanranyam) is where Sri Rama observed penance, lying on *darbha* grass here for three days. It is said that Adi Jagannatha appeared before Him, gave him the weapon called Divya Chapa, and blessed Him with success.

Five km south of Darbha Sayanam at Adi Setu is the **Adi Jagannatha Temple**. The Deity of Sri Vishnu here is in a reclining posture on Sesa Naga. It is said that King Dasaratha, the father of Rama, came here to pray for a child, when all his wives were childless. Hindu couples still visit this temple to pray for children. This temple is 8 km southeast of Ramnad (Ramanathapuram) Railway Station. The place where Sri Rama built His bridge is not far from here.

It is said that at the coastal town of **Devi Patnam (Navapashanam)** Lord Rama put nine stones standing upright in the shallow bay. They are supposed to represent the nine planets that He worshiped for success. This place is about 14 km northeast of Ramanathapuram on the mainland.

Other Places

There are many pastime places connected with the *Ramayana* in the area. There is a temple near the bridge that you cross to enter Rameswaram where there is a **floating rock**. When Lord Rama went to Lanka with the monkey army, they crossed the ocean on a bridge of floating rocks. The floating rock in this temple proves that floating rocks exist. Near this temple, close to the bridge, is **Lakshman Teertham** and **Rama Teertham**. Lord Rama is said to have bathed in these two tanks. **Kodi Teertham** is supposed to be a spring that Lord Rama created by shooting an arrow into the ground.

It is said that at **Jata Teertham**, Sri Rama washed His hair to get rid of any sins that He might have incurred in the battle at Lanka. This place is 4 km from Rameswaram, going toward Dhanushkodi. Next to this *teertham* is the **Papahareshwar Temple**.

At **Amba-samudram** there is a temple where King Kulasekhara worshiped the Deity of Lord Krishna. The King's *samadhi* is on the temple grounds.

Where To Stay

As this is a major pilgrimage town, sometimes lodging can be tight. If possible, reserve a room in advance from a Tourist Bungalow or at a Tamil Nadu Tourist Office. During a festival, if you arrive late in the day, it can be hard to find a place to stay. Also from the middle of December to the end of January you may have a problem getting a room here, especially late in the day.

The *Gujarati Dharamsala*, about a five-minute walk from the temple, was recommended to me as a cheap very basic place.

For a basic Indian type place that costs Rs 60/75 with attached bath there is the *Santhana Lodge*, South Car St; *Swami Ramanatha Tourist House*, *Santhya Lodge* and *Alankar Tourist Home* on West Car St. These places also have rooms with common bath for Rs 40/50. The *Alankar* is a little better than the rest. The *Santhya Lodge*, W Car St, has 22 rooms, some of them with A/C. Rooms at the *Devasthanam Lodge* (21241) are Rs 100/135.

The *Hotel Maharaja's* (21271), 7 Middle St (the street that goes west from the west temple gate), has good clean rooms for Rs 80/120 with attached bath. It also has some A/C rooms with TV for Rs 240. The *Hotel Venkatesh* (21296), Sithi Vinayagar Kovil St, has good rooms with bath for Rs 100/140. It also has a few rooms with A/C for Rs 210. These two places are a little better than the other hotels.

The highest class place in town is the *TTDC Hotel Tamil Nadu* (21277) in the northeast end of town, near the beach in a quiet area. Doubles with bath and hot water are Rs 150/175, and the best rooms have A/C and a TV for Rs 325. There are also dorm beds for Rs 20. All the rooms have a sea view. It has veg and non-veg restaurants.

Where To Eat

There are many cheap basic vegetarian places here. The *Sri Ganesh, Ashok Bhavan,* and *Hotel Ariya Bhavan* are simple *thali* places on West Car Street. There is a place run by the *Devasthanam Trust* located opposite the eastern gate of the temple. None of the places are very good, and you will have a problem getting food without onions. The *Vasantha Bhawan* is at the Central Bus Stand.

Travel

Air The closest airport is in Madurai, 167 km away.

Train There are trains to Madurai (5½- 7 hr, 5 daily), Chidambaram (11 hr, 1

daily), Coimbatore (12½ hr, 1 daily), and other places. There are two express trains, the Setu Express and the Rameswaram Express, that go to Madras daily (666 km, 15 hr). They do not stop in Madurai, but go through Tiruchirappalli. The daily Rameswaram-Madurai Passenger train goes directly to and from Madurai (164 km) in six and a half hours.

The Ramesvaram Exp #6102 (daily, 12.30 pm) takes 6½ to get to Tiruchirappalli. The Ramesvaram-Tirupati train #6800 departs to Tirupati at 6 am and arrives 23 hours later.

There are regular buses from the railway station to the Ramananthaswami Temple.

Bus The bus station is two km west of town. There are buses to Madras (14 hr), Madurai (4½ hr, 20 daily), Kanniyakumari (9 hr), and Tiruchirappalli. You can also catch a bus to Thanjavur and Pondicherry via Madurai. To get to Kerala it is easier and quicker to go by bus than to go by train. There are regular buses to Nagercoil, which is a major bus junction in southern Kerala, where you can connect to other places in Kerala.

From Rameswaram you can get a nonstop tourist bus to Madurai for Rs 75 that picks you up at your hotel and drops you off at a hotel in Madurai. It takes about 5 hours instead of 4½ by the local bus, but there is plenty of space for your luggage and it picks you up at your hotel, so it is relatively hassle free.

Sankaranayinar Koil

The deity in the **Sri Sankaranarayana Temple** is a *mrittika (earth) linga*. The *linga* is half Siva and half Narayana. The right portion is smeared with sandalwood paste and has the emblems of Siva, with a cobra, moon, etc.

The left side has a *sankha* (conch) and *cakra* (disc) carved on it and is Lord Vishnu. They are carved from one stone. There is also a *sphatika-linga* in the temple like at Chidambaram.

Naga Sunai, a sacred tank, is believed to be able to heal leprosy, piles, and other diseases. The huge *gopuram* is considered to be the third largest one in India. Sankaranayinar Koil is halfway between Madurai and Trivandrum, 52 km from Tirunelveli.

Tirunelveli

Population: 135,000, STD Code 0462

In Tirunelveli is the large 7th century **Kanthimathi Nellaiyappar Temple** dedicated to Parvati and Lord Siva. In the temple enclosure are two temples, the northern one dedicated to Lord Siva (Nellaiyappar) and the southern one to Parvati (Kanthimathi). Each of these two temples has enclosures of over 150m by 120m. The temple has musical pillars, a golden lily tank, and a 1000 pillar hall, with some beautiful sculptures. In the Mani Mandapam there are pillars that make unique musical sounds when struck. This temple has a large Nandi bull. There is a large Cart Festival in June/July. Tirunelveli is between Madurai and Kanniyakumari, about 90 km north of Kanniyakumari.

The **Krishnapuram Temple** is about 13 km from Tirunelveli. The Deity name is Thiruvenkatanatha. There are intricately carved life-size sculptures on this temple.

Tiruchendur

Population: 78,000, STD Code 04639

The Tiruchendur Temple is a gigantic seashore temple dedicated to Lord Subrahmanya (Kartikeya), the son of Lord Siva. Of the six major Subrahmanya temples this is considered the second most important, next to the temple at Palani. The 137-foot-high *gopuram* is on the western side of the temple instead of the east, because of the sea on the eastern side. Tiruchendur is 80 km northeast of Kanniyakumari.

It is said that Subrahmanya came here when he left Kailash to kill the demons who had a sea-fort called Mahendra-giri. From his camp here at Tiruchendur Lord Subrahmanya started his war with the demon Surapadman and his brother. There is a festival every year in Oct/Nov to celebrate this event.

There are Lord Vishnu Deities and many other deities in this temple. Lord Venkatesa Perumal Vishnu is standing facing east installed in a hollow of the rock. In another shrine is reclining Pallikonda Ranganatha (Vishnu) and Gaja Lakshmi. Near this shrine are shrines dedicated to the 12 Alwars devotees.

About 200 metres south of the temple on the seashore is a 14 foot well that has a flight of stairs with 34 steps. The water of this well is highly sulphurous in smell and somewhat salty. Inside this well is another small well that has crystal clear sweet water. The sea at Tiruchendur is good for swimming.

Practicalities

The *Hotel Tamil Nadu* has rooms for Rs 110 and Rs 225 with A/C. There is a rest house by the temple for pilgrims. Tiruchendur is about halfway between Rameswaram and Kanniyakumari on the seashore.

Sri Vaikuntham Area Temples

There are nine Vishnu Divya Desam temples called "Nava Tirupatis" in the area of Sri Vaikuntham, which can all be visited in one or two days by taxi. Sri Vaikuntham is about 80 km northeast of Kanniyakumari, between Tirunelveli and Tiruchendur.

A suggested itinerary to visit these temples is to start from Sri Vaikuntham and then go one after the other to Alwar Tirunagari, Tirukkolur, Tholaivilli-mangalam, Tirupperai, Tirukkulandai, Tiruppulingudi, and finish at Varagu-namangai.

The **Sri Vaikunthanatha Temple** is located one and a half km from the Sri Vaikuntham railway station. It is a large temple with some excellent sculptures on the stone pillars, on your right as you enter the temple.

Alwar Tirunagari (Thirukkurugoor), 33 km east of Tirunelveli and 28 km west of Tiruchendur, is where the famous **Adinatha Swami Temple** is located. It is dedicated to Lord Vishnu. This place is the birthplace of the famous Tamil saints Manavalamuni and Namm Alwar. Namm Alwar's birthplace is marked by a big tamarind tree called Toongapuli next to the Namm Alwar Shrine. There are some musical pillars in this temple.

Tirukkolur is three km east of Alwar Tirunagari. The Vishnu Deity in the temple here is called **Vaitthama Nidhi**.

The Tholaivillimangalam shrine is called Irattai Tirupati, because there are two shrines there a short distance apart, dedicated to **Srinivasa** and **Senthamarai Kannan**. In the list of Divya Desam temples they are treated as one place. This place is 3 km east of Alwar Tirunagari.

Five km southeast of Alwar Tirunagari is Tirupperai where there is the **Makara-nedungulaikkaadan Vishnu Temple**. There are some facilities to stay overnight in this town.

Tirukkulandai (Perunkulam) is 11 km northeast of Sri Vaikuntham. The Vishnu

Deity in the temple here is called **Sri Mayakuthan**.

Three km from the Sri Vaikuntham railway station is the **Kaisina Vendan Temple** at Thiruppulingudi.

One and a half km east of the town of Sri Vaikuntham is the **Vijayasanar Vishnu Temple** at Varagunamangai.

Practicalities

Sri Vaikuntham is on the Tirunelveli-Tiruchendur railway line. There are regular buses going and coming from Tirunelveli and Tiruchendur.

KANNIYAKUMARI
Population: 18,000, STD Code 04653

Kanniyakumari is located at the southernmost point of India, where the Bay of Bengal, the Indian Ocean, and the Arabian Sea meet. It is considered a holy place to bathe. The moonrise and sunset over the ocean here are impressive. During the full moon there is a dramatic sunset and moonrise here. On the full moon day in April you can see both the moon and sun on the same horizon

The extreme southern-most point of India is marked by two rocks half submerged in the sea called Pitru-tirtha and Matru-tirtha. Many people come to bathe at Kumari Ghat, which is right on the tip of the cape.

The sand at Kanniyakumari is different colors. It is said that Lord Siva married the goddess Parvati here, and the seven different colors of rice thrown at the wedding were turned into the seven colored sands of Kanniyakumari. There is an excellent view from the Lighthouse (3 to 7 pm).

Information and Tours

There are two main roads going through town. One goes north to the rail-

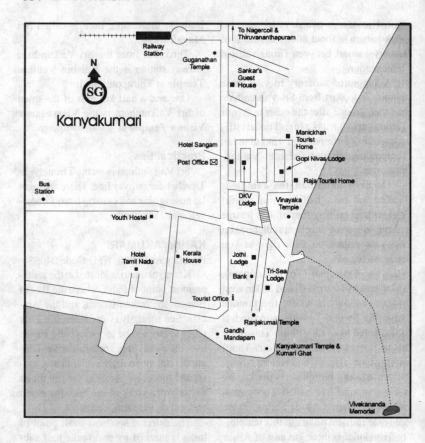

Kanyakumari

Railway Station
Guganathan Temple
To Nagercoil & Thiruvananthapuram
Sankar's Guest House
Manickhan Tourist Home
Hotel Sangam
Post Office
Gopi Nivas Lodge
Raja Tourist Home
Bus Station
DKV Lodge
Vinayaka Temple
Youth Hostel
Hotel Tamil Nadu
Kerala House
Jothi Lodge
Bank
Tri-Sea Lodge
Tourist Office
Ranjakumai Temple
Gandhi Mandapam
Kanyakumari Temple & Kumari Ghat
Vivekananda Memorial

way station, and the other goes west to the bus station. The main shopping area and the hotels are mainly near the junction of these two roads. The Kumari Amman temple is at the southern end of town, next to the shore.

The **tourist office** is at the Hotel Tamil Nadu on Beach Road, by the Gandhi Mandapa.

The Kerala Tourism Development Corporation (KTDC) conducts a **tour from Trivandrum** that leaves at 7:30 am and returns to Trivandrum around 9 pm. It covers Kovalam, Padmanabhapuram Palace, Suchindram, Nagercoil, and Kanniyakumari. You can start the tour at

Kovalam at 8.30 am. The bus does not return to Kovalam in the evening, but returns to Trivandrum.

Kumari Amman Temple

Located on the shore is the temple of the goddess Kanya (Parashakthi), the virgin goddess, who is doing penance. The sage Parasurama is said to have installed this deity. The history of this temple is that the demigods prayed to the goddess, an incarnation of Parvati, to destroy the demons. Soon after appearing, she was betrothed to Lord Siva. Knowing that if she married she would lose interest in killing demons, Narada Muni tricked

Lord Siva so that on the way to the wedding he turned back home to Kailash. So after destroying the demons, the goddess, a most charming deity to see, still waits in her temple for her husband. This temple was visited by Lord Caitanya.

The east gate of the temple is only open on special occasions. The temple is open 4.30 to 11.45 am and 5.30 to 8.45 pm. Non-Hindus are not allowed in the inner sanctum. Men must wear a dhoti and be bare-chested to enter the temple.

Other Places

There are two rocks, known as Pitru-tirtha and Matru-tirtha, about 500 metres from the coast, where Vivekananda meditated in 1892. There is a ferry that goes there. The **Vivekananda memorial** on the rock is open daily, except Tues, 7 to 11 am and 2 to 5 pm. The **footprints of Kanya Devi** are installed here in a small shrine, which marks the spot where she performed penance.

The **Gandhi Memorial** is constructed so that at noon on October 2 (Gandhi's birthday) the sun's ray falls on the spot where his ashes were kept for public view, before being put into the sea.

There is also the Vinayaka (Ganesh) Temple and Guganathan Temple in this town.

Where To Stay—Lower

It can be difficult to find a room, so it is best to get here early in the day, especially from December to February. During the high season (Dec/Jan) and during festivals, not only can the prices be more than double the prices quoted here, but it may be hard to find a room at all. Rooms are usually rented out for 24 hours. Over all, accommodation here is way overpriced and not such a good standard.

The *DKV Lodge* is about the best of the budget places. It has rooms with bath for Rs 100. The *Raja Tourist Home* and *Gopi Nivas Lodge* are north of the Vinayakar Kovil Temple and have decent rooms for Rs 80/100. On Main Road is the *Township Rest House*, which has rooms for Rs 80/100. The *Tri Sea Lodge* has rooms for Rs 110 with bath. The *Kaveri Lodge* and *Hotel Narmada* on Kovalam Rd have rooms for Rs 120.

Where To Stay—Middle

The *Hotel Sangam* (71351), on Main Road, has double rooms with hot water for Rs 160, some with balconies. Their front rooms are noisy. The *Hotel Tamil Nadu* (71257), west of the temple, is good, but usually fully booked. Rooms are Rs 275 and Rs 400 with A/C. You can get a room at the *Manickhan Tourist Home* (71387) for Rs 160 and a room with a view of the sea for Rs 180.

Kerala House (71229), Sea-front by Hotel Tamil Nadu, has standardized rooms with bath. Some rooms have a seaview. The *Cape* has double rooms for Rs 180 and rooms with A/C for Rs 220. Some rooms have a good view of the cape.

Where To Eat

In the center of town is the *Palace Hotel* with good cheap meals. The *Hotel Saravana* is supposed to have the best vegetarian meals in town. The *Sankar Guest House*, Main Rd, has a good vegetarian restaurant.

Travel

Air The closest airport is in Thiruvananthapuram (Trivandrum), 86 km north.

Train The weekly Himsagar Express #6017 (11.30 pm, Thursday) goes to Madras and then all the way to Delhi (72 hrs), and from there to Jammu (86 hr). This is the longest train trip in India. The daily passenger train to Thiruvananthapuram (Trivandrum) takes three hours. The train to Bombay, the Kanniyakumari Express #1081 (48 hr), departs at 3.35 am. It stops at Thiruvananthapuram (2¼ hr) on the way. The train station is about 1 km north of the center of town.

Bus The bus station is about a half a km (15 minute walk) west of the center of town. There are buses to Madras (703 km, 16 hr, 7 daily), Thiruvananthapuram (Trivandrum, 2½ hr), Rameswaram (409 km, 9 hr), and Madurai (245 km, 6 hr, 3 daily). There are regular local buses to Nagercoil and Kovalam. Nagercoil is a major bus junction, with two large bus stations. You can get buses for all over South India from there.

Maruda Malai

This is a mountain 6 miles from Kanniyakumari. *Maruda* means "medicine", and *malai* means "mountain". Laksmana, the younger brother of Lord Rama, was wounded during the battle with Ravana. Hanuman was asked to get some herbs from a mountain in the Himalayas to cure him. When he arrived there he could not figure out exactly what herbs were needed, so he picked up the entire mountain and brought it back to Lanka. It is said that part of the mountain fell down at this spot. Many herbs used for Ayurvedic medicine grow here.

Suchindram Temple

This beautiful temple, built mainly in the 17th century, is 13 km from Kanniyakumari. It contains a *linga*, known as Sthanumalaya Swami, the triple aspect of God. This *linga* is **Siva, Vishnu, and Brahma in one form**. When you enter the temple, you see a laurel (*konnayadi*) tree that is about 2000 years old. In the hollow of the tree there is a *linga* of the Trimurtis—Brahma, Vishnu, and Siva. It is said that the sage Atri and his wife resided here and the three gods—Brahma, Vishnu, and Siva—appeared here in the forms of Chandra, Dattatreya, and Durvasa Muni, thus answering their prayers. They are then said to have assumed the form of the Maha-linga, which represents the Trimurti. The bottom of the Maha-linga represents Brahma; the middle, Vishnu; and the top, Siva.

The 7-story *gopuram* (entrance gate) is 134 feet high. There is a huge white carved Nandi bull in this temple, said to be over 800 years old. At the entrance to the main temple are two large doorkeepers, and on two nearby pillars are two huge *yalis*. A *yali* is a lion with an elephant trunk.

It is said that **Indra** was advised to perform penance here to be relieved of the curse of Gautama Muni. He was cursed for misbehaving with Gautama Muni's wife, Ahalya. He worshiped the Trimurti here and is said to have been passed through burning ghee to purify himself. Because it is believed that Indra comes to worship the Trimurti from midnight to dawn, the daily rituals are over by dusk, so the night is free for him to perform worship. *Suci* means "purified" and *indram* means "Indra". Suchindram means "the place where Indra was purified."

There are about 30 shrines in this temple. By the side of the inner sanctum, there is the main Deity of Vishnu, made of eight metals. To the right as you enter the temple are **Sita-Rama Deities**. Across from them is an 18-foot-high **Hanuman** (including his tail). As you enter the temple, to your left is a Ganesh temple.

In front of this shrine is the **Navagraha Mandapa** which has carvings of the nine planets and the signs of zodiac on the ceiling.

There are numerous sculptures of the *Ramayana* and *Mahabharata* carved on the temple. In the Alangara Mandapa, which is to your right as you enter the temple, there are four **musical pillars** carved out of a single block of granite. Each pillar gives the sounds of a different instrument, mridanga, sitar, tambura, and jalataranga. On Friday there is a special sunset ceremony. Non-Hindus can enter this temple.

Nagercoil

Population: 190,000, STD Code 04652

Nagercoil is a major junction for buses coming in and out of Kerala. It is 18 km northwest of Kanniyakumari.

The main deity in the temple here is **Nagaraja** (king of the snakes), who is silver-plated and garlanded. There is also a Deity of Lord Krishna. There are snakes inside a small hut, behind the temple. There is a sacred pipal tree, which pilgrims circle here.

The **Tirukkurulappan Temple** is 3 km north of Nagercoil in Tiruvannparisaram (Tiruppatisaram). It is a one of the 108 Divya Desam temples. The Lord's name is Tirukkurulappan and the goddess's name is Kamalavalli Nacchiar.

Where To Stay

Tower Lodge, near Tower Junction, which is not far from the bus terminal, and *Azad Lodge* are recommended places. There is also the *Sri Swaminatha Lodge* by the long distance bus station. The *Rajam Hotel* (04652/24581), MS Road, near the center of town, two km for the railway station, is the best place in town with rooms for Rs 240 and Rs 390 with A/C. It has a roof garden.

Travel

Rail There are trains to Trivandrum (2½ hr), Quilon, Cochin, Madras, Delhi (58 hr, Fri only), and Bombay (48 hr, twice weekly).

Bus Nagercoil is a major bus junction and has two busy bus stands—one for local buses and the other for long distance ones. There are buses to all over Tamil Nadu, such as Rameswaram (8 hr) and Madurai (5 hr), as well as buses to Kerala to such places as Kovalam (2 hr), Trivandrum (2 hr), and Quilon. If you are going from Trivandrum or Kovalam to Madurai, you can easily get a bus to Nagercoil and from there get one of the frequent buses to Madurai.

The nearby Padmanabhapuram Palace is a popular tourist place. To get there from Nagercoil you take bus #11 or #29. There is a direct bus to the Adi-kesava temple from Nagercoil.

CHAPTER TWENTY

Kerala

Kerala is on the west coast of India extending from south of Mangalore in Karnataka to the southern tip of India. It is slightly smaller than Switzerland and about twice the size of Massachusetts. It was the first place in the free world to elect a communist government (in 1957), which has been in and out of power ever since.

It is said that Kerala was created by **Lord Parasurama**, one of the ten avatars (incarnations) of Lord Vishnu. He threw His battle axe into the sea. The sea then receded up to the point where the axe had fallen and created the landmass of Kerala.

Bali Maharaja is said to have ruled here before Vamanadeva banished him to the lower worlds. The Onam festival is a reliving of his reign, when there was prosperity for everyone.

The Guruvayur Temple, dedicated to Lord Krishna, near Thrissur, is one of the most popular and important temples in India. Also important is the Sri Padmanabhaswami Temple in Thiruvananthapuram. The Janardana Temple in Varkala and the Adi Kesava Temple in Tiruvatar were both visited by Lord Caitanya on His South Indian tour. The problem with most of the temples in Kerala is that they will not admit non-Hindus. But they will admit ISKCON devotees or converted Hindus. Some temples require that you wear a dhoti or sari to enter the inner sanctum and view the Deity.

Some of the towns in Kerala have recently been renamed. Most important is Trivandrum, which is now named Thiruvananthapuram. Also Cochin is now called Kochi, and Trichur is now Thrissur.

THRISSUR (TRICHUR)
Population: 275,000, STD Code 0487

Situated 74 km north of Ernakulam, Thrissur is the closest main city to the **Guruvayur Temple**. You could stay overnight in a hotel here and make a day trip to Guruvayur, which is about an hour away.

In August-September there is the Onam festival to welcome Maharaja Bali back from exile. There are spectacular elephant processions and fireworks during this festival. On the second and most important day of the festival, Thiruonam, there are many festivities.

The Pooram Festival in April-May is one of the biggest events in India with a thirty elephant procession and fireworks. There is also an elephant festival in January. You can get information about this festival from any Kerala tourist office.

Information
The point of orientation is the Round, a road subdivided into North, South, East, and West. It goes around the maidan (park) that surrounds the Vadakkunnathanan Temple.

The railway station is 1 km southwest of Round South. The KSRTC long-distance bus stand and many of the hotels are in this area near the railway station.

There is a **tourist office** at the KTDC Yatri Niwas (27383), Stadium Rd. The State Bank of India, opposite the Paramekkavu Temple, Round East, changes dollars and sterling, but not travellers' cheques. The Bank of Travancore, next to the Paramekkavu Temple, changes only American Express travellers' cheques.

Vadakkunnathanan Temple

This temple is in the park, right in the center of the city. It is one of the largest temples in Kerala and has excellent carved woodwork. On the walls there are excellent murals of the *Mahabharata* and Lord Vishnu reclining on Ananta.

It has three main shrines. One is dedicated to **Vadakkunnathan** (Lord Siva) and another to **Sankara Narayana**. South of these two shrines is a shrine dedicated to **Lord Rama**. Vadakkunnathan (Ten-Kailasanath) is a Maha-linga that is covered with offerings of ghee (clarified butter) hundreds of years old. The *linga* cannot be seen because the traditional *abhisheka* (bathing) with cow ghee over centuries has formed a 3m (9 ft) mound around the *linga*, which makes it difficult for the priest to walk around the inner sanctum. The shrine dedicated to Sankara Narayana has beautiful paintings of the *Mahabharata*. There is also a Deity of **Krishna** in the temple. There is a **Ganesh** deity between the two northern altars.

The famous *kuttambalam,* or theater hall, is on the left of the entrance. Non-Hindus are not allowed in the temple except for during the Pooram festival, when the restrictions are lifted. This temple is open from 4 to 10.30 am and 4 to 8.30 pm.

Pooram Festival

The major festival of the year is the Pooram Festival in April-May. This festival is celebrated in the Thekkinkadu Maiden (park) where the Vadakkunnathanan Temple is located. There is a thirty elephant procession and fireworks. It is celebrated by thousands of enthusiastic people. During this festival, deities from nine surrounding temples are brought to the Vadakkunnathan Temple. Several other temples in town celebrate this festival, but particularly the Paramekkavu and Thiruvambadi Temples. During this festival there is a huge procession with elaborately decorated elephants that comes to the Vadakkunnathan Temple. On the last day of the festival contingents from two temples have a competition to decide who has the best-decorated elephants.

Other places

The **Thiruvambadi Temple** is a Krishna temple in the middle of town.

There is an important temple dedicated to Lord Rama, the **Tiruvilamala Temple**, 30 km from Thrissur at Triprayar. It has excellent sculptures and woodcarvings. The **Kutalmanikyam Temple** dedicated to Bharata, Rama's brother, is located at Irinjalakuda, which is 21 km from Thrissur. It is the one of the only temple in India dedicated to Bharata.

Kalamandalam, 30 km north, has a Kathakali dance school.

Where To Stay – Lower

Many of the hotels are booked months in advance for the Pooram festival.

The cheaper places are close to the bus

station and railway station. These include the *Shanti Tourist Home*, Station Rd; *Chandy's Tourist Home*, Station Rd; and the *Jaya Lodge* on Kurrupam Rd. Rooms at these places are about Rs 30/50. The *Pathan's Lodging* (25623), off Round South, is a budget place in the center of town with a vegetarian restaurant. Rooms are Rs 90/150.

Where To Stay – Middle

The *Alukkas Tourist Home* (24067), Railway Station Rd, has rooms for Rs 75/150 and Rs 300 for an A/C room.

The *KTDC Yatri Niwas* (332-333), Stadium Road, in a secluded area, has clean rooms for Rs 125/175 and Rs 200/250 with A/C. The *Hotel Luciya Palace* (24731), Marar Rd, has rooms for Rs 120/190 and 275/350 with A/C.

The *Manapuram Hotel* (25891), Kuruppam, a few minutes from the railway and KSRTC bus stations, is a new well-managed place that has good modern rooms for Rs 250. It also has a vegetarian restaurant.

The *Hotel Elite* (pronounced Ee-light) International (21033), Chembottil Lane, off Round South, is centrally located and has rooms for Rs 260 and Rs 480 with A/C. Some rooms overlook the park where the Vadakkunnathanan Temple is located.

The best hotel in town is the *Casino Hotel* (24699), T B Rd, about a five minute auto-rickshaw ride from the railway station and bus station. There are rooms here for Rs 325/350 and Rs 475/500 with A/C. It has a bookshop.

Where To Eat

The *Hotel Bharath* is a clean vegetarian place. The *Manapuram Hotel*, near the KSRTC bus stand, has a vegetarian restaurant.

Travel

Train There are about seven trains daily to Thiruvananthapuram (Trivandrum, 8 hr). There are also direct trains to Kochi/Ernakulam (2½ hr, 5 daily), Bangalore, Hyderabad, Bombay, New Delhi, Madras (12 hr, 2 daily), Calcutta, Trichy, and Varanasi. The daily Madras Exp #6042 (6.40 pm) takes 11½ hours to reach Madras.

Bus There are three bus stands—the KSRTC long-distance bus stand by the railway station, the North (Priya Darshin) bus stand, north of the center of town, and Sakthan Thampuram (local) bus stand, which is two km south of the center of town. KSRTC has frequent buses to major towns in Kerala. There are express buses to **Thiruvananthapuram** (every half hour, Rs 85). There are also direct buses to Madras (13 hr), Bangalore (10 hr), Coimbatore, Madurai, and Palani.

The best way to get to and from **Mysore** (8 hr) is by bus. There is a morning bus that leaves from Mysore and stops at Guruvayur (7 hr). Frequent buses to **Irinjalakuda** depart from the Shakthan Thampuran bus stand, Pattalam Rd, 2 km from Round South.

About five buses go each hour to **Guruvayur** (1 hr, 29 km). This is a much better way to go than taking a train. You can get one of the regular buses to Guruvayur near the train station or ask at your hotel where to get a bus, as they depart from different places in the city.

Tiruvilamala

There are two temples next to each other in Tiruvilamala. One is dedicated to Lord Rama (facing west) and the other to Laksmana (facing east). Each has a Deity of Vishnu with four arms. The Deity of Lord Rama is said to be *swayambhu*, or self-manifested. Tiruvilamala is 29 km from Thrissur.

About 3 km from this temple is a cave called **Punarjanani,** which is supposed to have been built by Visvakarma on the request of Parasurama. Passing through this cave is said to relieve one from taking one of his destined births. This should be done on the day of the Guruvayur Ekadasi festival (Nov-Dec), because on other days the cave is said to be haunted by ghosts.

Triprayar

There is an important **Lord Rama** temple here. He holds a conch, chakra (disc), bow, and garland in His hands. It is an architecturally attractive old temple with ancient woodcarvings. On the **Ekadasi day** in Nov-Dec there is a major festival wherein Lord Rama is taken on procession with as many as 21 elephants. This temple is located about 10 km south of Thrissur.

Irinjalakuda

Located here is the **Kutalmanikyam Temple,** which is one of the only temples dedicated to **Bharata,** the brother of Lord Rama. The Deity is a four-armed form of Lord Vishnu. He holds a disc, conch, club, and *japa-mala* in His hands. The flower offerings at this temple include lotuses, *tulasi,* and *chetti*—no other flowers. The story of the Deity is that there was a local chieftain named Vakkey Kaimal who had a dream that four Deities had washed on the beach by the nearby shore. The Deities were found and installed at four temples: Rama at Triprayar, Laksmana at Moozhikulam, Bharata at Irinjalakuda, and Satrughna at Payammel. These temples are all near Thrissur. It is supposed to be especially

beneficial to worship at all four of these temples on the same day. This temple has a large eastern gateway (*gopuram*).

Irinjalakuda is located 20 km south of Thrissur. You can get a bus here from the Shakthan Thampuram bus stand at Thrissur. Irinjalakuda is 8 km from the Irinjalakuda railway station on the Trichur-Ernakulam line. The train is inconvenient, as the railway station is 8 km east of town.

GURUVAYUR
STD Code 0487

Guruvayur is known as the Dwarka of the South and is famous for the Sri Krishna Temple. Guruvayur is 30 km west of Thrissur and 80 km north of Ernakulam. It is a nice peaceful city with a spiritual atmosphere.

During the mid-morning hours many wedding ceremonies take place, one after another. Devoted couples believe that being married at the Guruvayur Temple is a great blessing, so they come here from all over South India.

Sri Krishna Temple (Guruvayurappan Temple)

This is the most important Krishna temple in Kerala and one of the most important and richest temples in all of South India. Lord Krishna is known here as **Guruvayurappan.** The name of the Deity means the Lord (Appan) of Guru and Vayu. Guruvayur is known as **Bhuloka Vaikuntha,** "where the spiritual world meets the earth".

The Deity of Lord Krishna in this temple is said to forgive all sins and grant liberation to His devotees. The Deity is believed to fulfill one's desires. According to the story about the temple, this Deity of Lord Krishna is over 5000 years old.

The Deity of Sri Krishna is made of the rare stone **patala anjanam**. He has four arms carrying a conch, disc, mace, and lotus, and He is adorned with a *tulasi* garland and pearl necklaces.

The temple schedule begins at 3 am with *nirmalayam darshan* (viewing the Deity), followed by *abhiseka* (bathing the Deity). The 3 am *darshan* is particularly auspicious. Worship and *darshans* continue until 10 pm when the Deity takes rest for the night. *Uchcha Puja* takes place at midday. The temple is closed between 1 and 4.30 pm.

Bilvamangala Thakur, who wrote *Sri Krishna-karnamrita*, frequently visited the Guruvayur Temple.

Tulabharam is a common vow in which devotees donate to the Deity a quantity of some article equal in weight to their body. Devotees are weighed on a scale against their choice of items such as silver, bananas, sugar, jaggery, or coconuts. On an average about 100 *tulabharams* are offered a day, but on major days the number goes over 200. The proceeds from *tulabharams* were Rs 2.25 crores ($600,000) in 1990-1991.

The temple worship is done by **Nambudri Brahmins**, who are expected to live within the temple precincts during their term of worship. They bathe in the temple tank next to the temple.

This temple has over Rs 45 crores in fixed deposits, 3 tons of silver articles, 600 kgs of gold articles, some priceless diamonds, and other jewelry.

Men must wear dhotis (tied-on cloth) and take off their shirts to enter the temple. You cannot carry a bag in the temple. You can check a bag in at the cloak room to the right of the eastern entrance. Only Hindus are allowed in the temple, but ISKCON devotees and converted Hindus may enter.

Temple Architecture

This temple is comparatively small in size compared to other South Indian temples. The attraction of this temple is the beautiful Deity of Lord Krishna. The temple faces east and is usually entered from that direction. The eastern gateway (*nada*), which is known as **Bhuloka Vaikuntham**, is the main entrance. In the outer enclosure, or *matilakam*, is a 33.5 metres (110 feet) high gold-plated *dhwajastambam*, or flag post. By the eastern entrance, on either side of the flag post, are seven metres (22 feet) high **dipastambhas**, or **pillar of lamps**, whose 13 circular receptacles provide a gorgeous spectacle when lit at night.

In the middle of the temple is the central shrine called the **Srikoil**. Within the Srikoil is the **garbha-griha** (sanctum sanctorum), where the main Deity of Lord Krishna resides. The walls of the Srikoil have paintings depicting the pastimes of Sri Krishna. Surrounding the Srikoil is the **Nalambalam enclosure,** which encircles the inner sanctum (altar). This is where the devotees view the Deity. As you enter the Nalambalam enclosure, the altar of Sri Krishna is located directly in front of you in the *garbha-griha*.

In the southwest part of the Nalambalam enclosure is a room which is totally closed up. It is called the "Mystery Cell," because no one knows what is in it. It is believed that inside there are precious jewels and ornaments that are guarded by serpents called **Panchanagas**. No one even dares to open this room. Next to this cell is the **Saraswati ara** (*ara* means room), where Saraswati is worshiped. Sacred books are also worshiped here during the Navaratri festival. The Ganesh shrine is in the southwest corner of this enclosure. Next to the Ganesh shrine is the place where the Head

Priest (Melsanti) distributes *prasadam*, sandal paste, and flowers to those who offer worship. Devotees exit the inner enclosure by the northern door. This door is referred to as **Swargavasal**, or "passageway to heaven."

The courtyard outside the inner temple area is called the **Matilakam**. This is the courtyard you enter when you first come into the temple. In the southeast corner of this courtyard is a shrine dedicated to Lord Sasta, who is said to be the son of Hari and Hara. On the outside of the northern wall surrounding the inner enclosure is the **Vilakkumatam,** which is 11 rows of 6614 tiny lamps that are lit on festivals. In the middle of the western wall of the inner enclosure, by the west entrance, is a beautiful sculpture of **Anantasayanam,** Lord Vishnu reclining on Ananta Sesa.

At the north side of the temple is the temple tank called **Rudra-tirtha**. The Deity is bathed here at the end of the ten day festival in Feb/March. The present tank is smaller than when the Deity was first brought here. Next to the tank is the shrine dedicated to the goddess of the temple, named **Edatharikathu Kavil Bhagavati**. The temple story states that her image was originally installed where the present Deity of Guruvayurappan is located. The goddess was waiting there for the arrival of the Deity from Dwarka. She welcomed Guru and Vayu when they arrived and requested them to install the Lord in her place, and then she moved a short distance to the left.

Next to the passage that leads to the temple tank is the stage where Krishnattam dance performances are held. In the northeast area of the enclosure is the temple well, the water of which is reputed to have digestive and curative properties. The upper story of the build-

ing in the northwest corner of the temple is where the Melsanti, Head Priest, lives during his six-month term of service. He is not supposed to leave the temple enclosure during his period of service.

Story of the Deity

According to the *Narada Purana*, this Deity was originally worshiped by Lord Brahma and was given to Vasudeva, the father of Krishna. Eventually, the Deity was worshiped by Krishna Himself in Dwarka. Lord Krishna later gave the Deity to Uddhava to help relieve his feelings of separation, as Krishna was preparing to leave the planet.

As the sea began to submerge the city of Dwarka, the Deity was transported by Guru (Brihaspati) and Vayu (the air-god) to the present location. Guru and Vayu were entrusted to find a suitable holy place for the Deity. They came to Kerala under the direction of Lord Parasurama, who led them to a lake full of lotuses—the present temple tank called Rudra-tirtha. They found Lord Siva (Rudranath) meditating by the lake, where he had previously enlightened the Pracetas. The Deity was installed there and called Guruvayurappan, or the Lord of Guruvayur.

At another time, King Janamejaya, the son of Pariksit Maharaja, got leprosy after performing a snake sacrifice to kill all the snakes on earth to avenge his father's death. No medicine could help him, so he was advised by the sage Dattatreya to worship Sri Krishna at Guruvayur. Janamejaya did so devoutly for four months and was cured from the leprosy.

Deity Darshan

The Deity can be viewed from 3 am to 12.30 pm and 4.30 to 10 pm. There are two entrances to the temple, one from

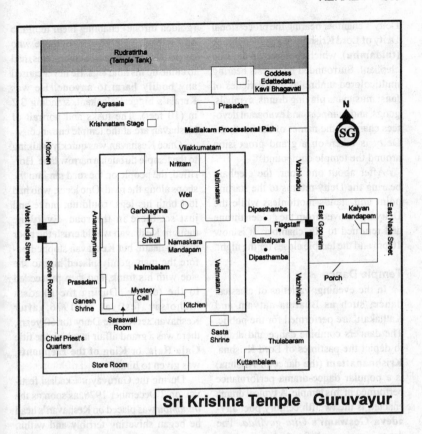

Sri Krishna Temple   Guruvayur

Map labels:
Rudratirtha (Temple Tank); Goddess Edattedattu Kavil Bhagavati; Agrasala; Prasadam; Krishnattam Stage; Matilakam Processional Path; Vilakkumatam; N SG; Kitchen; Nrittam; Vadlimatam; Vazhivadu; Kalyan Mandapam; West Nada Street; Anantasayanam; Well; Dipasthamba; East Gopuram; East Nada Street; Garbhagriha; Flagstaff; Srikoil; Namaskara Mandapam; Belikalpura; Nalmbalam; Dipasthamba; Store Room; Prasadam; Vadimatam; Porch; Ganesh Shrine; Mystery Cell; Kitchen; Saraswati Room; Chief Priest's Quarters; Sasta Shrine; Thulabaram; Store Room; Kuttambalam

the east, where the main bus stand is located, and another to the west, the back entrance. The main entrance may have a half-hour to hour wait, which can be avoided by going in the back western entrance. It is, however, traditional to enter the temple from the eastern entrance. Once you enter the temple you have to wait in one of two lines, one for men and the other for women, which take about a half-hour on a normal day. When you enter the inner sanctum you begin to view the Deity and are normally allowed just a few seconds directly in front of the Deity. Even when you get as close to the Deity of Sri Krishna as possible, you are

still a good distance away.

Deity Procession

The evening brings the main event of the day, a **Deity procession**. Every evening between 7 and 8 pm, the Deity of Lord Krishna, in His four-armed Narayana form, sits on His golden throne while riding on top of a gold-bedecked elephant. The Deity is also brought out on an elephant around six-thirty in the morning.

After elaborate preparations are made for the arrival of the Deity, a devotee blows three blasts on a conchshell. The priests then quickly emerge from the

Deity's chamber bearing the processional Deity of Lord Krishna on a golden throne (**thidambu**), which is placed on the lead elephant. Surrounded by priests bearing multicolored umbrellas and varieties of fans; musicians playing drums, cymbals, gongs, and trumpets; and exuberant devotees chanting the names of the Lord; the Deity is taken on a grand procession around the temple compound.

After about one hour, the elephant bearing the Deity returns to the starting point and stands motionless while the Deity is removed from the golden throne and returned to His chamber. It is now 10 pm and the temple closes for the night.

Temple Dance

In the evening, varieties of classical dance, such as Bharata-natyam and Kathakali, are performed for the public. The dancers combine dance and drama to depict the pastimes of Lord Krishna. **Krishnanattam** (the dance of Krishna) is a popular dance-drama performance performed in this temple. A typical drama enacted is the twelfth century poet **Jayadeva Goswami's** *Gita-govinda*. The dance is performed after the temple closes at night on a stage in the north part of the temple compound. It is completed before the temple opens in the morning at 3 am.

Keshavan the Elephant

Keshavan was donated by the King of Nilambur in 1916 at the age of 10. He served the Deity at Guruvayur his entire lifetime of 72 years. He behaved so well that he was loved by the local people. He was the regular carrier for the *utsava-vigraha*, the small processional Deity of Sri Krishna. He took part in every ceremony at the temple for 54 years. Keshavan would only bend his front-legs before those who held the Lord's *thidambu*

(golden throne) enabling them to climb on his back. Everyone else, those who carried the umbrella and other items, had to climb up his hind legs. He never caused any bodily harm to anyone. He was Kerala's biggest elephant, standing 3.2 m (10 feet). The tusks and portrait of Keshavan are at the temple entrance.

Once Keshavan was quickly walking to the temple through a narrow lane. Horrified, the people on the road ran into the shops along the road. One leper, who had lost both his legs, could not move and just sat there in the road. Everyone thought Keshavan would crush the poor man to death, but Keshavan stopped before the man, gently placed him to the side with his trunk, and then proceeded to the temple. During the Ekadasi Mahotsav festival in 1976, after Keshavan served the Deity for 60 years, there was a grand affair in which the title **Gaja Raja**, or **King of the Elephants**, was given to him.

During the Guruvayur Ekadasi festival, on 2 December 1976, as soon as the *thidambu* was placed on Keshavan's head he began shivering terribly and within minutes could not hold himself up. The *thidambu* was then changed to another elephant. He left this earth (breathed his last) at 3 am in the morning, passing away at what is considered to be an auspicious time of day. He was given a cremation befitting a noble person. He was 72 years old when he left this world.

A life-size, 12 foot tall, statue of Keshavan was made as a memorial and placed in front of the Panchajanyam Rest House. The temple administration decided to celebrate his death anniversary, which they designated as **Gaja Din,** or the **Day of the Elephant**. On that day all the Guruvayur elephants get ceremonially dressed and taken on a procession that ends at the statue of Keshavan. The tallest elephant then places a wreath of flowers on the statue.

Other Places

The **Parthasarathi Temple** is dedicated to Lord Krishna as the charioteer of Arjuna. This temple is a few minutes' walk from the eastern entrance of the Sri Krishna Temple. The Deity of Parthasarathi is believed to be over 1000 years old and was discovered in the ruins of the temple in 1972. The former temple had lain in ruins for years. The Deity was re-installed in a new temple in 1981.

Punnathur Kotta (4 km) is an ancient fort that houses over **40 elephants** belonging to the Guruvayur Temple.

Half a km northeast of the Parthasarathi Temple is a temple dedicated to **Venkatachalapati**, who is also known as Tiruvenkatam of Tirupati. The image of goddess **Bhagavati** is installed in this temple.

At **Mammiyur,** about a half km northwest of Guruvayur, is a Siva temple that is supposed to be older than the Guruvayur Temple. A half km north of Mammiyur is a temple dedicated to the **Goddess Narayani**, who is Vishnumaya.

There is a pleasant beach 3 km away in **Chavakkad.**

Festivals

The **Ekadasi festival**, celebrated in the month of Vrischikam (Nov/Dec), during the Mandalam season, is the most important temple festival. The Ekadasi festival starts almost a month in advance with a daily festival of lights called **Vilakku**. The lights on the **Vilakkumatam** around the Nalambalam (inner temple area) and the lights of the **dipastambhams** are lit during this festival. There are regular elephant processions. The last three days—Navami, Dasami, and Ekadasi—attract the largest crowds. A highlight of the festival is the day when the memorial service of the late Guruvayur Keshavan, who was the head of the elephants, is performed. All 40 elephants start at Punnathur and walk to the main temple, stopping at the Parthasarathi Temple on the way. They are then fed a sumptuous feast of bananas, jaggery, sugar, and *prasada*. On the Ekadasi day there is a grand elephant procession around the temple. As part of the Ekadasi Festival there is an 11 day **Chembai music festival** in which over 2000 Carnatic musicians perform.

The ten-day-long **Utsavam Festival** in Feb-March is an important festival that starts with an elephant race. The elephants race a good distance, starting from Manjulal and ending at the temple. The first five to eight elephants that arrive run into the temple. The elephant that arrives first is given royal treatment. On the tenth night the Deity is taken to the temple tank and bathed there. It is auspicious to bathe in the tank at the same time Krishna is bathed. There is also a grand elephant procession around the temple and tank. Over 6000 people a day are fed during this festival.

The **Pooram Festival** in April-May is a big festival with fireworks. **Ashtami Rohini** (Janmastami) in Aug/Sept is a large festival here.

Where To Stay

Guruvayur can be a very busy place, especially on the weekends when many marriages are performed. It can therefore be difficult to get a room. I was there on a Sunday in December and most of the places were full. Instead of staying in Guruvayur overnight you could stay in

Thrissur, which is about an hour away by bus. You could then make a day trip to Guruvayur. Beside the hotels in Guruvayur, there are much cheaper dharamsalas. It would be a good idea to call and reserve a room in advance, especially if you are coming here during a festival.

The *Govind Tourist Hotel*, North Nada, by the temple tank, has rooms with hot water for Rs 125. *Nandini Tourist Home* (556-509), East Nada, has normal rooms for Rs 115 and A/C rooms for Rs 300.

Hotel Nandanam (556-266), East Nada, has rooms for Rs 125 and A/C rooms for Rs 275. The *Poornima Tourist Home* (6690), East Nada, has normal rooms for Rs 150. *RVK Tourist Home* (556-204), East Nada, has rooms for Rs 200 and rooms with A/C for Rs 400.

The *Elite Tourist Home* (556-215), East Nadu, is one of the best places in town. It has rooms for Rs 165 with bath and Rs 350 with A/C. The *Hotel Vyshakh* (556-188), by the temple tank, has good rooms with hot water for Rs 275 and Rs 525 with A/C. It is one of the better places in town.

The two-star modern *Hotel Vanamala Kusuman* (556-702), South Nada, has rooms for Rs 250/325 and Rs 300/375 with A/C. It has a 3 pm checkout time. It is usually booked months in advance. It has the *Vishakham Thali Restaurant*.

Most of the eating places I saw in town were vegetarian *thali* places. I did not see any places that served side orders.

Travel

Air The nearest airport is in Kochi (Cochin), 90 km away.

Train Thrissur, 29 km away, is where the nearest long-distance railway station is located. If you are coming south from Mangalore, you can get off the train at **Kuttipuram**, 52 km north of Guruvayur, instead of going to Thrissur. From there you can get a bus. There are a few local trains between Thrissur and Guruvayur, but the bus is much more convenient.

There is one direct long distant train to and from Trivandrum from Guruvayur. The Guruvayur-Nagercoil Exp #6305 (9.25 pm) goes to Nagercoil (9 hr) via Trivandrum (7 hr). The Nagercoil-Guruvayur Exp #6306 departs Trivandrum at 9.40 pm and arrives in Guruvayur at 4.35 am going via Trichur.

Bus About five buses go each hour to and from Thrissur (1 hr, 29 km). You can get the bus to Guruvayur from Thrissur by the train station and at many other locations in the city. The morning bus from Mysore (7 hr) stops at Guruvayur on the way to Thrissur. As Guruvayur is a very important pilgrimage site, the bus station can be hectic.

KALADI
STD Code 04857

Adi Sankaracarya was born here on the bank of the Periyar River in 788. It is 45 km northeast of Kochi, 55 km southeast of Trichur, and 271 km north of Trivandrum. Sankaracarya was the only son of Sivaguru and Aryamba, a Kerala Brahmin couple. He completed his studies of the *Vedas* at the age of 16. He is said to have diverted the course of the Poorna River one and a half km from his house so his aged mother could have daily bath in the river without walking too far. He left his body at the age of 32 after establishing important maths in Sringeri, Dwarka, Joshimath, and Puri.

The **Sringeri Math** has a small complex of temples. There are two shrines here, one in memory of Sri Sankaracarya,

Dakshinamurti, and the other dedicated to the goddess Sharada. The Sringeri Math is believed to be located at the place where Sankaracarya's house was located. The black pole to the left of the entrance is said to mark the exact place where Sankaracarya was born. It is open 5.30 am to 12.30 pm and 3.30 to 8 pm.

There is a memorial which marks the place where Sankaracarya's mother, Aryamba, was cremated. **Crocodile Ghat**, the bathing ghat outside the temple, is said to be the place where Sankara was caught by a crocodile. He took the opportunity to ask his mother if he could take *sannyasa* (the renounced order). When she said yes, the crocodile let him go.

Next to the Sringeri Math is the ancient **Sri Krishna Temple**, which was Sankaracarya's family temple. It is open 5 to 8.30 am and 5 to 7.30 pm.

The 45 metre, nine story, Sri Adi Sankara **Keerthi Sthamba Mandapa** has illustrations in it that tell the story of Sankara's life. As you ascend the winding steps there are framed relief paintings that narrate the story of Sankaracarya. There are several large statues of Ganapati and Adi Sankara. It is open 7 am to 7 pm.

Located nearby are the **Manichamangalam Temple,** one km north of Kaladi, and two km away is the **Vellimanthulli Temple**, which is dedicated to the goddess Durga.

Practicalities

There are guest houses and choultries maintained by the *Sringeri Math* and *Ramakrishna Advaita Ashram*. There is also a *Government Rest House* and some private lodges.

The nearest airport is in Kochi (48 km). The closest railway stations are in Angamali (10 km) and Alwaye (23 km).

It takes about two hours to get from Trichur to Kaladi by bus. The temples are about two km from the bus stand.

SABARIMALA
STD Code 04739

The **Ayyappan Temple** is located at an elevation of 950m, deep in the forests of the Sahyadri mountain range and 190 km north of Trivandrum. The people dressed in black that you see all over South India are doing austerities to come to this temple. This temple is dedicated to Dharma Sasta as Ayyappa.

This is the most visited temple in all of India, even though it is totally in the middle of nowhere and it is closed part of the year. Over **25 million pilgrims** went there in 1990, an increase of 10 million since 1987. More and more people are going each year. On **Makara Vilakku** day over 2 million people visit this temple. The pilgrim season is from November to March. From mid-November to the end of December the temple is opened for 41 days. Makara Sankranti (mid-January) is the most crowded time of the year here. The temple is also open during mid-April, Prathistha day (May/June), and during the Onam festival (Aug/Sept).

Young women, between 15 and 50, are not supposed to come to this temple, because Ayyappa is an avowed celibate.

Ayyappan Temple

Ayyapa is said to be the son of Lord Siva and Mohini. He is a very strict bachelor. Lord Siva wanted to test the power of Mohini and asked to see Her. When he saw Her, he began to chase Her and he passed semen. From this semen, it is said that Ayyapa was born. He is called Hariharaputra, or the son (*putra*) of

Vishnu (Hari) and Siva (Hara), and is regarded as the third son of Siva. *Ayyappa* derives from Aryan (one worthy of reverence) and *appa*, which means "father" in Malayalam. The deity is about one-and-a-half feet tall and is made of an alloy of five metals called Panchaloha. The present temple was mainly built in 1951, after a devastating fire.

The temple is open to all regardless of religion, caste, creed, or status. It can take hours of waiting to see the Deity.

There are **18 steps** that lead to the temple that are said to be a ladder to heaven. To walk on the steps, the pilgrim must have observed 41 days of penance and carried the Irumudi (a cloth bag containing *puja* and personal paraphernalia) on his head. The steps can be used only twice during the pilgrim's visit—once when entering the sanctum with the Irumudi and again when leaving. At other times the steps on the north and west sides of the temple are used.

Pilgrimage Vow

People make a vow to dress in black, blue, or ochre clothes, wear a *rudraksha* or a *tulasi* garland, remain celibate, eat only vegetarian food, visit temples, and worship for a period of time before coming to this temple. They do not take meat, drugs, or alcohol. The period is usually 41 days. Only people who follow these strict vows for at least 41 days can step onto the "**patinettampadi**" (flight of 18 steps) that leads to the deity.

The pilgrim carries a cloth bag on his head called **Irumudi**, which has two compartments. The front portion contains a coconut filled with ghee along with camphor, rice, etc. The ghee is poured on the deity at the end of the pilgrimage. The rear part of the bag contains the pilgrim's personal items. This bag is supposed to be the only item that the pilgrim carries.

Persons on this pilgrimage call each other Swami. They chant "Swamiye, Saranam Ayyappa", or "Lord Ayyappa, I come to you for refuge."

Practicalities

There are three major routes to the temple. There is no road to the temple, as it is believed an effort must be made to get there. The Chalakayam route is just 8 km and is the most popular route. The Erumeli route, which is about 72 km, is the most traditional. The Vandiperiyar route is 95 km. You can also take a vehicle to Pampa and from there it is a 5 km trek.

There are many pilgrim dharamsalas run by the temple management to house pilgrims.

If you cannot climb up the hill you may be carried by bearers.

VARKALA

Population: 39,000, STD Code 04724

Varkala is on the seashore about 54 km northwest of Trivandrum and 20 km south of Quilon (Kollam). It has nice beaches and is not as crowded as Kovalam. It is popular with travelers. Many people told me it was a good place to relax. It has a private but fairly crowded small beach, so it will not be ideal for someone looking for total seclusion. There is a mineral water spring on the beach.

The spiritual reason for coming here is to go to the well-known **Janardhana Swami Temple**.

Sri Janardhana Temple

This famous Lord Vishnu temple is a few km from the town, on the edge of a coconut forest, by a low cliff overlooking the sea. The temple is about a km from the sea. The four-armed **Sri Janardhana** stands four feet high and wears the dress of various incarnations. After *mangala-arati* the doors stay open while the Deity is bathed before the assembled devotees. This good-sized temple is said to be over 2000 years old. Lord Caitanya came here on His South Indian tour.

The famous **Papanasam spring** rises at the foot of the steps on the north side of the temple. It then flows into the temple tank and then gently flows a half km into the sea. The area by the temple is a peaceful place.

Information

The **State Bank of Travancore** will exchange travellers' cheques, but will not exchange cash.

The Scientific **School of Yoga and Massage** (695-141) offers a ten-day yoga and massage course taught by an English speaking doctor. It also has a shop that sells Ayurvedic oils and other items.

The Sri Janardhana Temple and the beach are a five-minute auto-rickshaw ride from the downtown.

Where To Stay

Most of the hotels are on the cliff above the beach. Some people rent basic private houses.

The *Government Guest House* (2227), near the beach bus stand, has seven simple rooms. This place used to be a summer residence for a Maharaja. It is best to book a room here in advance. The *ITDC Tourist Home* is a basic cheap clean place. The *Hill Top Beach Resort* is a new clean place that overlooks the beach in a quiet location. Rooms are Rs 125 to Rs 150. *Mamma Hotel*, pass the Akshay by the beach, is a converted farmhouse with shared toilets. Directly opposite is the

Beach Palace, which has a good location, but is really basic. Rooms are Rs 50/80.

The *Varkala Beach Resort* (Taj), 500m from the beach, is the best place in town. It has an excellent view, a pool, and a landscaped garden. The *Varkala Marine Palace* is a recommended middle-class place with modern comfortable rooms for Rs 125 overlooking the beach. It is a good value. The *Akshay Beach Resort* (2668) has good rooms that are a bit small for Rs 150. It is a good middle-class place just 200m from the beach.

The *J A Tourist Home* (2453), in the town of Varkala, has rooms for Rs 100. It is a good value. The *Anandan Tourist Home* (2135), opposite the railway station, has rooms for Rs 50/80 and some A/C rooms for Rs 245. The *Babuji Lodge* (2243) is a basic place with rooms for Rs 55/70, but it is not a good value.

Travel

Varkala is a 50 minute train ride from Trivandrum. It is then a 2 km ride (Rs 15) to the temple from the station. There are eight trains a day to Thiruvananthapuram and two trains a day to Kanniyakumari—at 11.10 am and 2.05 pm.

There are regular buses to Varkala from Thiruvananthapuram's **Thampanoor Bus Stand** (1½ hr). From Varkala there are buses to Kovalam and Kollam (40 min). A taxi cost about Rs 300 to get to Varkala from Thiruvananthapuram.

THIRUVANANTHAPURAM (TRIVANDRUM)

Population: 825,000, STD Code 0471

The city derives its name from Thiru-anantha-puram—**the city, or puram, of Anantha,** the sacred serpent. Lord Padmanabha reclines on Ananta here in the famous Sri Padmanabhaswami Temple.

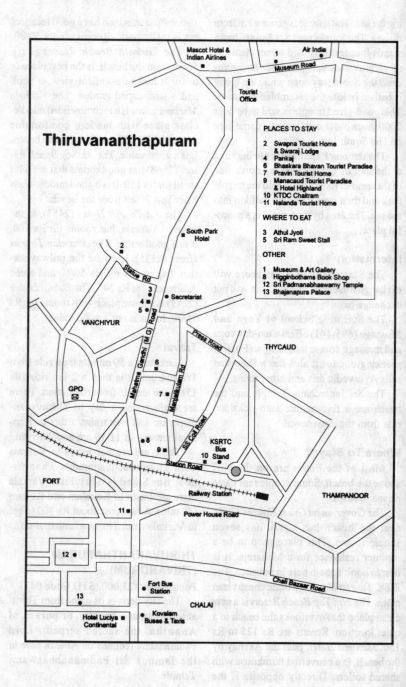

Thiruvananthapuram

Mascot Hotel & Indian Airlines

Air India

Museum Road

Tourist Office

PLACES TO STAY

2 Swapna Tourist Home & Swaraj Lodge
4 Pankaj
6 Bhaskara Bhavan Tourist Paradise
7 Pravin Tourist Home
9 Manacaud Tourist Paradise & Hotel Highland
10 KTDC Chaitram
11 Nalanda Tourist Home

WHERE TO EAT

3 Athul Jyoti
5 Sri Ram Sweet Stall

OTHER

1 Museum & Art Gallery
8 Higginbothams Book Shop
12 Sri Padmanabhaswamy Temple
13 Bhajanapura Palace

South Park Hotel

Statue Rd

Secretariat

VANCHIYUR

Press Road

THYCAUD

Mahatma Gandhi (M.G) Road

Manjalikulam Rd

GPO

SS Col Road

FORT

KSRTC Bus Stand

Station Road

THAMPANOOR

Railway Station

Power House Road

Chali Bazaar Road

CHALAI

Fort Bus Station

Kovalam Buses & Taxis

Hotel Luciya Continental

Many foreign tourists come to this city on their way to the beach town, Kovalam, which is 18 km away.

The town is built quadrilaterally around the **Sri Padmanabhaswami Temple**, which is oriented toward the four points of the compass, according to the Vedic scriptures.

Getting Your Bearings

Trivandrum is spread out over a fairly large area. The most important places are mainly on or just off MG Road, which runs north-south through the center of town. The railway station and bus station, in the southern part of town, are a few blocks east of MG Road. The Padmanabhaswami Temple is also in the southern part of the city, south of the railway station. The museums and zoo are on Museum Road, which is just off north MG Road. The Indian Airlines office and the Mascot Hotel are on north MG Road.

You can get a good city map from Pai and Company bookshop on MG Road.

Information

The **Tourist Information Center** (61132), Museum Rd, is off the north end of MG Rd, by the museum. It is a good source of information. They have good literature both for free and for a small charge on Kerala, Tamil Nadu, and Karnataka. Tours are not arranged from here, but from the office at the Chaithram Hotel.

There is also a **Tourist Reception Center** (75031) on Station Rd in front of the Chaithram Hotel near the railway station. They have only basic information, so it is best to go to the center on Museum Rd.

Tours

These tours are operated by **KTDC**

Tourism. You book the tours at their office by the Chaithram Hotel near the train station. You cannot book these tours at the tourist office by the museum.

The **Kanniyakumari** tour costs Rs 125. It leaves at 7.30 am and returns at 9 pm. It goes to Kovalam, Padmanabhapuram Palace (not on Monday), and Kanniyakumari. You can be picked up in Kovalam at 8.30 am for this tour, but they will not drop you off there. This tour is very popular so you may have to book it a few days in advance.

There is a **Trivandrum** tour that goes to the local sites. There is a **Sabarimala Tour** (Ayyappa Temple), which departs the last day of the Malayalam month as well as every day during Mandala Puja and the Makaravilakku season. It departs at 9.30 pm and returns 8.30 pm the next day.

Post and Banks

The GPO is on a side street off MG Road, by the Sri Padmanabhaswami Temple. It is open from 8 am to 8 pm and has a poste restante. There is a tailor who can seal your package for you just across the street.

Travellers' cheques can be changed at the *State Bank of India* on MG Road, near the Secretariat.

Visa Extensions

You can apply for a visa extension at the *Commissioner of Police* office on Residency Rd. The extension takes three days to a week. It is open Monday to Saturday from 10 am to 5 pm.

Shopping

Higginbotham's Bookshop and *Pai & Co* on Mahatma Gandhi Road are the best bookshops in town, but both have a limited selection of books.

The *Kairali Government Emporium,* opposite the Secretariat on MG Road, and *SMSM Handicrafts Emporium,* behind the Secretariat, are both good shops. *Chalai Bazaar* by the rail station is a good place to shop. The *Central Handicrafts Emporium* has a good selection of items.

Sri Padmanabhaswami Temple

The main Deity in this temple is **Lord Padmanabha,** who reclines on Ananta, the thousand-headed serpent. He is 18 feet long, so He is one of the largest Deities of Lord Vishnu in India. The Deity reclines in a large, dimly lit room. Devotees view Him through three large doors, one revealing His feet, another His midsection (with Brahma on the lotus), and the third His chest and head. The Lord's consort is Sri Hari Lakshmi Thayar.

This is a very ancient temple, believed to have been rebuilt by Marthanda Varma in 1733 AD. The temple is on an elevated part of the city, and its eastern tower (built in 1566) is seven stories high (30m). The temple is a blend of local Kerala style and Dravidian architecture. It is intricately carved in granite. In front of Lord Padmanabha is a raised stone platform, which is made of a single slab of granite, 2½ feet thick and 20 feet square.

The Deity is also called Ananta Padmanabha or Ananta Sayanam. He was originally formed from an iluppa tree, but was later replaced with **12,000 shala-gram-shilas**, which were brought on elephant back from the River Gandaki in Nepal. One book I read said that the *shilas* are held together with a paste made from gur (raw brown sugar) and ash, producing the present *murti* of some 18 feet long. Another book said He is held together by a mortar made of lime and granite covered with a paste of molasses and mustard.

It took 7 months for 4,000 stonecutters, 8,000 workers, and a hundred elephants to built the **Sreebalipura**, the rectangular corridor that surrounds the temple. There are 324 pillars in the temple corridor. It is 150m long on one side, 105m long on the other, and 25 feet wide.

After conquering the local area in 1729, **Marthanda Varma**, the ruler of Travancore, came to the temple and offered all his processions—his sceptre, sword, army, and people—to Lord Padmanabha. He symbolically placed the royal sword on the steps of the altar. He then received the sword back and ruled the state as "Padmanabha dasa", or servant of Lord Padmanabha, and ordained that his successors would do likewise.

The processional Deity of Lord Vishnu is taken at 4 pm on His daily procession around the temple grounds. There are several other deities in the temple including Sita, Rama, Laksman, and Hanuman. There is a temple dedicated to Lord Krishna in back of the main temple on the right hand side. By the south entrance of the inner sanctum is a Deity of Yoga Narasimha.

The temple tank, called Padma Teertham, is located just outside the main eastern entrance of the temple.

Temple Information

Timing of worship is 4 am, 5.15 am, 6.15 am to 6.45 am, 8.45 am to 9.30 am, and 5 pm to 7.15 pm. Only Hindus are allowed in this temple, but ISKCON devotees and converted Hindus can also go into the temple. Males have to wear a dhoti and be bare-chested to go in the temple. Women must wear saris. There is a booth by the temple entrance where you are supposed to leave any bag you have. Once you enter the temple you have to wait in line for about an hour to see the main Deity. There is a 5 rupee entrance fee.

Festivals

There are two main annual temple festivals—in March-April (Meenam) and Oct-Nov (Thulam). The **Utsavam Festival** is a ten-day festival at the Padmanabhaswami Temple. Each of the ten days there are festivities inside the temple (Hindus only).

During the **Arat** festival, the last day of the Utsavam festival, the Sri Padmanabha processional Deity is brought around the temple and then carried in a grand procession to Shangumugham Beach to be bathed there. The procession is lead by the Maharaja of Travancore with five gold-clothed elephants. The Maharaja, who walks the entire way, wears a simple white dhoti and has a bare chest. Before the procession begins there is a 21-gun salute. The procession leaves the temple accompanied by music at 5 pm and arrives at the beach about an hour later. After the ceremonies at the beach, the Deity returns to the temple by about 9 pm. The day ends with a fireworks display.

ISKCON Temple

It located on Hospital Road, a couple hundred feet from the W&C Hospital and Hotel Amritha. It is a small place with no place to stay overnight. There is nice *prasadam* lunch at 1 pm, but you may have to arrange it in advance. The phone number is 68197.

Museum, Gallery, and Zoo

These places are all in the park, at the north end of the city. The **Napier Museum** has a fine collection of 400 bronze deities and is worth seeing. There is a 9th century Deity of Lord Vishnu, with in-

laid crystal eyes, a 17th century bronze Vishnu and Garuda, and a wooden sculpture of Narasimha. There are also some elaborately carved wooden temple carts. It is open 9 am to 5 pm and is closed on Mondays. On Wednesday it is open 1 to 4.45 pm.

In the **Sri Chitra Art Gallery** are paintings of the Rajput and Tanjore schools. There are also some modern Indian paintings, especially ones painted by Ravi Varma. Also in the park is a good **zoo** and a botanical garden. The zoo is open 9 am to 5 pm daily, except Monday.

Kanakakunnu Palace

At night there is a performance of Kerala's temple rituals and arts. It is a devotional temple performance and a good show.

Where To Stay

The hotels here fill up by later in the day, so it may be difficult to find a room. Besides staying in Trivandrum, you can also stay in Kovalam (18 km), at the beach.

Where to Stay – Lower

Most of the cheap places are near the railway station and bus station, on or close to Station Road. Most of the hotels on Station Road are not very good and are noisy. A better area is along Manjalikulam Rd, which heads north off Station Road. This road is lined with hotels for about a km, from low-end to good mid-range hotels. It is also a quiet street.

The *Pravin Tourist Home* (330-443), Manjalikulam Rd, has clean quiet rooms for Rs 60/110 to Rs 150. The *Bhaskara Bhavan Tourist Paradise* (79662) isn't really a paradise, but the rooms are clean and cheap at Rs 40/75, with some rooms for Rs 100.

The *Sivada Tourist Home* (331-322) is good place with rooms for Rs 60/100 and Rs 225 with A/C. The *Manacaud Tourist Paradise* (695-001) has large rooms with bath for Rs 60/110.

The *Hotel Kyvalya* is a good place. It has double rooms with bath for Rs 250.

The *Taurus Lodge*, Statue Road, is a good place with clean rooms. Room 24 and 25 are the best rooms. The owner is full of interesting information.

Where to Stay – Middle

The *Hotel Regency* (330-377), Manjalikulam Cross Rd, has rooms for Rs 275/350 to Rs 450/600 with A/C. It has 24-hour hot water and is a good value. The *Hotel Highland* (78440), Manjalikulam Rd, is a tall building that can be seen from the railway station. It has comfortable rooms for Rs 140/180 and Rs 225/350 with A/C. The staff here is helpful.

The *Hotel Amritha* (63091), Thycaud, half a km from the railway station, has rooms for Rs 150/300 and Rs 300/375 with A/C.

The *Hotel Horizon* (66888), Aristo Rd, has comfortable rooms for Rs 350/500 and Rs 750/950 with A/C. *Residency Tower* (331-661), Press Rd, has rooms for Rs 275/350 and Rs 450/600 with A/C. It is clean and a good value.

The modern *Chaithram Hotel* (330-977), Station Rd, run by the Kerala Tourism Corporation, has rooms for Rs 275/375 to Rs 550/750 with A/C. There are also more expensive deluxe rooms. It is conveniently located by the bus and train station. It is fairly popular.

The *Hotel Pankaj* (76667), MG Rd, opposite the Secretariat, is a well-maintained comfortable place with rooms for Rs 400/550 and Rs 700/950 with A/C.

Where to Stay – High

The *KTDC Mascot Hotel* (438-990), Museum Road, is a three-star hotel which is located about 3 km north of the Padmanabhaswami Temple. It is a nice place to stay with hot water, A/C, and TV. Rooms are Rs 695/995 plus 20% luxury tax. It has a swimming pool and suites for Rs 1795. This is one of the best places in town and is a recommended place. It is best to see a few rooms before choosing one.

The three-star *Hotel Luciya Continental* (463-443), East Fort near the Sri Padmanabhaswami Temple, is a good modern place with rooms for Rs 995/1195 up to Rs 2500 for a suite. This place is centraly air-conditioned.

The four-star *South Park* (65666), MG Road, is a Welcomegroup hotel with comfortable A/C rooms for Rs 950/1150 up to Rs 1950 for a suite.

The well-managed *Hotel Fort Manor* (462-222), Power House Junction, half a km from the railway station, has clean rooms with A/C for Rs 750/950.

Where To Eat

The *Woodland Hotels* has the best restaurant in town and is a recommended place. When I was there it was closed for renovation.

The *Hotel Arulakam*, across the street and two blocks down from the railway station, has a vegetarian restaurant. Opposite the Secretariat on MG Road is the fairly good *Arul Jyothi* (78497). *Sri Ram Sweet Stall* (79395), near the Hotel Pankaj on MG, is a good place.

Further north is the *Ananda Bhavan Restaurant*, which is a basic South Indian place.

Except for the Woodlands Hotel (if it is open), all the other places are just average at best.

Travel

Air There are flights to Madras (daily), Delhi (daily), Bombay (2 daily), and Bangalore (four flights weekly).

From Thiruvananthapuram, Air India has flights to the Gulf, some of which continue on to Europe and New York. Gulf Air flies to the Middle East and connects from there to London and New York. There are three Indian Air flights weekly and four Air Lanka flights weekly to Colombo in Sri Lanka.

Airlines offices are: Indian Airline (436-870), Air Centre, Mascot Junction; Air India (434-837), Museum Rd, Velayambalam Circle; Gulf Air (67514) c/o Jet Air Travels, Panavila Junction; and Air Lanka (66495), Geethanjali Building, Geethanjali Hospital Rd, Vazhuthacaud.

Thiruvananthapuram Airport is on the beach, 6 km out of town. If you arrive on an international flight you can **change money** at the **bank** before going through customs. It gives a good rate of exchange. Local bus No 14 goes downtown.

Train The **reservation office** is on the first floor of the ticket office building. There is no tourist counter, so you should go to the Chief Reservations Supervisor's Office, counter 8, at the top of the stairs. They have a generous tourist quota. The reservation office is open from 7 am to 1 pm and 1.30 to 7.30 pm from Monday to Saturday and Sunday from 9 am to 5 pm. Counter 8 is for foreign tourist booking.

It is best to book your train as far in advance as possible, because sometimes it can be difficult to get a train out of Trivandrum, especially to the bigger cities like Bombay, Bangalore, Madras, and Delhi. Trains to the big cities can be booked a month in advance.

The daily Kerala Express #2625 (9.45 am) takes 54 hours to get to **Delhi**. The Himsagar Express #6017 (3.15 pm) departs only on Fridays to Delhi. The daily Trivandrum-Madras Mail #6320 (1.30 pm) takes 17 hours to reach **Madras**. The daily Kanniyakumari-Bangalore Exp # 6526 (10.20 am) takes 19 hours to get to **Bangalore**. The Kanniyakumari Express #1082 (7.30 pm) takes 45 hours to get to **Bombay.** There are direct trains to Mangalore, Ernakulam, Kanniyakumari, and many other places. There are about seven trains a day to **Thrissur** (Trichur) (8 hr). The train to **Madurai** departs about 7 pm and arrives in Madurai at 4 am.

The daily Malabar Express #6029 (5.40 pm, 16 hr) and the Trivandrum-Mangalore Exp #6349 (6.05 am, 15 hr) go along the coast to **Mangalore**. From Mangalore you can get a local train or bus to Udupi. There are 12 trains daily to Kollam (1¼ hr) via **Varkala** (45 min).

Bus Long-distance buses depart from the **Central Bus Station**, opposite the train station. For short or medium trips the buses are usually faster than the trains, but not as comfortable. For a long trip, such as to Madras, it is better to take a train.

There are buses to Kochi (Cochin) (5 hr), Madras (17 hr, 4 daily), and Madurai (7 hr, 10 daily). You can get a deluxe bus to Bangalore (18 hr) operated by Karnataka State Road Transport Corp (KSRTC). There are many buses to Nagercoil and Kanniyakumari (2 hr, 12 daily).

If you want to go to **Madurai**, as many travelers will, there are about 10 buses that go there, some on the way to Madras. You may be told that you cannot get a ticket until a half hour before the bus leaves. The problem is that some of the bus also go to Madras, and you can purchase a ticket in advance to go to Madras. So when you come back to get your ticket, a half hour before the bus leaves, there is a good chance the bus will be full. I saw this happen on two separate occasions. A good alternative is to take a bus to Nagercoil, about two hours away. Many of the buses travelling in South Kerala are routed through this town. There are many buses from Nagercoil to Madurai. It took me 7 hours to make the trip, which is the same time I was told it would take to go direct from Trivandrum to Madurai, if I could ever get on the bus. If you are staying in Kovalam, you do not necessarily have to come to Trivandrum to get to Madurai. You can take a bus direct to Nagercoil and save time and trouble.

Transportation To Kovalam

There are many buses going to Kovalam Beach every day. You catch bus No 111 from stand 19 at the **Fort Bus stand**. It is 100 yards south of the local bus stand on MG Rd, by the Hotel Luciya. The fare is Rs 4. At first the bus is usually very crowded, but it empties out quickly. If there is a long queue to get a ticket, you can get a boy to wait in line for you for a few rupees.

You can get a shared cab to Kovalam for Rs 20 a seat from the bus stand. An auto rickshaw costs Rs 70 to go to the lighthouse end of the beach.

In the Area

ADI KESAVA TEMPLE

This temple contains the Deity of Lord Kesava. This **Maha-Vishnu** Deity, lying on Sesa Naga, is **18 feet long** and viewed from three doors. This is where Lord Caitanya found a copy of *Brahma-samhita*. The Adi Kesava Temple is about 45 km southeast of Trivandrum in the town

of **Tiruvattar**. This place has a peaceful spiritual atmosphere. Few people visit this temple

The Deity faces west instead of east. The left hand of the Deity is down, while in most other Maha-Vishnu temples the right hand of the Deity is down. The priest of the temple says that Maha-Vishnu is facing west because this Deity is looking at the Deity of Sri Padmanabhaswami in Thiruvananthapuram. Also, this Deity does not have a Lord Brahma on a lotus flower coming out His naval, as found on the Padmanabhaswami Deity. The *pujari* first holds a lamp at one door and then at the other two doors. It is a large temple and is architecturally interesting, but it is not as large as the one in Thiruvananthapuram.

Practicalities

This temple is in the town of Tiruvattar, which is about 45 km southeast of Trivandrum. This is a very small town, and there are no facilities to stay overnight.

From Thiruvananthapuram you get here by first taking a bus to the town of Marthandum (35 km, 1½ hr, Rs 10). This town can be reached by getting a Nagercoil or Kanniyakumari bus. From there you get another bus to Tiruvattar (10 km, 20 min, Rs 3). You can also get a bus here from Nagercoil. The temple is about a ten-minute walk from where the bus lets you off. Both the Janardana Temple and this temple can be visited in one day, with a lot of traveling, even though both temples are in totally different directions. *Darshan* times are 5 to 8 am, 10 am to noon, and 5 to 8 pm.

Parasurama Temple

Located about halfway between Trivandrum and Kovalam at the junction of two roads is one of the only Parasurama temples in India.

Padmanabhapuram Palace

It is a beautiful palace made of granite and teakwood and surrounded by a huge town wall. Most of the palace dates from the 17th or 18th century, but some parts of the palace are said to date back to the 14th century. It is past Nagercoil, on the road from Kanniyakumari to Thiruvananthapuram (Trivandrum). It can be visited while going to or from Kanniyakumari. The Ramaswami Temple dates to the 18th century. It has 45 carved panels that tell the story of the *Ramayana*.

There is a Rs 500 charge to use a video camera here. The palace is closed on Mondays. It is compulsory to go on a tour with a guide. The Kanniyakumari tour that departs from Trivandrum comes here before going to Suchindram and Kanniyakumari. From the Thampanur station in Thiruvananthapuram buses going to Nagercoil and Kanniyakumari stop at Padmanabhapuram.

KOVALAM

Population: 3,000, STD Code 0471

Kovalam, 18 km south of Trivandrum, has a beautiful, clean beach. It is a half hour from Trivandrum Airport. Besides bathing, you can also get Ayurvedic massages and oil baths here. The busy time of the year is November to January, especially during the Christmas holiday.

There are four stretches of beaches, but two main areas. Lighthouse Beach is where the foreign tourists mainly stay. Nearby is Kovalam Beach, which is not as crowded. Lighthouse Beach is more built up and there are some vendors on the beach trying to sell things to you, but they are not too pushy.

It is hot here all year around. The best and coolest time to come is between December and March. It starts to get very hot in April. Between April and October the waves can be 6 metres high, and swimming can be extremely dangerous because of the undertow.

Getting Your Bearings

There are three beaches that extend over a 4 km stretch. The southern one is known as Lighthouse Beach, where the cheaper hotels are located. The north beach is not yet much developed and only has cottages. The Ashok Resorts is between the north beach and the middle beach. Kovalam village goes along the main road and has some small book shops, a post office, and other shops.

Information

You can change travellers' cheques at the *Central Bank of India* at the Ashok Radisson Beach Resort. It is open 10.30 am to 2 pm Monday to Friday and 10.30 to noon on Saturday. You can also change money at Wilson's Tourist Home. The **post office** is in Kovalam village.

Aries Travel, with an office in Thiruvananthapuram and Kovalam, is supposed to be a good travel agent.

There are many people giving massages here. You can get a good **Ayurvedic massage** (Rs 150) at the Seaweed Hotel. The man is professional and helped me a lot. The Neptune Hotel has a **Kathakali dance** three nights a week.

IMPORTANT The local water is very bad as there are many pit toilets that leak into the well water. It is advisable to only drink bottled water here.

CAUTION Swimming in the ocean here can be dangerous and many people drown. The lifeguards mark different areas of the sea as DANGEROUS. They are not kidding. If you are caught by the current (in an undertow), you are pulled both down and out. One person told me in the two weeks he was here, four people were said to have drowned.

It is important to swim with someone, and most people should not go past where they can touch the ground. If you are caught in an undertow, do not try to fight it. Call for help and use the incoming waves to get back to shore.

You also have to be careful of the **jellyfish**. The little orange ones are dangerous, and the purple one are harmless.

Where To Stay

Prices for hotels varies according to the season. December and January are the peak months. The price of a room in March can be half the price of the same room in January.

There are plenty of cottages along the beach for rent at cheap prices, starting at Rs 20 a day. The prices vary according to the season and how naive the customer is. It is best to inspect a few places before you choose one.

Where To Stay – Lower

The *Apsara Guest House* is a recommended cheaper place. The *Eden Seaside Resort*, like many of the places, is willing to charge about half their normal day rate if you stay for a month. Double rooms are Rs 150 in the high season and Rs 75 in the low.

The *Surya Tourist Home* is a cheap place that has rooms with common bath for Rs 100 and Rs 150 with bath in the low season and Rs 150 and Rs 200 during the high season. The *Thiruvonam Hotel*, on the beach, has good double rooms for Rs 300 to Rs 350.

Sergeant Guest House, inland from Lighthouse Beach, is a popular place managed by an interesting retired sergeant. *Hotel Achutha, Blue Sea Hotel, Hotel Thiruvathira* are all good cheaper places. *Wilson Tourist Home* (480-051) is a clean recommended place.

Where To Stay – Middle

The *Rockholm Hotel* (480-306, fax 480-607), Lighthouse Rd, is a very nice recommended place beside the lighthouse. It has a good view of the sea. In the busy season rooms are Rs 750/800. There is a 25% discount in the off season. The rooms on the roof can get very hot during the day.

The *Sea Weed Hotel* (480-391, fax 480-806) is a recommended place with rooms to fit all budgets. Rooms range from Rs 200/300 to Rs 600/700. It is very clean and is a really good place to stay. There is also a man here who gives very good professional Ayurvedic massages.

The *Varmas Beach Resort* (480-478) is another really good place. It has modern rooms from Rs 400 to Rs 700 and higher in the peak season. The *Hotel Samudra Tara* (54653) is also a good place with rooms for Rs 400 up to Rs 600 for a room with a balcony on the sea. The *Moonlight Tourist Home* (480-375), set back from the beach, has large modern rooms and is very clean. Rooms are Rs 250 to Rs 400 (low season) and Rs 500 to Rs 800 (high season).

Hotel Neptune (480-222) has rooms from Rs 400 to Rs 800. The rooms are half this price during the low season. There are Kathakali dances at this hotel. A friend of mine went and said they were good. The *Hotel Sea Rock* (480-422), right on the beach, has sea-facing rooms with balconies for Rs 750 (high season) and Rs 350 for a room in the back. In the low season the same rooms are Rs 350 and Rs 250. It is one of the best places on the beach.

Luxury

The *Kovalam Ashok Beach Resort* (480-101, fax 481-522) is a luxurious place with an excellent location. It has a swimming pool, a bookshop, and a Yoga and Health Center that offers Ayurvedic oil massages and baths. Rooms are Rs 2600/3000 and suites are Rs 4000 up to Rs 10,000 in the high season. They accept all major credit cards.

Travel

Air The closest airport is in Thiruvananthapuram (Trivandrum), a half hour from Kovalam.

Bus Usually the way to get here is to go to Trivandrum first. From Trivandrum buses depart every 40 minutes from the **Fort Bus Depot**, Platform 19 (bus No. 9D or No. 111). You can also get a shared taxi here for Rs 20 a person. The bus stand in Kovalam is on the main road by the **Ashok Resort**, in the northern part of town. You can get an auto-rickshaw to or from Trivandrum for Rs 70.

There are direct buses to Kanniyakumari, Ernakulum, and Quilon. If you are going to **Madurai**, you can get a bus to Nagercoil that takes two hours and from there get one of the regular buses to Madurai. This is better than going to Thiruvananthapuram to get the bus to Madurai, as many of the buses from Thiruvananthapuram to Madurai go through Nagercoil anyway. Plus it is easy to get a bus to Madurai from Nagercoil, but not from Thiruvananthapuram.

Aranmula

Aranmula is located 9 km from Chengannur on the bank of the Pampa River. There is the important **Parthasarathi Temple** here. This temple is considered to be one of the five most important Krishna temples in Kerala and it is one of the 108 Divya Desam temples referred to by the Alwars as especially sacred to Vaishnavas. The Deity in the temple is Parthasarathi, another name for Lord Krishna as the divine charioteer of Arjuna during the battle of Kurukshetra.

This place is known for the Aranmula Vallamkali (Utthrittathi) festival which is a boating event held on the last day of Onam (Aug-Sept). During this festival snake boats are rowed for about two hours. The 103-foot-long snake boats have 100 rowers and 25 singers, singing Vanchipattu or boat songs. The festival is to celebrate the crossing of the Yamuna River by Krishna, who is believed to be in all the boats simultaneously. It is not a competitive race and all the boats arrive at the same time.

Aranmula is about 125 north of Thiruvananthapuram. There are hotels in Alappuzha (Alleppey).

Ambalapuzha

The temple here is considered to be one of the three main Krishna temples in Kerala. The Deity was installed here in 1613. During the 1790 invasion of Sultan Tipu, the Deity of Lord Krishna was moved from Guruvayur and stayed here temporarily. The spot where the Deity was kept is still known as Guruvayurambalam, the temple of Guruvayur. This temple is famous for its offerings of *palpayasam*, a milk porridge of exceptional sweetness. Although worshiped as Unnikrishna, or child Krishna, the Deity looks like Parthasarathi with a whip in His right hand and a *sankha* (conch) in the left.

There is a ten day festival in March-April, during which there are a number of dance performances. Ambalapuzha is located 76 km south of Kochi (Cochin). The nearest rail junction is Tiruvalla Rd. Accommodation is in Alappuzha.

Tiruvangad

Located here is one of the three most famous Sri Rama temples in Kerala. It is a large temple area (6 acres) with a two acre tank. The temple is very old. The Deity in the temple is a four-armed form of Vishnu. The club is held upside down, which is unusual.

Tiruvangad is 2 km from Tellicherry station, 69 km north of Calicut on the seashore, in the north of Kerala.

Trichambaram Krishna Temple

In this temple there is a Deity of Lord Krishna as He appeared after killing Kamsa. This temple is said to have been established by Parasurama. It is about 2 km northeast of the Siva Temple at Taliparamba. The temple existed before the 11th century and has excellent wood-carvings.

CHAPTER TWENTY ONE

Nepal

Nepal is a beautiful country. It has a few important holy places such as Janakpur, the birthplace of Sita; Lumbini, the birthplace of Buddha; and Muktinatha, where many of the *shalagram-shilas* come from.

There are also many ancient temples in Nepal. Non-Hindus are not allowed to enter many of the temples in Nepal, and this is strictly enforced. The population of Nepal is about 18 million. It is mainly a Hindu nation.

One of the main reasons that people come to Nepal is because of the fantastic Himalayan mountains. One-third of the Himalayan mountains are within the borders of Nepal. This includes 10 of the 14 highest peaks above 8000 meters (24,000 feet).

Many of the prices in this section will be quoted in US dollars or Nepali rupees.

Tourist Visas & Trekking Permits

Except for Indians everyone needs a visa. You can get a visa in advance at a Nepal Embassy. You can also get a visa at the Kathmandu airport, which takes about an hour. If you arrive by bus, visas are quickly issued at the border. There is usually just a short line. You are expected to pay in US dollars, and Indian rupees are not accepted. You can also pay in Nepali rupees if you show a recent exchange certificate.

Visas are for 15, 30, or 60 days. A 15 day visas cost US$15, 30 day visas are US$25, and a double entry visa for 30 days is US$40, and a 60 days multiple-entry visa is US$60. You may extend your visa at a cost of US$1 a day up to a maximum five months in a year. Children under 10 do not pay a visa fee.

The Nepalese Embassy in New Delhi is on Barakhamba Rd, close to Connaught Place. It is open from 10 am to 1 pm, Monday to Friday. If you submit your application at the embassy before 12 noon, you can pick it up the next day.

You can extend your visa at the **Department of Immigration** (412-337, 418-573) in Kathmandu on Tridevi Marg, Thamel, between 10.30 am and 1 pm (12.30 pm in winter), Sunday through Thursday and 10 am to 12 pm on Friday.

The Department of Immigration also issues trekking permits, which are required to visit Nepal's interior regions (areas not connected by major roads). You need two different trekking permits to trek in two different areas of the country.

You can extend your visa and get trekking permits for the Annapurna region at the Pokhara Immigration Office, which is between the airport and Lakeside area in Pokhara.

Information

Nepal Standard time is 15 minutes ahead of Indian time. The electricity is 220 volts/50 cycles, the same as India. If you depart from the Kathmandu airport there is a **departure tax** of Nepal Rs 600 for SAARC countries (includes India) and Rs 700 for all other international destinations.

Post offices and other important offices are closed on Saturday in Nepal, not on Sunday. You should not use the mailboxes in major cities, but should make sure your letters and postcards have their stamps canceled in front of you at the post office. Otherwise the stamps may be removed from your letters. To send packages airmail takes 2 to 6 weeks, and seamail takes at least 3 months.

The yellow **maps** of Kathmandu and Pokhara are the best maps.

The Nepali word for toilet is *charpi*. Most people also understand the word toilet.

The number to dial for an English speaking local telephone operator is 180; the international operator number is 186 or 187; and the English speaking directory assistance is 197.

Medical and Eyeglasses

The Patan Hospital (5210-048), Lagankhel, Patan, is a good hospital. Two good clinics are the Nepal International Clinic (412-842), Naxal, at the top of Durbar Marg, a block and a half from the Royal Palace, and CIWEC (410-983), Baluwater.

Unless it is an emergency it is better to wait until you are back home to go to a hospital.

You can get eyeglasses at Optic Palace, Bagh Bazaar (226-673), or Euro Optic Centre (224-436), 22/234 Khicha Pokhari, near Durbar Square.

It is a good idea to bring a spare pair of eyeglasses from back home for your trip. If you are trekking or away from a Kathmandu Valley, it can be very difficult to get a spare set of glasses.

Money

The Nepali Rupee is about Rs 50 to the US dollar versus Rs 36 for the India Rupee.

Banks are open Sunday to Thursday, 10 am to 3 pm in the summer (10 am to 2.30 pm in the winter), and Friday, 10 am to 1 pm. The few banks that change money can take a long time, sometimes a few hours. Convenient banks are the Nepal Grindlay's Bank, opposite the Hotel Star in Thamel, the Nepal Bank, on Kantipath, and the R.B. Bank, at the corner of New Road and Sukrapath, a block from Durbar Square. The exchange receipt you receive may be needed for a visa extension, a trekking permit, or to ship something out of the country.

You can exchange money in the larger hotels quickly, but the rate is usually slightly less than the bank rate. For an extra dollar or two you can save an hour wait.

The black market in Kathmandu is very active for exchanging money, but illegal. The rate is two or three rupees more than the official rate.

There is an American Express office in front of the Hotel Mayalu, around the corner from the south end of Durbar Marg, on the road to Kantipath.

Weather

The coldest month in Kathmandu is January, when it can go to a low of 3° C (38° F) and a high of 18° C (65° F). In the winter, from the end of November till the end of February, you definitely need warm clothes. The sky is clear in December and January. It does not snow in the Kathmandu valley because December and January are the driest months, and also it does not usually go below freezing.

The weather is good in February,

March, and April, but visibility is not very good, although there are quite a few clear days. April is the hottest month with a high of about 30° C (86° F). The weather is best during the months of October and November when it is not too hot. There is no rain, and the sky is clear, so you can get a good view of the mountains.

The rainy season is from the end of June till the beginning of September. During the rainy season it does not usually rain all day, just an hour or two at a time. The weather is not bad from mid-June to September, but it is cloudy most of the time. It rains the most in July.

How Much Will It Cost

You can live for as cheaply as $5 a day, but the standard of living will be really basic. You can live fairly comfortably on $15 a day. The average expense for a simple traveler staying in middle range hotels is $20 to $30 a day. There are expensive hotels in Kathmandu costing over $100 a night. Except for the public transportation, it is more expensive in Nepal than India.

KATHMANDU

Population 350,000, Phone Code 01

This is the main city in Nepal, and if you arrive by air this is where you will arrive. It is an interesting city with many old buildings. You can easily stay busy just wandering the streets for a couple of days.

If you go to Nepal for less than a week, the Kathmandu valley may be the only place that you go, as there is a lot to do here. Beside Kathmandu, there are the two interesting towns of Patan and Bhaktapur. There are also several important Hindu temples and Buddhist holy sites. The Kathmandu valley is 1310m above sea level and is cold in the winter.

Tourist Offices

There is a **tourist office** (220818), on New Road, near Durbar Square, and at the Tribhuvan International Airport. They are both open Sunday to Friday from 9 am to 6 pm (5 pm in the winter). The airport tourist office usually has a better selection of maps and brochures, but the lady at the New Road office was helpful when I was there. They give out a free map of Kathmandu. The **Department of Tourism** (214-519), in Babar Mahal, hands out brochures and free posters.

Tours

Grayline has different tours around the city. One tour goes to Bhaktapur, Boudha, and Pashupatinath (3 hr) for Rs 195. The Patan and Swayambhunath tour (3 hr) cost Rs 195. To go to Nagarkot in the afternoon takes 4 hours and costs Rs 295. A trip to Dhulikhel takes 4 hours and costs Rs 275. To go and stay at Nagarkot overnight costs $59 per person. You can reserve a seat for these tours from many of the travel agents in town. There are morning and evening tours that depart from their Ram Shah Path office at 9 am and 2.30 pm.

Travel Agents

If you are booking a flight or plan to book an Indian railway train from Gorakhpur it could be a good idea to use a travel agent. *Student Travel & Tours* in Thamel, *Everest Travel Service* on Ganga Path, *Peace Travel & Tours* on Kantipath, and *Yeti Travels* in Durbar Marg are long-standing travel agents in Kathmandu. If you want to get an Indian train ticket you should give a travel agent a week to get it. Travel agents are useful to arrange high quality treks, airline flights, and special tours, especially during the high season.

If you have a travel agency arrange a

taxi, they charge much more than the regular fare. When I wanted to go to Nagarkot I asked a few travel agencies for a price. One told me Rs 1200 and the other said Rs 1300. The first taxi driver I asked told me Rs 900, and we settled for just Rs 800. The hotel managers may not help you get a cheap taxi either, because they get a percentage of what you pay for the taxi. They will arrange a taxi for Rs 1200, then pay the taxi driver Rs 800 and keep the other Rs 400 as their commission.

The travel agents in the hotels can be 25% to 100% more expensive than other travel agents, but I assume they are more trustworthy. When you ask the hotel clerk for advice on how to get somewhere, they will probably refer you to the travel agent in the hotel. These travel agents can then charge you a price that most taxi drivers would not believe anyone would pay. The travel agent in the hotel I was staying at was often charging double the real price. You can often save 25% to 200% by arranging your own travel facilities.

Books and Information

Nepal Traveller is a useful free magazine with tourist information about Nepal. It is available at the airport and the tourist office on New Road.

There are many bookshops where you can get a wide selection of used books. Kathmandu has one of the best selection of bookshops in Asia. Many bookshops will buy back books for 50% of the price you paid for them.

Tiwari's Pilgrims Book House, a few doors from Kathmandu Guest House, has one of the best selections of philosophical, yoga, and eastern medicine books anywhere. It is the best bookshop in town. The *Kailash Bookshop*, by the Hotel Yak & Yeti, also has an excellent selection.

Phone

You can use a private operator or call from the Central Telegraph Office, by the National Stadium and post office. The private operators charge about $3 to $3.50 a minute for international calls. If you plan to talk for a while it will be cheaper to call from the Central Telegraph Office. You can also call from your hotel, but it is best to first check the price. Calls made in a hotel are often more than double the normal price.

Taxis and Rickshaws

Taxi prices are not expensive, and they are a good way to get around. Most of the time the taxi meters are out of date and the taxi driver will charge you a certain percentage extra. Many times taxi drivers will try to overcharge, so it is a good idea to ask at your hotel what the fare adjustment charge is. Fares rise along with the price of fuel, which is expensive in Nepal. If you arrive at the airport, most taxi drivers will not use the meter. The auto-rickshaws are about half the price of the taxis.

The bicycle rickshaws are not cheap, and the rickshaw drivers can be tough to deal with. They often try to charge more than a taxi to go to the same place. You must agree on a price before you begin. At night be careful if a rickshaw driver is drunk, as they can be very difficult to deal with. If you want to take a cycle-rickshaw from the Kathmandu Guest House (Thamel) to Durbar Square, you will most likely be asked to pay Rs 50. The real price is Rs 20. In general you should pay less than half of the first quoted price.

Embassies and Consulates

The *US Embassy* (411-179), Maharajgunj, north of Thamel on an extension of Kantipath. *British Embassy* (411-590),

Lainchaur, Lazimpat, north of Thamel on an extension of Kantipath. *Australian Embassy* (411-578), Bhatbhateni, northeast of the Royal Palace. *Thai Embassy*, Jyoti Kendra Building, Thapathali.

Indian Embassy (410-900), Lainchaur. To get to the Indian Embassy from Thamel you walk pass the immigration office and turn left at the next street, at the circle. You walk 15 minutes, bearing to your right at the Y intersection. At the Hotel Ambassador you take the road that bears to your left and walk five minutes to the end of the road.

Shipping From Nepal

It not such a good idea to ship anything from Nepal, unless it is a large quantity of things. It is best to take whatever you purchase with you. If you ship something, besides shipping costs, there are customs charges, clearance, storage, and who knows what else. Add in all the work involved and it can cost you more to ship the goods then to bring them with you, even after paying overweight. Of course, that is, if you ever receive the items you ship. Sea freight is not much cheaper than air, as the goods first have to be shipped to Calcutta, which is an extra cost.

To post a package at the Foreign Post Section of the GPO takes about an hour and a half.

A good contact for shipping or purchasing things for resale is Oriental Express (526-466, Fax 977-1-220143), run by Dibya Joshi. His address is Post Box No 1690 in Kathmandu. Sharmason's (222-709), Kantipath, is a reliable shipper used by many foreigners.

Budhanilkantha Temple

Located here is a Deity of Lord Vishnu, Vishnu Jalasayana, lying on Ananta Sesa in the cosmic ocean. The Deity is over 1000 years old. Lord Vishnu is about 20 feet long and is lying in a 43 foot long tank, as if floating, with His legs crossed. Hindus can go touch His feet. His four hands hold the chakra (disc), club, conch shell, and lotus flower. The two main festivals at this temple are at the beginning and end of the monsoon season. Budhanilkantha is named after one of the Deity's former priests, whose name was Nilkantha and who worshipped the Lord into his old age (*budha*—old).

Budhanilkantha is about 8 km northeast of Kathmandu, at the base of Sivapuri hill. Buses and tempos to Budhanilkantha depart every half hour from near the National Theatre building at the northwest section of Rani Pokhari.

ISKCON (Hare Krishna) Temple

The ISKCON Temple (977-290-743) is located about a ten minute walk from the Budha-nilkantha Temple, in a beautiful rural setting.

Dhum Varahi Temple

In this temple is a 5th century Deity of Lord Varaha (Lord Vishnu as a boar) rescuing Prithvi, the earth goddess. It is about 5 km northeast of Kathmandu, in a school-yard just inside Ring Road, on the way to Budhanilkantha and the ISKCON Temple. If you go to Budhanilkantha by taxi, you can stop on the way.

Pharping

There is a temple here dedicated to Lord Vishnu as the dwarf Vamana. There is a holy tank next to the temple. It is located on the way to the Dakshinkali Temple, which is 12 miles south of Kathmandu.

Swayambhunath Stupa

Swayambhunath is an ancient Buddhist Stupa, three km west of downtown Kathmandu, said to be 2000 years old. On this Stupa, which is surrounded by over 200 prayer wheels, are the famous all seeing eyes of Buddha. Swayambhu is on top of a 77m (240 feet) hill. It takes about 20 minutes to walk up the more than 300 stairs. There is an excellent view of the Kathmandu valley and the surrounding mountains from here. Swayambhu means the "self-existent".

There are several temples on top of the hill. A large image of the Sakyamuni Buddha is in a monastery next to the Stupa. There is a temple dedicated to Hariti Devi, the goddess of smallpox. There is also a temple dedicated to the goddesses Yamuna and Ganga (Ganges).

At the base of the hill is a brightly painted gateway. Within the gatehouse there is a large prayer wheel, almost 12 feet tall, which strikes a bell when it goes around. It is believed that if you spin a prayer wheel that all the prayers written inside are recited and send upward to heaven.

National Museum

This museum is located at Chhauni, near Swayambunath. It houses the country's best collection of ancient religious art. Most of these works of arts are sculptures dating from the 1st to the 13th century. There is a metalwork room and a room containing wood carvings. There is also a weapon exhibit. The museum is open Wed to Mon, 10 am to 5 pm (4 pm in the winter).

Boudhanath

One of the largest stupas in South Asia is located at Boudhanath. It is the focal point for Tibetan Buddhism in Nepal. Around the stupa there is an entire village, inhabited mainly by Tibetans. Dilgo

Kyentse's Gompa is the most interesting monastery at Boudhanath.

Pashupatinath Temple and Area

It is said that Lord Siva came here because it was a perfect place for a holiday. Pashupatinath means "Lord of the Animals." Worship has been going on here for at least 1500 years, and there was a Siva temple here at least as far back as 879 AD. The present temple was built by King Bhupalendra Malla in 1653. It has a two-tiered gold-plated roof, silver doors, and fine quality wood carvings on its pagoda construction. Pashupatinath is on the way to Boudhanath, so both can be visited on the same day.

The Bagmati River flows next to the temple, and the Arya Ghat cremation grounds are near the temple. The Bagmati is considered holy because it flows into the Ganges. The ashes of persons cremated are sprinkled into the waters of the Bagmati, eventually to be carried to the Ganges. Non-Hindus are not allowed in the temple, but there is a good view from across the river.

Even if you cannot go into the temple, it is still worth going, because it is an ancient and interesting place. There are many temples in the area. The 6th century Bachhareshwari Temple, dedicated to Siva's consort Parvati, is south of the cremation ghats, on the western bank of the river. Further south are the Raj Rajeshwari and Nawa Durga Temples.

From across the river, on the west bank, you can get a good view of the Pashupatinath Temple. If you cross the river at the cremation grounds and then go south, which is to your right, you come to the Rama Temple. Further south is the Rama Janaki Temple, which has deities of Sita, Rama, and Hanuman. Janaki is another name for Sita. Next to this temple is the Lakshmi-Narayana Temple, which has a statue of Garuda in front of it.

Across the river and up the hill is the interesting Gorakhnath complex. To the southeast of this temple is the Vishswa-rupa Temple, which is dedicated to the universal form of Lord Vishnu.

If you continue on the path from the Gorakhnath Temple down the hill to the river, you reach the Guhyeshwari Temple, which is dedicated to goddess Kali. When Lord Siva was carrying away the body of Parvati after she burned herself to death, her yoni, the female sexual symbol, which is the counterpart of the *linga*, fell here. Non-Hindus cannot enter this temple. From Guhyeshwari Temple you can return to Pashupatinath or continue on to Boudhanath, which is about a km away.

A four-hour guided tour of the Pashu-patinath area costs about Rs 200 ($4). Buses from Kathmandu leave from Rani Pokhari, and the stop for Pashupatinath is called Gosala. Non-Hindus cannot enter most of these temples, and this is strictly enforced. This really means non-Asian looking people.

Changu Narayan Temple

This temple is said to be the most ancient Vishnu temple in the Kathmandu Valley. The original temple was built around the 3rd century. The present pagoda-style temple was rebuilt in 1702. It has many old stone, wood, and metal carvings. On the struts of the temple are the ten incarnations of Vishnu. There is a sixth century stone statue of the universal form of Lord Vishnu and another of Lord Vamana. A life-size Garuda, the carrier of Lord Vishnu, kneels before the temple. Garuda is said to date from the 5th century.

During the Mila Punhi festival, held on the full moon day of the month of Magh (Jan/Feb), the silver *kalash* of the Deity is carried in procession to be greeted by the goddess Kumari at the Taleju Temple, in Kathmandu.

The Changu Narayan Temple is a couple of hours drive east of Kathmandu (22 km). It is north of Bhaktapur (4 km). It is on a hill overlooking the valley. To walk here from Bhaktapur takes about two hours. The walk is not difficult except for the last climb near the temple. If you walk down from Nagarkot to Bhak-tapur you can stop at this temple on the way.

Kathmandu Durbar Square

There are more than 50 temples and shrines within a few blocks here. This is the site of the old palace of the king of Nepal. Durbar means "palace".

The ancient buildings here are interesting, and this is probably the most visited place in Kathmandu. There is a Krishna Temple here with a beautiful Deity of Krishna, but non-Hindus are not allowed in the temple. The three-storied Jagannatha Temple is also dedicated to Lord Krishna. There is a Hanuman Temple and many other temples in the square. Kastha Mandap is a wooden temple from which Kathmandu gets its name. It is located in the southwest corner of the square.

At the far end of the square is the **Kumari Bahal**, where the Kumari, or the "living goddess," lives. She is considered a living incarnation of the goddess Parvati by the Hindus and an incarnation of Tara by the Buddhist. She is selected from a group of three-to-five years old girls by esoteric rites. When she reaches puberty, another girl takes her place. During her period as the goddess she lives in seclusion. Visitors are allowed to enter the courtyard, from where the Kumari may sometimes be seen standing by a first floor window. You are expected to give a small donation, and no photographs are allowed.

The **Hanuman Dhoka** is the former Royal Palace of the Malla kings of Kantipur and sequentially of the Shah dynasty. There are several complexes connected together, that were built in the 16th century. King Pratap Malla enlarged the original building in the 17th century, adding many of the temples. The royal residence is now located at Narayan Hitti Palace, in the northern part of Kathmandu. The old palace, however, still has its importance, as various ceremonies, including the king's coronation, are held here. Suvarnadwar is the main entrance to the Durbar, or palace. To the left of the palace entrance is a 17th century statue of Hanuman.

There is a Lord Narasimha statue made of black stone inlaid with silver in the left side of the lobby. The 3-storied temple dedicated to Taleju is by the Malla palace.

Other Places

The **Balaju Water Gardens**, northwest of Kathmandu in the town of Balaju, has fountains, gardens, and fish ponds. There is a copy of the Lord Vishnu Deity at Budhanilkantha here. The king of Nepal is not allowed to see the Deity at Budhanilkantha, so he comes here to see this Vishnu Deity.

Gokarna Jungle Resorts, two km past Boudhanath Stupa, can be toured from on top of an elephant. It is open daily, 7 am to 6 pm. **Jawalakhel Zoo**, Patan, has Bengal tigers and a snow leopard. You can have an elephant ride inside the zoo. It is open from 10 am to 5 pm.

Mountain Flight

You can take a plane ride over the Himalayas for $99. The ride goes over Mt. Everest and takes about an hour. It leaves around 9 am, because the morning is usually the clearest time of the day. You can arrange a ticket with most travel agents. The airlines that conduct flights are Everest Air, Nepal Airways, and Necon Air. The flights are every day from September to May. From June to the beginning of September it is usually too cloudy to see anything.

Antiques

There are many antique shops on Durbar Marg and in Patan. Many objects sold as antiques are not real antiques, but are made to look old by putting some chemical on them or burying them for several months. This does not mean that there is nothing worth buying, but you should not pay extra for these supposed antiques.

It is illegal to take Nepali antiques, over 100 years old, out of the country. It is legal to export Tibetan, Indian, and Bhutanese antiques if you get an export stamp. If an object looks even remotely like an antique it should be cleared with the Department of Archaeology (213-701), Babar Mahal, as your baggage can be thoroughly searched by customs when you leave the country.

Where To Stay

There are no shortage of hotels in Kathmandu—from basic to luxury. Hotel prices in Kathmandu are a bit higher than the same hotels in India. This section divides the hotels into lower, middle, and higher. Lower price rooms range from $2 (Rs 100) to $10 (Rs 500). Middle-class rooms range from $10 (Rs 500) to $40 (Rs 2000). Higher priced rooms go from $40 to $160 or more. Many hotels have different priced rooms, some in the lower range and others in the middle range. These hotels have been placed in the lower group.

Middle and higher priced hotels all charge a luxury tax, between 10% and 15%, depending on the star rating of the hotel. Most higher priced hotels quote their rates in US dollars and only accept payment in foreign currency or Nepali rupees with an encashment receipt.

As many hotels have new additions and are constantly making renovations, it is a good idea to ask to see a few different rooms in a hotel, as there can be a big difference between rooms in the same hotel. One may be very gloomy and another very agreeable.

The Thamel area is the happening place to stay in Kathmandu. It is full of budget and good middle class hotels. It is a good sized area, north of the center of town and Durbar Square.

There are no shortage of touts (hotel commission agents) at the airport and bus station to greet you when you arrive. They may get as much as 50% or more of the price of the room for bringing you to the hotel of their choice. This commission will be added onto your bill, so avoid them if you can. You can always take a taxi to a restaurant in Thamel, ask to leave your bags there and then go find a room from there.

The busy months of the year are Oct, Nov, Feb, March, and April. Outside of the peak seasons prices are negotiable, and you can sometimes get a 50% discount. Many hotels offered me a 40% or 50% discount off their quoted price in August. To get a discount you have to first act like you are not really interested and then wait for them to offer a discount as you are leaving. If you are not offered a discount, you can just ask for one.

Where to Stay Lower – Thamel

The *Kathmandu Guest House* (413632), Thamel Area, is a good and extremely popular place that has rooms with common bath for $9/12 ($6/10 during the off-season) and $17/20 to $25/30 for a room with attached bath. A 12% tax is added to the bill. You receive a 10% discount if you stay more than seven days in the higher priced rooms. This is a highly recommended place. It is so famous that it is the central landmark for the area. It is centrally located, it has a pleasant garden, a storage area for luggage, money changing facilities, travel facilities, and a phone office. There is also a first-class lobby, which is a good place to meet fellow travellers. Most of the rooms are clean and well-maintained, but it is a good idea to ask to see a few rooms, as many of them are different. During the busy season you may have to book a room one month in advance.

Right next door is the popular *Takche Peak Guest House* (01-215-739), which has rooms for $4/5 (Rs 200/250). The *Ned Kelly Guest House*, Thamel, has rooms that are a good value for $3/4 (Rs 150/200). The *Hotel Star* (01-414-000), by the Kathmandu Guest House in Thamel, has basic rooms with common bath for $4 and with attached bath for $8. It could be used if the Kathmandu Guest House is full. The *Pheasant Lodge* (01-417-416), further down the side-road from the *Hotel Star*, is a good-valued cheaper place with rooms for $3/4. It is often full. It has a nice courtyard and is situated down an alley, so it is quiet. A little north and around the corner from the Kathmandu Guest House is the *Capital Guest House* (414-150), Thamel, which has rooms for Rs 150/200 and Rs 250/300 with bath.

The *Marco Polo Guest House* (01-227-914), Tridevi Marg in Thamel, has good rooms for $3/4 with common bath and $5/6 with bath. The rooms in the back are the best. It is a good place, and I would suggest it. *My Mom's House* (01-417-184), Thamel, has clean rooms for $3/4 with common bath and $5/6 with bath. It can be noisy up to 10 pm. The *Hotel Horizon* (220-904), off the main street, south of the Kathmandu Guest House, has rooms with common bath for $6 and with attached bath for $15. It is a decent value.

The *Mustang Guest House* (01-416-596), in the Paknajol area, north Thamel, is a good value with rooms during the busy season for $5/8 and $8/12 with bath. During the off-season you can get a room with bath for $3/4 (Rs 150/200). The *Lonely Planet Guest House* (412-715), north Thamel, is a decent place with rooms from Rs 150 to Rs 250. A little further north is the *Tibet Peace Guest House* (415-026), Thamel, which has rooms with bath for $7/8 up to $20. Nearby is the *Kathmandu Peace Guest House* (415-239), north Thamel, which has good rooms with a good view of the mountains for $4 and $6. It is a nice place.

The popular *Potala Guest House* (01-220-467), Chhetrapati area, has rooms for $8/12. It has a garden and hot water. The *Park Hotel* (01-211-753) has good rooms, some with a view of Swayambunath. Rooms are $4 (Rs 200) and $5/6 with bath. This place is often full. The *Shambala Guest House* (01-225-986) has a roof garden with a good view and is well-managed. Rooms are $6/8 to $10/18.

The friendly *Hotel Earth House* (01-418-436), off Tridevi Marg, in Bhagwan Bahal area in northeast Thamel, is a recommended place with rooms from $4/6 up to $10/16. It has a rooftop garden. The

rooms in the back are the best, so you should ask to see a few rooms before choosing one. You can get a good discount in the off-season. The *Souvenir Guest House* (410-277), further north, past Hotel Earth House, has a good location and a garden. Rooms are $4/6 with common bath and $8/12 with bath.

Where to Stay – Freak St

The Freak St and Durbar Square area have a bunch of really cheap hotels. Most of these places have seen better days, as most of the tourists now stay further north in the Thamel area. The popular *Century Lodge* (01-215-769), Freak St, is a good-valued place with rooms for $3 with bath. The *Hotel Sugat* with rooms from Rs 90 to Rs 275 is one of the better places in this area. The *Kathmandu Lodge* is popular and has rooms for $3/4 and $4/5 with bath. The *Annapurna Lodge* (01-213-684), Jhochhen, is about the best of the cheaper places in the area. Rooms with bath are Rs 150/200.

Where to Stay Middle – Thamel

The *Hotel Garuda* (01-416-776), Thamel, near the Kathmandu Guest House, is clean, well-managed, and has a good view of the mountains from the roof. A room with a bathroom and hot water is $13/17 up to $18/22. It is a recommended good-valued place. *Hotel Blue Diamond*, (01-226320), Jyatha, is a nice place that has rooms with A/C, or heat in the winter, for $16/18. It is quiet and a suggested place. On the off-season you can negotiate for a lower price, especially if you stay there a while.

The *Hotel Thamel* (01-417-643), just north of the Thamel taxi-stand, has standard rooms for $20 and $30 for a deluxe A/C room. You can bargain down the price during the off-season. The *Hotel*

Namche (01-413-503) has a rooftop garden and nice rooms for $20/25.

The well-managed quiet *Mustang Holiday Inn* (01-226-794), Jyatha, Thamel, down a side-road, has good rooms for $8/12 with common bath and $16/20 up to $30 with bath. You can bargain down the price, maybe 30%. It is a recommended place. Next door is the *Imperial Guest House* (229-339), which is a good place with rooms for $7/15. The *Hotel Utse* (01-228-952), Jyatha, Thamel, is new and a good value. It is very clean and comfortable and is a recommended place with rooms for $13/20 up to $22/29.

In the Chhetrapati area, south of Thamel, there are two good places. The *Tibet Guest House* (214-383) is a recommended place that has rooms with common bath for $7, with bath for $10, and with A/C for $20. It is a good place. The *Hotel Trans Himalayan* (214-683) is also a good place with rooms for $12/18 up $25.

Where to Stay Middle – Other Areas

The *Hotel Ambassador* (01-413-641), Lazimpat, just north of Thamel near the Indian Embassy, has an assortment of good rooms for $25/30 and $35 for a suite. You can get a good discount during the off-season. The rooms on the west side of the building are quieter because they are off the main street. You should ask to see some rooms before you choose one.

The *Hotel Vajra* (01-272-719), Bijeshwari area, going toward Swayambhunath, is an excellent place with Newari architecture using traditional materials and design. It is surrounded by gardens and trees and has a rooftop garden. It is a recommended good-valued place with a peaceful location. It has an

art gallery and a theater in which classical Nepalese dance is performed. Rooms are $33/38 up to $53/61. There are rooms without bath for $14/18. During the off-seasons you may be able to get 30% off the price of the room. The only problem with this place is that it is out of the way and it can be hard to get a taxi from here.

Where to Stay – Higher

The top-end hotels cost from $40 to more than $175. Most of them are away from the center of town, but they usually offer free bus service into town.

Where to Stay – Central

The *Yak & Yeti Park Royal Hotel* (01-226-635), Durbar Marg, is the most famous place in town. It is set off from the road in a quiet area of town. Part of the hotel used to be a Rana palace and now has the Naachgaar Theatre Restaurant in it. Carved wood and local textiles are used in the well-designed and well-maintained rooms. Rooms start at $150/160 and go up to $225.

The new three-star *Hotel Manang* (01-410-993), Paknajol, Thamel, is a very good place. It is well-designed and some rooms have a great view of the surrounding mountains. Standard rooms are $35/50 and the deluxe rooms are $65/75. The nearby *Hotel Marshyangdi* (01-414-105) is also a good place with standard rooms for $50/60 and deluxe rooms for $65/75.

The five-star *Hotel de l'Annapurna* (01-221-711) has a large swimming pool and is centrally located on Durbar Marg. The rooms overlooking the pool are the best. You should ask for one of the recently refurnished rooms. Rooms go for $125/135. Nearby is the *Hotel Woodland* (01-220-123), which has a swimming pool and rooms for $60/65.

The *Hotel Malla*, Lekhnath Marg, at

the northern end of Thamel, has a spacious garden and good rooms with large windows for $100/120. The *Hotel Shanker* (977/1-410-151), Lazimpat, is a former Rana palace with a large well-kept garden, set back from the road. Ask to see an assortment of rooms, as they are totally different. Rooms are $90/105.

Other Areas

The five-star *Soaltee Holiday Inn Crowne Plaza* (01-272-550), in the western part of town, is a large hotel with rooms for $150/160. The *Hotel Everest* (01-220-567), in the eastern part of town by the airport, has some great views, especially from the northern side of the hotel. Rooms are $175/200. The *Hotel Shangri-La* (01-412-999), north of Thamel, is an excellent place with first-class rooms and service. It has an excellent garden with a pool. Rooms are $95/110.

The *Dwarika's Hotel* (01-470-999), near the airport and Pashupatinath, is built in the traditional Newar style. The owner has collected thousands of antique carvings from buildings in the area and built them into the hotel. It is like a cross between a hotel and a museum. The large high standard rooms cost $70 to $90.

Places To Eat

Many of the vegetarian restaurants serve eggs. Often the noodles also contain eggs, so you should ask about this. *Tripti Restaurant*, Ranjana Cinema, just off New Rd, across from the Nepal Bank, is a good recommended Indian style pure vegetarian restaurant.

Mangalore Coffee House, on Durbar Marg by the corner, is a cheap South Indian vegetarian restaurant.

Three minutes down the road from the Kathmandu Guest House, on the left in Thamel, is the *Skala Restaurant,* which has a peaceful garden. *Nirmala*, a three minute walk north of the Kathmandu Guest House, is a good place. The noodles in the lasagne have eggs in them. The *Stupa View Restaurant*, on the third floor of a building on the north side of the Boudhanath Stupa, has among other things, brown rice and Greek salads on its menu.

Travel

Air There are regular flights to New Delhi ($142) and Calcutta on Indian Airlines and RNAC (Nepal Air). RNAC has flights to Bombay, Dubai, Hong Kong, Bangkok, Singapore, London, Frankfurt, and Colombo. Indian Airlines has a daily flight to Varanasi ($75). There is a 25% discount for travelers under 30 years of age on flights between Kathmandu and India.

Thai Airways flies from Los Angeles to Kathmandu via Bangkok. Singapore Airlines flies from Los Angeles via Singapore to Kathmandu. Lufthansa flies from several USA cities via Frankfurt to Kathmandu.

There is a Rs 600 ($12) departure tax when you fly to SAARC countries and a Rs 700 tax to all other international countries.

You should check-in at least two hours early for international flights because many flights are overbooked. You can be bumped off a flight if you arrive too late, even if you have a confirmed ticket. You should reconfirm your flight within 72 hours of departure. Domestic flights should be booked at least a week in advance. Many domestic flights are cancelled because of the weather, so you should not be too pushed for time.

The airport is 4 km east of Kathmandu. A taxi from the airport costs about

Rs 200. There is a prepaid taxi stand at the airport, where you pay a fixed price in advance. Many hotels have a courtesy pick-up service for their guests. There are a lot of touts (hotel commission agents) at the airport who want to bring you to a hotel of their choice, so they can get a good commission on what you pay for a room.

I have heard that the X-ray machines at the Kathmandu Airport are not film safe.

Flights to Janakpur cost $55 and to Pokhara $61.

Bus Most of the buses arriving from outside Kathmandu Valley arrive at the New Bus Station, north of town. It is about a 15-minute taxi (Nepali Rs 70) or auto-rickshaw (Nepali Rs 40) ride to Thamel or Durbar Marg. If you arrive in Kathmandu on a tourist bus from Pokhara or Chitwan, you will most likely be let off at the junction of Kantipath and Tridevi Marg, not far from the Thamel area.

Travel Between India and Nepal

There are several ways to arrive from India on the ground. Most take a long time (24 hours or more), but are cheap. **Sunauli** is a popular crossing point for travelers coming from Delhi or Varanasi. It takes 16 hours by train to go from Delhi to Gorakhpur and 7 hours from Varanasi to Gorakhpur. From Gorakhpur to the border towns of Sunauli/Bhairawa (Indian Rs 30) is a three hours bus ride. In Gorakhpur you will be approached by travel agents to take special buses to Kathmandu. They may try to charge you Rs 250 one way from India to Kathmandu. The actual cost is Indian Rs 30 to Sunauli and another Indian Rs 80 to get from Sunauli to Kathmandu, or a to-

tal of Indian Rs 110. I know someone who paid Indian Rs 650 to go round trip from Gorakhpur to Kathmandu. The actual price is Indian Rs 220. There is absolutely no reason or advantage to book a bus in Gorakhpur to Kathmandu with a travel agent in Gorakhpur.

There are direct tourist buses from Varanasi to Sunauli (Rs 100, 9 hr).

When you cross the border at Sunauli it is just a few minutes walk to the bus station where you get the bus to Kathmandu (Nepali Rs 118). Buses leave regularly in the morning up to around 11 am and from 4.30 to 7.30 pm. The bus ride from Sunauli to Kathmandu takes 9 to 12 hours. You could stop at Lumbini, the birthplace of Buddha, after crossing the border. It is only 22 km from Bhairawa.

You can get a train from either the New Delhi (15 hr) or Agra Fort Stations (16 hr) to Gorakhpur. Frequent buses depart from the old bus stand in **Mathura** to Agra Fort Bus Stand which is a few minutes, rickshaw ride (Rs 10) from the Agra Fort Station, where the trains to Gorakhpur depart.

From **Gorakhpur** it can be hard to get a same day train to either Delhi or Agra. If you get the 8 am bus from Sunauli you will arrive in Gorakhpur at 11.30 am. There is a train to Agra at 1.30 pm, but there is a good chance by the time you arrive there will be no tourist quota tickets available. From the travel agents across from the railway station you can purchase a ticket to Agra for Rs 300. The actual price was Rs 165. It is not a good idea to purchase a train ticket from the travel agents in Sunauli, as there is a good chance that a mistake will be made and you will be charged a higher commission. If you want to get an immediate train out of Gorakhpur, most of the travel agents across the street need only a couple of hours to get a quick ticket. It is a very bad idea, however, to purchase a bus ticket to Kathmandu from them, as it is easier to buy your own ticket at the bus station. Then you can also choose what bus you want to take at the border.

You can also cross the border at **Raxaul/Birganj** via Patna, Bihar, if you are coming from the east, such as Calcutta. The bus from Patna to Raxaul takes about 7 hours. From Birgani a direct bus to Kathmandu takes 11 hours. There are both day and night buses. There is some interesting scenery on the way.

From **Darjeeling** you can take a bus to Siliguri, then another bus to Raniganj, which is at the border of India. This part of the trip takes about 6 hours. You then cross the border to **Kakarbhitta** and from there get a 17-hour bus to Kathmandu. It could be a good idea to break your journey at Janakpur, the birthplace of Lord Rama's wife, Sita, as it is basically on the way and is a nice town.

Only if you are in a major hurry or plan to book an Indian railway train is it a good idea to use a travel agent in Kathmandu. *Student Travel & Tours* in Thamel, *Everest Travel Service* on Ganga Path, and *Yeti Travels* on Durbar Marg are long-standing travel agents in Kathmandu.

It is usually best to arrange your own transportation, rather than go through a travel agent. A travel agent will charge you a higher price (maybe three times the normal price) and just put you on the transportation that you could have easily arranged yourself. You will also be restricted to whatever they have arranged for you and will not be able to adjust your situation. Also I have heard and seen that many travel agents will outright lie. For instance, they will say that they will book

you a first-class ticket from Gorakhpur to New Delhi, connecting from a bus from Kathmandu. When you arrive, there will only be a second-class ticket waiting for you, even though you paid for a first-class ticket. When you pick up the ticket, the travel agent will tell you that he was told to give you that ticket by the travel agent in Kathmandu. What can you do?

KATHMANDU VALLEY

BHAKTAPUR (BHADGAON)

Bhaktapur was originally built by Raja Ananda Malla in the 12th century. There are many ancient temples and an ancient palace in the Durbar Square here. It costs about Rs 300 to go by taxi from Kathmandu to Bhaktapur or Rs 650 round trip with a stay of three hours. For a full day out, you could go to Bhaktapur in the morning, then north of Bhaktapur to the Changu Narayana Temple, and then to Nagarkot for a good view of the Himalayan sunset. This is a very interesting town.

Patan Durbar Square (Lalitpur)

There are several temples and other interesting buildings in Patan Durbar Square. There is a Royal Palace and the Krishna Temple (17th century) here. Many scenes from *Ramayana* and *Mahabharata* are carved on the Krishna Temple. Patan is on the other side of the Bagmati River from Kathmandu. It takes about twenty minutes to get to Patan from the Thamel area and costs about Rs 100 by taxi.

Mountain Ranges

The Himalayan Mountains stretch across 800 kilometres of northern Nepal and are known as the Nepal Himalayas. There are more than 250 peaks that are higher than 6,000m (18,000 ft). Nepal has 22 of the world's 31 mountains over 7,600m and eight of the 14 highest mountains, including Mount Everest (Sagarmatha). The Siwalek and Churia Hills, which would be mountains anywhere else, run parallel to the Himalayas, north of Kathmandu.

Nagarkot

Nagarkot is 32 kilometres east of Kathmandu at an elevation of 2,175m. On a clear day you can see Mt. Everest (Sagarmatha) from Nagarkot. You can also see Manaslu (8,463m), Ganesh Himal (7,111m), and Langtang (7,246m). It is best to view the mountains in the early morning, because it is more likely to be clear. You can go to Nagarkot in the afternoon and stay overnight and view the mountains at sunrise.

Nagarkot can be much colder than Kathmandu, especially in the winter. There is a coffee shop there where you can sit inside. You can usually get a good view of the mountains between October and March.

If you plan to stay overnight it is best to book your hotel room on arrival, as they are often full later in the day. You have to pass through Bhaktapur to get here, so you could go to Bhaktapur in the early afternoon then go to Nagarkot for the sunset or to stay overnight. Tourist buses leave from Thamel at 1.30 pm (Rs 110 one way and Rs 185 return). You can get a ticket at most travel agents. A round-trip taxi costs about Rs 1000.

Kakani

Kakani is located 29 km northwest of Kathmandu at an elevation of 1982m. You can see the northwestern Himalayan ranges from Kakani. The sunset is an interesting site here. You can see Ganesh

Himal (7,111m), Manaslu (8,163m), Garuishanker (7,134m), and Annapurna I (8,091m). The one and a half hour journey from Kathmandu goes up a beautiful scenic road. There is one hotel here with rooms for about $25.

JANAKPUR

Janakpur is the birthplace of Sita, daughter of King Janaka and the wife of Lord Rama. It is said to be the site of Lord Rama and Sita's wedding. Lord Rama won Sita's hand in marriage by picking up Lord Siva's bow and breaking it here. Janakpur is charged with a devotional mood and is an interesting holy city to visit.

Janakpur was the capital of the ancient state of Mithila, which used to be part of India.

It is located 128 km southeast of Kathmandu next to the Indian border. For the most part motorized traffic is banned from the city center, and there is almost no tourist hustle. So it is a peaceful place.

You can stop in Janakpur on the way from Kakarbhitta to Kathmandu, as it is just 30 km south of the Mahendra Highway, which is the road you take to get from Kathmandu to Kakarbhitta.

Information and Orientation

There is a **tourist office** (041-20755) at Bhanu Chowk. It is open from 10 am to 5 pm, Monday to Friday. It closes an hour earlier from November to January. The **Nepal Air** (RNAC) office (10 am to 4 pm) is right next to the tourist office.

Janakpur is a maze of mostly narrow streets, so it is difficult to know what direction you are going in. You can get your bearings from the telecommunications tower and the large concrete water tank. Janaki Mandir is just south of the water tank. The bus station is southwest of the temple by the telecommunications tower. The train station is a twenty-minute walk northeast of the water tank.

Janaki Mandir (Temple)

Janaki is another name for Sita, the wife of Rama. This massive marble temple in the center of town was built in 1911 by an Indian queen. It is believed to be where King Janaka found Sita lying in a ploughed field. The Deities in the temple are Sita, Rama, and Rama's brothers—Laksmana, Bharata, and Satrughna. This temple is open to everyone. You can climb the stairs to the roof of the outer building and get a good view of the courtyard.

Rama Sita Vivaha Mandapa

This is a new temple that honors the wedding of Sita and Rama. Lord Rama and Sita wear full make-up and wedding attire. It is next to the Janaki Mandir where Sita and Rama are said to have been married.

Rama Mandir

This Nepalese pagoda style temple was built in 1882. It is southeast of the Janaki Mandir, and right next to Dhanush Sagar. This temple is the centerpoint for the Rama Navami festival.

Dhanush & Ganga Sagar Tanks

These tanks are located at the spot where one of three pieces of Lord Siva's bow fell when Lord Rama broke it. Including these tanks, there are 24 sacred tanks in the city. Dhanush Sagar is next to the Rama Mandir, just southeast of the Janaki Mandir.

Sankat Mochan Temple

This temple is dedicated to Hanuman and is also called the Big Monkey Temple. Hanuman is worshipped here in the form of a live rhesus monkey. The monkey is kept in a cage and constantly fed by the pilgrims. Sankat Mochan means one who relieves all troubles.

Dhanusa

Dhanusa is the place where Rama is said to have strung Siva's bow. It is about 15 km north of Janakpur.

Festivals

The **Bibhaha (Vivah) Panchami** festival reenacts the wedding of Rama and Sita. Over 100,000 pilgrims come for this festival. There is a procession with elephants, horses, decorated chariots, and beating drums. It is on the fifth day of the waxing moon in November or early December.

Rama's appearance day, in March-April, is also an important festival that draws over 100,000 people. There is an annual one day *parikrama* (circumambulation) of the city in the first week of March. Many people offer prostrated obeisances along the entire eight km route.

Where To Stay

The *Hotel Welcome* (041-20224) is the only decent place to stay in town. The rooms are bad, but there is no real competition. They have rooms with common bath for $2, with bath for $3/4, and with A/C for $9/12. Ask to see several rooms, as some are really bad. The *Hotel Rama*, at the edge of town, has featureless rooms for $3/4 (Rs 150/200).

If you plan to come here during a major festival, you should book a room months in advance.

Travel

Air You can fly from Kathmandu one

way for $55. There are three flights a week.

Bus From Kathmandu there are both day and overnight private and government buses to Janakpur that cost about $3 (Rs 150, 12 hr). Most of the buses to Janakpur leave in the early morning or late afternoon from the New Bus Station, about 15 minutes north of the Thamel area of Kathmandu. Even though Janakpur is close to the border, foreign tourists are not allowed to cross the border at this point.

Private buses depart from Janakpur to Kakarbhitta, on the extreme eastern Nepal border, on the way to Darjeeling. They depart every half hour from 4.30 to 10 am and cost Rs 125 ($2.50). The trip takes 7 hours. The bus station is a short rickshaw ride from the city center.

MUKTINATH AND AREA

Muktinath means the "Lord of Liberation," which is another name of Lord Vishnu. There is a Vishnu temple here called Jiwala Mayi, which has a tiered roof. This temple is one of the 108 Vishnu Divya Desam Temples and is considered to be a very important temple. Near the main temple is another temple with sacred natural gas flames that are mentioned in the *Mahabharata*. These flames burn on rock and water. If you give a small donation to the priest they will show you the flames, which are behind a curtain. There are 108 waterspouts here, from which sacred water flows. Muktinath is at an elevation of 12,000 feet (3,749m). It can be very cold here, so it is best to come here in the summertime.

Damodara Kund (also called the Forbidden Lake) is a nine or ten day journey from Muktinath. It can only be reached in the late summer. This is considered to be the source of the Gandaki River and a major source of *shalagram-shilas*.

Shalagram-shilas are self-manifested Deities of Lord Vishnu, appearing as small stones. They are considered non-different from Lord Vishnu and His incarnations. These forms of Lord Vishnu require no installation ceremony. They are considered always non-different from Lord Vishnu Himself. Lord Caitanya told Gopal Bhatta Goswami to come here from Vrindavana to find Sri Hari in the form of a *shalagram-shila*.

In the *Bhavisya Purana*, Lord Krishna says to His devotee, Tulasi: "In the form of small stones, I live always on the banks of the Gandhaki River. The millions of worms who live in that place adorn those stones with the sign of My cakra, by carving Them with their small teeth."

Where To Stay

There are several guest houses in Muktinath. The *Himalaya Hotel* and *Hotel Muktinath* are about the best. On the way from Jomsom to Muktinath you pass the town of Jharkot, which has places to stay. The *Hotel Jarkot* and *Himali Hotel*, which has solar heating, are passable places.

In Jomsom, The *Alka Guest House* is one of the better places.

Travel

To get to Muktinath you first have to go to Jomsom, which is about 250 km northwest of Kathmandu. Muktinath is about a half hour past the small village of Ranipowa, a days walk from Jomsom. Muktinath and the Gandaki River are visited by people doing the famous Annapurna circuit trek.

Air There is a direct flight from Kathmandu to Jomsom ($120). There are also flights from Pokhara to Jomsom ($50, 3 flights daily, weather permitting).

Bus and Trek From Pokhara you can take a plane to Jomsom, and from there it is a one-day walk to Muktinath. Many people walk to Muktinath via Jomsom from Pokhara. There are some spectacular views along the way. This is the most traveled trekking route in Nepal. A guide is not necessary, and the food and lodging are at a relatively high standard. The round trip from Pokhara to Muktinath takes two weeks, but there are shorter and longer variations of this trek. From Pokhara you can take a bus to Birethanti and from there start the trek. For this trek you need warm clothes and rain gear.

If you cannot make the walk from Jomsom to Muktinath, you can ride up on a pony (Rs 1200 up and back). A couple of hours from Jomsom is the interesting medieval fortress town of Kagbeni. It takes about 6 hours to walk down from Muktinath to Jomsom.

Ridi Bazaar

This town is at the confluence of the Kali Gandaki (a tributary to the Ganges) and the Ridi Rivers. It is a holy town because *shalagram-shilas* are found here. There is an important Vishnu temple here dedicated to Lord Hrishikesh. The Deity in this temple is a large *shalagram-shila*. It is said that if you fast and worship here and then take bath in the Kali Gandaki, all your sins are taken away. Ridi Bazaar is 28 km from Tansen by bus (2 hr), or you can walk 13 km off the road to get there from Tansen. Tansen is 75 km northwest of Pokhara.

POKHARA

Pokhara is a big tourist spot, because it has a beautiful lake and great mountain scenery. It is 200 km west of Kathmandu, close to the 8000m Annapurna and Dhaulagiri mountain ranges. Machhapuchhare (fishtail peak), which is one of the most beautiful mountains in the world, is right next to the city. It is not as cold here in the winter as Kathmandu, because it is at a lower elevation. Near Pokhara is Sarangkot, where you can get an excellent view of the mountains.

On a small island in the middle of the lake is the **Varahi Temple**, dedicated to Varaha, the boar incarnation of Lord Vishnu. **Bhimsen Temple** is located on the main road in the northern part of the bazaar. In the north part of town, on a small hill, is the **Binde Basini Temple**. In this temple is Durga (Parvati), manifested in the form of a *shalagram*.

The **Seti Gandaki River** flows through Pokhara, but in some places it flows completely underground. *Seti* means white, as the water has turned a milky color because of the limestone in the soil. You can get a good view of the river at the north end of the bazaar, from the bridge near the old Mission Hospital. You can get an even better view of the river from the other side of the airport runway.

Where To Stay – Damside, Pardi

The *Hotel Pagoda* (061-21802) is a very good value with clean rooms for $3/4 and $9/12 with bath. The *Hotel Peaceful* has rooms for $3/4 and more comfortable rooms with bathrooms for $7/9. The *Hotel Pokhara View* (061-20189) has rooms with common bath for $5/6 and rooms with bath for $10/12. Some of the rooms have great views.

The *Ashok Guest House* (061-612-0374) is a recommended place with a beautiful garden. The rooms are $20/25 with a view and $15/20 without a view. From the park next door there is a good view of the mountains and lake. The

Mona Lisa is about the same standard as the Ashok with rooms for $20/25.

The *Hotel Tragopan* (061-21708) has good rooms for $35/40. This hotel has a nice garden, and there are good views from the comfortable rooms. The *Dragon Hotel* has comfortable rooms for $40/50.

Where To Stay – Lakeside

The *Dharma House* and *View Corner Lodge* have decent cheap rooms for Rs 125. The well-managed *New Pokhara Lodge* (061-20875) has rooms for $12/18. The *Gurkha Lodge* is a small clean place with good rooms for $14. The *Stay Well Guest House* is a small clean place with good rooms for $14/24.

The *Hotel Kantipur* (061-20886) has a good location, but it is somewhat run down. Rooms are $18/24 and $45/55 for a deluxe room. The *Hotel Osho* is a good place with comfortable rooms for $8/12.

The *Hotel Hungry-Eye* (061-20908) is a popular place with rooms for $24/34. The nearby *Snowland Hotel* (061-20384) is another popular place with rooms for $25/30. The *Tranquillity Lodge* (061-21030) has a nice garden and large good rooms for $18/28.

The *Temple Villa* (061-21203) is a clean place with a good location. The comfortable rooms are $12/18 and $18/28 with bath. The *Hotel Mountain Top* (061-20779) has good rooms with a great view for $24/32 and $35/45.

The *Base Camp Resort* (061-21226) is a good option if the Fish Tail is booked. It is a first-class place with a good garden and rooms for $51/55.

Where To Stay – High

The *Fish Tail Lodge* (977/612-0071) has a great location. This place has a beautiful garden. From the garden, when the sky is clear, you get a view of the Annapurnas and Machhapuchhare look-

ing over the Phewa Lake. The only problem with this place is that not all the rooms have views, so you should request a room with a view. The luxurious rooms cost $75/80. This is the place to stay in Pokhara.

Travel

Air There are two or three Royal Nepal Airline flights a day from Kathmandu. It takes about 35 minutes. You have a great view of the Himalayan range on the right hand side of the plane when traveling from Kathmandu to Pokhara. The fare is $61 one way. Flights from Jomsom to Muktinath cost $50.

Bus It takes about 9 hours to reach Pokhara from Kathmandu. For Rs 175 you can get a morning tourist bus that takes about seven hours. You can book this bus with one of the many travel agents in Kathmandu.

Chitwan National Park

This park is 120 km southeast of Kathmandu. There are many wild animals in the park, including rhinoceros, tigers, leopards, wild boars, and crocodiles. An attempt to view these animals can be made while riding on the back of an elephant. From Kathmandu it takes a day to get here and a day to return, so you need at least three days for a trip from Kathmandu. While here you can also do a river raft trip, spending three days on the Trishuli River or Seti Khola.

LUMBINI

This is the birthplace of Buddha, Siddhartha Gautama. It is a peaceful place located in the western terai of Nepal, close to the Indian border and the towns of Bhairawa and Sunauli. Emperor Ashok (249 BC) visited Lumbini and erected an inscribed pillar on the spot of Buddha's birth. The inscription on the pillar declares that Ashoka granted Lumbini tax-free status in honor of Buddha's taking birth there.

There is a temple here dedicated to **Maya Devi**, Buddha's mother. Parts of the temple are over 2000 years old. The ornate brickwork on the west side dates to the Gupta period (4th to 7th centuries). There is a bas-relief sculpture of Buddha's birth that is said to be as old as the third century BC. There is a pond next to the temple where Maya Devi is said to have bathed before (some say after) the delivery.

There are heavily restored brick foundations of stupas and buildings, which date from the second century BC to the ninth century AD. There are two modern monasteries, one Tibetan and the other Nepali.

Buddha Jayanti (Buddha's birthday) is celebrated in April/May. The government has set aside a large area of land to build a large pilgrimage center consisting of monasteries, gardens, fountains, and a tourist village. Some work has already been done.

There is a **tourist information booth** at the site. It only takes a couple of hours to see everything.

Where To Stay

Most people come just for a day trip and usually stay the night in Bhairawa or Sunauli, 22 km away. The *Lumbini Village Lodge*, Lumbini Mehalbar, about 2 km east of the main site, has simple rooms for $3/5. The *Lumbini Hokke Hotel* (977/ 071-20236), several km north of the main site, is a luxury hotel with rooms for $90/ 130. It is managed by Japanese and mainly used by Japanese Buddhist pilgrims. It is one of the best hotels in Nepal.

Travel

Air The closest airport is in Bhairawa. There are flights from there to Kathmandu ($80) and Pokhara ($40).

Bus Every half hour there are buses from Bhairawa (2 hr, Rs 10), which is 22 km away. You have to walk one km from where the buses let you off. The last bus from Lumbini to Bhairawa is 5.30 pm. Buses from Bhairawa depart from near the main intersection, across the street from the Hotel Yeti.

A taxi is a much more convenient way to get to Lumbini than the bus. Taxis cost Rs 500 ($10) and an auto-rickshaw is Rs 250 ($5). This includes the trip there and back and two hours waiting time.

You can get a bus from Bhairawa to Kathmandu or Pokhara. There are also buses to Varanasi and Gorakhpur (where you get the train to Delhi) from Sunauli.

Bhairawa and Sunauli

Sunauli is a small really nowhere town that you have to pass through to get from Varanasi or Delhi to Nepal by bus. It is right on the Nepal/India border. Bhairawa, four km north of the border, is much bigger, but about as exciting. You may stay in Bhairawa if you are visiting nearby Lumbini (22 km). There is a good chance you will have to stop here for the night on the way between Nepal and India, as the border closes at 7 pm and many of the buses arrive after this.

Information

The **Nepal immigration** and customs offices are open from 6 am to 7 pm.

India rupees are accepted in Sunauli and Bhairawa, but not usually beyond these towns. You can **change money** at the Nepal Rastra Bank in Sunauli between 7 am and 6 pm. They change money at the official government rate, which is slightly lower than the legal commercial rate given by private banks. This bank does not re-exchange Nepalese rupees. The bank on the Indian border opens at 10 am, after the buses have left. There are also black market operators, who do not give good rates.

When you cross the border into Nepal there is a useful **tourist office**, which hands out "*A Visitor's Guide*" and "*Travellers' Information*" booklets. You can also ask them for information on the best and cheapest way to get to where you are going.

Bhairawa and Sunauli are a twenty-minute bus (Rs 3) or auto-rickshaw ride apart.

Where to Stay – Bhairawa

Shree Pashupati Lodge, Narayana Path, about a 10 minute walk from the bus stand, is a recommended budget place with rooms for $2. The best place in town is the *Hotel Yeti* (071-20551), Bank Rd and Siddhartha Highway, with rooms for $12/16. It is by a bus stand so it can be noisy. The *Hotel Himalaya Inn* (977/071-20347), on New Road, a little out of town, is a decent place with rooms for $10/14. The *Sayapati Guest House*, by the Sajha Yatayat bus stop on Bank Rd, is very basic with rooms for Rs 60/100.

Where to Stay – Sunauli

The *Nepal Guest House* has rooms with bath and hot water for $2 (Rs 100). It is probably the best place in town, which doesn't mean much in this case. You should ask to see the rooms, as it is a fairly big place and there are many different varieties. It has a decent vegetarian restaurant. The travel agent here is a fast talker and not reliable. The *Hotel Mamta*, across the street, is all right. It

has rooms with bath for Rs 100. There is a good chance you will stay here, if you got a prearranged ticket from a travel agent.

Where To East

The *Kasuti Restaurant*, by the Shree Pashupati Lodge in Bhairawa, is a very good vegetarian place and is recommended.

Travel

Everyone changes buses at the border, even if you booked a "through" ticket from a travel agent. There are no "tourist" buses to Kathmandu from Sunauli.

To/From Nepal There are four RNAC (071-20175) flights a week between Bhairawa and Kathmandu ($80).

Most buses heading north to Kathmandu or Pokhara start their journey in Sunauli and then stop in Bhairawa. So it is best to get on the bus in Sunauli to get a good seat. The bus companies' offices are near the intersection of Bank Rd and Siddartha Highway. The Sajha Yatayat booking office is opposite the Yeti Hotel. Their buses are recommended, but they only go to Kathmandu. There are several day and night buses to Kathmandu and Pokhara. The day buses are slightly quicker. The buses to Kathmandu leave in the morning and after 4.30 pm. There are no buses between 11.30 am and 4.30 pm.

To/From India You get buses to Indian cities on the India side of the border. There are direct buses to Varanasi (9 hr) for Rs 100. This bus goes through Gorakhpur. The public bus to Gorakhpur (3 hr) costs Rs 30, and the tourist buses cost Rs 35. On the tourist buses they will ask you for an extra Rs 5 for each bag you have. The public bus is less crowded and has more leg room.

From Gorakhpur, buses depart to Sunauli every half hour between 5 am to 7 pm. You need to catch the 5 am bus to get to Sunauli in time to guarantee getting a day bus to Kathmandu.

GLOSSARY

acchha - good, OK, all right.

acharya - a guru, spiritual teacher or guide, one who teaches by example.

Agni - fire; the fire-god.

ahimsa - nonviolence.

Alwars - Tamil Nadu saints who were devotees of Lord Vishnu

amrita - immortality, nectar.

ananda - happiness.

ananta - unlimited.

Annapurna - Durga manifested in her form of supplier of food.

Apsara - heavenly damsels or dancing girls who sometimes attract rishis.

arati (arotika) - ceremonial offering of incense and lamps in the temples, accompanied by bell-ringing and chanting.

Archa-vigraha - the form of God manifested through material elements, as in a statue of Krishna or Vishnu. Actually present in this form, the Lord accepts worship from His devotees.

Aristasura - a demon who took the form of a bull and tried to kill Lord Krishna.

Aryan - a follower of Vedic culture. A person whose is spiritually advanced.

Arjuna - one of the five Pandavas from the Mahabharata. Krishna spoke the *Bhagavad-gita* to him on the battlefield of Kurukshetra.

asana - seat, or throne.

Ashoka - a king who spread Buddhism in India in the 3rd century BC.

ashrama - living quarters at a temple or holy place; usually a very basic place. Another meaning has to do with the four spiritual orders of life according to the Vedic social system. This includes *brahmacarya* (student life), *grhastha* (married life), *vana-*

prastha (retired life), and *sannyasa* (renounced order).

asura - a demon, or one who is envious of God.

avatara - literally means "one who descends." A partially or fully empowered incarnation of God who comes to the world for a particular mission.

ayurvedic medicine - natural herbal medicine prescribed in the Vedas.

baba - religious master, a term of respect.

bagh - garden.

baksheesh - tip, donation, or bribe.

Balarama - the older brother of Krishna. Also known as Balabhadra or Baladeva.

Bali Maharaja - the king of the demons who gave 3 paces of land to Vamanadeva, the dwarf incarnation of Lord Vishnu, and thereby lost his entire kingdom.

bandar - monkey.

banyan tree - a sacred tree of the fig family with self-rooting branches.

bazaar - market, shopping area.

Bhadrakali - another name of Durga.

Bhagavad-gita - Song of God. This is the sacred scripture in which Lord Krishna, the Supreme Personality of Godhead, instructs Arjuna about spiritual life and the importance of devotional service. This is considered the main spiritual scripture of India, as the *Bible* is considered in the Christian religion.

Bhagiratha - the king who performed austerities to bring the Ganges to earth to save his ancestors.

Bhairava - the terrifying aspect of Lord Siva, who chopped off the fifth head of Brahma.

bhajana-kutir - a place where a saintly person does personal mediation.

bhakta - devotee.

bhakti - devotional service to God.

Brahma - the first created being in the universe. Directed by Vishnu, he creates all life forms in the universes. He also rules the mode of passion.

Bharata - half-brother of Rama, he ruled Ayodhya when Rama was in exile.

Bhima - one of the Pandavas, known for his strength and strong appetite.

Bhudevi - consort of Lord Vishnu.

Bo (Bodhi) **tree** - the tree under which Buddha attained enlightenment.

brahmana (Brahmin) - a teacher, a member of the highest order in Vedic society according to occupational divisions.

brahmacari - celibate student, first of the four *asramas*.

Buddha - the founder of Buddhism who lived during the 5th century BC.

Caitanya-caritamrita - biography of Sri Caitanya Mahaprabhu written and compiled by Krishnadasa Kaviraja Goswami.

Caitanya Mahaprabhu - He appeared in Navadvipa, West Bengal, in the late 15th century and inaugurated the congregational chanting of the holy names of the Lord. Lord Caitanya is understood by Gaudiya Vaishnavas to be Lord Krishna Himself.

cantonment - former British administrative area of a city or town.

Chakra - disc weapon of Lord Vishnu. On the top of Vishnu temples there is usually a chakra.

chalo, chalo - let's go, let's go.

chance list - waiting list for an Indian Airline flight.

Chandra - the moon-god, or the moon.

chappals - sandals.

chadar - cotton or wool cloth worn on the upper half of the body, worn by temple priests during worship.

chaukidar (chowkidar) - night watchman; guard.

Cholas - South Indian rulers from the Tamil Nadu area.

choli - sari blouse.

choultry - dharamshala in the south; pilgrim accommodation.

crore - 10 million.

dacoit - a thief, particularly an armed robber.

daitya - demons who fought against the demigods.

Damodara - a name for Krishna in His form of a young child with a rope tied around His waist.

darshan - viewing the Deity.

darwaza - door.

Dasaratha - the king of Ayodhya and father of Ramachandra.

dharamshala - basic pilgrim accommodation.

dhobi - a man who washes clothes.

dhoti - a 5 yard piece of fabric, traditional Hindu men's dress.

Divya Desam temples - 108 important Vishnu temples sung about by the 12 Alwar devotees of Tamil Nadu.

Draupadi - wife of the five Pandavas brothers, her story is found in the *Mahabharata*.

Dravida - South India.

durbar - royal court, meeting place.

Durga - Lord Siva's wife in a fierce form, riding a tiger.

Ganesh - the son of Lord Siva and Parvati. He has an elephant head and is the god of prosperity (wealth) and wisdom. He has a rat for a carrier.

Ganga - another name for the sacred Ganges River. This river sprang from the toe of Lord Vishnu.

Garbhodakasayi Vishnu - He enters every universe and creates diversity.

garh - fort.

gari - vehicle.

Garuda - The bird carrier of Lord Vishnu. He is often found atop a pole facing the entrance of Vishnu temples.

ghat - steps that lead down to holy river, lake or kunda.

giri - hill.

godown - warehouse, storage room.

goonda (gunda) - hired thug.

Gopala - a name of Krishna as a young boy.

gopis - the cowherd girls of Vrinda-vana.

gopuram - highly carved, soaring tower over the gate of a temple.

goswami (gosvami) - a swami, one fully in control of his senses.

Govinda - one of Krishna's names.

gurdwara - Sikh temple.

guru - spiritual master, spiritual instructor.

Hanuman - the monkey follower and greatest devotee and servant of Lord Rama.

Hara - a name of Lord Siva.

Hari - a name of Lord Vishnu.

hathi - elephant

Hiranyakasipu - the demon king who was killed by Narasimha (the half-man, half-lion form of Lord Vishnu).

Hoysala - South Indian dynasty that ruled part of South India.

Indra - the chief demigod of heaven and presiding deity of rain.

Jagannatha - Lord of the universe. The main place of His worship is at Puri in Orissa.

Janaka - father of Sita, the wife of Rama.

ji - honorific suffix added to almost any name as a term of endearment.

Jyotir-linga - one of the 12 self-manifested Siva-lingas.

Kailasa - the home of Lord Siva in the Himalayas.

Kali - the black intense form of Lord Siva's wife. She wears a necklace of skulls.

Kali-yuga - the "Age of Quarrel and Hypocrisy." It began 5,000 years ago and lasts for a total of 432,000 years.

Kaliya Serpent - he is a snake that Krishna punished for poisoning the Yamuna River.

Kalki - He is the tenth incarnation of Lord Vishnu. He arrives on a white horse at the end of Kali-yuga to bring the world to an end.

Kanyakumari - The virgin maiden; another name of the wife of Lord Siva.

Karanodakasayi Vishnu (Maha-Vishnu) - He lies within the Causal Ocean and breathes out innumerable universes.

karma - material activities. The concept that whatever you do creates a reaction that you will receive in the future.

Kartikkeya - the son of Lord Siva. The god of war. Also known as Subrahman-ya or Skanda.

Kathakali - Keralan religious dance.

khadi - homespun cloth.

kovil - temple in Tamil Nadu.

Krishna - The Supreme Personality of Godhead; also known as Govinda or Gopala.

Ksirodakasayi Vishnu - the Super-soul; He enters into the heart of every created being and into every atom.

kumbha - pitcher.

kunda - small lake, or pond.

kurta - Indian shirts, pullover.

Kuvera (Kubera) - the god of wealth.

lakh - One hundred thousand, written as 1,00,000.

Lakshman - the younger half-brother of Rama, he went with Rama to the forest.

Laksmi (Laxmi) - Vishnu's consort;

the goddess of wealth and good fortune.

Linga (Lingam) - Phallic symbol which is used in the worship of Lord Siva.

lila - A transcendental "pastime" or activity performed by God or his devotee.

lorry - truck.

Madana-mohana - Krishna, who is the enchanter of even Cupid.

Mahabharata - the great epic history that includes the incidences leading up to and including the battle of the Pandavas and the Kauravas and Lord Krishna's narration of *Bhagavad-Gita*.

Mahadeva - Lord Siva.

mahal - palace or house.

maharaja - king, ruler, *sannyasi*..

maharani - wife of the king or the ruler in her own right.

mahatma - great soul, saintly person.

Maha-Vishnu - Lord Vishnu reclining on Adi-Sesa..

Mahisha - buffalo demon who was killed by Durga.

maidan - open square or park.

mandir - temple.

mantra - a transcendental sound or Vedic hymn, a prayer or chant.

Maratha - ruling group from Maharashtra in the 16th and 17th centuries.

marga - road.

mata - mother.

math - monastery.

maya - that which is not, unreality, deception, forgetfulness, material illusion. Under illusion a man thinks he can be happy in this temporary material world. The nature of the material world is that the more a man tries to exploit the material situation, the more he is bound by *maya*'s complexities.

mela - fair, festival.

Moghul - the Muslim dynasty of Indian Emperors starting from Babur.

moksa - liberation.

monolith - a monument, statue or temple carved out of a single stone.

monsoon - rainy season from June to October.

muni - a sage.

murti - the form of the deity on the altar in temples.

nadi - river.

Nanda Maharaja - the leader of the cowherd men of Vrindavana, father of Lord Krishna.

Nandi - the bull carrier of Siva, found in many Siva temples.

namaste - Hindu greetings, meaning "obeisances."

Narasimha (Narsingha) - half-man half-lion incarnation, who killed Hiranyakasipu and saved Prahlada Maharaja.

Narayana - the four-armed form of Lord Krishna, who presides over the Vaikuntha planets; Lord Vishnu.

Nataraja - Siva as the cosmic dancer.

navagraha - nine planets.

nawab - Muslim ruler or a big landowner.

nirvana - freedom from material existence.

padayatra - foot journey; to go on pilgrimage by foot.

paise - 100 paise equals one rupee.

palanquin - a seat that can be carried by four men, usually used to transport great personages or ladies.

Pallavas - South Indian dynasty of rulers.

Pandavas - the five sons of King Pandu—Yudhisthira, Bhima, Arjuna, Nakula and Sahadeva; the heroes of the Mahabharata.

panda - a Brahmin guide at temples and holy places

pandita - learned scholar or priest.

Pandyas - South Indian dynasty of rulers.

Parasurama - the sixth incarnation of Lord Vishnu who killed all the *ksatriyas* (warriors) 21 times.

Parvati - another name for Siva's wife, meaning daughter of the mountain.

Prabhupada - Founder Acarya of the International Society for Krishna Consciousness (ISKCON).

pradesh - state.

prasada, prasadam - sanctified food; food offered with devotion to Lord Krishna or Lord Vishnu.

puja - offering of worship.

pujari - one who offers puja or worship, a priest in a temple.

pakka - ripe, mature, reliable.

puram - town.

Puranas - the eighteen historical supplements to the Vedas written in Sanskrit.

purusa-avataras - the primary expansions of Lord Vishnu who effect the creation, maintenance and destruction of the material universes.

Radha - the favorite consort of Krishna in Vrindavana, situated on Lord Krishna's left on altars and pictures.

railhead - town or station at the end of the railway line; ending point.

Raja - rule or sovereignty. Used to describe the British rule

raja - king or prince.

Rama - Lord Ramacandra, an incarnation of Lord Vishnu who appeared in Ayodhya as the perfect king.

Ramayana - the story of Rama and Sita.

ratha - temple cart or chariot, used during religious festival to carry the Deities.

Ravana - the ten-headed demon king of Lanka who was killed by Rama for kidnapping Sita.

rickshaw - three wheeled passenger vehicle.

rishi - a sage.

Rukmini - the chief of Lord Krishna's wives.

Rupa Gosvami - one of the principal followers of Sri Caitanya Mahaprabhu.

rupee - main unit of currency used in India.

sadhu - a saint or Krishna conscious person. A wandering holy man.

sagar - lake.

sahib - "Lord"; title given to any gentlemen and usually to Europeans. This is a compliment.

Saivaite - followers of Lord Siva.

samadhi - trance; complete absorption in God consciousness. A great saint's tomb or memorial.

sampradayas - disciplic succession.

sangam - meeting point of two or more rivers.

Sankaracarya (Sankara) - the great philosopher, who established the doctrine of *advaita* (non-dualism). He stressed the impersonal feature of God and the identity of all souls with the impersonal (undifferentiated) Brahman.

sankirtana - congregational chanting of the holy names of God.

Sanskrit - It is the oldest language in the world. The *Vedas*, or India's holy scriptures, are written in Sanskrit.

sannyasa - the renounced order of life.

sannyasi - a person in the renounced order of life.

Saraswati - wife of Brahma, the goddess of learning. She usually sits on a white swan and holds a veena (stringed instrument) in her hands.

sari - traditional Indian dress worn by Hindu women - six yards long as a rule.

sastra - revealed scriptures; Vedic literature.

sati - when a widow burns herself in

her husband's cremation/funeral fire.

Sati - the wife of Siva who burned herself alive when her father insulted her husband, Lord Siva.

shakti - energy.

shalagram-shilas - sacred stones that are non-different from Lord Krishna or Lord Vishnu and His incarnations. Very often they are gotten from the Gandhaki River in Nepal.

sikhara - temple spire.

Sita - the wife of Rama who was abducted by Ravana.

Siva - the demigod who supervises the material mode of ignorance (*tamo-guna*) and who annihilates the material cosmos. He is also considered the greatest Vaishnava, or devotee, of Lord Krishna.

Sri (sree, shree, shri) - honorific prefix, to be used before the Deities name.

Srimad Bhagavatam - the topmost *Purana* written by Vyasadeva; the complete science of God that establishes the supreme position of Lord Krishna.

Subhadra - sister of Krishna. She is the yellow Deity found between Lord Jagannatha and Baladeva.

Subrahmanya - Kartikkeya, the son of Lord Siva. The god of war. Also known as Skanda.

sudra - a member of the laborer class of men.

Surya - the sun-god.

svami (swami) - one fully in control of his senses; a person in the renounced order of life.

tempo - three-wheeler vehicle used like a small bus.

tilaka - sacred clay which is put on a person's body and forehead to show he is a follower of Vedic culture.

tirtha (teertha) - a sacred place associated with a pastime of an incarnation of God, such as a holy river, a temple of the Lord, or the residence or place of meditation of a holy sage or saintly person.

tonga - two-wheeled horse carriage.

Upanisads - 108 philosophical treatises that appear within the Vedas.

Vaikunthas - the eternal planets of the spiritual world.

Vaishnava - a devotee of Lord Krishna or Lord Vishnu.

Vamana - Lord Vishnu in His fifth incarnation as a dwarf-brahmana.

vaisya (Vaishyas)- member of the mercantile or agricultural class.

vanaprastha - a man who has retired from married life to cultivate renunciation.

Varaha - the boar incarnation of Lord Vishnu.

varnasrama-dharma - the Vedic social system, which recognizes human society as consisting of four occupational and four spiritual divisions.

Vedas - the religious scriptures.

Yamaraja - god of death, who passes judgment on non-devotees at the time of death.

Vishnu - The Supreme Godhead.

TEMPLE GLOSSARY

antarala pillared hall.

chaitya - Buddhist temple, Buddhist hall of worship.

chakra - Vishnu's disc, which is found on top of a Vishnu temple.

darwaza - door, gateway.

dhvajastambha - flagstaff.

diwan-i-am - Hall of Public Audience.

diwan-i-khas - Hall of Private Audience.

deul - In Orissan temples it corresponds to the *vimana* or towered sanctum. It is a cubical inner apartment where the main Deity is located, with a tower over it.

dwarapala - the doorkeeper sculptures by the doorways of Hindu and Buddhist temples.

garbha-griha - inner sanctuary or altar room that contains the main Deity of the temple. The literal meaning is "womb-chamber."

gopuram (gopura) - highly carved soaring towers over the gates of the temples.

gurdwara - Sikh religious complex, which usually includes a temple and guest house.

mandapam (mandapa) - halls of the temple, often with many pillars. They are one or more entrance porches or halls that lead to the *vimana*, or inner sanctum.

nandavana - flower garden.

nrita-mandapa - dance hall.

prakara - the high walls surrounding the temple grounds.

pitha - the pedestal or altar of the Deity. The *pitha* is in the sanctum sanctorum (inner sanctum).

sanctum sanctorum - inner sanctuary or altar room that contains the main Deity of the temple.

shikhara - curved temple tower or spire. The roof of the sanctum sanctorum. It is crowned by a cakra in a Lord Vishnu temple and a trident in a Lord Shiva temple.

stupa - hemispheric Buddhist monument of worship.

vahana mandapa - where the mount of the Deity (*vahana*) such as Lord Vishnu carrier's Garuda or Siva's bull Nandi is located.

vihara - Buddhist monastery.
vimanam - it is the tower over the sanctum of the deity

Food Glossary

alu - potato.
bhindi - ladies' finger, okra.
bandh gobhi - cabbage
biryani - mild fancy rice, sometime with a sauce.
chai - tea.
channa - chick peas (garbanzo beans).
chapati - unleavened Indian bread.
curd - yogurt.
dal - lentil (bean, pulse) soup.
dosas - a very large, thin pancake, made of fermented rice flour. They are often wrapped round a spiced potato filling and are then called *masala dosa*.
ghee - clarified butter, used for cooking.
idli - steamed dumpling made of ground, fermented rice flour or with lentil dal, usually eaten with coconut chutney.
lassi - a sweet or salty yogurt drink.
kaju - cashew.
mattar - peas.
nan - baked leavened bread.
nimbu paani - fresh lemonade drink.
paani - water.
palak - spinach.
paneer - Indian cheese, curd.
phul gobhi - cauliflower
sabji - vegetables.
thali - vegetarian meal which includes many different preparations, usually all you can eat.

Key Dates

BC

3000	Kurukshetra War and *Bhagavad-gita* spoken
599	Appearance of Mahavir
563	Appearance of Gautama Buddha
327-325	Alexander invades North India
324	Chandragupta defeats the Greeks and founds Mauryan Dynasty
292-232	Reign of Ashoka

AD

100	Mahayana Buddhism founded
320	Chandra Gupta founds Gupta Dynasty
600	Gupta Dynasty ends, period of small India states
600	Chalukyan Dynasty in central Deccan & Pallavas in Tamil Nadu
750	Rashtrakutas rule central Peninsula
788-820	Shankaracarya
816-1192	Rajput kingdoms in Rajasthan
950	Khajuraho temples started
1001-1026	Mahmud of Ghazni invades India
1017-1137	Ramanujacarya
1193	Qutbuddin Aibak conquers Delhi
1193-1526	Various Muslim dynasties rule from Delhi
1198	Konark temple built
1100-1130	Rise of poet Jayadeva Goswami
1239-1319	Madhvacarya
1336-1565	Vijayanagar Empire rules most of South India
1398	Timur the Lame invades India
1434	Appearance of Advaita Acarya
1441	Appearance of Saci Mata
1450	Birth of Haridasa Thakura
1455	Advaita Acarya visits Vrindavana and finds the Madana Gopala Deity. Later Sanatana Goswami built a temple for this Deity called Madana Mohana.
1469-1538	Guru Nanak, founder of Sikhism
1465	Birth of Sanatana Goswami and Ramananda Raya
1470	Birth of Rupa Goswami
1473	Appearance of Nityananda Prabhu and Vallabhacarya
1479	Madhavendra Puri finds and establishes the worship of Gopala Raya. (Sri Nathaji)
1486	Appearance of Sri Caitanya Mahaprabhu
1487	Appearance of Gadadhara Pandit

1494	Birth of Raghunatha Goswami
1498	Vasco da Gama lands in Calicut
1510	Nimai takes *sannyasa*
1511	Birth of Jiva Goswami
1514	Sri Caitanya spends two months in Vrindavana
1515	Rupa Goswami and Sanatana Goswami came to Vrindavana to uncover pastimes places of Radha and Krishna
1526-1530	Reign of Babur, founder of Mughal dynasty
1534	Disappearance of Sri Caitanya
1556-1605	Reign of Akbar
1573	Jiva Goswami meets Emperor Akbar in Vrindavana.
1603	Guru Granth Sahib compiled
1627-1658	Rule of Shah Jahan, builder of Taj Mahal
1646	Birth of Visvanatha Cakravarti Thakura
1658-1707	Aurangzeb Emperor
1677	Shivaji and Marathas
1757	Battle of Plassey
1857	Indian uprising
1858	India comes under British government
1947	India becomes independent

Hindi

A good book that was recommended to me by a Hindi teacher was *Teach Yourself Hindi,* by Mohini Rao, which costs only Rs 35. This book also comes with two tapes. The book along with the two tapes costs Rs 150.

A few good phrase books are *Hindustani For the Tourist,* published by Jaico books, which costs just Rs 35, and the *Hindi/Urdu Phrase Book,* published by Lonely Planet.

Knowing just a few key Hindi words can help a lot. It is especially impressive to Indians when foreigners make an effort to communicate with them in their own tongue. Often this can make them go out of their way to be more helpful. For instance, the words *sabse acchha,* indicating the highest quality, is very useful, because for some reason many Indians can't believe you want to see the highest quality, and therefore, most expensive item first.

It is important to say the Hindi words correctly. Vowels are both short and long. The best way to learn is by hearing. Stress is also important. Even while speaking English you have to put the stress on words the way Indians do, not as you would normally do in your own country. It may also be necessary for you to speak with an Indian accent to be properly understood.

absolutely	*bilkul*
bad	*kharab*
best (quality)	*sabse acchha*
better	*zyada acchha*
big	*bara*
bill, please	*bill layiye*
breakfast	*nashtaa*
bring	*la-iye*

clean	*saf*
cold	*thanda*
costly (expensive)	*mehanga*
dirty	*gandaa*
enough	*kafi*
evening	*shaam*
fast	*tez, jaldi*
fat	*mota*
go	*jaaiye*
good, agreed	*acchha*
good	*shubh*
happy	*sukhi, khush*
heavy	*bhari*
hello/goodbye	*namaste*
holy	*pavitra*
hot	*garam*
how	*kaisee*
how many	*kitane*
how much	*kitana*
I	*mai*
large	*bada*
less	*kum*
many	*bahut*
medicine	*davai*
month	*mahina*
more	*zyada*
next	*agla, dusra*
night	*raat*
no	*nahin*
noon	*dopahar*
please	*kripaya*
price	*keemat / daam*
right (correct)	*thik*
right (hand)	*dahina, dayan*
room	*kamra*
small (quantity)	*thora, kuch*
small (size)	*chhota* (male)
small (size)	*chhoti* (female)
some	*kuch*
take	*lo*
thank you	*dhanyavad/shukriya*
very good	*bahut accha*
we	*hum*
week	*hafta*

what	*kyaa*
where	*kahaan*
yes	*han*
you	*aap*

Food

apple	*seb*
banana	*kela*
black pepper	*kali mirch*
bread	*chapati/roti/nan*
butter	*makkan*
cabbage	*band gobhi*
cashew	*kaju*
cauliflower	*phul gobhi*
food	*khanaa*
fruit	*phal*
grapes	*angur*
green pepper	*hara mirch*
ice	*baraf*
lime	*nimbu*
mango	*aum*
milk	*dudh*
papaya	*papita*
pea	*mattar*
peanuts	*mungphali*
pomegranate	*anannas*
potato	*aloo*
rice	*chawal*
salt	*namak*
sugar	*chini*
tangerine	*santara*
tea	*chai*
water	*pani*
vegetables	*sabji*
yogurt	*dahi*

How much?
kitna paise? kitne hai?

What is you good name?
apka shubh nam kya hai?

My name is ___.
mera naam ___ hai

My home is in ___.
Mera ghar ___ mein hain

Where is the ___ ?
___ kidhar hai

How far is ___ ?
kitne dur hai?

How do I get to ___?
___ kaise pahunch sakte hain?

Where do you live?
Aap kidhar rehte hain?

I am here for ___ days.
Mein ___ din ke liye yahan hun.

How much does this cost?
Iski keemat kya hai?

This shop is very expensive.
vak dukan bahut mahangi hai

This is expensive
yeh bahut mehange hai

Too much (cost)
jada hai

Lower the cost
kum karo

How are you?
ap kaise hain

Very well, thank you.
bahut achche shukriya

Can you speak Hindi?
ap Hindi bol sakate hain

What is that?
woh kyaa hai

What time is it?		60		sath
kitne baje hain		65		painsath
		70		sattar
Show me the menu.		75		pachhattar
Mujhe minu kikhayee		80		assi
		85		pachasi
I want something to drink.		90		nabbe
Mujhe kuch pina chayiye		95		pachanabbe
		100		ek so
Give me the bill.		200		do so
Bill de dijiyee		300		tin so
		1,000		ek hazar
Do not add ice.		2,000		do hazar
baraf matt daaliye		100,000		lakh
		10,000,000		crore

Numbers

1	ek
2	do
3	tin
4	char
5	panch
6	chhe
7	saat
8	aath
9	nau
10	das
11	gyarah
12	barah
13	terah
14	choda
15	pandrah
16	solah
17	satrah
18	aththarah
19	unnis
20	bis
21	ikkis
22	bais
25	pachis
30	tis
35	paintis
40	chalis
45	paintalis
50	pachas
55	pachpan

Index

MAP INDEX

India's spiritual richness is vast and incomparable, but often the physical difficulties make them less easy to appreciate. Jada Bharata has given nice practical advice on how to survive the difficulties, to find the spiritual essence that is the real India. I recommend this book. Buy it.

Bhakti Vikasa Swami England

I would like to congratulate Sriman Jada Bharata Prabhu on the publication of his book, Holy Temples and Places of India. This outstanding book will fulfill the desires of many sincere visitors to India by guiding them safely and intelligently to the real treasures of India, the holy places. I wish him all success in his continuing project of providing the best spiritual guidebook available.

His Holiness Hrdayananda dasa Gosvami

You have done a great service in writing your book, Holy Places and Temples of India. All the practical information on dealing with India is as welcome as the information on the holy sites.

W. Fox, Maharishi Institute of Management

I used Holy Places and Temples of India as my one and only guidebook while on an extended pilgrimage in India. When you have the best, what need is there for the second rate. A chock full, jammed packed, overflowing encyclopedia of reliable information on negotiating your way through spiritual India. For those jaded travelers who are tired of the hype and pressures of the Taj Mahal type tourist beat, this book guides you, lifts you, and directs you perfectly to and through India's spiritual destinations.

Gita Nagari Dasa

Your book is great. It is really you.

Gaura Purnima Dasi

Your book is great. The first tip that I got from your book saved me twice the value of the book.

Braja Bihari Dasa·
Vaishnava Institute of High Education, India

I am real enjoying your book.

Sandamani Dasi Tucson, AZ